D0848522

CHRISTIE'S

World Encyclopedia of

Champagne
& sparkling wine

CHRISTIE'S

World Encyclopedia of

Champagne & sparkling wine

TOM STEVENSON

RECEIVED

JUN 2 8 2001

MINNESOTA STATE UNIVERSITY LIBRARY
MANKATO, MN 56002-8419

WINE APPRECIATION
GUILD
San Francisco

EDITOR:
RUTH ARNOLD
EDITORIAL ASSISTANT:
JAMIE AMBROSE

ART DIRECTOR:
IAN MIDDLETON
DESIGNER:
KEITH WATSON
VISUAL CO-ORDINATOR AND
INTERNATIONAL LIAISON: SONIA CHAGUIBOFF

CARTOGRAPHY: STEVE MUNNS
PRODUCTION MANAGER:
CHRISTINE LEECH
PICTURE EDITOR: MATT INWOOD

FIRST PUBLISHED IN THE UNITED STATES IN 1999
BY THE WINE APPRECIATION GUILD LTD
360 SWIFT AVENUE, SOUTH SAN FRANCISCO CA 94080
(650) 866 3020
E-MAIL: WINEAPPRECIATION.COM

FIRST PUBLISHED IN GREAT BRITAIN IN 1998
BY ABSOLUTE PRESS, SCARBOROUGH HOUSE,
29 JAMES STREET WEST, BATH, BA1 2BT
T: 44 (0) 1225 316013 F: 44 (0)1225 445836
E-MAIL: SALES@ABSOLUTEPRESS.DEMON.CO.UK

COPYRIGHT © ABSOLUTE PRESS 1998
TEXT COPYRIGHT © TOM STEVENSON 1998

COVER AND MAIN IMAGE PHOTOGRAPHY: CEPHAS

ALL RIGHTS RESERVED. NO PART OF THIS PUBLICATION
MAY BE REPRODUCED, STORED IN A RETRIEVAL SYSTEM
OR TRANSMITTED IN ANY FORM OR BY ANY MEANS,
ELECTRONIC OR OTHERWISE, WITHOUT THE PRIOR
PERMISSION OF THE COPYRIGHT OWNER.

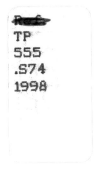
Ref
TP
555
.S74
1998

BRITISH LIBRARY CATALOGUING IN PUBLICATION DATA

STEVENSON, TOM
    CHRISTIE'S WORLD ENCYCLOPEDIA OF CHAMPAGNE
    & SPARKLING WINE
    1. CHAMPAGNE (WINE) - ENCYCLOPEDIAS
    2. SPARKLING WINES - ENCYCLOPEDIAS
    I. TITLE II. WORLD ENCYCLOPEDIA OF CHAMPAGNE
    & SPARKLING WINE
    641.2'22'4'03

    ISBN 1 899791 98 1

REPRODUCED BY GLOBAL COLOUR, MALAYSIA
PRINTED AND BOUND BY BUTLER & TANNER,
FROME, ENGLAND

AUTHOR'S ACKNOWLEDGEMENTS

First and foremost my thanks must go to Jon Croft, who is the most gentlemanly publisher I have ever worked with. His deal with Könemann Verlag of Munich to publish 150,000 copies in major European languages made this book a viable proposition before I wrote a single word. Thanks also to Amanda, Bron and especially Matt at Absolute Press.

My humblest apologies to Ruth Arnold! I enjoyed working with her so much when she was editor of WINE magazine and its sister trade publication *Wine & Spirit International* that I dragged her out of maternally-enforced semi-retirement to edit the Encyclopedia and put her through Hell and back before completing it. Ian Middleton, the art director, is the co-owner of Colville Place Gallery, one of the world's first galleries dedicated to digital art and design. His innovative approach has, I believe, brought a fresh, elegant dimension to the design of this book.

At Christie's, Michael Broadbent has been wonderfully supportive, as has Christopher Burr and David Elswood. My thanks also to everyone else behind the scenes at Christie's.

It is impossible to list everyone else who has assisted in the production of a book such as this, and I am sure that I must have missed out many who have been very helpful, but the following certainly should be singled out: Maureen Ashley MW (for freelance services on behalf of Italian producers), Luis Avides Moreira (Wines of Portugal), Owen J. Bird (Consultant Winemaker), Vicky Bishop (Victoria Bishop PR & Marketing), Nelly Blau Picard (UPECB, Burgundy), Daniel Brennan (formerly of Wines from Spain), Steve Burns (Washington Wine Institute), Colin Cameron (Caxton Tower for Dragon Seal, China), Stéphane Chaboud (Syndicat des Vignerons de Saint Péray), Tina Cody (Wines of South Africa), Christine Coletta (British Columbia Wine Institute), Maria do Cé Hespanha (Wines of Portugal), Nicole Dufour (CIVAS, Anjou-Saumur), Rachel Dutton (Seagram), Dawnine Dyer (Domaine Chandon, USA), Mme Faure (Syndicat de Die), Roger Fisher (T&CVA for English and Welsh sparkling wines), Monty Friendship (wine journalist, Zimbabwe), Peter Gamble (Canadian Wine Institute), Rémy Gauthier (Varichon & Clerc, Seyssel), Dieter Greiner (Deutsches Weininstitut), Jeff Grier (Villiera Estate, South Africa), Horst Groll (Henkell & Söhnlein), Rosemary Hall (Wines of Austria), Sarah Hately (Westbury Blake for Wines of Canada), Graham Hines (Wines from Spain), Jane Hunt MW (formerly of Wines of South Africa), Jane Hunter (Hunter's Wines, New Zealand), Carla Innes (Moët & Chandon London), Tony Keys (formerly of Australian Wine Bureau), Mark Lewis (Quality Wines of Naarden, Netherlands), Jon Leighton (Thames Valley Vineyards), Kit Lindlar (former English winemaker), Daniel Lorsen (CIVC, France), Cathérine Manac'h (Sopexa, London), Georgina McDermott (Syndicat des Maisons de Saumur), Lisa McGovern (New Zealand Wine Guild), Maggie McNie (formerly of the Greek Wine Bureau), Steffen Maus (The German Wine Information Service), Françoise Peretti (Champagne Information Bureau), Hazel Murphy and Georgie Beach (Australian Wine Bureau), Cherry Pattison (logistics), Jeff Porter (Evenlode Press), Georg Riedel (Riedel, Austria), Emma Roberts (SOPEXA, France), Doreen Schmid (Domaine Chandon, USA), Michael Schmidt (German wine consultant), Olivier Sohler (SPCA, Alsace), Pat Stevenson (for everything from PA to dog's body), Jenny Stewart (Seagram), Alex & Claire Taylor (Canto Perlic, Gaillac), James S Trezise (New York Wine & Grape Foundation), Barbara Tysome (German Wine Information Service), Michelle Vernoux (SVR Bordeaux), Emma Wellings (formerly Westbury Blake for Wines of Canada), Victoria Williams (Wines of Chile).

THIS BOOK IS DEDICATED TO MY MOTHER, WHO WAS THE FIRST PERSON TO DRIVE ME TO DRINK, AND TO MY FATHER, WHO CAME BACK WHEN HE REALISED HE HAD NOT SAID GOODBYE!

PUBLISHER'S ACKNOWLEDGEMENTS

The briefest inspection of this book will make apparent the requirement to thank so many people for all of their hard work and support over the last two years.
Absolute Press is grateful indeed to the following: Luis Avides, Adrienne Asher-Gepford, Tim Banks, Kirsty Bridge, James Craig-Wood, Frederick Frank, Rosemary Hall, Gladys Horiuchi, Kirk Irwin, Lynne Lubin, Catherine Manac'h, John Maclaren, Valerie Murphy, Justin Llewellyn, Su Lyn Ong, Gilbert van Reenen, Kevin Robinson, Meg Scantlebury, Jane Schneider, Sarah Schoen, Judith Scott, Rollin Soles, Odile Triplet, Jenny Williamson, Sheila Xander; and to each of the many individuals, wineries, bureaux and agencies worldwide, whose help has been invaluable.

CONTENTS

INTRODUCTION

SPARKLING WINES OF THE WORLD

FRANCE

EUROPE

AFRICAN CONTINENT

AMERICAN CONTINENT

ANTIPODES

ASIA 310

HOW TO USE THIS BOOK

FOLLOWING THE INTRODUCTORY SECTION, THE ENCYCLOPEDIA IS ARRANGED IN A COUNTRY-BY-COUNTRY FORMAT. WITHIN EACH COUNTRY THERE ARE TWO BASIC TYPES OF TEXT: GENERAL INTRODUCTION, AND PRODUCER PROFILES LISTED IN ALPHABETICAL ORDER. TO LOCATE A PARTICULAR COUNTRY, CONSULT THE CONTENTS. TO FIND A SPECIFIC PRODUCER: [I.] IF YOU KNOW THE COUNTRY IN QUESTION, THEN TURN TO THAT CHAPTER AND LOCATE BY ITS ALPHABETICAL LISTING, OR [II.] IF YOU KNOW THE NAME OF THE PRODUCER BUT ARE NOT SURE OF THE COUNTRY, REFER TO THE INDEX.

PRODUCER PROFILES

1 GLOBAL RANKING

A personalised percentile-based ranking that applies globally, thus a producer scoring 80 points anywhere in the world is the equivalent in quality (though different stylistically) to a Champagne producer scoring 80 points.

N/A *Where no ranking has been given, [a] because ownership or the winemaker of the property has recently changed, [b] where the author has insufficient experience of the wines or [c] where the producer is new to the market and therefore has no existing track record in terms of overall quality over a number of years.*

40 *If they are clean, the character of the wines must be dire.*

50 *Clean but boring.*

60 *Probably some potential, but usually cool-fermentation has produced an amylic style in which individual character is lost. Frankly this is as good as it gets in some areas.*

70 *The point at which any sparkling wine other than Champagne starts to become interesting, as far as I am concerned.*

75 *Any sparkling wine other than Champagne that receives this score is not just interesting, but one that is good enough to grace the table of a self-confessed Champagne addict.*

80 *Because Champagne has such intrinsic advantages over sparkling wines produced in less favourable terroirs, this is the level at which I start to take interest in an inexpensive BOB or secondary brand.*

85 *The sort of quality that Champagne has to be to warrant inclusion in my cellar. If a non-Champagne sparkling wine producer scores this high, it is of exceptional quality indeed.*

90 *Serious quality Champagne producer whose products have every right to demand a significant premium over the rest of the market. Be prepared to give these wines additional cellarage to reveal their true potential.*

95 *The greatest Champagne producers of all; their wines will often require at least 10 years' cellarage.*

98 *Only seven entries in this book: Krug (the only producer receiving this score for its entire range); Bollinger Vieilles Vignes Françaises; Clos des Goisses; Cuvée Dom Pérignon; Grand Siècle "La Cuvée"; Pol Roger Vintage; and Salon.*

100 *Perfection – impossible!*

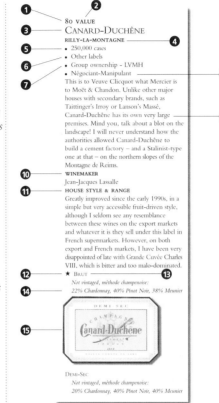

2 VALUE

Awarded to producers whose best wines generally stand within their category. As far as I'm concerned, value exists at 50 pounds or dollars, just as it does at five pounds or dollars, although the depth of your pocket will decide whether you can afford the value found at the top end of the market.

3 TRADING NAME

4 LOCATION

5 PRODUCTION OR SALES

It is a moot point whether a winery's annual production is the same as its sales, although in the case of a mature venture it often is. This figure relates to a producer's sparkling wines only, and for the sake of this book a case is defined as the equivalent of 12 x 75cl bottles.

6 OTHER LABELS

Primarily secondary brands, although in some instances this will include a primary brand when it is different from the trading name under which it is listed.

7 GROUP OWNERSHIP

Either the parent company that owns the winery or, if it is the parent company, any other operations belonging to it.

8 COMMERCIAL STATUS

Champagne only: in most cases this indicates whether the producer is a house (négociant-manipulant), grower (récoltant-manipulant), or cooperative (coopérative-manipulant). For details of other possibilities, see Types of Producer, p.44.

9 BACKGROUND INFORMATION

A thumbnail sketch of relevant details.

10 WINEMAKER

The person with overall responsibility for making the wines.

11 HOUSE STYLE

A general description of the house style, this often includes specific descriptions of individual cuvées.

12 STAR-RATING

These ratings are not global, but apply to wines that stand out within their own class, style or origin.

★ *Wines that are well above average quality.*

★★ *Extraordinarily exceptional.*

★★★ *So stunning that I have been unable to award this to any wines other than the seven greatest Champagnes.*

Half-stars indicate intermediate ratings.

13 NAME OF INDIVIDUAL WINE

14 CUVÉE DETAILS

Whether vintaged or not, method of production, grape varieties and other relevant information. Where it is stated 'grape varieties not revealed', these details are either uncertain or have not been forthcoming.

I have used 'bottle-fermented' where it has not been possible to discern whether a wine has been made by the méthode champenoise or transfer method. Every possible care has been taken to ensure the accuracy of this information, but I can only pass on what I have been told and there have been many occasions when it has been difficult to unravel the ambiguities of the details provided by producers despite several faxes and telephone calls.

15 LABEL

Labels should not be taken as a form of special recommendation; they are merely meant to represent a collective look of each country's sparkling wines.

FOREWORD

THIS IS AN ASTONISHINGLY COMPLETE WORK. NOT A SINGLE FACT OR DETAIL SEEMS TO BE LACKING, NOT ONLY UPDATING AND EXPANDING ON THE CHAMPAGNE SCENE IN THE TEN YEARS SINCE PUBLICATION OF HIS CLASSIC WORK 'CHAMPAGNE' BUT, MORE PROVOCATIVELY AND USEFULLY, INCLUDING THE WIDER WORLD OF SPARKLING WINES. MORE THAN A MAGNUM OPUS, THIS IS SURELY TOM STEVENSON'S 'JEROBOAM' OPUS!

Of all wines, Champagne has had the most consistently prestigious image. The real stuff has always been fashionable, often elitist, yet even when consumed at more popular levels, it maintains an air of exclusivity. Through Christie's unique catalogue archives, we can follow both fashions in Champagne consumption and prices. Although wine featured in James Christie's first sales in December 1766, two years of auctions elapsed before *champaigne* (sic) made an appearance. This was in February 1768. Other catalogue entries around that time include *White Champaigne* in 1770, *Red Champagne* in 1778 and, in 1788, the first reference to a specific district, renowned then, as now, *Aiy, white* and, the most fashionable of all, *Sillery*, part of a comprehensive cellar of wines being sold on behalf of the French Ambassador, the Comte d'Adhemar.

Champagne in hampers, 100 bottles each appears in 1796 (wine in bottle was normally shipped in hampers – wicker chests containing between 50 and 100 bottles); *Sweet Champagne d'Aye* is recorded in 1812 and, in an 1820 catalogue, I have found the first reference to *Superior White Creaming Champagne.*

Sparkling wines from other countries are not as recent newcomers as some may think. A catalogue of wines sold in 1828 lists *German Champagne* – Christie's would be sued for this description now! Also very popular in the 19th century was *St Peray, Sparkling*, the first mention of which appears in 1834.

Before leaving my home ground, let me just record that the most costly wine sold at Christie's between 1766 and the Autumn of 1966 was Champagne; in 1885 over 30 dozen bottles of Perrier Jouët's Cuvée de Réserve II 1874 vintage fetched 410 shillings per dozen. That's nearly three times the price of 1804 Lafite, which was reported to be the best red Bordeaux of the century.

At a less lordly level, Champagne and sparkling wines have also been the pre-eminent wine of celebration: at births, christenings, weddings, upon landing a new job, on retirement; launching ships of course and, symbolic and equally wasteful, on the podium at the end of every motor racing grand prix.

Breakfast time, mid morning, before and during lunch, after work, before going to bed: these superb bubbles have the ability to raise the spirit, reaffirm one's optimism for life, create, sustain, renew and enrich friendships. There's nothing to compare.

This encyclopedia goes to the very beginnings of sparkling wine and Champagne production and follows it through to the present day, travelling all over the world in the process. For all lovers of Champagne and sparkling wines, all lovers of life, it is essential reading.

MICHAEL BROADBENT

DIRECTOR, CHRISTIE'S

AUTHOR'S INTRODUCTION

THE HISTORY OF SPARKLING WINE IS AS LONG AS A PIECE OF STRING, AND IN THE FIRST EDITION OF *CHRISTIE'S WORLD ENCYCLOPEDIA OF CHAMPAGNE & SPARKLING WINE* I HAVE ONLY JUST BEGUN THE TASK OF WINDING IT IN.

The subject is so vast, involved and fast-moving that it will take a lifetime to elaborate on some of its more obscure areas, but this book should at least provide readers with a better understanding of the various types, styles and origins of sparkling wine. It should also give an indication where each wine stands in the pecking order within its own appellation or category. Certainly it could not have been written ten years ago, when there were so many dull, boring and blatantly bad products that it would not have encouraged anyone to explore sparkling wines beyond Champagne itself.

Indeed, the first sparkling wine produced in the New World to equal the quality of a good Champagne was the second release of Roederer Estate, which was made in 1987, but did not surface until the early 1990s. Prior to that it was simply a relief to get good, clean fizz outside Champagne that could boast a modest mouthful of fruit and refreshing acidity. But since the emergence of Roederer Estate, the premium sparkling wine sector has really taken off. Even Britain has produced world-class fizz since 1992, albeit under New World ownership at Nyetimber.

The one country that is lagging behind in the fizz stakes is, ironically, France. With the obvious exception of Champagne, the French still treat sparkling wine as a convenient means of getting rid of unripe or substandard grapes, and this results in some of the nastiest sparkling wines produced anywhere in the world. One day, hopefully, the French will take sparkling wine alternatives seriously; most wine regions in France could do battle with the best fizz the New World has to offer, and I would much rather fill this encyclopedia with exciting finds than words of caution.

TOM STEVENSON, AUGUST 1998

Spirit off wine & stir it about, some add a little salt well dryed. This fines y wine in 24 hours.

To keep must a year. Take must, put it into a Cask pitched within & without half full, stop y bung close with mortar. Others sow y Cask in a skine & sink it for 30 days into a well or river. Or els a garland of polium montanum hung in y vessel, or rub y inside of y vessel with chees. All these preserve & hinder must as y Scholiast on Dodonæus in Dutch.

Alume put into a hogs bladder keeps wine from turning flat faint or brown, & beaten with y whites of Eggs removes it's ropishnes.

Flat wines recovered with spirit of wines raysins & Sugar or Molossey & Sacks by drawing them on fresh lees ~~~~~~~

Our wine coopers of later times use vast quantities of Sugar & Molossey to all sorts of wines to make them drink brisk, & sparkling & to give them spirit as also to mend their bad tacks, all which raysins & Cute & stum perform.

Country vintners feed their fretting wines with raw beef, & her their Canaries with Malago which is added more or less to all Canaries.

The composition of wines is manifold, the vintners usually drawing out of 2 or 3 Casks for one pint to accomodate it to y palats of those y drink it. Most of y Canaries made with Malago & zeres sack.

I shall conclude with 2 common compounded wines Muscaden & Hippocras y former usually made with 30 gallons of Cute (which is wine boild to y consumption of ½) to a But of wine, or y lees & droppings boild & clarified, its flavour is made of Coriander seed prepared & shavings of Cypress wood. Some instead of cute make it of sugar molossey & honey, or mix them with y Cute.

This following is an Hippocras of my own making & y best I have tasted. Take of Cardamons Carpobalsamum an ½ an ounce Coriander seed prepared nutmegs ginger of each 2 ounces Cloves 2 drams, bruise & infuse them 48 hours in zeres & white wine an a gallon often stirring them then add thereto of milk 3 pints stroyn through an Hippocras bag & sweeten it with a pound of Sugar candy

THE FIRST DOCUMENTED DESCRIPTION OF WHAT WAS TO BECOME KNOWN AS THE MÉTHODE CHAMPENOISE – THE ADDITION OF SUGAR TO A FINISHED WINE WITH THE DELIBERATE INTENTION OF MAKING IT SPARKLING – IS FOUND IN LONDON, NOT REIMS OR EPERNAY, AT THE ROYAL SOCIETY, WHERE IT HAS BEEN PRESERVED SINCE DECEMBER 17, 1662. IT WAS PART OF AN EIGHT-PAGE PAPER READ OUT TO THE NEWLY-FORMED SCIENTIFIC BODY SIX YEARS BEFORE DOM PÉRIGNON SET FOOT IN HAUTVILLERS

A LITTLE HISTORY

IT IS IMPOSSIBLE TO PIN DOWN WHEN THE FIRST SPARKLING WINE WAS MADE BECAUSE IT MUST HAVE BEEN ACCIDENTAL; FIZZINESS IN WINE WAS ORIGINALLY PERCEIVED AS A FAULT, JUST AS FIZZINESS IN FRUIT JUICE IS TODAY. TRYING TO UNEARTH THE FIRST SPARKLING WINE IS THUS LIKE LOOKING FOR THE FIRST OXIDISED OR CORKED WINE — HARDLY SOMETHING WORTHY OF DOCUMENTATION, AS IT WAS SOMETHING THE EARLIEST WINEMAKERS WANTED TO ERADICATE, NOT REPLICATE. THE FIRST SPARKLING WINE OF ANY HISTORICAL IMPORTANCE HAS TO BE THE FIRST IN WHICH THE FIZZINESS WAS DELIBERATELY INDUCED BY A METHOD THAT COULD BE REPLICATED. WITH THIS FACT IN MIND, IT MAY GALL THE FRENCH TO DISCOVER THAT IT WAS ACTUALLY THE ENGLISH AND NOT THE FRENCH WHO INVENTED CHAMPAGNE.

THE ENGLISH PARADOX

Until the 18th century Champagne was, of course, a still wine. France did not have the technology to make sparkling Champagne until 1695 or thereabouts. The first French document to mention sparkling Champagne was written in 1718, and refers to its emergence some 20 years earlier. Thus we can be fairly accurate in dating the arrival of this purpose-made effervescing wine between 1695 and 1698. Yet some 20 years earlier sparkling Champagne was not only available in England, it had become so popular that dramatists were waxing lyrical about it. The very first mention of sparkling Champagne in any language is in English, not French, when in 1676 Sir George Etherege wrote, in *The Man of Mode*:

> To the Mall and the Park
> Where we love till 'tis dark,
> Then sparkling Champaign
> Puts an end to their reign;
> It quickly recovers
> Poor languishing lovers,
> Makes us frolic and gay, and drowns all sorrow;
> But, Alas, we relapse again on the morrow.

How could sparkling Champagne be recorded in English literature two decades before even the French admit the first sparkling Champagne was made? The answer is not time travel, it is simply that the English had sparkling wine technology and they used it to make still French wines fizzy.

So why didn't France have sparkling wine technology until circa 1695? Not much was needed: a glass bottle that could withstand the internal pressure of a sparkling wine, and an effective seal to maintain it. However, French glass was too weak and cork-stoppers had been 'lost' during the decline of the Roman Empire. Instead the French used wooden bungs wrapped in hemp, which would hardly keep the draught out, let alone the fizz in.

Although the French did not rediscover cork until 1685 at the earliest, the English, who also lost the cork after the Romans left, had come across it again much earlier. Again English literature provides documentary evidence because more than 130 years before the French started using corks again,

HISTORIC BOTTLE,
FROM VEUVE CLICQUOT'S
HERITAGE CENTRE IN REIMS

JAMES I OF ENGLAND
WHOSE ROYAL
PROCLAMATION PLAYED A
KEY PART IN THE
DEVELOPMENT OF
REINFORCED GLASS

Rosalind said to Celia in William Shakespeare's *As You Like It*:

> 'I would thou wouldst stammer, that thou mightest pour this concealed man out of my mouth, as wine comes out of a narrow-mouth'd bottle – either too much at once, or not at all. I pray thee take thy cork out of thy mouth, that I may drink thy tidings.'

All wines in Shakespeare's time were shipped to England in casks, and the English habitually bottled the wines themselves from the late 16th century onwards. This practice did not become traditional in France until the late 17th century, one of the reasons being that French glass was wood-fired and intrinsically weak, another being the absence of cork stoppers.

By 1615 English glass was much stronger than French glass, although this was more by luck than design. Worried that the decimation of English forests by charcoal burners would jeopardise British shipbuilding and thereby threaten the future of the fleet, Admiral Sir Robert Mansell convinced James I that charcoal burners were effectively endangering the security of the nation, and that he should issue a royal proclamation banning wood-fired furnaces. Because coal was the only viable alternative fuel and it burned at a much higher temperature, English glass instantly became a vastly stronger product.

Mansell retired two years later, built a new glassworks, and in 1623 obtained a royal patent granting him a monopoly for all coal-fired glassware. This might be opportunism or a well-deserved reward for his defence of the realm, depending on the reader's viewpoint, but it is certain that Mansell was instrumental in strengthening English glass. This was a role he once more unwittingly added to when, in an attempt to make coloured glass by adding a combination of iron and manganese, he succeeded in toughening it, thus inventing reinforced glass. Mansell's reinforced glass was the precursor to common bottle glass, which English winemerchants began using in the early 1630s, exactly one century before its commercial production in France, where it was known as *verre anglais*.

From this series of events it is clear that the English had the means to preserve the effervescence of a sparkling Champagne long before its first recorded mention by Sir George Etherege, but how and why did still wine from Champagne end up sparkling?

Obviously there were many occurrences of accidental refermentation causing a wine to become fizzy. The most common cause for such 'faulty' wines was the cold northerly situation of Champagne, where we can be sure that fermentation would have prematurely stopped at the first snap of winter, only to recommence once the wine was bottled and stored in the warmth of an English tavern. However, accidentally sparkling wines have been a fact of life since biblical times, as evidenced by references such as *'wine ... when it moveth itself'* (Proverbs 23:31) and, particularly apt, *'Neither do men put new wine into old skins; else the skins break'* (Matthew 9:17), but such incidents are an irrelevance to historians searching for the first deliberately-made sparkling wine.

Moët & Chandon would have us believe that Dom Pérignon invented Champagne but, while he can be credited with inventing the classic Champagne blend, it is generally held that he spent most of his life trying to eradicate bubbles that appeared naturally in his wines. This suggests that he did not understand why they were appearing and therefore could not have deliberately replicated the process.

If Champagne is an invention, then conclusive proof can only be demonstrated by documentary evidence describing the most rudimentary element of the *méthode champenoise* – the addition of sugar to a finished wine to induce a second fermentation for the specific intention of making it not just 'gay', 'brisk' or 'lively' (words often thought to infer effervescence), but unequivocally sparkling. Such a document exists, not in Reims or Epernay, but in London, where an eight-page paper entitled *'Some observations concerning the ordering of wines'* was presented on 17 December 1662 to the newly formed Royal Society by one Christopher Merret, who stated *'...our wine-coopers of recent times use vast quantities of sugar and molasses to all sorts of wines to make them drink brisk and sparkling'*.

The English therefore invented Champagne, and did it six years before Dom Pérignon set foot in Hautvillers, more than 30 years before the French made their first sparkling Champagne, and over 70 years before the oldest Champagne house was established.

THE EVOLUTION OF THE *MÉTHODE CHAMPENOISE*

Merret's paper demonstrates that Dom Pérignon did not invent sparkling Champagne, and although there is no proof that he even produced one sparkling wine, the consensus of opinion is that he probably did. Certainly that is what Dom Grossard, the last cellarmaster of Hautvillers believed. In a letter to the deputy mayor of Aÿ, Dom Grossard wrote: 'As you know, Monsieur, it was the celebrated Dom Pérignon who found the secret of making white sparkling wine'. This was, however, written more than 100 years after Dom Pérignon's death, and the great monk's immediate successor, Frère Pierre, did not mention

STATUE TO THE MEMORY OF DOM PÉRIGNON AT THE MOËT & CHANDON HEADQUARTERS

sparkling Champagne, let alone adding sugar to a finished wine to make it effervescent, even though in 1724 he devoted a 35-chapter *Traité de la culture des vignes de Champagne* to the man's achievements.

On the first page of this amazing document, Frère Pierre describes himself as *Elève et Successeur de Dom Pérignon* and his text records that his mentor 'scrupulously concerned himself with details that to others appeared insignificant', a point reiterated later in the text when Pierre stresses that Pérignon insisted on various practices that other winegrowers considered 'impossible, even ridiculous'. Frère Pierre's list of Dom Pérignon's accomplishments include: being the first person to produce a well-coloured red wine; the first person to produce a perfectly limpid white wine from black grapes; conceiving the concept of cool harvesting (the forerunner to night-harvesting techniques which were developed by New World countries in the 1970s); picking in several *tries* or passes to obtain the ripest and healthiest grapes; inventing the traditional Champagne coquard press; conceiving the art of *assemblage* to create a consistent and superior *cuvée* from numerous different vineyards; reintroducing the cork-stopper in France; pioneering the use of *verre anglais*.

It does seem odd that if Dom Pérignon had purposely produced a sparkling Champagne, such a meticulous student as Frère Pierre did not make note of it in his lengthy treatise. Unless, that is, fizziness was still considered a fault, which Pérignon was trying to avoid, not induce. There would have been little point in Frère Pierre mentioning a common fault, particularly if his former master had failed to overcome it.

So even if the consensus is right, perhaps Dom Pérignon made sparkling Champagne by accident, as many others had, and his experiments with *verre anglais* and cork stoppers were merely to contain the wild beast of refermentation. We do not have any notes written by Dom Pérignon himself. No doubt such a scrupulous person would have recorded his findings, if only to pass on to his successors, but apart from a handful of letters to customers, any such papers are presumed to have perished in one of the many lootings of Hautvillers. Maybe they still exist in a dusty pile in a dark corner of somebody's attic waiting to be discovered. If they are, then one day we will know for sure. But even if Dom Pérignon did not purposefully make sparkling Champagne, such wines did begin to emerge *circa* 1695, contemporary with the famous monk's other achievements.

Although the *Méthode Champenoise* should be known as 'Merret's Method' or the *Méthode Anglaise*, it was inevitable that it would be named after the earliest and most famous sparkling wine in the world. Sir George Etherege did after all write of *sparkling Champaign* in *The Man of Mode*, not sparkling English wine. Furthermore, Merret spoke of only the most rudimentary aspect of the *Méthode Champenoise*. It never was a revolutionary process, but an evolutionary one and one that took almost 200 years to unfold on a truly commercial scale, and continues to evolve to this day.

To take Merret's embryonic method, which can be equated to discovering the wheel, and develop it into the industrialised process that was in place in Champagne by the late 19th century took a series of sophistications. The three most important of these were:

1. **The *liqueur de tirage***
   The addition of sugar and yeast at the time of bottling to promote and guarantee a second fermentation.
2. **The concept of *dégorgement***
   Removing sediment from the bottle after the second fermentation, which required the invention of *remuage*.
3. ***Liqueur d'expédition***
   Added after disgorgement to sweeten the final product.

With these three embellishments, the *méthode champenoise* essentially came of age, guaranteeing that an absolutely limpid sparkling wine could be made with a predetermined strength of mousse and to the degree of sweetness desired.

THE *LIQUEUR DE TIRAGE*

As Merret pointed out in 1662, the English invented the concept of adding sugar to a finished wine in order to provoke a second fermentation, but it would always be a hit-or-miss affair until both the amount of sugar added could be quantified (Chaptal, 1801), and the basic function of yeast in the fermentation process was recognised (Pasteur, 1857).

The first reference in Champagne to the addition

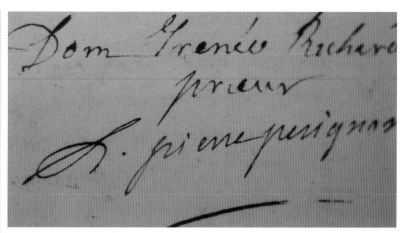

THE FAMOUS SIGNATURE OF DOM PÉRIGNON

of a crude *liqueur* prior to bottling was in 1877, when Professor Robinet of Epernay described the operation in his manual *Fabrication des Vins Mousseux*. He referred to it as the *liqueur de titrage*, which literally means 'the liquor that determines the strength of a wine', but with common usage the term was soon transformed into *liqueur de tirage* or 'bottling liquor'. Robinet discusses the subject as though it were common practice at the time, thus the *liqueur de tirage* must have been in use well before 1877. Most historians believe this practice was adopted in the early to mid-19th century, probably shortly after 1836 when Professor François invented a device called the *sucre-oenomètre*. This allowed the amount of sugar to be easily quantified in a practical environment, rather than under laboratory conditions. Thus for its first 140 years, sparkling Champagne was not the product of a second fermentation, but merely a continuation of the first fermentation. It was not until the 1880s that the use of a *liqueur de tirage* became widespread in the Champagne industry and took on board not just sugar, but yeast (to replace the natural yeast, most of which drops out prior to bottling).

THE CONCEPT OF *DÉGORGEMENT*, INCLUDING *REMUAGE*

Dégorgement literally means disgorgement, to dispel, and in Champagne specifically refers to the disposal of sediment caused by a second fermentation, the trick being to remove all of the sediment without losing any of the wine. Although *dégorgement* was thought to be practised by Dom Pérignon, albeit in a crude, intermediate sense, the technique was first documented by André Jullien in *Manuel du Sommelier* (1813). Apparently, when Hautvillers was renovated by Moët & Chandon, bottles were discovered stored with their necks stuck in a bed of sand. If this were indeed the case, then they were obviously kept like this to encourage the sediment to drift down to the base of the cork. However there is no suggestion that Dom Pérignon recorked his wines, thus it seems this was just a convenient way of getting rid of the sediment immediately prior to drinking.

Although developed after *dégorgement*, the technique known as *remuage* is inseparable from it, as its sole

purpose is to expedite the act of disgorgement on a commercial scale. Simply inverting bottles was inadequate because certain particles in the sediment would not descend to the base of the cork and remained firmly stuck to the inner surface of the bottle. The sediment created during second fermentation is composed of various waste products, several types of which possess a sticky character. To encourage these more cohesive particles to descend to the base of the cork requires a certain amount of physical persuasion. *Remuage* was developed by Veuve Clicquot at the very beginning of the 19th century as a method of supplying this encouragement.

Upon the death of her husband in 1805, the 27-year-old widow Nicole-Barbe Clicquot Ponsardin found herself in control of a major Champagne firm. She took personal charge of the cellars and, well aware of the problem posed by the obstinate particles of sediment which refused to fall easily, spent night and day trying to rid herself of this nuisance. It was her kitchen table that finally provided the ingenious solution. Taking it down to her cellars she cut holes in its surface to accommodate the inverted bottles of Champagne. Then she would periodically remove the inverted bottles from their positions, oscillate them, then replace them in the holes. By 1806 the Widow or *Veuve* as she was known, and her kitchen table were the talk of Reims, and by 1813 Jullien had included *remuage* in his description of *dégorgement*.

Although the system worked, it did not work well enough to satisfy the *Grande Dame*, so in 1810, she hired the services of a skilful *chef de caves* by the name of Antoine Müller, who involved himself in her experiments. In 1818 it was Müller, not Clicquot, who hit upon the supreme importance of cutting the holes in the table at an angle of 45°, a fact confirmed by a letter from Alfred Werlé, the son of one of the widow's associates. The angled cut of the hole enabled each bottle to start off at an angle of 45°, yet finish perpendicular. From this table-top operation to the far more efficient *pupitre* would seem a natural progression with hindsight, but it was not one Veuve Clicquot made either easily or quickly.

REPLICA OF THE ORIGINAL TABLE USED FOR REMUAGE (ABOVE LEFT) INVENTED BY THE VEUVE CLICQUOT (BELOW). ABOVE RIGHT SHOWS MODERN DAY PUPITRES

A *pupitre* consists of two heavy rectangular boards hinged together at the top to form an inverted V-shape. Each board contains 60 holes cut at 45°, which is exactly the same angle as the holes in Clicquot's table-top, but because the hinged boards also stand at an angle, the bottles go through almost 90° before ending up in a virtually perpendicular position, which allows more freedom and flexibility for the remuage. The pupitre can also process more bottles in less space. It is not certain who invented the pupitre or exactly when, but it was adopted by several Champagne houses just after Veuve Clicquot's *chef de caves* resigned in 1822, which suggests it was most probably Antoine Müller.

THE *LIQUEUR D'EXPÉDITION*

Long before 1801, when Chaptal advised on the addition of sugar to fermenting grape juice to increase a wine's potential alcohol, winemakers habitually added sugar after fermentation to sweeten the finished product. This was particularly prevalent in a northerly region like Champagne, where grapes struggled to ripen and wines could sometimes be green and tart.

It should also be understood that sparkling Champagne was originally a sweet wine. From the very beginning, its place at a meal was with the dessert, pushing to one side the former favourites of Lunel, Banyuls and Frontignan. Even when drier styles emerged, the habit of serving this wine at the end of the meal remained strong, which explains the Gallic perversion of drinking *brut* Champagne with sweet desserts today.

In *Oenologie Français*, which was published in 1827, Cavoleau declares that a dosage of sugar had been systematically applied to Champagne for at least 130 years, dating the *liqueur de tirage* from the very beginning of sparkling wine. Pierre-Jean-Baptiste Legrand d'Aussy declared in *Histoire de la vie privée de François depuis l'origine de la nation jusqu'à nos jours* (1782) that the second fermentation in bottle removed all trace of sugar from the wine, making it undrinkable unless adjusted with a little sugar. To add sugar, it first has to be dissolved in a wine of similar or compatible character, then a measured dose applied to each bottle of Champagne. This is a difficult operation because it causes excessive frothing, thus even though the practice was a common, stretching back to the earliest days of sparkling Champagne, it could not be applied on a commercial scale until 1844, when the first *dosage* machine was invented.

As soon as the *liqueur d'expédition* was firmly integrated in the manufacturing method, producers realised that they could dramatically change the taste of a Champagne by incorporating various esoteric ingredients. The classic components, however, were described by Charles Tovey in 1870 as the 'very finest sugar candy, the best Champagne, and the oldest and finest cognac', and of these, sugar was of paramount importance. Brandy was specifically used in those days because Champagnes were so sweet. Such a vast quantity of sugar had to be used for the sweetest Champagnes that the alcoholic strength was greatly diminished and this was redressed by incorporating an ingredient of disproportionately high alcoholic strength: brandy.

For the *dosage* of sweet Champagnes, therefore, brandy was as vital as sugar, but it was not very long before the champenois were trying out all sorts of esoteric additives. In *Traité théorie et practique du travail des vins* (1873), Maumené listed the following additional ingredients 'normally found' in the *liqueur d'expédition*: Port, Cognac, *Fismes dye* [elderberry], kirsch, raspberry brandy and saturated solutions of alum, tartaric acid and tannin. And although by this time the English had no need to use the Merret Method to make Champagne brisk and sparkling, because it already was, the English were still meddling with their imported wines. As William Thackeray, the famous 19th century novelist observed, 'Incomparably the best champagne I know is to be found in England. It is the most doctored, the most brandied, the most barley-sugared, the most winey wine in the world.' With all the bits and pieces that Maumené noted, sweet Champagne in England must have contained precious little Champagne *per se*, although the vogue for drier styles would eventually result in a much more natural product.

INDUSTRIALISATION OF THE *MÉTHODE CHAMPENOISE*

The rudimentary *méthode champenoise* that existed at the beginning of the 19th century was adequate for that era's annual production of just 600,000 bottles, but as soon as the first *dosage* machines appeared in the 1840s, the output of sparkling Champagne surged upwards to six million bottles. However, it took the industry-wide use of a measured *liqueur de tirage* and the development of a bulk form of *dégorgement* for production to reach 20 million bottles by the 1880s. At this juncture, the *méthode champenoise* was, for all intents and purposes, as complete as it is today, and all the sophistications that have occurred since have not been developed to perfect the product, but rather to increase its scale of production, decrease the amount of time it takes to produce a marketable

SEDIMENT COLLECTED IN THE NECK OF THE BOTTLE (ABOVE) IS REMOVED BY DISGORGEMENT (RIGHT AND BELOW)

product, thereby reducing the amount of capital tied up in stocks, and lowering labour and other costs.

Dégorgement à la glace was the Rubicon in terms of developments in the *méthode champenoise*, raising standards in the limpidity of Champagne on the one hand, yet enabling the industry to grow at a tremendous rate. As output started to soar prior to this pivotal invention, the largest firms found that old-style *dégorgement à la volée* caused serious hold-ups in the production process and, because the operation demanded a certain skill, the number of *dégorgeurs* could not easily be increased. What was needed was a new, faster form of *dégorgement* that could be performed by unskilled workers, and such a system was devised in 1884 by a Belgian called Armand Walfart.

Walfart invented *dégorgement à la glace*, which involves a shallow, refrigerated bath that is filled with brine and kept at a temperature well below freezing. The necks of the inverted bottles are dipped in to this brine for a minute or so, which freezes the wine and sediment collected at the base of the cork. It is not frozen solid, rather a frosty film coats the inside neck of the bottle, enveloping the sediment over the base of the cork. This enables the *dégorgeur* to bring the bottle back to its upright position without disturbing the sediment. The frosty film retains sufficient tension to remain adhered to the bottle while the cork is extracted, but when the cork is removed, the internal pressure ejects the sediment as a pellet of half-frozen slush. The freezing temperature creates a localised effect on the internal pressure, subduing it so that the rest of the wine does not escape, hence there is no spray of foam and the bottle may be topped up and recorked with a minimal loss of wine or pressure.

Anybody seeing this operation in the modern bottling halls of Champagne today will find it difficult to imagine that it was invented in the 19th century. But the house of Henri Abelé (which Antoine Müller became joint owner of in 1834) first used *dégorgement à la glace* in 1884 and by 1891 Moët & Chandon and Gallice et Cie (later to become Perrier Jouët) had also adopted the process, although Walfart did not patent it until 1896.

By the end of the century, production had increased to 30 million bottles, Champagne was enjoying a golden era, and *dégorgement à la glace* was sufficiently well established for it to be described by Ernest and Arthur Vizetelly in their book *Wines of France*. It remains the most widely practised form of *dégorgement* today.

HOW SPARKLING WINES ARE MADE

ALL WINES, WHETHER STILL OR SPARKLING, ARE THE RESULT OF FERMENTATION, WHEN YEAST CELLS CONVERT SUGAR INTO ALCOHOL AND CARBONIC GAS. BUT THE PRODUCTION OF SPARKLING WINES USUALLY INVOLVES TWO SEPARATE FERMENTATIONS, THE SECOND OF WHICH IS CONDUCTED IN A SEALED CONTAINER TO ENSURE THAT THE CARBONIC GAS DOES NOT ESCAPE. BY PUTTING A LID ON A VAT OR A CORK IN A BOTTLE, THE CARBONIC GAS REMAINS DISSOLVED IN THE WINE ITSELF UNTIL THAT LID OR CORK IS REMOVED. WHEN THE PRESSURE IS RELEASED, THE GAS RUSHES OUT OF THE WINE IN THE FORM OF BUBBLES. THE PRODUCTION OF ALMOST ALL SPARKLING WINES IS BASED ON THIS BASIC PRINCIPLE, AND USES ONE OF THE FOUR FOLLOWING METHODS.

1. THE *MÉTHODE CHAMPENOISE*

Also referred to as *méthode traditionnelle, méthode classique, méthode traditionnelle classique* or one of the *crémant* appellations (France), *metodo classico, metodo tradizionale* or *Talento* (Italy), *Método tradicional* (Spain), *Flashengärung nach dem Traditionellen Verfahren, Klassische Flashengärung* or *Traditionnelle Flashengärung* (Germany) and *Cap Classique* (South Africa).

This term indicates a sparkling wine which has undergone a second fermentation in the bottle in which it is sold. It is sometimes referred to as 'bottle-fermented', which is an easily understood term that has a certain quality ring to it, and would make an expressive universal term in English speaking countries if it were enforced by law to mean, and only to mean 'Individually fermented in this bottle'. Unfortunately there is currently no legal definition, and the term 'bottle-fermented' can often be found on wines which have been made by the 'transfer method' (*see below*).

Ironically, the term *méthode champenoise* is not permitted to be used in any member state of the European Union for any sparkling wine other than Champagne. Ironically because, of course, winemakers in Champagne do not need to use the term, and never do.

TRADITIONAL FERMENTATION IN BARRELS IN THE CELLARS OF CHAMPAGNE KRUG

While there are some poor wines made by the *méthode champenoise*, all the best brut style sparkling wines are made by this method because it is the only one that possesses a quality connotation. *See A Step-By-Step Guide To Méthode Champenoise, p.16.*

2. *TRANSVASAGE* OR TRANSFER METHOD

This refers to a wine produced through a second fermentation in bottle, but (and this is the catch) not the bottle in which it is sold. It is fermented in one bottle, transferred into a vat where it is filtered, then transferred into another bottle. The wine is kept under pressure at all times, but inevitably there is some loss of gas.

Transfer method is used either for commercial quality sparkling wines (which in the New World are sometimes confusingly described as bottle-fermented) or in Champagne where normal-sized bottles are used to fill airline splits (quarter-bottles), which are so small they are too impractical to riddle. *Transvasage* is also used in Champagne to fill Jeroboam size bottles or larger, which are disproportionately expensive, yet have a relatively high incidence of breakage when fermentation takes place in bottle. They are also as difficult to riddle as the tiny airline splits, but for the opposite reason. A few houses do ferment in very large bottles, but none ferments in anything smaller than a half-bottle (and most of those are filled by *transvasage* machines).

3. *CUVE CLOSE, CHARMAT* OR TANK METHOD

This is used for the bulk production of inexpensive sparkling wines that have undergone second fermentation in large tanks prior to filtration and bottling under pressure. Contrary to popular belief, there is no evidence to suggest that this is an intrinsically inferior method of sparkling wine production. It is entirely because this is a bulk production method that it attracts mediocre base wines and encourages a quick throughput. Also, contrary to classic *méthode champenoise*, the second fermentation is often conducted at a higher temperature than the first. A *cuve close* produced from the finest base wines, put through a slow, cool second fermentation, and given the autolytic benefit

of at least three years on its lees before bottling could well be indistinguishable from the 'real thing'.

4. THE RUSSIAN CONTINUOUS METHOD

An ingenious adaptation of *cuve close*, the Russian Continuous Method involves a series of interconnected pressurised tanks. Still base wine and a measured dose of yeast and sugar are fed on a continuous basis into the first tank, where they are mixed, and fermentation commences. The fermenting wine then passes into a number of tanks containing wood shavings, which are there to collect the dead yeast cells from current and previous fermentations. This process, although not very long, also adds an element of lees character to the wine.

Some writers have suggested that the Russian Continuous Method is intrinsically superior to *cuve close* because the wine has more contact with the dead yeast cells, but as it takes just three weeks to go through the entire series of tanks, it is in fact intrinsically inferior. Both methods are for bulk production, thus low quality base wines are used. If top quality base wines are used, a *cuve close* product can be improved by keeping the wine in tank for two years or more, and stirring up the lees with a paddle to effect greater contact, whereas the Russian Continuous Method cannot. If it could, it would not be continuous!

There are two further methods of producing sparkling wine which do not involve a second fermentation.

5. *MÉTHODE ANCESTRALE*

Historically known as the *méthode rurale*, this was the precursor of *méthode champenoise*, involving no second fermentation as such, merely a continuation of the first fermentation, the wine having been bottled prior to its termination. Variants of this format are still used today, albeit for a few obscure wines restricted primarily to southern France (Limoux in Languedoc–Roussillon, Die in the Rhône, Gaillac in southwest France, Bugey in Savoie).

PRESSURE TANKS FOR MAKING ASTI SPUMANTE AT MARTINI & ROSSI, PIEMONTE, ITALY

WINES MADE BY THE RUSSIAN CONTINUOUS METHOD AT J M FONSECA, AZEITO, PORTUGAL

6. CARBONATION

The cheapest method of putting bubbles into wine is, simply, by injecting it with carbon dioxide. Because this is the method used to make lemonade, it is incorrectly assumed that the bubbles achieved through carbonation are large and short-lived. They can be, especially in fully sparkling wines made by this method, since the release of carbonated gas at fully sparkling wine pressure results in a quick and uneven flow of carbon dioxide, but at *pétillant* and lower pressures, modern carbonation plants have the ability to induce the tiniest of bubbles, even to the point of imitating the 'prickle' of wine bottled *sur lie*.

FERMENTATION TANKS AT DOMAINE MUMM, CALIFORNIA

1. VITICULTURE: THE VENDANGE   2. VINIFICATION: CLARIFYING AND BLENDING   3. REMUAGE IN PUPITRES AND DISGORGEMENT

A STEP-BY-STEP GUIDE TO MÉTHODE CHAMPENOISE

THE MÉTHODE CHAMPENOISE IS THE MANNER BY WHICH A WINE IS MADE SPARKLING THROUGH THE INVOCATION OF A SECOND FERMENTATION INSIDE THE BOTTLE IN WHICH IT IS SOLD. ALTHOUGH AT ITS MOST BASIC LEVEL THIS PRODUCTION PROCESS WAS PRACTISED AS EARLY AS 1662, THE MORE SOPHISTICATED COMBINATION OF TECHNIQUES THAT COMPRISE THE MÉTHODE CHAMPENOISE TODAY WERE ACCUMULATED DURING THE 250 YEAR-LONG PERFECTION PROCESS OF CHAMPAGNE ITSELF. THEY INCLUDE A NUMBER OF VARIATIONS THAT ARE PRACTISED BY PRODUCERS OF SPARKLING WINES THROUGHOUT THE WORLD.

YEASTS

The yeasts used for fermentation may be divided into two categories: natural yeasts and cultured yeasts. Natural yeasts are found adhering to the *pruina*, a waxy substance that covers the skin of ripe grapes and other fruits. Cultured yeasts are thoroughbred strains of formerly natural wine yeasts which have been raised in a laboratory. Some cultured yeasts, such as those used for Champagne, have been developed for particular situations. There are numerous specialist Champagne yeasts available and they have various different properties, but they all share one thing in common – an aptitude for low-temperature, high-pressure fermentation in bottle. They are also quite adept at performing regular fermentations, thus most *méthode champenoise* producers, both in Champagne and throughout the rest of the world, tend to use cultured Champagne yeasts for both first and second fermentations. Indeed, unless a sparkling wine is the product of a single vineyard or estate, there is little point in using natural yeast for the first fermentation.

THE FIRST FERMENTATION

The initial fermentation takes place *en masse* in all manner of vessels, from huge, temperature-controlled, stainless-steel vats to small oak barrels, the latter being far less common these days, although they are currently enjoying a mini-vogue in Champagne itself. Anyone tasting the wine at this stage would be unmoved, dismayed even, by its ordinariness, even at the greatest Champagne houses. The wine is dry and tart, very acid to taste and relatively neutral in character. It must have no residual sugar since this would interfere with the precise amount of sugar

DÉGORGEMENT BY HAND, TOP, AND FERMENTING WINES IN STAINLESS STEEL TANKS, BOTTOM

added for the second fermentation; the acidity needs to be high to keep the wine fresh throughout the long bottle-ageing process; and there should be no distinctive aromas or flavours to inhibit the subtle effects of autolysis (*see* p.18).

The first fermentation is short and simple, while the second should be as long, cool and complex as possible. Although the complexity of a fine quality sparkling wine must be inherent in the grapes used, it should never manifest itself in the base wine. True complexity is a long-term process, and in a sparkling wine it is kick-started by the second fermentation.

Many sparkling wines undergo malolactic fermentation, which is known as MLF for short. This is not a true fermentation, but another biochemical process involving various bacteria rather than yeasts. MLF converts hard malic acid to soft lactic acid. Carbonic gas (carbon dioxide) is also produced, giving the impression of a true alcoholic fermentation as it bubbles away. Very few Champagne houses do not use MLF, but Bollinger, Gratien, Krug and Lanson are the most notable exceptions.

MLF is often used in the New World to impart some instant complexity, but the results can be clumsy. This is not merely because the build-up of complexity should be a long-term process. New World grapes are often harvested early in order to achieve the same alcoholic degree and total acidity as Champagne grapes. They therefore possess far more malic acid, consequently the resulting wines undergo too much MLF and this destroys the elegance and finesse. Some New World winemakers are more aware of this problem than others, and the very best producers now apply MLF with a much lighter touch than before.

DESPITE THE INDUSTRIALISATION OF THE MÉTHODE CHAMPENOISE, THE PROCESS REMAINS ESSENTIALLY THE SAME AS ILLUSTRATED IN THIS SERIES OF 19TH CENTURY MOSAICS THAT ADORN THE STREET ENTRANCE TO JACQUART'S OLD CELLARS

4. CORKING AND ATTACHING THE WIRE MUZZLE

5. HABILLAGE: LABELLING AND PACKING

ASSEMBLAGE – THE CONSTRUCTION OF THE *CUVÉE*

The blending of the base wine from its many component parts is called the *assemblage*. Few sparkling wine producers take the *assemblage* quite as seriously as the champenois, who will construct a non-vintage *cuvée* from as many as 70 different base wines. These wines vary by virtue of their different grape varieties and the villages or *crus* they come from, plus various reserve wines (see later) from previous vintages. Most Champagne producers have developed their own distinctive house style over the years, and the *assemblage* is their means of achieving a consistent product from wines that can differ radically every year. It may sound impossible and sometimes it is, but paradoxically the greater the number of wines and the wider the variation amongst them, the easier it is to achieve a similar product from year to year. This is why the best Champagne houses ferment the greatest number of wines separately.

The art of the sparkling winemaker is not just to blend a consistent product, but to achieve a quality that is greater than the sum of its parts. Furthermore he or she has to blend a product that is intrinsically out of balance because it will only achieve its correct balance after the second fermentation – which adds 1.5% of alcohol to the structure, up to six atmospheres of carbonic gas, and accentuated acidity – has taken place and the sugar that will be part of the dosage of even a brut-style Champagne has been added.

While the champenois will literally blend fractions of numerous vats, and entirely reject some wines (although they will be used for a different *cuvée*, marketed under a cheaper brand, or sold off in bulk), the concept of blending generally encountered elsewhere is often no more involved than the thought of mixing together the contents of all available tanks. Such winemakers have yet to learn that the intricacies of true *assemblage* are not only necessary for crafting the same style of non-vintage sparkling wine on an annual basis, but are also vital to achieve the desired structure and style of any sparkling wine, even one made from a single variety, vintage and vineyard. Indeed, the more restricted the basic components are, the more the winemaker must strive to create every conceivable form of building block. This can be achieved by separating the same variety grown on different rootstocks, different soils, or in different parts of the vineyard.

In Champagne, the *assemblage* usually takes place

BASE WINES FROM VEUVE CLICQUOT: AS MANY AS 60 MAY BE USED IN ANY ONE BLEND

in the first few months of the year following the harvest. At its most basic, it is a matter of balancing the characteristics of two or more of the three available grape varieties: Chardonnay, Pinot Noir and Meunier. Chardonnay is often steely in its youth, and has the most potential longevity, keeping Champagne fresh as it matures. It also has the greatest finesse, although arguably it is less complex than the Pinot Noir. Pinot Noir is no ephemeral beast itself, and does not lack a certain finesse but, perhaps more importantly, what it does provide is much of the backbone, body and structure of a classic Champagne. Meunier has flowery notes on the nose, and a youthful fruitiness on the palate.

When blending these three grapes, the winemaker not only has to take into account their different basic characteristics, but must also bear in mind that while the Meunier develops almost immediate appeal, the Pinot Noir takes over after a couple of years, with the Chardonnay being the last variety to kick-in. While the Meunier gives way to the Pinot Noir, the latter remains strong and the Chardonnay has to nudge in to share the stage with its classic partner. In Champagne, the numerous villages with their different soils and micro-climates exert different influences over each variety, all of which the winemaker must be aware.

In almost every wine region of the world, Chardonnay and Pinot Noir represent the most widely used varieties for the production of premium quality sparkling wine. Sometimes their roles of finesse vis-à-vis body are reversed, and the role of Meunier is often played by other grapes.

Reserve wines are quite literally wines kept in reserve from previous years. They are essential for the blending of non-vintage *cuvées*, particularly in Champagne where they can only be used in non-vintage blends because a vintage *cuvée* must be made entirely from the year in question. Outside of Champagne, however, the regulations for vintage authenticity vary (*eg*, 85% of the year indicated in the EU, 95% in the USA) and reserve wines can be just as useful in the blending of vintage sparkling wine as non-vintage.

The job of reserve wine is similar to that of the *dosage* in that they both make the sparkling wine easier to drink at a younger age. Reserve wines also provide a certain mellowness and complexity, which is why it is generally considered that the more added the better. But for every iota of instant mellowness and complexity received, there is a loss of autolytic influence, and thus a trade-off in potential finesse.

Reserve wines are kept in several ways: in tank under inert conditions, in casks of various size or, in the case of Champagne Bollinger, they are bottled in magnums with a tiny amount of sugar and yeast to promote a slight *pétillance* for added freshness, once a common practice throughout Champagne.

The importance of an intricate and meaningful *assemblage* is only just being appreciated by premium quality sparkling wine producers outside of the Champagne region.

THE SECOND FERMENTATION

After the *assemblage*, the wine undergoes a gentle fining and a day or two later, after it has thrown a light sediment, it is racked into a clean vessel. It is here that the *liqueur de tirage* – a mixture of still Champagne, sugar, selected yeasts, yeast nutrients and a clarifying agent such as bentonite – is added. The amount of sugar used depends on the degree of effervescence required (*pétillant, crémant* or fully *mousseux*). The wines are then bottled and sealed with a crown-cap, which holds in place a small plastic pot to catch the sediment. The second fermentation is often referred to as the *prise de mousse* (indeed some Champagne yeasts are even sold by that name), which literally means 'capturing the sparkle'.

POIGNETAGE AND REMUAGE

The duration of the second fermentation depends primarily on temperature; the cooler it is the longer it takes, and the longer it takes the more complex it becomes. A fast first fermentation results in more biochemical processes occurring. If this is followed by a cool, slow second fermentation, the result will be a more complex wine. In Champagne the temperature is always under 12°C, and quite often 10°C or cooler. In most cases the second fermentation lasts for between ten days and three months.

Progress of the fermentation of a particular *cuvée* can be monitored by the use of a special pressure gauge that fits into the bottle-neck. When fermentation is complete, the bottles can be transferred to *pupitres* or pallets to undergo *remuage*. However some producers, particularly in Champagne, age the wines for several more months, or even years before this stage. In this case, the bottles are stacked horizontally; traditionally in Champagne such wines were built into huge space-saving piles, each layer separated by thin wooden lathes or *lattes*, hence the wines at this stage are referred to as *vins sur lattes*, and they are still known as *vins sur lattes* even when they are stored horizontally in pallets.

It was customary to dismantle and rebuild these vast piles of *vins sur lattes* occasionally, shaking each bottle in the process, which helps the autolysis and prevents the sediment sticking fast to the inner surface of the bottle. Called *poignetage*, this used to be a dangerous task, as imperfect bottles could shatter and cellarworkers

MAGNUMS OF CHAMPAGNE MATURING ON THEIR LEES IN THE BOLLINGER CELLARS

would often wear protective iron masks. Although not as romantic, *poignetage* can be performed by the pallet-load today as cellarworkers move and re-stack them using forklifts which they drive around the cellars at maniacal speeds.

After ageing *sur lattes* the wines are either put into *pupitres*, which are described in *The Concept of Dégorgement (see p. 11)*, or moved from storage pallets to *girasols* or computer-controlled gyropalettes. In the latter case, the most efficient wineries use the same palettes for *sur lattes* as they do for *remuage* in the gyropalette machines, which cuts down the manual labour of emptying one palette to fill another. But gyropalettes are made of metal and are not only more expensive but also less efficient in terms of the vertical space they occupy, unless a winery is specifically designed and built to accommodate them.

The Gyropalette is a champenois development of the *girasol*, a Catalan invention of the 1970s. The *girasol* consists of a palette sitting on a hexagonal frame, which a cellarworker occasionally nudges from time to time. The gyropalette uses a computer program to replicate this unskilled labour for many machines and can, of course, be working 24 hours a day – it is thus quicker, and more efficient, (although no more intelligent). Both devices, computerised and manual, replicate the effects – not the movements – of *remuage*, which riddles the bottles to loosen the sediment, encouraging it to move to the neck of the bottle, where it is allowed to collect. Manual *remuage*, turning bottles in *pupitres*, takes about eight weeks to complete, while *remuage* using gyropalettes or *girasol* takes just eight days.

There is another technique which avoids the process of *remuage* altogether. Porous yeast capsules, called *billes*, are added to the wine with the *liqueur de tirage* before the second fermentation. These little balls attract the sediment which sticks to them. The bottles are then simply inverted and the sediment-laden *billes* descend into the neck in a matter of seconds, ready to be disgorged.

YEAST AUTOLYSIS

After *remuage*, the wine may undergo a further period of ageing *sur point* (in a fully inverted position) before the sediment is removed. Depending on the intrinsic quality of a sparkling wine and its suitability to lees-ageing, the longer it is aged *sur lattes* or *sur point* the better. The benefits of lees-ageing are derived from autolysis, which is the enzymatic breakdown of dead yeast cells that occurs several months after the second fermentation. Autolysis usually lasts for between four and five years, but has been known to continue for as long as ten years. The process produces several effects:

1. Releases reducing enzymes which inhibit oxidation.
   Reduces the need for sulphur dioxide.
2. Absorbs certain essential yeast nutrients.
   The main reason why the dosage does not re-ferment.

3 Increases amino acids and other nitrogenous matter.

These are the precursors to the inimitable 'champagne' character, which includes the acacia-like aroma and finesse noticed in a recently disgorged Champagne.

4 Produces acetal compounds.

Possibly adds a biscuity or brandy-like complexity.

5 Produces mannoprotein MP32.

Eliminates or reduces tartrate precipitation.

If a sparkling wine is kept on its lees after autolysis has finished, it merely remains fresher than the same wine disgorged at an earlier date. However, the longer it is kept in this state, the more rapid its evolution will be after it is disgorged. This is because the older a sparkling wine gets, the more sensitive it becomes to the sudden shock of exposure to the air during the disgorgement process. So, although a great Champagne kept on its lees for 20 years will be infinitely fresher after it has been disgorged than a bottle of the same wine that was disgorged when only five years old, after a further five years, when they are both 25 years old, the late-disgorged example will already seem older than the normally disgorged version. The late-disgorged Champagne could be over the hill by its 30th or 35th year, whereas the normally disgorged version might slowly improve until it is 50 years old or more. If the same Champagne happened to be disgorged at 50 years, instead of 20, then it could deteriorate in a matter of months or even weeks.

At 20 years old, the normally disgorged Champagne would be very toasty or biscuity, whereas the Champagne kept on its lees and not disgorged until 20 years old would have none of these mellowing aromas which are essentially created after the oxidative effect of disgorgement. A Champagne left on its lees until 50 years would probably have some, albeit discreet, toasty nuances.

DISGORGEMENT AND CORKING

With the sediment collected in the plastic pot at the bottom of the inverted bottle, it now has to be disposed of with a minimal loss of wine. The method used today is known as *dégorgement à la glace*, which involves the immersion of the bottle neck in

REMUAGE BY HAND AT CHAMPAGNE ROEDERER, ABOVE; AND USING GYROPALLETES, BOTTOM LEFT

SPARKLING WINE CORKS, FROM LEFT TO RIGHT, MUMM CUVÉE NAPA (CALIFORNIA), CHAMPAGNE, AND FERRARI (TRENTO, ITALY)

SEDIMENT FROZEN IN THE NECK OF A BOTTLE, WAITING TO BE DISGORGED

a shallow bath of freezing brine *(see Industrialisation of the Méthode Champenoise, p.13).*

After disgorgement, before corking, the bottles are topped up to the same level and the *liqueur d'expédition* is added. In all cases except Extra Brut, this will include a small amount of sugar: the younger the wine, the greater the *dosage* of sugar required to balance its youthful acidity. High acidity is crucial to any fine quality brut-style sparkling wine as it keeps the wine fresh during its lengthy bottle-ageing method of production and during any additional cellaring by the consumer. It also carries the flavour to the palate through the tactile effect caused by thousands of minuscule bursting bubbles. Acidity rounds out with age, thus the older the wine is when it is disgorged, the smaller the *dosage* required. However, some sugar is always necessary for the development of classic post-disgorgement aromas.

Although a sparkling wine cork has a distinctive mushroom-like appearance, prior to bottling it looks like any other cork, although significantly fatter. A metal cap is placed on top of the cork, and the cork is inserted for half its length into the neck of the bottle. The cork is then pounded so that the top half is too fat to go any further into the neck, and a wire muzzle secures it to the bottle. The bottle is then shaken to homogenize the wine and *liqueur*.

The best *cuvées* are kept for at least a further three months prior to shipment, as this helps marry the *liqueur*, but it will take a further two years or more for a truly fine sparkling wine to develop mellow, toasty and biscuity aromas. Just as autolysis is crucial prior to disgorgement, so *Reaction Maillard* is essential for the development of post-disgorgement aromas.

Commonly associated with part of the raisining effect that darkens dried fruit, the importance of Reaction Maillard in the marrying of the *dosage*, and the complex aromas that slowly develop afterwards, has only recently been recognised. It involves a reaction between sugars and amino acids in the wine, producing numerous compounds, some of which are now believed to be responsible for the toasty, roasted, and vanilla aromas in wines that have been given some bottle age.

THE ELUSIVE QUALITY FACTOR

SOME PEOPLE BELIEVE THERE IS NO SUCH THING AS INTRINSIC QUALITY IN WINE. THEY SAY THAT PREFERENCES ARE ENTIRELY A MATTER OF PERSONAL TASTE AND ARGUE THAT IF ONE PERSON LIKES WINE A WHILE ANOTHER PREFERS WINE B, NO ONE HAS THE RIGHT TO SAY WHICH IS THE BETTER QUALITY. SPLITTING HAIRS BETWEEN WINES OF SIMILAR QUALITY, THEY SAY, MERELY CONFUSES THE ISSUE. BUT QUALITY IS INTRINSIC TO VIRTUALLY EVERYTHING, INCLUDING THE BASIC STAPLES. IF THERE ARE SUCH THINGS AS GOOD AND POOR QUALITY CABBAGES, POTATOES AND CEREALS, THEN THERE ARE GOOD AND POOR QUALITY GRAPES, AND IF QUALITY IS INTRINSIC TO GRAPES, IT MUST ALSO BE INTRINSIC TO WINE.

Most experienced tasters would accept that a fine quality wine must have natural balance and finesse, and show a definite, distinctive and individual character within its own type or style. In sparkling wines of the classic brut style, the longer the wine needs to age on its lees and develop autolytic characters before it can be disgorged, the greater its quality. Likewise, the longer a wine takes to develop the mellow, complex, post-disgorgement bottle-aromas, the greater its quality. (Paradoxically, some wine will not improve by longer ageing.) This does not mean that early-drinking sparkling wines cannot be good quality, or that we should not enjoy them; they may not be of great quality, but it can sometimes be very easy to enjoy them. Indeed, early-drinking is almost always synonymous with easy-drinking.

QUALITY STARTS IN THE VINEYARD

The quality of grapes at harvest time represents the maximum potential of any wine that can be made from them. Every action taken after the moment of picking can only detract from that quality; the winemaker has no magical power to improve, only to limit the damage.

After a certain amount of damage-limitation, the effort required to claw back a few percentage points of potential quality is disproportionate to any improvement in the wine. However, it is relatively easy to substantially raise the intrinsic quality of the grapes themselves via viticultural practices.

Strangely, yield is one of the least important quality factors for sparkling wines. High yields are generally less harmful to the quality of white wines than they are to reds, and even less detrimental to that of sparkling whites, always providing the grapes attain reasonable sugar levels. This has been Champagne's saviour because, due to the vagaries of the region's knife-edge climate, the champenois tend to prune for a larger crop than necessary. Thus, when disaster hits, as it so often does, they are hopefully left with a normal size crop of fairly decent quality. Of course it is also true that when conditions are exceptional, the whole lot ripens, which explains why most great Champagne vintages have also been bumper harvests.

Viticultural factors that improve the quality of sparkling wines include the following:

CHARDONNAY GRAPES

PINOT NOIR GRAPES

Sparkling wine designated vineyards
This represents the most fundamentally important quality factor for sparkling wine. The natural balance of grapes grown specifically for sparkling wine is entirely different from the natural balance of the same varieties grown for still wine. This does not mean that for the ultimate quality sparkling wine an entire estate has to be devoted exclusively to it, or that a sparkling wine producer has to grow his own grapes – just that the vines used for sparkling wine production should be grown expressly and specially for that purpose.

Grape varieties must be relatively neutral for a classic brut-style sparkling wine, although more aromatic varieties are suited to the sweeter styles. Chardonnay and Pinot Noir are the greatest exponents of the brut style, and Chardonnay is often the most successful in regions that are least suited climatically to sparkling wine production. Meunier is a very good variety, but has been underrated because for many years the champenois tended to look down their noses at it, and are only now acknowledging its importance. Depending on the vineyard's location, other proven secondary varieties include Pinot Blanc, Pinot Gris, and Gamay.

For more information, *see Sparkling Wine Grape Varieties, p.317.*

Ripe grapes are essential for sparkling wine. The widespread misconception that early-harvested or even unripe grapes are suitable for sparkling wine originated in famous New World wine regions. With climates too hot for this style, the grapes ripen far too quickly, with sugars increasing and acidity dropping at such a rapid rate that any grapes required for sparkling wine had to be harvested early.

Harvesting must be by hand. Taking into account all the pros and cons of machine-harvesting, and despite the technological advancements found in the latest equipment, the one wine for which grapes should never be machine-harvested is a top quality sparkling wine. Bunches should be collected in small crates which do not crush the grapes when stacked, and delivered to the press house as quickly as possible.

1. THE VILLAGE OF BARR, ALSACE WITH GRAND CRU VINEYARDS BEHIND
2. HARVESTING GRAPES IN THE DOMAINE CHANDON VINEYARDS, CALIFORNIA

3. LATE AUTUMN AT THE BRANCOTT ESTATE VINEYARDS, IN MONTANA, MARLBOROUGH, NZ, WITH SNOW ON THE MOUNTAINS IN THE BACKGROUND

SPARKLING WINE VINEYARDS AROUND THE WORLD

4. AUTUMNAL VINES ON THE SLOPES IN OLTROVO PAVESE, ITALY
5. PINOT NOIR OUTSIDE THE VISITOR CENTRE AT DENBIES, ENGLAND

6. CHARDONNAY GROWING IN THE CHALK RICH SOIL OF THE CHAMPAGNE REGION
7. BODEGAS SANT SADURNI D'ANOIA, CATALONIA, SPAIN

Pressing must be of whole bunches only, and performed as quickly and as softly as possible. Sparkling wine grapes are never de-stemmed because the fibrous material creates a network of canals through which the juice rapidly drains – particularly advantageous for black grape varieties, as it avoids coloration. The best press for this job is Champagne's traditional *coquard* press, despite its 17th century technology (itself merely a flattened adaption of the Mediaeval basket press), followed closely by modern pneumatic presses. A pneumatic press has a large central or lateral, taste-free rubber balloon which inflates, gently yet rapidly crushing the grapes against the inner sides of the press from where the juice swiftly drains away along channels and through ducts. Sparkling wine presses are programmed with a CIVC-chip to replicate the *coquard*'s complex series of pressing and breaking-up operations.

Natural settling of the grape juice prior to the first fermentation is essential. In Champagne this is called *débourbage*, or cleansing, and consists of gently chilling the juice, which encourages particles of grapeskin and other impurities to settle, after which the clearer juice is drained off.

Minimum fining and filtration should be used as these procedures remove too much of the solids in the wine, and solids are required for the more complex biochemical processes of the second fermentation and autolysis. A double *débourbage* prior to the first fermentation is always preferable to fining after the fermentation, as all unwanted solids drop out in the sediment after the second fermentation anyway.

Base wines with an alcohol level of 10.5 – 11% are the ideal for brut-style sparkling wines, since any lower and the wines will lack body, yet any higher and the second fermentation, which adds a further 1.5% of alcohol, could be problematical.

Chaptalisation? It is an intriguing thought that we have probably become conditioned to expect and appreciate the artificial body that chaptalisation (the addition of sugar to increase a wine's alcoholic strength) gives to Champagne, especially non-vintage, the alcoholic strength of which is increased by some 2% through this practice. Chaptalisation affects the balance of alcohol to fruit, and no doubt contributes to Champagne's famed 'lean' structure in the sense that it has less ripe-fruit plumpness than one would otherwise expect for its alcoholic strength. This is where the boundary between intrinsic quality and conditioned taste inevitably overlap.

High, ripe acidity is essential. Providing the grapes are physiologically ripe, it does not matter how high the acidity is, as this can always be balanced with the *dosage*. No form of deacidification other than MLF is ever applied to a top quality sparkling wine *(see Moderate malolactic and Balanced dosage below)*.

ESSENTIAL STEPS TO
CONTROL QUALITY:

HARVESTING BY HAND

PRESSING SOFTLY

CONTROLLED
FERMENTATIONS

APPROPRIATE AGEING
ON THE LEES

ACCURATE DOSAGE

GOOD MOUSSE
RETENTION

A fast and furious first fermentation is the most underestimated factor that can affect the quality of a premium quality sparkling wine. By fermenting at 18-20°C (65-68°F), which would be considered cool for a red wine, but quite warm for a white wine, the fermentation is relatively quick, and the base wine is kept simple for the potential of its complexity to be exploited during the later stages of the second fermentation, yeast autolysis, and post disgorgement ageing.

A low-temperature first fermentation should be avoided, as this depletes the wine of its essential solids and creates amylic (peardrop, bananas, bubblegum) aromas that prevent the crafting of any individual character and inhibit the development of mellow, complex post-disgorgement aromas.

Avoid using heavily toasted oak barrels for the first fermentation. Any toastiness in a sparkling wine should be a slow-developing post-disgorgement aroma. Instant toast on an inexpensive or a medium-priced still wine is fine, but it results in a blowsy sparkling wine that lacks finesse and will be prone to rapid ageing after disgorgement.

Moderate malolactic fermentation is essential, if any MLF is necessary at all, for finesse. MLF can add complexity to a sparkling wine, but it should never be too obvious. This is another reason why early-harvested or underripe grapes are unsuitable because with so much malic acid present the MLF is over-used and the result is too heavy-handed, undermining any finesse the wine might have. One of the most prominent by-products of MLF is diacetyl, the butteriness of which may be fine for still Chardonnay wines, but it should be avoided like the plague in Champagne, where a special cocktail of MLF bacteria is used to produce the lowest possible diacetyl content.

A meaningful *assemblage* is vital for any top quality sparkling wine. Unfortunately there is little evidence of this in many premium sparkling wines, not just from the New World, but also French sparkling wine appellations outside of Champagne.

A slow second fermentation at around 10°C, preferably lower, but never higher than 12°C, is *de rigueur* for a classic, slow developing, brut-style sparkling wine, but it has to follow a fast, relatively warm first fermentation.

Good mousse retention is sought by all sparkling wine producers, and some natural elements in wine, such as proteins, are good for the development of the mousse. This is another reason why base wines should undergo minimum processing. Winemakers who lack experience in making sparkling wine are victims of their own training, part of which encourages them to produce protein-stable wines.

However, many of the greatest Champagnes are protein-unstable prior to the second fermentation, and this causes no problem, as unstable proteins drop out in the sediment. Certain Champagne yeast cultures have been selected to promote mousse-positive compounds during autolysis.

Tiny bubbles signal quality in a sparkling wine because the smaller and more numerous they are the smoother the mousse. After disgorgement a sparkling wine should be star-bright, but the most gifted makers of sparkling wine are never concerned about minuscule amounts of suspended matter, as microscopic tartrate crystals, yeast wall cells, bentonite or *kieselguhr* and other colloids will act as the nuclei from which bubbles will form and lazily rise to the surface.

In Champagne, the level of bentonite in the *liqueur de tirage* used to be calculated on limpidity alone but since the early 1990s, the presence of desirable microscopic nuclei and mousse-positive compounds (*see above*) have been prime factors in adjusting the amount deemed necessary.

Appropriate ageing on the lees. This does not mean a minimum of three years, five years or any rigid amount of time. Although autolysis usually lasts for between four and five years, if it has not started within a year, it probably never will occur (normally due to over processing of the base wine). If it does start, most of the effects of the process occur during the first 12 months, and many wines cannot take, or do no benefit, from more than 18 to 24 months on their lees. Other than the legal minimum limits in Champagne, there are no fixed ageing periods which is why, for example, Bollinger released its 1982 Grande Année after three years, when its vintage Champagnes are usually at least five years old before they are sold. This is a lesson in flexibility that New World winemakers should learn from the champenois.

Balanced *dosage* is essential, but some sparkling wine producers seem to be frightened of sugar. Sparkling wines that receive minimal *dosage* not only have much less texture than those which receive a good brut *dosage* (up to 15g/l of residual sugar), they are also potentially less complex. Although the primary role of a *dosage* is to counter the acidity, and the younger the wine, the more aggressive the acidity, thus the more sugar required, this is not its only task. Recent research has shown that many of the post-disgorgement aromas that give a mature Champagne its complexity are the product of a biochemical process called Reaction Maillard *(see Disgorgement and corking, p.19)*.

Minimum post-disgorgement ageing is essential for a great Champagne or sparkling wine to achieve its full potential. Such wines, however, go through several stages before they reach this peak and some people prefer to drink them at a younger age. It is

RIPE CHARDONNAY GRAPES IN THE VINEYARD OF CODORNÍU NAPA, CALIFORNIA

understandable, therefore, that producers will want to get their products onto the shelf when they still appeal to these customers, which is why they are shipped three to six months after disgorgement, when the *dosage* has had little time to marry. The burden of ageing the best Champagnes and sparkling wines must therefore be borne by the consumer. I am somebody who appreciates perfectly matured Champagnes of great quality, but I also find some modest Champagnes immensely enjoyable immediately they are released, although it is true to say that as far as I am concerned most of the Champagnes I drink benefit from at least 12 months' additional cellaring.

Footnote
Having listed all the factors necessary for producing the best quality sparkling wines, I should advise readers that I have seen many producers doing the right things only to produce lousy wines. But what is really humbling is to discover, as I have, those who do it all wrong and yet occasionally manage to craft a delicious sparkling wine. When it comes to quality, man is the joker in the pack, and the only thing that links the winemakers who produce great wines by the most inappropriate means with those who do it correctly is passion. Not surprisingly, most of those who do things correctly yet produce boring wines tend to be devoid of this passion – they are qualified but cold, uncaring technocrats. This may be a very unscientific observation, but I believe it is true. When I tell people that I know of winemakers who sleep in sleeping bags next to their vats during the fermentation period, they are inclined to think I am exaggerating. In fact this is common in every winemaking country.

PUTTING ON THE STYLE

CONTRARY TO BELIEF IN SOME PARTS OF THE WORLD, CHAMPAGNE IS NOT A GENERIC TERM FOR ANY SPARKLING WINE; IT IS THE PROTECTED NAME OF A SPARKLING WINE PRODUCED FROM CERTAIN GRAPE VARIETIES GROWN WITHIN A SPECIFIC, DEMARCATED AREA OF NORTHERN FRANCE. IF NOT ALL SPARKLING WINES ARE CHAMPAGNE, THEN IT IS EQUALLY TRUE THAT CHAMPAGNE IS NOT JUST ONE STYLE OF WINE. THERE ARE MANY DIFFERENT STYLES, FROM THE MOST BASIC DIVISION BETWEEN VINTAGE AND NON-VINTAGE, TO BLANC DE BLANCS, BLANC DE NOIRS, ROSÉ, CRÉMANT, NON-DOSAGE (EXTRA BRUT), PRESTIGE CUVÉES, RED, SWEETER STYLES AND AROMATIC STYLES. THIS APPLIES TO SPARKLING WINES WHEREVER THEY ARE PRODUCED.

NON-VINTAGE

In theory this is a blend of wines from two or more years, although many Champagne growers also sell a wine from a single year as non-vintage, which is perfectly legal because they are not actually claiming it comes from any particular year. Non-vintage sparkling wines are common in Europe, especially Champagne, but they are almost non-existent in parts of the New World where the connotation of a vintage is such that a product not bearing one is automatically deemed inferior.

In Champagne a non-vintage blend is always based on wines made from the current harvest, to which the reserve wines are added, so providing the second most fundamental level of potential complexity to a sparkling wine (the first level being achieved by blending different grapes and areas), and a certain instant maturity. The amount and age of the reserve wines used can vary from just five or ten per cent of wine from the previous year, to 40 or 50 per cent from six or seven vintages going back 15 years or more.

The term 'non-vintage' sounds derogatory to many people, yet a blend of different years is the most classic of Champagnes, and the equivalent French term of *sans année* or 'without year' provides a subtle but important difference in emphasis. All good non-vintage Champagnes benefit from an extra year or two cellarage and the very greatest (often prestige *cuvées* that are referred to as a multi-vintage or a blend of vintage years) can improve for as long as a great vintage Champagne.

THE TINY WALLED VINEYARD OF CLOS DU MESNIL, OWNED BY KRUG AND PLANTED WITH CHARDONNAY TO MAKE THE WORLD'S MOST EXPENSIVE CHAMPAGNE

VINTAGE

Vintage Champagne must by law be 100% from the year indicated, but other sparkling wines in the EU need only be 85% (which, ironically, is more of a blend than some non-vintage Champagne *cuvées*!). Elsewhere it varies; 95% in California, 85% in Australia, 75% in South Africa and so on. The vintage of any wines produced in a country with regulations that are not as strict as those in the EU must, however, be at least 85% if they are imported into any EU member state. The opposite applies in the USA where any imported wine merely has to conform to the standards set in the country of origin, even if they are inferior to domestic American regulations.

The implication of a vintage in Champagne is that the harvest in question was especially good and the wine produced does not require blending with other years. Some Champagne houses stick rigidly to declaring a vintage in only the greatest years, but many, sadly, do not, which is why we have seen vintage Champagnes from less than ideal years like 1978, 1980 and even 1984. There are certain cooperatives and growers who produce vintage Champagne virtually every year and in such circumstances the year merely becomes an indication of age, not quality. However, even in an authentic vintage, vintage Champagne is the result of selection and is thus a deliberate exaggeration, rather than a reflection, of the year in question. If vintage Champagne is superior to non-vintage, logic dictates that it is only because superior wines have

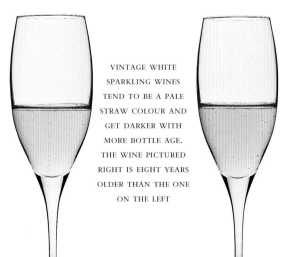

VINTAGE WHITE SPARKLING WINES TEND TO BE A PALE STRAW COLOUR AND GET DARKER WITH MORE BOTTLE AGE. THE WINE PICTURED RIGHT IS EIGHT YEARS OLDER THAN THE ONE ON THE LEFT

NON-VINTAGE WHITES TEND TO BE PALER IN COLOUR NO MATTER WHERE THEIR PROVENANCE

been selected for its production; volume-selling non-vintage Champagnes are still produced in even the greatest vintages. Any reserve wines added in the blending of non-vintage Champagnes are supposed to improve the product, thus the only difference between vintage and non-vintage Champagnes produced from the same year can only be the selection process of the base wine.

The character of a vintage Champagne is more autolytic than a non-vintage of the same age because it has no reserve wine mellowness. If you like those biscuity or toasty bottle aromas then you must store the vintage until it is eight to ten years from the date of harvest and has had at least three years ageing after it was purchased.

All the following styles of wine can also be either vintage or non-vintage.

BLANC DE BLANCS

Literally 'white of whites', a *blanc de blancs* simply means a white wine produced from white grapes, and it does not have to be sparkling. In Champagne this wine is produced entirely from Chardonnay, but for sparkling wines produced elsewhere it may be made from any white grape, either as a pure varietal or a blend.

A *blanc de blancs* Champagne possesses the greatest ageing potential of all sparkling wines, and although it may be made from grapes grown in any district of the region, the best examples are made with grapes from a small part of the Côte des Blancs between Cramant and Le Mesnil-sur-Oger. Like the Côte des Blancs, the Côte de Sézanne also specialises in grapes for *blanc de blancs* Champagne, but the wines made from these grapes are much more precocious, with attractive, tropical fruit flavours.

A classic *blanc de blancs* from the Côte des Blancs is a much tighter, more reserved style of wine that can appear to be austere and lacking in fruit in its youth. However, with sufficient age it develops a toasty richness that fills the mouth with a singular intensity of its fruit. Some of the classiest *blanc de blancs* from the best area of the Côte des Blancs develop a biscuity creaminess with complex aromas of hazelnuts, walnuts or brazil nuts.

Outside Champagne, pure Chardonnay *blanc de blancs* are generally the most successful classic brut style sparkling wines.

MOËT & CHANDON
VINEYARD AT AY,

BLANC DE NOIRS

Literally 'white of blacks', a *blanc de noirs* simply means a white wine produced from black grapes, and it does not have to be sparkling. In Champagne this wine is produced from either Pinot Noir or Meunier, or a blend of the two, but for sparkling wines produced elsewhere it may be made from any black grape, either as a pure varietal or a blend.

Throughout the New World, and in California in particular, *blanc de noirs* is used to describe slightly coloured wines that range from a sunset gold through various shades of rosé. But in France, where the term originated, the skill has always been to produce as light and as white a wine as possible by natural means.

In Champagne, a golden hue is acceptable, but any hint of pink would be regarded as clumsy by professional winemakers. The yardstick *blanc de noirs* Champagne is Bollinger's incredibly expensive Vielles Vignes Françaises, a unique example of super-ripe grapes from ungrafted Pinot Noir vines. This famous wine has given people the notion that all *blanc de noirs* are big, burly wines, but nothing can compare with it, and most other *blanc de noirs* Champagnes are unremarkable.

BLANC DE BLANCS WINES CAN VARY IN COLOUR CONSIDERABLY, DEPENDING ON THE BLEND AND PROVENANCE OF THE GRAPES

THERE CAN BE GREAT COLOUR VARIANCE IN THE COLOUR OF BLANC DE NOIRS CUVÉES DEPENDING ON THE CEPAGES USED IN THE BLEND

ROSÉ

Champagne rosé is an anomaly in EU wine law, as it is the only pink wine that may be made by blending white wine with a little red. All other rosés, whether still or sparkling, must be produced by macerating the juice and skins to extract pigments just as red wine itself is produced, but for a much shorter period. Some rosé Champagnes are, in fact, produced by maceration of the skins, but most are produced by adding a little red wine. Some critics believe that maceration is superior to blending white with red, but this is simply not true. It is possible to find good and poor quality examples produced by both methods, just as one can find rosé Champagnes that are light or dark in colour, and rich or delicate in flavour. Whenever I hear someone claim that maceration is intrinsically superior, I always issue a challenge: I'll set up a blind tasting of 20 rosé Champagnes and you tell me which ones have been made by maceration – no one has ever taken me up on it!

If there are any fairly common traits to pink Champagnes, whatever their method of production, it is that they have slightly less acidity than white Champagnes and are best drunk as young as possible. There are exceptions of course, but the lower acidity is due to the higher Pinot content and/or the addition of red wine. The reason why most rosé Champagnes should be drunk young is not because they won't last, but because they generally have a delicate, floral, perfumed style that has nothing to gain from laying down other than turning orange.

Many houses simply add a little red wine to their basic non-vintage or vintage Champagne *cuvées*, which is a cop-out and generally tends to produce the least inspiring wines of this category. Pink Champagne is a style, albeit a most varied one, and every winemaker has a duty to make something specific. Furthermore, if the non-vintage or vintage *cuvée* is a balanced product, it cannot be properly balanced again after red wine has been added.

The trouble is that most champenois do not take pink Champagne seriously – not even those who make the greatest pink Champagnes. In other sparkling wine areas the quality of this style is second only to that of *blanc de blancs*, but generally there is an inverted snobbery about rosé wines, whether they are still or sparkling.

THERE'S NO MISTAKING A SPARKLING RED!

PINK COVERS A WHOLE RANGE OF COLOURS FROM PALEST BLUSH TO SMOKED SALMON PINK AS THESE TWO VINTAGED ROSÉS DEMONSTRATE

CRÉMANT

Although a traditional champenois term, *crémant* disappeared from Champagne labels in the early 1990s by voluntary agreement. This occurred after the term was adopted for various French sparkling wines appellations, such as Crémant d'Alsace and Crémant de Bourgogne, following the EU ban on the use of the term *méthode champenoise*. Since only a small number of Champagne producers were actually using the term *crémant* at the time (just Besserat de Bellefon, Alfred Gratien, Abel Lepitre, Mumm de Cramant, and De Venoge spring to mind), having to drop it was of little commercial consequence, although historically it is a pity that it is no longer used in its appellation of origin. The few Champagne *crémants* that did exist are still made in the same style, and have merely been renamed. The most famous, Mumm's Crémant de Cramant, for example, is now sold as Mumm de Cramant.

A *crémant* should have a softer mousse; most Champagnes are fully sparkling or *grand mousseux*, with an internal pressure of between five and six atmospheres, but the old regulations determined that a Champagne *crémant* should have a pressure of just 3.6 atmospheres. To be a true *crémant*, however, it was not sufficient to have just a lower pressure; the word itself literally means 'creaming' and the mousse should unfold slowly, leaving a creamy *cordon* at the top of the wine around the inside of the glass, something that is very difficult to achieve. Beyond the various French sparkling wine appellations, the term is occasionally seen elsewhere, but few producers have a reputation for the style.

NON-*DOSAGE* (EXTRA BRUT)

This was a fad of the early 1980s, but not an entirely new one, as Laurent-Perrier sold *'Grand Vin Sans Sucre'* over a century ago. Officially designated throughout the EU as Brut Extra or Extra Brut, this style has been commercially labelled variously as *Brut Zéro, Brut Sauvage, Ultra Brut* and *Sans Sucre*. The late 20th century fashion for these wines emerged when consumers began seeking lighter, drier wines and were influenced by wine snobs who despised *Demi-Sec* and thought that Champagnes without any *dosage* must somehow be superior. Although such Champagnes still exist (most notably Laurent-Perrier Ultra-Brut and Piper-Heidsieck Brut Sauvage), most *cuvées* were austere, and lacked generosity, being tart

NON-VINTAGE ROSÉS ALSO VARY IN COLOUR. THESE EXAMPLES SHOW A MORE AMBER PINK ON THE LEFT COMPARED WITH A REDDER PINK ON THE RIGHT

SWEETNESS CHART

FRENCH TERMS ARE USED ON A FAIRLY INTERNATIONAL BASIS TO INDICATE THE LEVEL OF SWEETNESS IN SPARKLING WINES, THUS THE CHART BELOW LEADS WITH THESE DESCRIPTORS.

FRENCH TERM	RESIDUAL SUGAR (g/l)	LITERAL TRANSLATION	REALISTIC DESCRIPTION	EQUIVALENT TERMS
Extra Brut	0–6	Extra Raw	Usually very dry, but if the wine is properly balanced, it should never be austere	Brut de Brut (Fr), Brut Intégral (Fr), Brut Natur (Sp), Brut Nature (Fr & Sp), Brut Non-Dosé (Fr), Brut Sauvage (Fr), Brut Zéro (Fr), Extra Herb (Germ), Non Dosage (Fr)
Brut	0–15	Raw or Bone Dry	Varies between dry and very dry, but can still be ripe and succulent on the finish	Bruto (Port & Sp), Herb (Germ)
Extra-Sec	12–20	Extra Dry	Off-dry to medium-dry	Extra Trocken (Germ)
Sec	17–35	Dry	Medium dry	Secco (It), Seco (Port & Sp), Trocken
Demi-Sec	35–50	Medium Dry	Sweet	Abboccato (It), Halbsüss (Austrian), Halbtrocken (Germ), Meio-Seco (Port), Riche (Fr), Semi-Dulce (Sp)
Doux	50-plus	Sweet	Intensely sweet, but virtually non-existent	Doce (Port), Dolce (It), Dulce (Sp), Mild (Germ)

and unpleasant to drink. Furthermore, without a *dosage* a Brut Extra *cuvée* does not develop the mellow, complex bottle-aromas that devotees of mature Champagnes adore *(see the reference to Reaction Maillard in Disgorgement and corking, p.19)*. Not surprisingly the trend for these wines died a quick death, and the style has not taken off anywhere else.

PRESTIGE CUVÉES

These are the most expensive *cuvées* sold by sparkling wine producers. In Champagne, prestige *cuvées* are epitomised by the likes of Dom Pérignon, Roederer Cristal and Belle Epoque, but are they the greatest sparkling wines you can buy or just a marketing opportunity to increase profit margins?

The most important common factor that defines a prestige *cuvée* is selection. It is, or should be, the ultimate expression of the strictest selection that a particular producer can undertake. If vintage Champagne is superior to non-vintage only because higher quality wines have been selected for its production, then selection must be even more important for a prestige *cuvée*. And whereas the wines selected for a vintage Champagne logically result in a deliberate exaggeration of the year in question, then it is rational to assume that the wines chosen for a prestige *cuvée* are selected to exaggerate the house style or winemaker's philosophy. This is why prestige *cuvées* are produced in tiny quantities which inevitably determines their high price.

The expensive price is not, therefore, a ploy to increase profit margins, although whether the wine is worth the money is another matter entirely. The best most certainly are, but intensive selection alone cannot produce a great sparkling wine. Selection for selection's sake easily leads to *cuvées* that are over-refined and lack the vibrant balance that makes great sparkling wine so exciting. Perversely, there comes a point when the greater the selection, the more difficult it is to blend a sparkling wine of any finesse. The key to any prestige *cuvée* is selection, selection, selection, but a great prestige *cuvée* still requires a great winemaker.

RED

This style is illegal in Champagne, where only rosé or white wines are permitted. However, there are no colour intensity parameters written into the regulations, thus the dividing line between a dark rosé and a light red wine is a matter of opinion. Veuve Clicquot's 1976 Rosé was the deepest coloured Champagne I had come across until I discovered Leclerc-Briant's huge, crimson 1989 Rosé Rubis.

The earliest sparkling red wines were probably made in Burgundy in the 1820s, and the style has always been light and soft. Henry Vizetelly, who tasted a number of such wines as a juror at the Paris Exposition in 1878, stated that, 'Although red wines, they had the merit of being deficient in that body which forms an objectionable feature in sparkling wines of a deep shade of colour'.

There are today many sparkling red wines

produced in France and beyond, but the most famous and probably the most serious is Australia's sparkling Shiraz. This style started off as so-called Sparkling Burgundy, which a company called Auldana first produced in 1881. It was much lighter in both body and colour than today's sparkling Shiraz which, as a generic style, can loosely be taken to include sparkling red wines made from Cabernet Sauvignon, Merlot and other grape varieties, both pure and blended. They are deep purple-red colour, pungently-flavoured, full-throttle wines that invariably have a somewhat sweet finish and come in two distinct styles: oaky/fruity or fruity/fruity, with all the tannin and body that Vizetelly found so objectionable.

MYRIAD AROMAS ARE ATTRIBUTED TO SPARKLING WINES, INCLUDING FRUITS SUCH AS STRAWBERRIES AND PEACHES, AND NUTS LIKE ALMONDS AND BRAZILS

SWEETER STYLES

As Brut sparkling wines should have a balanced *dosage*, they rarely taste as austere as the term suggests, and the next level up – extra-sec or extra dry – is obviously sweeter *(see Sweetness Chart, p. 27)*. Some retailers have cottoned on to this and, knowing how many people 'Talk dry, drink sweet', they have deliberately imported Champagnes and sparkling wines at this level of sweetness instead of brut. When the *dosage* is properly balanced, extra-sec *cuvées* can be excellent, and the word *'sec'* or *'dry'* helps psychologically for people who want to be seen to be drinking a dry wine.

The same could be said for sparkling wines sold as *sec* or dry, which are sweeter still. But on its own, the word *sec* hints at Sekt, with all its bad connotations *(see Germany, p.179)*. The additional word 'extra' does allude to something extra, better, improved, thus *sec* is not used as heavily as *extra-sec*.

In theory the sweetest Champagne style is *doux* or sweet, which must contain at least 50 grams of residual sugar, but this style has not been widely available since the turn of the century, and the very last commercial production was made by Roederer in 1983 under its famous Carte Blanche label. That wine had 60 grams of residual sugar, which is not really sweet by *doux* standards, although ten years earlier Roederer's Carte Blanche was an 80 gram wine, while 100 years ago it was 180 grams.

Roederer's Carte Blanche today is just 45 grams, which puts it at the high end of the *demi-sec* range. A *demi-sec* Champagne may contain between 33 and 50 grams of residual sugar, but most average just 35g, although a few are as high as Roederer's Carte Blanche. Although a *demi-sec* is indeed sweet, it is not as intensely sweet as, say, a top Sauternes, which in great years will average 90-108g of residual sugar. It is thus neither one thing nor the other and because most who buy it are more concerned with experiencing a certain sweetness rather than a definite quality, the champenois have gradually been able to get away with using more and more inferior base wines.

The term *demi-sec* is now so debased that few houses take it seriously. A tiny number of quality-conscious houses have tried to raise the profile of this style, yet even they have been forced to market their products as *rich,* rather than *demi-sec*. Veuve Clicquot, for example, launched a vintage Champagne Rich in 1996. These are not dessert Champagnes, but when the quality is as exceptional as Veuve Clicquot's Rich, they work remarkably well with first and main course dishes which are essentially savoury yet utilise fruits and other sweetish ingredients.

AROMATIC STYLES

The use of aromatic grapes for a dry sparkling wine will always be difficult for regular Champagne drinkers to come to terms with, but once the style is accepted for what it is, the best examples shine out.

The most important dry sparkling wine made from an aromatic grape is of course Riesling Sekt, but until very recently the number of these wines showing any quality at all was very small indeed. There has, however, been a surge in the quality of some of these wines recently, although they still represent a tiny minority of the Sekt industry as a whole. Most of them are produced by small, go-ahead wine estates rather than the old-established Sekt factories and they are invariably bottle-fermented.

Keeping wines made from aromatic grape varieties on their yeast does nothing to help or increase the quality. In fact it detracts. Yeast-contact merely obscures the varietal purity of aromatic grapes, thus such wines should be disgorged as soon as possible after the second fermentation. Even the best of the new breed of Sekt could be made just as well by *cuve close*, but Sekt is so cheap that it is not considered a serious wine, even by those who drink it, thus the producers of the best Riesling Sekt have to use bottle-fermentation in order to persuade consumers that the wines are worthy of far higher prices than their competitors.

The easiest way for a Champagne drinker to enjoy the best quality Riesling Sekt is to forget Champagne and think of a fine Riesling because in the Sekt format the classic petrolly and honeyed character of a mature Riesling comes through.

The greatest sweet sparkling wine in the world is, without doubt, Asti. Although it is a fraction of the price of a *demi-sec* Champagne, the best Asti is ten times the quality, making it one of the great fine-wine bargains of the world. Virtually every bottle of Asti is made by *cuve close*, which is far superior to *méthode champenoise* for an aromatic, as mentioned above. This is particularly so for a sweet sparkling wine because, in all but a few exceptions, freshness of fruit is the key to a great sweet sparkling wine. No extra quality is gained from extended yeast contact.

The best Asti wines have a fine mousse of tiny bubbles, a fresh, grapey aroma, a luscious sweetness and a light yet rich, flowery fruitiness that should be vivacious and mouth-watering. The greatest examples will be reminiscent of peaches, and may even have a hint of orange, but Asti is not a wine that should be kept. One of the most important compounds in the Moscato aroma is geraniol, which is wonderful when fresh but which, with bottle-age, assumes an unpleasantly pungent geranium odour.

STORING AND SERVING

THE QUALITY OF ALL WINE CAN BE AFFECTED BY THE WAY IT IS BOTH STORED AND POURED. IN SPARKLING WINE, THE ADDITION OF BUBBLES INCREASES THE NEED FOR GOOD STORAGE CONDITIONS AND EXTRA CARE WHEN SERVING. EVEN THE SHAPE OF THE GLASS CAN HAVE AN EFFECT ON THE INTRINSIC AROMAS AND FLAVOURS IN THE WINE

STORAGE CONDITIONS

While 11°C (52°F) is supposed to be the perfect storage temperature, in fact anything between five and 18°C (40-65°F) will suffice for most styles of wines, providing there is no great temperature variation over a relatively short period of time. However, sparkling wines are somewhat more sensitive to temperature than other wines. While it will be no problem keeping sparkling wine, including Champagne, for a year or two at a constant temperature between 12 and 18°C (40-65°F), long term storage does require a cooler environment, ideally between 9°C and 11°C (48-52°F).

Higher temperatures increase the rate of oxidation in a wine, thus a bottle of wine stored at 18°C (65°F) will gradually get 'older' than the same wine stored at 11°C (52°F), but a constant 15°C (59°F) is far kinder to a wine than erratic temperatures that often hit 11°C (52°F), but jump between 5°C and 18°C (40-65°F) from one day to the next.

All wines are affected by the ultra-violet end of the light spectrum but sparkling wines seem to be particularly prone and, whereas some, if not all, of the photo-chemical effects of ultra-violet light can be reversed by cellaring an affected wine in darkness for a few months, this remedy is less effective for sparkling wines. It is one thing to buy a wine for everyday drinking off a well-lit supermarket shelf, but if you want to lay a wine down, particularly a sparkling wine, you should avoid buying any bottles which have been displayed in sunlight or under artificial lighting. Ask instead for bottles of the same wine that are still in the storeroom.

Similarly, unless you have a cellar or room in which the darkness can be maintained for most of the time, you should keep sparkling wine in any wrapping inside a box, even if it is not the box it was shipped in. If you store wine in a rack for any length of time, make sure you keep the wrapping, particularly if the bottle is clear and covered in coloured cellophane, such as the yellow anti-UV cellophane in which Roederer Cristal is wrapped. Brown glass bottles offer better protection against ultra-violet light than green glass, and dead-leaf or dark green is less prone than light or bright green.

STORING BOTTLES

There is no reason why sparkling wine bottles should be stored horizontally. All other wines should be stacked individually or in cases on their sides to keep the corks moist, thus fully swollen and airtight. This is because in time a bottle stored upright will end up with a shrunken, dried-out cork, which will expose the wine to air, causing oxidation. Tests in Champagne have demonstrated, however, that sparkling wine may be safely stored in an upright position because the CO_2 in the space between the wine and the base of the cork provides more than sufficient humidity to keep a sparkling wine cork moist and swollen. The added safeguard of storing such wines in an upright position is, of course, that by not keeping the cork in contact with the wine, the incidence of corked wine is significantly reduced.

Having said all this, I have to say that I have seen the cellars of some of the researchers involved, and they still store their bottles horizontally. Furthermore so does the author! Storing any wine in an upright position is not very efficient as far as space is concerned, and the aesthetic pleasure of seeing my own bottles laying horizontally in cases, bins and racks far exceeds any potential saving in the number of corked wines I might experience.

SERVING

Traditionally, white wines have been served chilled, while red wines have been served at room temperature (*chambré*), and although these practices have real effects on how the wine tastes, it could be argued that we appreciate these effects because we have become conditioned by them. Serving a white wine chilled retains the carbonic gas which makes it crisp and fresh and lively. Serving red wines at room temperature releases the more volatile, odorous compounds, giving more bouquet, and softening the texture of the wine, making it seem more mellow. However, there could be another world or an alternative earth where the inhabitants, through conditioning, enjoy mellow whites and crisp reds.

On the other hand, the temperature at which sparkling wine is served is the only one that can be scientifically justified. The bubbles are part of the wine and must be steadily released, otherwise there is no point having them

in the first place, and the rate at which they are released is determined by temperature. Serve *chambré* and the bottle would be dangerous to open, after which the wine would quickly froth up and go flat. Anything between 4.5 and 7°C (40-45°F) is ideal for a slow release of the mousse, but I am not one for thermometers, and prefer to advise simply putting a chill on a sparkling wine, just as I advise taking the chill off a red wine, as most people have the common sense to know when a wine is at a comfortable temperature.

In some restaurants, white wines, particularly sparkling wines, are served far too icy. Quite often a bottle is already at the ideal serving temperature prior to service, only for this to be ruined when the sommelier puts it into an ice-bucket for ten or 15 minutes before opening it. As this not only spoils the wine but can also do unpleasant things to your teeth, you should always feel the bottle first; if it seems well-chilled to you, then ask the sommelier not to put it in the ice-bucket. It can always go in later, if the restaurant is warm and it begins to lose its chill.

If you are picnicking beside a lake, river or the sea, tie the bottle securely to a length of strong cord and throw it into the deepest spot possible. At home on a frosty night, just leave the bottle outside for an hour or two. It is okay to chill wine in a refrigerator for a couple of hours, but try not to leave it longer than a day because not only might the cork stick, but the refrigeration process actually extracts moisture from a cork, causing it to shrink.

Emergency chilling of a sparkling wine by putting it in the coldest part of a deep-freeze for 15 minutes has never done a wine any harm (and has absolutely nothing to do with the long-term, cumulative effect of large temperature variations). Some people believe that this 'burns' the flavour of the Champagne, but no-one has so far been able to identify deep-freeze 'burnt' Champagne under blind conditions.

A bucket of ice and water (never just ice) is still one of the quickest ways to chill a bottle of fizz, but quicker still are the gel-filled jackets that are kept in the deep freeze and slip over the bottle itself. They take just six minutes, and the ones with draw-strings are the most efficient, especially over fatter-shaped bottles.

Whether you use these instant-chill sleeves or an ice-bucket, remember to invert the bottle gently a couple of times before opening because the wine in the neck is the least chilled, and the nearest to your jacket or dress when the cork comes out.

STORAGE TEMPERATURE	ENVIRONMENT	SERVING	
SHORT TERM: 12–18°C	OUT OF DIRECT LIGHT	4.5–7°C (40-45°F)	glass first, then go back
LONG TERM: 9–11°C	HORIZONTAL OR VERTICAL	When serving sparkling	and top each one up to
	STORAGE	wine, pour a little into each	between two-thirds and
			three-quarters full.

THE PERFECT CHAMPAGNE GLASS

TWO GLASSES HAVE BEEN SYNONYMOUS WITH CHAMPAGNE THROUGHOUT HISTORY: THE COUPE AND THE FLUTE.

The *coupe* was created circa 1663 by Venetian glass-makers at the Duke of Buckingham's glass factory in Greenwich (the duke having taken over Sir Robert Mansell's monopoly on glassmaking. In deference to its Italian inventors, this style of glass was originally called a *tazza* (cup), but the name faded during its 200-year climb to global popularity.

The Anglo-Italian *tazza* had been designed specifically for Champagne, but it was not until early Victorian commerce marketed it as a Champagne *coupe* that it became widely known in fashionable English society, and shortly thereafter in America. The *raison d'être* for its rise to fame was the remarkable success of pink Champagne, the brightly coloured spectacle of which, in these saucer-shaped crystal glasses, contrasted with the snow-white mousse and was so beguiling that both pink Champagne and the *coupe* soon became *de rigueur* in certain circles.

The flute is of a much earlier origin, dating back to Gallo-Roman times. Fine examples made at Murano near Venice became immensely popular

CLASSIC ENGLISH CHAMPAGNE FLUTE, CIRCA 1750, WITH A DRAWN TRUMPET BOWL AND MULTI-SPIRAL AIR-TWIST STEM.

during the 16th century, stimulating exports and generating the production of copies in the Netherlands and in England. At the court of Charles II the exiled St-Evrémond constantly tried to promote the flute as 'the glass of fashion' and, indeed, it became universally accepted for Champagne in France and England throughout the eighteenth century.

No serious wine lover today would dream of using a *coupe* for any sparkling wine, let alone a fine Champagne. The surface area of such a wide-brimmed glass is so large for the volume of wine that it encourages the bubbles to escape, rapidly rendering the wine flat, while the open shape is incapable of retaining any bouquet. The taller, narrower and more elegant flute is evidently superior in both respects, but even it is still not ideal, although some designs of flute are evidently better than others.

The perfect generic vessel for drinking any wine, still or sparkling, is the tulip-shaped glass; its bulbous base and gently-inward sloping sides concentrate the aromas in the top of the glass, allowing the drinker the full benefit of the wine's bouquet. Size is important:

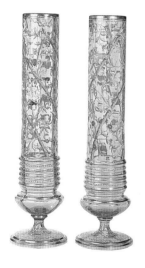

OPTIC BLOWN FLUTES, 42CM HIGH, CREATED BY JOSEF RIEDEL FOR THE JEWELLERS JABLONEC, AND ENAMELLED AT THE WORKSHOPS OF VINENZ POHL IN NEUWELT, BOHEMIA IN 1881.

ORNATE, TRANSPARENT GREEN FLUTES, 47CM HIGH, CREATED BY JOSEF RIEDEL FOR THE JEWELLERS JABLONEC, WITH COLOURLESS GLASS ADORNMENTS AND ENAMELLED WITH VINES, HERALDIC MOTIFS AND GILT AT THE WORKSHOPS OF VINENZ POHL IN NEUWELT, BOHEMIA IN 1882.

GREEN GLASS FLUTES, 38CM HIGH, CREATED BY JOSEF RIEDEL FOR THE JEWELLERS JABLONEC, AND PRODUCED AT THE HARRACHOV GLASSWORKS IN NEUWELT, BOHEMIA, IN 1893.

COLOURLESS, GILDED GLASS CHAMPAGNE FLUTES, 36CM HIGH, CREATED BY JOSEF RIEDEL FOR THE JEWELLERS JABLONEC, AND PRODUCED AT THE HARRACHOV GLASSWORKS IN NEUWELT, BOHEMIA, BETWEEN 1893 AND 1901.

THE IDEAL TASTING GLASS

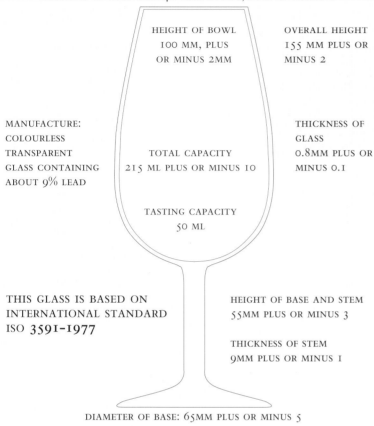

DIAMETER OF OPEN TOP: 46 MILLIMETERS, PLUS OR MINUS 2

HEIGHT OF BOWL
100 MM, PLUS
OR MINUS 2MM

OVERALL HEIGHT
155 MM PLUS OR
MINUS 2

MANUFACTURE:
COLOURLESS
TRANSPARENT
GLASS CONTAINING
ABOUT 9% LEAD

TOTAL CAPACITY
215 ML PLUS OR MINUS 10

THICKNESS OF
GLASS
0.8MM PLUS OR
MINUS 0.1

TASTING CAPACITY
50 ML

THIS GLASS IS BASED ON
INTERNATIONAL STANDARD
ISO 3591-1977

HEIGHT OF BASE AND STEM
55MM PLUS OR MINUS 3

THICKNESS OF STEM
9MM PLUS OR MINUS 1

DIAMETER OF BASE: 65MM PLUS OR MINUS 5

the glass must be sufficiently large to ensure that a 'good glassful' barely takes up more than half of the glass, thus leaving room above for the aromas to circulate. It is no coincidence that a tulip-shaped glass of specific dimensions has been accepted internationally as the standard ISO tasting glass.

Although generically the flute is not the ideal shape for tasting, it is nevertheless a very good one, and from an aesthetic point it can be more appealing than a 'perfect' ISO glass for drinking – as opposed to tasting – a fine quality Champagne. Aesthetics are a serious consideration for any hedonistic pursuit, particularly one as subjective as wine. The proportions of a glass, especially the fineness of the glass at its rim play an important role in the appreciation of wine.

Put a *cru classé* Bordeaux in a squat Paris goblet with a bulbous, rolled rim and drinking it will not be as pleasurable as drinking the same wine from, say, a Bordeaux Grand Cru glass from Riedel's handmade Sommelier range. Although a *vin de table* cannot be transformed into a *grand cru*, an inexpensive, good value wine can be seemingly infused with a certain class and finesse – those most subjective of qualities – by the quality-enhancing effects of a great glass when served at a flattering temperature. In addition to these aesthetic qualities, one high-quality glass manufacturer believes that there is a scientifically-based reason why certain glass shapes amplify or lessen specific characteristics in wine. The manufacturer in question is Riedel, and the design of every one of its glasses is based on this concept.

In the 19th and early 20th centuries the so-called traditional styles of wine glass evolved on a regional basis, but these shapes were primarily for recognition purposes, in much the same way as the different regional shapes of wine bottle were developed. Their suitability to the wines in question was not considered to be as relevant as the ability to discern what glass which wine should be poured into at the table. Riedel has not only redesigned glasses for all the classic wine regions based on their suitability, the firm has in many cases taken this concept to its logical conclusion and designed glasses to enhance the style of specific grape varieties and individual wine styles.

THE RIEDEL CONCEPT

The basis of each Riedel design hinges on the position of the tongue's four taste zones: sweetness is detected on its tip, sourness or acidity on the sides, bitterness at the back and top, and saltiness on the front and sides. It is hard to accept, but we smell all

ONE OF THE TWO EIGHTEENTH-CENTURY SÈVRES PORCELAIN COUPES THAT ONCE ADORNED THE QUEEN'S DAIRY TEMPLE AT THE CHÂTEAU DE RAMBOUILLET. SOME WRITERS HAVE CAST ASPERSIONS ON THE IDEA THAT THESE VESSELS WERE MODELLED ON THE BREASTS OF MARIE-ANTOINETTE, BUT IT IS NOT A RUDE RUMOUR, AS THE COLOURED NIPPLE IN THE BASE OF THE BOWL OF THE SOLE SURVIVING COUPE CLEARLY ILLUSTRATES. INDEED, THE CONCEPT WAS NOT EVEN NOVEL; A GREEK DRINKING CUP CALLED A MASTOS WAS MADE OF POTTERY IN THE FORM OF A WOMANS BREAST, COMPLETE WITH NIPPLE, AND COPIED IN GLASS BY THE ROMANS AS EARLY AS THE 4TH CENTURY.

other tastes through a sensory organ between our eyes called the olfactory bulb. This detects and catalogues aromas according to their origin; those picked up on the nose are accurately discerned as aromas, while those originating from the palate are perceived by our brain as tastes. Sometimes the same aroma emanates from both the nose and palate, thus the confusion between or overlap of some aromas and flavours.

Since the shape of a glass determines how and where the wine flows onto the tongue, it is logical to assume that it can emphasise or diminish the effect of these characteristics. Thus Riedel's premise is that glass design can manipulate in a very fundamental way how we perceive a wine. In theory, anyway. In practice, however, it is more likely to affect how we discern the balance of a wine than adjust our perception of the flavour.

Sweetness, acidity and tannin are the major factors affecting the balance of a wine, whereas, as explained, our perception of flavour is created by a multiplicity of aromas. Furthermore, although the shape of a glass determines how and where the wine hits the tongue, any effect must be extremely short-lived, as the wine does not stay in that one spot, but almost instantly flows over the tongue around the palate. Is the effect thus negligible, or is the first impression relatively of much more importance than its fleeting existence may suggest?

To answer these and other intriguing questions surrounding the effect of glass design on our perception of wine, I decided to test nine Riedel

THE FOUR TASTE ZONES OF THE TONGUE

BITTER

SALT

ACID

SWEET

glasses developed specifically for Champagne and sparkling wine. I assessed the affect of each glass on 100 different Champagnes and sparkling wines. Even with ten glasses of each design, this was a formidable task, comprising ten sessions, each involving the analyses of 90 different permutations of glass design and wine. Each glass was designed to achieve specific aims (described in italics beside each picture below); I wanted to find out whether these aims have been achieved, what perceptions are altered, if any, and if any glasses suited a particular style of Champagne or sparkling wine.

LOOKING BUBBLY

Although it is impossible to discern the true quality of a wine's mousse visually, I needed to guarantee that there would be comparable mousse in each glass for my series of tests, thus requested Riedel to etch a small spot to act as a nucleus at the bottom of every glass.

This idea was first promoted by the legendary André Simon, who used to engrave a star in the bottom of all his Champagne glasses. Riedel sells all of its glasses either etched or plain. There is much pleasure to be gained from seeing a lovely mousse beading to the surface of any fine sparkling wine, and nothing more disappointing than pouring out a good Champagne that looks flat.

BASIC CHAMPAGNE FLUTE

MACHINE-BLOWN, POTASH GLASS.

Designed for heavy commercial use, the short stem makes this the most dishwasher-friendly flute available. Its bowl is modelled on the Vinum Prestige Champagne flute, and it possesses a thin polished rim, which is rare in this category of glass, most having a rolled rim which presents a barrier to the flow of wine.

Not surprisingly the Basic Champagne Flute replicated every characteristic of Riedel's Vinum Prestige, and although the shorter stem did not provide as much pleasure when handling the glass, this made it far easier to use in restricted situations. I tested the glass on two flights, and came to the firm conclusion that this makes a first class standard tasting glass.

OVERTURE CHAMPAGNE FLUTE

MACHINE-BLOWN, POTASH GLASS.

Shorter and smaller than the Sommeliers flute, this glass nevertheless delivers an intense bouquet, and creamy texture, accentuating the fruitiness of a wine.

This glass generates a fast flow of very fine bubbles, creating a cushiony mousse feel in the mouth. It does not accentuate the fruitiness, as suggested, but rather brings out the minerally finesse in a wine. It knocks any elegance out of toasty aromas, and reveals the reductive faults in mature Champagnes, yet refines malolactic aromas. A sparkling red wine looks incongruous in many fizz glasses, but suits this tulip-shape and this glass also enhances the heady aromas of such wines. Very good for youthful *blanc de blancs* Champagnes, but without doubt the ideal Sparkling Shiraz glass.

VINUM CHAMPAGNE FLUTE

MACHINE-BLOWN, LEAD CRYSTAL.

When the Vinum range was introduced in 1986, machine-blown technology was not capable of utilising a pulled stem, and only the classic flute shape gave a comfortable appearance with an attached stem. The tasting experience is similar to that of the Sommeliers Champagne Flute.

Contrary to Riedel's assertion, the difference between the Vinum and Sommelier Champagne Flutes was such that I had to conduct separate comparisons literally blindfolded before I could believe my own results. This glass generates a fast release of bubbles, reduces amylic aromas, and emphasises flowery, minerally finesse in preference to fruitiness. The perfect glass for fruity New World fizz.

VINUM PRESTIGE CHAMPAGNE FLUTE

MACHINE-BLOWN, LEAD CRYSTAL.
With its wider bowl and tapered rim, this glass should generate a more complex aroma and focus the full spectrum of flavours, while preserving the elegance and effervescence of the wine.

This glass generates a fast flow of small bubbles, softens acidity and brings out elegance and fruitiness in Extra Brut styles, but it mutes the sweetness in sweeter wines, makes some Sekt seem almost corked on the nose, is worse than the Vinum for toasty aromas, and makes Pinot Noir *cuvées* seem unduly coarse. However, it finds finesse in the most malolactic-dominated wines, and adds a flowery elegance to sparkling Shiraz. A good glass for Sparkling Shiraz, but a great one for Extra Brut Champagne.

SOMMELIERS CHAMPAGNE FLUTE

HAND-BLOWN, LEAD CRYSTAL.
A classically shaped flute that was developed for light, fresh, dry, Champagnes. Designed so that the tingle of delicate bubbles can be experienced on the tip of the tongue. Also suitable for Cava and Prosecco.

In a different class to the Vinum Flute, this generates a medium-fast flow of tiny bubbles, retains its head the longest of all the glasses tested, and softens the tactile effect of the mousse on the palate. It has by far the thinnest rim and this physically heightens the impression of finesse as soon as it touches the lips. It brings freshness and elegance to sparkling Chenin wines, malolactic-dominated *cuvées*, and the heaviest oak characteristics. The best all-round glass for fizz, and my favourite for the greatest Champagnes.

SOMMELIERS VINTAGE CHAMPAGNE FLUTE

HAND-BLOWN, LEAD CRYSTAL.
When just one-third full, this flute concentrates the unique yeasty bouquet of great Champagnes, and prevents the bubbles from dominating the palate. The bubbles are smoothly integrated into the creamy texture of the mousse, forming part of the overall pleasure of the wine.

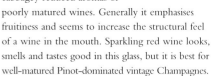

One of the three best glasses for generating a lazy, spiralling mousse of tiny bubble, it faithfully reflects all good aromas, but miraculously subdues some less attractive ones, such as heavy-handed malolactic and even the cabbagey reduced aromas of poorly matured wines. Generally it emphasises fruitiness and seems to increase the structural feel of a wine in the mouth. Sparkling red wine looks, smells and tastes good in this glass, but it is best for well-matured Pinot-dominated vintage Champagnes.

SOMMELIERS SPARKLING WINE FLUTE

HAND-BLOWN, LEAD CRYSTAL.
Originally custom made for a German Sekt company. The aim was to highlight the effervescence, and promote the pleasure of drinking Sekt from a narrow-lipped flute. The design of this glass makes the coarser Sekt bubbles seem smaller and the mousse creamier.

A fun-shaped glass for receptions, but the wine warms quickly in the hand. Contrary to Riedel's claim, I found this to be the worst for bubble size, although it suited the Sekt style very well, as it takes a ton of terpenes to show through what must be the world's worst design for capturing the bouquet of a wine. This does, however, have its advantages, as it neatly subdues amylic and heavy malolactic aromas, and somehow finds the fruit in the toastiest fizz. It is also an Asti glass *par excellence*.

WILLSBERGER CHAMPAGNE FLUTE

HAND-BLOWN, LEAD CRYSTAL.
Developed in 1984 by Hans Willsberger, publisher of Gourmet magazine, this was a revolutionary design at the time. When filled to the point where the bowl curves, the aromas linger, emphasising the finest aromas of the best Champagnes.

One of the three best glasses for generating a lazy, spiralling mousse, and the one that produces the most tiny bubbles. The bulbous top captures, concentrates and exaggerates aromas, including those that do not always benefit, such as amylic aromas, heavy malolactic and some terpenes. It does make Chenin finer and more flowery, brings out a minerally finesse in most sparkling wines, adds elegance to toasty aromas in New World wines, and is good for Asti, but I like it best for drinking top quality Saumur sparklers.

RODENSTOCK CHAMPAGNE FLUTE

HAND-BLOWN, LEAD CRYSTAL.
Developed in 1989 as part of a series of hand-blown glasses for the personal use of Hardy Rodenstock, who has been described by the Wine Spectator as 'the world's most extravagant wine collector'. The design of this glass focuses on the complexity and intensity of bouquet.

One of the three best for generating a lazy, spiralling mousse of tiny bubbles. The bulbous top exaggerates aromas good and bad, making amylic or heavy malolactic wines hard and bitter on the palate. It makes Chenin finer and more flowery, but it enhances fruitiness rather than minerally finesse, and plucks out the terpenes from toasty New World wines. Although even better than the Willsberger for Asti, this is my choice for Prestige Cuvée Champagnes.

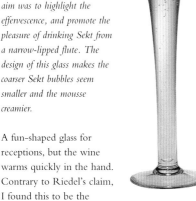

APPRECIATING SPARKLING WINE

The difference between a still and a sparkling wine is, of course, its bubbles, yet even professional tasters can sometimes ignore, misunderstand or fail to appreciate the mousse.

There are two basic attributes of a mousse: its strength or pressure, and the size of its bubbles, but these characteristics cannot be discerned by looking at the wine in a glass. When the same sparkling wine is poured into 12 seemingly identical glasses, it can give the appearance of up to 12 different qualities of mousse. These can vary from the wine seeming to be flat, through degrees of big and uneven bubbles, to the most splendid mousse of ultrafine bubbles, and the rate at which the bubbles are released can also fluctuate from furiously fast to a lazy cascade. Yet some, quite possibly all, of these impressions may be false.

Bubbles form wherever there are nuclei – infinitesimal imperfections on the inner surface of the glass or microscopic matter suspended in the wine itself. If there are no suitable nuclei, the bubbles will not form and the wine will look flat, although the first sip will soon reveal a prickly sensation of the mousse in the mouth. Not all nuclei enhance the mousse; the tension created by some glass imperfections can be such that they do not release a stream of tiny bubbles, but instead allow the gas to build until the bubbles are big and ungainly. However, that is the fault of the glass, or how it has been cleaned, not the wine.

The only way to assess the true qualities of a mousse is in the mouth, and this is much simpler than it sounds because we are not trying to articulate the imagined complexity of a combination of aromas, merely the prickly tactile impression of bursting bubbles. It is as easy to perceive as difference between various textures of cloth. If you can distinguish between pure silk and rough sackcloth when they glide across your skin, you should have no difficulty recognising the difference between high and low pressures of mousse, or the coarse and fine size of bubbles which make up the mousse.

When you roll the wine around your mouth, you will feel the strength of mousse by the degree of fizziness, which ranges from firm and assertive for a fully *mousseux* product, to soft and gentle for a lightly *crémant* style. The size of bubble also takes very little experience to calculate; the larger the bubbles, the more coarse the mousse feels, even when it is soft and gentle in pressure, whereas the smaller the bubbles, the smoother the mousse feels, with the most minuscule bubbles creating a silky, creamy texture on the finish.

Although the palate is the only reliable instrument for assessing the mousse, if a wine does show its mousse well in a glass, the sight can be mesmerising. Under such circumstances, the sign of a high quality mousse is when the tiniest of bubbles cascade lazily to the surface of the wine. The rate the bubbles are released should be slow, even in a fully *mousseux* sparkling wine, and the hallmark of a great Champagne is when the bubbles collect on the surface to form a creamy cordon, which adheres to the inside of the glass like a smooth, white ring.

PRESSURE TACTICS

THE DEGREE OF EFFERVESCENCE IS DETERMINED BY THE AMOUNT OF CARBONIC GAS DISSOLVED IN THE WINE AND IS NORMALLY QUANTIFIED BY A SCALE OF ATMOSPHERIC PRESSURE. ONE ATMOSPHERE IS 15LBS PSI (PER SQUARE INCH), WHICH IS THE PRESSURE OUR BODIES ARE SUBJECTED TO AT SEA-LEVEL. A SPARKLING WINE CAN BE ANYTHING UP TO SIX ATMOSPHERES, WHICH IS 90LBS PSI – THE EQUIVALENT OF THE PRESSURE IN A DOUBLE-DECKER BUS TYRE. THE ACTUAL PRESSURE AT SERVING TEMPERATURE, HOWEVER, IS MUCH LOWER, SO ALTHOUGH CARE MUST ALWAYS BE TAKEN WHEN OPENING A BOTTLE OF FIZZ, IT IS NOT AS SCARY AS THE THOUGHT OF AN EXPLODING BUS TYRE. A FULLY SPARKLING WINE OF SIX ATMOSPHERES WILL, FOR EXAMPLE, BE JUST 2.5 ATMOSPHERES AT 6°C.

A sparkling wine of a designated pressure is achieved by calculating the amount of sugar necessary to produce the required amount of carbonic gas. For further information, see *Liqueur de tirage* in the Glossary.

PERLANT

Less than 2.5 atmospheres
Usually cheap and more often than not artificially carbonated, this low-pressure style has been adopted to avoid the so-called tax on bubbles. In many countries sparkling wine carries a significantly higher rate of duty than still wines, and this is cost-prohibitive for bulk-produced commercial products. Thus *perlant* wines have been deliberately kept to a pressure just below that where the bubble-tax kicks in. Can range from barely a prickle to a light mousse.
EQUIVALENT TERMS INCLUDE *FRIZZANTINO* (IT.), *PERLÉ* (FR.), *PERLWEIN* (GERM.), *PRICKLE* (ENG.), *VINO DE AGUJA* (SP.).

PÉTILLANT

Between 2.5 and 3.5 atmospheres
An underrated style, particularly in the Loire, where it could be put to good use if the grapes for sparkling wine were generally of a better quality. *Pétillant* wines should have a definite, if very light, mousse, and the tiniest of bubbles.
EQUIVALENT TERMS INCLUDE *FRIZZANTE* (IT.), *SEMI-SPARKLING* (ENG.), *SPRITZIG* (GERM.).

CRÉMANT

Classically 3.6 atmospheres
This term is not legally defined, but is generally considered to include wines between 3.5 and 4 atmospheres. Some might edge this range up as high as 4.5 atmospheres, but that detracts from the contrast with a fully *mousseux* product (*see below*).
   Crémant was originally used in Champagne, where it traditionally applied to wines with just 3.6 atmospheres of pressure, although a true *crémant* was never merely a question of pressure, but also inferred a soft and literally creamy mousse. However, the term was phased out in Champagne as part of a bargain struck with producers of other French sparkling wines, who agreed in return to drop the term *méthode champenoise*. Because of the original connotation, a *crémant* is perceived as having a soft and gentle mousse, but the minimum pressure required by law for all the French *crémant* appellations is the same as that for Champagne, and in one case, Crémant d'Alsace, it is even higher.
CRÉMANT IS NOT DIRECTLY TRANSLATABLE; SOME COUNTRIES SUCH AS ITALY USE THE SAME WORD, WHILE OTHERS DO NOT HAVE A CATEGORY BETWEEN *PÉTILLANT* AND *MOUSSEUX*.

MOUSSEUX

3.5 – 6 atmospheres
This merely means sparkling, thus it is usually qualified as *fully mousseux* or, as in France, *grand mousseux*, both of which refer to wines with between five and six atmospheres of pressure, which is the average found in Champagne, even though a *mousseux* wine may legally be as low as 3.5 atmospheres.
EQUIVALENT TERMS INCLUDE *ESPUMANTE* (PORT.), *ESPUMOSO* (SP.), *SPARKLING* (ENG.), *SPUMANTE* (IT.).

DANGER: CLEANLINESS CAN KILL!

DETERGENT KILLS BUBBLES, BUT IT IS IMPOSSIBLE TO CLEAN GLASSES PROPERLY WITHOUT DETERGENT, THUS GLASSES SHOULD ALWAYS BE THOROUGHLY RINSED IN HOT WATER AT LEAST TWICE.

If using a dishwasher, do not mix glasses with any other items, and follow manufacturer's instructions to avoid 'milking', which also kills bubbles. Whether washed by hand or machine, allow the glasses to drain and dry as much as possible from residual heat (some dishwashers have a special drying programme), and merely wipe the rims with a clean glass cloth. The most imperceptible smear of grease can also ruin a mousse, so never use a glass cloth for anything other than glasses. Wash glass cloths separately, ensuring they are thoroughly rinsed, and use no perfumed softeners in the process. Never polish glasses just before serving because the action builds up static, which can play havoc with the formation of the mousse, often killing it. If polishing is necessary, then ensure this is carried out at least four hours prior to serving, to allow the static to dissipate.

SOIL AND CLIMATE

THE CHAMPENOIS HAVE LONG ASSERTED THAT IT IS THEIR UNIQUE COUPLING OF CHALKY SOIL AND COOL CLIMATE WHICH ALLOWS THEM TO MAKE THE BEST SPARKLING WINES IN THE WORLD. OF COURSE WINEMAKERS IN OTHER PARTS OF THE WORLD ARE BOUND TO DISAGREE.

The Champenois argue that it is *terroir*, that splendid word which has no direct equivalent in the English language, and which incorporates soil, climate, aspect, elevation and a number of other factors, which makes their sparkling wines unique in the world in terms of quality and ageability. *Terroir* is perhaps best understood as encompassing all the various elements in a vine's existence which owe little or nothing to the influence of man.

The factors cited as most important in the *terroir* of Champagne are the soil and the climate. The chalk subsoil which underlies all the vineyards (except those in the Aube region) holds enough water for the vines to survive dry spells, yet is sufficiently porous to prevent the roots becoming waterlogged. The northerly latitude and the cooling (and dampening) influence of the Atlantic combine to produce a climate such that, except in the warmest years, grapes struggle to ripen, while retaining high acidity. Wines from such fruit, tart to the point of being almost undrinkable with very little of note in the flavour department, may not pass muster as still wines, but are ideal material for turning into first class sparklers.

So the argument that the driving force behind Champagne is *terroir* is strong. However, so too is the opposing view that man is more important. If *terroir* is the be all and end all, why are there so few single vineyard wines, which should after all be the ultimate expression of *terroir*? Why do the styles of wines differ so much depending on the proportions of the various grape varieties? What about the winemaker's decision as to how much reserve wine to blend in, and how long a Champagne should spend on its lees? What if different varieties were to be used?

The truth, as with all top class wines, is that for greatness, man and nature must work in harmony. If Champagne currently has no rivals as the premium sparkling wine region in the world, it may be because

ABOVE: NEWLY CULTIVATED VINEYARD SITES IN THE CÔTE DE VERTUS, MARNE, WITH CHALKY SUBSOIL SHOWING THROUGH.

CHALKY SOIL: IDEAL FOR VINES AND POPPIES

its inhabitants have spent hundreds of years perfecting its wines. However, a testimony to the potential which the Champenois see for sparkling wine outside their region is the degree to which they have become involved in ventures in various other parts of the world, with the majority of them focussing on high quality rather than quantity. 'In theory,' says Jean-Marie Barillère, Vice President of Champagne Group Operations for Seagram, owner of Mumm and Perrier-Jouët, 'once you find the right soil types and the right climate in the same ratio, and plant the right varieties, it should be possible to make a wine of a similar quality to Champagne anywhere in the world'.

On the other side of the world, Dr Tony Jordan, MD of Moët & Chandon's Australian operation, Domaine Chandon, doesn't see the need for such rigid conditions. 'To make high quality sparkling wines from Chardonnay, Pinot Noir and Pinot Meunier that have elegance and length of flavour, cool climates are necessary, but it is not necessary to have a carbon copy of the Champagne climate or soil type. I believe there are now a number of *méthode traditionelle* sparkling wines from the New World that are as good as top quality Champagnes but of course they are different because they are grown in different *terroirs*. It is not an issue of the New World wine being less good than the French wine because it does not taste exactly the same.

So while nowhere else currently compares with Champagne in terms of the quality and quantity of its sparkling wine, that doesn't mean that there won't be some regions coming to the fore in the future. Frederic Panaiotis, winemaker at Veuve Clicquot says, 'The areas outside Champagne which I think are making the best sparkling wines are northern Italy, the northern parts of California such as Anderson Valley, Marlborough in New Zealand, Australia's Yarra Valley and, closer to home, Burgundy. But I don't feel that anything can compete with us yet on length, complexity, texture, richness and ageability.'

AND WHAT OF THE FUTURE?

If Champagne is on the northern limit of grape production, what of the country across the Channel? Several parts of southern England share the same chalky soil that Champagne does, and producers such as Nyetimber Vineyard have demonstrated that it is not too cold to grow Chardonnay and Pinot Noir successfully in such a climate. Is this a sign of global warming? Ten years ago, some climatologists were predicting that average global temperatures could increase by as much as 3°C by 2035. The map below

VIEW OVER THE VINEYARDS AT DOMAINE CHANDON IN AUSTRALIA WHERE, DR TONY JORDAN BELIEVES, SPARKLING WINES OF AS GOOD QUALITY AS CHAMPAGNE CAN BE MADE

shows what effect such a warming would have on the world in terms of climates suitable for grape growing, with viticulture becoming possible as far north as Scotland and Scandinavia. This has subsequently proved to be an extravagant estimate, and indeed data from NASA satellite measurements shows a slight cooling trend in the past 18 years.

It would seem that the most enjoyable way of reversing this downward trend in world temperatures is to reach for a bottle of your favourite fizz and release those lovely bubbles – the greenhouse gas carbon dioxide – into the atmosphere.

THE MAP BELOW SHOWS HOW, WITH GLOBAL WARMING, THE REGIONS OF THE WORLD WHERE THE CLIMATE CURRENTLY LENDS ITSELF TO SUCCESSFUL GRAPE GROWING, START TO BECOME TOO WARM AND HOW THE CLIMATE IN OTHER PARTS OF THE WORLD, WHICH ARE CURRENTLY TOO COOL TO GROW GRAPES, BECOME FEASIBLE PLANTING AREAS. TEN YEARS AGO SCIENTISTS WERE PREDICTING A WARM-UP OF 1°C EVERY DECADE. EVEN IF THAT FIGURE WERE HALVED, IT IS EASY TO SEE HOW PLACES THAT ARE CURRENTLY ON THE FRINGE OF SERIOUS GRAPE GROWING, SUCH AS ENGLAND, COULD MOVE INTO THE MAINSTREAM. AT THE SAME TIME, MANY AREAS THAT ARE SUCCESSFUL GRAPE GROWING REGIONS NOW, PARTICULARLY FOR SPARKLING WINES, COULD BECOME TOO WARM.

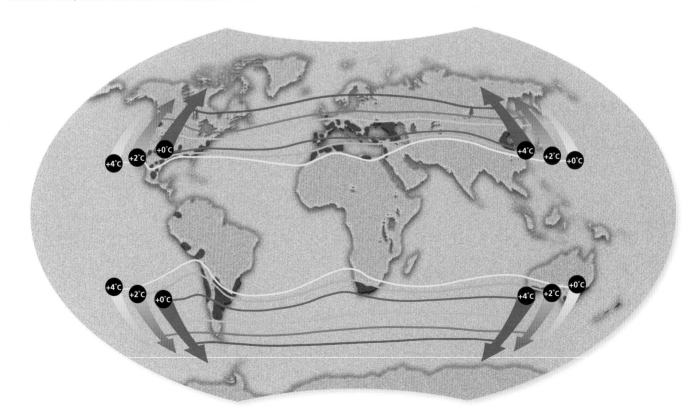

CHAMPAGNE

SOME PEOPLE THINK THAT CHAMPAGNE IS SIMPLY A GENERIC NAME THAT MAY APPLY TO ANY SPARKLING WINE. BUT, IN FACT, ONLY SPARKLING WINES MADE FROM GRAPES GROWN WITHIN A LEGALLY DEFINED AREA OF NORTHERN FRANCE MAY RIGHTFULLY CLAIM THE CHAMPAGNE APPELLATION. AND DESPITE THE NUMBER OF WINES THAT ARE LEGALLY PERMITTED TO USE THE NAME CHAMPAGNE WITHIN THEIR OWN COUNTRY OF ORIGIN, GLOBALLY IT REMAINS A UNIQUELY FRENCH PRODUCT, JUST AS REAL SHERRY ONLY COMES FROM SPAIN AND STILTON CHEESE IS UNQUESTIONABLY ENGLISH.

The wines of Champagne were originally still, and barely a pale *vin gris*; the intention being to make a red wine, but this proved difficult so far north where the grapeskins have relatively little pigment. The wines were, however, renowned for their delicacy and, in 1558, Paulmier described those of Aÿ as 'the ordinary drink of kings and princes'. Forty years earlier the first wine to reach England from Champagne was a shipment of 'vin d'Ay' sent to Cardinal Wolsey.

Although sparkling Champagne was consumed with relish by the English well before 1662, when Merret described how such wines were made *(see p.9)*, it did not appear in France itself until the end of the 17th century. French gourmands despised it; to them Champagne was a still wine, just like Bordeaux or Burgundy and, not unreasonably, they regarded fizziness as a fault. It is debatable just what Dom Pérignon, the mythical 'inventor' of Champagne did

CHAMPAGNE IS UNIQUE AMONGST FRENCH AOC WINES SINCE IT IS THE ONLY SUCH WINE THAT DOES NOT HAVE TO INDICATE 'APPELLATION CONTRÔLÉE' ON THE LABEL. THE NAME CHAMPAGNE WAS THOUGHT TO BE GUARANTEE ENOUGH.

achieve; there is no evidence that he made any sparkling wine and it is quite probable that he actually spent his life trying to solve this winemaking fault.

In the 18th century the habit of drinking sparkling Champagne spread throughout Europe as it sold to Germany, Italy, Holland, Flanders, Switzerland, Denmark, Sweden, Norway and Russia. However, the vast majority of Champagne produced was still rather than fizzy and remained so until the end of the 18th century.

America took to fizzy Champagne after George Washington served it to Senator Johnson of South Carolina in 1790, but it was not until the 19th century, when Champagne was exported under the marques of famous houses by characters such as Charles-Camille Heidsieck, that the entire world began to drink it in quantity. By the 1850s America and England were jointly consuming more Champagne than all other countries put together.

THE CHAMPAGNE REGION

THE CHAMPAGNE APPELLATION CONSISTS OF A LACEWORK OF 34,500 HECTARES SPREAD OVER 301 VILLAGES SITUATED IN FIVE DÉPARTEMENTS - MARNE, AISNE, AUBE, HAUT-MARNE AND SEINE-ET-MARNE. ALMOST 75% OF THE VINES ARE LOCATED WITHIN THE MARNE DÉPARTEMENT AND ONLY ONE-TENTH OF ONE PER CENT OF THE TOTAL AREA UNDER VINE IS IN THE HAUT MARNE AND SEINE-ET-MARNE. WITHIN THE LIMITS OF THE APPELLATION ARE FIVE MAJOR DISTRICTS, EACH PRODUCING DISTINCTLY DIFFERENT BASE WINES WHICH, WHEN BLENDED IN VARIOUS PROPORTIONS, CAN RESULT IN CHAMPAGNES OF WIDELY CONTRASTING CHARACTER, WHICH IS HOW EACH HOUSE HAS DEVELOPED ITS OWN DISTINCTIVE STYLE. THE BEST WAY TO APPRECIATE HOW THESE REGIONAL INFLUENCES CONTRIBUTE TO THE STYLE OF THE FAMOUS BRANDS IS TO SEEK OUT GROWER-PRODUCER CHAMPAGNES IN EACH DISTRICT. TO THIS END I HAVE INDICATED A FEW (OF THE MANY) GROWERS WHOSE WINES ARE EXPRESSIVE OF THEIR LOCALITY.

CÔTE DES BLANCS

Grape varieties: 96% Chardonnay, 3% Pinot Noir, 1% Meunier

The name of this area is derived from its almost exclusive cultivation of white Chardonnay grapes. The wines produced from these grapes have become the most sought after in all Champagne. The best four villages are clustered together in the heart of the Côte des Blancs: Cramant, Avize, Oger and le Mesnil-sur-Oger. The wines from these villages contribute finesse and delicacy to a blend, yet in their pure form can mature to an unequalled creamy-intensity of flavour, with fabulous biscuity, nutty (walnut, hazelnut, brazil nut) complexity.

EXPRESSIVE GROWERS:

Larmandier-Bernier (Vertus), Guy Charlemagne (le Mesnil-sur-Oger), Lilbert (Cramant), Jacques Selosse (Avize)

THE AUBE

Grape varieties: 8% Chardonnay, 85% Pinot Noir, 7% Meunier

Ripe, fruity wines are produced in this southern part of Champagne, which is closer to Chablis than to the classic vineyards of the Marne. This should be a Chardonnay district (not that Champagne needs more of that variety) but up until the Second World War it was planted with Gamay and, when that grape was phased out, Pinot Noir seemed to be the natural successor. The wines are cleaner in style and of a far better quality than the same vines grown in the outer areas of the Vallée de la Marne around Château-Thierry. The Union Auboise super-cooperative (Vve Devaux) at Bar-sur-Seine is the most dynamic, fastest improving cooperative in the Champagne region.

EXPRESSIVE GROWERS:

Grande Sendrée (not a grower, but Drappier's single-vineyard Champagne from Urville), Horiot (les Riceys), Serge Mathieu (Avirey-Lingey)

MONTAGNE DE REIMS

Grape varieties: 28% Chardonnay, 56% Pinot Noir, 16% Meunier

The Montagne de Reims is a massive, forest-capped formation between Epernay and Reims. It can be divided into northern and southern *Montagnieu*, but both are renowned for Pinot Noir, despite the influx of Chardonnay in recent decades.

The grapes in the vineyards of the northern *montagne* would not ripen but for the fact that the chilled night air slips away, down the slopes onto the plain, to be replaced by the convection of warmer air from a thermal zone that builds up above the *montagne* during the day.

The villages of the northern *montagne* include Rilly-la-Montagne, Mailly-Champagne, Verzenay and Verzy, and the vines grown here generally produce darker coloured, bigger bodied wines than those from southern *montagne*. The Southern *montagne* includes Ambonnay and Bouzy, the wines of which are generally not quite as dark as those of the northern *montagne*, but can have even more depth, extract and aromatic finesse.

EXPRESSIVE GROWERS

Michel Arnould (Verzenay), Paul Bara (Bouzy), Henri Goutorbe (Aÿ-Champagne), Jean Hanotin (Verzy), Mailly-Champagne (cooperative, not récoltant), Vilmart (Rilly-la-Montagne)

Map labels

Rethel
Soissons
Fismes
Reims
Verzy
Suippes
Ste-Menehould
Verneuil
Damery
Bouzy
A4
Dormans
Épernay
Charly
Château-Thierry
Cramant
Châlons-en-Champagne
La Ferté-sous-Jouarre
Orbais
Bergères-les-Vertus
Revigny-sur-Ornain
Montmirail
La Ferté-Gaucher
Sézanne
Sommesous
Vitry-le-François
Barbonne-Fayel
St-Dizier
Béthon
Arcis-sur-Aube
Provins
Romilly-sur-Seine
Brienne-le-Château
Nogent-sur-Seine
Troyes
Arsonval
Blaise
Bar-sur-Aube
Bayel
Bar-sur-Seine
Essoyes
les Riceys
Châtillon-sur-Seine

0   20 km
0   10 miles

KEY

Aube Vineyards
Côte des Blancs
Côte de Sézanne
Montagne de Reims
Vallée de la Marne
— Delimited AOC Region of Champagne

VALLÉE DE LA MARNE

Grape varieties: 10% Chardonnay, 27% Pinot Noir, 63% Meunier

Wines produced using these grapes tend to be essentially easy-drinking, fruity and forward with an extremely high proportion of Meunier which, because of its late bud-break and early ripening, is cultivated in the frost-prone valley vineyards .

It is debatable whether Aÿ-Champagne and the western half of Mareuil-sur-Aÿ are in fact Vallée de la Marne or Montagne de Reims, and certainly the Pinot Noir wines from these two villages are a class apart, having far more in common with southern *montagne* villages like Bouzy and Ambonnay.

The next division is formed by the vineyards of Dizy, Hautvillers and Cumières which overlook Epernay to the south. The further west you go beyond these three villages, the lesser the quality, particularly on the left bank, where the vines face north. Exceptions to this rule are Ste-Gemme and Leuvrigny, both of which have earned acclaim for the superior quality of their Meunier, and to a lesser degree Festigny and Villers-sur-Châtillon.

EXPRESSIVE GROWERS:

Goutorbe (Aÿ-Champagne), Gaston Chiquet (Dizy), Clos des Goisses (not a grower, but Philipponnat's single vineyard Champagne from Mareuil-sur-Aÿ), René Geoffroy (Cumières), Locret-Lachaud (Hautvillers).

CÔTE DE SÉZANNE

Grape varieties: 70% Chardonnay, 21% Pinot Noir, 9% Meunier

A rapidly developing area 10 miles southwest of the Côte des Blancs, the Sézannais also favours the Chardonnay grape, but its wines are more fruity, and can be quite exotic and musky. These wines lack the finesse of a Côte des Blancs blanc de blancs, but are ideal for modern consumers who enjoy New World sparkling wines, yet have difficulty coming to terms with the more classic style of Champagne. However, Pinot Noir is becoming increasingly important with some producers who are keen to develop more traditional blends.

The most southerly village of Villenauxe-la-Grande is in fact in the Aube département, but way up in the northwestern corner, far removed from the Aube Champagne district.

EXPRESSIVE GROWERS:

Pierre Jamain (Villenauxe-la-Grande), Triolet (Bethon).

VINEYARDS AT LA CELLE CHANTEMERLE, IN AUBE, CÔTE DE SÉZANNE

VINEYARDS AT NOÉ-LES-MALLETS, AUBE

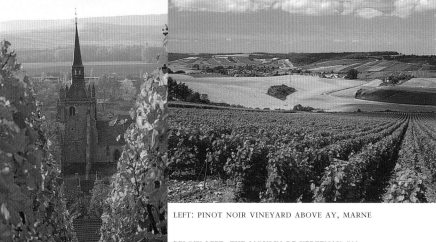

LEFT: PINOT NOIR VINEYARD ABOVE AY, MARNE

BELOW LEFT: THE MOULIN DE VERZENAY ON THE MONTAGNE DE REIMS

AUTUMNAL VINEYARDS ON THE CÔTE DES BLANCS NEAR CRAMANT

THE VILLAGES

ALL THE VINEYARDS OF CHAMPAGNE ARE QUALITY-RATED ON A VILLAGE-BY-VILLAGE BASIS BY A PERCENTILE SYSTEM KNOWN AS THE *ÉCHELLE DES CRUS*. THOSE VILLAGES THAT HAVE BEEN AWARDED THE MAXIMUM ÉCHELLE OF 100% ARE CLASSIFIED AS *GRANDS CRUS*, WHEREAS THOSE RATED BETWEEN 90 AND 99% ARE *PREMIERS CRUS*, AND THE LOWEST-RATED VILLAGES ARE CURRENTLY 80%. IT WOULD BE UNREALISTIC TO EXPECT SUCH A CLASSIFICATION TO START AT 1%, SINCE NO VILLAGE WITH ONE-HUNDREDTH THE POTENTIAL OF A *GRAND CRU* WOULD MERIT THE CHAMPAGNE APPELLATION, BUT THE *ÉCHELLE DES CRUS* WAS ORIGINALLY A TRUE PERCENTILE SYSTEM, WITH VILLAGES RANKED AS LOW AS 22.5% AND A SPREAD OF VILLAGES IN THE MIDDLE GROUND. HOWEVER, DUE TO VARIOUS AD HOC RE-CLASSIFICATIONS AND POLITICAL POSTURING, THE MINIMUM ÉCHELLE HAS GRADUALLY INCREASED AND, IN TRUTH, THE PRESENT SYSTEM IS NO MORE THAN A 20-POINT SCALE.

GRANDS CRUS

There are 17 villages classified as *grands crus*, and all are located in the Marne *département*. They account for some 3,000 hectares or 8.6% of AOC Champagne.

Ambonnay
Avize
Aÿ-Champagne
Beaumont-sur-Vesle
Bouzy
Chouilly★
Cramant
Louvois
Mailly-Champagne
le Mesnil-sur-Oger
Oger
Oiry
Puisieulx
Sillery
Tours-sur-Marne★★
Verzenay
Verzy

THE VILLAGE OF CRAMANT SITS OVERLOOKING ITS GRAND CRU VINEYARDS

THE PREMIER CRU VILLAGE OF CUIS

LE MESNIL-SUR-OGER IS A GRAND CRU VILLAGE

PREMIERS CRUS

There are 41 villages that qualify as *premiers crus*, and these too are all located in the Marne *département*. They include two *grand cru* villages (Chouilly and Tours-sur-Marne) that are rated 100% for just one variety, and two villages (Etréchy and Grauves) that are *premiers crus* for one variety only. Together they account for some 7,500 hectares or almost 22% of AOC Champagne.

99% Mareuil-sur-Aÿ
     Tauxières

95% Bergères-les-Vertus
     Billy-le-Grand
     Bisseuil
     Chouilly★★
     Cuis★
     Dizy
     Grauves★
     Trépail
     Vaudemanges
     Vertus
     Villeneuve-Renneville
     Villers-Marmery
     Voipreux

94% Chigny-les-Roses
     Cormontreuil
     Ludes
     Montbré
     Rilly-la-Montagne
     Taissy
     Trois-Puits

93% Avenay
     Champillon
     Cumières
     Hautvillers
     Mutigny

90% Bezannes
     Chamery
     Coligny★
     Cuis★★
     Ecueil
     Etréchy★
     Grauves★★
     Jouy-les-Reims
     Pargny-les-Reims
     Pierry
     Sacy
     Tours-sur-Marne★
     Villedommange
     Villers-Allerand
     Villers-aux-Noeuds

Note: Villages★ are classified at this rank for white grapes only, while villages★★ are classified for black grapes only.

GRANDS & PREMIERS CRUS

THE MAP BELOW SHOWS HOW THE HIGHEST CLASSIFIED VILLAGES ARE LOCATED IN ONE SMALL AREA OF THE DESIGNATED CHAMPAGNE APPELLATION. ALL 17 GRANDS CRUS AND 41 PREMIERS CRUS ARE SITUATED IN THE MARNE DÉPARTEMENT

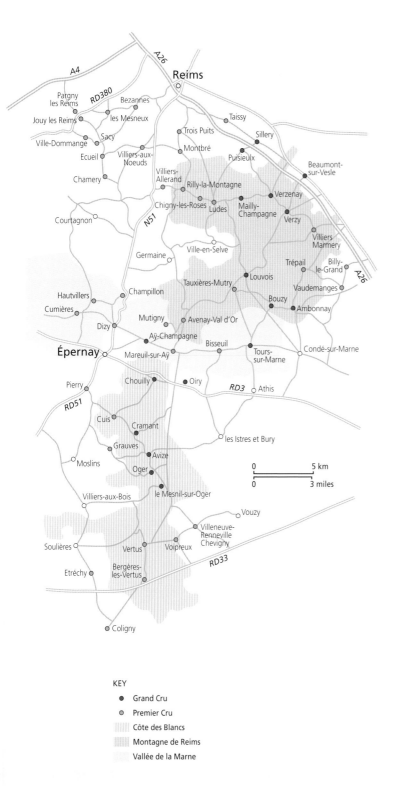

KEY
- ● Grand Cru
- ○ Premier Cru
- Côte des Blancs
- Montagne de Reims
- Vallée de la Marne

THE PRODUCERS

THERE ARE 19,000 SMALL GROWERS; 5112 OF THEM SELL CHAMPAGNE UNDER THEIR OWN LABEL

ALTHOUGH IT IS A COMPARATIVELY SMALL AREA, THE CHAMPAGNE VINEYARD AS A WHOLE IS DIVIDED INTO HUNDREDS OF TINY PARCELS INDIVIDUALLY OWNED AND MAINTAINED BY GROWERS. THESE GROWERS THEMSELVES FALL INTO MANY DIFFERENT CATEGORIES, MAKING CHAMPAGNE ONE OF THE MOST COMPLEX WINE AREAS OF THE WORLD.

There are 261 houses, 44 cooperatives, and 5,112 growers working within the Champagne appellation. A Champagne house is an informal name for a **négociant-manipulant**, the only producer permitted to purchase grapes in volume (Champagne growers are allowed to purchase grapes, but they are restricted to a maximum equivalent to 5% of their harvest).

The 261 houses own just 12% of the vineyards, yet are responsible for 71% of Champagne sales, thus their existence is dependant upon the purchase of grapes from the growers. The houses account for more than 88% of all Champagne exports and this rises to 97% outside of Europe, as few growers have the wherewithal to market their wines so far afield. Just 97 houses account for more than 95% of négoce sales. Of these houses, 10 account for 55%, and one, Moët & Chandon, produces more than 13% of all négociant-

HARVESTED GRAPES WAITING TO BE PRESSED

manipulant Champagne. These 261 houses sell Champagne under 1,316 different brand names.

There are a great many **cooperatives**, but only 44 make and sell Champagne under their own label. Although they account for just over seven per cent of total Champagne sales, the champenois cooperative movement as a whole processes more than half of all the Champagne produced at one stage or another (ie, pressing, still wine, Champagne sur-lattes). These 44 cooperatives sell Champagne under 231 different brand names.

Of the 19,000 **growers** in Champagne, only 5,112 sell Champagne under their own label and of these, just 2,124 actually make what they sell (but under 7,526 different brand names), accounting for just 18% of grower Champagne sales. Other growers have their Champagne made by a cooperative, thus there are literally thousands of grower brands which appear to be different products but are simply the same wine with a different label.

The growers together with the cooperatives are known collectively as the vignoble. Champagne growers own 88% of the vineyards, but account for just 22% of sales (29% including the cooperatives), thus they are reliant on the sale of grapes to the houses. Only 30 growers own more than 12 hectares and produce in excess of 80,000 bottles of Champagne, with a mere handful marketing as many as 200,000 bottles (which is more than the smallest houses produce).

PRODUCERS AND THEIR BRANDS

THERE ARE 9,206 BRANDS OF CHAMPAGNE MARKETED TO ONE DEGREE OR OTHER BY LESS THAN 2,500 TRUE PRODUCERS (HOUSES, GROWERS AND COOPERATIVES) AND MORE THAN 3,000 GROWERS, FIRMS AND INDIVIDUALS WHO ACT AS MIDDLE-MEN.

IN ADDITION TO THIS, THERE ARE A FURTHER 3,001 BUYER-OWN-BRANDS (SOLD BY RESTAURANTS, SUPERMARKETS, WINE MERCHANTS ETC WITH THEIR OWN NAME ON THE LABEL), MAKING A TOTAL OF 12,207 SEEMINGLY DIFFERENT BRANDS. SINCE EACH BRAND CONSISTS ON AVERAGE OF FOUR CUVÉES, THERE ARE WELL OVER 50,000 'DIFFERENT' CHAMPAGNES PRODUCED IN ANY ONE YEAR.

TYPES OF PRODUCER

THE INITIALS IN FRONT OF A SMALL CODE OR NUMBER ON THE LABEL, USUALLY AT THE BASE OF THE LABEL, IS THE KEY TO WHETHER THE CHAMPAGNE HAS BEEN PRODUCED BY A HOUSE (NM), A GROWER (RM) OR A COOPERATIVE (CM).

NM: NÉGOCIANT-MANIPULANT
A producer who buys grapes in volume from growers to make Champagne.

RM: RÉCOLTANT-MANIPULANT
A grower who sells grapes to the Houses as well as buying grapes from other growers and making his own Champagne.

CM: COOPÉRATIVE-MANIPULANT
A cooperative of growers who also make and sell Champagne under their own labels

RC: RÉCOLTANT-COOPÉRATIVE
A grower who sells a cooperative-produced Champagne under his own name. Although almost 4,000 RC brands are registered, they are seldom encountered even in France, and many of these cooperative clones are still sold with RM numbers.

SR: SOCIÉTÉ DE RÉCOLTANTS
A firm set up by two or more growers - often related - who share premises to make and market their Champagne under more than one brand.

ND: NÉGOCIANT DISTRIBUTEUR
A company selling Champagne it did not make.

MA: MARQUE D'ACHETEUR
A brand name owned by the purchaser, such as a restaurant, supermarket or wine merchant.

THE RULES OF CHAMPAGNE

ALTHOUGH THE MAKING OF CHAMPAGNE IS DEALT WITH IN SOME DETAIL IN THE OPENING CHAPTERS, THE FRENCH LOVE THEIR RULES AND CHAMPAGNE HAS MORE THAN MOST APPELLATIONS.

They start with the pressing, which is divided into the first pressing or cuvée and the second pressing or taille, both of which are misnomers because several pressings are necessary to extract the juice in both cases.

1 In a traditional coquard press, which has a capacity of 4000 kilos of grapes (known as a marc), only 2,550 litres of juice may be extracted - the first 2050 litres being the cuvée, the last 500 litres the taille. This rate of extraction was tightened up in 1992, prior to which an additional 166 litres of taille could be pressed.

2 A non-vintage Champagne must not be sold until at least 12 months after January 1st following the year of harvest, and a vintage at least 36 months. However, most non-vintage Champagne is aged for 18 to 30 months and, as the actual year of vintage Champagnes being sold will reveal, they are usually much more than three years old.

3 A vintage Champagne must be made using 100% of grapes grown in the year indicated (whereas the rule for other wines throughout the EU is 85%). To ensure the quality of non-vintage cuvées, no more than 85% of the grapes harvested in any one year may be sold as vintage (ie., 15% of the grapes from any one year must be used for non-vintage Champagne).

WHAT IS A GRANDE MARQUE?

A *GRANDE MARQUE* LITERALLY MEANS A GREAT OR FAMOUS BRAND, AND THIS FAME MAY BE DERIVED FROM EITHER QUALITY OR VOLUME: FORD AND ROLLS ROYCE ARE BOTH EQUALLY FAMOUS AND A SIMILAR EXAMPLE IN CHAMPAGNE MIGHT BE MOËT AND KRUG. QUALITY ALONE IS INSUFFICIENT: THE QUALITY MUST RESULT IN FAME FOR A BRAND TO BECOME A *GRANDE MARQUE*. MONSIEUR BLANC COULD MAKE THE GREATEST CHAMPAGNE IN THE WORLD, BUT IF FEW PEOPLE HAVE HEARD ABOUT IT, CHAMPAGNE BLANC WOULD NOT BE A *GRANDE MARQUE*.

Particular weight is given to the term *grande marque* in English-speaking countries, where the term has evolved into some sort of 'official' classification akin to the concept of a *grand cru*. The definition of *grande marque* became even more ambiguous when, in 1964, the Syndicat du Commerce des Vins de Champagne changed its name to the Syndicat de Grandes Marques de Champagne.

The Syndicat du Commerce des Vins de Champagne was established in 1882 to defend the Champagne name and by 1884 its membership amounted to 61 houses – practically everybody who was anybody in Champagne in those days. However, this membership declined as the less illustrious producers felt sidelined by the more famous names and, in 1912, a second, alternative organisation was formed, the Syndicat des Négociants en Vins de Champagne.

Those remaining in the original *syndicat* took the view that they comprised the elite – the *grandes marques* of Champagne in all but name and in 1964 they immodestly renamed themselves as such.

At that time the membership included Ayala, Billecart-Salmon, Bollinger, Veuve Clicquot, Delbeck, Deutz, Heidsieck & Co. Monopole, Charles Heidsieck, Irroy, Krug, Lanson, Massé, Moët & Chandon, Montebello, Mumm, Perrier-Jouët, Joseph Perrier, Piper-Heidsieck, Pol Roger, Pommery, Prieur (Napoleon), Roederer, Ruinart, Salon and Taittinger. Five new members were elected: Canard-Duchène and Henriot (because they were taken over by Veuve Clicquot), Mercier (because it was taken over by Moët), Laurent-Perrier and Gosset.

Twelve of these houses also belonged to the Champagne Shippers Association, a sort of Old Boys club that sponsored bright young things in the British wine trade to spend a couple of weeks going from house to house to learn 'all there is to know' about Champagne. One thing they did not learn, however, is that the official membership of the Syndicat de Grandes Marques de Champagne totalled 25-30 brands (the exact number depending on the year in question, of course). Consequently, as these lucky few distilled their new-found knowledge back into the trade whence they came, the idea emerged that there were only 12 *grandes marques*. When these house were referred to as the only *grandes marques* it used to so annoy Claude Taittinger (whose house was not a member of the Association of Champagne Shippers at the time) that he threatened to sue on more than one occasion.

In 1997 the Syndicat de Grandes Marques de Champagne disbanded itself. This was a direct result of a poll published in the 1991 Champagne supplement for *Wine & Spirit International* magazine in the UK. Every *grande marque* house was asked whether being a member of this *syndicat* was - or should be - a declaration of superior quality and if so, ought there to be some sort of quality criteria that members should abide by. They were also asked what those criteria should be and whether the *syndicat* should be opened up to any producer, regardless of status (because only houses belonged).

Bollinger was almost alone in answering affirmatively to all questions and when Christian Bizot, then head of Bollinger, read the answers of his peers, he did not know what was worse: those who said that membership of the *syndicat* was not a declaration of superior quality; those who said it was but thought it unnecessary to impose quality criteria for members; or those who thought quality criteria were necessary but didn't want to open the club to other producers who fulfilled such criteria and thought it unnecessary to kick out any members who failed to meet the terms.

Bizot was so ashamed of his colleagues that he declared he felt he had 'more in common with the growers than the *négoce*' and seriously considered resigning from the Syndicat de Grandes Marques de Champagne and joining the Syndicat Général du Vignerons instead. He did not, but to counteract the poor message his fellow members were communicating, Bizot launched 'Bollinger's Charter of Ethics & Quality', a two-page document which he published in various magazines. It soon became apparent, though, that no matter how fine the words of this document were, they meant nothing to the consumer unless they comprised a written guarantee on every bottle. Hence the development of Bollinger's back label to this effect.

It was De Venoge, however, that was first off the mark with such a warranty, and since then Deutz, Devaux and a whole host of others - the most significant being Moët - have all brought out their own versions.

It took four years from the date of *Wine & Spirit's* poll before we saw the avalanche of back label guarantees. During this time the Syndicat de Grandes Marques de Champagne elected a new chairman, Jean-Claude Rouzaud of Roederer, who promised a rebirth of the Syndicat with 'quality criteria and more open membership' or he would resign. Some critics wondered why he bothered: why not create a smaller club with the likes of Bollinger, Krug and other houses whose quality was assured, but his failure was not simply a matter of the smaller houses at loggerheads with the larger ones. After an exhaustive audit of every member of the Syndicat, it became clear that some of even the best quality Champagne houses simply did not have the financial, administrative or technological resources to guarantee the quality criteria that Rouzaud wished to set. Between the small, quality-conscious houses and the large, commercial bottlers there were those who wanted to comply but couldn't, and those who could have complied but didn't want to.

In the end it was not just Rouzaud who resigned, the whole lot did. At the time, in 1997, there were 24 *grandes marques*, accounting for 60% of all the Champagne sold by the 256 *négociants-manipulants*:

Ayala
Billecart-Salmon
Bollinger
Canard-Duchène
Deutz
Gosset
Charles Heidsieck
Heidsieck & Co Monopole
Krug
Lanson
Laurent-Perrier
Mercier
Moët & Chandon
Mumm
Joseph Perrier
Perrier-Jouët
Piper-Heidsieck
Pol Roger
Pommery
Roederer
Ruinart
Salon
Taittinger
Veuve Clicquot

The term *grande marque* will persist and, I suspect, another organisation might be resurrected after all the hullabaloo of the Millennium. It will be much easier to start afresh and, no matter how elitist the founding members may be, they must not make the fundamental error of calling themselves *grandes marques*. Houses deserving that accolade will always be decided by the market. Any new club must instead concern itself with guaranteeing a minimum quality that is significantly superior to an AOC that encompasses the lowest quality *premier prix*. The *négoce* must disown the prejudices of the past and open membership to any producer that satisifes its quality criteria, whoever they may be. Only then would the endorsement of such an organisation be worthy of a substantial price premium.

VINTAGE FARCE

ALTHOUGH NOT QUITE AS FANATICAL AS BOLLINGER'S PRACTICE OF DISGORGING EVERY BOTTLE NO MORE THAN 12 WEEKS PRIOR TO SHIPMENT, THE DISGORGING OF VINTAGE CHAMPAGNE TO ORDER IS A MATTER OF GRAVE CONCERN FOR THE ENTIRE INDUSTRY.

If Champagne wants the equivalent respect and reportage around the world as the great *crus classés* of Bordeaux, then every bottle of any specific vintage has to be disgorged at the same time, although when such disgorgements take place should still be up to the producer to get right or wrong.

This does not mean that the producers should be forced to disgorge every single bottle in one go, but any wines disgorged at a later date should carry a different label, to inform the customer that the wine is different from the regular vintage and, like Bollinger's RD, this could well demand a premium on the price paid.

But until a vintage tasted at any time in France is exactly the same as the one tasted at any time in the UK, USA, Australia et al, who is to know whether the wines described by, say, Michel Bettane, Michael Broadbent, Robert Parker, James Halliday or, indeed, this author are based on the same (disgorged) product. Indeed, the likelihood at the moment is that they will not.

There is an optimum moment to disgorge Champagne, just as there is an optimum moment to bottle a still wine, and the window of opportunity varies from vintage to vintage. Nearly everyone in Bordeaux had learned this lesson by the 1950s, but almost no one in Champagne appreciates its relevance 40 years later and the resistance to change is due purely to short-term commercial precautions. Not everyone likes the toasty, biscuity character of a mellow, mature Champagne, say the champenois. What about the majority of our customers, who prefer to drink Champagne as fresh as possible? they ask.

What about them? I reply. The majority of Champagne consumers

drink non-vintage Cuvées, whereas vintage Cuvées represent just 15-20 per cent of all Champagne sales. If some customers want to drink vintage Champagne freshly disgorged, then it is up to the producers to educate them. I don't mean change their taste, that would be arrogant, but advise them that if they want to drink a vintage Champagne freshly disgorged then, for the sake of producing one universally comparable product, they will only be able to do this when the vintage is first released, and they might have to wait two or three years for the next.

Until the great names of Champagne come around to this way of thinking, their best vintages will never earn the same respect as a great vintage from one of the *cru classé* châteaux of Bordeaux.

THERE IS AN OPTIMUM MOMENT TO DISGORGE CHAMPAGNE, JUST AS THERE IS AN OPTIMUM MOMENT TO BOTTLE A STILL WINE, AND THE WINDOW OF OPPORTUNITY VARIES FROM VINTAGE TO VINTAGE.

DID YOU KNOW?

THERE ARE 250 MILLION BUBBLES IN AN AVERAGE BOTTLE OF CHAMPAGNE. IT TAKES 1.2KGS OF GRAPES TO PRODUCE A BOTTLE OF CHAMPAGNE OR 1.5KGS IF IT IS PURE CUVÉE

85 VALUE
HENRI ABELÉ
REIMS

- 27,000 cases
- Group ownership - Freixenet
- Négociant-Manipulant

One of the oldest houses in Champagne, established by Théodore Vander Veken. He passed on ownership to his son, Remi, who handed it on to his nephew, Auguste Ruinart de Brimont, in 1828. In 1834, Brimont was joined by his brother-in-law, Antoine Müller, who had been the *chef de caves* at Veuve Clicquot, where he had helped the Widow develop the process of *remuage*.

From this partnership, the house passed on to François Abelé de Müller, whose son Henri took over and in 1903 changed the name of the house to Abelé-Vander Veken. In 1942, the house was sold to the Compagnie Française des Grands Vins, which was founded in 1908 by Eugène Charmat, the inventor of *cuve close*. It was purchased in 1985 by the giant Spanish group Freixenet, and the wines are now marketed under the Henri Abelé brand.

WINEMAKER
Hervé Ruin

HOUSE STYLE & RANGE
Soirées Parisiennes was introduced after the acquisition by Freixenet in response to the perceived swing in public taste towards lighter, fresher styles. However, Abelé is at its best when mature and toasty.
BRUT
Not vintaged, méthode champenoise: equal parts Chardonnay, Pinot Noir, Meunier
BRUT ROSÉ
Not vintaged, saignée, méthode champenoise: 30% Chardonnay, 45% Pinot Noir, 25% Meunier
★ LE SOURIRE DE REIMS ROSÉ
Not vintaged, saignée, méthode champenoise: 100% Pinot Noir
BRUT
Vintaged, méthode champenoise: 40% Chardonnay, 30% Pinot Noir, 30% Meunier
SOIRÉES PARISIENNES
Vintaged, méthode champenoise: 42% Chardonnay, 33% Pinot Noir, 25% Meunier
★ LE SOURIRE DE REIMS
Vintaged, méthode champenoise: 80% Chardonnay, 20% Pinot Noir

82
ADAM-GARNOTEL
RILLY-LA-MONTAGNE

- 30,000 cases
- Négociant-Manipulant

A little-known house established in 1899 by Louis Adam, with nine hectares of vineyards.
WINEMAKER
Garnotel family

HOUSE STYLE & RANGE
Deep; rich; with a simple, sprightly fruitiness.
★ BRUT
Not vintaged, méthode champenoise: 30% Chardonnay, 30% Pinot Noir, 40% Meunier
BRUT
Vintaged, méthode champenoise: 80% Chardonnay, 20% Pinot Noir
CUVÉE LOUIS ADAM
Vintaged, méthode champenoise: 90% Chardonnay, 10% Pinot Noir

83
AGRAPART
AVIZE

- 6,000 cases
- Récoltant-Manipulant

With nine hectares of vineyards in Avize, Cramant, Oger and Oiry, Pascal and Fabrice Agrapart are one of the larger growers.
WINEMAKER
Pascal Agrapart

HOUSE STYLE & RANGE
These Champagnes are richly flavoured with light dosage, but they can sometimes be too heavily influenced by malolactic fermentation, even when it is applied partially. The non-vintage *cuvées* have good bottle-age.
BRUT BLANC DE BLANCS, GRAND CRU
Not vintaged, 33% barrique-aged reserves from previous year, méthode champenoise: 100% Chardonnay
BRUT RÉSERVE, BLANC DE BLANCS, GRAND CRU
Not vintaged, two years older, 33% barrique-aged reserves from previous year, méthode champenoise: 100% Chardonnay
★ CUVÉE DES DEMOISELLES, BRUT ROSÉ, GRAND CRU
Not vintaged, addition of red wine, méthode champenoise: 93% Chardonnay, 7% Pinot Noir
★ L'AVIZOISE, BRUT BLANC DE BLANCS, GRAND CRU
Vintaged, vieilles vignes, partial malolactic, méthode champenoise: 100% Chardonnay
MILLÉSIME, BRUT BLANC DE BLANCS, GRAND CRU
Vintaged, méthode champenoise: 100% Chardonnay

LÉONCE D'ALBE
See VVE A DEVAUX

ARIDIS
See ARISTON

70
ARISTON
BROUILLET

- 5,500 cases
- Other labels - Aridis (but not used)
- Récoltant-Manipulant

After five generations as *vignerons*, the Ariston family established their own brand in 1970. Packaging is smart and unfussy.
WINEMAKER
Bruno Ariston

HARVESTING IN THE VINEYARD BELOW THE MOULIN DE VERZENAY ON THE MONTAGNE DE REIMS

HOUSE STYLE & RANGE

Clean, correct and respectable, if a bit pear-droppy. The Yellow Label is slightly fatter.

BRUT (WHITE LABEL)

Not vintaged, méthode champenoise:
40% Chardonnay, 40% Pinot Noir, 20% Meunier

BRUT (YELLOW LABEL)

Not vintaged, méthode champenoise:
40% Chardonnay, 40% Pinot Noir, 20% Meunier

ARLIT & CIE

See ALBERT LE BRUN

88
MICHEL ARNOULD

VERZENAY

• 6,700 cases

• Récoltant-Manipulant

Vignerons for five generations, the Arnoulds started making their own Champagne in 1961, specialising in pure Grand Cru Verzenay.

WINEMAKER

Patrick Arnould

HOUSE STYLE & RANGE

Rich but exquisitely balanced *blanc de noirs*.

★☆ BRUT GRAND CRU

Not vintaged, méthode champenoise: 100% Pinot Noir

★ BRUT ROSÉ GRAND CRU

Not vintaged, addition of red wine, méthode champenoise: 100% Pinot Noir

★☆ BRUT RÉSERVE GRAND CRU

Not vintaged, méthode champenoise; 30% Chardonnay, 70% Pinot Noir

★★ CUVÉE GRAND CRU 'AN 2000'

Not vintaged, méthode champenoise: 15% Chardonnay, 85% Pinot Noir

N/A
JEAN ARNOULT

BAR-SUR-SEINE

• 12,500 cases

• Négociant-Manipulant

The first house to be established in the Aube district, Jean Arnoult was founded in 1919 by its namesake when he was almost 60 years old. It was not until 1925, however, that the Jean Arnoult brand was first used. Not tasted for some time.

75
VINCENT D'ASTRÉE

PIERRY

• 8,500 cases

• Coopérative-Manipulant

A third of this collective's total production is returned to its members for commercialisation under their own individual labels, while another third is sold to the *négoce*.

WINEMAKER

Patrick Boivin

HOUSE STYLE & RANGE

Clean, fruity and straightforward.

BRUT 1ER CRU

Not vintaged, méthode champenoise: 20% Chardonnay, 80% Meunier

★ CUVÉE DE RÉSERVE, BRUT 1ER CRU

Not vintaged, méthode champenoise: 60% Chardonnay, 40% Pinot Noir

★ BRUT 1ER CRU

Vintaged, méthode champenoise: 100% Chardonnay

NICOLE D'AURIGNY

See VVE A DEVAUX

82 VALUE
AYALA

AY-CHAMPAGNE

• 50,000 cases

• Group ownership – also owns Château La Lagune in the Médoc

• Other labels – Montebello

• Négociant-Manipulant

This house has never been one of the truly great *grandes marques*, but it used to be one of the best value-for-money fizzes until the late 1980s, when the non-vintage brut started to deteriorate. Happily, the quality has since taken a turn for the better, and it is now back on good value form.

WINEMAKER

Nicolas Klym

HOUSE STYLE & RANGE

Light, fresh and pleasant, with a nice, cushiony mousse. The rosé is the least impressive, but the *grande cuvée* can be serious quality indeed.

★ BRUT

Not vintaged, méthode champenoise: 25% Chardonnay, 60% Pinot Noir, 15% Meunier

DEMI-SEC

Not vintaged, méthode champenoise: 10% Chardonnay, 30% Pinot Noir, 60% Meunier

ROSÉ BRUT

Not vintaged, addition of red wine, méthode champenoise: 10% Chardonnay, 90% Pinot Noir

★ BRUT

Vintaged, méthode champenoise: 25% Chardonnay, 75% Pinot Noir

BLANC DE BLANCS BRUT

Vintaged, méthode champenoise: 100% Chardonnay

★☆ GRANDE CUVÉE BRUT

Vintaged, méthode champenoise: 80% Chardonnay, 20% Pinot Noir

70
BARANCOURT

BOUZY

• 60,000 cases

• Group ownership - Vranken

• Négociant-Manipulant

The quality and individuality of these once-expressive Champagnes deteriorated under the original ownership of Jean-Paul Brice (*see* BRICE), Pierre Martin (*see* DELBECK) and Raynald Tritant, and sadly this has not abated under the ownership of Vranken, which took over Barancourt in 1994. The presentation has improved, but stylish bottles do not make stylish wines, and any devotees of authentic-style Barancourt *mono-crus* should look to Brice and Delbeck to bring back the happy memories. The last top-notch Champagne from Barancourt was the 1985 Cuvée des Fondateurs, but it was an even greater bargain sold *sur lattes* under the Chanoine label!

WINEMAKER

Arnaud Gallois

HOUSE STYLE & RANGE
Vrankenised.

BRUT RÉSERVE
Not vintaged, méthode champenoise:
30% Chardonnay, 70% Pinot Noir

CUVÉE DES FONDATEURS BRUT
Not vintaged, méthode champenoise:
20% Chardonnay, 80% Pinot Noir

CUVÉE DES FONDATEURS ROSÉ BRUT
Not vintaged, addition of red wine, méthode
champenoise: 5% Chardonnay, 95% Pinot Noir

RÉSERVE BRUT ROSÉ
Not vintaged, addition of red wine, méthode
champenoise: 15% Chardonnay, 85% Pinot Noir

★ BOUZY BRUT
Vintaged, méthode champenoise: 5% Chardonnay,
95% Pinot Noir

★ CUVÉE DES FONDATEURS BRUT
Vintaged, méthode champenoise: 5% Chardonnay,
95% Pinot Noir

85
BARDOUX
VILLEDOMMANGE

- 2,000 cases
- Récoltant-Manipulant

Vignerons in Villedommange since Pierre
Bardoux planted his first vine in 1684, the
Bardoux family started making their own
Champagne in 1929 under Jules and Prudent
Bardoux. The current incumbent is Pascal
Bardoux, who graduated from the Beaune
School of Viticulture in 1973 and describes
his Champagne as a 'classic malolactic style'.

WINEMAKER
Pascal Bardoux

HOUSE STYLE & RANGE
Rich and fruity, with as many as four
different vintages on offer.

★ BRUT 1ER CRU
Not vintaged, méthode champenoise: 20%
Chardonnay, 15% Pinot Noir, 65% Meunier

★ BRUT RÉSERVE, 1ER CRU
Not vintaged, méthode champenoise: 40%
Chardonnay, 20% Pinot Noir, 40% Meunier

★ BRUT 1ER CRU
Vintaged, méthode champenoise: 30% Chardonnay,
35% Pinot Noir, 35% Meunier

70
E BARNAUT
BOUZY

- 650 cases
- Other labels - Louis François
- Récoltant-Manipulant

This family enterprise was established by
Edmond Barnaut in 1874, and the brand is
still in use by his grandchildren, the Secondé
family. Barnaut's 14.5 hectares of vineyards
(which include 2.5 hectares in the Marne
Valley used exclusively for the Louis François
label) could theoretically yield approximately
10,000 cases per year, which makes the
actual production of 650 cases pale by
comparison. But like so many *vignerons*,
Philippe Secondé sells a proportion of the
harvest to the *négoce* – in this case, a very
large proportion indeed. Secondé harvests a
little later than the norm for the rest of
Bouzy and always by a succession of *tries*, or
sweeps, through the vineyards, picking out
only the ripest, healthiest grapes.

WINEMAKER
Philippe Secondé

HOUSE STYLE & RANGE
Ripeness allows for a light *dosage*. When
successful, the wines are made in a classic,
complex style, but all too often they lack
finesse. The rosé is best-known, but the
Sélection Brut is the most successful.

BLANC DE NOIRS, BRUT GRAND CRU
Not vintaged, average of five years' bottle-age,
méthode champenoise: 100% Pinot Noir

BRUT ROSÉ, GRAND CRU
Not vintaged, reverse saignée, méthode champenoise:
10% Chardonnay, 90% Pinot Noir

CUVÉE DOUCEUR SEC, GRAND CRU
Not vintaged, average of five years' bottle-age,
méthode champenoise: 30% Chardonnay,
70% Pinot Noir

GRANDE RÉSERVE, BRUT GRAND CRU
Not vintaged, average of five years' bottle-age,
méthode champenoise: 30% Chardonnay,
70% Pinot Noir

★ SÉLECTION EXTRA, BRUT GRAND CRU
Not vintaged, two years older than above, méthode
champenoise: 10% Chardonnay, 90% Pinot Noir

N/A
ROGER BARNIER
VILLEVENARD

- 3,250 cases
- Récoltant-Manipulant

The Barnier family first made Champagnes
under their own brand in 1932, but have
been *vignerons* for five generations, with
seven hectares of vines at Villevenard and the
Congy district. Villevenard is at the northern
extreme of the Sézanne district, and is known
as much for its Meunier as Chardonnay.

WINEMAKER
Frédéric Berthelot

HOUSE RANGE
BRUT CARTE NOIRE

Not vintaged, minimum 20% réserve wine, méthode
champenoise: 40% Chardonnay, 20% Pinot Noir,
40% Meunier

BRUT
Vintaged, méthode champenoise: 50% Chardonnay,
50% Pinot Noir

DEMI-SEC
Vintaged, méthode champenoise: 50% Chardonnay,
50% Pinot Noir

BRUT EXQUISE CUVÉE
Not vintaged, barrique-aged, partial malolactic,
méthode champenoise: 60% Chardonnay,
40% Meunier

BRUT ROSÉ
Not vintaged, addition of red wine, méthode
champenoise: 30% Chardonnay, 50% Pinot Noir,
20% Meunier

COLLECTION 'AN 2000'
Not vintaged, decorated bottle, méthode champenoise:
40% Chardonnay, 20% Pinot Noir, 20% Meunier

BRUT
Vintaged, méthode champenoise: 50% Chardonnay,
50% Pinot Noir

BRUT BLANC DE BLANCS
Vintaged, Vertus mono-cru, méthode champenoise:
100% Chardonnay

DEMI-SEC
Vintaged, méthode champenoise: 50% Chardonnay,
50% Pinot Noir

80
BARON ALBERT
CHARLY–SUR–MARNE

- 350,000 cases
- Other labels - Jean de la Fontaine
- Négociant-Manipulant

Vignerons since the 16th century, the Baron
Albert family established this firm in 1947,
and now owns 30 hectares of Marne Valley
vineyards on the western fringes of
Champagne.

The Jean de la Fontaine label is a prestige
cuvée (not a second brand), and is named after
the famous French poet who was born at
Château-Thierry in 1621, and wrote *The
Coach and the Fly* while travelling through
these vineyards.

A feature of Champagne Baron Albert is
that none of the wines go through
malolactic, and the *dosage* liquor for all its
cuvées is matured in oak casks.

WINEMAKER
Claude Baron

HOUSE STYLE & RANGE
Oddly enough, this house has succeeded in
off-years and disappointed in great vintages.
The 1987 Jean de la Fontaine was, for
example, one of the best Champagnes
produced that year. Can be too amylic, but
has definitely improved over the last five
years or so, and when successful, is always
good value in a straightforward, fruity style.

★ BRUT ROSÉ

Not vintaged, addition of red wine, méthode champenoise: 50% Chardonnay, 10% Pinot Noir, 40% Meunier

CARTE D'OR BRUT

Not vintaged, méthode champenoise: 50% Chardonnay, 50% Meunier

★ BRUT

Vintaged, méthode champenoise: 50% Chardonnay, 25% Pinot Noir, 25% Meunier

PRÉFÉRENCE BRUT

Vintaged, méthode champenoise: 70% Chardonnay, 15% Pinot Noir, 15% Meunier

JEAN DE LA FONTAINE BRUT

Vintaged, méthode champenoise: 60% Chardonnay, 20% Pinot Noir, 20% Meunier

70
BAUCHET
BISSEUIL

- 4,000 cases
- Other labels - Chatelin, Dom Casimir, Comte de Lisseuil, Saint Niçaise
- Récoltant-Manipulant

One of the largest growers, with 38 hectares of vineyards in Bisseuil, Grauves, Avize and the Aube, although production under the Bauchet label did not commence until 1975.

WINEMAKER

Lionel Legras

HOUSE STYLE & RANGE

Plenty of rustic richness, but a lack of finesse on the nose of most *cuvées* suggests that improvements could be made in the pressing.

RÉSERVE BRUT, 1ER CRU

Not vintaged, méthode champenoise: 70% Chardonnay, 30% Pinot Noir

SÉLECTION BRUT, 1ER CRU

Not vintaged, méthode champenoise: 60% Chardonnay, 40% Pinot Noir

BRUT MILLÉSIME

Vintaged, méthode champenoise: 70% Chardonnay, 30% Pinot Noir

---

SAINT NIÇAISE BRUT ROSÉ

Vintaged, addition of red wine, méthode champenoise: 85% Chardonnay, 15% Pinot Noir

SAINT NIÇAISE CUVÉE PRESTIGE, BLANC DE BLANCS, BRUT 1ER CRU

Vintaged, méthode champenoise: 100% Chardonnay

BRUT ROSÉ, 1ER CRU

Vintaged, addition of red wine, méthode champenoise: 85% Chardonnay, 15% Pinot Noir

65
BAUGET-JOUETTE
EPERNAY

- 130,000 cases
- Négociant-Manipulant

A vinegrower since 1822, Bauget-Jouette produced its first grower Champagne in 1949; by the early 1980s, it had become one of the largest *récoltants-manipulant*. Today, this firm is a fully-fledged *négociant-manipulant*, and its 14 hectares of vineyards provide as much as 80% of its total requirements.

WINEMAKER

Jean-Pierre & Gerard Bauget

HOUSE STYLE & RANGE

Still in amylic mode.

CARTE BLANCHE BRUT

Not vintaged, three years old, méthode champenoise: 40% Chardonnay, 20% Pinot Noir, 40% Meunier

GRANDE RÉSERVE BRUT

Not vintaged, extra year's ageing, méthode champenoise: 60% Chardonnay, 20% Pinot Noir, 20% Meunier

ROSÉ BRUT

Not vintaged, méthode champenoise: grape varieties not revealed

BRUT

Vintaged, méthode champenoise: 70% Chardonnay, 30% Pinot Noir

BLANC DE BLANCS BRUT

Vintaged, méthode champenoise: 100% Chardonnay

CUVÉE JOUETTE

Vintaged, méthode champenoise: 60% Chardonnay, 40% Pinot Noir

BCC

This stands for Boizel Chanoine Champagne, which replaced Paillard Baijot Investments (PBI) in 1996, when the group increased its 54.6% ownership of Champagne Boizel to 100%, and the Roques-Boizel family became an equal partner with Bruno Paillard and Philippe Baijot.

In addition to Boizel, this group includes Philipponnat and Abel Lepitre, but not Champagne Bruno Paillard, which has always been independently owned.

87
ANDRÉ BEAUFORT
AMBONNAY

- 2,000 cases
- Récoltant-Manipulant

Established in 1933 by André Beaufort and run today by Jacques Beaufort, whose seven hectares of vineyards include a few parcels in the Aube. All the vines are grown bio-dynamically and, like many growers, Beaufort offers four or five different vintages at the same time.

WINEMAKER

Claude Beaufort

HOUSE STYLE & RANGE

Such weird aromas have been present in some of these wines in the past that the odd, amylic-style *cuvée* has been a relief, but the quality and character of these wines have stabilised since the 1990 vintage.

★ BRUT

Not vintaged, méthode champenoise: 33% Chardonnay, 67% Pinot Noir

★★ BRUT GRAND CRU

Not vintaged, méthode champenoise: 33% Chardonnay, 67% Pinot Noir

★★ BRUT MILLÉSIME

Vintaged, méthode champenoise: 33% Chardonnay, 67% Pinot Noir

★★ ROSÉ BRUT GRAND CRU

Not vintaged, addition of red wine, méthode champenoise: 30% Chardonnay, 70% Pinot Noir

N/A
CLAUDE BEAUFORT
AMBONNAY

- Récoltant-Manipulant

Claude Beaufort is, at the time of writing, the mayor of Ambonnay.

WINEMAKER

Claude Beaufort

HOUSE STYLE & RANGE

Not impressed in the past, but not tasted recently; thus judgement reserved.

BLANC DE BLANCS BRUT

Not vintaged, méthode champenoise: 100% Chardonnay

CUVÉE RÉSERVE BRUT

Not vintaged, méthode champenoise: 85% Chardonnay, 15% Pinot Noir

BRUT ROSÉ

Vintaged, méthode champenoise: 50% Chardonnay, 50% Pinot Noir

84
CLAUDE BEAUFORT & FILS
TREPAIL

- 3,000 cases
- Récoltant-Manipulant

The Beaufort family have been *vignerons* in Trépail for five generations, and Champagne Claude Beaufort & Fils is today under the direction of Arnaud Beaufort.

WINEMAKER

Arnaud Beaufort

HOUSE STYLE & RANGE

Malolactic fermentation is usually avoided, producing crisp wines that require several years to fill out.

BLANC DE BLANCS BRUT

Not vintaged, méthode champenoise: 100% Chardonnay

BRUT ROSÉ

Not vintaged, méthode champenoise: grape varieties not revealed

CUVÉE RÉSERVE BRUT/EXTRA DRY

Not vintaged, méthode champenoise: 80% Chardonnay, 20% Pinot Noir

★★ BRUT PREMIER CRU

Vintaged, méthode champenoise: 70% Chardonnay, 30% Pinot Noir

VINEYARDS OUTSIDE THE VILLAGE OF BOUZY

85
HERBERT BEAUFORT
BOUZY

- 12,000 cases
- Récoltant-Manipulant

The Beaufort family have been *vignerons* in Bouzy since 1820, and today own almost 17 hectares of vineyards entirely within the village boundaries.

WINEMAKER

Henry Beaufort

HOUSE STYLE & RANGE

The delicious, non-vintage Carte d'Or is double the quality of the basic Carte Blanche for just an extra ten per cent on the price, but the alliteration of Bouzy Blanc de Blancs rolls off the tongue far more smoothly than Herbert Beaufort's Cuvée du Mélomane.

CARTE BLANCHE BRUT

Not vintaged, méthode champenoise: 30% Chardonnay, 70% Pinot Noir

★ CARTE D'OR BRUT

Not vintaged, méthode champenoise: 100% Pinot Noir

CUVÉE DU MÉLOMANE

Not vintaged, méthode champenoise: 100% Chardonnay

★★ BRUT

Vintaged, méthode champenoise: 100% Pinot Noir

★ BRUT ROSÉ

Vintaged, saignée, méthode champenoise: 100% Pinot Noir

JACQUES BEAUFORT
See ANDRÉ BEAUFORT

80
BEAUMET
EPERNAY

- 50,000 cases
- Other labels - Jeanmaire, Oudinot, Chaurey, Freminet
- Group ownership - small group of three brands owned by Jacques, Michel & Franck Trouillard
- Négociant-Manipulant

Not so much a small group of three houses as large premises with three entrances. Originally established in 1878 at Pierry, Beaumet moved to Châlons-sur-Marne, which is now called Châlons-en-Champagne, and was taken over by Chaurey in the 1950s. Then, as Beaumet-Chaurey, it passed through the hands of Charbaut and Leclerc-Briant and in the process found itself back in Épernay (Pierry is virtually a suburb). It was acquired in 1977 by Jacques Trouillard, and in 1980, Beaumet moved into Parc Malakoff, a two-hectare site and its current address.

In 1981, Jacques Trouillard sold the Trouillard-de-Venoge group to Joseph Henriot, and purchased Oudinot and Jeanmaire. According to the firm itself, the *cuvées* of Beaumet, Jeanmaire and Oudinot are exactly the same – the different labels merely make it easier to trade with different sectors of the market so that, for example, the brand sold through supermarkets does not devalue the one purchased by restaurants. You can imagine my consternation, therefore, when every year they used to send me the complete range of all three brands. I used to wonder if they had decided to make some of the *cuvées* different and were testing me to see if I noticed. Either that, or they had an evil sense of humour!

WINEMAKER

Denis Colombier

HOUSE STYLE & RANGE

Generally fresh and clean, but often too amylic. Old vintages are the best value, particularly of the *blanc de blancs*. *Cuvées* below refer to Jeanmaire and Oudinot as well as Beaumet.

BRUT 1ER CRU

Not vintaged, méthode champenoise: 30% Chardonnay, 40% Pinot Noir, 30% Meunier

BLANC DE BLANCS BRUT

Not vintaged, méthode champenoise: 100% Chardonnay

DEMI-SEC

Not vintaged, méthode champenoise: 30% Chardonnay, 40% Pinot Noir, 30% Meunier

ROSÉ BRUT

Not vintaged, saignée, méthode champenoise: 70% Pinot Noir, 30% Meunier

BLANC DE NOIRS GRAND CRU BRUT

Vintaged, méthode champenoise: 100% Pinot Noir

GRAND CRU BRUT

Vintaged, méthode champenoise: 40% Chardonnay, 60% Pinot Noir

ROSÉ BRUT

Vintaged, saignée, méthode champenoise: 100% Pinot Noir

CUVÉE DU CENTENAIRE BLANC DE BLANCS BRUT

Mature vintages, méthode champenoise: 100% Chardonnay

★★ CUVÉE MALAKOFF/ELYSÉE/PARTICULIÈRE BLANC DE BLANCS

Vintaged, méthode champenoise: 100% Chardonnay

★★ CUVÉE MALAKOFF/ELYSÉE/PARTICULIÈRE ROSÉ

Vintaged, saignée, méthode champenoise: 100% Pinot Noir

★★ RÉSERVES ELYSÉE BRUT

Mature vintages up to 30 years old, méthode champenoise: 100% Chardonnay

87 VALUE
BEAUMONT DES CRAYÈRES
MARDEUIL

- 40,000 cases
- Other labels - Charles Leprince
- Coopérative-Manipulant

A co-op of 210 growers, with 80 hectares of vineyards concentrated in Vauciennes, Cumières, Verneuil and Mardeuil. These are not *grand cru* villages (and only Cumières is a *premier cru*), but most of the members own very small vineyards which are looked after at weekends and tended to like gardens, without resort to machines or chemicals. With such quality-conscious members it's not quite so surprising that Beaumont des Crayères makes Champagne beyond the quality of its *echelle*.

WINEMAKER

Jean-Paul Bertus

HOUSE STYLE & RANGE

Ripe grapes ensures richness and allows for a light dosage. Top *cuvées* can be bursting with richness.

★★ CUVÉE DE PRESTIGE BRUT

Not vintaged, partly barrique-vinified, méthode champenoise: 15% Chardonnay, 40% Pinot Noir, 15% Meunier

★ CUVÉE DE RÉSERVE BRUT/DEMI-SEC

Not vintaged, méthode champenoise: 25% Chardonnay, 55% Pinot Noir, 20% Meunier

★ ROSÉ PRIVILÈGE BRUT

Not vintaged, méthode champenoise: equal parts Chardonnay, Pinot Noir, Meunier

★★ NOSTALGIE BRUT

Vintaged, partly barrique vinified, méthode champenoise: 70% Chardonnay, 30% Pinot Noir

75
BESSERAT DE BELLEFON

EPERNAY

- 90,000 cases
- Group ownership - Marne et Champagne
- Négociant-Manipulant

WINEMAKER

Vincent Malherbe

HOUSE STYLE & RANGE

Since this brand was purchased by Marne et Champagne, I have not been as excited by these *cuvées* as often as I have by the many exceptional BOBs produced by Marne et Champagne – even though they are made by the same winemaker in the same premises.

BRUT GRANDE TRADITION

Not vintaged, méthode champenoise: 35% Chardonnay, 35% Pinot Noir, 30% Meunier

★ CUVÉE DES MOINES BRUT

Not vintaged, méthode champenoise: 20% Chardonnay, 55% Pinot Noir, 25% Meunier

CUVÉE DES MOINES ROSÉ BRUT

Not vintaged, addition of red wine, méthode champenoise: 20% Chardonnay, 60% Pinot Noir, 20% Meunier

BRUT MILLÉSIME

Vintaged, méthode champenoise: 60% Chardonnay, 25% Pinot Noir, 15% Meunier

ROSÉ MILLÉSIME

Vintaged, addition of red wine, méthode champenoise: 30% Chardonnay, 50% Pinot Noir, 20% Meunier

★ GRANDE CUVÉE BLANC DE BLANCS

Vintaged, méthode champenoise: 60% Chardonnay, 40% Pinot Noir

BILLECART-SALMON

See p. 53

86
HENRI BILLIOT

AMBONNAY

- 3,400 cases
- Récoltant-Manipulant

Pure *mono-cru* Champagnes from tiny two-hectare vineyard in Ambonnay.

WINEMAKER

Serge Billiot

HOUSE STYLE & RANGE

Classic, power-packed, non-malo style that requires considerable bottle-age to show its real potential.

★ BRUT RÉSERVE

Not vintaged, méthode champenoise: 25% Chardonnay, 75% Pinot Noir

BRUT ROSÉ

Not vintaged, addition of red wine, méthode champenoise: 15% Chardonnay, 85% Pinot Noir

BRUT TRADITION

Not vintaged, méthode champenoise: 25% Chardonnay, 75% Pinot Noir

★★ BRUT MILLÉSIME

Vintaged, méthode champenoise: 20% Chardonnay, 80% Pinot Noir

★ CUVÉE LAETITIA

Not vintaged, méthode champenoise: 40% Chardonnay, 60% Pinot Noir

79
BINET

RILLY-LA-MONTAGNE

- 25,000 cases
- Group ownership - Germain
- Négociant-Manipulant

Repackaged and launched in the mid-1990s, Binet is aimed at those parts of the restaurant market that parent company Germain cannot reach. Until then, this was little more than a *sous-marque* of H Germain, except in Great Britain, where it has been shipped without break since 1887 by Berry Bros & Rudd.

WINEMAKER

Hervé Laduce

HOUSE STYLE & RANGE

Ironically, given the above, the style is fruit-driven; thus these are not food wines.

BRUT ÉLITE

Not vintaged, méthode champenoise: 15% Chardonnay, 50% Pinot Noir, 35% Meunier

BRUT ROSÉ

Not vintaged, addition of red wine, méthode champenoise: 15% Chardonnay, 85% Pinot Noir

★ CUVÉE SÉLECTION

Not vintaged, méthode champenoise: 23% Chardonnay, 67% Pinot Noir

BRUT

Vintaged, méthode champenoise: 25% Chardonnay, 60% Pinot Noir, 15% Meunier

★ BLANC DE BLANCS BRUT

Vintaged, méthode champenoise: 100% Chardonnay

80
DE BLEMOND

CUIS

- 8,000 cases
- Coopérative-Manipulant

Small cooperative of 100 growers owning 40 hectares in the northwestern hinterland of the Côte des Blancs.

WINEMAKER

Pierre Munier

HOUSE STYLE & RANGE

Value-for-money, fruit-driven non-vintage; less impressive at the top end of the range.

BRUT 1ER CRU

Not vintaged, méthode champenoise: 20% Chardonnay, 40% Pinot Noir, 40% Meunier

BRUT 1ER CRU SÉLECTION GRANDE RÉSERVE

Not vintaged, méthode champenoise: 40% Chardonnay, 30% Pinot Noir, 30% Meunier

BLANC DE BLANCS BRUT

Vintaged, méthode champenoise: 100% Chardonnay

85
HENRI BLIN

VINCELLES

- 42,000 cases
- Coopérative-Manipulant

Tony Rasselet has worked hard to make the best possible wine from the good but limited quality of 110 hectares of *petit crus* vineyards in the Marne Valley which belong to this co-op's 95 members. He came good with the wines produced from 1986 onwards. A high-tech press-house was built in 1990.

WINEMAKER

Tony Rasselet

HOUSE STYLE & RANGE

Fresh, clean and fruity in general, but the best *cuvées* develop a nice biscuity complexity after a couple of years additional bottle-age, particularly when in magnum.

BRUT CHARDONNAY

Not vintaged, méthode champenoise: 100% Chardonnay

★ BRUT RÉSERVE

Not vintaged, méthode champenoise: 20% Chardonnay, 80% Pinot Noir

BRUT ROSÉ

Not vintaged, addition of red wine, méthode champenoise: 50% Pinot Noir, 50% Meunier

BRUT TRADITION/DEMI-SEC

Not vintaged, méthode champenoise: 5% Pinot Noir, 95% Meunier

★ BRUT MILLÉSIME

Vintaged, méthode champenoise: 50% Chardonnay, 50% Pinot Noir

85
BLONDEL

LUDES

- 8,400 cases
- Négociant-Manipulant

Founded in 1904, this small family-owned

house owns ten hectares of vineyards and is run by Brigette and Thierry Blondel, whose wines show particularly well in French consumer publications.

WINEMAKER
Thierry Blondel

HOUSE STYLE & RANGE
A capable producer with a fine, fruity rosé and an interesting selection of old vintages going back to 1974 (on request), but the basic Carte Or Brut is rather light and neutral.

BRUT ROSÉ

Not vintaged, méthode champenoise: 20% Chardonnay, 80% Pinot Noir

CARTE OR BRUT

Not vintaged, méthode champenoise: 30% Chardonnay, 70% Pinot Noir

CUVÉE 'AN 2000'

Not vintaged, méthode champenoise: 45% Chardonnay, 55% Pinot Noir

BLANC DE BLANCS

Vintaged, méthode champenoise: 100% Chardonnay

VIEUX MILLÉSIME

Vintaged, méthode champenoise: 100% Chardonnay

85 VALUE
BOIZEL

EPERNAY
- 230,000 cases
- Other labels – Kremer, Camuset, Montoy, Veuve Borodin, Veuve Delaroy
- Group ownership – BCC
- Négociant-Manipulant

Like many Champagne houses, Boizel suffered a severe cash-flow problem due to the recession in the early 1990s. Rumours of a Japanese investment in the company were rife by 1994, but in fact it was Paillard Baijot Investments (PBI) which bailed out the company.

Ironically, after two years of heavy losses, Boizel made a profit in 1994. Luckily the Roques-Boizel family had retained almost 46% of Boizel's shareholding which it was later able to exchange for equal partnership within Boizel Chanoine Champagne (BCC), which replaced PBI; thus, it now owns part of four different Champagne houses, including the recently acquired Philipponnat and Abel Lepitre.

All in all, the Roques-Boizels have not

95
BILLECART-SALMON

MAREUIL-SUR-AY
- 60,000 cases
- Other labels – Charles le Bel (made from the *tailles*, mostly sold in France)
- Négociant-Manipulant

The Billecart family has lived in Mareuil-sur-Aÿ since the 16th century. Pierre Billecart was Parliamentary Counsellor to Louis XIII, and it was his son, Nicolas-François Billecart, who established this house with the help of his brother-in-law, Louis Salmon, in 1818.

A small, family-owned house that always produces high-quality Champagne of great finesse, Billecart-Salmon is particularly renowned for the delicate style of its rosé, which accounts for one in every five bottles it sells. The essence of the Billecart-Salmon style has always been its meticulous production, from the double *débourbage,* or cleansing of the must, through the use of its own cultured yeast (from the best natural yeasts of Avize, Cramant and Verzenay), to its long, slow, very cool fermentation.

Billecart-Salmon was exceptional years ago and, due to the acquisition of ten hectares of vineyards and a constant upgrade in the source of purchased grapes, the wines are even better today.

WINEMAKER
François Domi

HOUSE STYLE & RANGE
A delight for those who enjoy a purity and ripeness of fruit in their Champagnes, yet want them to be capable of ageing well.

★★☆ BRUT RÉSERVE

Not vintaged, méthode champenoise: 30% Chardonnay, 35% Pinot Noir, 35% Meunier

★★☆ BRUT ROSÉ

Not vintaged, addition of red wine, méthode champenoise: 30% Chardonnay, 35% Pinot Noir, 35% Meunier

★★★☆ BLANC DE BLANCS BRUT

Vintaged, méthode champenoise: 100% Chardonnay

★★★☆ GRANDE CUVÉE BRUT

Vintaged, méthode champenoise: 80% Chardonnay, 20% Pinot Noir

★★★☆ ELIZABETH SALMON ROSÉ

Vintaged, addition of red wine, méthode champenoise: 42% Chardonnay, 58% Pinot Noir

★★★☆ NICOLAS-FRANÇOIS BILLECART

Vintaged, méthode champenoise: 45% Chardonnay, 55% Pinot Noir

done badly despite the hard times, and Evelyn Roques-Boizel remains in day-to-day control of her former family firm.

WINEMAKER

Christophe Roques-Boizel

HOUSE STYLE & RANGE

After a period in the late 1980s when the individual personality of these wines was destroyed by amylic aromas, the previously established quality-for-money ratio has returned with a vengeance.

The Brut Chardonnay is one of the most underrated *blanc de blancs* Champagnes, and the Joyeau de France is fine quality by any standards.

★★⚹ BRUT CHARDONNAY

Not vintaged, méthode champenoise: 100% Chardonnay

★ BRUT RÉSERVE

Not vintaged, méthode champenoise: 30% Chardonnay, 55% Pinot Noir, 15% Meunier

⚹ BRUT ROSÉ

Not vintaged, méthode champenoise: 10% Chardonnay, 50% Pinot Noir, 40% Meunier

★ BRUT GRAND VINTAGE

Vintaged, méthode champenoise: 30% Chardonnay, 60% Pinot Noir, 10% Meunier

★★ JOYEAU DE FRANCE, BRUT

Vintaged, méthode champenoise: 35% Chardonnay, 65% Pinot Noir

96
BOLLINGER

AY–CHAMPAGNE

- 100,000 cases
- Bollinger also owns Langlois in the Loire, and is in collaboration with Brian Croser at Petaluma in Australia, and Allied-Hiram and Antinori at Atlas Peak in California.
- Négociant-Manipulant

I am one of Bollinger's greatest fans, but this house's strict disgorgement policy is a bone of contention. Every bottle of Bollinger, whether vintage or not, is disgorged 12 weeks before shipment. This is to ensure that each bottle reaches the customer in the freshest condition possible.

Such a philosophy is fine for the Special Cuvée, as most non-vintage Champagne is consumed shortly after purchase. Also, the fresh, acacia-like aromas of a disgorgement add a thread of continuity to the style of each *cuvée*, no matter what year it is based on. For a vintage product, however, the effect is quite the reverse, as it denies the wine the very consistency that should occur naturally in all examples of the same vintage.

Disgorging to order makes as little sense for Bollinger Grande Année as it would for Château Margaux: there is an optimum moment to bottle a red wine just as there is to disgorge a sparkling wine. Economically, however, whether winemakers carry out these operations at the best possible moment is less important than doing them at the same time.

This disgorgement policy not only makes it impossible for wine enthusiasts and critics to assess each vintage of Grande Année on a universal basis, it also obscures Bollinger's RD concept. A registered trademark, RD stands for *récemment dégorgé*, and was used to indicate a vintage that had been disgorged several years after it was first released.

This should provide a fascinating comparison of how the same wine matures when aged for, say, eight or ten years on its yeast, compared to four or five, when the vintage was originally marketed. At these two soundly spaced, well-defined junctures, the wine will be radically different. Yet if, as Bollinger now does, the vintage is disgorged to order numerous times, the myriad of intermediate variations dilutes and blurs the RD effect.

This eroding of the RD concept is a pity as far as Bollinger is concerned, but the disgorging of vintage Champagne according to when it will be shipped rather than its intrinsic quality is also a widespread practice that undermines the potential reputation of the entire industry.

Bollinger is, however, a house *par excellence* for vintage Champagne, and my advice to lovers of toasty, mature Champagne is to buy the vintage by the case when it is first released so that you can follow its true development, and leave those who prefer the flowery disgorgement aromas to pay twice the price for the RD *cuvées*.

WINEMAKER

Gerard Liot

HOUSE STYLE & RANGE

Classic, Pinot-dominated Champagnes of great potential longevity and complexity, Bollinger tends to go toasty rather than biscuity, due no doubt to the influence of oak, rather than of Chardonnay, which plays a relatively minor role. There is a huge difference between Bollinger's non-vintage and vintage styles, and even the non-vintage varies according to whether you buy it by the bottle or magnum.

At least half of the wines used for the Special Cuvée are cask-fermented, making it one of the most complex non-vintage Champagnes

MAISON BOLLINGER IN AY–CHAMPAGNE, THE HEADQUARTERS FOR THIS FAMOUS CHAMPAGNE HOUSE

on the market, with a lean, austere, acidic, even unforgiving character, with oaky echoes on the finish. Although dominated by the mature, oxidative aromas of reserve wines going back 15 years or so, these represent just six to eight per cent of the blend, the main component of which is very young indeed. Thus, with three years' further ageing its oxidative nature doesn't increase; rather, the wine becomes silky-smooth, toasty and mellow.

Magnums of Special Cuvée are always much softer, extremely fruit-driven and far more accessible. There are no oxidative aromas, yet they mature to great complexity and finesse over a much longer period. The vintage *cuvées* are classic and complex, never austere, and some might say the Vieilles Vignes Françaises Blanc de Noirs is not classic Champagne in any sense of the term – although all would agree that it is in a class of its own.

✫ SPECIAL CUVÉE (BOTTLES)
Not vintaged, méthode champenoise:
25% Chardonnay, 60% Pinot Noir, 15% Meunier

★✫ SPECIAL CUVÉE (MAGNUMS)
Not vintaged, méthode champenoise:
25% Chardonnay, 60% Pinot Noir, 15% Meunier

★★✫ GRANDE ANNÉE
Vintaged, méthode champenoise: 39% Chardonnay,
61% Pinot Noir

★★✫ RD
Vintaged, same as Grande Année, but with more age
on yeast

★ GRANDE ANNÉ ROSÉ
Vintaged, same as Grande Année, but with the
addition of red wine

★★★ VIEILLES VIGNES FRANÇAISES,
BLANC DE NOIRS
See p.57

90
BONNAIRE
CRAMANT
● 15,000 cases
● Récoltant-Manipulant
Founded in 1932 by Fernand Bouquement, this producer was known as Bonnaire-Bouquement during the transition to the Bonnaire side of the extended family. Jean-Louis Bonnaire is the third generation of *récoltants-manipulants* to run this house, and owns 22 hectares, 13.5 of which are in Cramant, with the rest in the Marne Valley.

WINEMAKER
Jean-Louis Bonnaire

HOUSE STYLE & RANGE
Occasionally spoiled by dominant malolactic tones, most wines are a pure joy, with beautifully focused fruit and a luxuriantly creamy finish. The best *cuvées* possess extraordinary richness and offer great potential longevity.

★✫ BRUT BLANC DE BLANCS
Not vintaged, méthode champenoise: 100% Chardonnay

★ BRUT TRADITION
Not vintaged, méthode champenoise: equal parts
Chardonnay, Pinot Noir, Meunier

★ BRUT TRADITION
Not vintaged, addition of red wine, méthode
champenoise: 90% Chardonnay, 10% Pinot Noir

★★ CRAMANT GRAND CRU
Vintaged, méthode champenoise: 100% Chardonnay

★★ SPECIAL CLUB BRUT
Vintaged, méthode champenoise: 100% Chardonnay

VINEYARD ABOVE RICEY-BAS, LES RICEYS, AUBE

80
ALEXANDRE BONNET
LES-RICEYS
● 55,000 cases
● Négociant-Manipulant
Ambitious Aubois grower who owns some 40 hectares of vineyards, and makes some good *cuvées*. However, it is the collective run by Alexandre Bonnet that is of greatest importance, enabling him to supply almost any style, quality or price of Champagne required.

WINEMAKER
Alain Pailley

HOUSE STYLE & RANGE
Very soft and fruity, although some *cuvées* have been rather amylic.

★ BRUT PRESTIGE
Not vintaged, méthode champenoise:
30% Chardonnay, 70% Pinot Noir

★ BRUT ROSÉ
Not vintaged, méthode champenoise: 100% Pinot Noir

BRUT TRADITION
Not vintaged, méthode champenoise: 100% Pinot Noir

MADRIGAL, BRUT
Vintaged, méthode champenoise: 50% Chardonnay,
50% Pinot Noir

81 VALUE
F BONNET
REIMS
● 100,000 cases
● Other labels – Brossault
● Group ownership – Rémy-Cointreau

● Négociant-Manipulant
This house is used as a source of BOB Champagnes. The Bonnet range itself was revamped in 1996–97 to make Bonnet a strong challenger brand in the key European markets. This was a good marketing plan, but Rémy-Cointreau did not need F Bonnet to fulfil either role; instead, it could have been the first house to create the concept of a super-estate.

Since Rémy-Cointreau purchased De Venoge, which itself is a challenger brand with a well-established BOB business, there seems little point in maintaining Bonnet's current strategy. If Rémy-Cointreau removed Bonnet's ten hectares from the group's melting pot, and used it as the core to buy and build up a super-estate on a hitherto unheard of scale, they could then revert to *récoltant-manipulant* status, and ask Daniel Thibault to fashion individual Champagnes that are vividly expressive of this *terroir* or parts of it.

Imagine what a super-sized grower Champagne could achieve if it was marketed with the experience, muscle and established distribution system of a *grande marque* group like Rémy-Cointreau.

WINEMAKER
Dominique Dufour (Cécile Rivault for Princesse de France)

HOUSE STYLE & RANGE
The BOBs bearing the F Bonnet name in small print can vary as much as any other BOB supplier, but some of the better BOB *cuvées* can outshine the new Brut Héritage, which is a dullard compared to the old Carte Blanche (80% Chardonnay and 20% Pinot Noir), and the same applies to the Rosé.

★ BLANC DE BLANCS
Not vintaged, méthode champenoise: 100% Chardonnay

BRUT HÉRITAGE
Not vintaged, méthode champenoise:
18% Chardonnay, 32% Pinot Noir, 50% Meunier

ROSÉ BRUT
Not vintaged, méthode champenoise:
80% Chardonnay, 20% Pinot Noir

★ PRINCESSE DE FRANCE, GRANDE RÉSERVE
Vintaged, méthode champenoise: 20% Chardonnay,
60% Pinot Noir, 20% Meunier

98

BOLLINGER
VIEILLES VIGNES FRANÇAISES, BLANC DE NOIRS

CONTRARY TO POPULAR BELIEF, THERE ARE MANY BLANC DE NOIRS CHAMPAGNES, ALTHOUGH UNTIL RECENTLY VERY FEW WERE LABELLED AS SUCH. NONE, HOWEVER, HAS THE SPECIFICITY OF BOLLINGER'S VIEILLES VIGNES FRANÇAISES, BUT BECAUSE PINOT NOIR GENERALLY MAKES THE BIGGEST, CHEWIEST, MOST COMPLEX BASE WINES – AND THIS PARTICULARLY INTENSE CUVÉE SINGLE-HANDEDLY ESTABLISHED THE REPUTATION OF BLANC DE NOIRS – THIS STYLE OF CHAMPAGNE IS ALWAYS EXPECTED TO BE BIG, CHEWY AND COMPLEX. IN PRACTICE, THE STRUCTURE, TEXTURE AND COMPLEXITY OF OTHER BLANC DE NOIRS SELDOM DIFFER FROM REGULAR BLENDS.

• 170 cases

It is because Bollinger's Vieilles Vignes Françaises is made in minute quantities from ungrafted vines that it is in a completely different class from any other *blanc de noirs*. These vines are grown by the *à l'avance* variant of *en foule*, which literally means 'in a crowd'. This is descriptive of the congested carpet of new canes that results from layering the vine each year (*see En foule* in the glossary for a detailed general explanation).

However, the most important factor in this particular case is that Bollinger's *en foule* vineyards consist of some 30,000 vines per hectare compared to less than 7,000 commonly found in a normally grafted Champagne vineyards. Even when unchecked, each ungrafted vine yields far fewer grapes than a grafted vine (thus the juice is more concentrated), but the overall production per hectare can be very similar because there are significantly more plants per hectare.

However, in Bollinger's case, each ungrafted vine is severely pruned to restrict the number of bunches to just two or three. Thus, the yield per hectare is as much as 35% less, and the juice produced is even more concentrated than the super-rich wine normally expected from an *en foule* vineyard.

The smaller yield per vine also brings another very important quality factor into play because it encourages the grapes to ripen a full week earlier than those in the

BOLLINGER TAKES ITS PINOT NOIR GRAPES FROM ONLY THREE VINEYARDS

surrounding vineyards. As the date of harvest in Champagne is strictly controlled on a village-by-village basis, the grapes cannot be picked until the date given, thus all the vintages of Vieilles Vignes Françaises have been made from grapes that are not only super-rich, but significantly overripe. Indeed, in some years, the grapes have been dangerously overripe. When Bollinger first started making the wine, the company put in requests for a special dispensation to harvest its *en foule* vines a week earlier, but on each occasion it was refused.

This bureaucratic stupidity was, however, the making of the wine because such super-ripe grapes have given Vieilles Vignes Françaises a unique concentration and style. Any further attempts to harvest early would be a recipe for disaster.

Bollinger grows ungrafted vines at three tiny *lieux-dits,* or named sites: Clos St-Jacques in Aÿ-Champagne (a walled garden on the western outskirts of the village itself, 15 ares, all ungrafted, but only 50% *en foule*); Chaudes Terres, also in Aÿ-Champagne (another walled garden, this one being Bollinger's own back garden, 21 ares, entirely *en foule*); and Croix Rouge in Bouzy (if driving

WHY IS VIEILLES VIGNES FRANÇAISES SO SPECIAL?

1. It is made exclusively from Pinot Noir vines
2. It is restricted to three exceptional sites, including two authentic *clos*, in two of the greatest *Grands Crus* villages: Aÿ-Champagne and Bouzy.
3. The vines are ungrafted; thus, the yield is very small and the grapes ripen early.
4. The wine is made from overripe grapes and is massively concentrated.
5. It is vinified in small, four-year-old, oak casks.
6. No malolactic fermentation is permitted.

A WILD BEAST OF WINE, VIEILLES VIGNES FRANÇAISES HAS BRED THE LIE THAT ALL BLANC DE NOIRS ARE BIG. THIS, HOWEVER, IS NOT JUST BIG, IT IS A MASSIVELY CONCENTRATED, WINEY-WINE OF HUGE COMPLEXITY.

Bollinger's chairman, Ghislain de Montgolfier, was surprised when I requested a vertical tasting of Vieilles Vignes Françaises. It was, after all, something that no one at Bollinger had ever done.

Gérard Liot, Bollinger's quiet, unassuming winemaker, is the man responsible for making some of Champagne's most profound *cuvées*, including the uniquely styled Vieilles Vignes Françaises.

from Louvois to Bouzy, and you take the left turn into the village itself, the triangular patch of vines on the left is the only vineyard to be signposted as 'Bollinger's Vieilles Vignes': 16 ares, entirely *en foule*).

These three sites total 52 ares, or a smidgen over half a hectare, which, under normal circumstances, could produce as much as 8,500 bottles. But due to Bollinger's strict quality-control and the disproportionate losses of keeping such a small quantity of grapes separate, production never actually exceeds 3,000 bottles – which explains the price as much as the quality.

Vieilles Vignes Françaises is not a classic Champagne, but it is a great wine. Contrary to Bollinger's initial beliefs, it is a wine that ages exceedingly well. If my vertical tastings have demonstrated anything, it is that Vieilles Vignes Françaises shows infinitely better after warming up in the glass – so never over-chill it.

VIEILLES VIGNES FRANÇAISES, BLANC DE NOIRS
HOW THE VINTAGES COMPARE, FROM THE FIRST ONE IN 1969 TO THE PRESENT

1996 Not yet released, and not yet tasted.

1992 Not yet released, and not yet tasted.

1990 Not yet released, and not yet tasted.

1989 ★★☆ Full, rich and lush, the aroma is already complex, but not yet defined, although decidedly fine. The fruit on both nose and palate is marked with the broad brush-strokes of ripeness. It has a structure of extraordinary firmness for such a big wine, with vanilla and oak coming through on the finish.

1988 ★★ Dominated by the acacia-like, flowery finesse of recent disgorgement. Rich, dry, intense flavour, high acidity and peppery after-aromas.

1986 ★★ Although truly brut, the *dosage* is prominent, but it has lovely, cushiony fruit. Not one of my favourite Champagne vintages generally, but a great success here.

1985 ★★ This vintage is strangely disjointed on nose and palate when first poured, but develops a pleasing coffee aroma after 20 minutes in the glass and is probably going through a change of life.

1982 ★★☆ Initially dumb, but quickly opens into a wonderfully complex, beautifully balanced wine that seems complete, yet very young. Made from the ripest grapes of any vintage of Vieilles Vignes Françaises, with no less than 13% natural alcohol by volume.

1981 ★★ It is hard to believe this wine appears foursquare and ribby (all alcohol and acidity, no fruit or finesse) when first tasted at a nicely chilled temperature, but it gradually comes together, revealing a touch of coffee and toast on the nose and more flesh on the palate.

1980 ★★ Another initially foursquare wine that develops lovely fruit in the glass, with a toasty-biscuity finish beginning to build. I could not

believe myself marking any Champagne from the 1980 vintage so high, but it merely verifies the early Roederer Cristal philosophy that the best sites – when severely pruned – can produce great Champagnes even in poor years.

1979 ★★☆ This wine still has quite a youthful aroma and succulent fruit on the palate, together with complex nuances of toast and coffee showing on the nose and finish, and great finesse.

1975 ★☆ The aroma of fresh-cut mushrooms pervaded the last example of this vintage I tasted, but it was obviously a manifestation peculiar to that bottle. Previous tastings have been marked by a vividly pure Pinot fruit character. High acidity gives it a very crisp finish.

1973 ★★☆ Rich and toasty, with lovely fruit and high acidity giving great length and finesse to the toastiness on the finish. From the start, this has always had a superior balance of acidity, and is second only to the 1970 (which technically has the worst acidity balance!).

1970 ★★★ The toasty finesse on this wine stands out head and shoulders above the rest from the moment it is poured. Although others improved, it was easily the best wine at the end of the tasting. I remember this being so big and beefy in its youth that it was cumbersome and unbalanced, requiring strong flavoured dishes to prop it up. Now, it is soft, sensuous and full of succulently toasty fruit. Pure *velouté*.

1969 Only tasted once, a recently disgorged bottle direct from Bollinger's own cellars. Although it showed an echo of the penetrating flavour it must once have had, it was definitely too oxidised and dried out. This vintage was the first Vieilles Vignes Françaises and could simply be over the hill, but it has an extraordinary reputation, and the bottle I tasted might not be representative, so I will réserve judgement until I have tasted it a few more times.

VEUVE BORODIN
See BOIZEL

80
BOUCHÉ
PIERRY, EPERNAY
- 42,000 cases
- Négociant-Manipulant

Pierre and José Bouché currently run this small, family-owned house which was established in 1945. Today, it owns some 35 hectares in a wide spread of *crus*.

WINEMAKER
José Bouché
HOUSE STYLE & RANGE
Soft, fresh, fruity style.
BRUT BLANC DE BLANCS
Not vintaged, méthode champenoise:
100% Chardonnay

BRUT CUVÉE RÉSERVÉE
Not vintaged, méthode champenoise:
50% Chardonnay, 30% Pinot Noir, 20% Meunier
BRUT CUVÉE SAPHIR
Not vintaged, méthode champenoise:
60% Chardonnay, 40% Pinot Noir
BRUT ROSÉ
Not vintaged, méthode champenoise:
10% Chardonnay, 30% Pinot Noir, 60% Meunier
BRUT GRANDE RÉSERVE
Vintaged, méthode champenoise: 45% Chardonnay,
35% Pinot Noir, 15% Meunier
ROSÉ SPECIAL CUVÉE
Vintaged, méthode champenoise: 45% Chardonnay,
35% Pinot Noir, 15% Meunier

75
BOUCHER FILS
CHAMPILLON
- 4,500 cases
- Other labels - Boucher-Caruel
- Récoltant-Manipulant

Growers since 1806, the Boucher family first made and sold Champagne under its own name in 1911.

WINEMAKER
Sylvain Boucher
HOUSE STYLE & RANGE
Lots of character but little finesse, although this is of less importance for the Cuvée Fin de Siècle, which simply overwhelms the palate with its incredible concentration of flavour.

BOUCHER-CARUEL BRUT/SEC/DEMI-SEC
Not vintaged, méthode champenoise: 50% Pinot
Noir, 50% Meunier
CARTE BLANCHE
Not vintaged, méthode champenoise:
50% Chardonnay, 50% Pinot Noir
★ CUVÉE FIN DE SIÈCLE, PRESTIGE
Not vintaged, méthode champenoise:
50% Chardonnay, 25% Pinot Noir, 25% Meunier

85
RAYMOND BOULARD
LA NEUVILLE AUX LARRIS
- 15,000 cases
- Other labels - L'Année de la Comète
- Négociant-Manipulant

The late Raymond Boulard was a character indeed. I once asked him at what level the pressing should be set in Champagne, and he said 'Booff!' (well, I hope that's what he said). 'Forget the pressing, good wine comes from good grapes - the rest is poetry!'

WINEMAKER
Francis & Dominique Boulard
HOUSE STYLE & RANGE
In recent years there has been a move from succulently fruity Champagnes to an amylic style, although the Tradition, Grand Cru and Millésime are currently free of this ubiquitous peardrop aroma.

BLANC DE BLANCS - VIEILLES VIGNES BRUT
Not vintaged, méthode champenoise:
100% Chardonnay
★ CUVÉE TRADITION BRUT
Not vintaged, méthode champenoise:
50% Chardonnay, 30% Pinot Noir, 20% Meunier
✭ GRAND CRU BRUT
Not vintaged, mono-cru from Mailly, méthode
champenoise: 10% Chardonnay, 90% Pinot Noir
✭ RÉSERVE BRUT/DEMI-SEC
Not vintaged, méthode champenoise:
20% Chardonnay, 35% Pinot Noir, 45% Meunier
RÉSERVE/DEMI-SEC
Not vintaged, méthode champenoise:
20% Chardonnay, 35% Pinot Noir, 45% Meunier
ROSÉ DE SAIGNÉE BRUT
Not vintaged, méthode champenoise: 60% Pinot
Noir, 40% Meunier
L'ANNÉE DE LA COMÈTE - 2,000 BRUT
Vintaged, méthode champenoise: 50% Chardonnay,
25% Pinot Noir, 25% Meunier
★ MILLÉSIME BRUT
Vintaged, méthode champenoise: 50% Chardonnay,
25% Pinot Noir, 25% Meunier

85 VALUE
CHÂTEAU DE BOURSAULT
BOURSAULT
- 5,000 cases
- Négociant-Manipulant

Château de Boursault is a truly majestic 17th-century house that once belonged to

the great Widow Clicquot, but is today owned by the Fringhian family. Within its high walls is a vineyard which, due to the microclimate of this authentic *clos*, has the potential to outclass Boursault's modest village *echelle de cru* of 84%. Harald Fringhian, the present incumbent, has slowly but consistently produced Champagnes of increasing finesse, particularly since 1990.

WINEMAKER
Harald Fringhian
HOUSE STYLE & RANGE
Light, fresh and elegant. The rosé has always been the most successful, with the fruit really coming out if aged two years after purchase.
★ BRUT
Not vintaged, méthode champenoise:
30% Chardonnay, 35% Pinot Noir, 35% Meunier
✭ BRUT PRESTIGE
Not vintaged, méthode champenoise:
30% Chardonnay, 35% Pinot Noir, 35% Meunier

★ BRUT ROSÉ
Vintaged, méthode champenoise: 50% Pinot Noir,
50% Meunier

75
G BOUTILLEZ VIGNON
VILLERS-MARMERY
- 2,250 cases
- Récoltant-Manipulant

Members of the Boutillez family have been *vignerons* in Villers-Marmery since 1524.

WINEMAKER
Gérard Boutillez
HOUSE STYLE & RANGE
The Millésime goes biscuity rather than toasty, while the Cuvée Prestige has an oxidative tendency.
✭ CUVÉE PRESTIGE
Not vintaged, méthode champenoise:
60% Chardonnay, 40% Pinot Noir
✭ MILLÉSIME
Vintaged, méthode champenoise: 100% Chardonnay

82
BRICE
BOUZY
- 12,000 cases
- Négociant-Manipulant

Jean-Paul Brice was one of the three original partners in the Bouzy-based Champagne

Barancourt, now part of Vranken-Monopole. Brice has returned to the original Barancourt philosophy of producing a range of non-vintage *mono-cru* Champagnes that age well.

WINEMAKER
Michel Joly

HOUSE STYLE & RANGE
The basic Brut Premier Cru is a smooth, light, elegant *cuvée*, whereas the *mono-cru* Champagnes are expressive of their *terroir* – with the singular exception of the first release of Verzenay, all samples of which have been badly oxidised.

★ AŸ BRUT
Not vintaged, méthode champenoise:
10% Chardonnay, 90% Pinot Noir

★ BOUZY BRUT
Not vintaged, méthode champenoise:
20% Chardonnay, 80% Pinot Noir

✭ BRUT PREMIER CRU
Not vintaged, méthode champenoise:
80% Chardonnay, 20% Pinot Noir

BRUT ROSÉ
Not vintaged, méthode champenoise:
25% Chardonnay, 75% Pinot Noir

CRAMANT BRUT
Not vintaged, méthode champenoise:
100% Chardonnay

VERZENAY BRUT
Not vintaged, méthode champenoise:
25% Chardonnay, 75% Pinot Noir

80
BRICOUT

AVIZE
- 335,000 cases
- Group ownership - Delbeck
- Négociant-Manipulant

This house dates back to 1820, when Charles Koch came from Heidelberg to establish Koch & Fils in Avize. His three sons took over in 1858, and towards the end of the century they merged their business with the Épernay-based house of Bricout. Arthur Bricout, a former technical director at Champagne de Venoge, had married the

1985 CHAMPAGNE AT CHAMPAGNE BRICOUT

daughter of Christian Adalbert Kupferberg, the famous Sekt producer in Mainz, in 1869.

Kupferberg gained majority ownership of Bricout & Koch, and quietly dropped the Koch from its labels in the early 1990s when the house was under the day-to-day control of Andreas Kupferberg. For a number of years, however, it was known that Kupferberg wished to relinquish ownership of Bricout and in July 1998 it was sold to the ambitious Delbeck 'group'. The firm occupies the renovated Ancien Château d'Avize, and its production is very large for a Côte des Blancs house.

WINEMAKER
Philippe Pomi

HOUSE STYLE & RANGE
Light, fresh and uncomplicated in general, it is well worth paying the relatively small premium for the vastly superior Cuvée Prestige, which is not a prestige *cuvée* as such – merely an upmarket non-vintage. The real prestige *cuvée* is Cuvée Arthur Bricout, which can be excellent and, when successful, ages gracefully.

★ CUVÉE PRESTIGE BRUT
Not vintaged, méthode champenoise:
40% Chardonnay, 60% Pinot Noir

CUVÉE RÉSERVE BRUT
Not vintaged, méthode champenoise:
40% Chardonnay, 30% Pinot Noir, 30% Meunier

ROSÉ BRUT
Not vintaged, méthode champenoise:
80% Chardonnay, 20% Pinot Noir

BRUT
Vintaged, méthode champenoise: 60% Chardonnay, 40% Pinot Noir

★ CUVÉE ARTHUR BRICOUT
Vintaged, méthode champenoise: 70% Chardonnay, 30% Pinot Noir

N/A
LOUISE BRISON

NOE-LES-MALLETS
- 580 cases
- Récoltant-Manipulant

Although members of this family have been growers since the end of the 19th century, they did not start making their own Champagnes until 1991.

WINEMAKER
Francis Brulez

HOUSE STYLE & RANGE
I recently tasted these wines for the very first time, so it is impossible to make a definitive judgement. Furthermore, since this grower has limited winemaking experience, there is bound to be a learning curve, but the Cuvée Tendresse has a hard, metallic taste, and the only common denominator in the other wines is a flowery perfume I normally associate with Meunier, although none of the wines contain that grape.

✭ BRUT
Vintaged, barrique-fermented, no malolactic, méthode champenoise: 40% Chardonnay, 60% Pinot Noir

✭ CUVÉE GERMAIN BRULEZ, MAGNUM
Vintaged, barrique-fermented, no malolactic, méthode champenoise: 40% Chardonnay, 60% Pinot Noir

CUVÉE TENDRESSE
Vintaged, barrique-fermented, no malolactic, méthode champenoise: 100% Chardonnay

85
BROCHET-HERVIEUX

ECUEIL
- 7,500 cases
- Récoltant-Manipulant

An old-established family of growers which first made and sold Champagne under its own name in 1945. Current incumbents Alain and Vincent Brochet own 15 hectares.

WINEMAKER
Alain Brochet

HOUSE STYLE & RANGE
Rich, fat, ripe sweetness of fruit, tending to go biscuity, sometimes malty-biscuity.

★ BRUT EXTRA
Not vintaged, méthode champenoise:
12% Chardonnay, 85% Pinot Noir, 3% Meunier

★ CUVÉE HBH
Vintaged, méthode champenoise: 30% Chardonnay, 70% Pinot Noir

N/A
BROGGINI
RILLY-LA-MONTAGNE
- 5,000 cases
- Négociant-Manipulant

A small, quality-conscious grower with four hectares of vineyards and a sense of style.

WINEMAKER
Jacki Broggini

HOUSE STYLE & RANGE
Infrequently tasted, but the prestige Cuvée Emeraude can be full and rich.

BLANC DE BLANCS BRUT
Not vintaged, méthode champenoise: 100% Chardonnay

BRUT 1ER CRU
Not vintaged, méthode champenoise: 15% Chardonnay, 10% Pinot Noir, 75% Meunier

BRUT ROSÉ 1ER CRU
Not vintaged, addition of red wine, méthode champenoise: 20% Pinot Noir, 80% Meunier

ROSÉ SUBLIME
Not vintaged, addition of red wine, méthode champenoise: 20% Pinot Noir, 80% Meunier

BRUT EXTRÈME
Vintaged, méthode champenoise: 20% Chardonnay, 30% Pinot Noir, 50% Meunier

BRUT 1ER CRU CUVÉE EMERAUDE
Vintaged, méthode champenoise: 40% Chardonnay, 60% Pinot Noir

BROSSAULT
See F BONNET

86
EDOUARD BRUN & CO
AY-CHAMPAGNE
- 16,700 cases
- Négociant-Manipulant

Edouard Brun made his first bottles of Champagne in 1875, but did not establish this house until 1898. In 1939, he teamed up with Edmond Lefèvre, and in 1968 the house became the property of Lefèvre's daughter and son-in-law, Madame & Monsieur Delescot Lefèvre.

WINEMAKER
Philippe & Norbert Delescot

HOUSE STYLE & RANGE
Over the last ten years or so, Edouard Brun has gone from a very traditional Champagne to a more fruit-driven style.

BLANC DE BLANCS BRUT
Not vintaged, méthode champenoise: 100% Chardonnay

★ CUVÉE SPÉCIALE BRUT
Not vintaged, méthode champenoise: 14% Chardonnay, 36% Pinot Noir, 50% Meunier

★ RÉSERVE 1ER CRU BRUT
Not vintaged, méthode champenoise: 30% Chardonnay, 70% Pinot Noir

★ ROSÉ BRUT
Not vintaged, méthode champenoise: 25% Chardonnay, 50% Pinot Noir, 25% Meunier

CUVÉE DU CENTENAIRE BRUT
Vintaged, méthode champenoise: 50% Chardonnay, 50% Pinot Noir

80
ROGER BRUN
AY-CHAMPAGNE
- 3,000 cases
- Récoltant-Manipulant & Négociant-Manipulant

Roger Brun, whose great-great grandfather was a godson of Napoleon, manages all the Piper-Heidsieck vineyards in Aÿ as well as his own 18 hectares, and is helped in the running of this family firm by daughter Caroline.

WINEMAKER
Roger Brun

HOUSE STYLE & RANGE
The basic non-vintage is simple and fruity, but the rosé is a delightful, soft and silky *cuvée* with oodles of strawberry fruit. The Cuvée des Sires is classic and biscuity, rather than toasty.

BRUT
Not vintaged, méthode champenoise: grape varieties not revealed

★ CUVÉE DES SIRES
Not vintaged, Chardonnay is barrel-fermented, méthode champenoise: 67% Chardonnay, 33% Pinot Noir

★ ROSÉ BRUT
Not vintaged, addition of red wine, méthode champenoise: grape varieties not revealed

BRUT
Vintaged, méthode champenoise: grape varieties not revealed

80
ALBERT LE BRUN
CHALONS-EN-CHAMPAGNE
- 25,000 cases
- Other labels - Arlit & Cie
- Négociant-Manipulant

Just down the road from Joseph Perrier, Albert le Brun is the only other Champagne producer in Châlons-en-Champagne, although Duval-Leroy has cellars in the town for storage purposes only. All three companies share Jacquesson's old cellars, which were so magnificent when built that Napoleon awarded the company a special medal. There is not, however, any free passage between the three entities today.

WINEMAKER

François le Brun

HOUSE STYLE & RANGE
Entirely different from that of Joseph Perrier, there being no vineyards around the town and thus no Châlons style as such. Albert le Brun is not in the same league as Joseph Perrier, but its Champagnes are consistently well-made and the best *cuvées* share an ability to age well. They are traditionally vinified, well-matured and good value.

★ BLANC DE BLANCS BRUT
Not vintaged, méthode champenoise: 100% Chardonnay

CUVÉE RÉSERVÉE BRUT
Not vintaged, méthode champenoise: 65% Chardonnay, 35% Pinot Noir

★ VIEILLE FRANCE BRUT
Vintaged, méthode champenoise: 45% Chardonnay, 55% Pinot Noir

VIEILLE FRANCE ROSÉ BRUT
Vintaged, addition of red wine, méthode champenoise: 20% Chardonnay, 80% Pinot Noir

80
LE BRUN DE NEUVILLE
BETHON
- 35,000 cases
- Other labels - Saint Simon and Clovis
- Coopérative-Manipulant

The larger of the two Sézannais cooperatives, Le Brun de Neuville comprises 145 growers owning 140 hectares of vineyards.

WINEMAKER
Giles Baltazart

HOUSE STYLE & RANGE
Not as consistent as it used to be. Once upon a time, you could count on Le Brun de Neuville for creamy, rich, exotically fruity Champagne. It might not have been classic, but it was always enjoyable and made a very user-friendly introduction to the world of Champagne for those weaned on New World fizz. Now the wines are sometimes closer to a fat Chablis style.

★ BLANC DE BLANCS CUVÉE CHARDONNAY BRUT
Not vintaged, méthode champenoise: 100% Chardonnay

CUVÉE SÉLECTION BRUT
Not vintaged, méthode champenoise: 72% Chardonnay, 28% Pinot Noir

★ MILLÉSIME BRUT
Vintaged, méthode champenoise: 95% Chardonnay, 5% Pinot Noir

87
PIERRE CALLOT
AVIZE
- 7,000 cases
- Récoltant-Manipulant

The Callot family have been *vignerons* since 1784, when Louis Callot established this family concern.

WINEMAKER

Thierry Callot

HOUSE STYLE & RANGE

Fermented in large oak barrels to produce fruity wines of some depth and the potential to age well.

★ AVIZE BLANC DE BLANCS GRAND CRU

Not vintaged, méthode champenoise:
100% Chardonnay

★✩ GRANDE RÉSERVE BLANC DE BLANCS
GRAND CRU

Not vintaged, méthode champenoise:
100% Chardonnay

CAMUSET
See BOIZEL

80 VALUE
CANARD-DUCHÊNE
RILLY-LA-MONTAGNE

• 250,000 cases
• Group ownership - LVMH
• Négociant-Manipulant

This is to Veuve Clicquot what Mercier is to Moët & Chandon. Unlike other major houses with secondary brands, such as Taittinger's Irroy or Lanson's Massé, Canard-Duchêne has its own very large premises. Mind you, talk about a blot on the landscape! I will never understand how the authorities allowed Canard-Duchêne to build a cement factory – and a Stalinist-type one at that – on the northern slopes of the Montagne de Reims.

WINEMAKER

Jean-Jacques Lassalle

HOUSE STYLE & RANGE

Greatly improved since the early 1990s, in a simple but very accessible fruit-driven style, although I seldom see any resemblance between these wines on the export markets and whatever it is they sell under this label in French supermarkets. However, on both export and French markets, I have been very disappointed of late with Grande Cuvée Charles VIII, which is bitter and too malo-dominated.

★ BRUT

Not vintaged, méthode champenoise:
22% Chardonnay, 40% Pinot Noir, 38% Meunier

BRUT ROSÉ

Not vintaged, addition of red wine, méthode
champenoise: 25% Chardonnay, 35% Pinot Noir,
30% Meunier

DEMI-SEC

Not vintaged, méthode champenoise:
20% Chardonnay, 40% Pinot Noir, 40% Meunier

GRANDE CUVÉE CHARLES VII

Not vintaged, méthode champenoise:
40% Chardonnay, 50% Pinot Noir, 10% Meunier

★ BRUT

Vintaged, méthode champenoise: 30% Chardonnay,
45% Pinot Noir, 15% Meunier

CARLIN
See CATTIER

80 VALUE
DE CASTELLANE
EPERNAY

• 210,000 cases
• Other labels - Maxim's, Ettore Bugatti, Jacques Cattier, A Mérand
• Group ownership - Laurent-Perrier
• Négociant-Manipulant

This underrated house was established in 1890 by Vicomte Florens de Castellane, who was of Provençal origins and adorned his label with the red cross of St André, the standard of the oldest regiment in Champagne. The cupola-topped tower of de Castellane is such an oddity on Épernay's skyline that no visitor has any excuse for not finding this house. De Castellane has an interesting museum charting the development of the *méthode champenoise*; there is also the wonderful Jardin des Papillons: a garden heated to tropical temperatures with 400 exotic European, American, Asian and African butterflies allowed to flutter about the place in complete freedom (worth a visit just for this experience).

WINEMAKER

Patrick Dubois

HOUSE STYLE & RANGE

Plenty of freshness and fruit, not lacking in intensity or length, and absolutely clean. Brilliant value for money. Age-worthy top *cuvées* of very high quality indeed, with creamy, citrous, fruit-driven Chardonnay a speciality of the house.

★ CHARDONNAY BRUT

Not vintaged, méthode champenoise:
100% Chardonnay

CROIX ROUGE ST. ANDRÉ ROSÉ

Not vintaged, addition of red wine, méthode
champenoise: 40% Chardonnay, 60% Pinot Noir

✩ TRADITION BRUT

Not vintaged, 15-20% reserve wines stored one year
in wood, méthode champenoise: 35% Chardonnay,
40% Pinot Noir, 25% Meunier

✩ VICOMTE DE CASTELLANE (CAPPIELLO)
BRUT/CROIX ROUGE ST ANDRÉ BRUT

Not vintaged, 15-20% reserve wines stored one year
in wood, méthode champenoise: 30% Chardonnay,
40% Pinot Noir, 30% Meunier

CHAMPAGNE DE CASTELLANE'S TOWER, EPERNAY

★ BRUT

Vintaged, méthode champenoise: 40% Chardonnay,
50% Pinot Noir, 10% Meunier

★★ CUVÉE COMMODORE BRUT

Vintaged, méthode champenoise: 30% Chardonnay,
70% Pinot Noir

★✩ CUVÉE COMMODORE ROSÉ

Vintaged, addition of red wine, méthode
champenoise: 20% Chardonnay, 80% Pinot Noir

★ CUVÉE FLORENS DE CASTELLANE BRUT

Vintaged, méthode champenoise: 90% Chardonnay,
10% Pinot Noir

★✩ CUVÉE ROYALE BRUT

Vintaged, méthode champenoise: 100% Chardonnay

87 VALUE
CATTIER
CHIGNY-LES-ROSES

• 35,000 cases
• Other labels - Laurent Desmazières, Carlin, Courrèges
• Négociant-Manipulant

Deservedly famous for its Clos du Moulin (*see p.68*), little else used to excite me about Cattier until its superb trio of vintages 1988, 1989 and 1990. Producing these three stunning wines seems to have kick-started Cattier into turbo-charging some of its other *cuvées*, such as its non-vintage *blanc de blancs* and Cuvée Renaissance. The latter did nothing for me when first released, but has been excellent since the 1989 vintage.

WINEMAKER
Jean Jacques Cattier

HOUSE STYLE & RANGE
Ignoring the basic brut and rosé, the style elsewhere is serious and fruit-driven, and it is getting richer by the minute.

★★ BRUT BLANC DE BLANCS 1ER CRU
Not vintaged, méthode champenoise:
100% Chardonnay

BRUT 1ER CRU
Not vintaged, méthode champenoise:
25% Chardonnay, 40% Pinot Noir, 35% Meunier

BRUT ROSÉ 1ER CRU
Not vintaged, addition of red wine, méthode champenoise: 10% Chardonnay, 50% Pinot Noir, 40% Meunier

★★ BRUT 1ER CRU
Vintaged, méthode champenoise: 35% Chardonnay, 35% Pinot Noir, 30% Meunier

★★★ CLOS DU MOULIN BRUT
See p. 68

CUVÉE MILLARIUM BRUT
Vintaged, reserved for a trilogy of vintages (1995, the last vintage of this millennium and the first of the next millennium), méthode champenoise: 40% Chardonnay, 30% Pinot Noir, 30% Meunier

★★ CUVÉE RENAISSANCE BRUT 1ER CRU
Vintaged, méthode champenoise: 40% Chardonnay, 40% Pinot Noir, 20% Meunier

JACQUES CATTIER
See DE CASTELLANE

86
CHARLES DE CAZANOVE
EPERNAY
- 290,000 cases
- Other labels - H Lanvin, Magenta
- Négociant-Manipulant

Founded at Avize in 1811 by Charles-Gabriel de Cazanove, who was one of a family of ten children and the father of five himself. However, it was his son, Charles Nicolas, the vice-president of the Marne Valley Horticultural Society and a member of the committee charged with fighting the dreaded phylloxera, who did most to establish the reputation of this house.

Charles Nicolas de Cazanove's descendents ran the firm until 1958, when it was purchased by Martini, which in turn sold it to the Moët-Hennessy group in 1979. It was purchased by its present owners, the Lombard family, in 1985. The Lombard family was and is still the owner of a BOB business by the name of SAME (also known as Magenta), and had purchased another house, Champagne Marie Stuart, in 1972 (although this has recently been sold to Alain Thienot).

WINEMAKER
Olivier Piazza

HOUSE STYLE & RANGE
These wines have been gaining in finesse for the last five or six years, and there now appears to be a move from a fruit-driven to a more biscuity, malolactic style.

★★ BRUT AZUR 1ER CRU
Not vintaged, méthode champenoise:
60% Chardonnay, 30% Pinot Noir, 10% Meunier

★ BRUT CLASSIQUE
Not vintaged, méthode champenoise:
30% Chardonnay, 50% Pinot Noir, 20% Meunier

BRUT ROSÉ
Not vintaged, addition of red wine, méthode champenoise: 95% Chardonnay, 5% Pinot Noir

DEMI-SEC
Not vintaged, méthode champenoise:
30% Chardonnay, 50% Pinot Noir, 20% Meunier

★ BRUT MILLÉSIME
Vintaged, méthode champenoise: 40% Chardonnay, 60% Pinot Noir

★ BRUT AZUR 1ER CRU MILLÉSIME
Vintaged, méthode champenoise: 80% Chardonnay, 20% Pinot Noir

★★ STRADIVARIUS BRUT
Vintaged, méthode champenoise: 70% Chardonnay, 30% Pinot Noir

85 VALUE
CHANOINE
REIMS
- 42,000 cases
- Group ownership - BCC
- Négociant-Manipulant

In 1730, just one year after Ruinart was established, Chanoine Frères was founded, making it the second-oldest sparkling Champagne house, but it ended up as nothing more than a label belonging to Canard-Duchêne, which itself was a subsidiary of Veuve Clicquot.

The brand was purchased by Bruno Paillard and Philippe Baijot, although it has always been more Baijot's baby than Paillard's, and it is now a fully integrated member of the BCC group, which is jointly owned by Baijot, Paillard and the Roques-Boizel family.

When Chanoine relaunched in 1991, it was only supposed to be a superior supermarket Champagne, but the bottles were beautifully presented with reproduction labels, and the quality of the wines was far too good for supermarkets (the truly exceptional 1985 was in fact Barancourt's first and greatest vintage of Cuvée Fondateurs, but sold under the Chanoine label for half the price!).

Chanoine could have continued as a supermarket brand from different sources but, although supermarkets remain its primary outlet, it has since built up respect as a brand in its own right, encouraging BCC to build a vast new high-tech winery around the corner from Champagne Bruno Paillard, which makes the future for this label look very promising.

WINEMAKER
Laurent Guyot

HOUSE STYLE & RANGE
Until Chanoine built its own winery, the style jumped around a bit according to where the wines were sourced, but the quality was far more consistent (always fair, sometimes quite exciting). Since Chanoine's own-produced *cuvées* came onto the market in 1997, the style of the non-vintage has been fresh, easy and surprisingly light for such a high proportion of Pinot Noir.

The vintages released so far were all made before Chanoine was relaunched, and although they have been noticeably richer, with a full, satisfying succulent finish, we'll have to wait a few years to see what Chanoine's own-produced vintage style is like. The new prestige *cuvée* Tsarine has an upfront, fruit-driven style, yet packs an intense punch, making it enjoyable for immediate drinking, yet promising to improve if kept a few years.

★ BRUT
Not vintaged, méthode champenoise:
15% Chardonnay, 70% Pinot Noir, 15% Meunier

★ BRUT ROSÉ
Not vintaged, addition of red wine,
55% Chardonnay, 35% Pinot Noir, 10% Meunier

★ BRUT
Vintaged, méthode champenoise: 30% Chardonnay, 50% Pinot Noir, 20% Meunier

★★ TSARINE BRUT
Vintaged, méthode champenoise: 50% Chardonnay, 25% Pinot Noir, 15% Meunier

74
CHARBAUT
EPERNAY

- 100,000 cases
- Group ownership - Vranken-Monopole
- Négociant-Manipulant

Established as a *récoltant-manipulant* in 1948 by André Charbaut in Mareuil-sur-Aÿ, the firm became *négociants* in 1955, moving to Épernay as ownership passed to André's sons, Guy and René. The house was purchased in 1995 by the Vranken group, and its splendid premises in Épernay's avenue de Champagne now boast another Vranken brand, Heidsieck & Co Monopole, relegating Charbaut to little more than a secondary label.
See also GUY CHARBAUT.

WINEMAKER
Thierry Gomirieux

HOUSE STYLE & RANGE
The quality was always patchy at the bottom end of the range, and the basic non-vintage brut had not been good for quite a while prior to this firm's acquisition, so the blame is not entirely Vranken's. Indeed, the Certificate Blanc de Blancs and Certificate Rosé (Charbaut was reputed for its rosé above all else) were superb wines by any standards, requiring more than ten years to show their true potential – yet the last great vintage was 1985, ten years before Paul Vranken got his hands on this brand. Everything has now been Vrankenised.

BLANC DE BLANCS BRUT
Not vintaged, méthode champenoise: 100% Chardonnay

BRUT
Not vintaged, méthode champenoise: 50% Chardonnay, 50% Pinot Noir

SÉLECTION BRUT
Not vintaged, méthode champenoise: 20% Chardonnay, 60% Pinot Noir, 20% Meunier

CERTIFICATE BLANC DE BLANCS BRUT
Vintaged, méthode champenoise: 100% Chardonnay

CERTIFICATE ROSÉ BRUT
Vintaged, méthode champenoise: 90% Chardonnay, 10% Pinot Noir

N/A
GUY CHARBAUT
MAREUIL-SUR-AY

- 10,000 cases
- Récoltant-Manipulant

If you are an old Charbaut fan, this is where to find the family-produced Champagnes. Champagne Guy Charbaut was established in 1995, when Vranken purchased the *négociant* business in Épernay.

WINEMAKER
Guy Charbaut

HOUSE STYLE & RANGE
Too early to say, but the vintage shows lots of richness, and the rosé is made by the *saignée* method in true Charbaut fashion. If Guy ever gets back to making classic, slow-maturing *blanc de blancs* and rosé like the good old vintage of Certificate, he could always market them as 'Charbaut Diplôme'.

BLANC DE BLANCS BRUT PREMIER CRU
Not vintaged, méthode champenoise: 100% Chardonnay

BRUT
Not vintaged, méthode champenoise: 33% Chardonnay, 67% Pinot Noir

CUVÉE DE RÉSERVE BRUT
Not vintaged, méthode champenoise: 33% Chardonnay, 67% Pinot Noir

ROSÉ BRUT PREMIER CRU
Not vintaged, saignée, méthode champenoise: 10% Chardonnay, 90% Pinot Noir

★★☆ BRUT
Vintaged, méthode champenoise: 33% Chardonnay, 67% Pinot Noir

89
GUY CHARLEMAGNE
LE MESNIL-SUR-OGER

- 10,000 cases
- Récoltant-Manipulant

Although most grower Champagnes are a relatively recent phenomenon, father and son have worked together to produce and sell Champagne under the Charlemagne name since 1892. Guy and Philippe Charlemagne currently cultivate 15 hectares in Le Mesnil-sur-Oger, Oger, Sézanne, Mancy and Cuis.

WINEMAKER
Philippe Charlemagne

HOUSE STYLE & RANGE
Wines of indisputable complexity and finesse, very elegant, and beautifully focused, with only occasional lapses in some lesser vintages.

★☆ BRUT EXTRA
Not vintaged, méthode champenoise: 80% Chardonnay, 20% Pinot Noir

BRUT ROSÉ
Not vintaged, addition of red wine, méthode champenoise: 70% Chardonnay, 30% Pinot Noir

★★☆ RÉSERVE BRUT, GRAND CRU, BLANC DE BLANCS
Not vintaged, méthode champenoise: 100% Chardonnay

★★ CUVÉE CHARLEMAGNE, GRAND CRU, BLANC DE BLANCS
Vintaged, méthode champenoise: 100% Chardonnay

★★ MESNILLÉSIME, CUVÉE DE PRESTIGE, GRAND CRU BLANC DE BLANCS BRUT
Vintaged, méthode champenoise: 100% Chardonnay

N/A
JACKY CHARPENTIER
VILLERS-SOUS-CHÂTILLON

- 6,750 cases
- Récoltant-Manipulant

Jacky Charpentier heads the Syndicat Général des Vignerons de la Champagne, a professional organisation catering for the needs of its 4,700 Champagne growers, more than half of which are *récoltants-manipulants*. His family have been growers since the beginning of this century. His father first sold Champagne under the Charpentier name in 1954, but this is a separate family enterprise, which Jacky (a common name in this part of France) and his wife Claudine established in 1974.

WINEMAKER
Jacky Charpentier

HOUSE STYLE & RANGE
I have not tasted the entire range regularly; thus, no overall score is given. Those I have tasted have been rustic, Meunier-dominated Champagnes from Marne valley vineyards.

BRUT PRESTIGE
Not vintaged, méthode champenoise: 20% Chardonnay, 60% Pinot Noir, 20% Meunier

BRUT RÉSERVE
Not vintaged, méthode champenoise: 10% Chardonnay, 10% Pinot Noir, 80% Meunier

BRUT ROSÉ
Not vintaged, addition of red wine, méthode champenoise: 10% Chardonnay, 10% Pinot Noir, 80% Meunier

BRUT TRADITION
Not vintaged, méthode champenoise: 5% Chardonnay, 5% Pinot Noir, 90% Meunier

EXTRA BRUT
Not vintaged, méthode champenoise: 10% Chardonnay, 10% Pinot Noir, 80% Meunier

COMTE DE CHENIZOT
Not vintaged, méthode champenoise: Equal parts Chardonnay, Pinot Noir, Meunier

BRUT MILLÉSIME
Vintaged, méthode champenoise: 50% Pinot Noir, 50% Meunier

85
CHARTOGNE-TAILLET
MERFY

- 6,000 cases
- Récoltant-Manipulant

The Taillets have been *vignerons* in Merfy since the 17th century, but the seeds of this family enterprise began in 1870, when Oscar Chartogne arrived in the village, and purchased his first vineyard. In 1920, his daughter Marie married Etienne Taillet, and the two families have been associates ever since, *cont. p. 66*

98

CLOS DES GOISSES

SINGLE VINEYARD CHAMPAGNE

MAREUIL-SUR-AŸ, CÔTE DES BLANCS

- Owned by Philipponnat
- 2,500 cases (just 300 in some years)

Since I was introduced to Clos des Goisses by the late Colin Fenton, it has always been a favourite of mine, but it is a very special wine and you have to know why to appreciate it. Not because the knowledge miraculously changes your perception of the wine, but because you will know when to drink it. Most vintages of Clos des Goisses need ten to 15 years before they even start to show their full potential, and true aficionados will seldom drink a vintage less than 20 years old.

Colin Fenton was a Master of Wine with a particular passion for and a great knowledge and experience of Champagne Salon. He believed that anyone who could not understand and enjoy Salon at its peak would not appreciate Clos des Goisses, and vice versa. Although there are great differences and contrasts between the two Champagnes – one being a Marne Valley Pinot Noir dominated blend, the other a Côte des Blancs Chardonnay – they both share a specificity that makes them special.

The famous part of Clos des Goisses is its fully south-facing slope. It is so straight-sided, with no deviation from its southerly aspect, that it is often referred to as south-south facing. The Clos des Goisses slope is very steep indeed, and can hardly be missed as one approaches the village from Tours-sur-Marne. Its reflection in the Marne canal is renowned for its uncanny resemblance to a bottle lying on its side.

This steep slope is, however, just a part of the entire *clos*, which stretches out northwards behind the famous escarpment for a considerable distance. It actually encompasses 5.5 hectares and is planted with both Chardonnay and Pinot Noir, enabling Philipponnat to employ a unique degree of flexibility in the blending of this single-vineyard Champagne.

The micro-climate of Clos des Goisses is such that it is

RECENTLY TAKEN OVER BY BCC, PHILIPPONNAT'S NEW CHAIRMAN IS BRUNO PAILLARD (LEFT), WITH EX-MOËT MAN FRANÇOIS RENDINGER (RIGHT) IN DAY-TO-DAY CONTROL, AND NORBERT THIÉBERT (CENTRE), PHILIPPONNAT'S LONG-SERVING WINEMAKER

WHY IS CLOS DES GOISSES SO SPECIAL?

1 The extremely steep, south-south facing front slope gives the wine its indelible flavour.

2 Over five hectares of gently sloping east-facing vines provide exceptional blending flexibility.

3 It is made from a classic 70% Pinot Noir, 30% Chardonnay mix.

possible to select wines from the south-south slope with enough fruit to balance the acidity of even the meanest years.

Few years in Champagne have been quite as mean as 1951, yet a magnum of Clos des Goisses 1951 kept *sur pointes* until 1981, when I tasted it, was nothing short of remarkable. A lightly dosaged magnum consumed in 1991 was even better.

That such a wine was possible is a testament to the ripening capacity of this sun-blessed, south-south facing slope. In hot years, however, the grapes can literally roast on the vine before they are allowed to be harvested, which is when the rest of the 5.5 hectares of Clos des Goisses, which gently slopes in an east-facing direction, really come into their own, enabling winemaker Norbert Thiébert to effect a perfect balance.

CLOS DES GOISSES IN 1910, WHEN THE CONFIGURATION OF TREES WAS SUCH THAT IT NOT ONLY LOOKED LIKE A CHAMPAGNE BOTTLE, BUT IT APPEARED TO HAVE A MUSHROOM-SHAPED CORK EMERGING FROM THE NECK, WHICH SPORTS A FINE BAGUE CARRÉ

LA CHAMPAGNE

MAREUIL (SUR AŸ) — Un Paysage Champenois — La Bouteille

THE VINTAGES

INITIALLY FRESH AND FRAGRANT, WITH STRONG, RIPE FRUIT, CLOS DES GOISSES ASSUMES A QUIET, SLOW-RISING MOUSSE AND GREAT DEPTH OF FLAVOUR AFTER A COUPLE OF DECADES, WHEN IT REVEALS A RIVETING BOUQUET, WITH COMPLEX AROMAS OF BROKEN, CREAMY BISCUITS, HAZELNUTS, TOAST, HONEY AND VANILLA.

1996 Not yet released.

1995 Not yet released.

1993 Not yet released.

1991 ★★ Not yet released, this was extraordinarily easy to drink when young, with a delicious pineapple fruit that appears to be light-years away from this Champagne's truly complex potential.

1990 ★★★ Not yet released. This *cuvée* has a pure acacia aroma, with elegant, intensely flavoured, pineapple fruit on the palate. It is a shame to drink this now, yet very hard to resist.

1989 ★★☆ Fat aromas are contrasted by tight, elegant pineapple fruit on the palate. This *cuvée* has recently started to develop richness and give some hint of its eventual complexity.

1988 ★★★ Although a truly great Champagne, it does appear as if Clos des Goisses changed its style as from this vintage. It might be due to the limited number of times I have managed to taste this single-vineyard wine from its very earliest days and follow each vintage up to and through release, but it strikes me that, from 1988 onwards, this *cuvée* is easier to drink when young, having an elegance and generosity that was lacking in Clos des Goisses vintages of the past. It could simply be the effect of three exceptional vintages, but they all seem to have delicious pineapple fruit from their earliest days, whereas fruit of any description used to be noticeable by its absence in young Clos des Goisses. This vintage is not fat like the 1989, but very rich indeed, with an aromatic finesse that will one day make a profoundly complex, utterly beguiling, mature Champagne.

1986 ★★ Not the class of 1985 Clos des Goisses, but extraordinary finesse and quality for year.

1985 ★★☆ Classic Clos des Goisses, with a huge, rich, deep flavour and slow-building complexity that is only just beginning to form.

1983 ★★☆ Disappointing a few years ago, this vintage has just started to put on weight, with some biscuitiness building on the palate. It should be drinking nicely by its 20th birthday.

1982 ★★☆ This has such a youthful light colour, with toast developing rather than the biscuitiness of the 1983. Very rich, ripe fruit makes it ready for drinking, but it is still in its formative stage – a very long way from its peak.

1980 ★★☆ This really surprised me with its coffee and toast aromas. Although not great Clos des Goisses, it is one of the three best 1980 vintages made in Champagne. It is equal to the 1980 Dom Pérignon Rosé, but not quite in the same league as the 1980 Cuvée Louise Pommery Rosé. (As both of those wines are significantly better than their sister brut *cuvées* of the same vintage, perhaps the addition of some red wine makes up for the inadequacy of the 1980 vintage, so a Clos des Goisses rosé might have trumped the lot!)

1979 ★★☆ I've had a couple of maderised bottles of this otherwise excellent vintage, which has beautifully ripe, mellow, elegant fruit, but has only just started to develop complex aromas.

1978 My latest tasting of this vintage involved two bottles, both of which were heavily maderised.

1976 ★★★ This did not show at all well at a WINE magazine blind tasting of 1975 and 1976 vintages, but the bottle was obviously not in good condition: prior to and after that event, the 1976 has consistently proved itself to one of the greatest vintages of Clos des Goisses. With seductive coffee and toast aromas, but all ripe fruit on the palate, there is still a way to go before it enters its third and final stage of true complexity. Heaps of finesse.

1975 ★★★ Pure fruit. Delightful to drink now, this is the only vintage prior to 1988 that has pineapple fruit. Frankly, it is too seductive because it will take another decade to develop its true complexity and finesse, and I doubt many people will be able to keep their hands off this until then. I would have to taste this side by side with the 1966, '64, '61 and '59 to decide which is best, and only time will tell whether the 1988 and 1990 will match such legendary Champagnes.

1973 ★★ The last time I tasted this, it was all fresh mushrooms. Connoisseurs of mature Champagne will know that is no insult, but I'm not sure whether it has just developed this character and it pervades the entire batch, or whether it affects just some of the bottles. With or without it, this is a very refined and focused wine.

1971 ★★☆ It is a long time since I last tasted this vintage; thus, I have no specific notes for it. It used to have an edge over both the 1973 and 1970.

1970 ★★☆ I have not tasted this vintage for a long time; thus no specific notes.

1966 ★★★ Although this vintage has classic Clos des Goisses richness and fullness, it is lighter, fresher and younger than the 1964. When consumed on its own, this definitely has the edge over the 1964, which is better with food, and as it seems much younger than the two year difference, 1966 is theoretically superior.

1964 ★★★ Deeper and toastier than the '66, but although that vintage is lighter and fresher, this is also extraordinarily light for such depth of flavour, and it certainly does not lack freshness.

1961 ★★★ I have not tasted this vintage for a long time, so again, there are no specific notes for it, but it used to have the edge over the '59.

1959 ★★★ I have not tasted this vintage for a time, thus no specific notes. It used to be on par with the 1964.

1952 ★★★ The best Clos des Goisses I've tasted, although the '64 might give it a run for its money in 20 years. Firmly structured yet elegant, with rich, succulent fruit and an amazing array of vanilla, toast and coffee aromas of increasing complexity.

with Philippe and Elizabeth Chartogne the current owners.

WINEMAKER

Philippe Chartogne

HOUSE STYLE & RANGE

Never lacking richness or weight, most *cuvées* start off creamy, quickly acquiring a mellow toastiness. Occasionally the rosé can be too mature; I prefer to age my wines myself.

★ CUVÉE FIACRE TAILLET BRUT

Not vintaged, oldest vines, méthode champenoise: 60% Chardonnay, 40% Pinot Noir

★★✰ CUVÉE SAINTE ANNE BRUT

Not vintaged, méthode champenoise: 40% Chardonnay, 40% Pinot Noir, 20% Meunier

✰ CUVÉE SAINTE ANNE BRUT ROSÉ

Not vintaged, addition of red wine, méthode champenoise: 40% Chardonnay, 50% Pinot Noir, 10% Meunier

★★✰ CUVÉE SAINTE ANNE BRUT MILLÉSIME

Vintaged, méthode champenoise: 60% Chardonnay, 40% Pinot Noir

82

CHASSENAY D'ARCE

VILLE–SUR–ARCE

- 100,000 cases
- Négociant-Manipulant

This Aube co-op was founded in 1956 by a dozen local growers. It now consists of 160 growers owning more than 325 hectares. Forty per cent of the production is sold under the co-op's own brand (primarily Chassenay d'Arce).

WINEMAKER

Patrick Bourgeon

HOUSE STYLE & RANGE

Cuvée Sélection is a light, fruity, sweetish non-vintage brut, but the Cuvée Privilège is a much fuller wine, with a nice hint of biscuit that develops well; Cuvée Spéciale is even more age-worthy. The rosé is very fruity in a pure Pinot Noir style, despite a little Chardonnay.

✰ CUVÉE PRIVILÈGE BRUT

Not vintaged, méthode champenoise: 40% Chardonnay, 60% Pinot Noir

CUVÉE SÉLECTION BRUT/DEMI-SEC

Not vintaged, méthode champenoise: 12% Chardonnay, 88% Pinot Noir

★ ROSÉ BRUT

Not vintaged, addition of red wine, méthode champenoise: 10% Chardonnay, 90% Pinot Noir

CHARDONNAY BRUT

Vintaged, méthode champenoise: 100% Chardonnay

★ CUVÉE SPÉCIAL BRUT

Vintaged, méthode champenoise: 50% Chardonnay, 50% Pinot Noir

82

GUY DE CHASSEY

LOUVOIS

- 2,000 cases
- Négociant-Manipulant

AUTUMNAL VINEYARDS ON THE SLOPES OF THE MONTAGNE DE REIMS ABOVE BOUZY

Run by the daughter of the late Guy de Chassey.

WINEMAKER

Lucien Beaufort

HOUSE STYLE & RANGE

Weighty, well-structured *grand cru* Champagnes that are rich and assertive, and often reveal a touch of spicy complexity.

BRUT DE BRUT

Not vintaged, méthode champenoise: 35% Chardonnay, 65% Pinot Noir

★ BRUT RESERVÉE

Not vintaged, méthode champenoise: 35% Chardonnay, 65% Pinot Noir

GRAND CRU BRUT

Not vintaged, méthode champenoise: 5% Chardonnay, 95% Pinot Noir

★ BRUT MILLÉSIME

Vintaged, méthode champenoise: 50% Chardonnay, 50% Pinot Noir

CHATELIN

See BAUCHET

70

CHAUDRON & FILS

VAUDEMANGES

- 5,000 cases
- Other labels - Louis Laurent
- Négociant-Manipulant

A producer capable of making some good Champagnes, but the quality can be erratic. This *marque* was relatively unknown until Luc Chaudron purchased Georges Goulet, since when it has had even less commercial impact due to the greater fame of that brand. *See also* GEORGES GOULET.

WINEMAKER

Luc Chaudron & Lucien Quatresol

HOUSE STYLE & RANGE

Chaudron is much lighter, fruitier and simpler than Goulet, with amylic aromas on occasions.

BRUT

Not vintaged, méthode champenoise: grape varieties not revealed

BRUT

Vintaged, méthode champenoise: grape varieties not revealed

ROSÉ BRUT

Vintaged, méthode champenoise: grape varieties not revealed

N/A

JEAN-LOUIS CHAURÉ

BASSUET

- 1,250 cases
- Récoltant-Manipulant

The Chaurés have been *vignerons* for five generations, yet like most growers, they sold grapes, not Champagne. It was not until 1987 that Jean-Louis Chauré first made and sold his own wines.

WINEMAKER

Jean-Louis Chauré

HOUSE STYLE & RANGE

I do not have sufficient experience of these Champagnes to give a rating or discern a house-style, other than that it is evidently Chardonnay-dominated.

BLANC DE BLANCS RÉSERVE BRUT

Not vintaged, méthode champenoise: 100% Chardonnay

BRUT ROSÉ

Not vintaged, addition of red wine, méthode champenoise: 90% Chardonnay, 10% Pinot Noir

CUVÉE PRESTIGE BRUT

Not vintaged, méthode champenoise: 100% Chardonnay

86

CHAUVET

TOURS-SUR-MARNE

- 10,000 cases
- Group ownership
- Négociant-Manipulant

Chauvet is situated opposite Laurent-Perrier and is the only other Champagne house in

Tours-sur-Marne. Run by the Paillard-Chauvet family, under the day-to-day control of Jean François Paillard, who is a cousin of Pierre Paillard of Bouzy and Bruno Paillard of Reims, and a nephew of Antoine Gosset, the former owner of Champagne Gosset in Aÿ.

WINEMAKER
Arnaud Paillard

HOUSE STYLE & RANGE
These Champagnes are surprisingly fine and complex. All age gracefully with the exception of the Grand Rosé, which is a delight – but only when it is young and fresh.

★ BRUT
Not vintaged, méthode champenoise:
35% Chardonnay, 65% Pinot Noir

★☆ CARTE VERTE BLANC DE BLANCS BRUT
Not vintaged, méthode champenoise: 100% Chardonnay

★ BRUT
Vintaged, méthode champenoise: 85% Chardonnay,
15% Pinot Noir

☆ GRAND ROSÉ BRUT
Vintaged, addition of red wine, méthode
champenoise: 85% Chardonnay, 15% Pinot Noir

82
CHEURLIN & FILS

GYE–SUR–SEINE
- 21,500 cases
- Négociant-Manipulant

The largest and most ambitious of the Aube's ubiquitous Cheurlin Champagne producers, Cheurlin & Fils is also the most active in developing its export trade.

WINEMAKER
Pascal Cheurlin

HOUSE STYLE & RANGE
Most *cuvées* have fresh, tangy fruit, and are quite fat and soft. The Brut Originel is an example of enthusiastic experimentation with oak. Rather too oaky at the time of writing, but there is a learning curve to these things...

☆ GRANDE CUVÉE BRUT
Not vintaged, méthode champenoise:
20% Chardonnay, 80% Pinot Noir

★ PRESTIGE BRUT
Not vintaged, méthode champenoise:
30% Chardonnay, 70% Pinot Noir

BRUT ORIGINEL
Vintaged, méthode champenoise: 50% Chardonnay,
50% Pinot Noir

VEUVE CHEURLIN

CELLES–SUR–OURCE
- 12,500 cases
- Négociant-Manipulant

Owner-winemaker Alain Cheurlin also sells Champagne under the Jean Arnoult label. *See also* JEAN ARNOULT.

85
GASTON CHIQUET

DIZY
- 15,000 cases
- Récoltant-Manipulant

The Chiquet family first planted vines in Dizy in 1746, but it was not until 1935 that brothers Ferdinand and Gaston Chiquet produced their first Champagne. Cousins to Jean-Hervé and Laurent Chiquet of Jacquesson, current incumbents Antoine and Nicolas Chiquet own vineyards in the nearby villages of Aÿ, Mareuil-sur-Aÿ and Hautvillers.

WINEMAKER
J-C Therasse

HOUSE STYLE & RANGE
Ranges from succulent and creamy, with juicy fruit to a more mature, full, malolactic style.

CARTE BLANCHE BRUT
Not vintaged, méthode champenoise:
10% Chardonnay, 10% Pinot Noir, 80% Meunier

DEMI-SEC
Not vintaged, méthode champenoise:
35% Chardonnay, 20% Pinot Noir, 45% Meunier

ROSÉ BRUT
Not vintaged, addition of red wine, méthode
champenoise: 30% Chardonnay, 30% Pinot Noir,
40% Meunier

TRADITION BRUT
Not vintaged, méthode champenoise:
35% Chardonnay, 20% Pinot Noir, 45% Meunier

★★ BLANC DE BLANCS D'AŸ BRUT
Vintaged, méthode champenoise: 100% Chardonnay

★★ BLANC DE BLANCS D'AŸ BRUT, MAGNUM
Vintaged, méthode champenoise: 100% Chardonnay

★★ CARTE D'OR BRUT
Vintaged, méthode champenoise: 40% Chardonnay,
60% Pinot Noir

SPÉCIAL CLUB BRUT
Vintaged, méthode champenoise: 70% Chardonnay,
30% Pinot Noir

AMÉLIE CLÉMENT
See MONIQUE DAUBANTANT

85
CLÉRAMBAULT

MUSSY–SUR–SEINE
- 100,000 cases
- Coopérative-Manipulant

This cooperative was formed under the auspices of Pierre Gillet in 1951, by a group of 38 growers cultivating 44 hectares of exclusively Gamay vines. Clérambault now consists of 60 growers owning a total of 140 hectares, with hardly a Gamay vine in sight. Most of the production is sold to other producers, primarily the Union Auboise, a group of cooperatives to which Clérambault belongs.

WINEMAKER
Claude Thibaut

HOUSE STYLE & RANGE
A very fruity, easy-to-drink fizz; the better *cuvées* are more succulent, with riper fruit.

☆ CUVÉE CARTE NOIRE BRUT
Not vintaged, méthode champenoise:
20% Chardonnay, 60% Pinot Noir, 20% Meunier

☆ CUVÉE TRADITION BRUT
Not vintaged, méthode champenoise: 100% Pinot Noir

★ ROSÉ BRUT
Not vintaged, addition of red wine, méthode
champenoise: 100% Pinot Noir

★★ BLANC DE BLANCS BRUT
Vintaged, méthode champenoise: 100% Chardonnay

★ CARTE OR GRAND MILLÉSIME BRUT
Vintaged, méthode champenoise: 50% Chardonnay,
50% Pinot Noir

★★ GRANDE EPOQUE BRUT
Vintaged, méthode champenoise: 50% Chardonnay,
50% Pinot Noir

★ ROSÉ BRUT
Vintaged, addition of red wine, méthode
champenoise: 100% Pinot Noir

85
ANDRÉ CLOUET

BOUZY
- 5,500 cases
- Société de Récoltant

Highly respected grower with traditional views.

WINEMAKER
Jean-François Clouet

HOUSE STYLE & RANGE
High-quality, rich *cuvées* with well-extracted, Pinot-dominated flavours that are sometimes spoiled by an overly oxidative approach.

BRUT/DEMI-SEC
Not vintaged, méthode champenoise:
40% Chardonnay, 60% Pinot Noir

★ BRUT GRANDE RÉSERVE
Not vintaged, méthode champenoise: 100% Pinot Noir

BRUT ROSÉ
Not vintaged, addition of red wine, méthode
champenoise: 100% Pinot Noir

☆ SILVER BRUT
Not vintaged, not dosaged, méthode champenoise:
100% Pinot Noir

90
CLOS DU MOULIN

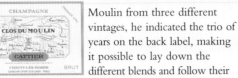

CHIGNY-LES-ROSES

- 1,500 cases
- Produced by Champagne Cattier

The Cattiers have grown grapes since 1763, but did not make their own Champagne until 1911. However, the most important date in this producer's history is undoubtedly 1951, when Jean Cattier bought a 2.2 hectare parcel of land called Clos du Moulin.

Once the property of Allart de Maisonneuve, an officer of Louis XV, the original windmill and its surrounding wall was obliterated during two world wars. Less than half a hectare of vines had survived, the remainder of the parcel consisting of bomb craters. Jean Cattier bought the land for a song and planted the entire *clos* with vines within the year. Since then, it has been completely replanted – half in 1981, the remainder in 1984.

Cattier made a tiny quantity of Clos du Moulin in 1952. Apart from that first year, this Champagne has always been a blend, originally of two years, but now of three. I have tasted the 1961/59 and 1969/66 *cuvées* with old Jean Cattier; although the latter was very fine with fresh, toasty fruit, I think even Jean would agree that these old wines cannot be compared with the special quality of Clos du Moulin today.

It was Jean's son, Jean-Jacques, who elevated this great Champagne to its current status. When he decided to blend Clos du

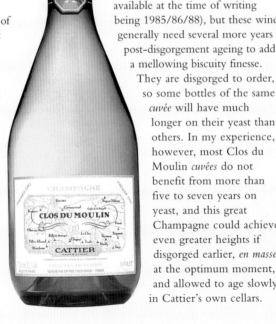

Moulin from three different vintages, he indicated the trio of years on the back label, making it possible to lay down the different blends and follow their development as one would a vintage Champagne. A brilliantly simple way of giving a great blended *cuvée* the same respect as a vintage Champagne without compromising the integrity of a traditional blend. The first Clos du Moulin to carry a back label was the 82/80/79 blend.

The very high quality of the wines is achieved through a rigorous selection process that yields fewer than 25,000 bottles (each bottle is numbered). I also believe the blending of three truly vintage years is responsible for the exceptional finesse of this *mono-cru* Champagne. Clos du Moulin is usually already complex when released as it has had up to ten years' yeast contact (the *cuvée* available at the time of writing being 1985/86/88), but these wines generally need several more years post-disgorgement ageing to add a mellowing biscuity finesse.

They are disgorged to order, so some bottles of the same *cuvée* will have much longer on their yeast than others. In my experience, however, most Clos du Moulin *cuvées* do not benefit from more than five to seven years on yeast, and this great Champagne could achieve even greater heights if disgorged earlier, *en masse*, at the optimum moment, and allowed to age slowly in Cattier's own cellars.

★★☆ CATTIER CLOS DU MOULIN (1990/89/88)
Vintaged, méthode champenoise: 50% Pinot Noir, 50% Chardonnay

★★☆ CATTIER CLOS DU MOULIN (1988/86/85)
Vintaged, méthode champenoise: 50% Pinot Noir, 50% Chardonnay

★★☆ CATTIER CLOS DU MOULIN (1986/85/83)
Vintaged, méthode champenoise: 50% Pinot Noir, 50% Chardonnay

★★ CATTIER CLOS DU MOULIN (1985/83/82)
Vintaged, méthode champenoise: 50% Pinot Noir, 50% Chardonnay

★★ CATTIER CLOS DU MOULIN (1983/82/80)
Vintaged, méthode champenoise: 50% Pinot Noir, 50% Chardonnay

★★☆ CATTIER CLOS DU MOULIN (1982/80/79)
Vintaged, méthode champenoise: 50% Pinot Noir, 50% Chardonnay

★★ BRUT MILLÉSIME
Vintaged, méthode champenoise: 50% Chardonnay, 50% Pinot Noir

CLOVIS
See LE BRUN DE NEUVILLE

85
MICHEL COCTEAUX

MONTGENOST

- 8,000 cases
- Récoltant-Manipulant

Established in the Sézanne since 1968, Cocteaux's 8.5 hectares of vineyards (6.5ha Chardonnay, 2ha Pinot Noir) are situated in Villenauxe-la-Grande and Montgenost.

WINEMAKER

Michel Cocteaux

HOUSE STYLE & RANGE

Usually ripe and succulent, even at basic non-vintage level, although there have been lapses into the ubiquitous, ultra-fresh amylic style. The vintage *cuvées* are very rich and biscuity, with typically exotic Sézannais fruit on the aftertaste.

☆ BRUT
Not vintaged, méthode champenoise: 100% Chardonnay

★☆ BRUT
Vintaged, méthode champenoise: 50% Chardonnay, 50% Pinot Noir

83
RAOUL COLLET

AY-CHAMPAGNE

- 50,000 cases
- Coopérative-Manipulant

Underrated, low-profile co-op in one of the greatest *grands crus*, also known as COGEVI (Coopérative Générale des Vignerons), this co-op has been making and selling Champagne under its own label since 1921, and has long had a relationship with the Clérambault co-op which supplies it with wines from the Aube.

WINEMAKER

Jean Pierre Depaquis

HOUSE STYLE & RANGE

Lightly structured, with flowery/peppery aromas and a touch of biscuitiness. The more upmarket the *cuvée*, the more intensity of fruit. The vintage wines are lean but biscuity-rich.

☆ CARTE NOIRE
Not vintaged, méthode champenoise: 50% Pinot Noir, 50% Meunier

★ CARTE PERLE
Not vintaged, méthode champenoise: grape varieties not revealed

CARTE ROUGE
Not vintaged, méthode champenoise: 35% Chardonnay, 65% Pinot Noir

ROSÉ
Not vintaged, addition of red wine, méthode champenoise: 100% Pinot Noir

★ CARTE D'OR
Vintaged, méthode champenoise: 50% Chardonnay, 50% Pinot Noir

85
JACQUES COPINET
MONTGENOST

- 4,000 cases
- Other labels - Charles Desfours, Jean Larrey
- Récoltant-Manipulant

Established in 1975, Jacques Copinet is one of the most highly organised growers on the Côte de Sézanne, where he and his wife Brigitte own six hectares of vineyards. Virtually all of their vines are Chardonnay, with less than one-third of a hectare planted with Pinot Noir.

WINEMAKER
Jacques Copinet

HOUSE STYLE & RANGE
The basic non-vintage has typical Sézannais exuberance and exotic fruit, and the vintage *cuvées* can be even fatter.

★ BLANC DE BLANCS BRUT
Not vintaged, méthode champenoise: 100% Chardonnay

★★ BLANC DE BLANCS, CUVÉE MARIE ETIENNE
Not vintaged, méthode champenoise: 100% Chardonnay

★★ BRUT
Vintaged, méthode champenoise: 100% Chardonnay

★ BRUT EXTRA QUALITY
Vintaged, méthode champenoise: 80% Chardonnay, 20% Pinot Noir

★ BRUT ROSÉ
Vintaged, méthode champenoise: 70% Chardonnay, 30% Pinot Noir

CVC
The Centre Vinicole de la Champagne, commonly known as CVC, is the largest cooperative in Champagne – a vast collective of 85 co-ops whose total membership consists of 4,900 growers owning over 1,900 hectares among them. Although annual production exceeds 1.3 million cases, Champagne sold under CVC's own labels (primarily Nicolas Feuillatte) comes to just 230,000 cases. The CVC is a major contract producer for its own adherent co-ops, a number of *récoltants-coopérateurs*, many famous houses (usually under the supervision of their own winemakers) and, of course, it makes a lot of BOBs.
See NICOLAS FEUILLATTE.

85 VALUE
COMTE AUDOIN DE DAMPIERRE
CHENAY

- 10,000 cases
- Other labels - Elayne de Biron
- Marque d'Acheteur

This English-loving, lovingly eccentric, classic-car fanatic of an aristocrat is one of those larger-than-life characters who is simply too charming and polite to ignore. At the time of writing, Dampierre was offering 2,000 magnums of truly excellent 1990 Blanc de Blancs Brut Grand Cru, sealed in the ancient way with the cork tied down by string and wax, but I would keep it a little longer and instead use his sumptuous, biscuity-rich 1985 to toast in the year 2000.

WINEMAKER
M Cohargue

HOUSE STYLE & RANGE
Elegant and fruity, most *cuvées* are nicely aged for current drinking, although some vintages are selected for their age-worthy potential.

★ BLANC DE BLANCS BRUT
Not vintaged, méthode champenoise: 100% Chardonnay

★★ CUVÉE DES AMBASSADEURS BRUT
Not vintaged, méthode champenoise: 50% Chardonnay, 50% Pinot Noir

★ GRANDE CUVÉE BRUT
Not vintaged, méthode champenoise: 50% Chardonnay, 50% Pinot Noir

★★ BLANC DE BLANCS GRAND CRU BRUT
Vintaged, méthode champenoise: 100% Chardonnay

★ BRUT
Vintaged, méthode champenoise: 35% Chardonnay, 65% Pinot Noir

★ BRUT ROSÉ OEIL DE PERDRIX
Vintaged, méthode champenoise: 88% Chardonnay, 12% Pinot Noir

COMTE DE LISSEUIL
See BAUCHET

COURRÈGES
See CATTIER

N/A
MONIQUE DAUBANTON
RIZAUCOURT-BUCHEY

- 2,400 cases
- Other labels - Amélie Clement
- Récoltant-Coopérateur

A grower since 1982, with 2.6 hectares of vines, Monique Daubanton started selling Champagne under her own label in 1990. Champagnes under the *négociant-distributeur* Amélie Clement label are bought in.

WINEMAKER
Jean-Pierre Vincent (CVC)

HOUSE STYLE & RANGE
The *cuvées* I have tasted have lacked elegance, but I have little experience of this new brand, so I must reserve judgement.

BRUT
Not vintaged, méthode champenoise: 20% Chardonnay, 40% Pinot Noir, 40% Meunier

BRUT ROSÉ
Not vintaged, méthode champenoise: 10% Chardonnay, 60% Pinot Noir, 30% Meunier

CUVÉE VICTORIEN BRUT
Vintaged, méthode champenoise: 40% Chardonnay, 30% Pinot Noir, 30% Meunier

85
H DAUVERGNE
BOUZY

- 3,000 cases
- Négociant-Manipulant

Growers for three generations, the Dauvergne family currently cultivates some six hectares.

WINEMAKER
Hubert Dauvergne

HOUSE STYLE & RANGE
Big, rich, excellent non-vintage, deep-hued rosé of great Bouzy character, and a mouth-filling prestige *cuvée* called Fine Fleur de Bouzy.

BRUT
Not vintaged, 30% reserve wine from previous three years, méthode champenoise: 15% Chardonnay, 85% Pinot Noir

★ CUVÉE ROSÉ BRUT
Not vintaged, méthode champenoise: 100% Pinot Noir

AUTUMNAL VINEYARDS ABOVE AY, CHAMPAGNE WHERE RAOUL COLLET'S VINEYARDS ARE SITUATED

★✩ CUVÉE FINE FLEUR DE BOUZY
Vintaged, méthode champenoise: 100% Pinot Noir

90
DELAMOTTE
LE MESNIL-SUR-OGER
- 30,000 cases
- Group ownership - Laurent-Perrier
- Négociant-Manipulant

Founded in 1760, Delamotte is the sixth-oldest house in Champagne and the true origin of Lanson (the cross on every bottle of Champagne Lanson is in fact Nicolas Louis Delamotte's cross of the Knight of the Order of Malta). This is a small, quality-conscious producer located next to Salon, one of the greatest houses in Champagne which, like Delamotte, is part of the Laurent-Perrier group.

WINEMAKER
Alain Terrier

HOUSE STYLE & RANGE
With the exception of the rosé, these elegantly rich, superior quality *cuvées* are always dominated by Le Mesnil Chardonnay, particularly the prestige *cuvée* Nicolas-Louis Delamotte, which contains 90% (in 1998, for example, this was all from the mature 1983 vintage). The vintage *blanc de blancs* is 50% Le Mesnil, plus Oger and Avize, the next two *grand cru* villages to the north; thus, although they are not *mono-cru* Champagnes as such, they are always expressive of the locality.

BLANC DE BLANCS
Not vintaged, méthode champenoise: 100% Chardonnay

★ BRUT
Not vintaged, méthode champenoise: 50% Chardonnay, 30% Pinot Noir, 20% Meunier

★★ NICOLAS-LOUIS DELAMOTTE
Not vintaged, méthode champenoise: 90% Chardonnay, 10% Pinot Noir

★★✩ ROSÉ
Not vintaged, addition of red wine, méthode champenoise: 20% Chardonnay, 80% Pinot Noir

★★ BLANC DE BLANCS
Vintaged, méthode champenoise: 100% Chardonnay

VEUVE DELAROY
See BOIZEL

N/A
ANDRÉ DELAUNOIS
RILLY-LA-MONTAGNE
- 5,000 cases
- Récoltant-Manipulant

A family venture established in 1925. Current incumbents Alain Toullec and Eric Chanez cultivate eight hectares of vines planted in equal amounts of all three grape varieties.

WINEMAKER
Alain Toullec & Eric Chanez

HOUSE STYLE & RANGE

I have enjoyed a biscuity-rich Cuvée du Fondateur in the recent past.

CARTE BLANCHE PREMIER CRU BRUT
Not vintaged, méthode champenoise: equal parts Chardonnay, Pinot Noir, Meunier

CARTE D'OR PREMIER CRU BRUT
Not vintaged, méthode champenoise: 42% Chardonnay, 58% Pinot Noir

CUVÉE DU FONDATEUR BRUT
Not vintaged, méthode champenoise: 90% Chardonnay, 10% Pinot Noir

CUVÉE SUBLIME
Not vintaged, méthode champenoise: Pinot Noir, Meunier

87
DELBECK
REIMS
- 12,500 cases
- Négociant-Manipulant
- Ownership – recently purchased Bricout

One of the earliest Champagne houses, founded in 1799 by Frédéric-Désiré Delbeck, a banker's son. Champagne Delbeck achieved its greatest height of fame in 1838, when it was appointed exclusive supplier to the French Court (hence the *fleurs de lys* on the neck label today); but by 1964, it was nothing more than a secondary label under the ownership of Piper-Heidsieck.

After François d'Aulan sold Piper-Heidsieck to Rémy-Cointreau in 1990, he bought back the Delbeck brand, which he lavishly repackaged and relaunched. It was then sold to Bruno Paillard, who later sold all but ten per cent of his shareholding to Pierre Martin, one of the three original owners of Barancourt (now part of Vranken). Bruno Paillard later sold his remaining share to Martin's partner, Olivier de la Giraudière. Delbeck has since purchased Waris & Chenayer in Avize, where the wines are now made, although the offices remain in Reims.

WINEMAKER
Pierre Martin

HOUSE STYLE & RANGE
This firm's unsettled past explains why it has yet to establish a style. Since being relaunched with purchased stock, its Champagnes have been sourced from at least three different locations. When Waris & Chenayer was bought, 350,000 bottles had to be disposed of, so even now some Delbeck is still effectively purchased stock (to be fair, Martin and Giraudière have isolated these different *cuvées*). I have tasted forthcoming *cuvées* and all the ratings below are based on what Delbeck will be when the purchased stock has worked its

way out of the system. The basic non-vintage requires some fine-tuning, but the style of Delbeck's best *cuvées* is (or will be) full, rich and reminiscent of Barancourt in the good old days.

★★✩ BOUZY GRAND CRU
Not vintaged, méthode champenoise: 20% Chardonnay, 80% Pinot Noir

★ BRUT HÉRITAGE/DEMI-SEC
Not vintaged, méthode champenoise: 30% Chardonnay, 70% Pinot Noir

★★✩ CRAMANT GRAND CRU
Not vintaged, méthode champenoise: 100% Chardonnay

★★ ORIGINE BRUT
Not vintaged, a blend of Avize, Bouzy and Cramant the origin of Martin's estate of vineyards, méthode champenoise: 50% Chardonnay, 50% Pinot Noir

★ ROSÉ HÉRITAGE
Not vintaged, addition of red wine, méthode champenoise: 10% Chardonnay, 90% Pinot Noir

★★ VINTAGE BRUT
Vintaged, méthode champenoise: 30% Chardonnay, 70% Pinot Noir

78
MAURICE DELOT
CELLES-SUR-OURCE
- 6,000 cases
- Récoltant-Manipulant

Serious winemakers with ten hectares in the Aube, Vincent and Philippe Delot are active in export markets, where they sell a significant proportion of their production.

WINEMAKER
Philippe Delot

HOUSE STYLE & RANGE
Delot's Grande Reserve shows the warmth and fruitiness expected of its southern Aube origins. The Cuvée la Champenoise offers more finesse, but the single-vineyard Montre-Cul *cuvée* is too fat and too young.

★✩ GRANDE RÉSERVE BRUT
Not vintaged, méthode champenoise: grape varieties not revealed

MONTRE-CUL BRUT
Not vintaged, méthode champenoise: grape varieties not revealed

★ CUVÉE LA CHAMPENOISE BRUT
Vintaged, méthode champenoise: grape varieties not revealed

N/A
DELOUVIN-NOWACK
VANDIERES
- 6,000 cases
- Récoltant-Manipulant

An old, established family of *vignerons* apparently dating back to 1500. The first Champagnes to be produced and sold here were by Bertrand Delouvin's father in 1949.

WINEMAKER
Bertrand Delouvin

HOUSE STYLE & RANGE
The non-vintage has good Meunier perfume, but no elegance, and the one vintage I have tasted (1991) was very strange indeed.

★ BRUT CARTE D'OR
Not vintaged, méthode champenoise: 100% Meunier

BRUT ROSÉ
Not vintaged, addition of red wine, méthode champenoise: 100% Meunier

BRUT TRADITION
Not vintaged, méthode champenoise: 100% Meunier

BRUT EXTRA SÉLECTION
Vintaged, méthode champenoise: 50% Chardonnay, 50% Meunier

DEMOISELLE
See VRANKEN

√A
MICHEL DERVIN
CUCHERY
• 3,000 cases
• Négociant-Manipulant
Small producer with five hectares of vines, Michel Dervin also produces Domaine J Laurens sparkling wines in Limoux. Not tasted recently.
See J LAURENS

CHARLES DESFOURS
See COPINET

LAURENT DESMAZIÈRES
See CATTIER

88 VALUE
PAUL DÉTHUNE
AMBONNAY
• 2,500 cases
• Récoltant-Manipulant
The Déthune family have been *vignerons* since 1610, and currently cultivate seven hectares of vines, producing an excellent range of elegantly presented Champagnes.

WINEMAKER
Pierre Déthune

HOUSE STYLE & RANGE
Rich, stylish, Pinot-driven wine, with creamy, succulent fruit. Pierre Déthune vinifies in oak.

★☆ BRUT
Not vintaged, méthode champenoise: 50% Chardonnay, 50% Pinot Noir

★ BRUT GRAND CRU
Not vintaged, méthode champenoise: 100% Pinot Noir

★☆ PRINCESSE DES THUNES BRUT
Vintaged, méthode champenoise: 100% Pinot Noir

89
DEUTZ
AY–CHAMPAGNE
• 75,000 cases
• Group ownership - Louis Roederer
• Négociant-Manipulant
The profitability of Deutz suffered from under-funding until Roederer acquired it in 1993, but there was no danger of it becoming a mere *sous marque*, as that would do as much harm to Roederer's reputation as to Deutz. Compared to some brands that have been taken over by large groups, Roederer chairman Jean-Claude Rouzaud has been almost philanthropic, but he does not give money away. Roederer is the most cash-rich, non-bank-dependent house in Champagne, and its acquisition of Deutz was definitely profit-minded.

Under the day-to-day control of Fabrice Rosset, Rouzaud's brilliant protegé, Deutz's global viticultural ventures have been curtailed to focus capital and energy on Champagne. He has signed a ten-year contract with Montana in New Zealand to continue production of Deutz Marlborough, but sold its interest in Maison Deutz, California, in December 1997.

That the quality of these wines is back on form and the style now reminiscent of Deutz a couple of decades ago is not a miracle-cure by either Roederer or Rosset. Things started to come right in the bottle from 1990, just before recession hit. Rosset is the sort of man who will, however, make certain that Deutz maintains this quality and, with Odilon de Varine retained as winemaker, the perpetuation of the true Deutz style should be assured.

WINEMAKER
Odilon de Varine

HOUSE STYLE & RANGE
Firm, flavour-packed wines of increasing finesse, the vintages – particularly those of Cuvée William Deutz – have the capacity to attain great complexity over many years. The rich yet delicate vintage rosé is a speciality.

★ BRUT CLASSIC
Not vintaged, méthode champenoise: 30% Chardonnay, 38% Pinot Noir, 32% Meunier

ROSÉ BRUT
Not vintaged, addition of red wine, méthode champenoise: 25% Chardonnay, 40% Pinot Noir, 35% Meunier

★☆ BLANC DE BLANCS
Vintaged, méthode champenoise: 100% Chardonnay

★☆ BRUT
Vintaged, méthode champenoise: 30% Chardonnay, 40% Pinot Noir, 30% Meunier

★★ BRUT ROSÉ
Vintaged, méthode champenoise: 100% Pinot Noir

★★ CUVÉE WILLIAM DEUTZ
Vintaged, méthode champenoise: 30% Chardonnay, 60% Pinot Noir, 10% Meunier

★★☆ CUVÉE WILLIAM DEUTZ ROSE
Vintaged, méthode champenoise: 100% Pinot Noir

85 VALUE
VVE A DEVAUX
BAR SUR SEINE
• 200,000 cases
• Other labels - Léonce d'Albe, Nicole d'Aurigny
• Coopérative-Manipulant
Vve A Devaux is the marketing initiative of Union Auboise des Producteurs de Vins de Champagne, a collective of 12 Aube co-ops with a combined membership of 800 growers owning a total 1,000 hectares. Relative to the intrinsic quality of the Aube, which – contrary to what some Champagne snobs might think – is not, of course, comparable to the best *grands crus* and *premiers crus*, this is the best, fastest-improving and most innovative co-op in the region. Do not believe the *grandes marques* when they say they don't use Aube wines in their blends. A few might not (for the wrong reasons in my mind), but statistics prove that most *grande marque* non-vintage *cuvées* contain up to 15% Aube wine, virtually all of it from this co-op or one of its members.

WINEMAKER
Claude Thibaut

HOUSE STYLE & RANGE
Not just fruit-driven, although the fruit displays the ripeness of its southern origin. The wines attain more biscuity finesse with each year.

☆ BLANC DE NOIRS BRUT
Not vintaged, méthode champenoise: 100% Pinot Noir

★☆ CUVÉE ROSÉ BRUT
Not vintaged, addition of red wine, méthode champenoise: 25% Chardonnay, 75% Pinot Noir

☆ GRANDE RÉSERVE BRUT
Not vintaged, méthode champenoise: 25% Chardonnay, 75% Pinot Noir

★ OEIL DE PERDRIX TRADITION BRUT
Not vintaged, méthode champenoise: 25% Chardonnay, 75% Pinot Noir

★ CUVÉE DISTINCTION BRUT
Vintaged, méthode champenoise: 50% Chardonnay, 50% Pinot Noir

★ CUVÉE DISTINCTION ROSÉ BRUT
Vintaged, addition of red wine, méthode champenoise: 50% Chardonnay, 50% Pinot Noir

★★ MILLÉSIME BRUT
Vintaged, méthode champenoise: 100% Chardonnay

98

CUVÉE DOM PÉRIGNON

PRESTIGE CUVÉE CHAMPAGNE
- Owned by Moët & Chandon
- 200,000 cases (estimated)

The crowning glory in fostering the legend of Dom Pérignon was the decision by Moët & Chandon to launch the very first prestige *cuvée* in 1936, and to name it after him.

The concept of a prestige *cuvée* was unknown at this time, for although the origins of Roederer Cristal go back much further, that wine was created at the personal request of Tsar Alexander II. The first commercially available vintage of Cristal was 1945, whereas the first Cuvée Dom Pérignon to be launched was 1921; thus, Moët not only created a new sector of the market, but had this to itself for almost a quarter of a century.

The idea of a super-luxury *cuvée* costing twice the price of a top vintage would have been audacious at any juncture of Champagne's previous history, but in 1936, with France

ONE OF MOËT'S BRIGHTEST YOUNG STARS, RICHARD GEOFFROY IS NOT ONLY A ROVING OENOLOGICAL CONSULTANT TO THE COMPANY'S VARIOUS INTERNATIONAL VENTURES, BUT HAS BEEN THE WINEMAKER FOR CUVÉE DOM PÉRIGNON SINCE THE 1990 VINTAGE

WHY IS CUVÉE DOM PÉRIGNON SO SPECIAL?

1. It was the first prestige *cuvée,* and the legend that Moët has built up for Dom Pérignon the person rubs off on Dom Pérignon the wine.
2. It uses the same source of grapes (*see box*) for each vintage.
3. A very rigorous selection process in both the vineyard and winery.
4. Seamless balance of Chardonnay and Pinot Noir in roughly equal proportions, the aim being not to allow one variety to dominate.
5. Such impeccable blending that you could swear that reserve wines have been used.
6. Beautifully understated, offering characteristic smoothness.

still reeling from the Great Depression, and with the price of Champagne plummeting, it must have seemed like madness. As things turned out, it wasn't, but whether due to circumstance or the existence of an intrinsic method to Moët's madness, we shall never know.

A few years ago, at a Christie's auction in London, a bottle of 1926 Dom Pérignon was catalogued as the second vintage released of this great Champagne. But no such vintage ever officially existed: Moët followed 1921 with the legendary 1928. Curiously, the 1926 was not a fake. It looked exactly like Dom Pérignon, in the same replica 18th-century bottle, with an identical shield-type label written in the same script. In fact, the words *Dom Pérignon* were not mentioned anywhere on the label. What it did say was *'Champagne specially shipped for Simon Brothers & Co's Centenary 1835-1935'* and it was one of 300 bottles commissioned by Moët's English agents to send to 150 of their best customers.

Word of this special Champagne filtered through the upper echelons of American society, generating a number of requests from across the Atlantic, so 100 cases were shipped to New York in November 1936. They could not use the London agent's centenary label, of course; hence a new brand had to be created.

THE IDEA OF USING THE REPLICA 18TH CENTURY BOTTLE FOR A SPECIAL CUVÉE CAME FROM AN ENGLISH JOURNALIST, LAURENCE VENN, WHO WAS ACTING AS ADVISOR TO THE FORERUNNER OF THE SYNDICAT DE GRANDES MARQUES

It was Moët's marketing director, Robert-Jean de Vogüé, who decided to name it after Dom Pérignon. It was also a nice touch to choose the 1921 vintage – a greater, more mature year.

The 1926 was therefore really the precursor to Dom Pérignon; when it was announced at the Christie's auction that it had been shipped one year before the 1921 and in a fraction of the quantity, its uniqueness and rarity value pushed bidding far beyond the catalogue price. De Vogüé could not have used the name Dom Pérignon but for Pierre Gabriel Chandon, who acquired the Abbey of Hautvillers and its vineyards between 1823 and 1825. The Dom Pérignon brand belonged to Mercier, which never used it. It was presented as a gift to Moët & Chandon in 1927, when Francine Durand-Mercier married Paul Chandon-Moët

But how could Moët go back to the 1921 vintage of a wine in a specially commissioned bottle when there was no intention for the 1926 to be anything other than a one-off anniversary *cuvée*? The answer is simple: the wines were *transvasaged*. In fact, Simon Brother's centenary *cuvée* and the Dom Pérignon vintages of 1921 1928, 1929 and 1934 were all *transvasaged*. The first Cuvée Dom Pérignon to be fermented inside its famous bottle was, in fact, 1943.

THE VINEYARDS OF DOM PÉRIGNON

For many years, Dom Pérignon has been produced exclusively from the vineyards owned by the Abbey of Hautvillers at the time of Dom Pérignon, and purchased by Moët & Chandon in the 1820s. In theory, this story has not changed, but after the acquisition of Lanson by Moët in 1990 and the subsequent selling of the brand to Marne et Champagne, Yves Bénard, then PDG of Moët, stated that Lanson's vineyards, which the firm had retained, would enable it 'to increase the production of Dom Pérignon and Moët vintage *cuvées* without sacrificing quality'. However, the Hautvillers vineyards below remain the heart and sole of Cuvée Dom Pérignon:

VILLAGE	LIEUX-DITS
GRANDS CRUS	
Aÿ-Champagne	Bourdeleuse, Côte d'Aÿ, Vouzelles
Bouzy	Les Assises, Les Brousses, Les Dames, Les Pertes
Cramant	Les Buissons, Les Busons, Les Payennes, Saran
Le Mesnil-sur Oger	Joyettes, Les Moulins
Verzenay	Les Chardonnières, Les Croix Rouges
PREMIER CRU	
Hautvillers	Les Basses Prières, Les Chantes de Linotte, Les Côtes-à-Bras, Les Hautes Prières

THE VINTAGES

WHEN FIRST RELEASED, DOM PÉRIGNON HAS AN ULTRA-SMOOTH CREAMINESS OF FRUIT WITH PERFECT MID-PALATE WEIGHT.
IT AGES SO GRACEFULLY THAT THE SLOW-BUILDING, TOASTY AROMAS ALWAYS POSSESS GREAT FINESSE.

1992/3 Not yet released, and not tasted.

1990 This immaculate cuvée, with its creamy velouté of fruit and mouthwatering, ripe acidity has the edge over the 1988, and promises to have two lives – like the 1982, but significantly superior. Probably equal in terms of quality to the 1975.

1988 Floral, toasty aromas mingle beautifully with the firm, pineapple fruit, with a distinct perception of acidity on the finish. The Chardonnay from Dom Pérignon vineyards must have been very powerful in 1988, because the proportion in this blend was reduced to 45% – yet it is still dominating the 55% Pinot Noir. In theory, the older the Champagne, the more dominant the Chardonnay should become, but I get the impression the Pinot will eventually exert itself. Either the blend will assume a typical seamless Dom Pérignon balance, or it will tip towards biscuity Pinot.

1985 ★★☆ A great intensity of Pinot fruit, still very tight and supremely focused, and although this cuvée is now showing in toasty vein, the massive concentration on the finish will gradually become biscuity and eventually assume a Christmas cake complexity.

1983 ★★☆ The best Champagne produced in this vintage, with a more classic structure than the 1982. I have always given the two wines equal scores, even under blind conditions. The older they get, the more obvious it is that they are the same quality, albeit of radically different character.

1982 ★★☆ While the 1993 has mellowed with age, this vintage, which was so creamy and delicious when first released, has tightened up with citrous instead of peachy fruit. A supremely elegant Champagne, pervaded by soft, gentle, toasty aromas.

1980 ★ This toasty-mature Champagne is too simple and ordinary to warrant a Dom Pérignon vintage, although recently disgorged bottles do improve with more bottle-age.

1978 ★★ Like 1980, this is not a true vintage for the Champagne region as a whole, but individual cuvées of high quality can

be produced through strict selection in almost any year – as this wine proves with its luscious, silky-soft, creamy-vanilla fruit. Both this and the 1975 are in the same basic mould despite a huge difference in harvest conditions.

1976 ★★☆ Some people rate this above the '75 but, although I adore the '76's exotic fruit, I have consistently marked the 1975 higher.

1975 ★★★ Even at this high level, special wines stand out and 1975 is one. How can Moët cram so much succulent, delicious fruit into one bottle and yet produce a Champagne of incomparable finesse and charm? Absolutely complete, with a creamy, vanilla richness backed up by toasty acidity, this vintage is still in fruit-driven mode and will take a long time to build up an extraordinary complexity.

1973 ★★☆ When freshly disgorged, this is all acacia and spices on the nose, with exquisitely fine fruit, highlighted by 1973's characteristic point of acidity. In terms of development on yeast, this is the least-evolved, youngest Dom Pérignon that has been produced. It's amazing to think that it is 25 years old. Normally released bottles reveal, however, how vital post-disgorgement ageing is. A well-cellared '73 has coffee and toast aromas with creamy, walnutty richness of Le Mesnil Chardonnay.

1971 ★★☆ It is a long time since I last tasted this vintage, so I have no specific notes but it always had the edge over the '73.

1970 ★★☆ Not one of the greatest Dom Pérignon vintages, yet magnums disgorged in 1988 drink very well, and, if kept, develop a charming toasty finesse after five years' post-disgorgement ageing.

1969 ★★☆ Marked by toasty acidity, as so many great 1969s are, the fruit in this cuvée has gone from honeyed lemon to peach-stone in recent years, particularly on the finish.

1966 ★★★ Looking back over almost 20 years of tasting notes, I have consistently marked this higher than the 1964. Sometimes the margin has

BORDEAUX-BORN JEAN-MARIE LABORDE TOOK OVER THE CONTROL OF MOËT & CHANDON, MERCIER AND RUINART IN 1996.

been quite small, but never have I rated them the other way around. This vintage is just entering its third stage of development. When I first tasted this wine, the fruit was beguiling and, for the past five years or so, the toastiness, although showing plenty of finesse, has been intense. The core of that intensity is now opening up and developing into great complexity, although only the coconut richness is showing through at the moment, plus the original fruit.

1964 ★★☆ Non-dosaged examples disgorged at Moët have always tasted much drier than other non-dosaged vintages of Dom Pérignon, although there is an intriguing sweetness on both the nose and the aftertaste. Under such conditions, the 1964 currently stands out as different from all other Dom Pérignon vintages, with a grippy, austere texture to the fruit. Without detracting from anything I have said about the 1966 above, I would not be surprised if in another 20 years the relative merits of the two wines might be reversed.

1962 ★★☆ It is a long time since I tasted this (so no specific notes), but it used to be one of the most seductive Dom Pérignons.

1961 ★★★ The best Dom Pérignon I have ever tasted. This is textbook stuff, with fabulous length and depth for such a relatively light-bodied wine, with wonderfully mellow aromas of coffee, toast, macaroons and peaches. Great complexity, but even greater finesse.

1959 The trouble with this vintage is not the wine, but the bottle: the neck in many bottles and magnums was slightly warped. This meant that only part of the cork gripped, reducing its effectiveness as a seal. The last time I was at Dom Pérignon, we wasted three magnums: all were spoiled by the treacle aroma of oxidation. This was a great Champagne, but if you are ever disappointed by a 1959 Dom Pérignon, slide your finger down the inside of the neck. If you can feel a warp, you will know why.

DOM CASMIR

See BAUCHET

N/A
DOQUET-JEANMAIRE

VERTUS

- 6,700 cases
- Société de Récoltants

This grower has the same origins as Champagne Jeanmaire, which was established in 1933 by Pascal Doquet's grandfather, André Jeanmaire. After expanding and buying up Oudinot, he sold both brands to the Trouillard family. Jeanmaire retained 2.5 hectares of superbly situated vines on the middle slopes of Le Mesnil-sur-Oger, to which Doquet's father added vineyards in Vertus, Bergères-les-Vertus, Voipreux and on Mont Aimé in Val-de-Marais. The family estate now totals 14 hectares, and Pascal Doquet joined his father in 1982, after graduating from the viticultural school in Avize.

WINEMAKER

Pascal Doquet

HOUSE STYLE & RANGE

Although I have recently tasted the full range, it was my first experience of these wines; hence judgement is reserved. At best, they can be soft and creamy, although some *cuvées* have an oxidative tendency.

BLANC DE BLANCS RÉSERVE DEMI-SEC
Not vintaged, méthode champenoise: 100% Chardonnay

CARTE OR, BLANC DE BLANCS BRUT
Not vintaged, méthode champenoise: 100% Chardonnay

ROSÉ BRUT
Not vintaged, addition of red wine, méthode champenoise: 85% Chardonnay, 15% Pinot Noir

SÉLECTION, BLANC DE BLANCS BRUT
Not vintaged, méthode champenoise: 100% Chardonnay

COEUR DE TERROIR, BLANC DE BLANCS BRUT
Vintaged, méthode champenoise: 100% Chardonnay

MILLÉSIME, BLANC DE BLANCS BRUT
Vintaged, méthode champenoise: 100% Chardonnay

N/A
ROBERT DOYARD

VERTUS

- 2,500 cases
- Récoltant-Manipulant

It was Maurice Doyard who, with Robert-Jean de Vogüé, cleverly persuaded the Germans to establish the CIVC by suggesting that the Third Reich had more important things to do than to get bogged down in the day-to-day machinations of the Champagne industry. This not only enabled the Champenois to run their own industry under the noses of their invaders, but also resulted in the most powerful interprofessional organisation in the French wine industry, although this power has declined in 1990s.

WINEMAKER

Yannick Doyard

HOUSE STYLE & RANGE

Over the years, these *cuvées* have varied between a promising youthful intensity and some very strange brews, but the samples promised for an update tasting did not materialise. Judgement is reserved.

EXTRA BRUT
Not vintaged, méthode champenoise: 100% Chardonnay

★ PREMIER CRU BLANC DE BLANCS RÉSERVE
Not vintaged, méthode champenoise: 100% Chardonnay

PREMIER CRU ROSÉ BRUT
Not vintaged, addition of red wine, méthode champenoise: 90% Chardonnay, 10% Pinot Noir

BRUT
Vintaged, méthode champenoise: 100% Chardonnay

89 VALUE
DRAPPIER

URVILLE

- 60,000 cases
- Other labels - Recamier
- Négociant-Manipulant

Charles de Gaulle's favourite Champagne comes from the most dynamic independent producer in the Aube. Drappier also vies with Serge Mathieu as this southerly district's very best producer. The company also has cellars in Reims, but the production is still heavily influenced by Aube fruit. Some *cuvées* are pure Aube – which makes a nonsense of the claim by some *grande marque* snobs that the Aube should not even be part of the Champagne appellation. One pure Aube *cuvée* is in fact Drappier's best Champagne: Grande Sendrée. This is not just pure Aube, or even a *mono-cru*, but one of Champagne's rare single-vineyard wines. It is made from 70-year-old vines, and derives its name from a corruption of *cendrée*, the vineyard having been woodland until it was burned down in 1838, infusing the soil with ash, which should give Madeira aficionados a sense of *déjà vu*.

WINEMAKER

Michel Drappier

HOUSE STYLE & RANGE

Ultra-fruity Champagnes that quickly attain a lovely biscuity complexity due to the low-sulphur regime employed in making them.

★✷ CARTE D'OR BRUT
Not vintaged, méthode champenoise: 7% Chardonnay, 90% Pinot Noir, 3% Meunier

★✷ ROSÉ BRUT
Not vintaged, méthode champenoise: 100% Pinot Noir

★✷ SIGNATURE, BLANC DE BLANCS BRUT
Not vintaged, méthode champenoise: 100% Chardonnay

★✷ CARTE D'OR BRUT
Vintaged, méthode champenoise: 10% Chardonnay, 90% Pinot Noir

★★ GRAND SENDRÉE BRUT
Vintaged, méthode champenoise: 45% Chardonnay, 55% Pinot Noir

★✷ GRAND SENDRÉE ROSÉ
Vintaged, méthode champenoise: 100% Pinot Noir

★✷ CUVÉE DE L'AN 2000 BRUT
Vintaged, méthode champenoise: 40% Chardonnay, 55% Pinot Noir, 5% Meunier

84
J DUMANGIN

CHIGNY-LES-ROSES

- 7,500 cases
- Other labels - M Dumangin Fils, Alexis Dumangin, Dumangin & Goulard, Olivier Walsham
- Récoltant-Manipulant

A grower Champagne that was established at the beginning of the 20th century. Only those *cuvées* sold under the J Dumangin label carry an RC number, and are thus exclusively produced from this grower's own vineyards. All the other brands carry ND numbers.

WINEMAKER

Jacky Dumangin

HOUSE STYLE & RANGE

Sometimes firm, sometimes soft, but always fruit-driven, tending to go biscuity rather than toasty.

✷ BRUT CARTE D'OR
Not vintaged, méthode champenoise: 25% Chardonnay, 25% Pinot Noir, 50% Meunier

BRUT GRANDE RÉSERVE
Not vintaged, méthode champenoise: 25% Chardonnay, 25% Pinot Noir, 50% Meunier

BRUT ROSÉ
Not vintaged, addition of red wine, méthode champenoise: 25% Chardonnay, 25% Pinot Noir, 50% Meunier

✷ DEMI-SEC CARTE D'OR
Not vintaged, méthode champenoise: 25% Chardonnay, 25% Pinot Noir, 50% Meunier

✭ Brut Millésime

Vintaged, méthode champenoise: 60% Chardonnay, 40% Pinot Noir

Cuvée 2000

Vintaged, méthode champenoise: 60% Chardonnay, 40% Pinot Noir

85
DANIEL DUMONT
RILLY-LA-MONTAGNE

• 5,000 cases
• Récoltant-Manipulant

This highly respected grower is from the same village as Vilmart, where his family is also practised in the art of the *pépiniériste,* or nurseryman, selling every clone of Chardonnay, Pinot Noir and Meunier recommended by the CIVC.

WINEMAKER
Jean-Michel Dumont

HOUSE STYLE & RANGE
Rich and full in fruit, sometimes a touch sprightly, but always capable of attaining a creamy, biscuity complexity with age.

★ Brut Grande Réserve

Not vintaged, méthode champenoise: 30% Chardonnay, 40% Pinot Noir, 30% Meunier

✭ Brut Rosé

Not vintaged, addition of red wine, méthode champenoise: 30% Chardonnay, 40% Pinot Noir, 30% Meunier

Brut Tradition

Not vintaged, méthode champenoise: equal parts Chardonnay, Pinot Noir, Meunier

Demi-Sec

Not vintaged, méthode champenoise: equal parts Chardonnay, Pinot Noir, Meunier

★ Brut Cuvée d'Excellence

Vintaged, méthode champenoise: 50% Chardonnay, 50% Pinot Noir

Brut Grande Réserve Millésime

Vintaged, méthode champenoise: 30% Chardonnay, 40% Pinot Noir, 30% Meunier

88
DUVAL-LEROY
VERTUS

• 500,000 cases
• Other labels - Baron de Beaupré, E Michel, Henri de Varlane, Paul Vertay
• Négociant-Manipulant

While not in the premier league, Duval-Leroy has always been a good-value producer, but these Champagnes have improved at such an impressive rate that they have progressed way beyond the realms of just good value. This is now a seriously underrated, high-quality house, and the jump from this to premier-league status is not really that great. Indeed, it is probably much less than Duval-Leroy has already achieved in the 1990s. The decisive factor on how to progress successfully from here will have less to do with what is in the bottle than how the brand is presented in markets worldwide. It is an intriguing thought that Duval-Leroy is better-known on more markets now than Clicquot-Ponsardin was before the famous Widow took over.

There are few family-owned houses in Champagne today where a widow could emulate the *grande dame,* and there are even fewer houses that have the financial stability to make success a real possibility, but Duval-Leroy is one and Carol Duval is the toughest Champagne widow I have ever seen. Furthermore, at her side is the quietly spoken, highly talented Hervé Jestin who, with the investments made by the Duval family, has created a superbly equipped press-house and state-of-the-art winery. He has skilfully employed these facilities to achieve a level of quality that no Duval in his or her right mind could possibly have expected. Jestin is to Carol Duval what Müller was to the Widow Clicquot, having given her the sort of quality required to conquer the modern-day equivalent of the mighty Russian market. With luck, if Carol Duval is half as successful as Nicole-Barbe Clicquot, Jestin will stay longer than Müller did.

WINEMAKER
Hervé Jestin

HOUSE STYLE & RANGE
Elegance, purity of fruit and a linear-like focus creates a consistency of style throughout the entire range that is not surpassed in Champagne, and rarely equalled. A new prestige *cuvée* is in the pipeline to replace the de-listed Cuvée des Roys. It is a superb wine and will be presented in a lovely bottle with beautifully understated labelling, but I'm not so sure about the proposed name, and hope it will be changed before it is released.

★✭ Fleur de Champagne Blanc de Blancs

Not vintaged, méthode champenoise: 100% Chardonnay

★✭ Fleur de Champagne Blanc de Noirs

Not vintaged, méthode champenoise: 60% Pinot Noir, 40% Meunier

★ Fleur de Champagne Brut

Not vintaged, méthode champenoise: 73% Chardonnay, 27% Pinot Noir

VINES SURROUND THE BUILDINGS OUTSIDE EPERNAY

Fleur de Champagne Demi-Sec

Not vintaged, méthode champenoise: 30% Chardonnay, 50% Pinot Noir, 20% Meunier

★ Fleur de Champagne Saignée Rosé

Not vintaged, addition of red wine, méthode champenoise: 100% Pinot Noir

★✭ Fleur de Champagne Blanc de Blancs

Vintaged, méthode champenoise: 100% Chardonnay

★★ Fleur de Champagne Brut

Vintaged, méthode champenoise: 75% Chardonnay, 25% Pinot Noir

78
CHARLES ELLNER
EPERNAY

• 83,000 cases
• Other labels - Charles de Floricourt, Veuve M Page, Marquis d'Estrand, De Pompadour, Ph d'Albecourt
• Négociant-Manipulant

Charles-Emile Ellner came from a family of growers, and it was his son Pierre who established the *négociant* status of this house in 1972. In hard times, it is Charles Ellner's *patrimoine* of 52 hectares of vineyards and its sales of BOB and *sous marque* that help keep this family-owned firm afloat while so many others are threatened by huge losses.

WINEMAKER
Jacques Ellner

HOUSE STYLE & RANGE
Known for its soft, fruity, Pinot Noir dominated rosé and the Cuvée de Réserve, which is rich with quite broad flavours and lavishly packaged with a reproduction painting for its award-winning label.

Blanc de Blancs

Not vintaged, méthode champenoise: 100% Chardonnay

Brut Rosé

Not vintaged, addition of red wine, méthode champenoise: 50% Pinot Noir, 50% Meunier

Carte Or Brut

Not vintaged, méthode champenoise: 60% Chardonnay, 40% Pinot Noir

★ Cuvée de Réserve Brut

Not vintaged, méthode champenoise: 60% Chardonnay, 40% Pinot Noir

BRUT

Vintaged, méthode champenoise: 75% Chardonnay, 25% Pinot Noir

★ CHARLES ELLNER BRUT

Vintaged, méthode champenoise: 70% Chardonnay, 30% Pinot Noir

★ SÉDUCTION BRUT

Vintaged, méthode champenoise: 70% Chardonnay, 30% Pinot Noir

78 VALUE
ESTERLIN
EPERNAY

- 83,400 cases
- Other labels – d'Alencourt, Victor Lejeune
- Coopérative-Manipulant

Established in Mancy in 1948, Esterlin did not start commercialising its own Champagne until as recently as 1985.

My first visit to this co-op is memorable. I had tasted some surprisingly good Champagnes and wondered whether they were good by design or luck. If the former, why was Esterlin not better known? My visit was to Esterlin's original building in Mancy, where I was met by the *directeur*, Michel Plantagenet, who now runs plush new premises on the avenue de Champagne in Épernay.

As the whole point of my visit was to taste Esterlin's wines as comprehensively as possible, I was somewhat flummoxed when Michel Plantegenet apologised for not being able to give me any tasting whatsoever. When I pressed him on the subject, he insisted it would be impossible to organise because the workers pinch the wines from his refrigerator! It was my time to insist, later to my regret, to taste whatever may be left in the fridge. Just two wines were left, and they were obviously the ones the discerning workers refused to steal: the non-vintage brut was maderised and the rosé would have been better had it been. Monsieur Plantagenet now has a much larger fridge in the brand new, high-tech winery and offices. He actually designed these premises and as far as I can tell he missed just one thing: a padlock for his fridge.

WINEMAKER
Sébastien Barbier

HOUSE STYLE & RANGE
Good wines can be made here, as the 1985 vintage and some *cuvées* of the *blanc de blancs* have been quite superb in an upfront, rich and utterly delicious style. The wines are dominated by Sézannais Chardonnay which, when successful, gives them their user-friendliness.

★ BLANC DE BLANCS

Not vintaged, méthode champenoise: 100% Chardonnay

BRUT

Not vintaged, méthode champenoise: 60% Chardonnay, 5% Pinot Noir, 35% Meunier

RAINY WEATHER AT HARVEST TIME, AY

ROSÉ

Not vintaged, addition of red wine, méthode champenoise: 55% Chardonnay, 15% Pinot Noir, 30% Meunier

MILLÉSIME

Vintaged, méthode champenoise: 100% Chardonnay

78
NICOLAS FEUILLATTE
EPERNAY

- 230,000 cases
- Other labels – St Nicholas, St Maurice, Desroches, Camille d'Haubaine, Henri Macquard, Philippe de Nantheuil
- Coopérative-Manipulant

The marketing arm of the massive CVC super-cooperative, Nicolas Feuillatte has enough high-quality vineyards to make it capable of producing very good Champagne, but although it has improved over the last ten years or so, the performance is still patchy.

WINEMAKER
Jean-Pierre Vincent

HOUSE STYLE & RANGE
It looked as if these Champagnes might have started to pick up with the launch of the excellent 1985 Palmes d'Or, but subsequent vintages have been disappointing, and most wines tend to lack elegance. Even when a good *cuvée* is produced, there seems to be something missing.

BRUT RÉSERVE PARTICULIÈRE

Not vintaged, méthode champenoise: 20% Chardonnay, 40% Pinot Noir, 40% Meunier

★ BRUT BLANC DE BLANCS

Vintaged, méthode champenoise: 100% Chardonnay

★ BRUT CUVÉE SPÉCIALE

Vintaged, méthode champenoise: 40% Chardonnay, 40% Pinot Noir, 20% Meunier

BRUT PREMIER CRU

Vintaged, méthode champenoise: 20% Chardonnay, 40% Pinot Noir, 40% Meunier

BRUT PREMIER CRU ROSÉ

Vintaged, addition of red wine, méthode champenoise: 10% Chardonnay, 60% Pinot Noir, 30% Meunier

GRANDE CUVÉE PALMES D'OR

Vintaged, méthode champenoise: 60% Chardonnay, 40% Pinot Noir

72
GHISLAIN FIÈVET
NOGENT-LABBESSE

- 840 cases
- Récoltant-Manipulant

One of the few Champagnes available from Mont Berru, an anomalous area of Chardonnay vineyards growing north of the northern Montagne. Most of the growers in the three villages on Mont Berru belong to the cooperative, which does not even sell grapes or juice to the *négoce* but insists on vinifying the wine itself and thus deters those houses who like to control the vinification. Fièvet is an exception.

WINEMAKER
Joël Fièvet

HOUSE STYLE & RANGE
The basic non-vintage is an oxidative style, but the Cuvée de Réserve has more mellow fruit, although can be dominated by creamy, caramel malolactic.

BRUT

Not vintaged, méthode champenoise: 100% Chardonnay

CUVÉE DE RÉSERVE BRUT

Not vintaged, méthode champenoise: 100% Chardonnay

GRANDE CUVÉE

Not vintaged, méthode champenoise: 100% Chardonnay

ROSÉ

Not vintaged, addition of red wine, méthode champenoise: 85% Chardonnay, 15% Pinot Noir

85
ROLAND FLINIAUX
AY-CHAMPAGNE

- 7,000 cases
- Other labels – Henri IV, A Foursin
- Négociant-Manipulant

A small, traditional house with just four hectares, but this is enough to supply a quarter of its needs, especially as they are all *grand cru* Aÿ-Champagne.

WINEMAKER
Régis Fliniaux

HOUSE STYLE & RANGE
Unashamedly full of bold Pinot Noir flavour and complexity. Sometimes oxidative aromas and occasionally noticeable sulphur content, but always capable of a nutty complexity, although the potential longevity is medium-term rather than great.

★ CARTE NOIR BRUT
Not vintaged, méthode champenoise: 20% Chardonnay, 80% Pinot Noir

★ CUVÉE DE RÉSERVE BRUT
Not vintaged, méthode champenoise: 20% Chardonnay, 80% Pinot Noir

★★ BRUT
Vintaged, méthode champenoise: 100% Pinot Noir

★★ ROSÉ BRUT
Vintaged, méthode champenoise: 100% Pinot Noir

80
G FLUTEAU
GYE-SUR-SEINE

- 4,600 cases
- Négociant-Manipulant

This small Aubois house is called Herard et Fluteau, but markets its Champagne under the G Fluteau label. Thierry Fluteau and his American wife Jennifer own eight hectares of vineyards and claim to be the smallest *négociant-manipulant* house in Champagne. Indeed, Fluteau is smaller even than Salon (although that great Champagne is not produced every year).

WINEMAKER
Thierry Fluteau

HOUSE STYLE & RANGE
Rich and fruity, with good weight, and a gentle mousse.

★ CARTE BLANCHE BRUT
Not vintaged, méthode champenoise: 100% Pinot Noir

CARTE RUBIS ROSÉ
Not vintaged, saignée, méthode champenoise: 100% Pinot Noir

★ CUVÉE PRESTIGE
Vintaged, méthode champenoise: 100% Chardonnay

★ CUVÉE RÉSERVÉE
Not vintaged, méthode champenoise: 100% Pinot Noir

72
FORGET-BRIMONT
LUDES

- 8,300 cases
- Other labels – 'a lot' but none specified
- Négociant-Manipulant

Forgets have been *vignerons* in Ludes, Mailly and Chigny-les-Roses for six generations, but Eugène Forget was the first to make and sell his own Champagne in 1920. Michel Forget currently owns nine hectares of vineyards.

WINEMAKER
Michel Forget

HOUSE STYLE & RANGE
Some *cuvées* are rich and ripe on the palate, but too many are dull and lack finesse.

BRUT ROSÉ, 1ER CRU
Not vintaged, addition of red wine, méthode champenoise: 25% Chardonnay, 60% Pinot Noir, 15% Meunier

CARTE BLANCHE BRUT, 1ER CRU
Not vintaged, méthode champenoise: 25% Chardonnay, 60% Pinot Noir, 15% Meunier

CARTE BLANCHE DEMI-SEC, 1ER CRU
Not vintaged, méthode champenoise: 25% Chardonnay, 60% Pinot Noir, 15% Meunier

★ CARTE BLANCHE EXTRA BRUT, 1ER CRU
Not vintaged, méthode champenoise: 25% Chardonnay, 60% Pinot Noir, 15% Meunier

CUVÉE PRESTIGE BRUT, 1ER CRU
Vintaged, méthode champenoise: 50% Chardonnay, 50% Pinot Noir

LOUIS FRANÇOIS
See E BARNAUT

N/A
MICHEL FURDYNA
CELLES-SUR-OURCE

- 4,200 cases
- Récoltant-Manipulant

A small Aubois grower established in 1974, Michel Furdyna owns eight hectares of vineyards in Celles-sur-Ource, Landreville, Loches-sur-Ource and Neuville-sur-Seine.

WINEMAKER
Michel Furdyna

HOUSE STYLE & RANGE
Apart from Furdyna's excellent non-vintage Réserve Brut, I have seldom tasted these Champagnes; hence no overall judgement.

CARTE BLANCHE BRUT/DEMI-SEC
Not vintaged, méthode champenoise: 5% Chardonnay, 85% Pinot Noir, 10% Meunier

★ RÉSERVE BRUT
Not vintaged, méthode champenoise: 100% Pinot Noir

ROSÉ BRUT
Not vintaged, addition of red wine, méthode champenoise: 100% Pinot Noir

PRESTIGE BRUT
Vintaged, méthode champenoise: 30% Chardonnay, 70% Pinot Noir

N/A
GAILLARD GIROT
MARDEUIL

- 1,250 cases
- Récoltant-Manipulant

This family enterprise is new to me, but has apparently been making and selling its own Champagne since the end of the 19th century.

WINEMAKER
Sandrine Gaillard

HOUSE STYLE & RANGE
Only the basic non-vintage brut tasted, so I cannot give an overall rating, but it was rich, fruity and tasty, with creamy, biscuity finesse building on the finish.

BRUT
Not vintaged, méthode champenoise: grape varieties not revealed

BRUT DE BRUT
Not vintaged, méthode champenoise: grape varieties not revealed

DEMI-SEC
Not vintaged, méthode champenoise: grape varieties not revealed

86
GALLIMARD
LES RICEYS

- 6,500 cases
- Other labels – Arnaud de Beauroy
- Négociant-Manipulant

Jean and Didier Gallimard are fifth-generation *vignerons*; the a family first made and sold Champagne in 1930. They own eight hectares of vineyards and recently received some well-deserved attention in the French press.

WINEMAKER
Didier Gallimard

HOUSE STYLE & RANGE
Fine and flowery with some finesse, and a long finish; tending to go biscuity with a little age.

AN 2000
Not vintaged, méthode champenoise: 20% Chardonnay, 80% Pinot Noir

BRUT ROSÉ
Not vintaged, addition of red wine, méthode champenoise: 100% Pinot Noir

★ CUVÉE RÉSERVE BRUT
Not vintaged, méthode champenoise: 100% Pinot Noir

★ CUVÉE PRESTIGE BRUT
Vintaged, méthode champenoise: 10% Chardonnay, 90% Pinot Noir

85
GARDET
CHIGNY-LES-ROSES

- 80,000 cases
- Other labels - Saint Flavy
- Négociant-Manipulant

Since the beginning of the 20th century, Gardet & Cie has traditionally sold its Champagne as Georges Gardet in the UK and as Charles Gardet in France, but there is now a tendency to focus on Gardet and use the Charles Gardet name for its prestige *cuvée*. The reputation of this house is particularly strong in Britain, thanks to the fanaticism of the incorrigible Michael Peace MW.

WINEMAKER
Jean Philippe Gardet

HOUSE STYLE & RANGE
These Champagnes used to be too oxidative, and some *cuvées* have suffered from too much yeast-contact, but Jean-Philippe Gardet has been attempting a much fresher and fruitier style over the last few years.

BRUT
Not vintaged, méthode champenoise:
30% Chardonnay, 70% Pinot Noir
BRUT ROSÉ
Not vintaged, méthode champenoise: 100% Pinot Noir
★ BRUT
Vintaged, méthode champenoise: 33% Chardonnay,
33% Pinot Noir, 33% Meunier
★ CUVÉE CHARLES GARDET
Vintaged, méthode champenoise: 67% Chardonnay,
33% Pinot Noir

85
GATINOIS
AY-CHAMPAGNE

- 2,500 cases
- Récoltant-Manipulant

A small producer with a high reputation, owner Pierre Cheval can trace back his family line to Nicolas le Cacheur, a *vigneron* in Aÿ in 1696. Like many growers today, Cheval sells part of his production to various houses, including Bollinger, but increasingly makes more of his own Champagne.

WINEMAKER
Pierre Cheval-Gatinois

HOUSE STYLE & RANGE
Tradition Brut is an easy-drinking *cuvée*, but

needs 18 to 24 months to smooth down its raw floral notes. These are not present in the Réserve Brut, although it is exactly the same wine with longer yeast-contact. I have yet to be convinced by the vintage *cuvées*.
★★ RÉSERVE BRUT, GRAND CRU
Not vintaged, méthode champenoise:
10% Chardonnay, 90% Pinot Noir
ROSÉ BRUT, GRAND CRU
Not vintaged, addition of red wine, méthode
champenoise: 100% Pinot Noir
★ TRADITION BRUT, GRAND CRU
Not vintaged, méthode champenoise:
10% Chardonnay, 90% Pinot Noir
TRADITION DEMI-SEC, GRAND CRU
Not vintaged, méthode champenoise:
10% Chardonnay, 90% Pinot Noir
MILLÉSIME BRUT
Vintaged, méthode champenoise: 100% Pinot Noir

N/A
MICHEL GENET
CHOUILLY

- 4,150 cases
- Récoltant-Manipulant

Vincent and Antoine Genet own 6.5 hectares of vines in Chouilly, Cramant and Épernay.

WINEMAKER
Vincent Genet

HOUSE STYLE & RANGE
An inconsistent producer in my experience.
BRUT, GRAND CRU
Not vintaged, méthode champenoise: 100% Chardonnay
GRAND RÉSERVE, GRAND CRU
Vintaged, méthode champenoise: 100% Chardonnay

85
RENÉ GEOFFROY
CUMIERES, DAMERY

- 9,000 cases
- Récoltant-Manipulant

René and Jean-Baptiste Geoffroy trace family ownership of their vineyards in Cumières back to the 17th century. They are extremely quality-conscious, both in the vineyard and in the winery, harvesting grapes in *tries*, using oak *foudres*, and preventing malolactic fermentation.

WINEMAKER
Jean-Baptiste Geoffroy

HOUSE STYLE & RANGE
The house style is soft and smooth, with fine flavours, and a gentle mousse of tiny bubbles. I have not yet tasted the new Cuvée R de Geoffroy.

★ CUVÉE DE RÉSERVE BRUT
Not vintaged, méthode champenoise:
10% Chardonnay, 40% Pinot Noir, 50% Meunier
★ BRUT ROSÉ
Vintaged, saignée, méthode champenoise:
100% Pinot Noir
★★ CUVÉE PRESTIGE BRUT
Vintaged, méthode champenoise: 67% Chardonnay,
33% Pinot Noir
CUVÉE DE R. GEOFFROY
Vintaged, fermented in small oak barriques, méthode
champenoise: 70% Chardonnay, 30% Pinot Noir
★★ CUVÉE SÉLECTIONNÉE BRUT
Vintaged, méthode champenoise: 33% Chardonnay,
67% Pinot Noir

N/A
HENRY GERMAIN
RILLY-LA-MONTAGNE

- 150,000 cases
- Other labels - Binet, Collery
- Group ownership - Frey Group
- Négociant-Manipulant

Established by Henri-Antoine Germain in 1898, this house took over the old, established firm of Binet in 1985, and was itself purchased in 1988 by Frey, a local furniture company. Germain owns Collery in Aÿ-Champagne, and has a partnership with Champagne Dehours of Cerseuil.

WINEMAKER
Hervé Ladouce

HOUSE STYLE & RANGE
Patchy quality, hence no overall rating. Bottom-rung *cuvées* that can be too amylic, but when on song, they are rich and succulently fruity Champagnes of extremely good value. Star-ratings apply to *cuvées* when on form.
BRUT
Not vintaged, méthode champenoise:
15% Chardonnay, 50% Pinot Noir, 35% Meunier
★ BRUT RÉSERVE
Not vintaged, méthode champenoise:
20% Chardonnay, 60% Pinot Noir, 20% Meunier
BRUT ROSÉ
Not vintaged, addition of red wine, méthode
champenoise: 85% Chardonnay, 15% Pinot Noir
★★ PRESIDENT SIGNATURE, BRUT
Not vintaged, méthode champenoise:
50% Chardonnay, 50% Pinot Noir
★ TÊTE DE CUVÉE, BRUT
Not vintaged, méthode champenoise:
30% Chardonnay, 60% Pinot Noir,
10% Meunier
BRUT ROSÉ
Vintaged, addition of red wine, méthode champenoise:
20% Chardonnay, 60% Pinot Noir, 2
0% Meunier
★★ MILLÉSIMÉ BRUT
Vintaged, méthode champenoise: 40% Chardonnay,
60% Pinot Noir

★★☆ PRESIDENT, GRAND CRU BLANC DE BLANCS, BRUT
Vintaged, méthode champenoise: 100% Chardonnay

90
PIERRE GIMONNET
CUIS
- 15,000 cases
- Other labels - Larmandier Père & Fils
- Récoltant-Manipulant

The Gimonnets have been growers in Cuis since 1750, but not until 1935 did Pierre Gimonnet became the first to produce and sell Champagne under his own label. This house now owns 26 hectares of vineyards (in conjunction with Larmandier Père & Fils), all Chardonnay, in Cuis (a *premier cru*), and the *grands crus* of Chouilly and Cramant.

An exclusively Chardonnay domaine is rare even on the Côtes des Blancs, where a little Pinot Noir is normally grown for rosé, but the Gimonnets are fanatical in their pursuit of Champagnes that are expressive of their origins. More than half the vines are over 40 years old, which reduces the yield and increases the ripeness; hence, in years such as 1989, 1990 and 1992, the wines did not have to be chaptalised (and the vast majority of Champagne has to be).

In Cramant, the Gimonnets cultivate a vineyard in a *lieu-dit* called La Terre des Buissons, where their vines exceed 80 years of age. I have long urged Gimonnet to produce a single-vineyard Champagne in ultra-minute quantities from this vineyard to sell at the same price as Salon.

WINEMAKER
Didier & Olivier Gimonnet

HOUSE STYLE & RANGE
A classy combination of succulent, pristine Chardonnay fruit, richness and finesse. All are excellent, but my favourite varies from year to year. At the moment, it is the 1990 Fleuron.

★☆ CUIS 1ER CRU, BLANC DE BLANCS BRUT
Not vintaged, méthode champenoise: 100% Chardonnay
★★ FLEURON, 1ER CRU, BLANC DE BLANCS BRUT
Vintaged, méthode champenoise: 100% Chardonnay
★★ GASTRONOME, 1ER CRU, BLANC DE BLANCS BRUT
Vintaged, méthode champenoise: 100% Chardonnay

★★ OENOPHILE, 1ER CRU, BLANC DE BLANCS MAXI-BRUT
Vintaged, méthode champenoise: 100% Chardonnay

♦ Preparing to open a Megaboam ♦

★★ SPECIAL CLUB, BLANC DE BLANCS BRUT
Vintaged, méthode champenoise: 100% Chardonnay
★★ SPECIAL CLUB, GRAND CRU CHARDONNAY BRUT
Vintaged, méthode champenoise: 100% Chardonnay

N/A
PAUL GOBILLARD
PIERRY
- 12,500 cases
- Négociant-Manipulant

Although the Gobillards have been *vignerons* in Pierry since the early 19th century, it was not until 1941 that Paul Gobillard became the first member of the family to make and sell Champagne under his own name. Today, father and son, Jean-Paul and Bruno Gobillard, own some five hectares of vineyards, and run their enterprising family firm from the charming Château de Pierry, which houses La Maison du Millésime: a tasting venture with audio-visual facilities and a small museum. La Maison du Millésime provides the rare experience of tasting older vintages of Champagne in perfect condition from the cellars of various famous houses. You can taste by arrangement old vintages of Krug, Pol Roger, Bollinger, Taittinger... the list goes on.

WINEMAKER
Jean-Paul & Bruno Gobillard

HOUSE STYLE & RANGE
Often weighty wines, yet crisp acidity gives an elegant balance. Normally excellent, but some disappointing *cuvées* were made in the late 1980s, and I have yet to be convinced that Gobillard has turned things around, except for the Cuvée Régence.

BLANC DE BLANCS BRUT
Not vintaged, méthode champenoise: 100% Chardonnay
CARTE BLANCHE BRUT
Not vintaged, méthode champenoise: 25% Chardonnay, 75% Pinot Noir

★☆ CUVÉE RÉGENCE BRUT
Not vintaged, méthode champenoise: 30% Chardonnay, 70% Pinot Noir
RÉSERVE BRUT
Not vintaged, méthode champenoise: 30% Chardonnay, 70% Pinot Noir
ROSÉ BRUT
Not vintaged, méthode champenoise: 10% Chardonnay, 90% Pinot Noir
MILLÉSIME BRUT
Vintaged, méthode champenoise: 50% Chardonnay, 50% Pinot Noir

87
PAUL GOERG
VERTUS
- 15,000 cases
- Other labels - Goutte d'Or
- Coopérative-Manipulant

Established in 1950, La Goutte d'Or cooperative now comprises of more than 100 growers owning 120 hectares of vineyards, including some 95 hectares of Chardonnay, with an average *échelle des crus* of 97%.

WINEMAKER
Daniel Aubertin

HOUSE STYLE & RANGE
Rich, well-focused flavours that promise to develop complexity and finesse with a little bottle-age.

★ BLANC DE BLANCS BRUT
Not vintaged, méthode champenoise: 100% Chardonnay
BRUT ROSÉ
Not vintaged, addition of red wine, méthode champenoise: 87% Chardonnay, 13% Pinot Noir
BRUT TRADITION
Not vintaged, méthode champenoise: 60% Chardonnay, 40% Pinot Noir
★★ CUVÉE DU CENTENAIRE BRUT
Not vintaged, méthode champenoise: 93% Chardonnay, 7% Pinot Noir
★ MILLÉSIME BRUT
Vintaged, méthode champenoise: 100% Chardonnay

DID YOU KNOW?

THE LONGEST DISTANCE OVER WHICH A CORK HAS BEEN EJECTED FROM A CHAMPAGNE BOTTLE IS 177 FEET, 9 INCHES. THIS WAS RECORDED BY PROF. EMERITUS HEINRICH MEDICUS AT WOODBURY VINEYARD WINERY IN CHATAUQUA COUNTY, IN THE STATE OF NEW YORK ON JUNE 5TH, 1988

N/A
MICHEL GONET
AVIZE

- 25,000 cases
- Other labels - Marquis de Sade, André Bonin, Comte d'Harmont
- Group ownership - Gonet also owns Château Lesparre in the Graves de Vayres area of Bordeaux, where sparkling wine has been produced since 1986
- Récoltant-Manipulant

The Gonets have been *vignerons* for seven generations, and are very important growers today, with 40 hectares of vineyards in Le Mesnil-sur-Oger, where the family originated, as well as Oger and Avize. If Michel Gonet reached the high notes he is capable of more often and more consistently, this would be a very worthwhile grower Champagne indeed.

WINEMAKER
Michel Gonet

HOUSE STYLE & RANGE
When on form, these Champagnes have exuberant fruit and show nice finesse. Note that star-ratings apply to *cuvées* when on form.

★★✰ BLANC DE BLANCS, GRAND CRU, BRUT
Not vintaged, méthode champenoise: 100% Chardonnay
BRUT RÉSERVE
Not vintaged, méthode champenoise: 70% Chardonnay, 30% Pinot Noir
BRUT ROSÉ
Not vintaged, addition of red wine, méthode champenoise: 100% Pinot Noir
★★✰ BLANC DE BLANCS, GRAND CRU, BRUT
Vintaged, méthode champenoise: 100% Chardonnay
★★✰ SPECIAL CLUB, BLANC DE BLANCS GRAND CRU
Vintaged, méthode champenoise: 100% Chardonnay

N/A
PHILIPPE GONET
Le-Mesnil-sur-Oger

- 8,500 cases
- Other labels - Ch Pierre Cellier
- Récoltant-Manipulant

Cousins to Michel Gonet, this part of the family still resides in Le Mesnil-sur-Oger, but its 19 hectares of vineyards are spread over a much wider area, although a third of the estate centres on Le Mesnil and Oger.

WINEMAKER
Pierre Gonet

HOUSE STYLE & RANGE
I have had much less experience of these Champagnes than I have of those made by cousin Michel (above), which is why I have not given this producer an overall rating. However, the most recently tasted vintage had a lovely creamy, nutty style marked by a low *dosage*.

★ BLANC DE BLANCS BRUT
Not vintaged, méthode champenoise: 100% Chardonnay
BLANC DE BLANCS DEMI-SEC
Not vintaged, méthode champenoise: 100% Chardonnay
RÉSERVE BRUT
Not vintaged, méthode champenoise: 30% Chardonnay, 60% Pinot Noir, 10% Meunier
ROSÉ BRUT
Not vintaged, addition of red wine, méthode champenoise: 100% Pinot Noir
★★✰ BLANC DE BLANCS, GRAND CRU BRUT
Vintaged, méthode champenoise: 100% Chardonnay
SPÉCIAL CLUB, BLANC DE BLANCS GRAND CRU BRUT
Vintaged, méthode champenoise: 100% Chardonnay

90
GOSSET
AY–CHAMPAGNE

- 50,000 cases
- Other labels - Ivernel
- Négociant-Manipulant

Although Ruinart is the oldest Champagne house (*ie* commercial producer of sparkling Champagne), Gosset is the oldest known producer of wine in Champagne, tracing its origins back to Pierre Gosset in 1584. Ironically, in 1992 Gosset became the first new *grande marque* for more than 30 years – ironically, because the Syndicat de Grandes Marques de Champagne was disbanded in 1997. Then, in 1994, after 410 years of family ownership, the house was sold to the Cointreau family, and is now under the direct control of Béatrice Cointreau. The *chef de caves* and oenologist remain the same, as do the winemaking techniques, which involve the use of some wood and an avoidance of malolactic fermentation, and the level of production is unchanged, being just over 500,000 bottles, which is similar in size to Krug.

Readers who also have *The New Sotheby's Wine Encyclopedia* will be pleased to know that the query that hung over Gosset in the first print-run of that book can now be disregarded. The quality is as good as it has ever been, and the confusion was all my own fault. I often 'taste ahead', but because forthcoming vintages and non-vintage *cuvées* are specially disgorged for this purpose, they do not always show as they eventually will. This is due to various reasons, the three most important being [1] it might not be the optimum moment for

disgorgement, [2] a non-commercial dosage is always guesswork, and [3] such wines seldom receive enough time between disgorgement and tasting; consequently the *dosage* might not be well integrated and there can be some sulphur pick-up. If, despite these problems, a Champagne shows great promise, its future success is virtually guaranteed and I am happy to write about it. However, if a Champagne does not show well, there are so many reasons why this might be that it is best not to mention the wine at all. The Gosset *cuvées* I was rather concerned about happened to be forthcoming *cuvées*. When the fully commercial products were released, they turned out to be excellent, with none of the aromas I found so distressing.

WINEMAKER
Jean Pierre Mareignier

HOUSE STYLE & RANGE
There is nothing wrong with the fresh, sweet, easy-drinking, fruity Brut Excellence, but it is simply not in the same league as the rest of the range, consequently lowering the overall rating from what might otherwise be around the 92 mark. There is such a huge step up to the Grande Réserve Brut, which is refined, with a lovely depth of flavour. This profoundly serious wine is heaped in finesse, capable of great complexity of smooth, biscuity richness, and is the perfect flagship for the Gosset style.

✰ BRUT EXCELLENCE
Not vintaged, méthode champenoise: 45% Chardonnay, 45% Pinot Noir, 10% Meunier
★★★ GRANDE RÉSERVE BRUT
Not vintaged, méthode champenoise: 46% Chardonnay, 38% Pinot Noir, 16% Meunier
★★✰ CELEBRIS BRUT
Vintaged, méthode champenoise: 70% Chardonnay, 30% Pinot Noir
★★✰ GRAND MILLÉSIME BRUT
Vintaged, méthode champenoise: 66% Chardonnay, 34% Pinot Noir
★★✰ GRAND ROSÉ BRUT
Vintaged, addition of red wine, méthode champenoise: 80% Chardonnay, 20% Pinot Noir

86
GOSSET–BRABANT
AY–CHAMPAGNE

- 2,500 cases
- Récoltant-Manipulant

Cousins to the former owners of the famous Champagne Gosset, also in Aÿ-Champagne, Michel and Christian Gosset can trace their roots back 17 generations to Jean Gosset, Seigneur d'Aÿ in 1531. The oldest known *vigneron* in the family was Claude Gosset (1555), and it was Pierre Gosset who became the oldest wine producer in Champagne (1584).

WINEMAKER
Michel & Christian Gosset

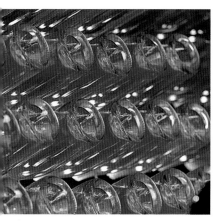

ROSÉ CHAMPAGNE IN PUPITRE IN THE CELLARS OF CHAMPAGNE GOSSET, AY

HOUSE STYLE & RANGE

The non-vintage lacks length and can have strawlike aromas, but the better *cuvées* are well-structured with expressive, creamy-rich fruit.

BRUT 1ER CRU TRADITION

Not vintaged, méthode champenoise:
20% Chardonnay, 70% Pinot Noir, 10% Meunier

★ CUVÉE DE RÉSERVE, 1ER CRU BRUT

Not vintaged, méthode champenoise:
20% Chardonnay, 70% Pinot Noir, 10% Meunier

★⯪ GRAND CRU CUVÉE GABRIEL BRUT

Vintaged, méthode champenoise: 40% Chardonnay,
60% Pinot Noir

N/A
GEORGE GOULET
REIMS

- 125,000 cases
- Group ownership - Chaudron
- Other labels - Henry Goulet
- Négociant-Manipulant

Goulet Frères was founded in 1834 by François André Goulet, but he abandoned the business in 1849. It was re-established in 1867 as George Goulet by the founder's third son. This Champagne was most famous in England, and received royal warrants from both King George IV and King George V.

In 1960, George Goulet was acquired by Abel Lepitre, and shortly afterwards an umbrella company called Le Société des Grandes Champagnes de Reims was formed to embrace Abel Lepitre, George Goulet and de Saint Marceaux (another great, long-lost Champagne). Goulet has since been sold to Lionel and Luc Chaudron who, since 1990, have produced these *cuvées* from their own vineyards.

This is the Champagne that the late David Niven confessed (in his autobiography *The Moon's a Balloon*) to selling in New York in 1933, just prior to Prohibition being lifted. His FBI mug-shot still adorns the legitimate offices of '21's today, with the caption 'First and worst salesman'!

WINEMAKER
Luc Chaudron & Lucien Quatresol

HOUSE STYLE & RANGE

Used to be renowned for its big, full-flavoured rosé capable of ageing several decades. Just after Chaudron purchased the brand, it launched a stunningly complex, age-worthy non-vintage *cuvée;* since then, however the wines have been too inconsistent, hence no overall rating.

BRUT

Not vintaged, méthode champenoise:
33% Chardonnay, 67% Pinot Noir

ROSÉ BRUT

Not vintaged, méthode champenoise:
30% Chardonnay, 70% Pinot Noir

BRUT

Vintaged, méthode champenoise: variable

90
HENRI GOUTORBE
AY–CHAMPAGNE

- 10,000 cases
- Récoltant-Manipulant

With 15 hectares of vineyards, Henri Goutorbe is one of the more important growers in Champagne. Like many growers, he offers a number of older vintages.

WINEMAKER
René Goutorbe

HOUSE STYLE & RANGE

Generally excellent rich, well-structured Champagnes – always satisfying to drink. Goutorbe's Grand Cru Special Club is in a different class, and his 1990 Grand Cru Special Club is the best he has ever made.

★⯪ CUVÉE PRESTIGE BRUT

Not vintaged, méthode champenoise:
30% Chardonnay, 70% Pinot Noir

★ CUVÉE TRADITIONNELLE BRUT

Not vintaged, méthode champenoise:
30% Chardonnay, 65% Pinot Noir, 5% Meunier

★★ SPECIAL CLUB 1990 BRUT

Vintaged, méthode champenoise: 25% Chardonnay,
75% Pinot Noir

89
ALFRED GRATIEN
EPERNAY

- 12,500 cases
- Group ownership - Gratien, Meyer, Seydoux & Cie in the Loire
- Négociant-Manipulant

In 1864, the firm of Gratien & Meyer set up business in Épernay and Saumur. The holding company today is Gratien, Meyer, Seydoux et Cie, which sells Saumur under the Gratien & Meyer label, and Champagne under the Alfred Gratien brand. Methods here are traditional – fermentation in wood, hand-riddling, manual disgorgement – but the grapes are bought in.

WINEMAKER
Jean-Pierre Jaeger

HOUSE STYLE & RANGE

In the early 1990s, the non-vintage swung from over-oxidative to over-amylic, but has since regained its original full, complex style, yet with more freshness. The vintage has never failed to amaze me; if rated on that alone, Gratien could easily notch up 91 points. These wines have a tremendous freshness; the 1973, 1975 and 1979, for instance, have all been drinking beautifully for the last nine years or so. The Cuvée Paradis is a strange thing, made to appeal when fresh and young, but it is rather bland and actually repays ageing a few years while it builds up mellow, toasty aromas.

★⯪ BRUT RÉSERVE

Not vintaged, méthode champenoise:
45% Chardonnay, 10% Pinot Noir, 45% Meunier

★★ BRUT

Vintaged, méthode champenoise: 60% Chardonnay,
30% Pinot Noir, 10% Meunier

★ CUVÉE PARADIS BRUT

Not vintaged, méthode champenoise: 60%
Chardonnay, 10% Pinot Noir, 30% Meunier

★ CUVÉE PARADIS BRUT ROSÉ

Not vintaged, méthode champenoise: 55%
Chardonnay, 20% Pinot Noir, 25% Meunier

N/A
EMILE HAMM
AY–CHAMPAGNE

- 8,000 cases
- Other labels - Vve Duverger
- Négociant-Manipulant

Emile Hamm was born in Mareuil-sur-Aÿ, and married the daughter of a *vigneron* in neighbouring Aÿ-Champagne. He managed his father-in-law's vineyards until 1910, then started making and selling Champagne under his own name, becoming a *négociant-manipulant* in 1930. Present incumbents Claude and Michel Hamm own four hectares of vineyards.

WINEMAKER
Michel Hamm

HOUSE STYLE & RANGE

Underrated house whose wines are elegant, rich and aromatic, but not tasted recently.

BRUT SÉLECTION

Not vintaged, méthode champenoise:
10% Chardonnay, 30% Pinot Noir, 60% Meunier

DEMI-SEC SÉLECTION

Not vintaged, méthode champenoise:
10% Chardonnay, 30% Pinot Noir, 60% Meunier

RÉSERVE BRUT

Not vintaged, méthode champenoise: 40%
Chardonnay, 40% Pinot Noir, 20% Meunier

ROSÉ BRUT

Not vintaged, addition of red wine, méthode
champenoise: 60% Chardonnay, 40% Pinot Noir

SIGNATURE BRUT

Not vintaged, méthode champenoise: 40%
Chardonnay, 40% Pinot Noir, 20% Meunier

N/A
HEIDSIECK & CO MONOPOLE
EPERNAY

- 100,000 cases
- Group ownership - Vranken
- Négociant-Manipulant

Like Charles Heidsieck, Heidsieck & Co Monopole can trace its origins back to Florenz-Ludwig Heidsieck, who founded the company in 1785. This house did not establish its own identity until 1834, when Henri-Louis Walbaum, the first of the nephews brought into the original firm by Florenz-Ludwig, started up in business as Walbaum, Heidsieck & Co. The famous Monopole brand was registered in 1860, but did not form part of the trading name until 1923, when Edouard Mignot of Comtoirs Français purchased this house from the Walbaum family.

Heidsieck & Co Monopole became part of the Seagram group in 1972, but in the early 1990s, it became clear that the parent company wanted to dispose of this brand. The obvious target was Rémy-Cointreau, already owner of the other two Heidsieck companies, but the Cognac-based group was unwilling to pay the price Seagram wanted. Germain was once tipped as a dark horse, and it was no coincidence that this possibility occurred when Bernard Walbaum was running the company. Yet although Germain was purportedly willing to cough up more than Rémy-Cointreau, again, it was insufficient. The deal, you see, did not include the firm's 110 hectares of vineyards, nor the famous Moulin à Verzenay. No one in their right mind, it seemed, would pay the price Seagram was asking just for a brand and stocks – even if that brand was technically a *grande marque*. Then Paul-François Vranken, the Belgian-born entrepreneur, did just that in October 1996. acquiring 130 hectares of vineyards in the process (though none of the firm's great sites). Indeed, the only vineyards that actually belonged to Heidsieck & Co Monopole were its lowest-rated ones in Savigny-sur-Ardre at 86% *échelle de cru*. This once-famous firm now operates from Charbaut's old premises on Épernay's avenue de Champagne.

HOUSE STYLE & RANGE
This will not be determined until the purchased stocks are exhausted and Vranken starts producing its own Heidsieck & Co Monopole. Currently, purchased stock of non-vintage Blue Top Brut is light, fresh and easy to drink, while the current 1989 vintage has creamy fruit supported by high acidity. Diamant Bleu used to be one of the best value prestige *cuvées* available, but had lost its quality even under Mumm, whose 1976 was the last great vintage.

BLUE TOP BRUT
Not vintaged, méthode champenoise:
24% Chardonnay, 48% Pinot Noir, 28% Meunier
RED TOP SEC

Not vintaged, méthode champenoise:
28% Chardonnay, 36% Pinot Noir,
36% Meunier
DIAMANT BLEU BRUT
Vintaged, méthode champenoise:
40% Chardonnay, 60% Pinot Noir

91
CHARLES HEIDSIECK
REIMS

- 170,000 cases
- Group ownership - Rémy-Cointreau
- Négociant-Manipulant

As with all Heidsieck firms, this house can trace its origins back to Florenz-Ludwig Heidsieck in 1785. The Charles Heidsieck brand itself did not appear until 1851 and takes its name from Charles-Camille Heidsieck, one of Florenz-Ludwig's great nephews and the legendary 'Champagne Charlie': a nickname derived from his flamboyant life-style. The oft-quoted verse from George Leybourne's famous music-hall song rarely mentioned Heidsieck, as, for a shilling, he would fit in any Champagne name:

> *Champagne Charlie was my name,*
> *Champagne drinking gained my fame,*
> *So as of old when on a spree,*
> *Moet and Shandon's [sic] the wine for me.*

Charles-Camille Heidsieck's brother-in-law and co-founder of Champagne Charles Heidsieck was Ernest Henriot. He left the firm in 1875 to take over the reins at Veuve Henriot Aîné, a Champagne house established in 1808 by his widowed grandmother. In 1976, almost 101 years to the day after Ernest Henriot left, his descendant, Joseph Henriot, returned to buy up Charles Heidsieck. Yet Joseph Henriot had bigger fish to fry (his famous 'reverse-takeover' of Veuve Clicquot; *see* HENRIOT), and in 1985 sold the firm to Rémy Martin, the family-owned Cognac house that already owned Krug.

Charles Heidsieck's Daniel Thibault is the acknowledged maestro of master blenders; the genius winemaker who transformed Charles Heidsieck's good-value Brut into the top-performing Brut Réserve. He did this by building up massive stocks of reserve wines to the detriment of sales, yet Rémy Martin (now Rémy-Cointreau) bravely backed him to the hilt at a time when the rest of Champagne was in a selling frenzy.

These were not so-called reserve wines from the previous year or two, but true reserves ranging across no fewer than eight different vintages, and Thibault planned to use an unprecedented 40% in each and every *cuvée*.

DANIEL THIBAULT, WINEMAKER FOR CHARLES HEIDSIECK, IN THE CELLARS OF THE OLD GALLO-ROMAN CHALK CRAYÈRES OF REIMS

He succeeded in producing a spectacularly rich, complex non-vintage with a distinct hint of vanilla – even though this stainless-steel fermented *cuvée* never saw so much as a stave of oak. This was, however, much less impressive than the fact that he has replicated this quality and character year-in and year-out ever since.

The critical success of the Brut Réserve was recognised even by Charles Heidsieck's major competitors, yet in 1997, the firm decided to relaunch it. As the Americans say, 'If it ain't broke don't fix it', but it has now been relaunched in three versions under the so-called *Mis en Cave* concept. It is still a brilliant *cuvée*; in fact, in a very fundamental way it has not changed. The *Mis en Cave* concept merely indicates the date of bottling, and the first three to be released were Mis en Cave 1992 (the 1991-based Brut Réserve), Mis en Cave 1993 (1992-based), and Mis en Cave 1994 (1993-based). The composition of the *cuvée* has not changed; it still contains 40% reserve wines from up to eight vintages. Indeed, if anything, Charles Heidsieck is merely being open and honest about what is actually on the market because there are probably three different *cuvées* of every famous non-vintage in distribution somewhere.

When a *cuvée* based on a different year is released, the majority already in distribution will obviously be based on the previous year, while a small percentage of outlets with slow turnovers will still have stocks of the *cuvée* prior to that. Some of us prefer a more mature style, while others like their Champagne as fresh as possible. Charles Heidsieck is simply trying to point us in the right direction.

The trouble is, it could all be a bit too confusing. Although simple enough once explained, the problem is the fact that it actually needs explaining. The *Mis en Cave* is a nice idea, but it is more of an instructive exercise than a commercial proposition. It might have been better to have launched it as separate *cuvées* or in a limited release.

In terms of an instructive exercise, a more relevant concept would be to disgorge the same blend in three consecutive years to illustrate the significant difference post-disgorgement ageing has – but again as a limited release. I just hope that by issuing three versions of the house non-vintage the reputation and image of Brut Réserve is not fractionalised to the point that it will divide its otherwise loyal customers.

WINEMAKER
Daniel Thibault

HOUSE STYLE AND RANGE
The full, rich Brut Réserve with its super-smooth, vanilla-hued complexity was so exceptional that there was no discernible step up in terms of quality to the vintage – only in the price. This changed with the release of the stunning 1990, the first vintage that Thibault radically revamped. Quite what he has done, I'm not sure, but it has twice the fruit of any previous vintage yet it is very much a serious wine – not merely fruit-driven – and it now shows exceptional finesse. The vintage rosé is a wine that benefits from ageing but often has a short window of opportunity for optimum drinking, when it is flame-gold in colour and the ripeness of fruit is perfectly *à point*. Note that the former prestige *cuvée*, Champagne Charlie, is included below because a number of old vintages are due to be re-released for the millennium.

★★☆ BLANC DES MILLÉNAIRES
Vintaged, méthode champenoise: 100% Chardonnay

★★☆ BRUT MILLÉSIME
Vintaged, méthode champenoise: 30% Chardonnay, 70% Pinot Noir/Meunier
★★ BRUT RÉSERVE
Vintaged, méthode champenoise: 25% Chardonnay, 75% Pinot Noir/Meunier
★ BRUT ROSÉ MILLÉSIME
Vintaged, addition of red wine, méthode champenoise: 30% Chardonnay, 70% Pinot Noir/Meunier
★★☆ CHAMPAGNE CHARLIE
Vintaged, méthode champenoise: 50% Chardonnay, 50% Pinot Noir

80
D HENRIET-BAZIN
VILLERS–MARMERY
- 5,000 cases
- Récoltant-Manipulant

Growers for four generations, the Henriet-Bazin family owns six hectares in Villers-Marmery, Verzy and Verzenay.

WINEMAKER
Daniel Henriet-Bazin

HOUSE STYLE AND RANGE
I recently taste several *cuvées* from this producer, and they are like chalk and cheese, ranging from sprightly fruit to butterscotch.
★ BRUT GRAND CRU
Not vintaged, méthode champenoise: 30% Chardonnay, 70% Pinot Noir
CARTE D'OR, BRUT 1ER CRU
Vintaged, méthode champenoise: 40% Chardonnay, 60% Pinot Noir
★ MN HENRIET, BLANC DE BLANCS, BRUT 1ER CRU
Vintaged, méthode champenoise: 100 % Chardonnay

87
HENRIOT
REIMS
- 65,000 cases
- Négociant-Manipulant

Founded in 1808 by Appoline Henriot, *née* Godinot, the widow of Nicolas-Simon Henriot, whose family owned vineyards since 1640. It was her grandson, Ernest Henriot, who helped Charles-Camille Heidsieck to establish his own house before assuming control of this family firm in 1875.

Ernest Henriot expanded sales and purchased some 75 hectares of prime vineyards on the Côte des Blancs. Just over a century later, in 1976, Joseph Henriot purchased Charles Heidsieck, but sold it again to Rémy Martin in December 1985; one month later, he exchanged Champagne Henriot and its magnificent estate of 125 hectares for 11% of Veuve Clicquot stock. This was the start of a commercial strategy that has been dubbed the 'reverse takeover' of Veuve Clicquot.

Henriot's 11% made him the most important minority shareholder in Veuve Clicquot and, as part of the package, he became chairman designate of the company. It was due to a boardroom rift with his chairman, Alain de Vogüé, that Henriot sided with Henry Racamier, the chairman of Louis Vuitton and, in doing so, helped Louis Vuitton succeed in its bid to take over Clicquot. Henriot was also on the board of Louis Vuitton at the time and owned shares in the company. Needless to say, under Louis Vuitton, Joseph Henriot soon replaced de Vogüé as chairman. So by selling out to Veuve Clicquot, Joseph Henriot ended up running the company.

It was through Henriot's position on the board of Louis Vuitton and his alliance with Racamier that Veuve Clicquot and Moët-Hennessy were brought together within the framework of LVMH (Louis Vuitton-Moët Hennessy). In a very short time, Henriot brought Veuve Clicquot into the modern world, improving its image, finances and trading, but his days in charge were numbered after Bernard Arnault took over as chairman of LVMH in 1989.

Henriot once described Veuve Clicquot as 'the most beautiful of the large Champagne houses' – just as well, for he was held hostage for two days in his office by Veuve Clicquot workers, who were protesting against imminent lay-offs due to the restructuring of the company – something many houses were forced to undertake during the crisis of the early 1990s.

Joseph Henriot left Veuve Clicquot in 1994, taking his family brand with him. At the time, the French press stated that it had cost Henriot and his family 'at least 130m francs' to repurchase the brand from Veuve Clicquot, but Henriot has since claimed that he never sold the brand to Clicquot in the first place. 'When we were discussing the sale of Henriot, Alain de Vogüé told me, "Your vineyards are lovely, and we like your stock, but you know, Joseph, your brand is worth nothing," to which I replied, "At that price Monsieur de Vogüé, my brand is not for sale!".'

The Henriot wines are made at Veuve Clicquot under the personal supervision of Philippe Thieffry, who works for both houses.

WINEMAKER
Philippe Thieffry

HOUSE STYLE AND RANGE
Many houses ship somewhat more mature *cuvées* to the UK market compared to those they sell in France, where the preference is for younger and more recently disgorged Champagne. The contrast of Henriot tasted in the UK and France is, however, greater than most – although the quality is exactly the same. The youthful French style is fresh and elegant, but lacks the richness and creamy, biscuity complexity that British customers expect from Henriot.
★ BLANC DE BLANCS
Not vintaged, méthode champenoise: 100% Chardonnay

★★☆ BRUT SOUVERAIN
Not vintaged, méthode champenoise: 40% Chardonnay, 60% Pinot Noir
★ BRUT
Vintaged, méthode champenoise: 45% Chardonnay, 55% Pinot Noir

★ BRUT ROSÉ
Vintaged, addition of red wine, méthode champenoise: 48% Chardonnay, 52% Pinot Noir

★★ CUVÉE DES ENCHANTELEURS
Vintaged, méthode champenoise: 55% Chardonnay, 45% Pinot Noir

84
HÉRARD
NEUVILLE-SUR-SEINE

- 15,000 cases
- Négociant-Manipulant

The Hérard family have been *vignerons* in the Aube district for generations and created this house in 1925. Since then, it has established a well-deserved reputation as a reliable producer of good-value Champagne.

WINEMAKER
Philippe Hérard

HOUSE STYLE & RANGE
Best-known for its bright and breezy *blanc de noirs*, ultra-fruity and strawberryish, but also capable of a very good *demi-sec*.

★ BRUT RÉSERVE
Not vintaged, 30% reserves, méthode champenoise: 25% Chardonnay, 75% Pinot Noir

★ BLANC DE NOIRS, BRUT
Not vintaged, méthode champenoise: 100% Pinot Noir

★ BRUT BLANC DE NOIRS, DEMI-SEC
Not vintaged, méthode champenoise: 100% Pinot Noir

N/A
JACQUES HOSTHOMME
CHOUILLY

- 10,000 cases
- Négociant-Manipulant

Michel and Jacques Hostomme own 12 hectares of vineyards, all located within the *grand cru* of Chouilly, although three hectares are planted with Pinot Noir and Meunier, which can claim only *premier cru* status.

WINEMAKER
Jacques Hostomme

HOUSE STYLE & RANGE
Tasted too few times to make an overall rating, but those I have tasted lacked the sort of finesse expected from a *grand cru* Champagne.

BLANC DE BLANCS BRUT
Not vintaged, méthode champenoise: 100% Chardonnay

BLANC DE NOIRS BRUT
Not vintaged, méthode champenoise: 80% Pinot Noir, 20% Meunier

GRANDE RÉSERVE BRUT
Not vintaged, méthode champenoise: 100% Chardonnay

ROSÉ BRUT
Not vintaged, addition of red wine, méthode champenoise: 50% Chardonnay, 50% Pinot Noir

BRUT
Vintaged, méthode champenoise: 100% Chardonnay

IRROY
REIMS

Once a truly great *grande marque*, Irroy is now nothing more than a *sous-marque* of Taittinger.
See TAITTINGER

IVERNEL
AY-CHAMPAGNE

Originally established in 1955 by Bernard Ivernel, this brand was sold in 1989 to Gosset, which really wanted to buy the house, but the Ivernel family has lived in it since the 15th century, and it was not for sale. Gosset does not actively promote Ivernel, but has kept the brand alive for a loyal following of customers.
See GOSSET

JACKMANN & CO
See MEDOT

85 VALUE
JACQUART
REIMS

- 400,000 cases
- Other labels - Ritz, Amilquart
- Coopérative-Manipulant & Négociant-Manipulant

The Coopérative Régionale des Vins de Champagne, to give its full title, was created as recently as 1962, yet it is now the fifth-largest producer of Champagne, with 850 growers owning over 1,000 hectares of vineyards in 160 different villages, averaging 94% *échelle des crus*.

When the Jacquart brand was launched in the 1970s, a separate company was created to market the wine. To avoid being lumbered by the typical co-op image, all the growers were made shareholders in the firm, thus enabling it to assume the mantle of *négociant-manipulant* rather than co-op – hence the NM initials before the matriculation number on the label. One of its *cuvées*, the Brut Tradition, actually states *Appellation Champagne Contrôlée* on the label! Although all Champagne is indeed classified as AOC, it is the only wine that does not have to indicate its appellation on the label (traditionally, the name *Champagne* was considered sufficient guarantee), and it is rare indeed to find it so mentioned. Why Jacquart considered it necessary is a mystery, but why Jacquart mentions the appellation on this *cuvée* and not the others is an even bigger conundrum.

WINEMAKER
Richard Dailly

HOUSE STYLE & RANGE
Extremely underrated, very reliable brut non-vintage, both Tradition and Mosaïque, but the vintage varies according to the year. Jacquart still has a co-op mentality when it

comes to declaring vintage-producing years such as 1987 which, although fine for the year, really should not have been vintaged. The vintaged Mosaïque Blanc de Blancs made a very promising start, but the 1990 has tasted like three different Champagnes. The vintaged Mosaïque Rosé can be a dark horse, but with a short window of opportunity for optimum drinking; the first vintage, 1986, was tight for a very long time, then became beautifully *à point* in 1997, but had lost its vitality by 1998, although it was by no means over the hill.

La Cuvée Nominée Brut has consistently disappointed, but the rosé usually excels, although there is no mention of its rosé style anywhere on the bottle, and can only be recognised by the bronze-pink colour of its presentation.

★ BRUT MOSAÏQUE
Not vintaged, méthode champenoise: 45% Chardonnay, 40% Pinot Noir, 15% Meunier

★ BRUT TRADITION
Not vintaged, méthode champenoise: equal parts Chardonnay, Pinot Noir, Meunier

BLANC DE BLANCS, CUVÉE MOSAÏQUE
Vintaged, méthode champenoise: 100% Chardonnay

★ BRUT MILLÉSIMÉ, CUVÉE MOSAÏQUE
Vintaged, méthode champenoise: 50% Chardonnay, 50% Pinot Noir

LA CUVÉE NOMINÉE BRUT
Vintaged, méthode champenoise: 40% Chardonnay, 60% Pinot Noir

★★ LA CUVÉE NOMINÉE ROSÉ
Vintaged, addition of red wine, méthode champenoise: 35% Chardonnay, 65% Pinot Noir

★★ ROSÉ MOSAÏQUE
Vintaged, addition of red wine, méthode champenoise: 40% Chardonnay, 50% Pinot Noir, 10% Meunier

87
ANDRÉ JACQUART
LE MESNIL-SUR-OGER

- 10,000 cases
- Récoltant-Manipulant

An important grower with 18 hectares of vineyards, 11 in Le Mesnil-sur-Oger, and seven in the Marne Valley and the Aube.

WINEMAKER
André Jacquart

HOUSE STYLE & RANGE
Well-aged, basic non-vintage, but it is the

classic Grand Cru Blanc de Blancs from Le Mesnil-sur-Oger that you seek out. Incredibly rich and full-bodied for pure Chardonnay from the Côte des Blancs, they age gracefully.

BRUT ROSÉ
Not vintaged, méthode champenoise: 90% Chardonnay, 10% Pinot Noir

CARTE BLANCHE BRUT
Not vintaged, méthode champenoise: 40% Chardonnay, 30% Pinot Noir, 30% Meunier

CUVÉE EXTRA DRY
Not vintaged, méthode champenoise: 40% Chardonnay, 30% Pinot Noir, 30% Meunier

★★ BLANC DE BLANCS SPÉCIAL CLUB BRUT
Vintaged, méthode champenoise: 100% Chardonnay

★★ CUVÉE SPÉCIAL BLANC DE BLANCS BRUT
Vintaged, méthode champenoise: 100% Chardonnay

N/A
JACQUINET-DUMEZ
LES MESNEUX
- 5,000 cases
- Récoltant-Manipulant

WINEMAKER
Olivier Jacquinet

HOUSE STYLE & RANGE
My first experience of Champagnes from this family grower was in 1997; thus I reserve overall judgement, but I very much enjoyed the depth and finesse of L'Excellence. I was less impressed with the simple fruit of the non-vintage brut, and the malo-dominated, sprightly fruit in the Grande Réserve.

BRUT
Not vintaged, méthode champenoise: 60% Pinot Noir, 40% Meunier

BRUT GRANDE RÉSERVE
Not vintaged, méthode champenoise: 80% Pinot Noir, 20% Meunier

★☆ CUVÉE SPÉCIALE, L'EXCELLENCE DE JACQUINET
Vintaged, méthode champenoise: 10% Chardonnay, 80% Pinot Noir, 10% Meunier

85 VALUE
PIERRE JAMAIN
LA CELLE-SOUS-CHANTEMERLE
- 2,000 cases
- Récoltant-Manipulant

Elisabeth Jamain creates stunning Champagne from her three hectares of vineyards – among the first planted in the Sézannais.

WINEMAKER
Elisabeth Jamain

HOUSE STYLE & RANGE
Excellent acidity gives the rich, ripe, sometimes exotic fruit in these Champagnes a scintillating intensity and freshness.

★☆ BRUT
Not vintaged, méthode champenoise: 100% Chardonnay

BRUT
Vintaged, méthode champenoise: 100% Chardonnay

DIZY
- 25,000 cases
- Négociant-Manipulant

The *SS Niantic* was carrying a consignment of Champagne Jacquesson when, on July 4, 1849, it dropped anchor in San Francisco Bay to allow its passengers (all gold miners) to disembark. The captain awoke the next morning to find his entire crew had deserted to join the gold rush.

The captain of the *Niantic* was not alone in this experience, for gold fever was so infectious that by the early 1850s no fewer than 700 such ships had been abandoned in the waters of Yerba Buena Cove. Some were later sailed away; others were deliberately sunk and quite a number – including the *Niantic* – were beached and used for all sorts of purposes, from churches to jails, general stores to hotels, and warehouses to whorehouses.

Beached at the end of Clay Street, the *Niantic* was first a warehouse, but in 1851, one of the numerous fires that swept the city razed her to the keel. Almost before the ashes had cooled, a wooden three-storey building was constructed over them; the upper two floors comprised the Niantic Hotel. When this building was demolished in the 1870s, some 35 baskets of Champagne Jacquesson were found. The wine, which had originally been in the ship's hold, had been submerged in mud and water and had thus survived the fire 19 years earlier. Newspaper clippings on file in the San Francisco Museum reported this wine had been 'so completely covered as to be almost excluded from the air, and some of the wine effervesced slightly on uncorking, and was of a very fair flavour'.

After Adolphe Jacquesson died in 1875, his family showed little interest in winemaking. Sales dwindled, and by the 1920s, Jacquesson belonged to Léon de Tassigny, a broker who moved the firm from its famous cellars in Châlons-sur-Marne (now Châlons-en-Champagne) to Reims. However, it was not until 1974,

95
JACQUESSON

when Jacquesson was bought by the Chiquet family, that the foundations of today's superb quality were laid down.

Jean-Hervé and Laurent Chiquet own vineyards in Aÿ, Dizy, Hautvillers and Avize which provide the core character of the Jacquesson style, while large oak *foudres* used for both vinification and storage of reserve wines contribute to the wines' complexity.

In 1997 Jacquesson produced a Champagne made from 100% Petit Meslier. One of the region's ancient varieties, the Petit Meslier had become almost extinct, but the Chiquet family planted 20 ares (half an acre) in its Dizy vineyard in 1959 'just for fun'. It had only just been bottled at the time of writing so it will be a couple of years at least before a tasting is possible.

WINEMAKER
Laurent Chiquet

HOUSE STYLE & RANGE
Qualitatively, these wines can be compared to Billecart-Salmon: they are equally sumptuous, but with more emphasis on complexity and less on elegance – although both have both, of course.

★☆ PERFECTION BRUT
Not vintaged, méthode champenoise: 35% Chardonnay, 30% Pinot Noir, 35% Meunier

★★ PERFECTION BRUT ROSÉ
Not vintaged, addition of red wine, méthode champenoise: 25% Chardonnay, 55% Pinot Noir, 20% Meunier

★★☆ BLANC DE BLANCS
Vintaged, méthode champenoise: 100% Chardonnay

★★☆ DÉGORGEMENT TARDIVE
Vintaged, méthode champenoise: grape varieties vary - the 1985 in regular 75cl bottles, for example, is 41% Chardonnay, 37% Pinot Noir, 22% Meunier, whereas in magnum it is 100% Chardonnay

★★☆ SIGNATURE
Vintaged, méthode champenoise: 50% Chardonnay, 50% Pinot Noir

★★☆ SIGNATURE ROSÉ
Vintaged, addition of red wine, méthode champenoise: 47% Chardonnay, 53% Pinot Noir

N/A
JAMART
ST-MARTIN DALBOIS

- 6,000 cases
- Other labels - A Mootz, Mootz Lefèvre & Rudolf Richards
- Négociant-Manipulant

Established in 1934 by Emilien Jamart, the baker and mayor of St-Martin d'Albois.

WINEMAKER
Bernard Richet

HOUSE STYLE
Not outstanding, but not tasted recently, with no information forthcoming about the different *cuvées*.

N/A
JANISSON-BARADON
EPERNAY

- 4,000 cases
- Récoltant-Manipulant

Georges Baradon began making and selling its own Champagne in 1922. Richard and Cyril Janisson are the fourth and fifth generation of growers in this family, which owns vineyards in the Vallée de la Marne and Montagne de Reims.

WINEMAKER
Richard Janisson

HOUSE STYLE & RANGE
Not tasted, but I had heard some good reports and duly requested samples, which were promised – yet failed to turn up.

BRUT SÉLECTION
Not vintaged, méthode champenoise:
50% Chardonnay, 45% Pinot Noir, 5% Meunier

CUVÉE GEORGES BARADON BRUT
Vintaged, méthode champenoise: 70% Chardonnay,
30% Pinot Noir

CUVÉE R JANISSON BRUT
Vintaged, méthode champenoise: 100% Chardonnay

87 VALUE
ANDRÉ JARRY
BETHON

- 4,000 cases
- Récoltant-Manipulant

High-quality Sézannais producer with 12 hectares of vineyards, all planted with Chardonnay.

WINEMAKER
André Jarry

HOUSE STYLE & RANGE
Excellent basic non-vintage in a style that falls between the exotica of his native Sézannais and the classic character of the Côte des Blancs. Jarry's Cuvée Spécial, which comes from 40-year-old vines, is about as *vin de garde* as can be found in the Côte de Sézanne, requiring it to be cellared for several years to show its full potential of biscuity richness, with an aftertaste of vanilla and peaches.

BRUT
Not vintaged, méthode champenoise:
100% Chardonnay

CUVÉE SPÉCIAL BRUT
Not vintaged, méthode champenoise:
100% Chardonnay

JEANMAIRE
EPERNAY

- 120,000 cases
See BEAUMET

75
JEEPER
DAMERY

- 4,000 cases
- Négociant-Manipulant

Named after the jeep that Armand Goutorbe used to drive around in, this grower-turned-merchant is related to the Goutorbe family of Aÿ. Now run by Armand's son, Christian, who owns 32 hectares of vineyards in the Marne Valley and the Côte de Sézanne.

WINEMAKER
Christian Goutorbe

HOUSE STYLE & RANGE
These Champagnes have an amylic tendency and can be so clinically clean that they will never evolve, although the occasional *cuvée* has developed some biscuity bottle-aromas after two or three years.

CUVÉE DUCALE BRUT
Not vintaged, méthode champenoise:
40% Chardonnay, 20% Pinot Noir, 40% Meunier

CUVÉE DUCALE BRUT ROSÉ
Not vintaged, addition of red wine, méthode
champenoise: 60% Chardonnay, 40% Pinot Noir

★ GRANDE RÉSERVE BRUT
Not vintaged, méthode champenoise:
100% Chardonnay

★ BLANC DE BLANCS BRUT
Vintaged, méthode champenoise: 100% Chardonnay

★ DOM GROSSARD BRUT
Vintaged, méthode champenoise: 60% Chardonnay,
40% Pinot Noir

JOLLY LANG
See LANG-BIÉMONT

98
KRUG
See p. 88

N/A
JEAN LALLEMENT
VERZENAY

- 2,000 cases
- Récoltant-Manipulant

The Lallements first made and sold Champagne under their own name in 1936, and have vineyards in Verzenay and Verzy.

WINEMAKER
Jean-Luc Lallement

HOUSE STYLE & RANGE
The brut is a blend of Verzenay and Verzy, while the brut réserve is a pure Verzenay *mono-cru*, but in my limited experience they are too oxidative to possess any finesse. Jean-Luc Lallement uses natural yeast to express the *terroir* in the first fermentation, and he neither filters his wines nor puts them through cold stabilisation – evidence of someone obviously passionate about his Champagne. In deference to this passion and my recent, limited exposure to these wines, I must reserve my judgement, thus no overall rating is given.

BRUT
Not vintaged, méthode champenoise:
20% Chardonnay, 80% Pinot Noir

BRUT RÉSERVE
Vintaged, méthode champenoise: 20% Chardonnay,
80% Pinot Noir

N/A
LAMIABLE
TOURS-SUR-MARNE

- 4,000 cases
- Récoltant-Manipulant

Most of these Champagnes are elaborated at the giant CVC cooperative in Chouilly (*see* NICOLAS FEUILLATTE), although at least one *cuvée*, the Special Club, carries an RM matriculation number; presumably Dr Pierre Lamiable, who owns six hectares of *grand cru* vineyards, makes some Champagne himself.

HOUSE STYLE & RANGE
Just one *cuvée* tasted (once) and very recently: an undemanding, basic non-vintage that seemed very sweet for a brut Champagne. I need to taste more *cuvées* before I can make any rational assessment, but the Special Club, which is a blend of 40% Cramant and 60% Tours-sur-Marne, seems the most interesting Champagne in the range.

GRAND CRU, BRUT
Not vintaged, one-third reserve wine from the
previous year, méthode champenoise: 30%
Chardonnay, 70% Pinot Noir

GRAND CRU, ROSÉ BRUT
Not vintaged, addition of red wine, one-third reserve
wine from the previous year, méthode champenoise:
30% Chardonnay, 70% Pinot Noir

GRAND CRU, SPECIAL CLUB BRUT
Vintaged, méthode champenoise: 40% Chardonnay,
60% Pinot Noir

LAMORLAYE
See MARIE STUART

LAMOTTE
See MONTAUDON

84
A LANCELOT-PIENNE
CRAMANT
- 7,500 cases
- Récoltant-Manipulant

Albert Lancelot's family have been growers in Champagne for more than 120 years. Father and son Albert and Gilles Lancelot own just over five hectares of vineyards, and export a quarter of their production.

WINEMAKER
Gilles Lancelot

HOUSE STYLE & RANGE
An extreme case of sprightly fruit in the Brut Sélection, but the *blanc de blancs* has lovely fresh, zingy, zippy, sherbety fruit with a mouthwateringly crisp finish.

BLANC DE BLANCS BRUT
Not vintaged, méthode champenoise: 100% Chardonnay
SÉLECTION BRUT
Not vintaged, méthode champenoise: 35% Chardonnay, 15% Pinot Noir, 50% Meunier

N/A
LANG-BIÉMONT
OIRY
- 40,000 cases
- Other labels - Jolly Lang
- Négociant-Manipulant

This small family firm now belongs to Chaudron, owner of the George Goulet brand.

WINEMAKER
Rémi Rozok

HOUSE STYLE & RANGE
Once capable of producing several truly excellent *cuvées*, especially the Cuvée d'Exception and Cuvée 111 Blanc de Blancs, but not tasted under new ownership.

BRUT CUVÉE RÉSERVÉE
Not vintaged, méthode champenoise: 90% Chardonnay, 10% Pinot Noir
BRUT ROSÉ
Not vintaged, addition of red wine, méthode champenoise: 33% Chardonnay, 67% Pinot Noir
BLANC DE BLANCS BRUT
Vintaged, méthode champenoise: 100% Chardonnay

CUVÉE EXCEPTION BLANC DE BLANCS BRUT
Vintaged, méthode champenoise: 100% Chardonnay
CUVÉE 111 BRUT
Vintaged, méthode champenoise: 100% Chardonnay

87
LANSON
REIMS
- 500,000 cases
- Group ownership - Marne et Champagne
- Other labels - Baron Edouard Masse, Albert Etienne
- Négociant-Manipulant

This famous *grande marque* dates back to 1760, when François Delamotte began making and selling Champagne. In 1828, his son took on Jean-Baptiste Lanson as a partner. When Delamotte died in 1837, the firm's name was changed to Veuve Delamotte-Barrachin and Lanson's two nephews, Victor-Marie and Henri, entered the business.

In 1856, Delamotte's widow died and shortly afterwards the Lansons gained full control of the firm, changing its name to Lanson Père et fils. The pastis firm of Ricard purchased a 48% share in 1970; in 1980, the Gardinier Group, which owned Pommery and already had a significant holding in Lanson (the connection being that Pierre Lanson had married Hélène Gardinier in 1960), purchased Ricard's share and took control.

Lanson and Pommery were sold to BSN, the giant French food group, in 1983. The two houses were purchased by LVMH in December 1990; four months later, Marne et Champagne purchased Lanson, minus its vineyards, but with its own premises, four years' stocks, and the same winemaker.

WINEMAKER
Jean-Paul Gandon

HOUSE STYLE & RANGE
None of these Champagnes undergo malolactic fermentation. The Black Label has longer yeast-contact than it used to, but is pretty much the same: not worth opening – unless, that is, you keep it a few years; then it can really shine. If a Champagne is produced without malolactic, it doesn't matter whether it receives two, three or four years on its yeast: it won't be worth drinking. Krug illustrates that, to drink nicely, a non-malolactic Champagne needs seven years rather than five. Lanson Black Label would be better served cutting back one year on yeast and keeping an additional year after disgorgement.

The first vintage under the new ownership is 1993, and it is rather soft and forward, but that is due more to the vintage itself than to Gandon's efforts to replicate the Lanson style without its old vineyards. It will not be until truly great vintages such as 1995 and (particularly) 1996 have some maturity (in,

VIEW OVER THE STAINLESS-STEEL FERMENTING AND STORAGE TANKS AT CHAMPAGNE LANSON, REIMS

say, 2005-2006) that we will be able to gauge how successful Gandon has been.

★ BLACK LABEL BRUT
Not vintaged, méthode champenoise: 35% Chardonnay, 50% Pinot Noir, 15% Meunier
BRUT ROSÉ
Not vintaged, addition of red wine, méthode champenoise: 32% Chardonnay, 53% Pinot Noir, 15% Meunier
★ DEMI-SEC
Not vintaged, méthode champenoise: 35% Chardonnay, 50% Pinot Noir, 15% Meunier
★★ BLANC DE BLANCS BRUT
Vintaged, méthode champenoise: 100% Chardonnay
★★★ GOLD LABEL BRUT
Vintaged, méthode champenoise: 48% Chardonnay, 52% Pinot Noir
★★★ NOBLE CUVÉE
Vintaged, méthode champenoise: 60% Chardonnay, 40% Pinot Noir

87
LARMANDIER
CRAMANT
- 3,000 cases
- Group ownership - Pierre Gimonnet
- Récoltant-Manipulant

Jules Larmandier established this family house in 1889, and built up an important client base in Paris at a time when very few growers made and sold their own Champagne. The Champagnes of Larmandier Père & Fils are now made by Pierre Gimonnet, the two houses having formed a partnership through the marriage of Françoise Gimonnet-Larmandier.

WINEMAKER
Didier Gimonnet

HOUSE STYLE & RANGE
A fresh, vibrant, style that always shows great purity of fruit, this producer is best known for its Perlé, a light *blanc de blancs* that was first created in 1920 by Jules Larmandier for his Parisian customers to drink with their oysters.

Continues on page 90

⁹⁸

KRUG

THE SMALL WALLED
VINEYARD OF CLOS DU
MESNIL, PLANTED
SOLELY WITH
CHARDONNAY USED
FOR THE WORLD'S
MOST EXPENSIVE
CHAMPAGNE

REIMS
- 40,000 cases
- Group ownership - Rémy-Cointreau
- Négociant-Manipulant

WINEMAKER
Henri Krug

The founder Johann-Josef Krug (Gallicised to Joseph Krug) cut his teeth at Champagne Jacquesson in 1834, and within months was made a partner. When he married Emma Anne Jaunay, the English sister-in-law of Adolphe Jacquesson, in 1841, it was presumed he would remain with the family firm for life. But in September 1842, Joseph Krug told Jacquesson he was leaving not just the firm, but Châlons-sur-Marne.

There was much to stay for, not least the family ties. However, from correspondence it appears that Joseph Krug was not happy with the quality of Jacquesson's wines and was restless to start up his own Champagne house. There is also suggestion of a rift caused by Krug having worked on the side for Hippolyte de Vivès, a competitor in Reims. His wife desperately wanted to keep the extended family together and tried to dissuade him from starting up on his own. But Krug was determined and left Jacquesson in October 1842, taking his wife and baby to Reims. More than a year went by before he set up business, as he negotiated an equal share in de Vivès' wine concern, which he changed to Krug et Cie – and so the House of Krug was born.

Krug is the most expensive, least consumed Champagne in existence – hence its reputation is more legendary than actual. As such it evokes mixed emotions, even at the heart of the wine trade. Krug is there to be shot down, but many who take a shot have never tasted it. On the other hand, some of Krug's most ardent supporters often delight in the fact that they never drink any other brand. Put the knockers and Krugists together, and we have two blind people arguing the difference between purple and mauve.

At one time I used to think the Krugs themselves had become too Krugist. In *Champagne* (Sotheby's Publications, 1986), I accused the Krugs of playing with words when they claimed that their Grande Cuvée was not a basic non-vintage, but a prestige *cuvée*. Rémi Krug replied, 'If Grande Cuvée is a basic non-vintage, then a Rolls Royce is just a car and the Pope a priest.' The flaw in his analogy was, of course, that Rolls Royce is the name of a brand, and even Rolls Royce offers a basic model, whereas the Pope is evidently not just a priest, but the head priest, the top of the range.

From this exchange grew Krug's multi-vintage concept, but it was not until Henri Krug later revealed that he made his wines back to front that I saw the light. If what he says is true, then Krug does not have a basic non-vintage because Henri Krug claims the Grande Cuvée is blended first and is given preference over any vintage that may or may not be produced in any given year. This is the opposite to what happens in other houses, where a vintage is the first selection.

Whether or not Grande Cuvée is Krug's basic non-vintage, there was never any doubt about it being a prestige *cuvée*. It sells at the price of a prestige *cuvée* – indeed, Krug Grande Cuvée and Dom Pérignon set the standard for prestige *cuvée* prices. Furthermore, when tasting and comparing quality, it would be extremely unfair to pitch Grande Cuvée against basic non-vintage Champagnes at a third of the price.

If every house followed the Krug philosophy, Champagne would become so elitist it would be meaningless for most wine lovers, but there should be at least one Krug in every great wine appellation, and the prestige *cuvée* quality it produces across the board makes Krug the only producer to rate 98% for the entire range.

WHY IS KRUG SO SPECIAL?

1. Since Joseph and Paul Krug in the 1860s, each father-and-son winemaking team has worked several decades together, developing and passing on the family style.
2. The high price permits a ruthless degree of selection.
3. All wines are fermented in small barriques of weathered Argonne oak.
4. Rapid first fermentation, no malolactic and a very slow second fermentation.
5. The Grande Cuvée receives 35-50% reserve wines from six to ten vintages spanning 15 years or more.
6. Such quality demands long ageing and Grande Cuvée, the youngest Champagne in the range, has at least five to seven years' yeast-contact.

AFTER MANY YEARS
LEARNING FROM HIS FATHER,
PAUL KRUG II, HENRI KRUG
(LEFT) TOOK OVER FULL
WINEMAKING RESPONSIBILITY
IN 1977. BUT PAUL'S GREAT
EXPERIENCE WAS CALLED
UPON DURING THE
BLENDING OF EVERY CUVÉE
THROUGHOUT THE LAST
20 YEARS OF HIS LIFE.

THE NEXT GENERATION OF KRUG IS REPRESENTED BY OLIVIER (RIGHT),
THE SON OF HENRI, AND CAROLINE, THE DAUGHTER OF RÉMI.

THE KRUG STYLE & RANGE

THE KRUG STYLE CANNOT BE SUMMED UP IN A SINGLE SENTENCE AS EACH CUVÉE HAS ITS OWN UNIQUE PERSONALITY. SUFFICE IT TO SAY THAT QUALITY REGARDLESS OF POPULAR TASTES IS PARAMOUNT: KRUG IS KRUG IS KRUG.

GRAND CUVÉE

★★★ *Not vintaged, méthode champenoise: 25-35% Chardonnay, 45-55% Pinot Noir, 15-20% Meunier*
The most important Champagne in the range; Henri Krug's first task each year is to select the very best wines from which to blend it. On average, this involves up to 50 wines of widely varying proportions from 20 to 25 villages, of which Le Mesnil-sur-Oger and Avize are most important for Chardonnay, Aÿ-Champagne and Ambonnay for Pinot Noir, and Leuvrigny and Ste-Gemme for Meunier. Typically some 35% to 50% of reserves from six to ten vintages are added. While it is generally accepted in Champagne that the better the primary base wine, the fewer reserves required, the opposite often applies to Grande Cuvée, where the more distinctive the vintage character, the more reserves are needed to overwhelm it and impose the Krug style (1985 required 49% reserves; 1988 needed 59%).

All Krug's base wines are vinified in 205-litre barriques made from weathered Argonne oak, which is relatively neutral (tasted with other Champagnes, Krug's oakiness is distinctive, but rarely discernible when drunk on its own). Typically, the wine has a beautiful pale-golden colour, a soft yet invigorating mousse of slow-rising, ultra-fine bubbles, elegant aromas of toast, roasted nuts, and dried fruits. The palate is profoundly rich, the fruit ripe yet beautifully dry and mellow, with great finesse and complexity. Wonderful to drink when first released, when the mellow richness is lifted by the flowery, acacia aromas of autolysis; if kept at least two years, the fruit becomes honeyed. It ages beautifully, gaining more depth and complexity over five years, improving up to ten.

ROSÉ

★★ *Not vintaged, addition of red wine, méthode champenoise: 20-30% Chardonnay, 50-55% Pinot Noir, 15-20% Meunier*
Very pale and refined, with exquisitely clean summer-fruit and exceptional length for its light balance. A great rosé with a serious style that improves with one or two years in bottle.

VINTAGE

★★★ *Vintaged, méthode champenoise: 25-35% Chardonnay, 30-55% Pinot Noir, 15-30% Meunier*
The above grape mixes are approximate: the Chardonnay has been as high as 50% (1981) and the Meunier has reached 30% (1953).

The **1989**, released prior to the 1988, has opulent, creamy, walnutty fruit, with a silkiness on the palate and soft acidity on the finish, making it a gorgeous mouthful when young, yet with plenty of development ahead.

The **1988** had not been released at the time of writing, but its dazzling ripe acidity will ensure this is one of Krug's greatest. (Rumour has it the 1990 is even better!)

When the **1985** was first released, its class and complexity stood out with an exotic, oak-fermented fruit background and an almost tannic finish, indicating that much would happen to this wine after its first flush of fruit. By the time of writing, it had clammed up, and should be left to mature until at least 2002, when it might just be starting to develop the honeyed richness and mellowed complexity typical of a Krug Vintage in its second life.

The **1982** is legendary: a massive wine with big, toasty aromas and broad, multilayered flavours. This vintage has been drinking fabulously for years, yet it is nowhere near its peak and is completely overshadowed by the stunning **1981**, one of the three greatest Champagnes produced in the last 30 years.

The flowery, toasty **1979** is the epitome of breed and finesse, and the creamy, honeyed **1976** is one of the classiest, most elegant of that blistering-hot vintage. The exquisite richness in the impeccably balanced **1975** is permeated by ultra-fine, slow-beading bubbles. The **1973** is very pale and youthful due to its high but ripe acidity, succulence of fruit and sweet, creamy, oaky notes. Divine. Krug **1971** vies with Dom Pérignon as the second-greatest Champagne of this vintage – only Salon is better. I have tasted back to 1928 and have favourite vintages for each decade, but I think Krug is at its best between 20 and 30 years of age.

COLLECTION

Exactly the same as for Vintage, only these are later releases of the vintages in question
Krug has no interest in disgorgement dates, recent or otherwise. Almost all the older vintages have been disgorged at the same time as the bulk of the vintage stock. The Collection concept is to offer old vintages that have never been moved from Krug's cellars. The age at which they are offered is not so much chronological as evolutionary, since Henri Krug waits for a vintage to enter what he terms its 'second life' before releasing it. Collection wines have gone back as far as 1928.

CLOS DU MESNIL

★★★ *Vintaged, méthode champenoise: 100% Chardonnay*
Clos du Mesnil is just 1.87 hectares situated in part of the built-up area of Le Mesnil-sur-Oger. Its *terroir*, however, is completely cut off from the surrounding buildings by its very high walls, giving the vines growing on its gently inclined, east-facing slope a unique environment.

Krug bought and replanted it in 1971, but it was not ready to produce a wine of the quality Krug demanded until **1979**. That first vintage showed great class and complexity as soon as it was released, yet within a few years the fruit had become so exotic that the wine was vulgar and seemed to be going over. By 1993, however, the '79 was back on form, boasting incredible elegance for such a great concentration of creamy, oaky, walnutty, biscuity fruit. It now ranks with the straight Krug 1981 vintage as one of the best three Champagnes produced in the last 30 years.

The **1980** is unbalanced, and should never have been released, with too much acidity for its weight of fruit, and a strange malty bouquet. By contrast, the **1982** is truly great, with huge, compact flavours that will require decades to open out. The **1983** has luxurious, creamy, biscuity fruit, making it a very good Clos du Mesnil, but not a great one. The **1985** possesses an explosive combination of bright, ripe, creamy fruit flavours.

In 1998 Krug released the hitherto unheard of **1986** and although this is a notch up on the 1980, it shares the same malty character and is not in the same class as the other vintages.

The **1988** was not released at the time of writing (the Krugs decided to put the '89 on the market first), but there is no mistaking its quality – at least as good as '79. One of the greatest wines I have tasted, with luscious, vanilla-infused, acidity-charged fruit, and the sort of balance that will take 20 years to reveal its true potential.

The **1989** is not quite in the same class, yet it is superior to the '82, and only the '88 and '79 are better. Pale, young and fresh – the finest 1989 Champagne I have encountered so far.

★★ BRUT, CRAMANT GRAND CRU
Not vintaged, méthode champenoise:
100% Chardonnay

★ BRUT 1ER CRU, BLANC DE BLANCS
Not vintaged, méthode champenoise:
100% Chardonnay

★★☆ BRUT PERLÉ DE LARMANDIER
Vintaged, méthode champenoise: 100% Chardonnay

★★ BRUT SPÉCIAL CLUB MILLÉSIMÉ,
GRAND CRU
Vintaged, méthode champenoise: 100% Chardonnay

85
GUY LARMANDIER
VERTUS

- 6,000 cases
- Récoltant-Manipulant

Guy Larmandier, who owns almost nine
hectares of vineyards, has been making his
own Champagne since 1977, assisted by his
son, François.

WINEMAKER
François & Guy Larmandier

HOUSE STYLE & RANGE
Floral, fruity aromas of some finesse, with clean,
precise, elegant fruit and a well-focused finish;
the rosé is particularly rich and succulent.

★ BRUT CUVÉE PERLÉE
Not vintaged, méthode champenoise:
100% Chardonnay

★ BRUT PREMIER CRU
Not vintaged, méthode champenoise:
100% Chardonnay

★★ BRUT ROSÉ
Not vintaged, addition of red wine, méthode
champenoise: 80% Chardonnay, 20% Pinot Noir

★★☆ CRAMANT GRAND CRU, BLANC DE BLANCS,
BRUT
Not vintaged, méthode champenoise:
100% Chardonnay

★★☆ MILLÉSIME CUVÉE PRESTIGE
Vintaged, méthode champenoise: 100% Chardonnay

91
LARMANDIER-BERNIER
VERTUS

- 8,000 cases
- Récoltant-Manipulant

The Larmandier and Bernier families have
been vineyard owners on the Côte des Blancs
since the Revolution, when the land was
parcelled out. This grower traces the origins
of making and selling Champagne under the
family name back to Jules Larmandier, just as
Larmandier Père & Fils in Cramant does.
Elisabeth Larmandier-Bernier and Pierre
Larmandier own 11 hectares of vineyards in
Cramant, Chouilly, Oger, Avize and Vertus.
With more than 45% of their Champagnes
exported, this mother-and-son team is carrying
on the family tradition of creating a reputation
far beyond the cellar door, where most growers

are content to limit their sales. This is one of
the top six producers on the Côte des Blancs.

WINEMAKER
Pierre Larmandier

HOUSE STYLE & RANGE
Luscious, crisp, creamy fruit that is wonderfully
fresh and pure when first released, but slowly
builds a creamy, walnutty richness and finesse.

★★☆ BLANC DE BLANCS BRUT, 1ER CRU
Not vintaged, méthode champenoise:
100% Chardonnay

★★ GRAND CRU BLANC DE BLANCS BRUT
Vintaged, méthode champenoise: 100% Chardonnay

★★★☆ GRAND CRU VIEILLES VIGNES DE
CRAMANT, EXTRA-BRUT
Vintaged, méthode champenoise: 100% Chardonnay

★★★☆ SPECIAL CLUB BLANC DE BLANCS BRUT
Vintaged, méthode champenoise: 100% Chardonnay

JEAN LARREY
See JACQUES COPINET

89
LAUNOIS PÈRE
LE MESNIL-SUR-OGER

- 15,000 cases
- Other labels - Veuve Clémence
- Récoltant-Manipulant

An old, established grower Champagne that
has been marketed since 1872. Current
incumbents Bernard and Dany Launois own
21 hectares of vineyards, and have built an
interesting museum that houses (among
many other things) examples of 17th and
18th century presses.

WINEMAKER
Bernard Launois

HOUSE STYLE & RANGE
Ranging from creamy, rich *cuvées* for current
drinking to tight, compact wines that
become quite luscious with age.

☆ BLANC DE BLANCS CAROLINE DE CHESTILLON
Not vintaged, méthode champenoise: 100% Chardonnay

★ GRAND CRU CUVÉE RÉSERVÉE BLANC DE
BLANCS BRUT
Not vintaged, méthode champenoise: 100% Chardonnay

★★ GRAND CRU SPECIAL CLUB BLANC DE
BLANCS BRUT
Not vintaged, méthode champenoise: 100% Chardonnay

★★☆ GRAND CRU BLANC DE BLANCS BRUT
Vintaged, méthode champenoise: 100% Chardonnay

LOUIS LAURENT
See CHAUDRON

90 VALUE
LAURENT-PERRIER
TOURS-SUR-MARNE

- 500,000 cases
- Other labels - Lemoine
- Group ownership - also owns de Castellane,
Delamotte, Joseph Perrier, and Salon.

ANTIQUE POSTCARD SHOWING HAND RIDDLING IN
THE LAURENT-PERRIER CELLARS

- Négociant-Manipulant

This firm dates back to 1812, when the
Laurent family moved from their native village
of Chigny-les-Roses on the Montagne de
Reims, gave up their trade as coopers and
began making and selling Champagne from the
remains of an 11th-century abbey at Tours-sur-
Marne. When their son, Eugène Laurent, who
had married Mathilde Émile Perrier, died in
1887, the firm's name was changed to Veuve
Laurent-Perrier. Mathilde Laurent-Perrier died
without heirs, and the firm was purchased by
Marie-Louise de Nonancourt, sister of Victor
and Henri Lanson.

But the seeds of Laurent-Perrier's fame
were not sown until after the Second World
War, when Nonancourt's son, Bernard, took
over. At that time it was ranked a mere 98th
among the producers of Champagne; now it
is one of the top houses, and owns a
controlling interest in several others, making
it the fifth largest group in the industry.

At one time, Laurent-Perrier's sprawling
wine empire included Bordeaux shipper
Dubois Frères, Château Malartic-Lagravière
in Graves-Léognan, Château Treilles,
Château Quattre and Domaine de Guingal
in Cahors, and Antonin Rodet in Burgundy.
However, these outposts have recently been
disposed of, so the company can concentrate
its efforts and finances on its Champagne
holdings. The only foreign property left over
at the time of writing is a large tract of land
in Oregon, USA, where Laurent-Perrier was
going to plant vines (now going cheap!). The
capital recouped from these sell-offs has enabled
the Nonacourt family to buy back IDV's
22.4% shareholding in Laurent-Perrier and
the nominal one per cent IDV held in the
holding company, Vve Laurent-Perrier & Co.

WINEMAKER
Alain Terrier

HOUSE STYLE & RANGE
I tend to think of the basic non-vintage brut
in the same light as Taittinger's, since both can
occasionally wander off the track (when they
might be lucky to scrape in with ☆). Yet when
on form, they are capable of offering some of
the greatest value *grande marque* Champagnes in
the light, pure, elegantly fruity, Chardonnay-

influenced style (when they easily warrant ★★). When young, some Laurent-Perrier *cuvées* have an intriguing pepperiness which is not classic and used to worry me – but not any more, as this characteristic tends to disappear after a little additional bottle-age. I am halfway to becoming convinced that in this producer's case, pepperiness is a precursor to a certain complexity and finesse. The Ultra Brut is a particular favourite of Alain Terrier's, but the complexity is rather coarse, and lacks the finesse it might otherwise have with a proper *dosage*. However, Laurent-Perrier produced a *Grand Vin Sans Sucre* as long ago as 1889, and I respect the homage paid to its origins when this style was relaunched in 1981.

The straight vintage can be a dark horse but, contrary to its widespread fame, I am not that impressed with the Cuvée Rosé Brut: it can seem one-dimensional when first released, although it gains depth and finesse with an extra year or two in bottle. Grand Siècle 'La Cuvée' is the epitome of finesse *(see following page)*, but the vintaged Grand Siècle Exceptionellement Millésime requires at least three years' additional ageing to even begin to show its true potential.

Grand Siècle Alexandra Rosé is beautiful to drink as soon as it is released.

★ BRUT LP
Not vintaged, méthode champenoise:
45% Chardonnay, 40% Pinot Noir, 15% Meunier

★ CUVÉE ROSÉ BRUT
Not vintaged, saignée, méthode champenoise:
100% Pinot Noir

★ ULTRA BRUT
Not vintaged, méthode champenoise:
55% Chardonnay, 45% Pinot Noir

★★ BRUT
Vintaged, méthode champenoise: 55% Chardonnay,
45% Pinot Noir

★★★ GRAND SIÈCLE ALEXANDRA ROSÉ
Vintaged, saignée, méthode champenoise:
20% Chardonnay, 80% Pinot Noir

★★★ GRAND SIÈCLE 'LA CUVÉE'
See p. 93

★★★ GRAND SIÈCLE EXCEPTIONELLEMENT
MILLÉSIME
Vintaged, méthode champenoise: 50% Chardonnay,
50% Pinot Noir

LECHERE
See UNION CHAMPAGNE

85 VALUE
LECLERC BRIANT
EPERNAY
- 21,000 cases
- Négociant-Manipulant

The Leclercs have been *vignerons* since 1664, but did not produce Champagne under the family name until 1872. Pascal Leclerc Briant, the current owner, owns 30 hectares of vineyards in the Montagne de Reims and Vallée de la Marne, which he farms bio-dynamically. He holds the world record for the largest Champagne fountain, built from 14,404 glass flutes at the Biltmore Hotel, Los Angeles on June 18, 1984. It had 44 levels of glasses, reached 28 feet, eight inches high and was made to flow successfully with Champagne from the top glass into those beneath.

If you ever visit his cellars, Leclerc Briant will offer you the choice of the stairs or to abseil through a hole in the floor!

WINEMAKER
Roger Hodgkinson

HOUSE STYLE & RANGE
Pascal Leclerc's most expressive Champagne is his Rubis Rosé des Noirs, made from 100% Pinot Noir. The 1989 was so dark that it was deeper than many red sparkling wines from Bordeaux and Burgundy. Although sparkling red Champagne is illegal, the flaw in the law is that there exists no legal definition of the colour difference between pink and red Champagne. I am normally against dark coloured rosés because they tend to lack the elegance expected from this Champagne style, but Rubis has a remarkable perfume of pure cherry fruit that blows away all prejudice. It may look as if it will be heavy and coarse, but it is deliciously soft and surprisingly delicate.

The best Champagne, however, is Cuvée Divine which, if you can put up with the kitsch presentation, is the most succulent and accessible *cuvée* in the Leclerc Briant range.

★ BLANC DE BLANCS
Not vintaged, méthode champenoise: 100% Chardonnay

★ BRUT EXTRA
Not vintaged, méthode champenoise:
70% Pinot Noir, 30% Meunier

★ CUVÉE RÉSERVE BRUT
Not vintaged, méthode champenoise:
30% Chardonnay, 70% Pinot Noir

DEMI-SEC
Not vintaged, méthode champenoise:
70% Pinot Noir, 30% Meunier

★ LES CHÈVRES PIERREUSES, LES AUTHENTIQUES
Not vintaged, méthode champenoise:
40% Chardonnay, 60% Pinot Noir

★ LE CLOS DES CHAMPIONS, LES AUTHENTIQUES
Not vintaged, méthode champenoise:

30% Chardonnay, 70% Pinot Noir

★ LES CRAYÈRES, LES AUTHENTIQUES
Not vintaged, méthode champenoise: 90% Pinot
Noir, 10% Meunier

COLLECTION HISTORIQUE, XVÈME CENTENAIRE
DU BAPTÊME DE CLOVIS
Vintaged, méthode champenoise: 25% Chardonnay,
75% Pinot Noir

★★ CUVÉE DIVINE
Vintaged, méthode champenoise: 50% Chardonnay,
50% Pinot Noir

CUVÉE DU SOLSTICE 2000
Vintaged, méthode champenoise: 50% Chardonnay,
50% Pinot Noir

★ ROSÉ CUVÉE RUBIS DE NOIRS
Vintaged, addition of red wine, méthode
champenoise: 100% Pinot Noir

N/A
LEFEBVRE
HOURGES
- 12,000 cases
- Négociant-Manipulant & Récoltant-Manipulant

This small producer founded his brand in 1928 and owns vineyards on the south-facing slopes of the Massif de St-Thierry, west of Reims.

WINEMAKER
Jean Marie Lefebvre

HOUSE STYLE & RANGE
Not tasted recently.

BRUT
Not vintaged, méthode champenoise: 25%
Chardonnay, 50% Pinot Noir, 25% Meunier

83
R&L LEGRAS
CHOUILLY
- 20,000 cases
- Négociant-Manipulant

A small house dating back to the end of the 18th century, when Honoré Legras bought a vineyard in Chouilly. The family remained growers rather than Champagne-makers until the 20th century, achieving *négociant-manipulant* status in 1972. Today, R&L Legras owns 14 hectares of vineyards (13 in Chouilly, one in Ambonnay). The house speciality is its production of Champagne for a number of good restaurants throughout France.

WINEMAKER
Vincent Legras *Continues on page 94*

GRAND SIÈCLE, 'LA CUVÉE'

- 40,000 cases

After a preview at Tours-sur-Marne for restaurateurs from the Côte d'Azur in 1957 (which is often erroneously quoted as the launch date for Grand Siècle), this prestige *cuvée* was officially released on 9th September 1960, the 300th anniversary of the marriage of Louis XIV.

The era of the Sun King is known as Le Grand Siècle because he brought unprecedented prosperity to France and, according to Voltaire, 'his name can never be pronounced without summoning the image of an eternally memorable age'. The Champagne is named after this period, and the bottle, with its broad base and long, elegant neck is a replica of one blown in 1705, in the midst of Louis XIV's reign.

Apart from Dom Pérignon and the then relatively new Roederer Cristal, the concept of a prestige *cuvée* was unknown when Grand Siècle was conceived. Bernard de Nonancourt, still a very active owner today, was then in charge of a very small house and he probably had no idea Taittinger was simultaneously working on Comtes de Champagne, which would be launched with the 1952 vintage, and it was almost two decades before Perrier-Jouët would launch the illustrious Belle Epoque.

That Nonancourt thought it appropriate for such an obscure house to produce a prestige *cuvée* is evidence of the man's confidence and foresight, but even in retrospect it does seem odd that he chose not to vintage Grand Siècle. He was in fact the first to conceive the notion of a 'blend of vintage years', a phrase that has only recently been superseded by Krug's 'multi-vintage' terminology. According to Nonancourt Grand Siècle was an exercise 'to study the science of assemblage', but quite why and how he hit upon the idea of making it a strict blend of three vintage years is hard to discern at this juncture.

Three, however, turned out to be a very lucky number because, if you look back over every group of three consecutive vintages (not necessarily consecutive years) on record, you will discover three different, often radically different, styles of Champagne, each of which strangely compliments the other two. Blending is necessary in the general scheme of things if a classic quality sparkling wine is to be wrenched from the uncertain grip of Champagne's northern, Atlantic-influenced climate. But the degree of that

BERNARD DE NONANCOURT OR 'LE GRAND BERNARD' AS HE IS AFFECTIONATELY KNOWN, HAS GUIDED LAURENT-PERRIER FROM OBSCURITY SINCE JUST AFTER THE SECOND WORLD WAR TO BECOME ONE OF THE LARGEST CHAMPAGNE PRODUCERS

quality is always determined by how strict the selection is and, by insisting on vintage-quality wines exclusively from *grand cru* vineyards, Nonancourt had hit upon the ultimate expression of *assemblage*.

Grand Siècle is composed of Chardonnay and Pinot Noir in almost equal proportions, Chardonnay having a very slight emphasis. An accurate average composition would be something like 52% Chardonnay, 48% Pinot Noir, although the Chardonnay has occasionally been as high as 58%. The Pinot Noir comes from some of the best vineyards in Ambonnay, Bouzy and Tours-sur-Marne, whereas the Chardonnay is primarily from le Mesnil-sur-Oger, Oger, Avize and Cramant.

WHY IS GRAND SIÈCLE 'LA CUVÉE' SO SPECIAL?

1. An *assemblage* of three vintage years and exclusively *grand cru* grapes.
2. Chardonnay has an edge over Pinot Noir in a roughly 50/50 blend.
3. Peerless blending skill.
4. Sealed with a cork and agrafe for the second fermentation.
5. Usually a minimum of seven years yeast-contact.
6. Manual disgorgement allows an additional quality check on the nose for each individual bottle.

LAURENT-PERRIER'S EXCEPTIONALLY GIFTED WINEMAKER, THE BORDEAUX-BORN ALAIN TERRIER, IS UNIQUELY FEATURED IN TWO OF THE VERY GREATEST SPARKLING WINES IN THIS BOOK THE OTHER INSTANCE BEING CHAMPAGNE SALON

There have been just two winemakers: Edouard Leclerc, who retired in 1981, and Alain Terrier.

In the USA, where a vintage date rules supreme, Laurent-Perrier sacrificed the principle of Grand Siècle's expression of *assemblage* by marketing a pure vintage version, and later made it globally available with the 1985 Grand Siècle Exceptionellement Millésimé. Although these wines have been superb, they are not Grand Siècle: indeed, they make a mockery of the original concept. Champagne lovers are not seduced by the four digits of a vintage and the USA has plenty of genuine Champagne lovers. Laurent-Perrier was merely pandering to the market as a whole.

However, as the tasting notes below reveal, Grand Siècle is not just a great Champagne, but a Champagne of great longevity, thus the question Laurent-Perrier should have asked itself was how could it remain true to Grand Siècle's philosophy, while at the same time allowing serious Champagne collectors to cellar, follow and compare the evolution of its different *cuvées*.

The answer to this conundrum was not very difficult and one that a small house on the Montagne de Reims hit upon in the mid 1980s, when Cattier released the first Clos du Moulin to be produced from three vintage years and simply indicated those years on the back label. Grand Siècle and its followers deserve no less respect.

THE VINTAGES

GRAND SIÈCLE, 'LA CUVÉE' IS A BEAUTIFULLY MATURE CUVÉE OF GREAT FINESSE, WITH AN EXQUISITE, WONDERFULLY DELICATE RICHNESS AND SLOW-BUILDING COMPLEXITY.

★★★ GRAND SIÈCLE 'LA CUVÉE' (1995/93/90)
Not yet released.
Tasted in November 1997, this was the youngest Grand Siècle I had experienced, but with almost 18 months since it was bottled, I was surprised to find quite so many raw-ferment odours still present. It was a bit like tasting a Champagne with less than 12 months on its yeast, which is a testament to the slow rate of its fermentation and maturation, key factors in the development of Grand Siècle's extraordinary finesse. The most outstanding quality I noticed in this youthful cuvée was its wonderful acidity.

★★★ GRAND SIÈCLE 'LA CUVÉE' (1993/90/88)
Not yet released.
The finesse here is already evident, despite a firmness of fruit that seems to be characteristic of 1988, and an underlying pepperiness, which I often find in Laurent-Perrier's basic vintage and non-vintage cuvées when young.

★★★ GRAND SIÈCLE 'LA CUVÉE' (1990/88/85)
Not released at the moment of tasting, but should be by the time of publication.
Although I had tasted Grand Siècle vertically before, this was the first time I had gone from forthcoming, through current, to past cuvées, and it was as plain as day why Laurent-Perrier gives these wines so much yeast contact. After two cuvées that were a long way from being ready, this one had the smoothness on the finish that is so typical of Grand Siècle, with the slow-building complexity immediately noticeable. There are so many great Grand Siècle cuvées, but this must rate as one of the very finest.

★★★ GRAND SIÈCLE 'LA CUVÉE' (1988/85/82)
This cuvée was currently available when tasted but the end of its distribution was in sight, and the toasty post-disgorgement aromas had started to dominate the wine. It needs another three years for the finesse to reassert itself, and five or more for the second phase of complexity to kick in.

★★★ GRAND SIÈCLE 'LA CUVÉE' (1985/82/81)
This assemblage was really quite yeasty when first released but has developed tremendous finesse since going off the market. Possibly as good as the 1990/88/85 blend.

★☆ GRAND SIÈCLE 'LA CUVÉE' (1983/82/79)
Currently dominated by a distinctive, chocolatey character of mature Pinot Noir on the finish, this assemblage opens up in the glass but shows more still wine aromas than Champagne. Preferred when released on the market for general distribution, it does not seem to have developed the finesse and complexity of other old cuvées and although this could merely be a phase, it has to be rated on current performance.

★★ GRAND SIÈCLE 'LA CUVÉE' (1982/79/78)
Well-balanced, enjoyable, but not exceptional, although it has more complexity and richness than the 1983/82/79 blend.

★★★ GRAND SIÈCLE 'LA CUVÉE' (1979/78/76)
Verification that Grand Siècle does go through awkward stages in its development, this cuvée was overly strong and cumbersome at the same age as the 1983/82/79, when it was more disappointing than that wine, but it is currently quite superb, with a perfect balance of richness and finesse, and a spicy-toasty hint to the complexity. Certainly as good as the 1985/82/81 blend.

★★★ GRAND SIÈCLE 'LA CUVÉE' (1978/76/75)
This cuvée has always been so complete it has never really needed a dosage. Its profound depth of finesse and complexity for such a delicately balanced wine initially put it well ahead of the 1979/78/76, but that cuvée has since caught up and they are now probably on level pegging.

★★★ GRAND SIÈCLE 'LA CUVÉE' (1976/75/73)
Very rich, with a succulent coconutty complexity and an impeccable mousse.

GRAND SIÈCLE 'LA CUVÉE' (1975/73/70)
A lovely cuvée when it was in distribution, it has become rather blurred with age. No specific fault as such, but lacking the focus and finesse of a great wine, although I would never rule out the potential of any Grand Siècle cuvée.

★★☆ GRAND SIÈCLE 'LA CUVÉE' (1973/70/69)
A rarity for Grand Siècle, this assemblage contains base wines made in a year that was never declared a vintage by Laurent-Perrier, but 1969 was by a good number of other houses and its intrinsically hard acidity has kept most of those Champagnes alive for almost 30 years. This cuvée has a particularly satisfying, toasty aroma.

★★★ GRAND SIÈCLE 'LA CUVÉE' (1970/69/66)
Another assemblage containing the undeclared 1969, this has a very fresh aroma, with relatively little toast developing prior to disgorgement. The palate is suffused with fresh mushrooms as can happen in some old Champagnes, and this may or may not be present in every bottle. The finish is so delicately rich and creamy that it reminds me of a triple cream cheese called Boursault.

★★★ GRAND SIÈCLE 'LA CUVÉE' (1969/66/64)
Wonderfully rich with coffee aromas just beginning to build. If I had to be super critical, I would have to say that the finish is not as persistent as it could be, but this is great, mature Champagne, make no mistake.

★★★ GRAND SIÈCLE 'LA CUVÉE' (1966/64/62)
This is so rich, with luscious fruit of great finesse, and seductive coffee and toasty aromas, that only the very first cuvée (1955/53/52) is better.

GRAND SIÈCLE 'LA CUVÉE' (1966/64/61)
Unless it is going through a developmental phase, a gamey, puffed-wheat aroma pervades this assemblage, robbing it of finesse.

★★★ GRAND SIÈCLE 'LA CUVÉE' (1955/53/52)
The fruit is still so pure and luscious, with such an array of complex aromas that it would be misleading to try to describe them. A sumptuous, mature Champagne of great finesse.

HOUSE STYLE & RANGE

Thoroughly respectable, although not outstanding, these Champagnes have a classic, lean structure, and show good fruit.

★ BRUT BLANC DE BLANCS
Not vintaged, méthode champenoise: 100% Chardonnay

DEMI-SEC BLANC DE BLANCS
Not vintaged, méthode champenoise: 100% Chardonnay

★★ PRÉSIDENCE BRUT
Vintaged, méthode champenoise: 100% Chardonnay

★★ SAINT-VINCENT BRUT
Vintaged, méthode champenoise: 100% Chardonnay

N/A
RC LEMAIRE
VILLERS-SOUS-CHÂTILLON

• 6,000 cases
• Récoltant-Manipulant

Established in 1945 by Roger Constant Lemaire, whose son-in-law Gilles Tournant-Lemaire runs the business today. Production is from ten hectares in Cumières, Hautvillers, Reuil, Leuvrigny and Binson-Orquigny.

WINEMAKER
Gilles Tournant

HOUSE STYLE & RANGE

The three *cuvées* below were all tasted recently, but there was no finesse, and none impressed. It is, however, my first encounter with this producer; thus I reserve overall judgement.

BRUT CUVÉE TRIANON
Not vintaged, méthode champenoise:
45% Chardonnay, 55% Pinot Noir

BRUT SÉLECT RÉSERVE
Not vintaged, méthode champenoise: 100% Meunier

BRUT ROSÉ
Vintaged, addition of red wine, méthode
champenoise: 50% Pinot Noir, 50% Meunier

LEMOINE
See LAURENT-PERRIER

85 VALUE
LENOBLE
Damery

• 25,000 cases
• Other labels - Charles Kindler
• Négociant-Manipulant

A small house with a low profile, Lenoble was founded by Armand-Raphael Graser, a native of Alsace who served a few years' apprentice-ship at Champagne Chanoine before becoming a broker. After his premises had been destroyed in the First World War, he was helped by another broker called Léon de Tassigny (who took over Jacquesson in 1920). While still a broker, Graser sold Champagnes under his own brand, but did not set up this house until 1941. He called the firm AR (for Armand Graser) Lenoble – a play on the noble status of Champagne within the world of wine. Today, Lenoble is run by Graser's grandson, Jean-Marie Malassagne, his daughter Anne and son Antoine. They own 18 hectares of vineyards in Chouilly, Bisseuil and Damery.

WINEMAKER
André Houte

HOUSE STYLE & RANGE

Very ripe, creamy, rich fruit is the key to these wines. The only criticism is that the fruit is so gluggy that it is almost too easy to drink – but that can't be so bad!

★★ BLANC DE BLANCS, GRAND CRU
Not vintaged, méthode champenoise: 100% Chardonnay

★ BRUT RÉSERVE
Not vintaged, méthode champenoise:
40% Chardonnay, 30% Pinot Noir, 30% Meunier

★ BRUT ROSÉ
Not vintaged, addition of red wine, méthode
champenoise: 85% Chardonnay, 15% Pinot Noir

★★ BRUT MILLÉSIME
Vintaged, méthode champenoise: 40% Chardonnay,
60% Pinot Noir

★★ GRANDE CUVÉE GENTILHOMME
Vintaged, méthode champenoise: 100% Chardonnay

83 VALUE
ABEL LEPITRE
REIMS

• 25,000 cases
• Group ownership - BCC
• Négociant-Manipulant

When BCC purchased Philipponnat from Marie Brizard in 1997, it also acquired Abel Lepitre, which some commentators believed it would sell off pretty quickly to help finance the deal – particularly as sales had dropped from 40,000 cases. The premises probably will go, but there are no immediate plans to sell them, and absolutely no chance that the brand will be sold. Few people realise that Philippe Baijot and Bruno Paillard, BCC's founders, have a sentimental attachment to Abel Lepitre. Philippe Baijot's first job in the industry was with this firm, and the very first Champagne sold under the Bruno Paillard name was sourced from Lepitre. By a quirk of fate, they literally owe their current success to Abel Lepitre. Furthermore, although its sales have dropped off, its core customers would provide a useful sales medium for any small, rapidly expanding group.

WINEMAKER
Norbert Thiébert

HOUSE STYLE & RANGE

Under the previous ownership, these Champagnes had a very middle-of-the-road image, but Abel Lepitre often produced very good-value *cuvées* and occasionally turned out a real stunner. Lepitre's most consistent fine wine has always been its prestige *cuvée*, which was originally called Prince A de Bourbon-Parme, and was renowned for its delicate aromas and a gentle vanilla richness of flavour. When Marie Brizard took over, it unimaginatively renamed it Cuvée Reservée. The quality was maintained at the same high standard, but the name was lost in a sea of Réserve this and Réservée that. New owners BCC has now rationalised the range, kicking out the old vintage brut, and making the former prestige *cuvée* Abel Lepitre's regular vintage – which is a beautifully understated way of pushing the brand upmarket. This firm's other speciality used to be *blanc de blancs*, particularly its *crémant*, which had a flowery, fragrant style similar to that of Mumm's Crémant de Cramant (now Mumm de Cramant). After the *crémant* term was voluntarily banned, Lepitre sold the *cuvée* as Réserve 'C', but it failed to make any impact, thus BCC, which is keen to re-establish the firm's reputation for this style, has renamed it Chardonnay Demi-Mousse.

★ BRUT RÉSERVE
Not vintaged, méthode champenoise:
25% Chardonnay, 60% Pinot Noir, 15% Meunier

BRUT ROSÉ
Not vintaged, méthode champenoise:
25% Chardonnay, 60% Pinot Noir, 15% Meunier

★★ CHARDONNAY DEMI-MOUSSE BRUT
Not vintaged, méthode champenoise: 100% Chardonnay

★★ BRUT
Vintaged, méthode champenoise: 65% Chardonnay,
35% Pinot Noir

LÉONCE D'ALBE

The earliest brand of Union Auboise, the largest co-op in the Aube, this was originally spelt Léonze d'Albe, reflecting the fact that Union Auboise originally consisted of 11 Aube co-ops. Although still the largest-selling brand of the Union Auboise, it has been regarded as something of a second label since the launch of the Vve Devaux brand, which has grown so rapidly that its sales will eventually be larger.
See VVE DEVAUX

LECLERC BRIANT LES AUTHENTIQUES

IN THE EARLY-1990S, LECLERC BRIANT LAUNCHED THREE SINGLE-VINEYARD CHAMPAGNES UNDER THE 'LES AUTHENTIQUES' LABEL. THEY WERE ALL, IN FACT, PURE VINTAGE WINES – NOT FROM ANY OLD YEAR, BUT THE TOP-PERFORMING 1990 VINTAGE. BUT PASCAL LECLERC BRIANT DELIBERATELY CHOSE NOT TO INDICATE THE VINTAGE ON THESE OR ANY FUTURE *CUVÉES*, MAINLY BECAUSE HE WAS ASKED NOT TO BY FRENCH *SOMMELIERS* WHO HELPED HIM DEVELOP THE CONCEPT.

If the wines carried a vintage, the *sommeliers* would have to charge more for them, even if Leclerc Briant did not. Rightly or wrongly, there are accepted price bands for vintage and non-vintage, just as there are for *grandes marques* and lesser brands. Very few restaurants are willing to deviate from this banding and, having carved himself a nice niche in the French restaurant market, Leclerc Briant was not about to price himself out of it.

However, what is the point of the specific nature of a single-vineyard Champagne if customers cannot follow its development? Not much, of course, so for anyone wishing to identify the age of these *cuvées*, here is how to crack the code.

Check out the EU lot number, which differs according to each producer; in this particular case, the two letters identify the vineyard of origin (CH for Les Chèvres Pierreuses, CL for Clos des Champions, and CR for Les Crayères), while the two numbers indicate the year of bottling. Leclerc started with 43 for the first three *cuvées*, which were all bottled in 1991, after which the lot numbers jumped ten digits per year; thus, 53 indicates a wine bottled in 1992, 63 in 1993, 73 in 1994, etc.

Since Champagne is bottled in the spring following the harvest, the year prior to this bottling date will, in most instances, be the vintage of the wine in question. Indeed, the first three *cuvées* were all pure 1990 wines, even though the customer was unaware of any vintage on the label. Occasionally, however, due to the vagaries of Champagne's climate, insufficient wine for a pure vintage is produced in the smallest vineyards (Clos des Champions and Les Crayères); thus a blend is possible, although from the date of bottling you will at least have some idea of the age of such wines.

For example, the 1991 and 1992 wines from the two smallest vineyards were blended together; hence L63CH (Chèvres Pierreuses) and L63CR (Crayères) were both 1991-'92 blends bottled in 1993. To be aware of this, anyone following these wines would have to notice that no L53CH or L53CR were sold, whereas both L53CL and L63CL were marketed from the much larger Clos des Champions vineyard.

Although this is quite simple to work out once you understand how these lot numbers work, it is a pain trying to explain it to other people. Why does Leclerc Briant make the chronology is vague? There is no need to be so arcane about coding these lot numbers when the simplest solution would be to use actual vintage years, such as L92CR, for example, to indicate a pure 1992 Les Crayères, and L9192CL for a blend of 1991 and 1992 Clos des Champions.

LES CHÈVRES PIERREUSES

Not vintaged, méthode champenoise:
60% Pinot Noir, 40% Chardonnay
At 2.8 hectares this is the largest of the three vineyards. It is located 700kms west of Cumières on a south-facing slope in the middle of the *côte* with a slightly greater incline than the other two. When freshly disgorged, this wine has lovely autolytic character, a firm mousse of tiny bubbles and beautiful fruit/acidity balance. Of the three *cuvées*, this shows the most finesse.

LES CRAYÈRES

Not vintaged, méthode champenoise:
90% Pinot Noir, 10% Pinot Meunier
This *lieu-dit* is 1.07 hectares, located 1.5kms west of the village on a gentle south-facing slope with the most chalky soil of all three vineyards. This has marked floral aromas – particularly acacia – reflected on the palate, which is soft and flowery, proving that not all *blanc de noirs* wines are necessarily massive. The mousse is firm, with the tiniest bubbles of all three *cuvées* (yet Chardonnay is always supposed to give the finest bubbles, Pinot Noir the largest).

LE CLOS DES CHAMPIONS

Not vintaged, méthode champenoise:
70% Pinot Noir, 30% Chardonnay
At just 0.49 hectares, Clos des Champions is the smallest of Leclerc Briant's three *lieux-dits*. It is situated a mere 300 metres northwest of the village, on a gentle south-facing slope of calcareous clay soil. The wine made from this site, however, is very aggressive in style when first disgorged, but it has the richest fruit, and the biggest structure.

75
JEAN-CLAUDE LÉPITRE
COULOMMES-LA-MONTAGNE

- 1,200 cases
- Récoltant-Manipulant

In 1940, Gérard Lépitre became the first grower in this family, but it was not until 1979 that Jean-Claude Lépitre, who owns six hectares of vineyards, made and sold Champagne under the Lépitre name.

WINEMAKER
Jean-Claude Lépitre

HOUSE STYLE & RANGE
Rather rustic, lacking finesse, but the vintage has a certain oxidative complexity.

BRUT
Not vintaged, méthode champenoise:
25% Chardonnay, 25% Pinot Noir, 50% Meunier

CUVÉE DE RÉSERVE
Not vintaged, méthode champenoise:
25% Chardonnay, 25% Pinot Noir, 50% Meunier

BRUT PRESTIGE
Vintaged, méthode champenoise: 70% Chardonnay,
15% Pinot Noir, 15% Meunier

CHARLES LEPRINCE
See BEAUMONT DES CRAYÈRES

N/A
PIERRE LESAGE
CRAMANT

- Récoltant-Manipulant

Not tasted recently, but his *blanc de blancs* used to be very elegant and shows finesse; the basic non-vintage brut was just another amylic *cuvée*. Production from the Côte de Sézanne, as well as Cramant, the village on the label.

N/A
LÉTÉ-VAUTRAIN
CHATEAU-THIERRY

- 3,400 cases
- Récoltant-Manipulant

Established in 1968 by the parents of Frédéric and Michèle Lété, the current owners. Their five hectares of Marne Valley vineyards are dominated by the American Monument on Côte 204 in remembrance of the American troops who, in 1918, lost their lives in the second battle of the Marne. The vines actually grow where those Americans (and French and British soldiers too) fought and died; hence the American Monument motif on the labels of these Champagnes.

WINEMAKER
Michèle Lété

HOUSE STYLE & RANGE
I have only tasted these Champagnes once, hence no overall rating. Both were acceptable, although the Traditionnel Brut had a rather off-putting, explosive foaminess to the mousse. It was, however, my

preference of the two wines tasted, with an attractively flowery nose, very rich and fruity on the palate, and a creamy finish. The Réserve Brut had a light, creamy, malo style.

☆ GRANDE RÉSERVE BRUT
Not vintaged, méthode champenoise:
20% Chardonnay, 30% Pinot Noir, 50% Meunier

☆ TRADITIONNEL BRUT
Not vintaged, méthode champenoise:
20% Chardonnay, 30% Pinot Noir, 50% Meunier

89
LILBERT-FILS
CRAMANT

- 2,500 cases
- Récoltant-Manipulant
Winegrowers since 1746.

WINEMAKER
Georges Lilbert

HOUSE STYLE & RANGE
A consistent producer of classic, firm *blanc de blancs* that show finesse and age gracefully – particularly the vintage *cuvées*.

★☆ BRUT
Not vintaged, méthode champenoise: 100% Chardonnay

★☆ BRUT PERLÉ
Not vintaged, méthode champenoise: 100% Chardonnay

★★ BRUT MILLÉSIME
Vintaged, méthode champenoise: 100% Chardonnay

COMTE DE LISSEUIL
See BAUCHET

82
LOCRET-LACHAUD
HAUTVILLERS

- 8,400 cases
- Other labels – De L'Abbatiale
- Récoltant-Manipulant
Brothers Eric and Philippe Locret belong to a family of growers dating back to 1620.

WINEMAKER
Philippe Locret

HOUSE STYLE & RANGE
Although the Locret brothers have produced a Champagne Cuvée Karate, the only wine have got a kick out of recently is the De l'Abbatiale, which has good acidity, and some creaminess of the nose and palate.

BRUT, 1ER CRU
Not vintaged, méthode champenoise:
26% Chardonnay, 41% Pinot Noir, 33% Meunier

BRUT ROSÉ, 1ER CRU
Not vintaged, addition of red wine, méthode
champenoise: 22% Chardonnay, 32% Pinot Noir,
46% Meunier

☆ DE L'ABBATIALE, BRUT 1ER CRU
Not vintaged, méthode champenoise: 43%
Chardonnay, 43% Pinot Noir, 7% Meunier

82
MICHEL LORIOT
FESTIGNY

- 3,500 cases
- Other labels – Henri Loriot, Le Loriot
- Négociant-Manipulant

This small family business traces its origins back to Léopold Loriot, who supplied Moët & Chandon with grapes until 1908, when he decided it would be better for the quality and more profitable to install the first press in Festigny, rather than the long and detrimental task of transporting the grapes to Épernay. In 1931, he went one step further and started making his own Champagne. Michel and Martine Loriot own six hectares of vineyards in Festigny and adjoining villages.

WINEMAKER
Michel Loriot

HOUSE STYLE & RANGE
These Champagnes are among the most expressive examples of Meunier

DECORATIVE BARRELS AT THE VILLAGE OF CRAMANT ON THE CÔTE DES BLANCS

currently available.

BRUT ROSÉ
Not vintaged, méthode champenoise: 100% Meunier

CARTE BLANCHE BRUT
Not vintaged, méthode champenoise: 100% Meunier

★ **BRUT**
Vintaged, méthode champenoise: 100% Meunier

★ **LE LORIOT BRUT**
Vintaged, méthode champenoise: 100% Meunier

LVMH

Short for Louis Vuitton-Moët-Hennessy, LVMH is the largest conglomerate in the Champagne industry, comprising Moët & Chandon, Mercier, Ruinart, Pommery, Veuve Clicquot, and Canard-Duchêne.

86 VALUE
MAILLY GRAND CRU

MAILLY–CHAMPAGNE

- 35,000 cases
- Coopérative-Manipulant

This unique, *mono-cru* cooperative was established in 1929 by Gabriel Simon, who grouped together 24 growers with vineyards located exclusively within the *grand cru* village of Mailly-Champagne. Since the early 1980s, there have been 70 members owning 70 hectares of vineyards, all within the village boundary.

Mailly Grand Cru produced Champagnes of exceptional value and character throughout the 1970s and much of the 1980s, but there has been a lack of finesse in some of the *cuvées* during the early-to-mid 1990s. This cooperative is, however, back on form, producing its best Champagnes in over ten years and, now that it is, Mailly Grand Cru should give thought to how it can progress.

For a producer whose reputation is inextricably linked to the *terroir* of just one village, there would seem to be just one option: a project that will explain what the characteristics of that *terroir* are. The top Champagnes here can be very good, but they are often less expressive of the *terroir* than the more basic *cuvées*. The most consistent expression of Mailly is, in fact, the *blanc de noirs*, which is not surprising as Pinot Noir reigns supreme on the Montagne de Reims. Any Chardonnay grown in this village is merely a convenience; it helps to produce a more diverse range of Champagnes which, in general terms, is a good thing – but this is not white-grape country (until 1972 Mailly Chardonnay could not even claim *grand cru* status).

Within each named individual site, or *lieu-dit,* there are smaller plots called *galipes*, some of which this cooperative has vinified separately for several years now, before blending them together. Mailly Grand Cru

should use this *galipe*-by-*galipe* knowledge to produce three Champagnes from the three most diverse (but mutually compatible) *galipes,* all Pinot Noir, and make one Champagne blended from all three. To emphasis the difference, the grapes must be from a low yield, in a very ripe year, thus these four Champagnes will have to be vintaged, and produced only in the finest years - maybe only two or three times a decade. If these new wines were sold in a case of six – one of each *galipe* and three of the blend – it would create a newsworthy vehicle through which Mailly's characteristics of *terroir* could be explained, and it would also inform consumers that even a *mono-cru* is a product of selection and blending.

WINEMAKER
Hervé Dantan

HOUSE STYLE & RANGE
These Champagnes are currently showing great typicity of *terroir*, with fine, flowery, Pinot aromas followed by rich fruit of some finesse, with the capacity to build a biscuity complexity, although some of the more mature *cuvées* also take on some toasty aroma.

★★ **BLANC DE NOIRS, GRAND CRU**
Not vintaged, méthode champenoise: 100% Pinot Noir

★ **BRUT RÉSERVE**
Not vintaged, méthode champenoise: 25% Chardonnay, 75% Pinot Noir

BRUT ROSÉ
Not vintaged, addition of red wine, méthode champenoise: 10% Chardonnay, 90% Pinot Noir

★ **EXTRA BRUT**
Not vintaged, méthode champenoise: 25% Chardonnay, 75% Pinot Noir

★ **BRUT**
Vintaged, méthode champenoise: 25% Chardonnay, 75% Pinot Noir

★★ **CUVÉE DES ECHANSONS**
Vintaged, méthode champenoise: 25% Chardonnay, 75% Pinot Noir

★★ **CUVÉE DU 60e ANNIVERSAIRE**
Vintaged, méthode champenoise: 60% Chardonnay, 40% Pinot Noir

★★ **L'INTEMPORELLE**
Vintaged, méthode champenoise: 60% Chardonnay, 40% Pinot Noir

85 VALUE
HENRI MANDOIS

PIERRY

- 25,000 cases
- Other labels - Comte de la Rochefoucauld, Comte de Lantage
- Négociant-Manipulant

Jimmy Boyle's favourite Champagne! An important grower when Victor Mandois first made Champagne under the family name, this is now a small, successful house with 35 hectares of vineyards spread across 12 different villages.

WINEMAKER

Henri Mandois

HOUSE STYLE & RANGE
Elegant Champagnes which have a satisfying length of attractive, creamy fruit, and a fine balance. Mandois does not make wines that will attain great complexity, but they do represent great value.

★ **BRUT ROSÉ, PREMIER CRU**
Not vintaged, méthode champenoise: 50% Chardonnay, 10% Pinot Noir, 40% Meunier

★ **CUVÉE DE RÉSERVE BRUT**
Not vintaged, méthode champenoise: 50% Chardonnay, 10% Pinot Noir, 40% Meunier

★★ **CHARDONNAY BRUT, PREMIER CRU**
Vintaged, méthode champenoise: 100% Chardonnay

★ **CUVÉE DES TROIS GÉNÉRATIONS**
Vintaged, méthode champenoise: grape varieties can vary but usually 100% Chardonnay

★★ **CUVÉE VICTOR MANDOIS**
Vintaged, méthode champenoise: 70% Chardonnay, 15% Pinot Noir, 15% Meunier

★★ **MILLÉSIME BRUT, PREMIER CRU**
Vintaged, méthode champenoise: 40% Chardonnay, 30% Pinot Noir, 30% Meunier

★★ **ROSÉ DE SAIGNÉE**
Vintaged, saignée, méthode champenoise: 50% Pinot Noir, 50% Meunier

85 VALUE
MANSARD-BAILLET

EPERNAY

- 167,000 cases
- Négociant-Manipulant

How this little-known producer has grown half as big again as Bollinger is a mystery, but the Mansard family owns some 70 hectares of vineyards, of which the company owns 17 hectares; thus it can rely on a good source of raw materials to supplement grapes bought-in.

WINEMAKER
M Mansard

HOUSE STYLE & RANGE
The basic *cuvées* are lightly structured, but have an ultra-fruity aroma and flavour, with a fresh finish. The higher up the scale, the firmer these Champagnes become, Tradition de Mansard being the firmest of all.

★ **BRUT**
Not vintaged, méthode champenoise: 50% Chardonnay, 25% Pinot Noir, 25% Meunier

★★ **BRUT PREMIER CRU**
Not vintaged, méthode champenoise: 70% Chardonnay, 15% Pinot Noir, 15% Meunier

BRUT ROSÉ

> *Not vintaged, méthode champenoise:*
> *65% Pinot Noir, 35% Meunier*

DEMI-SEC

> *Not vintaged, méthode champenoise:*
> *50% Chardonnay, 25% Pinot Noir, 25% Meunier*

★★ BLANC DE BLANCS, GRAND CRU BRUT

> *Vintaged, méthode champenoise: 100% Chardonnay*

CUVÉE DES SACRES BRUT

> *Vintaged, méthode champenoise: 65% Chardonnay,*
> *35% Pinot Noir*

★☆ TRADITION DE MANSARD, GRANDE CUVÉE
BRUT

> *Vintaged, méthode champenoise: 90% Chardonnay,*
> *10% Pinot Noir*

80
MARGAINE
VILLERS-MARMERY

- 5,000 cases
- Récoltant-Manipulant

This grower owns seven hectares of vineyards, 90% of which are planted with Chardonnay, despite being on the Montagne de Reims.

WINEMAKER
Arnaud and Bernard Margaine

HOUSE STYLE & RANGE
Basic *cuvées* are often too amylic, but the Cuvée Club is a good buy, with very rich fruit, yet lean structure and excellent acidity.

BRUT CUVÉE TRADITIONNELLE

> *Not vintaged, méthode champenoise:*
> *90% Chardonnay, 10% Pinot Noir*

BRUT ROSÉ

> *Not vintaged, addition of red wine, méthode*
> *champenoise: 85% Chardonnay, 15% Pinot Noir*

★★☆ CUVÉE SPECIAL BLANC DE BLANCS BRUT

> *Not vintaged, méthode champenoise: 100% Chardonnay*

N/A
MARGUET-BONNERAVE
AMBONNAY

- 10,000 cases
- Other labels - Gallaxie
- Récoltant-Manipulant

The Bonnerave brothers first made and sold Champagne under the Bonnerave Frères label in 1870. When current winemaker Christian Marguet married Françoise Bonnerave, the name changed to Marguet-Bonnerave. The firm was well established by the early 1980s, and currently owns 12 hectares in the *grands crus* of Ambonnay, Bouzy and Mailly.

WINEMAKER
Christian Marguet

HOUSE STYLE AND RANGE
Very fresh, light and zesty at the basic level. The better wines are fatter with less acidity, and a noticeable creamy-malolactic character, which can take on toffee and caramel flavours. Entire range not tasted; hence no overall rating.

SNOW COVERING THE VINEYARDS ABOVE EPERNAY, HOME TO MARNE ET CHAMPAGNE

★☆ BRUT GRAND CRU

> *Not vintaged, two years' yeast-contact, méthode*
> *champenoise: 30% Chardonnay, 70% Pinot Noir*

BRUT PRIVILÈGE

> *Not vintaged, five years' yeast-contact, méthode*
> *champenoise: 50% Chardonnay, 50% Pinot Noir*

★ BRUT RÉSERVE

> *Not vintaged, three years' yeast-contact, méthode*
> *champenoise: 45% Chardonnay, 55% Pinot Noir*

BRUT ROSÉ

> *Not vintaged, addition of red wine, two years' yeast-*
> *contact, méthode champenoise: 85% Chardonnay,*
> *15% Pinot Noir*

DEMI-SEC GRAND CRU

> *Not vintaged, two years' yeast-contact, méthode*
> *champenoise: 30% Chardonnay, 70% Pinot Noir*

BLANC DE BLANCS BRUT

> *Vintaged, four years' yeast-contact, méthode*
> *champenoise: 100% Chardonnay*

★☆ BRUT

> *Vintaged, méthode champenoise: 75% Chardonnay,*
> *25% Pinot Noir*

N/A
MARIE STUART
REIMS

- 105,000 cases
- Other labels - Raynal, De Lamorlaye, Charles de Braine
- Group ownership - Alain Thienot
- Négociant-Manipulant

This house was established in 1867, and the Marie Stuart brand was registered in 1909, named after the Scottish queen, who has

always been greatly admired in France.

The firm was acquired in 1927 by André Garitant, sold in 1954 to Champagne Trouillard, and sold again in 1962 to Prat-Fontaine & Longuet. In 1972, it was purchased by the Lombard family, who did little more than allow it to tick over, preferring to concentrate their investments in Charles de Cazanove. Little surprise, then, that the firm sold Marie Stuart to Alain Thienot in 1994.

After such a chequered existence, and sorely in need of modernisation, it is hoped that Thienot will make the requisite investment to revitalise this *marque*; with sale already established at two-and-a-half times that of his own eponymous brand, it would seem the logical commercial decision. Thienot already has his own high-tech winery and warehousing, so the Marie Stuart premises need only be revamped for offices and visiting facilities.

WINEMAKER
Laurent Fedou

HOUSE STYLE & RANGE
Only one wine appears to have changed so far – the basic non-vintage brut – but Thienot's Brut 1er Cru is, if anything, even more disappointing than the Lombard's Brut Tradition. This may simply be due to teething troubles, but in any case, the overall rating must be reserved until Thienot has established his own track record with every *cuvée* here – and that will probably take a decade from the date of his acquisition.

★ BRUT BLANC DE BLANCS
Not vintaged, méthode champenoise:
100% Chardonnay

BRUT 1ER CRU
Not vintaged, méthode champenoise:
25% Chardonnay, 60% Pinot Noir, 15% Meunier
BRUT ROSÉ
Not vintaged, méthode champenoise:
80% Chardonnay, 20% Pinot Noir
★★ CUVÉE DE LA REINE
Not vintaged, méthode champenoise:
90% Chardonnay, 10% Pinot Noir
★ MILLÉSIME
Vintaged, méthode champenoise: 80% Chardonnay,
20% Pinot Noir

85 VALUE

MARNE ET CHAMPAGNE
ÉPERNAY

- Almost 1 million cases excluding Lanson and Besserat de Bellefon
- Other labels - *see below*
- Group ownership - owns Lanson (including Massé) and Besserat de Bellefon
- Négociant-Manipulant

Even without its acquisition of Lanson, this low-profile company ranks as the second-largest house in Champagne. How come? Because Marne et Champagne markets its wines through more than 200 different labels, not one of which is the company's name. Its reputation is not even diffused, it is non-existent – and deliberately so. In fact, many Champenois living in Épernay have not even heard of this company, although it is an important employer.

Over the years, however, Marne et Champagne has come to the attention of the specialist press, which has labelled it the Champagne industry's 'life-support system'. This is because the *grandes marques* sell their *vins de taille* to Marne et Champagne, so that they may claim their wines are made exclusively from *vins de cuvée*. But, when stocks are low and demand high, most *grandes marques* have been forced at one time or another to buy ready-made Champagnes *sur lattes* – most of this has come from Marne et Champagne, and a fair few *vins sur latte* contain *vins de tailles*.

WINEMAKER
Vincent Malherbe

HOUSE STYLE & RANGE
In addition to approximately 100 own-label Champagnes (none of which are *premier prix*),

some 70% of Marne et Champagne's production is sold under its own brands, which number almost 200, and the 20 most important are listed below.

Marne et Champagne essentially makes three basic qualities. The best is pure *vin de cuvée*. The second quality involves the use of ten to 15% *vin de taille*, which is about average for most non-vintage brut Champagnes throughout the region, and the third as much as 40% to 50% *vin de taille*. Malolactic fermentation is prevented.

The first quality is one of the most consistent *vin de garde* Champagnes produced, and, at the top of the tree, Alfred Rothschild is produced in a full range of *cuvées*. The second quality is very fruit-driven, but builds up flattering, toasty aromas relatively quickly, and wins a surprising number of blind-tasting events (as does the first quality, of course).

Second-quality Champagnes are made in both vintage and non-vintage styles. Third-quality Champagnes are almost invariably non-vintage, light in colour and weight, with a soft, clean, inoffensive, but hardly gripping character.

It is impossible to make a definitive statement about the quality of every brand, as logistics and deals can change things on certain markets at various times, but you can be sure that the following, at least, are always of the same first quality: Alfred Rothschild, Pol Gessner, Eugène Cliquot, Geismann & Co, Gauthier. Certain first-quality brands do not even make the top 20. Giesler & Cie, for example, is the first brand that founder Gaston Burtin purchased. Because of this history, it is always maintained as one of Marne et Champagne's first-quality brands, but the market is so price-conscious that the slight premium to cover its marketing back-up is sufficient to keep sales relatively small.

MARNE ET CHAMPAGNE TOP 20 BRANDS
1. **Alfred Rothschild et Cie**
   Sales: 187,500 cases
2. **Colligny Père & Fils**
   Sales: 100,000 cases
3. **Leprince-Royer**
   Sales: 70,000 cases
4. **Delacoste & Fils**
   Sales: 50,000 cases
5. **Mary Martin**
   Sales: 48,000 cases
6. **Baron de Brou**
   Sales: 35,000 cases
7. **Roger Perreau**
   Sales: 20,000 cases
8. **Marquis de Prevel**
   Sales: 19,000 cases
9. **Vve Pasquier & Fils**
   Sales: 12,000 cases

10. **Laurence Duvivier**
    Sales: 10,500 cases
11. **Pol Gessner**
    Sales: 10,000 cases
12. **Bourgeois**
    Sales: 10,000 cases
13. **Georges Martel**
    Sales: 5,000 cases
14. **Eugène Cliquot**
    Sales: 4,500 cases
15. **Roger Perroy**
    Sales: 2,500 cases
16. **Geismann & Co**
    Sales: 2,000 bottles
17. **Gauthier**
    Sales: 2,000 bottles
18. **De Bracieux**
    Sales: 1,750 bottles
19. **Pol Albert**
    Sales: 1,700 bottles
20. **Vve Guérin**
    Sales: 1,700 bottles

N/A
JEAN-PIERRE MARNIQUET
VENTEUIL

- Récoltant-Manipulant

For some reason, Cuvée Eclat is labelled JP Marniquet, whereas for all the others, Jean-Pierre is spelt out in full.

HOUSE STYLE & RANGE
My experience of these Champagnes is too recent and too little to make an objective overall assessment, but I found the basic Cuvée Tradition Brut to have an unusual exotic, Muscat-like character – not classic by any means, but not unattractive, either, although the Brut 1er Cru was just another amylic clone.

The vintages Cuvée de Millésime and Eclat promised were 1986, but those received and tasted were both 1985. Cuvée de Millésime was rather dark and *passé*, while the Eclat was extraordinarily fresh.
BRUT 1ER CRU
Not vintaged, méthode champenoise:
35% Chardonnay, 15% Pinot Noir, 50% Meunier
CUVÉE RÉSERVE BRUT
Not vintaged, méthode champenoise:
35% Chardonnay, 15% Pinot Noir, 50% Meunier
CUVÉE ROSÉ BRUT
Not vintaged, addition of red wine, méthode champenoise:
90% Chardonnay, 5% Pinot Noir, 5% Meunier
★ CUVÉE TRADITION BRUT
Not vintaged, méthode champenoise:
35% Chardonnay, 15% Pinot Noir, 50% Meunier
★ CUVÉE ECLAT BRUT
Vintaged, méthode champenoise: 60% Chardonnay,
40% Pinot Noir
CUVÉE DE MILLÉSIME, RÉSERVE BRUT
Vintaged, méthode champenoise: 35% Chardonnay,
15% Pinot Noir, 50% Meunier

MARQUIS DE SADE

See MICHEL GONET

80
GH MARTEL

EPERNAY

- Other labels – E Rapeneau, Mortas, Comte de Lamotte
- Négociant-Manipulant

This house dates back to 1869, when a *vigneron* in Avenay produced Champagne under the GH Martel name (although it was a young man called André Tabourin who did most to develop the brand in the 1920s). When Tabourin died in 1979, the business was acquired by Rapeneau & Cie, which had been established by Ernest Rapeneau in 1901, since when GH Martel has become its primary brand. This house has recently increased its vineyard holdings from an already healthy 50 hectares to 100 hectares, increasing production by 50% over the same period, thus reducing its overall dependency on grapes purchases. It is now a major player in the Champagne industry, but although GH Martel is its principal brand, it still only accounts for less than 20% of total sales and on some markets represents less than two per cent of sales, emphasising that it specialises in BOB, *sous marque* and *sur latte* sales.

WINEMAKER

Lionel Sausy

HOUSE STYLE & RANGE

There never used to be anything outstanding under the Martel label, but since the 1989 vintage, Cuvée Victoire has been rich and succulent. Although GH Martell's prestige *cuvée*, it is significantly cheaper than most *grande marque* vintage Champagnes, making it an excellent buy.

BRUT BLANC DE BLANCS CHARDONNAY
  Not vintaged, méthode champenoise:
  100% Chardonnay
BRUT CUVÉE GRANDE RÉSERVE
  Not vintaged, méthode champenoise:
  30% Chardonnay, 70% Pinot Noir
BRUT CUVÉE PRESTIGE
  Not vintaged, méthode champenoise:
  30% Chardonnay, 70% Pinot Noir
BRUT ROSÉ
  Not vintaged, addition of red wine, méthode
  champenoise: 10% Chardonnay, 90% Pinot Noir
DEMI-SEC EXTRA
  Not vintaged, méthode champenoise: equal parts
  Chardonnay, Pinot Noir, Meunier
BRUT
  Vintaged, méthode champenoise: 40% Chardonnay,
  60% Pinot Noir
BRUT ROSÉ
  Vintaged, addition of red wine, méthode
  champenoise: 10% Chardonnay, 90% Pinot Noir
★✫ CUVÉE VICTOIRE BRUT
  Vintaged, méthode champenoise

THE VISITOR CENTRE AT CHAMPAGNE MERCIER, WITH THE VINEYARD IN THE FOREGROUND

MASSÉ

See LANSON

88
SERGE MATHIEU

AVIREY-LINGEY

- 7,500 cases
- Récoltant-Manipulant

This small, immaculately equipped grower first started making and selling Champagne under its own name in the 1970s, and has firmly established itself as one of the two best producers in the Aube today. Go to Drappier for complexity, Mathieu for elegance.

WINEMAKER

Serge Mathieu

HOUSE STYLE & RANGE

Elegance is not the only characteristic of these wines; they also show a refreshing richness of fruit, along with a fine, fluffy mousse of ultra-fine bubbles.

★ BRUT ROSÉ
  Not vintaged, addition of red wine, méthode
  champenoise: 100% Pinot Noir
★★✫ BRUT SELECT, TÊTE DE CUVÉE
  Not vintaged, méthode champenoise:
  30% Chardonnay, 70% Pinot Noir
✫ CUVÉE TRADITION, BLANC DE NOIRS BRUT
  Not vintaged, méthode champenoise:
  100% Pinot Noir
★ CUVÉE BRUT PRESTIGE

  Not vintaged, méthode champenoise:
  30% Chardonnay, 70% Pinot Noir
★✫ BRUT
  Vintaged, méthode champenoise: 30% Chardonnay,
  70% Pinot Noir

MAXIM'S

See DE CASTELLANE

75
MEDOT

PARGNY-LE-REIMS

- 13,000 cases
- Other labels – Philippe Guidon
- Négociant-Manipulant

The firm's origins date back to 1897, when Jules Pascal made and sold Champagne, mainly *sur lattes*, and not under any particular brand. It was Pascal's daughter, Léonie (wife of Jules Medot), who was the first to sell Champagne under a family-owned brand. Current owners are Philippe and Patricia Guidon.

WINEMAKER

Philippe Guidon

HOUSE STYLE & RANGE

Some *cuvées* have been amylic, but the non-vintage brut can be soft and mellow. The Clos des Chaulins has been disappointing the few times I have tasted it.

BRUT
  Not vintaged, méthode champenoise:
  10% Chardonnay, 10% Pinot Noir, 80% Meunier
BRUT 1ER CRU CLOS DES CHAULINS
  Not vintaged, méthode champenoise:
  5% Chardonnay, 80% Pinot Noir, 15% Meunier
BRUT
  Vintaged, méthode champenoise: 50% Chardonnay,
  20% Pinot Noir, 30% Meunier

VEUVE DE MEDTS

See UNION CHAMPAGNE

6 VALUE
MERCIER
ÉPERNAY

- 500,000 cases
- Group ownership - LVMH
- Négociant-Manipulant

Established in 1858 by Eugène Mercier, who combined five houses (Berton, Philippe Gourlon, Dufaut Père & Fils, René Lesecq and Veuve Soyez) into one called Maison Mercier Union de Propriétaires, based in Paris. An imposing figure of ancient Champagne stock, Mercier successfully marketed his wines to the population as a whole, rather than to a select group of privileged customers. He never missed an opportunity to draw attention to his wines, and is best remembered for his use of a team of 24 white oxen to haul a huge and fabulous carved cask through Paris on May 7, 1889, during the Paris Exhibition when the streets were crowded with sightseers. The cask was almost 1,000 times the size of a traditional Champagne barrel and took 20 years to build. Mercier was taken over by Moët & Chandon in 1970, since when it has been seen by many as a downmarket *sous marque* of the region's largest producer. But it is Mercier – not Moët – that is the brand-leader in France, and it always has been.

WINEMAKER
Parentheon

HOUSE STYLE & RANGE
Generally fuller and fatter than Moët, with unashamed Aube fruit ripeness. Generally less elegant, too, although some of the vintages can excel, and the rich, flavour-packed Cuvée du Fondateurs offers extraordinary value for money.

BRUT
Not vintaged, méthode champenoise: 10-15% Chardonnay, 45-50% Pinot Noir, 40% Meunier
BRUT ROSÉ
Not vintaged, addition of red wine, méthode champenoise: 60% Pinot Noir, 40% Meunier
DEMI-SEC
Not vintaged, méthode champenoise: 55% Pinot Noir, 45% Meunier
DEMI-SEC ROSÉ
Not vintaged, addition of red wine, méthode champenoise: 60% Pinot Noir, 40% Meunier
★☆ CUVÉE DE FONDATEUR, EUGÈNE MERCIER BRUT
Not vintaged, méthode champenoise: 10% Chardonnay, 55% Pinot Noir, 35% Meunier

★ VENDANGE
Vintaged, méthode champenoise: 50% Chardonnay, 35% Pinot Noir, 15% Meunier

87
DE MERIC
AŸ-CHAMPAGNE

- 16,500 cases
- Other labels - Baron Martin
- Négociant-Manipulant

Edmond Besserat founded Besserat de Bellefon in 1843, but in 1959 the house was sold to Cinzano which, four years later, moved the business out of Aÿ-Champagne to new premises at Murigny, on the outskirts of Reims. It was taken over by Ricard in 1976, and the brand disposed of to Marne et Champagne in 1991. Christian Besserat established this small, quality-conscious house one year after his father and uncle sold out to Cinzano. He owns ten hectares of vineyards, and is assisted by his son, Patrick.

WINEMAKER
Christian & Patrick Besserat

HOUSE STYLE & RANGE
Brut Sélection is simple, but elegant and fruity. The non-vintage *blanc de blancs* is fine and fragrant yet firm and ages gracefully, but of all the basic non-vintage *cuvées*, it is the rosé that delights me the most, with its pale-gold colour and an exquisitely delicate, soft, fruity flavour. Straight vintages can be very elegant, but the greatest Champagne produced here is de Meric's Cuvée Prestige Cathérine de Medici – a very special wine that shows best with food, and offers true aficionados sublime finesse and seductively mellow bottle-aromas.

★☆ BLANC DE BLANCS BRUT
Not vintaged, méthode champenoise: 100% Chardonnay
★ BRUT SÉLECTION
Not vintaged, méthode champenoise: 30% Chardonnay, 70% Pinot Noir
★★ BRUT SÉLECTION ROSÉ
Not vintaged, addition of red wine, méthode champenoise: 15% Chardonnay, 85% Pinot Noir
★★☆ BRUT
Vintaged, méthode champenoise: 30% Chardonnay, 70% Pinot Noir
★★★☆ BRUT CATHÉRINE DE MEDICI
Vintaged, méthode champenoise: 50% Chardonnay, 50% Pinot Noir

87 VALUE
LE MESNIL
LE MESNIL-SUR-OGER

- 10,000 cases
- Négociant-Manipulant

Only an occasional glitch mars the exceptional quality potential of this cooperative, located in one of the Côte des Blancs' greatest growths.

WINEMAKER
M Lebouef

HOUSE STYLE & RANGE
Smooth and rich, with fine acidity at basic level, the vintage quality is a significant step up, with crisper, richer, fuller fruit that will develop a toasty finesse. However, it is this cooperative's so aptly named prestige *cuvée*, Sublime, that offers the highest degree of richness, complexity and finesse.

★ BLANC DE BLANCS BRUT
Not vintaged, méthode champenoise: 100% Chardonnay
★★ RÉSERVE SÉLECTION, BLANC DE BLANCS BRUT
Vintaged, méthode champenoise: 100% Chardonnay
★★ SUBLIME, BLANC DE BLANCS BRUT
Vintaged, méthode champenoise: 100% Chardonnay

E MICHEL
See DUVAL LEROY

N/A
GUY MICHEL
PIERRY

- 2,500 cases
- Récoltant-Manipulant

Vincent Michel is the fifth generation of the Michel family to work as a *vigneron*, and currently owns 20 hectares in ten different villages. I am flummoxed by this grower, who owns so many hectares, yet produces relatively little Champagne in a bewildering number of styles.

WINEMAKER
Vincent Michel

HOUSE STYLE & RANGE
The only wine I tasted recently was the basic 1990 brut. Although it was not very good at all, it could well be an anomaly, and I could not possibly give an objective, overall appraisal of this astonishingly large and varied range on such limited experience.

BLANC DE BLANC BRUT
Not vintaged, no malolactic, méthode champenoise: 100% Chardonnay

BRUT
Not vintaged, méthode champenoise: 30% Chardonnay, 26% Pinot Noir, 44% Meunier
BRUT ROSÉ
Not vintaged, saignée, méthode champenoise: 100% Pinot Noir

DID YOU KNOW?

RED CHAMPAGNE – NOT COTEAUX
CHAMPENOISE – OFFICIALLY EXISTS,
ALBEIT AS A FIGMENT OF A
BUREAUCRAT'S MIND, AS THE ONLY
RED WINE THAT MAY BE ADDED TO
WHITE IN ORDER TO PRODUCE PINK
CHAMPAGNE HAS TO BE AOC
CHAMPAGNE, ACCORDING TO A DECREE
OF LAW DATED JUNE 17, 1938

BRUT SÉLECTION
> Not vintaged, méthode champenoise: 55%
> Chardonnay, 10% Pinot Noir, 35% Meunier

DEMI-SEC
> Not vintaged, méthode champenoise: 100% Chardonnay

BRUT MILLÉSIMÉ
> Vintaged, no malolactic, méthode champenoise:
> 15% Chardonnay, 10% Pinot Noir, 75% Meunier

BRUT TRADITION
> Vintaged, méthode champenoise: 30% Chardonnay,
> 70% Meunier

CUVÉE DU PRIEURÉ
> Vintaged, no malolactic, méthode champenoise:
> 50% Chardonnay, 50% Meunier

PARIS FOLIES
> Vintaged, méthode champenoise: 40% Chardonnay,
> 60% Meunier

VIEUX CHAMPAGNE LIQUOREUX
> Vintaged, méthode champenoise: 100% Chardonnay

75
PIERRE MIGNON
LE BREUIL
- 20,000 cases
- Négociant-Manipulant

This family-owned producer was established
in 1906, and today owns ten hectares, of
which 80% are planted with Meunier, as
befits their location. Pierre Mignon
Champagnes have been served at the Elysée
palace and the *Matignon* (official residence of
the Prime Minister), and the firm specialises
in personalised labels for private customers.

WINEMAKER
Pierre Mignon

HOUSE STYLE & RANGE
Although they have the floral expressiveness of
Meunier, the wines are rustic and lack finesse.

BRUT PRESTIGE
> Not vintaged, méthode champenoise:
> 15% Chardonnay, 15% Pinot Noir, 70% Meunier

BRUT PRESTIGE ROSÉ
> Not vintaged, addition of red wine, méthode
> champenoise: 10% Pinot Noir, 90% Meunier

BRUT ROSÉ
> Not vintaged, addition of red wine, méthode
> champenoise: 15% Chardonnay, 15% Pinot Noir,
> 70% Meunier

CUVÉE RÉSERVE BRUT
> Not vintaged, méthode champenoise:
> 10% Chardonnay, 10% Pinot Noir, 80% Meunier

GRANDE RÉSERVE BRUT
> Not vintaged, méthode champenoise:
> 10% Chardonnay, 10% Pinot Noir, 80% Meunier

BLANC DE BLANCS BRUT
> Vintaged, méthode champenoise: 100% Chardonnay

CUVÉE IRIS BRUT
> Vintaged, hand-painted bottle, méthode champenoise:
> 20% Chardonnay, 30% Pinot Noir, 50% Meunier

CUVÉE DE MADAME BRUT
> Vintaged, méthode champenoise: 20% Chardonnay,
> 30% Pinot Noir, 50% Meunier

GRANDE RÉSERVE BRUT
> Vintaged, méthode champenoise: 10% Chardonnay,
> 10% Pinot Noir, 80% Meunier

80
MIGNON & PIERREL
EPERNAY
- 15,000 cases
- Négociant-Manipulant

This house proudly claims to have gained a
reputation for its 'daring packaging' – and
suppose you have to be daring to shrink-
wrap your best Champagnes in pink, blue
or green floral-patterned plastic (but not
half as daring as those who buy it!). There
are good Champagnes in some of these
shrink-wrapped bottles, and the pity is that
without the floral decor, the labels would be
very stylish indeed.

WINEMAKER
Dominique Pierrel

HOUSE STYLE & RANGE
If you can bring yourself to buy the blue
floral-patterned bottle, then you will be
well-rewarded with the light but satisfying
richness of this non-vintage *cuvée*, which is
serious Champagne with a creamy, biscuity
finish. I have not tasted the pink-clad
Cuvée Floral Rosé for some time, but the
1992 Cuvée Floral Brut was not very
impressive.

★✦ CUVÉE FLORALE BRUT
> Not vintaged, méthode champenoise:
> 60% Chardonnay, 40% Pinot Noir

CUVÉE FLORALE ROSÉ
> Not vintaged, addition of red wine, méthode
> champenoise: 90% Chardonnay, 10% Pinot Noir

CUVÉE TRADITION BRUT
> Not vintaged, méthode champenoise: grape varieties
> not revealed

CUVÉE TRADITION ROSÉ
> Not vintaged, addition of red wine, méthode
> champenoise: 90% Chardonnay,
> 10% Pinot Noir

CUVÉE FLORALE BRUT
> Vintaged, méthode champenoise:
> 100% Chardonnay

CUVÉE TRADITION, BLANC DE BLANCS
> Vintaged, méthode champenoise: 100% Chardonnay

GRANDE CUVÉE TRADITION
> Vintaged, méthode champenoise: 90% Chardonnay,
> 10% Pinot Noir

80
JEAN MILAN
OGER
- 5,000 cases
- Récoltant-Manipulant &
  Négociant Distributeur

Established in 1964, the Milan family have been winegrowers for five generations. Current incumbent Henry-Pol Milan owns five hectares of vineyards, and has continued to market Champagne under his father's name (Jean Milan). For a few years, he has also used his son's name – Champagne Jean-Charles Milan – which will eventually replace it.

WINEMAKER

Henri-Pol Milan

HOUSE STYLE & RANGE

Traditional producer who uses oak barrels for some of its *cuvées*, but I have yet to taste one that I can praise, whereas I thoroughly recommend the cheapest Champagne, which sees no oak and is very fresh, with fine aromas and nice, lean fruit.

★✭ BRUT SPÉCIAL
  Not vintaged, méthode champenoise:
  100% Chardonnay

CUVÉE DE RÉSERVE
  Not vintaged, oak-aged, méthode champenoise:
  100% Chardonnay

CUVÉE TENDRESSE
  Not vintaged, méthode champenoise:
  100% Chardonnay

DEMI-SEC
  Not vintaged, méthode champenoise:
  100% Chardonnay

TERRE DE NOËL
  Vintaged, méthode champenoise: 100% Chardonnay

87
MOËT & CHANDON
EPERNAY
- 2 million cases
- Group ownership - LVMH
- Négociant-Manipulant

This house was established in 1743 by Claude Moët, a *courtier en vin* since 1716, and the owner of vineyards in the Marne Valley.

According to the late Patrick Forbes, a director of Moët & Chandon and a respected historian, some people claim the first Moët was a 15th-century Dutchman called Le Clerc (which sounds terribly French to me), who ran at the head of a crowd at Rémois, shouting *'Het moet zoo zijn'* ('It must be so'), when the English were trying to prevent Charles VII from entering the city. Apparently he did this 'so lustily that the English vanished, and he was known forever as 'M Moët' – which seems a more logical explanation for the origin of the term 'double-Dutch' than the name Moët.

A few years ago, when the *grande marque's* share on export markets began to slide, and it became obvious that the interest in grower Champagnes and different *crus* was on the increase, it was suggested to Moët that the houses could play the growers at their own *terroir* game by releasing a set of *mono-cru* Champagnes. With all the base wines that pour through Moët & Chandon each year, it ought to be simple to produce limited quantities of half-a-dozen *grands crus* that would be expressive of their own particular village. The principle difference between a grower Champagne from, for instance,

Cramant and Avize is invariably the grower (the different techniques he or she employs), which is part of the endless fascination of grower Champagnes. However, if one winemaker produced *cuvées* from, say, Ambonnay, Aÿ, Bouzy, Cramant, Avize, and Le Mesnil, they would offer the first realistic insight to the intrinsic differences of the *terroirs* concerned.

Coincident with this suggestion, Moët was developing an excellent new *cuvée* called Brut Premier Cru, which is not expressive of any *terroir*, but should open up sales to those who refuse to be seen drinking Moët & Chandon Brut Impérial. A significant proportion of Champagne drinkers believe that this producer's basic non-vintage brut is inconsistent, due to its huge production. This is not true, as explained below, but even those who hold this myopic view do recognise that Moët can – and does – produce great Champagne in the form of Dom Pérignon. The only way to penetrate this market is to release a new non-vintage that proclaims a much greater degree of selection – hence Brut Premier Cru.

The Brut Impérial name is both the key to Moët's success among the masses, and the obstacle to its progress for the younger, more discerning and knowledgeable (if sometimes mistaken or misinformed) base of new Champagne drinkers. The same argument could therefore be applied to Moët's vintage Brut Impérial. And it might well be, but Brut Premier Cru could also be a stepping-stone to a fully-fledged range of *mono-cru* Champagnes, if other houses do not beat this slumbering giant to the punch.

After the most exhaustive tasting, I am convinced that, contrary to popular belief, Moët's Brut Impérial is exceptionally consistent in quality and character. I was given the freedom of all its storage depots to select bottles to taste under laboratory conditions. Accompanied by Richard Geoffroy, I chose samples from the bottom of pallets, from the back of rows, as well as from the bottling line, and from shipments due to be flown to numerous countries around the world. At one point, as a container lorry was pulling away from the export depot, Richard said, jokingly, 'Do you want me to stop the lorry and get you a sample?', to which I replied, 'Now that's a good idea,' and the lorry was duly stopped, a pallet removed, and a case taken off.

Back at the laboratory, I added samples sent to me by colleagues from all around the world. Moët was unaware of this until I produced the samples, but had no objection to my including them in the tasting. Until this event, I had been one of Brut Impérial's

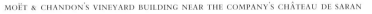

MOËT & CHANDON'S VINEYARD BUILDING NEAR THE COMPANY'S CHÂTEAU DE SARAN

104 | FRANCE

biggest critics. Having experienced the odd toasty wonder at competitive blind tastings, I, too, subscribed to the inconsistency theory, but this event changed my view completely. Brut Impérial has an amazing consistency; the reason for its apparent differences lies in the construction of the *cuvée*.

Although Moët won't admit it in so many words, Brut Impérial is deliberately made in a soft, light, fresh but somewhat bland style to make it amenable to the masses and offend no one. This is why it rarely stands out in blind tastings. But it is the very lightness and softness of its structure that makes Brut Impérial so prone to full, toasty aromas within 12 to 18 months of release. When Moët submits bottles for a tasting, they will always be fresh samples, but sometimes samples are purchased off the shelf for competitive events, and occasionally one will be from slightly older stock – hence the odd occurrence of an award-winning Brut Impérial.

WINEMAKER
Dominique Foulon (Moët & Chandon) & Richard Geoffroy (Dom Pérignon)

HOUSE STYLE & RANGE
If judged for drinking on purchase, the world's greatest-selling non-vintage *cuvée*, Moët's Brut Impérial, might just scrape in as a decent BOB. If kept for 12 months, however, it quickly picks up toasty aromas and achieves a nice, mellowed elegance. Brut Premier Cru is not bigger or richer, but has an extra dimension of finesse, making it a delight for any knowledgeable consumer to drink on purchase. The new non-vintage Brut Rosé is a wonderfully fresh, delicately floral Champagne that is long and elegant with less depth than the established vintage rosé, but more finesse – making it significantly superior in my judgement. The vintage version has an accent on perfumed Pinot aromas, with a mellow richness of fruit on the palate. Vintage Brut Impérial is, as every aficionado knows, one of the best-bargain vintage Champagnes on the market, while Dom Pérignon Brut and the much rarer Dom Pérignon Rosé are sublime.

★ BRUT IMPÉRIAL
Not vintaged, méthode champenoise: 10% Chardonnay, 50% Pinot Noir, 40% Meunier

★★☆ BRUT 1ER CRU
Not vintaged, méthode champenoise: equal parts Chardonnay, Pinot Noir, Meunier

★★ BRUT ROSÉ
Not vintaged, addition of red wine, méthode champenoise: equal parts Chardonnay, Pinot Noir, Meunier

★★☆ CUVÉE DOM PÉRIGNON ROSÉ
Not vintaged, méthode champenoise: 40% Chardonnay, 60% Pinot Noir

★★ BRUT IMPÉRIAL
Vintaged, méthode champenoise: 40% Chardonnay, 45% Pinot Noir, 15% Meunier

★★☆ BRUT IMPÉRIAL ROSÉ
Vintaged, addition of red wine, méthode champenoise: 38% Chardonnay, 52% Pinot Noir, 10% Meunier

★★★ CUVÉE DOM PÉRIGNON BRUT
See p. 73

80
MONTAUDON
REIMS

- 100,000 cases
- Other labels – Lamotte, Vander Gucht
- Négociant-Manipulant

Auguste-Louis Montaudon, winemaker at Bouvet-Ladubay in Saumur, was sent to look after the cellars of Union Champenoise, a subsidiary located in Épernay where, in 1891, he established his own Champagne house. The firm moved to Reims, and is run today by Luc Montaudon, who owns 35 hectares of vineyards, exclusively planted with Pinot Noir, in Les Riceys.

WINEMAKER
Michel Rozeaux

HOUSE STYLE & RANGE
The non-vintage and vintage have always been passable but not special, but the Chardonnay has some toasty potential. The Grande Rosé is excellent in some years (1990 for example), but it can be very disappointing in others.

BRUT
Not vintaged, méthode champenoise: 25% Chardonnay, 50% Pinot Noir, 25% Meunier

★ CHARDONNAY PREMIER CRU BRUT
Not vintaged, méthode champenoise:

DEMI-SEC
Not vintaged, méthode champenoise: 25% Chardonnay, 50% Pinot Noir, 25% Meunier

BRUT MILLÉSIME
Vintaged, méthode champenoise: 40% Chardonnay, 60% Pinot Noir

GRANDE ROSÉ BRUT
Vintaged, méthode champenoise: 50% Chardonnay, 50% Pinot Noir

70
MARC MORIZET
CRAMANT

- 250 cases
- Récoltant-Manipulant

Parfait Morizet was the first in this grower's family to make and sell Champagne in 1905.

WINEMAKER
Jean-Marc Morizet

HOUSE STYLE & RANGE
The Brut Réserve is rather oxidative, with straw-like fruit underneath. Although the basic Grand Cru is better, it is not special.

GRAND CRU, BLANC DE BLANCS BRUT
Not vintaged, méthode champenoise: 100% Chardonnay

GRAND CRU, BLANC DE BLANCS BRUT RÉSERVE
Vintaged, méthode champenoise: 100% Chardonnay

MONTEBELLO
This brand belongs to Ayala, but it has an interesting history as well as the once-magnificent, now quite dilapidated, Château de Mareuil – all of which could be exploited to great fortune, rather than simply relegated to a *sous-marque*.
See AYALA

A MOOTZ
See JAMART

MOOTZ LEFEVRE
See JAMART

80
MOUTARD
BUXEUIL

- 45,000 cases
- Other labels – François Diligent
- Négociant-Manipulant

Although these Champagnes are sold under the Moutard Père et Fils label, the full name of this house is Moutard-Diligent.

The Diligents can trace their roots in Buxeuil back to 1642, and have been winegrowers in this area for centuries. It was not until 1927, however, that François Diligent first made and sold Champagne under the family name. The business is run today by his daughter and her husband, François Moutard, who own 20 hectares of vineyards.

WINEMAKER
François Moutard

HOUSE STYLE & RANGE
I like the daring things this small house is trying to do, but the ideas are often more interesting than the results, which often lack finesse and are sometimes quite dire. Cuvée Arbane is a good example. What a brilliant idea to produce a *cuvée* from this ancient, almost extinct variety which, through a quirk in the regulations, is still technically permissible in Champagne. This is in fact the first example I have come across of Arbane (also spelt Arbanne), which is so renown for the specificity of its floral aroma that local producers are supposed to be able to identify

a minuscule amount of this variety in a huge vatful of wine with just one sniff. 'Ah, Arbane!' they would say – although that was not quite the exclamation I used when I came across this wine in one of my blind tastings. If only Moutard could inject into these wines as much finesse as enthusiasm, they would be very exciting indeed. Cuvée de l'An 2000 was not released nor had been tasted at the time of writing.

BRUT
Not vintaged, méthode champenoise: 100% Pinot Noir

★ **BRUT RÉSERVE**
Not vintaged, méthode champenoise: 100% Chardonnay

BRUT GRANDE RÉSERVE
Not vintaged, no malolactic fermentation, méthode champenoise: 100% Chardonnay

★✠ **BRUT ROSÉ**
Not vintaged, saignée, méthode champenoise: 100% Pinot Noir

CUVÉE ARBANE VIEILLE VIGNE
Not vintaged, méthode champenoise: 100% Arbane

✠ **CUVÉE EXTRA-BRUT**
Not vintaged, wines aged 5-7 years, méthode champenoise: 50% Chardonnay, 50% Pinot Noir

CUVÉE PRESTIGE
Not vintaged, wines aged 5-7 years, méthode champenoise: 50% Chardonnay, 50% Pinot Noir

★ **BRUT**
Vintaged, méthode champenoise: 100% Chardonnay

CUVÉE DE L'AN 2000
Vintaged, méthode champenoise: 100% Chardonnay

84 VALUE
JEAN MOUTARDIER
LE BREUIL
- 17,000 cases
- Négociant-Manipulant

Run by Englishman Jonathan Saxby, who gave up a career with Rank Hovis McDougal when he married into the Moutardier family. Although Claude Barré is the winemaker, Jonathan took his new role seriously enough to study oenology at the famous Champagne school in Avize.

The Moutardiers have been growers since 1650, although they did not make and sell their own Champagne until 1920. They currently own 16 hectares of vineyards in Le Breuil, one of the best sites in Champagne

for Meunier. Although it is the *cuvées* Moutardier makes with just Chardonnay and Pinot Noir that have proved to be consistently the best, I very much support his 100% Meunier Champagnes. However, these are the best-selling basic house vintage, non-vintage and rosé, and it would be nice to think that Jonathan Saxby might one day make a pure Meunier prestige *cuvée*. Somebody somewhere will eventually have a bash at trying to make the greatest-ever pure-Meunier Champagne: why not Moutardier? What would it be like if made from truly old *vieilles vignes* in a favoured *lieu-dit*, using only the *coeur de cuvée*, with perhaps an understated use of new oak and no malolactic fermentation? This might be overkill, but it would be a good way to start.

WINEMAKER
Claude Barré

HOUSE STYLE & RANGE

★ **CARTE D'OR**
Not vintaged, méthode champenoise: 100% Meunier

★✠ **CENTENAIRE**
Not vintaged, méthode champenoise: 85% Chardonnay, 15% Pinot Noir

✠ **ROSÉ**
Not vintaged, addition of red wine, méthode champenoise: 100% Meunier

★ **SÉLECTION**
Not vintaged, méthode champenoise: 50% Chardonnay, 50% Pinot Noir

★ **MILLÉSIME**
Vintaged, méthode champenoise: 100% Meunier

80
PH MOUZON-LEROUX
VERZY
- 5,900 cases
- Other labels - Y Mouzon-Leclère, R Mouzon-Juillet, Mouzon Père et Fils
- Récoltant-Manipulant & Négociant-Manipulant

A family enterprise established by Cécile and Roger Mouzon in 1938. The current incumbents are Pascal and Philippe Mouzon, who own nine hectares of vines, almost entirely in Verzy, with less than half a hectare in Villers-Marmery.

Ph Mouzon-Leroux is made exclusively from the firm's own vineyards, as are the *sous marques* Y Mouzon-Leclère and R Mouzon-Juillet, while the Mouzon Père et Fils label is restricted to Champagnes blended from purchased grapes.

WINEMAKER
Philippe Mouzon

HOUSE STYLE & RANGE
Some *cuvées* can be spoiled by an amylic aroma or a certain rusticity, although they can be saved by the richness of flavour.

✠ **BRUT GRANDE RÉSERVE/DEMI-SEC**
Not vintaged, méthode champenoise: 25% Chardonnay, 75% Pinot Noir

✠ **BRUT ROSÉ**
Not vintaged, addition of red wine, méthode champenoise: 30% Chardonnay, 70% Pinot Noir

CUVÉE MOUZON-JUILLET
Not vintaged, oak-matured, méthode champenoise: 90% Chardonnay, 10% Pinot Noir

✠ **CUVÉE BRUT PRESTIGE**
Vintaged, méthode champenoise: 80% Chardonnay, 20% Pinot Noir

80
MUMM
REIMS
- 625,000 cases
- Group ownership - Seagram
- Négociant-Manipulant

This house was founded in 1827 by two Germans, Peter Arnold de Mumm and Frederick Giesler, who together formed PA Mumm, Giesler & Co. After ten years, Giesler left to start Giesler & Co at Avize, which attained great fame but is now simply a *marque* belonging to Marne et Champagne.

The firm was confiscated during the First World War because, unlike the other German founders of Champagne houses, the Mumms had not sought naturalisation. In 1920 GH Mumm & Co was purchased by a group of investors, one of which was Dubonnet; René Lalou, whose wife was a Dubonnet, took control of the firm. As chairman, he successfully guided Mumm until 1973, building it into one of the largest Champagne houses, acquiring Perrier-Jouët in 1959, Chauvet Frères in 1969, and Heidsieck & Co Monopole in 1972. In the same year that it purchased Chauvet, Mumm itself was taken over by one of its shareholders, the giant Canadian-based multi-national Seagram Group. In 1996, Seagram sold off Heidsieck & Co Monopole, something it had been trying to do for many years.

Although Perrier-Jouët is the more prestigious brand (and probably financially sound in its own right), Mumm is the leading house due to its historical position as the parent company and its significantly larger sales – despite its heavy losses. These financial problems are compounded by the

HARVESTING PINOT NOIR
GRAPES FOR CHAMPAGNE
MUMM BELOW THE
MOULIN DE VERZENAY
ON THE MONTAGNE
DE REIMS

uncertainty of Seagram's commitment to Champagne, making rumours rife that the multinational group will eventually sell off the company.

Mumm has to re-establish its credibility among discerning Champagne consumers if it is to become profitable – it must for long-term survival, whoever owns it. The disposal of Heidsieck & Co Monopole removed an unnecessary drain on its resources, while the disposal of the lower echelons of its viticultural holdings has helped focus a smaller production on a higher quality level. Add to this the fact that Mumm still has a very high turnover in the number of bottles sold (albeit significantly lower than it used to be), and it would appear that Mumm could use the millennium boom to boost its sales and reputation.

What it does require, however, is an irrefutable statement that any change for the good will be permanent, and the best way to achieve that would be to emphasise the roots of its style and quality. Those roots take us to Cramant, and what better statement of purpose would there be than to sell off its expensive Reims premises, and build a high-tech winery on the plain beneath Cramant unlike anything Champagne has seen thus far? It would take both Mumm and Champagne into the 21st century.

WINEMAKER
Dominique Demarville
HOUSE STYLE & RANGE
Previous winemaker Pierre-Yves Harang had a difficult job weeding out the decent wines from the morass of dross left by his former mentor, the once-gifted André Carré. The wines were so heavily influenced by malolactic fermentation that they stank of sauerkraut. The real watershed occurred with the 1996 harvest, but the non-vintage *cuvées* based on that year will not be in distribution until late 1999, and the vintage Champagnes much later. The 1995s were much cleaner, and

should be circulating as this book hits the shelf, but it is the 1996s that indicate a return to the light, pure, fluffy style for which Mumm used to be renowned. A young oenologist by the name of Dominique Demarville was essentially responsible for producing the wines from those two harvests, and he has been chief winemaker since the beginning of 1997, when Pierre-Yves Harang retired.

CORDON ROSÉ
  Not vintaged, addition of red wine, méthode
  champenoise: 28% Chardonnay, 50% Pinot Noir,
  22% Meunier

★ CORDON ROUGE
  Not vintaged, méthode champenoise:
  28% Chardonnay, 50% Pinot Noir, 22% Meunier
CORDON VERT DEMI-SEC
  Not vintaged, méthode champenoise:
  10% Chardonnay, 55% Pinot Noir, 35% Meunier
★ MUMM DE CRAMANT
  Not vintaged, méthode champenoise: 100% Chardonnay
★ CORDON ROUGE
  Vintaged, méthode champenoise: 25% Chardonnay,
  75% Pinot Noir
★ GRAND CORDON
  Vintaged, méthode champenoise: 46% Chardonnay,
  54% Pinot Noir

NAPOLÉON
See CH & A PRIEUR

N/A
DE NAUROY
REIMS
• 10,000 cases
• Group ownership - Bruno Paillard

• Négociant-Manipulant
De Nauroy Champagne has been sold for 40 years, but it was a co-op-produced clone until the late 1980s, when Eric and Raymond Rudloff started making their own creamy, rich, biscuity Champagnes not dissimilar in style to Roederer Brut Premier, and stole the show at the London Wine Trade Fair in 1992. They also happened to be made according to strict kosher rules.

Launching a Champagne brand is difficult enough at the best of times, but trying to do it in the economic depression of the early 1990s proved too much for De Nauroy. The typical response was 'lovely Champagne, beautiful label, but nobody knows the name', and De Nauroy was unable to achieve a reasonable price for its quality, even though it was outstanding. So in 1997, the Rudloff family sold the brand and stocks to Bruno Paillard (personally – not to BCC).

The Rudloff's 5.5 hectares of vineyards were not part of the deal, although Paillard has contracted to purchase their grapes for future *cuvées* which will be made at Champagne Bruno Paillard in Reims, not at the old De Nauroy premises in Prouilly. That Paillard will make good Champagne is not in doubt, but whether it will retain the De Nauroy style remains to be seen. Still, if he sticks to the family vineyards, then it is certain that he will not, because it was the grapes that Rudloff purchased from Bouzy and (in particular) Cramant that gave De Nauroy its creamy, rich, biscuity quality.

Presumably De Nauroy will remain Rudloff-produced Champagne until at least 2001, but already the range has been stripped of its best *cuvée*, the Black Label, which sold for a premium over the Green Label. I'd love to know where those stocks will end up.
WINEMAKER
Laurent Guyot
HOUSE STYLE & RANGE
The Rudloff-produced Champagnes all have the ability to attain a characteristic creamy, biscuitiness with a little bottle-age, and are rated below on the assumption that they will remain Rudloff-produced Champagnes for the time being. The overall ranking must, however, be subject to question, if only to draw attention to the fact that a change in production is imminent.
★ BRUT
  Not vintaged, méthode champenoise:
  20% Chardonnay, 35% Pinot Noir, 45% Meunier
★★ BRUT ROSÉ
  Not vintaged, méthode champenoise:
  5% Chardonnay, 60% Pinot Noir, 35% Meunier
★★ BRUT
  Vintaged, méthode champenoise: 30% Chardonnay,
  60% Pinot Noir, 10% Meunier

85
MICHEL NOIROT
LES RICEYS
- 7,000 cases
- Récoltant-Manipulant

Established as recently 1968 by Maurice Noirot, current incumbent Michel Noirot cultivates 8.5 hectares of vines on his Le Clos St-Roch estate in Les Riceys.

WINEMAKER
Michel Noirot

HOUSE STYLE & RANGE
With plenty of curranty fruit at the basic level, the Cuvée du Clos St-Roch has an excellent concentration of fruit, but the Cuvée Blanche Clos St-Roch is lighter, with not quite so much finesse.

★ BRUT TRADITION
Not vintaged, méthode champenoise: 20% Chardonnay, 80% Pinot Noir

★★ CUVÉE CENDRÉE DE ROSE
Not vintaged, addition of red wine, méthode champenoise: 70% Chardonnay, 30% Pinot Noir

★ EXTRA BRUT
Not vintaged, méthode champenoise: 20% Chardonnay, 80% Pinot Noir

★ BRUT MILLÉSIME
Vintaged, méthode champenoise: 80% Chardonnay, 20% Pinot Noir

★ CUVÉE BLANCHE CLOS ST-ROCH
Vintaged, méthode champenoise: 100% Chardonnay

★★ CUVÉE DU CLOS ST-ROCH
Vintaged, méthode champenoise: 90% Chardonnay, 10% Pinot Noir

OUDINOT
EPERNAY
- 85,000 cases
See BEAUMET

88 VALUE
BRUNO PAILLARD
REIMS
- 25,000 cases
- Group ownership - also owns De Nauroy
- Négociant-Manipulant

This is the 'chicken or the egg' house that broke the mould of the bad old days of Champagne, when only those producers who had sold Champagne the year before could qualify to buy grapes. This old contract kept the club of houses – not just *grandes marques* – nice and cosy, because without grapes, you cannot make Champagne to sell, and without selling Champagne, you cannot buy the grapes to make it. Furthermore, the bad old contract kept the status quo by basing the amount of grapes which could be purchased on the amount of Champagne that was sold the previous year. Thus, the big houses remained on top, and the pecking order could not be changed.

BRUNO PAILLARD: FIRST TO START A CHAMPAGNE HOUSE FROM SCRATCH IN THE MODERN ERA

If you had enough money, you could simply buy a house, and if you are a grower you can apply to become a *négociant-manipulant*, but Bruno Paillard was the first person to start up a house from scratch in the modern era by a combination of circumstance and attitude.

A Champenois by birth, Paillard began work in the Champagne trade by selling BOBs for his father and, shortly afterwards, for Marne et Champagne. On occasion, he would come across a small lot of Champagne that was simply too good to sell anonymously under a supermarket brand. In fact, it was so good that he put his signature on the label to show that he personally recommended the Champagne. After a few years, he had established a range of Champagnes, all under his own name, so he presented the authorities with this egg and demanded they make him into a fully fledged chicken. It was a grey area, but Paillard was something of a Young Turk in those days. As one much older member of the trade told me, 'We knew that Paillard would not let it drop, and he could have made things difficult. As our American friends say, it was considered "wiser to have him inside the tent pissing out, than outside pissing in".' How wise they were: since Bruno Paillard became a *négociant-manipulant* in 1984, he has become a pillar of the very establishment he once threatened.

WINEMAKER
Laurent Guyot

HOUSE STYLE & RANGE
Light, delicately rich fruit of increasing elegance, Bruno Paillard always prefers finesse to complexity, although his best *cuvées* possess complexity as well. Premier Cuvée also happens to be one of the most consistent non-vintages on the market. Look out for the launch of a prestige *cuvée* in 1999. The details were under wraps at the time of writing, but I know the first vintage will be 1990, composed exclusively of *grands crus* and barrique-fermented.

★★ BRUT PREMIÈRE CUVÉE
Not vintaged, méthode champenoise: 33% Chardonnay, 45% Pinot Noir, 22% Meunier

★★ CHARDONNAY RÉSERVE PRIVÉE
Not vintaged, méthode champenoise: 100% Chardonnay

★★ ROSÉ PREMIÈRE CUVÉE
Not vintaged, méthode champenoise: 15% Chardonnay, 85% Pinot Noir

★★ BRUT
Vintaged, méthode champenoise: 40% Chardonnay, 60% Pinot Noir

86 VALUE
PALMER
REIMS
- 25,000 cases
- Coopérative-Manipulant

Although when established in 1947, this cooperative was located in Avize, its members have always owned more vineyards in the *grands crus* of the Montagne de Reims than the Côte des Blancs. Officially called the *Société Co-opérative de Producteurs des Grands Terroirs de Champagne*, the origin of the Palmer brand name has always been a bit of a mystery. Some say that each letter of the name stands for qualities the original founders or their wines aspired to or reflected: P (for *précision* and *poésie*), A (for *assemblage* and *amour*), L (for *limpidité* and *légèreté*), M (for *maîtrise* and *majesté*), E (for *erudition* and *élégance*) and R (for *recherche* and *raffinement*), but this is typical of Gallic poetic licence.

Another theory is that the name is an acronym of the initials of its founding members; although there were seven of them and only six letters in Palmer, this story does at least contain a grain of truth. Apparently, the founders tried to make an acronym from their initials, but found it impossible and were at a loss over what to do when one of them was inspired by a packet of Huntley & Palmer biscuits. I kid not – although Jean-Claude Colson, the current manager, might have done so when he told me. He did not, however, appear to be jesting, and it is true that, having been deprived of imports during the war, the *rémois* bestowed packets of Huntley & Palmer biscuits with something akin to a *grande marque* status in the late 1940s.

Why Champagne Palmer rather than Champagne Huntley, I have no idea, but the brand was not appreciated by the owners of a certain *château* in Bordeaux, and there was a protracted exchange of letters. But however much Champagne Palmer tried to explain that it had no intention of exploiting the name of Château Palmer, the problem just would not go away. Until, that is, someone suggested sending their Bordelais cousins a case of Champagne Palmer. Apparently, it was so well appreciated that all objections were dropped.

Some 230 members today own more than 400 hectares of vineyards spread across 50 different villages, although still dominated by the *grands crus* of the Montagne de Reims. Palmer also has one of the best reputations among the Champagne houses – hard-won respect, considering they have to deal with co-ops on a continuous basis.

WINEMAKER
Michel Davesne
HOUSE STYLE & RANGE
Palmer is typically dominated by rich, expansive, often highly perfumed Pinot Noir fruit. Old vintages are a speciality, although in my experience, they offer more medium-term than long-term pleasure, and I often find they develop better if purchased when young. They should be rich, smooth and biscuity, but some years are noticeably less successful than others. The quality of the Amazone de Palmer started off a bit wobbly, but it is now a seamless blend of Pinot Noir and Chardonnay, and has become this producer's most consistent *cuvée*.

BRUT
  *Not vintaged, méthode champenoise:
  50% Chardonnay, 45% Pinot Noir, 5% Meunier*
★★ BRUT AMAZONE DE PALMER
  *Not vintaged, méthode champenoise:
  50% Chardonnay, 50% Pinot Noir*
BRUT ROSÉ CUVÉE RUBIS
  *Not vintaged, addition of red wine, méthode
  champenoise: 45% Chardonnay, 50% Pinot Noir,
  5% Meunier*
★☆ BRUT
  *Vintaged, méthode champenoise: 50% Chardonnay,
  50% Pinot Noir*
BRUT BLANC DE BLANCS
  Vintaged, méthode champenoise: 100% Chardonnay

85 VALUE
PANNIER
CHATEAU THIERRY
• 250,000 cases
• Other labels - De Brienne
• Coopérative-Manipulant
Originally established at Dizy in 1899 by Louis Eugène Pannier, whose son Gaston had to move to larger premises at Château-Thierry in 1937 to cope with growing sales. In 1971, Gaston's heirs sold the business to a group of growers who had been long-time suppliers to Pannier and who wished to ensure the brand's future. They formed the

Coopérative de Champagnisation des Coteaux du Val de Marne, or COVAMA for short, and set about attracting the membership of other local growers. This co-op has grown rapidly – particularly in the last few years– and it now consists of 300 growers owning 560 hectares of vineyards in the three principal districts of Champagne.

Pannier makes an ideal stopover for anyone motoring into Champagne from Paris or the Channel. Its cellars were originally quarried in AD720 to provide stone for the castle of the Merovingian ruler Theodoric IV, also known as Thierry IV, the puppet king of the Franks under Charles Martell. These rough-hewn caves were converted into two-tier vaulted cellars in the 12th century, and are different to anything else you will see in Champagne. After a good night's rest, take a leisurely drive along the vine-clad banks of the Marne Valley from Château Thierry to Épernay, and your first sight of Champagne will be the city of Reims.

WINEMAKER
Philippe Dupuis
HOUSE STYLE & RANGE
The problem here is the modest quality of the vineyards belonging to the cooperative's members. However, the proportion of grapes coming from the classic areas of the Marne has gradually increased, and there has been a noticeable increase in finesse since 1990. At one time I could not recommend the basic brut here, but the 1990-based non-vintage *cuvées* were excellent. Subsequent blends have not been quite up to that standard; due to the crops in question, they outclass anything Pannier made prior to 1990 and have all been thoroughly recommendable. This co-op has two prestige *cuvées*, which might seem a bit confusing, but they have different aims; Louis Eugène is the ultimate expression of Pannier's house style, whereas Egérie is an extreme example of the vintage in question.

★ BRUT ROSÉ
  *Not vintaged, addition of red wine, méthode champenoise:
  37% Chardonnay, 25% Pinot Noir, 38% Meunier*

★ BRUT TRADITION/SÉLECTION
  *Not vintaged, méthode champenoise:
  38% Chardonnay, 25% Pinot Noir, 37% Meunier*

DEMI-SEC
  *Not vintaged, méthode champenoise:
  38% Chardonnay, 25% Pinot Noir, 37% Meunier*
★★ EGÉRIE
  *Vintaged, méthode champenoise: 48% Chardonnay,
  24% Pinot Noir, 28% Meunier*
★☆ LOUIS EUGÈNE
  *Not vintaged, méthode champenoise: 42%
  Chardonnay, 36% Pinot Noir, 22% Meunier*
★☆ LOUIS EUGÈNE ROSÉ
  *Not vintaged, saignée, méthode champenoise: 39%
  Chardonnay, 43% Pinot Noir, 18% Meunier*
★ VINTAGE
  *Vintaged, méthode champenoise: 36% Chardonnay,
  24% Pinot Noir, 40% Meunier*

83
JEAN-MICHEL PELLETIER
PASSY-GRIGNY
• 750 cases
• Récoltant-Manipulant
Established as recently as 1982, Jean-Michel Pelletier owns four hectares of vineyards on a south-facing spur overlooking the confluence of the Semoigne and Brandouille rivers. These vineyards are located within the boundaries of the three villages of Passy-Grigny, Verneuil and Ste-Gemme, and more than 80% of the vines planted are Meunier.

WINEMAKER
Jean-Michel Pelletier
HOUSE STYLE & RANGE
Although some *cuvées* are marked with an unwelcome wet-straw character, when successful, these wines are generally soft and smooth. The extremely rich-flavoured Cuvée Anaëlle is a serious and satisfying Champagne of some class.

BRUT ROSÉ
  *Not vintaged, addition of red wine, méthode champenoise:
  20% Chardonnay, 40% Pinot Noir, 40% Meunier*

☆ BRUT SÉLECTION
  *Not vintaged, méthode champenoise:
  20% Chardonnay, 30% Pinot Noir, 50% Meunier*
BRUT TRADITION
  *Not vintaged, méthode champenoise: 10% Pinot
  Noir, 90% Meunier*
DEMI-SEC
  *Not vintaged, méthode champenoise: 10% Pinot
  Noir, 90% Meunier*

GRANDE RÉSERVE BRUT
*Not vintaged, méthode champenoise: 20%
Chardonnay, 30% Pinot Noir, 50% Meunier*

★★ CUVÉE ANAËLLE
*Vintaged, oak-aged Chardonnay, méthode
champenoise: 50% Chardonnay, 50% Meunier*

87 VALUE
JOSEPH PERRIER
CHALONS-EN-CHAMPAGNE

- 50,000 cases
- Group ownership - Laurent-Perrier
- Négociant-Manipulant

Founded in 1825 by Joseph Perrier, who in 1870, left his grandson Gabriel Perrier a thriving business, but he had little inclination to run a Champagne house and it was eventually sold to Paul Pithois in 1888. It is currently run by Jean-Claude Fourmon, a direct descendant, although the Laurent-Perrier group owns a majority shareholding.

WINEMAKER
Claude Dervin

HOUSE STYLE & RANGE
Very consistent (Dervin is the third generation in his family to blend Joseph Perrier), with rich, creamy fruit and a noted capacity to age well; these Champagnes generally turn biscuity when mature. The non-vintage *blanc de blancs* definitely repays cellaring, picking up a wonderful creamy, biscuity, walnutty complexity after three years or more. The rosé has a tendency to be rather clumsy, but occasionally excels in a much lighter, more elegant style.

★★ CUVÉE ROYALE BRUT
*Not vintaged, méthode champenoise:
35% Chardonnay, 35% Pinot Noir, 30% Meunier*

★★ CUVÉE ROYALE BRUT BLANC DE BLANCS
*Not vintaged, méthode champenoise:
100% Chardonnay*

CUVÉE ROYALE DEMI-SEC
*Not vintaged, méthode champenoise:
35% Chardonnay, 35% Pinot Noir, 30% Meunier*

CUVÉE ROYALE BRUT ROSÉ
*Not vintaged, addition of red wine,
méthode champenoise: 25% Chardonnay,
75% Pinot Noir*

★★ CUVÉE JOSÉPHINE
*Vintaged, méthode champenoise: 45% Chardonnay,
55% Pinot Noir*

★★ CUVÉE ROYALE BRUT
*Vintaged, méthode champenoise: 50% Chardonnay,
48% Pinot Noir, 2% Meunier*

90
PERRIER-JOUËT
EPERNAY

- 250,000 cases
- Group ownership - Seagram
- Négociant-Manipulant

This firm was established in 1811 by Pierre Nicolas-Marie Perrier, the uncle of Joseph Perrier, and he added his wife's maiden name to his own surname to create the Perrier-Jouët brand. Pierre soon created a healthy export demand for his product, but it was his son, Charles Perrier, who did most to build up the reputation of this Champagne, supplying it to the courts of Napoleon III, King Leopold of the Belgians and Queen Victoria. He built Château Perrier opposite Maison Perrier-Jouët in the avenue de Champagne, which is used today as the local library and museum. Ownership of Perrier-Jouët passed on to Charles Perrier's nephew, Henri Gallice, thence to Louis Budin, who was married to a member of the Gallice family. Louis Budin's son, Michel, took over in 1959, the same year the house was acquired by the Mumm Group. Under the auspices of the Seagram group, Perrier-Jouët is run today by Michel Budin's son, Thierry.

WINEMAKER
Hervé Deschamps

HOUSE STYLE & RANGE
There was a time in the early 1990s when Perrier-Jouët was going down the same unfortunate route as Mumm, but the quality has since been reasserted. Perrier-Jouët has always been light, elegant, and true-brut in style, with heaps of fruit. The amount of Chardonnay in these wines is often thought to be considerably higher than it actually is, because Perrier-Jouët's vineyards in Cramant yield such dominant fruit. Blason de France, which was launched five years before Belle Epoque, is always worth the premium, and Perrier-Jouët's basic vintage is legendary for its quality and longevity (the 1929 is peerless).

★★ BLASON DE FRANCE
*Not vintaged, méthode champenoise:
35% Chardonnay, 35% Pinot Noir, 30% Meunier*

★★ BLASON DE FRANCE ROSÉ
*Not vintaged, addition of red wine, méthode
champenoise: 25% Chardonnay, 45% Pinot Noir,
30% Meunier*

★ GRAND BRUT
*Not vintaged, méthode champenoise:
20% Chardonnay, 40% Pinot Noir, 40% Meunier*

★★★ BRUT MILLÉSIME
*Vintaged, méthode champenoise: 30% Chardonnay,
40% Pinot Noir, 30% Meunier*

★★★ LA BELLE EPOQUE
See p.110

★★★ LA BELLE EPOQUE ROSÉ
See p.110

87 VALUE
PHILIPPONNAT
MAREUIL-SUR-AY

- 40,000 cases
- Group ownership - BCC
- Négociant-Manipulant

Bruno Paillard purchased this house on behalf of BCC in November 1997, and he did so in a flamboyantly unexpected fashion. Just one week before signing contracts, he walked out of talks with the then-owner, Marie Brizard, because the unions refused to accept his deal, which included halving the workforce to make Philipponnat profitable. The unions threatened to take to court any owner who made its members redundant, even though the ailing Marie Brizard group no longer had the financial resources to keep Philipponnat afloat. Without a new owner, the company would have gone bust, with every person it employed losing their jobs.

Even after Paillard had walked out and no other realistic offers were forthcoming, the unions did not budge, so it surprised everyone when Paillard ignored the inevitability of a messy legal battle and purchased Philipponnat on his own terms within days of withdrawing from negotiations. At the time of writing, BCC faced 20 separate legal cases – although their outcome is presumably assured, since the company has apparently paid redundancy money in excess of the legal minimum.

The deal also included Abel Lepitre, but the jewel in the crown was Philipponnat's Clos des Goisses, a single-vineyard Champagne that is on par with Salon. *Chef de cave* Norbert Thiébert has been retained, so there should be no discontinuity in winemaking style, and ex-Moët man François de Rendinger is in day-to-day charge.

WINEMAKER
Norbert Thiébert

HOUSE STYLE & RANGE
This has always been an underrated house offering good quality and excellent value. The house style is generally elegant and fresh, with plenty of easy-going fruit and a soft, smooth mousse. Philipponnat also boasts one of Champagne's greatest wines: Clos des Goisses. Although Clos des Goisses requires extreme age to achieve its fabulous complexity (*see p.64*), and another *cuvée*, Le Reflet, contains 50% Pinot Noir from Clos des Goisses (plus 50% Chardonnay from the Côte des Blancs), Le Reflet requires no ageing whatsoever. It is like a quick-fused second

Continues on page 111

PERRIER-JOUËT LA BELLE ÉPOQUE

Many houses produced elaborately enamelled bottles in the Belle Époque era (1890s-1914), but only Perrier-Jouët uses such extrovert handiwork to commercialise Champagne today. I remember an old bottle overlaid with an attractive enamel mosaic in a display cabinet at Pol Roger some 20 years ago, but it is Perrier-Jouët's bottle, with its flowers painted in pink, gold and green enamel, that is so evocative of the *joie de vivre* of the Belle Époque.

Champagne Belle Époque was Pierre Ernst's idea. Ernst was Michel Budin's associate, and ran the company before Thierry Budin took over. He found a dusty old bottle in a cupboard at Perrier-Jouët. It was decorated with an enamelled arabesque of anemones and signed by Emile Gallé, the great art nouveau glassmaker and cabinet-maker of Nancy. Gallé had created the design for Perrier-Jouët in 1902, just two years before his death, to evoke the Gay Nineties, and Ernst thought it would make an ideal *cuvée* to sell through Maxim's restaurant in Paris.

The first vintage was 1964, launched

MAGNUMS OF BELLE ÉPOQUE IN THE CELLARS OF PERRIER-JOUËT, EPERNAY

in 1969, and was sold exclusively through Maxim's and Fauchon, the elite grocery store. In the early 1980s, Belle Époque Rosé was launched with the 1976 vintage.

Some critics have accused Perrier-Jouët of putting more effort into the bottle than the quality of the Belle Époque Champagne, but anyone who has followed these *cuvées* will know this is not true. Not only is the quality extraordinarily high, but

no other prestige *cuvée* can match the consistency of style that Belle Époque stamps upon every vintage.

The character of each vintage is nicely stated, but the overriding style is Belle Époque, which is itself determined by the influence of great Cramant Chardonnay. Not only does Cramant provide every Belle Époque vintage with supreme finesse; it is so distinctive that, after 20 years or so, both Belle Époque Brut and Belle Époque Rosé become virtually indistinguishable. Even the colours merge into one another, as the brut deepens to old gold and the rosé lightens through flame-gold to exactly the same hue, for all hint of the pink pigment drops out.

THE CHAMPAGNES

LA BELLE ÉPOQUE BRUT

Vintaged, méthode champenoise:
50% Chardonnay, 45% Pinot Noir, 5% Meunier
★★☆ This *cuvée* is typically very pale when first released, with a delightful but deceptive lightness of fruit that is so elegant, and has a delicate creaminess on the finish. The finesse is so great that it is evident from the very start. Gradually, the colour deepens and the flavour lengthens, with toasty aromas beginning to emerge after the third year. Eventually, Belle Époque assumes an old-gold hue, with complex aromas of coffee and vanilla mingling with the toast, while the fruit attains an extraordinary richness and depth for what is still a light and very elegant wine. The years declared so far are 1964, 1969, 1971, 1973, 1975, 1976, 1978, 1979, 1982, 1983, 1985, 1988, 1989 and 1990 – all of which fully deserve a ★★☆ rating, and the 1978 is far and away the greatest Champagne of that generally lacklustre vintage.

LA BELLE ÉPOQUE ROSÉ

Vintaged, addition of red wine, méthode champenoise:
45% Chardonnay, 50% Pinot Noir, 5% Meunier
★★☆ Here, the anemones are enamelled onto clear glass, revealing the colour of this wine, which is always a salmon pink – never a pink rosé, although some years are deeper than others. This *cuvée* is initially very fresh and delicate, sometimes revealing red-fruit aromas such as wild strawberries, but it takes on a mellowing ripeness of fruit after just two or three years (from disgorgement). Cramant Chardonnay starts to assert itself at about ten years from the date of harvest, when the colour has yellowed to an apricot-salmon, and by 20 years of age, there is very little difference between this wine and Belle Époque Brut in colour, aroma or flavour.

RÉSERVE LA BELLE ÉPOQUE

55% Chardonnay, 45% Pinot Noir
★★☆ A limited edition of 2,000 individually numbered jeroboams (the equivalent of four bottles) of a special 1995 Belle Époque selling at $2,000 each. This might not sound like good value, but it is probably the biggest Champagne bargain ever because the price also includes dinner and an overnight stay for two at Perrier-Jouët's fabulous Maison Belle Époque. This small *château* in Épernay is decorated and furnished exclusively in art nouveau, with priceless pieces by such masters as Marjorelle, Gruber, Carabin, Vallin, Guimard, Lallique, Rodin and, of course, Gallé. The Maison Belle Époque has always been a privilege that money could not buy, and with just 2,000 jeroboams for the entire world, not many people will be able to purchase the privilege. Because demand would outstrip supply, the only advertising has been by word of mouth – until I opened mine!

HARVESTING
GRAPES IN
PIPER
HEIDSIECK'S
VINEYARDS

wine of Clos des Goisses, whose charms show from the very moment it is released, and do not benefit in the slightest from further maturation. The Grand Blanc works in some years (1990), but not in others (1986).

★✰ LE REFLET
Not vintaged, méthode champenoise:
50% Chardonnay, 50% Pinot Noir

✰ RÉSERVE ROSÉ BRUT
Not vintaged, addition of red wine, méthode
champenoise: 35% Chardonnay, 55% Pinot Noir,
10% Meunier

✰ ROYALE RÉSERVE BRUT
Not vintaged, méthode champenoise:
30% Chardonnay, 55% Pinot Noir, 16% Meunier

✰ BRUT RÉSERVE SPÉCIALE
Vintaged, méthode champenoise: 35% Chardonnay,
65% Pinot Noir

GRAND BLANC BRUT
Vintaged, méthode champenoise: 100% Chardonnay

★★★ CLOS DES GOISSES
See p.64

80

PIERRE PINARD
Sézanne
• 1,700 cases
• Récoltant-Manipulant
Although this grower's substantial 15 hectares of vineyards are located in the heart of the Côte de Sézanne, his Champagnes contain 30% Pinot Noir – unusual for a district where the norm is 100% Chardonnay.

WINEMAKER
Jacques Pinard

HOUSE STYLE
The very rich, fennel fruit in these Champagnes is indeed different from other Sézannais wines, and tends to turn biscuity within a couple of years. The structure is also different – not bigger, just different.

N/A

PIERSON WHITAKER
AVIZE
• 840 cases
• Récoltant-Coopérateur

Small family business set up by Didier Pierson and Imogen Whitaker, a couple who run a small B&B house in Avize.

WINEMAKER
Didier Pierson

HOUSE STYLE & RANGE
Not yet established.

BLANC DE BLANCS
Not vintaged, méthode champenoise: 100% Chardonnay

BRUT
Not vintaged, méthode champenoise:
30% Chardonnay, 70% Pinot Noir

RÉSERVE
Not vintaged, méthode champenoise:
50% Chardonnay, 50% Pinot Noir

85 VALUE

PIPER-HEIDSIECK
REIMS
• 420,000 cases
• Group ownership - Rémy-Cointreau
• Other labels - Heidsieck
• Négociant-Manipulant

Like the other Heidsieck & Co Monopole and this firm's sister company Charles Heidsieck, Piper-Heidsieck can trace its roots back to Florens-Ludwig Heidsieck in 1785, but its origins as a separate entity really date from 1834, when Christian Heidsieck formed his own company. From that juncture, this house is the only one allowed to use the brand 'Heidsieck', plain and simple, although obviously its greatest sales are under the Piper-Heidsieck label.

The Piper connection stems from 1837, when Christian Heidsieck's widow married Henri-Guillaume Piper, her brother-in-law. Under his control, the business changed its name to H Piper & Co, but continued selling its Champagne under the Heidsieck brand. In 1845, however, the firm began selling its Champagne as 'Piper-Heidsieck' in deference to its American customers, who insisted on calling it 'Piper-Heidsieck'.

When Henri Piper died in 1870, he left the business to his partner Jean-Claude Kunkelmann, and Kunkelmann et Cie

remained the firm's legal title until as recently as 1988, although ownership passed into the hands of the d'Aulan family as long ago as 1930. The Marquis François d'Aulan sold Piper-Heidsieck to Rémy-Cointreau, already owner of Charles Heidsieck, in 1990.

WINEMAKER
Daniel Thibault

HOUSE STYLE & RANGE
Due to the severity of its non-malolactic, low-dosage, relatively young style, Piper-Heidsieck was often misunderstood in the d'Aulan family era, but the ugly duckling non-vintage brut changed into a lovely Champagne if aged two or three years after purchase. The old Piper style also made for vintages which were extremely robust: I remember the *chef de cave* in 1980 opening a bottle of 1961 that had been kicking around in the bottom of his locker for ten years, and it was wonderful. However, since 1990, master blender Daniel Thibault has been working his magic on these Champagnes, all of which now go through a full malolactic fermentation.

Obviously the non-vintage brut took a leap in style in 1990, but the real jump in quality came with the 1992-based blend, which hit the shelves in 1996, while its smart new red label has given this Champagne a more classy appearance since 1997. It does not have the depth and complexity of Charles Heidsieck's Brut Réserve, nor does it have the class, but Thibault's reborn Piper is richer than the old-style *cuvée* and has more upfront fruit. You do not have to age, but if you do lay down a few bottles for two or three years, it develops a curious Charles-like, creamy–vanilla richness. Try it and see what you think. The Brut Sauvage tastes more low-*dosage* than non-*dosage*, which is a tribute to Thibault's blending skills. The Piper Rare has always been one of the most underrated prestige *cuvées*.

✰ BRUT
Not vintaged, méthode champenoise:
15% Chardonnay, 55% Pinot Noir, 30% Meunier

✰ BRUT ROSÉ
Not vintaged, addition of red wine, méthode
champenoise: 15% Chardonnay, 45% Pinot Noir,
40% Meunier

DEMI-SEC
Not vintaged, méthode champenoise:
15% Chardonnay, 55% Pinot Noir, 30% Meunier

✰ BRUT
Vintaged, méthode champenoise: 30% Chardonnay,
70% Pinot Noir

★✰ BRUT SAUVAGE
Vintaged, méthode champenoise: 30% Chardonnay,
70% Pinot Noir

★★ RARE
Vintaged, méthode champenoise: 65% Chardonnay,
35% Pinot Noir

86 VALUE
PLOYEZ-JACQUEMART
LUDES
- 11,000 cases
- Négociant-Manipulant

Marcel Ployez came from the Aube *département* to marry Yvonne Jacquemart, and established this small house in the Montagne de Reims in 1930. When Marcel Ployez died in 1957, his widow took control of the business and ran it for ten years until her two sons, Gérard and Jacques, were able to enter the firm. In 1975, Gérard Ployez and his wife Claude took over the running of the business, including 1.8 hectares of vineyards in Mailly and Ludes.

WINEMAKER
Laurence Ployez-Krommydas

HOUSE STYLE & RANGE
The Extra Brut always used to be reliable and peaked in the early 1990s, when it typically had fragrant, creamy, lemony fruit, but has become rather rustic since then. However, this producer's most exciting *cuvée* remains L d'Harbonville which, since 1988, has been *barrique*-fermented, without malolactic fermentation, and is neither fined nor filtered. The results have been wines which are stunning in their youth, turning towards a great Burgundian style with age.

★☆ BLANC DE BLANCS BRUT
   Not vintaged, méthode champenoise: 100% Chardonnay
★ BRUT
   Not vintaged, méthode champenoise:
   30% Chardonnay, 40% Pinot Noir, 30% Meunier
EXTRA QUALITY
   Not vintaged, méthode champenoise:
   50% Chardonnay, 35% Pinot Noir, 15% Meunier
SÉLECTION ROSÉ
   Not vintaged, méthode champenoise:
   35% Chardonnay, 35% Pinot Noir, 30% Meunier
★★ L D'HARBONVILLE
   Vintaged, méthode champenoise: 70% Chardonnay,
   25% Pinot Noir, 5% Meunier

96 VALUE
POL ROGER
EPERNAY
- 108,500 cases
- Négociant-Manipulant

The Pol-Roger family name used to be Roger, but was changed in 1900 to honour the founder, Pol Roger, who was just 19 when he established this house in 1849. He started off by making Champagne for other houses, but by the time his two sons, Maurice and Georges, took control in 1899, the business was well established under the Pol Roger name. So well established, in fact, that they decided to append their father's Christian name to their surname. Unlike other countries, in France it is not very easy

DÉGORGEMENT AT POL ROGER

to change your name, and the two brothers were required to seek a presidential decree.

When the Germans occupied Épernay in September 1914, it was for only seven days, but in that time Prince Mecklenburg, Prince William of Prussia (the Kaiser's son) and General von Moltke each set up their own headquarters in the town. The police and municipal authorities moved out just before the Germans arrived, and the only French official left to face the invaders was Maurice Pol-Roger, who was mayor of Épernay.

He withstood German threats to shoot him and to burn the town to the ground and this earned him the eternal gratitude of his fellow citizens. He was presented with a leather-bound book containing the signature of every inhabitant who had remained behind when the Germans took Épernay. The townspeople also showed their thanks by voting him mayor so many times that, in 1935, he declined the office and so they made him honorary mayor for life.

Upon his death, the house of Pol Roger passed to his son Jacques and his nephew Guy. Since 1964, the firm has been run by Christian de Billy and Christian Pol-Roger, who are both great-grandsons of the founder and over the last decade they have been increasingly helped by Christian de Billy's son Hubert. As Serena Sutcliffe MW once put it: 'The Pol-Roger clan are Épernay people... they do not merely respect history, they are usually around when it is being made.'

The house of Pol Roger remains family-owned and, until 1955, it possessed no vineyards whatsoever. It currently owns 85 hectares, mostly located in the Épernay area: Chavot-Courcourt, Chouilly, Cramant, Cuis, Grauves, Mardeuil, Moussy, Pierry and, of course, Épernay itself.

WINEMAKER
James Coffinet

HOUSE STYLE & RANGE
This firm's basic non-vintage is known for obvious reasons as White Foil. White Foil is typically full of flowery Meunier sweetness when first released, but it should be kept a year or two, after which time the Pinot Noir starts to take a grip, the flavour deepens, and the structure firms up. It is not a particularly long-lived non-vintage *cuvée*, and never has been. However, if you catch it while the Pinot Noir is in ascendance (but before it actually dominates), and the freshness of the Meunier remains, it shows true Pol Roger class and finesse.

Although the *demi-sec* is exactly the same blend, but with a much higher *dosage*, it can and should be kept for up to five years, as I found to my delight when judging at the International WINE Challenge. Despite a natural inclination of most tasters on my table to make rude remarks when faced with a row of sweet Champagnes, we were all smitten by the gorgeous complexity of one obviously mature *cuvée*. They were all tasted blind, of course, but we discovered later that the wine in question was Pol Roger Demi-Sec.

The Blanc de Blancs de Chardonnay is so sumptuous and creamy when first released that there is little point in ageing it, although it can develop nicely for a further three to five years.

The rosé is exquisitely perfumed with strawberry, peach and raspberry, and always reminds me of the bubbly, rosy-cheeked Christian de Billy. The Réserve Spéciale PR is abundantly rich in fruit, with every bit as much class, complexity and finesse as Cuvée Sir Winston Churchill – and in some vintages the Pinot Noir is so dominant that I think the old boy might have preferred it.

Note that at this house, 'extra-dry' (legally 12-20g/l), which has traditionally been used on the UK market, is synonymous with 'brut' (up to 15g/l), and the normal *dosage* is in fact 12g/l

★ BRUT/EXTRA-DRY
   Not vintaged, méthode champenoise: equal parts of
   Chardonnay, Pinot Noir, Meunier
★ DEMI-SEC
   Not vintaged, méthode champenoise: equal parts of
   Chardonnay, Pinot Noir, Meunier
★★ BLANC DE BLANCS DE CHARDONNAY
   Vintaged, méthode champenoise: 100% Chardonnay
★★ BRUT ROSÉ
   Vintaged, addition of red wine, méthode
   champenoise: 40% Chardonnay, 60% Pinot Noir
★★☆ RÉSERVE SPÉCIALE PR
   Vintaged, méthode champenoise: 50% Chardonnay,
   50% Pinot Noir
★★★ BRUT VINTAGE
   See p.114
★★☆ CUVÉE SIR WINSTON CHURCHILL
   See p.116

POL ROGER VINTAGE

40% Chardonnay, 60% Pinot Noir
  30,000 cases (estimated)

My first recollection of Champagne *per se* was my father telling me (then aged just six) why he used to drink Pol Roger 1928 from a silver tankard before the war. I have been asked so many times about the cryptic dedication alluding to this story in my book *Champagne* that it might be prudent to elaborate on it here.

I had no idea, of course, what Champagne tasted like at such a tender age, but on that particular occasion I was drinking Vimto (which dates me!) from my father's tankard, and my teeth were on edge from the experience. It must have been this unpleasant physical sensation that has kept the incident alive in my mind because I remember thinking that Champagne, which I knew to be fizzy (having already seen plenty of bottles opened), must be worse than Vimto when drunk from anything metallic.

My father told me that it was when he was helping out at his father's restaurant, The Grand, in Hastings, before the war that he acquired the habit of drinking Champagne from a tankard (it was only later that I discovered the Champagne in question was Pol Roger 1928, and that 'before the war' was specifically 1938).

At the back of The Grand there was a very large, high-ceilinged room where the Court Players used to rehearse. The Court Players became quite well-known in their time, with various companies existing around the country. The company in Hastings used to perform at the White Rock Pavilion, and was managed by a character called Jack Kingdom – and but for Jack I might never have specialised in Champagne. He liked a drink or two, but his boss, Harry Hansen, who owned the Court Players, tolerated this weakness provided that Jack drank nothing stronger than beer. Harry's favourite tipple was, however, Pol Roger, and in 1938, my grandfather stocked the 1928 vintage.

Harry Hansen used to turn up at the odd rehearsal in a chauffeur-driven car, which my father thought very pretentious for someone who 'employed a bunch of men in tights', so it took little persuading to help the more down-to-earth Kingdom to hoodwink Hansen. In those days, it was possible to buy draught ale at a place like The Grand, but only in silver tankards, which made the perfect cover for Kingdom's Champagne. He insisted

that my father do likewise, and thus every bottle of Pol Roger 1928 that Jack purchased was split between the two tankards. When Harry Hansen rolled up, he would be openly relieved at the sight of Harry's tankard, yet still told my father, 'Just make sure he sticks to pints,' to which my father would raise his tankard, take a mouthful of Champagne and

say, 'Don't worry, Mr Hansen. We always drink the same brew.' Ever since I was six, that story has made Champagne a little bit special for me, but I count myself lucky that Kingdom drank Pol Roger. No other house has a better record for producing vintage Champagne of great quality and exceptional longevity.

CHRISTIAN DE BILLY (LEFT) AND SON HUBERT WITH CHEF DE CAVES AND WINEMAKER JAMES COFFINET (RIGHT). HAVING ESTABLISHED THE MODERN-DAY REPUTATION OF BILLECART-SALMON BEFORE TAKING ON THE CHALLENGE AT POL ROGER IN 1985, COFFINET ACCOMPLISHED A SMOOTH TRANSITION WITH EASE

WHY IS POL ROGER VINTAGE SO SPECIAL?

I honestly don't know! Certainly the temperature of Pol Roger's cellars have something to do with it because, at 9.5°C, they are a half to one-and-a-half degrees colder than most other cellars in Champagne. Although a seemingly small difference, this will significantly slow down the second fermentation and retard the maturation process, causing greater finesse and longevity, but this is relative to the intrinsic quality of the wine. The cellar cannot create great finesse and longevity, it can only ensure that more of the potential finesse and longevity is retained. In other words, put Cava into Pol Roger's cellars and it will end up better Cava, not Pol Roger.

The curious thing is, however, that when the origin of the wines used to make Pol Roger are analysed, they are not particularly outstanding. In truth, only Cramant is; the rest are frankly ordinary. This does not disappoint me; quite the opposite, in fact, because it means that the blender's art here is practised with such skill that the end result truly is greater than the sum of its parts. The Pol Roger family – be they Pol-Roger or de Billy – have always decided the blend. Like most family-owned Champagne houses, the *chef de caves* does much of the groundwork, setting up the tastings to include the most likely possibilities, but the family – and only the family – decides. When carried out properly, the so-called family palate is handed down from generation to generation, with members of at least two generations on hand for every decision. I can personally vouch that the Pol Roger family palate has successfully passed from father to son to nephew or whatever from 1892 to at least 1995. Hopefully, Hubert de Billy will do his bit for the future.

THE VINTAGES

1996
60% Pinot Noir, 40% Chardonnay
Not yet released and not tasted, but in theory should be better than the 1995.

1995
60% Pinot Noir, 40% Chardonnay
★★★ Not yet released, but an advance disgorgement was showing beautifully in early 1998, when its elegantly balanced fruit, ripe acidity and fine mousse demonstrated that it will have as much finesse as the 1988, although the two vintages could not be more different. This is much softer than the 1988, with none of the flintiness that vintage displayed at the same age.

1993
60% Pinot Noir, 40% Chardonnay
★★☆ Not yet released, this has delicate fruit aromas, but is quite fat on the finish, having already developed some creamy, biscuity complexity by early 1998. Probably on par with 1989, and definitely has the edge over 1986.

1992
60% Pinot Noir, 40% Chardonnay
Not tasted, this year is not considered a top vintage, even within Pol Roger, and its distribution will be limited in the same manner as the 1989 and 1983.

1990
60% Pinot Noir, 40% Chardonnay
★★★ Seductively soft and exquisitely perfumed, this is a hedonistic delight, with impeccable balance and cushiony mousse. It is one of Pol Roger's greatest vintages. It should firm up by the year 2000, when it should be left for at least five years, by which time it should be showing great complexity and finesse.

1989
60% Pinot Noir, 40% Chardonnay
★★☆ Like the 1983 and 1992, this was not released on all markets, and even when it was exported, distribution was often restricted. This wine is very fruity when disgorged, but quickly develops a creamy, walnutty, biscuity complexity.

1988
Brut 60% Pinot Noir, 40% Chardonnay
★★★ Firm yet sensuous, this vintage is classic, slow-developing Pol Roger, with smooth vanilla-finesse only just beginning to build in 1998.

1986
60% Pinot Noir, 40% Chardonnay
★★ This has always had lovely fruity aromas with good creamy fruit on the palate. It has some class and is one of the top performers in 1986, but it lacks the complexity and finesse of a true Pol Roger vintage.

1985
60% Pinot Noir, 40% Chardonnay
★★★ Initially showed great class, became quite fat and unctuous by the time the 1986 was well-distributed, and has slowly converted that into succulent richness.

1983
60% Pinot Noir, 40% Chardonnay
★★ Released in France, but not exported to major markets, this was not one of the top performers in 1983, although it definitely has the edge over Pol Roger's 1986, even though that was one of the top performers of its vintage.

1982
60% Pinot Noir, 40% Chardonnay
★★★ Great finesse when first released, this is still wallowing around in its second, purely fruit-driven stage, although the Chardonnay is now more dominant, whereas it used to be all Pinot Noir. This will still be lovely in a few decades.

1979
60% Pinot Noir, 40% Chardonnay
★★★ Classic 1979, classic Pol Roger, this *cuvée* has a beautifully lean structure with a light balance, yet slow-building, creamy, richness and a seemingly endless capacity for complex after-aromas.

1976
60% Pinot Noir, 40% Chardonnay
★★★ In 1985, this was disappointing (it was heavy and oxidative). Eight years later, the wine had developed a Devon-toffee character, as if heavily dominated by malolactic flavours, which was disturbing. But another five years on, it has transformed into a pure, seductive Champagne with perfumed aromas and full, rich, toasty, coconutty fruit. To many people's surprise, the 1976 will be one of Pol Roger's longest-lived vintages.

1975
60% Pinot Noir, 40% Chardonnay
This vintage promised to be one of Pol Roger's greatest from the day it was released, and no-one predicted its strange behaviour. By 1987, it had a mushroomy aroma, but was wonderfully fresh with no hint of any imminent demise. I started to feel things were no quite right in 1993, when I tasted a sample disgorged and sent direct from Pol Roger's cellars, and I have not found a good bottle since. It is possible that the problem is limited to part of a batch and that some bottles will make a treasure trove in the future, but it seems this once promising *cuvée* has gone over at the age of 23 – akin to infant mortality for a Pol Roger vintage.

1973
60% Pinot Noir, 40% Chardonnay
★★★ Brilliant contrasts, with a very pale colour evoking lightness and youth, a savoury, toasty aroma suggesting fullness and maturity, and deliciously pure, fresh fruit on the palate.

1971
60% Pinot Noir, 40% Chardonnay
★★★ Beautifully preserved, quite pale with wonderful mellow, rich fruit. Some bottles have taken on a fresh mushroom character but, although delightful in itself, I prefer more purity of fruit.

1966
65% Pinot Noir, 35% Chardonnay
★★★ This vintage has always had a deep and full nose, and it now has rich, spicy aromas. This seems riper than many other 1966s, with excellent freshness, and is very rich in extract. Complexity still building.

1964
60% Pinot Noir, 40% Chardonnay
★★★ I drank this great wine many times in the late 1970s and early 1980s, but it has been so long since I last taste it, a description would be meaningless.

1959
60% Pinot Noir, 40% Chardonnay
★★★ Old disgorged bottles are wonderfully honeyed, with heaps of toasty, coconut fruit. A freshly disgorged example recently was far less exciting, although it still had intense fruit and an interesting fresh-mushroom aroma.

1955 *60% Pinot Noir, 40% Chardonnay*
★★★ A truly beautiful Champagne; fresh-mushroom aromas mingling with rich, ripe fruit. This will go on for decades.

1952 *70% Pinot Noir, 30% Chardonnay*
★★★ In 1986, this was the best Champagne I had ever tasted. Twelve years later, it still rates in my top ten. This has a typical *goût anglaise*, which does not mean (as so many French think) an old maderised style. In fact, the English preference is for the freshest, oldest Champagnes, and this 1952 has a legendary vigour indeed.

1949 *60% Pinot Noir, 40% Chardonnay*
★★★ A specially disgorged example had an appealing fresh-mushroom nose, although of the several normally disgorged bottles of this vintage I have encountered in recent years, none has had a hint of mushroom. All have a splendid richness of ripe, peachy fruit, and biscuity, vanilla complexity.

1947 *70% Pinot Noir, 30% Chardonnay*
★★★ One of my favourite Pol Roger vintages, this *cuvée* is still dominated by a delicious richness and purity of fruit. When recently disgorged there is a touch of fresh mushroom, but the intensity of flavour on the finish is stunning, and it is still capable of developing more complexity.

1937 *80% Pinot Noir, 20% Chardonnay*
★★★ First tasted in early 1998, recently disgorged at Pol Roger itself, this certainly ranks as one of this producers best-preserved vintages. Very fresh aromas, with a dry, intense fruit that builds deliciously in the mouth. It is extremely rich, with nuances of vanilla and coconut, and a touch of bitterness on the finish, which promises even more complexity to come.

1928 *80% Pinot Noir, 20% Chardonnay*
Tasted only three times, all old normally disgorged stock, and none very memorable – which might be surprising for what is arguably the greatest vintage of the century – but that is always the chance you take with old bottles (but *see below*).

1928 *100% Chardonnay*
★★★ A reserve wine made more than 30 years before Pol Roger's first commercial *blanc de blancs*, this *cuvée* was originally given a very light *liqueur d'expédition* to provide at most a *crémant*-like mousse – just enough *pétillance* to keep the wine fresh for use in future non-vintage blends – yet it still retains more fizz than most *grand mousseux* Champagnes of this age. Furthermore the colour is not just very pale, it still has a tinge of green. When I tasted this wine I was amazed and turned to James Coffinet, who said, 'I know. The first time I tasted I could not believe its age either, but there is a pile of them and they're all the same!' This remains the youngest-tasting oldest Champagne I have ever encountered.

1921 *80% Pinot Noir, 20% Chardonnay*
★★★ A wonderful, totally beguiling nose of coffee and fresh wild mushrooms, the latter pervading every aspect of this Champagne through to finish and aftertaste.

1919 *80% Pinot Noir, 20% Chardonnay*
★★★ A beautifully pure, succulent and compellingly complex Champagne full of rich, mellow toasty fruit. This vintage ranks with the 1914, and above the 1921, despite the latter's well-deserved legendary status.

1914 *80% Pinot Noir, 20% Chardonnay*
★★★ All the surviving stock was disgorged in 1944, yet after more than 50 years on its second cork, this death-defying Champagne is still on stunning form, with still-delicious fruit. An amazingly long-lived, incredibly fresh Champagne which, in 2014, will no doubt rival the 1892.

1906 *80% Pinot Noir, 20% Chardonnay*
Deep and sweet, with lovely coffee aromas, but the toffee is an indication of oxidation which, combined with its lack of mousse, makes this more of an historical experience rather than a truly great Champagne today, although it must have been at one time.

1892 *80% Pinot Noir, 20% Chardonnay*
★★★ Tasted in 1993, when it was 101 years old. I have tasted a number of much older Champagnes, but this remains the oldest to still possess a healthy mousse which, after foaming up on pouring, remained in the form of a positive spritz for up to ten minutes. Most 19th-century Champagnes not only have lost their fizz, but have oxidised to the point that they look, smell and taste like a mature sherry, whereas Pol Roger 1892 not only has a fizz, it is blessed with a fabulous honeyed-coffee aroma, great length, class and finesse.

MAISON POL ROGER IN EPERNAY, WHERE SIR WINSTON CHURCHILL'S FAVOURITE CHAMPAGNES WERE, AND STILL ARE, MADE

95
POL ROGER CUVÉE SIR WINSTON CHURCHILL

Pol Roger is inextricably linked to Winston Churchill, who met Odette Pol-Roger in November 1944, at a luncheon party hosted by Lady Diana Cooper at the British Embassy. She was one of General Wallace's three strikingly beautiful daughters – known affectionately as the 'Wallace Collection' – and the great man was instantly captivated by her wit, charm and intelligence. He even named one of his racing horses Odette Pol-Roger, although it always ran simply as Pol-Roger. Much to everyone's delight, it won the Black Prince Stakes at Kempton on the very day that Queen Elizabeth II was crowned in 1953.

In 1992, Bill Gunn MW, the managing director of Pol Roger UK, discovered an invoice in the Churchill Archives showing that Winston Churchill was drinking Pol Roger as early as 1908 (a case of 1895 for the princely sum of 96 shillings). His meeting in 1944 was not, therefore, his first introduction to Pol Roger, but merely put the icing on the cake of his relationship with this house, which like Topsy, 'just growed' afterwards, and this Champagne became his first choice for the rest of his life. When Churchill died in 1965, Pol Roger placed a black border

around the label of the White Foil shipped to England, and in 1984, the firm launched Cuvée Sir Winston Churchill, one of the greatest prestige *cuvées* of modern times.

Pol Roger refuses to reveal the composition of this Champagne, no matter who asks. This is not because Pol Roger is deliberately trying to be uncooperative, but because a promise was made to the Churchill family when the idea was first proposed. It is supposed to be made in a style that the great man would have appreciated, and as his favourite vintages were 1895, 1928 and 1947, it should in theory be 70% to 80% Pinot Noir, 20% to 30% Chardonnay, although some vintages – particularly the first three (1975, 1979 and 1982) – taste as if these percentages are transposed.

At the launch of Cuvée Sir Winston Churchill in 1984, Lady Soames said of her father's passion for Pol Roger, 'I saw him many times the better for it, but never the worse.'

1975 ★★★
1979 ★★★
1982 ★★★⯪
1985 ★★★
1988 ★★★⯪

WHEN CHURCHILL'S SON-IN-LAW, THE LATE LORD SOAMES, CALLED A PRESS CONFERENCE IN THE MIDST OF THE RHODESIAN PEACE TALKS, HE WAS ASKED HOW LONG THE NEGOTI-ATIONS WERE LIKELY TO LAST. 'THIRTY DAYS,' REPLIED SOAMES. 'HOW CAN YOU BE SO PRECISE?' THE REPORTER ASKED. 'BECAUSE I HAVE ONLY 30 BOTTLES OF POL ROGER LEFT,' HE REPLIED. THE EXCHANGE IS ON RECORD, BUT I ASKED POL ROGER WHETHER SOAMES ACTUALLY HAD ANY OF THEIR CHAMPAGNE, THINKING THAT PERHAPS IT WAS JUST A CLEVER QUIP, AND WAS TOLD THAT AS SOON AS SOAMES ARRIVED IN SALISBURY, HE ORDERED FIVE CASES OF POL ROGER TO BE FLOWN OUT. THE MAN OBVIOUSLY HAD HIS PRIORITIES.

'I AM EASILY SATISFIED WITH THE BEST' — SIR WINSTON CHURCHILL

88 VALUE
POMMERY
REIMS
• 500,000 cases
• Group ownership - LVMH
• Négociant-Manipulant

This house dates its origins from 1836, when Narcisse Greno took over the house of Dubois-Gosset. Louis Alexandre Pommery became an associate in 1856, investing so heavily in the firm that, when he died two years later, his widow Jeanne Alexandrine Louise Pommery took over the house. Greno retired in 1860 on health grounds.

Until her husband died, Madame Pommery had confined her attentions to her family and had no business experience whatsoever, but, like the Widow Clicquot almost half a century earlier, she stepped into her husband's shoes and did an even better job. There are many widows throughout the history of Champagne, and it almost became fashionable to append the term *veuve* to the name of a firm, but the two greatest Champagne widows were without doubt the *veuves* Clicquot and Pommery.

Madame Pommery's most notable accomplishment was, of course, the creation of a truly great *grande marque*, but she is also remembered for various specific achievements, such as her cellars, the extraordinary buildings above, and her pioneering of the brut style. It is also interesting to note that well into the second half of the 19th century, one of her first decisions was to concentrate production on sparkling, rather than still, Champagne.

When the Germans occupied Reims in the Franco-Prussian War, the Prince of Hohenhoe used the Pommery house for six months as his headquarters as the governor of the city. At a dinner, the prince remarked how pleased he was that all the civilians had at last been disarmed and, it is reputed, Madame Pommery casually produced a tiny revolver from her bag to show how wrong he was. When the Germans pleaded that she not do such a thing in the governor's house, she pointed out that it was her house, and claimed that hidden within it was her family's own arsenal. The weapons were hidden beneath the floorboards of the room in which they were dining, and she recklessly dared them to mount a search. According to the story, the silence that followed this outburst was eventually broken by Graf von Waldersee, who proclaimed], 'Madame, it is not we who disarm the ladies, it is they who disarm us!'

Shortly after the German left Reims, Madame Pommery acquired 60 hectares of land on what was known as the Butte St Niçaise. This was composed of 120 Gallo-Roman *crayères*, which she connected with a series of tunnels, forming 18 kilometres of cellars. The *crayères* were supported with Gothic- and Norman-style arches, and the chalk faces were decoratively carved in strategic places.

Above these cellars, builders set to work on an eight-year task to construct a grand house to Madame Pommery's own design. Whether she had the builders work in isolation and ignorance of one another's allotted function is not known, but the resulting strange conglomeration of towers, spires and domes in brick and stone might suggest this was so. It is said to have been inspired by the stately homes of Madame Pommery's five most important customers in England and Scotland. Those who were invited to the opening in 1878 were reported to be dumbfounded by the sight of what looked like five separate buildings stuck together to create a most magnificent folly.

Pommery claims that its 1874 Nature, which was exclusively shipped to England, was the first brut style of Champagne. It is difficult to make any judgement on the matter, but *sec,* or dry, Champagne was sold as early as 1855, and *extra-sec* by 1865. On the one hand, we might think these terms literally meant 'dry' and 'extra-dry', unlike their legal definitions today, but on the other, Champagne was initially a sweet dessert wine; thus they could merely have been relative to the accepted *dosage* of the day, and thus the reason why the modern legal limits seem such a sham.

Certainly, the term *brut* itself was not used until 1876 and England, where the 1874 was destined, was the key market in the evolution of this style. There is certainly no denying that Pommery 1874 Nature made an incomparable impact on the English from the following *Ode to Pommery 1874*, which was written by Richard John Lloyd Price, and published in *Vanity Fair* on December 27, 1894:

Farewell, then, Pommery Seventy-Four!
With reverential sips
We part and grieve that never more
Such wine may pass our lips.

In 1879, Madame Pommery married her daughter Louise to Prince Guy de Polignac, whose family could be traced back over 40 generations, through 11 centuries, to Armand I who, in 860, was Vicomte de Polignac, and known as the 'King of the Mountains' in Velay. The Polignacs are cousins of the Grimaldis of Monaco, and it was Prince Jules de Polignac who, as prime minister, pursued the ultra-royalist policy that provoked the revolution of 1830.

The house of Pommery remained in the hands of the Polignac family until 1979, when it was sold to Xavier Gardiner, who already

PRINCE ALAIN DE POLIGNAC, A DIRECT DESCENDENT OF MADAME POMMERY, IN THE POMMERY CELLARS BENEATH A FAMOUS FRESCO CARVED INTO THE LIMESTONE BY HENRI NAVET

owned Lanson. In 1984, barely a year after building a £2 million *cuverie* that still looks ultra-modern today, Gardinier sold both houses to BSN, the giant French food and beverage group, which in turn sold them on to LVMH in 1990. Prince Alain de Polignac remains Pommery's oenologist.

WINEMAKER
Thierry Gasco & Alain de Polignac
HOUSE STYLE & RANGE
Pommery's image has suffered from too high sales at too cheap prices, and the introduction of the brilliant new Apanage *cuvée* would seem to confirm this. The total production was recently almost 600,000 cases – twice the volume it was when the Polignac family sold up. The lighter the style, the harder it is to produce Champagne in large quantities, and with Pommery's light, elegant style, the increase in its sales was obviously stretching things too far. I used to wonder whether there was any strategic policy at LVMH because the obvious solution from the group's point of view would be to halve Pommery's production and double Ruinart's.

The current production of both these houses is still out of balance, but, as sales have moved in the right direction, LVMH should be given the benefit of any doubt. If the group's board of directors are themselves in any doubt, then they need only drink a few bottles of Apanage, and imagine what the image (and therefore asking price) of Pommery would be if its customers could rely on this quality of Champagne for its house non-vintage.

Pommery has a huge estate of some of the best-sited vineyards in the region, impeccable production facilities and fabulous cellars, and

its two talented winemakers, Prince Alain de Polignac and Thierry Gasco, should be allowed to express this potential without having to produce truckloads of fizz at knockdown prices. They have just shown what can be done through true selection by introducing two new seasonal *cuvées* – the fresh, delicious, lime-scented Summertime *blanc de blancs*, and Wintertime, a *blanc de noirs*, both made mostly from Pommery's own vineyards with a high percentage of *grands crus*. Cuvée Louise Pommery has already established itself as a great prestige Champagne, and has been re-launched as Louise with even classier packaging. Which only leaves one thing: to delist the Brut Royal (selling off the stocks *sur lattes*) and promote Apanage as the house non-vintage. Occasionally, the Brut Royal can be good, as it was for a while in the mid-1990s, but it is too much of a handicap for what should be one of Champagne's greatest houses. Indeed, if it did not exist, Pommery would rate an overall score in the early 90s.

★★ BRUT ROSÉ
Not vintaged, addition of red wine, méthode champenoise: 40% Chardonnay, 35% Pinot Noir, 25% Meunier
BRUT ROYAL
Not vintaged, méthode champenoise: 35% Chardonnay, 35% Pinot Noir, 30% Meunier
★★ BRUT ROYAL APANAGE
Not vintaged, méthode champenoise: 45% Chardonnay, 35% Pinot Noir, 20% Meunier
★★ SUMMERTIME BLANC DE BLANCS
Not vintaged, méthode champenoise: 100% Chardonnay
★★ BRUT MILLÉSIME
Vintaged, méthode champenoise: 50% Chardonnay, 50% Pinot Noir
★★ LOUISE
Vintaged, méthode champenoise: 60% Chardonnay, 40% Pinot Noir
★★★ LOUISE ROSÉ
Vintaged, méthode champenoise: 45% Chardonnay, 55% Pinot Noir
WINTERTIME BRUT
Vintaged, méthode champenoise: 20% Meunier, 80% Pinot Noir

85
CH & A PRIEUR
VERTUS
• 12,500 cases
• Négociant-Manipulant
Established in 1825 by Jean-Louis Prieur, it

was his sons, Charles and Alfred, who gave their initials to the firm's present title, and it was Charles' sons, the founder's grandsons, Louis-Charles and Alfred M Ernest, who conceived the Napoléon, after assuming control of the company in 1898.

The first Napoléon Champagne was a small shipment sent to Volgograd in Russia at the turn of the century, since when the Prieurs have had the sole right to use the name of Napoléon on a Champagne bottle.

WINEMAKER
Vincent Prieur

HOUSE STYLE & RANGE
The Réserve Carte Vert has improved over the years, and is now a Champagne of individual character and quality, but the Tradition Carte Or is still impressively richer and more mature, with some biscuity complexity. The Prieurs traditionally sell more mature vintages, the style of which is definitely in the Carte Or mould.

★ NAPOLÉON BRUT ROSÉ
Not vintaged, méthode champenoise:
40% Chardonnay, 60% Pinot Noir

NAPOLÉON RÉSERVE CARTE VERT DEMI-SEC
Not vintaged, méthode champenoise: 25%
Chardonnay, 8% Pinot Noir, 66% Meunier

★ NAPOLÉON RÉSERVE CARTE VERT BRUT
Not vintaged, méthode champenoise:
25% Chardonnay, 8% Pinot Noir, 66% Meunier

★ NAPOLÉON TRADITION CARTE OR BRUT
Not vintaged, méthode champenoise:
50% Chardonnay, 50% Pinot Noir

NAPOLÉON TRADITION CARTE OR DEMI-SEC
Not vintaged, méthode champenoise:
50% Chardonnay, 50% Pinot Noir

★★ NAPOLÉON BRUT
Vintaged, méthode champenoise: 45% Chardonnay,
55% Pinot Noir

RÉMY-COINTREAU

This family-owned, Cognac-based group includes Charles-Heidsieck, Piper-Heidsieck, F Bonnet and De Venoge. It also includes Krug, although Henri and Rémi Krug sit on the main board, and the running of this house is virtually autonomous.

87
R RENAUDIN
DOMAINE DES CONARDINS, MOUSSY

- 15,000 cases
- Other labels – de Lossy
- Récoltant-Manipulant

This domaine used to boast a fine *château* which was destroyed in 1799, but the owners still bear the title of *Seigneurs des Conardins*. According to Dominique Tellier, grandson of the founder, Raymond Renaudin was not related to Paul Renaudin who, with Jacques Bollinger, established Renaudin, Bollinger &

Co (the name Renaudin appeared on the Bollinger label until as recently as 1984). Tellier says that Renaudin is a common surname in the Champagne region. He and his brother Christophe own 24 hectares of vineyards and run the business on behalf of their mother. A proportion of their Champagne is produced according to strict kosher rules.

WINEMAKER
Bruno Krein

HOUSE STYLE & RANGE
An overtly rich and fruity style that has a tendency to go biscuity, Renaudin also produces age-worthy rosé.

BRUT RÉSERVE
Not vintaged, méthode champenoise:
20% Chardonnay, 10% Pinot Noir, 20% Meunier

★★ BRUT GRANDE RÉSERVE
Vintaged, méthode champenoise: 70% Chardonnay,
10% Pinot Noir, 20% Meunier

★★ BRUT ROSÉ
Vintaged, addition of red wine, méthode
champenoise: 20% Chardonnay, 10% Pinot Noir,
70% Meunier

★★ RÉSERVE SPECIALE CD
Vintaged, méthode champenoise: 80% Chardonnay,
5% Pinot Noir, 15% Meunier

87
ALAIN ROBERT
LE MESNIL-SUR-OGER

- 7,150 cases
- Récoltant-Manipulant

An old winegrowing family since the 17th century, the present incumbent owns vineyards in seven villages, but it is the Champagnes made exclusively from Le Mesnil-sur-Oger that have earned Alain Robert his fine reputation.

WINEMAKER
Alain Robert

HOUSE STYLE & RANGE
The basic non-vintage Champagnes can be overly oxidative, lacking finesse, but the vintage *cuvées* from Le Mesnil-sur-Oger itself have such an intensity of ripe, peachy fruit and exquisitely high acidity that they age far more slowly, gradually assuming a wonderfully toasty maturity.

BLANC DE BLANCS BRUT
Not vintaged, méthode champenoise: 100% Chardonnay

BLANC DE BLANCS SÉLECTION
Not vintaged, méthode champenoise: 100% Chardonnay

MESNIL SÉLECTION
Not vintaged, méthode champenoise: 100% Chardonnay

MESNIL SÉLECTION 'VIEUX DOSÉ'
Not vintaged, méthode champenoise: 100% Chardonnay

★★ CUVÉE SÉDUCTION
Vintaged, méthode champenoise: 100% Chardonnay

★★ MESNIL RÉSERVE
Vintaged, méthode champenoise: 100% Chardonnay

★★ MESNIL TRADITION
Vintaged, méthode champenoise: 100% Chardonnay

83 VALUE
THÉOPHILE ROEDERER
REIMS

- Group ownership – Louis Roederer
- Négociant-Manipulant

Originally a separate firm, Théophile Roederer was established in 1864, but purchased by the house of Louis Roederer as far back as 1907. As an independent producer, Théophile Roederer never owned any vineyards and always purchased grapes, which it still does under Louis Roederer ownership, in the form of juice from various cooperatives in the region. Although the quality of these raw materials determines Théophile's relatively modest quality and style, its *cuvées*, which are made and stored separately from those of Louis Roederer's, nevertheless benefit from the *grande marque's* expertise, making them an eminently drinkable alternative for Louis Roederer customers who happen to be strapped for cash.

96 VALUE
LOUIS ROEDERER
REIMS

- 216,700 cases
- Group ownership – also owns Deutz, Roederer Estate (California), Ramos-Pinto (Port), Château Haut-Beauséjour (St-Estèphe), Château de Pez (St-Estèphe)
- Négociant-Manipulant

The origins of this house stem from the founding in 1760 of a firm called Dubois Père & Fils, which passed into the hands of Nicolas-Henri Schreider who, in 1827, sought the assistance of his nephew Louis Roederer. The latter took over when his uncle died in 1833, and the house became known as Louis Roederer. His greatest achievement was in conquering the Russian market. The Tsar became his best customer – although this was later to rebound on the firm's fortunes.

In 1876, at the request of Alexander II, Louis Roederer's eponymous son created the now famous Cristal (then an extremely sweet style), which was presented in a special bottle of clear crystal. Louis Roederer II died suddenly in 1880, leaving the thriving business to his sister Léonie Olry, but she died eight years later, and the firm passed into the hands of her two sons, Louis-Victor and Léon, who obeyed their mother's dying wish to append Roederer to their surname.

The October Revolution of 1917 dealt a serious blow to Roederer, depriving the firm of its principal market and leaving it with the Tsar's outstanding bills, which the new regime had no intention of paying. It also left a considerable stock of sweet Champagne in very expensive, clear crystal bottles to dispose of. It took a while, but eventually the entire stock was sold to a buyer with a sweet tooth in South America.

In 1932, Léon Olry-Roederer died, and the following year his widow, Madame Camille Olry-Roederer, took control, directing the firm with great energy for a period of some 42 years. After her death, it passed to her daughter, whose son Jean-Claude Rouzaud is in charge today. Rouzaud was one of many of his generation to inherit a family-owned Champagne house but one of the few to retain that ownership, and the only one that is profitable today. He has had, of course, the advantage of a magnificent estate of vineyards, which now totals 190 hectares and represents more than 80% of the house's total needs – but then, other family-owned firms have been similarly blessed.

Louis Roederer has a tremendous reputation for quality, but again: so have others. So what has been the secret of Roederer's success?

Firstly Cristal, which has become nothing less than a licence to print money (particularly in the US); secondly, Rouzaud's penny-pinching economy, where a lick of paint and office heating are not considered strictly necessary.

WINEMAKER
Michel Pansu

HOUSE STYLE & RANGE
The Brut Premier is always a good buy for a rich, creamy, biscuity non-vintage, as is the straight vintage, and Cristal (both brut and the even more rare rosé are, of course, sublime). However, it is the *blanc de blancs* that offers Champagne buffs the biggest bargain, as some vintages of this rich and succulent *cuvée*, with its classy, complex, creamy, walnutty fruit can rival Cristal. The last time I tasted the *cuvées* side-by-side, the 1985 *blanc de blancs* was on par with the 1985 Cristal, and the 1986 was infinitely superior, although that was an atypically disappointing year for Cristal.

Cristal 2000 is a methuselah of 1990 vintage produced in a limited quantity of 2000 of these giant-sized bottles, but it is not the same *cuvée* as the regular 1990 Cristal. There is often a slight variation from the normal recipe given below, and in 1990, the regular Cristal was 42% Chardonnay, 58% Pinot Noir, while the special Cristal 2000 was a blend of 51% Chardonnay, 49% Pinot Noir. While nine per cent might not seem much overall, the selection of *crus* (Le Mesnil-sur-Oger and Avize) disproportionately emphasises the

Chardonnay. Tasting the two *cuvées* together, I thought the Cristal 2000 not only differed considerably from the regular 1990 Cristal, but was unlike any Roederer I have ever tasted – more like a pure *blanc de blancs*, but unlike Roederer *blanc de blancs*. I told Jean-Claude Rouzaud that if Prince Alain de Polignac were to create a pure *blanc de blancs* version of Pommery's Cuvée Louise, I could well imagine that it would end up tasting something like this. He was not offended, and happily accepted the allusion. Specifically, he was pleased there was such a difference between the two Cristal *cuvées*: he was, after all, selling these Methuselahs for $2,000. At least he wont have to put up with anyone suggesting they buy eight bottles of Cristal 1990 instead!

★★ BRUT PREMIER
Not vintaged, méthode champenoise:
34% Chardonnay, 62% Pinot Noir, 8% Meunier

★★☆ CARTE BLANCHE
Not vintaged, demi-sec style, méthode champenoise:
34% Chardonnay, 62% Pinot Noir, 8% Meunier

★★☆ EXTRA DRY
Not vintaged, méthode champenoise:
34% Chardonnay, 62% Pinot Noir, 8% Meunier

★★☆ GRAND VIN SEC
Not vintaged, méthode champenoise:
34% Chardonnay, 62% Pinot Noir, 8% Meunier

★★★☆ BLANC DE BLANCS
Vintaged, méthode champenoise: 100% Chardonnay

★★ BRUT MILLÉSIMÉ
Vintaged, méthode champenoise: 66% Chardonnay,
34% Pinot Noir

★★★☆ CRISTAL
Vintaged, méthode champenoise: 45% Chardonnay,
55% Pinot Noir

★★★☆ CRISTAL ROSÉ
Vintaged, addition of red wine, méthode
champenoise: 30% Chardonnay, 70% Pinot Noir

★★ ROSÉ MILLÉSIMÉ
Vintaged, addition of red wine, méthode
champenoise: 30% Chardonnay, 70% Pinot Noir

N/A
ROYER
LANDREVILLE
• 12,000 cases
• Récoltant-Manipulant
This Aubois grower owns 20 hectares of hillside vineyards outside Landreville.

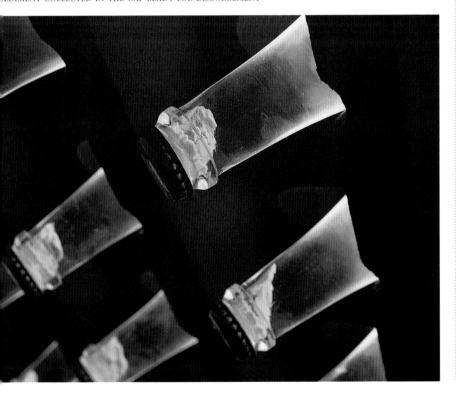

THE NECKS OF BOTTLES OF ROEDERER CRISTAL IN PUPITRES IN THE CELLARS OF LOUIS ROEDERER, WITH SEDIMENT COLLECTED IN THE CAP READY FOR DISGORGEMENT

WINEMAKER

JP Royer

HOUSE STYLE & RANGE

I have only occasionally come across these Champagnes, so I have no overall impression, but on a recent tasting I enjoyed the rich elegance of Royer's *blanc de blancs*. This demonstrates the potential of Chardonnay in the Aube, which is closer to Chablis than the rest of Champagne, and has the same soil. The Cuvée de Réserve had dull, straw-like fruit, and I was not impressed by the rosé.

★ CUVÉE BLANC DE BLANCS

Not vintaged, méthode champenoise: 100% Chardonnay

CUVÉE PRESTIGE BRUT

Not vintaged, méthode champenoise: 100% Chardonnay

CUVÉE DE RÉSERVE BRUT/DEMI-SEC

Not vintaged, méthode champenoise:
25% Chardonnay, 75% Pinot Noir

CUVÉE ROSÉ BRUT

Not vintaged, addition of red wine, méthode
champenoise: 100% Pinot Noir

91 VALUE

RUINART

REIMS

- 167,000 cases
- Group ownership - LVMH
- Négociant-Manipulant

The oldest sparkling Champagne house, established in 1729 by Nicolas Ruinart, nephew of Dom Thierry Ruinart, who was a friend and confidant of Dom Pérignon. Nicolas Ruinart started in the linen trade, and it became his custom to present his customers with Champagne as a token of goodwill, but it was so well appreciated that eventually the trade in linen was replaced by Champagne.

RUINART'S CHAIRMAN ROLAND DE CALONNE

JEAN-FRANÇOIS BAROT, CHEF DE CAVES FOR CHAMPAGNE RUINART

Ruinart's eldest grandson, Irénée, was particularly active, selling Champagne to royalty all over Europe. He also sold Ruinart to the Empress Josephine, but she refused to pay her bills after her divorce. Irénée's son, Edmond, was received by President Jackson at the White House in Washington DC, and his son Edgar opened up the Russian market in 1860. Edgar's brother Charles was a pioneer of aviation who sponsored, with others, the first cross-Channel air race.

When the firm's buildings were destroyed by shelling during the Battle of the Marne, André Ruinart literally went underground, conducting the firm's affairs from one of Ruinart's spectacular *crayères*. When further shelling flooded his cellars, he simply lashed the office furniture to a wooden platform and it was business as usual from a raft floating around a massive gallery 80 feet below ground.

In 1950, Ruinart required an injection of capital from Baron Philippe de Rothschild, and in 1963, the company was purchased by Moët & Chandon, which later became LVMH. Although sales quadrupled during its association with Rothschild, and have doubled again under LVMH, the scale of production is still relatively modest.

WINEMAKER

Jean-François Barot

HOUSE STYLE & RANGE

A Chardonnay-influenced house, Ruinart is best known for Dom Ruinart, but its basic 'R' de Ruinart *cuvées* are all too often overlooked, yet represent amazing value – especially the standard non-vintage brut, which is always rich and satisfying. The non-vintage 'R' rosé has recently been relaunched in a new, fat, upmarket bottle-shape, but the difference is not merely cosmetic, as the wine inside has more pure-tasting fruit in an impressively lighter, fresher, easier-drinking style.

The vintage 'R' tends to go very toasty, much like the Dom Ruinart, but without its class or complexity.

★★ 'R' DE RUINART BRUT

Not vintaged, méthode champenoise:
40% Chardonnay, 50% Pinot Noir, 10% Meunier

★★ 'R' DE RUINART BRUT ROSÉ

Not vintaged, addition of red wine, méthode
champenoise: 41% Chardonnay, 36% Pinot Noir,
23% Meunier

★★ 'R' DE RUINART BRUT

Vintaged, méthode champenoise: 42% Chardonnay,
58% Pinot Noir

★★★ DOM RUINART BLANC DE BLANCS

See p.121

★★★ DOM RUINART BRUT ROSÉ

See p.121

SACOTTE

See VRANKEN

N/A

LOUIS DE SACY

VERZY

- 15,000 cases
- Other labels - Laurent Dauphin
- Négociant-Manipulant

A lesser-known house belonging to a family that have been *vignerons* in Verzy since 1663. Pierre-Louis Sacy became Louis de Sacy in 1697 by royal decree from Louis XIV for his exploits fighting against the English. It was the current owner, André de Sacy, who established this small house in 1969, and he currently owns 20 hectares in five villages.

WINEMAKER

André & Alain Sacy

HOUSE STYLE & RANGE

I have been tasting these Champagnes on and off for almost 20 years and although I was not initially impressed, in the early 1990s the prestige *cuvée* Grand Soir was really quite good. Since then, however, the wines have swung from amylic to oxidative.

BRUT

Not vintaged, méthode champenoise:
40% Chardonnay, 40% Pinot Noir, 20% Meunier

ROSÉ

Not vintaged, addition of red wine, méthode
champenoise: 80% Pinot Noir, 20% Meunier

MILLÉSIMÉ

Vintaged, méthode champenoise: 30% Chardonnay,
30% Pinot Noir, 40% Meunier

GRAND SOIR

Vintaged, méthode champenoise: grape varieties
not revealed

DE SAINT GALL

See UNION AVIZE

SAINT NIÇAISE

See BAUCHET

84 VALUE
ST-RÉOL

AMBONNAY

• 40,000 cases
• Coopérative-Manipulant

Less than a quarter of this cooperative's
production is sold under the St-Réol label,
the balance being returned to the members
to sell under their own labels. There are
150 members, who collectively own 150
hectares.

WINEMAKER

René Martinet

HOUSE STYLE & RANGE

A very good range, from a gentle, easy-drinking
non-vintage brut to a very fruity straight
vintage, and the aptly named Cuvée Elégance.

★ BRUT BLANC DE BLANCS, 1ER CRU

Not vintaged, méthode champenoise:
100% Chardonnay

★ BRUT GRAND CRU

Not vintaged, méthode champenoise:
30% Chardonnay, 70% Pinot Noir

BRUT ROSÉ GRAND CRU

Not vintaged, méthode champenoise:
85% Chardonnay, 15% Pinot Noir

★ PRESTIGE D'ARGENT

Vintaged, méthode champenoise: 60% Chardonnay,
40% Pinot Noir

★☆ ELÉGANCE

Vintaged, méthode champenoise: 75% Chardonnay,
25% Pinot Noir

95
DOM RUINART

• 10,000 cases (estimated)
The most inexplicable
aspect of Ruinart is
how underrated its
wines are (*see p. 120*).
Although Champagne
aficionados know only
too well the exquisite
quality of this house, its name is one of the
least recognised by the general public,
particularly outside France. If Ruinart is
widely rated for anything, though, it is for
its prestige *cuvées* Dom Ruinart Blanc de
Blancs (first vintage: 1959) and Dom
Ruinart Rosé (first vintage: 1962). Of
these, it is the *blanc de blancs* that is best
known and has succulent ripe fruit that
develops full, toasty, smoky aromas after a
few years additional age in bottle.

Such a textbook Chardonnay, Dom
Ruinart Blanc de Blancs is more wine than
Champagne, due no doubt to its origins: a
blend of Avize, Cramant, Chouilly, Le
Mesnil-sur-Oger, Sillery and Verzenay.
The fact that almost half this *cuvée* is
produced from Chardonnay grown on the
Montagne de Reims accounts for its
exceptional weight and vinosity,
and the Burgundian tones it
acquires after maturation in
bottle.

The Dom Ruinart Rosé is,
however, at least as classy –
some years more so – with its
immediately beguiling bouquet
of red summer fruits that is so redolent of
Pinot Noir. Even for those who know the
facts well, it is difficult to believe that this
is in fact pure Dom Ruinart Blanc de
Blancs to which a small proportion of red
wine has been added. The varietal
character is so strong that few pure Pinot
Noir *cuvées* can rival it for *typicité*,
particularly after some additional ageing.

I prefer the rosé at ten or 12 years old,
when it has a superb golden-marmalade
colour, and toasty aromas are beginning to
mingle with the red fruits. At this juncture,
it goes superbly with food, especially warm
smoked-salmon dishes, but both Dom
Ruinart *cuvées*, which are exclusively *grand
cru* wines, are food wines, and the *blanc de
blancs* also benefits immensely if cellared for
three years or more after purchase.

BOTTLES HELD IN PUPITRES IN RUINART'S GALLO-ROMAN CHALK CELLARS

THE VINTAGES

★★☆ DOM RUINART BLANC DE BLANCS
100% Chardonnay

1961 ★★★	1981 ★★★
1964 ★★★	1982 ★★★
1966 ★★★	1983 ★★☆
1969 ★★★	1985 ★★☆
1973 ★★☆	1986 ★★
1975 ★★☆	1988 ★★☆
1976 ★★☆	1990 ★★★
1979 ★★★	

★★☆ DOM RUINART BRUT ROSÉ
Vintaged, addition of red wine, méthode champenoise:
80% Chardonnay, 20% Pinot Noir

1973 ★★☆
1975 ★★☆
1976 ★★★
1981 ★★★
1982 ★★☆
1986 ★★☆
1986 ★★☆
1988 ★★☆

98

SALON

LE MESNIL-SUR-OGER

- 10,000 cases
- Group ownership - Laurent-Perrier
- Négociant-Manipulant

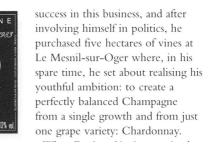

This tiny house on the Côte des Blancs is known only to the most dedicated amateurs of great Champagne. Located at Le Mesnil-sur-Oger, Salon produces just 20,000 bottles a year. When it produces anything at all, that is; it must be the only winery in the world that does not make wine every year.

Salon is a wine of very singular nature indeed: just one *cuvée* is produced and it comes from one grape variety grown in one village during one year. In years when a vintage is not declared, Salon's sister company and neighbour Delamotte gets first refusal on the grapes, after which they are used by Laurent-Perrier, its parent company, which also owns De Castellane, Lemoine, Joseph Perrier and, of course, Delamotte.

Salon was established in 1921 by Eugène-Aimé Salon, who was born in 1867 at Pocancy, a small agricultural village on the plains of Champagne, to the east of Le Mesnil-sur-Oger. Eugène-Aimé spent much of his boyhood assisting his brother-in-law, Marcel Guillaume, in his work as *chef de caves* for a small firm producing a single-vineyard Champagne called Clos Tarin. In due course Marcel was to establish a co-op called the Union des Producteurs de la Côte des Blancs.

Although Salon's boyhood experience kindled an enthusiasm for winemaking, he did not enter the trade for some years. Trained as a teacher, he rejected that profession in favour of commerce and joined a Parisian firm of furriers called Chapel. After achieving

success in this business, and after involving himself in politics, he purchased five hectares of vines at Le Mesnil-sur-Oger where, in his spare time, he set about realising his youthful ambition: to create a perfectly balanced Champagne from a single growth and from just one grape variety: Chardonnay.

When Eugène-Aimé entertained his associates, he offered them his own unlabelled Champagne; soon, he was besieged with requests for supplies, which he declined at first since he was still principally a furrier. As the requests mounted, however, he released a few bottles, business accumulated and he found himself running a Champagne firm.

Eugène-Aimé enlarged his vineyard and started buying grapes from other growers in Le Mesnil-sur-Oger. He used only the best fruit and only the *vin de cuvée*; all else was sold off. Furthermore, he only produced vintage Champagne so wines of undeclared years were also sold off. Salon appears to have been the first house to exploit commercially a *blanc de blancs* Champagne.

Salon was Maxim's house wine during the 1920s and, throughout that decade and the 1930s, it achieved its pinnacle of fame. Since Eugène-Aimé Salon died in 1943, the reputation of this exceptional Champagne has never reached the level achieved in its earlier years, although the quality of the wine has not deteriorated in the slightest.

Acquired by Besserat de Bellefon in 1963, it was re-launched as Cuvée S by Besserat's chairman, Paul Bergeot, in 1976. As Bergeot was impatient to launch Salon in the new, fatter bottle, he ordered what remained of the 1971 and 1973 vintages to be decanted, mixed with a light *liqueur de tirage* and re-bottled. This

caused a third fermentation, and was illegal, as the two *liqueurs* exceeded the maximum sugar allowed for the *liqueur de tirage*, but no one realised it at the time. There are thus 'old' and 'new' versions of the two vintages, and their merits are always fascinating to compare.

Salon was acquired by Laurent-Perrier in 1989; shortly afterwards, it came under the helm of Bertrand de Fleurian, who has done more than anyone (other than Eugène-Aimé Salon) to assure the ascendancy of this great house. At the end of 1997, de Fleurian was promoted to *directeur générale* of the entire Laurent-Perrier group for his efforts at Salon now run by Didier Depond. A smooth transition is ensured by the presence at Salon of Alain Terrier, Laurent-Perrier's *chef de caves* , and one of Champagne's most intelligent winemakers.

DECLARED VINTAGES

According to most sources, 25 vintages of Salon were produced up to and including the unreleased 1990, but an investigation of the cellars reveal no fewer than 31. This included some curiosities such as 1956, 1951 and 1925, which were very poor years – not exactly vintages to publicise – yet the 1951 Salon was a miracle.

What is strange is not so much the off-years that Salon did make, but the excellent vintages it did not. I can understand that there might not be any 1981, because although the year produced some of the very greatest Champagnes (Krug in particular), very little was made, and the quality was not even, so perhaps it was not that special for Salon. Yet why no 1975, 1970, 1962, 1945, 1933 or 1929?

ALAIN TERRIER: ONE OF CHAMPAGNE'S MOST INTELLIGENT WINEMAKERS

WHY IS SALON SO SPECIAL?

1. It is made entirely from Chardonnay grown in Le Mesnil-sur-Oger, one of the greatest and most distinctive *crus* of the Côte des Blancs.
2. Only grapes from vines in excess of 40 years old, growing on the mid-slopes, are used. The restricted yield from these vines is responsible for Salon's extraordinary intensity of fruit.
3. It is the only wine in the world that is not made every year (wines made in undeclared years go to Delamotte first, Laurent-Perrier second).
4. Normally, no malolactic fermentation is allowed, which increases potential longevity.
5. It has extended yeast contact – often ten years or more.
6. Manual disgorgement allows an additional quality check on the nose for each individual bottle.

THE VINTAGES

...URE CLASS, EXQUISITE FRUIT, AND A SUPER-SOFT MOUSSE OF MINUSCULE BEADS THAT RISE LAZILY TO THE SURFACE...
...ALON EVOLVES SO SLOWLY THAT IT NEEDS AT LEAST TEN YEARS BEFORE IT IS DRINKABLE, AND DOES NOT START TO INTEREST
...RUE ENTHUSIASTS UNTIL IT IS 20 OR 30 YEARS OLD. THEN IT DEVELOPS GREAT DEPTH AND LENGTH, WITH A MYRIAD OF
...OMPLEX AROMAS AND FLAVOURS THAT TYPICALLY INCLUDE COCONUT, MACAROONS, WALNUTS, VANILLA AND COFFEE.

1990★★★ (Not yet released) Tasted four times. Obviously exceptional, promising to be exquisite, from the elegant, flowery aromas to the beautifully ripe acidity.

1988★★★ (Not yet released) Tasted four times. Initially, the very pale 1988 had an edge over the 1990, but the latter has since demonstrated its superiority. Yet this is still a great vintage, with complex, citrus fruit that is so tight it will take time, even by Salon's standards, to unfold. When it does, it will be stunning.

1985★★★ Very fine, elegant and pure. Delightful now, but will mature gracefully for another 30 years or more.

1983★★☆ Initially firm and very brut, with a prunelike character gaving way to a creamy coconut, hazelnut and walnut complexity after a spurt of maturation in the mid-1990s. Great intensity, but evolving relatively fast and not in the same class as the '82.

1982★★★ When recently disgorged, this is very austere, with a mouth-puckering, lemony toastiness. After a few years, it assumes a luscious, peachy fruitiness, with toasty vanilla aromas and a silky finish, yet acidity keeps it fresh.

1979★★★ This still has a kernel of undeveloped extract and needs at least 20 years more.

1976★★★ Long, rich and fat, with peachy, ripe fruit, hazelnut complexity and fine acidity. Astonishing finesse, freshness.

1973★★★ Shows a seductive, flowery, hazelnut fragrance.

1973★ (Thrice-fermented, new presentation) Revitalised when first released, but is now 'older' and breaking up.

1971★★★ Beautifully à point for several years and gives the impression it will stay this way for a long time. Rich, harmonious and complex, with great finesse.

1971★★★ (Thrice-fermented, new presentation) Fresher than the original bottling when first released, but gradually growing more alike. Far more successful than the thrice-fermented '73.

1969★★★ Disappointingly coarse and oxidative when tasted in October 1994, but probably atypical as all previous bottles have been exceptionally fine, keeping fresh as a daisy due to firm acidity.

1966★★★ Walnut complexity; fine, flowery autolytic finesse and just a touch of toast. By 1997, the toastiness had increased, but this has taken so long to develop that no matter how powerful it becomes, the wine will always have finesse and never become overblown.

1966(Experimental bottling) Just after the acquisition by Besserat de Bellefon, the prospect of expanding production by turning Salon into a blend was a serious consideration. Thankfully, this disastrously dark, fat, jammy, maderised mélange of 55% Salon '66, 20% Salon '64 and 25% Pinot d'Aÿ (home of the Besserat family) put a stop to that.

1964★★★ This wine is flawless. Sumptuous, with great finesse and wonderfully rich, succulent, peachy fruit, providing enormous length and stunning youth.

1961★★★ A bottle opened in October 1994 had lost most of its fizz, but none of its life, while the same vintage tasted at Salon a few months earlier had masses of soft, lively, creamy mousse.

1959★★★ Once sensational and, apart from a couple of tastings, revealing a maderised toffee character, which I put down to bottle variation, this is still an extra-ordinary wine. Last tasted in late 1997,when it had a vanilla-tinged, coffee finesse, and seemed obscenely young!

1955★★★ In 1986, this was fresh, luscious and still in its fruit stage, despite being 30 years old. By late 1997, it had developed a toasty intensity, with a long, fruity finish and fine acidity making it seem younger than the 1966 in the same tasting.

1956Not tasted.

1952Previously thought not to have existed, but Bertrand de Fleurian reports having seen a 1952 Salon label in Berlin.

1953★★ Not tasted since 1986, but this was ageing faster than the 1955, although in a fuller, firmer style.

1951★★★ A very poor vintage in Champagne, as in everywhere else in France, yet the Salon 1951 I have tasted (June '94) showed great honeyed finesse, knocking spots off the 1949 tasted side by side. One of only three '51s I am aware of.

1949★★★ Until tasting a superb bottle in 1997, I had to go back to '87 to find a note to merit the legendary reputation of this wine. One tasted in 1994 was good, but a shadow of its stunningly rich former self. I thought it had peaked and was on a gradual decline, but it must have been an unfortunate run of bottle variation, because, tasted in 1997, it had luxurious rich fruit and toffee-caramel on the finish.

1948Tasted once, many years ago, when it was disappointing. No way of knowing whether it was a good bottle.

1947★★★ Stunning, deep, cream flavour with an indelible finish of walnuts, hazelnuts and macaroons. Ranks with the 1964.

1943Tasted once, in 1996, when it was richand complex, with huge length and fabulous finesse.

1942, 1937, 1934 Not tasted

1928★★★ Some say that 1928 is the greatest vintage of the century. I say that Salon is the greatest 1928 I have tasted.

1925 1923 1921 Not tasted.

N/A
CRISTIAN SENEZ
FONTETTE

- 187,500 cases
- Négociant-Manipulant

Cristian Senez was a cheese-maker, lumberjack and grave-digger before he purchased and planted his first hectare of vines in 1955 – just in time for the entire vineyard to be wiped out by the horrendous frosts of 1956. Nevertheless he persevered, becoming the *chef de cave* of the local co-op at Fontette, but it was not until 1973 that he produced and marketed a Champagne under his own name.

In 1985, he achieved the status of *négociant-manipulant*, and he now owns 32 hectares of all three classic varieties, mostly Pinot Noir, but also one hectare of Pinot Blanc.

WINEMAKER
Frédéric Roger

HOUSE STYLE & RANGE
Too inconsistent to have an overall rating, Cristian Senez has however produced some very interesting Champagnes, making it essential for me to follow him. Indeed, the first Champagne I ever tasted from this producer was his stunning 1981, and I bought a case. How frustrating, then, that his 1982 should be so disappointing! Since then, I have occasionally enjoyed some nice Champagnes from Senez, the most recent being his 1989 vintage, but his 1990 is too exotic, and his non-vintage Fontette Brut a curious combination of plastic and coconut. I'm still hoping for another 1981.

BRUT CARTE BLANCHE
Not vintaged, méthode champenoise:
10% Chardonnay, 90% Pinot Noir
BRUT CARTE VERTE
Not vintaged, méthode champenoise:
50% Chardonnay, 50% Pinot Noir
BRUT GRANDE RÉSERVE
Vintaged, méthode champenoise: 25% Chardonnay,
75% Pinot Noir
BRUT MILLÉSIME
Vintaged, méthode champenoise: 75% Chardonnay,
25% Pinot Noir
BRUT ROSÉ MILLÉSIME
Vintaged, addition of red wine, méthode
champenoise: 20% Chardonnay, 80% Pinot Noir

75
DE SOUSA
AVIZE

- 4,200 cases
- Récoltant-Manipulant

Although from a family of growers for three generations, the Champagnes of De Sousa & Fils were established as recently as 1986, and by husband-and-wife team Erik and Michelle, rather than father and son. They own 5.5 hectares of vineyards in Avize, Cramant and Oger, the average age of which is 30 years, with more than three-quarters being considerably older.

WINEMAKER
Erick de Sousa (James Darsonville consulting)

HOUSE STYLE & RANGE
The vintage *blanc de blancs* is usually excellent (although not the 1993), but the non-vintage *blanc de blancs* lacks finesse, as does the oxidative, floral non-vintage Tradition.

BRUT DEMI-SEC
Not vintaged, méthode champenoise:
50% Chardonnay, 40% Pinot Noir, 10% Meunier
BRUT RÉSERVE, BLANC DE BLANCS
Not vintaged, méthode champenoise: 100% Chardonnay
BRUT TRADITION
Not vintaged, méthode champenoise:
50% Chardonnay, 40% Pinot Noir, 10% Meunier
ROSÉ BRUT
Not vintaged, addition of red wine, méthode
champenoise: 92% Chardonnay, 8% Pinot Noir
★✦ BRUT MILLÉSIMÉ, BLANC DE BLANCS
Vintaged, méthode champenoise: 100% Chardonnay
CUVÉE DU MILLÉNAIRE 2000
Vintaged, méthode champenoise: 100% Chardonnay

80
PATRICK SOUTIRAN
AMBONNAY

- 3,300 cases
- Récoltant-Manipulant

From a family of five generations of *vignerons*, Patrick Soutiran started making Champagne in 1971, and currently owns three hectares of vineyards in Ambonnay and Trépail.

WINEMAKER
Patrick Soutiran

HOUSE STYLE & RANGE
Good potential, with rich, smooth, biscuity fruit, but whereas the style used to be soft and perfumed, it has recently taken on an oxidative character, which makes these Champagnes unnecessarily rustic. This needs to be toned down if the finesse is to return.

BRUT BLANC DE BLANCS
Not vintaged, méthode champenoise: 100% Chardonnay
BRUT BLANC DE NOIRS
Not vintaged, méthode champenoise: 100% Pinot Noir
BRUT ROSÉ
Not vintaged, addition of red wine, méthode
champenoise: 88% Chardonnay, 12% Pinot Noir

BRUT MILLÉSIME
Vintaged, méthode champenoise: grape varieties not revealed
BRUT PRESTIGE D'ARGENT
Vintaged, méthode champenoise: grape varieties not revealed
PRESCIEUSE D'ARGENT
Vintaged, méthode champenoise: 100% Chardonna

85
SOUTIRAN-PELLETIER
AMBONNAY

- 10,000 cases
- Other labels - Vve Victorine Mongardien Angeline Godel
- Négociant-Manipulant

From an old-established family of *vignerons*, it was Alain Soutiran who established this small house in 1955. The family also run a Champagne gift shop called La Palette de Bacchus in the centre of Ambonnay.

WINEMAKER
Alain Soutiran

HOUSE STYLE & RANGE
Best to buy this producer's wonderfully cream *blanc de blancs* and, while the Brut used to be disappointing, it is now rich and biscuity.

★★ BRUT BLANC DE BLANCS GRAND CRU
Not vintaged, méthode champenoise: 100% Chardonna
★ BRUT GRAND CRU
Not vintaged, méthode champenoise:
25% Chardonnay, 75% Pinot Noir
BRUT ROSÉ GRAND CRU
Not vintaged, addition of red wine, méthode
champenoise: 100% Pinot Noir
BRUT MILLÉSIMÉ GRAND CRU
Vintaged, méthode champenoise: 50% Chardonnay,
50% Pinot Noir

TAILLEVENT
See RENAUDIN

90 VALUE
TAITTINGER
REIMS

- 355,000 cases
- Group ownership - also owns Bouvet in Saumur and Domaine Carneros in California, as well as a French hotel chain and Baccarat crystal
- Other labels - Saint-Evremond, Irroy
- Négociant-Manipulant

This firm was originally established by Jacque

Continues on page 12

96
TAITTINGER: COMTES DE CHAMPAGNE

The *Comtes*, or Counts, of Champagne date back to the Counts of Troyes, whose existence was first recorded in the mid-ninth century and who were hereditary vassals of Burgundy by 877. When Troyes was acquired by Heribert of Vermandois in 940, he broke with Burgundy. Vermandois was also the Count of Meaux, and his two *comtés* (earldoms) plus the links by marriage to the counts of Blois and Chartres, formed the geopolitical basis of what was later to be Champagne.

The Vermandois line died out between 1019 and 1023, and Eudes II of Blois and Chartres became Count of Troyes and Meaux. Historians consider him to be Eudes I of Champagne, and thus the first Count of Champagne, although this title did not exist until 1077. It was not until the beginning of the 13th century that Champagne replaced Troyes as the primary designation.

With the death of Eudes in 1037, Troyes and Meaux were divided among his heirs, and the strength of Blois declined. Champagne was reunited with Blois in 1125 under Thibaut IV, who became Thibaut II of Champagne and was also known as Thibaut the Great. He was the most powerful man in France after the king, and a bitter rivalry developed between them. The conflicts, first with Louis VI and then with Louis VII, ended only when Joan of Navarre, heiress to the *comté* of Blois-Champagne, married the future king of France, Philip Augustus.

The next count of any significance was Thibaut IV of Champagne, son of Thibaut III and Blanche of Navarre, who was born at Troyes in 1201. After his father's death, he moved his court to Reims. Thibaut IV was a musician and probably the most famous of the aristocratic *trouvères,* the epic poets of Northern France. It was rumoured that he was the lover of Blanche of Castile, Louis VII's widow and the regent of France, and that many of his poems were addressed to her.

Champagne was prospering at this time from the great trade fairs held under the auspices of the Counts of Champagne. In times of war, Champagne's location between the Frankish and German kingdoms rendered it prone to the ravages of invading armies, but in times of peace, it was ideally situated at the crossroads to the great trade centres of Europe. Several fairs were held throughout the year; there was the 'Warm' June Fair and the 'Cold' October Fair of Troyes, the May Fair and the September Fair of St-Ayoul in Provins, the Lent Fair of Bar-sur-Aube and

TAITTINGER'S CHÂTEAU LA MARQUETTERIE, PIERRY

the January Fair of Lagny. Each fair lasted 49 days and formed a meeting place for merchants from Spain, Italy, England, the Low Countries and other parts of France. The Counts of Champagne were quick to recognise these fairs as lucrative sources of income; they consequently dropped any inhibiting feudal dues, guaranteed the safety of the merchants, and generally policed the fairs. Copious quantities of Champagne wine were consumed by such a large influx of visitors that the vineyards flourished and the *vignerons* prospered, leading to the export of both the wine and its reputation throughout the emerging markets of Europe.

Both of Thibaut's sons succeeded him, after which the line died out and his grandaughter, Joan, married Philip the Fair, who became Philip IV of France. When Joan died, the *comté* of Champagne passed to her son Louis, who united it with the crown when he became Louis X of France.

With the ancient home of the Counts of Champagne under family ownership since just after the First World War, Taittinger's use of the name *Comtes de Champagne* for a prestige *cuvée* was not unexpected. It was launched to pay homage to

Thibault IV, for he moved his court to Reims, and it is also fitting that such a classic Champagne should honour a romantic poet.

Comtes de Champagne Blanc de Blancs (first vintage: 1952) is a blend of six or seven growths, with Avize, Chouilly, Cramant, Le Mesnil-sur-Oger, Oger and Pierry the most regular constituents, so it is almost pure *grand cru* and almost pure Côte des Blancs. Unusually for a prestige *cuvée,* only half the grapes come from the producer's own vineyards, although the various sources that comprise the balance are all under long-term contract.

The wines always undergo malolactic fermentation, and a tiny percentage is matured for two or three months in new or recently used oak *barriques* (no more than five per cent, I'm informed, although some vintages give the appearance of more oak-influence than that). The style is full, lush and succulent, with wonderfully broad-textured, creamy fruit. Some vintages have shown a tendency to go very exotic with some bottle-age (1976 is a classic example, and 1989 is heading in the same direction), but it is a crime to drink this Champagne before its tenth birthday; 15 to 20 years is the optimum window to show both freshness and complexity, and the best vintages keep improving for at least 30 years.

Comtes de Champagne Rosé (first vintage: 1966) is blended exclusively from the *grands crus* of Ambonnay and Bouzy on the southern *montagne,* and made by the *saignée* method. It always possesses great potential, although it quite often neglects to display this when first released. Indeed, it can be simplistic, even dull or heavy when young, with a very noticeable *dosage* (which is no greater than that used for the *blanc de blancs*), but with age, this *cuvée* never fails to turn into a great food wine, with an amazing depth of chewy, cherry Pinot fruit.

COMTES DE CHAMPAGNE BLANC DE BLANCS	
100% Chardonnay	
1961 ★★	1979 ★★✫
1964 ★★★	1981 ★★★✫
1966 ★★✫	1983 ★★★✫
1970 ★★★✫	1985 ★★★✫
1971 ★★★	1986 ★★★✫
1973 ★★★✫	1988 ★★★✫
1975 ★★★✫	1989 ★★★✫
1975 ★★★✫	1990 ★★★
1976 ★★★	

COMTES DE CHAMPAGNE ROSÉ	
100% Pinot Noir	
1966 ★★★	1982 ★★★✫
1970 ★★★✫	1983 ★★★✫
1971 ★★★✫	1985 ★★★✫
1973 ★★★✫	1986 ★★★✫
1975 ★★★✫	1991 ★★★✫
1976 ★★★✫	
1979 ★★★✫	
1981 ★★★✫	

Fourneaux under his own name in 1743, making it the third-oldest Champagne house.

Jacques Fourneaux came from a family of important vineyard owners in Rilly-la-Montagne. He was succeeded by his son Jérôme Fourneaux, who was the constant advisor to the young widowed Nicole-Barbe Clicquot, and he blended all the Veuve Clicquot wines between 1805 and 1810.

The formative years of this house were relatively uneventful compared to the post-war period when it has enjoyed phenomenal success, having been purchased in 1932 by Pierre Taittinger from Lorraine. He changed the firm's name to Ets Taittinger Mailly & Cie and, like a number of other houses that have built up some of Champagne's most magnificent estates, he bought vineyards at a time when the economy was depressed and land was exceedingly cheap. His most notable acquisition was Château la Marquetterie, which gained its name from its history of cultivating alternating plots of black and white grapes. It was at La Marquetterie that Brother Jean Oudart made wine at the same time as Dom Pérignon and for 27 years after the famous monk's death.

In 1933, the firm was transferred from Mailly to the ancient home of the Counts of Champagne in Reims, which the Taittinger family had purchased and restored just after the First World War. It was built in the 13th century for Thibault IV, a descendant of Charlemagne and heir to the Counts of Champagne and the kingdom of Navarre. When François Taittinger took control in 1942, he moved the business to its present premises in place St-Niçaise, keeping the ancient home for special banquets and ceremonies.

The cellars at place St-Niçaise contain traces of the 13th-century St-Niçaise Abbey, which was visited by Tsar Peter the Great in 1717. These are showpiece cellars for Taittinger and are reserved for the prestige *cuvée* Comtes de Champagne, the working cellars being located in the rue de la Justice.

Claude Taittinger took the helm in 1960, since when his nephew Pierre-Emmanuel Taittinger has joined the firm as joint managing director with Philippe Court.

WINEMAKER
Maurice Morlot

HOUSE STYLE & RANGE
Taittinger has always aimed for elegance and purity of fruit, rather than character or complexity. Although the Brut Réserve has occasionally been disappointing, when it's on form, it is one of the best value *grande marque* Champagne – and this house has been on stunning form for a couple of years.

At the time of writing, the Brut Réserve shows Taittinger's typically light and elegant balance, yet the fruit is rich and creamy, with a real lusciousness that promises to go beautifully biscuity. Wedged between the volume-selling non-vintage and the famous Comtes de Champagne *(see p. 125)*, Taittinger's straight Brut Millésime is often overlooked, but while it might not be the greatest or longest-lived Champagne, it is very reliable and the best years easily improve for 12 years or more.

The Vintage Collection comprises a series of vintage Champagnes that are decorated by a selected artist each year. Only the first two releases (1978 and 1981) were different to the regular Brut Millésime, and it is not the bottle itself but the plastic cladding in which it is encased that is decorated. If the bottles were tastefully decorated and the wine blended to reflect the artist's work, then the Vintage Collection would indeed be special, but I cannot see why anyone would want to pay a hefty premium over the Brut Millésime just for some kitsch plastic.

★ BRUT CUVÉE PRESTIGE ROSÉ
Not vintaged, addition of red wine, méthode champenoise: 70% Pinot Noir, 30% Meunier

★★ BRUT MILLÉSIME
Vintaged, méthode champenoise: 40% Chardonnay, 60% Pinot Noir

★★ BRUT RÉSERVE
Not vintaged, méthode champenoise: 38% Chardonnay, 42% Pinot Noir, 20% Meunier

★★★☆ COMTES DE CHAMPAGNE BLANC DE BLANCS
Vintaged, méthode champenoise: 100% Chardonnay

★★★☆ COMTES DE CHAMPAGNE ROSÉ
Vintaged, addition of red wine, méthode champenoise: 100% Pinot Noir

★★☆ VINTAGE COLLECTION
Vintaged, méthode champenoise: 40% Chardonnay, 60% Pinot Noir

78
TARLANT
OEUILLY
- 7,500 cases
- Récoltant-Manipulant

A family of *vignerons* since 1687, the first Champagne sold under the Tarlant name was by Adrien and Julia Tarlant in 1929. The Tarlants currently own 12 hectares of vineyards spread across five Marne Valley villages. Half the range is classically presented; the other half is labelled with cheap, transparent transfers.

WINEMAKER
Jean-Mary Tarlant

HOUSE STYLE & RANGE
All straight, stainless-steel fermented Champagnes, with the exception of Cuvée Louis, which is fermented in new oak, supposedly from the Vosges, but its coconut character is more reminiscent of American oak.

BLANC DE BLANCS BRUT
Not vintaged, méthode champenoise: 100% Chardonnay

BRUT ROSÉ
Not vintaged, addition of red wine, méthode champenoise: 80% Chardonnay, 20% Pinot Noir

★ CUVÉE LOUIS BRUT
Not vintaged, barrique-fermented, méthode champenoise: 50% Chardonnay, 50% Pinot Noir

THE CELLARS OF TAITTINGER, WITHIN THE REMAINS OF THE MEDIAEVAL ABBEY OF ST NIÇAISE

RÉSERVE BRUT

Not vintaged, méthode champenoise: equal parts of Chardonnay, Pinot Noir, Meunier

RÉSERVE BRUT ZÉRO

Not vintaged, méthode champenoise: equal parts of Chardonnay, Pinot Noir, Meunier

RÉSERVE DEMI-SEC

Not vintaged, méthode champenoise: equal parts of Chardonnay, Pinot Noir, Meunier

TRADITION BRUT

Not vintaged, méthode champenoise: 30% Chardonnay, 50% Pinot Noir, 20% Meunier

PRESTIGE BRUT

Vintaged, méthode champenoise: 60% Chardonnay, 40% Pinot Noir

ROSÉ PRESTIGE BRUT

Vintaged, addition of red wine, méthode champenoise: 80% Chardonnay, 20% Pinot Noir

N/A
J DE TELMONT

DAMERY

- 110,000 cases
- Other labels - Ch de Fellecourt, H de Bellecroix
- Négociant-Manipulant

Henri Lhopital first made and sold Champagne under his family's name in 1920, but it was André Lhopital who established this firm in 1952. In the early 1980s, when most houses were experimenting with 506-bottle *gyropalettes* to automate *remuage* but were too coy to admit it (because they thought it took away some of the romance of Champagne), the Lhopital family was openly using a 4,000-bottle *gyropalette*. This house owns 30 hectares of vineyards in Cumières, Damery, Fleury-la-Rivière and Romery, but 80% of its needs from 40 different *crus* throughout the region.

WINEMAKER
Bertrand Lhopital

HOUSE STYLE & RANGE
When Serge Lhopital was the winemaker and Gilles Seveon the *chef de caves*, J de Telmont offered a consistently good product of remarkable value. The Grande Réserve was always a joy to drink – in fact, for many years I never a bad bottle, and the *blanc de blancs* was an age-worthy *cuvée* indeed. The Grand Vintage and Grand Couronnement were the only temperamental Champagnes in the range, but it was worth putting up with the off-years to pounce on such phenomenal pound-savers as the 1985 Grand Vintage and the 1992 Grand Couronnement.

Recently, the quality of the entire range has been doubtful, to put it mildly, but I don't know whether this is a temporary glitch or simply that Serge's son, Bertrand Lhopital, and *chef de caves* Monsieur Jondreville are not of the same calibre. Only time will tell. I, for one, would like to see the next generation succeed.

GRANDE RÉSERVE BRUT

Not vintaged, méthode champenoise: 34% Chardonnay, 34% Pinot Noir, 32% Meunier

GRAND ROSÉ BRUT

Not vintaged, addition of red wine, méthode champenoise: 89% Chardonnay, 11% Pinot Noir

GRAND VINTAGE BRUT

Vintaged, méthode champenoise: 40% Chardonnay, 40% Pinot Noir, 20% Meunier

BLANC DE BLANCS BRUT

Vintaged, méthode champenoise: 100% Chardonnay

CUVÉE GRAND COURONNEMENT BRUT

Vintaged, méthode champenoise: 100% Chardonnay

N/A
ALAIN THIENOT

REIMS

- 25,000 cases
- Group ownership - also owns Marie Stuart
- Other labels - Billiard, Castille, Petitjean
- Négociant-Manipulant

Alain Thienot used to be a successful Champagne broker. He took over Champagne Castille (on which he cut his teeth) before launching his own brand in 1980. He then concentrated all his efforts on establishing Champagne Alain Thienot, with little enthusiasm for his other three brands, which were serviced rather than promoted.

Thienot built a brand-new winery that cannot be missed when entering Reims by autoroute from Châlons-sur-Marne but, despite having produced some very good *cuvées*, he has discovered just how hard it is to establish a Champagne house in modern times. In 1994, he purchased Marie Stuart and, although Thienot is unlikely to relegate his eponymous *marque* to the secondary status of Billiard, Castille and Petitjean, I wouldn't be surprised to see it go on the back burner for a while.

WINEMAKER
Laurent Fedou

HOUSE STYLE & RANGE
Even when these Champagnes were on top form, they always performed better on export markets such as the UK, where the wines were more mature and the well-focused fruit was underscored by rich, toasty bottle-aromas. In France, they have seemed much less impressive, but there has been considerable inconsistency throughout the range over the last five years or so. This has

coincided with Thienot's pursuit and purchase of Marie Stuart, yet he does not appear to have ignored this range (which has been smartly repackaged), and he has been dabbling with some new oak. Currently, the position is confused and the fairest I can be is to withhold overall judgement of this brand until Thienot knows where he is going with Marie Stuart.

BRUT

Not vintaged, méthode champenoise: 30% Chardonnay, 45% Pinot Noir, 25% Meunier

BRUT

Vintaged, méthode champenoise: 40% Chardonnay, 60% Pinot Noir

BRUT GRANDE CUVÉE

Vintaged, méthode champenoise: 40% Chardonnay, 60% Pinot Noir

BRUT ROSÉ

Vintaged, méthode champenoise: 40% Chardonnay, 50% Pinot Noir, 10% Meunier

86
MARCEL TRIOLET

BETHON

- 2,500 cases
- Récoltant-Manipulant

One of the very best growers in the Sézannais, Marcel Triolet owns nine hectares of vines, nearly all of which are Chardonnay.

WINEMAKER
Marcel Triolet

HOUSE STYLE & RANGE
The biscuity complexity of these wines puts them at the very top of Sézannais Champagnes. Triolet's style – which is more classic than the local tendency for overtly fruity Champagne – used to be creamy-biscuity, but in recent years, it has taken on a more oxidative biscuitiness which should be toned down.

★ BRUT

Not vintaged, méthode champenoise: 80% Chardonnay, 15% Pinot Noir, 5% Meunier

★★ BRUT SÉLECTION

Not vintaged, méthode champenoise: 100% Chardonnay

80
TROUILLARD

EPERNAY

- 20,000 cases
- Other labels Charles Collin, Defontsoyes, Fleur de Muret
- Négociant-Manipulant

Bertrand Trouillard is from the same family that owns Beaumet, Oudinot and Jeanmaire, but when they split from the family firm in 1980, Bertrand and his father René continued trading under the family name. One year later, they sold the firm to Joseph Henriot, who stripped it of much of its stock, selling the brand on to Navigation Mixte in 1983, which sold it one year later to Bertrand Trouillard. It has been under family ownership ever since.

WINEMAKER
Bertrand Trouillard

HOUSE STYLE & RANGE
Remarkably similar to Beaumet, *et al.*

BLANC DE BLANCS BRUT
Not vintaged, méthode champenoise: 100% Chardonnay

DIAMANT BRUT
Not vintaged, méthode champenoise: 40% Chardonnay, 60% Pinot Noir

EXTRA SÉLECTION BRUT
Not vintaged, méthode champenoise: 30% Chardonnay, 40% Pinot Noir, 30% Meunier

★✦ CUVÉE FONDATEUR BRUT
Vintaged, méthode champenoise: 100% Chardonnay

DIAMANT BRUT
Vintaged, méthode champenoise: 40% Chardonnay, 60% Pinot Noir

GRANDE RÉSERVE BRUT
Vintaged, méthode champenoise: 40% Chardonnay, 60% Pinot Noir

85 VALUE
UNION CHAMPAGNE
AVIZE
- 100,000 cases
- Other labels - René Florancy, Lechere, Chevalier de Melline, Pierre Vaudon, de Saint Gall, Veuve de Medts
- Coopérative-Manipulant

Established as recently as 1966, this super-cooperative comprises ten cooperatives with a combined membership of 1,200 growers owning 1,000 hectares, more than 80 per cent of which is on the Côte des Blancs. In total, Union Champagne processes the equivalent of almost one million cases, but most of this is produced directly for various large houses, particularly Moët & Chandon and Mercier, with 'just' 100,000 sold under the cooperative's own labels, of which de Saint Gall, the largest-selling brand, accounts for some 20%.

WINEMAKER
Alain Coharde

VIEW FROM UNION CHAMPAGNE VINEYARDS TOWARDS AVIZE

HOUSE STYLE & RANGE
In general, these Champagnes are made in an easy-drinking style, with plenty of light, fresh, sweet, ripe fruit. The vintage *cuvées* can attain a lovely creamy, biscuity richness that makes them splendid value for money. In certain years, such as 1985, Cuvée Orpale is a class act of great magnitude.

BRUT BLANC DE BLANCS
Not vintaged, méthode champenoise: 100% Chardonnay

BRUT DEMI-SEC
Not vintaged, méthode champenoise: 60% Chardonnay, 40% Pinot Noir

BRUT ROSÉ
Not vintaged, addition of red wine, méthode champenoise: 85% Chardonnay, 15% Pinot Noir

✦ BRUT SÉLECTION
Not vintaged, méthode champenoise: 60% Chardonnay, 40% Pinot Noir

★ BRUT BLANC DE BLANCS
Vintaged, méthode champenoise: 100% Chardonnay

★★ CUVÉE ORPALE BLANC DE BLANCS
Vintaged, méthode champenoise: 100% Chardonnay

VANDER GUCHT
See MONTAUDON

PIERRE VAUDON
See UNION CHAMPAGNE

N/A
MARCEL VAUTRAIN
DIZY
- 2,500 cases
- Récoltant-Manipulant

I know very little about the background of this grower, although I have come across the odd bottle during the last 15 years or so.

WINEMAKER
M Vautrain

HOUSE STYLE & RANGE
I do not know these Champagnes well enough to give an overall mark but, apart from the occasional encounter, I did manage to taste three wines recently. The Cuvée Prestige was rather foursquare, but under blind conditions, hundreds of wines apart, I noted a distinctive apricot quality in the other two *cuvées*. Unfortunately, the Grande Réserve was spoilt by an unpleasant plastic aroma, and the very jammy apricot fruit in the 1990 was marred by a coarse, oxidative character.

BRUT CUVÉE PRESTIGE
Not vintaged, méthode champenoise: 100% Chardonnay

BRUT GRANDE RÉSERVE BLANC DE BLANCS
Not vintaged, méthode champenoise: 100% Chardonnay

BRUT RÉSERVE BLANC DE BLANCS
Not vintaged, méthode champenoise: 100% Chardonnay

CARTE BLANCHE BRUT
Not vintaged, méthode champenoise: grape varieties not revealed

CARTE BLANCHE DEMI-SEC
Not vintaged, méthode champenoise: grape varieties not revealed

BRUT MILLÉSIME
Vintaged, méthode champenoise: 75% Chardonnay, 20% Pinot Noir, 5% Meunier

85
VAZART-COQUART
CHOUILLY
- 6,500 cases
- Récoltant-Manipulant

I had lost touch with this grower until 1995, when Martin Brown of The Grape Shop in Boulogne reintroduced me via an excellent bottle of 1988 Grand Bouquet. I first came across Vazart-Coquart in 1983, when I tasted an old 1957-based, non-vintage version of Grand Bouquet. Chouilly has never been one of my favourite growths (I never understood why it was elevated to *grand cru* when the significantly superior Mareuil-sur-Aÿ was not), 1957 was a lousy year, the wine was 26 years old, I had never heard of Vazart-Coquart and grower Champagnes were generally much poorer in those days, so you can imagine I was not expecting much. But I was charmed by this soft, stylish and very honeyed old Champagne.

WINEMAKER
Jacques Vazart

HOUSE STYLE & RANGE
Capable at the top end of rich, satisfying, creamy, biscuity Champagne of real quality.

BRUT RÉSERVE
Not vintaged, méthode champenoise: 100% Chardonnay

BRUT ROSÉ
Not vintaged, méthode champenoise: 90% Chardonnay, 10% Pinot Noir

★★ GRAND BOUQUET
Vintaged, méthode champenoise: 100% Chardonnay

✓A
JEAN VELUT
MONTGUEUX
● 1,700 cases
● Récoltant-Manipulant

Five generations of the Veluts family have been *vignerons* at Montgueux, near Troyes, the ancient capital of Champagne, but the first person to make and sell Champagne rather than grapes was Jean Velut in 1976. His son, Denis, runs the business today.

WINEMAKER
Denis Velut

HOUSE STYLE & RANGE
I have only just encountered this small grower, so cannot make any overall judgement, but I found the basic non-vintage brut very rustic, and although the Cuvée Spéciale initially showed plenty of creamy fruit, it left an unpleasant aftertaste.

BRUT
Not vintaged, méthode champenoise:
75% Chardonnay, 25% Pinot Noir

BRUT BLANC DE BLANCS, CUVÉE SPÉCIALE
Not vintaged, méthode champenoise: 100% Chardonnay

DEMI-SEC
Not vintaged, méthode champenoise:
75% Chardonnay, 25% Pinot Noir

ROSÉ
Not vintaged, addition of red wine, méthode
champenoise: 70% Pinot Noir, 30% Meunier

85 VALUE
DE VENOGE
ÉPERNAY
● 90,000 cases
● Group ownership - Rémy-Cointreau
● Négociant-Manipulant

Established in 1837 by Henri-Marc de Venoge at Mareuil-sur-Aÿ, the firm moved to Épernay in 1839. The de Venoge family was of Swiss origin and took its name from the river that flows into Lake Geneva.

This house achieved its greatest success between 1845 and 1869, under Henri's son Joseph, who cultivated the custom of various young European princes to go on shooting picnics. The story is that these princes, being such highborn folk, were reluctant to see their Champagne served in common bottles, so they asked for it to be bottled in crystal decanters. If you think this sounds familiar (Roederer Cristal), then join the queue, but unlike the other better-known story, you won't find any documentary evidence to back this one up. We're just supposed to swallow it, which I wouldn't mind except that the bottle in which the excellent Champagne des Princes is commercialised in is awfully kitsch.

THE HEADQUARTERS FOR DE VENOGE ON THE AVENUE DE CHAMPAGNE, EPERNAY

De Venoge has had several owners in recent years, and not one of them has had the sense to repackage this *cuvée*, yet the bottles are costly, and due to their teardrop shape, they are very awkward and expensive to handle.

In January 1981, the Trouillard-de-Venoge group was sold to Joseph Henriot; two years later, it was sold on to Navigation Mixte. De Venoge has never been considered a classic Champagne house, and its owners have never pretended to make great wines (although the Champagne des Princes sometimes has been). Yet under Navigation Mixte's Thierry Mantoux, it gained a reputation as a consistent producer of well-made, good-value fizz.

Navigation Mixte, however, felt Mantoux received more coverage than De Venoge, and promoted him sideways to become the area manager of one of its sugar factories. The ultimate sweetener, no doubt, but Navigation Mixte failed to realise that De Venoge received no attention prior to the arrival of their self-promoting managing director.

The gossip under Navigation Mixte was that De Venoge was for sale, but the huge investment in renovating its premises on the avenue de Champagne, and installing a brand-new *cuverie* gave the impression that its corporate owner had at least got one thing right: it realised the Champagne business is cyclical, and buying a house is a long-term investment. Not so, apparently. After the removal of Mantoux, De Venoge seemed to be directionless and in 1996 was purchased by the Rémy-Cointreau group. Quite why Rémy-Cointreau wanted to buy what is described as a 'challenger' brand, when it already had Champagne Ferdinand Bonnet earmarked for that role, was

a bit of a mystery, although rumour had it that both Navigation Mixte and Rémy-Cointreau shared the same bank, Rémy-Cointreau wanted to invest heavily in its other houses, and the bank wanted to make sure the future of De Venoge was assured.

WINEMAKER
Eric Lebel

HOUSE STYLE & RANGE
The basic Cordon Bleu has improved enormously, and is now a quaffing, fruity style that quickly develops a nice, creamy richness. The vintage is richer, tending to go creamy/biscuity with toasty, floral aromas. The *blanc de blancs* is a traditional favourite of the British market, where older stocks are usually found and anyone doubting the potential quality and longevity of Champagne des Princes should try a mature bottle at Chez Pierrot in Épernay. I still have 1979 and 1976 in my cellar.

★ CORDON BLEU BRUT SELECT
Not vintaged, méthode champenoise:
25% Chardonnay, 50% Pinot Noir, 25% Meunier

★ CORDON BLEU DEMI-SEC
Not vintaged, méthode champenoise:
25% Chardonnay, 50% Pinot Noir, 25% Meunier

★ ROSÉ PRINCESSE
Not vintaged, addition of red wine, méthode
champenoise: 20% Chardonnay, 60% Pinot Noir,
20% Meunier

★★ BLANC DE BLANCS
Vintaged, méthode champenoise: 100% Chardonnay

★ BLANC DE NOIRS
Vintaged, méthode champenoise: 80% Pinot Noir,
20% Meunier

★★ CHAMPAGNE DES PRINCES
Vintaged, méthode champenoise: 100% Chardonnay

★★☆ MILLÉSIMÉ

Vintaged, méthode champenoise: 15% Chardonnay, 68% Pinot Noir, 17% Meunier

85
GEORGES VESSELLE
BOUZY

- 12,000 cases
- Récoltant-Manipulant

Georges Vesselle used to manage Mumm's vineyards (the quality of which has never been in doubt), but also established his own grower brand in 1951. He currently owns 17.5 hectares of vineyards, primarily Pinot Noir and mostly in Bouzy.

WINEMAKER

Georges Vesselle

HOUSE STYLE & RANGE

Perfumed Pinot Noir aromas, the fruit requires a little bottle-age to lengthen on the palate and gradually builds toasty aromas over the richness of this fruit. The vintage Champagnes are brilliant at the table, particularly with uncomplicated meat dishes.

★ BRUT GRAND CRU

Not vintaged, méthode champenoise: 10% Chardonnay, 90% Pinot Noir

★ BRUT ROSÉ GRAND CRU

Not vintaged, méthode champenoise: 10% Chardonnay, 90% Pinot Noir

★★☆ BRUT GRAND CRU

Vintaged, méthode champenoise: 10% Chardonnay, 90% Pinot Noir

★★ BRUT GRAND CRU JULINE

Vintaged, méthode champenoise: 10% Chardonnay, 90% Pinot Noir

★ BRUT ZÉRO GRAND CRU

Vintaged, méthode champenoise: 10% Chardonnay, 90% Pinot Noir

N/A
JEAN VESSELLE
BOUZY

- 7,000 cases
- Négociant-Manipulant

Well known, and at least as good as Georges Vesselle. Possibly has potential to be one of the greatest producers in Bouzy.

WINEMAKER

Delphine Vesselle

HOUSE STYLE & RANGE

These wines have always been rich, mature and distinctive, but Delphine Vesselle has yet to establish her own track record.

BRUT

Not vintaged, méthode champenoise: 100% Pinot Noir

BRUT OEIL DE PERDRIX

Not vintaged, méthode champenoise: 100% Pinot Noir

BRUT

Vintaged, méthode champenoise: 100% Pinot Noir

BRUT ROSÉ

Vintaged, méthode champenoise: 100% Pinot Noir

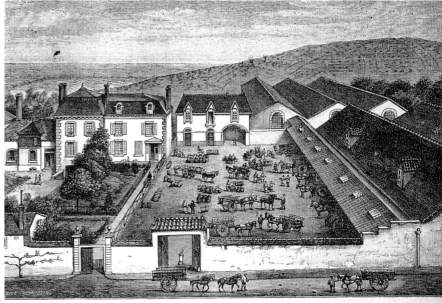

Fig. 7. — Vendangerie de Verzenay.

ANTIQUE POSTCARD SHOWING THE CLICQUOT ESTATE (ABOVE) AND A DRAWING OF LA GRANDE DAME (BELOW)

91
VEUVE CLICQUOT PONSARDIN
REIMS

- 83,000 cases
- Group ownership – LVMH
- Négociant-Manipulant

This house dates its founding from 1772, when Philippe Clicquot Muiron opened a trading house in Reims, dealing mainly in fabrics and banking with very modest transactions concerning Champagne. The total Clicquot production in those early years amounted to some 5,000 bottles, made from six hectares of vines at Bouzy and Ambonnay. In 1799, Clicquot's son, François, married Nicole-Barbe Ponsardin, daughter of a famous baron, and it soon became evident that François' preference was for wines, not drapery or banking.

A daughter, Clementine, was born in 1800, but five years later François died, aged only 30, after suffering malignant fever for two weeks. His father had retired four years earlier and was too heartbroken to run the business again, especially in the wake of the disastrous harvest of 1805. He wanted to sell up, but Madame Clicquot had no intention of doing so, taking control of the company and running it in quite the most remarkable way.

She not only ran things with a degree of skill that would have pleased and probably amazed her late husband, she made Veuve Clicquot into a *grande marque* that was second to none. She died peacefully at her luxurious Château de Boursault in 1866, aged 88, leaving

the business to Edouard Werlé (very sensibly, *see* LA GRANDE DAME, p. 131).

In 1884, the house of Clicquot passed to Edouard's son Alfred, who had married the grandaughter of the Duc de Montebello. For 50 years, the firm was controlled by Alfred's son-in-law, Comte Bertrand de Mun, whose own son-in-law, Comte Bernard de Vogüé, ran Clicquot until Joseph Henriot's so-called reverse-takeover, which brought the house into the LVMH group, where it is skilfully run by Philippe Pascal.

WINEMAKER

Jacques Peters

HOUSE STYLE & RANGE

I once wrote, 'The greatest tribute I can pay Veuve Clicquot is to say that this house is proof it is possible to sell eight million bottles a year and still maintain the highest

Continues on page 133

HARVESTING THE GRAPES IN THE 19TH CENTURY

96
VEUVE CLICQUOT: LA GRANDE DAME

Champagne's greatest *dame* was Nicole-Barbe Clicquot-Ponsardin whose husband died in 1805 after just seven years of marriage, thereby thrusting an inexperienced, 27-year-old woman into one of the most competitive, male-dominated businesses of the times. She not only turned out to be an astute merchant, but one of Champagne's greatest entrepreneurs and innovators.

In the wake of Napoleon's defeats, yet before peace was finally achieved, the house of Clicquot took the calculated risk of shipping the 1811 vintage to Russia through the Allied blockade in 1814, although it was her late husband's principal associate, Louis Bohne, who took the physical risk of accompanying the shipment. At Bohne's first stop, Königsberg in Prussia, he wrote in a letter dated July 1814: *'They worship my wine... of all the wines that have turned Northern heads, the cuvée of Madame Clicquot's 1811 has no equal. Delicious to taste, it is a real assassin, and whoever wishes to know it should tie themselves to the chair, otherwise they may find themselves under the table with the crumbs!'*

Prior to this, Bohne had severely criticised the quality of Madame Clicquot's Champagne: *'This is a terrible thing that gets up and goes to bed with me: toad's eyes! I like large eyes everywhere, except in Champagne.'* But in 1810, when the firm was on a good financial footing, Madame Clicquot relinquished the services of Jérôme Fourneaux, another associate of her late husband (the principal one, in fact) and engaged a skilful *chef de caves* by the name of Antoine Müller.

The departure of Fourneaux and the arrival of Müller thus marked a dramatic change in the quality – and thereby an increase in the reputation – of Champagne Clicquot, but Müller was also instrumental in developing the system of *remuage*, which the Clicquots had been working on since at least 1806. According to Alfred Werlé, the son of Comte Edouard Werlé (an employee of Madame Clicquot's since 1821 and her partner from 1831), it was Antoine Müller who, in 1818, hit upon the supreme importance of cutting the holes in the racks in such a way that the bottles undergoing *remuage* are racked at an angle of 45 degrees.

Madame Clicquot's daughter Clementine married the penniless Comte Louis de Chevigné in 1817 – not a wise choice, but both mother and daughter were charmed by the Comte's personality and felt sorry for his circumstances (his father had been killed

during the royalist rising in the Vendée and his mother thrown into prison with her six children, including the newborn Louis). Although Louis de Chevigné had been denied the grandeur to which his birth should have entitled him before the Revolution, he had been well-trained by his mentor, Richard Castel, in the practice of extravagant living, and the art of ingratiating himself into the company of those who could afford to pay for such luxuries. Married to Clementine and ensuring that he was adored by his mother-in-law, he had secured a bottomless cash-box from which to meet his gambling debts and pay his other excessive expenses.

It was upon Chevigné's urging that Madame Clicquot purchased and lavishly renovated the Château de Boursault. She would probably have been led into many other reckless ventures had it not been for Edouard Werlé. In 1828, a famous bank in Paris (with which the Clicquot capital was deposited) collapsed. Without disclosing his intention to Madame Clicquot, Werlé set off to the city to trade in his own private fortune to pay off the creditors, who had

started demanding immediate settlement of their debts. Although rich, Werlé was merely an employee, but when the widow heard of this gesture, she made him a partner and put him in charge of the day-to-day running of the house.

Now it was the sombre-faced Werlé who Louis de Chevigné had to approach when he wanted money, not his adoring mother-in-law. The amount of money going into Chevigné's pocket was drastically reduced, but, although this enabled the house of Clicquot to prosper, it did not completely foil the wiley Comte. He set about writing a rather risqué book of poems entitled *Les Contes Rémois*, which he reprinted every time he required some money, knowing his mother-in-law would buy up each edition to keep such licentious work off the bookstalls!

The first vintage of La Grande Dame was 1969, launched in 1977 to celebrate the firm's bicentenary, and the grapes used come exclusively from the eight *grand cru* vineyards originally owned by the great lady herself in Ambonnay, Avize, Aÿ-Champagne, Bouzy, Le Mesnil-sur-Oger, Oger, Verzenay and Verzy. La Grande Dame has always been one of the greatest prestige *cuvées*, but suffered from the image presented by its dumpy, waisted bottle until Joseph Henriot re-launched the 1985 with its current stylish bottle. There were two versions of 1985: one in the old bottle, which was excellent as usual; and one in the new bottle, which was even better, with more elegance and finesse.

In fact, it is the extra dimension of elegance and finesse that differentiates this *cuvée* in general from Veuve Clicquot vintage. La Grande Dame Rosé is the same blend as the original brut *cuvée* to which is added up to 15% of red wine made from one of Clicquot's top Bouzy vineyards, Clos Colin. It is very early days, but the vintages produced so far rank among the very greatest rosé Champagnes ever made, in a style that is all succulence and finesse.

LA GRANDE DAME	
40% Chardonnay, 60% Pinot Noir	
1973 ★★✰	1985 ★★✰
1975 ★★✰	1988 ★★✰
1976 ★★✰	1989 ★★★
1979 ★★✰	1990 ★★★
1983 ★★✰	

LA GRANDE DAME ROSÉ
38% Chardonnay, 62% Pinot Noir
1988 ★★★
1990 ★★★

95
VILMART & CIE

RILLY-LA-MONTAGNE

- 7,500 cases
- Other labels - R Vilmart
- Récoltant-Manipulant & Négociant-Manipulant

The Vilmarts have been *vignerons* in Rilly-la-Montagne for generations and produced Champagne under their own name as early as 1890, achieving their current superstar status relatively recently.

When I first tasted Vilmart in the early 1980s it was nothing special, but by 1991 I was declaring it to be 'the greatest grower Champagne I know' (*WINE* magazine). I have since tasted wines made before my first acquaintance with this grower to see if I missed any promise of the quality to come, but I did not. The sea-change must have occurred in the mid-1980s to be noticeable at the turn of that decade, but what caused it I am still struggling to comprehend. All I can say is that it coincided with the culmination of René Champs' winemaking experience.

René is still the owner (his wife was born a Vilmart), and was at that time the winemaker. He is an artist and craftsman of great skill and fastidious patience, as can be gleaned from his home he built from scratch, right down to the stained-glass windows, each of which took him 200 hours to create. The house is full of the results of his artistic passion. I can imagine him being a bit like Dom Pérignon, who was determined to master every facet of the winemaker's art. Perhaps by the mid-1980s everything just clicked.

Vilmart owns 11 hectares, which are all farmed bio-dynamically, but it is the restricting of the yield that is the basis of this grower's great quality, and this potential has always been there, even if it was not fully exploited until 15 years ago. In the cellars are large, 5,000-litre, oval-shaped wooden casks that one might see in Germany or Alsace, but not Champagne, although since 1989 there has also been the presence of more and more new 225-litre barriques. All *cuvées* are oak-fermented, but only the top wines are *barrique*-fermented, and they are not filtered, although they do undergo a light fining.

WINEMAKER

Laurent Champs

HOUSE STYLE & RANGE

It is the small yields of northern *montagne* fruit that provide immense richness of fruit with a degree of ripe acidity that electrifies some of Vilmart's *cuvées*. The Brut Réserve and *blanc de blancs* are for current drinking and are full of unashamed, upfront creamy fruit. They might age, but with every other *cuvée* in the range having great potential longevity, why bother to find out?

The Grand Cellier is where the complexity and true ageing potential in the Vilmart range begins, with its classic structure of fine fruit and a slow-building biscuitiness. Forget the fact that it is non-vintage; just make a note on the bottle when it was purchased and lay it down for a few years.

With the launch of Coeur de Cuvée, the Grand Cellier d'Or seldom gets the attention it deserves, but this was the top of the range when I first declared Vilmart to be the greatest grower Champagne I knew and the quality has not dropped – although it has become vintaged (1988 being the first). Grand Cellier d'Or matures into a mini-Krug, whereas the new oak influence in Coeur de Cuvée creates a Champagne that has nothing in common with the famous *grande marque*. *Coeur de cuvée* means 'heart of the *cuvée*', and that is literally what this is because from every 2000 litres of *vin de cuvée* produced, Vilmart plucks out the very best 800 litres and vinifies it in small *barriques* of new oak. The first vintage was 1989, which at the time of writing had only just lost the heavy, oxidative character that had spoilt the wine when first released. It is now showing beautiful finesse and obviously should have been released after the 1990, which is an even better wine, but has always been accessible. The 1990 Coeur de Cuvée is one of the three greatest Champagnes made in the last 25 years, with its fabulously rich, creamy, brioche nose, and fruit that is incredibly luscious due to the huge, ripe acidity having been skilfully balanced by a generous *dosage* (a lesson to sparkling wine producers everywhere: never be frightened to use a large *dosage* if it is balanced, and never de-acidify).

Vilmart got carried away with new oak in the 1991 (a learning curve no doubt), but it should not have been disgorged until 2001, and my advice to anyone in possession of this vintage is to leave it in the cellar as long as possible, because the more post-disgorgement aromas there are, the less oakiness that will show through.

However, in comparison to Vilmart's 1990 Cuvée Création, the 1991 Coeur de Cuvée could have been vinified in stainless steel! The new oak in this special *cuvée* is so dominant that it tastes like an Australian Chardonnay with bubbles, and having now tasted it five times, I am convinced that the oakiness is increasing. In a New World fizz tasting I might well give this a very high score, qualified by the comment 'for its type', but it is so far off the wall for Champagne, and the base wine so unlike anything else in the current Vilmart range, that I must reserve judgement and follow this wine's development over the next four or five years.

★ BLANC DE BLANCS BRUT
Vintaged, méthode champenoise: 100% Chardonnay

★ BRUT RÉSERVE
Vintaged, méthode champenoise: 80% Chardonnay, 20% Pinot Noir

★★★ COEUR DE CUVÉE
Vintaged, méthode champenoise: 80% Chardonnay, 20% Pinot Noir

CUVÉE CRÉATION
Vintaged, méthode champenoise: 80% Chardonnay, 20% Pinot Noir

★★ GRAND CELLIER
Vintaged, méthode champenoise: 80% Chardonnay, 20% Pinot Noir

★★★ GRAND CELLIER D'OR
Vintaged, méthode champenoise: 80% Chardonnay, 20% Pinot Noir

SHAKING BOTTLES OF LA GRANDE DAME BEFORE PUTTING THEM INTO PUPITRES IN THE OLD GALLO-ROMAN CHALK CRAYÈRES OF REIMS

quality.' Well, now it is selling ten million bottles and the quality has never been better.

You will have to lay down the non-vintage for two or three years in order to obtain the biscuity complexity for which Clicquot is so well-known. Veuve Clicquot vintage needs food to accompany it when first released, and requires at least two years for its complexity to start revealing itself. Unlike the non-vintage, this *cuvée* has a tendency to go toasty rather than biscuity, and, contrary to the reputation Veuve Clicquot has for making big, rich vintages of great longevity, it does not rank among Champagne's longest-lived. Apart from a few notable exceptions (1961, 1955, 1949, 1929 and – to a lesser extent – 1921), Veuve Clicquot vintages usually show their most finesse between ten and 20 years old. However, this does not mean it is not a great Champagne. Indeed, some years can be superior to Veuve Clicquot's Grande Dame, albeit by a hair's breadth; the most recent of these include 1979 and 1973.

★★☆ BRUT
Not vintaged, méthode champenoise: 30% Chardonnay, 55% Pinot Noir, 15% Meunier

★ DEMI-SEC
Not vintaged, méthode champenoise: 30% Chardonnay, 55% Pinot Noir, 15% Meunier

★★ RICH RÉSERVE
Vintaged, méthode champenoise: 33% Chardonnay, 67% Pinot Noir

★★ ROSÉ RÉSERVE
Vintaged, addition of red wine, méthode champenoise: 28% Chardonnay, 72% Pinot Noir

★★ VINTAGE RÉSERVE
Vintaged, méthode champenoise: 33% Chardonnay, 67% Pinot Noir

★★☆ LA GRANDE DAME BRUT
See p.131

★★☆ LA GRANDE DAME ROSÉ
See p.131

N/A
VILMART PERE & FILS
RILLY-LA-MONTAGNE
• Récoltant-Manipulant

Not be confused with Vilmart & Cie, this is the grower Champagne of Franck Vilmart. Not tasted recently.

60
VOLLEREAUX
PIERRY
• 33,000 cases
• Other labels – Domaine Corrigot
• Négociant-Manipulant
A low-profile, family-owned house that owns 40 hectares of vineyards.

WINEMAKER
Pierre Vollereaux

HOUSE STYLE & RANGE
Not very impressive generally.

BRUT
Not vintaged, méthode champenoise: equal parts Chardonnay, Pinot Noir, Meunier

BRUT BLANC DE BLANCS
Not vintaged, a blend of three consecutive years, méthode champenoise: 100% Chardonnay

BRUT ROSÉ
Not vintaged, méthode champenoise: 100% Pinot Noir

BRUT
Vintaged, méthode champenoise: too variable to average

CUVÉE MARGUERITE BRUT
Vintaged, méthode champenoise: 25% Chardonnay, 75% Pinot Noir

N/A
VRANKEN
EPERNAY
• Négociant-Manipulant
Paul-François Vranken is one of the cleverest businessmen in Champagne, having built up a small empire from virtually nothing. In addition to Champagnes sold under the Vranken label, he also owns Barancourt, Demoiselle, Charles Lafitte, Charbaut and, his latest acquisition, Heidsieck & Co Monopole. He owns subsidiaries in his native Belgium, produces Port under the Quinta do Convento, Quinta do Paco, and São Pedro labels in Portugal, and Señora & Vranken Cavas in Spain, where he also produces Santora under a joint venture with Seagram.

DID YOU KNOW?

THE MAXIMUM YIELD FOR CHAMPAGNE IS CONTROLLED ON AN ANNUAL BASIS BUT MUST NEVER BE IN EXCESS OF 13,000KGS PER HECTARE OR 83 HECTOLITRES PER HECTARE

OTHER FRENCH SPARKLING WINES

THE 'SECRET' OF PUTTING BUBBLES INTO WINE LEAKED OUT FROM CHAMPAGNE INTO MOST WINE REGIONS OF FRANCE IN ABOUT 1820. THERE ARE VAGUE CLAIMS THAT SPARKLING WINES WERE PRODUCED IN THE JURA IN THE 18TH CENTURY, BUT THEY ARE UNSUBSTANTIATED. IT IS GENERALLY THOUGHT THAT JEAN ACKERMAN WAS THE FIRST TO MAKE A FRENCH FIZZ OUTSIDE OF THE FAMOUS CHAMPAGNE REGION ITSELF IN 1811. BY THE 1870s THERE WAS HARDLY A WINE IN FRANCE THAT SOMEBODY HAD NOT FIZZED UP – NOT JUST ALL THE SPARKLING WINES WE KNOW TODAY, BUT ALSO THE MOST UNLIKELY CLASSICS, SUCH AS SAUTERNES AND CÔTE RÔTIE.

The claim that the 'oldest' French sparkling wine is Blanquette de Limoux also turns out to be unsubstantiated. Numerous authorities have quoted 1531 as the date when the Benedictine monks of St-Hilaire first produced sparkling wine, not accidentally, but deliberately, albeit by a continuation of the first fermentation in what would be the very first example of the *méthode rurale*. In checking out these claims, it seems the records date from 1544, not 1531. Furthermore, there is no mention of the wine being sparkling, nor even any use of words that could be construed to mean the slightest effervescence. When I queried why the producers of Limoux maintain that the wine documented was sparkling, I was told it was because the price was high and the bottles were differently-shaped. But a high price merely infers the wines were superior in quality, and very little can be read into the 'different' bottle when almost every French wine region developed its own characteristic bottle shape.

BOTTLES OF FRENCH CRÉMANT, A PREFIX WHICH IS CURRENTLY ALLOWED ON SEVEN SPARKLING WINE APPELLATIONS, WITH MORE IN THE PIPELINE

DEMISE OF *MÉTHODE CHAMPENOISE*, EMERGENCE OF *CRÉMANT*

Seven sparkling wine appellations are currently prefixed with the term *crémant*, and more are in the pipeline. The growth of *crémant* appellations is part of a deal struck by the *Champenois* whereby other French sparkling wines could gain exclusive use of *crémant* for their appellations in return for the entire EC wine community dropping the term *méthode champenoise*.

Although the first two *crémant* appellations, Crémant de Bourgogne and Crémant de Loire, appeared as early as 1975, it was this agreement, prompted by the champenois in 1985 that lead to a swelling of the *crémant* ranks.

Officially it was a compromise that was floated after the EC authorities had spent three years trying to agree on the definition of *méthode champenoise*. Readers would be forgiven for thinking that this is a simple task and that 'Second fermentation in this bottle' says it all, but the search for an acceptable definition was complicated when certain parties stipulated that it must cover every aspect of the process. Inevitably the definitions became too long and unwieldy. The *Champenois* were determined to do away with the term because, they claimed, consumers were confused by it

and thought that wines labelled *méthode champenoise* were in fact Champagne.

Although this is doubtful (most people realise would that no Champagne would describe itself as 'Champagne method'), it was nevertheless decided at the end of 1985 that since a definition of *méthode champenoise* could not be agreed, the term should be banned. The timing of this decision was no coincidence, as Spain was due to become a member state of the EC on January 1, 1986, and Cava was the single largest *méthode champenoise* appellation in the world. If they had not managed to get the ban approved prior to Spain's entry, it is quite likely that the Spanish could have blocked any future attempts.

The irony for many *crémant* producers today is that the *Champenois* could not have succeeded without their connivance, and they are beginning to worry whether their own identities are becoming lost amid a plethora of *Crémant de* something-or-other appellations. Before they got into bed with the *Champenois*, the *méthode champenoise* term was at least secondary to their own historic names. Now they find it very difficult to build up their own individual reputation, and a growing number of *crémant* producers wonder whether they were duped into this situation by the *Champenois*. Frankly, I don't think the *Champenois* have demonstrated they are that clever, although if I were a *crémant* producer I might be more paranoid about it.

FRENCH SPARKLING WINES – A MAJOR INDUSTRY THAT COULD DO BETTER

Of the two billion bottles of sparkling wine produced in the world each year, France accounts for almost a quarter, and half of this comes from areas outside Champagne itself. In terms of revenue, French sparkling wines are extremely important, yet more than two-thirds of the wines are well below standard. Although there are some very nice French sparkling wines that make good value alternatives to Champagne, they are few and far between.

This criticism applies across the board, but it is particularly disturbing to find such poor quality under the Crémant de Bourgogne appellation. Other sparkling wines are made from grape varieties that might have local reputation but are not internationally recognised as classic choices for sparkling wine. It could be argued that unless you have grown accustomed to the fizzy product of such grapes, you cannot appreciate the quality. But Crémant de Bourgogne is made from Pinot Noir and Chardonnay grapes, so its producers are unable to make such a claim.

The truth is that the poor standard of French sparkling wine seldom has anything to do with the variety of vines grown and usually has everything to do with the dire quality of grapes used. A clue to the reason why the quality of the grapes is so poor is found in the disproportionate number of these wines which have throat-choking levels of sulphur. Due to the inherently reductive process and the reducing enzymes produced during autolysis, fizz needs a much lower level of sulphur than any other style of wine, thus the only explanation for an excessively sulphured example is that the grapes contained high levels of rot or that the base wine was in some other way faulty, requiring some sort of treatment in the winery prior to the secondary fermentation.

This suggests that producers still think the only soluton for unhealthy grapes or poor quality base wines is to make the wine fizzy, but bubbles do not hide defects. Substandard base wines simply make substandard sparkling wines. No sparkling wine will fulfil its true potential if it is merely perceived as a convenient dumping ground for inferior wines made from rotten grapes, yet there is evidence that this practice is rife in many French fizz appellations.

ALSACE: SIGN FOR CELLARS OF CHARLES SCHWARTZ, BAS-RHIN, FRANCE

The other fundamental reason why French sparkling wine alternatives are so disappointing concerns those producers who are at least doing the right thing: growing grapes specifically for sparkling wine. Yet they are either relying too heavily on unsuitable varieties or, if they are suitable, then they are growing the wrong clones for this style of wine. The problem does not stop there because too many wines have unripe flavours suggesting the grapes have been picked too early.

ALSACE

The earliest Alsace sparkling wine I have come across is from a small grower called Dirler, in Guebwiller, who made a *vin mousseux* as early as 1880. But it was Dopff Au Moulin who effectively established this region's sparkling wine trade in Alsace in 1900, and Dirler stopped making sparkling Alsace wine in 1939.

Although there are plenty of grape varieties to choose from, early-picked Pinot Blanc growing on the plain is far and away the most popular. The fertile plain of Alsace is not often suited to high quality varietal wines, but it does provide one of the best *terroirs* in the region for Crémant d'Alsace. However, as a rule, the grapes are picked far too early and the committee of professionals that advises when the grapes should be harvested, the CIVA (Comité Interprofessionnel du Vin d'Alsace) is as much to blame as the growers themselves. The result, apart from green fruit, is an insubstantial structure and a lack of ripe acidity.

The extra richness and higher acidity of Pinot Gris usually makes a superior sparkling wine than a pure Pinot Blanc *cuvée*, but its significantly higher price has prevented the widespread use of this grape. Pinot Gris costs 40% more than Pinot Blanc, yet a pure Pinot Gris Crémant d'Alsace cannot attract a 40% premium, thus it is not exactly economical. When it is used, Pinot Gris is often confined to a small percentage of the *cuvée*, but it plays a disproportionate role in boosting the quality.

Chardonnay is popping up in an increasing number of *cuvées*, but it invariably makes a small wine in every sense of the word. Whether it is the wrong clone, unsuitable *terroir*, how it is grown or harvested, it is impossible for a solitary observer to discern, but there has only ever been one successful Crémant d'Alsace made from Chardonnay and that was by Kuentz-Bas, who no longer produces it.

Pure Riesling Crémant d'Alsace is not very common; when you do encounter it it is naturally much drier than Deutscher Riesling Sekt, but the quality is much less exciting than the best German *cuvées*.

Crémant Rosé is the region's most underrated sparkling wine, with its soft, elegant, pure strawberry or cherry fruit. This style can be made only from the Pinot Noir and as a result it is far more consistent than white Crémant d'Alsace.

Another underrated pure Pinot Crémant is *blanc de noirs*. More use could be made of Pinot Noir to firm up Pinot Blanc blends and no one has thought to produce a sweet Muscat fizz to rival Clairette de Die *méthode ancestrale*. Most Crémant d'Alsace is best consumed within six to 18 months of purchase.

BORDEAUX

Although Cordeliers, the oldest sparkling Bordeaux wine manufacturer still in production, dates back to 1890, the boom in French sparkling wine had reached this region by at least the 1870s, when the survival of Sauternes was threatened by the bubbly bandwagon. At this juncture, vast quantities of these sweet wines were transported to Messers Normandin Sparkling Sauternes Manufactory near Angoulème, in Charentes, where it was turned into award-winning sparkling wine.

The quality of Bordeaux Mousseux has always been decent, if not exactly exciting, but despite the marked increase in the number of producers since the introduction of Crémant de Bordeaux in 1990 (although Bordeaux Mousseux was not done away with until 1995), there has not been much noticeable improvement in quality.

BURGUNDY

Although Crémant de Bourgogne has superseded Bourgogne Mousseux, red sparkling wines are still sold under the latter appellation. There are three major districts of production for Crémant de Bourgogne: the Yonne (Chablis), the Region de Mercurey (Chalonnaise), and the Mâconnais.

There are some exciting wines, but the improvement that was expected as the Crémant de Bourgogne appellation got underway did not happen. Most Crémant de Bourgogne producers still need to be persuaded to cultivate grapes specifically for sparkling wines rather than relying on excess production or inferior grapes as has traditionally been the case in Burgundy.

However, when Crémant de Bourgogne is good it is usually very good and always a bargain. They are invariably pure Chardonnay sparklers and the styles range from full and toasty (often from the Yonne), through rich and smooth (best usually from the Côte Chalonnaise) to fresh, light and vivacious (Mâconnais). The rosé style is not as interesting, unless it is made from 100% Pinot Noir, when it can be very attractive, in a fuller, more serious style than Crémant d'Alsace rosé.

Most good quality Crémant de Bourgogne is best consumed within two years of purchase.

VINEYARD ON THE SOUTHERN SLOPES BELOW THE HISTORIC MARKET TOWN OF VEZELAY, YONNE IN BURGUNDY

LIMOUX

According to copies of the oldest documents supplied to me by a Limoux producer, the first mention of this wine was on October 25, 1544 when Bertrand Pellet the King's Officer in Limoux, supplied a consignment of wine, including four *pinctes* and two *flacons* of Blanquette, to the Sieur d'Arques for 28 *sous*. There is no description of the wine, let alone anything sparkling, and even the local Sieur d'Arques cooperative admits the bottles were sealed with wooden bungs, which could not possibly keep a wine fizzy (especially when transported by cart along rough tracks). At some time, however, the wine apparently developed a sparkle, having been bottled, one assumes, before it had ceased fermenting. This was most probably due to the sudden snap of winter bringing a temporary halt to the process (yeast cells stop producing the fermenting enzymes at -3°C, at which temperature the partially-fermented wine would fall bright).

The earliest reference I can find to sparkling Limoux is 1680, when Duval, geographer to Louis XIV, described the wines of both Limoux and Gaillac as sparkling. I have yet to see the document in question, and would be surprised if the word used was *mousseux* (sparkling) or even *mousse* (froth), since that would predate its hitherto first known documented use (applicable to wine) by 38 years, in the treatise circa 1718 that has been attributed to Godinot. The first mention of either of these two terms by a French dictionary was in 1724, in the *Dictionnaire Universel de la France Ancienne e Moderne*, which refers to the *'vin du Champagne qui fai beaucoup de mousse'* ('the wine of Champagne that makes a lot of froth') in its definition for the adjective *mousseux*.

Although *mousseux* and *mousse* are more precise than words such as *vif* (lively) in French or 'brisk' in English, they would still not be proof of an intentionally sparkling wine. If the definition of the first mention of the *méthode champenoise* is the addition of sugar to a finished wine with the stated intention of making it

LIMOUX: VINEYARDS BELOW THE ROCK OF SOLUTRE IN THE MACONNAIS

sparkling, then the definition of the first mention of the *méthode rurale* would be the bottling of a wine before the fermentation has finished with the stated intention of making it sparkling. Merret thus first defined the *méthode champenoise* in London in 1662 (*see p.10*), but any trace of the first *méthode rurale* remains as elusive as ever.

Blanquette de Limoux has always had a certain rusticity about it, even though it is exceptionally fine for a sparkling wine produced in such sunny climes. It has, however, improved even further over the last decade, moving away from its distinctive aroma of fresh-cut grass to adopt much finer characteristics. In 1989 a new appellation, Crémant de Limoux, was introduced, and five years allowed for producers to decide whether they wanted to adopt this permanently or retain their traditional Blanquette de Limoux AOC.

As Blanquette de Limoux relied primarily on the Mauzac grape and Crémant de Limoux required a combined minimum of 30% Chardonnay and Chenin Blanc, the choice was not merely about a name, but what direction and style Limoux producers wished to follow. It was thought that Mauzac-based Blanquette de Limoux would wind down while the Chardonnay-influenced *crémant* would slip into the fast lane. But Crémant de Limoux did not take off as anticipated. By 1993, the year before the deadline when the producers were supposed to decide which appellation to keep, just a 20th of Limoux's sparkling wine harvest was being sold under the *crémant* appellation.

Thus for the foreseeable future it appears that we will have two styles of fizzy Limoux, one traditional, the other modern, which means more choice for consumers. However, the most exciting sparkling Limoux is its oldest style, *Blanquette Méthode Ancestrale*. Formerly called Vin de Blanquette, this wine is bottled when partially fermented, and does not undergo a second fermentation, but achieves its sparkle through a continuation of its first fermentation. This lusciously sweet bubbly has a low alcoholic content, making it comparable to Asti, although it is much softer, with a more delicate aroma (often of very ripe apple). Its silky-soft, sweet finish makes it ideal for drinking on a balmy summer afternoon, although it is also the perfect accompaniment to *foie gras* or fresh fruit. Just a few years ago, you would have great difficulty finding Vin de Blanquette in the region itself, as barely a handful of producers made it, and what little there was would be consumed by family and friends. With the advent of the change of name, tiny amounts are beginning to trickle onto export markets and hopefully this means we will see more *méthode ancestrale* in the future.

LOIRE VALLEY

Unless you are brought up on fizz from the Loire, it is difficult to get to grips with these wines, due to the primary variety used, Chenin Blanc, which is too aromatic for a classic brut-style. The distinctive character of this grape fights the subtle development of autolysis before disgorgement and hinders the mellowing effect of bottle aromas after disgorgement. There are, of course, exceptions, but even well-made Loire bubblies can seem too aggressive and there are far

LOIRE: HARVESTING CHARDONNAY GRAPES AT GRATAY, SAONE-ET-LOIRE

too many wines made from overcropped or poor quality Chenin Blanc.

Saumur is the largest French sparkling wine appellation outside of Champagne, and its tufa limestone soil, together with the regulations that allow the use of up to 20% Chardonnay and Sauvignon Blanc, should make it one of the most successful appellations, qualitatively as well as quantitatively. Unfortunately they do not. Until recently I have been inclined to suggest that the percentage of Chardonnay should be increased. Crémant de Loire has no restrictions on this or any other of its permitted varieties, and wines made here with a significant Chardonnay content have proved to have the greatest quality potential of all Loire sparklers.

However, I have recently had the chance to taste under blind conditions a large number of Saumur and Crémant de Loire *cuvées* with various proportions of Chardonnay. The Chardonnay used in the Crémant de Loire proved infinitely superior to that used for the Saumur. There could be various reasons for this, but the most likely is that all the superior locations in Saumur are devoted to Chenin Blanc, which is that region's traditional variety. If this is true, then unless Saumur growers dedicate some of their better sites to Chardonnay, they might as well not grow this classic variety at all: inferior Chardonnay is no use whatsoever.

I am constantly appalled by the poor quality of all forms of Vouvray other than the truly magnificent, succulently sweet *moelleux*. It seems to me that growers in this famous region cannot be bothered with the other styles, and *mousseux* comes very low on their list of priorities. On the other hand, Montlouis appears to be far more successful, particularly the *pétillant*, but this might simply be due to the fact that there are relatively few of them, thus those who decide to make sparkling Montlouis actually care about the product.

Touraine is the dark horse of Loire bubbly; a potentially excellent appellation due to the wide range of permitted grape varieties and a large production area to blend from.

AN A-Z OF OTHER FRENCH SPARKLING WINES

Beyond the boundary of Champagne, no fewer than 38 other sparkling wines are produced throughout the country, in addition to which these wines boast 14 alternative designations, thus you can find French fizz under 52 seemingly different appellations. Just four of these are VDQS, the rest claim full AOC status. The sparkling wines of Cheverny ceased to exist in 1993, when the still wines of this appellation were upgraded to AOC, although for three years following this wine's promotion, any remaining fizz could still be sold as Cheverny VDQS.

On the face of it, French wines are the most tightly controlled in the world, but these regulations often have little impact on the quality standards they are supposed to protect. In terms of yield, for example, the limits given are subject to a *Plafond de Classement* or PLC, which is a sort of leeway, normally set at 20%. Should a grower harvest beyond the PLC, the wine will be declassified down to *vin de table*. If the maximum yield is, say, 50hl/ha, a grower may harvest up to 60hl/ha without running foul of the authorities, but 61hl/ha or above and the whole lot will be declassified.

This sounds reasonable enough from both the growers' and the authorities' point of view, but it is really a French farce. The optimum yield varies according to many factors, such as grape variety, soil, climate and the style of wine to be produced, but in general terms, the lower the yield, the higher the quality. However, when the AOC authorities claim to restrict yields, they are merely preventing the grower from harvesting his entire crop. It does not matter how much fruit the vines have actually produced. To take the same example, a grower with a maximum yield of 50hl/ha could grow the equivalent of 150hl/ha or, indeed, any amount (providing the vines have been pruned according to the AOC's regulations), but as long as he harvest only 60hl/ha the yield is legal and the wines duly classified.

Note that discrepancies between minimum sugar content of grapes and minimum alcohol levels is due to the varying degrees of chaptalisation permitted. Although chaptalisation has to be agreed on an annual basis, and is strictly controlled, it happens to one degree or another more times than not. Where no minimum ageing controls are noted, this is specific to the appellation in question, as all méthode champenoise in the EU must be aged for at least nine months on their lees before disgorgement.

NAME, APPELLATION AND GRAPE VARIETIES	MINIMUM VINE PLANTING DENSITY	MAXIMUM YIELD	MINIMUM SUGAR CONTENT	ALCOHOL CONTENT 2ND FERMENTATION		PRESSURE	NOTES
				BEFORE	AFTER		
ANJOU LOIRE VALLEY Because *mousseux* has 'cheap fizz' connotations, the wines officially designated as Anjou Mousseux are often marketed simply as Anjou. *See* ANJOU MOUSSEUX							
ANJOU MOUSSEUX (WHITE AND ROSÉ) LOIRE VALLEY The Anjou district encompasses the vineyards of Saumur, thus Saumur may be sold as Anjou, but not vice versa. As this *méthode champenoise* wine is softer than its Saumur equivalent, it suggests that it rarely comes from the communes within Saumur itself, despite the fact that it may legally do so. **GRAPE VARIETIES PERMITTED** FOR WHITE WINE: *a minimum of 40% Chenin Blanc plus Cabernet Sauvignon, Cabernet Franc, Malbec, Gamay, Grolleau, Pineau d'Aunis* FOR ROSÉ WINE: *Cabernet Sauvignon, Cabernet Franc, Malbec, Gamay, Grolleau, Pineau d'Aunis*	5000/ha (2023/acre)	55hl/ha	162g/l	9.5%	10.5%	- -	*2nd ferm. must be in bottle. All production must be in area of origin. No controls over pressure or yeast conta*
ANJOU PÉTILLANT (WHITE AND ROSÉ) LOIRE VALLEY Little-used appellation for gentle *méthode champenoise* wines with a minimum of nine months bottle-age, which must be sold in ordinary still wine bottles with regular corks. The rosé version may be labelled *Anjou Pétillant, Anjou Rosé Pétillant or Rosé d'Anjou Pétillant.* **GRAPE VARIETIES PERMITTED** FOR WHITE WINE: *Mimimum 80% Chenin Blanc, maximum 20% Chardonnay and Sauvignon Blanc* FOR ROSÉ WINE: *Grolleau, Cabernet Franc, Cabernet Sauvignon, Pineau d'Aunis, Gamay, Malbec*	5000/ha (2023/acre)	55hl/ha	162g/l	9.5%	10.5%		*2nd ferm. must be in bottle. All production must be in area of origin. No controls over pressure or yeast conta*
ARBOIS MOUSSEUX (WHITE) JURA A *méthode champenoise* wine seldom seen outside Arbois. This appellation will be phased out in favour of the all-encompassing Crémant du Jura AOC as from December 1999. **GRAPE VARIETIES PERMITTED** FOR WHITE WINE: *Sauvignon, Chardonnay, Pinot Blanc*	5000/ha (2023/acre)	65hl/ha	153g/l	10%	13%		*As above*

AME, APPELLATION AND GRAPE VARIETIES	MINIMUM VINE PLANTING DENSITY	MAXIMUM YIELD	MINIMUM SUGAR CONTENT	ALCOHOL CONTENT 2ND FERMENTATION BEFORE	AFTER	PRESSURE	NOTES
BLANQUETTE DE LIMOUX (WHITE) **LANGUEDOC-ROUSSILLON** Although this has always been a surprisingly good *méthode champenoise* for such sunny southern vineyards, the best Limoux have improved by leaps and bounds over the last decade. **GRAPE VARIETIES PERMITTED** FOR WHITE WINE: *Minimum 90% Mauzac, plus Chardonnay, Chenin Blanc*	4000/ha 1619/acre	50hl/ha	153g/l	10% (9.5% natural) ie: before chaptalisation	13%	3.5atmospheres	*2nd ferm. in bottle. All production in area of origin. Nine months on yeast.*
BLANQUETTE MÉTHODE ANCESTRALE (WHITE) **LANGUEDOC-ROUSSILLON** *Blanquette Méthode Ancestrale was formerly known simply as Vin de Blanquette.* It is this wine that some claim was invented by the monks at the Abbey of St-Hilaire in 1531. This ancient *méthode rurale* should not only be preserved, but should be experimented with and perfected, so that it can be used as a prestige *cuvée* for every sparkling wine producer in Limoux. **GRAPE VARIETIES PERMITTED** FOR WHITE WINE: *Mauzac*	4000/ha	50hl/ha	153g/l	*There is no second fermentation, only a continuation of the first. The wine is bottled when partially fermented, usually at 4-5% alcohol. No liqueur de tirage is added and there is no control over final alcoholic strength other than it must have a 'potential' minimum of 10%, inferring a finished strength of 5-6%. There is thus a potential for 68-85g/l residual sugar – doux in sweetness terms. No control over pressure or age on yeast.*			
BOURGOGNE MOUSSEUX (RED) **BURGUNDY** Since December 1985, this AOC has been limited to, and remains, the only appellation for sparkling red Burgundy. Although a favourite in the pubs of pre-war Britain, this sweetish red fizz is very much out of step with today's consumers, but could be back in favour if Australia's sparkling Shiraz, which originally mimicked sparkling Burgundy in the late 19th century, does make a breakthrough as an internationally acceptable style. **GRAPE VARIETIES PERMITTED** FOR RED WINE: *Pinot Noir, Gamay, plus, in the Yonne (Chablis) César and Tressot*	*None*	55hl/ha	135g/l	9.5%	10.5%	-	*2nd ferm. must be in bottle. All production in area of origin. No controls over pressure or yeast contact*

CLAIRETTE DE DIE (WHITE) **RHÔNE VALLEY**

This dry version of Clairette de Die will be phased out in favour of Crémant de Die as from December 1998, although stocks of this wine will remain in distribution until they are sold out. Although some sort of change was necessary to clarify which was the dry and the sweet style of fizz from this bubbly outpost of the Rhône, the situation is now more confused than ever. Die is the place where these wines come from, Clairette is a type of grape. By a classic example of Gallic logic, the only wine to mention Clairette does not have to contain a single grape of that variety, whereas the one wine that must be 100% Clairette does not mention the variety! *See* CRÉMANT DE DIE AOC.

CLAIRETTE DE DIE MÉTHODE DIOISE ANCESTRALE (WHITE) **RHÔNE VALLEY** Formerly Clairette de Die Tradition, this wine may contain Clairette, but it is essentially a sparkling Muscat. Contrary to what the appellation suggests, most *cuvées* contain very little Clairette, and the best examples none at all. The so-called *Méthode Dioise Ancestrale* is an updated variant of the *méthode rurale*, and produces a very fresh, deliciously fruity wine of at least *demi-sec* sweetness, with an outrageously ripe, peachy flavour. **GRAPE VARIETIES PERMITTED** FOR WHITE WINE: *At least 75% Muscat à Petits Grains (this went up in 1993 from a minimum of 50%), plus Clairette*	1818/ha (736/acre)	55hl/ha	136g/l	*No second fermentation★ (see below),*			

★No second fermentation, just a continuation of the first, the wine is bottled when partially-fermented. Must have minimum 55g/l of residual sugar when bottled, (4.5% alcohol). Some producers traditionally bottle at 3%, thus assuring a much sweeter wine with a lower alcoholic strength when finished. No liqueur de tirage is added and when the bottle-fermentation phase is complete, the finished wine should have at least 35 grams per litre of residual sugar. It can then be disgorged, although usually filtered under pressure. Can only be topped up with the same cuvée, as it must be corked without the any addition of any liqueur d'expédition. All production must be completed in area of origin. Degree of pressure not controlled, but the 20g/l difference between the wine at the time of bottling and commercialisation, with no dosage permitted, infers minimum pressure 4.5 atmospheres (at 20°C). No controls over yeast contact.

CÔTES DU JURA MOUSSEUX (WHITE) **JURA** This will be phased out in favour of the all-encompassing Crémant du Jura AOC from December 1999. **GRAPE VARIETIES PERMITTED** For white wine: *Savagnin, Chardonnay, Pinot Blanc*	5000/ha (2023/acre)	55hl/ha	144g/l	9.5%	13.5%	No controls	*2nd ferm. must be in bottle. No control over yeast contact.*
CRÉMANT D'ALSACE (WHITE AND ROSÉ) **ALSACE** Due to a clerical error, the designation *Vin Mousseux d'Alsace* was denied equal status when the AOC laws were drawn up for this region in 1962, and the situation wasn't rectified until 1976, when *AOC Crémant d'Alsace* was introduced for *méthode champenoise* wines. *Continues*	*None*	100hl/ha (Maximum extraction during pressing is 100 litres per 150kg)	145g/l	8.5%	None	3.5 atmospheres	*2nd ferm must be in bottle. At least nine months on yeast.*

NAME, APPELLATION AND GRAPE VARIETIES	MINIMUM VINE PLANTING DENSITY	MAXIMUM YIELD	MINIMUM SUGAR CONTENT	ALCOHOL CONTENT 2ND FERMENTATION BEFORE	AFTER	PRESSURE	NOTES

(Continued) GRAPE VARIETIES PERMITTED

FOR WHITE WINE: *Pinot Blanc, Pinot Gris, Pinot Noir, Auxerrois, Chardonnay, Riesling*

FOR ROSÉ WINE: *Pinot noir*

CRÉMANT DE BORDEAUX (WHITE AND ROSÉ) BORDEAUX

| | None | 65hl/ha | 136g/l (144g/l for black varieties destined for red wine cuvées) | 8.5% | 13% | 3.5 atmospheres | 2nd ferm. must be in bottle. Mu spend at least 9 months on yeast. |

This appellation was introduced in 1990 to replace the old *Bordeaux Mousseux* AOC, which was phased out on December 31, 1995. Although preferable to a lot of poorly produced Loire wines, there is nothing special about Bordeaux bubbly. For a region that is supposed to have the best climate in the world for winemaking, Bordeaux performs very poorly when it comes to sparkling wines, although this has more to do with mentality than the weather. Like most other French sparkling wines, there are precious few sparkling wine designated vineyards and a belief that the Crémant appellation makes a useful dumping ground for unripe or poor quality grapes. Changing the appellation hasn't altered this attitude because, like the old Bordeaux Mousseux, Crémant de Bordeaux is a modest and inoffensive fizz at best. It lacks the spirit and expressiveness to stand out.

GRAPE VARIETIES PERMITTED

FOR WHITE WINE: *Sémillon, Sauvignon Blanc, Muscadelle, Ugni Blanc, Colombard, Cabernet Franc, Cabernet Sauvignon, Carmenère, Merlot, Malbec, Petit Verdot*

FOR ROSÉ WINE: *Cabernet Sauvignon, Cabernet Franc, Carmenère, Merlot, Malbec, Petit Verdot*

CRÉMANT DE BOURGOGNE (WHITE AND ROSÉ) BURGUNDY

| | None | 50hl/ha (Maximum extraction during pressing is 100 litres per 150kg grapes) | 136g/l | 8.5% | 13% | 3.5 atmospheres | 2nd ferm. must be in bottle. At least 9 months on yeast. |

Introduced in 1975, this was the first 'Crémant' appellation in France, It was created to supersede the *Bourgogne Mousseux* AOC, which had failed to inspire a quality image because of the cheap and nasty image of the term *mousseux*. Bourgogne Mousseux now applies to sparkling red wines only. The three major production centres for Crémant de Bourgogne are the Yonne, Region de Mercurey and the Mâconnais. There are many exciting wines, but there are also a lot of disappointing ones. However, quality will improve when producers grow grapes specifically for sparkling wines, rather than relying on excess or inferior grapes, as has traditionally been the case.

GRAPE VARIETIES PERMITTED

FOR WHITE AND ROSÉ WINE: *Pinot Noir, Pinot Gris, Pinot Blanc, Chardonnay, Sacy, Aligoté, Melon de Bourgogne and a maximum of 20% Gamay*

CRÉMANT DE DIE (WHITE) RHÔNE VALLEY

| | 1818/ha (736/acre) | 50hl/ha (Maximum extraction during pressing is 100 litres per 150kg grapes) | 136g/l | 9% | 12.5% | 3.5 atmospheres | 2nd ferm. must be in bottle. At least 9 months on yeast. |

This dry sparkling wine was introduced in 1993 to replace *Clairette de Die Mousseux*, which will be phased out by January 1999. Like the old *Clairette de Die Mousseux* appellation, Crémant de Die must be made by the *méthode champenoise*, but whereas the former may have included up to 25% Muscat à Petit Grains, the latter must be 100% Clairette.

GRAPE VARIETIES PERMITTED

FOR WHITE WINE: *Clairette*

CRÉMANT DE LIMOUX (WHITE AND ROSÉ) LANGUEDOC–ROUSSILLON

| | 4000/ha (1619/acre) | 50hl/ha | 153g/l | 9.5% | none | 3.5atmospheres | 2nd ferm. must be in bottle. At least 9 months on yeast. |

Introduced in 1989 to allow producers to decide the future name of their appellation (Blanquette de Limoux or Crémant de Limoux), it now appears that these two appellations will co-exist with one another.

GRAPE VARIETIES PERMITTED

FOR WHITE WINE: *Mauzac plus a minimum of 30% Chardonnay and Chenin Blanc (neither of which may exceed 20%)*

CRÉMANT DE LOIRE (WHITE AND ROSÉ) LOIRE VALLEY

| | None | 50hl/ha | 137g/l | 8% | none | 3.5atmospheres | 2nd ferm. must be in bottle. At least 9 months on yeast. |

Of all the Loire's wines, Crémant de Loire probably is the most underrated, yet has the greatest potential because it can be blended from two districts (Anjou-Saumur & Touraine) and the widest range of grape varieties. The best white wine *cuvées* are normally a blend of Chenin Blanc in the main,

NAME, APPELLATION AND GRAPE VARIETIES	MINIMUM VINE PLANTING DENSITY	MAXIMUM YIELD	MINIMUM SUGAR CONTENT	ALCOHOL CONTENT 2ND FERMENTATION BEFORE	AFTER	PRESSURE	NOTES

with a good dash of Cabernet Franc and Chardonnay. They have yet to establish the best Chardonnay clones in the Loire, but at least it is widely used for sparkling wines, whereas Pinot Noir is not which is a mystery, as it is a proven variety in the region. As for rosé fizz, the most successful usually contain a high proportion of Cabernet Franc and Grolleau Noir. Cabernet Franc makes the most distinctive wine, often deeply coloured and with pungent raspberry aromas. A pure Pinot Noir *crémant* rosé would be interesting - more strawberry than raspberry - and could easily be made within the regulations.

GRAPE VARIETIES PERMITTED

FOR WHITE AND ROSÉ WINE: *Chenin Blanc, Cabernet Franc, Cabernet Sauvignon, Pineau d'Aunis, Pinot Noir, Chardonnay, Arbois, Grolleau Noir, Grolleau Gris*

CRÉMANT DU JURA MOUSSEUX (WHITE) JURA

The Jura's latest sparkling wine appellation, this was introduced in 1995 and may be used for any wine conforming to the *vin mousseux* AOCs of the Côtes du Jura, Arbois and L'Etoile. It may also be applied retrospectively to any such wines produced from 1991 onwards. This should be a more variable version of *Côtes de Jura Mousseux* as it now includes sparkling wines formerly made under the Arbois and L'Etoile appellations, but we have to wait and see what the effect will be of an expansion of grape varieties to include Trousseau, Pinot Gris and Pinot Noir (although Pinot Blanc has been dropped).

GRAPE VARIETIES PERMITTED

FOR WHITE WINE: *Chardonnay, Pinot Gris, Pinot Noir, Savagnin, Trousseau*

- Minimum vine planting density: 5000/ha (2023/acre)
- Maximum yield: 65hl/ha
- Minimum sugar content: 136g/l (144g/l for black grapes used in red cuvées)
- Alcohol content before: 8.5%
- After: 12.5%
- Pressure: 3.5 atmospheres
- Notes: 2nd ferm. must be in bottle. At least nine months on yeast.

GAILLAC SOUTHWEST FRANCE

Because *mousseux* has 'cheap fizz' connotations, the wines officially designated under three Gaillac Mousseux appellations are often marketed simply as 'Gaillac'. Although the *Gaillac Sec Perlé* AOC no longer exists, various producers make a very slightly *pétillant* wine called *Perlé* under the Gaillac appellation. Traditionally this style has been made by what could be described as a hint of *méthode rurale* – the wines are bottled at the very last moment, just before the fermentation is due to finish. There have been allegations that less reputable producers sparge the wines with CO2 at the time of bottling, and this probably contributed to the official demise of *Gaillac Sec Perlé. See the various* GAILLAC MOUSSEUX AOCs

---

GAILLAC MOUSSEUX méthode DEUXIÈME FERMENTATION (WHITE AND ROSÉ) SOUTHWEST FRANCE

Sparkling wine made by *méthode champenoise*. Expect to see a phasing out of the term *mousseux* on these and other Gaillac sparkling wine regions. Few producers care very much about the appellation, and those who do have a sense of pride seldom make anything interesting, although there is no reason why this area cannot produce decent sparkling wine.

GRAPE VARIETIES PERMITTED

FOR WHITE WINE: *At least 15% (each or in total) of Len de l'El and Sauvignon Blanc, plus Mauzac, Mauzac Rosé, Muscadelle, Ondenc, Sémillon*
FOR ROSÉ WINE: *At least 60% Duras, plus Fer, Gamay, Syrah, Cabernet Sauvignon, Cabernet Franc, Merlot*

- Minimum vine planting density: 3500/ha (1416/acre)
- Maximum yield: 60hl/ha
- Minimum sugar content: 153g/l
- Alcohol content before: 10%
- After: 13%
- Pressure: no controls
- Notes: 2nd ferm must be in bottle. No control over duration of yeast contact.

GAILLAC MOUSSEUX MÉTHODE GAILLACOISE (WHITE AND ROSÉ) SOUTHWEST FRANCE

Sparkling wines made by the *méthode rurale*, involving just one fermentation, with no addition of a *liqueur de tirage*. The wine is bottled before the fermentation stops and no *liqueur d'expédition* is added prior to distribution, thus any residual sweetness comes entirely from the original grape sugars. Styles include *brut* and *demi-sec*. A *doux* is also available, but is governed by stricter rules and given its own denomination
(See GAILLAC MOUSSEUX méthode GAILLACOISE DOUX AOC).
(Continued)

- Minimum vine planting density: None
- Maximum yield: 60hl/ha
- Minimum sugar content: 153g/l
- Notes: No 2nd ferm. The wine is bottled when partially fermented. Maximum potential alcohol strength when finished is 14%. There are no controls over degree of pressure or duration of yeast contact.

NAME, APPELLATION AND GRAPE VARIETIES	MINIMUM VINE PLANTING DENSITY	MAXIMUM YIELD	MINIMUM SUGAR CONTENT	ALCOHOL CONTENT 2ND FERMENTATION BEFORE	AFTER	PRESSURE	NOTES
(Continued) GRAPE VARIETIES PERMITTED FOR WHITE WINE: *At least 15% (each or in total) of Len de l'El and Sauvignon Blanc, plus Mauzac, Mauzac Rosé, Muscadelle, Ondenc, Sémillon* FOR ROSÉ WINE: *At least 60% Duras, plus Fer, Gamay, Syrah, Cabernet Sauvignon, Cabernet Franc, Merlot*							
GAILLAC MOUSSEUX MÉTHODE GAILLACOISE DOUX (WHITE AND ROSÉ) **SOUTHWEST FRANCE** Sparkling wine made by the *méthode rurale* (*see* previous entry) from riper grapes (minimum of 11%) than are used in any other Gaillac sparkling wine appellation, and a minimum of 45 grams per litre of residual natural grape sugar. These wines are not as exotic as, say, *Clairette de Die Méthode Dioise Ancestrale*, but delicious, sweet, grapey and fragrant *cuvées* are occasionally encountered. I have never come across a Gaillac *doux* rosé, but it would be an interesting experience. **GRAPE VARIETIES PERMITTED** FOR WHITE WINE: *At least 15% (each or in total) of Len de l'El and Sauvignon Blanc, plus Mauzac, Mauzac Rosé, Muscadelle, Ondenc, Sémillon* FOR ROSÉ WINE: *At least 60% Duras, plus Fer, Gamay, Syrah, Cabernet Sauvignon, Cabernet Franc, Merlot*	None	45hl/ha	178g/l				*No 2nd ferm. The wine is bottled when partially fermented. Maximum potential alcohol strength when finished is 14%. There are no controls over degree of pressure or duration of yeast contact.*
L'ETOILE MOUSSEUX (WHITE) **JURA** Not quite up to the standard of *Côtes du Jura Mousseux*, but this *méthode champenoise* had more potential than *Arbois Mousseux*. However, both appellations (and *Côtes du Jura Mousseux*, which was the most promising of all) will be phased out in favour of the all-encompassing *Crémant du Jura AOC* as from December 1999. **GRAPE VARIETIES PERMITTED** FOR WHITE WINE: *Chardonnay, Poulsard, Savagnin*	5000/ha (2023/acre)	65hl/ha	153g/l	10%	13.5%	no controls	*2nd ferm. must be in bottles. No control over duration of yeast contact*

MONTLOUIS **LOIRE VALLEY**
Because *mousseux* has 'cheap fizz' connotations, the wines officially designated as *Montlouis Mousseux* appellation are often marketed simply as Montlouis. *See* MONTLOUIS MOUSSEUX

NAME, APPELLATION AND GRAPE VARIETIES	MINIMUM VINE PLANTING DENSITY	MAXIMUM YIELD	MINIMUM SUGAR CONTENT	ALCOHOL CONTENT 2ND FERMENTATION BEFORE	AFTER	PRESSURE	NOTES
MONTLOUIS MOUSSEUX (WHITE) **LOIRE VALLEY** In poor vintages the grapes are used to make *méthode champenoise* versions of Montlouis. The medium-dry (*demi-sec*) styles of *Montlouis Mousseux* AOC are very popular in France.	6000/ha (2428/acre)	55hl/ha	136g/l	9.5%	13.5%	No control	*2nd ferm. must be in bottle. No control over yeast contact*

MONTLOUIS PÉTILLANT (WHITE) **LOIRE VALLEY**
Consistently one of the most successful *pétillant* wines in France, the details, including grape varieties, are the same as for *Montlouis Mousseux*, except that the maximum alcoholic strength after second fermentation is 13% rather than 13.5% and the wines must be aged on yeast for at least nine months.

MOUSSEUX DE BUGEY **SAVOIE**
Alternative designation for the *Vin du Bugey Mousseux* appellation. *See* VIN DU BUGEY MOUSSEUX

MOUSSEUX DE SAVOIE **SAVOIE**
Alternative designation for the *Vin du Savoie Mousseux* appellation. *See* VIN DU SAVOIE MOUSSEUX

PÉTILLANT DE BUGEY **SAVOIE**
Alternative designation for the *Vin du Bugey Pétillant* appellation. *See* VIN DU BUGEY PÉTILLANT

PÉTILLANT DE SAVOIE **SAVOIE**
Alternative designation for the *Vin du Savoie Pétillant* appellation. *See* VIN DU SAVOIE PÉTILLANT

ROSÉ D'ANJOU
Unofficial alternative designation for rosé-style wines under the *Anjou Mousseux* appellation. *See* ANJOU MOUSSEUX

NAME, APPELLATION AND GRAPE VARIETIES	MINIMUM VINE PLANTING DENSITY	MAXIMUM YIELD	MINIMUM SUGAR CONTENT	ALCOHOL CONTENT 2ND FERMENTATION BEFORE	AFTER	PRESSURE	NOTES

ROSÉ D'ANJOU PÉTILLANT

Alternative designation for the rosé-style wines under the *Anjou Pétillant* appellation. *See* ANJOU PÉTILLANT

ST-PÉRAY RHÔNE VALLEY

Because *mousseux* has 'cheap fizz' connotations, the wines officially designated as *St-Péray Mousseux* are often marketed simply as St-Péray. *See* ST-PÉRAY MOUSSEUX

	MINIMUM VINE PLANTING DENSITY	MAXIMUM YIELD	MINIMUM SUGAR CONTENT	BEFORE	AFTER	PRESSURE	NOTES
ST-PÉRAY MOUSSEUX (WHITE) **RHÔNE VALLEY**	None	45hl/ha	136g/l	9%	13%	No control	2nd ferm. must be in bottle. No control over duration of yeast contact.

The first sparkling St-Péray was produced in 1825 by a Champenois *caviste* and opened with a little pomp and much ceremony at Château de Crussol, the ruins of which the young Napoleon once climbed as a dare. A *méthode champenoise* wine made from the wrong grapes grown on the wrong soil, St-Péray is a cumbersome, rustic fizz with a coarse mousse and an earthy taste that lacks finesse.
GRAPE VARIETIES PERMITTED
FOR WHITE WINE: *Marsanne, Roussanne*

SAUMUR LOIRE VALLEY

Because *mousseux* has 'cheap fizz' connotations, the wines officially designated as *Saumur Mousseux* are often marketed simply as *Saumur* or the *Saumur d'Origine* designation that producers have created to market these wines under. *See* SAUMUR MOUSSEUX

SAUMUR D'ORIGINE

Not an appellation as such, although it might as well be, as this designation is aggressively marketed in preference to the *Saumur Mousseux* AOC.

	MINIMUM VINE PLANTING DENSITY	MAXIMUM YIELD	MINIMUM SUGAR CONTENT	BEFORE	AFTER	PRESSURE	NOTES
SAUMUR MOUSSEUX (WHITE AND ROSÉ) **LOIRE VALLEY**	None	60hl/ha	136g/l	8%	13%	No control	2nd ferm. must be in bottle. At least nine months yeast contact.

This is the technically correct appellation for all fully sparkling white and rosé Saumur wines made by the *méthode champenoise*. But producers have shied away from the down-market term *mousseux*, selling the wines simply as *Saumur* or their market-oriented *Saumur d'Origine* 'appellation'. There is no allowance for this in the regulations, but it is so widespread that the authorities might as well integrate these wines in the basic Saumur AOC or officially embellish the Saumur d'Origine 'appellation'. Although the production per hectare of this wine is one-third more than for its Anjou equivalent, Saumur is - or at least should be - better in quality and style due to its Chardonnay content and the tufa-limestone soil. Most wines are white and made in a true, bone-dry, brut style, although the full gamut is allowed and wines up to *demi-sec* sweetness are relatively common. The vast majority of these wines have a thin greengage character, lack finesse and do not pick up toasty or biscuity bottle-aromas. Pink Saumur can be made from several varieties, but many are pure Cabernet Franc and an increasing number are showing very well these days. However, the aggressive potential of this grape can quickly turn a thrilling raspberry flavoured fizz into something hideously tart and pungent. Pure Cabernet Sauvignon rosés can also be very good, although much smoother, less overt and not as intrinsically Saumur as a Cabernet Franc *cuvée*. A significant amount of red *méthode champenoise* is also produced, but this cannot claim AOC status.
GRAPE VARIETIES PERMITTED
FOR WHITE WINE: *Chenin Blanc plus maximum 20% Chardonnay and Sauvignon Blanc and up to 60% Cabernet Sauvignon, Cabernet Franc, Malbec, Gamay, Grolleau, Pineau d'Aunis, Pinot Noir*
FOR ROSÉ WINE: *Cabernet Sauvignon, Cabernet Franc, Malbec, Gamay, Grolleau, Pineau d'Aunis, Pinot Noir*

	MINIMUM VINE PLANTING DENSITY	MAXIMUM YIELD	MINIMUM SUGAR CONTENT	BEFORE	AFTER	PRESSURE	NOTES
SAUMUR PÉTILLANT (WHITE AND ROSÉ) **LOIRE VALLEY**	5000/ha (2023/acre)	55hl/ha	162g/l	9.5%	10.5%	No control	2nd ferm. must be in bottle. At least nine months yeast contact.

Little-used appellation for gently *méthode champenoise* wines with minimum nine months bottle-age, which must be sold in ordinary still wine bottles with regular corks. These dry to *demi-sec*, light-bodied, fruity wines, similar to the fine wines of the *Montlouis Pétillant* appellation, should be revived.
GRAPE VARIETIES PERMITTED
FOR WHITE WINE: *Minimum 80% Chenin Blanc and maximum 20% Chardonnay and Sauvignon Blanc*

NAME, APPELLATION AND GRAPE VARIETIES	MINIMUM VINE PLANTING DENSITY	MAXIMUM YIELD	MINIMUM SUGAR CONTENT	ALCOHOL CONTENT 2ND FERMENTATION		PRESSURE	NOTES
				BEFORE	AFTER		
SEYSSEL MOUSSEUX (WHITE) **SAVOIE** It was Varichon & Clerc that first carved a niche for *Seyssel Mousseux* in the export market. **GRAPE VARIETIES PERMITTED** FOR WHITE WINE: *Molette, Chasselas, plus a minimum of 10% Roussette*	6000/ha *(2428/acre)*	65hl/ha	136g/l	8.5%	13.5%	*No control*	*2nd ferm. must be in bottle. No control over duration of yeast conta*

TOURAINE **LOIRE VALLEY**

Because *mousseux* has 'cheap fizz' connotations, the wines officially designated as *Touraine Mousseux* are often marketed simply as *Touraine*. *See* TOURAINE MOUSSEUX

NAME, APPELLATION AND GRAPE VARIETIES	MINIMUM VINE PLANTING DENSITY	MAXIMUM YIELD	MINIMUM SUGAR CONTENT	BEFORE	AFTER	PRESSURE	NOTES
TOURAINE MOUSSEUX (RED, WHITE AND ROSÉ) **LOIRE VALLEY** Very good-value *méthode champenoise* wines. While the grapes for the white and rosé versions can come from the entire AOC Touraine area, those for red Touraine Mousseux may only come from Bourgueil, St-Nicolas-de-Bourgueil and Chinon. **GRAPE VARIETIES PERMITTED** FOR RED & ROSÉ WINE: *Cabernet Franc* FOR WHITE WINE: *Primarily Chenin Blanc but may include Arbois and up to 20% Chardonnay and a combined maximum of 30% Cabernet, Pinot Noir, Pinot Gris, Pinot Meunier, Pineau d'Aunis, Malbec and Grolleau*	None	60hl/ha	136g/l *(153g/l for black varieties for red cuvées)*	8.5% *(9.5% for red cuvées)*	9.5% *(13% for red cuvées)*	*No controls*	*2nd ferm. must be in bottle. No control over duration of yeast conta*
TOURAINE PÉTILLANT (WHITE AND ROSÉ) **LOIRE VALLEY** Refreshing, slightly effervescent white and rosé wines made from the same grape varieties as Touraine Mousseux. None are exported and they are mostly drunk in the locality. **GRAPE VARIETIES PERMITTED** FOR RED & ROSÉ WINE: *Cabernet Franc* FOR WHITE WINE: *Chenin Blanc, Arbois, Sauvignon Blanc and up to 20% Chardonnay*	4500/ha *(1821/acre)*	60hl/ha *(45hl/ha for black varieties for red cuvées)*	136g/l	8.5% *(9.5% for red cuvées)*	13%	*3.5atmospheres*	*2nd ferm. must be in bottle. At least nine months on yeast.*
VIN DU BUGEY-CERDON MOUSSEUX VDQS (RED AND WHITE) **SAVOIE** Of the 64 villages that comprise this appellation, only five may add their name to the Vin du Bugey VDQS and, of these, only Cerdon may add its name to the appellation for *mousseux* or *pétillant* wines. **GRAPE VARIETIES PERMITTED** FOR RED AND WHITE WINE: *Gamay, Pinot Noir, Pinot Gris, Poulsard*	None	40hl/ha	144g/l *(153g/l for black varieties for red cuvées)*	9.5%	13%	*No controls*	*2nd ferm. must be in bottle. No control ove duration o yeast conta*

VIN DU BUGEY-CERDON PÉTILLANT VDQS (RED AND WHITE) **SAVOIE**

Same details including grape varieties as for *Vin du Bugey-Cerdon Mousseux*, but this is a semi-sparkling version. *See* VIN DU BUGEY-CERDON MOUSSEUX

NAME, APPELLATION AND GRAPE VARIETIES	MINIMUM VINE PLANTING DENSITY	MAXIMUM YIELD	MINIMUM SUGAR CONTENT	BEFORE	AFTER	PRESSURE	NOTES
VIN DU BUGEY MOUSSEUX VDQS (RED, WHITE AND ROSÉ) **SAVOIE** Brillat-Savarin was born in Bugey, an area that has produced sparkling wines since at least the late-19th century. **GRAPE VARIETIES PERMITTED** FOR RED WINE & ROSÉ: *Gamay, Pinot Noir, Poulsard, Mondeuse, plus up to 20% (in total) of Chardonnay, Roussette, Aligoté, Mondeuse Blanche, Jacquère, Pinot Gris and Molette* FOR WHITE WINE: *Chardonnay, Roussette, Aligoté, Mondeuse Blanche, Jacquère, Pinot Gris, Molette*	None	45hl/ha	136g/l	9%	13%	*No controls*	*2nd ferm. must be in bottle. No control over duration of yeast conta*

VIN DU BUGEY PÉTILLANT VDQS (WHITE AND ROSÉ) **SAVOIE**

Same details including grape varieties as for *Vin du Bugey Mousseux*, except that this is a semi-sparkling version. *See* VIN DU BUGEY MOUSSEUX

NAME, APPELLATION AND GRAPE VARIETIES	MINIMUM VINE PLANTING DENSITY	MAXIMUM YIELD	MINIMUM SUGAR CONTENT	BEFORE	AFTER	PRESSURE	NOTES
VIN DE SAVOIE AYZE MOUSSEUX (WHITE) **SAVOIE** Very promising *méthode champenoise* wines from Ayze and the neighbouring villages of Bonneville and Marignier. The sparkling wines of Ayze are typically marked by aromas of violets or jasmine, with a	6000/ha *(2428/acre)*	65hl/ha	136g/l	9%	12.5%	*No controls*	*No control over duration of yeast conta*

AME, APPELLATION AND GRAPE VARIETIES	MINIMUM VINE PLANTING DENSITY	MAXIMUM YIELD	MINIMUM SUGAR CONTENT	ALCOHOL CONTENT 2ND FERMENTATION BEFORE	AFTER	PRESSURE	NOTES

touch of white peach on the palate.
GRAPE VARIETIES PERMITTED
FOR WHITE WINE: *Gringet, Roussette, plus up to 30% Roussette d'Ayze*

✓IN DE SAVOIE AYZE PÉTILLANT (WHITE) **SAVOIE**

Same details including grape varieties as for *Vin de Savoie Ayze Mousseux*, but this is a semi-sparkling version. *See* VIN DE SAVOIE AYZE MOUSSEUX

✓IN DE SAVOIE MOUSSEUX (WHITE) **SAVOIE** A very consistent and undervalued generic *méthode champenoise*. **GRAPE VARIETIES PERMITTED** FOR WHITE WINE: *Aligoté, Roussette, Jacquère, Chardonnay, Pinot Gris, Mondeuse Blanche, plus Chasselas (Ain and Haute-Savoie), Molette (Haute-Savoie, Isère), Gringet and Roussette d'Ayze (Haute-Savoie), Marsanne and Verdesse (Isère)*	6000/ha (2428/acre)	65hl/ha	136g/l	9%	12.5%	No controls	*2nd ferm. must be in bottle. No control over duration of yeast contact.*

✓IN DE SAVOIE PÉTILLANT (WHITE) **SAVOIE**

Same details including grape varieties as for *Vin de Savoie Mousseux*, except that this is a semi-sparkling version. *See* VIN DE SAVOIE MOUSSEUX

✓OUVRAY **LOIRE VALLEY**

Because *mousseux* has 'cheap fizz' connotations, the wines officially designated as *Vouvray Mousseux* are often marketed simply as *Vouvray*. *See* VOUVRAY MOUSSEUX

VOUVRAY MOUSSEUX (WHITE) **LOIRE VALLEY** In years when the grapes do not ripen properly they are converted into wine, using the *méthode champenoise*, and are blended with reserve wines from better years to ensure they are of consistent quality. **GRAPE VARIETIES PERMITTED** FOR WHITE WINE: *Chenin Blanc and Arbois*	6000/ha (2428/acre)	55hl/ha	136g/l	9%	13% 9.5% min.)	No controls	*2nd ferm. must be in bottle. No control over duration of yeast contact*

✓OUVRAY PÉTILLANT (WHITE) **LOIRE VALLEY**

)ften more stylish and consistent than fully sparkling Vouvray, although relatively little is produced. Same details including grape varieties as for *Vouvray Mousseux*, xcept that this is a semi-sparkling version. *See* VOUVRAY MOUSSEUX

HEDGING OF VINES IN EARLY SUMMER AT THE CHAPELLE DES MOINES, BERZE-LA-VILLE, SAONE-ET-LOIRE

ALSACE

70
LES CAVES J B ADAM
AMMERSCHWIHR, ALSACE

- 6,700 cases
- Other labels - Veuve Joseph Pfister, Schroedel

A family enterprise for 14 generations, JB Adam is a well-known but seriously underrated producer of rich, upfront varietal wines that have been traditionally vinified in large oak casks and age extremely well. Adam first produced Crémant d'Alsace in 1991.

HOUSE STYLE & RANGE
The Extra Brut is light and elegant, yet really quite rich on the nose and finely structured on the palate. The Brut is sometimes spoiled by strawlike aromas that detract from its finesse, but it has sufficient fruit on the palate to make it more satisfying than the average Crémant d'Alsace.

CRÉMANT D'ALSACE BRUT
Not vintaged, méthode champenoise: 100% Pinot Blanc

★ CRÉMANT D'ALSACE EXTRA BRUT
Not vintaged, méthode champenoise: 100% Pinot Blanc

N/A
BAUMANN-ZIRGEL
MITTELWIHR, ALSACE

- 340 cases

A grower with five hectares, Baumann-Zirgel has produced some attractive varietal wines, but started making sparkling wine in 1991.

WINEMAKER
Jean-Jacques Zirgel

HOUSE STYLE & RANGE
Tasted recently for the first time, this wine was bitter and foursquare.

CRÉMANT D'ALSACE BRUT
Not vintaged, méthode champenoise: 100% Pinot Blanc

80
CHARLES BAUR
EGUISHEIM, ALSACE

- 1,350 cases

This Eguisheim grower consistently produces elegant Riesling Gewurztraminer from Grand Cru Eichberg, and since producing his first *cuvée* in 1982, he has become quite adept at Crémant d'Alsace.

WINEMAKER
Armand Baur

HOUSE STYLE & RANGE
Lovely intensity of fruit.

CAVE VINICOLE DE BEBLENHEIM HEADQUARTERS

★★ CRÉMANT D'ALSACE BRUT
Vintaged, méthode champenoise: 100% Pinot Blanc

70
CAVE VINICOLE DE BEBLENHEIM
BEBLENHEIM, ALSACE

- 33,500 cases
- Other labels - Baron de Hoen

An export label belonging to the Beblenheim cooperative, the Baron de Hoen range accounts for a quarter of its production. This cooperative was established in 1953 and today comprises 150 members owning 250 hectares of vineyards, not just in Beblenheim, but also Riquewihr, Zellenberg, Mittelwihr, Bergheim, St-Hippolyte, Ostheim and Rorschwihr. Cave Vinicole de Beblenheim produced its first sparkling wine in 1975.

HOUSE STYLE & RANGE
The basic Brut is an elegant sparkling wine with ripe fruit and a succulent finish that is not too brut. It is much preferred to the sprightly fruitiness found in the Baron de Hoen Blanc de Noirs.

★ BARON DE HOEN CRÉMANT D'ALSACE BRUT
Vintaged, méthode champenoise: grape varieties not revealed

BARON DE HOEN BLANC DE NOIRS CRÉMANT D'ALSACE BRUT
Vintaged, méthode champenoise: grape varieties not revealed

N/A
BECK - DOMAINE DU REMPART
DAMBACH LA VILLE, ALSACE

- 420 cases

This producer is also known as Gilbert Beck, René Beck and René & Gilbert Beck. Beck was the eighth grower to produce Crémant d'Alsace, but his reputation is firmly based on Riesling and Pinot Noir, not sparkling wine.

WINEMAKER
Gilbert Beck

HOUSE STYLE & RANGE
Wet straw aroma and slightly mouldy taste.

BRUT DU REMPART CRÉMANT D'ALSACE
Not vintaged, méthode champenoise: 100% Pinot Blanc

BELAMOUR
See CAVES DE WISSEMBOURG

60
CAVE VINICOLE DE BENNWIHR
BENNWIHR, ALSACE

- 42,000 cases
- Other labels - Caves Klug, Lentz, Victor Preiss

Established in 1946, Cave Vinicole de Bennwihr now consists of 200 growers who in total own 340 hectares of vineyards. This cooperative first produced sparkling wine in 1987 and has a modest but growing reputation for its varietal wines.

WINEMAKER
Michel Pinsun

HOUSE STYLE & RANGE
The Blue Label is an amylic, straw-like combination that does not work, whereas the Gold Label is an obviously older *cuvée* with mature toasty aromas, but short and lacking mouthfill. I prefer the pure Riesling, even though the structure is not quite right; it needs a slightly higher *dosage*. This cooperative's sparkling wines were better focused and more promising five years ago.

CRÉMANT D'ALSACE BRUT (BLUE LABEL)
Not vintaged, méthode champenoise: grape varieties not revealed

CRÉMANT D'ALSACE SIGILLE (GOLD LABEL)
Not vintaged, méthode champenoise: grape varieties not revealed

CRÉMANT D'ALSACE ROSÉ
Not vintaged, méthode champenoise: 100% Pinot Noir

★ RIESLING CRÉMANT D'ALSACE
Not vintaged, méthode champenoise: 100% Riesling

N/A
CLAUDE BERGER
MITTELWIHR, ALSACE

- 420 cases

Formerly known as Frédéric Berger, this small grower produces traditionally vinified wines and is known for Riesling, Gewurztraminer and Tokay-Pinot Gris, especially from the Grand Cru Sonnenglanz. First produced sparkling wine in 1982.

WINEMAKER
Claude Berger

HOUSE STYLE & RANGE
My first and only experience of this wine found it to be coarse and fundamentally unattractive.

CRÉMANT D'ALSACE BRUT
Not vintaged, méthode champenoise: 100% Pinot Blanc

72
DOMAINE PAUL BLANCK
KIENTZHEIM, ALSACE

- 840 cases

Established in 1922 by Paul Blanck, this domaine's claim to fame is Riesling from the *grands crus* of Furstentum and Schlossberg. Although enthusiastic sparkling wine producers since 1980, the Blanck's skills are

...etter demonstrated in their crafting of classic ...arietal wines.

WINEMAKER

...rédéric Blanck

HOUSE STYLE & RANGE

...estrained malo-aroma followed by malo-
...ominated fruit on the palate. I've tasted
...etter from Blanck, and no sparkling wine of
...ny finesse has malolactic aromas dominating
... Malolactic should merely be part of a
...ear-subliminal creamy complexity.

... CRÉMANT D'ALSACE EXTRA BRUT

Vintaged, méthode champenoise: 100% Pinot Blanc

...5
...MILE BOECKEL

...ITTELBERGHEIM, ALSACE

... 5,000 cases

...love the picturesque village of
...littelbergheim and find Emile Boeckel to be
... very charming person, but I always struggle
... discover the same charm in any of his
...eautifully labelled wines. This firm was
...ounded in 1853 by Frédéric Boeckel, but
...ne Boeckel family have been winegrowers
...nce 1530. Boeckel first produced sparkling
...ine in 1980.

WINEMAKER

...mile Boeckel

HOUSE STYLE & RANGE

...hese sparkling wines generally lack the
...orrect lean structure, leaning towards flabby
...nd lacking freshness. Chardonnay is probably
...ne worst *cuvée*, although Boeckel has been
...aking it for almost 20 years. The Blanc de
...lancs is the freshest fizz in the range, and
...ne 1995 was a huge improvement on the
...994, promising to develop some biscuity
...omplexity with a little age.

...LANC DE BLANCS CRÉMANT D'ALSACE BRUT

Vintaged, méthode champenoise: 100% Pinot Blanc

...LANC DE NOIR CRÉMANT D'ALSACE BRUT
...XTRA

Vintaged, méthode champenoise: 100% Pinot Noir

...HARDONNAY CRÉMANT D'ALSACE BRUT
...XTRA

Vintaged, méthode champenoise: 100% Chardonnay

...RUT ROSÉ CRÉMANT D'ALSACE

Not vintaged, méthode champenoise: 100% Pinot Noir

...NNE BOECKLIN

...ee CAVE VINICOLE DE KIENTZHEIM-
...AYSERSBERG

...A
...OMAINE DU BOUXHOF

...ITTELWIHR, ALSACE

... 440 cases

...Iy first opportunity to taste several *cuvées* from
...his producer was as recent as 1997, although
...e has made sparkling wine since 1989.

WINEMAKER

François Edel

HOUSE STYLE & RANGE

Lots of sprightly pineapple fruitiness gives this
wine a real richness, but it has the acidity to
support it.

★ DOMAINE DU BOUXHOF CRÉMANT
D'ALSACE BRUT

*Not vintaged, méthode champenoise: grape varieties
not revealed*

N/A
PAUL BUECHER

WETTOLSHEIM, ALSACE

• 5,850 cases

This family enterprise was founded at the
end of the 17th century and today comprises
some 20 hectares of vineyards in Husseren-les-
Châteaux, Eguisheim, Wettolsheim,
Wintzenheim, Turckheim, Ingersheim and
Colmar. Sparkling wine has been produced
here since 1978.

WINEMAKER

Henri Buecher

HOUSE STYLE & RANGE

The rich, fruity and well-structured Prestige
cuvée is the best sparkling wine that Buecher
has produced in the last five years, but the
Prestige Rosé is flabby, while the
Chardonnay is too fat and has no finesse.

CHARDONNAY CRÉMANT D'ALSACE BRUT

Not vintaged, méthode champenoise: 100% Chardonnay

★ PRESTIGE CRÉMANT D'ALSACE BRUT

*Not vintaged, méthode champenoise: grape varieties
not revealed*

PRESTIGE CRÉMANT D'ALSACE ROSÉ BRUT

Not vintaged, méthode champenoise: 100% Pinot Noir

70
DOMAINE JOSEPH CATTIN

VOEGTLINSHOFFEN, ALSACE

• 5,000 cases

Joseph Cattin first produced sparkling wine
in 1980, and the only reason there is any
inconsistency in the style of his Crémant
d'Alsace is because he keeps changing the
cépage, otherwise it is always an interesting
wine, albeit the most rustic in his range.

WINEMAKER

Joseph Cattin

HOUSE STYLE & RANGE

Lots of sprightly, strawberry'ish fruitiness, but
finishes rather fat and needs more acidity.

★ CRÉMANT D'ALSACE

*Not vintaged, méthode champenoise: grape varieties
not revealed*

GF CAVALIER

See CAVES DE WISSEMBOURG

N/A
CAVE VINICOLE DE CLÉEBOURG

CLEEBOURG, ALSACE

• 12,500 cases
• Other labels - Clérotstein

Founded in 1946 by Georges Rupp, this
cooperative at the northern extreme of the
Alsace appellation consists of just under 200
growers owning a total of 150 hectares of
vineyards in the villages of Cléebourg, Rott,
Oberhoffen and Steinseltz. Although one of
the most underrated cooperatives in the
region, particularly for various Pinot varietal
wines, Cave Vinicole de Cléebourg has yet
to master its sparkling wine style.

HOUSE STYLE & RANGE

Although previous Crémant d'Alsace from
this cooperative have failed to impress, they
were made exclusively from Auxerrois, whereas
this *cuvée* is entirely Pinot Gris. Unfortunately
the only bottle I have tasted was corked.

CLÉROTSTEIN TOKAY PINOT GRIS CRÉMANT
D'ALSACE BRUT

*Vintaged, méthode champenoise: 100% Tokay
Pinot Gris*

CLÉROTSTEIN

See CAVE VINICOLE DE CLÉEBOURG

N/A
CLAUDE DIETRICH

KIENTZHEIM, ALSACE

• 600 cases

This relatively new venture was established
in 1987 by Claude Dietrich and his wife
Elizabeth, who is the sister of Philippe
Blanck (of Domaine Paul Blanck).

WINEMAKER

Claude Dietrich

HOUSE STYLE & RANGE

Some classy aromas on the nose, but
unfortunately they are not reflected on the
palate, which is rather workmanlike, without
possessing the finesse promised on the bouquet.

CRÉMANT D'ALSACE BRUT

Vintaged, méthode champenoise: 100% Pinot Blanc

60
DOPFF & IRION

RIQUEWIHR, ALSACE

• 10,000 cases
• Other labels - Charles Jux, Ernest Preiss

From the same roots as cousins Dopff au
Moulin (*see below*), this company was formed
in 1945 by René Dopff and remained family-
owned until the late 1980s. Until the early
1990s, this firm still had an excellent
reputation for the understated style of its own
domaine wines, but this was being undermined

by the cheaper volume-selling wines in the range, and the various Crémant d'Alsace *cuvées* have never been consistent in quality or style.

HOUSE STYLE & RANGE

Currently the non-vintage is showing best, with some biscuity-malo complexity, the Rosé is something and nothing, and the last two vintages tasted were both maderised.

✮ CRÉMANT D'ALSACE BRUT
Not vintaged, méthode champenoise: grape varieties not revealed

CRÉMANT D'ALSACE BRUT
Vintaged, méthode champenoise: grape varieties not revealed

CRÉMANT D'ALSACE ROSÉ BRUT
Not vintaged, méthode champenoise: 100% Pinot Noir

74
DOPFF AU MOULIN
RIQUEWIHR, ALSACE

• 10,000 cases

Both this company and Dopff & Irion trace their roots back to the same 16th century origins, namely one Jean Daniel Dopff, but the family and business split in two at the end of the Second World War, and only Dopff au Moulin remains in family hands. Although growers such as Dirler had made sparkling Alsace wine since at least 1880, 20 years before Dopff au Moulin's first *cuvée*, it was this firm that was responsible for creating and maintaining a fully commercial sparkling wine industry in Alsace. The most exciting wines here, however, remain the domaine-bottlings of varietal wines.

HOUSE STYLE & RANGE

There has been a noticeable lowering of standards in the last few years, as the fruit in some of these wines has become worryingly unripe. There are still good wines, but not as many as there used to be, and they no longer stand out as they once did. Cuvée Julien typically has good weight of fruit for correctly lean structure, but Cuvée Bartholdi is one of this producer's best three sparkling wines, with its richly flavoured, vivacious fruit and a better than average ageing capability.

Bartholdi is only produced in the best years and is always a strict selection of the best grapes from two vineyards, Froehn in Riquewihr and the Hardt just outside Colmar. The Blanc de Noirs is usually one of the other two top-of-the-range fizzes, and gets that rating, even though the 1994 was a disgrace by the standard set by previous vintages. The third of Dopff au Moulin's three best *cuvées* is Wild Brut (formerly Brut Sauvage), a non-*dosage* wine of some finesse.

The latest Rosé *cuvée* possesses a strange combination of amylic character and underripe fruit, which never works in any wine, and is particularly incongruous for a rosé. The

Chardonnay is green, underripe, flavourless and bears no resemblance to the variety we know.

★ CUVÉE BARTHOLDI CRÉMANT D'ALSACE BRUT
Vintaged, méthode champenoise: 50% Chardonnay, 50% Pinot Blanc

✮ DOPFF AU MOULIN, CUVÉE JULIEN
CRÉMANT D'ALSACE BRUT
Not vintaged, méthode champenoise: Pinot Auxerrois, Pinot Blanc

CRÉMANT D'ALSACE ROSÉ BRUT
Not vintaged, méthode champenoise: 100% Pinot Noir

★ CRÉMANT D'ALSACE BLANC DE NOIRS BRUT
Vintaged, méthode champenoise: 100% Pinot Noir

★ CRÉMANT D'ALSACE WILD BRUT
Vintaged, méthode champenoise: Pinot Auxerrois, Pinot Blanc

CRÉMANT D'ALSACE CHARDONNAY BRUT
Vintaged, méthode champenoise: 100% Chardonnay

N/A
JEAN PAUL ECKLÉ
KATZENTHAL, ALSACE

• 1,000 cases

This grower owns a small plot of vines on the Grand Cru Wineck-Schlossberg, from which he produces good Riesling and Muscat, but a recent tasting was my first experience of his Crémant d'Alsace, even though he has made this style since 1984.

WINEMAKER

Jean Paul Ecklé

HOUSE STYLE & RANGE

Sprightly fruit and plenty of flavour, this wine suggests promise, but currently lacks finesse.

CRÉMANT D'ALSACE BRUT
Not vintaged, méthode champenoise: grape varieties not revealed

FRANÇOIS EDEL
See DOMAINE DU BOUXHOF

N/A
ANDRÉ EHRHART
WETTOLSHEIM, ALSACE

• 670 cases

A small grower with a reputation for his Riesling and Gewurztraminer from the Grand Cru Hengst, but I have only just come across Ehrhart's Crémant d'Alsace, which he has made since 1982.

WINEMAKER

Antoine Ehrhart

HOUSE STYLE & RANGE

I have only recently tasted wines from this single-vineyard Crémant d'Alsace and I am impressed by the nice touch of biscuity complexity and sweet malty fruit in this *cuvée*, which I intend to follow in future.

★ CRÉMANT D'ALSACE BRUT, ROTENBERG
Not vintaged, méthode champenoise: grape varieties not revealed

N/A
FERNAND ENGEL
RORSCHWIHR, ALSACE

• 2,500 cases

A small family enterprise with vineyards at the foot of Haut-Koenigsbourg, where they have produced sparkling wine since 1985.

WINEMAKER

Fernand Engel

HOUSE STYLE & RANGE

The Tradition had a touch of Chablis-like fruit, with firm structure and assertive acidity but it was at least approachable, whereas the green, unripe fruit in the Chardonnay *cuvée* was not.

✮ TRADITION CRÉMANT D'ALSACE BRUT
Not vintaged, méthode champenoise: 100% Pinot Blanc

CHARDONNAY CRÉMANT D'ALSACE BRUT
Vintaged, méthode champenoise: 100% Chardonnay

N/A
MICHEL FAHRER
ORSCHWILLER, ALSACE

• 340 cases

This grower has a certain reputation for Rouge de St-Hippolyte, but only just passes muster for his Crémant d'Alsace, which he has produced since 1985.

RIQUEWIHR VIEWED FROM THE GRAND CRU SCHOENENBOURG VINEYARD, HAUT-RHIN, FRANCE

WINEMAKER
Michel Fahrer

HOUSE STYLE & RANGE
Commendably fresh fruit, but needs to be more individually expressive in style.

CRÉMANT D'ALSACE BRUT
Not vintaged, méthode champenoise: grape varieties not revealed

N/A
FREY-SOHLER
SCHERWILLER, ALSACE
● 2,500 cases
Founded by grandpa Frey, this 20-hectare estate is a truly family affair, gainfully employing all members of the Sohler family.

WINEMAKER
Nicolas Sohler

HOUSE STYLE & RANGE
I recently tasted these wines for the first time, so I cannot give an overall judgement, but both were disappointingly foursquare. Although the structure of the Riesling was wrong and it lacked acidity, it did at least have an attractive peachiness to the fruit, making it preferable to the Blanc de Blancs, a wine that was particularly unpleasant on the nose.

BLANC DE BLANCS CRÉMANT D'ALSACE BRUT
Not vintaged, méthode champenoise: grape varieties unrevealed

RIESLING CRÉMANT D'ALSACE BRUT
Not vintaged, méthode champenoise: 100% Riesling

N/A
MARCEL FREYBURGER
AMMERSCHWIHR, ALSACE
● 250 cases
There are a few Freyburgers in Alsace, and this is probably the least known of all of them. Apart from a fine, spicy Gewurztraminer Kaefferkopf, I have had little experience of Marcel Freyburger's wines.

WINEMAKER
Marcel Freyburger

HOUSE STYLE & RANGE
I tasted this producer's Crémant d'Alsace for the first time very recently. Furthermore the wine I tasted was Freyburger's first sparkling wine *cuvée*, so no overall judgement would be fair, but I was not impressed by its straw-like aromas, which were followed by sprightly apricot fruit and a rather heavy finish.

CRÉMANT D'ALSACE BRUT
Vintaged, méthode champenoise: grape varieties not revealed

N/A
PIERRE FRICK
PFAFFENHEIM, ALSACE
● 585 cases
A small bio-dynamic producer who makes excellent, expressive varietal wines without

any chaptalisation, but I have yet to be convinced about the Crémant d'Alsace.

WINEMAKER
Jean-Pierre Frick

HOUSE STYLE & RANGE
Although this *cuvée* has an interesting apricot character, it lacks the sort of substance required of an non-*dosage* wine.

BRUT DE BRUT CRÉMANT D'ALSACE
Vintaged, méthode champenoise: grape varieties not revealed

JEAN GEILER
See CAVE VINICOLE D'INGERSHEIM

GIERSBERGER
See CAVE VINICOLE DE RIBEAUVILLÉ

70
WILLY GISSELBRECHT
DAMBACH-LA-VILLE, ALSACE
● 8,350 cases
● Other labels - Antoine Heinrich
Louis Gisselbrecht's more talented cousin first produced sparkling wine in 1981.

HOUSE STYLE & RANGE
The Rosé has attractive soft, pure Pinot fruit, but the well-flavoured Brut is spoilt by wet-straw aromas.

CUVÉE PRESTIGE CRÉMANT D'ALSACE BRUT
Not vintaged, méthode champenoise: 100% Pinot Blanc

★ PRESTIGE BRUT ROSÉ CRÉMANT D'ALSACE
Not vintaged, méthode champenoise: 100% Pinot Noir

77
DOMAINE JOSEPH GRUSS
EGUISHEIM, ALSACE
● 1,700 cases
A few wines from this Eguisheim grower have come my way, including a charming Pinot Noir, but it is Gruss's Crémant d'Alsace, which has been steadily improving since he made his first *cuvée* in 1982, that impresses me the most.

WINEMAKER
Joseph Gruss

HOUSE STYLE & RANGE
The Brut has a very fruity aroma, sherbety fruit, cushiony mousse, and a fresh, breezy finish, but the Brut Prestige is even better, with lovely, fat and sassy fruit and a nice cushiony mousse.

★ CRÉMANT D'ALSACE BRUT
Not vintaged, méthode champenoise: grape varieties not revealed

★★ BRUT PRESTIGE CRÉMANT D'ALSACE
Not vintaged, méthode champenoise: grape varieties not revealed

HARTENBERGER
See CAVE VINICOLE DE PFAFFENHEIM

HEIM
See CAVES WESTHALTEN

ANTOINE HEINRICH
See WILLY GISSELBRECHT

N/A
LÉON HEITZMANN
AMMERSCHWIHR, ALSACE
● 1,000 cases
A capable producer of varietal wines, particularly Pinot Gris and *Vendange Tardive* style, Léon Heitzmann started producing Crémant d'Alsace in 1981.

WINEMAKER
Léon Heitzmann

HOUSE STYLE & RANGE
My first, recent and so far only experience of Heitzmann's Crémant d'Alsace was a pleasant one because, despite the straw-like aroma, there is a nice, fat, fruity flavour, with a hint of spice and good acidity.

★ CRÉMANT D'ALSACE BRUT
Not vintaged, méthode champenoise: grape varieties not revealed

72
ALBERT HERTZ
EGUISHEIM, ALSACE
● 420 cases
● Other labels - Prince Albert
A top Alsace grower for beautifully focused varietal wines.

WINEMAKER
Albert Hertz

HOUSE STYLE & RANGE
This Crémant d'Alsace used to be a blend of 20% Auxerrois, 40% Chardonnay and 40% Pinot Blanc, but the latest *cuvée* tastes more like sparkling Muscat. Whatever it is, it needs some sweetness, and would be an absolute stunner if produced in a rich *demi-sec* style.

★ PRINCE ALBERT CRÉMANT D'ALSACE BRUT
Not vintaged, méthode champenoise: grape varieties not revealed

BARON DE HOEN
See CV BEBLENHEIM

70
CAVE VINICOLE DE HUNAWIHR
HUNAWIHR, ALSACE
- 8,340 cases

This small cooperative does not always hit the high notes expected from the superior village of Hunawihr, but its wines are usually above average and can sometimes be minor gems.

HOUSE STYLE & RANGE
Consistently fresh, finely balanced and elegant.

★ CALIXTE CRÉMANT D'ALSACE BRUT
Not vintaged, méthode champenoise: grape varieties not revealed

45
CAVE VINICOLE D'INGERSHEIM
INGERSHEIM, ALSACE
- 25,000 cases
- Other labels - Jean Geiler, Weingartner

This cooperative first produced sparkling wine in 1981.

HOUSE STYLE & RANGE
The mousse is good, and there is a sweetness to the fruit, but this wine is spoilt by a foursquare aroma and finish.
CRÉMANT D'ALSACE BRUT
Not vintaged, méthode champenoise: grape varieties not revealed

CHARLES JUX
See DOPFF & IRION

55
CAVE VINICOLE DE KIENTZHEIM-KAYSERSBERG
KIENTZHEIM, ALSACE
- 5,000 cases
- Other labels - Anne Boecklin

This cooperative first produced sparkling wine in 1981.

HOUSE STYLE & RANGE
The Tradition has good acidity, but rather soapy aromas, whereas the Anne Boecklin is fresh, sweet and simple. Cave Vinicole de Kientzheim-Kaysersberg used to produce much better, more mature sparkling wines.

ANNE BOECKLIN CRÉMANT D'ALSACE BRUT
Not vintaged, méthode champenoise: grape varieties not revealed
TRADITION CRÉMANT D'ALSACE BRUT
Not vintaged, méthode champenoise: grape varieties not revealed

N/A
DOMAINE KLEIN
ROSEHEIM, ALSACE
- 585 cases

I have only tasted wines from this grower once. He has been producing sparkling wine since 1979.

WINEMAKER
Rémy Klein

HOUSE STYLE & RANGE
Wet straw aroma, otherwise very ordinary.
CRÉMANT D'ALSACE BRUT, 1ER CÔTES DE ROSEHEIM
Not vintaged, méthode champenoise: grape varieties not revealed

N/A
GEORGES KLEIN
ST-HIPPOLYTE, ALSACE
- 1,400 cases

This producer first made Crémant d'Alsace in 1981, but his best wine is Rouge de St-Hippolyte.

WINEMAKER
Georges Klein

HOUSE STYLE & RANGE
The sprightly fruitiness in this wine suggests an easy to drink style, but the mousse is a bit too firm and attacks the tip of the tongue, making it difficult to enjoy.
CRÉMANT D'ALSACE BRUT, 1ER CÔTES DE ROSEHEIM
Not vintaged, méthode champenoise: grape varieties not revealed

N/A
ROBERT KLINGENFUS
MOLSHEIM, ALSACE
- 840 cases

This grower owns 15 hectares, but comes from a family of coopers rather than vignerons.

HOUSE STYLE & RANGE
Only recently had my first experience of this wine, thus no overall rating can be given. This *cuvée* is not very inspiring, being a dull, flabby, malolactic-dominated wine with no Chardonnay character showing whatsoever.
CHARDONNAY CRÉMANT D'ALSACE BRUT
Not vintaged, méthode champenoise: 100% Chardonnay

CAVES KLUG
See CAVE VINICOLE DE BENNWIHR

N/A
JEAN-MARIE KOEHLY
KIENTZHEIM, ALSACE
- 840 cases

Not to be confused with Charles Koehly (Rodern), this grower produces brilliant Pinot Noir, but I have only recently tasted his sparkling wines thus am unable to give an overall rating.

WINEMAKER
Jean-Marie Koehly

HOUSE STYLE & RANGE
The richness and ripeness of his Pinot Noir varietal wine comes through in Koehly's sparkling Rosé *cuvée*, which has an attractive aroma of creamy cherries, a soft and easy palate, with fat fruit dominating a very pleasant finish.
★ CRÉMANT ST-URBAIN ROSÉ CRÉMANT D'ALSACE BRUT
Not vintaged, méthode champenoise: 100% Pinot Noir
CRÉMANT ST-URBAIN CRÉMANT D'ALSACE BRUT
Not vintaged, méthode champenoise: grape varieties not revealed

70
GUSTAVE LORENTZ
BERGHEIM, ALSACE
- 2,500 cases

One of Alsace's best-known producers, from the beautiful village of Bergheim, Gustave Lorentz has produced sparkling wine since 1989.

HOUSE STYLE & RANGE
Terpene aromas suggest Riesling, although there is no indication of any variety on the bottle. Good acidity.

★ CRÉMANT D'ALSACE BRUT
Not vintaged, méthode champenoise: 100% Pinot Blanc

LENTZ
See CAVE VINICOLE DE BENNWIHR

MADAME SANS-GÊNE
See CAVES WESTHALTEN

MARÉCHAL LEFEBVRE
See CAVES WESTHALTEN

MEISTER
See CAVES WESTHALTEN

75
A ET P MERCKLÉ
AMMERSCHWIHR, ALSACE
- 840 cases

Although I have been disappointed with Pierre Mercklé's Crémant d'Alsace in the past, even when it had won a gold medal at Dijon, I am delighted to say that the quality has at last come good. Sparkling wines have been produced here since 1982.

WINEMAKER
André Mercklé

HOUSE STYLE & RANGE
Good fruity acidity gives a tangy, pineapple finish, which should go toasty with a year or two bottle-age.

★ ANDRÉ MERCKLÉ CRÉMANT D'ALSACE BRUT
Not vintaged, méthode champenoise: grape varieties not revealed

C MEYER
See CAVES WESTHALTEN

N/A
MEYER-FONNÉ
KATZENTHAL, ALSACE
- 670 cases

This producer started making Crémant d'Alsace as recently as 1992 and has not established a proven track record.

WINEMAKER
François Meyer

HOUSE STYLE & RANGE
Fresh, fizzy Chablis style.

★ CRÉMANT D'ALSACE BRUT EXTRA
Not vintaged, méthode champenoise: grape varieties not revealed

P MITTNACHT
See CAVES WESTHALTEN

N/A
DOMAINE CLAUDE MORITZ
ANDLAU, ALSACE
- 420 cases

This grower owns vineyards in the *grands crus* of Kastelberg and Wiebelsberg, and has produced sparkling wine since 1984.

WINEMAKER
Claude Moritz

HOUSE STYLE & RANGE
My recent initial experience of these *cuvées* was not a pleasant one, as both the Brut and the Rosé had a sickly smelling nose beyond which it was difficult to enjoy the wines.

CRÉMANT D'ALSACE BRUT
Not vintaged, méthode champenoise: 100% Pinot Blanc
CRÉMANT D'ALSACE ROSÉ BRUT
Not vintaged, méthode champenoise: 100% Pinot Noir

DOMAINE DU MOULIN DE DUSENBACH
See BERNARD SCHWACH

N/A
CHARLES MULLER
TRAENHEIM, ALSACE
- 1,700 cases

A rewarding first encounter with this producer, who has been making sparkling wine since 1982.

HOUSE STYLE & RANGE
The basic Brut is rather sweet, but the Rosé offers soft cherry and strawberry fruit, with a smooth mousse of tiny bubbles.
CRÉMANT D'ALSACE BRUT RÉSERVE
Not vintaged, méthode champenoise: 100% Pinot Blanc
★ ROSÉ CRÉMANT D'ALSACE BRUT
Not vintaged, méthode champenoise: 100% Pinot Noir

70
RENÉ MURÉ
ROUFFACH, ALSACE
- 6,700 cases

A great estate, dating back to 1630, when it was founded by Michel Muré, this producer is best-known for its *Vendange Tardive* styles. Muré has struggled, however, to equal the excellence of the pure Riesling Crémant d'Alsace Brut '0' produced in 1982. When that wine was disgorged in 1987, it retained an exquisite varietal aroma, despite its five years yeast-contact, which would blur most Riesling Crémant d'Alsace.

WINEMAKER
René Muré

HOUSE STYLE & RANGE
Presented in a classy Krug-like bottle, this is fresh, elegant and fruity, with a fine mousse.

★ CRÉMANT D'ALSACE BRUT
Not vintaged, méthode champenoise: grape varieties not revealed

N/A
GÉRARD NEUMEYER
MOLSHEIM, ALSACE
- 670 cases

Although I have had a few wines from this producer in Molsheim, none was particularly special, so I was pleasantly surprised to see Neumeyer's name on this *cuvée* when the covers came off at a recent blind tasting. A producer of sparkling wine since 1980.

WINEMAKER
Gérard Neumeyer

HOUSE STYLE & RANGE
Creamy, malo nose and creamy, rich fruit on the palate, underpinned by very good acidity.
★ CUVÉE MILLÉSIMÉE CRÉMANT D'ALSACE BRUT
Vintaged, méthode champenoise: grape varieties not revealed

N/A
CAVE VINICOLE DE PFAFFENHEIM
PFAFFENHEIM, ALSACE
- 17,000 cases
- Other labels - Hartenberger

Founded in 1957, this cooperative consists of more than 200 growers owning 190 hectares not just in Pfaffenheim, but also Gueberschwihr, Rouffach, Hattstatt, Herrlisheim, Obermorschwihr and Voegtlinshoffen. The Cave Vinicole de Pfaffenheim first produced sparkling wine in 1981 and its products normally rank among the best Crémant d'Alsace, but its quality has been dubious of late and it pains that I cannot rate this co-op on the excellence of its past performance.

HOUSE STYLE & RANGE
The Blanc de Blancs is usually the least interesting *cuvée*, but currently ranks as its best, with rich and ripe fruit that is quite fat, providing good mouthfill and a rather sweet finish, but needs more acidity for a higher score. The Pinot Gris is usually in a class of its own, but the 1994 vintage of this *cuvée* and the Blanc de Noirs are a disgrace, having maderised in less than four years. The current *cuvées* are below par, but hopefully Hartenberger will bounce back.
★ HARTENBERGER, BLANC DE BLANCS CRÉMANT D'ALSACE BRUT
Not vintaged, méthode champenoise: 100% Pinot Blanc
HARTENBERGER BLANC DE NOIR CRÉMANT D'ALSACE BRUT
Vintaged, méthode champenoise: 100% Pinot Noir
HARTENBERGER PINOT GRIS CRÉMANT D'ALSACE BRUT
Vintaged, méthode champenoise: 100% Pinot Gris

VEUVE JOSEPH PFISTER
See LES CAVES J.B. ADAM

ERNEST PREISS
See DOPFF & IRION

VICTOR PREISS
See CAVE VINICOLE DE BENNWIHR

PRINCE ALBERT
See ALBERT HERTZ

RIBEAUVILLE AT THE FOOT OF THE GRAND-CRU
GIESBERG VINEYARD, HAUT-RHIN

70
CAVE VINICOLE DE RIBEAUVILLÉ
RIBEAUVILLÉ, ALSACE
- 10,000 cases
- Other labels - Giersberger, Martin Zahn
One of the oldest cooperatives in France, the
Cave Vinicole de Ribeauvillé was established
in 1895 and is best-known today for its Clos
du Zahnacker, a classic still wine blend from
a region renowned for its pure varietal wines.
A producer of sparkling wine since 1981.
HOUSE STYLE & RANGE
The Riesling has good fruit and although a
recent sample was spoilt by a whiff of sulphur,
this will go toasty with time. While toasty
Riesling might seem strange, this wine certainly
has the acidity to take it. The Giersberger Brut
has an oxidative complexity and attractively
sweet fruit on the palate. A recent sample of
the Giersberger Brut de Noirs was spoilt by a
smelly nose, but it has such lovely, fat, sassy
fruit and cushiony mousse, I'm inclined to
forgive it.

✭ GIERSBERGER CRÉMANT D'ALSACE BRUT
  *Not vintaged, méthode champenoise: grape varieties
  not revealed*
✭ RIESLING CRÉMANT D'ALSACE BRUT
  Not vintaged, méthode champenoise: 100% Riesling
GIERSBERGER BRUT DE NOIR CRÉMANT
D'ALSACE
  Not vintaged, méthode champenoise: 100% Pinot Noir

N/A
ANDRÉ RIEFFEL

MITTELBERGHEIM, ALSACE
- 1,250 cases
This producer has made sparkling wine since
1981, but his reputation has been built on
Klevner, which is always excellent value, and
Riesling Grand Cru Zotzenberg, which is not.
WINEMAKER
André Rieffel
HOUSE STYLE & RANGE
The Cuvée Judith is just fierce fizz, while the
Cuvée Chardonnay has no varietal character.
CRÉMANT D'ALSACE CUVÉE CHARDONNAY
BRUT
  Not vintaged, méthode champenoise: 100% Chardonnay
CUVÉE JUDITH CRÉMANT D'ALSACE BRUT
  Not vintaged, méthode champenoise: 100% Pinot Blanc

70
RUHLMANN
DAMBACH-LA-VILLE, ALSACE
- 1,250 cases
Established in 1668, this grower owns ten
hectares of vineyards, and produced his first
sparkling wine in 1986.
WINEMAKER
André Ruhlmann
HOUSE STYLE & RANGE
Attractively fresh, fat and fruity, with very
good acidity.
✭ CRÉMANT D'ALSACE BRUT
  Vintaged, méthode champenoise: 100% Pinot Blanc

70
EDGARD SCHALLER
MITTELWIHR, ALSACE
- 3,000 cases
Edgard Schaller has produced sparkling wine
since 1979, but is better-known for his
varietal wines, particularly Riesling Grand
Cru Mandelberg.
WINEMAKER
Edgard Schaller
HOUSE STYLE & RANGE
The Blanc de Noirs is Schaller's best *cuvée*
here, with its crisp fruit, a sturdy structure,
and capable of ageing. The Extra Brut is made
in an oxidative style with straw-like aromas. The
last example of S de Schaller 0 had a cabbagey
smell, which I hope was a one-off fault.
✭ BLANC DE NOIR CRÉMANT D'ALSACE BRUT
  Not vintaged, méthode champenoise: 100% Pinot Noir
CRÉMANT D'ALSACE EXTRA BRUT
  Not vintaged, méthode champenoise: 100% Pinot Blanc

S DE SCHALLER BRUT 0 CRÉMANT D'ALSACE
  Not vintaged, méthode champenoise: 100% Pinot Blanc

N/A
THIERRY SCHERRER
AMMERSCHWIHR, ALSACE
- 420 cases
This grower first produced Crémant d'Alsace
as recently as 1993.
WINEMAKER
Thierry Scherrer
HOUSE STYLE & RANGE
Encountered recently for the first time, I
could taste the *dosage* as a separate element in
the wine, but perhaps it was recently
disgorged. Judgement reserved.
CUVÉE THIERRY CRÉMANT D'ALSACE BRUT
  *Not vintaged, méthode champenoise: grape varieties
  not revealed*

N/A
XAVIER SCHOEPFER
WINTZENHEIM, ALSACE
- 500 cases
This grower first produced Crémant d'Alsace
in 1983.
WINEMAKER
Xavier Schoepfer
HOUSE STYLE & RANGE
Tasted recently for the first time, the only
available sample had an unclean flavour that
hung at the back of the throat, thus I must
reserve judgement as far as an overall rating
is concerned.
XS BRUT CRÉMANT D'ALSACE
  *Not vintaged, méthode champenoise: grape varieties
  not revealed*

SCHROEDEL
See LES CAVES J.B. ADAM

N/A
BERNARD SCHWACH
RIBEAUVILLÉ, ALSACE
- 2,100 cases
- Other labels - Domaine du Moulin de
  Dusenbach
There are at least three Alsace producers by
the name of Schwach, all from Hunawihr,
but Bernard Schwach is the best-known,
especially for his Gewurztraminer and Rouge
d'Alsace, which are sold under the Domaine
du Moulin de Dusenbach label. He has
produced sparkling wines since 1982.
WINEMAKER
Bernard Swach
HOUSE STYLE & RANGE
The basic Brut is a bit thin, but the Réserve
has promising acidity and structure.
✭ BRUT RESERVE CRÉMANT D'ALSACE
  *Not vintaged, méthode champenoise: grape varieties
  not revealed*
CRÉMANT D'ALSACE BRUT
  *Not vintaged, méthode champenoise: grape varieties
  not revealed*

N/A
DOMAINE SEILLY
OBERNAI, ALSACE

This family domaine was established in 1865 and owns some of the best slopes in Obernai. Best-known for its rather uninspiring 'Vin de Pistolet'.

WINEMAKER
Marc Seilly

HOUSE STYLE & RANGE
The non-vintage Brut is dull and foursquare, and the vintage Brut smells of cabbage and is too old.
CRÉMANT D'ALSACE BRUT
Not vintaged, méthode champenoise:
100% Pinot Blanc
CRÉMANT D'ALSACE BRUT
Vintaged, méthode champenoise:
100% Pinot Blanc

70
DOMAINE SIFFERT
ORSCHWILLER, ALSACE
• 500 cases

It is Siffert's Pinot Noir Coteaux du Haut-Koenigsbourg that usually stands out, but his Crémant d'Alsace, which he has produced since 1981, also shows promise.

WINEMAKER
Maurice Siffert

HOUSE STYLE & RANGE
This wine has a beautiful Riesling aroma, but the fruit is rather fat and the structure, although firm, could be leaner.
CRÉMANT D'ALSACE BRUT
Not vintaged, méthode champenoise:
100% Riesling

N/A
DOMAINE SIPP MACK
HUNAWIHR, ALSACE
• 850 cases

This domaine was established in 1698, exactly 300 years ago, and is today a great producer of still Riesling wines, both generic and *grand cru*, but I'm not convinced by its fizz, which has been made since 1985.

WINEMAKER
Jacques Sipp

HOUSE STYLE & RANGE
Strangely fat yet tart fruit, with fresh, terpene aromas suggesting some Riesling content.

CRÉMANT D'ALSACE BRUT
Not vintaged, méthode champenoise: grape varieties
not revealed

N/A
SPECHT
MITTELWIHR, ALSACE
• 670 cases

First produced Crémant d'Alsace in 1982.

WINEMAKER
Jean-Paul & Denis Specht

HOUSE STYLE & RANGE
Rich, succulent fruit underpinned by a nice cushiony mousse, this is the first Specht Crémant d'Alsace I have tasted, and it turned out to be the only wine of their's I have enjoyed. Either the Specht brothers are making better wines nowadays, or fizz is their forté; in either case, this is a *cuvée* I will follow.
★ CRÉMANT D'ALSACE BRUT
Not vintaged, méthode champenoise: grape varieties
not revealed

N/A
CHARLES STOEFFLER
BARR, ALSACE
• 1,000 cases

This producer has been making sparkling wine since 1981, although I have only had the chance to taste his *cuvées* once.

WINEMAKER
Vincent Stoeffler

HOUSE STYLE & RANGE
Rather sweet for a brut, but nice fruity style.
★ BLANC DE BLANCS CRÉMANT D'ALSACE BRUT
Vintaged, méthode champenoise: grape varieties not
revealed

N/A
ANTOINE STOFFEL
EGUISHEIM, ALSACE
• 670 cases

My first encounter with Antoine Stoffel from Eguisheim, and I was greatly impressed by his *crémant*, which he has been making since 1988.

WINEMAKER
Antoine Stoffel

HOUSE STYLE & RANGE
Fresh and fruity with a seductively soft, cushiony mousse, minuscule bubbles and refreshingly ripe acidity.
★★ CRÉMANT D'ALSACE BRUT
Not vintaged, méthode champenoise: grape varieties
not revealed

N/A
JOS. STRAUB
BLIENSCHWILLER, ALSACE
• 670 cases

This grower first produced sparkling wine in 1984, and I tasted it recently for the first time but Straub is better known for his very rich *Vendange Tardives* under the Domaine de La Tour label.

HOUSE STYLE & RANGE
An interesting wine, with toasty aromas mixed with hints of coffee grounds on the nose, and toasty fruit on the palate. A good wine that could have been better if the structure were leaner without losing any ripeness of fruit.
★ CUVÉE JEAN-SÉBASTIEN CRÉMANT D'ALSACE BRUT
Not vintaged, méthode champenoise: grape varieties
not revealed

N/A
ANDRÉ TEMPÉ
AMMERSCHWIHR, ALSACE
• 420 cases

My first opportunity to taste several *cuvées* from this producer, who has been making sparkling wine since 1984.

WINEMAKER
André Tempé

HOUSE STYLE & RANGE
Although this wine has ubiquitous fresh, amylic aromas on the nose, the palate has more finesse than most of this style, and better acidity.
★ CRÉMANT D'ALSACE BRUT
Not vintaged, méthode champenoise: grape varieties
not revealed

N/A
JEAN PIERRE VORBURGER
VOEGTLINSHOFFEN, ALSACE
• 500 cases

This grower produced his first sparkling wine as recently as 1994.

HOUSE STYLE & RANGE
Vorburger has not had time to learn the art, let alone establish a style, but the wine I have tasted lacks finesse, although the bottle proudly proclaims a Gold Medal.
CRÉMANT D'ALSACE BRUT
Vintaged, méthode champenoise: 100% Pinot Blanc

N/A
BERNARD WEBER
MOLSHEIM, ALSACE
• 250 cases

This small domaine was established sometime in the 18th century, and made its first Crémant d'Alsace in 1983.

WINEMAKER
Bernard Weber

HOUSE STYLE & RANGE
I have tasted the Crémant d'Alsace Blanc de Blancs a few times over the last seven or eight years, and it was always one of the few wines from Weber that stood out. Not so much a great wine, but certainly a curious one, with its exotic, almost botrytised tropical fruits and vanilla. I was never sure whether I actually liked the wine, but it certainly grabbed my attention. Unfortunately I cannot say that about the current *cuvée*, which is foursquare

with a dull straw-like aroma. The rosé has a worryingly over-mature orange colour.

CRÉMANT D'ALSACE BLANC DE BLANCS BRUT

Not vintaged, méthode champenoise: grape varieties not revealed

CRÉMANT D'ALSACE ROSÉ BRUT

Not vintaged, méthode champenoise: 100% Pinot Noir

WEINGARTNER

See CAVE VINICOLE D'INGERSHEIM

N/A
GÉRARD WEINZORN
NIEDERMORSCHWIHR, ALSACE

This grower produced his first sparkling wine in 1989.

WINEMAKER

Gérard Weinzorn

HOUSE STYLE & RANGE

My first experience of this wine was not a pleasant one. At first I thought it was just foursquare, but then a mustiness started to build at the back of my throat and hung there.

CRÉMANT D'ALSACE BRUT

Not vintaged, méthode champenoise: grape varieties not revealed

N/A
CAVES WESTHALTEN
WESTHALTEN, ALSACE

• 16,700 cases

• Other labels – Heim, Maréchal Lefebvre, Madame Sans-Gêne, Meister, C Meyer, P Mittnacht

This co-op's first sparkling wine was produced in 1974. Heim was once a producer in its own right, but is now just a brand belonging to and marketed by the Westhalten cooperative.

HOUSE STYLE & RANGE

The Westhalten cooperative usually produces good quality sparkling wines, but I have been unimpressed by its *cuvées* of late. Maréchal Lefebvre is the best that I have tasted recently, but that is merely a light and fruity fizz that will go toasty. The last vintage of Sans-Gêne is dull, foursquare and won't improve. The

THE TOWN OF EGUISHEIM, ALSACE, HOME TO WOLFBERGER

vintage Heim Brut is like fizzy, cheap Chablis and the Heim Rosé is just, well, sort of stark, and lacking in any charm whatsoever.

★ CUVÉE MARÉCHAL LEFEBVRE CRÉMANT D'ALSACE BRUT

Not vintaged, méthode champenoise: grape varieties not revealed

HEIM IMPERIAL D'ALSACE CRÉMANT D'ALSACE BRUT

Not vintaged, méthode champenoise: grape varieties not revealed

HEIM IMPERIAL D'ALSACE CRÉMANT D'ALSACE ROSÉ BRUT

Not vintaged, méthode champenoise: 100% Pinot Noir

CUVÉE MADAME SANS-GÊNE CRÉMANT D'ALSACE BRUT

Vintaged, méthode champenoise: grape varieties not revealed

HEIM IMPÉRIAL D'ALSACE CRÉMANT D'ALSACE BRUT

Vintaged, méthode champenoise: grape varieties not revealed

ARTHUR WEYSBECK

See WOLFBERGER

60
CAVES DE WISSEMBOURG
WISSEMBOURG, ALSACE

• Other labels – GF Cavalier, Belamour

A vast bubble factory close to the border with Germany, with quality ranging from dross through low-alcohol fizz up to fresh, clean and uncomplicated. Wines are sourced from almost anywhere legally permitted for the production of *vins mousseux*.

70
WOLFBERGER
EGUISHEIM, ALSACE

• 300,000 cases

• Other labels Aussay, Arthur Weysbeck

Wolfberger is the brand name for the Eguisheim cooperative, which is the largest producer in Alsace both in general and of *crémant*. First produced sparkling wine in 1972.

HOUSE STYLE & RANGE

The basic non-vintage Brut is dull and foursquare. The Demi-Sec is a simple, sweetish fizz of no interest, but could be so much better with a good dollop of Muscat. The vintaged Brut was 1988 at the time of writing and far too old. The Riesling has a petrolly aroma, which follows onto the palate, with nice honeyed, petrol richness, but the wine finishes a bit too soft, requiring more acidity for a higher score. The Rosé has nice cherry-Pinot aromas, with soft fruit lifted by the effervescence on the palate, but again needs more acidity. The Blanc de Noirs has lovely sweet, ripe fruit and a better acidity balance that the previous two *cuvées*. The Chardonnay gets no marks for varietal character, but good apricot fruit, although it could do with more finesse. The Prestige usually has the best balance of all Wolfberger sparkling wines, due to its Riesling content, which also contributes to the wine's fruitiness. The Tokay Pinot Gris needs a bit more work, especially to its structure, which should be leaner, but it is nevertheless a promising, pure varietal fizz.

★ BLANC DE NOIRS CRÉMANT D'ALSACE BRUT

Not vintaged, méthode champenoise: 100% Pinot Noir

CHARDONNAY CRÉMANT D'ALSACE, EXTRA BRUT

Not vintaged, méthode champenoise: 100% Chardonnay

CRÉMANT D'ALSACE BRUT

Not vintaged, méthode champenoise: 100% Pinot Blanc

CRÉMANT D'ALSACE BRUT

Vintaged, méthode champenoise: 100% Pinot Blanc

CRÉMANT D'ALSACE DEMI-SEC

Not Vintaged, méthode champenoise: grape varieties not revealed

★ PRESTIGE CRÉMANT D'ALSACE

Not vintaged, méthode champenoise: Pinot Blanc, Pinot Gris, Pinot Noir, Riesling

★ RIESLING CRÉMANT D'ALSACE BRUT

Not vintaged, méthode champenoise: 100% Riesling

★ ROSÉ CRÉMANT D'ALSACE BRUT

Vintaged, méthode champenoise: 100% Pinot Noir

TOKAY PINOT GRIS CRÉMANT D'ALSACE BRUT

Not vintaged, méthode champenoise: 100% Tokay Pinot Gris

MARTIN ZAHN

See CAVE VINICOLE DE RIBEAUVILLÉ

N/A
J-J ZIEGLER-MAULER
MITTELWIHR, ALSACE

• 42 cases

Sparkling wine has been produced here in tiny quantities since 1988.

HOUSE STYLE & RANGE

This *cuvée* is dull with a straw-like aroma.

CRÉMANT D'ALSACE BRUT

Not vintaged, méthode champenoise: grape varieties not revealed

BORDEAUX

AIMI
See UNION DES PRODUCTEURS (BORDEAUX)

N/A
BALARD
CASTILLON LA BATAILLE, BORDEAUX
• 840 cases
This brand is used by the Union Vignerons d'Aquitaine cooperative in Castillon, which commenced sparkling wine production as recently as 1995. *See also Compagnie du Crémant de Bordeaux.*
HOUSE STYLE & RANGE
A crisp and refreshing fizz, which is more than can be said of most Crémant de Bordeaux.

☆ CRÉMANT DE BORDEAUX BRUT
Not vintaged, méthode champenoise: 10% Muscadelle, 90% Sémillon

N/A
JEAN-LOUIS BALLARIN
HAUX, BORDEAUX
• 17,000 cases
• Other labels – Marquis de Haux
This small producer apparently makes his own sparkling wine, although it is not clear when he first started production. There is also a non-AOC Jean-Louis Ballarin Méthode Traditionnelle.
WINEMAKER
Jean-Louis Ballarin
HOUSE STYLE & RANGE
An impressive Krug-like bottle raises hopes, only for them to be quickly dashed by boring almondy fruit and an unsuitable balance. Tasted only once therefore judgement is reserved.
CUVÉE ROYALE CRÉMANT DE BORDEAUX BRUT
Not vintaged, méthode champenoise: Muscadelle, Sémillon

N/A
BARON D'ESPIET
ESPIET, BORDEAUX
• 1,700 cases
• Other labels – Seigneur des Ormes
This cooperative, which was established in 1932, started producing Crémant de Bordeaux as recently as 1992, contracting

out the process to local specialists Brouette Petit Fils.
WINEMAKER
Brouette Petit Fils
HOUSE STYLE & RANGE
Tasted recently for the first time, this was full and rich in style, with some pepperiness, but showed borderline acceptability as far as quality goes.
BARON D'ESPIET CRÉMANT DE BORDEAUX BRUT
Not vintaged, méthode champenoise: Muscadelle, Sémillon

N/A
VIGNOBLES BOUDON
SOULIGNAC, BORDEAUX
• 750 cases
• Other labels – Le Bourdieu
Established in the Entre-Deux-Mers district in 1920, Vignoble Boudon has marketed its own sparkling wine since 1955, becoming a fully bio-dynamic operation in 1963. Red and white still wines are sold under the Domaine du Bourdieu, Domaine Sainte Anne and Château Haut-Mallet labels.
WINEMAKER
Ets Lateyron
HOUSE STYLE & RANGE
Tasted recently for the first time, this wine was so ordinary that it had no character or style to speak of.
LE BOURDIEU CRÉMANT DE BORDEAUX BRUT
Not vintaged, méthode champenoise: 70% Sémillon, 30% Ugni Blanc

MARC BOUSSEAU
See CHÂTEAU DE L'HURBE

N/A
MAISON RÉMY BRÈQUE
SAINT GERVAIS, BORDEAUX
• 840 cases
One of the oldest producers of sparkling Bordeaux wines, Maison Rémy Brèque has specialised in this style since 1927.
HOUSE STYLE & RANGE
Tasted recently for the first time, I prefer the basic Brut to Rémy Brèque's Cuvée Prestige. Both wines have straw-like aromas, but the basic Brut has ripe fruit underneath, whereas the Cuvée Prestige unfortunately tastes dried out.

☆ CRÉMANT DE BORDEAUX BRUT
Not vintaged, méthode champenoise: 35% Muscadelle, 30% Sauvignon, 35% Sémillon
CUVÉE PRESTIGE CRÉMANT DE BORDEAUX BRUT
Not vintaged, méthode champenoise: 50% Muscadelle, 50% Sémillon

73
BROUETTE PETIT FILS
BOURG SUR GIRONDE, BORDEAUX
• 27,000 cases
One of the largest producers of Crémant de Bordeaux, Brouette also acts as a contract sparkling winemaker for numerous other brands, and is involved in the production of AOC fizz in the Loire Valley and Limoux.
HOUSE STYLE & RANGE
The Tradition Blanc de Blancs is fresh and easy with good fruit and acidity. Brouette's prestige Cuvée de L'Abbaye is too fat and lacking in acidity, but although the Rosé has an off-putting mature orange colour, it has plenty of perfumed fruit on the palate, with a delicately fruity finish.
CRÉMANT DE BORDEAUX CUVÉE DE L'ABBAYE BRUT
Not vintaged, méthode champenoise: 50% Muscadelle, 50% Sémillon

☆ CRÉMANT DE BORDEAUX TRADITION BLANC DE BLANCS BRUT
Not vintaged, méthode champenoise: 20% Muscadelle, 80% Sémillon
☆ ROSÉ CRÉMANT DE BORDEAUX BRUT
Not vintaged, méthode champenoise: 20% Cabernet Sauvignon, 80% Merlot

CATHÉRINE DE FRANCE
See CHÂTEAU SAINTE CATHÉRINE

N/A
COMPAGNIE DU CRÉMANT DE BORDEAUX
CASTILLON LA BATAILLE, BORDEAUX
• 4,200 cases
• Other labels – Paul Ribes
This offshoot of the Castillon cooperative was established in 1994 to focus on Bordeaux's developing sparkling wine market, and its first *cuvée* was produced the following year.
WINEMAKER
Union Vignerons d'Aquitaine
HOUSE STYLE & RANGE
Tasted recently for the first time, this wine

had off-putting wet-straw aromas followed by high-tone fruit on the palate, and was nothing like the Crémant de Bordeaux made by the Union Vignerons d'Aquitaine from exactly the same grape variety composition.

PAUL RIBES BRUT

Not vintaged, méthode champenoise: 10% Muscadelle, 90% Sémillon

45
LES CORDELIERS
ST-EMILION, BORDEAUX

• 75,000 cases

The oldest and most famous of all sparkling Bordeaux wine producers, this firm was established in 1890, producing its first sparkling wine two years later. This firm has its showcase cellars beneath the ruined cloisters of Clos des Cordeliers in St-Emilion.

WINEMAKER
Patrick Verge

HOUSE STYLE & RANGE
The quality always used to be decent, if not exactly exciting, but it has been particularly disappointing of late. The only interesting wine in the range recently has been Les Cordeliers 1892-1992 anniversary *cuvée*, which has plenty of rich, clean fruit, although even that needs more acidity to achieve some finesse. The Cuvée Saint-Jean is very fruity, but flabby – acidity again proving to be the villain. The basic Brut is just light and lacking.

COLLIER NOIR

Not vintaged, non-AOC, méthode champenoise: grape varieties not revealed

COLLIER ROUGE

Not vintaged, non-AOC sparkling red, méthode champenoise: grape varieties not revealed

✯ LES CORDELIERS 1892-1992 CRÉMANT DE BORDEAUX BRUT

Not vintaged, méthode champenoise: Cabernet Franc and Cabernet Sauvignon, Merlot, Muscadelle, Sauvignon Blanc, Sémillon

CRÉMANT DE BORDEAUX BRUT

Not vintaged, méthode champenoise: Cabernet Franc and Cabernet Sauvignon, Merlot, Muscadelle, Sauvignon Blanc, Sémillon

CRÉMANT DE BORDEAUX ROSÉ

Not vintaged, méthode champenoise: Cabernet Franc and Cabernet Sauvignon, Merlot, Muscadelle, Sauvignon Blanc, Sémillon

CUVÉE PRESTIGE BLANC DE BLANCS BRUT

Not vintaged, méthode champenoise: Muscadelle, Sémillon

CUVÉE PRESTIGE BLANC DE BLANCS DEMI-SEC

Not vintaged, méthode champenoise: Muscadelle, Sémillon

CUVÉE SAINT-JEAN BLANC DE BLANCS BRUT/DEMI-SEC

Not vintaged, méthode champenoise: Muscadelle, Sémillon, Ugni Blanc

CRISTAL DE MELIN
See CLAUDE MODET

GRANDE CATHÉRINE
See CHÂTEAU SAINTE CATHÉRINE

N/A
CHÂTEAU DE L'HURBE
ST-LAURENT D'ARCE, BORDEAUX

• 210 cases

This *petit château* was established in 1921 and has produced its own sparkling wine since 1994.

WINEMAKER
Marc Bousseau

HOUSE STYLE & RANGE
Succulent fruit intermingles with toasty aromas on both nose and palate. Very good for one of the first *cuvées*, but needs more finesse on the finish for a higher score.

✯ CHÂTEAU DE L'HURBE CRÉMANT DE BORDEAUX BRUT

Not vintaged, méthode champenoise: Sémillon

LOUIS LAFON
See ANDRÉ QUANCARD

N/A
SA LATEYRON
MONTAGNE, BORDEAUX

• 33,500 cases
• Other labels - Paulian

This family-owned enterprise is the second-oldest producer of sparkling Bordeaux wine, having been established in 1897.

HOUSE STYLE & RANGE
Tasted recently for the first time, this wine is most intriguing. Although lime is commonly found in top quality Australian Sémillon, I have never encountered such a distinctive lime aroma and flavour in a Bordeaux wine before. When I tasted it blind I thought it was pure Sémillon, but later discovered it to be 70%, and many others have 90% or more, without even the barest hint of lime, which makes me suspect that the Sémillon in this wine was very much riper than is the norm for this appellation.

★ PAULIAN CRÉMANT DE BORDEAUX BRUT

Not vintaged, méthode champenoise: 20% Cabernet Franc, 10% Muscadelle, 70% Sémillon

N/A
CHÂTEAU LESPARRE
BORDEAUX

HOUSE STYLE & RANGE
Tasted recently for the first time, the only available sample of this wine was oxidised.

BLANC DE BLANCS BRUT

Vintaged, méthode champenoise: grape varieties not revealed

N/A
CHÂTEAU DE LISENNES
TRESSES, BORDEAUX

• 350 cases

Established in 1938, the first sparkling wines produced under this label were made as recently as 1996. The grapes are purchased and the wines produced under contract.

WINEMAKER
Union Vignerons d'Aquitaine

HOUSE STYLE & RANGE
Tasted recently for the first time, this wine was rather strange on the nose, which would deter me from drinking it, which is a pity because it is not bad on the palate, having rich fruit and uncommonly good acidity for Crémant de Bordeaux.

CRÉMANT DE BORDEAUX BRUT

Not vintaged, méthode champenoise: 10% Muscadelle, 90% Sémillon

LUCCIOS
See UNION DES PRODUCTEURS

MARQUIS DE HAUX
See JEAN-LOUIS BALLARIN

N/A
CLAUDE MODET
BAURECH, BORDEAUX

• 500 cases
• Other labels - Cristal de Melin

Established in 1971, sparkling wines have been produced under contract since 1992.

WINEMAKER
Jean-Louis Ballarin

HOUSE STYLE & RANGE
Tasted recently for the first time, this wine was not very impressive, having a mean, straw-like aroma and dull, almondy fruit. The only good thing was the acidity.

CRISTAL DE MELIN CRÉMANT DE BORDEAUX BRUT

Not vintaged, méthode champenoise: Sémillon

N/A
GAEC DU MOULIN BORGNE
MARCENAIS, BORDEAUX

• 1,340 cases
• Other labels - Domaine de la Nouzillette

This family-owned estate has sold sparkling wines under the Domaine de la Nouzillette label since 1979.

WINEMAKER
Brouette Petit Fils

HOUSE STYLE & RANGE
Tasted recently for the first time, the Blanc de Blancs had a certain perfumed attraction to the nose, but the palate was totally dominated by unripe Sauvignon fruit. The Rosé was more acceptable despite its orange hue and mature, jammy fruit.

DOMAINE DE LA NOUZILLETTE BLANC DE BLANCS, CRÉMANT DE BORDEAUX BRUT
Not vintaged, méthode champenoise: 30% Colombard, 70% Sauvignon Blanc

DOMAINE DE LA NOUZILLETTE, CRÉMANT DE BORDEAUX ROSÉ BRUT
Not vintaged, méthode champenoise: 70% Cabernet Sauvignon Blanc, 30% Merlot

DOMAINE DE LA NOUZILLETTE
See GAEC DU MOULIN BORGNE

PAULIAN
See S A LATEYRON

N/A
ANDRÉ QUANCARD
ST ANDRÉ DE CUBZAC, BORDEAUX
• 2,500 cases
• Other labels - Louis Lafon

WINEMAKER
Louis Lafon

HOUSE STYLE & RANGE
Tasted recently for the first time, this wine was mature but not particularly expressive.
LOUIS LAFON CRÉMANT DE BORDEAUX BRUT
Not vintaged, méthode champenoise: 10% Muscadelle, 50% Sauvignon Blanc, 40% Sémillon

PAUL RIBES
See COMPAGNIE DU CRÉMANT DE BORDEAUX

N/A
CHÂTEAU SAINTE CATHÉRINE
PAILLET, BORDEAUX
• 5,000 cases
• Other labels - Cathérine de France, Grande Cathérine
This 12th century chapel was converted into a *château* and established as a wine estate in 1987. Château-bottled Crémant de Bordeaux has been produced since 1990.

HOUSE STYLE & RANGE
Tasted recently for the first time, the Brut

had straw-like aromas and the Rosé was pleasant but not special.
CRÉMANT DE BORDEAUX ROSÉ BRUT
Vintaged, méthode champenoise: 50% Cabernet Sauvignon, 50% Merlot

CRÉMANT DE BORDEAUX BRUT
Vintaged, méthode champenoise: 20% Cabernet Sauvignon, 10% Merlot, 70% Sémillon

SEIGNEUR DES ORMES
See BARON D'ESPIET

N/A
TOUR DU ROY
ST-EMILION, BORDEAUX
• 1,650 cases
Château du Roy has produced sparkling wines since 1886, making it one of the oldest sparkling wine producers in Bordeaux.

HOUSE STYLE & RANGE
Although situated in St-Emilion, these sparkling wines are sourced from the Entre-Deux-Mers district. Tasted recently for the first time, when only the Brut was tasted, thus no general rating is possible, but it had a creamy rich aroma, with sweet fruit and good acidity.
✭ CRÉMANT DE BORDEAUX BRUT
Not vintaged, méthode champenoise: 20% Sauvignon, 80% Sémillon

CRÉMANT DE BORDEAUX DEMI-SEC
Not vintaged, méthode champenoise: 20% Sauvignon, 80% Sémillon

CRÉMANT DE BORDEAUX ROSÉ
Not vintaged, méthode champenoise: grape varieties not revealed

CRÉMANT DE BORDEAUX ROSÉ DEMI-SEC
Not vintaged, méthode champenoise: grape varieties not revealed

N/A
ELISABETH TROCARD
LES ARTIGUES DE LUSSAC, BORDEAUX
• 500 cases
This Crémant de Bordeaux has been made under contract by Cordeliers in St-Emilion since 1965.

WINEMAKER
Les Cordeliers

HOUSE STYLE & RANGE
Tasted recently for the first time, thus no rating is possible, but this was a succulently fruity *cuvée* with a touch of class on the finish. Certainly worth watching in the future.
CRÉMANT DE BORDEAUX CUVÉE TRADITION BRUT
Not vintaged, méthode champenoise: grape varieties not revealed

N/A
UNION DES PRODUCTEURS
CASTILLON LA BATAILLE, BORDEAUX
• 2,100 cases
• Other labels - Aimi, Luccios
This cooperative was established in 1949 and, since 1990, it has contracted Les Cordeliers to produce Crémant de Bordeaux from a small proportion of its production.

WINEMAKER
Les Cordeliers

HOUSE STYLE & RANGE
The peppery, citrous Luccios is on the borderline of acceptability, but the Aimi is cloying and quite appalling.
AIMI CRÉMANT DE BORDEAUX RÉSERVE BRUT
Not vintaged, méthode champenoise: 10% Muscadelle, 90% Sémillon

LUCCIOS BLANC DE BLANCS CRÉMANT DE BORDEAUX BRUT
Not vintaged, méthode champenoise: 10% Muscadelle, 90% Sémillon

UNION VIGNERONS D'AQUITAINE
See BALARD

40
VEUVE DU VERNAY
MÉRIGNAC, BORDEAUX
• 2 million cases
The brand that became so big it took over the firm, Veuve du Vernay was designer-made for the British market in the late 1960s by Robert Charmat, son of Eugène Charmat, inventor of the *cuve close* method of sparkling wine production. It is now a major international brand, but brands of no fixed origin are becoming *passé* and Veuve du Vernay will find it increasingly hard to maintain its market share.

In 1993 Veuve du Vernay was 'restyled and relaunched to reflect a growing demand for lighter, fresher styles' and in 1997 it was 'reblended and relaunched to suit the change in tastes'. Prior to that, there was a 1984 relaunch, but there are probably others I have missed. Tastes had not in fact changed much between 1993 and 1997, but brands are often relaunched when the distributor is changed, and they have to give some sort of reason.

Coinciding with the last relaunch, it was announced that Angela Muir had been contracted to advise on improvements to the blend. Muir is the redoubtable British MW who in the 1980s almost single-handedly modernised Spain's bulk-wine production practices. If anyone can make Veuve du Vernay fit for the next millennium, Muir can, but her biggest difficulty will be sourcing better quality wines within the tight-fisted budget demands faced by a big brand with high marketing overheads and a low unit price.

Her problems do not stop there because the way this wine is produced is, like many huge-volume *cuve close* brands, the complete reverse of how it should be, and the reason for this stems from the price above which it is not prepared to pay for base wines. With low-grade base wines on the one hand, and a huge number of bottles produced on the other, Veuve du Vernay cannot take any chances, thus the first fermentation is cold and slow. Too cold and too slow, while the second fermentation is warmer and faster to get the bottle out of the winery and onto the shelf as quick as possible. This is not only back-to-front, it will continue to produce a fizz that is dominated by bland, hard-fruit aromas of apples and pears, when Veuve du Vernay needs more luscious, soft-flesh fruit aromas.

The days of bland *cuve close* are numbered. Veuve de Vernay requires a richer flavour with low-key tropical notes and crisper acidity if it is to combat New World fizz, its new adversary. The only way that Veuve du Vernay will survive will be by a quality upgrade, not a marketing retread, and the only way to fund that is by edging its selling price up to just below the lower end of the premium sector.

HOUSE STYLE & RANGE

A very fresh and soft, but bland amylic-style fizz that is typical of the technically correct, stylistically boring category of French *cuve close* with no fixed-abode. The difference between the wines currently available and those that resulted from the previous relaunch is that Chardonnay, Chenin Blanc and Folle Blanche have been replaced by Sauvignon Blanc and Colombard, and whereas the Charentes and Loire remain two of the three most important sources, Gascony is now preferred to Bordeaux for the third. On the face of it, this might seem like a retrograde step, but you can buy good quality Colombard for the price of a very poor Chardonnay. Similarly, why pay through the nose for rubbish in Bordeaux when you can find better wines for much less from Gascony? The result is still, however, far from exciting, although in 1998, six months after they were relaunched, Angela Muir had yet to put her seal of approval on any of the *cuvées*. So far the Rosé remains the same, with no plans to reblend or relaunch.

BRUT
> *Not vintaged, cuve close: Chardonnay, Colombard, Sauvignon Blanc, Ugni Blanc*

DEMI-SEC
> *Not vintaged, cuve close: Chardonnay, Colombard, Sauvignon Blanc, Ugni Blanc*

ROSÉ
> *Not vintaged, cuve close: Cinsault, Syrah*

VINEYARDS AT ST CYR-LES-COLONS, YONNE, BURGUNDY

BURGUNDY

N/A
VEUVE AMBAL
RULLY, BURGUNDY

- 260,000 cases
- Other labels – Charles Ninot, Paul Robin, Charles Roux

This house was established in 1898, since when it has specialised in *méthode champenoise*.

HOUSE STYLE & RANGE

Cuvée Marie Ambal is light and easy with sweetish, almondy fruit, Cuvée Saint Charles is flabby with too much malolactic character, and the Tête de Cuvée is decidedly foursquare.

CUVÉE MARIE AMBAL CRÉMANT DE BOURGOGNE BRUT
> *Not vintaged, méthode champenoise: 30% Chardonnay, 70% Pinot Noir*

CUVÉE SAINT CHARLES CRÉMANT DE BOURGOGNE BRUT
> *Not vintaged, méthode champenoise: 70% Chardonnay, 30% Pinot Noir*

TÊTE DE CUVÉE CRÉMANT DE BOURGOGNE BRUT
> *Not vintaged, méthode champenoise: 60% Chardonnay, 30% Pinot Noir*

70
CAVES DE BAILLY
SAINT BRIS LE VINEUX, BURGUNDY

- 100,000 cases
- Other labels – Meurgis

Also known as SICA du Vignoble Auxerrois, this cooperative on the outskirts of the Chablis district was founded in 1972 and produced its first sparkling wine in 1974.

HOUSE STYLE & RANGE

Despite the fullness suggested by the Blanc de Noirs term, Cave de Bailly's rendition of this style is light and elegant, with perfumed aromas and an exceptionally fine mousse. The rosé has a darkish *clairet* colour and gives the impression that it will age, but it lacks finesse. However, this *cuvée* represents a minute part of Caves de Bailly's production and thus has relatively little effect on the overall rating.

MEURGIS BLANC DE NOIRS CRÉMANT DE BOURGOGNE BRUT

> *Vintaged, méthode champenoise: 20% Gamay, 80% Pinot Noir*

MEURGIS CRÉMANT DE BOURGOGNE ROSÉ BRUT
> *Vintaged, méthode champenoise: 20% Chardonnay, 80% Pinot Noir*

N/A
BARTNICKI
BURGUNDY

- Other labels – Princesse de Vix, Comte de Saint Robert

Little known about this producer, whose wines I have recently encountered.

HOUSE STYLE & RANGE

The basic Brut had a strawlike aroma and sweet fruit, the Princesse de Vix was disconcertingly yellow, but with rich, sweet fruit.

COMTE DE SAINT ROBERT CRÉMANT DE BOURGOGNE BRUT
> *Not vintaged, méthode champenoise: grape varieties not revealed*

CRÉMANT DE BOURGOGNE BRUT
> *Not vintaged, méthode champenoise: grape varieties not revealed*

PRINCESSE DE VIX CRÉMANT DE BOURGOGNE BRUT
> *Not vintaged, méthode champenoise: grape varieties not revealed*

N/A
ALAIN BERTHAULT
MOROGES, BURGUNDY

- 300 cases

This grower has been making sparkling wine since 1984.

WINEMAKER
Alain Berthault

HOUSE STYLE & RANGE

Tasted recently for the first time, this wine comes from the Coteaux du Mont St-Avril in Moroges, and is clean, rich and fruity with some malolactic complexity.

✱ CRÉMANT DE BOURGOGNE BRUT
> *Not vintaged, méthode champenoise: 10% Aligoté, 10% Gamay, 80% Pinot Noir*

N/A
CAVE DE VIGNERONS DE BISSEY

BISSEY SOUS CRUCHAUD, BURGUNDY
- 6,000 cases

This cooperative has produced sparkling wine since 1980. The Rosé does not actually mention *rosé* on the bottle, but has a pink coloured foil for those in the know.

HOUSE STYLE & RANGE

Tasted only once, therefore no overall rating, but these were all dull, foursquare wines. The Rosé tasted of greengages, the Blanc de Blanc was straw-like and oxidative, and the Brut was unclean.

CRÉMANT DE BOURGOGNE BRUT
Vintaged, méthode champenoise: 60% Aligoté, 10% Chardonnay, 30% Pinot Noir

CRÉMANT DE BOURGOGNE BLANC DE BLANCS BRUT
Vintaged, méthode champenoise: 100% Chardonnay

CRÉMANT DE BOURGOGNE ROSÉ BRUT
Vintaged, méthode champenoise: 60% Aligoté, 10% Gamay, 30% Pinot Noir

N/A
LOUIS BOUILLOT
NUITS-SAINT-GEORGES, BURGUNDY
- 17,000 cases
- Group ownership - Varichon et Clerc (Savoie)

Made at the same address as Chevalier, which is owned by Boisset.

HOUSE STYLE & RANGE

Tasted recently for the first time, the only sample had an overpowering sweet-sickly smell.

CRÉMANT DE BOURGOGNE BRUT
Not vintaged, méthode champenoise: 75% Chardonnay, 25% Pinot Noir

N/A
DOMAINE GILBERT ET RÉGINE BRIGAND
MASSINGY, BURGUNDY
- 1,500 cases

This family-owned domaine has produced sparkling wine since 1975.

HOUSE STYLE & RANGE

The only sample I have tasted was spoilt by clean, but excessive sulphur.

CARTE NOIRE CRÉMANT DE BOURGOGNE BRUT
Not vintaged, méthode champenoise: equal parts Chardonnay, Pinot Blanc, Pinot Noir

70
CHANSON PÈRE & FILS
BEAUNE, BURGUNDY

One of the six oldest *négociant* houses in Burgundy, Chanson has something of a reputation for its red Bourgogne Mousseux.

HOUSE STYLE & RANGE

Light, elegant and sweetly stylish, with soft varietal flavours of cherries and strawberries.

★ BOURGOGNE MOUSSEUX
Not vintaged, méthode champenoise: 100% Pinot Noir

N/A
GUY CHAUMONT
ROSEY, BURGUNDY
- 500 cases

A producer of sparkling wine since 1987.

WINEMAKER

Guy Chaumont

HOUSE STYLE & RANGE

Oxidative, wet-straw aroma with full, rich fruit on palate.

CRÉMANT DE BOURGOGNE BRUT
Not vintaged, méthode champenoise: 40% Aligoté, 40% Chardonnay, 20% Pinot Noir

PHILIPPE CHAUTARD
See MAISON LOUIS PICAMELOT

40
CHEVALIER
NUITS-SAINT-GEORGES, BURGUNDY
- 9,200 cases

Acquired by Boisset (along with almost everything else in Burgundy) in June 1994, Chevalier moved into its current ultra-modern facility at Nuits-Saint-Georges in 1995. In addition to Crémant de Bourgogne, Chevalier also produces *méthode traditionelle* and large volumes of anonymous *cuve close*.

HOUSE STYLE & RANGE

The Prestige Brut is basic and foursquare.

PRESTIGE CRÉMANT DE BOURGOGNE BRUT
Not vintaged, méthode champenoise: 80% Chardonnay, 20% Pinot Noir

N/A
BERNARD ET ODILE CROS
MOROGES, BURGUNDY
- 1,250 cases

A producer of sparkling wine since 1946.

HOUSE STYLE & RANGE

While the 1994 is dull and foursquare, the '93 is a fresh, citrous style with a very firm mousse.

CRÉMANT DE BOURGOGNE BRUT
Vintaged, méthode champenoise: 65% Aligoté, 35% Pinot Noir

88
DOMAINE DELIANCE
DRACY-LE-FORT, BURGUNDY
- 250 cases

The two highest-scoring Crémants de Bourgogne and they both come from the same grower, which under blind conditions speaks volumes. Domaine Deliance makes a total of just 250 cases per year, produced from Côte Chalonnaise grapes.

HOUSE STYLE & RANGE

If only all Crémant de Bourgogne *cuvées* had the class and finesse of these two wines. The Ruban Mauve is virtually a *blanc de noirs* and a beautiful wine it is too, with gorgeous fluffy fruit brimming with sherbety freshness

and great life-preserving ripe acidity. The Ruban Vert is closer to a *blanc de blancs* and has lovely Burgundian Chardonnay fruit, and is obviously well selected and skilfully made, with the potential to age.

★★ RUBAN MAUVE CRÉMANT DE BOURGOGNE BRUT
Not vintaged, méthode champenoise: 10% Chardonnay, 90% Pinot Noir

★★ RUBAN VERT CRÉMANT DE BOURGOGNE BRUT
Not vintaged, méthode champenoise: 80% Chardonnay, 20% Pinot Noir

72
ANDRÉ DELORME
RULLY, BURGUNDY
- 30,000 cases

This firm is very important in the Côte Chalonnaise, where it owns 60 hectares of vineyards and has a consistent standard in both *négociant* and domaine-bottled Burgundies. Jean-François Delorme was one of the original members of the technical committee that laid down the foundations of the Crémant regulations prior to the decree that established the first of these appellations in 1975.

WINEMAKER

Jean-François Delorme

HOUSE STYLE & RANGE

Generally soft and buttery, although sometimes the fruit can have a strange combination of richness and underripeness. Although the Rosé is fruit-driven, it does have a rather noticeable malolactic taste on the finish. The Blanc de Noirs is best, with better fruit, structure and finesse than the other *cuvées*. Delorme was once one of the front-runners, not only among Crémant de Bourgogne, but also for any sparkling wine alternative to Champagne, but its *cuvées* no longer stand out internationally. I doubt there has been any drop in quality, merely that others have moved on a lot faster, particularly outside France.

BLANC DE BLANCS CRÉMANT DE BOURGOGNE BRUT
Not vintaged, méthode champenoise: 40% Aligoté, 60% Chardonnay

BLANC DE NOIRS CRÉMANT DE BOURGOGNE BRUT
Not vintaged, méthode champenoise: 20% Gamay, 80% Pinot Noir

CRÉMANT DE BOURGOGNE ROSÉ BRUT

Not vintaged, méthode champenoise: 10% Gamay, 90% Pinot Noir

CELLIER DENISE
See DOMAINE GONET

LUCIEN DENIZOT
See DOMAINE DES MOIROTS

N/A
THIERRY ET CORINNE DROUIN
JERGISSON, BURGUNDY
- 270 cases

This small domaine consists of some seven hectares of Mâconnais vineyards and has produced a sparkling wine since 1991.

WINEMAKER
Thierry Drouin

HOUSE STYLE & RANGE
My first encounter with this wine found some richness, but it was not special.
CRÉMANT DE BOURGOGNE BRUT

Not vintaged, méthode champenoise: 100% Chardonnay

70
CHARLES DE FÈRE
NUITS-ST-GEORGES
- 42,000 cases

This brand was established by Champenois Jean-Louis Denois (see Domaine de l'Aigle) at Fère-en-Tardenois, where he produced non-AOC sparkling wine from Chardonnay and Pinot Noir growing just outside the Champagne appellation. He later supplemented these with grapes from his own vineyard in Limoux, then sold out to Boisset who moved the production to its ultra-modern facility in Nuits-St-George. Although Denois no longer has any formal connection with the company, Charles de Fère's winemaker, Marcel Maillet, maintains contact on an official basis, and the two regularly conduct comparitive tastings of their respective products.

WINEMAKER
Marcel Maillet, Grégoire Pissot

HOUSE STYLE & RANGE
There are three primary sources for these wines: the Loire, Langeudoc and Limoux. The Tradition and Tradition Chardonnay are well-structured wines that pick up biscuity richness with a little additional bottle-age. Although this is a serious *Vin Mousseux de Qualité*, and deserves a good rating, Charles de Fère has always lacked finesse and still does.

CUVÉE JEAN LOUIS

Not vintaged, cuve close: grape varieties not revealed

RESERVE BLANC DE BLANCS BRUT

Not vintaged, bottle-fermented: 40% Chardonnay, 15% Chenon Blanc, 15% Ugni Blanc plus others

★ TRADITION BRUT

Not vintaged, bottle-fermented: Chardonnay, Pinot Noir

★ TRADITION CHARDONNAY BRUT

Not vintaged, bottle-fermentd: 100% Chardonnay
BRUT ROSÉ

Not vintaged, bottle-fermented: Cabernet Franc, Groslot, Pinot Noir

N/A
DOMAINE FRANCIS FICHET
IGÉ, BURGUNDY
- 1,000 cases

This family-owned domaine started producing Crémant de Bourgogne in 1988.

HOUSE STYLE & RANGE
The Brut has a floral, peppery aroma followed by peppery fruit on the palate. I have not tasted the Rosé Demi-Sec.
CRÉMANT DE BOURGOGNE BRUT

Not vintaged, méthode champenoise: 80% Chardonnay, 20% Pinot Noir

CRÉMANT DE BOURGOGNE ROSÉ DEMI-SEC

Not vintaged, méthode champenoise: 100% Pinot Noir

N/A
CHÂTEAU DE FUISSÉ
FUISSÉ, BURGUNDY
- 500 cases

This is the famous tried and tested master of Pouilly-Fuissé. He first produced Crémant d'Alsace in 1992.

WINEMAKER
Jean-Jacques Vincent

HOUSE STYLE & RANGE
Tasted recently for the first time, thus no overall rating, but as an admirer of Château de Fuissé's Mâconnais wine, I am desperately disappointed by M. Vincent's Crémant de Bourgogne. It is not bad, but it is not special either, and I was rather hoping it would be, given its maker's ability to produce excellent still white wines.
CHÂTEAU FUISSÉ CRÉMANT DE BOURGOGNE BRUT

Not vintaged, méthode champenoise: 100% Chardonnay

N/A
DOMAINE GONET
BURGUNDY
★ Other labels - Cellier Denise

VINEYARDS IN THE SNOW AT CAVE DE LUGNY

Owned by Gonet Ph. & Fils of Le-Mesnil-sur-Oger in Champagne.

HOUSE STYLE & RANGE
Only tasted once, when it was overblown and maderised.
CELLIER DENISE CRÉMANT DE BOURGOGNE BRUT

Not vintaged, méthode champenoise: grape varieties not revealed

75
LES VIGNERONS DE HAUTE BOURGOGNE
CHATILLON-SUR-SEINE, BURGUNDY
- 2,500 cases

This cooperative started producing Crémant de Bourgogne as recently as 1994.

HOUSE STYLE & RANGE
The latest *cuvée* of basic Brut was spoilt by burnt-toffee tones on the finish, but it has been a decent fizz in the past. The Demi-Sec is a lovely wine, with creamy, biscuity malolactic complexity on the nose, and rich, sweet, vanilla and caramel fruit on the palate. Assuming this cooperative has not gone overboard on malolactic, it deserves its rating.
CRÉMANT DE BOURGOGNE BRUT

Not vintaged, méthode champenoise: 30% Chardonnay, 70% Pinot Noir

CRÉMANT DE BOURGOGNE DEMI-SEC

Not vintaged, méthode champenoise: 30% Chardonnay, 70% Pinot Noir

73
LES CAVES DES HAUTES-CÔTES
BEAUNE, BURGUNDY
- 15,000 cases

This cooperative started making sparkling Burgundy in 1979, and exclusively uses grapes grown in the Hautes-Côtes de Nuits and Hautes-Côtes de Beaune.

HOUSE STYLE & RANGE
The non-vintage Brut shows some biscuity maturity on the nose, with good acidity underpinning plenty of light, elegant fruit on the palate. The non-vintage Blanc de Blancs is one of the more serious Crémants de Bourgogne, with creamy, biscuity aromas, good length of flavour, and ripe, fruity acidity.
CRÉMANT DE BOURGOGNE BLANC DE BLANCS BRUT

Not vintaged, méthode champenoise: grape varieties not revealed

CRÉMANT DE BOURGOGNE BRUT

Not vintaged, méthode champenoise: grape varieties not revealed

CRÉMANT DE BOURGOGNE BRUT

Vintaged, méthode champenoise: grape varieties not revealed

CRÉMANT DE BOURGOGNE ROSÉ BRUT

Not vintaged, méthode champenoise: grape varieties not revealed

N/A
EARL d'HEILLY-HUBERDEAU
MOROGES, BURGUNDY
- 325 cases
- Other labels – d'Heilly, Pierre et Martine Huberdeau, Pierre d'Heilly et Martine Huberdeau

Producer of domaine-bottled, bio-dynamic Crémant d'Alsace since 1990.
WINEMAKER
Pierre d'Heilly-Huberdeau
HOUSE STYLE & RANGE
Tasted recently for the first time, thus judgement is reserved. The rich, biscuity fruit in this wine is spoilt by its straw-like aroma, which unfortunately detracts from the wines underlying finesse.
CRÉMANT DE BOURGOGNE BRUT
Not vintaged, méthode champenoise: equal parts Aligoté, Chardonnay, Pinot Noir

PIERRE ET MARTINE HUBERDEAU
See EARL d'HEILLY-HUBERDEAU

N/A
LES VIGNERONS D'IGÉ
IGÉ, BURGUNDY
- 11,250 cases

This Mâcon cooperative first produced sparkling wine in 1977.
HOUSE STYLE & RANGE
Recently tasted for the first time, the non-vintage had a not unattractive pepperiness to its fruit, whereas the Rosé shows a little amylic character on the palate.
CRÉMANT DE BOURGOGNE BRUT
Not vintaged, méthode champenoise: 80% Chardonnay, 20% Pinot Noir
CRÉMANT DE BOURGOGNE ROSÉ BRUT
Not vintaged, méthode champenoise: grape varieties not revealed

0
KRITER
BEAUNE, BURGUNDY
- Group ownership - Patriarche Père & Fils
- 1.2 million cases

These sparkling wines are said to contain some Burgundian Aligoté, but that is hardly something to boast about.
HOUSE STYLE & RANGE
Technically correct, but dull and boring, these wines might as well be made by the *cuve close*. They taste to me as if they contain a large amount of wines from the Loire and Charentes.
BRUT DE BRUT
Not vintaged, transfer method: grape varieties not revealed
CARTE D'OR DEMI-SEC
Not vintaged, transfer method: grape varieties not revealed

ROSÉ
Not vintaged, transfer method: grape varieties not revealed
IMPÉRIAL BRUT
Vintaged, transfer method: grape varieties not revealed

NOËLLIE LABORDE
See MAISON ALBERT SOUNIT

JOSEPH LEFEVRE (SOME EXPORT MARKETS)
See MOINGEON LA MAISON DU CRÉMANT

N/A
THIERRY LESPINASSE
ROSEY, BURGUNDY
This family-owned enterprise first made sparkling wine in 1982.
HOUSE STYLE & RANGE
Tasted only once, the style seemed quite perfumed, but the only sample available was unfortunately corked, thus it was difficult to discern what its true style should be.
CRÉMANT DE BOURGOGNE BRUT
Not vintaged, méthode champenoise: 100% Chardonnay

70
CAVE DE LUGNY
LUGNY, BURGUNDY
- 37,500 cases

This well-known cooperative has been producing sparkling wine since 1975.
HOUSE STYLE & RANGE
Initially these wines seem to be very much fruit-driven, but all too often it is just the aroma that is fruity, and the wines lack fruit and finesse on the palate. In most cases, these *cuvées* are best drunk as young and fresh as possible. The only exception is the Rosé, Cave de Lugny's best fizz, which is lovely and fresh when young, with lots of red fruit on the palate, a hint of vanilla on the finish, turning toasty after a further 12 months ageing.
CRÉMANT DE BOURGOGNE BRUT
Not vintaged, méthode champenoise: 50% Chardonnay, 50% Pinot Noir
CRÉMANT DE BOURGOGNE BLANC DE BLANCS BRUT
Not vintaged, méthode champenoise: 100% Chardonnay

★ CRÉMANT DE BOURGOGNE BRUT ROSÉ, CAVE DE LUGNY
Vintaged, méthode champenoise: grape varieties not revealed

CRÉMANT DE BOURGOGNE CUVÉE MILLÉSIMÉE BRUT
Vintaged, méthode champenoise: Chardonnay, Pinot Noir

N/A
CAVE DES VIGNERONS DE MANCEY
MANCEY, BURGUNDY
HOUSE STYLE & RANGE
This *cuvée* tastes as if the base wine was kept too long before bottling.
CRÉMANT DE BOURGOGNE BLANC DE BLANCS BRUT
Not vintaged, méthode champenoise: grape varieties not revealed

N/A
DOMAINE MATHIAS
CHAINTRE, BURGUNDY
- 200 cases

This family-owned domaine started to produce sparkling wine as recently as 1995.
HOUSE STYLE & RANGE
My first taste of this wine was very recent, and it was the first *cuvée* produced by this domaine, thus an overall judgement would not be fair, but I was not impressed by this foursquare, straw-like fizz.
CUVÉE RÉSERVÉE CRÉMANT DE BOURGOGNE BRUT
Not vintaged, méthode champenoise: 100% Chardonnay

MEURGIS
See CAVES DE BAILLY

N/A
MOINGEON LA MAISON DU CRÉMANT
NUITS-ST-GEORGES, BURGUNDY
- 165,000 cases
- Other labels - Joseph Lefevre (some export markets)

The house of Moingeon was established more than 100 years ago and commenced sparkling wine production in 1975, when the Crémant de Bourgogne appellation was established. In 1995 the company was taken over by Mark and Eva Siddle, proprietors of Domaine Bertagna in Vougeot. They have since renovated and re-equipped this winery in order to specialise in sparkling wine production exclusively by the *méthode champenoise*.
HOUSE STYLE & RANGE
A fizz full of simple, sprightly fruit, but I expect the quality and complexity of these wines to increase dramatically as the effect of the new equipment kicks in, and more sophisticated techniques are employed. The presentation is already excellent.
CRÉMANT DE BOURGOGNE BRUT
Not vintaged, méthode champenoise: 10% Aligoté, 70% Chardonnay, 20% Pinot Noir

VIN MOUSSEUX DE QUALITÉ BRUT

Not vintaged, méthode champenoise: mostly Chardonnay

N/A
DOMAINE DES MOIROTS
BISSEY-SOUS-CRUCHAUD, BURGUNDY

- 900 cases
- Other labels - Lucien Denizot

A family-owned estate that has produced domaine-bottled sparkling wines since 1976.

WINEMAKER
Lucien Denizot

HOUSE STYLE & RANGE
Perfumed with some pepperiness on the palate.

CRÉMANT DE BOURGOGNE BRUT

Not vintaged, méthode champenoise: 35% Aligoté, 65% Pinot Noir

N/A
DOMAINE MOISSENET-BONNARD
POMMARD, BURGUNDY

- 175 cases

This small domaine started producing Crémant de Bourgogne as recently as 1995.

HOUSE STYLE & RANGE
Tasted recently for the first time, this wine was rich and toasty, but short on the finish.

CRÉMANT DE BOURGOGNE BRUT

Not vintaged, méthode champenoise: 100% Pinot Noir

75
DOMAINE HENRI NAUDIN-FERRAND
MAGNY-LES-VILLERS, BURGUNDY

- 300 cases

This family estate has an excellent reputation for its beautifully focused Burgundies, and has produced small quantities of excellent domaine-bottled Crémant de Bourgogne since 1991.

HOUSE STYLE & RANGE
Rich fruit aroma and flavour; not a profound wine, but it is a profoundly correct and enjoyable one.

CRÉMANT DE BOURGOGNE BRUT

Not vintaged, méthode champenoise: equal parts Aligoté, Chardonnay, Pinot Noir

CHARLES NINOT
See VEUVE AMBAL

N/A
PARIGOT
MELOISEY, BURGUNDY

HOUSE STYLE & RANGE
My first experience of these wines, the Crémant Blanc has a firm structure, good depth of flavour, and a firm mousse, and the Crémant Rosé is a plump, almost fat and fruity wine, hinting of strawberries. The only sample of the Crémant Millésimé (1992) I have tasted was cabbagey.

✭ CRÉMANT BLANC CRÉMANT DE BOURGOGNE BRUT

Not vintaged, méthode champenoise: grape varieties not revealed

✭ CRÉMANT ROSÉ CRÉMANT DE BOURGOGNE BRUT

Not vintaged, méthode champenoise: grape varieties not revealed

CRÉMANT MILLÉSIMÉ CRÉMANT DE BOURGOGNE BRUT

Vintaged, méthode champenoise: grape varieties not revealed

80
MAISON LOUIS PICAMELOT
RULLY, BURGUNDY

- 4,250 cases
- Other labels - Philippe Chautard

Maison Louis Picamelot has been making sparkling wine since 1926, and this wealth of experience is evident in its best Crémant de Bourgogne, the Cuvée Jeanne Thomas.

WINEMAKER
Philippe Chautard

HOUSE STYLE & RANGE
The basic Brut is an elegant fizz that is full of perfumed fruit that seems to be Pinot Noir, but Cuvée Jeanne Thomas is a truly top Crémant de Bourgogne, boasting toasty, oaky fruit aromas of some finesse, with excellent acidity supporting the palate.

✭ CRÉMANT DE BOURGOGNE BRUT

Not vintaged, méthode champenoise: 25% Aligoté, 25% Chardonnay, 50% Pinot Noir

★★ CRÉMANT DE BOURGOGNE, CUVÉE JEANNE THOMAS BRUT

Not vintaged, méthode champenoise: 10% Aligoté, 90% Chardonnay

1926 CUVÉE ANNIVERSAIRE CRÉMANT DE BOURGOGNE BRUT

Not vintaged, méthode champenoise: equal parts Aligoté, Chardonnay, Pinot Noir

PRINCESSE DE VIX
See BARTNICKI

50
GROUPEMENT DE PRODUCTEURS DE PRISSÉ
PRISSÉ, BURGUNDY

- 10,500 cases

Also known as Cave de Prissé, this cooperative is well known for its good value Mâcon, and has sold sparkling wines under its own label since 1975.

HOUSE STYLE & RANGE
Straightforward peppery fruit.

CRÉMANT DE BOURGOGNE BLANC DE BLANCS BRUT

Not vintaged, méthode champenoise: 100% Chardonnay

N/A
DOMAINE MICHEL PRUNIER
MEURSAULT, BURGUNDY

- 500 cases

This grower produces brilliant Auxey-Duresses and has made sparkling wine since 1982.

WINEMAKER
Michel Prunier

HOUSE STYLE & RANGE
I have recently encountered this Crémant de Bourgogne for the first time. Unfortunately the sample I tasted was unclean and over-sulphured. Considering the quality of his still wines, I would like to believe it was not representative and I will thus reserve judgement.

CRÉMANT DE BOURGOGNE BRUT

Not vintaged, méthode champenoise: 60% Aligoté, 10% Gamay, 30% Pinot Noir

PAUL ROBIN
See VEUVE AMBAL

N/A
DOMAINE DU ROTISSON
ST-GERMAIN SUR L'ARBRESLE, BURGUNDY

- 750 cases

This grower has produced domaine-bottled sparkling wine from his Beaujolais vineyard since 1993.

WINEMAKER
J. Paul Peillon

HOUSE STYLE & RANGE
Perfumed, almondy fruit.

CRÉMANT DE BOURGOGNE BRUT

Not vintaged, méthode champenoise: 100% Chardonnay

CHARLES ROUX
See VEUVE AMBAL

COMTE DE SAINT ROBERT
See BARTNICKI

JEAN-CLAUDE SIMONNET
See SIMONNET-FEBVRE

N/A
SIMONNET-FEBVRE
CHABLIS, BURGUNDY

- 6,650 cases
- Other labels - Jean-Claude Simonnet

This producer has been making *méthode champenoise* sparkling wine since 1840, selling it as Chablis Mousseux, a wine that was in vogue at the turn of the century.

WINEMAKER
Jean-Claude Simonnet

HOUSE STYLE & RANGE

The basic Brut has become insipid of late. The Carte Blanche and Blanc de Blancs are not AOC wines, although the Chardonnay used for the former comes from the Chablis region.

BLANC DE BLANCS BRUT
Not vintaged, méthode champenoise: 100% Ugni Blanc
CARTE BLANCHE BRUT
Not vintaged, méthode champenoise: 100% Chardonnay
CRÉMANT DE BOURGOGNE BRUT
Not vintaged, méthode champenoise: 25% Chardonnay, 75% Pinot Noir
CRÉMANT DE BOURGOGNE ROSE
Not vintaged, méthode champenoise: 100% Pinot Noir

70
MAISON ALBERT SOUNIT
RULLY, BURGUNDY

• 7,500 cases
• Other labels – Noëllie Laborde

Founder Albert Sounit started making sparkling wine in the 1930s.

HOUSE STYLE & RANGE

This producer's best sparkling wine, Cuvée Chardonnay, is sourced from the Mâconnais and Beaujolais. Although it has a typically amylic aroma, there is also some finesse, which could mean the peardrop character will dissipate after a while, making way for a dry, light-bodied fizz with fine acidity. The Brut de Brut tastes as if the grapes were not ripe enough for a non-*dosage* style.

CRÉMANT DE BOURGOGNE BRUT DE BRUT
Not vintaged, méthode champenoise: 25% Chardonnay, 75% Pinot Noir
★ CRÉMANT DE BOURGOGNE, CUVÉE CHARDONNAY
Not vintaged, méthode champenoise: 100% Chardonnay
CRÉMANT DE BOURGOGNE PRESTIGE BRUT
Not vintaged, méthode champenoise: 35% Chardonnay, 65% Pinot Noir

UPITRES AT MAISON ALBERT SOUNIT

N/A
CÉLINE ET LAURENT TRIPOZ
LOCHÉ, BURGUNDY

• 100 cases

This tiny family enterprise in Mâcon was founded as recently as 1986, when Céline and Laurent Tripoz exploited just two hectares of vines, but they now own eight hectares. The first sparkling wine was produced in 1991.

WINEMAKER

Laurent Tripoz

HOUSE STYLE & RANGE

The unripe fruit on the non-vintage Brut has been given a superficial creamy, malolactic veneer, while the vintage Brut is ripe, but even more malolactic-dominated, with creamy-caramel aromas and mint toffees on the finish.

CRÉMANT DE BOURGOGNE BRUT
Not vintaged, méthode champenoise: 100% Chardonnay
CRÉMANT DE BOURGOGNE BRUT
Vintaged, méthode champenoise: 100% Chardonnay

N/A
CAVE DE VERZÉ
VERZÉ, BURGUNDY

A minor Mâcon cooperative.

HOUSE STYLE & RANGE

Green and unripe.

CRÉMANT DE BOURGOGNE BRUT
Vintaged, méthode champenoise: 100% Chardonnay

N/A
CAVE DE VIRÉ
VIRÉ, BURGUNDY

• 17,000 cases

This successful cooperative, located in one of Mâcon's most ubiquitous village appellations, has produced sparkling wine since 1975.

HOUSE RANGE

CRÉMANT DE BOURGOGNE BRUT
Vintaged, méthode champenoise: 100% Chardonnay

80
VITTEAUT-ALBERTI
RULLY, BURGUNDY

• 20,000 cases

Established in 1951, this family firm first produced sparkling wine in 1975, and today owns eight hectares of vineyards in the Haute-Côtes de Beaune and the Côte Chalonnaise.

WINEMAKER

Gérard Vitteaut

HOUSE STYLE & RANGE

The basic Brut is not bad, but not special, and the Rosé is foursquare. However, you can taste the selection in the lovely fruit-driven Blanc de Blancs, which has a succulent fruity finish that is not too brut, and a silky-soft mousse of ultrafine bubbles.

BLANC DE BLANCS BRUT, CRÉMANT DE BOURGOGNE
Not vintaged, méthode champenoise: 20% Aligoté,

80% Chardonnay
CRÉMANT DE BOURGOGNE BRUT
Not vintaged, méthode champenoise: 20% Aligoté, 40% Chardonnay, 40% Pinot Noir
CRÉMANT DE BOURGOGNE ROSÉ BRUT
Not vintaged, méthode champenoise: 100% Pinot Noir

N/A
EMILE VOARICK
SAINT-MARTIN-SOUS-MONTAIGU, BURGUNDY

• 1,000 cases

First sparkling wines were produced in 1991.

HOUSE STYLE & RANGE

I recently encountered this producer's sparkling wine for the first time, thus it would be unfair to generalise, but the sample I tasted was too heavy, and lacked finesse.

CRÉMANT DE BOURGOGNE BRUT
Not vintaged, méthode champenoise: 100% Chardonnay

CORBIÈRES

N/A
MAISON LA MOTTE
NARBONNE

A one-off release of a single-vineyard, pure Chardonnay sparkling wine from grapes grown at Domaine de la Motte in 1992, which is best-known for James Herrick's brilliant still Chardonnay wines, and his up-and-coming Cuvée Simon red. Although officially deemed a *Vin Mousseux de Qualité*, this was for all practical purposes a *méthode champenoise* Vin de Pays d'Oc, and a darn sight better than most wines claiming the Crémant de Bourgogne appellation. Maison la Motte fizz has not been repeated, and Herrick doubts that it ever will be, which is a pity.

GAILLAC

N/A
CANTO PERLIC
GAILLAC

• 250 cases

British couple Claire and Alex Taylor bought this small estate in 1991, the year of the frost, a quirk of nature that forged their interest in sparkling wine. Due to the frost, the grapes were so acid that Alex decided to make Gaillac Mousseux; fizz has been his main interest ever since. Whether his winemaking is up to scratch has yet to be established, but he shows more enthusiasm about raising the profile of Gaillac than all the other French owners put together.

WINEMAKER

Alex Taylor

HOUSE STYLE & RANGE

Tasted for the first time recently, therefore no overall rating, but either Taylor is getting it totally wrong, or the only available bottle was not representative because he thinks 'it's brilliant', yet the wine I tasted had an oxidised nose and a heavy, rather clumsy, palate.

CUVÉE CLAIRE BRUT DE BRUT

Vintaged, méthode champenoise: 45-35% Len de l'El, 55-65% Mauzac

N/A
VIGNOBLES JEAN CROS
CAHUZAC-SUR-VÈRE, GAILLAC

• Other labels - Château Laroze, Domaine Jean Cros

The Cros family own two properties in the Coteaux de la Rive Droite area of Gaillac, the 17-hectare Château Laroze, and the 25-hectare Domaine Jean Cros.

WINEMAKER
Jean-Etienne Cros

HOUSE STYLE & RANGE
Not tasted recently, but usually one of the appellation's better producers.

GAILLAC MÉTHODE GAILLACOISE

Vintaged, méthode rurale: 33% Len de l'El, 67% Mauzac

GAILLAC PERLÉ

Vintaged, vin pétillant, méthode rurale: 33% Len de l'El, 67% Mauzac

N/A
DOMAINE D'ESCAUSSES
SAINTE-CROIX, GAILLAC

An important-sized family enterprise with 24 hectares of vineyards in the Coteaux de la Rive Droite area of the Gaillac appellation.

WINEMAKER
Denis Balaran

HOUSE RANGE
GAILLAC BRUT

Vintaged, méthode champenoise: grape varieties not revealed

GABERLÉ
See CAVE DE LABASTIDE DE LEVIS

N/A
DOMAINE DE GRADDÉ
CAMPAGNAC, GAILLAC

One of the few Gaillac bubblies produced from vineyards on the Plateau Cordaia, Domaine de Graddé is situated at the northwestern tip of the appellation.

WINEMAKER
Etienne Coursières

HOUSE RANGE
GAILLAC PERLÉ

Vintaged, vin pétillant, méthode rurale: Len de l'El, Mauzac

N/A
DOMAINE DE LABARTHE
CASTANET, GAILLAC

Historic domaine that has been in the Albert family since the 16th century, Domaine Labarthe comprises 40 hectares at the northeastern corner of the Coteaux de la Rive Droite.

WINEMAKER
Jean Albert

HOUSE RANGE
GAILLAC BRUT

Vintaged, méthode champenoise: grape varieties not revealed

GAILLAC PERLÉ

Vintaged, vin pétillant, méthode rurale: 100% Mauzac

N/A
CAVE DE LABASTIDE DE LEVIS
MARSSAC-SUR-TARN, GAILLAC

• Other labels - Gaberlé
Slightly sparkling wines from one of Gaillac's three cooperatives.

HOUSE STYLE & RANGE
Although the Gaillac Sec Perlé denomination for *pétillant* dry white wines has been dropped, Gaillac Perlé still seems to flourish in wines such as these. The grapes are grown on the Terrasses de la Rive Gauche area of the appellation.

GABERLÉ

Not vintaged, vin pétillant, méthode rurale: Len de l'El, Mauzac

GABERLÉ ROSÉ

Not vintaged, vin pétillant, méthode rurale: grape varieties not revealed

N/A
DOMAINE DE LACROUX
CESTAYROLS, GAILLAC

• 670 cases
The Derrieux family who run this property in the Coteaux de la Rive Droite show more interest in the sparkling wines of their appellation than most other producers, but I have yet to be convinced by the quality.

WINEMAKER
Jean & Philippe Derrieux

HOUSE STYLE & RANGE
Although I was not impressed, I have tasted only the Brut and that just once, so it would be unfair to make an overall assessment.

GAILLAC BRUT

Vintaged, méthode champenoise: 100% Len de l'El

GAILLAC DEMI-SEC

Vintaged, méthode champenoise: 100% Len de l'El

CHÂTEAU LAROZE
See VIGNOBLES JEAN CROS

N/A
CHÂTEAU LASTOURS
LISLE-SUR-TARN, GAILLAC

This 18th century château comprises 38 hectares of vineyards in the Coteaux de la Rive Droite area of Gaillac and produces the entire range of wines permitted.

WINEMAKER
Hubert & Pierric de Faramond

HOUSE RANGE
GAILLAC BRUT

Vintaged, méthode champenoise: grape varieties not revealed

GAILLAC DEMI-SEC

Vintaged, méthode champenoise: grape varieties not revealed

GAILLAC PERLÉ

Vintaged, vin pétillant, méthode rurale: Len de l'El, Mauzac

N/A
CHÂTEAU DE MAYRAGUES
CASTELNAU DE MONTMIRAL, GAILLAC

• 210 cases
This property was purchased by the current owners in 1980.

WINEMAKER
Alan Geddes

HOUSE RANGE

GAILLAC BRUT

Not vintaged, méthode champenoise: 70% Len de l'El, 30% Mauzac

N/A
CHÂTEAU MIRAMOND
GAILLAC

This property in the Coteaux de la Rive Droite area of Gaillac produces dessert-style fizz by the classic *méthode gaillaçoise* from the same variety as Blanquette Méthode Ancestrale in Limoux.

WINEMAKER
Hubert & Pierric de Faramond

HOUSE RANGE
GAILLAC PERLÉ

Vintaged, vin pétillant, méthode rurale: 100% Mauzac

N/A
DOMAINE DE PERCHES
GAILLAC

• 330 cases
This vineyard was established as recently as 1993 and a sparkling wine was produced from the first harvest in 1994.

WINEMAKER
Charlotte Fraser

HOUSE STYLE & RANGE
A first effort from such young vines, it would be unfair to make a generalised judgement, but the sample I tasted had an unclean finish that caught at the back of the throat. There is, however, more enthusiasm here than in

most other Gaillac properties, and I hope this results in a rapid improvement.

GAILLAC BRUT

Not vintaged, méthode champenoise: 60% Len de l'El, 40% Mauzac

78
ROBERT PLAGEOLES
CAHUZAC-SUR-VÈRE, GAILLAC

• Other labels - Domaine Très-Cantous

This grower and his son own two domaines, Roucou and Très-Cantous, although it is the latter that produces fizz and the family name takes slight precedence over the domaine. However, it is the style of wine, often focusing on a pure varietal, that takes centre stage in the labelling of these wines. Robert Plageoles comes from a family who have been *vignerons* for half a millennium and he is surely one of Gaillac's greatest producers, combining innovation and tradition to produce some of the most fascinating wines in Southwest France.

WINEMAKER
Robert Plageoles

HOUSE STYLE & RANGE
Big, full and rich, with a light mousse of ultrafine bubbles, and a long, soft sweet finish with more emphasis on character than finesse.

★ MAUZAC NATURE EFFERVESCENT DOMAINE TRÈS-CANTOUS

Not vintaged, méthode rurale: 100%

72
DOMAINE DES TERRISSES
GAILLAC

A small producer in the Coteaux de la Rive Droite area of Gaillac.

WINEMAKER
Brigette & Alain Cazottes

HOUSE STYLE & RANGE
Consistently fresh and fruity.

GAILLAC BRUT

Vintaged, méthode champenoise: grape varieties not revealed

★ GAILLAC MÉTHODE GAILLAÇOISE

Vintaged, méthode rurale: grape varieties not revealed

N/A
DOMAINE LA TOUR BOISSEL
BOISSEL, GAILLAC

Vincent Fiault is the fifth generation of *vignerons* to run this property, where he produces the entire range of wines permissible.

WINEMAKER

VINEYARDS NEAR GAILLAC

Vincent Fiault

HOUSE RANGE
GAILLAC BRUT

Vintaged, méthode champenoise: grape varieties not revealed

GAILLAC DEMI-SEC

Vintaged, méthode champenoise: grape varieties not revealed

GAILLAC PERLÉ

Vintaged, vin pétillant, méthode rurale: Len de l'El, Mauzac

DOMAINE DE TRÉS-CANTOUS
See ROBERT PLAGEOLES

N/A
CAVE DES TROIS CLOCHERS
LISLE-SUR-TARN, GAILLAC

Owned and run by the fifth generation of a family of *vignerons*, Caves des Trois Clochers is situated in the Coteaux de la Rive Droite where a new winery was built in 1995.

WINEMAKER
Jean-Pierre & Thierry Pages

HOUSE RANGE
GAILLAC MÉTHODE TRADITIONNELLE BRUT

Not vintaged, méthode champenoise: grape varieties not revealed

GAILLAC PERLÉ

Not vintaged, vin pétillant, méthode rurale: Len de l'El, Mauzac

N/A
DOMAINE DE LA TRONQUE
CASTELNAU DE MONTMIRAL, GAILLAC

• 250 cases

This domaine was established in 1976 and became fully bio-dynamic in 1988.

WINEMAKER
Claude Leduc

HOUSE STYLE & RANGE
Not impressed, but tasted only once.

BERLE D'ANTAN MÉTHODE GAILLAÇOISE

Not vintaged, méthode rurale: 100% Mauzac

CUVÉE AMÉLIE, GAILLAC BRUT, CUVÉE TRADITIONNELLE

Not vintaged, méthode champenoise: Muscadelle, Sauvignon Blanc

JURA

70
ROLET
ARBOIS, JURA

These are the favourite non-Champagne guzzlers of Doctor Patricia Norman, an MD who is so passionate about the health benefits of drinking wine that she spends more time selling it than practising medicine.

HOUSE STYLE & RANGE
The Brut is an oxidatively-driven *cuvée* with no finesse, but not unpleasant in a rustic way. The Rosé is also rustic, without much finesse, but much better, with bruised plums on the nose contrasting with perfumed fruit on the palate.

CRÉMANT DU JURA BRUT

Not vintaged, méthode champenoise: grape varieties not revealed

★ CRÉMANT DU JURA BRUT ROSÉ

Not vintaged, méthode champenoise: grape varieties not revealed

LIMOUX

70
DOMAINE DE L'AIGLE
ROQUETAILLADE, LIMOUX

Jean-Louis Denois' family had been growers in Cumières, Champagne, for six generations but, after qualifying from the Beaune school of viticulture and oenology, he sought practical experience in Australia, New Zealand and California before taking up a job in South Africa in 1979.

Returning to France, he set up production of non-AOC sparkling wine at Fère-en-Tardenois, just outside Champagne, creating the premium sparkling wine label of Charles de Fère. In 1984 he entered into a ten year consultancy agreement to produce sparkling wine with Jeff Grier of Villiera in South Africa. In 1989 he purchased Domaine de l'Aigle in Limoux, and this must be the place he had been searching for because Denois has been reasonably settled ever since. His winemaking is as innovative as ever.

WINEMAKER
Jean-Louis Denois

HOUSE STYLE & RANGE
The Brut Tradition is full-bodied and well-structured, but rather heavy on the nose, which has a touch of toffee that detracts from the finesse of the wine, which undergoes its first fermentation in old barrels.

The Crémant de Limoux is lighter and fresher in style, with peppery fruit of some elegance, but the finish is very soft and almost soapy.

BRUT CRÉMANT DE LIMOUX

Not vintaged, méthode champenoise: 20% Chardonnay, 20% Chenin Blanc, 60% Mauzac

TRADITION BRUT CHARDONNAY-PINOT NOIR

Not vintaged, non-AOC, méthode champenoise: 30% Chardonnay, 70% Pinot Noir

AIMERY
See SIEUR D'ARQUES

ALDERIC
See SIEUR D'ARQUES

ANNE DE LA RENARDIÈRE
See SCEA CONCOURSON

75
GEORGES & ROGER ANTECH
LIMOUX

This relatively large family-owned Limoux house owns some 60 hectares of vineyards, and is one of the most dedicated producers in the appellation.

WINEMAKER

Georges Antech

HOUSE STYLE & RANGE

The Crémant de Limoux is fresh and crisp with a fine, lean structure, the Blanquette de Limoux somewhat fatter and less fine, but fresher, finer and crisper than most others examples of that appellation. The Maître Blanquetiers vies with the Crémant de Limoux for lightness and elegance, yet has a longer, finer and more intense finish. The Cuvée Saint-Laurent is dedicated to the patron saint of cooks, and is supposed to have more strength and fullness of flavour in order to cope with the task of accompanying food.

CUVÉE CARTE BLANCHE BLANQUETTE DE LIMOUX BRUT

Not vintaged, méthode champenoise: 5% Chardonnay, 5% Chenin Blanc, 90% Mauzac

CUVÉE CARTE BLANCHE BLANQUETTE DE LIMOUX DEMI-DOUX

Not vintaged, méthode champenoise: 5% Chardonnay, 5% Chenin Blanc, 90% Mauzac

CUVÉE CARTE BLANCHE BLANQUETTE DE LIMOUX DEMI-SEC

Not vintaged, méthode champenoise: 5% Chardonnay, 5% Chenin Blanc, 90% Mauzac

★ CUVÉE CARTE NOIRE BLANQUETTE DE LIMOUX BRUT

Not vintaged, méthode champenoise: 5% Chardonnay, 5% Chenin Blanc, 90% Mauzac

CUVÉE CARTE NOIRE BLANQUETTE DE LIMOUX DEMI-SEC

Not vintaged, méthode champenoise: 5% Chardonnay, 5% Chenin Blanc, 90% Mauzac

★★ FLASCON DES MAÎTRE BLANQUETIERS BLANQUETTE DE LIMOUX BRUT

Not vintaged, méthode champenoise: 5% Chardonnay, 5% Chenin Blanc, 90% Mauzac

CUVÉE CARTE OR BLANQUETTE DE LIMOUX BRUT

Vintaged, méthode champenoise: 5% Chardonnay, 5% Chenin Blanc, 90% Mauzac

★ CUVÉE CARTE OR PRESTIGE CRÉMANT DE LIMOUX BRUT

Vintaged, méthode champenoise: 20% Chardonnay, 20% Chenin Blanc, 60% Mauzac

★ CUVÉE SAINT-LAURENT CRÉMANT DE LIMOUX BRUT

Vintaged, méthode champenoise: 20% Chardonnay, 20% Chenin Blanc, 60% Mauzac

★ GRANDE CUVÉE CRÉMANT DE LIMOUX BRUT

Vintaged, méthode champenoise: 20% Chardonnay, 20% Chenin Blanc, 60% Mauzac

72
ROBERT
PIEUSSE, LIMOUX

One of the more commercially aware growers of Limoux.

HOUSE STYLE & RANGE

Fresher and richer than most Limoux, the Crémant de Limoux has finer, more elegant fruit.

CARTE IVOIRE BLANQUETTE DE LIMOUX BRUT

Not vintaged, méthode champenoise: Chardonnay, Chenin Blanc, Mauzac

CARTE NOIRE BLANQUETTE DE LIMOUX BRUT

Not vintaged, méthode champenoise: Chardonnay, Chenin Blanc, Mauzac

★ CRÉMANT DE LIMOUX BRUT

Not vintaged, méthode champenoise: Chardonnay, Chenin Blanc, Mauzac

★ DAME ROBERT BLANQUETTE DE LIMOUX BRUT

Not vintaged, méthode champenoise: Chardonnay, Chenin Blanc, Mauzac

★ MAÎTRE BLANQUETIERS BLANQUETTE DE LIMOUX BRUT

Not vintaged, méthode champenoise: Chardonnay, Chenin Blanc, Mauzac

CHÂTEAU DE GAURE
See SIEUR D'ARQUES

DAME D'ARQUES
See SIEUR D'ARQUES

LE PROPRIÉTAIRE
See SIEUR D'ARQUES

70
SIEUR D'ARQUES
LIMOUX

- 670,000 cases
- Other labels - Aimery, Alderic, Château de Gaure, Dame d'Arques, Le Propriétaire, Sieur d'Arques, Vanel

The local Limoux cooperative is one of the most confusingly named wine operations in the world, referring to itself variously as [a] Les Caves du Sieur d'Arques, [b] Aimery Les Caves du Sieur d'Arques, [c] Aimery Producteur, and [d] Société des Producteurs de Blanquette de Limoux. By whatever name, this cooperative produces 80% of all the Blanquette de Limoux.

BOTTLES OF CRÉMANT DE LIMOUX UNDERGOING REMUAGE AT SIEUR D'ARQUES

Established in 1946, this cooperative today consists of 600 members who between them own 1,000 hectares of vineyards, and boast one of the most modern wineries in France.

HOUSE STYLE & RANGE

The Alderic is a full, well-structured, standard-quality Blanquette de Limoux. Sieur d'Arques ranks among the best of the dry Limoux, whether Blanquette de Limoux or Crémant de Limoux, as in this case. It often has most finesse, the tiniest bubbles and the most accessible fruit. The Grande Cuvée Renaissance has a full, buttery, caramel aroma, but the fruit is too thin and bitter, and cannot take this level of malolactic (quite apart from the fact that its acidity does not need to be lowered!). Un Soir Ame du Vin is a semi-sparkling novelty wine that is advertised as 'anti-conventional but socially correct'. The Dame d'Arques is a wonderfully luscious *méthode ancestrale* with 70g/l of residual sugar (which is technically *doux*, yet tastes more like a *demi-sec*), with a silky succulence on the finish. Le Propriétaire offers a similar style from an

individual producer, whose details are indicated
in the label. Although Le Propriétaire is
sealed with a traditional mushroom-shaped
cork, it is also affixed with a levered stopper
to help retain the fizz after opening the bottle.
This used to be quite common, particularly
on soft drinks, many years ago, but it has
fallen by the wayside and it was clever of the
Sieur d'Arques cooperative to re-invent it. I
wonder if it will take off?

➤ ★ **DAME D'ARQUES BLANQUETTE
MÉTHODE ANCESTRALE TRADITION**
Not vintaged, méthode rurale: 100% Mauzac
**GRANDE CUVÉE RENAISSANCE CRÉMANT DE
LIMOUX**
*Not vintaged, méthode
champenoise: 20% Chardonnay,
20% Chenin Blanc, 60%
Mauzac*
**LE PROPRIÉTAIRE
BLANQUETTE MÉTHODE
ANCESTRALE FRUITÉ**
*Not vintaged, méthode rurale: 100%
Mauzac*
**UN SOIR AME DU VIN CÉPAGE CHARDONNAY,
VIN DE PAYS DE LA HAUTE VALLÉE DE L'AUDE**
*Not vintaged, semi-sparkling, carbonated: 100%
Chardonnay*
BLANQUETTE DE LIMOUX ALDERIC BRUT
*Vintaged, méthode champenoise: 10% Chardonnay,
10% Chenin Blanc, 80% Mauzac*
CHÂTEAU DE GAURE BLANQUETTE DE LIMOUX
Vintaged, méthode champenoise: 100% Mauzac
CHÂTEAU DE GAURE BLANQUETTE DE LIMOUX
*Vintaged, méthode champenoise: 15% Chardonnay,
15% Chenin Blanc, 70% Mauzac*
CRÉMANT DE LIMOUX, CUVÉE DE DOM NEUVE
*Vintaged, méthode champenoise: 20% Chardonnay,
20% Chenin Blanc, 60% Mauzac*
**CRÉMANT DE LIMOUX, DUC DE QUERIBUS
BRUT**
*Vintaged, méthode champenoise: 20% Chardonnay,
20% Chenin Blanc, 60% Mauzac*
DIAPHANE BLANQUETTE DE LIMOUX BRUT
Vintaged, méthode champenoise: 100% Mauzac
★ **SIEUR D'ARQUES CRÉMANT DE LIMOUX
BRUT**
*Vintaged, méthode champenoise: 20% Chardonnay,
20% Chenin Blanc, 60% Mauzac*
VANEL CRÉMANT DE LIMOUX BRUT
*Vintaged, méthode champenoise: 20% Chardonnay,
20% Chenin Blanc, 60% Mauzac*
**VANEL CRÉMANT DE LIMOUX CUVÉE
EXCELLENCE**
*Vintaged, méthode champenoise: 30% Chardonnay,
10% Chenin Blanc, 60% Mauzac*
VANEL CRÉMANT DE LIMOUX EXTRA BRUT
*Vintaged, méthode champenoise: 20% Chardonnay,
20% Chenin Blanc, 60% Mauzac*

VANEL
See SIEUR D'ARQUES

VIEW OVER
VINEYARDS TO THE
CHAPELLE DES
MOINES AT BERZE-
LA-VILLE, SAONE-
ET-LOIRE

LOIRE

N/A
ACKERMAN
ST-HILAIRE-ST-FLORENT, LOIRE VALLEY
- 500,000 cases
- Other labels - Louis Ackerman
- Group ownership - Rémy-Pannier
Established in 1811 by Jean Ackerman, a
Belgian who founded the sparkling Saumur
industry. Thought to be the oldest French
sparkling wine producer outside Champagne,
this firm's full title is Ackerman-Laurance
(named after Jean Ackerman's wife, Emilie
Laurance), but there has been a move away
from the double-barrel name in recent years.
WINEMAKER
Jean Paul Malinge
HOUSE STYLE & RANGE
The 1811 Brut used to be one of the best
Saumur *cuvées* around, but now offers no more
than standard greengage fruit in a typically
chunky style. The Cuvée Jean-Baptiste is
supposed to be top of the range, but it is
nothing special. The whole sparkling wine
range has been disappointing of late, whereas
the still wines, which never used to be exciting,
have dramatically improved. Ackerman also
produces sparkling wines under the Crémant
d'Alsace, Crémant de Bordeaux and
Crémant de Bourgogne appellations.
1811 CUVÉE DE L'AIGLON SAUMUR BRUT
*Not vintaged, méthode champenoise: 10% Cabernet
Franc, 10% Chardonnay, 80% Chenin Blanc*
1811 CUVÉE DE L'AIGLON SAUMUR DEMI-SEC
*Not vintaged, méthode champenoise: 10% Cabernet
Franc, 10% Chardonnay, 80% Chenin Blanc*
1811 CUVÉE DE L'AIGLON SAUMUR ROSÉ
*Not vintaged, méthode champenoise: primarily
Cabernet Franc*
**CHARDONNAY BRUT, VIN MOUSSEUX DE
QUALITÉ**
Not vintaged, méthode champenoise: 100% Chardonnay

CHENIN BRUT, VIN MOUSSEUX DE QUALITÉ
*Not vintaged, méthode champenoise: 100% Chenin
Blanc*
CRÉMANT DE LOIRE BRUT
*Not vintaged, méthode champenoise: grape varieties
not revealed*
CRÉMANT DE LOIRE ROSÉ
Not vintaged, méthode champenoise: Cabernet Franc
VOUVRAY BRUT, MÉTHODE TRADITIONNELLE
*Not vintaged, méthode champenoise: 20% Chardonnay,
80% Chenin Blanc*
CUVÉE JEAN-BAPTISTE SAUMUR BRUT
*Vintaged, méthode champenoise: 20% Chardonnay,
80% Chenin Blanc*

N/A
ALLIAS
VOUVRAY, LOIRE VALLEY
- 840 cases
A family-owned winery, established in 1922,
when the Allias family purchased Clos du
Petit Mont. The first sparkling wines were
produced in 1929.
WINEMAKER
Cave des Producteurs de Vouvray
HOUSE STYLE & RANGE
Fresh, soft and easy-drinking fizz.
★ **VOUVRAY BRUT**
*Not vintaged, méthode champenoise: 100% Chenin
Blanc*
★ **VOUVRAY PÉTILLANT**
*Not vintaged, méthode champenoise: 100% Chenin
Blanc*

50
CFVM VEUVE AMIOT
ST-HILAIRE ST-FLORENT, LOIRE VALLEY
- 250,000 cases
- Other labels - Cadre Noir, J. de Villaret,
  Vouvray Club, Muscador Opéra, Baron
  Charmeuil, Montparnasse
Established in 1884 by a young widow
(*veuve*) called Elisabeth Amiot, two years after
the death of her husband. In 1971, after three

generations as a family-owned company, Veuve Amiot became part of the Martini & Rossi group. It is now jointly owned by Bacardi Martini of the USA and R Faber of Germany.

WINEMAKER

Gérard Labonde, Gilles Foulon

HOUSE STYLE & RANGE

Most of the Veuve Amiot *cuvées* are merely OK, but not something I would bother to drink. The Rosé has cherry rather than raspberry fruit that is normally found in most pink Loire bubblies made exclusively from Cabernet Franc. The Vouvray Club is also very ordinary. The Cadre Noir used to be a great value fizz, but it has lost its edge and the last *cuvée* I tasted was decidedly unclean. Muscador Opéra, Baron Charmeuil and Montparnasse are all labels for cheap *cuve close*.

CADRE NOIR SAUMUR BLANC BRUT

> *Not vintaged, méthode champenoise: 10% Cabernet Franc, 10% Chardonnay, 80% Chenin Blanc*

CRÉMANT DE LOIRE BLANC BRUT

> *Not vintaged, méthode champenoise: 20% Chardonnay, 80% Chenin Blanc*

SAUMUR CUVÉE RÉSERVÉE BRUT

> *Not vintaged, méthode champenoise: 20% Chardonnay, 80% Chenin Blanc*

SAUMUR HAUTE TRADITION BRUT

> *Not vintaged, méthode champenoise: 15% Chardonnay, 80% Chenin Blanc, 5% Sauvignon Blanc*

SAUMUR ROSÉ BRUT

> *Not vintaged, méthode champenoise: 100% Cabernet Franc*

VOUVRAY CLUB BLANC BRUT

> *Not vintaged, méthode champenoise: 100% Chenin Blanc*

SAUMUR CUVÉE ELISABETH BRUT

> *Vintaged, méthode champenoise: 20% Chardonnay, 80% Chenin Blanc*

80
DOMAINE DES BAUMARD
ROCHEFORT, LOIRE VALLEY

- 4,000 cases

Before his retirement Jean Baumard was the Loire's greatest exponents of Chenin Blanc. He was one of those rare, gifted winemakers who could make this grape sing, even in the driest still wines, and his son Florent shares some of his father's outstanding abilities. Much of the Baumard magic can be put down to sensible crop levels, gentle pressing (Jean Baumard's first pneumatic press was purchased in 1966, which made him almost 20 years ahead of his time), and clean, non-oxidative, basic winemaking techniques. Florent's father produced this domaine's first sparkling wine in 1957 (Carte Turquoise) and he remains his favourite consultant to this day.

WINEMAKER

Florent Baumard

HOUSE STYLE & RANGE

The Carte Turquoise is drier than the Carte Corail, with less perfume, but a more food-friendly structure. The Carte Corail is dry, easy-going and accessible, with a perfumed aftertaste. Its deliciously tangy fruit is as clean as a whistle, making this rosé a delight to drink. It might seem strange that I rate Baumard's vintage below the cheaper non-vintage *cuvées*, but it is at least three years older than his current non-vintage *cuvée* and the rate of improvement is such that the more recent wine is better. If you matched the vintage against the non-vintage produced in the same year, I am sure the vintage would be significantly superior. There is also the difference in grape varieties; Baumard favours Chardonnay to back up his Chenin Blanc for his vintage, while Cabernet Franc plays this role for the non-vintage Carte Turquoise.

★★✩ CARTE CORAIL CRÉMANT DE LOIRE BRUT

> *Not vintaged, méthode champenoise: Cabernet Franc*

★★✩ CARTE TURQUOISE CRÉMANT DE LOIRE BRUT

> *Not vintaged, méthode champenoise: Cabernet Franc, Chenin Blanc*

★ CRÉMANT DE LOIRE BRUT

> *Vintaged, méthode champenoise: Chardonnay, Chenin Blanc*

N/A
CHÂTEAU DE BEAUREGARD
LE PUY-NOTRE-DAME, LOIRE VALLEY

- 2,500 cases

A family estate established in 1927 by the incumbent's grandfather, Château de Beauregard started making sparkling wine as recently as 1993 and got all the basics right very quickly.

WINEMAKER

Philippe & Alain Gourdon

HOUSE STYLE & RANGE

Very fresh and very clean, with deliciously refreshing fruit and a lively finish.

★ SAUMUR BRUT

> *Vintaged, méthode champenoise: 20% Chardonnay, 80% Chenin Blanc*

70
BLANC FOUSSY
ROCHECORBON, LOIRE VALLEY

- 13,000 cases
- Other labels - Robert de Schlumberger, Veuve Oudinot
- Group ownership - Schlumberger (Austria)

This firm has devoted its production to *méthode champenoise* sparkling wine since it was established in 1970, and gets its rating in spite of the decline of Blanc Foussy itself.

WINEMAKER

Jean-Pierre Dargent

HOUSE STYLE & RANGE

The basic Blanc Foussy *cuvée* used to be one of the Loire's best value bubblies, but although it does not have the stingy greengage character of so much cheap and nasty Chenin Blanc fizz it is merely a decent, clean sparkling wine with a certain firmness and basic fruit. Although the deep flavour and high acidity of the Robert de Schlumberger would seem to suggest a wine fit for ageing, this is definitely made ready for drinking. Veuve Oudinot is fresh and rich with bright flavours underpinned by high acidity to produce a wine for ready drinking in a vif and lively style.

BLANC FOUSSY TOURAINE BRUT

> *Not vintaged, méthode champenoise: 10% Chardonnay, 90% Chenin Blanc*

★ ROBERT DE SCHLUMBERGER TOURAINE BRUT

> *Not vintaged, méthode champenoise: 20% Chardonnay, 80% Chenin Blanc*

★ VEUVE OUDINOT TOURAINE BRUT

> *Not vintaged, méthode champenoise: 100% Chenin Blanc*

75
BOUVET-LADUBAY
ST-HILAIRE ST-FLORENT, LOIRE VALLEY

- Other labels - Bouvet, Mlle Ladubay
- Group ownership - Taittinger

Founded in 1851, Bouvet-Ladubay is the second-oldest sparkling Saumur house, and is currently run by Patrice Monmousseau. Some of the wines are sold simply as Bouvet and others Bouvet-Ladubay. The simplified Bouvet label started when the company made its first export to the USA, where the importers wanted an easier name to market. There is yet a third variation, Mlle Ladubay, which Patrice Monmousseau introduced ten years ago for the supermarket trade.

Monmousseau would like one day to focus on just one label, the original Bouvet-Ladubay, but market pressures apparently prevent him from doing so at the moment.

WINEMAKER

Patrice Monmousseau, Michel Rochard

HOUSE STYLE & RANGE

The standard Bouvet Saumur Brut has basic fruit with a hint of pepperiness, but is otherwise not outstanding. Excellence has a longer finish and is more perfumed than the basic Brut, making it the entry level *cuvée* for serious Bouvet consumers. The Saphir Brut is much richer and softer than most Saumur, with a liquorice intensity to the fruit. When

CHENIN BLANC
VINEYARD AT
VOUVRAY IN THE
LOIRE VALLEY

Trésor Brut was first released, the fruit was much riper, and more exotic, and the oak leapt out of the glass. Many experienced wine consumers thought it was a New World fizz when they first tasted it, and people either loved it or loathed it, especially as it was extremely expensive for a Loire fizz. Now it is half the price and half the wine. It probably has a wider appeal, but there is nothing exotic or oaky, even though it is still barrique-fermented. It is just peppery and firm, and many might wonder what all the fuss was about. The Trésor Rosé also shows little sign of its barrique-fermentation, but it is rather 'pretty' with delicate fruit underpinned by a fine mousse of minuscule bubbles and good, ripe acidity, which gives the wine excellent length in the mouth. The Demi-Sec is fresher and more elegant than most Loire wines of this style, with plenty of sweet fruit.

★ BOUVET EXCELLENCE CRÉMANT BRUT
   Not vintaged, méthode champenoise: 20% Chardonnay, 80% Chenin Blanc
★ BOUVET LADUBAY TRÉSOR BRUT, SAUMUR
   Not vintaged, méthode champenoise: 20% Chardonnay, 80% Chenin Blanc
★ BOUVET LADUBAY TRÉSOR ROSÉ BRUT, SAUMUR
   Not vintaged, méthode champenoise: 100% Cabernet
★ BOUVET SAPHIR BRUT VINTAGE
   Vintaged, méthode champenoise: 5% Chardonnay, 95% Chenin Blanc
BOUVET SAUMUR BRUT
   Not vintaged, méthode champenoise: 100% Chenin Blanc
★ BOUVET SAUMUR DEMI-SEC
   Not vintaged, méthode champenoise: 5% Chardonnay, 95% Chenin Blanc

MAURICE BONNAMY
See CAVE DES VIGNERONS DE SAUMUR

45
CAVE DE LA BOUVRAIE
INGRANDES-SUR-LOIRE, LOIRE VALLEY
• Other labels - Grandin

Established in 1880 and purchased by the Berger group in 1979. The company claims 'authentic French origin' for all its *vins mousseux* of no fixed abode, although it is merely typical anonymous *cuve close* quality. Also produces Crémant de Loire.

70
MARC BRÉDIF
ROCHECORBON, LOIRE VALLEY
• 20,000 cases
This famous old firm has belonged to Ladoucette of Château du Nozet (Pouilly Fumé fame) since 1980.
HOUSE STYLE & RANGE
Fresh, rich and longlived.
★ VOUVRAY BRUT
   Not vintaged, méthode champenoise: 100% Chenin Blanc
★ VOUVRAY PÉTILLANT
   Not vintaged, méthode champenoise: 100% Chenin Blanc

N/A
DOMAINE DE BRIZÉ
MARTIGNÉ-BRIAND, LOIRE VALLEY
• 1,350 cases
This family domaine was formed in 1755 and has produced sparkling wines since 1960.
WINEMAKER
Luc Delhumeau
HOUSE STYLE & RANGE
The deep, full nose on the Crémant de Loire hints at botrytis and, as strange as that might seem on a sparkling wine, it does make it more interesting than the overwhelming number of boring *cuvées* made in the Loire Valley. It also has plenty of fruit, which gives the impression more of New World ripeness than Old. The Saumur alas does not stand out.
★ CRÉMANT DE LOIRE BRUT
   Not vintaged, méthode champenoise: Chardonnay, Chenin Blanc
SAUMUR BLANC BRUT
   Not vintaged, méthode champenoise: Chardonnay, Chenin Blanc

72
PAUL BUISSE
MONTRICHARD, LOIRE VALLEY
• 5,000 cases
In 1989 former chef Paul Buisse took over the family *négociant* business, purchased vineyards and started making his own domaine-bottled wines.
HOUSE STYLE & RANGE
The Crémant de Loire is packaged in a heavier, more expensive bottle than the so-called Prestige *cuvées* from Touraine, and is richer and more succulent than either of them. The Prestige Touraine Brut is attractively fresh, sweet and peppery, but not in the same class as the Crémant de Loire, although it does have the edge over the Prestige Touraine Rosé, which has an old-gold colour, a malo-dominated nose and simple, peppery fruit.
★ CRÉMANT DE LOIRE BRUT
   Not vintaged, méthode champenoise: 40% Chardonnay, 60% Chenin Blanc
★ PRESTIGE TOURAINE BRUT
   Not vintaged, méthode champenoise: 100% Chenin Blanc
PRESTIGE TOURAINE ROSÉ BRUT
   Not vintaged, méthode champenoise: 60% Grolleau, 40% Pineau d'Aunis

DE BUSSY
See CAVES DE GRENELLE

CADRE NOIR
See CFVM VEUVE AMIOT

N/A
LE CAPITAINE
ROCHECORBON, LOIRE VALLEY
• 1,700 cases
This family-owned firm has produced sparkling wine since 1990.
WINEMAKER
Alain & Christophe Capitaine
HOUSE STYLE & RANGE
What little fruit there is mid-palate is lost on the finish.
VOUVRAY BRUT
   Not vintaged, méthode champenoise: 100% Chenin Blanc

70
DIDIER CHAMPALOU
VOUVRAY, LOIRE VALLEY
• 1,700 cases
Didier Champalou is ahead of the pack, but still has some fine-tuning to do if he is to reveal the true quality of this *cuvée*.
WINEMAKER
Didier Champalou
HOUSE STYLE & RANGE
The finesse on the nose of this wine makes it stand out from the morass of dull and deadly

aromas that pervade so many Loire bubblies, but although the fruit is initially attractive and tangy in the mouth, it is let down by a hint of dry-straw on the finish.

☆ VOUVRAY BRUT
Not vintaged, méthode champenoise: 100% Chenin Blanc

BARON CHARMEUIL
See CFVM VEUVE AMIOT

DOMAINE DE LA CHÂTAIGNERAIE
See BENOÎT GAUTIER

N/A
FRANÇOIS CHIDAINE
MONTLOUIS, LOIRE VALLEY
• 840 cases
WINEMAKER
François Chidaine
HOUSE STYLE & RANGE
The samples I have tasted of this wine showed an unpleasant nose with bitter greengage fruit on the palate.
MONTLOUIS BRUT
Not vintaged, méthode champenoise: 100% Chenin Blanc

N/A
SCEA CONCOURSON
LOIRE VALLEY
• Other labels - Anne de la Renardière
HOUSE STYLE & RANGE
My recent and sole experience of this wine can only be described as strange.
ANNE DE LA RENARDIÈRE SAUMUR BRUT
Not vintaged, méthode champenoise: 100% Chenin Blanc

75
CRAY
LUSSAULT-SUR-LOIRE, LOIRE VALLEY
• 25,000 cases
Owned by Paul Boutinot, an English wine merchant with strong opinions that are often right, and never boring.
WINEMAKER
Paul Boutinot, Pierre Laroche
HOUSE STYLE & RANGE
The 1990 vintage of Cray Brut had a rather soapy aroma and lacked fruit. The 1992 was too highly rated by some critics, but although it was not a bad wine and certainly represented better value than most inexpensive Loire bubblies, it favoured character more than finesse. Tasting the 1992 Brut next to the 1993 Rosé, the latter was clearly different, more zesty, and obviously better. It turned out that when Boutinot purchased the property, the 1992 base wines had already been made. These base wines were rather full and not entirely to Boutinot's taste,

but with the *assemblage*, he made a wine close to how he wanted it. In 1993, however, Boutinot was able to make the wines from scratch and consequently produced a lighter, more elegant wine, marked by a zesty finesse. This is a wine to watch. There could possibly be a single-vineyard *cuvée* in a few years time.

★ CRÉMANT DE LOIRE BRUT
Vintaged, méthode champenoise: equal parts Chardonnay, Chenin Blanc, Pinot Noir
★ CRÉMANT DE LOIRE ROSÉ
Vintaged, méthode champenoise: 100% Pinot Noir

DAHEUILLER
See DOMAINE DES VARINELLES

73
PASCAL DELALEU
VERNOU, LOIRE VALLEY
• 3,350 cases
Consistently successful sparkling wine producer over the last five years or so.
HOUSE STYLE & RANGE
Very fresh with delicate fruit lifted by a fine mousse of tiny bubbles.
☆ VOUVRAY CUVÉE CLÉMENT BRUT
Not vintaged, méthode champenoise: 100% Chenin Blanc

MARC ET LUC DELHUMEAU
See DOMAINE DE BRIZÉ

DEPREVILLE
See LACHETEAU

N/A
DOMAINE DULOQUET
LES VERCHERS SUR LAYON, LOIRE VALLEY
• 170 cases
This domaine was established as recently as 1991, and made its first sparkling wine the following year.
WINEMAKER
Hervé Duloquet
HOUSE STYLE & RANGE
Fresh, but not expressive.
SAUMUR BRUT
Vintaged, méthode champenoise: 40% Chardonnay, 30% Chenin Blanc, 30% Grolleau

N/A
DOMAINE DUTERTRE
LIMERAY, LOIRE VALLEY
• 2,500 cases

Owned by Jacques Dutertre, vice-president of the association of Crémants de Loire, although sparkling wine production did not commence here until as recently as 1989.
WINEMAKER
Gilles Dutertre
HOUSE STYLE & RANGE
The quality of these wines does not impress.
CRÉMANT DE LOIRE ROSÉ BRUT
Not vintaged, méthode champenoise: grape varieties not revealed

CUVÉE SAINT GILLES CRÉMANT DE LOIRE BRUT
Not vintaged, méthode champenoise: 25% Cabernet Franc, 25% Chardonnay, 25% Chenin Blanc, 25% Pinot Noir
TOURAINE PÉTILLANT MÉTHODE TRADITIONNELLE BRUT/DEMI-SEC
Not vintaged, méthode champenoise: grape varieties not revealed
TOURAINE PÉTILLANT MÉTHODE TRADITIONNELLE ROSÉ BRUT/DEMI-SEC
Not vintaged, méthode champenoise: grape varieties not revealed

N/A
DOMAINE DE LA FONTAINERIE
VOUVRAY, LOIRE VALLEY
• 840 cases
This old domaine was established in 1712 and today consists of five hectares. Sparkling wine was first produced in 1990.
WINEMAKER
Cathérine Dhoye-Deruet
HOUSE STYLE & RANGE
Only tasted recently for the first time, but this typical Chenin Blanc fizz did not impress, although regular consumers of Loire bubbly seem to be satisfied.
VOUVRAY BRUT
Vintaged, méthode champenoise: 100% Chenin Blanc

80
PHILIPPE FOREAU
VOUVRAY, LOIRE VALLEY
• 3,400 cases
One of Vouvray's best growers, Foreau's sparkling version is rarely encountered, but his is a *vin de garde* that is worth digging out. His father André made even longer-lived Vouvray Mousseux.
WINEMAKER
Philippe Foreau

HOUSE STYLE & RANGE
Brilliantly clean fruit flavours that remain fresh and lively for many years.

★★ VOUVRAY BRUT
Not vintaged, méthode champenoise: 100% Blanc

LOUIS FOULON
See LACHETEAU

72
DOMAINE SYLVAIN GAUDRON
VERNOU, LOIRE VALLEY
• 4,200 cases
The small family enterprise was established in 1958, and has been making sparkling wines since 1971.

WINEMAKER
Gilles Gaudron

HOUSE STYLE & RANGE
I used to enjoy the sparkling Vouvray from this domaine ten or 15 years ago, and I am glad to find both these *cuvées* to be soft, easy and elegant, with gentle, creamy fruit and a smooth mousse.

★ VOUVRAY BLANC DE BLANCS BRUT
Not vintaged, méthode champenoise: 100% Chenin Blanc

★ VOUVRAY PÉTILLANT DEMI-SEC
Not vintaged, méthode champenoise: 100% Chenin Blanc

N/A
BENOÎT GAUTIER
ROCHECORBON, LOIRE VALLEY
• 3,350 cases
• Other labels - Domaine de la Châtaigneraie, Domaine de la Racauderie
The Gautier family have been *vignerons* since 1669, but established their own domaine-bottled enterprise as recently as 1981, making their first sparkling wine the same year.

WINEMAKER
Benoît Gautier

HOUSE STYLE & RANGE
Two wines tasted once very recently, when the hint of oxidation on the nose of the Brut was its best attribute (the flavour was awful) and the Demi-Sec had a finish like old straw.

VOUVRAY DOMAINE DE LA CHÂTAIGNERAIE BRUT
Not vintaged, méthode champenoise: 100% Chenin Blanc

VOUVRAY DOMAINE DE LA CHÂTAIGNERAIE DEMI-SEC
Not vintaged, méthode champenoise: 100% Chenin Blanc

N/A
DOMAINE DE LA GLORIETTE
LE PUY-NOTRE-DAME, LOIRE VALLEY
• 3,350 cases
This family-owned domaine started producing sparkling wine as recently as 1990.

WINEMAKER
Jean-François Crépaux

HOUSE STYLE & RANGE
The Cuvée de Prestige Crémant de Loire has similar botrytis-like hints on the bouquet to those of Domaine de Brizé, but without any of the 'New World' fruit on the palate, although it is still very fruity. It is much preferred to this domaine's Saumur which, unfortunately, is rather dull, heavy and cumbersome.

★ CUVÉE PRESTIGE, CRÉMANT DE LOIRE BRUT
Not vintaged, méthode champenoise: 95% Chardonnay, 5% Chenin Blanc

SAUMUR BRUT
Not vintaged, méthode champenoise: 30% Cabernet Franc, 10% Chardonnay, 60% Chenin Blanc

HENRI DE GRAMEY
See GRATIEN & MEYER

EUGÈNE GRANDET
See CHÂTEAU MONCONTOUR

GRANDIN
See CAVE DE LA BOUVRAIE

REMUAGE ON MÉTHODE TRADITIONELLE SPARKLING WINES IN THE CELLARS OF CHÂTEAU DE BEAULIEU, NEAR SAUMUR

72
GRATIEN & MEYER
SAUMUR, LOIRE VALLEY
• 8,350 cases
• Other labels - Henri de Gramey, Heritage
• Group ownership - Champagne Alfred Gratien (sister company)
Holding company Gratien, Meyer and Seydoux owns both this firm and Champagne Alfred Gratien, and is itself owned by the Seydoux family, who are related to the Krugs of Champagne. The Saumur business was established in 1864 by Albert Jean Meyer, whose family was Swiss and had migrated via Alsace. At some indeterminate date, Meyer teamed up with Alfred Gratien, the founder of the Champagne firm, with ownership of both houses passing into the Seydoux family (cousins of the Krugs) through the marriage of Meyer's daughter.

WINEMAKER
Nicolas François

HOUSE STYLE & RANGE
The Cuvée Royal Brut has a very rich, fresh and fruity aroma, making it much better value than Gratien & Meyer's basic Saumur Cuvée. The Harmonie Dry proved to be the freshest of all the *sec* I tasted in 1997, and it is as rich and sweet as a *demi-sec* on the palate, with nicer, more juicy fruit than Gratien & Meyer's Délice Demi-Sec. The Cuvée Flamme Brut is this producer's prestige *cuvée* and is indeed the best wine in the Gratien & Meyer range, with its apricots and custard nose, followed by elegant apricot fruit with a twist of tangerine on the palate. The well-structured Cuvée Flamme Rosé is not in the same class, although it is definitely a good wine and one that is capable of improving in bottle.

Old vintages sold under the Collection label are a curiosity, not least because they appear to be a late-disgorged version of a vintaged Saumur that does not exist! However, any so-called non-vintage blend that contains at least 85% of a single year may indicate that vintage on the label. These are serious wines with creamy fruit aromas and flavours, but they do not possess much complexity or finesse and they therefore merely age rather than mature.

I'm not totally convinced that Chenin Blanc makes a worthwhile youthful fizz (wines like Cuvée Flamme are the exception), let alone one that benefits from ageing, but true devotees of Loire sparkling wines are likely to rate Gratien & Meyer's Collection *cuvées* much higher than I do. The Cardinal Noir de Noirs is an impressively dark, deep feast of tannic, black fruit flavours, with a long, very sweet finish. Henri de Gramey is a value-for-money Saumur *sous marque*, while Heritage is a non-AOC bargain-basement fizz.

AURORE ROSÉ SAUMUR BRUT

Not vintaged, méthode champenoise: 100% Cabernet Franc

★ CARDINAL NOIR DE NOIRS DEMI-SEC, VIN ROUGE MOUSSEUX

Not vintaged, méthode champenoise: 100% Cabernet Franc

★☆ CUVÉE FLAMME, SAUMUR BRUT

Not vintaged, méthode champenoise: 15% Cabernet Franc, 10% Chardonnay, 75% Chenin Blanc

☆ CUVÉE FLAMME, SAUMUR ROSÉ

Not vintaged, méthode champenoise: 100% Cabernet Franc

☆ CUVÉE ROYALE, CRÉMANT DE LOIRE BRUT

Not vintaged, méthode champenoise: 10% Cabernet Franc, 90% Chenin Blanc

DÉLICE SAUMUR DEMI-SEC

Not vintaged, méthode champenoise: 25% Cabernet Franc, 75% Chenin Blanc

☆ HARMONIE DRY, SAUMUR

Not vintaged, méthode champenoise: 25% Cabernet Franc, 75% Chenin Blanc

HENRI DE GRAMEY SAUMUR BRUT

Not vintaged, méthode champenoise: 20% Chardonnay, 80% Chenin Blanc

HÉRITAGE BLANC DE BLANCS BRUT

Not vintaged, méthode champenoise: Chardonnay, Chenin Blanc

SOLEIL SAUMUR BRUT

Not vintaged, méthode champenoise: 25% Cabernet Franc, 75% Chenin Blanc

☆ COLLECTION, SAUMUR BRUT

Vintaged, late-disgorged, méthode champenoise: 100% Chenin Blanc

70
CAVES DE GRENELLE
SAUMUR, LOIRE VALLEY

• 120,000 cases

• Other labels Louis de Grenelle, Comte de Montmorency, De Bussy, Charles de Valois

Family-owned enterprise established in 1859, producing its first sparkling wine that same year. It also makes sparkling wines under contract for 60 growers throughout the region.

WINEMAKER
Monsieur Flao

HOUSE STYLE & RANGE
The Saumur is tight, with lemony fruit. Not a great wine, but an expressive one, and for once the theoretically superior Saumur appellation has proved better than the Crémant de Loire, which is exceptionally boring. The Saumur Rosé Sec is fresh and sweetish, with very clean, easy-drinking fruit.

SAUMUR CHÂTEAU ABOVE THE RIVER LOIRE

LOUIS DE GRENELLE BLANC DE BLANCS BRUT

Not vintaged, méthode champenoise: Chardonnay, Chenin Blanc, Sauvignon

LOUIS DE GRENELLE CRÉMANT DE LOIRE BRUT

Not vintaged, méthode champenoise: 5% Cabernet Franc, 25% Chardonnay, 70% Chenin Blanc

☆ LOUIS DE GRENELLE SAUMUR BRUT

Not vintaged, méthode champenoise: 20% Chardonnay, 80% Chenin Blanc

☆ LOUIS DE GRENELLE SAUMUR ROSÉ SEC

Not vintaged, méthode champenoise: 100% Cabernet Franc

LOUIS DE GRENELLE VIN MOUSSEUX ROUGE DEMI-SEC

Not vintaged, non-AOC, méthode champenoise: 80% Cabernet Franc, 20% Cabernet Sauvignon

N/A
GRÉSILLE
LOIRE VALLEY

My first opportunity to taste several *cuvées* from this producer.

HOUSE STYLE & RANGE
A slight oxidative complexity adds a dimension of interest to clean, lean fruit in this wine. Good length.

☆ ANNE DE LA GRÉSILLE CRÉMANT DE LOIRE BRUT

Not vintaged, méthode champenoise: grape varieties not revealed

70
CAVE DU HAUT-POITOU
NEUVILLE DE POITOU, LOIRE VALLEY

• 10,000 cases

This cooperative was established in 1948 and has been the driving force behind the up-and-coming Haut-Poitou VDQS since the early 1980s. Although all eyes have been on the red wines (primarily Gamay) since Georges Duboeuf, the 'King of Beaujolais', took control of the cooperative, the non-appellation sparkling wine, the production of which is contracted out to the Saumur

cooperative, has been one of its most consistent value-for-money products.

WINEMAKER
Cave des Vignerons de Saumur

HOUSE STYLE & RANGE
The Blanc de Blancs is a cheap thrill for those who like toasty fizz and cannot afford anything better, whereas the Brut Rosé is more fruit-driven and upfront.

☆ DIANE DE POITIERS BLANC DE BLANCS BRUT

Not vintaged, méthode champenoise: 100% Chardonnay

☆ DIANE DE POITIERS BRUT ROSÉ

Not vintaged, méthode champenoise: 100% Gamay

DOMAINE DES HAUTES DE SANZIERS
See HOUËT & TESSIER

HÉRITAGE
See GRATIEN & MEYER

65
HOUËT & TESSIER
SANZIERS, LOIRE VALLEY

• 8,340 cases

• Other labels – Domaine des Hautes de Sanziers

This estate was founded in 1822 by Eugène Tessier and exclusively produced red and white Saumur until 1970, when the first sparkling wines were made.

WINEMAKER
Dominique Tessier

HOUSE STYLE & RANGE
Recently tasted for the first time, this Saumur has just above average fruit and length, which might not sound like much, but puts it in the top ten per cent of Loire fizz.

SAUMUR BRUT

Not vintaged, méthode champenoise: 20% Cabernet Franc, 20% Chardonnay, 60% Chenin Blanc

72
GASTON HUET
VOUVRAY, LOIRE VALLEY

• 2,500 cases

The most famous domaine in Vouvray makes some of the most splendid wines of the appellation, especially the single-vineyard *cuvées* but some of Huet's *lieux-dits* are better than others, and although the sparkling wine has one of the best reputations, quality is variable

WINEMAKER
Noël Pinguet

HOUSE STYLE & RANGE
Fresh when on form, turning toasty with age

☆ VOUVRAY BRUT

Not vintaged, méthode champenoise: 100% Chenin Blanc

★ VOUVRAY PÉTILLANT

Vintaged, méthode champenoise: 100% Chenin Blanc

LaCheteau

DOUÉ-LA-FONTAINE, LOIRE VALLEY

● 100,000 cases
● Other labels - Louis Foulon, Leon Leroi, Montgueret, Montvermeil, Charles de Thouars, Depreville, Vendôme

LaCheteau is a family-owned firm that first produced sparkling wine in 1988 and has worked with two 'flying winemakers' – Australian Matt Pellew in 1996 and New Zealander Shayne Cox in 1997.

WINEMAKER

Gilles Bertrand

HOUSE STYLE & RANGE

The Louis Foulon is raisiny, yet the Léon Leroi is fresh, albeit not special, while the Montgueret Saumur Brut is dominated by creamy, malolactic aromas, which seem really weird on an average Loire fizz. The Montgueret Crémant de Loire Brut is dull with a straw-like aroma. The Montvermeil has ripe fruit aromas, but it is a bit sweet and basic on the palate. There is no mistaking the dominance of Chenin Blanc in the Foulon Demi-Sec and although that puts me off (not because of the variety *per se*, but how it reacts with secondary fermentation), it is the staple diet of many Loire aficionados, so if you are one of them, do not let this comment distract you because apart from that it is perfectly OK.

★ LÉON LEROI CRÉMANT DE LOIRE BRUT
Not vintaged, méthode champenoise: 20% Chardonnay, 80% Chenin Blanc

LOUIS FOULON SAUMUR BRUT
Not vintaged, méthode champenoise: 10% Cabernet Franc, 10% Chardonnay, 80% Chenin Blanc

LOUIS FOULON SAUMUR DEMI-SEC
Not vintaged, méthode champenoise: 10% Cabernet Franc, 10% Chardonnay, 80% Chenin Blanc

MONTGUERET SAUMUR BRUT
Not vintaged, méthode champenoise: 10% Cabernet Franc, 10% Chardonnay, 80% Chenin Blanc

MONTVERMEIL CRÉMANT DE LOIRE BRUT
Not vintaged, méthode champenoise: 20% Chardonnay, 80% Chenin Blanc

MONTGUERET PRESTIGE SAUMUR BRUT
Vintaged, méthode champenoise: 20% Chardonnay, 80% Chenin Blanc

N/A
JEAN-PIERRE LAISEMENT

VOUVRAY, LOIRE VALLEY

● 5,000 cases

This producer is well-known for his excellent Vouvray *moelleux*, and has produced sparkling wines since 1960.

WINEMAKER

Jean-Pierre Laisement

HOUSE STYLE & RANGE

I have enjoyed Laisement's fizzy Vouvray in the past, although it has recently been bitter,

dull and foursquare. His Touraine Rosé was unknown to me until very recently, and after his dismal Vouvray I am particularly delighted by how well it performed at a recent tasting. Not great in any classic sense, it is however rich and succulent in an easy to drink style.

★★ TOURAINE ROSÉ BRUT
Not vintaged, méthode champenoise: 60% Gamay, 30% Grolleau, 10% Pinot d'Aunis

TOURAINE ROSÉ DEMI-SEC
Not vintaged, méthode champenoise: 60% Gamay, 30% Grolleau, 10% Pinot d'Aunis

VOUVRAY BRUT
Not vintaged, méthode champenoise: 100% Chenin Blanc

VOUVRAY DEMI-SEC
Not vintaged, méthode champenoise: 100% Chenin Blanc

VOUVRAY PÉTILLANT
Not vintaged, méthode champenoise: 100% Chenin Blanc

N/A
YVES LAMBERT

MONTREUIL-BELLAY, LOIRE

● 4,200 cases

This grower has been making sparkling wines since 1983.

WINEMAKER

Yves Lambert

HOUSE STYLE & RANGE

Fresh and clean, with light-bodied greengage fruit that is best drunk young.

CRÉMANT DE LOIRE BRUT
Vintaged, méthode champenoise: 5% Cabernet Sauvignon, 30% Chardonnay, 65% Chenin Blanc

74
LANGLOIS-CHATEAU

SAUMUR, LOIRE VALLEY

● 25,000 cases

Established in 1885 by Edouard Langlois, the Chateau part of this producer's title refers not to a building, but the maiden name of the founder's wife, Jeanne Chateau.

Sparkling wine was made by Langlois from the very beginning of this domaine's existence. Now co-owned by the founder's family and Champagne Bollinger, Langlois-Château places much emphasis on blending a wide selection of wines from a diversity of *terroirs*, hence its use of the Crémant de Loire appellation in preference to Saumur. The eagerly awaited

launch of Quadrille de Langlois-Château was one of the greatest anti-climaxes of the wine world. It should have been the Bollinger of the Loire, yet sadly was not.

WINEMAKER

Bernard Leroux

HOUSE STYLE & RANGE

The firm, assertive flavour of the Brut is nicely set off against a soft mousse, and underpinned by an intense finish. The Réserve has lovely biscuity aromas, illustrating the sort of bottle-aged complexity expected from a mature sparkling wine, but it does not quite follow through on the palate. A good, but not great effort. The Rosé is a serious wine with firm fruit, and made in typical Bollinger food-wine fashion. The first release of Quadrille de Langlois has a nasty taste that catches at the back of the throat.

★ LANGLOIS CRÉMANT DE LOIRE BRUT
Not vintaged, méthode champenoise: 15% Cabernet Franc, 15% Chardonnay, 65% Chenin Blanc, 5% Grolleau

★ LANGLOIS ROSÉ CRÉMANT DE LOIRE BRUT
Not vintaged, méthode champenoise: 70% Cabernet Franc, 30% Grolleau

QUADRILLE DE LANGLOIS-CHATEAU CRÉMANT DE LOIRE BRUT
Not vintaged, méthode champenoise: 15% Cabernet Franc, 5% Cabernet Sauvignon, 30% Chardonnay, 50% Chenin Blanc

★ RÉSERVE CRÉMANT DE LOIRE BRUT
Vintaged, méthode champenoise: 20% Cabernet Franc, 10% Chardonnay, 65% Chenin Blanc, 5% Grolleau

LEON LEROI

See LACHETEAU

N/A
DOMAINE LEVASSEUR

MONTLOUIS, LOIRE VALLEY

● 3,000 cases
● Other labels - Claude Levasseur

A top grower of Montlouis *moelleux* but currently on disappointing form as far as his fizzy wines go, although he has made sparkling wines since 1962.

WINEMAKER

Claude Levasseur

HOUSE STYLE & RANGE

The Crémant de Loire is ordinary, with no appeal, while the Montlouis is more correct than special, with more of a sugariness than any true sensation of ripe fruit. The sparkling wines today bear no resemblance to the truly excellent Montlouis Pétillant I have had from this grower in the past.

CLAUDE LEVASSEUR BRUT, MONTLOIS

Not vintaged, méthode champenoise: 100% Chenin Blanc

CLAUDE LEVASSEUR CRÉMANT DE LOIRE BRUT

Not vintaged, méthode champenoise: 32% Chardonnay, 50% Chenin Blanc, 18% Pinot Noir

N/A
CHÂTEAU MONCONTOUR
VOUVRAY, LOIRE VALLEY

• 8,000 cases
• Other labels - Eugène Grandet, La Pilonnière
This famous Vouvray *château* is one of the oldest estates in France, some of its vineyards having been in production as early as the fourth century. The wines had a natural tendency to sparkle as early as the 18th century, but this was merely by accidental refermentation, brought on by the warmth of spring. The first *méthode champenoise* was produced at the end of the 19th century by Baron Jules de Königswarter. In the 1960s this property had the dubious honour of supplying base wines by the train-load for Germany's Sekt industry. It was purchased by Dr. Feray, a retired hip-surgeon.

WINEMAKER
Messieurs Grandchamp and Loisy
HOUSE STYLE & RANGE
I have not tasted the Château Moncontour *cuvées* for a while, but they were always dependable, which makes it all the more disappointing that La Pilonnière should be so ordinary, and that the Eugénie Grandet should be so off-putting on the nose. On current showing this producer warrants an overall score of no more than 40, but I will reserve judgement in the hope that these wines will return to form.

CHÂTEAU MONCONTOUR TÈTE DE CUVÉE BRUT

Vintaged, méthode champenoise: 100% Chenin Blanc

CHÂTEAU MONCONTOUR CUVÉE PREDILECTION BRUT

Vintaged, méthode champenoise: 100% Chenin Blanc

LA PILONNIÈRE VOUVRAY BRUT

Not vintaged, méthode champenoise: 100% Chenin Blanc

EUGÉNIE GRANDET BLANC DE BLANCS TOURAINE BRUT

Vintaged, méthode champenoise: 5% Chardonnay, 95% Chenin Blanc

70
MONMOUSSEAU
MONTRICHARD, LOIRE VALLEY

• 59,000 cases

Founded in 1886, Monmousseau began to specialise in *méthode champenoise* wines in 1930. At one time Monmousseau was a sister company of Bouvet (run today by Patrice Monmousseau) under the ownership of Taittinger, but the firm was fairly recently sold to the Luxembourg-based Bernard Massard group.

WINEMAKER
Joël Galland
HOUSE STYLE & RANGE
The Cuvée J.M. Blanc de Blancs is nice and lean, with ripe fruit that maintains its freshness longer than most Loire fizz, and the fresh flavoured Printemps has intense fruit and is ideal for those who prefer less fizz and a less sweet *demi-sec*, but the Vouvray Brut was bitter, and the Brut Etoile dominated by dull, greengage Chenin Blanc fruit.

BRUT ETOILE

Not vintaged, méthode champenoise: 25% Chardonnay, 65% Chenin Blanc, 10% UgniBlanc

★ PRINTEMPS GRAND VIN PÉTILLANT VOUVRAY DEMI-SEC

Not vintaged, méthode champenoise: 100% Chenin Blanc

VOUVRAY BRUT

Not vintaged, méthode champenoise: 100% Chenin Blanc

★ CUVÉE J M BLANC DE BLANCS BRUT, TOURAINE

Vintaged, méthode champenoise: 100% Chenin Blanc

MONTGUERET
See LACHETEAU

COMTE DE MONTMORENCY
See CAVES DE GRENELLE

MONTPARNASSE
See CFVM VEUVE AMIOT

MONTVERMEIL
See LACHETEAU

MOULIN ROUGE
See DOMAINE DE LA PERRUCHE

MUSCADOR OPÉRA
See CFVM VEUVE AMIOT

NEMROD
See CHÂTEAU DES ROCHETTES

65
DOMAINE DE NERLEUX
SAINT-CYR-EN-BOURG, LOIRE VALLEY

• 4,250 cases
Better-known for Saumur-Champigny, although this producer has been making sparkling wines since 1955.

HOUSE STYLE & RANGE
There is tangy, peppery fruit in the Crémant de Loire but the Saumur is dull and boring.

★ CRÉMANT DE LOIRE BRUT

Not vintaged, méthode champenoise: 30% Chardonnay, 70% Chenin Blanc

SAUMUR BRUT

Not vintaged, méthode champenoise: 100% Chenin Blanc

50
DE NEUVILLE
ST-HILAIRE, LOIRE VALLEY

• 84,000 cases
• Group ownership - Rémy-Pannier
Established in 1856 by the Coquebert de Neuville family.

WINEMAKER
Jean-Paul Malinge
HOUSE STYLE & RANGE
Generally unexciting wines.

CRÉMANT DE LOIRE

Not vintaged, méthode champenoise: grape varieties not revealed

SAUMUR SPARKLING, EXTRA QUALITY BRUT

Not vintaged, méthode champenoise: Cabernet Franc Cabernet Sauvignon, Chenin Blanc

SPARKLING BRUT

Not vintaged, cuve close: grape varieties not revealed

VEUVE OUDINOT
See BLANC FOUSSY

70
DOMAINE DE LA PALEINE
LOIRE VALLEY

My first opportunity to taste several *cuvées* from this producer was in early 1997.
HOUSE STYLE & RANGE
Very fresh, easy-going and clean for Saumur.

★ SAUMUR BRUT

Not vintaged, méthode champenoise: 100% Chenin Blanc

50
RÉMY-PANNIER
ST-HILAIRE, LOIRE VALLEY

• 42,000 cases
• Group ownership - also owns Ackerman and De Neuville
Established in 1885 by the Remy family.
WINEMKAER
Eric Laurent
HOUSE STYLE
Generally unexciting wines.

CHARDONNAY

Not vintaged, cuve close: 100% Chardonny

CHÂTEAU DE SAINTE RADEGONDE,

CRÉMANT DE LOIRE

Not vintaged, Méthode champenoise: grape varieties not revealed

SAUMUR SPARKLING

Not vintaged, méthode champenoise: Cabernet Franc, Cabernet Sauvignon, Chenin Blanc

N/A
CHÂTEAU DE PASSAVANT
LOIRE VALLEY
Recently tasted for the first time.
HOUSE STYLE & RANGE
An invigorating fizz with fresh, lemony fruit.
★ CRÉMANT DE LOIRE BRUT

Not vintaged, méthode champenoise: grape varieties not revealed

N/A
DOMAINE DE LA PERRUCHE
MONTSOREAU, LOIRE VALLEY
• 840 cases
• Other labels - Moulin Rouge
WINEMAKER
Bernard Pélé
HOUSE STYLE & RANGE
The Saumur Brut has a dull, straw-like nose and is too hefty on the palate and finish.
SAUMUR BRUT

Not vintaged, méthode champenoise: 20% Chardonnay, 80% Chenin Blanc

SAUMUR ROSÉ BRUT

Not vintaged, méthode champenoise: 100% Cabernet Franc

LA PILONNIÈRE
See CHÂTEAU MONCONTOUR

70
PASCAL PIBALEAU
AZAY-LE-RIDEAU, LOIRE VALLEY
• 420 cases
One of the best producers of Touraine Azay-le-Rideau, since 1990 Pascal Pibaleau has been making a better than average stab at fizz.
WINEMAKER
Pascal Pibaleau
HOUSE STYLE & RANGE
Very fresh fruit with a juicy-ripe pear flavour makes this a nice, soft-styled aperitif wine.
★ BRUT CRÉMANT DE LOIRE

Not vintaged, méthode champenoise: 20% Cabernet Franc, 60% Chenin Blanc, 20% Grolleau

N/A
CHÂTEAU DE PUTILLE
LA POMMERAYE, LOIRE VALLEY
• 3,000 cases
This family-owned property began making sparkling wine in 1984 with Anjou Mousseux.

WINEMAKER
Pascal Delaunay
HOUSE RANGE

CRÉMANT DE LOIRE BRUT

Not vintaged, méthode champenoise: grape varieties not revealed

DOMAINE DE LA RACAUDERIE
See BENOÎT GAUTIER

N/A
LIONEL RENARD
ST-LÉGER DE MONBRILLAY, LOIRE VALLEY
• 330 cases
A producer of sparkling Saumur since 1993.
WINEMAKER
Lionel Renard
HOUSE STYLE & RANGE
Rather dull *cuvée*.
SAUMUR BRUT

Not vintaged, méthode champenoise: 100% Chenin Blanc

N/A
CHÂTEAU DES ROCHETTES
CONCOURSON SUR LAYON, LOIRE VALLEY
• 420 cases
• Other labels - Nemrod
Having tasted some very good Coteaux du Layon, Anjou Rouge and Coteaux de l'Aubance from this producer, his sparkling wine is extremely disappointing.
WINEMAKER
Jean Douet
HOUSE RANGE
NEMROD SAUMUR BRUT

Not vintaged, méthode champenoise: 20% Chardonnay, 80% Chenin Blanc

74
ALAIN ROHART
VOUVRAY, LOIRE VALLEY
• 1,700 cases
Established in 1987 when Alain Rohart was made redundant after 20 years as a factory technician. At the age of 40, he went back to school to learn how to make wine and somebody should tell him that he is doing a much better job at it that many formerly famous Vouvray producers who have rested on their laurels for far too long.
WINEMAKER
Alain Rohart
HOUSE STYLE & RANGE

Two wines that prove good quality Chenin Blanc grapes can make successful sparkling wine. The non-vintage Tête de Cuvée is rich and lively, with perfumed fruit. The vintaged Coeur de Cuvée might be too assertively Chenin for my personal taste, but it is very good for its type, with a particularly rich finish – a style that should please Loire purists.
★ VOUVRAY TÊTE DE CUVÉE BRUT

Not vintaged, méthode champenoise: 100% Chenin Blanc

★ VOUVRAY, COEUR DE CUVÉE BRUT

Vintaged, méthode champenoise: 100% Chenin Blanc

75
CAVE DES VIGNERONS DE SAUMUR
SAINT-CYR-EN-BOURG, LOIRE VALLEY
• 75,000 cases
• Other labels - Maurice Bonnamy, Charles de Villeneuve
Established in 1957, this cooperative made its first sparkling wine in 1975, and was the very first producer of Crémant de Loire. Professor Guimberteau of Bordeaux University consults here, and British-based, Australian-trained flying winemaker John Worontschak also has an agreement with this cooperative. It is difficult to give an overall rating to a producer of so many sparkling wine *cuvées*, the worst of which is clean, decent and above average, with the best individually deserving scores in the 80s.
WINEMAKER
Jacques-Antoine Toublanc
HOUSE STYLE & RANGE
Does this cooperative really make as many different *cuvées* as this? Unfortunately I cannot recommend one of its pure Saumur *cuvées*. This has nothing to do with the level of winemaking skill, which is patently high. Indeed, some of its Crémants de Loire are equivalent in quality to fairly decent Champagne and here we have a clue as to what is wrong. Tasting these wines blind and mixed in random order with sparkling wines from other Loire producers,

VINEYARDS ABOVE THE LOIRE, EAST OF SAUMUR

CHENIN BLANC VINEYARD IN LA VALLEE DE NOUY AT VOUVRAY

it is clear that the more Chardonnay in this cooperative's Crémant de Loire, the better it is, yet the same percentage of Chardonnay in the Saumur has little effect.

Obviously the Chardonnay in the Crémant de Loire is superior to that used in the Saumur. As Crémant de Loire can come from the Anjou-Saumur and Touraine districts, it would seem that either Touraine and areas of Anjou outside Saumur itself are better suited to Chardonnay or the best areas of Saumur have been stubbornly preserved for Chenin Blanc. If Saumur *vignerons* cannot grow good enough Chardonnay or refuse to plant this variety in at least some of its best locations, they should not bother with it at all.

Even within the Crémant de Loire wines of this one producer, the quality of the Chardonnay used differs. The most recent *cuvée* of non-vintage Brut Spécial is one of the best Loire sparkling wines I have ever tasted, with the Chardonnay providing a lovely, soft texture, freshness and finesse, whereas the non-vintage Maurice Bonnamy Médaille Pierre Premier, with exactly the same percentage of Chardonnay, is extraordinarily peppery and although not a bad wine, it has none of Brut Spécial's finesse. It is the vintaged version of Brut and Spécial that shows the increasing quality that good Chardonnay can bring to Crémant de Loire. The 1988 was just 10% Chardonnay, and not a wine to recommend. By 1993 it had reached 15% and it was still nothing special. In 1994 the cooperative produced a Brut Spécial with 50% Chardonnay and it was stunning for all reasons mentioned above, yet the Brut at 15% was ordinary by comparison, although infinitely superior to the Saumur with 15% Chardonnay, which was also produced in 1994, and the same pattern emerged in 1995.

In 1995 the Cave des Vignerons produced five different vintaged Saumur *cuvées*, four numbered and one Brut Spécial. All working

well within the maximum 20% Chardonnay permitted for this appellation, No.1, No.2 and No.4 all possess just 5% and only the winemakers knows what constitutes any difference between these *cuvées*. No.1 and No.2 taste similar, lacking both interest and texture, whereas No.4 has the sort of pepperiness that I have come to associate with low-grade Loire Chardonnay. No.3 has 10% Chardonnay and is also peppery, and the Saumur Brut Spécial has 6% and a bitterness on the finish. The Crémant de Loire Rosé Brut is a very fresh fizz with lively raspberry fruit, whereas the Sec version of this *cuvée* is surprisingly dry, only a tad fatter than the Brut. The Mousseux Rouge Demi-Sec is really deep and dark, with luscious sweet, raspberry fruit.

CAVE MAURICE BONNAMY CRÉMANT DE LOIRE BLANC BRUT
Not Vintaged, méthode champenoise: 20% Chardonnay, 80% Chenin Blanc

CAVE MAURICE BONNAMY CRÉMANT DE LOIRE BLANC BRUT MÉDAILLE PIERRE PREMIER
Not vintaged, méthode champenoise: 50% Chardonnay, 50% Chenin Blanc

CAVE MAURICE BONNAMY SAUMUR BLANC BRUT NO.1/NO.2
Not vintaged, méthode champenoise: 5% Chardonnay, 95% Chenin Blanc

★★✩ CRÉMANT DE LOIRE BLANC BRUT SPÉCIAL
Not vintaged, méthode champenoise: 50% Chardonnay, 50% Chenin Blanc

✩ CRÉMANT DE LOIRE ROSÉ BRUT
Not vintaged, méthode champenoise: 100% Cabernet

✩ CRÉMANT DE LOIRE ROSÉ SEC
Not vintaged, méthode champenoise: 100% Cabernet

★ MOUSSEUX ROUGE DEMI-SEC
Not vintaged, méthode champenoise: 100% Cabernet

SAUMUR BLANC BRUT SPÉCIAL
Not vintaged, méthode champenoise: 100% Chenin Blanc

CRÉMANT DE LOIRE BLANC BRUT
Vintaged, méthode champenoise: 15% Chardonnay, 85% Chenin Blanc

★★✩ CRÉMANT DE LOIRE BLANC BRUT SPÉCIAL
Vintaged, méthode champenoise: 50% Chardonnay, 50% Chenin Blanc

SAUMUR BLANC BRUT NO.1/NO.2/NO.4
Vintaged, méthode champenoise: 5% Chardonnay, 95% Chenin Blanc

SAUMUR BLANC BRUT NO.3
Vintaged, méthode champenoise: 10% Chardonnay, 90% Chenin Blanc

SAUMUR BLANC BRUT NO.4
Vintaged, méthode champenoise: 6% Chardonnay, 90% Chenin Blanc

SAUMUR BLANC BRUT SPÉCIAL
Vintaged, méthode champenoise: 15% Chardonnay, 85% Chenin Blanc

ROBERT DE SCHLUMBERGER
See BLANC FOUSSY

CHARLES DE THOUARS
See LACHETEAU

CHARLES DE VALOIS
See CAVES DE GRENELLE

N/A
DOMAINE DES VARINELLES
VARRAINS, LOIRE VALLEY
• 2,500 cases
This domaine was founded in 1850 and has made good Saumur-Champigny and Rosé de Loire but, although they have been produced since the late 1980s, I have only tasted these sparkling wines once, thus no overall rating.
WINEMAKER
Laurent Daheuiller
HOUSE STYLE & RANGE
This zesty fizz is decent enough, and that makes it superior to the vast majority of Loire bubblies.

✩ CRÉMANT DE LOIRE BRUT
Not vintaged, méthode champenoise: 10% Cabernet Franc, 30% Chardonnay, 60% Chenin Blanc

VENDÔME
See LACHETEAU

J. DE VILLARET
See CFVM VEUVE AMIOT

CHARLES DE VILLENEUVE
See CAVE DES VIGNERONS DE SAUMUR

N/A
CAVE DES PRODUCTEURS DE VOUVRAY
VOUVRAY, LOIRE VALLEY
Although this cooperative was established in 1953, its first sparkling wine was made from the previous year's harvest. A small co-op of 50 growers who together own 250 hectares.

WINEMAKER
Philippe Thierry
HOUSE STYLE & RANGE
Harsh, bitter and peppery.
VOUVRAY EXTRA RÉSERVE BRUT
Not vintaged, méthode champenoise:
100% Chenin Blanc

VOUVRAY CLUB
See CFVM VEUVE AMIOT

RHÔNE

55
EARL DU BIGUET
TOULAUD, SAINT PÉRAY
• 1,670 cases
The only St-Péray producer that Bettane and
Desseauve are prepared to recommend in *Le*
Classement 1998 and they award this top marks.
WINEMAKER
Jean-Louis Thiers
HOUSE STYLE & RANGE
Rich, full and well-made, with good bottle
development on the palate, yet absolutely fresh
and clean. This is probably the best St-Péray
I have ever tasted, but it still needs acidity, and
could have been much better had the same
wine been fermented in the New World
where its quality could have been enhanced
in the absence of inhibiting AOC regulations.
SAINT-PÉRAY BLANC DE BLANC BRUT
Not vintaged, méthode champenoise: 100% Marsanne

N/A
CHAI BUFFARDEL
DIE, RHÔNE VALLEY
Some people reckon Buffardel, with its
Champenois roots, makes the best wines in
the appellation.
HOUSE STYLE & RANGE
Occasional vintaged *cuvées* can be sensational.
★ CLAIRETTE DE DIE MÉTHODE DIOISE
ANCESTRALE
Not vintaged, méthode rurale: 25% Clairette, 75%
Muscat à Petit Grains
★★ CLAIRETTE DE DIE MÉTHODE DIOISE
ANCESTRALE
Vintaged, méthode rurale: 25% Clairette, 75%
Muscat à Petit Grains

40
JEAN-FRANÇOIS CHABOUD
ST-PÉRAY, RHÔNE VALLEY
One of the oldest family-owned domaines in
St-Péray.
HOUSE STYLE & RANGE
Despite being one of the appellation's better
producers, the wines are dull, heavy and coarse.
ST-PÉRAY BRUT
Not vintaged, méthode champenoise: 100% Marsanne

ST-PÉRAY CUVÉE PRESTIGE
Not vintaged, méthode champenoise: 50% Marsanne,
50% Roussanne

CAVE THIERS
See EARL DU BIGUET

JEAN-LOUIS THIERS
See EARL DU BIGUET

N/A
UJVR – UNION JEUNE VITICULTEURS RÉCOLTANTS
VERCHENY, RHÔNE VALLEY
• 33,500 cases
A group of nine young growers clubbed
together in 1961 and with their 60 hectares
of half-and-half Clairette and Muscat vines,
they have become the second-largest producer
of Clairette de Die and Crémant de Die.
HOUSE STYLE & RANGE
I have tasted the Clairette de Die when it was
Tradition, and excellent it was too. This co-
op has since invested in a brand new winery,
which should mean the wines have got better
rather than worse, but not tasted recently.
CRÉMANT DE DIE BRUT
Not vintaged, méthode champenoise: 100% Clairette
CLAIRETTE DE DIE MÉTHODE DIOISE
ANCESTRALE
Not vintaged, méthode rurale: 10% Clairette,
90% Muscat à Petit Grains

80
UNION DE PRODUCTEURS (DIE)
DIE, RHÔNE VALLEY
• 540,000 cases
Trading under the name of Sud Est
Appellations, this cooperative is the largest
producer of Clairette de Die, accounting for
80% of the appellation.
HOUSE STYLE & RANGE
No Crémant de Die, or the Clairette de Die
Mousseux it replaced, has so far demonstrated
that it could possibly achieve a worthwhile
score, thus the overall rating for this producer
is based exclusively on its Clairette de Die
Méthode Dioise Ancestrale, especially its superb
new Clairdissime, one of the most luscious
dessert-style bubblies produced in France.
Infinitely preferable to 90% of Champagne
demi-sec, and nowhere near as expensive,
Clairdissime is a luxury everybody can afford.
CAPELLA CLAIRETTE DE DIE MÉTHODE
DIOISE ANCESTRALE
Not vintaged, bio-dynamic, méthode rurale: 25%
Clairette, 75% Muscat à Petit Grains
★ CLAIRDIE CLAIRETTE DE DIE MÉTHODE
DIOISE ANCESTRALE
Not vintaged, méthode rurale: 25% Clairette, 75%
Muscat à Petit Grains

★★ CLAIRDISSIME CLAIRETTE DE DIE
MÉTHODE DIOISE ANCESTRALE
Not vintaged, méthode rurale: 10% Clairette, 90%
Muscat à Petit Grains
CRÉMANT DE DIE BRUT
Not vintaged, méthode champenoise: 100% Clairette

SAVOIE

PIERRE BONIFACE
See DOMAINE DES ROCAILLES

N/A
DOMAINE DES ROCAILLES
MONTMELIAN, SAVOIE
• 1,500 cases
This grower owns 18 hectares of vineyards
and has produced sparkling wine since 1976.
WINEMAKER
Pierre Boniface
HOUSE STYLE & RANGE
I have had some good still wines from this
producer in the past, but I have not tasted
the fizz.
BRUT DE SAVOIE
Not vintaged, méthode champenoise: 5% Altesse and
Chardonnay, 95% Jacquère

70
MAISON MOLLEX
SEYSSEL, SAVOIE
• 3,400 cases
The Mollex family have been resident in
Seyssel since 1359 and today own 25 hectares.
HOUSE STYLE & RANGE
Fragrantly dry with refreshing acidity.

SEYSSEL BRUT
Not vintaged, méthode champenoise: 10% Altesse,
90% Molette

N/A
JEAN ET ERIC VALLIER
BONNEVILLE, SAVOIE
• 3,500 cases
This family enterprise has produced
domaine-bottled sparkling wine from seven
hectares of vines since 1988.
WINEMAKER
Eric Vallier
HOUSE RANGE
AYZE EXTRA BRUT
Vintaged, méthode champenoise: 70% Gringet,
30% Roussette

EUROPE, EXCLUDING FRANCE

MOST COUNTRIES IN EUROPE WHICH MAKE STILL WINES ALSO MAKE SPARKLING *CUVÉES*. THESE NOT ONLY INCLUDE WESTERN EUROPEAN COUNTRIES SUCH AS AUSTRIA AND SWITZERLAND BUT ALSO THOSE AS FAR TO THE EAST AS RUSSIA AND THE UKRAINE, AS SOUTH AS GREECE AND MALTA AND AS UNLIKELY AS THE NETHERLANDS.

GERMANY 179

FAR LEFT: VIEW OVER THE GOLDTROPFCHEN VINEYARD TO PIESPORT AND THE MOSEL.

GREAT BRITAIN 204

TOP: THE 18 ACRE WICKHAM VINEYARD IN HAMPSHIRE, ENGLAND

ITALY 211

LEFT: HIGH-TRAINED VINES AT CAVALLERI, ERBUSCO, LOMBAD

PORTUGAL 220

MIDDLE LEFT: THE ESTATE OF CASA DA TAPADA, FISCAL, PORTUGAL

SPAIN 226

BOTTOM LEFT: CAVAS CHANDON, THE SPANISH BRANCH OF MOET ET CHANDON, SUBIRATS, CATALONIA, SPAIN

AUSTRIA AND THE REST OF EUROPE 236

BOTTOM: THE PREMISES OF LEN MOSER, ROHRENDORF, KAMTAL, AUSTRIA

BOTTOM: IN THE VINEYARDS, MOLDOVA, EASTERN EUROPE

GERMANY

THE FIRST FULLY DOCUMENTED GERMAN SPARKLING WINE WAS PRODUCED IN 1826 BY GEORG KESSLER AT ESSLINGEN ON THE NECKAR RIVER IN WÜRTTEMBERG. THERE IS AN EVEN EARLIER RECORDED MENTION OF GERMAN SPARKLING WINE; IN A PUBLICATION CALLED *INTELLIGENZIABLATT* (PAPER FOR THE INTELLIGENTSIA), WHICH WAS WRITTEN BY JOH. MAX. JOS. FUNCKE IN KOBLENZ IN 1791. THE AUTHOR MOMENTARILY DIGRESSES FROM A DISCUSSION ABOUT FRENCH CHAMPAGNE TO MENTION THAT SPARKLING WINE HAD BEEN MADE IN THE RHINE IN 1783, ALTHOUGH NO SPECIFIC PRODUCER IS NAMED.

Until someone uncovers the identity of Funcke's mysterious fizz producer, Kessler must go down as the man who established Germany's sparkling wine industry in 1826. He had been an employee of Madame Clicquot since 1807, just two years after she was forced to take over the firm after the death of her husband.

Recommended by Clicquot's partner Louis Bohne, Kessler was originally employed to look after the company books, but little by little he became responsible for the cellars which were being run on an ad hoc basis by Jérôme Fourneaux. When Fourneaux's services were relinquished in 1810, and Antoine Müller was hired as the full-time *chef de caves*, Kessler assumed the responsibility for purchasing wines. In 1821 he persuaded Madame Clicquot to buy an estate at Heilbronn in Württemberg called Neuhoff, and later to establish more premises at Esslingen.

In 1826, Kessler and Veuve Clicquot parted company, enabling him to found the firm of G.C. Kessler, which is still in existence and is considered to be the oldest Sekt house in Germany.

GERMAN CUCKOOS NESTING IN CHAMPAGNE

Kessler may have established Germany's sparkling wine industry in 1826, but the first German to make sparkling wine (as opposed to the first person to make German sparkling wine) was Florenz-Ludwig Heidsieck in 1785, and the pivotal influence of Germans on the early evolution of the Champagne trade should not be underestimated.

There are three reasons why so many Germans were hired by Champagne houses in the 19th century. The first is because the French were then as lazy at learning foreign languages as the British are now. Consequently Germans, who were renowned for their linguistic prowess, were employed to sell Champagne abroad. The second reason is that members of the French aristocracy considered commerce so lowly that they did not wish their family name to be connected with a business. They preferred instead to use others, often Germans, to act as front men. Thirdly, Germans were considered to have a fastidious mind for detail and a particularly legible hand, thus they were often employed for their bookkeeping and basic clerical skills.

However, this innate thoroughness was such that the German employees soon knew

THE ORIGIN OF THE WORD 'SEKT'

What possible connection could there be between Philip II of Spain and the adoption by the German wine industry of the name Sekt almost 300 years later? Well, if Philip had not ordered the invasion of England, Sir Francis Drake would not have raided Cadiz in 1587 and taken away with him 3,000 casks of 'sack'.

The term sack had been in use since the beginning of the 16th century, and derived from the Spanish verb *sacar*, to take away or take out, and came to refer to exported sherry, specifically an oloroso style of sherry, although whether this was because the first oloroso the English drank was sacked or exported is difficult to say.

If the word sack was not widely utilised by the English prior to Drake's raid, then

it certainly was afterwards, when 'authentic Cadiz sack' was sold from every tavern in the country. Within less than 10 years of Drake's adventure, Shakespeare had immortalised sack as Falstaff's favourite drink.

We now leap forward to Berlin in 1825, when Ludwig Devrient, Germany's most original actor of the Romantic period, entered his favourite restaurant, Lutter & Wegener, and jocularly quoted from his Falstaff role 'Give me a cup of sack, rogue'. Unaware of the meaning of the quote or indeed of sack, the waiter did not realise that Devrient wanted a sherry, and served the great actor a glass of his usual fizz. By the time this story was told and retold around the Berlin restaurant

circuit, which was not known for it grasp of Shakespeare, *sack* had become *sekt*, and by 1890 this new term was widely used for German sparkling wine.

According to Weinfach-Notizkalender (Diemer, 1885) 'Sekt is really a wine made from *Trockenbeeren* grapes, but the term is strangely yet frequently used for *Schaumwein*', although today we find it far more strange that Sekt ever applied to a *Trockenbeerenauslese*. However, Myers Grosses Conversakon Lexikon (1907) also refers to Sekt as a *'Trockenbeer'* (sic) wine, and mentions that its use for sparkling wine has been quite common since Devrient's famous sack story was misquoted, especially in parts of northern Germany.

more about the businesses than their owners. They conducted confidential correspondence with customers, building up a network of contacts in all the major foreign markets and took it upon themselves to learn the so-called secrets of Champagne making. Many ended up running the firms they were employed by, and eventually came to own them. Others left to set up their own houses. Thus from humble clerks to captains of industry, these commercial cuckoos soon established a plethora of Germanic-sounding Champagne houses:

Josef-Jacob-Placide Bollinger, later known as Jacques Bollinger, came from Württemberg. He worked for a small house called Müller-Ruinart until 1829, when the Comte de Villermont offered to fund a new house under Bollinger's own name.

Frederick Delbeck married Balsamie Ponsardin, the niece of the Veuve Clicquot, and established a house under his own name in 1832.

William Deutz and **Pierre Geldermann**, both from Aachen, established the house of Deutz & Geldermann in 1838, after working as clerks for Bollinger.

Friederich Giesler came from the Rhineland to be one of the five founding partners in PA Mumm & Co (now GH Mumm & Co), which was founded in Reims in 1827. He left in 1837 to establish his own house, Giesler & Co, in Avize.

Florenz-Ludwig Heidsieck from Westphalia worked as a foreign-language correspondent before establishing the original firm of Heidsieck & Co in 1785, which itself gave birth to the three Heidsieck brands we know today (Charles Heidsieck, Piper Heidsieck and Heidsieck & Co Monopole).

G. Heuser was one of the original partners of PA Mumm & Co (now GH Mumm & Co, but then named after Peter Arnold Mumm, who had died in 1797), but little is known about him other than the fact that he managed the company.

Georg Kessler of Württemberg worked first as a bookkeeper at Veuve Clicquot.

Charles Koch came from Heidelberg in 1820 to establish a house in Avize with Artur Bricout.

Die Quelle der Freude

Johann-Josef Krug, born in Mainz, worked at Jacquesson & Fils, marrying Adolphe Jacquesson's English sister-in-law, before founding Krug & Co in 1843.

Jean-Claude Kunkelmann came from a German family, represented H Piper & Co (now Piper-Heidsieck) in America, became a partner in the business in 1850, inheriting it in 1870, when the title was changed to Kunkelmann & Cie, which has remained as the firm's official name to this day.

Jean-Baptiste Lanson came from a German family that had settled in the Ardennes

Jacobus, Gotlieb & Philipp Mumm, whose father Peter Arnold had established the house of P.A. Mumm & Co in Cologne and Frankfurt as early as 1761, were three of the original five partners in the firm of PA Mumm & Co (now GH Mumm & Co), which they founded in Reims in 1827.

Antoine Müller helped the Widow Clicquot invent the process of *remuage*, before leaving in 1822 to set up a small house called Müller-Ruinart, now known as Henri Abelé.

Louis Roederer came from a German family that had settled in Strasbourg, took over the house of Dubois Père & Fils from his uncle Nicolas-Henri Schreider.

Pierre Taittinger came from a German family settled in Lorraine, took over the low-key firm of Forest-Fourneaux & Cie just after the First World War, turning it into a thriving *grande marque* under his name.

Edouard Werlé, formerly Wehrle, was the son of a Hessian postmaster and the first and most faithful of Veuve Clicquot's partners, as well as mayor of Reims.

Remove these names from Champagne's history, and it would be stripped bare of much that was important in the development of the world's greatest sparkling wine, yet in Germany the progress of sparkling wine was painfully slow.

By 1849 there were as many as 43 producers, but they were making less than 1.3 million bottles of fizz. The real boom occurred in the 1850s, when the term Sekt became widely used, and a much greater number of houses sprung up. Many of these disappeared as quickly as they had emerged, but by 1872 production had risen to four million bottles, and the industry was of sufficient importance to field 12 Sekt houses at the World Exhibition in Vienna.

By 1902 production was up to 11 million bottles and Sekt had caught the attention of the German exchequer, which was under pressure to fund the expansion of its armed forces. A Sekt Tax was introduced by Wilhelm II to help pay for the building of a new German fleet. This was later added to by the Banderole Tax, the Sliding Tax and Value Tax, so that no less than 55% of the price of a bottle went straight into the exchequer's coffers.

Between the two wars, the only time that Sekt was not burdened by crippling taxes was at the height of the depression, when of course there was no market for a celebratory product. It was even worse after the war, when what little Sekt was being sold was subjected to a War Surcharge of three Reichsmark per bottle. As soon as this was reduced to one Mark in 1952, sales began to climb, and although taxes were raised in 1966

GRAPES GROWING ON THE SLOPES AT DURBACH, BADEN

THE ULTIMATE *CUVE CLOSE* SEKT

I had already come to the conclusion by the early 1980s that there was nothing wrong with *cuve close* itself. If these vats were fitted with a large propeller to stir up the yeast lees every now and then to promote autolysis, and top quality base wines were aged on these lees in tank for two or three years before bottling, the results I imagined could be indistinguishable from the 'real thing'. I thought this would remain purely hypothetical; after all, who would be crazy enough to fit a propeller inside a vat and take it out of general production for a couple of years? But Wegeler-Deinhard experimented with just such a vat, using base wines from their famous Bernkasteler Doctor vineyard and did it three times, in 1978, 1980 and 1984, tying up the tank for no less than six years.

Although these were some of the worst vintages in Germany, Deinhard produced some of the greatest Sekt I have ever tasted. In fact, Wegeler-Deinhard chose these years because the grapes failed to reach Spätlese ripeness, the minimum requirement the company demanded for its Bernkasteler Doctor Kabinett. The grapes were not unripe *per se*, just underripe for the minimum level that Wegeler-Deinhard itself had demanded from its greatest vineyard, whereas in sparkling wine terms, they were virtually vintage-ripe.

At that juncture, the family-owned firm of Deinhard (now part of the Henkell & Söhnlein group) was, and still is, an important Sekt house. Thus, at a time when a few fledgling estate Sekte were utilising the *méthode champenoise* to secure premium prices, this sparkling wine producer bravely aimed to make the ultimate quality of *cuve close*. The results were stunning, and in the early to mid 1980s sold for DM60-80 in Germany, and $60 in the USA.

(to 1.5 Marks) and 1982 (two Marks), sales continued to go up. The market had built up such momentum in the late 1950s and early 1960s that these increases only slowed down the expansion momentarily.

Sales jumped from 137 to 238 million bottles between 1970 and 1977. By 1987 they were up to 338 million bottles, 1991 saw 438 million of Sekt, and just three years later sales topped half a billion bottles, which is almost twice that of Champagne. But exports have not followed this pattern. In fact, very little Sekt has been exported, making its brand names virtually unknown outside of Germany itself.

There is no mystery about this. The vast majority of Sekt is produced by *cuve close* or tank method (although it started as a bottle-fermented product, of course), and over 85% is not even German, but a blend of dregs from various European countries. In short, Sekt is a very low grade product of no individual character, and is thus of no interest to discerning drinkers on the international market. How so much Sekt can be consumed by the Germans themselves is a real mystery.

The fact that Sekt is primarily a *cuve close* product is not in itself a reason for poor quality. Contrary to popular belief, *cuve close*, which involves a second fermentation in tanks, not bottles, is not intrinsically inferior as a method of sparkling wine production. Because it is a bulk production method, it tends to attract mediocre base wines and encourage a quick throughput; if all *cuve close* products used the finest base wines, we might not regard the process with such disdain.

Because of the nature of the beast, Sekt factories (which is how the companies themselves describe these facilities) search out wines made from underripe rather than overripe grapes, and prefer to sell the end products when they are just months old because of their limited shelf-life. To cover this tart-green mishmash, a liberal *dosage* is required. This is the fizzmaker's ultimate cosmetic and, as the big brands are invariably *trocken*, they contain between 17 and 35 grams per litre of residual sugar, which takes the wines right up to the fringe of *demi-sec* sweetness, despite the so-called 'dry' designation. Is it any wonder then that such bland dross of no specific origin and no ageing potential is of little interest outside Germany?

Until 1986 Deutscher Sekt was not obliged by law to contain a single drop of German wine and even though it must be 100 per cent German origin today, well over 85% of Sekt is still blended from the dregs of several anonymous countries - if you look closely, the largest Sekt factories have simply dropped the word *Deutscher* from the labels of their volume-selling brands. Even genuine 100 per cent German Deutscher Sekt is no guarantee of satisfaction since most of these are simply blended from the dregs of German production. They are also the products of *cuve close*, and the end result is little better than ordinary Sekt of no fixed abode

But it is not all bad news, in fact there is some very good news and it promises even better things to come. A clue to these glad tidings is that while Sekt production increased from 400 to 500 million bottles in the 1990s, the number of Sekt producers rose from 200 to more than 1,300. A 550% growth in producers resulting in 25% expansion in production can only mean that there is a new breed of producers making Sekt on a tiny scale. In fact, there are 1,164 producers who turn over less than 2,000 cases each a year, which means that 90% of the industry make less than one per cent of the wines.

SINKING THE BISMARCK

One night at Potsdam, so the story goes, Wilhelm II was entertaining Bismarck, when the Chancellor took one sip of the German 'champagne' served to him and put down his glass. The Kaiser looked at him enquiringly, and the great statesman admitted that he found it impossible to drink Sekt. The Kaiser apparently regretted that he could not serve the Chancellor's favourite Heidsieck for reasons of both economy and patriotism, to which Bismarck announced 'Your Majesty, I am very sorry, but my patriotism stops short of my stomach.'

This illustrates a very radical change in the industry, the effect of which is both minimal and maximal. Minimal because 85% of the production remains Eurosekt. Maximal because although the new wave consists of less than one per cent of the production, this is spread over almost 1,200 brands, offering consumers outside Germany a vast range of far more interesting Sekte than ever before. Most of these new Sekt producers are small, go-ahead wine estates, producing bottle-fermented (primarily *méthode champenoise*) from classic grapes and of specific origin.

Estate-bottling of Sekt is by itself no guarantee of quality: a lot is in fact dross. However, a small and growing band of truly quality-conscious estates have been crafting excellent sparkling wines since the early 1990s. The least surprising development has been the emergence of some very fine pure Riesling Sekt.

Although an aromatic variety such as Riesling cannot possibly produce a classic brut style fizz, because the relatively subtle effects of autolysis and post-disgorgement aromas are overwhelmed by its powerful varietal character, there is no reason why it cannot produce a sparkling wine of its own unique style. As yeast contact has such little effect, logic tells us that a

PIESPORT CHURCH
WITH GOLDTROPFCHEN
AND FLAKENBURG
VINEYARDS

second fermentation in the bottle offers little advantage over *cuve close*. However, nearly all the best Riesling Sekte currently available have been bottle-fermented, even if most are transfer method rather than *Traditionelle Flashengärung* (*méthode champenoise*).

The fact is that *cuve close* Sekt has such a cheap image, the only way a producer can hope to obtain the premium his sparkling wine deserves is to use the term *Traditionelle Flashengärung*, which instantly puts it into a different price category. There are no guarantees in the wine world worth the paper they are printed on, but bottle-fermentation, even by the transfer method, should also act as some sort of safeguard for the consumer because of the 'who would bother' factor. Who would bother to put inferior wine through a costly, labour-intensive process like bottle-fermentation? Some I suppose, but apart from hardened rip-off artists, most users of cheap, low-quality base wines want to get the stuff through the system as quickly and as cheaply as possible. The best of these pure Riesling Sekte fall into three distinct categories: petrolly-mature, peachy-ripe, and flowery-elegant. There is even a Sekt made from Riesling Eiswein (*see* Schales).

Probably the most unlikely sparkling wine style that Germany's new breed of Sekt producers have come up with is pure Pinot Noir rosé, the quality of which should bowl over the fiercest Sekt-haters. The best Crémant d'Alsace rosés possess a rare purity of Pinot Noir fruit, but the most successful German *cuvées* are at least their equal. This is a style that can bridge the divide between aromatic Sekt and classic brut style sparkling wine far more successfully than any German fizz made from Pinot Blanc, Chardonnay or Auxerrois.

The only obstacle preventing most of us from enjoying these exciting wines is the small size of their production. Hopefully it will not be very long before the best specialist importers on major export markets pick up on the bright new potential of Sekt. While that is happening, however, the big Sekt producers (*see box left*) have the chance to show the rest of the world that they are not solely interested in churning out the cheapest Sekt possible. If they have any sense, let alone pride, the largest producers will want to upgrade the image and therefore the price of Sekt.

The industrialised process of sparkling wine production actually makes it easier for large, well-equipped wineries to make a better quality of sparkling wine than it is for small, non-specialist wine estates, so all they have to do is follow the lead of the pioneering producers. Will they bother? Some of the smaller, privately owned Sektkellerei, such as Brogsitter, have already taken up the challenge. A number of cooperatives have too, but although these large, faceless collectives have been justly criticised in the past, a few are excelling at the art of Sekt-making. For several years they have produced some of the country's finest fizz, and deserve the credit for this.

The biggest problem with Sekt is its euroblend image, but the *raison d'être* of a cooperative is to make local German products. Put this way, it is only logical that cooperatives are leading the Sekt revolution and, if nothing else, the Germans are logical.

GERMANY'S LARGEST SEKT PRODUCERS

The size of Germany's Sekt industry is mindboggling, with the production of just two groups, Henkell & Söhnlein and Reh Kendermann, the equivalent in size to the entire Champagne industry. However it should be remembered that Sekt is not a geographical appellation like Champagne. Most Sekt is not even German in origin, its production being sourced from various different European countries.

Group	Cases	Most important brands
1. Henkell & Söhnlein	12.5m	Henkell, Söhnlein, Rüttgers, Carstens, Deinhard
2. Reh Kendermann	8.3m	Faber, Feist
3. Seagram	3.3m	Mumm, MM
4. Rotkäppchen	2.8m	Rotkäppchen
5. Racke	1.0m	Kupferberg, Blanchet

TOP 10 BEST-SELLING SEKT BRANDS

Champagne's top-selling brand Moët & Chandon would rank sixth in the following table, and two Sekt brands, Söhnlein and Faber, are both larger in volume than Moët, Mercier and Pommery combined.

	Brand	Cases	Group
1.	Söhnlein	4,320,000	Henkell & Söhnlein
2.	Faber	3,125,000	Reh Kendermann
3.	Rotkäppchen	2,833,000	Rotkäppchen
=4.	Deinhard	2,166,000	Henkell
=4.	Mumm	2,166,000	Seagram
6.	Rüttgers	1,860,000	Henkell & Söhnlein
7.	Henkell	1,460,000	Henkell & Söhnlein
8.	Feist	1,250,000	Reh Kendermann
9.	MM	1,167,000	Seagram
10.	Kupferberg	875,000	Racke

50
CARL ADELSECK
MUNSTER–SARMSHEIM, NAHE

● 1,000 cases

The winery, which was first mentioned in the 11th century, first produced sparkling wine in 1981.

WINEMAKER
Jens Adelseck

HOUSE STYLE & RANGE
Small quantities of commercial quality fizz.
MÜNSTERER PITTERSBERG RIESLING TROCKEN
Vintaged, Sekt bA, bottle-fermented: 100% Riesling

55
AFFENTALER WG
BUHL–EISENTAL, BADEN

● 4,200 cases

Established in 1908, this cooperative consists of 980 growers in the Bühl-Eisental area, and made its first Sekt in 1977.

WINEMAKER
Leo Klär

HOUSE STYLE & RANGE
The Rieslings are rather sweet and soft, with apple and almond aromas.
AFFENTALER PINOT ROSÉ EXTRA TROCKEN
Vintaged, Sekt bA, bottle-fermented: 100% Pinot Noir
AFFENTALER RIESLING EXTRA TROCKEN
Vintaged, Sekt bA, bottle-fermented: 100% Riesling
AFFENTALER RIESLING 'KLOSTERFÜRST'
BADISCHER SEKT BRUT
Vintaged, Sekt bA, bottle-fermented: 100% Riesling

N/A
WG ALDE GOTT
SASBACHWALDEN, BADEN

● 5,850 cases

This co-op was established in 1948 for growers in the Sasbachwalden area, who

currently number 420 and own 230 hectares of vineyards. Sekt was first made here in 1987.

WINEMAKER
Hermann Bähr

HOUSE STYLE & RANGE
Wines tasted recently from this property were old and tired, and were quickly oxidising, even though they were just three years old. I have insufficient previous experience of these Sekts to give an objective overall rating.
SASBACHWALDENER PINOT EXTRA BRUT
Vintaged, Sekt bA, méthode champenoise:
100% Pinot Noir

60
GEBRÜDER ANSELMANN
EDESHEIM, PFALZ

● 3,350 cases

This recently formed private company was established in 1988 by brothers Gerd and Ralf Anselmann, who also have commercial links to San Felipe wines of Gran Canaria in the Canary Islands.

WINEMAKER
Gerd Anselmann

HOUSE STYLE & RANGE
The red is sweet, weird and fizzy, but the Riesling is a wine of some intensity, with plenty of petrolly and peppery aromas, although it does seem somewhat lacking in finesse.
EDENKOBENER SCHLOSS LUDWIGSHÖHE
DORNFELDER TROCKEN
Vintaged, Sekt bA, méthode champenoise:
100% Dornfelder

NOTES

1 The following terms located in the details for each *cuvée* are unique to the German chapter:
Deutscher Sekt – 100% German origin
Sekt bA – The sparkling wine equivalent of QbA, this denotes a quality wine originating from a delimited region such as the Rheingau, the Pfalz, Mosel-Saar-Ruwer, etc. The name of the *cuvée* will indicate if this has come from a specific village or vineyard.

2 If neither of the above terms are indicated, the origin of the wine has not been revealed and is thus Sekt of no fixed abode. In the past, most of this has been a blend of wines from Italy (often Emilia-Romagna and Trentino) and France (often Loire and Charentes), but since Spain joined the EU it has supplied increasing amounts of base wines and, as the EU widens its membership, so the origin of basic Sekt is likely to expand, particularly when the cheapest East European wines become available.

3 Bottle-fermented – only those wines the producers have unequivocally stated as being made by *méthode champenoise* or transfer method are listed as such, the rest being designated bottle-fermented.

4 The following abbreviations are for terms that are usually synonymous with 'cooperative':
Wg (*Weingärtner, Weingärtnergenossenschaft* or *Winzergenossenschaft*)
Wv (*Winzerverein*)

✦ EDESHEIMER ORDENSGUT
RIESLING BRUT
Vintaged, Sekt bA, méthode champenoise:
100% Riesling

AFFALTRACH
See SCHLOSSKELLEREI AFFALTRACH

GABRIEL VON ARKEN
See HANSE SEKTKELLEREI WISMAR

50
WG AUGGEN
AUGGEN, BADEN

● 4,200 cases

Established in 1922 for growers in Auggen, this cooperative first produced sparkling wine in 1988, and has links with flying winemakers Nick Butler and Jürgen von der Mark.

WINEMAKER
Reinhard Zöllin

HOUSE STYLE & RANGE
Not very impressive: sweetish fizz with almondy aromas.
AUGGENER SCHÄF 'SCHLÖSSLEGARTEN'
GRAUERBURGUNDER EXTRA TROCKEN
Vintaged, Sekt bA, bottle-fermented: 100% Pinot Gris
KLOSTERFÜRST WEISSBURGUNDER BRUT
Vintaged, Sekt bA, bottle-fermented: 100% Pinot Blanc

50
AUGUSTUS
LEIWEN, MOSEL–SAAR–RUWER

Part of the Reh Kendermann group, this firm is under the personal direction of Niclaus Graf von Plettenberg, and produces a commercial quality Sekt under the St Augustus label.

50
BARON LANGWERTH VON SIMMERN'SCHES
ELTVILLE, RHEINGAU

Small production of unexceptional estate fizz.

BARON ZU KNYPHAUSEN
See FREIHERR ZU KNYPHAUSEN

BAUMANN
See SCHLOSSKELLEREI AFFALTRACH

BEETHOVEN
See GESCHWISTER KÖWERICH

N/A
BERNARD-MASSARD
TRIER, MOSEL–SAAR–RUWER

● 270,000 cases
● Group ownership – Hoehl, Langenbach
● Other labels – Graf Luxemburg

Established in 1919 by Jean Bernard-Massard in the historic 15th-century Palais Pillhof in the centre of Trier. Two years later, he

AUTUMNAL VINES AT PIESPORT, MOSEL

founded Bernard-Massard in Luxembourg. Today, both companies are owned by one joint-stock company in Luxembourg, the main shareholders of which are the Clasen family (which manages Bernard-Massard in Luxembourg) and the Immelnkemper family (which manages this firm). Bernard-Massard is also active in the BOB Sekt market.

WINEMAKER
Waldemar Baum

HOUSE STYLE & RANGE
The Cuvée Zero Saar-Kristall Riesling Brut Extra could be better focused on the nose, but it is clean, with nice, flowery, peachy fruit that is evocative of the variety on the palate.
CABINET BRUT
Vintaged, cuve close: grape varieties & origin not revealed
CABINET GOLD ROYAL TROCKEN
Vintaged, cuve close: grape varieties & origin not revealed
CABINET HALBTROCKEN
Vintaged, cuve close: grape varieties & origin not revealed
CABINET SILBER EXTRA DRY
Vintaged, cuve close: grape varieties & origin not revealed
DIAMANT HALBTROCKEN
Vintaged, bottle-fermented: grape varieties and origin not revealed
ELBLING BRUT
Vintaged, Sekt bA, bottle-fermented: 100% Elbling
GRAF LUXEMBOURG HALBTROCKEN/MILD
Vintaged, plastic stopper, cuve close: grape varieties and origin not revealed
HERRENKLASSE RIESLING TROCKEN
Vintaged, Deutscher Sekt, bottle-fermented: 100% Riesling
LIFESTYLE DEMI SEC
Vintaged, cuve close: grape varieties/origin not revealed
LIFESTYLE CHARDONNAY EXTRA DRY
Vintaged, cuve close: 100% Chardonnay
SAAR-KRISTALL RIESLING EXTRA BRUT
Vintaged, Sekt bA, bottle-fermented: 100% Riesling
SPÄTBURGUNDER TROCKEN
Vintaged, cuve close: 100% Pinot Noir
TRADITION TROCKEN/HALBTROCKEN/MILD
Vintaged, plastic stopper, cuve close: grape varieties and origin not revealed

WINZERSEKT SAAR-RIESLING BRUT
Vintaged, single-estate, méthode champenoise: 100% Riesling

N/A
BEZIRKSKELLEREI MARKGRÄFLERLAND
EFRINGEN, BADEN
• 5,000 cases
Established in 1953 as a co-op for growers in the Markgräflerland region, this firm produced its first sparkling wine in 1990.

WINEMAKER
Günter Ehret

HOUSE STYLE & RANGE
My only experience of this cooperative's Sekt is the Nobling, which still had fermentation odours at three years of age. This was not necessarily a bad omen; indeed, it could be a good sign, perhaps indicating that, unlike so many German sparkling wines, this *cuvée* needed more yeast-contact prior to disgorgement or more time afterwards. However, it was not possible to discern what the potential quality would be if given this additional ageing.
BINZENER SONNHÖHLE NOBLING BRUT
Vintaged, Sekt bA, bottle-fermented: 100% Nobling

50
BICKENSOHL
VOGTSBURG–BICKENSOHL, BADEN
Established in 1924, this cooperative's members currently own 170 hectares of vineyards. The fizz produced has not been outstanding so far.

N/A
WG BISCHOFFINGEN
BISCHOFFINGEN, BADEN
• 225,000 cases
Established in 1924, this cooperative of growers in the Bischoffingen area made its first sparkling wine in 1985.

WINEMAKER
Werner Hassler

HOUSE STYLE & RANGE
I have insufficient experience to make an objective overall rating; not impressed so far.
PINOT BRUT
Not vintaged, Sekt bA, bottle-fermented: 100% Pinot Blanc
PINOT BRUT ROSÉ
Not vintaged, Sekt bA, bottle-fermented: 100% Pinot Noir

78
BISCHÖFLICHE WEINGÜTER TRIER
TRIER, MOSEL-SAAR-RUWER
• 6,700 cases

This producer has been making Sekt *cuvées* since 1986.

WINEMAKER
Richard Müller

HOUSE STYLE & RANGE
Perfumed Riesling aroma with soft, peachy fruit on the palate, and fine acidity for freshness.
★★ SCHARZHOFBERGER RIESLING BRUT
Vintaged, Sekt bA, méthode champenoise: 100% Riesling
★ SCHARZHOFBERGER RIESLING EXTRA BRUT
Vintaged, Sekt bA, méthode champenoise: 100% Riesling

BLANCHET
See RACKE

BLACK TOWER SEKT
See KENDERMANN

BLUE NUN SEKT
See H SICHEL SÖHNE

50
ALFRED BONNET
FRIEDELSHEIM, PFALZ
• 2,500 cases
Winemakers for ten generations, the Bonnet family first produced Sekt in 1981. This is one of a tiny number of producers who annoyingly twist the wire holding the cork in a different direction to that of the rest of the world.

WINEMAKER
Alfred D Bonnet

HOUSE STYLE & RANGE
The quality of these wines has not impressed.
CHARDONNAY EXTRA TROCKEN
Not vintaged, Sekt bA, méthode champenoise: 100% Chardonnay
RIESLING EXTRA TROCKEN
Not vintaged, Sekt bA, méthode champenoise: 100% Riesling

N/A
WG BRACKENHEIM
BRACKENHEIM, WÜRTTEMBERG
• 3,200 cases
This cooperative was established in 1925 for the growers of Brackenheim, the largest wine city in the viticultural region of Württemberg and the birthplace of Theodor Heuss, first president of the Federal Republic of Germany. Wg Brackenheim made its first Sekt in 1984.

WINEMAKER
Friedrich Hammel

HOUSE STYLE & RANGE
Only two cuvées tasted, thus this producer has no overall rating. The rosé is merely of a basic commercial quality but it is preferable to the brut, my experience of which included unappealing chemical aromas.

BRACKENHEIMER ZWEIFELBERG LEMBERGER BRUT
Vintaged, Sekt bA, bottle-fermented: 100% Lemberger
BRACKENHEIMER ZWEIFELBERG LEMBERGER
TROCKEN ROSÉ
Vintaged, Sekt bA, bottle-fermented: 100% Lemberger

76
BROGSITTER PRIVAT SEKTKELLEREI

GRAFSCHAFT-GELSDORF, AHR

● 25,000 cases

● Other labels - Rotsekt, Sankt Peter

The Brogsitter family, which has owned vineyards and made wine in the Ahr district since 1600, started producing Sekt in 1950.

WINEMAKER

Elmar Sermann

HOUSE STYLE & RANGE

It is not surprising that an Ahr producer should specialise primarily in red and rosé sparkling wines. Some *cuvées* are ordinary and amylic, but Brogsitter's Spätburgunder is certainly its best fizz (despite an appalling label), with plenty of elegant, cherry, Pinot fruit supported by a soft, cushiony mousse.

BLANC DE NOIRS BRUT
Vintaged, Sekt bA, bottle-fermented: 100% Pinot Noir
★☆ SPÄTBURGUNDER BRUT
Vintaged, Sekt bA, bottle-fermented: 100% Pinot Noir

N/A
REICHSRAT VON BÜHL

DEIDESHEIM, PFALZ

● 3,350 cases

Established in 1849, the first sparkling wine was produced in 1983.

WINEMAKER

Frank John

HOUSE STYLE & RANGE

This Sekt generally appears to need another year in bottle whenever I have tasted it, but as I have never had the inclination to store a bottle or the opportunity to taste the same wine one year later, it is impossible to give this producer an objective overall rating.

RIESLING BRUT
Vintaged, Sekt bA, méthode champenoise: 100% Riesling

65
BÜRGERSPITAL ZUM HL GEIST

WURZBURG, FRANKEN

● 1,000 cases

The Bürgerspital is one of the oldest and largest wine estates in Germany, having been founded in 1319 as a home for the poor and elderly of Würzburg. The estate consists of

140 hectares of vineyards and produced its first Sekt in 1987, but it is more highly regarded for its still wines, particularly its Würzburger Stein and Pfaffenberg.

WINEMAKER

Robert Braungardt

HOUSE STYLE & RANGE

Only pure varietal, single-vineyard Sekt is produced. The Riesling is fat and satisfying, but the nose lacks finesse and the finish would benefit from more acidity.

BÜRGERSPITAL KERNER EXTRA TROCKEN
Vintaged, Sekt bA, bottle-fermented: 100% Kerner
BÜRGERSPITAL RIESLING BRUT
Vintaged, Sekt bA, bottle-fermented: 100% Riesling

74
BURG HORNBERG

NECKARZIMMERN, BADEN

● 250 cases

Owned by the Baron von Gemmingen-Hornberg family for 400 years, Burg Hornberg produced its first sparkling wine in 1920.

WINEMAKER

Baron Dajo von Gemmingen-Hornberg

HOUSE STYLE & RANGE

Made in a true-white *blanc de noirs* style, rather than the New World synonym for rosé, this pure Meunier fizz is really quite refined and one of the few Sekts that could take some ageing.

★ SCHWARZRIESLING BLANC DE NOIRS BRUT
Vintaged, Sekt bA, bottle-fermented: 100% Meunier

BURG SPONECK

See JECHTINGER

N/A
BURG WEISENAU

SPEYER, PFALZ

● 250,000 cases

● Group ownership - Henkell & Söhnlein

A specialist in regional Sekt brands, this firm was founded by Luwig Christian Cantor in 1852, when it was called E&F Cantor. Its name was changed to Burg Weisenau in 1936, and the company was purchased by the Oetker family in 1963, merging with Kurpfalz Sektkellerei in 1997.

See KURPFALZ SEKTKELLEREI

DR ALBERT BÜRKLIN

See DR BÜRKLIN-WOLF

72
DR BÜRKLIN-WOLF

WACHENHEIM, PFALZ

● 2,100 cases

● Other labels - Dr Albert Bürklin

This famous family estate started making Sekt in 1978.

WINEMAKER

Fritz Knorr

HOUSE STYLE & RANGE

Satisfying and well-balanced, with easy-drinking Riesling fruit.

★☆ GEHEIMRAT DR ALBERT BÜRKLIN WOLF RIESLING BRUT
Vintaged, Sekt bA, méthode champenoise: 100% Riesling

N/A
CANTOR

● 250,000 cases

● Group ownership - Henkell & Söhnlein

CARSTENS

● 270,000 cases

See HENKELL

CASTELLER

See FÜRSTLICH CASTELL'SCHES DOMÄNENAMT

76
FÜRSTLICH CASTELL'SCHES DOMÄNENAMT

CASTELL, FRANKEN

● 2,500 cases

● Other labels - Schloss Castell, Casteller Herrenberg

Some Castell vineyards were documented as early as 1258, and the Castell-Castell family have been vineyard owners for 27 generations, first producing Sekt in 1973.

WINEMAKER

Christian Friess, Reinhard Firnbach

HOUSE STYLE & RANGE

I have found the Schloss Castell to be musty, but the leesy, rich Casteller Herrenberg is a very good sparkling wine. Its petrolly character is very Riesling in style – even though it is a Riesling/Sylvaner cross.

SCHLOSS CASTELL BRUT
Not vintaged, Sekt bA, transfer method: 50% Kerner, 50% Bacchus
★☆ CASTELLER HERRENBERG RIESLANER BRUT
Vintaged, Sekt bA, transfer method: 100% Rieslaner

CASTEL-STAADTER

Merely the place-name used by Michael Hausen-Mabilon for one of his Sekte, but its prominence on the label compared to the small print used for the producer's name could lead some readers to think this is the primary brand name.

See HAUSEN

N/A
CHANDON

MUNICH, BAYERN

- 175,000 cases
- Group ownership – LVMH (France)

This part of the sprawling Chandon sparkling wine empire lags behind the fizz Chandon produces in South America.

50
MATH JOS CLUSSERATH

MEHRING, MOSEL–SAAR–RUWER

Standard, unexciting commercial fizz.

74
WV DEIDESHEIM

DEIDESHEIM, PFALZ

- 270 cases

Founded in 1898, this is the local co-op for the growers of Deidesheim, who have been making Sekt since 1979.

WINEMAKER

Ludwig Eichberger

HOUSE STYLE & RANGE

Fresh, peachy, pure Riesling fruit, with a nice, juicy finish.

★ DEIDESHEIMER PARADIESGARTEN EXTRA BRUT
Vintaged, Sekt bA, méthode champenoise: 100% Riesling

✴ SPÄTBURGUNDER ROTSEKT TROCKEN
Vintaged, Sekt bA, transfer method: 100% Pinot Noir

N/A
DEINHARD

KOBLENZ

- 2.5 million cases
- Group ownership – Henkell & Söhnlein

Founded 1794. This export house remained in family hands for over 200 years, until it was taken over by Henkell & Söhnlein in 1996.

HOUSE STYLE & RANGE

All the wines are made by *cuve close*, from the inexpensive and very commercial Cabinet, through the recently launched Yello (*sic*) to the well-established Lila Imperial. Its three *cuvées* of Bernkasteler Doctor Sekt prove that Deinhard is capable of producing the highest quality via tank fermentation. However, no overall judgement can be made until it has established a track record under new ownership.

CABINET
Not vintaged, cuve close: grape varieites not revealed
CLUB DE BRUT
Not vintaged, cuve close: grape varieites not revealed
LILA
Not vintaged, cuve close: 100% Riesling
SILVER RIDGE
Not vintaged, cuve close: Chardonnay and Riesling

80
MATTHIAS DEIS

LEHMEN, MOSEL–SAAR–RUWER

- 840 cases

This family-owned enterprise was founded in 1580, and has produced hand-riddled Sekt by *méthode champenoise* since 1985. Volume barely exceeds 100 cases for each *cuvée*.

WINEMAKER

Matthias Deis

HOUSE STYLE & RANGE

The Trocken in particular has a fine, fresh Riesling style, with vanilla on the finish.

★ RIESLING BRUT
Vintaged, Sekt bA, méthode champenoise: 100% Riesling

★★ RIESLING TROCKEN
Vintaged, Sekt bA, méthode champenoise: 100% Riesling

68
JOSEF DEPPISCH

ERLENBACH BEI MARKTHEIDENFELD, FRANKEN

- 850 cases

A private winery and estate established in 1872, and run by the Deppisch family ever since, with Theo and Johannes representing the fifth generation of owners. The first sparkling wine here was produced in 1981.

WINEMAKER

Johannes Deppisch, Günter Schubert

HOUSE STYLE & RANGE

The Silvaner is fat, basic and uninteresting, but the Pinot has an apricot-and-custard touch that is sometimes found when ripe Pinot (or Chardonnay) grapes undergo a little malolactic fermentation.

✴ PINOT BRUT
Vintaged, Sekt bA, transfer method: 10% Pinot Noir, 50% Pinot Blanc, 40% Pinot Gris
SILVANER BRUT
Vintaged, Sekt bA, transfer method: 100% Silvaner

55
WG DEUTSCHES WEINTOR

ILBESHEIM, PFALZ

The Gebiets-Winzergenossenschaft Deutsches Weintor is a vast, regional co-op close to the French border. The size of its Sekt production is unspecified.

HOUSE STYLE & RANGE

Fresh, fat and sassy.

✴ CHARDONNAY BRUT
Not vintaged, Sekt bA, méthode champenoise: 100% Chardonnay

DEUTZ & GELDERMANN

See GELDERMANN PRIVATSEKTKELLEREI

DOMÄNENWEINGUT SCHLOSS SCHÖNBORN

See SCHLOSS SCHÖNBORN

N/A
MATTHIAS DOSTERT

NITTEL, MOSEL–SAAR–RUWER

- 5,000 cases

A family-owned business, established in 1625 which first produced sparkling wine in 1982.

WINEMAKER

Matthias Dostert

HOUSE STYLE & RANGE

The Elbling Brut is musty (not corked), while the Elbling Trocken is tangy, but not special. Too little experience to give an overall rating.

ELBLING BRUT
Not vintaged, Sekt bA, méthode champenoise: 100% Elbling
ELBLING TROCKEN
Not vintaged, Sekt bA, méthode champenoise: 100% Elbling

DR MAYER

See ST JOHANNER

50
EWALD THEO DRATHEN

ALF, MOSEL–SAAR RUWER

- Other labels – Schloss Avras

This large bottler of export wines is based in Alf, and produces a large range of cheap, commercial-quality, *cuve close* fizz.

50
JOSEF DRATHEN

ZELL, MOSEL–SAAR RUWER

This is a completely different firm to Ewald Theo Drathen, with production facilities located at Zell, rather than Alf. It produces Sekt that is equally commercially oriented.

THE PREMISES OF SEKTKELLEREI DEIDESHEIM IN THE PFALZ, WHICH PRODUCES THE STARRED DEIDERSHEIMER PARADIESGARTEN EXTRA BRUT, MADE WITH 100 PER CENT RIESLING GRAPES

85
DURBACHER WG
DURBACH, BADEN
- 5,000 cases

Founded 1928, the Durbacher Winzer-genossenschaft is the local co-op for the growers of Durbach, who have produced Sekt since 1973.

WINEMAKER
Josef Wörner

HOUSE STYLE & RANGE
This co-op makes a delightful, pure Pinot Noir rosé, old-gold in colour, with hues of a setting sun. It has a fine varietal perfume and gorgeous rich, yet wonderfully light, Pinot fruit, nicely cushioned by an impeccable mousse of tiny pinhead bubbles. The 1994 vintage was one of the five best German Sekte I have ever tasted.

★★☆ DURBACHER KOCHBERG BRUT ROSÉ
Vintaged, Sekt bA, méthode champenoise:
100% Pinot Noir

EDELGRÄFLER
See WILHELM ZÄHRINGER

N/A
EGERT
OESTRICH WINKEL, RHEINGAU
- 420 cases

A small family-owned winery dating back to the 18th century, Weingut Egert made its first *méthode champenoise* in 1993, since when it has won various domestic awards.

WINEMAKER
Herr Solter

HOUSE STYLE & RANGE
Very rich in style, with ripe fruit.

HATTENHEIMER HASSEL RIESLING EXTRA TROCKEN
Vintaged, Sekt bA, méthode champenoise:
100% Riesling

75
CHRISTIAN UND RICHARD EMRICH
BAD KREUZNACH, NAHE
- 1,000 cases

Established for over 300 years, the Emrichs started making sparkling wine just 20 years ago.

WINEMAKER
Steffen Montigny

HOUSE STYLE & RANGE
Generally soft with gentle fruit, the rosé is particularly successful, with soft, elegant, cherry fruit and fine acidity which nicely offsets its off-dry finish.

★ KREUZNACHER BLAUER SPÄTBURGUNDER
EXTRA TROCKEN ROSÉ
Vintaged, Sekt bA, bottle-fermented: 100% Pinot Noir

★ KREUZNACHER WINZERSEKT RIESLING
TROCKEN
Vintaged, Sekt bA, bottle-fermented:
100% Riesling

ERBEN
See FW LAGGUTH ERBEN

50
GUT ERBES
SPIESHEIM, RHEINHESSEN
- 350 cases

Small estate dating back 300 years, but only started sparkling wine production in 1987.

WINEMAKER
Heribert Erbes

HOUSE STYLE & RANGE
Basic-quality fizz with a peppery touch.

RIESLING BRUT
Vintaged, méthode champenoise: 100% Riesling

ESER CABINET
See JOHANNISHOF

50
FABER
TRIER, MOSEL-SAAR-RUWER
- 3.1 million cases
- Group ownership - Reh Kendermann
- Other labels - Feist

Established in 1950, Faber produced its first sparkling wine two years later, and very quickly became Germany's largest Sekt brand. However, sales of Faber have dropped one million cases over the last ten years, although it still ranks as number two.

HOUSE STYLE & RANGE
Basic commercial quality.

KRÖNUNG HALBTROCKEN
Not vintaged, cuve close: grape varieties and origin
not revealed

ROTLESE HALBTROCKEN
Not vintaged, red fizz, cuve close: grape varieties and
origin not revealed

FEIGENWÄLDCHEN
See NAEGELSFÖRST, GUT

FEIST
This group produces around 1.3 million cases of Feist Belmont and Feist Riesling.
See FABER

70
FISCHBORN-SCHENK
BIEBELSHEIM, RHEINHESSEN
- 420 cases

This small, privately owned estate was established in 1833. It began producing sparkling wine in 1981, moving over exclusively to *méthode champenoise* in 1994.

WINEMAKER
Hans-Werner Schenk

HOUSE STYLE & RANGE
The Riesling brut is quite satisfying, though it would improve with a little more ageing, but the Riesling Trocken (which bears the same vineyard designation), with a larger *dosage*, seems very basic by comparison.

★ BIEBELSHEIMER KIESELBERG RIESLING BRUT
Vintaged, Sekt bA, méthode champenois:
100% Riesling

BIEBELSHEIMER KIESELBERG RIESLING TROCKEN
Vintaged, Sekt bA, méthode champenoise:
100% Riesling

N/A
WG FLEIN-TALHEIM
FLEIN, WURTTEMBERG
This co-op was established in 1923 by 56 growers in Flein, and merged in 1972 with the Talheim co-op. Flein-Talheim is large and still expanding, now boasting 400 growers. Production size remains unspecified.

WINEMAKER
Roland Hönnige

HOUSE STYLE & RANGE
The Riesling is basic commercial fizz, as is the Samtrot – though it does have some semi- Pinot character, which is not unexpected for a Meunier mutation.

SANKT VEIT RIESLING BRUT
Vintaged, Sekt bA, méthode champenoise:
100% Riesling

VILLAGE OF DURBACH
IN BADEN, SURROUNDED
BY VINEYARDS, WHERE
THE DURBACHER CO-OP
IS SITUATED

SANKT VEIT TALHEIMER KIRCHENWEINBERG SAMTROT TROCKEN
Vintaged, Sekt bA, méthode champenoise: 100% Samtrot

FREIHERR HEINRICH
See GRÄFLICH VON KAGENECK'SCHE

FREIHERR VON SCHLEINITZ
See SCHLEINITZ, FREIHERR VON

50
JOSEF FRIEDERICH
ZELL, MOSEL–SAAR–RUWER
Makes standard commercial fizz under the Friedericus Trocken label.

FRIEDERICUS
See JOSEF FRIEDERICH

70
H-J FRIES
MARING–NOVIAND, MOSEL–SAAR–RUWER
• 250 cases
Established in 1747, this privately owned producer first made Sekt in 1984. Today, it uses grapes exclusively from its own, steep-sloping Riesling vineyard and part-vinifies in wood for the first fermentation.
WINEMAKER
Hans-Josef Fries
HOUSE STYLE & RANGE
Rather herbaceous, yet strangely satisfying, some wines need time in bottle to develop.
✶ MARING-NOVIANDER KLOSTERBERG RIESLING BRUT
Vintaged, Sekt bA, méthode champenoise: 100% Riesling

MARING-NOVIANDER KLOSTERBERG RIESLING EXTRA BRUT
Vintaged, Sekt bA, méthode champenoise: 100% Riesling

N/A
RUDOLF FÜRST
BURGSTADT, FRANKEN
• 850 cases
Founded in 1632, the vineyards of Rudolf Fürst are impeccably maintained, and Paul Fürst makes splendid still wines. However, the Sekte leave much to be desired.
WINEMAKER
Paul Fürst
HOUSE STYLE & RANGE
I don't have enough experience of his Sekt

to give this producer an overall rating, but I tasted two different vintages of the same wine and found both of them coarse and far too almondy for any finesse.
SPÄTBURGUNDER BRUT BLANC
Vintaged, Sekt bA, bottle-fermented: 100% Pinot Noir

FÜRST VON METTERNICH
See METTERNICH, FÜRST VON

FÜRST ZU HOHENLOHE-OEHRINGEN
See HOHENLOHE-OEHRINGEN, FÜRST ZU

FUERST BLUECHER
See ZIMMERMAN-GRAEFF & MÜLLER

65
ERNST GEBHARDT
SOMMERHAUSEN, FRANKEN
This old-established estate was purchased at the end of the 19th century by the Hügelschäffer family, the current proprietors.
HOUSE STYLE & RANGE
The best Sekt I have tested here was the Frankensekt Marktbreiter Sonnenberg, which is very rich, with a herbal twist to the petrolly, Riesling fruit. However, the Franken Privat Kerner is merely clean and fizzy, while the amylic Franken Privat Silvaner is far too soft and lacking in acidity.
✶ FRANKENSEKT MARKTBREITER SONNENBERG RIESLING BRUT
Vintaged, Sekt bA, cuve close: 100% Riesling
FRANKEN PRIVAT KERNER EXTRA BRUT
Vintaged, Sekt bA, cuve close: 100% Kerner
FRANKEN PRIVAT SILVANER EXTRA BRUT
Vintaged, Sekt bA, cuve close: 100% Silvaner

GEBRÜDER WEISS
See KESSLER

N/A
GEORG GEILING
BACHARACH, MITTELRHEIN
• 50,000 cases
Established 1890, when it made Sekt from base wines transported in bulk from Champagne. This firm uses various methods of production for its different labels and qualities, but seldom produces anything special.

50
GELDERMANN PRIVATSEKTKELLEREI
BREISACH, BADEN
• 250,000 cases
• Other labels - Odeon, Wappen von Breisach Grande Classé
Established at Breisach in 1925 by Deutz & Geldermann of Champagne fame, this Sekt house makes sparkling wine by *cuve close*,

transfer method and *méthode champenoise*, but the clean and simple commercial style seems to pervade wines made by all three methods. No longer connected with Deutz (formerly Deutz & Geldermann) in Champagne.

50
JAKOB GERHARDT
NIERSTEIN, RHEINHESSEN
• 200,000 cases
Significant producer of commercial *cuve close* wines, of which the volume-seller is a basic Euroblend, but Deutscher Sekt is also made

N/A
A GILLOT & SÖHNE
OPPENHEIM, RHEINHESSEN
• 50,000 cases
Small, privately owned Sekt house using grapes grown in its own vineyards for some of the production; exclusively Deutscher Sekt

N/A
PAUL RAINER GILLOT
OPPENHEIM, RHEINHESSEN
• 50,000 cases
A different brand to the above, Paul Rainer Gillot is related to Adam Gillot, but there are no commercial links between the two firms.

N/A
FREIHERR V GLEICHENSTEIN
OBERROTWEIL, BADEN
• 400 cases
A well-known wine estate established in 1634. Produced its first sparkling wine in 1988.
WINEMAKER
Frank Müller
HOUSE STYLE & RANGE
Almondy fizz. I much prefer this estate's still wine, particularly its Amolterner Steinhalde.

BADISCHER WINZERSEKT PINOT EXTRA BRUT
Vintaged, Sekt bA, bottle-fermented: 33% Pinot Blanc, 33% Pinot Noir, 33% Pinot Gris

50
GOLDHAND SEKTKELLEREI
MAINZ, RHEINHESSEN
• 100,000 cases
Privately owned house producing a basic-quality *cuve close* fizz.

GOLDLACK
See LANGENBACH

SEKTKELLEREI CARL GRAEGER
BINGEN, RHEINHESSEN
- 125,000 cases
- Owned by Volker Valerius

HOUSE STYLE & RANGE
The intensity of the Pinot Noir fruit is so satisfying and mellow it is almost gamey, but most of the production here is basic-quality cuve close.
★ PRIVAT RESERVE HEPPENHEIMER SCHLOSSBERG
  PINOT NOIR BRUT
  Not vintaged, Sekt bA, bottle-fermented:
  100% Pinot Noir

GRAF ARTOS
See HERRES

GRAF LUXEMBOURG
See BERNARD-MASSARD

N/A
GRÄFLICH V KAGENECK'SCHE
BREISACH, BADEN
- 200,000 cases
- Other labels - Freiherr Heinrich, Greiffenegg Schlössle, Schloss Munzingen

A co-op founded in 1974, Kageneck produces a large range of bottle-fermented varietal Sekt that used to be competently made, but not any longer from recent tasting.

GREIFFENEGG SCHLÖSSLE
See GRÄFLICH VON KAGENECK'SCHE

N/A
KF GROEBE
BIEBELSHEIM, RHEINHESSEN
- 500 cases

A small family-owned estate founded in 1763, KF Groebe owns seven hectares of hillside vineyards around Westhofen, and has links with Julien Meyer in Nothalten, Alsace.

WINEMAKER
Friedrich Groebe

HOUSE STYLE & RANGE
The Groebe + Prinze, which is the product of a joint venture with Fred Prinz Hallgarten, does not impress me, but Groebe's own Riesling is fresh and zesty.
GROEBE + PRINZ BRUT
  Vintaged, Sekt bA, bottle-fermented: 100% Riesling
★ RIESLING BRUT
  Vintaged, Sekt bA, bottle-fermented: 100% Riesling

PETER LOUIS GUNTRUM
DEXHEIM, RHEINHESSEN
Standard commercial fizz from a firm that should not be confused with Louis Guntrum.

GUT ERBES
See ERBES, GUT

GUT NAEGELSFÖRST
See NAEGELSFÖRST, GUT

76
WV HAGNAU
HAGNAU, BADEN
- 1,700 cases

Founded in 1881 by Dr Heinrich Hansjakob, Winzerverein Hagnau is the local cooperative for the growers of Hagnau. The first sparkling wine was produced here in 1988.

WINEMAKER
Robert Markheiser

HOUSE STYLE & RANGE
The Kerner is not one of my favourite grapes, but Hagnau produces the best fizzy rendition of this variety that I've ever encountered: a fresh, flowery, off-dry style that is appealing in an undemanding way.
★★ HAGNAUER BURGSTALL EXTRA TROCKEN
  Vintaged, Sekt bA, méthode champenoise 100% Kerner

70
HAMBACHER SCHLOSS
NEUSTADT, PFALZ
- 50,000 cases

The Hambacher Schloss winery was established in 1902, and is the co-op for growers in the Hambach locality, who currently number 150 and own some 80 hectares of vineyards.

WINEMAKER
Andreas Nöh

HOUSE STYLE & RANGE
The Dornfelder is a curious (yet not unpleasant) red-winey fizz, but the fresh, flowery Weisser Burgunder is more satisfying.
HAMBACHER REBSTÖCKEL DORNFELDER TROCKEN
  Vintaged, Sekt bA, transfer method: 100% Dornfelder
★ WEISSER BURGUNDER EXTRA BRUT
  Vintaged, Sekt bA, transfer method: 100% Pinot Blanc

72
HAMMEL
KIRCHHEIM, PFALZ
- 420 cases

Founded in 1723, the entire Hammel family is employed by the estate that it owns, and first produced sparkling wine in 1967, changing to *méthode champenoise* in 1988.

WINEMAKER
Christoph Hammel

HOUSE STYLE & RANGE
The Pinot Noir is a soft and frothy *blanc de noirs*, with tiny bubbles and nice high acidity. The petrolly Riesling is pleasantly dry.
★ KLEINKARLBERGER HERRENBERG PINOT
  BLANC DE NOIRS BRUT
  Vintaged, Sekt bA, méthode champenoise:
  100% Pinot Noir

★ KIRCHHEIMER RÖMERSTRASSE
  RIESLING TROCKEN
  Vintaged, Sekt bA, méthode champenoise:
  100% Riesling

75
HANSE
WISMAR, MOSEL-SAAR-RUWER
- 150,000 cases
- Other labels - Gabriel von Arken, Schloss Schwerin

This privately owned winery was first mentioned as Weinhaus Michaelis in 1648 and has produced sparkling wine since 1958.

WINEMAKER
Helmuth Westphal

HOUSE STYLE & RANGE
The Trocken is not as fresh or as crisp as the Brut, but both have lovely petrolly aromas, and the Brut has a particularly fine balance, with a very smooth finish.
★ HANSE SELECTION RIESLING BRUT
  Vintaged, Deutscher Sekt, méthode champenoise:
  100% Riesling
★ HANSE TRADITION RIESLING TROCKEN
  Vintaged, Deutscher Sekt, méthode champenoise:
  100% Riesling

N/A
HAUSEN
KASTEL-STAADT, MOSEL-SAAR-RUWER
- 6,700 cases

Staadter Sektkellerei Michael Hausen-Mabilon, to give it its full title, is a private Sekt house established as recently as 1986.

WINEMAKER
Michael Hausen-Mabilon

HOUSE STYLE & RANGE
Fresh and perfumed, but with amylic aromas that trivialise what might have been an excellent Riesling Sekt.
KASTEL-STAADTER MAXIMINER PRÄLAT
  RIESLING BRUT
  Vintaged, Sekt bA, méthode champenoise:
  100% Riesling

MARTIN HEIM
See HEIM'SCHE PRIVAT-SEKTKELLEREI

75
HEIM'SCHE PRIVAT-SEKTKELLEREI
NEUSTADT, PFALZ
- 92,000 cases

This privately owned Sekt house has been producing a strange but remarkable fizz from Gewürztraminer grapes since 1989.

WINEMAKER
Martin Heim

HOUSE STYLE & RANGE
One of only two German sparkling wines made from the Gewürztraminer grape, I

have tasted. Although it is difficult to come to grips with such an unaccustomed style, it is far better balanced than one might imagine. Its clean, spicy fruit has true varietal pungency.

★ MARTIN HEIM GEWÜRZTRAMINER TROCKEN
Vintaged, Sekt bA, méthode champenoise:
100% Gewürztraminer

55
HENKELL
WIESBADEN, RHEINGAU

- 4 million cases
- Group ownership - Henkell & Söhnlein
- Other labels - Carstens SC, Adam Henkell, Lutter & Wegner, Rüttgers Club, Schloss Biebrich, Schloss Rheinberg

This house was established as a general wine merchant in 1832 by Adam Henkell, who built a sparkling-wine facility in Mainz in 1856. The company launched Henkell Trocken in 1894, moved to new cellars in Birbrich, Wiesbaden, in 1909; the following year, it became the market-leading Sekt brand. In 1948, the firm came under the control of 25-year-old Otto Henkell II, who restructured the business, launched the Rüttgers brand in the 1950s and purchased Carstens in 1975, retiring in 1982. Henkell and Söhnlein Rheingold merged in 1987. Although the headquarters of Henkell & Söhnlein are Henkell's old premises in Wiesbaden, the group is the exclusive property of the Oetker family, owner of Söhnlein prior to the merger. Henkell Trocken is also produced by Henkell & Söhnlein in Austria.

HOUSE STYLE & RANGE
Adam Henkell Rosé is marketed as the top-of-the-range wine, but although it is infinitely preferable to Henkell Trocken, it does not impress. A Sekt, not Deutscher Sekt (although its Côtes de Toul origin in the former province of Lorraine was once German), Adam Henkell Rosé is fresh, but very ordinary in character.
ADAM HENKELL ROSÉ
  Not vintaged, cuve close: 50% Gamay, 50% Pinot Noir
HENKELL TROCKEN
  Not vintaged, cuve close: varieties/origin not revealed
HENKELL TROCKEN PIKKOLO
  Not vintaged, cuve close: small bottle version of above

ADAM HENKELL
See HENKELL

HENKELL & SÖHNLEIN
WIESBADEN, RHEINGAU

- 12.5 million cases
- Group ownership - Henkell, Söhnlein, Carstens SC, Adam Henkell, Lutter & Wegner, Mattiacus, Rüttgers Club, Schloss Biebrich, Schloss Rheinberg, Kurpfalz Sektkellerei, Burg Weisnau, Hungarovin (Hungary), Balatonboglàr (Hungary)

This group formed when Henkell merged with Söhnlein in 1987. The administrative headquarters are located at Henkellsfeld in Wiesbaden, but the group is exclusively owned by the Oetker family, who has been the proprietor of Söhnlein since 1958.
See INDIVIDUAL BRANDS

55
HERRES
TRIER, MOSEL-SAAR-RUWER

- 625,000 cases
- Other labels - Graf Artos, Römer

Established in 1954, this well-known Sekt house has grown quite rapidly over the last ten years. In 1994, it became the first firm in the industry whose quality-control qualified for the ISO 9001 standard (an internationally accredited rating), although the subjective quality of its products leaves much to be desired. The Wiltinger Scharzberg stands out, but most Sekt is ordinary and sold under the Römer label.

N/A
HEUCHELBERG-KELLEREI
SCHWAIGERN, WURTTEMBERG

- 4,200 cases

The cooperative for the growers of Schwaigern was founded in 1925 and commenced sparkling-wine production in 1986.

WINEMAKER
Dieter Steinbrenner

HOUSE STYLE & RANGE
I am not impressed by the Gewürztraminer (Dieter Steinbrenner should take a look at Martin Heim's rendition – not a great sparkling wine *per se*, but the best fizzy version of this grape I have encountered.) I find the Schwarzriesling bland apart from what appears to be the influence of oak (although no oak is used according to the information I have).
SCHWAIGERNER GRAFENBERG GEWÜRZTRAMINER
  TROCKEN
  Vintaged, Sekt bA, méthode champenoise:
  100% Gewürztraminer
SCHWAIGERNER GRAFENBERG SCHWARZRIESLING
  TROCKEN

Vintaged, Sekt bA, méthode champenoise:
100% Meunier

75
HIESTAND
GUNTERSBLUM, RHEINHESSEN

- 210 cases

The Hiestand family emigrated from Switzerland in the 17th century, established this small estate in 1733, and produced their first *méthode champenoise* wine as recently as 1990.
WINEMAKER
Erich Hiestand

HOUSE STYLE & RANGE
The Steig-Terrassen Riesling is coarse, but the Eiserne Hand Pinot Blanc is crisp, clean and very pale, with a gentle, slow-rising bead, and makes a fine food wine, neatly presented in its tall Rhine bottle.

★ GUNTERSBLUMER EISERNE HAND WEISSER
  BURGUNDER BRUT
  Vintaged, Sekt bA, méthode
  champenoise:
  100% Pinot Blanc
GUNTERSBLUMER STEIG-
TERRASSEN RIESLING
  TROCKEN
  Vintaged, Sekt bA, méthode champenoise:
  100% Riesling

50
HOEHL
TRIER, MOSEL-SAAR-RUWER

- 42,000 cases
- Group ownership - Bernard-Massard
- Other labels - Schloss Herrenfels

Brothers Phillip Carl and Bernard Hoehl established this Sekt house at Geisenheim in 1868. It was taken over by Matheus Müller in 1917, and came under Seagram ownership in 1987. It was then purchased in 1992 by Joachim Immelnkemper, proprietor of Bernard-Massard, who moved production to Trier. Like Bernard-Massard, Hoehl specialises in BOB.
WINEMAKER
Waldemar Baum

HOUSE STYLE & RANGE
The top-of-the-range Hoehl Riesling has some varietal aroma, but is basically dull, lacking in freshness, focus and vitality.
DIPLOMAT TROCKEN/HALBTROCKEN
  Vintaged, cuve close: grape varieties/origin not revealed
RIESLING EXTRA DRY
  Vintaged, cuve close: 100% Riesling

N/A
DR HÖFER
BURG LAYEN, NAHE

- 16,700 cases

A family-owned wine estate founded in 1775. It is run today by Dr Thomas Höfer, who owns 23 hectares of vineyards spread

...ver nine villages.

WINEMAKER
...ndreas Engelmann

HOUSE STYLE & RANGE
...wo Sekte in the range are made with Grauer ...urgunder. The brut is basic, with an ...mondy flavour, while the *Trocken* has a ...ulphury nose and lacks finesse. Also produces ...are varietal Sekt from Riesling, Silvaner and ...Veissburgunder.

...VINZENHEIMER HONIGBERG GRAUER
  BURGUNDER BRUT
  Vintaged, Sekt bA, bottle-fermented: 100% Pinot Gris
...VINZENHEIMER HONIGBERG GRAUER
  BURGUNDER TROCKEN
  Vintaged, Sekt bA, bottle-fermented: 100% Pinot Gris

N/A
...TAATLICHER HOFKELLER ...WÜRZBURG
...ÜRZBURG, FRANKEN
• ...840 cases
...ncient wine estate dating back to 1128, ...hen it belonged to the Prince-Bishops of ...Vürzburg. Secularised in 1803, it is owned ...y the state of Bavaria.

WINEMAKER
...Dr Rowald Hepp

HOUSE STYLE & RANGE
...he wine is of basic commercial quality.

...REUZWERTHEIMER KAFFELSTEIN SPÄTBURGUNDER
  WEISSHERBST BRUT
  Vintaged, Sekt bA, bottle-fermented: 100% Pinot Noir
...REUZWERTHEIMER KAFFELSTEIN RIESLING BRUT
  Vintaged, Sekt bA, bottle-fermented: 100% Riesling

...O
...FÜRST ZU HOHENLOHE-...OEHRINGEN
...OEHRINGEN, WÜRTTEMBERG
• ...250 cases
...irst documented in 1342, this private estate ...nade its sparkling-wine debut in 1978.

WINEMAKER
...Siegfried Röll

HOUSE STYLE & RANGE
...olid and fruity, but not special.

...ERRENBERGER VERRENBERG BRUT
  Vintaged, Sekt bA, méthode champenoise:
  60% Chardonnay, 40% Meunier

...HÖLLENBERG
...e KLOSS & FOERSTER

...MPERSONATOR
...e KLOSS & FOERSTER

...4
...WG JECHTINGER
...ASBACH-JECHTINGER, BADEN
• ...3,000 cases
• Other labels - Burg Sponeck

This co-op was established in 1924, and started production of sparkling wine in 1980.

WINEMAKER
Bill Arno

HOUSE STYLE & RANGE
Good, full, fruity style, with an expansive palate and a soft, cushiony mousse.

★ PINOT BRUT
  Vintaged, Sekt bA, méthode champenoise: 40%
  Pinot Gris, 40% Pinot Noir, 20% Pinot Blanc

N/A
JOHANNISHOF
JOHANNISBERG, RHEINGAU
Owned by the Eser family, who sell Sekt under the Eser-Cabinet label.

JOHANN MAXIMILIAN
See HANS LANG

KAGENECK
See GRÄFLICH VON KAGENECK'SCHE

40
GRÄFLICH V KAGENECK'SCHE
BREISACH, BADEN
• 150,000 cases
Established in 1974, first production in 1978. Switzerland, France.
• Other labels: Schloss Munzingen.

WINEMAKER
Reiner Rosswog, Manfred Vitt

HOUSE STYLE & RANGE
The Schloss Munzingen is very basic in quality, and the Kageneck has an unpleasant chemical character.

KAGENECK EXTRA RIESLING BRUT
  Vintaged, Sekt bA, bottle-fermented: 100% Riesling
SCHLOSS MUNZINGEN PINOT BLANC DE
  NOIRS BRUT
  Not vintaged, Sekt bA, bottle-fermented:
  100% Pinot Noir

75
ALBERT KALLFELZ
ZELL, MOSEL-SAAR-RUWER
• 4,200 cases
Family-owned winery that was established in 1907, but did not make its first Sekt until 1986.

WINEMAKER
Albert Kallfelz, Rüdiger Nilles

HOUSE STYLE & RANGE
Satisfying, peachy fruit with a fresh floweriness on the finish.

★ RIESLING BRUT
  Vintaged, Sekt bA, bottle-fermented: 100% Riesling

★ RIESLING EXTRA BRUT
  Vintaged, Sekt bA, bottle-fermented: 100% Riesling

N/A
KAPELLENHOF
SELZEN, RHEINHESSEN
Private producer of *Winzersekt* (grower's Sekt).

74
KARTHÄUSERHOF
TRIER-EITELSBACH, MOSEL-SAAR-RUWER
• 340 cases
• Other labels - Tyrell
Owned by Christoph Tyrell, who produced Karthäuserhof's first Sekt in 1987.

WINEMAKER
Ludwig Breiling

HOUSE STYLE & RANGE
Fresh, unashamed, fruit-driven style.

★ TYRELL RIESLING BRUT
  Vintaged, Sekt bA, bottle-fermented:
  100% Riesling

80
KASSNER-SIMON
FREINSHEIM, PFALZ
• 340 cases
A family-owned winery established in 1949. The first sparkling wine here was produced in 1990 by Willi Simon.

WINEMAKER
Willi Simon

HOUSE STYLE & RANGE
Essentially an elegant, flowery, fruity style, the Riesling Extra Trocken has extra richness, but also increased sulphur, taking its rating down a peg or two.

★★ RIESLING EXTRA BRUT
  Vintaged, Sekt bA, méthode champenoise:
  100% Riesling
★ RIESLING EXTRA TROCKEN
  Vintaged, Sekt bA, méthode
  champenoise:
  100% Riesling

N/A
KATHARINENHOF
DURKHEIM, PFALZ
• 420 cases
Established in 1980, this firm first started Sekt production in 1988.

WINEMAKER
Volker Hauer

HOUSE STYLE & RANGE
The Scheurebe is overpowered by a cat's pee aroma and it is over-*dosaged*, but the rosé has nice, sweet Pinot fruit.

★ DÜRKHEIMER FEUERBERG SPÄTBURGUNDER
  ROSÉ TROCKEN
  Vintaged, Sekt bA, bottle-fermented: 100% Pinot Noir
DÜRKHEIMER FRONHOF SCHEUREBE BRUT
  Vintaged, Sekt bA, bottle-fermented: 100% Scheurebe

KENDERMANN

BINGEN, RHEINHESSEN

- Group ownership - Reh Kendermann

Famous (or infamous) for Black Tower Liebfraumilch, still one of the world's largest-selling brands despite the downturn in the Liebfraumilch market. Sales of sparkling Black Tower have always been minuscule by comparison, and it remains to be seen what will happen to this brand of Sekt now that the company has become part of the Reh Kendermann group.

N/A
REICHSGRAF VON KESSELSTATT

TRIER, MOSEL-SAAR-RUWER

- 1,500 cases

Founded 1820, this great wine estate made its first sparkling wine under the Majoratsfüllung brand at the beginning of the 20th century.

WINEMAKER

Bernward Keiper

HOUSE STYLE & RANGE

The Majoratsfüllung shows nice, fat, rich apricoty fruit, but the Palais Kesselstatt is too smooth, needing more freshness and zest.

★ MAJORATSFÜLLUNG RIESLING BRUT
Vintaged, Sekt bA, méthode champenoise: 100% Riesling

PALAIS KESSELSTATT RIESLING BRUT
Vintaged, Sekt bA, méthode champenoise: 100% Riesling

N/A
KESSLER

ESSLINGEN, WURTTEMBERG

- Other labels - Gebrüder Weiss

Founded 1826 by Georg Kessler, who once worked for Veuve Clicquot, this is Germany's oldest Sekt house, and the first Sekt producer on record (although sparkling wines were probably made on the Rhein as early as 1883). Still family-owned, this firm uses various methods of production, but all wines under the Kessler label are bottle-fermented, and highly regarded on the domestic market. Gebrüder Weiss wines are all *cuve close*.

50
WG KIECHLINSBERGEN

ENDINGEN-KIECHLINSBERGEN, BADEN

- 1,100 cases

Established in 1930 for the growers in the Kiechlinsbergen area, this cooperative has been making Sekt since the late 1980s.

WINEMAKER

Ens Hans

HOUSE STYLE & RANGE

Commercial quality fizz.

KIECHLINSBERGER ÖLBERG BLANC DE NOIRS BRUT
Vintaged, Sekt bA, bottle-fermented: 100% Pinot Noir

78
KIRSTEN

KLUSSERATH, MOSEL-SAAR-RUWER

- 400 cases

A family concern established by the current owner's grandfather, the first Sekt was made in 1987.

WINEMAKER

Bernhard Kirsten

HOUSE STYLE & RANGE

The Weisser Burgunder has a very flowery aroma with soft, elegant fruit on the palate, but it is the classy, ripe, peachy Riesling fruit that makes this *cuvée* stand out.

★ WEISSER BURGUNDER BRUT
Vintaged, Sekt bA, méthode champenoise: 100% Pinot Noir

★★ RIESLING BRUT
Vintaged, Sekt bA, méthode champenoise: 100% Riesling

N/A
KISTENMACHER-HENGERER

HEILBRONN, WURTTEMBERG

- 170 cases

Established in 1958, this company's first production of sparkling wine was in 1987.

WINEMAKER

Hans Hengerer

HOUSE STYLE & RANGE

One often receives a good whiff of free sulphur on the Pinot Brut, but the Muskattrollinger Brut Rosé is fresh and very elegant, although too soft. It would score much higher with more acidity to give it extra structure.

HEILBRONNER STIFTSBERG PINOT BRUT
Vintaged, Sekt bA, bottle-fermented: 40% Pinot Noir, 30% Pinot Gris, 30% Meunier

★ HEILBRONNER WARTBERG MUSKATTROLLINGER BRUT ROSÉ
Vintaged, Sekt bA, bottle-fermented: 100% Muskattrollinger

65
KLOSS & FOERSTER

RUDESHEIM, RHEINGAU

- 200,000 cases
- Other labels - Höllenberg, Impersonator, OHLIG, Wappen

An old-established Sekt house that originated in eastern Germany in 1856, Kloss & Foerster exclusively produces sparkling wine and uses both *cuve close* and *méthode champenoise*.

WINEMAKER

Karl-Heinz Bubeck

HOUSE STYLE & RANGE

Mostly basic in quality, although some of the Deutscher Sekt and Sekt bA *cuvées* can be interesting, such as the Spätburgunder Weissherbst, which is fat and rich. However, the Riesling Brut lacks finesse, although it ha good structure with nice petrol aromas.

RÜDESHEIMER BISCHOFSBERG RIESLING BRUT
Vintaged, Sekt bA, méthode champenoise: 100% Riesling

★ SPÄTBURGUNDER WEISSHERBST BRUT
Vintaged, Deutscher Sekt, cuve close: 100% Pinot Noir

KLOSTERBERGFELSEN

See NAEGELSFÖRST, GUT

KLOSTERFÜRST

See WG AUGGEN

76
KLOSTERMÜHLE ODERNHEIM

ODERNHEIM, NAHE

- 420 cases

Dr Peter Becker, Christian Held, Michael Ritzan and Max Hoch jointly established th company as recently as 1992, producing the first Sekt the following year.

WINEMAKER

Thomas Zenz

HOUSE STYLE & RANGE

The Monfort Brut is a very clean and well-focused rosé, with elegant red-fruit pastilles on the nose and crisp acidity on the palate. A touch of tannin detracts from the elegance of the Monfort Trocken.

★★ MONTFORT BRUT
Vintaged, Sekt bA, bottle-fermented: 100% Pinot No
MONTFORT TROCKEN
Vintaged, Sekt bA, bottle-fermented: 100% Pinot No

88
FREIHERR ZU KNYPHAUSEN

ERBACH, RHEINGAU

- 250 cases

Founded as Klosterhof Drais by Cistercian monks in 1141, this estate was purchased in 1818 by the Knyphausen family. Seven generations later, it is run by Gerko Freiherr zu Knyphausen, whose Sekt is made in tiny quantities of brilliant quality.

WINEMAKER

Rainer Rüttiger

HOUSE STYLE & RANGE

Made from *Spätlese* grapes, the Riesling Extr Brut is richly flavoured and seriously gluggable despite low *dosage*. It takes at least five years to develop classic petrol bottle-aromas, then a peachy ripeness builds on the finish. Its class and elegance demolish the opposition, placing Knyphausen into a class f its own as far as commercially available, ry style, pure Riesling Sekt is concerned.

★★☆ BARON ZU KNYPHAUSEN RIESLING
EXTRA BRUT
Vintaged, Sekt bA, bottle-fermented: 100% Riesling

KOMUTREI
See MOSELLAND

'4
GESCHWISTER KÖWERICH
ÖWERICH, MOSEL-SAAR-RUWER
● 500 cases

he Köwerichs include Beethoven's mother 1 their family line; thus, when they started aking Sekt in 1989, they named this *cuvée* fter the great man.

WINEMAKER
Marcus Regnery

HOUSE STYLE & RANGE
ery ripe, round and perfumed.

★ LUDWIG VAN BEETHOVEN RIESLING BRUT
Vintaged, Sekt bA, méthode champenoise: 100% Riesling

N/A
KRUGER-RUMPF
MÜNSTER-SARMSHEIM, NAHE
● 500 cases

ounded by Karl Kruger in 1790, producing s first sparkling wine in 1992. Between 1988 nd 1997, Kruger-Rumpf has been placed in he 100 best producers in Germany.

WINEMAKER
tefan Rumpf

HOUSE STYLE & RANGE
election Lisa-Maria needs more bottle-age, nd might turn out quite well; the Silvaner is ust amylic and fat, lacking zest and freshness.

MÜNSTERER PITTERSBERG RIESLING
EXTRA TROCKEN
Vintaged, Sekt bA, bottle-fermented: 100% Riesling
' TROCKEN
Vintaged, Sekt bA, bottle-fermented: 100% Silvaner

★ SELECTION LISA-MARIA EXTRA BRUT
Vintaged, Sekt bA, bottle-fermented: 40% Chardonnay, 40% Pinot Noir, 20% Pinot Blanc

O
KUPFERBERG
MAINZ, RHEINHESSEN
● 875,000 cases

● Group ownership - Racke
● Other labels - Casino

This well-known Sekt house was established in 1850 by Christian Adalbert Kupferberg, who, two years later, sold his first bottle of Kupferberg Gold – still the firm's best-selling brand. In 1869, Kupferberg's daughter married Arthur Bricout, technical director at Champagne de Venoge. He established Champagne Bricout, which now belongs to the Racke group and is currently presided over by Andréas Kupferberg. The quality is above average.

KUPFERBERG GOLD
Not vintage, cuve close: local grape varieties
KUPFERBERG ROT
Not vintage, cuve close: mainly Pinot Noir
KUPFERBERG ROSÉ
Not vintaged, cuve close: local grape varieties
KUPFERBERG RIESLING BRUT
Not vintaged, cuve close: 100% Riesling

N/A
KURPFALZ SEKTKELLEREI
SPEYER, PFALZ
● 350,000 cases
● Group ownership - Henkell & Söhnlein
● Other labels - Burg Weisenau (Burgverlies, Goldlack, Schwarzlack, Weisslack, Weisssiegel), Kurpfalz (Jubiläumssekt, Krone, Kurfürst Friedrich)

Established at Bad Dürkheim in 1921, Kurpfalz Sektkellerei moved to its current location just two years later. Henkell & Söhnlein purchased a majority shareholding in 1995, so that Kurpfalz could work the regional brand with Burg Weisenau, which had been part of the group for more than 30 years, and now operates out of the same premises. Kurpfalz Sektkellerei is the largest Sekt producer in the Pfalz, and is particularly proud of its ties with Germany's top restaurants, most of which buy their own-label Sekt from this company.

LAGENSEKT
See WG WACHTENBURG-LUGINSLAND

50
FW LAGGUTH ERBEN
TRABEN-TRARBACH, MOSEL-SAAR-RUWER
Large export house established in 1798; makes commercial-quality fizz under the Erben label.

73
HANS LANG
ELTVILLE-HATTENHEIM, RHEINGAU
● 2,500 cases

Family-owned estate founded in 1953 by Hans Lang, who made his first Sekt in 1968. Hans Lang died prematurely in 1972 and was succeeded by his son, Johann Maximilian, the current incumbent, who wastes nothing. After bottling the estate's best wines, he not

only distils the leftovers for *Weinbrand* (brandy), but also the skins and pips for *Testerbrand* (grappa), and even the yeast for *Hefebrand* (yeast-brandy).

WINEMAKER
Johann Maximilian Lang

HOUSE STYLE & RANGE
The malolactic influence on the Chardonnay & Weissburgunder Extra Brut is overdone, with big, blowsy butterscotch aromas. This wine would benefit from a more classic malolactic culture. It is a curiosity, but not an unpleasant one. The best fizz here is the Johann Maximilian Riesling Extra Brut, a fluffy wine with fresh, sherbety fruit and a satisfying almondy complexity on the finish.

★ CHARDONNAY/WEISSBURGUNDER EXTRA
BRUT
Vintaged, Sekt bA, méthode champenoise: 60% Chardonnay, 40% Weissburgunder
★ JOHANN MAXIMILIAN RIESLING EXTRA BRUT
Vintaged, Sekt bA, méthode champenoise: 100% Riesling

N/A
LANGENBACH
TRIER, MOSEL-SAAR-RUWER
● 83,000 cases
● Group ownership - Bernard-Massard

Established at Worms by Julius Langenbach in 1852, this large bottler of export wines recently became part of the Reh Kendermann group. Confusingly, the wines sold in Germany, Belgium, Netherlands and Luxembourg are made by the Bernard-Massard group, which has owned the brand in these countries since 1992.

WINEMAKER
Waldemar Baum

HOUSE STYLE & RANGE
I was a bit wary when a *cuve close* of no fixed abode was submitted to a recent tasting as this brand's best fizz, but it was infinitely better than all the other Deutscher Sekt made from Chardonnay in that tasting.

Although not great by any means, this *cuvée* has good varietal fruit and a fresh, elegant style. Apparently it is made with grapes which come exclusively from Trentino, which probably explains the success of this varietal Sekt.

★ JULIUS LANGENBACH RIESLING-TRADITION
TROCKEN
Not vintaged, cuve close: 100% Riesling
★ 'CHARDY' CHARDONNAY EXTRA BRUT
Vintaged, cuve close: 100% Chardonnay
GOLDLACK CHARDONNAY EXTRA DRY
Vintaged, cuve close: 100% Chardonnay
LILIPUT TROCKEN/HALBTROCKEN
Vintaged, plastic stopper, cuve close: small bottle version of Weisslack
PURPUR SPÄTBURGUNDER HALBTROCKEN
Vintaged, cuve close: 100% Pinot Noir

VIEW ACROSS THE KLOSTERGARTEN VINEYARD, OVER THE MOSEL TO TRITTENHEIM

RIESLING BRUT
Vintaged, Deutscher Sekt, cuve close: 100% Riesling
WALDRACHER RIESLING BRUT
Vintaged, Deutscher Sekt, cuve close: 100% Riesling
WEISLACK BRUT/TROCKEN/HALBTROCKEN/DOUX
Vintaged, plastic stopper, cuve close: grape varieties and origin not revealed
WINZERSEKT SAAR-RIESLING BRUT
Vintaged, single-estate, méthode champenoise: 100% Riesling

N/A
LANGENBACH
WORMS, RHEINHESSEN

The original winery of this large export house is owned by the Reh Kendermann group, which owns the rights to the Langenbach brand in all countries except for Belgium, the Netherlands, Luxembourg and Germany itself, where the wines are made and sold by the Bernard-Massard group (*see* previous entry). Only one Sekt appears to be available for the majority of the world under this label at the time of writing: Langenbach Sparkling, although I have no experience of it.

73
WG LAUFFEN
LAUFFEN, WURTTEMBERG

● 8,400 cases
This cooperative was founded in 1935 and first made Sekt in 1989.
WINEMAKER
Alfred Gaiser
HOUSE STYLE & RANGE
The Blanc de Noirs is fresh and fruity, good quality wine and this house would score a higher overall rating were it not for the Riesling which, unfortunately, is not a very impressive wine.
LAUFFENER KATZENBEISSER RIESLING TROCKEN
Vintaged, Sekt bA, transfer method: 100% Riesling
★✦ LAUFFENER KATZENBEISSER
SCHWARZRIESLING BLANC DE NOIRS BRUT
Vintaged, Sekt bA, transfer method: 100% Meunier

N/A
LERGENMÜLLER
HAINFELD-NUSSDORF, PFALZ

● 2,500 cases
This 30-hectare estate has made *méthode champenoise* since 1986, using only brut *dosage*, with a minimum of three years on its yeast.
WINEMAKER
Jürgen Lergenmüller
HOUSE STYLE & RANGE
The only Sekt I have tasted is the Grande Cuvée. It spends six years on its yeast and is very fresh, sharp and crisp, requiring some post-disgorgement ageing.
✦ PINOT BRUT GRANDE CUVÉE
Vintaged, Sekt bA, méthode champenoise: 100% Pinot Noir

LIECHTENSTEIN
See HERMANN SCHNAUFER

LILA IMPERIAL
See DEINHARD

LILLIPUT
See LANGENBACH (TRIER)

LISA-MARIA
See KRUGER-RUMPF

50
HEINRICH LORCH
BAD BERGZABERN, PFALZ

Commercial-quality fizz under the Lorch Privat Cuvée label.

LUDWIG VAN BEETHOVEN
See GESCHWISTER KÖWERICH

LUTTER & WEGNER
This Berlin-based brand was taken over by Söhnlein between 1960 and 1961, and is now part of the Henkell & Söhnlein group. *See* SÖHNLEIN RHEINGOLD

MAJORATSFÜLLUNG
See KESSELSTATT, REICHSGRAF VON

72
KONRAD MARINGER-THEES
TRITTENHEIM, MOSEL–SAAR–RUWER

● 192 cases
An old wine-growing family founded this estate in the mid-18th century, making its first sparkling wine in 1975. The entire Sekt production is bottle-fermented, estate-bottle and stored for between two and five years in cellars at 12°C.
WINEMAKER
Konrad Maringer-Thees
HOUSE STYLE & RANGE
The Rosé Extra Trocken is not very impressive (hence the low overall rating), but the Riesling is of generally good quality, especially the extraordinarily fresh ten-year-old *cuvée* tasted recently. OK, maybe it is sweet for a so-called brut, but it is very rich and concentrated with an amazing freshness of fruit.
ROSÉ EXTRA TROCKEN
Not vintaged, Sekt bA, méthode champenoise: 100% Pinot Noir
★ TRITTENHEIMER ALTÄRCHEN RIESLING BRUT
Vintaged, Sekt bA, méthode champenoise: 100% Riesling

MATTIACUS
See HENKELL & SÖHNLEIN

55
MÄURER
DACKENHEIM, PFALZ

● 7,500 cases
This family-owned winery was founded way back in 1695 but only made its first Sekt in 1984. Renate and Willy Mäurer are the current owners.
WINEMAKER
Willy Mäurer
HOUSE STYLE & RANGE
The *blanc de noirs* is supposed to be Mäurer's classic *cuvée*, but I find it fat and blowsy, despite having no *dosage*.
BLANC DE NOIRS BRUT
Vintaged, Sekt bA, bottle-fermented: 100% Pinot Noir
RIESLING BRUT
Vintaged, Sekt bA, bottle-fermented: 100% Riesling
ROSÉ PINOT BRUT
Vintaged, Sekt bA, bottle-fermented: 85% Pinot Noir, 15% Meunier
WEISSER BURGUNDER BRUT
Vintaged, Sekt bA, bottle-fermented: 100% Pinot Blanc

JOHANN MAXIMILIAN
See HANS LANG

DR MAYER
See ST JOHANNER

MENGER-KRUG

DEIDESHEIM, PFALZ

33,000 cases

This Sekt estate was founded in 1981, and uses wines made exclusively from vineyards owned by the Menger-Krug family. Since there is a minority shareholding by Rémy-Cointreau, the Menger-Krugs presumably are related to the famous Krug family of Champagne Krug (owned by Rémy-Cointreau).

WINEMAKER

R Acker, E Birk

HOUSE STYLE & RANGE

It's a good job Rémy-Cointreau is a minority shareholder, otherwise Champagne Krug might have felt compelled to take action against this firm, whose fizz is presented in a very Krug-like bottle. The best thing Menger-Krug could do would be to request a regular consultancy from Rémy-Cointreau's maestro Champagne-maker, Daniel Thibault, because the best wine I have tasted is the amylic rosé, while the Pinot Brut has a nasty oil-refinery smell (both bottles). If this weren't my first encounter with these wines, Menger-Krug would have received one of the lowest rating in this book. However, I reserve judgement.

ROSÉ BRUT

Not vintaged, Sekt bA, bottle-fermented: 85% Pinot Noir, 15% Meunier

PINOT BRUT

Vintaged, Sekt bA, bottle-fermented: 20% Pinot Noir, 40% Pinot Blanc, 40% Pinot Gris

PETER MERTES

BERNKASTEL, MOSEL-SAAR-RUWER

300,000 cases

Germany's largest private winery for generic wines, Peter Mertes produces Sekt for a number of export houses which cannot be bothered to make the stuff themselves.

FÜRST VON METTERNICH

735,000 cases

Group ownership - Henkell & Söhnlein

The first Metternich to own Schloss Johannisberg was Klemens von Metternich, foreign minister to Austria from 1809 to 1848.

Born in 1773 and christened Klemens Wenzel Nepomuk Lothar von Metternich-Winneburg-Beilstein, he was the son of Franz Georg Karl, Graf von Metternich-Winneburg and Countess Beatrix Kagenegg. Although a descendant of ancient Rhenish nobility, it was his marriage in 1795 to Countess Eleonore Kaunitz that provided the link to Austrian nobility – which was necessary for the high imperial office he sought.

Emperor Francis I appointed von

Metternich minister of foreign affairs in 1809, bestowing the hereditary title of Prince on him in 1813, in recognition of his services at the Treaty of Reichenbach, which enabled Austria to re-arm.

In 1816, after von Metternich's brilliant moderation at the Congress of Vienna 1814-1815, a grateful Emperor Francis I presented him with Schloss Johannisberg.

After the death of his wife in 1825, von Metternich married Baroness Antoinette Leykam (1827), and after her death in 1829, he married Countess Melanie Zichy-Ferraris (1831). Klemens died in 1859, four years after his third wife passed away, and the very same year that Richard, his son by his second wife, became the Austrian ambassador to France, later turning out to be one of the leading diplomats of his time. It was Richard Fürst von Metternich who signed an agreement with Johann Jacob Söhnlein to supply the Sekt firm with grapes.

In 1934, the von Metternichs granted Söhnlein (then Söhnlein Rheingold) permission to use 'Fürst von Metternich' as a brand name, and in 1971 Fürst von Metternich Riesling-Sekt was launched. Today, this brand is still produced exclusively from Riesling grapes grown on the legendary Rheingau estate of Schloss Johannisberg, the ownership of which remains with the von Metternich family. *See* SÖHNLEIN RHEINGOLD

MM

See MATHEUS MÜLLER

65
MARKUS MOLITOR

BERNKASTEL-WEHLEN, MOSEL-SAAR-RUWER

- 1,250 cases

The Molitor family have been running this privately owned winery for eight generations, and made its first Sekt in 1982.

WINEMAKER

Markus Molitor

HOUSE STYLE & RANGE

The grapes come from 40- to 60-year-old vines, giving good intensity of sharp-tasting fruit and a smooth finish.

★ RIESLING SEKT PRESTIGE BRUT

Vintaged, Sekt bA, méthode champenoise; 100% Riesling

SEKTKELLEREI MÖLLER

HAINFELD, PFALZ

- 840 cases

Gunter Möller started out as a 'flying Sektmaker' in 1986, and now makes over 8,000 cases of fizz for other wineries, in

addition to producing a limited number of bottles of his own.

WINEMAKER

Gunter Möller

HOUSE STYLE & RANGE

Although Möller makes nine different *cuvées*, I have tasted just the two indicated below, thus cannot give this producer an overall rating. Möller treated both these wines to first fermentation in Allier *barriques* and gave them just one filtration. Despite this attention, the Auxerrois is merely basic in quality, and the apricot-and-custard Chardonnay has curiosity value only.

AUXERROIS EXTRA BRUT

Vintaged, Deutscher Sekt, méthode champenois: 100% Auxerrois

CHARDONNAY BRUT

Vintaged, Deutscher Sekt, méthode champenoise: 100% Chardonnay

MONFORT

See KLOSTERMÜHLE ODERNHEIM

MOSELLAND

BERNKASTEL, MOSEL-SAAR-RUWER

- 20,000 cases
- Other labels - Komutrei, Nigra, Schloss Lieser

A large co-op comprising 4,500 growers and producing in total 3.5 million cases of wine, of which Sekt represents a tiny fraction. Most is cheap fizz sold under the Nigra label.

50
ADAM MÜLLER

LEIMEN, BADEN

- 4,200 cases

A family-owned firm since 1735, the Müllers made their first sparkling wine in 1927, but did not maintain production, restarting it in 1982.

WINEMAKER

Marcus Müller

HOUSE STYLE & RANGE

Basic commercial quality, the Weissburgunder has an amylic hint, while the Pinot Blanc is fatter and marginally more satisfying.

LEIMENER KREUZWEG PINOT BRUT

Vintaged, Sekt bA, méthode champenoise: 100% Pinot Noir

LEIMENER KREUZWEG WEISSBURGUNDER BRUT

Vintaged, Sekt bA, transfer method: 100% Pinot Blanc

MATHEUS MÜLLER

ELTVILLE, RHEINGAU

- 1.2 million cases
- Group ownership - Seagram

The date of this firm's origin is set at 1811, when Matheus Müller purchased Freiherrlich von Sohlern'sche Hof at Eltville, but sparkling wine production did not commence until 1837. The company's initials 'MM' were used as its brand from as early as the 1850s.

In 1917, Müller purchased Gebrüder Hoehl in Geisenheim (recently sold off to Bernard Massard). Two years later, Müller's vineyards at Jouy-Aux-Arches in Lorraine were forfeited as a result of the Treaty of Versailles. In 1922, Herman von Mumm, a director of Matheus Müller, arranged for the firm to produce Mumm Sekt on a contract basis; in 1984, Seagram, owner of Champagne Mumm in France, purchased Matheus Müller.

HOUSE STYLE & RANGE
The *Trocken* is a clean, half-decent fizz, although its plastic stopper does it no favours. The *Halbtrocken*, complete with its wretched plastic stopper, is just plain unpleasant.
MM EXTRA, HALBTROCKEN
  Not vintaged, plastic stopper, cuve close: grape varieties and origin not revealed
MM EXTRA, TROCKEN
  Not vintaged, plastic stopper, cuve close: grape varieties and origin not revealed

RUDOLF MÜLLER
See ZIMMERMANN, GRAEFF & MÜLLER

50
MUELLER
REES
Produces commercial-quality fizz under the Mondial label.

N/A
GH VON MUMM & CO
HOCHHEIM, RHEINGAU
- 2.2 million cases
- Group ownership - Seagram
- Other labels Burgeff, Schloss Hochheim

HOUSE STYLE & RANGE
The best wines here are the vintaged brut and Cuvée Rheingau Riesling Extra Dry. The brut has a typical peachy Rheingau Riesling character, but it is more recognisable than enjoyable, with bubbles that could be much smaller. The Extra Dry has an additional fatness to its peachy Riesling fruit, indicating a skilful application of its larger *dosage*.

However, the non-vintage Dry is decidedly unpleasant, and this negative quality is merely highlighted by its nasty plastic stopper. Seagram claims that Mumm Dry is a blend taken exclusively from different German regions – which makes me wonder why it doesn't say *Deutscher Sekt* on the label.
DRY
  Not vintaged, plastic stopper, cuve close: Riesling, Silvaner, Elbling
CUVÉE RHEINGAU RIESLING BRUT
  Vintaged, Sekt bA, cuve close: 100% Riesling

CUVÉE RHEINGAU RIESLING EXTRA DRY
  Vintaged, Sekt bA, cuve close: 100% Riesling

N/A
GUT NAEGELSFÖRST
BADEN-BADEN, BADEN
- 840 cases

This wine estate dates back to 1268, when it was founded by Cistercian monks. It is now owned by the Strickler family, who first produced sparkling wine in 1985.
WINEMAKER
Werner Benz
HOUSE STYLE & RANGE
Although the labels are not exactly stylish, Gut Naegelsförst pays attention to small details, such as intertwining gold and green wire to secure the cork. A pity, then, that the same fastidiousness has not been applied to the wines. This is my first encounter with this Sekt, with just two *cuvées* tasted (both 1994s) – hence no overall rating. The Riesling is oxidising on the nose and losing fruit on the palate, which is a pity because it gives the impression of once having been a nice wine (but there is no excuse for a sparkling wine to be breaking up when just over three years old). The Pinot is technically correct and not going over, but unfortunately it is basic in quality. Second samples were tasted to no avail (one was maderised).
PINOT BLANC DE NOIRS KLOSTERBERGFELSEN BRUT
  Vintaged, Sekt bA, bottle-fermented: 100% Pinot Noir
RIESLING FEIGENWÄLDCHEN BRUT
  Vintaged, Sekt bA, bottle-fermented: 100% Riesling

75
GRAF VON NEIPPERG
SCHWAIGERN, WURTTEMBERG
- 350 cases

The Counts of Neipperg have grown vines around their castle for more than 700 years, but began making Sekt only recently.
WINEMAKER
Bernd Supp
HOUSE STYLE & RANGE
A pure, elegant and fruity Meunier that tastes more like Pinot Noir than most Pinot Noir.

★ NEIPPERGER SCHLOSSBERG SCHWARZRIESLING TROCKEN
  Vintaged, Sekt bA, bottle-fermented: 100% Meunier

55
NIERSTEINER WG
NIERSTEIN, RHEINHESSEN
- 600 cases

Established in 1930 for the growers of Nierstein, this co-op began making Sekt in the late 1970s. Today, it has 180 members owning 170 hectares of vineyards.
WINEMAKER
Peter Eichler
HOUSE STYLE & RANGE
Fresh and correct, but not special.
NIERSTEINER SPIEGELBERG RIESLING BRUT
  Vintaged, Sekt bA, méthode champenoise: 100% Riesling

NIGRA
See MOSELLAND

N/A
WG NORDHEIM
NORDHEIM, WURTTEMBERG
- 200,000 cases

Established 1939, this cooperative consists of 250 members owning 155 hectares of vineyards in the Nordheim area.
WINEMAKER
Helmut Kilburg
HOUSE STYLE & RANGE
With products ranging from a chemical-tasting Pinot Blanc to the fourth-best Sekt tasted, the Nordheim co-op obviously has excellent potential, but its inconsistency makes an overall rating impossible. Although the Pinot is quite sweet for an extra brut and gives no label indication of being a red sparkling wine, its pure Pinot fruit is all cherries and strawberries, with a perfumed aftertaste.
PINOT BLANC EXTRA BRUT
  Vintaged, Sekt bA, méthode champenoise: 100% Pinot Blanc
★★ PINOT NOIR EXTRA BRUT
  Vintaged, Sekt bA, méthode champenoise: 100% Pinot Noir

N/A
NYMPHENBURG
MUNICH
- 250,000 cases

Family-owned firm established in 1955.
WINEMAKER
Reinhold Schwarz, Joseph Blum
HOUSE STYLE & RANGE
Blended from Riesling grapes grown in the Mosel-Saar-Ruwer and Pfalz regions, König Ludwig II is fresh and zesty, with true Riesling fruit, but lacks finesse.

NYMPHENBURG KÖNIG LUDWIG II EXTRA TROCKEN
Not vintaged, Deutscher Sekt, cuve close: 100% Riesling

ODEON
See GELDERMANN PRIVATSEKTKELLEREI

OHLIG
See KLOSS & FOERSTER

N/A
OPPMANN
WURZBURG, FRANKEN
- 740 cases
- Oppmann was established in 1865.

WINEMAKER
Josef Sauer

HOUSE STYLE & RANGE
I am unfamiliar with these wines, so there is no overall rating, but the Franken-Cuvée is a very basic commercial quality sekt, while I have only experienced maderised bottles of the Riesling.

FRANKEN-CUVÉE EXTRA TROCKEN
Not vintaged, Sekt bA, bottle-fermented: Kerner, Müller-Thurgau, Scheurebe, Silvaner
RIESLING BRUT
Not vintaged, Sekt bA, bottle-fermented: Riesling

PALAIS KESSELSTATT
See KESSELSTATT, REICHSGRAF VON

PURPUR
See LANGENBACH (TRIER)

N/A
RACKE
MAINZ, RHEINHESSEN
- 1 million cases
- Other labels: Kupferberg
Built upon the success of Kupferberg Gold Sekt, this group includes the Blanchet brand as well as Bricout in Champagne and Buena Vista in California.

75
RATZENBERGER
BACHARACH, MITTELRHEIN
- 670 cases
- A family-owned winery established in 1956, making its first sparkling wine in 1987.

WINEMAKER
Jochen Ratzenberger

HOUSE STYLE & RANGE
Really good, crisp style with lots of satisfying depth and length to the succulent, peachy fruit.

★✦ BACHARACHER KLOSTER FÜRSTENTAL
RIESLING BRUT
Vintaged, Sekt bA, méthode champenoise: 100% Riesling

N/A
REH KENDERMANN
BINGEN
- 8.3 million cases
- Group ownership - Augustus, Faber, Feist, Huesgen, Kendermann, Langenbach (Worms only), Carl Reh, Franz Reh, Günther Reh, Schloss Boechingen, Schloss Wachenheim
The foundation of this group is Faber, once the top-selling Sekt, but its recent merging of Reh with Kendermann and Schloss Wachenheim has made Reh Kendermann an even more formidable force – particularly in the Sekt market. The acquisition of Langenbach in Worms is complicated by the fact that Bernard-Massard also makes this brand, but its sales are restricted to the German market and Benelux countries (*see* LANGENBACH).

REICHSGRAF VON KESSELSTATT
See KESSELSTATT, REICHSGRAF VON

N/A
HANS RESCH
WILTINGEN, MOSEL-SAAR-RUWER
- 850 cases
This wine estate, which includes part of the famous Scharzhofberg vineyard, was founded in 1873, but didn't produce its first sparkling wine until almost a century later in 1972.

WINEMAKER
Franz-Andreas Resch

HOUSE STYLE & RANGE
Little experience of these wines, hence no overall rating. I am not impressed by the Cuvée Anna Lioba Brut, and alarmed by great wafts of malolactic influence on the Riesling!

CUVÉE ANNA LIOBA BRUT
Vintaged, Sekt bA, méthode champenoise: 94% Pinot Noir, 3% Pinot Blanc, 3% Chardonnay
RIESLING BRUT
Vintaged, Sekt bA, méthode champenoise: 100% Riesling

75
RESS & COMPAGNIE SEKT
ELTVILLE, RHEINGAU
- 840 cases
This Sekt house, which is linked to Balthasar Ress, produced its first sparkling wine in 1950.

WINEMAKER
Markus Boor

HOUSE STYLE & RANGE
The Spätburgunder is made in a rosé style and tastes like wine-gums with bubbles, yet it

has much more elegance than this description might suggest. The Riesling has a fine structure, with a high concentration of fruit.
★ RIESLING BRUT
Vintaged, Deutscher Sekt, méthode champenoise: 100% Riesling
★✦ SPÄTBURGUNDER BRUT
Vintaged, Deutscher Sekt, méthode champenoise: 100% Pinot Noir

REZZO
See WÜRTTEMBERGISCHE WEINGÄRTNER-ZENTRALGENOSSENSCHAFT

65
MAX FERD RICHTER
MULHEIM, MOSEL-SAAR-RUWER
- 840 cases
An old-established wine estate that dates back over 300 years. Its first Sekt was made in 1984, and production is in conjunction with the Saar-Mosel-Winzersekt cooperative.

WINEMAKER
Walter Hauth

HOUSE STYLE & RANGE
I know this producer's excellent still wines very well, particularly the Brauneberger Juffer and Brauneberger Juffer Sonnenuhr. Max Ferd Richter is famous for his superb Eiswein. Although his Sekt is OK in an age-rounded way, it is not special, as are the rest of his wines. He should either ensure that it is or not bother.

✦ MÜLHEIMER SONNENLAY RIESLING BRUT
Vintaged, Sekt bA, méthode champenoise: 100% Riesling

72
GERHARD RIENTH
FELLBACH, WURTTEMBERG
- 500 cases
Gerhard Rienth founded this small, family-owned winery in 1971, making his first Sekt in 1983.

WINEMAKER
Gerhard Rienth

HOUSE STYLE & RANGE
A nice, easy-going, fresh and fluffy Riesling Sekt, but the brut rosé is sickly sweet.

FELLBACHER GOLDBERG
BRUT ROSÉ
Vintaged, Sekt bA, bottle-fermented: 100% Trollinger
★ FELLBACHER GOLDBERG
RIESLING BRUT
Vintaged, Sekt bA, bottle-fermented: 100% Riesling

55
RILLING SEKT
STUTTGART-BAD CANNSTATT, WURTTEMBERG
- 475,000 cases
- Other labels - Schloss Rosenstein

A family-owned winery established in 1887, Rilling produced its first sparkling wines in 1935, and today markets 24 different varieties and types of Sekt.

WINEMAKER
Reinhard Stamm

HOUSE STYLE & RANGE
A large range of ordinary Sekt. Even at the top of the range, the best *cuvées* can best be described as fierce, with a certain earthiness.

EICHSTETTER LERCHENBERG PINOT BRUT
Vintaged, Sekt bA, bottle-fermented: 100% Pinot Blanc

SCHWARZRIESLING WEISSHERBST BRUT
Vintaged, Sekt bA, bottle-fermented: 100% Meunier

RITTERHOF
See RITTERHOF SEKTKELLEREI FITZ

74
RITTERHOF SEKTKELLEREI FITZ
BAD DURKHEIM, PFALZ
- 18,500 cases

The third-oldest Sekt-producing firm in Germany and the oldest in the Pfalz, Ritterhof has been in possession of the Fitz family since it was established in 1837.

WINEMAKER
Rolf Hanewald

HOUSE STYLE & RANGE
Despite *cuve close* and naff frosted bottles, these pure Riesling Sekts can have fresh, elegant fruit with a hint of peaches.

BRUT
Vintaged, Deutscher Sekt, cuve close: 100% Pinot Blanc

★ EXTRA BRUT
Not vintaged, Deutscher Sekt, cuve close: 100% Riesling

RÖMER
See HERRES

50
RÖMERHOF
TRABEN-TRARBACH, MOSEL-SAAR-RUWER
Commercial-quality fizz.

N/A
ROTKÄPPCHEN
FREYBURG, SAALE-UNSTRUT
- 2.8 million cases

A privately owned company established in 1856, Rotkäppchen produced its first sparkling wine in 1858, but has truly blossomed since the German reunification in 1989, its turnover having increased six-fold in just six years. As recently as 1992, sales of Rotkäppchen Sekt were around the 500,000 case mark. They are now close to three million and, if anything, the rate of growth seems to be increasing.

ROTSEKT
See BROGSITTER PRIVAT SEKTKELLEREI

N/A
RÜDESHEIMER WEINKELLEREI
RUDESHEIM, RHEINGAU
- 834,000 cases

This privately owned winery was established in 1863 by Johann Baptist Dietrich, who apparently learned the art of sparkling winemaking in Champagne. Today, the company is owned by Eberhard Elsässer.

WINEMAKER
Friedrich Beck

HOUSE STYLE & RANGE
The Spätburgunder Weissherbst has a metallic taste, but the Riesling has good varietal character – albeit lacking in finesse.

RHEINGAU RIESLING BRUT
Not vintaged, Sekt bA, cuve close: 100% Riesling

SPÄTBURGUNDER WEISSHERBST BRUT ROSÉ
Not vintaged, Sekt bA, cuve close: 100% Pinot Noir

74
FRIEDEL RUSSLER
WALLUF, RHEINGAU
- 1,000 cases

Although this family-owned winery has been established for 200 years, the Russlers did not make their first sparkling wine until 1982. Within the context of Germany's Sekt market, they receive premium prices for them.

WINEMAKER
Friedel & Frank Russler

HOUSE STYLE & RANGE
The brut is in fact a non-*dosage* wine, yet has a satisfying depth of fresh Riesling fruit, whereas the *dosage* in the Extra Trocken is so well balanced that it merely brings out a peachy tang rather than any overt sweetness.

★ WALLUFER WALKENBERG RIESLING BRUT
Vintaged, Sekt bA, bottle-fermented: 100% Riesling

★ WALLUFER WALKENBERG RIESLING EXTRA TROCKEN
Vintaged, Sekt bA, bottle-fermented: 100% Riesling

RUTTGERS
See HENKELL

'S'
See KRUGER-RUMPF

N/A
SAAR-MOSEL-WINZERSEKT
TRIER, MOSEL-SAAR-RUWER
- 42,000 cases
- Other labels SMW

A Sekt co-op of 130 growers from the Mosel-Saar-Ruwer (the Ruwer was left out because SMW is snappier than SMRW!). All sparkling wines are aged in barrels for six months, then for a further 12 months in

bottle on yeast, as opposed to the legal minimum of nine months.

WINEMAKER
Peter Jostock

HOUSE STYLE & RANGE
The 1992 Ürziger Schwarzlay Riesling is easy-going and rounded, while the 1987 Riesling Trocken is no means over the hill, with an interesting smoky, petrolly complexity.

✦ RIESLING TROCKEN
Vintaged, Sekt bA, méthode champenoise: 100% Riesling

SMW MOSEL RIESLING BRUT/TROCKEN
Vintaged, Sekt bA, méthode champenoise: 100% Riesling

SMW OBERMOSEL ELBLING BRUT/TROCKEN
Vintaged, Sekt bA, méthode champenoise: 100% Elbling

SMW SAAR RIESLING BRUT/TROCKEN
Vintaged, Sekt bA, méthode champenoise: 100% Riesling

ÜRZIGER SCHWARZLAY RIESLING BRUT
Vintaged, Sekt bA, méthode champenoise: 100% Riesling

ST AUGUSTUS
See AUGUSTUS

50
ST JOHANNER
RUDESHEIM, RHEINGAU
- Other labels - Dr Mayer, St Jacob

Commercial-quality fizz.

ST JACOB
See ST JOHANNER

SANKT PETER
See BROGSITTER PRIVAT SEKTKELLEREI

74
ST URBANS-HOF
LEIWEN, MOSEL-SAAR-RUWER
- 170 cases

Privately owned and run by the Weis family since 1947. Began making Sekt in 1989.

WINEMAKER
Rudolf Hoffmann

HOUSE STYLE & RANGE
A very soft and gentle expression of Riesling fruit of some finesse.

★ RIESLING BRUT
Vintaged, Sekt bA, bottle-fermented: 100% Riesling

SANKT VEIT
See WG FLEIN-TALHEIM

50
WG SASBACH AM KAISERSTUHL
SASBACH-AM-KAISERSTUHL, BADEN
- 1,700 cases

established in 1935 as a co-op for the growers of Sasbach-am-Kaiserstuhl, who currently number 313 and first produced Sekt in 1988.

WINEMAKER
Gerhard Staiblin

HOUSE STYLE & RANGE
There is an almondy character about these sparkling wines that demolishes any finesse there might have been.

IMBURG WEISSER BURGUNDER EXTRA BRUT
Vintaged, Sekt bA, méthode champenoise:
100% Pinot Blanc
PINOT BLANC DE NOIRS EXTRA TROCKEN
Vintaged, Sekt bA, bottle-fermented: 100% Pinot Noir

✓A
OTGER SCHELL
RECH, AHR
● 340 cases
Although this enterprise was established in 1921, the Schell family did not make any sparkling wine until as recently as 1993, yet they have already won a clutch of awards for their fizz.

WINEMAKER
Otger Schell

HOUSE STYLE & RANGE
The Riesling *Halbtrocken* has beautifully sweet, succulent fruit but, unfortunately, the Ahr-Frühburgunder-Spätburgunder does not impress, hence no overall rating.
★ RECHER HARDTBERG RIESLING HALBTROCKEN
Vintaged, Sekt bA, méthode champenoise;
100% Riesling
AHR-FRÜHBURGUNDER-SPÄTBURGUNDER TROCKEN
Vintaged, Sekt bA, méthode champenoise:
50% Pinot Magdelaine, 50% Pinot Noir

55
FREIHERR VON SCHLEINITZ
KOBERN-GONDORF, MOSEL-SAAR-RUWER
● 420 cases
This estate has been owned since 1956 by the Hähn family, whose winemaking activities date back to 1650. The current owner, Konrad Hähn, started production of these sparkling wines in 1984.

WINEMAKER
Konrad Hähn

HOUSE STYLE & RANGE
The brut is soft, easy, and rounded, but the Trocken is one of those that actually benefits from a higher *dosage*, giving the wine a succulence as well as sweetness of fruit.

90
SCHALES

FLÖRSHEIM-DALSHEIM, RHEINHESSEN
● 50 cases
This estate was established in 1783 by Christian Schales, and is still owned by the Schales family today, with Heinrich tending the vines while Kurt makes the wines.

Since 1964, this estate has developed something of a reputation for its *Eiswein*, where the grapes are harvested and pressed when frozen. When the ice has been skimmed off, the freshly pressed juice is effectively reduced to a significantly higher degree of sugar and acidity, providing a concentration of flavour that is reminiscent of a *Beerenauslese*.

In 1991, Schales made its first – indeed the world's first – sparkling wine from an *Eiswein*. This was a pure Silvaner, and in 1996 Schales went one better (presumably, although not tasted) by producing a Sekt from Riesling *Eiswein*. *Eiswein* is very expensive under any circumstances, but having gone through bottle-fermentation (effectively *méthode rurale*) and available in such a tiny quantities, it is not surprising that these rare sparkling wines are so expensive - DM140 per bottle at the time of going to press.

WINEMAKER
Kurt Schales

HOUSE STYLE & RANGE
Although *Eiswein* must conform to the same technical standard as *Beerenauslese*, these Sekts have closer to an *Auslese* level of sweetness because they have endured fermentation *en masse* and in bottle, resulting in an unusually high alcoholic strength for an *Eiswein*. The sweet, botrytis-like richness has a liquorice intensity of fruit on the finish and, for the moment at least, strikes this author as mighty odd for a fizzy style of wine.

It will take several tastings for me to arrive at an unprejudiced opinion for such extraordinary wines, but until then, the overall score has to remain high to reflect the exceptional quality of the raw materials used.
★ RIESLANER PREMIUM SEKT, EXTRA-DRY
Vintaged, Sekt bA, méthode champenoise:
100% Rieslaner
RIESLING EISWEIN SEKT
Vintaged, Sekt bA, méthode rurale: 100% Riesling
★★✗ SILVANER EISWEIN SEKT
Vintaged, Sekt bA, méthode rurale: 100% Silvaner

CELLARMASTER KURT SCHALES USES TRADITIONAL WOOD VATS. NEARLY 100,000 LITRES OF WINE CAN BE STORED IN OAK BARRELS ON THE SCHALES ESTATE IN RHEINHESSEN

KOBERNER SCHLOSSBERG RIESLING BRUT
Vintaged, Sekt bA, méthode champenoise:
100% Riesling
★ KOBERNER SCHLOSSBERG RIESLING TROCKEN
Vintaged, Sekt bA, méthode champenoise: 100% Riesling

SCHLOSS AVRAS
See EWALD THEO DRATHEN

SCHLOSS BOECHINGEN
See REH KENDERMANN

SCHLOSS CASTELL
See FÜRSTLICH CASTELL'SCHES DOMÄNENAMT

SCHLOSS HOCHHEIM
See GH VON MUMM & CO

N/A

SCHLOSS JOHANNISBERG

JOHANNISBERG, RHEINGAU

Dating back to 1720, this famous Rheingau estate claims to be the oldest Riesling vineyard in constant usage. It is here that *Spätlese* (wine made with late-picked grapes) is supposed to have originated in 1775. The story goes that the courier from the Prince-Bishop of Fulda was so late in arriving with authorisation for the growers to commence the harvest that year that the grapes had been attacked by what later became known as noble rot.

Schloss Johannisberg was secularised under Napoleon and presented by the Austrian Emperor to his foreign minister, Prince von Metternich. The property is still owned by the von Metternich family, but the vineyards are managed and the wines made and marketed by Söhnlein, whose premium Sekt brand Fürst von Metternich is produced exclusively from Riesling grapes grown on this estate.

See SÖHNLEIN RHEINGOLD

SCHLOSS LIESER

See MOSELLAND

SCHLOSS MUNZINGEN

See GRÄFLICH VON KAGENECK'SCHE

75

SCHLOSS ORTENBERG

ORTENBERG, BADEN

- 125 cases

Established in 1950 as a viticultural school.

WINEMAKER

Hans-Peter Dieffien

HOUSE STYLE & RANGE

Extremely ripe and rich, this is not only on the sweet side of brut, it is so richly sweet as to make the brut style a nonsense. In pure quality terms, however, this would make a very good *Halbtrocken*.

★ PINOT BRUT

Not vintaged, Sekt bA, méthode champenoise: 100% Pinot Blanc

SCHLOSS RHEINBERG

See HENKELL

N/A

SCHLOSS REINHARTSHAUSEN

GEISENHEIM, RHEINGAU

- 1,000 cases

This used to be a *cuve close* Riesling sparkler of competent if unexciting commercial quality, but it is now bottle-fermented. The 1990 was extremely acidic, but it is a while since I have tasted it and I really need more experience of these wines to give a rating.

SCHLOSS ROSENSTEIN

See LUDWIG RILLING

50

SCHLOSS SCHÖNBORN

ELTVILLE-HATTENHEIM, RHEINGAU

- 1,250 cases

This famous estate was established way back in 1349, and produced its first sparkling wine in 1958.

WINEMAKER

Gerhard Kirsch

HOUSE STYLE & RANGE

The Riesling has some petrolly varietal typicity but lacks finesse, making the lesser rosé (Deutscher Sekt, not Sekt bA), with its smooth, rich fruit the better fizz – although it is still merely OK, rather than anything special.

HATTENHEIMER PFAFFENBERG RIESLING BRUT

Vintaged, Sekt bA, méthode champenoise: 100% Riesling

★ RHEINGAU SPÄTBURGUNDER WEISSHERBST BRUT

Vintaged, Deutscher Sekt, méthode champenoise: 100% Pinot Noir

74

HEINRICH SCHMITGES

ERDEN, MOSEL-SAAR-RUWER

- 420 cases

Although this privately-owned enterprise was established in 1744, it was not until 1985 that Andreas Schmitges became the first winemaker in his family to produce a sparkling wine *cuvée*.

WINEMAKER

Andreas Schmitges

HOUSE STYLE & RANGE

Crisp, fresh and focused Riesling fruit.

★ ERDENER HERRENBERG RIESLING BRUT

Vintaged, Sekt bA, bottle-fermented: 100% Riesling

★ ERDENER HERRENBERG RIESLING EXTRA BRUT

Vintaged, Sekt bA, bottle-fermented: 100% Riesling

SCHLOSS SCHWERIN

See HANSE SEKTKELLEREI WISMAR

50

SCHLOSS VAUX

ELTVILLE, RHEINGAU

- 50,000 cases

Standard-quality *cuve close* and bottle-fermented fizz.

SCHLOSS WACHENHEIM

Merged with Faber, part of the Reh group, in 1996.

50

SCHLOSSKELLEREI AFFALTRACH

OBERSULM, WÜRTTEMBERG

- 230,000 cases
- Other labels - some 400!

This property dates back to the 13th century. More recently, it has been owned since 1928 by the Baumann family, who first produced Sekt in 1934. Grapes from the estate's own vineyards are supplemented by purchases to produce such a large production under various labels.

WINEMAKER

Heinz Voelcker

HOUSE STYLE & RANGE

Even at the top end of this uninteresting range there is little to choose between the amylic, almondy Riesling and the fat, sweet rosé.

BAUMANN RIESLING BRUT

Not vintaged, Sekt bA, transfer method: 100% Riesling

BAUMANN ROSÉ EXTRA TROCKEN

Not vintaged, Sekt bA, cuve close: 60% Pinot Noir, 40% Meunier

SCHLÖSSLEGARTEN

See WG AUGGEN

SCHLOSSMÜHLE DR HÖFER

See DR HÖFER

65

SCHMITT SÖHNE

LONGUICHM, MOSEL-SAAR-RUWER

The Ockfener Scharzberg Sekt stands out here

50

HERMANN SCHNAUFER

ALTHENGSTETT, WÜRTTEMBERG

- 250,000 cases

A significant production of commercial-quality *cuve close* Sekt, most of which is sold under the Liechtenstein label.

SCHÖNBORN

See SCHLOSS SCHÖNBORN

70

SCHUMANN-NÄGLER

GEISENHEIM, RHEINGAU

- 840 cases

This privately owned estate dates back to Niclas Schumann in 1438, and has been owned by the same family ever since. Sparkling wine production began in 1960.

WINEMAKER

Fred Schumann

HOUSE STYLE & RANGE

Quite fat and fruity.

★ GEISENHEIMER MÖNCHSPFAD RIESLING BRUT

Vintaged, Sekt bA, bottle-fermented: 100% Riesling

√A
SEAGRAM

3.3 million cases

The oldest house in this group, Matheus Müller, dates back to 1811, although it was not until 1837 that it first produced sparkling wine. In 1984, Matheus Müller was purchased by Seagram, which already owned Champagne Mumm and was thus eager to acquire a firm that had produced Mumm Sekt since 1922 (upon the instigation of Hermann von Mumm, a director of Matheus Müller). The Hoehl brand, which was purchased by Matheus Müller in 1968, was sold off in the early 1990s and now belongs to Bernard-Massard.

See MATHEUS MÜLLER

75
SELBACH-OSTER

ZELTINGEN, MOSEL-SAAR-RUWER

250 cases

This winery was established as a separate entity in 1964 by the Selbach family, whose vineyards can be traced back to 1661.

WINEMAKER

Hans Selbach, Klaus-Rainer Schäfer

HOUSE STYLE & RANGE

Very good length without being fat or too rich.

★ ZELTINGER HIMMELREICH RIESLING BRUT
Vintaged, Sekt bA, méthode champenoise: 100% Riesling

√A
SCHLOSS SOMMERHAUSEN

SOMMERHAUSEN, FRANKEN

1,250 cases

The castle of Sommerhausen was built between 1546 and 1575, but its winegrowing tradition dates from 1653, with sparkling wine first produced in 1982.

WINEMAKER

Heinrich Gutbrod

HOUSE STYLE & RANGE

Too little experience of these for an overall rating. I find the copper-coloured rosé coarse, and the Riesling of basic commercial quality.

AUXERROIS EXTRA BRUT
Vintaged, Sekt bA, bottle-fermented: 100% Meunier

RIESLING BRUT
Vintaged, Sekt bA, bottle-fermented: 100% Riesling

SCHWARZRIESLING BRUT ROSÉ
Vintaged, Sekt bA, bottle-fermented: 100% Meunier

75
SEKTHAUS ST LAURENTIUS

LEIWEN, MOSEL-SAAR-RUWER

3,500 cases

This producer's winegrowing tradition goes back 400 years, but it didn't start making sparkling wine until as recently as 1982. In addition to its own-label, St Laurentius Sekt,

SÖHNLEIN RHEINGOLD

ALTHOUGH NOT GIVEN A RATING, THIS PRODUCER HAS ONE OF THE MOST INTERESTING HISTORIES OF ALL GERMAN SEKT PRODUCERS

WIESBADEN
- 6 million cases
- Group ownership - Henkell & Söhnlein
- Other labels - Fürst von Metternich

This brand traces its origins back to 1864, when Johann Jacob Söhnlein and six other partners built a winery in Wiesbaden and four years later launched a sparkling wine called Rheingold, made from the 'basic wines' of the famous Rheingau estate of Schloss Johannisberg.

Rheingold won a gold medal at the Paris Exposition in 1876, the judges publicly declaring that it *'possesses all the characteristics for which the best brands of French Champagne are renowned, and thus combines all the fine flavours of the Schloss Johannisberg cabinet wines that are peculiar to these sparkling pearls of the Rheingau and which no wine of the Champagne can achieve.'* Wilhelm I ordained that *'henceforth and for all times, only the brand Rheingold shall be used for the purpose of christening at the launching of German warships'.*

Johann Jacob Söhnlein became the sole proprietor and, in 1877, he formalised the commercial link between Söhnlein and the von Metternich family, which owned Schloss Johannisberg, by entering into a long-term agreement to supply the Sekt firm with grapes. When the Imperial yacht *Meteor*, which had been built in New York, was launched in 1902, she was supposed to be christened with Rheingold, but a famous Champagne house (Moët & Chandon) allegedly slipped one of their bottles into the hands of the US president's daughter, Alice Roosevelt, just before she was to perform the launch, and she used that rather than the prescribed Rheingold. A public-relations battle ensued in which both wine producers made claims, counter-claims and denials. Eventually it went to court (Langericht Wiesbaden), with Söhnlein winning the

case. The verdict, announced on October 17, 1903, found Moët & Chandon guilty of bribery, and ordered the firm to pay costs. In 1907, the company changed its name from Söhnlein & Co to Rheingold Söhnlein, and this was later transposed to Söhnlein Rheingold.

In 1934, Söhnlein Rheingold entered into a new contract with Schloss Johannisberg which not only guaranteed the supply of grapes, but also granted permission for *Fürst von Metternich* to be used as a brand name for a premium Sekt (to be made exclusively from Schloss Johannisberg grapes) and to use the coat of arms of the house of *Fürst* (Prince) von Metternich-Winneburg for its neck label (this was the forerunner to the Fürst von Metternich Riesling-Sekt brand launched in 1971).

In 1958, Söhnlein was taken over by Rudolf August Oetker, a grocery entrepreneur, and in 1963, Söhnlein took over Burg Weisenau, a Sekt producer specialising in regional brands. Söhnlein merged with Henkell to form the Henkell & Söhnlein group in 1987, now 100% owned by the Oetker family.

HOUSE STYLE & RANGE

Fürst von Metternich is regarded as this producer's finest Sekt. A pure Riesling from the Rheingau's famous Schloss Johannisberg estate, it used to be one of the three best German sparkling wines – but no longer.

It is tangy and clean, with an unmistakably Riesling character, but unfortunately, it is not at all special. Has its quality gone downhill or as sparkling wines elsewhere have so rapidly improved, have our expectations risen?

SÖHNLEIN BRILLANT TROCKEN
Not vintaged, cuve close: grape varieties and origin not revealed

FÜRST VON METTERNICH RIESLING BRUT
Vintaged, cuve close: 100% Riesling

12,500 cases are made for other winegrowers from base wines.

WINEMAKER

Klaus Herros, Jürgen Basten

HOUSE STYLE & RANGE

The Riesling is very fresh and fruity, while the *barrique*-aged Pinot is soft and creamy

with a lovely mousse of minuscule bubbles.

★ PINOT BRUT
Vintaged, Deutscher Sekt, bottle-fermented: 40% Pinot Blanc, 45% Pinot Noir, 15% Riesling

★ RIESLING BRUT
Vintaged, Deutscher Sekt, bottle-fermented: 100% Riesling

N/A
SEKTKELLEREI CANTOR
SPEYER, PFALZ

- 1,700 cases

A non-alcoholic Sekt brand established in 1989 by Henkell & Söhnlein and Robin Harold Cantor, who named it in honour of Lugwig Christian Cantor, founder of Burg Weisenau.

50
H SICHEL SÖHNE
ALZEY, RHEINHESSEN

Producer of Blue Nun, the firm makes an equally bland sparkling version under contract.

SMW
See SAAR-MOSEL-WINZERSEKT

SPLENDID
See ZIMMERMANN-GRAEFF & MÜLLER

STAADTER SEKTKELLEREI MICHAEL HAUSEN-MABILON
See HAUSEN

STAATLICHER HOFKELLER WÜRZBURG
See HOFKELLER WÜRZBURG, STAATLICHER

76
STEIN
OBERHAUSEN, NAHE

- 7,500 cases

Established in 1801, this privately owned winery first made sparkling wine in 1960.

WINEMAKER
Edith Schneider & Rainer Hammer

HOUSE STYLE & RANGE
A smooth rosé of some finesse.

★ RIESLING EXTRA TROCKEN
 Vintaged, Sekt bA, cuve close: 100% Riesling

★★ SCHWARZRIESLING WEISSHERBST BRUT ROSÉ
 Vintaged, Sekt bA, cuve close: 100% Meunier

N/A
STUDERT-PRÜM MAXIMINHOF
BERNKASTEL-WEHLEN, MOSEL-SAAR-RUWER

- 250 cases

This small, family-owned estate dates to 1581, and made its first sparkling wine in 1992.

WINEMAKER
Stephan & Gerhard Studert

HOUSE STYLE & RANGE
Why the Brut should be spoilt by malolactic fermentation, yet not the Trocken, which is essentially basic in quality, I have no idea, but I have only tasted fizz from this estate once, so I will reserve judgement.

MAXIMINER CABINET RIESLING BRUT
 Vintaged, Sekt bA, méthode champenoise: 100% Riesling

MAXIMINER CABINET RIESLING TROCKEN
 Vintaged, Sekt bA, méthode champenoise: 100% Riesling

74
WWE DR H THANISCH
BERNKASTEL-KUES, MOSEL-SAAR-RUWER

This estate was first documented in 1636. Thanisch is one of the most famous producers of the even more famous Bernkastel Doctor, which dates back to 1360. Thanisch started making sparkling wine in 1974, and it is currently owned and run by Margaritt Müller-Burggraef, the fourth generation of women to manage this estate.

See also ZIMMERMANN-GRAEFF & MÜLLER

WINEMAKER
Hans Eduard Leiendecker

HOUSE STYLE & RANGE
Apricot fruit, with some vanilla creaminess.

★ LIESERER NIEDERBERG HELDEN RIESLING BRUT
 Vintaged, Sekt bA, bottle-fermented: 100% Riesling

74
WG THÜNGERSHEIM
THUNGERSHEIM, FRANKEN

- 1,700 cases

This cooperative of growers in the Thüngersheim area was established in 1939 and started making Sekt in 1977.

WINEMAKER
Norbert Gerhardt, Reinhold Full

HOUSE STYLE & RANGE
Elegant Pinot fruit.

★ RÜCKER SCHALK, RÜCKER JESUITENBERG PINOT NOIR TROCKEN
 Not vintaged, Sekt bA, bottle-fermented: 100% Pinot Noir

N/A
SEKTKELLEREI OTTO TREIS
ZELL-MARL, MOSEL-SAAR-RUWER

This winery was established in 1810 and made its first sparkling wine in 1907.

HOUSE STYLE & RANGE
This producer does not wish to reveal the level of its production – which is not an uncommon desire and may be understandable. But it also does not wish to have its winemaker's name revealed which seems a bit strange, until I tasted the wine. I cannot make an objective assessment of Sektkellerei Otto Treis on a single sample – hence I have given no overall rating – but if I were the winemaker of the bottle I tasted, I would not want to put my name to it, either.

MOSEL RIESLING TROCKEN
 Vintaged, Sekt bA, transfer-method: 100% Riesling

TYRRELL
See WGV KARTHÄUSERHOF

N/A
VOLK
SPAY, MITTELRHEIN

- 170 cases

This small, family-owned winery was established in 1900 (or thereabouts), and produced its first sparkling wine in 1989, when current incumbent Jürgen Volk decided to do so as a continuation of his winemaking studies at Geisenheim University. The Steuermann brand name makes use of what has been the village nickname for the Volk family since the time of Jürgen's great-grandfather, who was a helmsman.

WINEMAKER
Jürgen Volk

HOUSE STYLE & RANGE
Quite sweet for a brut, but a pleasant enough example.

STEUERMANN RIESLING WINZERSEKT BRUT
 Vintaged, Sekt bA, méthode champenoise: 100% Riesling

76
WG WACHTENBURG-LUGINSLAND
WACHENHEIM, PFALZ

- 10,000 cases
- Other labels - Lagensekt

This cooperative was established in 1900, and started making Sekt in 1984.

WINEMAKER
Günter Weiss

HOUSE STYLE & RANGE
Pleasant wines, with 'moreish' strawberry fruit

★ WACHENHEIMER BISCHOFSGARTEN SPÄTBURGUNDER EXTRA TROCKEN
 Vintaged, Sekt bA, transfer method: 100% Pinot Noir

★ WACHENHEIMER BISCHOFSGARTEN SPÄTBURGUNDER HALBTROCKEN
 Vintaged, Sekt bA, transfer method: 100% Pinot Noir

WAPPEN
See KLOSS & FOERSTER

WAPPEN VON BREISACH GRANDE CLASSÉ
See GELDERMANN PRIVATSEKTKELLEREI

50
GEBRÜDER WEBER
TRIER, MOSEL-SAAR-RUWER

Commercial-quality fizz sold under the Michael Weber label.

MICHAEL WEBER
See GEBRÜDER WEBER

50
EUGEN WEHRHEIM
NIERSTEIN, RHEINHESSEN

Commercial quality fizz.

WEINGÄRTNER

Each *Weingärtner* (co-op) is listed under its primary title or location.

WEINGÄRTNERGENOSSENSCHAFT

Each *Weingärtnergenossenschaft* (co-op) is listed under its primary title or location.

WEISLACK

See LANGENBACH (TRIER)

85
WILHELMSHOF

SIEBELDINGEN, PFALZ

- 2,500 cases

This family-owned winery produced its first Sekt in 1975, using only *méthode champenoise*.

WINEMAKER
Herbert Roth

HOUSE STYLE & RANGE
The Spätburgunder has an impeccable balance of succulent fruit and ripe, sherbety acidity – the best true *blanc de noirs* Sekt I have tasted.

★★☆ SPÄTBURGUNDER BLANC DE NOIRS BRUT, SIEBELDINGER KÖNIGSGARTEN
Vintaged, Sekt bA, méthode champenoise:
100% Pinot Noir

★ WEISSER BURGUNDER BRUT, SIEBELDINGER KÖNIGSGARTEN
Vintaged, Sekt bA, méthode champenoise:
100% Pinot Blanc

70
WINZERSEKT SPRENDLINGEN

SPRENDLINGEN, RHEINHESSEN

- 250,000 cases

This cooperative was established in 1981 and is dedicated to the production of Sekt. It was quite innovative in the mid-1980s, when it introduced a range of pure varietal *cuvées*.

WINEMAKER
Alfons Fleischer, Hermann Hembd, Hans Helbig

HOUSE STYLE & RANGE
Some Pinot Blancs can be too old, having developed Riesling-like terpenes. The Pinot Noir rosé is better structured, with good fruit acidity and a soft, cushiony mousse.

WINZERSEKT PINOT BLANC EXTRA BRUT
Vintaged, Sekt bA, bottle-fermented:
100% Pinot Blanc

★ WINZERSEKT PINOT NOIR EXTRA TROCKEN ROSÉ
Vintaged, Sekt bA, bottle-fermented:
100% Pinot Noir

80
WILHELM ZÜHRINGER

HEITERSHEIM, BADEN

- 1,700 cases
- Other labels - Edelgräfler

Established in 1844, Weingut Wilhelm

Zühringer is a member of Ecovin (an association of biodynamic wine producers), and produced its first sparkling wine in 1989.

WINEMAKER
Nli Klee

HOUSE STYLE & RANGE
An eclectic range of Sekt, from a dark-red fizz that must rank as Germany's answer to sparkling Shiraz, to a botrytis-tinged Pinot Blanc that is on the sweet side for a brut, but has lovely fruit and a very soft mousse of tiny bubbles.

★★ VIERLIG PINOT BLANC BRUT
Vintaged, Sekt bA, méthode champenoise:
100% Pinot Blanc

★★☆ ZÄHRINGER ECOVIN SPÄTBURGUNDER ROT SEKT BRUT
Vintaged, Sekt bA, méthode champenoise:
100% Pinot Noir

50
WG WILLSBACH

OBERSULM-WILLSBACH, WURTTEMBERG

- 1,250 cases

This winery was established in 1924 by the growers of Willsbach, who currently number 290 and own 210 hectares of vineyards.

WINEMAKER
Peter Euz

HOUSE STYLE & RANGE
General quality does not impress.

WILLSBACHER DIEBLESBERG SAMTROT ROSÉ TROCKEN
Vintaged, Sekt bA, transfer method: 100% Samtrot

N/A
SEKTKELLEREI WINTERLING

NIEDERKIRCHEN, PFALZ

- 5,000 cases

Founded in 1982 by Anne and Martin Winterling, who made their first sparkling wine the following year. Initially, the Winterlings purchased wines to make their Sekt, but since 1992, they have bought grapes only, enabling them to control the first fermentation as well as the second. Since 1996, they have begun buying their own vineyards, and no doubt one day intend to make estate-bottled Sekt.

WINEMAKER
Martin Winterling

HOUSE STYLE & RANGE
The Pinot Brut is very fruity, with a good hint of apricots, but it lacks elegance, whereas 'La Coulée d'Or' is just as fruity, but fuller, fatter, without any apricot character but with a touch more elegance.

I feel the Winterlings are still learning, but they certainly have the potential to make some excellent sparkling wines by international standards in the future.

★ CUVÉE 'LA COULÉE D'OR' BRUT
Not vintaged, Sekt bA, méthode champenoise;
50% Riesling, 25% Pinot Blanc, 25% Pinot Noir

PINOT BRUT
Vintaged, Sekt bA, méthode champenoise:
50% Pinot Noir, 25% Pinot Blanc, 25% Pinot Gris

WINZERGENOSSENSCHAFT

Each *Winzergenossenschaft* (cooperative) is listed under its primary title or location: ALDE GOTT, AUGGEN, BISCHOFFINGEN, DEUTSCHER WEINTOR, DURBACH, JECHTINGEN, KIECHLINSBERGEN, NIERSTEIN, SASBACH AM KAISERSTUHL, THÜNGERSHEIM, AND WACHTENBURG-LUGINSLAND.

WINZERVEREIN

Each *Winzerverein* (cooperative) is listed under its primary title or location.

N/A
WÜRTTEMBERGISCHE WEINGÄRTNER- ZENTRALGENOSSENSCHAFT

MULINGEN, WURTTEMBERG

- Other labels - Rezzo

The centralised cooperative for the Württemberg region.

ZIMMERMANN-GRAEFF

See ZIMMERMANN-GRAEFF & MÜLLER

N/A
ZIMMERMANN-GRAEFF & MÜLLER

ZELL, MOSEL-SAAR-RUWER

- 600,000 cases
- Other labels - Fuerst Bluecher, Splendid

A recent merging between Zimmermann-Graeff, which dates back to 1886, and Rudolf Müller, founded in 1919, the newly formed Zimmermann-Graeff & Müller (ZGM for short) also has shareholding connection with Wwe Dr Thanisch, whose Sekt has always been produced by Rudolf Müller, a function now performed by ZMG.

HOUSE STYLE & RANGE
The quality is quite ordinary under the Eurosekt 'Splendid' label, and some of the Deutscher Sekt is also disappointing. However, the pure Riesling fizz can excel, and when it does, it often has an attractive peachy sweetness.

★ RHEIN CUVÉE BRUT
Not vintaged, Deutscher Sekt, bottle-fermented:
100% Riesling

SPLENDID TROCKEN/HALBTROCKEN/MILD
Not vintaged, cuve close: grape varieties and origin not revealed

★ CLASSIC PRIVAT RIESLING EXTRA TROCKEN
Vintaged, Deutscher Sekt, bottle-fermented:
100% Riesling

RIESLING EXTRA TROCKEN
Vintaged, Deutscher Sekt, bottle-fermented:
100% Riesling

GREAT BRITAIN

FELSTED AND PILTON MANOR WERE THE FIRST ENGLISH VINEYARDS TO PRODUCE FIZZ IN 1976, BUT THE STYLE DID NOT TAKE OFF AND, AS RECENTLY AS JUST TEN YEARS AGO, LAMBERHURST AND CARR TAYLOR WERE THE ONLY ENGLISH SPARKLING WINES AVAILABLE ON A REGULAR BASIS. TODAY THERE ARE ALMOST 50 VINEYARDS PRODUCING SUCH WINES, AND THE REASON FOR THE DRAMATIC INCREASE IS THAT BRITAIN IS ONE OF THE FEW PLACES ON EARTH NATURALLY SUITED TO GROWING GRAPES FOR SPARKLING WINE. IF CHAMPAGNE'S KNIFE-EDGE *TERROIR* IS IDEAL FOR FIZZ, THEN BRITAIN IS JUST ON THE WRONG SIDE OF THAT KNIFE-EDGE.

The wrong side maybe, but it makes the vineyards in Britain much better suited to the production of fine quality fizz than those situated in either California or Australia, despite tremendous progress made in sparkling wine production in both those areas in recent years.

There is not such a wealth of viticultural and oenological expertise in Britain as there is in the New World but it is building, and, if English and Welsh vineyard owners undertake the task with the same degree of tenacity as the Californians and Australians, the results should be even more spectacular.

The most resounding success so far is **Nyetimber** which received such acclaim when it was launched in 1996 that within just 12 months it was selected for the Queen's Golden Anniversary lunch. Nyetimber is owned by an American couple, Stuart & Sandy Moss, who had a crazy ambition to make a top quality fizz from classic Champagne grape varieties in England. But when they sought so-called expert advice about growing vines, they were told there was no way that Chardonnay would ripen and Pinot Noir would just rot. With no such thing as an indigenous grape variety in Britain, they were advised to play it safe and plant hardy hybrids. This was never an option for the Mosses, who knew it would be impossible to establish a worthwhile reputation with grapes that are not even taken seriously by the majority of wine drinkers in Britain, let alone those on major markets abroad.

The Mosses did the damnedest thing; something the English had never dreamed of doing: they asked the champenois for help. Readers probably imagine that asking the champenois how to make sparkling wine would be one of the very first things any aspiring fizz-maker would do, and indeed it was for these two Americans. But the very thought was anathema to English winemakers, many of whom who had trained at Geisenheim, the home of Müller-Thurgau and the funny farm of all funny farms when it comes to creating a multitude of boring grape crosses. In the mid- to late 1980s the most radical thought in the English wine industry was to jump from German crosses to French hybrids, even though more than 30 years earlier Konstantin Frank had persuaded growers in the far less hospitable climes of New York State to give these up in favour of classic *vinifera* vines.

NYETIMBER: LEADING UK SPARKLING WINE

If English wine has any reputation at the moment, it is for the unfashionable grapes that have to be grown because of the country's inhospitable climate. This reputation will stick until most of the hybrids and crosses are grubbed up and only those vineyard sites with true potential are replanted. This is the only option for English wines if the industry wants to shake off its farmers-playing-at-winemakers image, but it took two Yanks to teach this to the Brits. Any doubters should just ask themselves one question: why was Nyetimber chosen for the Queen's Golden Anniversary rather than one of the Seyval Blanc and Müller-Thurgau blends that have been around much longer? Not because it is owned by a couple of Americans, that's for sure.

There are plenty of early-ripening clones of Chardonnay and Pinot Noir that can produce a good crop in England, as the champenois have demonstrated at Nyetimber, but the choice does not necessarily have to be restricted to the two greatest sparkling wine grapes. Any variety that wine drinkers are familiar with will suffice, as long as it is suitable. Gamay, Meunier, Pinot Blanc and Auxerrois have all shown promise in Britain, and there are many other varieties which have yet to be tried. The most important thing for Britain's fledgling sparkling wine industry is that it uses grapes from vineyards which are planted, trained and harvested specifically for sparkling wine, rather than using excess or rejected grapes grown initially for other wine production.

Important in this respect is the fact that Nyetimber's 40-acre vineyard is not alone: Ridgeview near Ditchling Common has 16 of its 26 acres planted exclusively for sparkling wine and, on a smaller scale, Davenport at Rotherfield has four acres. With these two new vineyards soon to come into production, the future for English sparkling wine could be bright, but the rest of the industry has to rid itself of crosses and hybrids, particularly the more aromatic varieties.

If and when that happens, the problems to surmount are not much different than in other aspiring sparkling wine areas: the grapes should be harvested at riper levels (or grow another crop); all de-acidification except malolactic fermentation should be avoided like the plague (if the grapes are worthy of sparkling wine, the acidity is never too high, and should simply be balanced by the *dosage*, however high that has to go); malolactic should be used with a light hand (buttery and caramel aromas should never be present in a sparkling wine, let alone allowed to dominate); the first fermentation temperatures should be increased (to get rid of amylic aromas); and lastly, the second fermentation temperatures should be decreased (to increase finesse).

NOTES FOR THE FOLLOWING VINEYARD PROFILES

1. As the industry is growing from practically zero, production figures would be totally meaningless in all instances except Carr Taylor, which has an established production stretching back almost 15 years.

2. In most instances the wines are 100% estate-produced as far as the first fermentation is concerned, and many of these estates bottle the wines for the second fermentation. However, the majority have been disgorged and dosaged at one of the larger wineries. The big players in this game are Chapel Down, Harvest Group and Three Choirs. It would be misleading to reveal who did what because there is a lot of chopping and changing going on, although a future edition may contain this information.

N/A
ASCOT
See THAMES VALLEY VINEYARD

N/A
BARKHAM MANOR
PILTDOWN, UCKFIELD, EAST SUSSEX

This sparkling wine has been made for a few years, but only started to show well with the 1995 vintage. Hopefully this will set a trend.

WINEMAKER
Mark & Lynn Lambert

HOUSE STYLE & RANGE
Amylic followed by rich fruit aromas; bitter, baked apple-pie juices on the palate; medium fine mousse of ultrafine bubbles. Very good acidity and length make this interesting to age.

BUBBLY BRUT
Vintaged: méthode champenoise, Pinot Noir and Bacchus

N/A
BARTON MANOR
EAST COWES, ISLE OF WIGHT

This vineyard produces a sparkling wine, but not tasted recently.

N/A
BEAULIEU
BROCKENHURST, HAMPSHIRE

Beaulieu was first planted with vines by Cistercian Monks in 1204, and became the site of the current English viticultural revival in 1958 when it was cultivated by Colonel Robert Gore-Browne. The vintage car-crazy Lord Montagu is a lover of all fine wines, and one of the strongest, longest supporters of English wine, but he has yet to prove himself serious about English sparkling wine. Quality apart, Bubbly Brut seems a frivolous name, and rather downmarket for a member of the Upper House. Perhaps, when the style is perfected, 'Vintage Classic' might be more appropriate.

WINEMAKER
Lord Montagu

HOUSE STYLE & RANGE
Persistent cordon of creamy mousse on the inside of the glass; something niggles on the palate. This could just indicate a duff bottle, thus judgement is reserved.

BUBBLY BRUT
Vintaged: méthode champenoise, grape varieties not revealed

N/A
BIDDENDEN
ASHFORD, KENT

This 20-acre, south-facing vineyard was established parcel by parcel between 1969 and 1987 on what was originally an apple orchard. With a string of award-winning wines to his name, Richard Barns could be expected to produce a good fizz, and he has, although I have not been informed about its content.

WINEMAKER
Richard Barns

HOUSE STYLE & RANGE
Distinctively English grassy-flowery aroma, very tangy on the palate, enhanced by a firm mousse of small bubbles and nice acidity. Good brut dryness.

BRUT
Not vintaged: méthode champemoise, grape varieties not revealed

N/A
BOTHY VINEYARD
FRILFORD HEATH, OXFORDSHIRE

If Roger Fisher can make other vintages of sparkling wine in a similar quality and style to his 1991, then he will be rated 75 in a future edition of this book.

WINEMAKER
Roger Fisher

HOUSE STYLE & RANGE
The 1991 vintage of this wine is one of the most distinctive English sparkling wines made to date. However, I would not touch the 1992 with a barge-pole. Quite simply, the 1991 is so uncannily like an effervescent version of a Pouilly-Fumé that it is fascinating. Hopefully Fisher will be able to repeat the phenomenon and never make anything like the 1992 again.

DRY
Vintaged: méthode champemoise, Perle, Albalonga and Kerner

N/A
BOZE DOWN
WHITCHURCH ON THAMES, READING, BERKSHIRE

Quite how much Chardonnay is growing at Boze Down is difficult to work out because some of the vines were initially thought to be Pinot Blanc. Vintages up to and including 1995 included some 40% Seyval Blanc.

WINEMAKER
Dick Conn

HOUSE STYLE & RANGE
Typically English with toasty bottle-aromas. The firm mousse is a bit out of kilter with the fruit-alcohol structure, giving the wine a bit of a schizophrenic character, but it is certainly one of the better English sparkling wines.

BRUT
Vintaged: Chardonnay and Pinot Blanc

N/A VALUE
BREAKY BOTTOM
RODMELL, LEWES, EAST SUSSEX

This wine has the potential for more finesse if given a warmer, quicker first fermentation, but a longer, cooler second fermentation.

WINEMAKER
Peter Hall

HOUSE STYLE & RANGE
Very amylic when first disgorged, but this backs off if rested for a few months, when it becomes an attractive, easy-drinking, light and fruity fizz.

CUVÉE RÉSERVÉE BRUT
Vintaged: méthode champemoise, 100% Seyval Blanc

N/A
BRECON COURT
LLANSOY, NEAR USK, GWENT

Desmond and Barbara McElney have the largest vineyard in Wales on their deer farm.

WINEMAKER
Barbara McElney

HOUSE STYLE & RANGE
The 1995 sparkling wine was an inauspicious start and cannot be recommended in 1998. But I have tasted worse first releases from wineries which have gone on to produce successful fizz.

PREMIER LANSOY, MEDIUM DRY
Vintaged: méthode champemoise, Seyval Blanc and Pinot Gris

N/A
BRUISYARD ST. PETER
SAXMUNDHAM, SUFFOLK

I have liked one or two wines from Bruisyard in the past, and Ian Berwick's fat, distinctive Müller-Thurgau is currently my favourite, so I will give his sparkling wine expertise the benefit of the doubt for a few more *cuvées* yet.

WINEMAKER
Ian Berwick

HOUSE STYLE & RANGE
Sweet, low-key, amylic aromas give way to fat, almost jam-like fruit on the palate. Particularly fat on the finish. Something catches at the back of the throat. Could do with more acidity, perhaps by manipulating the *dosage* with a base wine of high, but not unripe, acidity.

EXTRA BRUT
Not vintaged: méthode champemoise, grape varieties not revealed

BUBBLY
See BARKHAM MANOR, DOWN ST MARY, AND BEAULIEU

N/A VALUE
CAMEL VINEYARD
NANSTALLON, BODMIN, CORNWALL

A small, award-winning vineyard situated on the sunny slopes of the Camel river valley. Released its first fizz in 1997, which is good value but no overall rating can be given yet.

WINEMAKER
Bob Lindo

HOUSE STYLE & RANGE
One of the better, easy-drinking English sparkling wines with its fresh, delicate fruit.
BRUT
Vintaged, méthode champemoise: 100% Seyval Blanc

N/A
CANE END
READING, BERKSHIRE

A 12-acre vineyard producing elegantly presented wines. It is particularly well-known for its late-harvest Bacchus, but also makes an underrated generic medium white wine, and now it appears to be excelling with fizz, albeit with an unashamedly English style.

WINEMAKER
Edward Hordern

HOUSE STYLE & RANGE
Fresh, aromatic English aroma; typical 'English' style fruit on palate, but softened by the Pinot Noir to make a fattish finish, rather than 'English' zip. A clever blend.
SPARKLING DRY NV
Not vintaged, méthode champemoise: Pinot Noir and Seyval Blanc

CARIAD
See LLANERCH

45
CARR TAYLOR
WESTFIELD, EAST SUSSEX
• 8,000 cases

Established in 1971 by David and Linda Carr Taylor, who made their first fizz in 1983. The following year, Carr Taylor became the first English vineyard to set up production of *méthode champenoise* on a commercial scale, and benefited from a champenois consultancy for seven years. However this expertise was not to be extended to the vineyard.

I used to like the Medium Dry, German crosses and all, between 1987 and 1989, or thereabouts, when David Carr Taylor was ahead of the game, but despite the clutch of gongs he can wave in my face (or, when he reads this, bash me over the head with), the results of my tastings suggest that his vinification techniques have not even stood still, but dipped. The wines used to be clean and fresh, with apricot fruit that was nice and tangy, and verged on the exotic. Within the parameters of such a style, Carr Taylor was doing something that Britain could be proud of a decade ago. But the wines are no longer

clean and they fail to impress today.

Whether or not this has been due to the troubled times that culminated in Carr Taylor going from a family concern to a limited company in early 1997, I'm not sure. Maybe there are some old stocks, or they used old or lesser quality wines in the blending? I hope so. I hope that Carr Taylor sparkling wines can at least get back to their former quality and wish that they could gain the sort of finesse that today's serious sparkling wine drinkers demand.

WINEMAKER
David Carr Taylor

HOUSE STYLE & RANGE
Generally clean and fresh on the palate, the Vintage Reserve has a berry-fruit finish while the Dry Reserve has a simplistic finish and a perfumed aftertaste. The Rosé has an off-putting, deep orange hue with still wine aromas and a shrivelled berry taste that becomes quite fat, with baked-fruit flavours, a bitter finish and a sweet aftertaste giving a confused impression.

VINTAGE RESERVE MEDIUM DRY
Vintaged, méthode champemoise: Reichensteiner and Kerner
DRY RESERVE
Not vintaged, méthode champemoise: Reichensteiner and Kerner
ROSÉ RESERVE
Vintaged, méthode champemoise: Pinot Noir

N/A
CARTER'S VINEYARD
BOXTED, COLCHESTER

Formerly called Orion, the first sparkling wine from Carter's Vineyard changed names to Lovejoy in December 1997. Owner-winemaker Mary Mudd asked me not to be too hard on her first sparkling wine because she has learned a lot since it was made in 1995, but it was a darn sight better than the offerings from some winemakers with far more experience.

WINEMAKER
Mary Mudd

HOUSE STYLE & RANGE
A pre-commercial disgorgement in May 1997 suggested that this 1995-based wine could do with at least another year on yeast, and a fully commercialised product disgorged some seven months later confirmed this, but herbaceous aromas, perfumed fruit on the palate and herbaceous finish makes it very English.
LOVEJOY
Not vintaged, méthode champemoise: 80% Orion, 20% Chardonnay

65
CHAPEL DOWN
TENTERDEN, KENT

Chapel Down was established at Tenterden Vineyard in 1993. It produces wines sourced from over 20 different English vineyards under the auspices of David Cowderoy, who started off making wine at his father's Rock Lodge vineyard in Kent. He trained at Roseworthy College in Australia and has winemaking experience in New Zealand, Chile, Romania, Hungary and France.

There is no doubt about the potential of the sparkling wines from Chapel Down, especially when early-ripening Chardonnay and Pinot Noir clones are grown expressly for this purpose in some of the vineyards that supply its needs. Indeed a new *cuvée* from these grapes was in the works as I wrote this book. Chapel Down vies with The Harvest Group as the country's most important contact sparkling wine specialist, disgorging and dosaging for a number of small English vineyards.

WINEMAKER
David Cowderoy

HOUSE STYLE & RANGE
The Epoch NV has flowery, amylic fruit on the palate, with an elegant balance of acidity, and a medium-firm mousse of small, persistent bubbles. However, it is a rather dull, Sekt style. The Century is sweeter and more down-market but I prefer it. It's fresh, not dull, and at least the sweetness makes the fruit accessible. The 1990 Epoch Vintage is an uninteresting wine that lacks finesse. However, by the time of publication, Epoch should have moved onto the deliciously peachy 1993, after which we can look forward to the 1995, which is less peachy, but has additional violet, vanilla finesse.
CENTURY EXTRA DRY
Not vintaged: grape varieties not revealed

EPOCH BRUT
Not vintaged: Müller-Thurgau and Reichensteiner
VINTAGE BRUT
Vintaged: Reichensteiner and Müller-Thurgau

75 VALUE
CHILFORD HUNDRED
LINTON, CAMBRIDGE

This large vineyard was established in 1972, but did not produce its first sparkling wine until as recently as 1994. Only rosé produced so far, and one-tenth of the blend is barrel-fermented.

WINEMAKER

Chris Durant

HOUSE STYLE & RANGE

An old gold colour, apple-blossom aroma and a palate of ripe, green apples, Victoria plums and a touch of 'Muscat' on the finish.

ALURIC DE NORSEHIDE

Vintaged, méthode champemoise: Müller-Thurgau, Dornfelder

N/A
CHILTERN VALLEY
HENLEY-ON-THAMES, OXFORDSHIRE

It is too early to say whether this vineyard will develop a sparkling wine expertise.

WINEMAKER

David Ealand

HOUSE STYLE & RANGE

Fresh, flowery, sweet-fruit aroma, with a light, fresh, flowery, off-dry flavour that's rather inoffensive and commercial.

BRUT

Not vintaged, méthode champemoise: grape varieties not revealed

N/A
DAVENPORT VINEYARDS
ROTHERFIELD, EAST SUSSEX

Will Davenport is a graduate of Roseworthy College in Australia, and has worked for wineries in Alsace, California and South Australia before setting up in England in 1990. He has a still wine vineyard at Horsmonden in Kent, but Davenport Vineyard will be used exclusively for sparkling wine. Planted in 1993 with Pinot Noir and Auxerrois, Davenport came into production in 1997, with the first sparkling wines due to be released at the end of 1999.

40
DENBIES
DORKING, SURREY

These are not the worst English sparkling wines, but they should be a darn sight better, particularly as the huge size of these vineyards and designer visiting facilities make Denbies a showcase for English wine. Denbies sparkling wines desperately need a change of winemaking style and infinitely better presentation.

With Kiwi-trained Nick Patrick in charge since the 1997 harvest, perhaps we will see an improvement in the quality and style of the product when it hits the shelf in a couple of years. But even if Nick Patrick does push quality up, the effect will be diluted if he is forced to use the cheap, lightweight, bright green bottles and nasty wires and caps which his predecessors had to put up with.

WINEMAKER

Nick Patrick

HOUSE STYLE & RANGE

The Surrey Brut is nothing special while the 1993 Rosé has an unappealing apricot-yellow colour, with mellow cherry fruit aromas and a firm mousse. The inaugural 1992 vintage was better than 1993, with attractive strawberry/cherry Pinot Noir aromas. Both wines have a firm mousse.

CUVÉE SURREY BRUT

Vintaged, méthode champemoise: Pinot Noir, Riesling, Elbling

CUVÉE PINOT ROSÉ BRUT

Vintaged, méthode champemoise: 100% Pinot Noir

N/A
DOWN ST MARY
DOWN ST MARY, CREDITON, DEVON

I used to wonder how on earth Down St Mary could register 'Bubbly' as a Trademark, but if you look closely at the 'y' you will see it's not a letter at all: it's a glass. Despite the levity of the presentation, owner Simon Pratt is serious about his fizz.

WINEMAKER

Simon Pratt

HOUSE STYLE & RANGE

The early style of Down St Mary's sparkling wine was far too oxidative, although it won 'general approval' from Jancis Robinson in the *Financial Times*, so obviously it is a matter of opinion. However, from 1994, the style has been more fruit-driven, showing a degree of finesse missing from earlier wines, and promising to go toasty rather than simply oxidative.

BUBBLY DRY

Vintaged, méthode champemoise: Reichensteiner and Auxerrois

ELGAR
See TILTRIDGE VINEYARD

N/A
THE GREAT LODGE VINEYARD
BARDFIELD ESTATE, BRAINTREE, ESSEX

The idea that you can make fizz out of underripe grapes is a myth, but there is nothing worse than underripe herbaceous varieties, particularly when they are as underripe as the 1993 Brut and Extra Brut from this vineyard. Should this vineyard be growing rape seed rather than grapes, or have its owners learned a heck of a lot since 1993? If the latter, I look forward to tasting future vintages, rather than just nosing them.

WINEMAKER

L A Jordan

N/A
HALFPENNY GREEN VINEYARDS
STOURBRIDGE, WEST MIDLANDS

A vineyard with a charming name, Halfpenny

makes a good Madeleine Angevine still wine, which is something of an accomplishment for vines growing on the outskirts of Birmingham, so I'll give this sparkling wine *cuvée* a few more tries before giving up hope.

WINEMAKER

Clive Vickers

HOUSE STYLE & RANGE

Fresh, amylic aroma tends to quickly become murky and unclean. However, the palate is quite clean, albeit with a pithy, greengage style of fruit that is more reminiscent of Chenin than Pinot, Chardonnay or Seyval.

HALFPENNY GREEN

Vintaged, méthode champemoise: Pinot Noir, Chardonnay and Seyval Blanc

HARTLEY'S
See MEON VALLEY

HARVEST GROUP
See THAMES VALLEY VINEYARD

HERITAGE
See THAMES VALLEY VINEYARD

N/A
HIDDEN SPRINGS
HORSHAM, EAST SUSSEX

Hidden Springs wines have the most collectable labels in the business (especially Sussex Sunset, Decadence and Take It As Red), and joint-owners Martyn Doubleday and Chris Cammel have won the English Sparkling Wine Trophy in 1997 for their first fizz, which is good enough for Fortnum & Mason to stock.

WINEMAKER

John Worontschak

HOUSE STYLE & RANGE

A very pale *vin gris* colour with amylic aromas when first disgorged, this wine develops charming cherry-style Pinot Noir fruit on the nose and palate after a little while in bottle, and promises to age further.

PINOT ROSÉ

Not vintaged, méthode champemoise: 100% Pinot Noir

N/A
HORTON ESTATE
HORTON, WIMBORNE, DORSET

According to owner Brian Burch, who has been making Horton fizz since 1991, there is not a lot left for him to learn about the current theory of making and ageing sparkling wine. Unfortunately I cannot comment about how effectively he has put this theoretical knowledge into practice. His idea of turning Bacchus into an Asti-inspired sweet, aromatic style of sparkling wine is the best yet for any German cross – in theory, at least.

WINEMAKER
Brian Burch
HOUSE RANGE
BRUT
  Vintaged: 70% Kerner, 30% Reichensteiner

N/A
LLANERCH VINEYARD
HENSOL, PENDOYLAN, VALE OF GLAMORGAN
This Welsh vineyard wins awards for tourism as well as wine, so why not make a visit?
WINEMAKER
Peter Andrews
HOUSE STYLE & RANGE
Attractive, very pale salmon colour with an extremely amylic aroma when first disgorged, this peardrop character disappears after six months or so, leaving fresh, assertive jammy fruit, quite zesty, and underpinned by a medium-strength firm mousse of fine bubbles.
CARIAD GWRID BLUSH BRUT
  Vintaged, méthode champenoise: Seyval Blanc, Reichensteiner and Triomphe

LOVEJOY
See CARTER'S VINEYARD

N/A
MANSTREE
EXETER, DEVON
I had heard good things about a fizz called Essling, but two sparkling wines from Manstree tasted at Chapel Down in August 1997 were not at all special. Judgement reserved.
WINEMAKER
Gerry Symons
HOUSE STYLE & RANGE
A clean but boring 1993, and a dull 1994.
BRUT
  Vintaged: grape varieties not revealed

N/A
MEON VALLEY
SWANMORE, HAMPSHIRE
WINEMAKER
Chris Hartley
HOUSE STYLE & RANGE
A *vin de table* nose; old yet fresh fruit without any complexity or finesse derived from slow maturation. Tastes like an aged, unripe wine with an almondy overtone. It's early days yet, but the problem could well be deacidification.
HARTLEY'S SPARKLING ENGLISH WINE, BRUT.
  Vintaged, méthode champenoise: Meunier, Pinot Noir, Chardonnay and Seyval Blanc

N/A
MEOPHAM VALLEY
MEOPHAM, KENT
The 1995 Pinot Noir/Chardonnay needed at least another year on yeast when last tasted in May 1997, thus judgement must be reserved.
WINEMAKER
David Grey
HOUSE STYLE AND RANGE
MEOPHAM VALLEY BRUT
  Vintaged, méthode champenoise: Pinot Noir and Chardonnay

N/A
MONNOW VALLEY
MONMOUTH, WALES
Tasted just once, and little known about this Welsh operation, other than that the wine was submitted via Three Choirs.
HOUSE STYLE & RANGE
Deep yellow, yet fresh and aromatic aroma, but needs more fruit on palate, and a more gentle approach to the structure.
SPECIAL RESERVE BRUT
  Vintaged, méthode champemoise: 100% Seyval Blanc

N/A
MOORLYNCH VINEYARD
BRIDGEWATER, SOMERSET
This vineyard is situated on a sunny south-facing hillside that has, surprisingly for England, a somewhat dry microclimate. Owner-winemaker Peter Farmer hopes to gradually increase ageing on lees from the current three years to five but, although I have had little experience of his wines, I would frankly be amazed if this proved beneficial. The longest yeast-contact any English sparkling wine has needed so far has been 40 months for Nyetimber's 1992 Chardonnay. For a long while the Nyetimber wine simply was not ready, but at 40 months it cried out to be disgorged, and for six months all disgorgements were excellent. However, the window of opportunity slammed shut after four years, since when the disgorgements have yielded wines that are still nice, but not as good, with the finesse gradually ebbing away. Have a go Peter, by all means, but do not get fixed on any specific length of ageing. Longer is not necessarily better, just older. A new Faber-based pink fizz has recently been introduced, but not tasted by this author.
WINEMAKER
Peter Farmer
HOUSE STYLE & RANGE
Initially quite strong, typically English aroma, but this quickly maderises in the glass: before it does, however, one may enjoy the mid-palate weight and fruit-alcohol structure of the wine, although it can be a bit hot on the finish. This was Jancis Robinson's 'favourite'

in a recent English fizz article for the *Financial Times*, so one must assume there is bottle variance; I therefore reserve judgement.
SPECIAL RESERVE BRUT
  Vintaged, méthode champemoise: 100% Seyval Blanc

N/A
NORTHBROOK SPRINGS
BISHOPS WALTHAM, HAMPSHIRE
Young, up-and-coming vineyard with 13 acres of vines, offering good value, and proving adept at noble rot dessert wines as well as fizz.
WINEMAKER
Brian Cable
HOUSE STYLE & RANGE
Some flowery finesse on the nose, with rich, well-structured fruit on the palate, and a firm mousse of small bubbles. It would be interesting to age this (both on and off the yeast).
BRUT
  Vintaged, méthode champemoise: Reichensteiner and Kerner

NYETIMBER
See box opposite

N/A
OLDAKER
PLUCKLEY, KENT
Although insignificant in size, Oldaker is important historically, since it was the first English vineyard to be planted with Chardonnay, Pinot Noir and Meunier for the sole purpose of producing sparkling wine. This was in 1986, two years before Nyetimber. Furthermore, all three classic Champagne methods of vine training have been employed: Chablis for Chardonnay, Cordon de Royat for Pinot Noir, and Vallée de la Marne for Meunier. Although the wines are commercial products, it is very much a hobby for Martin Oldaker, who has contracted three different winemakers to make two vintages each: Carr Taylor in 1991 & 1992, Kit Lindlar in 1993 & 1994, and John Worontschak in 1995 & 1996. There was no crop in 1997.
HOUSE STYLE & RANGE
There is no varietal character in any of the vintages, and only John Worontschak has made a decent, clean product, thus he will be making Oldaker for the foreseeable future. Now that the methodology is on a sound footing, Martin Oldaker would be well advised to replant entirely with earlier-ripening, better quality clones.
BRUT
  Vintaged, méthode champemoise: Chardonnay, Pinot Noir and Meunier

ORION
See CARTER'S VINEYARD

Pant Teg
N/A
WALES

Tasted just once, and little known about this Welsh operation.

HOUSE STYLE & RANGE

Charmingly aromatic bouquet, like the freshest elderflower (no cat's pee), but lacks depth and length.

GWIN PEFRIOG CAIN CYMREIG BRUT
Vintaged, méthode champenoise: Kerner and Kernling

Premier Lansoy
See BRECON COURT

Ridgeview
N/A
UPPER FURZEFIELD, DITCHLING COMMON, SUSSEX

Owned by Christine and Mike Roberts, this newly planted vineyard consists of 16 acres planted with 13 clones of Chardonnay, Pinot Noir and Meunier devoted exclusively to estate-bottled sparkling wine. Ridgeview has two south-facing blocks: one on the crest of the estate, which is planted entirely with Chardonnay, and a lower vineyard, which is surrounded by woods and planted with Pinot Noir and Meunier. The vines are trained high to avoid frost and wide to avoid shade, resulting in a tall hybrid version of single Guyot. The silty, clay loam soil has been permeated with more than ten kilometres of underground pipes to ensure good drainage. There is a new, well-equipped winery with underground cellars. First planted in 1995, a minuscule crop was harvested in 1996, and a somewhat larger one in 1997, despite the spring frosts, but the first commercial sized crop will not be until 1998.

WINEMAKER

Mike Roberts

Sedlescombe
N/A
ROBERTSBRIDGE, EAST SUSSEX

A proudly organic vineyard that presents its wines very well, but needs to work on the style and quality of the wine.

WINEMAKER

Roy Cook

HOUSE STYLE & RANGE

The Organic Brut has an unusual fresh, garden herb aroma and rich fruit on the palate. The 1994 Rosé is unimpressive, but two of the grapes are unusual enough to make it worth seeking out by the been-there tasted-it brigade. Furthermore, growing a vine with *Vitis amurensis* sap from Siberia flowing through its canes (AZ15477) is probably difficult enough, let alone being one of the first to make a wine from its grapes. And sparkling wine

GAY STREET, WEST CHILTINGTON, WEST SUSSEX

Owned by American couple Stuart & Sandy Moss, who are not absentee landlords, but live at this idyllic estate. Nyetimber means 'new timber' building, and is so ancient that the house and its two lakes were recorded by the Norman conquerors in the *Domesday Book* (written between 1085 and 1086). Nyetimber is the largest sparkling wine vineyard in the country. Experimental planting began in 1988, but most of the 40 acres currently in production were planted in 1990 and 1991. The vineyard is south-facing, with a modest slope running down to a golf course, which acts as a frost drop, allowing the vines to be planted close to the ground and in a high density of 2,500 per acre (6,200 per hectare). There are several individual blocks of vines, each of which is entirely enclosed by fencing to prevent young shoots and ripe grapes being eaten by wildlife. The fencing extends under the ground to a depth that is sufficient to prevent ingress by burrowers such as rabbits.

Nyetimber has its own well-designed, impeccably equipped winery, all above ground and totally air-conditioned. Sandy Moss is the winemaker, with champenois consultancy maintained for both vineyard and vinification. Both vineyards and winery can undergo a 100% expansion if desired.

I have followed Nyetimber from two years before its first release and, having tasted a vertical of future vintages on three occasions, I can safely say that it is not a

techniques are the most difficult and longest to learn, so I will be following this one for a few *cuvées* before giving up all hope, even though there is a hell of a lot of room for improvement. The unwelcoming darkness to the hue could be ignored if the wine were to delight otherwise, but the aroma is unpleasantly pungent, and there is a medicinal hint to the fruit on the palate. The wine has an overly unctuous feel on the finish, which is too fat, lacks acidity, and is probably over-dosaged.

ORGANIC BRUT
Vintaged, méthode champenoise: Seyval Blanc and Reichensteiner
ORGANIC ROSÉ BRUT
Vintaged, méthode champenoise: Rondo, AZ15477 and Kerner

Nyetimber
80 VALUE

one-off. The 1993 Chardonnay-Pinot blend is even better than the 1992 Chardonnay that made this vineyard so famous in such a short space of time. The 1994 Chardonnay is even better, and the low-yield 1995 wines were very special in tank.

WINEMAKER

Sandy Moss

HOUSE STYLE & RANGE

England's first world-class sparkling wine. This has the class, complexity and finesse that even the best of the others lack. By comparison with most other English fizz, Nyetimber is fat, but that is a misleading description because the wine possesses a correctly lean structure, and simply seems fat when tasted amongst the herbaceousness of aromatic crosses and hybrids that are less than ripe. The fatness is actually nothing more than the satisfying feel in the mouth of riper grapes of a more neutral variety.

The inaugural 1992 vintage of this *cuvée* is one of the most successful first attempts at sparkling wine I have ever come across. Outside Champagne, Nyetimber is one of a rare breed of sparkling wines that needs at least three years on its yeast and, rarer still, a further two years after disgorgement to develop a mellow, biscuity, creamy, walnutty complexity. The 1993 shows some herbaceous, Colombard-like character, and the 1994 has consistently shown the best balance of all, with exceptional finesse.

★★ PREMIÈRE CUVÉE CHARDONNAY BRUT
Vintaged, méthode champenoise: 100% Chardonnay

Tenterden Vineyard
N/A
TENTERDEN, KENT

It is interesting that Stephen Skelton, who worships Seyval Blanc and who has claimed many times that Chardonnay does not ripen and that Pinot Noir will just rot, uses the latter for this wine, but he can do much better than this. Or is he just trying to fuel the hybrid cause?

WINEMAKER

Stephen Skelton

HOUSE STYLE & RANGE

A salmon-orange Anjou Rosé colour, fleeting amylic aromas, with some nice strawberry-style Pinot Noir fruit on the mid-palate. It does, however, lack freshness, and is quickly dominated by a buttery, caramel, malolactic character on the finish.

ROSÉ NV BRUT

Not vintaged, méthode champemoise: 100% Pinot Noir

75 VALUE
THAMES VALLEY VINEYARD
STANLAKE PARK, TWYFORD, BERKSHIRE

Headquarters of The Harvest Group, which is to Thames Valley what Chapel Down Wines is to Tenterden: a grouping of vineyards from which generic wines are sourced without impinging on the individual products of their owners.

The owner of Thames Valley Vineyard, Jon Leighton, cleverly provided his own winemaker, Jon Worontschak, with the facilities to set up The Harvest Group, and this also acts as a base for his flying-winemaker activities, working for major British supermarket groups in Argentina, Brazil, California, Mexico, Peru, South Africa, and Uruguay.

Australian born and trained, Jon Worontschak is the most skilful sparkling winemaker in the country, even if Nyetimber has the vineyard, grape varieties, and champenois input to remain a class apart.

WINEMAKER
Jon Worontschak

HOUSE STYLE & RANGE
Flowery finesse with good fruit and acidity and firm mousse of tiny bubbles. Compared to other English sparkling wines, Clocktower Gamay is more classic, less English in style, although when tasted blind against Champagnes, its Englishness sings through.

ASCOT BRUT

Not vintaged, méthode champemoise: Pinot Noir and Chardonnay

CLOCKTOWER GAMAY NV

Not vintaged, méthode champemoise: 100% Gamay

HERITAGE NV BRUT

Not vintaged, méthode champemoise: Reichensteiner, Seyval Blanc, Müller-Thurgau, Pinot Noir and Chardonnay

N/A
THREE CHOIRS
NEWENT, GLOUCESTERSHIRE

A large vineyard that has played an important role in the development of English wines generally, Three Choirs is one of the major players when it comes to disgorging and dosaging other sparkling wines, particularly from Wales and the west of England. A new non-vintage *cuvée* is due to be released as this book goes to press.

WINEMAKER
Martin Fowke

HOUSE STYLE & RANGE
The 1992 won a medal at Vinexpo in 1997,

but the 1995 smells of sweaty armpits, followed by green fruit on the palate.

VINTAGE RESERVE

Vintaged, méthode champemoise: 70% Seyval Blanc, 30% Pinot Noir

N/A
THROWLEY
THROWLEY, FAVERSHAM, KENT

I get the impression that the grapes in these wines could have made far better quality fizz if first fermentation techniques were improved.

WINEMAKER
Alan Smalley

HOUSE STYLE & RANGE
The 1990 has an aroma of prunes with a touch of caramel; the fruit is a bit fat and the *dosage* is too sweet for the maturity and balance of the wine, which has a medium-soft mousse of tiny bubbles.

RÉSERVE BRUT

Vintaged, méthode champemoise: Pinot Noir and Chardonnay

N/A
TILTRIDGE VINEYARD
UPTON-ON-SEVERN, WORCESTERSHIRE

As this vineyard did not start commercial production until 1990-91, it is too early to make any fair critical comment about what the future might bring, but the structure of the wines is good, and the mousse technically correct, and I have tasted good Huxelrebe still wine from here, so presumably Tiltridge can ripen grapes successfully so far north.

WINEMAKER
Peter & Sandy Barker

HOUSE STYLE & RANGE
The 1994 has a nice, creamy cordon that clings to the inside of the glass; a persistent amylic aroma and plain flavour, with an unripeness that takes on a green apple character on the finish.

ELGAR SPARKLING BRUT

Vintaged, méthode champemoise: Reichensteiner and Auxerrois

N/A
WHATLEY ST GEORGE
WHATLEY, FROME, SOMERSET

Just the first attempt, and much to be learned, especially about ripeness levels, but the malolactic process seems to be licked.

WINEMAKER
Michael Witt

HOUSE STYLE & RANGE
Nice fruit on the palate. Any whiff of free sulphur may distract, although the wine is clean and this should dissipate with time.

DRY

Vintage, méthode champemoise: Seyval Blanc and Reichensteiner

THE 18-ACRE WICKHAM VINEYARD PRODUCES AN EXCELLENT CLASSIC BRUT STYLE

N/A VALUE
WICKHAM
SHEDFIELD, HAMPSHIRE

An 18-acre vineyard that does outrageously well with Kerner, making an excellent, classic Brut style wine under its nicely presented Première Cuvée label. A pure Pinot Noir rosé fizz has just been produced.

WINEMAKER
John Charnley

HOUSE STYLE & RANGE
The Vintage Brut has an estery, amylic style with a 'muscatty' lilt, which comes out in the glass and travels through onto the palate. A soft, flowery, early-drinking style of fruity fizz. The Premier Cuvée Brut has the classic flowery finesse of autolysis on the nose, plus some class and a serious hint of vanilla complexity to the fruit on the finish.

BRUT

Vintaged, méthode champemoise: Kerner and a small percentage of Seyval Blanc

PREMIÈRE CUVÉE BRUT

Vintaged, méthode champemoise: 100% Kerner

ROSÉ BRUT

Vintaged, méthode champemoise: 100% Pinot Noir

N/A VALUE
WOOLDINGS
WHITCHURCH, HAMPSHIRE

Owner Charles Cunningham is serious about wine *per se*, but fizz in particular, herding fellow English winemakers out to Champagne to see how it should be done. He is gradually crafting an elegant, creamy-rich style, and learning from his mistakes, particularly in 1992, when he de-acidified far too heavily.

WINEMAKER
Charles Cunningham

HOUSE STYLE & RANGE
The 1994 is creamy-rich and tangy, like the 1992. Still needs a touch more finesse, but a resounding success compared to the 1993.

BRUT

Vintaged, méthode champemoise: mostly Pinot Noir, plus Chardonnay, Meunier and sometimes Pinot Gris

ITALY

No country has as many sparkling wine appellations as Italy, with its optional 'may be spumante' clauses cluttering up more than 100 of the country's DOCs (*Denominazione di Origine Controllata*, Italy's equivalent of the French *Appellation d'Origine Contrôlée* system). Even Frascati, Soave and Valpolicella can legally be made sparkling!

The irony is that despite this morass of 'maybe fizz', there was not a single Italian appellation specifically for classic brut sparkling wine until Franciacorta was elevated to DOCG (*Denominazione di Origine Controllata e Garantita*) in 1995. Furthermore, Franciacorta is still the only Italian appellation which must be made by the *metodo classico* (*méthode champenoise*).

The myriad of Italy's little-known, half-forgotten sparkling wine appellations are all *cuve close*, which might be ideal for sweet sparkling wines like Asti, but is the worst possible method for any classic brut style of sparkling wine that has the slightest aspiration of achieving international recognition or respect. This is not because *cuve close* is an intrinsically inferior method; in theory it should be able to produce dry sparkling wines that are every bit as good as those made by *méthode champenoise*, but in practice it does not. It is a bulk-production process and consequently attracts the cheapest base wines.

No producers bother to put a top quality base wine through *cuve close*, let alone keep it there for two or three years, and even if they did, they would have to adapt the equipment to stir the lees should they wish the wine to benefit from such ageing. On the other hand, no one bothers to go to the trouble and expense of applying *méthode champenoise* to the cheapest base wines. Bad bottle-fermented sparkling wines are quite common; method alone does not guarantee quality, but

VINEYARD BELONGING TO BELLAVISTA WITH THE HILLS THAT SURROUND THE LAGO D'ISEO IN THE DISTANCE

at least it encourages producers in the right direction, which is why the Italian Wine Law should require all DOC sparkling wines to be produced by the *metodo classico*. Until that happens, no Italian sparkling wine will be taken seriously.

FRANCIACORTA

Franciacorta comes from Chardonnay, Pinot Bianco (Pinot Blanc) and up to 15% Pinot Nero (Pinot Noir) grapes grown on hilly slopes near Lake Iseo, northeast of Milan. It is the first classic brut appellation and currently the only DOC or DOCG to stipulate that its wines must be made by *metodo classico*. Until September 1995, Franciacorta could be still or sparkling, like so many other Italian DOCs. In fact the red wines were quite impressive.

However, in a decision that put quality first (so rare that it remains unique in Italian wine legislation), the most successful style was elevated to its own super-appellation, its production restricted to the finest areas, its yield lowered, and its method of production tightened up. The still red and white wines retain their DOC status, but have been renamed Terre di Franciacorta. Only the sparkling wines may claim the Franciacorta DOCG. The area of production has been restricted to 19 of the 23 communes previously delimited, and the yield has not only gone down from 12.5 to ten metric tons per hectare, but the juice that can be extracted

ITALIAN FIZZ IN 1335?

In June 1998 a 14th century manuscript came up for auction at Sotheby's and some newspapers claimed its contents proved that the Italians invented sparkling wine as early as 1335. Upon examination of the text, however, it is clear that its author, Francesco Scacchi, did not describe how to make a sparkling wine at all, rather how to make a wine that 'surpasses all others in excellence'. He warned about bubbles being one of wines 'evil qualities' that 'upsets the humours of the body'.

Since the bubbles were not welcome, Scacchi was not deliberately making a sparkling wine – any fizziness was

accidental, a phenomenon that has occurred since biblical times. Indeed, Scacchi describes making the wine in a large open vat, which would obviously not be very adept at retaining the fizz. Scacchi refers to this wine being 'very sweet'and it is this, plus his health warning, and the recommendation that the wine is 'best drunk when the weather is cold' that give clues as to what this wine actually was, and the fact is it can still be found today.

It is perhaps best known in Austria, where it is called *Sturm*, the sweet, cloudy, still fermenting new wine that is sold in the weeks prior to St Martin's Day

(11 November). After this juncture, the fermentation will be complete, and most wines will be clear and dry, and can thus be sold in thousands of Heurigen throughout the country.

Visitors to Austria during October are warned against sampling the *Sturm* because it causes upset stomachs, although the locals have built up a resistance to its effects. A similar product called *vin moustillant* or *vin bourru* can occasionally be found in southwest France.

Scacchi's sparkling wine therefore turns out to be nothing more than a *Sturm* in a teacup.

CONFUSED BY MOSCATO?

Although Asti is a pure Moscato sparkling wine, Moscato d'Asti is an entirely different product, and sparkling Moscato, without any geographical designation, is another thing altogether. Moscato d'Asti is a different appellation to Asti; it is not supposed to be fully sparkling, just *frizzantino* or barely *pétillant*, and can sometimes be as still as any ordinary white wine. In recent times there has been an inclination to fizz them up so that they have a definite fizz, albeit not quite as strong as a fully sparkling wine. This tendency is a pity because it blurs the difference between what should be two distinctive styles made from the same grape and area. You can at least recognise a Moscato d'Asti by its normal cork, which is fully inserted into the neck of the bottle, with no mushroom top.

Wines that simply state *Moscato*, without *d'Asti* (or any other location) are cheap, inferior imitations of the real thing. However, the best can be attractive, if not as sweet, rich or tangy as a good Asti and, indeed, they will be preferred to poor quality Asti, which exists by the ocean-load. And because cheap, supermarket Moscato turns over quickly, it will be fresh, whereas good Asti sometimes hangs around, and even the greatest Asti is disgusting when old and geranium-like.

from these grapes has also been reduced. If this uncompromising attitude were applied to every single appellation in the country, Italy would not merely be the largest wine-producing nation in the world, as it is now, it would also be the greatest. With 25 months ageing on its lees (37 if *riserva*), Franciacorta has the potential for producing fine, biscuity, brut and lightly rich rosé sparkling wines.

ASTI

Although Asti is made by *cuve close* in a sweet style, the finest Asti are the greatest sweet sparkling wines in the world. A fraction of the price of *demi-sec* Champagne, but ten times the quality, the finest Asti also represent some of the greatest wine bargains in the world. They were formerly sold as Asti Spumante, but *spumante*, which, like *mousseux* in France, merely means sparkling, had become tarnished by the cheap products that also used the term, thus Spumante was dropped when it was promoted to DOCG in 1993.

Asti is made entirely from Moscato (Muscat) grapes, grown in 52 communes throughout the provinces of Asti, Cuneo and Alessandria in the Piedmont region of northwest Italy. The *cuve close* method of production is far superior to *méthode champenoise* for an aromatic, sweet sparkling wine like Asti because its most vital quality – the freshness of its fruit – gains nothing from extended yeast contact.

As soon as the second fermentation is complete, the wine needs to be removed from the yeast and bottled. The best Asti has a fine mousse of tiny bubbles, a fresh, grapey aroma, a luscious sweetness and a light, yet rich,

flowery, fruitiness that should be vivacious and mouth-watering. The greatest examples will be reminiscent of peaches, and may even have a hint of orange, but Asti is not a wine that should be kept. One of the most important compounds in the Moscato aroma is geraniol, which is wonderful when fresh, but with bottle-age can all too easily assume an unpleasantly pungent geranium odour.

LAMBRUSCO AND PROSECCO

After Asti, Lambrusco and Prosecco are Italy's most ubiquitous sparkling wines, and like Moscato, they can be a cheap, unclassified brew of no fixed abode or an official geographical appellation. Lambrusco Sorbara and Prosecco di Conegliano-Valdobbiadene offer the best prospects, although the vast majority of wines made in both DOCs are dross pure and simple.

Some experts on Italian wine accept that most Prosecco is ordinary, but are enthusiastic about a small number of the best producers. I am enthusiastic about an even smaller number of producers, as most of the so-called 'best' Prosecco wines undergo their first fermentation at far too low temperatures and, although clean and fresh, they are chock-a-block full of amylic aromas. If you want to know what amylic aromas smell like, buy a bottle of Prosecco.

I probably agree with most Italian-wine specialists about Lambrusco, as hardly anyone has much interest in all but a tiny few producers. A good Lambrusco Sorbara, however, can be fascinating, and the few quality-conscious producers should band together to create a new, superior, bottle-fermented DOC to upgrade their image.

WINTER VINEYARDS BELOW ISOLA D'ASTI, PIEMONTE

45
ADAMI
COLBERTALDO, VALDOBBIADENE, VENETO

● 20,000 cases

In 1920 Abele Adami purchased this estate, which had produced wine since at least 1606, from Count Balbi-Valier.

WINEMAKER

Armando & Franco Adami

HOUSE STYLE & RANGE

Abele Adami was instrumental in achieving recognition for Prosecco di Valdobbiadene, and we can be sure that it was not a cold-fermented, amylic wine like his grandson and great-grandson make today, along with almost everyone else in the appellation. All these *cuvées* are amylic with the exception of the Cartizze Dry, which is just plain and ordinary.

CARTIZZE PROSECCO DI VALDOBBIADENE SUPERIORE DRY

Vintaged, cuve close: 100% Prosecco

PROSECCO DI VALDOBBIADENE SPUMANTE BRUT

Vintaged, cuve close: 15% Chardonnay, 85% Prosecco

PROSECCO DI VALDOBBIADENE SPUMANTE EXTRA DRY

Vintaged, cuve close: 15% Chardonnay, 85% Prosecco

VIGNETO GIARDINO PROSECCO DI VALDOBBIADENE DRY

Vintaged, cuve close: 15% Chardonnay, 85% Prosecco

71
ANTEO
ROCCA DE GIORGI, OLTREPÒ PAVESE

● 10,000 cases

This producer specialises in Pinot Noir fizz, using 'almost organic' methods.

HOUSE STYLE & RANGE

The basic Pinot Nero Brut is rather mean, but the Metodo Classico Pinot Nero Brut is a more mature and more serious *cuvée* with some malolactic complexity on the nose, and creamy fruit on the palate. The Rosé is very pale in colour, with very little on the nose, but quite an intense, firm-style flavour. The Selezione del Gourmet is the best of the range, with a hint of almonds on the nose, and fruit that is so rich it is almost unctuous, but has the structure to take it.

ANTEO NATURE EXTRA BRUT

Not vintaged, méthode champenoise: predominantly Oltrepò Pavese Pinot Noir plus Chardonnay

★ METODO CLASSICO PINOT NERO BRUT, OLTREPÒ PAVESE

Not vintaged, méthode champenoise: predominantly Oltrepò Pavese Pinot Noir plus Chardonnay

★ PINOT NERO BRUT, OLTREPÒ PAVESE

Not vintaged, cuve close: predominantly Oltrepò Pavese Pinot Noir plus Chardonnay

PINOT NERO CHARMAT LUNGO BRUT

Not vintaged, cuve close: 100% Oltrepò Pavese Pinot Noir

★ ROSÉ BRUT PINOT NERO, OLTREPÒ PAVESE

Not vintaged, méthode champenoise: predominantly Oltrepò Pavese Pinot Noir plus Chardonnay

★ SELEZIONE DEL GOURMET PINOT NERO, OLTREPÒ PAVESE BRUT

Not vintaged, méthode champenoise: predominantly Oltrepò Pavese Pinot Noir plus Chardonnay

75
ANTICA CANTINA FRATTA
FRANCIACORTA, LOMBARDY

The first sparkling wine I have tasted from this lovely old villa.

HOUSE STYLE & RANGE

Very creamy nose, with succulent fruit on the palate, and a pungent strawberry aftertaste. Too sweet for a true brut, otherwise it would have scored higher, and those who drink *sec* in preference to brut should add a few points.

★ BRUT FRANCIACORTA

Not vintaged, méthode champenoise: grape varieties not revealed

70
ANTINORI
TUSCANY

This large, respected, aristocratic Chianti producer makes several sparkling wines, two of which stand out from the rest in terms of quality.

HOUSE STYLE & RANGE

The non-vintage Nature Brut is fresh, light and elegant, while the Brut Millesimato is a definite step up in an simple but attractive lemony style, with good balancing acidity on the finish.

★ NATURE BRUT

Not vintaged, méthode champenoise: grape varieties not revealed

★ BRUT MILLESIMATO

Vintaged, méthode champenoise: grape varieties not revealed

70
ARUNDA
MELTINA, BOLZANO, ALTO ADIGE

● 5,000 cases

● Other labels - Vivaldi

WINEMAKER

Josef Reiterer

HOUSE STYLE & RANGE

I have enjoyed Vivaldi wines in the past, but the most recent sample was uncharacteristically coarse and clumsy. The Riserva Extra Brut under the Arunda label has tangy fruit, and although it is a bit solid and fat, it has good acidity. The barrique-fermented Arunda Cuvée Marianna is disappointingly dull and foursquare.

ARUNDA CUVÉE MARIANNA EXTRA BRUT, SÜDTIROLER SEKT

Not vintaged, méthode champenoise: 80% Chardonnay, 20% Pinot Noir

★ RISERVA EXTRA BRUT, SÜDTIROLER SEKT

Not vintaged, méthode champenoise: 60% Chardonnay, 40% Pinot Noir

VIVALDI BRUT, SÜDTIROLER SEKT

Not vintaged, méthode champenoise: 50% Chardonnay, 30% Pinot Blanc, 20% Pinot Noir

VIVALDI EXTRA BRUT, SÜDTIROLER SEKT

Not vintaged, méthode champenoise: 80% Chardonnay, 20% Pinot Noir

74
BANFI
TAVERNELLE, TUSCANY

Villa Banfi's immaculate vineyards and high-tech winery help to make this one of Italy's more consistent sparkling wine producers.

WINEMAKER

Ezio Rivella

HOUSE STYLE & RANGE

The Pinot Vino is a fresh, light and fruity fizz for everyday drinking. The Brut Talento is a step up; it has a fat but very fresh aroma, with soft, satisfying vanilla fruit lifted by the effervescence. The sparkling red Brachetto d'Acqui has big, blowsy Pinot aromas followed by soft, sweet, strawberry fruit on the palate. Banfi's Asti is sweeter than most in the appellation, with very fresh, light and fluffy fruit. The Tener Sauvignon-Chardonnay is a fresh, crisp wine with a light balance. The fruit is dominated by Sauvignon, but it is not herbaceous, and a little Chardonnay input is noticeable.

★★ ASTI NV VINO SPUMANTE DOLCE

Not vintaged, cuve close: 100% Moscato

★ BRUT PINOT VINO SPUMANTE

Not vintaged, cuve close: Pinot Blanc, Pinot Noir

★ BRUT TALENTO

Not vintaged, méthode champenoise: grape varieties not revealed

★ TENER SAUVIGNON-CHARDONNAY, BANFI NV VINO SPUMANTE BRUT

Not vintaged, méthode champenoise, cuve close: Chardonnay, Sauvignon Blanc

★ BRACHETTO D'ACQUI, VINO SPUMANTE DOLCE

Vintaged, cuve close: 100% Brachetto

73
FRATELLI BERLUCCHI
BORGONATO, FRANCIACORTA, LOMBARDY

It is important to separate the two Berlucchi: Fratelli Berlucchi is run by Pia Berlucchi, produces only Franciacorta and is very traditionally packaged, whereas Berlucchi plain and simple is the best-selling brand that

80
BELLAVISTA

ERBUSCO, FRANCIACORTA, LOMBARDY

• 42,000 cases

This has been one of my favourite Italian sparkling wine producers for many years, and Bellavista's 1993 Gran Cuvée Brut Rosé is still the greatest dry Italian sparkling wine I have ever tasted.

WINEMAKER

Shihi Hakim

HOUSE STYLE & RANGE

The basic Cuvée Brut has a restrained nose with delicately ripe fruit on the palate and a fine, cushiony mousse, making it an elegant wine of some finesse. The Gran Cuvée Brut Rosé is a dream, with its golden-sunset colour, and delicious cushiony fruit

SHIHI HAKIM
CHECKS THE
POSITION OF THE
SEDIMENT IN
BOTTLES OF
BELLAVISTA GRAN
CUVEE

supported by lively acidity. The Gran Cuvée Brut has a fine, fresh, biscuity aroma, with a rich fruit flavour and good acidity for further development.

BELLAVISTA GRAN CUVÉE PAS OPERÉ, FRANCIACORTA

> *Not vintaged, méthode champenoise: 65% Chardonnay, 35% Pinot Noir*

BELLAVISTA GRAN CUVÉE SATÈN, FRANCIACORTA

> *Not vintaged, méthode champenoise: Chardonnay*

BELLAVISTA RISERVA VITTORIO MORETTI, FRANCIACORTA

> *Not vintaged, méthode champenoise: 50% Chardonnay, 50% Pinot Noir*

★✶ CUVÉE BRUT, FRANCIACORTA

> *Not vintaged, méthode champenoise: 80% Chardonnay, 10% Pinot Blanc, 10% Pinot Noir*

★ GRAN CUVÉE BRUT, FRANCIACORTA

> *Vintaged, méthode champenoise: 72% Chardonnay/Pinot Blanc, 28% Pinot Noir*

★★ GRAN CUVÉE BRUT ROSÉ, FRANCIACORTA

> *Vintaged, méthode champenoise: 40% Chardonnay, 60% Pinot Noir*

72
FRANCESCO BELLEI

BOMPORTO, EMILIA ROMAGNA

• 6,000 cases

This winery was established by Francesco Bellet in 1920, but it was his grandson, Giuseppe, who first applied the *méthode champenoise* to Lambrusco di Sorbara, which is the best of its type and stocked by all the best restaurants in the region.

WINEMAKER

Giuseppe & Christian Bellei

HOUSE STYLE & RANGE

Bomporto is a serious quality Chardonnay-Pinot. The mousse has a noticeably lower pressure, but extraordinarily fine bubbles. There is something missing from the mid-palate, which lowers the score, but the wine has nice vanilla finesse and complexity on the finish. However, it is Bellei's Lambrusco di Sorbara that is of greatest interest here, and applying the costly,

work-intensive *méthode champenoise* to this wine is a beautifully simple way of focusing the mind on quality. Even though Sorbara is the best Lambrusco appellation, most wines bearing the name are not anywhere near as good as this, with its deep, dry, intense, seriously flavoured, sour-cherry fruit. It might be interesting to age, but I will play safe and recommend this as a ready-to-drink fizz.

This is not a great wine *per se*, but it is a great Lambrusco, and if all Lambrusco were this good, it would not have such a bad name.

★ LAMBRUSCO DI SORBARA

> *Not vintaged, méthode champenoise: 100% Lambrusco Sorbara*

★✶ BOMPORTO EXTRA CUVÉE BRUT

> *Vintaged, méthode champenoise: 40% Chardonnay, 60% Pinot Noir*

is run by cousin Guido, who blends his sparkling wines from various sources, and does not produce any Franciacorta (at least, not yet).

Fratelli Berlucchi's labels are marvellously over-ornate, the sort of packaging that most large producers would have rationalised in the 1950s.

WINEMAKER

Pia Berlucchi

HOUSE STYLE & RANGE

The Brut is a fresh, easy-drinking fizz with a sweet twist of almondy fruit on the finish. The Rosé is rather deep, and could be brighter, but the fruit-acidity balance makes this a nice, easy drinking fizz too. Although

the Brut Reserve has a certain oxidative complexity on the nose, it is within limits and in no way detracts from the lovely, soft vanilla fruit on the palate, which makes this the best *cuvée* in the range.

★✶ BRUT, FRANCIACORTA

> *Vintaged, méthode champenoise: 90% Chardonnay, 10% Pinot Noir*

★ BRUT RESERVE, FRANCIACORTA

> *Vintaged, méthode champenoise: 90% Chardonnay, 10% Pinot Noir*

★✶ FRATELLI BERLUCCHI 1993 BRUT, FRANCIACORTA ROSÉ

> *Vintaged, méthode champenoise: Chardonnay, Pinot Blanc, Pinot Noir*

N/A
GUIDO BERLUCCHI

BORGONATO, FRANCIACORTA, LOMBARDY

• 375,000 cases

Guido Berlucchi is situated in the Alpine foothills of Lombardy, just a couple of miles northeast of Ca'del Bosco. Berlucchi has some 70 hectares planted with Pinot Blanc and Pinot Noir in the Franciacorta area, on top of which the firm buys in Pinot Noir from the Oltrepò Pavese, which is also in Lombardy, and both Pinot Blanc and Chardonnay from Trentino and the Alto-Adige in northeast Italy. Although these are all quality wine areas the resulting blend cannot claim DOC status.

WINEMAKER

Arturo Ziliani

HOUSE STYLE & RANGE

Berlucchi wines have always tended to be dominated by amylic first-fermentation odours, but the intrinsic richness of the wines regularly puts them in the top half-dozen dry *spumante* ranges in the country. Recent *cuvées* have, however, been hugely disappointing in quality and Berlucchi seems to have traded the ubiquitous amylic aroma for a dull, strawlike, oxidative character. While I'm not sorry to see the peardrops go, they were preferable to straw and oxidation. The non-vintage Imperiale Brut was the only amylic wine of the bunch, and the quality was just not there either.

CELLARIUS BRUT RISERVA SPECIALE

> *Not vintaged, méthode champenoise: Chardonnay, Pinot Blanc, Pinot Noir*

CUVÉE IMPERIALE BRUT

> *Not vintaged, méthode champenoise: Chardonnay, Pinot Blanc, Pinot Noir*

CUVÉE IMPERIALE BRUT EXTRÈME

> *Not vintaged, méthode champenoise: Chardonnay, Pinot Blanc, Pinot Noir*

CUVÉE IMPERIALE MAX ROSÉ

> *Not vintaged, méthode champenoise: Chardonnay, Pinot Blanc, Pinot Noir*

CUVÉE IMPERIALE PAS DOSÉ

> *Not vintaged, méthode champenoise: Chardonnay, Pinot Blanc, Pinot Noir*

CUVÉE IMPERIALE MILLESIMATO
Vintaged, méthode champenoise: Chardonnay, Pinot Blanc, Pinot Noir

FRANCIACORTA BRUT
Vintaged, méthode champenoise: Chardonnay, Pinot Blanc

CA' DEI FRATI
LUGANA DI SIRMIONE, FRANCIACORTA, LOMBARDY
• 1,650 cases
One of the two best producers of Lugana in the still form, Ca' dei Frati also makes a good attempt with this sparkling version.
HOUSE STYLE & RANGE
Rich, fruity aromas with fresh, easy-going fruit on the palate.
✭ CUVÉE DEI FRATI NV BRUT, LUGANA
Not vintaged, méthode champenoise: 10% Chardonnay, 90% Lugana

CA' DEL BOSCO
ERBUSCO, FRANCIACORTA, LOMBARDY
• 50,000 cases
Motorcycle-mad, multi-millionaire Maurizio Zanella is one of Italy's most consistent sparkling wine producers. At one time Ca' del Bosco was made in a full, complex style to emulate Champagne, but this often meant the wines sacrificed finesse for character. Now, however, Ca' del Bosco exhibits more freshness and increasing elegance. There is still a way to go, but at least these wines are going in the right direction.
WINEMAKER
Maurizio Zanella
HOUSE STYLE & RANGE
The basic non-vintage Brut has a fresh Mâcon-like aroma, with good fruit and acidity on the palate, but bubbles could be smaller. The vintaged Brut has some lemony finesse on the nose, with rich fruit on the mid-palate and a creamy finish, but the aftertaste lacks elegance, otherwise it would have a full star rating. The very fruity Rosé is a definite step up, as it is not over fruity, and dries to a nicely focused finish. The Satèn Brut has strong, sprightly fruit aromas on the nose, followed by a nice piquancy of fruit on the palate. Cuvée Annamaria Clementi Brut is, if anything, a bit too rich for its balance to be special, but it does make a lovely, ripe-fruity fizz for easy drinking without food.
✭ BRUT, FRANCIACORTA
Not vintaged, méthode champenoise: 45% Chardonnay, 30% Pinot Blanc, 15% Pinot Noir
✭ BRUT, FRANCIACORTA
Vintaged, méthode champenoise: 50% Chardonnay, 35% Pinot Blanc, 15% Pinot Noir

★✭ ROSÉ BRUT, FRANCIACORTA
Vintaged, méthode champenoise: 30% Chardonnay, 30% Pinot Blanc, 40% Pinot Noir
✭ SATÈN BRUT, FRANCIACORTA
Vintaged, méthode champenoise: 60% Chardonnay, 40% Pinot Blanc
★ CUVÉE ANNAMARIA CLEMENTI BRUT, FRANCIACORTA
Vintaged, méthode champenoise: 35% Chardonnay, 35% Pinot Blanc, 30% Pinot Noir
DOSAGE ZÉRO 1994, FRANCIACORTA
Vintaged, méthode champenoise: 50% Chardonnay, 35% Pinot Blanc, 15% Pinot Noir

73
CAVALLERI
ERBUSCO, FRANCIACORTA, LOMBARDY
• 16,700 cases
The Cavalleri family have been landowners in Erbusco since 1450, and started wine production in 1905, when Atillo and Giovanni Cavalleri inherited the property from their father. The first sparkling wines were produced in 1979 by the *méthode champenoise* and today the firm is a consistent producer of fine Franciacorta DOCG.
WINEMAKER
Pierluigi Calabria
HOUSE STYLE & RANGE
The non-vintage Blanc de Blancs has a full toasty aroma, with plenty of fruit on the palate, but needs more layers of flavour and finesse for a higher rating. The fresh, fruity Rosé is Italy's easy-drinking answer to Angas Brut Rosé.
✭ FRANCIACORTA
BLANC DE BLANCS BRUT
Not vintaged, méthode champenoise: 100% Chardonnay
FRANCIACORTA BLANC DE BLANCS CRÉMANT SATÈN
Not vintaged, méthode champenoise: 100% Chardonnay
FRANCIACORTA BLANC DE BLANCS PAS DOSÉ
Not vintaged, méthode champenoise: 100% Chardonnay
✭ BLANC DE BLANCS BRUT, FRANCIACORTA
Vintaged, méthode champenoise: 100% Chardonnay
✭ CAVALLERI 1993 ROSÉ, FRANCIACORTA
Vintaged, méthode champenoise: Chardonnay, Pinot Noir

73
MICHELE CHIARLO
CALAMANDRANA, ASTI
• 1,500 cases
Michele Chiarlo is better known for his Moscato d'Asti, his Gavi, and an outstanding Nebbiolo-Barbera blend called Barilot. He is now also beginning to establish himself as one of Italy's premier sparkling wine producers.
HOUSE STYLE & RANGE
The Extra Brut has complex biscuity

aromas, but like so many Italian sparkling wines, it lacks the correct acidity balance, thus misses out on the sort of length and finesse that would have earned it a full star rating. The EOS Extra Brut makes a fine, fresh, zesty fizz compared to most of the Italian competition, and from its zany presentation alone, it would make an ideal, albeit expensive own-label fizz for a top avant garde restaurant.
✭ EXTRA BRUT
Vintaged, méthode champenoise: 30% Chardonnay, 70% Pinot Noir
✭ EOS EXTRA BRUT
Vintaged, méthode champenoise: 50% Chardonnay, 50% Pinot Noir

N/A
GIULIO COCCHI
ASTI, PIEDMONT
Giulio Cocchi was a Florentine who, in 1891, established a confectionery business in Asti, expanding first into a distillery, then a sparkling wine producer.
HOUSE STYLE & RANGE
Some of these wines recently won a clutch of awards but I have not been able to taste them yet.
ASTI DOLCE
Not vintaged, cuve close: 100% Moscato
BRACHETTO SPUMANTE
Not vintaged, cuve close: 100% Brachetto
BRUT ROSÉ METODO CLASSICO
Not vintaged, méthode champenoise: 100% Pinot Noir
CHARDONNAY BRUT
Not vintaged, cuve close: 100% Chardonnay
COCCHI BRUT
Not vintaged, cuve close: 100% Pinot Blanc
EUPHORIA EXTRA BRUT
Not vintaged, cuve close: 100% Cortese
PRIMOSECOLO BRUT
Not vintaged, cuve close: 100% Chardonnay
BRUT MILLESIMO METODO CLASSICO
Vintaged, méthode champenoise: Chardonnay, Pinot Noir
BRUT RISERVA METODO CLASSICO
Vintaged, méthode champenoise: Pinot Noir

N/A
LE COLTURE
ST STEFANO DI VALDOBBIADENE, VENETO
• 14,700 cases
This privately-owned enterprise is run by Cesare and Renato Ruggeri, whose family have been winemakers since 1500.
HOUSE STYLE & RANGE
The Prosecco Extra Dry is fresh and OK, but not special.
FUNER PROSECCO DI VALDOBBIADENE EXTRA DRY
Not vintaged, cuve close: 100% Prosecco
PROSECCO DI VALDOBBIADENE BRUT
Not vintaged, cuve close: 15% Chardonnay, 85% Prosecco

PROSECCO DI VALDOBBIADENE EXTRA DRY

Not vintaged, cuve close: 10% Chardonnay, 90% Prosecco

SUPERIORE DI CARTIZZE PROSECCO DI VALDOBBIADENE DRY

Not vintaged, cuve close: 100% Prosecco

N/A
GIUSEPPE CONTRATTO
CANELLI, ASTI, PIEDMONT

• 17,000 cases

Established in 1867, this firm originally built its fame on 'Asti Champagne' and in the 1980s built up a reputation for exceptional dry sparkling wines. Now it is back re-inventing Asti. The drop in the quality of Contratto's dry wines is worrying, hence no overall rating.

WINEMAKER

Dott. Gian Carlo Scaglione

HOUSE STYLE & RANGE

With the exception of the fresh, peppery Riserva, I have been gravely disappointed by most of Contratto's dry sparkling wines lately, although they used to be outstanding. However, the bottle-fermented Asti, Contratto de Miranda, is absolutely stunning. Who would have thought that anyone would have bothered to put Asti through the full *méthode champenoise*?

In normal circumstances I would say that the fresh, succulently sweet, fruity style of Asti has nothing to benefit from fermentation in the bottle, but this specific *cuvée* is sensational. Everything about it is a class apart and much more intense than even very good Asti, from the colour to the richness, sweetness, balance and finesse. Gancia's special *cuvée*, Camilo Gancia, used to be the greatest Asti by far; now there are two Asti superstars.

BACCO D'ORO EXTRA DRY

Not vintaged, méthode champenoise: 20% Chardonnay, 80% Pinot Noir

BRUT

Not vintaged, méthode champenoise: 20% Chardonnay, 80% Pinot Noir

FOR ENGLAND PAS DOSÉ

Not vintaged, méthode champenoise: 100% Pinot Noir

BRUT RISERVA

Vintaged, méthode champenoise: predominantly Pinot Noir plus Chardonnay and Pinot Blanc

★★☆ CONTRATTO DE MIRANDA 1995 ASTI

Vintaged, méthode champenoise: 100% Moscato

☆ RISERVA GIUSEPPE CONTRATTO, SPUMANTE

Vintaged, méthode champenoise: 50% Chardonnay, 50% Pinot Noir

N/A
RICCI CURBASTRO
CAPRIOLO, FRANCIACORTA, LOMBARDY

German-based Tasmanian flying-winemaker Owen Bird has been consulting here for a few years. He also consults for Chard Farm's new sparkling wine project in New

Zealand's Central Otago region.

WINEMAKER

Owen J Bird

HOUSE STYLE & RANGE

The basic Brut is not at all pleasant on the nose, while the palate is dull, with terpenes showing through. The Satèn Brut has creamy, malolactic aromas and rich fruit, but although there is good acidity, it is not in harmony with the rest of the wine. The Demi Sec was just dull and sweet. Hopefully things will improve under the auspices of Owen Bird.

FRANCIACORTA BRUT

Not vintaged, méthode champenoise: 80% Chardonnay, 5% Pinot Blanc, 15% Pinot Noir

FRANCIACORTA EXTRA BRUT

Not vintaged, méthode champenoise: 80% Chardonnay, 5% Pinot Blanc, 15% Pinot Noir

FRANCIACORTA SATÈN BRUT

Not vintaged, méthode champenoise: 100% Chardonnay

SPUMANTE DEMI BRUT

Not vintaged, méthode champenoise: 60% Chardonnay, 40% Pinot Blanc

SPUMANTE DEMI SEC

Not vintaged, méthode champenoise: 60% Chardonnay, 40% Pinot Noir

73
ENDRIZZI
MEZZOCORONA, TRENTINO

I was suitably impressed by my first encounter with this producer.

HOUSE STYLE & RANGE

Satisfying clean richness of fruit, a firm mousse and very small bubbles, with correct structure and good acidity.

★ ENDRIZZI NV COLLEZIONE MASETTO BRUT

Not vintaged, méthode champenoise, cuve close: grape varieties not revealed

N/A
FACCOLI LORENZO
COCCAGLIO, FRANCIACORTA, LOMBARDY

• 2,350 cases

Family-owned estate with four hectares of vines.

HOUSE RANGE

FRANCIACORTA BRUT

Vintaged, méthode champenoise: 40% Chardonnay, 50% Pinot Blanc, 10% Pinot Noir

FRANCIACORTA EXTRA BRUT

Vintaged, méthode champenoise: 40% Chardonnay, 50% Pinot Blanc, 10% Pinot Noir

FRANCIACORTA ROSÉ BRUT

Vintaged, méthode champenoise: 40% Chardonnay, 40% Pinot Blanc, 20% Pinot Noir

74
DE FAVERI
BOSCO DI VIDOR, VENETO

• 42,000 cases

In over 100 Proseccos tasted recently, only six stand out. Two of those are from Lucio de Faveri including the best Prosecco I've ever tasted.

WINEMAKER

Lucio De Faveri

HOUSE STYLE & RANGE

The basic Prosecco di Valdobbiadene is similar to, but lighter than, the Prosecco di Valdobbiadene in the prestige-shaped bottle, with very fresh, Mâcon-style fruit on the nose and palate, the freshness and elegance following on through the finish to the aftertaste.

☆ PROSECCO DI VALDOBBIADENE VINO SPUMANTE BRUT

Not vintaged, cuve close: Prosecco plus 10-15% Pinot Blanc

★★☆ PROSECCO DI VALDOBBIADENE NV VINO SPUMANTE BRUT

Not vintaged, cuve close: Prosecco plus 10-15% Pinot Blanc

PROSECCO DI VALDOBBIADENE SUPERIORE DI CARTIZZE

Not vintaged, cuve close: Prosecco plus 10-15% Pinot Blanc

75
FERRARI
TRENTO, TRENTINO

• 250,000 cases

If it is not a contradiction in terms, Ferrari is acknowledged by many as the Rolls Royce of Italian fizz. This firm was established by Giulio Ferrari in 1902 and purchased by Bruno Lunelli in 1952.

HOUSE STYLE & RANGE

Although still very good in Italian fizz terms, Ferrari does not seem to be as outstanding as it used to. Having said that, the wines have a firm, rich flavour of some complexity, which can develop further in bottle.

★ BRUT, TRENTO

Not vintaged, méthode champenoise: 95% Chardonnay, 5% Pinot Noir

THE BAROQUE 17TH-CENTURY VILLA GETILOTTO VIEWED OVER CHARDONNAY VINES BELONGING TO FERRARI AT MATTARELLO, NEAR TRENTO, TRENTINO

ROSÉ
Not vintaged, méthode champenoise: predominantly
Pinot Noir plus Chardonnay

GIULIO FERRARI RISERVA DEL FONDATORE
Vintaged, méthode champenoise: 100% Chardonnay

PERLE
Vintaged, méthode champenoise: 100% Chardonnay

√A
FIRMATO
TRENTINO
HOUSE STYLE & RANGE
Rich, smooth fruit supported by firm
mousse, with a tasty finish.

★ BRUT, TRENTO
Not vintaged, méthode champenoise: grape varieties
not revealed

75
FONTANAFREDDA
CUNEO, PIEDMONT
• 350,000 cases
This well-known firm was founded in 1878
by Comte Emanuele Guerrieri, the son of
King Vittoria Emanuele II, and is probably
more famous for its excellent Barolo and
other still wines than it is for Asti, although it
is one of the big four (the others being
Gancia, Martini and Riccadonna).

HOUSE STYLE & RANGE
One of the richest and most lush, aromatic
Asti *cuvées* on the market.

★★ ASTI
Not vintaged, cuve close: 100% Moscato

85
NINO FRANCO
VALDOBBIADENE, VENETO
Some Italian specialists believe Nino Franco
is the best producer of Prosecco. They should
try these wines against those of De Faveri.

WINEMAKER
Primo Franco

HOUSE STYLE & RANGE
There is nothing wrong with any of these
wines; they are all faultless, but they are also
all amylic and so clean that surgical comes to
mind. I challenge anyone to tell which of at
least three of these wines is any different from
the other two. The banalising effect of amylic
aromas is one thing, but most of these wines
taste so similar that it seems pointless to label
them as different *cuvées*.

PRIMO BRUT
Not vintaged, cuve close: 100% Chardonnay
PROSECCO DI VALDOBBIADENE BRUT
Not vintaged, cuve close: 100% Prosecco
PROSECCO DI VALDOBBIADENE PRIMO FRANCO
Not vintaged, cuve close: 100% Prosecco
PROSECCO DI VALDOBBIADENE RUSTICO
Not vintaged, cuve close: 100% Prosecco
PROSECCO DI VALDOBBIADENE SUPERIORE DI

CARTIZZE
Not vintaged, cuve close: 100% Prosecco

70
GANCIA
CANELLI, PIEDMONT
• 1.7 million cases
Gancia is, of course, famous for its Asti and,
indeed, it was Carlo Gancia who, in 1865,
became Asti's founding father. Carlo must
have been something of a whizz-kid because
at the age of just 18, he was already running
a company called Dettoni in Turin. But he
was attracted by the idea of making a
sparkling wine in his native Piedmont, so he
went to Champagne, where he spent two
years learning about the process at Piper
Heidsieck.

Upon his return home, he formed the
Gancia Company with his brother Edouardo.
This was in 1850, when he also set about
adapting the techniques of bottle fermentation
to native Piedmontese grapes. His first
inclination was to try this with black grapes,
as he had witnessed in Champagne, but the
results were far from satisfactory, so he turned
his attention to the local Moscato, or Muscat.

It had been traditional to produce sweet
wines from the Moscato since the turn of the
14th century, so it simply did not occur to
Carlo Gancia that a sparkling Moscato should
be anything other than sweet. This presented
him with a problem of how to halt the second
fermentation once it had started, and thereby
provide the desired sweetness. In order to
ensure sufficient sugar for both the second
fermentation and the final sweetness, the wines
had to be bottled at a much lower alcoholic
degree, which ironically enabled the second
fermentation to continue far beyond that
possible in Champagne, where the alcoholic
level becomes too toxic for the yeast to survive.
The second fermentation thus continued to
build up the pressure until even the strongest
bottles were doomed to explode.

In the mid-19th century this was not easy,
but with the help of an oenologist called
Arnaldo Strucchi, Gancia reduced the
nitrogen level of the wine prior to bottling,
primarily by extensive settling and cleansing
of the must, and repeated filtration of the
wine through 'Dutch Sacks'. As nitrogen is
essential to the life of yeast cells, they will
die as soon as the reduced nitrogen content
has been exhausted, thus ending the second
fermentation. Gancia achieved this in 1865,
and within a very short while the wine was
being marketed as Moscato Champagne or
Italian Champagne, acquiring its Asti
Spumante appellation in 1932.

The rest, as they say, is history. Except
that since its recent upgrading from DOC

to DOCG, Asti has dropped the word
Spumante from its title. Although it simply
means sparkling, *spumante* became tarnished
by the cheap products that share this word,
just as *mousseux* has in France, and *Sekt* has in
Germany.

HOUSE STYLE & RANGE
When on form, the non-DOC Pinot de
Pinot has fresh, attractive sherbety fruit, but
easily tires. The Chardonnay Brut is
another non-DOC *cuve close*, but is
creamier than the Pinot de Pinot, although
this is more the effect of malolactic than
varietal character. The Prosecco
Chardonnay is fresh and crisply aromatic,
with delicate fruit that makes it easy to
drink. Riserva Carlo Gancia has attractive
creamy oak fruit. Gancia dei Gancia is light
and tight, but fresh and creamy. The
Brachetto is a very aromatic sparkling red
wine, with deliciously fresh, intensely sweet,
Moscato-like fruit. The Gran Dessert is not
Asti, but a non-DOC fizzy Moscato, and is
comparatively neutral on the nose, without
quite the zip and zing of Asti on the palate,
and somewhat less sweet than Asti Gancia.
Camilo Gancia is made only in exceptional
harvest conditions in tiny quantities. Until
Contratto launched Miranda, this stunning
Camilo Gancia was head and shoulders
above all the other Astis.

★ ASTI GANCIA
Not vintaged, cuve close: 100% Moscato
★ BRACHETTO ANTICA CASA MARCHESI SPINOLA
Not vintaged, cuve close: 100% Brachetto
★★★ CAMILLO GANCIA, ASTI
Not vintaged, cuve close: 100% Moscato
CASTELLO GANCIA PROSECCO CHARDONNAY
Not vintaged, cuve close: Chardonnay, Prosecco
GANCIA CHARDONNAY
Not vintaged, cuve close: 100% Chardonnay
GANCIA DEI GANCIA
Not vintaged, cuve close: 100% Chardonnay
GANCIA GRAN DESSERT
Not vintaged, cuve close: 100% Moscato
PINOT DELLA ROCHA, OLTREPÒ PAVESE PINOT
Not vintaged, cuve close: mostly Pinot Blanc
PINOT DI PINOT BRUT
Not vintaged, cuve close: 85% Pinot Blanc plus other
varieties
RISERVA CARLO GANCIA GRAND TRADIZIONE
BRUT
Vintaged, bottle-fermented: 80% Chardonnay, 20%
Pinot Noir

74
GIANNI
ASTI, PIEDMONT
HOUSE STYLE & RANGE
This succulently sweet, fresh, rich and
piquant *cuvée* has the most muscatty fruit I
have tasted in a long time.

★✫ GIANNI ASTI

Not vintaged, cuve close: 100% Moscato

N/A
GRUPPO ITALIANO VINI
CALMASINO, VERONA, VENETO

- Other labels – D'Arco

This sparkling wine is produced for Gruppo Italiano Vini by Cantina Sociale Mezzocorona, a cooperative in the Trentino region.

HOUSE STYLE & RANGE

This *cuvée* is a pleasant new experience for me, with its lively fruit acidity, which heightens the freshness and leaves a tingly, crisp finish.

CUVÉE ANDREA D'ARCO BRUT

Not vintaged, méthode champenoise: 90% Chardonnay, 10% Pinot Noir

✫ RISERVA NICOLÒ D'ARCO BRUT

Not vintaged, méthode champenoise: 90% Chardonnay, 10% Pinot Noir

N/A
GIORGIO LUNGAROTTI
TORGIANO, PERUGIA, UMBRIA

Lungarotti is most famous for its Rubesco Torgiano, whose reputation led to the establishment of the Torgiano DOC and, more recently, DOCG status for Torgiano Riserva. Lungarotti is also the clear leader when it comes to producing Umbria's excellent new-wave wines, but this was my first experience of its fizz.

HOUSE STYLE & RANGE

Tasted recently for the first time, this wine had a strange, but not unpleasant, combination of peppery fruit, blown wheat and apricots.

BRUT

Not vintaged, méthode champenoise: 50% Chardonnay, 50% Pinot Noir

55
MARTINI & ROSSI
TORINO, PIEDMONT

- 1.5 million cases
- Group ownership – Bacardi

Established in 1863, the name of this company is more likely to conjure up the sound of Martini, the clink of ice, roller-skating babes and vermouth before Asti comes to mind, but it is still one of the biggest sellers.

HOUSE STYLE & RANGE

Clean and grapey, but not one of the richest Asti *cuvées* on the market.

ASTI

Not vintaged, cuve close: 100% Moscato

OLTREPÒ PAVESE BRUT

Not vintaged, cuve close: 100% Welschriesling

RISERVA MONTELERA BRUT

Not vintaged, méthode champenoise: 100% Pinot Noir

45
MASOTTINA
TREVISO, VENETO

- 42,000 cases

HOUSE STYLE & RANGE

These wines all have an amylic style.

CARTIZZE SPUMANTE DRY

Not vintaged, cuve close: 100% Prosecco

MARZEMINO SPUMANTE DOLCE

Not vintaged, cuve close: 100% Marzemino

PINOT BRUT SPUMANTE

Not vintaged, cuve close: 80% Pinot Bianco, 20% Pinot Noir

PINOT CHARDONNAY SPUMANTE BRUT

Not vintaged, cuve close: 50% Chardonnay, 50% Pinot Blanc

PROSECCO DI CONEGLIANO E VALDOBBIADENE EXTRA DRY/DRY

Not vintaged, cuve close: 100% Prosecco

72
MONTE ROSSA
BORNATO, FRANCIACORTA, LOMBARDY

- 17,000 cases

A 16th-century villa with 30 hectares of vines.

HOUSE STYLE & RANGE

Not all the Monte Rossa wines can be recommended, but the three which can, offer an interesting contrast of styles. The basic non-vintage Brut is very fruity in an everyday drinking style. The non-vintage Brut Satèn has some creamy finesse showing through slow-building toasty aromas, with toast, coffee and a twist of lemon on the palate. The vintaged Brut has distinctive fresh pepperiness on the nose, and soft, sweet fruit on the palate.

✫ FRANCIACORTA BRUT

Not vintaged, méthode champenoise: 40% Chardonnay, 50% Pinot Blanc, 10% Pinot Noir

★ FRANCIACORTA BRUT SATÈN

Not vintaged, méthode champenoise: Chardonnay, Pinot Blanc

FRANCIACORTA ROSÉ BRUT

Not vintaged, méthode champenoise: 40% Chardonnay, 20% Pinot Blanc, 40% Pinot Noir

FRANCIACORTA SEC

Not vintaged, méthode champenoise: Chardonnay, Pinot Blanc, Pinot Noir

✫ FRANCIACORTA BRUT

Vintaged, méthode champenoise: 40% Chardonnay, 50% Pinot Blanc, 10% Pinot Noir

FRANCIACORTA CABOCHON BRUT

Vintaged, méthode champenoise: 70% Chardonnay, 30% Pinot Noir

N/A
MORIANO
TRENTINO

HOUSE STYLE & RANGE

My first and recent experience of this wine, the Moriano Brut is a good, if somewhat oaky *cuvée* that would benefit from a leaner structure and higher acidity.

✫ BRUT TRENTO

Not vintaged, méthode champenoise, cuve close: grape varieties not revealed

N/A
PISONI
TRENTINO

Well-established as one of the best producers of sparkling wine under the Trento DOC.

HOUSE STYLE & RANGE

Succulent and appealing fruit on the nose becomes much firmer on the palate.

✫ BRUT TRENTO

Not vintaged, méthode champenoise: grape varieties not revealed

N/A
POJER & SANDRI
FAEDO, TRENTO, TRENTINO

I have only recently tasted my first sparkling wine from this top Trentino producer, who makes an excellent range of still wines.

WINEMAKER

Mario Pojer

HOUSE STYLE & RANGE

Immaculate presentation and nice, fresh, apricot aromas on the nose, but lacks the depth and acidity for a top score.

✫ CUVÉE '93-'94, EXTRA BRUT

Not vintaged, méthode champenoise: 65% Chardonnay, 35% Pinot Noir

70
RICCADONNA
CANELLI, ASTI, PIEDMONT

- 1.2 million cases

Established in 1921 by Ottavia Riccadonna, this is one of the big four Asti producers (the others are Fontanafredda, Gancia and Martini).

HOUSE STYLE & RANGE

When fresh, the Asti can be good, although low-key and not as sweet as perhaps it should be. A number of dry non-DOC sparklers are produced, but they are of little interest.

ASTI

Not vintaged, cuve close: 100% Moscato

70
ROTARI
TRENTINO

Produced by the Cantina Sociale Mezzocorona

HOUSE STYLE & RANGE

The Riserva is fresh and fruity, with good acidity, but the fruit peters out shortly after the mid-palate, otherwise Rotari would have a higher rating over all.

★ ROTARI RISERVA 1993 BRUT, TRENTO
Vintaged, méthode champenoise: grape varieties not revealed

BLANC DE NOIR BRUT
Not vintaged, méthode champenoise: grape varieties not revealed

ARTE ITALIANA BRUT
Not vintaged, méthode champenoise: grape varieties not revealed

N/A
RUGGERI
VALDOBBIADENE, TREVISO, VENETO
Well thought of by some critics, but I am left cold by the entire range of wines from this producer.

HOUSE STYLE & RANGE
Mostly amylic, although the Extra Dry is the most intense and can ride this out, and the Brut is dominated by the caramel character of heavy-handed malolactic fermentation.

CARTIZZE
Not vintaged, cuve close: 100% Prosecco

PROSECCO DI VALDOBBIADENE BRUT
Not vintaged, cuve close: 100% Prosecco

PROSECCO DI VALDOBBIADENE EXTRA DRY
GIUSTINO BISOL
Vintaged, cuve close: 100% Prosecco

PROSECCO DI VALDOBBIADENE SPUMANTE DRY S.
STEFANO
Not vintaged, méthode champenoise: 100% Prosecco

PROSECCO DI VALDOBBIADENE SPUMANTE EXTRA
DRY ORO
Not vintaged, cuve close: 100% Prosecco

PROSECCO DI VALDOBBIADENE TRANQUILLO
Not vintaged, cuve close: 100% Prosecco

70
SOLDATI LA SCOLCA
GAVI LIGURE, PIEDMONT
La Scolca was purchased in 1919 as a summer retreat, and is the oldest winery in the Gavi area, most of which was destroyed during the Second World War.

HOUSE STYLE & RANGE
Soldati La Scolca does tend to lean more towards the heavy and characterful rather than light and elegant, and the wines could do with more finesse at times.

The basic non-vintage Brut is a rich and mature cuvée with hints of toast and lemon, and good acidity giving a crisp finish. The Gavi Brut has a creamy-malo nose with soft fruit, some peachiness and a creamy, menthol aftertaste, supported by a soft mousse of fine bubbles. The Gavi Pas Dosé is admirably ripe, with fruity aromas and good acidity to highlight the palate.

Brut Millesimato gets a high score because it is a mature vintage of around ten years

when released and survives well for Italian fizz, most of which are dead by this age. This longevity is due to its high acidity, but it is ripe acidity, and the wine has matured into an exotic, coconutty concoction with apricots and custard on the finish.

★ BRUT
Not vintaged, méthode champenoise: 100% Cortese

★ GAVI BRUT
Not vintaged, méthode champenoise: 100% Cortese

★ GAVI PAS DOSÉ
Not vintaged, méthode champenoise: 100% Cortese

RUGRÉ LA SCOLCA, GAVI
Not vintaged, méthode champenoise: 100% Cortese

SOLDATI LA SCOLCA MÉS-BRUT CRÉMANT
Not vintaged, méthode champenoise: 100% Cortese

★★ BRUT MILLESIMATO
Vintaged, méthode champenoise: 100% Cortese

N/A
CANTINA PRODUTTORI DI VALDOBBIADENE
VALDOBBIADENE, TREVISO, VENETO
This cooperative was established in 1952 and today comprises 600 growers owning 600 hectares of vineyards.

HOUSE STYLE & RANGE
Tasted recently for the first time, the Prosecco was amylic (aren't they all?) and the Pinot Chardonnay had a tight structure with an ordinary taste.

PINOT CHARDONNAY BRUT
Not vintaged, cuve close: Chardonnay, Pinot

PROSECCO DI VALDOBBIADENE BRUT
Not vintaged, cuve close: 100% Prosecco

PROSECCO DI VALDOBBIADENE BRUT/EXTRA DRY
Not vintaged, cuve close: 100% Prosecco

N/A
VILLA
MONTICELLI BRUSATI, FRANCIACORTA, LOMBARDY
• 6,250 cases
A well-known estate situated in an ancient village, with 20 hectares of impeccably maintained vineyards on the steep slopes of the Madonna della Rosa Hill.

HOUSE STYLE & RANGE
Tasted recently for the first time, I found these wines dull with oxidative, straw-like aromas and fruit.

FRANCIACORTA BRUT
Not vintaged, méthode champenoise: 70% Chardonnay, 20% Pinot Blanc, 10% Pinot Noir

FRANCIACORTA CUVETTE

Not vintaged, méthode champenoise: 80% Chardonnay, 5% Pinot Blanc, 15% Pinot Noir

FRANCIACORTA EXTRA BRUT
Not vintaged, méthode champenoise: 85% Chardonnay, 5% Pinot Blanc, 10% Pinot Noir

72
ZAMUNER
SONA, VERONA, VENETO
Established in 1981, Daniele Zamuner makes a rich and rustic Cabernet Sauvignon-Merlot called Valecchia, but she also makes a range of sparkling wines.

WINEMAKER
Daniele Zamuner

HOUSE STYLE & RANGE
I find a general theme of peppery fruit notes running through the range of wines from this producer. I am not impressed by the Brut, but I am fascinated by the Extra Brut, which has peanuts and chocolate – like drinking a Snickers Bar – but with good acidity. The Rosé Brut has fresh, peppery fruit going to cappuccino, with a zesty, uplifting finish.

BRUT
Not vintaged, méthode champenoise: 10% Chardonnay, 20% Meunier, 70% Pinot Noir

★ EXTRA BRUT, SPUMANTE CLASSICO
Vintaged, méthode champenoise: 10% Chardonnay, 20% Meunier, 70% Pinot Noir

★ ROSÉ BRUT, SPUMANTE TRADIZIONALE
Vintaged, méthode champenoise: Meunier, Pinot Noir

60
ZARDETTO
OGLIANO DI CONEGLIANO, TREVISO, VENETO
Made by a gnome called the 'King of Bubbly' who lives in the forests of the Venetian Alps. If you do not believe me, look on the bottle and you'll see his picture. It's a flute of fizz in his right hand, but don't ask what he's holding in his left hand or what he does with it.

HOUSE STYLE & RANGE
Only one wine recently tasted: the Brut, which was a fresh, light and fruity fizz that would be ideal for those who do not like their bruts too dry.

BRIOSO, PROSECCO DI CONEGLIANO
Not vintaged, cuve close: 100% Prosecco

EXTRA BRUT
Not vintaged, cuve close: 35% Pinot Blanc, 50% Prosecco, 15% Verdiso

★ PROSECCO DI CONEGLIANO BRUT
Not vintaged, cuve close: 5% Pinot Blanc, 90% Prosecco, 5% Verdiso

SUPERIORE DI CARTIZZE, PROSECCO DI
VALDOBBIADENE DRY
Not vintaged, cuve close: 100% Prosecco

ZERO VENTI, PROSECCO DI CONEGLIANO DRY
Not vintaged, cuve close: 10% Pinot Bianco, 90% Prosecco

PORTUGAL

MOST PORTUGUESE *MÉTHODE CHAMPENOISE* WINES ARE PRODUCED IN BAIRRADA, BUT THE INDUSTRY IS BEGINNING TO DEVELOP, PARTICULARLY IN THE UPPER DOURO AND IN THE VAROSA AREA NORTH OF LISBON.

The general quality of Portuguese fizz is pretty poor because the vast majority is sold on the domestic market (primarily through restaurants), and the standard expected of sparkling wine in Portugal falls a long way short of what is acceptable in, say, London, San Francisco or Sydney. Very little is exported, thus producers have no experience of competing against the lowest quality of cheap sparkling wine, let alone more upmarket products.

The revolution in bubbles has yet to arrive in Portugal, but it will come, I am sure. Ten years ago, the same could have been said about Portuguese red wines, which were totally devoid of fruit. But that has all changed over the last five years and, like all good revolutions, the transformation started at the bottom and worked upwards. We are still waiting for the same thing to happen with still white wines, and we will have to wait even longer for a revolution in fizz because the technology is far more sophisticated, and the learning curve much longer.

As much as 15% of Portuguese fully sparkling wine is red, and that does not include *Vinhos Verdes*, most of which are red. A red 'green wine' is not the contradiction it may sound because 'green' in this case merely means underripe. Vinhos Verdes must be included in an encyclopedia of sparkling wines, even if there is hardly a prickle in some of the wines at the lowest pressure levels, let alone a fizz. Most exported

VINES AT JP VINHOS AT PONTE DE LIMA ON THE SETUBAL PENINSULA

Vinhos Verdes are souped-up (sweetened with concentrate and fizzed-up (sparged with carbon dioxide prior t bottling), thus really do fall in the semi-sparkling categor

Genuine Vinho Verde is totally dry, although it ma be delicately dry or raspingly dry, and it should alway have a refreshing tang, which usually incorporates certain minerally aftertaste. Whether souped-up o authentic, virtually all Vinhos Verdes are best drun when they are as young as possible.

Vinho Verde comes from the Minho regior between the River Douro and the Atlanti coast where the vines virtually grow on tree trellises, up telegraph poles and along fences on anything, in fact, to take them above th ground. Training the vines in such a wa enables the smallholders – and there are mor than 60,000 of them in the Minho – to grov the cabbages, maize and beans that their familie survive on underneath, and at the same time t produce grapes, which they sell either to larg wineries such as Sogrape or Aveleda, or to loca winemaking co-ops who then sell the wine to tourist

In addition to these smallholdings, there are growing number of professionally run *quintas*, wher the vines are neatly trained on *cruzeta* trellises, seven o eight feet above the ground. Only in the Minho ca one see pickers going to the harvest with ladders, sight more reminiscent of hop-picking.

When picked, the grapes should not be fully ripe, fo Vinho Verde has a low alcohol content (about nine p cent, although the minimum permitted is seven p cent) and high acidity, which is why it is called *verde* o 'green'. Bottling takes place very early to retain as muc freshness as possible and to encourage a malolacti fermentation in the bottle, which results in some degre of *pétillance*, though this can be anything from a semi sparkle to barely a prickle.

50
AGULHA, VINHO VERDE

HOUSE STYLE & RANGE
A dry, commercially-blended Vinho Verde, with only a faint *pétillance*, sold in a stone bottle.
AGULHA VINHO VERDE
Not vintaged: grape varieties not revealed

AVELEDA
See QUINTA DA AVELEDA

75
AZEVEDO
BARCELOS
• Group ownership - part of Sogrape
This large Vinho Verde firm was created when Quinta da Aveleda went to part of the Guedes family that split away from Sogrape, leaving the largest wine producer without a Vinho Verde.

HOUSE STYLE & RANGE
The flagship Vinho Verde is a classic dry *cuvée* in Portugal, but all too often sweetened-up for

export markets. The other wines are some of the best commercially blended Vinhos Verdes; well-made with crisp fruit.
✮ QUINTA DE AZEVEDO, VINHO VERDE
Vintaged: Loureiro and Paderna
✮ CHELLO, VINHO VERDE
Not vintaged: grape varieties not revealed
✮ GAZELA, VINHO VERDE
Not vintaged: grape varieties not revealed
★★ MORGADIO DA TORRE ALVARINHO, VINHO VERDE
Vintaged: Alvarinho

50
BORGES & IRMÃO
OPORTO
Large producers of Port, still wine and Vinho Verde, with some interest in fully sparkling wines.

HOUSE STYLE & RANGE
Gatão is the largest-selling commercially-blended Vinho Verde in the world and can have a flowery-fresh aroma when young. The

other wines are clean but disappointing.
FITA AZUL
Vintaged: grape varieties not revealed
GAMBA, VINHO VERDE
Not vintaged: grape varieties not revealed
GATÃO, VINHO VERDE
Not vintaged: grape varieties not revealed
GATÃO, VINHO VERDE TINTO
Not vintaged: grape varieties not revealed
TROVADOR BRANCO
Not vintaged: grape varieties not revealed
TROVADOR ROSÉ
Not vintaged: grape varieties not revealed

N/A
CASA DA TAPADA
FISCAL
The first Vinho Verde producer to make fully sparkling wine – not a bad idea, but the grapes need to be riper and the techniques cleaner.

HOUSE STYLE & RANGE
Single-*quinta* Vinho Verde grown on southwest-facing slopes. Inconsistent, but can be good.

VINHO VERDE
Vintaged: Loureiro
RESERVA
Vintaged, méthode champenoise: predominantly Loureiro

O
CASA DE CABANELAS
USTELO
HOUSE STYLE & RANGE
A light, dry and aromatic single-*quinta* Vinho Verde.
VINHO VERDE
Vintaged: Azal, Loureiro, Trajadura and Pederna

5
CASA DE COMPOSTELA
LEQUIÃO, FAMALICÃO
HOUSE STYLE & RANGE
A light, fresh and fruity, cool-fermented single-quinta Vinho Verde.
VINHO VERDE
Vintaged: primarily Pederna with Loureiro and Trajadura

O
CASA DE OLEIROS
AMARANTE
HOUSE STYLE & RANGE
Correctly dry wines, the Vinho Verde has typical mineral qualities while the Tinto has some rich fruit.
★ VINHO VERDE
Vintaged: grape varieties not revealed.
★ VINHO VERDE TINTO
Vintaged: grape varieties not revealed.

O
CASA DE PENELA
ADAÚFE
HOUSE STYLE & RANGE
Single-quinta Vinho Verde with an aromatic and distinctive style.
VINHO VERDE
Vintaged: Loureiro and Trajadura

5
CASA DE RENDUFE
RESENDE
HOUSE STYLE & RANGE
A fruity single-quinta Vinho Verde with a delicate aroma, from the south bank of the River Douro.
VINHO VERDE
Vintaged: Avesso

O
CASA DE SANTA LEOCADIA
GERAZ DO LIMA
HOUSE STYLE & RANGE
A fine, aromatic single-quinta Vinho Verde, with a fruity character.
★ VINHO VERDE
Vintaged: Loureiro

75
CASA DE SEZIM
NESPEIRA, GUIMARÃES
• Other labels - Tia Chia
Owned by the same family since 1375.
HOUSE STYLE & RANGE
Good aroma and more weight than most, and many people believe this *quinta's* top *cuvée* to be the second-best Vinho Verde, after Palácio da Brejoeira.
★★ CASA DE SEZIM VINHO VERDE
Vintaged: mostly Loureiro, plus Trajadura, Pederna and a little Azal Branco

60
CASA DE VILA BOA
VILA BOA DE QUIRES
HOUSE STYLE & RANGE
Fresh, light and distinctive single-quinta.
VINHO VERDE
Vintaged: Azal

60
CASA DE VILACETINHO
ALPENDURADA
HOUSE STYLE & RANGE
Fresh, delicate and elegant single-quinta.
★ VINHO VERDE
Vintaged: Azal, Loureiro and Pederna

55
CASA DE VILA NOVA
SANTA CRUZ DO DOURO, BAIÃO
HOUSE STYLE & RANGE
Typical minerally single-*quinta*.
VINHO VERDE
Vintaged: Avesso and Pederna

55
CASA DE VILAVERDE
CAÍDE DE REI
HOUSE STYLE & RANGE
A light, clean and aromatic single-*quinta*.
VINHO VERDE
Vintaged: Loureiro, Pederna and Azal

55
CASA DOS CUNHAS
QUINTADO BELINHO
HOUSE STYLE & RANGE
The Vinho Verde is light, dry and aromatic while the Tinto is typically aggressive.
VINHO VERDE
Vintaged: Loureiro
VINHO VERDE TINTO
Vintaged: Espadeiro and Vinhão

50
CASA DO LANDEIRO
CARREIRA, BARCELOS
HOUSE STYLE & RANGE
Typically minerally.

VINHO VERDE
Vintaged: Loureiro and Trajadura

QUINTA DO CASAL BRANCO, ALMEIRIM

N/A
CASAL BRANCO, SOCIEDADE DE VINHOS SA
QUINTA DO CASAL BRANCO, ALMEIRIM
Beautifully understated orange label creates a stunning presentation
HOUSE STYLE & RANGE
Unusual lemon-jam flavour is more of a curiosity than something to enjoy.
MONGE BRUTO
Vintaged, méthode champenoise: grape varieties not revealed.

CASAL GARCIA
See QUINTA DA AVELEDA

50
CASALINHO
FELGUEIRAS, VIZELA
HOUSE STYLE & RANGE
Light, commercial blend; off-dry with a definite *pétillance*.
VINHO VERDE
Not vintaged: grape varieties not revealed

45
CAVES ALIANÇA
SANGALHOS
• 83,000 cases
Large, Bairrada-based firm specialising in sparkling wine, Dão and Bairrada.
HOUSE STYLE & RANGE
Commercially blended wines, consistent if uninteresting.
C MENDES
Not vintaged: grape varieties not revealed
CASAL MENDES, VINHO VERDE
Not vintaged: grape varieties not revealed

DANÚBIO BRUTO

Not vintaged, méthode champenoise: various white Bairrada grape varieties

MIRITA, VINHO VERDE

Not vintaged: grape varieties not revealed

★ TINTO BRUTO

Not vintaged, méthode champenoise: grape varieties not revealed

BAIRRADA BRUTO

Vintaged, méthode champenoise: Baga plus various white Bairrada grape varieties

BAIRRADA SUPER RESERVA BRUTO

Vintaged, méthode champenoise: Baga plus various white Bairrada grape varieties

N/A
CAVES IMPÉRIO
SANGALHOS
• 25,000 cases
Large family-owned producer of bottle-fermented sparkling wines since 1943.
WINEMAKER
António Pereira
HOUSE RANGE
PRINCIPE PERFEITO

Vintaged, méthode champenoise: Maria Gomes, Bical, Chardonnay

PRINCIPE REAL

Vintaged, méthode champenoise: Maria Gomes, Bical, Chardonnay

50
CAVES DA RAPOSEIRA
LAMEGO
• 200,000 cases
• Group ownership – part of Seagram
Sparkling wine specialist whose wines are appreciated on the domestic market as well as in Angola and throughout South America.
HOUSE STYLE & RANGE
Although they are above average for Portuguese fizz, they lack finesse.
MEIO SECO

Not vintaged, méthode champenoise: local varieties

SUPER RESERVA

Vintaged, méthode champenoise: Chardonnay, Pinot Blanc, Pinot Noir

SUPER RESERVA BRUTO

Vintaged, méthode champenoise: Chardonnay, Pinot Blanc, Pinot Noir

VELHA RESERVA,

Vintaged, méthode champenoise: Chardonnay, Pinot Blanc, Pinot Noir plus local varieties

75 VALUE
CAVES DE MONTANHA
ALIJÓ
Produced by Caves de Montanha for Caves Transmontanas in collaboration with Schramsberg of California.
HOUSE STYLE & RANGE
The first vintage, 1990, was not a very auspicious start, although it did get rave reviews in Portugal, but then most countries without any history of fine sparkling wines tend to go overboard about the first release of any collaboration with a foreign producer of any repute. I am glad to say that the 1994, however, is in a different class. Not a great sparkling wine, but an excellent one by Portuguese standards and at least the equal of Loridos Extra Bruto (JP Vinhos), although in a much lighter, more elegant style, with fluffy, creamy fruit.

★★ VÉRTICE

Vintaged: 50% Touriga Francesa, 15% Malvasia Fina, 12% Gouveio and 23% Códega

45
CAVES MESSIAS
MEALHADA
• 25,000 cases
This large Bairrada-based winery has been producing bottle-fermented sparkling wines since 1945.
WINEMAKER
António Dias Cardoso
HOUSE STYLE & RANGE
The best wines in the range have fruity aromas, but unfortunately all lack elegance and are bland.
MESSIAS, VINHO VERDE

Not vintaged, grape varieties not revealed

MESSIAS BAIRRADA ARINTO BRUT

Vintaged, méthode champenoise: Arinto

MESSIAS BAIRRADA BICAL BRUT

Vintaged, méthode champenoise:: Bical

MESSIAS BAIRRADA BLUE LABEL BRUTO

Vintaged, méthode champenoise: Bical

MESSIAS SANTOLA, VINHO VERDE

Not vintaged: grape varieties not revealed

55
CAVES MURGANHEIRA
OPORTO
This producer makes a large range of sparkling wines that get rave reviews in Portugal, but which most enthusiasts in the UK and New World countries would find mediocre. Having said that, I would like to taste one more Murganheira fizz, the Gewürztraminer Bruto, which was launched in 1997, if only out of curiosity.
HOUSE STYLE AND RANGE
Most of the wines in the range lack any real character, style or quality. The exceptions are the Rosé Bruto which has soft, gentle fruit, and the Tinto Bruto which has real red wine character while still retaining some finesse even in a dry sparkling wine format.

MURGANHEIRA CERCEAL BRUTO

Vintaged, méthode champemoise: Cerceal

MURGANHEIRA GRANDE RESERVA BRUTO

Vintaged, méthode champemoise: grape varieties not revealed

MURGANHEIRA RESERVA BRUTO

Vintaged, méthode champemoise: grape varieties not revealed

★ MURGANHEIRA ROSÉ BRUTO

Vintaged, méthode champemoise: grape varieties not revealed

MURGANHEIRA SUPER RESERVA BRUTO

Vintaged, méthode champemoise: Cerceal, Malvasia, Tinto Roriz, Touriga Nacional

BOTTLES OF
SPARKLING WINE
IN PUPITRES IN
THE CELLARS OF
CAVES
MURGANHEIRA IN
OPORTO

★ Murganheira Tinto Bruto
Vintaged, méthode champemoise: grape varieties not revealed

50
CAVES PRIMAVERA
ÁGUEDA

Best known for its red wines from Bairrada, Caves Primavera relies heavily on local grapes, particularly Baga, for its sparkling wine.

HOUSE STYLE & RANGE
The Chave D'Oiro shows a rare level of competence in the Portuguese sparkling wine industry; a cool-fermented, pears and apples concoction. But the other wines tend to be rather coarse or bitter.

Célebre Data Extra Bruto
Vintaged, méthode champemoise: Maria Gomes, Bical, Arinto

★ Chave D'Oiro Bruto
Vintaged, méthode champemoise: Baga, Maria Gomes, Bical, Arinto, Rabo de Ovelha

D. Duarte Bairrada Bruto
Vintaged, méthode champemoise: Baga, Bical and Maria Gomes

70
CAVES VELHAS
BUCELAS

Group ownership - owned by the state-controlled Sagres brewery.

Best known for Bucelas whites and *garrafeira* aged reds, Caves Velhas utilises the native Arinto grape of Bucelas for its venture into sparkling wine production. Interestingly it makes the sparkling wines in a *demi-sec* style, in total contrast to the austere dry Bucelas wines. Luis Pato is involved in the making of these wines.

HOUSE STYLE & RANGE
The 1995 is tiring, but the 1994 is delicious and fruity, with a liquorice intensity – a darn sight better than most Champagne *demi-sec.*

★ Arinto Meio Seco
Vintaged: Arinto

CEPA VELHA
See VINHOS DE MONÇÃO

CHELLO
See AZEVEDO

40
CONDES DE BARCELOS
BARCELOS

HOUSE STYLE & RANGE
Standard cooperative producing run-of-the-mill Vinho Verde.

Vinho Verde
Vintaged: Loureiro

50
CONVENTO DE ALPENDURADA
ALPENDURADA

A vineyard of south-facing slopes along the River Douro which has belonged to a convent since 1024.

HOUSE STYLE & RANGE
Traditionally vinified red.

Vinho Verde Tinto
Vintaged: grape varieties not revealed.

55
COOPERATIVA DE CASTELO DE PAIVA
CASTELO DE PAIVA

HOUSE STYLE & RANGE
A dry, dark red Vinho Verde which has fruit and body.

★ Vinho Verde Tinto
Vintaged: grape varieties not revealed.

70
COOPERATIVA DE MONÇÃO
MONÇÃO

HOUSE STYLE & RANGE
Award-winning Vinho Verde; mouthwateringly fresh and flavoursome.

★ Alvarinho, Vinho Verde
Vintaged: Alvarinho

45
DOM FERRAZ

A semi-dry, commercially-blended Vinho Verde with a fullish aroma, and typical minerally fruit.

75 VALUE
DOÑA PATERNA
MONÇÃO

HOUSE STYLE & RANGE
Deliciously refreshing with finesse and complexity. A serious contender for the best

Vinho Verde.

★★ Alvarinho, Vinho Verde
Vintaged: Alvarinho

70 VALUE
ENCOSTAS DE PADERNE
PADERNE

HOUSE STYLE & RANGE
Currently one of the most expressive Alvarinho Vinhos Verdes.

★ Alvarinho, Vinho Verde
Vintaged: Alvarinho

FITA AZUL
See BORGES & IRMÃO

FONSECA INTERNACIONAL
AZEITÃO

- 100,000 cases
- Group ownership - joint owned by IDV, the UK drinks giant.

Producer of white and rosé fizz by continuous Russian method, sold under the Lancers label, primarily to the US.

GAMBA
See BORGES & IRMÃO

GATÃO
See BORGES & IRMÃO

GAZELA
See AZEVEDO

GRINALDA
See QUINTA DA AVELEDA

75 VALUE
JP VINHOS
PONTE DE LIMA

One of Portugal's best wine producers. Well-equipped, with plenty of expertise, and

AMAZINGLY PALATIAL CELLARS AT JP VINHOS, ONE OF PORTUGAL'S BEST WINE PRODUCERS

making the only international class sparkling wine in the country.

HOUSE STYLE & RANGE
Creamy, complex aromas with clean, fresh or rich, toasty fruit. Well ahead of the competition.

★✫ LORIDOS BRUTO
Vintaged, méthode champemoise: Periquita and Fernão Pires

★★ LORIDOS EXTRA BRUTO
Vintaged, méthode champemoise: Chardonnay

✫ PAÇO DO CARDIDO, VINHO VERDE
Vintaged: Loureiro

LAGOSTA
See REAL VINICOLA

50
MEIRELES
A decent commercially-blended Vinho Verde made in a simple, but refreshing style.

55
MONTEFARO
QUINTA DE SEARA, ESPOSENDE
HOUSE STYLE & RANGE
Delicately aromatic.
VINHO VERDE
Vintaged: grape varieties not revealed

MURGANHEIRA
See CAVES MURGANHEIRA

50
PAÇO D'ANHA
ANHA, VIANA DO CASTELO
HOUSE STYLE & RANGE
Fresh, dry and fruity.
VINHO VERDE
Vintaged: predominantly Loureiro and Trajadura

N/A
PAÇO DE TEIXEIRO
TEIXEIRÓ, MESÃO FRIO
Set in the foothills of Serra do Marão, bordering the Minho and Douro regions, this single-quinta Vinho Verde has belonged to the innovative Champalimaud family (of Quinta do Côtto fame) since the 13th century.
HOUSE STYLE & RANGE
This is a distinctive and fragrant dry wine, but it can be inconsistent.
VINHO VERDE
Vintaged: Avesso

80
PALACIO DA BREJOEIRA
PINHEIROS, MONÇÃO
Housed in the vast neo-classical Palácio da Brejoeira on the Spanish border, this producer is famous for Portugal's finest and most prestigious Vinho Verde.
HOUSE STYLE & RANGE
A wine with finesse, a term not easily applied to any Vinho Verde, with a delicately tangy acidity and great length. It is a deliciously dry white wine which, most remarkable of all, has a capacity to remain fresh and vital for up to four years.
★★ VINHO VERDE
Vintaged: Alvarinho

65
LUIS PATO
AMOREIRA DA GÂNDARA
HOUSE STYLE & RANGE
The Bairrada has very good mouthfill and structure while the straight Luis Pato has delicate aromas but lacks some finesse on the palate.
✫ LUIS PATO
Vintaged, méthode champemoise: Baga
★ LUIS PATO BAIRRADA BRUTO
Vintaged, méthode champemoise: Baga

50
PONTE DE LIMA
PONTE DE LIMA
HOUSE STYLE & RANGE
Nothing special at this technically proficient winery, except the Tinto which is one of the few red Vinhos Verdes that non-Portuguese palates appreciate. Fresh fruit offsets the dry and slightly tannic flavour.
LOUREIRO, VINHO VERDE
Vintaged: Loureiro
★ VINHO VERDE TINTO
Vintaged: grape varieties not revealed
QUINTA DO AMEAL, VINHO VERDE
Not vintaged: grape varieties not revealed

PORTAL DO FIDALGO
See PROVAM

50
PROVAM
BARCELOS
HOUSE STYLE & RANGE
A solid producer making sparkling wines of good commercial quality.
VERANDA DO CONDE, VINHO VERDE
Vintaged: Alvarinho and Trajadura
PORTAL DO FIDALGO, ALVARINHO
Vintaged: Alvarinho

70 VALUE
QUINTA D'ALÉM
ALÉM

HOUSE STYLE & RANGE
Rich, creamy, almost New World style.
★ VINHO VERDE
Vintaged: grape varieties not revealed

60
QUINTA DA AVELEDA
PENAFIEL
An elaborate property owned by part of the Guedes family (the other half being the owners of Sogrape).
HOUSE STYLE & RANGE
Mostly bulk-blended and souped-up for export, but top wines have a fragrant nose with crisp, delicately rich fruit.
AVELEDA, VINHO VERDE
Not vintaged: grape varieties not revealed
✫ CASAL GARCIA, VINHO VERDE
Not vintaged: grape varieties not revealed
★ GRINALDA, VINHO VERDE
Vintaged: Loureiro and Trajadura
LOUREIRO DA AVELEDA, VINHO VERDE
Vintaged: Loureiro
★ QUINTA DA AVELEDA, VINHO VERDE
Vintaged: grape varieties not revealed

45
QUINTA DA FRANQUEIRA
BARCELOS
HOUSE STYLE & RANGE
Standard stuff, not special.
VINHO VERDE
Vintaged: grape varieties not revealed

65
QUINTA DA LIVRAÇÃO
LIVRAÇÃO, MARCOS DE CANAVESES
Vineyard situated on the River Tâmega slopes.
HOUSE STYLE & RANGE
Light and fragrant, with a delicate character that remains fresh for up to two years in bottle.
★ VINHO VERDE
Vintaged: grape varieties not revealed

55
QUINTA DA PORTELA
CARREIRA
Grapes here grow on southwest facing slopes
HOUSE STYLE & RANGE
Typically crisp and minerally, fairly decent Vinho Verde.
✫ VINHO VERDE
Not vintaged: grape varieties not revealed

50
QUINTA DA QUINTÃO
SÃO TOME DE NEGRELOS, SANTO TIRSO
HOUSE STYLE & RANGE
Dry and aromatic.
VINHO VERDE
Not vintaged: predominantly Loureiro

N/A
QUINTA DAS BAGEIRAS
FOGUEIRA, SANGALHOS
HOUSE STYLE & RANGE
Inconsistent quality from year to year.
BAIRRADA BRUTO GRANDE RESERVA
Vintaged, méthode champemoise: grape varieties not revealed.
BAIRRADA BRUTO SUPER RESERVA
Vintaged, méthode champemoise: Maria Gomes, Bical, Rabo de Ovelha and Cerceal
BAIRRADA ROSÉ BRUTO SUPER RESERVA
Vintaged, méthode champemoise: Baga

QUINTA DE AZEVEDO
See AZEVEDO

50
QUINTA DE CURVOS
ESPOSENDE
HOUSE STYLE & RANGE
Typically minerally.
VINHO VERDE
Vintaged: grape varieties not revealed

55
QUINTA DE SANTO CLAUDIO
ESPOSENDE
Terraced south-facing vineyard.
HOUSE STYLE & RANGE
Fuller, riper style
★ VINHO VERDE
Vintaged: Loureiro

65
QUINTA DO CRASTO
TRAVANCA, CINFÃES
Grown on the slopes of the River Paiva.
HOUSE STYLE & RANGE
Traditionally produced with a delicate and aromatic character.
★ VINHO VERDE
Vintaged: Pederna, Azal and Avesso

50
QUINTA DO MIOGO
GUIMARAES
HOUSE STYLE & RANGE
Light with a delicate aroma.
VINHO VERDE
Vintaged: Loureiro

N/A
QUINTA DO OUTEIRO DE BAIXO
AMARANTE
HOUSE STYLE & RANGE
Fine, fruity whites and typically aggressive reds.
★ VINHO VERDE
Vintaged: Azal and Pederna
VINHO VERDE TINTO
Vintaged: Espadeiro

N/A
QUINTA DOS ROQUES
Respected producer of Dão appellation fully sparkling wine. Not tasted.

60
QUINTA DO TAMARIZ
CARREIRA, BARCELOS
An estate-bottled Vinho Verde since 1939. Vines are low-trained on south facing slopes.
HOUSE STYLE & RANGE
Fine, fresh, well-balanced wines.
★ VINHO VERDE
Vintaged: Loureiro

45
REAL VINICOLA
Large Port producer which makes one of the better-known Vinhos Verdes on export markets.
HOUSE STYLE & RANGE
Souped-up, commercially-blended wines with a gassy *pétillance*.
LAGOSTA, VINHO VERDE
Not vintaged: grape varieties not revealed

SANTOLA
See CAVES MESSIAS

55
SOALHEIRO
MELGAÇO
HOUSE STYLE & RANGE
Fuller, more ripe and satisfying style than most Vinhos Verdes; fruity and accessible.
★ ALVARINHO, VINHO VERDE
Vintaged: Alvarinho

65
SOLAR DAS BOUÇAS
PROZELO, AMARES
HOUSE STYLE & RANGE
Characteristically light aroma, correctly crisp flavour, a very slight *pétillance* and a perfumed aftertaste reminiscent of orange-flower water.

SPARKLING WINE PRODUCTION USING THE RUSSIAN CONTINUOUS METHOD AT JM FONSECA

★ VINHO VERDE
Vintaged: Loureiro

50
SOLAR DE RIBEIRO
SANTO LOURENÇO DO DOURO
HOUSE STYLE & RANGE
Medium-dry with a fuller flavour than most.
VINHO VERDE
Not vintaged: grape varieties not revealed

TIA CHIA
See CASA DE SEZIM

45
TRES MARIAS
A sweetish commercially-blended Vinho Verde.

60
QUINTA DE TORMES
VILA NOVA DE GAIA
HOUSE STYLE & RANGE
Refreshing with a full aroma and a fragrant, deliciously dry and tangy flavour.
★ VINHO VERDE
Vintaged: Avesso

VERANDA DO CONDE
See PROVAM

VERTICE
See CAVES DE MONTANHA

60
VINHOS BORGES
FELGUEIRAS
HOUSE STYLE & RANGE
The Simaens is distinctively crisp and fruity, the Vilancette lean and minerally.
QUINTA DE SIMAENS, VINHO VERDE
Vintaged: Padernã
VILANCETE
Vintaged: grape varieties not revealed

60
VINHOS DE MONÇÃO
MONÇÃO
The wines are produced from Alvarinho grapes grown at Monção on the Spanish border.
HOUSE STYLE & RANGE
Commercially blended but slightly richer and firmer than most with a stronger, almost fat fruit flavour that retains its freshness for up to two years in bottle.
ALVARINHO DE MONÇÃO
Not vintaged: Alvarinho

SPAIN

IN 1340 FRANCESCO EIXIMENIS WROTE OF 'FORMIGALEJANTS' OR 'TINGLING' WINES, YET ANOTHER EXAMPLE OF ACCIDENTAL FIZZ, ALBEIT BARELY *PÉTILLANT* FROM THE SOUND OF IT. BUT THE DELIBERATE PRODUCTION OF SPARKLING WINE DID NOT OCCUR IN SPAIN UNTIL THE SECOND HALF OF THE 19TH CENTURY.

Until recently it was assumed that the very first Spanish sparkling wine was produced in 1872 by Josep Raventós, the head of Codorníu, but research by Antonio Ribas now suggests that it was 'invented' by Luis Justo Vilanueva and produced in 1862 by Antoni Gili. Whoever was first, there was no Spanish sparkling wine industry to speak of until after the Second World War.

It was not until 1974 that exports were significant enough to be officially recorded, and it probably is not coincidental that this closely followed Spain's agreement in 1970 to drop the name Champagne, or *Champaña,* in favour of a newly created appellation called *Cava.* When any wine industry abandons the practice of selling its products on the back of an historically famous name, it usually finds much greater success. When a wine industry stands on its own feet, not only does it gain self-respect, but its local customers find a new pride, and the result is an increase in both sales and quality.

Such was the growth in the production of Spanish sparkling wines that by the 1980s Cava had become the second-largest bottle-fermented appellation in the world. The word *Cava* simply means 'cellar' and when it was devised in 1970, it could be used by any Spanish sparkling wine made by the *méthode champenoise.* After Spain joined the Common Market in 1986, it became subject to the EC wine regime, which is based on the integrity of origin. Because Cava had no delimited area of production, the appellation could not continue in its existing format.

Then, as now, most Cava came from Catalonia, and most of that from Sant Sadurní d'Anoia in the Penedès region, but there were also tiny quantities of Cava produced by a number of wineries spread across the country. This presented the Spanish authorities with a problem because they had been charged with establishing a geographical area of production for Cava. They were also still smarting from being double-crossed by the EC over the protection of their sherry appellation and, ironically, this simplified the solution.

With a 3,000 year pedigree, sherry is probably the oldest wine appellation in the world and the Spanish were promised it would enjoy the full protection of the EC if they joined. They were also told that so-called 'sherry' produced by other member states would be banned. However, they were shamefully misled, I am bound to say, by Britain and Ireland. These two countries had lucrative industries where fortified wines made from imported grape concentrate were sold as British and Irish

VINEYARDS PLANTED MAINLY WITH CHARDONNAY AND PINOT NOIR, ARE LEASED TO CODORNÍU, NEAR POBLET, CATALONIA, SPAIN.

Sherry. They therefore used their combined veto to block the Community's attempt to prohibit these products.

Authentic sherry was eventually protected in 1996, exactly ten years later, but at the time the Spanish were annoyed that EU bureaucrats cared more about the letter of the law than its spirit. Was it coincidence then that they did exactly the same? Cava fell short of the EU's ethos which stated that all appellations must be geographically based. If a geographically based appellation was what the EU wanted, that was what the Spanish authorities would give them. Observing the letter of the law, they simply drew boundaries around the municipalities in which all the Cava producers were located. So, although 98% of Cava came from Catalonia, its officially delimited area of production covers 160 municipalities in 11 provinces spread across one-third of Spain.

CAVA'S SPANISH ROOTS

Production is dominated by two firms, Codorníu and Freixenet. The latter has always been violently opposed to the invasion of Cava by foreign grape varieties, although it might be cynical to wonder whether this position has been influenced by the fact that Codorníu was the first and most successful proponent of Chardonnay (initially with Raimat, after which it was used in the primary Codorníu brand). However, Freixenet's argument is certainly valid – that foreign grape varieties could erode Cava's Spanish character.

Cava is, after all, the only dry sparkling wine appellation of any repute outside of France and, of course, Spain has its own indigenous grape varieties, while California, Australia, New Zealand *et al*, which have no sparkling wine appellations, do not. While it might seem obvious for New World producers to try the Champagne varieties first, Cava producers have a certain heritage to defend.

The problem is that more than three-quarters of Cavas are boring or worse. Readers should not think that I am unfairly picking on the Spanish, elsewhere in this book I state that two-thirds of French sparkling wines are undrinkable, and that is a heinous crime because the climate and soil in regions like Burgundy and the Loire are far better suited to sparkling wine production than anywhere in Spain. These statements are my personal opinion, but the figures are not

plucked out of thin air, they are statistics derived from tasting thousands of such wines over a number of years.

The reason why so many Cava wines are generally boring is not so much the climate or soil (much less appropriate areas in the New World have, with skill, started to produce excellent sparkling wines) as three so-called traditional varieties Macabéo, Xarel-lo and Parellada. According to Cava gospel, Macabéo, which is usually, but not exclusively, the base of a Cava, provides the fruit; Xarel-lo the strength and body; and Parellada softness and aroma. In reality, Macabéo is not bad as a base wine; it does usually have good fruit and decent acidity. Xarel-lo is quite useful in small amounts for adjusting the structure of a Macabéo-based wine.

There are some good Cavas made predominantly with Parellada but on the whole it can't be considered as a good grape to use for fine quality sparkling wines. The average Parellada makes such a neutral base wine that it is virtually tasteless and has so little acidity that it turns litmus paper blue. The best Parellada comes from the highest vineyards, where the grapes take longer to ripen, but almost all Parellada is grown on high ground, yet most of the fruit is unsuitable for high quality sparkling wine. You would have to grow it on top of Montserrat to get sufficient acidity, and even then it is prone to rot, which is not exactly a bonus for the last Cava variety to be harvested. Furthermore, this rot can slip through the strictest physical examination at the winery reception area. Physically checking every bunch is a thing of the past, but even if it were not, the Parellada is so tight-packed that huge bunches can appear beautiful and healthy, when in fact they are rotten inside.

So why is Cava made from these varieties? Ask any Cava firm and the reply will be because Cava has always been made from Macabéo, Xarel-lo and Parellada, just as Champagne has always been made from Chardonnay, Pinot Noir and Meunier. However, Champagne was once planted with numerous varieties and it took three centuries of trial and error to decide which of these are the most appropriate. For example, it was only in 1927 that it was decided to uproot the Gamay which grew throughout the region, particularly the Aube. It is still theoretically possible to use Gamay in Champagne today and, at the last count, there were still 20 hectares, including a few on the illustrious Côte des Blancs.

If Champagne's three classic varieties are not exclusive to the region after 300 years, how can Cava producers be so sure that Macabéo, Xarel-lo and Parellada are even adequate, let alone the best varieties, for sparkling wine in their area?

The first sparkling Spanish wines were produced barely more than 100 years ago, and for the first 75 years there were just two producers of any relevance. The first fizz was made from grapes that just happened to be growing in the vicinity and obviously these were not planted specifically for sparkling wine. The first Cava regulations enshrined the tradition (established by two firms) and over the last 25 years, a large number of Cava firms have cropped up, and it seems as if they just fell into the habit of thinking that these varieties were indeed classic for Cava. This illustrates how premature

CAVA CORKS

it is for Cava's three so-called varieties to assume traditional, let alone classic, status.

As inadequate as Cava's holy trinity of grapes appears to be, some producers make decent fizz from them, and there is ample room to improve the quality of these wines without having to rely on other varieties. It will require the development of numerous new clones for each variety, so that growers can make appropriate selections for their own specific sites, and a lot of work still needs to be done on site selection, how each variety should be trained according to its location, and the effects of the controlling of yields. There is no doubt that the vineyard is the most important area for future development, but there is also still much more

CHARDONNAY

Although good quality Chardonnay undoubtedly adds a desperately needed plumpness to a Cava made from traditional varieties, by no means all the Chardonnay used by the industry is good. In fact, the situation is similar to Alsace and Saumur, where the vast majority of Chardonnay planted produces very poor wines indeed. One appeasement to the traditionalists would be to restrict the cultivation of this variety to specified clones in certain proven areas.

that could be achieved in the winery.

Furthermore, if the EU-constrained Cava producers could operate under a more flexible regime, it would be a fairer fight. If they could irrigate (admittedly some irrigation has recently been permitted during drought conditions, but this is strictly limited) and add acid, it would allow the grapes to be harvested riper, and the resulting wines have better fruit and balance. Too many Cavas are so soft that they have to have an extremely light *dosage*, they age far too rapidly and fail to develop any true finesse or complexity.

A lot of Cava drinkers claim that this softness is Cava's prime virtue. If that is what people want, it should not be taken away from them, and I do not advocate that Cava firms should stop making such wines. I do believe, however, that these companies could make much better wines that huge numbers of other consumers would appreciate, so why not broaden the range?

THE SEARCH FOR DIFFERENT GRAPE VARIETIES

As a major force in Cava and the leading traditionalist, Freixenet was woefully lax. It did nothing to prevent the introduction of Chardonnay, but after it had been established, the management of this giant group merely bleated its dissatisfaction, doing nothing constructive to validate its position for a decade or more. At a Cava shipper's dinner in 1991, when the company's chairman Manuel Duran admitted that the jury was still out on whether the three traditional varieties are ideally suited for sparkling wine, he was challenged not simply to find an indigenous substitute for Chardonnay, but to try to experiment with black Spanish varieties.

Cava's traditionalists have, for some bizarre reason, always considered black grapes in a white Cava to be sacrilegious, yet Duran picked up the gauntlet. The first variety Freixenet experimented with was Monastrell, which is authorised for rosé Cava and is perfectly legal for white, but being a black grape, no one had tried it. Although the first Cava produced using Monastrell was flabby, lacking in acidity and generally not a great success, this was due to insufficient expertise in using black grapes for white wines and Freixenet is gradually improving the product.

Garnacha (Grenache) is another grape permitted for rosé Cava, and Trepat was at one time the only non-Cava Spanish variety that was officially under trial for Cava (again for rosé). Mont Marçal has used Tempranillo while Can Ràfols dels Caus has even tried Merlot, both, of course, for pink Cava. Freixenet has been strangely mute about the use of these varieties, and other foreign interlopers such as Chenin Blanc, even though they are technically illegal.

Prior to Freixenet's Monastrell project, Codorníu was the only house to try black grapes in white Cava and succeeded beyond its wildest dreams, producing one of the most sumptuous Spanish sparkling wines ever. At the right price, it would knock the living

daylights out of all but the very best premium sparklers from the New World. However, while Pinot Noir remains experimental, the public will be denied such fantastic advances in the quality of Cava.

The future is black, and I mean that in the most positive sense. Whether it is Monastrell, Garnacha, Trepat, Tempranillo or some other Spanish grape, Cava wines will one day benefit from the use of indigenous black varieties and when that happens, Codorníu will, I am sure, use them. The company would be stupid not to. Then and only then will the traditionalists have any grounds for criticising Codorníu or any of its competitors for using foreign grape varieties.

CAVA'S FUTURE

Using foreign or traditional grapes is just one of several questions Cava producers have been posed for at least five years, and the industry really needs to make a decision if it is to move forward. That, however, means Freixenet and Codorníu will have to agree on a common strategy, and this seems less possible as each year goes by. The pity is that when the petty bickering between these two giants is brushed away, both obviously want the Cava appellation to succeed. They have opposite viewpoints, but both are valid and this could be to Cava's strength if they agreed to differ on each other's positions and cooperated for the sake of their appellation.

The two most important questions that the Cava industry must tackle are: [1] should Cava producers be complacent with their present level of quality or happy with the rate and direction of current efforts to improve it, and [2] should Cava stay as it is or should it compete with the New World in the rapidly expanding premium sector of the sparkling wine market?

I have already explained how I think Cava wines could be improved, whether using so-called traditional varieties, other Spanish grapes or foreign interlopers. The decision whether to compete with the New World is, I think, just as important because although Cava is the second-largest *méthode champenoise* appellation in the world, its sales on international markets will inevitably be eroded by the New World's more user-friendly fizz.

In the last few years some Cava houses have made noises about entering into the premium sparkling wine sector that has been so successfully established by New World producers, but it has been idle talk. The most that Cava houses have done is tried to position certain *cuvées* within this sector by adjusting price-points and repackaging the products. They have yet to learn that it is not simply a matter of price and packaging; consumers drink New World wines because of the style and consistency of quality that can be found at good value prices. The only way that Cava can penetrate this market is to develop a more upfront, fruit-driven style specifically for export markets where New World products are strong. Not to replace any existing *cuvées*, but to add to the range of Cavas currently offered.

PERFORMING REMUAGE ON BOTTLES OF CAVA IN THE CELLARS OF RAVENTOS I BLANC AT SANT SADURNÍ D'ANOIA, CATALONIA

N/A
VINOS DEL BIERZO
CACABELOS, LEÓN
• Other labels – Don Perejón

I am surprised that Moët has not sued this cooperative for mocking their sacred monk with this cheeky brand!

HOUSE STYLE & RANGE
Tasted recently for the first time, the brut and *semi seco* were not experiences I would like to repeat, but the Mencía Rosé, although merely decent fizz, has more accessible fruit than a lot of Cava, thus is more enjoyable to drink.

DON PEREJÓN BRUT
  Not vintaged, méthode champenoise: 100% Doña Blanca

DON PEREJÓN SEMI SECO
  Not vintaged, méthode champenoise: 100% Doña Blanca

DON PEREJÓN BRUT MENCÍA ROSÉ
  Not vintaged, méthode champenoise: 100% Mencía

80 VALUE
CAN FEIXES
CABRERA D'ANOIA, PENEDÈS
• Other labels – Huguet

A small, family-owned Cava firm that is well endowed with its own vineyards, Huguet is 100% estate-bottled and ranks among the best Cavas available.

HOUSE STYLE & RANGE
The Brut Nature is very tight and young, but develops well in bottle, whereas the fruit is so lush in the Brut Classic that there is no reason to age it.

★★ HUGUET CAVA GRAN RESERVA BRUT NATURE
  Vintaged, méthode champenoise: 14% Chardonnay, 24% Macabéo, 62% Parellada

★★ HUGUET CAVA GRAN RESERVA BRUT CLASSIC
  Vintaged, méthode champenoise: 14% Chardonnay, 24% Macabéo, 62% Parellada

45
CAN RÀFOLS DELS CAUS
AVINYONET DEL PENEDÈS, P ENEDÈS
• Other labels – Gran Caus

Although an excellent small estate for its Cabernet Sauvignon-Merlot red wine called Gran Caus, the Cavas of Can Ràfols dels Caus will fail to impress most sparkling wine drinkers outside Spain. It should be noted, though, that the wines are highly regarded on the home market.

HOUSE STYLE & RANGE
The Brut Nature is coarse and peppery, while the Extra Brut Reserva is not nice at all.

GRAN CAUS CAVA BRUT NATURE
  Vintaged, méthode champenoise: primarily Xarel-lo, plus Chardonnay, Chenin Blanc, Macabéo, Muscat

GRAN CAUS CAVA EXTRA BRUT RESERVA
  Vintaged, méthode champenoise: primarily Xarel-lo, plus Chardonnay, Chenin Blanc, Macabéo, Muscat

GRAN CAUS CAVA ROSADO
  Vintaged, méthode champenoise: primarily Xarel-lo, plus Chenin Blanc, Merlot, Muscat

70
CASTELLBLANCH
SANT SADURNÍ D'ANOIA, PENEDÈS
• Group ownership - Freixenet

Castellblanch produces a consistently above average quality of Cava.

HOUSE STYLE & RANGE
Cava Brut Zero is fresh and floral when first released, with good acidity and structure for a Cava, but it quickly gains a terpene character. The *rosado* has a fresh, easy-drinking style, but that puts it in Cava's elite, whereas the Dos Lustros swings between floral aromas with an incongruous, foursquare richness on the palate, to thin and characterless. I have tasted the Brut Maritim only once, in early 1997, when it had a lovely autolytic nose of fresh acacia, but the palate was dull, with a pervading hay-like character that suggested deterioration. The Cristal Seco is soft and clean with plenty of fresh, sweetish fruit.

★ CAVA BRUT ZERO
  Vintaged, méthode champenoise: 30% Macabéo, 10% Parellada, 60% Xarel-lo

★ CAVA BRUT MARITIM
  Vintaged, méthode champenoise: Macabéo, Parellada, Xarel-lo

★ CAVA ROSADO BRUT
  Vintaged, méthode champenoise: 60% Garnacha, 40% Monastrell

★ CRISTAL CAVA SECO
  Vintaged, méthode champenoise: 30% Macabéo, 30% Parellada, 40% Xarel-lo

DOS LUSTROS CAVA BRUT NATURE
  Vintaged, méthode champenoise: 40% Macabéo, 40% Parellada, 20% Xarel-lo

N/A
CASTELL DE VILARNAU
SANT SADURNÍ D'ANOIA, PENEDÈS
• Group ownership – González Byass

This small Cava firm was established in 1982 and is doing well on export markets.

HOUSE STYLE & RANGE
Not as consistent as it should be, but the Vintage Brut is capable of producing a richer, more complex Cava when on form (as in 1988 and 1993), but is not consistent. The deep-coloured Brut Rosado usually has strawberry aromas and bags of fruit, although a recent sample was too dry for regular *rosado* punters, and the wine lacked the sort of finesse that more serious drinkers look for. The fruit in the Demi-Sec is terribly green, as if they have harvested the grapes far earlier than normal to achieve enough acidity to balance the sugar; they might as well use lemon juice.

CAVA BRUT DE BRUT
  Vintaged, méthode champenoise: 60% Macabéo, 40% Parellada

★ CAVA BRUT ROSADO
  Vintaged, méthode champenoise: 50% Garnacha, 50% Monastrell

CAVA DEMI-SEC
  Vintaged, méthode champenoise: 60% Macabéo, 40% Parellada

VINTAGE CAVA BRUT
  Vintaged, méthode champenoise: 60% Macabéo, 35% Parellada, 5% Xarel-lo

70
CAVA CHANDON
SANT CUGAT DE SESGARRIGUES, PENEDÈS
• 350,000 cases
• Other labels – Torre del Gall
• Group ownership - LVMH

Established in 1987, Cava Chandon has been content to use part of the *grande marque* name on the fizz it sells in Spain, but like other outposts of Moët & Chandon's sparkling wine empire, the owners have qualms about doing this on an international basis. Each Chandon winery has therefore had to re-invent itself for export markets, and in this case they plumped for Torre del Gall (literally 'Tower of the Rooster'), the original 17th-century name of the farm where Cava Chandon now stands.

WINEMAKER
Manuel Via, Georges Blanck

HOUSE STYLE & RANGE
These wines were initially as dull as bulk-blended Sekt, but started to become interesting with *cuvées* made from 1992 onwards. They are clean and fresh, with good acidity for Cava, although best drunk young. The wines are exactly the same under both Cava Chandon and Torre del Gall labels, although some wines, particularly the Brut Nature, will be older on the Spanish market.

★ CAVA BRUT NATURE
  Not vintaged, méthode champenoise: Chardonnay, Macabéo, Parellada, Xarel-lo

★ CAVA BRUT RESERVA
  Not vintaged, méthode champenoise: Macabéo, Parellada, Xarel-lo

CAVA BRUT GRAN RESERVA
  Vintaged, méthode champenoise: Chardonnay, Macabéo, Parellada, Xarel-lo

CAVA CUVÉE RICHE
  Not vintaged, méthode champenoise: Macabéo, Parellada, Xarel-lo

75 VALUE
CIGRAVI
SANTA FÉ DEL PENEDÈS, PENEDÈS

- Other labels - Masía Parera, Bell Duc, Giró Ribot
- Group ownership - jointly owned by Rémy-Cointreau and the Giró Ribot family

Although CIGRAVI (Companía Internacional de Grandes Vinos) is jointly owned, the Paul Cheneau brand is 100% owned by Rémy-Cointreau, whereas Giró Ribot is, of course, 100% owned by the Giró Ribot family.

HOUSE STYLE & RANGE

Paul Cheneau was produced by Freixenet until 1992, when it was switched to CIGRAVI, although quite how the lush, elegant, fruity style was miraculously transplanted at the same time is anybody's guess. The Bel Duc is impressively sweet, toasty and fat and with plenty of sassy fruit. The most outstanding quality of the 1995 Masía Parera is that it has no Chardonnay, yet tastes as if it does, which is a refreshing change from all the so-called Chardonnay Cavas that do not. It has the creamy mouth-feel that Chardonnay is supposed to supply, and is a huge improvement on the sweet, boring, almondy 1994 vintage.

★ BELL DUC CAVA BRUT
   Vintaged, méthode champenoise: grape varieties not revealed

GIRÓ RIBOT CAVA BRUT
   Vintaged, méthode champenoise: 50% Macabéo, 20% Parellada, 30% Xarel-lo

★ MASIA PARERA CAVA BRUT
   Vintaged, méthode champenoise: 47% Macabéo, 20% Parellada, 33% Xarel-lo

★ PAUL CHENEAU CAVA BRUT
   Vintaged, méthode champenoise: 33% Macabéo, 20% Parellada, 47% Xarel-lo

73
COVIDES
SANT SADURNÍ D'ANOIA, PENEDÈS

- Other labels - Duc de Foix

A large cooperative formed in 1964, COVIDES (Cooperativa Vinícola del Penedès) consists of 800 members and three wineries. The other wineries are in Sant Cugat and Marti Sarroca.

HOUSE STYLE & RANGE

The Duc de Foix Brut is fatter and more elegant than most Cavas, with more fruit and better acidity, resulting in a more satisfying mouthfill. The Xenius Brut is a light-bodied *cuvée* that shows some elegance and ripeness, but essentially for those Cava drinkers who prefer a sweeter-styled brut.

★✮ DUC DE FOIX CAVA BRUT
   Not vintaged, méthode champenoise: 25% Macabéo, 25% Parellada, 50% Xarel-lo

✮ XENIUS NV CAVA BRUT
   Not vintaged, méthode champenoise: 30% Macabéo, 30% Parellada, 40% Xarel-lo

N/A
BODEGAS ESCUDERO
GRÀVALOS, RIOJA

Established in 1852, this is one of a number of Rioja firms who try their hand at fizz in what is demonstrably red wine country.

HOUSE STYLE & RANGE

Tasted recently for the first time, I was not impressed by the coarse fruit and clumsy balance in these wines.

BENITO ESCUDERO ABAD CAVA SEMI SECO
   Not vintaged, méthode champenoise: 100% Viura

BENITO ESCUDERO ABAD CAVA BRUT
   Not vintaged, méthode champenoise: 100% Viura

DIORO BACO CAVA EXTRA BRUT
   Vintaged, méthode champenoise: 100% Chardonnay

70
FAUSTINO MARTÍNEZ
OYÓN, RIOJA

Established in 1860, this is another Rioja winery producing Cava, but Faustino Martínez is more famous, and while I much prefer this firm's *reserva* and *gran reserva* red wines, its fizz is far better than most from this region.

HOUSE STYLE & RANGE

Fresh and simple with a tropical fruit flavour.

✮ CAVA EXTRA SECO
   Not vintaged, méthode champenoise: 100% Viura

N/A
JOSÉ FERRET MATEU
ELS MONJOS DEL PENEDÈS, PENEDÈS

Small producer whose wines attract a premium in Spain.

HOUSE STYLE & RANGE

Tasted recently for the first time, but not impressed by the oxidative style.

CAVA NARIA MATEU
   Vintaged, méthode champenoise: 40% Chardonnay, 60% Macabéo

73
FREIXENET
SANT SADURNÍ D'ANOIA, PENEDÈS

- 7 million cases (group total)
- Other labels - Castellblanch, Segura Viudas, Conde de Caralt, Canals Nubiola (*see individual entries*)

- Group ownership - Freixenet also owns sparkling wine operations in California and Mexico, plus the Champagne house of Henri Abelé

One of the two giants of Cava, the combined production of Freixenet's various brands vies with that of Codorníu. This company was founded in 1889 by Don Pedro Ferrer, who was born at the Freixeneda estate in Mediona, Alt Penedès. After marrying Doña Dolores Sala, from another traditional winegrowing family, Ferrer established Freixenet.

Over the last 20 years or so, the company has grown like Topsy, taking over other Cava firms, investing in California, Mexico and even Champagne. Freixenet is famous for its black bottle Cava, Cordon Negro, and is leader of the traditionalists in the industry, who do not want to see their appellation usurped by the Chardonnay buzz-word.

WINEMAKER

Josep Bujam

HOUSE STYLE & RANGE

The Cordon Negro in its famous black bottle is amylic and bland, although some *cuvées* of the vintaged version of Cordon Negro, called Brut Nature, can be extremely good in some years (the 1991 was the best since 1975, but the 1994 was one of the worst). Although Brut Nature would seem to infer no *dosage*, it is technically Brut Extra, which can range from zero to 6g/l of residual sugar, and Freixenet takes it to the very limit, just one gram below its standard 7/g/l Brut *dosage*.

The Monastrell-Xarel-lo is a ground-breaking *cuvée*: the first commercially-available white Cava to include black grapes in the blend, and the first white *cuvée* to include a Spanish variety other than Parellada, Macabéo and Xarel-lo. However, it still has a way to go. Although improving with each release, it is still far too soft. The Cuvée DS was named in honour of the late Doña Dolores Sala, widow of the founder. It is a Gran Reserva that is made in an old-fashioned style, with terpene-like characters. Its appeal beyond Cava groupies must be very limited.

CAVAS FREIXENET WINERY AT SANT SADURNÍ D'ANOIA, CATALONIA

Monastrell-Xarel-lo Cava Brut
Not vintaged, méthode champenoise: 50%
Monastrell, 50% Xarel-lo

★ Carta Nevada Brut Nature
Vintaged, méthode champenoise: 40% Macabéo,
30% Parellada, 30% Xarel-lo

★ Cava Brut Nature
Vintaged, méthode champenoise: 40% Macabéo,
30% Parellada, 30% Xarel-lo

Cordon Negro Brut
Vintaged, méthode champenoise: 35% Macabéo,
40% Parellada, 25% Xarel-lo

Cuvée DS Cava Brut
Vintaged, méthode champenoise: 40% Macabéo,
20% Parellada, 40% Xarel-lo

★ Rosado Cava Brut
Vintaged, méthode champenoise: 50% Garnacha,
50% Monastrell

75 VALUE
GRAMONA
SANT SADURNÍ D'ANOIA, PENEDÈS
This small family-owned firm has its own
vineyards, and regularly produces some of
the best Cavas.
HOUSE STYLE & RANGE
Good news: two wines that have
extraordinary finesse for Cavas are Cellar
Battle, which has lovely lemony, toasty fruit
and III Lustros, with its creamy, peachy,
vanilla fruit packed on the palate and sweet
vanilla finish. Bad news: they are expensive
– up there with expensive Champagne.
More bad news: they do not benefit from
extra ageing, quickly picking up terpene
aromas, which severely depletes their finesse.
The other *cuvées* command merely highish-
normal Cava prices. The Brut Imperial and
Vintage Gran Reserva are decent, tangy
sparklers, but not special, while the Gran
Reserva Dulce is a toffee-laden fizz that
picks up terpenes if kept a short while.

Cava Brut Imperial
Vintaged, méthode champenoise: Chardonnay,
Macabéo, Parellada, Xarel-lo

★★ Cellar Battle Cava Brut
Vintaged, méthode champenoise: Macabéo, Xarel-lo

Gran Reserva Cava Dulce
Vintaged, méthode champenoise: Macabéo, Parellada,
Xarel-lo

★ III Lustros Cava Brut
Vintaged, méthode champenoise: Macabéo, Xarel-lo

Vintage Cava Gran Reserva Brut
Vintaged, méthode champenoise: Macabéo, Parellada,
Xarel-lo

45
CAVAS HILL
MOJA, PENEDÈS
Although established in 1887, the origins of
this old Cava firm go back much further, to
the original Mr Hill, an Englishman who

SANT SADURNÍ D'ANOIA, PENEDÈS
- 10 million cases
- Other labels – Raimat

Founded by Don
Josep Raventós, who
is credited with
establishing the
Spanish sparkling
wine industry,
although recent
research suggests
that he was not
actually the first to
produce Spanish
sparkling wine.
Despite its
ancient origins,
Codorníu is the
most innovative
firm in the Cava
industry today, with one of the most
impressive wineries in Spain. Codorníu
started the foreign grape controversy by
introducing Chardonnay, initially through
its estate-bottled Raimat Cava from the
Conca de Barberà, then in its primary
branded range.
It cannot be denied that when grown in
the right area, Chardonnay does pump up
the quality, depth and finesse of Cava, but
there is opposition to non-traditional
grapes from those who fear they will erode
the intrinsically Spanish character of the
wine, and the prime antagonist in this
respect is Freixenet. Codorníu is again
stirring up local feelings by using Pinot
Noir, but I have to say that pure Pinot
experimental *cuvées* have been quite
sensational.
WINEMAKER
Miguel Gurpide
HOUSE STYLE & RANGE
The recently launched Cuvée Raventós is
clean, elegant and fruity, with a creamy-
citrussy finish. There used to be a Codorníu
Chardonnay and an Anna de Codorníu,
which did not mention Chardonnay, but
contained an increasing percentage of that
variety in each successive vintage. These
two *cuvées* were effectively merged into
Anna de Codorníu Chardonnay as from
the 1995 vintage, but it was not a smooth
transition. Essentially the 1995 was released
far too young, but both wines were
consistently excellent prior to the change,

CODORNÍU

A LIGHT SHOWS THE SEDIMENT IN THE NECK
OF A BOTTLE OF CAVA AT CODORNÍU

so Anna deserves her
star-rating on past
performance and will,
I am sure, return to
form. Raimat is the
original Chardonnay
blockbuster and is still
very good, with rich
varietal fruit and good
acidity. It tends to go
very toasty, but is
usually more rustic
than a properly aged
Anna de Codorníu.
When Raimat Gran
Brut was first released,
this barrel-fermented
cuvée had a lemony,
oaky nose and was
dominated by creamy,
coconutty oak despite
its extremely rich fruit.
A lovely wine, and certainly one of the top
half-dozen Cavas on the market at the
time, even though it was rather obvious.
Later releases of this *cuvée* have developed
remarkable finesse. Because Raimat Gran
Brut is not vintaged, it is difficult to discern
whether this is due to the wine settling
down in bottle or to the fact that Codorníu
might have moved on to a completely
different bottling. The oak is still noticeable,
but it is far more refined barrel-fermented
aromas that dance around the palate, rather
than a coconut stuffed down the throat.
These subtle aromas pervade every facet of
the delicious pineapple and other tropical
fruits filling the mouth. If any Cava can
beat the New World at its own game, this
is it. Raimat Gran Brut represents mindboggling value for money.

1551 Brut
Not vintaged, méthode champenoise:
20% Chardonnay, 45% Macabéo, 35% Xarello

★ Cuvée Raventós Cava Brut
Not vintaged, méthode champenoise:
50% Chardonnay, 25% Macabéo, 25% Xarello

★★★ Raimat Cava Gran Brut
Not vintaged, méthode champenoise:
100% Chardonnay

★ Raimat Chardonnay Cava Brut
Not vintaged, méthode champenoise:
100% Chardonnay

★★ Anna de Codorníu Chardonnay
Cava Brut
Vintaged, méthode champenoise: 85% Chardonnay,
15% Parellada

established a vineyard at Moja, just southwest of Vilafranca del Penedès.

HOUSE STYLE & RANGE

The Brut de Brut is nothing special, but the Reserva Oro Secco can be quite good (as in 1995), although it can also be lousy (1994), and even when on form, its lightweight fruit lacks texture. The Brutisimo is fruity, but lacks finesse.

CAVA BRUT DE BRUT

Vintaged, méthode champenoise: 45% Macabéo, 20% Parellada, 35% Xarel-lo

CAVA BRUT BRUTISIMO

Vintaged, méthode champenoise: 45% Macabéo, 25% Parellada, 30% Xarel-lo

CAVA RESERVA ORO BRUT

Vintaged, méthode champenoise: 45% Macabéo, 20% Parellada, 35% Xarel-lo

CAVA RESERVA ORO SECO

Vintaged, méthode champenoise: 45% Macabéo, 20% Parellada, 35% Xarel-lo

N/A
JULIÀ & NAVINÈS
GUARDIOLA DE FONT-RUBÍ, PENEDÈS

Established as recently as 1986.

HOUSE STYLE & RANGE

Tasted recently, but too infrequently in the past for an overall impression; the wines have not, however, been impressive. Generally they are coarse and lacking finesse. The prize-winning Brut has a certain fruitiness, but lacks freshness, and the Chardonnay has no varietal character whatsoever.

CAVA BRUT

Not vintaged, méthode champenoise: 31% Macabéo, 49% Parellada, 20% Xarel-lo

CAVA BRUT NATURA

Not vintaged, méthode champenoise: 30% Macabéo, 47% Parellada, 23% Xarel-lo

CAVA CHARDONNAY

Not vintaged, méthode champenoise: 100% Chardonnay

45
JUVÉ Y CAMPS
SANT SADURNÍ D'ANOIA, PENEDÈS

A respected, traditionally-run, family firm, whose wines attract good reviews and premium prices in Spain.

HOUSE STYLE & RANGE

I have consistently failed to discern any intrinsically superior qualities in these wines, but they continue to get rave reviews, so maybe it's just down to personal taste.

At a recent tasting the nose of the Reserva de la Familia was dominated by ferment odours and should not have been released at such an unready stage; the Brut Vintage was dull and almondy; and the Rosado dark, coarse and heavy. If I cannot comprehend the quality of the wines, I am even more puzzled about what the critics who hype

them up so much on the domestic market believe their intrinsic qualities to be.

BRUT VINTAGE

Vintaged, méthode champenoise: 45% Macabéo, 35% Parellada, 20% Xarel-lo

CAVA GRAND JUVÉ Y CAMPS

Vintaged, méthode champenoise: 40% Macabéo, 45% Parellada, 15% Xarel-lo

RESERVA DE LA FAMILIA CAVA BRUT NATURAL

Vintaged, méthode champenoise: 40% Macabéo, 40% Parellada, 20% Xarel-lo

ROSADO CAVA BRUT

Vintaged, méthode champenoise: 100% Monastrell

60
CAVAS LAVERNOYA
SANT SADURNÍ D'ANOIA, PENEDÈS

• Other labels - Lácrima Baccus

An old-established firm founded in 1890.

HOUSE STYLE & RANGE

The Brut Nature is all almonds and aldehydes, and not very pleasant at all, but the Reserva Brut makes an unusual spicy concoction. The Primerisimo and Summum are both relatively sweet for true brut wines, but can be quite rich, with a certain sweetness and sprightly fruit. The Reserva Semi Seco has real richness and depth of fruit, with excellent acidity.

LÁCRIMA BACCUS GRAN RESERVA CAVA BRUT NATURE

Vintaged, méthode champenoise: 40% Macabéo, 25% Parellada, 35% Xarel-lo

★LÁCRIMA BACCUS RESERVA CAVA BRUT

Vintaged, méthode champenoise: 40% Macabéo, 20% Parellada, 40% Xarel-lo

LÁCRIMA BACCUS PRIMERISIMO CAVA BRUT

Vintaged, méthode champenoise: 18% Chardonnay, 35% Macabéo, 17% Parellada, 30% Xarel-lo

SUMMUM LÁCRIMA BACCUS CAVA BRUT NATURE

Vintaged, méthode champenoise: 40% Macabéo, 25% Parellada, 35% Xarel-lo

★☆ Lácrima Baccus Reserva Cava Semi Seco

Vintaged, méthode champenoise: 40% Macabéo, 20% Parellada, 40% Xarel-lo

70
MARINO
SANT SADURNÍ D'ANOIA, PENEDÈS

• Group ownership - Berberana

This recently launched Cava is made for Rioja-based Berberana by the Martini & Rossi-owned Marqués de Monistrol.

HOUSE STYLE & RANGE

This has ranged from a gutsy mouthful of flavour, with a succulently fruity finish when first released to fresh and easy, but it has always been drinkable.

CAVA BRUT

Vintaged, méthode champenoise: 35% Macabéo, 35% Parellada, 30% Xarel-lo

VILLAGE OF MONISTROL D'ANOIA, THE MAJOR PART OF WHICH IS THE BODEGA OF MARQUÉS DE MONISTROL, NEAR SANT SADURNÍ D'ANOIA

75 VALUE
MARQUÉS DE MONISTROL
SANT SADURNÍ D'ANOIA, PENEDÈS

Owned by Martini & Rossi, this Cava firm was originally established in 1882, and currently owns over 400 hectares of vineyards. This producer makes Marino, a Cava for Berberana

HOUSE STYLE & RANGE

The basic Brut has excellent autolytic floral-finesse, with lemony fruit on the palate and good acidity, and the vintaged Brut Reserva is rich and full with good acidity, but while the Brut Selección is generally an easy-going *cuvée* in a light, elegant and fruity style, with good acidity underlining nice fresh flavours, a recent sample tasted of polythene. Gran Coupage is very sweet, even for a *semi-seco*, but people who buy the style expect a seriously sweet sparkler, and despite its high degree of sweetness, this *cuvée* is nicely light and elegant.

★ CAVA BRUT

Not vintaged, méthode champenoise: 30% Macabéo, 40% Parellada, 30% Xarel-lo

★★ GRAN COUPAGE CAVA SEMI SECO RESERVA

Not vintaged, méthode champenoise: grape varieties not revealed

★ CAVA BRUT RESERVA

Vintaged, méthode champenoise: 40% Macabéo, 40% Parellada, 20% Xarel-lo

★ CAVA BRUT SELECCIÓN

Vintaged, méthode champenoise: 40% Macabéo, 40% Parellada, 20% Xarel-lo

CAVA ROSADO

Vintaged, méthode champenoise: 100% Monastrell

75 VALUE
JOSEP MASACHS
TORRELLES DE FOIX, PENEDÈS

• Other labels - Louis de Vernier

Josep Masachs is a family-owned Cava firm owning more than 40 hectares of vineyards. It started sparkling wine production in 1940.

HOUSE STYLE & RANGE

The Louis de Vernier Blanc de Blancs is fresh, clean and uncomplicated with a fruit-driven style. The Gran Vernier is OK, but nothing special, and certainly not as good as the basic Blanc de Blancs, but the Carolina de Masachs is light, elegant and fruity, with good acidity.

★ CAROLINA DE MASACHS CAVA BRUT NATURE RESERVA

Not vintaged, méthode champenoise: 10% Chardonnay, 30% Macabéo, 60% Parellada

★ LOUIS DE VERNIER BLANC DE BLANCS CAVA BRUT

Not vintaged, méthode champenoise: 30% Macabéo, 40% Parellada, 30% Xarel-lo

GRAN VERNIER DE LOUIS DE VERNIER CAVA BRUT

Not vintaged, méthode champenoise: 35% Macabéo, 30% Parellada, 35% Xarel-lo

65
ANTONIO MASCARÓ CARBONELL
VILLAFRANCA DEL PENEDÈS, PENEDÈS

• Other labels - Mascaró

Don Narcisi Mascaró Marcé was born into a well-established family of distillers, but set up this winery in 1945 to exclusively produce sparkling wines.

HOUSE STYLE & RANGE

The Brut Nature is richly-flavoured with good depth and nice acidity, without the coarseness that blights so many other Cavas.

★ MASCARÓ CAVA BRUT NATURE

Not vintaged, méthode champenoise: 20% Macabéo, 80% Parellada

MASCARÓ CAVA BRUT ROSÉ

Not vintaged, méthode champenoise: 100% Garnacha

MASCARÓ CAVA BRUT

Vintaged, méthode champenoise: 20% Macabéo, 80% Parellada

GRAN BRUT ANTONIO MASCARÓ CAVA EXTRA BRUT

Vintaged, méthode champenoise: 30% Macabéo, 60% Parellada, 10% Xarel-lo

N/A
MASÍA CAN MAYOL
VILOBÍ DEL PENEDÈS, PENEDÈS

• Other labels - Loxarel

HOUSE STYLE & RANGE

Although tasted recently for the first time, the acidity was the only interesting character of the otherwise very ordinary Brut Daurat, but the Reserva Familia was simple and fruity.

LOXAREL BRUT DAURAT CAVA BRUT

Vintaged, méthode champenoise: 30% Macabéo, 30% Parellada, 40% Xarel-lo

LOXAREL CHARDONNAY CAVA BRUT NATURE

Vintaged, méthode champenoise: 100% Chardonnay

LOXAREL RESERVA FAMILIA CAVA BRUT

Vintaged, méthode champenoise: 20% Macabéo, 15% Parellada, 45% Xarel-lo

70
MESTRES
SANT SADURNÍ D'ANOIA, PENEDÈS

This estate dates back to at least 1312, although sparkling wines were not produced until 1928. The methods are extremely traditional, and the style very much the sort of thing that lovers of well-matured Cavas adore. Not being a lover of this genre, I find these single-vineyard Cavas little more than interesting curiosities which could have been so much better with higher ripe-acidity levels and less age. Most international consumers whose tastes range between the New World and Champagne will agree with me, but many aficionados of old-style Cava probably consider this producer deserves an overall score in the 80s, with each individual wine worthy of a star-rating. Although, as stated, I am not into old Cava, it is instructive nevertheless to note that when a small, estate producer such as Mestres wants to make sparkling wines of what traditionalists perceive as the highest quality and greatest possible longevity, Xarel-lo is the most important variety.

HOUSE STYLE & RANGE

The Coquet is the youngest and freshest, in a light, slightly amylic style. Los Coupage is firmer, tighter, and capable of some ageing. Clos Nostre is full of honeyed terpenes. Clos Damiana is also honeyed, but with a toffee richness, indicating greater oxidation (the presence of terpenes suggesting a more reductive ageing). The Reserva Mas Via has a ripe, mature sweetness with honeyed aromas.

COQUET CAVA BRUT NATURE

Not vintaged, méthode champenoise: 15% Macabéo, 20% Parellada, 65% Xarel-lo

★ LOS CUPAGES DES MESTRES CAVA BRUT NATURE

Not vintaged, méthode champenoise: 15% Macabéo, 20% Parellada, 65% Xarel-lo

CLOS DAMIANA 1987 CAVA BRUT NATURE

Vintaged, méthode champenoise: 25% Macabéo, 30% Parellada, 45% Xarel-lo

CLOS NOSTRE SENYOR 1990 CAVA BRUT NATURE

Vintaged, méthode champenoise: 15% Macabéo, 15% Parellada, 60% Xarel-lo

RESERVA MAS VIA CAVA BRUT

Vintaged, méthode champenoise: 10% Macabéo, 20% Parellada, 70% Xarel-lo

73
MONT MARÇAL
CASTELLVÍ DE LA MARCA, PENEDÈS

Owned by the Sancho y Hijas family, who founded this firm in 1975, and have quickly made a reputation for these Cavas.

HOUSE STYLE & RANGE

The Brut Nature is young and firm, with plenty of promise and a delightful cushiony mousse. It can be spoilt by amylic aromas, but they tend to drop out if stored for a few months. The Brut can be rather oxidative, and the Gran Reserva has creamy-malolactic aromas dominating rich, mellow fruit, but lacks finesse. The Rosado is amylic and the Demi Sec almondy. I have tasted the Palau Brut only once and enjoyed its carefree fruit and elegance.

CAVA BRUT

Vintaged, méthode champenoise: 40% Macabéo, 30% Parellada, 30% Xarel-lo

★ CAVA BRUT NATURE

Vintaged, méthode champenoise: 40% Macabéo, 30% Parellada, 30% Xarel-lo

GRAN RESERVA CAVA BRUT

Not vintaged, méthode champenoise: 30% Macabéo, 30% Parellada, 40% Xarel-lo

★ PALAU CAVA BRUT

Vintaged, méthode champenoise: 40% Macabéo, 30% Parellada, 30% Xarel-lo

ROSADO CAVA BRUT

Vintaged, méthode champenoise: 50% Cariṣena, 50% Merlot

N/A
CAVA RAMON NADAL GIRO
EL PLÁ DEL PENEDÈS, PENEDÈS

HOUSE STYLE & RANGE

Tasted recently for the first time, this *cuvée* was quite full and toasty, but not special.

ESPECIAL CAVA EXTRA BRUT

Vintaged, méthode champenoise: 48% Macabéo, 27% Parellada, 25% Xarel-lo

N/A
PARXET
TIANA, PENEDÈS

HOUSE STYLE & RANGE

The current *cuvée* of Brut Nature Chardonnay has a sweet, perfumed, amylic aroma, sweet fruit and a vinegary finish, whereas the previous release was totally closed on the nose, and fat on the palate, but neither wine showed much varietal character, and the traditional Brut Nature finishes much better. You could buy a top-notch *grande marque* non-vintage for the cost of Reserva Anniversario Brut Nature (and it is not the most expensive Cava available - you'd have to pay half as much again for a couple of Gramona *cuvée*s), but it is not what you would call value for money, and I'm not sure about its style, let alone quality. This *cuvée* appears to be numbered, the first I came across being 76, with high extract and perhaps some promise for the future, but the second, 77, was not at all nice on the nose. Anniversario is certainly eye-catching in its silver bottle, although it would look more at home between the shampoos and aftershave bottles than on the shelf of your local wine merchant. The Rosé Cuvée Dessert is an interesting project, but the wine is too heavily amylic, and needs far more acidity and sweetness. Parxet seems to be on the ball as far as developing and marketing its products go, but its wines are less exciting than they used to be. Judgement reserved.

CAVA BRUT

*Not vintaged, méthode champenoise: Macabéo,
Parellada, Xarel-lo*

CAVA BRUT NATURE

*Vintaged, méthode champenoise: 25% Macabéo,
25% Parellada, 50% Xarel-lo*

CAVA BRUT NATURE CHARDONNAY

Vintaged, méthode champenoise: 100% Chardonnay

CAVA BRUT RESERVA

*Vintaged, méthode champenoise: 30% Macabéo,
30% Parellada, 40% Xarel-lo*

CAVA BRUT ROSÉ

Not vintaged, méthode champenoise: 100% Monastrell

CAVA RESERVA SECO

*Not vintaged, méthode champenoise: Macabéo,
Parellada, Xarel-lo*

CAVA ROSÉ CUVÉE DESSERT

Not vintaged, méthode champenoise: 100% Monastrell

CAVA RESERVA ANNIVERSARIO BRUT NATURE

*Vintaged, méthode champenoise: grape varieties not
declared*

CAVA CUVÉE DESSERT DULCE

Vintaged, méthode champenoise: Chardonnay, Monastrell

50
CASTILLO DE PERELADA
PERELADA, GERONA

Located in the Ampurdán-Costa Brava
region north of Penedès, this Cava producer
was established as the Costa Brava Company
in 1925 and was at the centre of the famous
'Spanish Champagne' case in 1962. The
word objected to by the Champagne
authorities was *Champaña*, which means
Champagne, and they won. A just decision,
we all thought, but I wonder what the jury
at the Old Bailey would have thought had
they known that Moët & Chandon had just
started making and selling South American
fizz as *Champaña*? The facilities here include
a fabulous museum, library and even a casino.

HOUSE STYLE & RANGE
The Gran Claustro is typically dull, low-acid,
with terpenes, Brut Nature has good acidity
and structure, but is sometimes spoilt by an
oxidative finish, while the Brut Natura
Chardonnay is spoilt by amylic aromas over
light, prissy fruit.

CAVA BRUT NATURE RESERVA

*Not vintaged, méthode champenoise: 40% Macabéo,
30% Parellada, 30% Xarel-lo*

CAVA BRUT NATURE

*Vintaged, méthode champenoise: 40% Macabéo,
30% Parellada, 30% Xarel-lo*

CAVA BRUT NATURA CHARDONNAY

Vintaged, méthode champenoise: 100% Chardonnay

CAVA BRUT ROSADO

Vintaged, méthode champenoise: Garnacha, Monastrell

CAVA GRAN CLAUSTRO BRUT NATURE

*Vintaged, méthode champenoise: 25% Chardonnay,
35% Macabéo, 15% Parellada, 25% Xarel-lo*

80 VALUE
JOAN RAVENTÓS ROSELL
MASQUEFA, PENEDÈS

This offshoot of the Raventós family owns
60 hectares of vines at the foot of Montserrat,
and established its own Cava enterprise as
recently as 1985.

HOUSE STYLE & RANGE
These Cavas have always been some of the
most stylishly presented on the market, but
historically they were invariably disappointing
in tastings. Over the last few years, however,
the quality has become as stylish as the
packaging, and now offers delicious,
mouthfilling fruit of some finesse. Some of
these *cuvées* develop a curious blown-wheat
character in bottle, which is not unpleasant,
but the fresher they are the better.

★★☆ CAVA BRUT NATURE

*Vintaged, méthode champenoise: Macabéo, Parellada,
Xarel-lo*

☆ CAVA BRUT RESERVA

*Vintaged, méthode champenoise: Macabéo, Parellada,
Xarel-lo*

★ CAVA CLASS BRUT

*Vintaged, méthode champenoise: Macabéo, Parellada,
Xarel-lo*

75 VALUE
RAVENTÓS I BLANC
SANT SADURNÍ D'ANOIA, PENEDÈS

Josep María left his family's firm, Codorníu,
to set up his own Cava house in 1986. The
classy presentation stands out among most
other Cavas.

VINEYARDS OF J. RAVENTÓS ROSELL WITH
THE SIERRA DE MONTSERRAT BEYOND

HOUSE STYLE & RANGE
The Gran Reserva Personal has some
malolactic complexity peeping through its
richness of fruit, and goes biscuity with a little
bottle-age. The basic Gran Reserva is lighter
than the Gran Reserva Personal, in a much
easier, less complex style, with none of the
malolactic aromas showing. In general, these
wines are not the cheapest Cavas, but they
certainly represent value for money.

☆ CAVA GRAN RESERVA BRUT NATURE

*Vintaged, méthode champenoise: Chardonnay,
Macabéo, Parellada, Xarel-lo*

★ CAVA GRAN RESERVA PERSONAL BRUT
NATURE

*Vintaged, méthode champenoise: Chardonnay,
Macabéo, Parellada, Xarel-lo*

45
ROVELLATS
SANT MARTÍ SARROCA, PENEDÈS

Established in 1940, this small family firm with
large vineyard holdings exclusively produces
estate-bottled Cava. Highly thought of in Spain,
these Cavas fail to strike a chord with me.

HOUSE STYLE & RANGE
The Brut Especial has decent acidity, but is
just frothy, whereas Brut Imperial is very
rich with good acidity, but the fruit is coarse,
and lacking finesse. However, the Gran
Reserva Brut Nature is light, clean and easy.

CAVA BRUT ESPECIAL

*Vintaged, méthode champenoise: Macabéo, Parellada,
Xarel-lo*

CAVA BRUT IMPERIAL

*Vintaged, méthode champenoise: Macabéo, Parellada,
Xarel-lo*

CAVA ROSÉ BRUT

*Vintaged, méthode champenoise: Monastrell,
Tempranillo*

☆ CAVA GRAN RESERVA BRUT NATURE

*Not vintaged, méthode champenoise: Chardonnay,
Macabéo, Parellada, Xarel-lo*

N/A
SANDORA
SANDORA, PENEDÈS

New joint venture between two Champagne
groups, Seagram and Vranken-Monopole,
the synergy being that Vranken recently
purchased Heidsieck & Co Monopole from
Seagram, and Seagram has continued to
distribute the brand for Vranken-Lafitte. The
first *cuvée* was launched in December 1997.

HOUSE STYLE & RANGE
Not bad for a first effort, but not special.
The Chardonnay content does provide some
mouthfill, although the taste is a rather soapy
and youthful.

BLANC DE BLANCS CAVA BRUT

*Not vintaged, méthode champenoise: 35% Chardonnay,
65% Parellada*

75 VALUE
SEGURA VIUDAS
SANT SADURNÍ D'ANOIA, PENEDÈS

• Group ownership - Freixenet
• Other labels - Conde de Caralt

Freixenet's top-performing Cava brand.

HOUSE STYLE & RANGE

Although the red-labelled non-vintage Brut is sweetish and okay, it is not what it used to be, whereas the black-labelled vintaged Brut is invariably one of Cava's best staples. The Aria is not as outstanding as it used to be when launched five years ago. I still have a few bottles of the original *cuvée* and it is still drinking well, but the current stuff has a rather common touch. When on form, the Reserva Heredad has lots of satisfying sweetly ripe fruit flavour that will go toasty with a bit of extra bottle-age, and a soft, cushiony mousse. Although it deserves its star-rating, it can be annoyingly dull and bland at times. The reliable if unexciting Conde de Caralt Cava brand is a second label, helping Segura Viudas increase quality through selection.

ARIA CAVA BRUT
 Vintaged, méthode champenoise: 60% Macabéo, 20% Parellada, 20% Xarel-lo

★ CAVA BRUT RESERVA
 Vintaged, méthode champenoise: 50% Macabéo, 35% Parellada, 15% Xarel-lo

CONDE DE CARALT BLANC DE BLANCS CAVA BRUT
 Vintaged, méthode champenoise: 50% Macabéo, 30% Parellada, 20% Xarel-lo

CONDE DE CARALT CAVA BRUT
 Vintaged, méthode champenoise: 50% Macabéo, 30% Parellada, 20% Xarel-lo

★ RESERVA HEREDAD CAVA BRUT
 Not vintaged, méthode champenoise: 67% Macabéo, 33% Parellada

70
JAUME SERRA
VILANOVA I LA GELTRÚ, PENEDÈS

• Other labels - Cristalino

Jaume Serra was founded in 1926 and today utilises the not inconsiderable talent of Ignacio Recabarren, Chile's highest-profile winemaker, as consultant for these Cavas.

HOUSE STYLE & RANGE

The Cristalino has a fresh, fruit-driven style with a fine mid-palate feel.

CAVA BRUT
 Not vintaged, méthode champenoise: 55% Macabéo, 30% Parellada, 15% Xarel-lo

CAVA BRUT
 Vintaged, méthode champenoise: 65% Macabéo, 35% Parellada

★ CRISTALINO CAVA BRUT
 Not vintaged, méthode champenoise: grape varieties not revealed

N/A
AUGUSTÍ TORELLÓ
SANT SADURNÍ D'ANOIA, PENEDÈS

• Other labels - Aliguer, Kripta

This small, impeccably clean and superbly equipped, family-owned Cava firm, established in 1950, has only recently come to prominence. However, after many years in charge of Segura Viudas, Augustí Torelló should know something about running a Cava house, not to mention developing export markets.

HOUSE STYLE & RANGE

The Aliguer is flowery and amylic, but does manage some finesse, whereas the sweet and creamy fruit in the Mata Brut is let down by a lack of acidity. The talking point of this producer is, however, its prestige *cuvée*, Kripta, which is spelt on the label with a backward-facing 'K' and comes in a replica Roman bottle, having no flat bottom and must therefore be kept in an ice-bucket once opened. I can respect what Augustí Torelló is trying to do with Kripta (produce something of Krug-like dimensions), and the 1992 vintage is a considerable improvement on the 1991, which was not a very auspicious start for this new *cuvée*, but there is a long way to go yet. The 1992 is much cleaner and better focused, with fresh, sweet, vanilla fruit on the palate, but it needs far more acidity if it is to show any true degree of finesse.

ALIGUER 1994 CAVA BRUT
 Vintaged, méthode champenoise: 45% Macabéo, 30% Parellada, 25% Xarel-lo

MATA CAVA BRUT RESERVA
 Vintaged, méthode champenoise: 45% Macabéo, 30% Parellada, 25% Xarel-lo

MATA CAVA BRUT NATURE GRAN RESERVA
 Vintaged, méthode champenoise: 40% Macabéo, 35% Parellada, 25% Xarel-lo

✶ KRIPTA BRUT NATURE GRAN RESERVA CAVA
 Vintaged, méthode champenoise: 43% Macabéo, 30% Parellada, 27% Xarel-lo

60
MASÍA VALLFORMOSA
VILOBÍ DEL PENEDÈS, PENEDÈS

This family-owned Cava firm is supplied for the most part from its own vineyards, which are centred on the old Sala de Vallformosa estate, which date backs to 977, and today totals more than 300 hectares.

HOUSE STYLE & RANGE

The Brut has a dull nose, but the palate is more lively, with good, lemony acidity, while the last Gran Reserva Brut I came across had fermentation odours dominating the nose and should not really have been in distribution. The Extra Seco is oxidative, with a toasty finish. Although Semi Seco is not terribly sweet and won't appeal to those who usually make a bee-line for this style, it has plenty of fruit, with a refreshing citrussy flavour, which should give it a wider appeal. The Semi Seco saved this producer from an embarrassingly low overall rating.

★✶ CAVA SEMI SECO
 Not vintaged, méthode champenoise: 30% Macabéo, 40% Parellada, 30% Xarel-lo

CAVA BRUT
 Vintaged, méthode champenoise: 30% Macabéo, 35% Parellada, 35% Xarel-lo

CAVA BRUT VINTAGE
 Vintaged, méthode champenoise: 30% Macabéo, 35% Parellada, 35% Xarel-lo

CAVA EXTRA SECO
 Vintaged, méthode champenoise: 30% Macabéo, 40% Parellada, 30% Xarel-lo

GRAN RESERVA CAVA BRUT
 Vintaged, méthode champenoise: 30% Macabéo, 35% Parellada, 35% Xarel-lo

THE MASÍA VALLFORMOSA WINERY, VILOBÍ DEL PENEDÈS. THE ESTATE DATES RIGHT BACK TO 977

REST OF EUROPE

AUSTRIA

FIZZ IS NOT THE FIRST WINE THAT COMES TO MIND WHEN AUSTRIA IS MENTIONED, BUT WITH ITS CLOSE ASSOCIATION TO GERMANY, IT IS NOT SURPRISING TO DISCOVER THAT IT HAS A SIMILAR SORT OF SEKT INDUSTRY, ALTHOUGH NOWHERE NEAR THE SAME SIZE.

Austrian Sekt has suffered all the same problems as German Sekt. They are the problems inherent in any sparkling wine industry that went over to *cuve close en masse* when the technology became available: a gradual lowering of standards as the bulk-production method attracts cheaper raw materials. Within the country of origin the process is hardly noticed and eventually the entire wine drinking community develops a 'cellar palate', having been conditioned into accepting a lower standard of quality as the norm. Meanwhile outside the country in question, international standards have risen, as have the expectations of knowledgeable wine drinkers, creating more discriminating markets for finer quality sparkling wines.

The result, as in Germany, is that ultimately the domestic product becomes fit only for local consumption, even though those locals might in every other respect be some of the widest-travelled, most sophisticated people in the world. They can be the most discerning Champagne enthusiasts but, whether through false national pride or simple conditioning, they apply different standards to the product on which they have been bred. The result is a healthy home market with negligible exports.

The German words *Sekt* and *Schaumwein* are interchangeable terms for sparkling wine in Austria, where this style was first produced by one Robert Schlumberger in 1842. Although fizz of sorts is produced in most of the country's various wine regions, most comes from Weinviertel, which borders the Czech Republic to the north.

Traditionally, sparkling wine grapes have been grown either side of the so-called Brünerstrasse, a road linking Vienna with the Czech city of Brno. Poysdorf, the centre of Austria's Sekt industry, is often described as being on the same geographical latitude as Champagne. It is, however, only the same latitude as Sézanne, which is south of the classic Côte des Blancs, and Poysdorf is as far north as Austria's sparkling wine vineyards go.

The Austrian Sekt industry would have to travel to Brno, well into the Czech Republic, to reach the same latitude as Reims, and perhaps, at one point, it did. Perhaps that was the whole point of the Brünerstrasse. Yet, even if the Sekt industry did move to this area, the continental climate is totally different. These grapes along the Brünerstrasse are high in acidity and extract, but low in alcohol; the main varieties used are Welschriesling, Grüner Veltliner and Pinot Blanc.

SCHLOSS MAILBERG IN WEINVIERTEL, THE AREA ON THE CZECH BORDER WHERE MOST OF AUSTRIA'S SPARKLING WINES ARE MADE

75
WEINGUT BRÜNDLMAYER
LANGENLOIS, KAMPTAL
- 2,200 cases

The Bründlmayers have been vinegrowers and winemakers since the 17th century, currently owning 50 hectares of vines, making this one of the largest privately-owned domaines in Austria. Sparkling wine is, however, a recent innovation for Weingut Bründlmayer, with the first wine produced in 1989. Only the traditional *méthode champenoise* is used.

WINEMAKER
Willy Bründlmayer

HOUSE STYLE & RANGE
Currently vies with Weingut Platzer for the best Austrian sparkling wine, Bründlmayer is crisp, with fine acidity, and an elegant, slightly oxidative complexity.

★★☆ BRUT
Vintaged, méthode champenoise: Chardonnay, Pinot Blanc and Pinot Noir

CHARPENTIER
See WEINGUT R. ZIMMERMANN

70
CHORHERRENSTIFT KLOSTERNEUBURG
KLOSTERNEUBURG, DONAULAND
- 1,650 cases

With over 100 hectares, Klosterneuburg is the largest private owner of vineyards in Austria, and has been making sparkling wines since 1973.

HOUSE STYLE & RANGE
At the top of the range, the wines are made by *méthode champenoise*; the mousse is firm with tiny bubbles, the fruit all apples and pears, and somewhat amylic, but good acidity.

SEC
Not vintaged, méthode champenoise: Grüner Veltliner

DEMI-SEC
Not vintaged, méthode champenoise: Grüner Veltliner

ROSÉ
Not vintaged, méthode champenoise: St Laurent

GRAND RESERVE BRUT
Not vintaged, méthode champenoise: Pinot Blanc

★ GRANDE RESERVE MATHÄI
Not vintaged, méthode champenoise: Pinot Blanc (Kabinett quality)

N/A
SCHLOSSWEINGUT GRAF HARDEGG
SEEFELD-KADOLZ, WEINVIERTEL
- 1,600 cases

Uninspiring fizz produced from estate-grown, hand-picked grapes that undergo second fermentation at Schlumberger. It is difficult to tell whether it is the base wine that is wrong, or Schlumberger's handling of the bottle-fermentation, but I have tasted good still wines from Graf Hardegg (Grüner Veltliner Dreikreuzen Kabinett, and Grüner Veltliner Maximilian Kabinett).

WINEMAKER
Maximilian Hardegg

HOUSE STYLE & RANGE
Not faulty, but gives off strange aromas, and lacks finesse.
WEISSBURGUNDER BRUT
Vintaged, méthode champenoise: 88% Pinot Blanc, 12% Chardonnay

HOCHRIEGL
See KATTUS

45
KARL INFÜHR
KLOSTERNEUBURG, DONAULAND
- 250,000 cases

Founded in 1949, this is one of Austria's major players in the Sekt market, with some 12 different *cuvées*, mostly marketed under gimmicky names with tacky labels. The three listed here are the best of the range, which isn't saying much. The others are not generally available outside Austria.

WINEMAKER
Hans Inführ

HOUSE STYLE & RANGE
Suffers from thin, underripe fruit or amylic aromas, while the supposedly upmarket *cuve close* tried too hard to be complex, and ends up being unclean.
OESTERREICH GOLD BRUT
Not vintaged, méthode champenoise: 85% Grüner Veltliner, 15% Welschriesling
BLUE MAGIC SEKT BRUT
Not vintaged, méthode champenoise: Grüner Veltliner, Welschriesling
CHARDONNAY PINOT NOIR SEKT EXTRA BRUT
Not vintaged, cuve close: Chardonnay, Pinot Noir

N/A
KATTUS
VIENNA
Founded in 1857 by Johann Kattus II, who apparently worked at various Champagne houses to refine his knowledge of the *méthode champenoise*. The Hochriegl brand was named after the vineyard belonging to Kattus that supplied the grapes for the very first *cuvée*.

WINEMAKER
Josef & Franz Kattus

HOUSE RANGE
HOCHRIEGL TROCKEN/HALBÜSS
Not vintaged, transfer method: Grüner Veltliner, Welschriesling
HOCHRIEGL ALTE RESERVE BRUT
Not vintaged, barrique-aged, transfer method: Grüner Veltliner, Welschriesling
HOCHRIEGL RUBIN (RED)
Not vintaged, transfer method: grape varieties not revealed
GROSSER JAHRGANG BRUT
Vintaged, transfer method: Welschriesling

40
KIRCHMAYR
WEISTRACH, KAMPTAL
- 5,500 cases

Best-known for young, fresh Sekt made from pear juice. The only Kirchmayr sparkling wine made from grapes that I have tasted is a 12-year-old bottle-fermented Abtei-sekt, which is old rather than mature, and yellow, with unpleasant oxidised and maderised aromas.

HOUSE STYLE & RANGE
This producer's policy of producing Abtei-sekt with just 7.5% alcohol, and then ageing it for a minimum of five years would seem to be a recipe for disaster.
ABTEI-SEKT
Vintaged, méthode champenoise: Grüner Veltliner
RIESLING-SEKT
Vintaged, cuve close: Riesling

65
BRÜDER KLEINOSCHEG
GRAZ-GÖSTING, SÜDOSTEIERMARK
- 4,000 cases

The second-oldest sparkling wine producer in Austria, Ludwig and Anton Kleinoscheg produced their first fizz from Styrian grapes in 1849, just seven years after Robert Schlumberger had produced his in Vienna.

HOUSE STYLE & RANGE
The Chardonnay is quite fat, but with dried-fruit complexity, while the Schilchersekt could do with some fat to fill out its dry, peppery, raspberry flavour.
DERBY CHARDONNAY BRUT
Not vintaged, méthode champenoise: Chardonnay
SCHILCHERSEKT
Not vintaged, méthode champenoise: Blauer Wildbacher

55
FÜRST LIECHENSTEIN
WILFERSDORF, WEINVIERTEL
- 2,500 cases
- Group ownership - now belongs to Domäne Müller

This estate belonged to the Prince Liechenstein family from 1436 until 1990, when it was sold to pay off death duties.

HOUSE STYLE & RANGE
Petrolly bottle-aromas, quite fat, could be more elegant.
FL CUVÉE BRUT
Vintaged, cuve close: Grüner Veltliner

40
WEINGUT MALAT
PALT, KREMSTAL
Small producer making *méthode champenoise* sparkling wines since 1979.

WINEMAKER
Gerald Malat

HOUSE STYLE & RANGE
Lacks finesse.
MALAT EXTRA BRUT
Vintaged, méthode champenoise: Chardonnay, Pinot Noir

MALTESER RITTERORDEN
See LENZ MOSER

50
LENZ MOSER
RÖHRENDORF, KAMTAL
- 30,000 cases

The most famous Austrian name produces cheap, bulk-blended fizz under its own name, and supposedly more expressive sparkling wine from grapes grown on its rented Knights of Malta estate in Weinviertel.

HOUSE STYLE & RANGE
Dull and foursquare.
LENZ MOSER BRUT
Vintaged, cuve close: Welschriesling, Grüner Veltliner
SOUVEÄNER MALTESER RITTERORDEN BRUT
Vintaged, cuve close: Grüner Veltliner, Chardonnay

N/A
PM MOUNIER
VIENNA
- 10,000 cases
- Group ownership - acquired by Schlumberger in 1988

Established in 1914 by Paul-Marie Mounier, whose life was back-to-front for a monk, (but more logical for the rest of us mere mortals), having given up the austerity of monastic life to wallow in the luxury of material wealth.

HOUSE STYLE & RANGE
Disappointing on current tasting (like fizzed-up stale grape juice!) but I remember some much better *cuvées*, so I will reserve opinion.

MOUNIER BLEU BRUT

  Not vintaged, méthode champenoise: Pinot Blanc

35
DOMÄNE MÜLLER
GROSS ST FLORIAN,

- Group ownership - also owns Fürst
Liechenstein

It was in 1936 that Günter Müller's grandfather established this firm, which has become the most important producer of Styrian wines.

WINEMAKER
Günter Müller

HOUSE RANGE
STYRIAN SCHILCHER SEKT ULTRA BRUT

  Vintaged, cuve close: Blauer Wildbacher

STYRIAN WELSCHRIESLING BRUT

  Vintaged, cuve close: Welschriesling

67
PFRIMER
GRAZ, STYRIA

- 800 cases

Wine merchants since the 1850s.

HOUSE STYLE & RANGE
Although amylic, the light, clean style of this *cuve close* wine shows more elegance than most Austrian *méthode champenoise.*

★ GRAND SEIGNEUR

  Vintaged, cuve close: 75% Grüner Veltliner,
  25% Welschriesling

75
WEINHOF PLATZER
KLOCH, SÜDOSTEIERMARK

Small grower producing one of Austria's best sparkling wines.

HOUSE STYLE & RANGE
Elegant *méthode champenoise* sparkling wine with gentle fruit, a firm mouse, and well balanced acidity.

★★ PINOT CUVÉE

  Vintaged, méthode champenoise: Pinot Blanc

SAMMUS
See WEINGUT WOHLMUTH

52
WEINGUT SATTLERHOF
GAMLITZ, SÜDOSTEIERMARK

- 700 cases

This producer is the so-called 'founder of dry Styrian quality wines' yet it tends to make less than dry fizz.

WINEMAKER
Willi Sattler Jnr.

HOUSE STYLE & RANGE
Clean, but a bit sweet and bland.
BRUT

  Vintaged, méthode champenoise: 50% Chardonnay,
  50% Pinot Blanc

67
HERBERT SCHILLING
STREBERSDORF, VIENNA

- 1,100 cases

Although most of Schilling's wines are still sold through his *Heurige*, the amount of wine that is now being bottled and marketed through general distribution is growing at an even pace.

WINEMAKER
Herbert Schilling

HOUSE STYLE & RANGE
An unpretentious *cuve close* that is clean and fresh, with good acidity.

★ VIENNA CLASSIC SEKT BRUT

  Vintaged, cuve close: 40% Grüner Veltliner,
  40% Welschriesling, 20% Riesling

SCHLUMBERGER
VIENNA

- 500,000 cases
- Group ownership - now owns PM
Mounier

In 1842, after several years working for Champagne Ruinart, Robert Schlumberger took the *méthode champenoise* back to Vienna, where he set up shop and made the first Austrian sparkling wine.

HOUSE STYLE & RANGE
Disappointing quality, particularly at the bottom end of the range, the *cuvées* of which account for the vast majority of Schlumberger sales.

BLANC DE BLANCS BRUT

  Not vintaged, méthode champenoise: Welschriesling

ROSÉ BRUT

  Not vintaged, méthode champenoise: Pinot Noir

JUBILÄUM BRUT

  Not vintaged, méthode champenoise: Pinot Blanc

72
SZIGETI
GOLS, NEUSIEDLERSEE

- 25,000 cases

Up and coming sparkling wine producer established as recently as 1991 but already enjoying a decent reputation.

HOUSE STYLE & RANGE
The range from this producer includes a fresh Grüner Veltliner, inelegant Welschriesling (but then that describes the grape as much as any wine made from it), and one of the best dryish Muscat fizzes produced anywhere.

★ GRÜNER VELTLINER BRUT

  Vintaged, méthode champenoise: Grüner Veltliner

★★ MUSKAT OTTONEL EXTRA DRY

  Vintaged, méthode champenoise: Muscat Ottonel

WELSCHRIESLING BRUT

  Vintaged, méthode champenoise: Welschriesling

N/A
WINKLER-HERMADEN
SCHLOSS KAPFENSTEIN

- 250 cases

This privately-owned wine estate, founded in 1914, is close to the border with Slovenia and Hungary. It began production of bottle-fermented sparkling wine in 1991 and is a member of an association of six wineries who jointly market wines under the Vision brand.

HOUSE STYLE & RANGE
Coarse, but tasted just once, thus opinion reserved.

VISION BRUT WEISSBURGUNDER

  Vintaged, méthode champenoise: Pinot Blanc

69
WEINGUT WOHLMUTH
KITZECK, SÜDOSTEIERMARK

- 375 cases

A family-owned wine estate since 1803, but sparkling wine is a relatively recent addition.

WINEMAKER
Gehard Wohlmuth

HOUSE STYLE & RANGE
Quite fruity, with a touch of spice.

SUMMUS CHARDONNAY BRUT

  Not vintaged, méthode champenoise: Chardonnay

60
WEINGUT R ZIMMERMANN
KLOSTERNEUBURG, DONAULAND

- 1,200 cases

The Zimmermann family also owns a *Heurige* in the centre of Grinzling, Vienna, and always includes a sun motif on its labels to express life on earth.

HOUSE STYLE & RANGE
A clean *cuve close* blended from two vintages.

CHARPENTIER BRUT

  Not vintaged, cuve close: Chardonnay

BULGARIA

UNDER THE OLD COMMUNIST REGIME, ISKRASHTO VINO (SPARKLING WINE) WAS PRODUCED BY THE CONTINUOUS RUSSIAN METHOD AT REGIONAL COOPERATIVE WINERIES THROUGHOUT BULGARIA AND EXPORTED TO THE FORMER SOVIET UNION.

The most famous were *Iskra*-Chirpan (or Cirpan) and *Iskra*-Maritsa in Thrakiiska Nizina, and *Iskra*-Zvezditsa from the Varna winery in Tschernomorski Raion. Other sparkling wines were made at the Targovischte winery in Tschernomorski Raion, the Lyaskovets winery in Dunavska Raunina, the Perustica (or Perushtitza or Peroushtitza) winery in Thrakiiska Nizina, and the Slaviantzi winery in Podbalanski Raion.

It was from Slaviantzi that the first Bulgarian sparkling wine was produced for export. Called **Balkan Crown Brut**, it was made by the *cuve close* method from a blend of Chardonnay, Ugni Blanc and Riesling, and hit the British market in the 1980s. Although it was at least as good as the most successful *cuve close* produced in France, and Bulgarian Cabernet Sauvignon was the UK's best-selling red wine at the time, Balkan Crown Brut failed to make any impact.

The only *méthode champenoise* of any repute is **Magura**, which is made at the Rabisha winery in Dunavska Raunina, and comes in all shades of colour and sweetness but, as far as I am aware, it has never been exported. The only Bulgarian fizz currently exported is **Black Sea Gold Chardonnay** from the Varna winery, although the top-performing **Domaine Boyar** is due to produce 'export quality' sparkling wine in collaboration with the Chirpan winery as this book goes to press.

CZECH REPUBLIC

MORAVIA ACCOUNTS FOR THE MAJORITY OF CZECH VINEYARDS, AND *SUMIVÉ VÍNO* (SPARKLING WINE) IS MADE IN THE TOWNS OF MIKULOV AND BZENEC BY BOTH *CUVE CLOSE* AND CONTINUOUS RUSSIAN METHODS. HOWEVER, THE LARGEST PRODUCER OF MORAVIAN BUBBLY IS SITUATED IN BOHEMIA.

63
BOHEMIA SEKT
STARY PLZENEC, BOHEMIA
• 2.2 million cases

Established in 1942 as *Ceskomoravske Sklepy Sumivych Vin* (Czech-Moravian Sparkling Wine Cellars), this producer was originally housed in a former brewery and the first sparkling wines were fermented using brewing equipment and sold in 1945 under the Black Widow label.

The winery was soon more properly equipped and with the help of a French wine consultant, Louis Giradot, the volume of Bohemia Sekt production soared.

HOUSE STYLE & RANGE
Light, easy and clean.

AVANTI
Not vintaged, carbonated, low-alcohol, various shades of colour and sweetness: grape varieties not revealed

CHÂTEAU BELVEDER DEMI-SEC (RED)
Not vintaged, transfer method: grape varieties not revealed

CHÂTEAU RADYNE BRUT
Not vintaged, transfer method: grape varieties not revealed

FRIZZANTE
Not vintaged, carbonated, demi-sec: Spanish and Italian wines

REGIA BRUT/SEC/DEMI-SEC
Not vintaged, cuve close: Welschriesling, Grüner Veltliner

REGIA DEMI-SEC (RED)
Not vintaged, cuve close: St. Laurent, Limberger

SEKT DEMI-SEC
Not vintaged, cuve close: Welschriesling, Grüner Veltliner

SEKT ROSÉ DEMI-SEC
Not vintaged, cuve close: Welschriesling, Grüner Veltliner, St.Laurent

LOUIS GIRARDOT BRUT
Vintaged, méthode champenoise: Chardonnay, Pinot Gris, Welschriesling

GEORGIA

SOME SPARKLING WINES ARE MADE IN THE KAKHETIA REGION BY THE *MÉTHODE CHAMPENOISE*, USING CHINURI, GORULI, MTSVANE AND TASITSKA GRAPES.

GREECE

THE CAIR COOPERATIVE ON RHODES WAS FOR YEARS THE ONLY PRODUCER OF *MÉTHODE CHAMPENOISE* WINES IN GREECE, BUT THIS SITUATION HAS JUST BEGUN TO CHANGE.

When in the early 1990s the sons of winemaker fathers refused to produce the oxidised products that had plagued the Greek wine industry throughout the 20th century, the result was an unprecedented surge in quality of wines produced.

The respect the new wines received gave the new generation of winemakers something to be proud of and many have gone on to dabble with styles that have seldom been seen in Greece, one of these being bottle-fermented sparkling wine. But winemakers will find the learning curve for this style of sparkling wine far longer and more difficult than perhaps they imagined, although some will make it, I'm sure.

AUTOCRATORIKOS
See TSANTALIS

BOHEME
See CAIR

N/A
BOUTARIS
VRISSAKI, NAOUSA
Probably the best of the large old-style *négociant* type producers, Boutaris has been experimenting with sparkling wine, but has not yet produced a commercial *cuvée*. One to watch, hopefully.

55
CAIR S.A.
KAPODISTRIOU, RHODES
• 62,500 cases

The Rhodes cooperative was established in 1928 and under the CAIR label, this was the only source of *méthode champenoise* in the country for decades.

WINEMAKER
Mr Glynos

HOUSE STYLE & RANGE
Strong, coarse and fiercely fizzy, ideal as a mixer for Bucks Fizz.

BOHEME BRUT/DEMI SEC
Not vintaged, cuve close: Athiri

BRUT/DEMI-SEC
Not vintaged, méthode champenoise: Athiri

N/A
EMERY
EMPORANOS, RHODES
This high-tech winery, surrounded by

immaculate vineyards on the island of Rhodes, was established in 1974.

WINEMAKER
Dr Marengo (Italian consultant)
HOUSE RANGE
GRAND PRIX BRUT/DEMI-SEC
Not vintaged, méthode champenoise: grape varieties not revealed

GRAND PRIX
See EMERY

ODE PANOS
See SPYOPOULOS

75
SPYOPOULOS
ARTEMISIO, MANTINIA
• Group ownership
This is a fully organic, family-owned winery with excellent-looking vineyards in Mantinia. Spyopoulos has just released the most elegant sparkling wine currently produced in Greece.
WINEMAKER
Yannis Paraskevopoulos
HOUSE STYLE & RANGE
Pale and fresh, with creamy fruit tasting of apples and pears.
★★ ODE PANOS BRUT
Vintaged: Moschofilero

60
TSANTALIS
AGHIOS PAVLOS, CHALKIDIKI
This producer is just a whisper behind Boutaris in terms of technical proficiency, but has yet to produce a fully-fledged brut style *méthode champenoise*.
WINEMAKER
Pavlos Argyropoulos
HOUSE STYLE & RANGE
A clean and commercial wine, with fresh, flowery fruit, medium sweetness, and lively *pétillance*.
AUTOCRATORIKOS
Not vintaged: grape varieties not revealed

70
ZITSA
IOÁNNINA, EPIRUS
Cooperative for six smaller villages around Zitsa, northwest of Ioánnina. Here the vines grow at an altitude of some 600 metres in rugged terrain.
WINEMAKER
Vassilis Vaimakis
HOUSE STYLE & RANGE
Dry and semi-sweet, clean and delicately fruity wines in a *perlant* style.
★ SEMI-SPARKLING SEC/DEMI-SEC
Not vintaged: Debina

HUNGARY
THE FOUNDING OF HUNGARY'S SPARKLING WINE INDUSTRY IS LIKE THAT OF SO MANY OTHERS: LOCAL LAD BRINGS BACK *MÉTHODE CHAMPENOISE* FROM CHAMPAGNE.

In this case it was one József Törley, who learned the process in Reims and used this knowledge to set up the Törley Pezsgögyár (Törley Champagne Factory) at Budafok on the southwestern outskirts of Budapest in 1882, utilising grapes from Etyek, a little further to the southwest.

Four years later the Frenchman Louis François established his Transylvania 'champagne' house, also in Budafok.

The term *habzó* or 'sparkling' can refer to any method of production, but will probably be *cuve close*, whereas *pezsgö* often indicates a sparkling wine made by the *méthode champenoise*, but is also used on some *cuve close* (by Törley, for example).

50
BALATONBOGLÁR WINERY
BALATONBOGLÁR SZABADSAG
• 600,000 cases
• Group ownership - partnership with Henkell & Söhnlein of Wiesbaden
The BB, or Balatonboglár winery has made wines from its own vines on the southern shores of Lake Balaton for more than 40 years, but it did not start production of sparkling wines until 1982. Tasted under Chapel Hill and Silver Swan labels.
WINEMAKER
Gyözö Mészáros & Dénes Gádor
HOUSE STYLE & RANGE
Technically sound, but very basic.
BB DRY-SEC/DEMI-SEC/DOUX
Not vintaged, cuve close: Chardonnay, Welschriesling, Grüner Veltliner, Királyleányka, Riesling
BB SPUMANTE MUSKOTÁLY
Not vintaged, cuve close: Muscat

BB
See BALATONBOGLÁR WINERY

CHAPEL HILL
See BALATONBOGLÁR WINERY

FRANÇOIS
See HUNGAROVIN

HUNGARIA
See HUNGAROVIN

40
HUNGAROVIN
BUDAPEST, HÁROS

• 1.5 million cases
• Group ownership - partnership with Henkell & Söhnlein of Wiesbaden
Although they are the largest bottlers of Hungarian fizz, I have had bottles of Françoi in the past that were clean and interesting, with a nice fine mousse. However, François was unavailable for tasting at the time of writing, thus I can make no judgement on the current quality of this wine.
WINEMAKER
László Kiss & László Kemendy
HOUSE STYLE & RANGE
Quality across the range is not up to the usual Henkell & Söhnlein standard; some *cuvées* are not just unclean, but very dirty an unpleasant.
TÖRLEY SEC/DEMI-SEC
Not vintaged, cuve close: Chardonnay, Ezergó, Welschriesling, Grüner Veltliner, Riesling

TÖRLEY GÁLA SEC
Not vintaged, cuve close: Chardonnay, Ezergó, Welschriesling, Grüner Veltliner, Riesling
TÖRLEY TALISMAN DEMI-SEC
Not vintaged, cuve close: Chardonnay, Ezergó, Welschriesling, Grüner Veltliner, Riesling
TÖRLEY FORTUNA DEMI-SEC
Not vintaged, cuve close: Chardonnay, Ezergó, Welschriesling, Grüner Veltliner, Riesling
TÖRLEY CHARMANT DOUX
Not vintaged, cuve close: Chardonnay, Ezergó, Welschriesling, Grüner Veltliner, Riesling
TÖRLEY CHARMANT ROUGE DOUX
Not vintaged, cuve close: grape varieties not revealed
TÖRLEY MUSCATELLER DOUX
Not vintaged, cuve close: Muscat
TÖRLEY CHARDONNAY BRUT
Vintaged, méthode champenoise: Chardonnay
HUNGARIA DRY/EXTRA SEC/DOUX
Vintaged, cuve close: Chardonnay, Ezergó, Welschriesling, Grüner Veltliner, Riesling
HUNGARIA GRANDE CUVÉE EXTRA SEC
Vintaged, cuve close: Chardonnay, Ezergó, Welschriesling, Grüner Veltliner, Riesling
HUNGARIA ROUGE DOUX
Vintaged, cuve close: grape varieties not revealed
FRANÇOIS PRESIDENT BRUT
Vintaged, méthode champenoise: grape varieties not revealed

SILVER SWAN
See BALATONBOGLÁR WINERY

TÖRLEY
See HUNGAROVIN

ISRAEL

THIS COUNTRY DID NOT START PRODUCING AN INTERNATIONALLY ACCEPTABLE STANDARD OF WINE UNTIL 1987, WHEN THE GOLAN HEIGHTS WINERY ATTRACTED ATTENTION WITH ITS BRIGHT, CLEAN, FRUITY GAMLA CABERNET SAUVIGNON AND YARDEN SAUVIGNON BLANC, MADE BY A UC DAVIS TRAINED OENOLOGIST.

The Golan Heights is the most promising area within Galilee (or Galil), the country's premier wine region, where temperatures, even in the middle of summer, rarely rise above 25° (77°F). Since the late 1980s, these wines and others have not been as consistently fine as the first releases promised, but it is still early days as far as Israel's quality wines are concerned, although wine has of course been produced in this area since Biblical times. As readers will discover throughout this book, the development of sparkling wine always lags behind that of still wine in general, so it is not unexpected that shipments of **Yarden Blanc de Blancs**, a non-vintage *méthode champenoise*, have also varied. This sparkling wine has won awards on the international stage, and has a lightly rich malo style with elegant, mellow fruit.

LUXEMBOURG

THE FIRST *MÉTHODE CHAMPENOISE* IN LUXEMBOURG WAS PRODUCED BY BERNARD-MASSARD IN 1921. MOST LUXEMBOURG SPARKLING WINE IS *CUVE CLOSE* AND VERY BLAND IN STYLE, BUT EXTREMELY POPULAR, WITH EVERYONE HAVING THEIR OWN FAVOURITE BRAND.

Caves Gales/Caves St. Martin, Caves Desom, Krier and Mathes make up to 100,000 cases each, but **Bernard-Massard** is the Moët & Chandon of Luxembourg, and it is the only producer in the country interested in building up an international reputation. The Crémant de Luxembourg appellation was introduced in 1991 for *méthode champenoise* wines with up to four atmospheres of pressure. A number of growers have started to produce this style, but it is too early to make any judgements, although it would be nice to see what a good flying winemaker could do with the Crémant de Luxembourg appellation, particularly with Auxerrois grapes.

65
BERNARD-MASSARD

GREVENMACHER

- 250,000 cases
- Group ownership - the Fourcroy group is a major shareholder, and Bernard-Massard itself owns Monmousseau in the Loire and, of course, Sektkellerei Bernard-Massard in Germany.

Run by the Classon family, which is also a major shareholder, Bernard-Massard made Luxembourg's first sparkling wines in 1921, and tries very hard today, but really needs a consultant to bring the sort of finesse that I am sure Luxembourg fizz could easily possess.

WINEMAKER

Freddy Sinner

HOUSE STYLE & RANGE

The non-vintage *cuvées* are invariably fresher and more interesting than the vintage wines.
BRUT

> *Not vintaged, méthode champenoise: Pinot Blanc, Chenin Blanc, Riesling*

CUVÉE DE L'ECUSSON BRUT
> *Not vintaged, méthode champenoise: Pinot Blanc, Chardonnay, Pinot Noir*

CUVÉE DE L'ECUSSON ROSÉ
> *Not vintaged, méthode champenoise: Pinot Noir*

CUVÉE DE L'ECUSSON BRUT
> *Vintaged, méthode champenoise: Pinot Blanc, Chardonnay, Pinot Noir*

DOMAINE CLOS DES ROCHERS CRÉMANT DE LUXEMBOURG BRUT
> *Vintaged, méthode champenoise: Pinot Blanc, Riesling*

MALTA

JUST THREE SPARKLING WINES ARE PRODUCED IN MALTA, ALL BY EMMANUEL DELICATA, BUT ONLY ONE – GELLEWZA FRIZZANTE, A PÉTILLANT DEMI-SEC ROSÉ – IS MADE FROM MALTESE-GROWN GRAPES.

Delicata is a well-equipped modern winery that has made sparkling wine since 1995. There is a frizzante-styled dry Chardonnay and sweet Moscato wines from Italian-grown grapes, which are shipped as bunches in refrigerated containers to Malta where they are pressed and fermented. The method of production is carbonation, which is effective for low-

pressure styles, although plans are afoot to change to *cuve close*.

MOLDOVA

THE MOST REMARKABLE SPARKLING WINE FACILITY IN THE WORLD IS LOCATED AT CRICOVA, SOME 25 KILOMETRES NORTH OF CHISINAU. NOT THAT IT PRODUCES ANYTHING REMARKABLE IN THE WAY OF WINE, BUT IT IS SUCH A VAST UNDERGROUND COMPLEX THAT IT MAKES ONE WONDER ABOUT ITS ORIGINAL PURPOSE.

Hewn out of solid rock 80 metres below the ground, it is equivalent in area to 25 well spread out villages above Cricova. The 'official' explanation is that it was excavated for stone to build houses at Chisinau, and no doubt that is where much of the rock went, but Moldova's capital would have to be solid-rock itself to accommodate all of it.

The explanation would be more plausible if the Cricova winery, which occupies just a small part of this man-made cavern, happened to be the only thing down there, but it is not. It is an underground city and it is so enormous that it has 65 kilometres of roads; not just tracks for tippers to trundle along, but a sophisticated network of named highways which are illuminated by street lighting. Vehicles are strictly controlled by an integrated system of traffic lights and road signs, and off each major highway there are a series of minor streets leading to 120 kilometres of fully-powered storage bunkers.

It simply is not credible that the Cricova winery would need sufficient space to store the equivalent of a half-billion years of production, so the question must be asked, why is the entire

CRICOVA UNDERGROUND WINERY, MOLDOVA

underground complex fitted out? What was it originally intended to house?

The answer is obvious the moment anyone enters Cricova through its solitary two-lane access road, which can be sealed-off by a series of massive, electronically operated, blast-proof steel doors. Inside Cricova there are opulent reception halls, a dining room the like of which cannot be seen anywhere else in Eastern Europe, and a cellar boasting priceless old vintages of Mouton Rothschild, Latour, Romanée-Conti *et al*.

The penny literally drops when visiting the luxurious men's room with solid, gleaming marble on the floor, walls and ceiling. After all, who but the now defunct Politburo could afford gold-plated taps when most of the peasants above Cricova do not even have an outside loo? And having tasted the fizz, it is little wonder that they wanted to lay down such a magnificent cellar of foreign wines.

NETHERLANDS

ALTHOUGH THIS COUNTRY IS SITUATED TO THE NORTH OF BELGIUM, SOME OF ITS 59 LITTLE-KNOWN AND VERY TINY VINEYARDS ARE LOCATED EAST OF MAASTRICHT, WHICH IS IN FACT MORE SOUTHERLY THAN THE BELGIAN VINEYARDS OF BRABANT.

Most are in fact to be found to the north, including the country's largest vineyard, De Agthuysen, which also produces the Netherlands' only commercial sparkling wine under the **Hof Van Putten** label.

Winemaker Fred Lorshield utilises grapes from two vineyards he owns in Atlantic-lashed Zuidland, which is just southwest of Rotterdam. Winjngaard de Agthuysen and Domein de Vier Ambachten are both approximately three hectares, all the grapes are hand-picked, and only the *méthode champenoise* is used.

Some 200 cases of Hof Van Putton have been produced every year since 1994, and this will soon increase to 500 cases. The grape varieties are 30% Pinot Noir, 30% Chardonnay, 30% Pinot Blanc, and 10% other Pinot varieties, and come exclusively from Ambachten. The Cuvée

comes in two styles: *droog* (dry) and *extra droog* (extra dry).

As from 1996, a new *cuvée* has been blended from both vineyards. Called Cuvée 2000, it is a 50/50 blend of Kerner from Agthuysen, and Reichensteiner from Ambachten.

Another vineyard even further north, at Maarssen, in the southern suburbs of Amsterdam, called **Winjngaard de Kikvors** occasionally produces sparkling wine but does not bother to commercialise it. However, its location of 52.08°N is equivalent in the southern hemisphere to 392 miles south of the most southerly tip of New Zealand's South Island, which is so preposterous that Winjngaard de Kikvors is included for curiosity's sake.

RUSSIA

EACH YEAR RUSSIA PRODUCES FIVE MILLION CASES OF SPARKLING WINE, AROUND HALF OF WHICH IS MADE FROM IMPORTED WINE AND GRAPE CONCENTRATE. ALMOST ALL OF IT IS PRODUCED USING A SYSTEM THAT WAS INVENTED BY SOVIET TECHNICIANS IN THE MID-1950S.

Known as the 'Russian Continuous Flow Method', it was developed to make fizz by a natural second fermentation, but in the cheapest, easiest and quickest way possible (*see p.15*).

The largest sparkling wine production centres are in Moscow, Rostov-na-Donu, St Petersburg, Nizhniy Novgorod and Tsimlyansk, the latter being known for a red fizz called Tsimlyanskoe, which is made primarily from the Tsimlyansk grape bolstered by a little Plechistik.

There is very little *méthode champenoise*, but the best comes from **Abrau-Durso**, west of Krasnodar, where vines are grown on southwest-facing coastal slopes overlooking the Black Sea.

SERBIA

THESE VINEYARDS WERE RELATIVELY UNAFFECTED BY THE FIGHTING IN THE FORMER YUGOSLAVIA, BUT THERE IS VERY LITTLE TRADITION FOR SPARKLING WINE IN SERBIAN CULTURE, ALTHOUGH WHAT IS PRODUCED COMES PRIMARILY FROM VINEYARDS IN FRUSKA GORA, SMEDEREVO, VRANJE, AND JAGODINA.

N/A
NAVIP
ZEMUN
- 165,000 cases

The only sparkling wine producer of any repute, Navip was established in 1848. It owns 1,700 hectares of vineyards and also buys grapes from various cooperatives.
WINEMAKER
Ruzica Gojkovic
HOUSE STYLE & RANGE
All *demi-sec*, but not tasted recently.
MILION WHITE
Not vintaged, cuve close: Riesling, Sauvignon Blanc, Semillon, Smederevka
MILION RED
Not vintaged, cuve close: Merlot, Pinot Noir, Gamay, Prokupac
FRUSKOGORSKI BISER WHITE
Vintaged, carbonated: Smederevka, Riesling, Sauvigno
FRUSKOGORSKI BISER RED
Not vintaged, carbonated: Pinot Noir, Prokupac, Merl

SLOVAKIA

SPARKLING WINES HAVE BEEN MADE SINCE 1825 AT SERED, EAST OF BRATISLAVA, IN THE DANUBE DISTRICT AND ARE STILL MARKETED UNDER THE HUBERT BRAND, BUT THE QUALITY IS NOT PARTICULARLY HIGH.

SLOVENIA

THE WEALTHIEST PART OF THE FORMER YUGOSLAVIA, SLOVENIA HAS A PER CAPITA INCOME SIMILAR TO THAT OF NEIGHBOURING AUSTRIA PLUS NEGLIGIBLE INFLATION.

As the country suffered minimal damage in its fight for freedom in 1991, the vineyards are intact and producers have had little difficulty continuing their international commerce. Sparkling (*prneci*) and *perlant* (*biser*) wines have a more traditional role in Slovenia than in any other state of former Yugoslavia.

AVIA
See SLOVENIJAVINO

65
BARBARA INTERNATIONAL
LJUBLJANA
- 9,000 cases

Privately owned by the Istenic family, Barbara International is considered 'new' in Slovenian terms, although it was established in 1968, and has been producing single-vineyard *méthode champenoise* for 30 years from the stenic's own hillside domaine in Stara Vas.

WINEMAKER
Janez Istenic

HOUSE STYLE & RANGE
Clearly the best Slovenian sparkling wines, but not yet of true international standard.

BARBARA (SEC)
Not vintaged, méthode champenoise:
80% Welschriesling, 20% Sauvignon Blanc

CUVÉE PRINCESSE (DEMI-SEC)
Not vintaged, méthode champenoise:
80% Chardonnay, 20% Welschriesling

GOLF BRUT
Not vintaged, méthode champenoise:
70% Chardonnay, 30% Sauvignon Blanc

MICHELLE ROSÉ (DEMI-SEC)
Not vintaged, méthode champenoise:
70% Blaufrankisch, 30% Pinot Noir

MIHA (RED, DEMI-SEC)
Not vintaged, méthode champenoise:
80% Blaufrankisch, 20% Pinot Noir

NO.1 CUVÉE SPECIALE BRUT
Vintaged, méthode champenoise: 80% Chardonnay,
20% Welschriesling

CLUB SLOVIN
See JERUZALEM ORMOZ

CONTESSA BAGUERI
See KMETIJSKA ZADRUGA GORISKA BRDA

CUVÉE PRINCESSE
See BARBARA INTERNATIONAL

GOLF
See BARBARA INTERNATIONAL

50
JERUZALEM ORMOZ
ORMOZ
Named after a locally renowned site in the centre of the Ljutomer-Ormoz region, where this well-equipped, modern winery has its own vineyards.

WINEMAKER
Andreja Brglez

HOUSE STYLE & RANGE
Basic *cuve close* quality.

CLUB SLOVIN
Not vintaged, cuve close: grape varieties not revealed

SEKT JERUZALEM
Not vintaged, cuve close: grape varieties not revealed

50
KMETIJSKA ZADRUGA GORISKA BRDA
DUBROVO
A large cooperative with a modern winery in the western part of Slovenia, where grapes are grown under a Mediterranean climate.

VINEYARD AT NOVA GORA, NEAR KRSKO, 100KM
EAST OF LJUBLJANA, SLOVENIA

WINEMAKER
Irena Zezlin

HOUSE STYLE & RANGE
Basic *cuve close* quality.

CONTESSA BAGUERI
Not vintaged, cuve close: grape varieties not revealed

PENECA CHARDONNAY
Not vintaged, cuve close: Chardonnay

PENECA PINOT
Not vintaged, cuve close: Pinot Blanc, Pinot Gris

PENECA PROSECCO
Not vintaged, cuve close: Prosecco

PENECA REBULA
Not vintaged, cuve close: Ribolla

MICHELLE
See BARBARA INTERNATIONAL

MIHA
See BARBARA INTERNATIONAL

NO.1 CUVÉE SPECIALE
See BARBARA INTERNATIONAL

55
RADGONSKE GORICE
GORNJA RADOGNA
• 50,000 cases
The oldest and largest producer of sparkling wine in Slovenia, this firm was founded by a winemaker called Klenosek, who is credited with introducing *méthode champenoise* in 1852.

WINEMAKER
Filipic Alojz

HOUSE STYLE & RANGE
Not up to today's international standards.

RADGONSKA BISER
Not vintaged: method and grape varieties not revealed

SEBRINA RADGONSKA PENINA

Not vintaged, méthode champenoise:
90% Chardonnay, 10% Pinot Noir

ZLATA RADGONSKA PENINA
Not vintaged, méthode champenoise:
90% Chardonnay, 10% Pinot Noir

ZLATA RADGONSKA PENINA ROSÉ
Not vintaged, méthode champenoise: Pinot Noir

50
SLOVENIJAVINO
LJUBLJANA
Modern winery that sources its wines from a number of private and cooperative producers throughout Slovenia.

WINEMAKER
Joze Kovic

HOUSE STYLE & RANGE
Basic *cuve close* quality.

AVIA
Not vintaged, cuve close: grape varieties not revealed

VALVASOR
Not vintaged, cuve close: grape varieties not revealed

VALVASOR
See SLOVENIJAVINO

50
VINAG
MARIBOR
Sparkling wines produced from vines growing either side of the Drava river, just outside Maribor, and stored in 200-year-old cellars.

HOUSE STYLE & RANGE
Basic *cuve close* quality.

VINAG BRUT
Not vintaged, cuve close: grape varieties not revealed

50
VINAKOPER
KOPER
This large winery is in the Koper wine district, which is Refosco country, and is located in the Primorska region.

WINEMAKER
Iztok Klenar

HOUSE STYLE & RANGE
Basic *cuve close* quality.

PENECE VINO CAPRIS
Not vintaged, cuve close: grape varieties not revealed

55
VINO BREZICE
BREZICE
Better-known as the sole producer of Slovenian 'port' and Adria Cooler low-alcohol products.

HOUSE STYLE & RANGE
Not up to today's international standards.

BARON MOCSON (SEC)
Not vintaged, méthode champenoise: grape varieties
not revealed

BARON MOCSON (RED, DEMI-SEC)
Not vintaged, méthode champenoise: grape varieties not revealed

GRAJSKI BISER
Vintaged: method and grape varieties not revealed

VIPAVA 1894

VIPAVA

Various *cuve close* sparkling wines are produced by Lidija Vidmar under the Vipava label from grapes grown in the Primorska region, where the Mediterranean climate is tempered by Alpine influence.

SWITZERLAND

THE FIRST SWISS SPARKLING WINE WAS MADE BY LOUIS-EDWARD MAULER AT THE ABBEY OF ST-PIERRE IN MÔTIERS, NEUFCHÂTEL, IN 1829. BY THE LATE-19TH CENTURY THESE WINES HAD CREATED AN ENVIABLE REPUTATION IN GREAT BRITAIN AND THE USA.

In Britain's *Field* magazine (July 1878), the editor drew attention to the benefits of Mauler's Swiss Champagne (sic), which he started drinking on the recommendation of an eminent physician who had prescribed it for a stomach complaint. To his surprise he found that he preferred it to more expensive French Champagnes.

Things have obviously changed since then: Swiss sparkling wines now rank as some of the least inspiring bubblies in the world. There can be no argument about whether great French Champagnes were produced in the 19th century because a few old bottles are still available to taste at a number of *grande marque* houses, so either the quality of Swiss fizz has declined dramatically or the editor of *Field* in 1878 had an over-inflated opinion of these wines. The latter seems most likely.

The main obstacle to success for Swiss wines in general has been the excessive yields allowed in the vineyards. However, this does not appear to be the main problem with the country's sparkling wines. Some passable fizz does exist, but there are only a few producers and the common denominator among the less palatable fizzy wines seems to be a lack of winemaking expertise resulting, in some cases, in basically faulty wines.

That and the fact that the majority of sparkling wines, not even the most famous are not made with grapes of exclusively Swiss origin!

BACCARAT

See CAVE DE GENÈVE

55
LA CAVE DE GENÈVE

SATIGNY, GENÈVE

This producer of pure Swiss sparkling wines was established as recently as 1994, and purchases grapes exclusively from 150 growers in the canton of Genève. Fizz is just one of 60 different wines produced, but it is one of the best Swiss sparkling wines I have tasted, albeit in a modest, fruity style.

HOUSE STYLE & RANGE

The Blanc de Blancs is too amylic and foamy in the mouth, but the Rosé has no amylic character, and lovely depth of exuberant fruit.

BACCARAT BLANC DE BLANCS CHARDONNAY
Not vintaged, méthode champenoise: Chardonnay

BACCARAT BRUT ROSÉ PRESTIGE
Vintaged, méthode champenoise: Pinot Noir

50
MAULER & CIE

MÔTIERS, NEUFCHÂTEL

- 40,000 cases

The oldest and most famous producer of Swiss sparkling wines, Mauler concentrates exclusively on this style of wine and should therefore have developed a high level of expertise. But from an international point of view of what is an acceptable quality for non-Champagne sparkling wine, this company seems to be stuck in a time warp circa 1950s. Production comes from Mauler's own vineyards - 20 hectares on the lakeside of Neufchâtel, and 30 hectares in France.

WINEMAKER

Blaise Mauler

HOUSE STYLE & RANGE

Basic lines are best in a simple, fruity way, but more upmarket *cuvées* are dominated by the wrong sort of malolactic (too much diacetyl), or too much sulphur.

BLANC DE BLANCS
Not vintaged, méthode champenoise: Chardonnay

★ ROSÉ BRUT
Not vintaged, méthode champenoise: 10% Chardonnay, 50% Pinot Noir, 40% Cabernet Sauvignon

TRADITION BRUT
Not vintaged, méthode champenoise: 10% Chardonnay, 20% Reserve wines, 60% French Pinot Blanc and Chenin Blanc

CUVÉE EXCELLENCE
Vintaged, méthode champenoise: 30% Chardonnay, 70% Pinot Noir

★ CUVÉE DE RESERVE
Vintaged, méthode champenoise: 40% Chardonnay, 50% Pinot Noir, 10% French Pinot Blanc and Chenin Blanc

N/A
VALSANGIACOMO 1831

CHIASSO, TICINO

- 1,700 cases

Merlot del Ticino is consistently one of Switzerland's best red wines, and Valsangiacomo is one of the three top producers, but I have yet to be convinced that there is any merit in adding bubbles to it

WINEMAKER

Uberto Valsangiacomo

HOUSE STYLE & RANGE

Tasted only once, when it had nasty aromas, thus opinion reserved.

SPUMANTE TICINO EXTRA BRUT
Not vintaged, méthode champenoise: Merlot

TURKEY

IT MAY COME AS A SURPRISE TO DISCOVER THAT TURKEY HAS THE FIFTH-LARGEST AREA UNDER VINE IN THE WORLD.

However, because the population is mainly Muslim, the grapes produced are mostly used as fresh fruit, sultanas or currants. Any wines that are produced are often flabby, too heavy, alcoholic, over-sulphured and often oxidized

The most important producer of sparkling wine is the **Sevilen Vineyard and Winery**, a family-owned firm that was established in 1942, and sells 20,000 cases of fizz under the **Pirlanta** label every year. Sevilen's winemaker, Coskun Guner, uses 70% Sémillon, 20% Colombard and 10% local varieties from the company's own vineyards west of Anatolia. The production method is carbonation, the carbonic gas being injected into a full tank of wine held at 0°C and then bottled at this temperature to retain as much pressure as possible.

UKRAINE

THE CRIMEA, OR KRYM, IS THE FAMOUS PENINSULA THAT ENCLOSES THE SEA OF AZOV AND, UNLIKE THE REST OF THE UKRAINE, THE CRIMEAN WINE INDUSTRY IS PRIMARILY FOCUSED ON SPARKLING WINE PRODUCTION.

It was here, in the villages of Alushta and Sudak, that L S Golitsin made the first Ukrainian sparkling wine in 1799. Sparkling Krim is a *méthode champenoise* wine made in five styles, from brut through to sweet, and in a semi-sweet red version. The grapes used include Chardonnay, Pinot Noir, Rizling, Aligoté and Cabernet. The wines are coarse and old-fashioned, but the Brut and Demi-Sec Red, which used to be available in export markets before the fall of the Soviet empire, sold on novelty value.

Various other dubious quality sparkling wines are produced at Nikolayev-Kherson, just northeast of Krym, and Odessa.

AFRICA: SOUTH AFRICA

THE FIRST SOUTH AFRICAN SPARKLING WINE WAS CARBONATED: A BICYCLE-PUMP JOB, AS IT'S KNOWN IN THE TRADE. PRODUCED BY THE STELLENBOSCH FARMERS' WINERY IN 1929, IT WAS VERY SWEET AND CONSISTED OF STILL CHENIN BLANC AND CLAIRETTE BLANCHE WINES THAT HAD BEEN INJECTED WITH CARBONIC GAS, IN MUCH THE SAME WAY THAT COLA OR ANY OTHER FIZZY SOFT DRINK IS MADE. CALLED GRAND MOUSSEUX VIN DOUX, IT WAS THE MARKET LEADER FOR 60 YEARS, AND IT IS STILL A BIG SUCCESS TODAY, PARTICULARLY IN NAMIBIA.

A modest step up in the quality of South African fizz occurred in 1945, when Nederburg produced its Première Cuvée, the country's first *cuve close*. But any hint of the emergence of a serious sparkling wine industry had to wait until 1971, when Frans Malan produced the first *méthode champenoise* at Simonsig. It was called Kaapse Vonkel (which simply means 'sparkling wine') and the first *cuvée* was made primarily from Chenin Blanc. However, the South African market was in the grip of low-priced wines and no other producer dared follow Simonsig upmarket until Boschendal produced its first *méthode champenoise* in 1979.

The next turning point in South Africa's embryonic sparkling wine industry came in 1984, when Jeff Grier of Villiera entered into a ten-year partnership with champenois Jean-Louis Denois. More recently, Champagne Mumm has collaborated with Nicky Krone of Twee Jongegezellen, producer of Krone Borealis, one of South Africa's best sparkling wines.

The ostracism of South Africa during the final phase of its apartheid era stifled developments in its wine industry at a time when wine was generally going through one of its most active and progressive periods throughout the rest of the world. When the country eventually embraced a multiracial democracy, world markets suddenly opened up, and South African winemakers discovered that many of their wines were not up to the standards expected internationally. They were eager to learn, though, and started this process in the winery, where fairly instant results could be achieved through stricter grape selection and a massive investment in new wood and better equipment. However, it was the Cape's vineyards that were at the root of South Africa's quality problem.

After lengthy international isolation, the country's viticultural knowledge was lagging ten years behind, thus a research and improvement project was embarked upon to provide the country's wine industry with long-term stability. The face-lift taking place in wineries throughout the country might have had an instant effect, but the Vine Improvement Programme, or VIP as it has become known, was intended to leapfrog the end of the 20th century and firmly establish the Rainbow State's wine industry in the new millennium.

A substantial proportion of South Africa's growing export income was diverted into this VIP, phase one of which involved clonal selection and rootstock improvement. A vine needs three years before it yields a crop, and five years before the first inklings of its true potential can be discerned, thus the earliest effect of the initial phase one period is not due to kick in until the

BOSCHENDAL ESTATE IN THE GROOT DRAKENSTEIN VALLEY, FRANSCHHOEK, CAPE PROVINCE, SOUTH AFRICA

end of 1999. Furthermore, the main thrust of phase one is still underway, and phase two, which is to test the suitability of phase one clones and rootstock in the different *terroirs* of the Cape, is an ambitious and very long-term task. Although a number of South Africa's wines have noticeably improved, the real jump in quality will not start to materialise for a decade or more.

Improvements that have been made so far are confined to still wines because all immediate progress is restricted to the winery, and the learning curve for sparkling wine vinification is far more difficult than that for still wine. Sparkling wine simply takes much longer to produce. A winemaker can see the result of his or her work on a still wine within a year of its harvest, but it takes at least two years, often three and sometimes even longer before a serious quality sparkling wine can be taken off its yeast lees.

At the moment most sparkling wine is made by *cuve close*, and some have even been carbonated, while many of those made by *méthode champenoise* (called Cap Classique) are merely fruity fizz, but there is a fine structure and a certain delicacy of fruit about Cape grapes that promises an interesting future.

MYSTERY OF THE FIRST SOUTH AFRICAN MÉTHODE CHAMPENOISE

Although Simonsig claims to have made the country's first *méthode champenoise* sparkling wine, and other references support this, it is open to question. Even the most authoritative book on the history of South African wine, *The Complete Book of South African Wine* (John Kench, Phyllis Hands & David Hughes) is uncertain. On page 163 the authors state that Kaapse Vonkel 'is the first South African sparkling wine produced by the *méthode champenoise*' but then in the very next paragraph they claim 'In earlier days in the Cape, all sparkling wines were made this way, but with the perfection of tank fermentation, bottle fermentation all but disappeared'. As Nederburg's Première Cuvée was the first *cuve close* in 1945, this suggests that there were a number of *méthode champenoise* wines made prior to this date, and it certainly seems plausible that in any significant wine-producing country, someone somewhere would be attempting to make a *méthode champenoise* sparkling wine by the late 19th century. In the Cape, however, it remains a bit of a mystery.

AVON
See AVONTUUR

75
AVONTUUR
SOMERSET WEST, STELLENBOSCH

• 400 cases

This estate is famous for its upfront wines, particularly reds, and Le Blush, a pink Chardonnay that was accidentally made when someone in the winery put Chardonnay into a barrel that had previously been used for Merlot. Le Blush was so successful that Avontuur now repeats the process deliberately every year. Now this wine estate is moving into sparkling wine, and doing it pretty successfully too.

WINEMAKER

Jean-Luc Sweerts

HOUSE STYLE & RANGE

The Brut is fresh and crisp with zingy fruit and a good, dry finish. I have not tasted the Avon Blush.

AVON BLUSH, CAP CLASSIQUE
  Vintaged, méthode champenoise: 100% Pinot Noir

★ AVON BRUT, CAP CLASSIQUE
  Vintaged, méthode champenoise: 100% Chardonnay

78
BACKSBERG
KLAPMUTS, PAARL

• 2,000 cases

This estate was made famous by the late Sydney Back, who was three times Champion Estate Winemaker, and his son Michael has continued to produce some of South Africa's most consistent and classy wines. Backsberg launched its first vintage (1985) in 1988 to celebrate Sydney Back's 50th year as owner-winemaker.

WINEMAKER

Hardy Laubser

HOUSE STYLE & RANGE

Light yet rich, with creamy, biscuity fruit, this *cuvée* has a tendency to go through an awkward developmental stage during which the nose is not as inviting as the palate. However, the inherent quality always comes through in the end.

★ CAP CLASSIQUE BRUT
  Vintaged, méthode champenoise: 45% Chardonnay, 55% Pinot Noir

N/A
BARRYDALE
BARRYDALE, KLEIN KAROO

• 200 cases

This claims to be the only cooperative in South Africa to use the *méthode champenoise*, but see HELDERBERG.

WINEMAKER

Bob de Villers

HOUSE STYLE & RANGE

Tasted only once, I found the 1991 vintage to be too malty and one-dimensional, but must reserve judgement.

TRADOUW BLANC DE BLANCS, CAP CLASSIQUE
  Vintaged, méthode champenoise: 100% Chardonnay

80
GRAHAM BECK
MADEBA, ROBERTSON

Graham Beck produces budget fizz by transfer method under the Madeba label, while reserving his eponymous brand for more serious Cap Classique wines, which also sport a very stylish presentation.

WINEMAKER

Pieter Ferreira

HOUSE STYLE & RANGE

The Brut is slightly amylic, but is saved by the elegance of its fruit, which is very fresh and fluffy, and usually goes zesty and toasty after a year in bottle. The Chardonnay Sur Lie is also slightly amylic, but again it is saved by the elegance of its fruit, which has a more sherbetty feel than that of the Brut. It gains its name from being left *sur lie* (on its sediment) for six months prior to bottling.

There is nothing amylic about the Blanc de Blancs. Why should this be so? Well, half the wine is barrel-fermented, the temperature of which is almost certainly higher than that required to produce the peardrop aroma, on top of which the wine spends four years on its yeast rather than just one or two, thus any amylic aromas from the other half of the wine will be lost or hidden. The Blanc de Blancs has lovely lemony, toasty fruit, like a good, mature Chardonnay, and with an extra year in bottle, this becomes a citrussy, creamy, oaky humdinger of a wine.

The Madeba Cellars name appears on simpler *cuvées*, which are very fresh, fruity and easy to drink - look closely at the small print on some of the better British supermarket fizz from this country. British-based, Australian-trained flying winemaker John Worontschak has roosted here a couple of times, utilising reserves to produce a superior cheap fizz with mature, biscuity aromas, yet fresh, zesty fruit on the palate.

★ BRUT CAP CLASSIQUE
  Not vintaged, méthode champenoise: 50% Chardonnay, 50% Pinot Noir

★ MADEBA BRUT, ROBERTSON
  Not vintaged, transfer method: 20-40% Chardonnay 60-80% Pinot Noir

★★ BLANC DE BLANCS BRUT, CAP CLASSIQUE
  Vintaged, 50% barrique-fermented, méthode champenoise: 100% Chardonnay

★ CHARDONNAY SUR LIE, CAP CLASSIQUE
  Vintaged, méthode champenoise: 100% Chardonnay

N/A
BELLINGHAM
RANDBURG, PAARL

Under Graham Beck of Graham Beck Winery in Robertson, Bellingham has gone from a good value commercial brand sourced from wherever the price was right to a fine quality range of own-vineyard wines, priced a tad more upmarket, but even better value for money.

WINEMAKER

Charles Hopkins

HOUSE RANGE

BRUT
  Not vintaged, cuve close: predominantly Chardonnay

70
BERGKELDER
STELLENBOSCH

• 41,000 cases

• Other labels - Pongrácz, JC le Roux

This large winery is part of Rupert International, and is responsible for the maturation, bottling and marketing of wine from a fluctuating number of member estates, as well as making and marketing its own wines under the Fleur du Cap, Stellenryck, Pongrácz and JC le Roux labels.

Pongrácz is named after Desiderius Pongrácz, an officer-cadet in the Royal Hungarian Army who spent almost eight years in a Siberian labour camp. Repatriated after the death of Stalin, Pongrácz escaped Hungary during the 1956 uprising and sought refuge in South Africa, where he made his name as a consultant viticulturist and author of many books, including the small but seminal *Practical Viticulture* (1978).

WINEMAKER

Melanie Kriel

HOUSE STYLE & RANGE

The Pongrácz is a contradictory *cuvée* with rich, complex flavours that are coarsened by youthfully oxidative aromas, robbing the wine of its finesse. Gentler handling could bump the overall rating to 85 points at least. Both JC le Roux wines are also made in an oxidative style, the Pinot Noir having a big toffee finish, while the Chardonnay is a touch coarse and bitter. A new JC le Roux *cuvée* is due to be released in Autumn 1998.

PONGRÁCZ BRUT CAP CLASSIQUE
Not vintaged, méthode champenoise: 37% Chardonnay, 63% Pinot Noir

C LE ROUX CHARDONNAY, CAP CLASSIQUE
Vintaged, méthode champenoise: 100% Chardonnay

C LE ROUX PINOT NOIR, CAP CLASSIQUE
Vintaged, méthode champenoise: 10% Chardonnay, 90% Pinot Noir

N/A
BLOEMENDAL
URBANVILLE
● 700 cases
An up-and-coming winery with first-rate Cabernet Sauvignon, and a growing reputation for its fizz.
WINEMAKER
Jackie Coetzee
HOUSE STYLE & RANGE
Tasted just twice, and the burnt-toffee aftertaste on the second occasion left me unimpressed. Judgement reserved.

BLOEMENDAL BRUT CAP CLASSIQUE
Vintaged, méthode champenoise: 100% Chardonnay

N/A
BOLAND
HUGUENOT, PAARL
This cooperative is highly-praised for its excellent oak-aged Cabernet and now makes rich, toasty Chardonnay, but fizz is a new departure, and cooperative-produced carbonated Sauvignon Blanc seems to be a trend (see FRANSCHHOEK VINEYARDS).
WINEMAKER
Charl du Plessis
HOUSE RANGE
BRUT
Vintaged, carbonated: 100% Sauvignon Blanc

5
BON COURAGE
ROBERTSON
● 850 cases
Owner André Bruwer was Champion Estate Winemaker in 1985 and 1986, yet if anything the quality has gone up since his son Jacques took over. The first sparkling wine was produced in 1991, but the first *méthode champenoise* was made in 1995 and launched under the Jacques Bruère (a Gallicised version of Bruwer) label in 1997.
WINEMAKER
Jacques Bruwer
HOUSE STYLE & RANGE
The Jacques Bruère Blanc de Blancs is a

creamy, rich classic with slow-building, biscuity complexity of impressive finesse. Just ten per cent barrique-fermented wine used, which seems just about perfect to me. Certainly a wine to watch. The Brut Reserve has an excellent reputation, but I have not tasted it. The carbonated Blush is very sweet.

★★ JACQUES BRUÈRE BLANC DE BLANCS NV CAP CLASSIQUE
Not vintaged, méthode champenoise: 100% Chardonnay

VIN DOUX BLUSH SPARKLING
Not vintaged, carbonated: predominantly Pinot Noir plus a little Muscat

JACQUES BRUÈRE BRUT RESERVE CAP CLASSIQUE
Vintaged, méthode champenoise: 50% Chardonnay, 50% Pinot Noir

N/A
BOSCHENDAL
PAARL
● 10,000 cases
Vines have been growing at 'Bossendaal' (as it was originally known) since 1685, having been planted by Jean de Long, a Huguenot emigré. He sold the property in 1715 to Abraham de Villiers, another Huguenot, and it remained in the de Villiers family for over 160 years.

The economic depression caused by phylloxera forced the de Villiers family to sell Boschendal and within a few years it became one of the 30-odd estates owned by Cecil Rhodes as part of his grandiose Fruit Farm scheme. In 1969 Boschendal and all the estates belonging to Rhodes Fruit Farms were taken over by the Anglo-American Corporation, the current owners.

Best-known as one of the Cape's pioneering *méthode champenoise* producers, Boschendal made its first fizz in 1979, but also makes a large range of still wines. Many of these other wines are much more exciting than Boschendal's bubbly, but Mike Graham is a relatively new broom (1996), and hopefully he will sweep the place clean.
WINEMAKER
Mike Graham
HOUSE STYLE & RANGE
I have tasted some dodgy Boschendal fizz in the past and several samples of the shipments that coincided with the writing of this book were corked. When Grand Pavillon is on form it has a tangy richness of fruit, with a touch of biscuity complexity, but it has never been exciting, yet this is the fizz they tend to push on export markets. The Brut is usually better, although also not special (although it gets good reviews in South Africa), and I have had off-bottles of that *cuvée* too. What the talented Mike Graham will make of these wines is anyone's guess, but by my reckoning we should be due to find out as from 1999.

THE BOSCHENDAL WINERY, ESTABLISHED BY HUGUENOTS IN 1685

BRUT CAP CLASSIQUE
Not vintaged, méthode champenoise: 50% Chardonnay, 50% Pinot Noir

LE GRAND PAVILLON BRUT NV CAP CLASSIQUE
Not vintaged, méthode champenoise: Chardonnay, Cruchen Blanc, Sémillon

JACQUES BRUÈRE
See BON COURAGE

N/A
BUITENVERWACHTING
CONSTANTIA
● 1,100 cases
This is part of the historical Constantia estate; its cellars are over 200 years old and have had many owners, not all of them wine producers. By the 1970s, the vineyards were in very poor condition and the buildings in a state of disrepair, but the Müller family, who purchased the property, replanted the vineyards, renovated the buildings and have built a new winery. *Buitenverwachting* means 'beyond expectation' and as from 1985, which was the new owner's first vintage, this estate has performed according to its name, justifiably earning an outstanding reputation for wines of virtually every style. The first *méthode champenoise* was produced in 1988.
WINEMAKER
Hermann Kirschbaum
HOUSE STYLE & RANGE
The current *cuvée* is a perfumed yet rich and full sparkling wine in a non-classic, almost contradictory style. It is not an uninteresting wine, but the odd element is, I think, the Pinot Gris. Kirschbaum is in any case about to change the blend, hence no overall rating, as all *cuvées* will be 100% Pinot Noir in future.

★ BRUT CAP CLASSIQUE
Not vintaged, méthode champenoise: 20% Chardonnay, 40% Pinot Gris, 40% Pinot Noir

75
CABRIÈRE ESTATE
FRANSCHHOEK

• 30,000 cases

Highly regarded fizz from the Cabrière Estate, owned by Achim von Arnim, who used to be the winemaker at Boschendal until 1984, when he left to carve out his own brand from this mountainside vineyard.

WINEMAKER
Achim von Arnim

HOUSE STYLE & RANGE

The non-vintage Brut just scrapes in for its half-star rating on the fresh and fruity ticket, but it needs layering with more flavours and a touch of finesse to make the grade of a top estate fizz. Arnim's Blanc de Blancs fares much better despite the extraordinary mint-caramel character, which is distinctive, but detracts from the finesse of the wine. Goodness knows where the mint comes from: the effect of Cabrière's *terroir* on the Pinot perhaps? The caramel is, however, derived in part from malolactic and/or oak, and I say that knowing full well that Arnim steadfastly maintains his wines don't go through malolactic. Neither does Krug, but it is not so adamant that it never happens during or after the secondary fermentation, and the caramel in Arnim's Blanc de Blancs certainly seems like diacetyl to me.

If the mint-caramel provides this wine with some novelty value, then the higher acidity certainly gives it the edge over most other *cuvées*. For a winemaker hell-bent on avoiding malolactic, it seems strange that Arnim does not seem to mind if his *cuvées* display malolactic character. The Brut Sauvage, for example, would appear to have too much creamy, caramel malolactic influencing the nose and it matters very little if this is malolactic, oak or whatever, because it is too dominant and the effect is the same: it detracts from the potential finesse of the wine. The fruit is very rich and soft, with a fat, caramel and vanilla

flavour that needs more acidity. The least controversial and most immediately appealing of all the wines is the Rosé, which has a golden colour with barely any hint of pink, but plenty of soft, succulent fruit. Arnim's *cuvées* are fascinating concoctions, and they are wines that all devotees of New World sparkling wine must try. I will be following these wines with great interest - the quality of the fruit is there, a number of extraordinary wines are testament to Arnim's skill as a winemaker, and the man obviously has very fixed ideas about what he wants to achieve. I just have the feeling that his best *cuvées* have yet to be released.

✮ PIERRE JOURDAN CAP CLASSIQUE BRUT
Not vintaged, méthode champenoise: 60% Chardonnay, 40% Pinot Noir

★ PIERRE JOURDAN BLANC DE BLANCS CAP CLASSIQUE BRUT
Not vintaged, méthode champenoise: 100% Chardonnay

✮ PIERRE JOURDAN CAP CLASSIQUE BRUT SAUVAGE
Not vintaged, méthode champenoise: 60% Chardonnay, 40% Pinot Noir

★ PIERRE JOURDAN CAP CLASSIQUE CUVÉE BELLE ROSÉ
Not vintaged, méthode champenoise: 100% Pinot Noir

CAPE LEVANT
See SONOP WINERY

N/A
CHAMONIX
FRANSCHHOEK

This 35-hectare wine estate owned by Chris Hellinger has a growing following.

WINEMAKER
Peter Arnold

HOUSE RANGE
COURCHEVEL CUVÉE BRUT
Not vintaged, carbonated: 100% Clairette Blanche

LOUIS CHAUVIN
See STELLENBOSCH WINE FARMERS

PLASTIC CRATES READY FOR THE HARVEST AT CLOS CABRIÈRE, FRANSCHHOEK, CAPE PROVINCE

N/A
CINZANO
STELLENBOSCH

Produced under licence by Gilbeys, whose other brands include Alphen, Bertrams, Craighall, Mondial and Stellenvale.

HOUSE RANGE
SPUMANTE
Not vintaged, cuve close: grape varieties not revealed
VITTORIA
Not vintaged, cuve close: Chenin Blanc, Sauvignon Bla...

LA COTTE
See FRANSCHHOEK VINEYARDS

CUVÉE CAP FOR MUMM
See TWEE JONGEGEZELLEN

DE HELDERE
See HELDERBERG

N/A
EIKENDALE
STELLENBOSCH

Owned by Für Planatagen of Switzerland, Eikendale has developed a growing reputatio... for its wines in recent years, particularly its Chardonnay, Merlot and Classique, a Bordeaux-style blended red. It has only bee... producing sparkling wines since 1993.

WINEMAKER
Josef Krammer, Anneke Burger

HOUSE RANGE
MON DESIR CAP CLASSIQUE
Vintaged, méthode champenoise: 40% Chardonnay, 60% Pinot Noir

N/A
FAIRVIEW ESTATE
SUIDER-PAARL, PAARL

• 350 cases

Vines were grown here at the beginning of the 20th century, when it was known as Bloemkoolfontein and owned by the Hugo family. This property did not come into the possession of its current owners until 1937, when it was purchased by Charles Back, an immigrant from Lithuania. When he bough... Bloemkoolfontein, Back was already the owner of the Backsberg estate, thus when h... died in 1954, both his sons ended up with a... estate: Sydney took Backsberg, while Cyril took Fairview. The first wines under the Fairview label came from the 1974 vintage, and this estate is now run by Cyril's son, Charle...

Fairview is one of the most innovative wine estates in South Africa, offering a breathtakingly large and constantly expanding range of wine styles. The first sparkling wine was produced in the 1980s.

WINEMAKER
Charles Back

HOUSE STYLE & RANGE
have too little experience to make an overall judgement, but a recent *cuvée* had a strange aroma, but was okay, if not special, on the palate.

CHARLES GERARD BRUT CAP CLASSIQUE
Not vintaged, méthode champenoise: Chardonnay, Pinot Noir

FRANSCHHOEK VINEYARDS
FRANSCHHOEK

Other labels - La Cotte
An up-and-coming cooperative capable of good value wines, a number of which appear on British supermarket shelves.

WINEMAKER
Deon Truter, Driann van der Merwe

HOUSE STYLE & RANGE
Both are inexpensive; the Sauvignon being a very simple, fresh, amylic fizz, while the Demi-Sec is a semi-sweet, clean fizz with a touch of Muscat flavour from the Hanepoot grape used.

LA COTTE SAUVIGNON BRUT SPARKLING
Vintaged, carbonated: 100% Sauvignon Blanc
LA COTTE SPARKLING DEMI-SEC
Vintaged, carbonated: 50% Chenin Blanc, 50% Hanepoot

CHARLES GERARD
See FAIRVIEW ESTATE

JACQUES GERMANIER
See SONOP WINERY

HAUTE PROVENCE
FRANSCHHOEK

This small winery is owned by former journalist Peter Younghusband, and is better-known for good value Cabernet Sauvignon, but the winemaker is obviously not adverse to getting his bicycle pump out.

WINEMAKER
John Groschen

HOUSE RANGE
BRUT
Not vintaged, carbonated: 60% Sauvignon Blanc, 40% Sémillon
BRUT CHARDONNAY
Not vintaged, carbonated: 100% Chardonnay

HELDERBERG
FIRGROVE, STELLENBOSCH

This cooperative has always produced a large range of above average products, but since joining with three other cooperatives to form Stellenbosch Vineyards in 1996, a number of interesting small lots have been added to the range. The first sparkling wines

were produced in 1996.

WINEMAKER
Albie Treunicht

HOUSE STYLE & RANGE
Not tasted, and too early to make any overall judgement in any case.

DE HELDERE VONKEL BRUT, CAP CLASSIQUE
Vintaged, méthode champenoise: 100% Pinot Noir
DE HELDERE VONKEL SEC
Vintaged, carbonated: grape varieties not revealed

PHILIP JONKER
See WELTEVREDE

JOURDAN
See CABRIÈRE ESTATE

KRONE BOREALIS
See TWEE JONGEGEZELLEN

78
LABORIE
SUIDER-PAARL, PAARL
• 850 cases

This is KWV's flagship estate, but the wines with the Laborie label were not estate-bottled until recently. Now the wines are made, matured and bottled on the estate, using brand new facilities installed in 1995 and 1996.

WINEMAKER
Gideon Theron

HOUSE STYLE & RANGE
The Cap Classique is made in a classic biscuity style that builds up toasty aromas after an extra year in bottle, developing a violet, vanilla smoothness on the finish.

★ CAP CLASSIQUE
Vintaged, méthode champenoise: 80% Chardonnay, 20% Pinot Noir
BLANC DE NOIRS
Not vintaged, transfer method: Pinotage, Pinot Gris, Pinot Noir

LA COTTE
See FRANSCHHOEK VINEYARDS

LE PHANTOM
See SAXENBURG

LONGRIDGE
STELLENBOSCH
• 1,500 cases

This new winemaker-négociant on Helderberg Mountain quickly built a reputation by making excellent value wines of consistent

quality from bought-in grapes, but has recently purchased 80 hectares of its own vineyards. Some brilliant varietal wines have been produced by Danie Zeeman with help from Martin Prieur of the top-performing Burgundian estate Domaine Jacques Prieur. The sparkling is, however, produced under contract by Nicky Krone of Twee Jongegezellen.

WINEMAKER
Nicky Krone

HOUSE STYLE & RANGE
Initially I thought this sparkling wine showed promise, but the 1994 tasted in late 1998 was not impressive, so I must reserve judgement. If it does not come around, however, it will be one of Krone's rare failures.

BRUT CAP CLASSIQUE
Vintaged, méthode champenoise: 50% Chardonnay, 50% Pinot Noir

L'ORMARINS
SUIDER-PAARL, PAARL

Run by Toni Rupert, the son of Anton Rupert, the second richest man in South Africa. With unlimited finance at his disposal, Rupert has quickly established L'Ormarins at the very top of Cape winemaking.

WINEMAKER
Josef Minkowitsch

HOUSE RANGE
MÉTHODE CHAMPENOISE JEAN ROI
Vintaged, méthode champenoise: 50% Chardonnay, 50% Pinot Noir

MADEBA
See GRAHAM BECK

MON DESIR
See EIKENDALE

MÔRESON
FRANSCHHOEK, PAARL
• 550 cases

Acquired by Richard Friedman in 1985, the 35-hectare vineyard was planted the following year.

WINEMAKER
John Laubser

HOUSE STYLE & RANGE
The first Soleil du Matin was produced in

1995 and I have tasted the wine just once, so judgement must be reserved, but I was not particularly impressed by it. It was fresh, with an admirably long flavour for such a light-bodied wine, but no special character stood out, although it is obviously young, and no one knows how it will develop.

SOLEIL DU MATIN BRUT, CAP CLASSIQUE

Not vintaged, méthode champenoise: 90% Chardonnay, 10% Chenin Blanc

N/A MORGENNOF

STELLENBOSCH

This relatively recent renovation of an historic wine estate has been undertaken by French emigrés Alain and Anne Huchon, who have family connections in Champagne and Cognac.

WINEMAKER

Jean Daneel

HOUSE STYLE & RANGE

The Huchons have made some super varietals (particularly Cabernet Sauvignon, Chardonnay, Merlot and Sauvignon Blanc), but their first sparkling wine (1993) was unpleasantly unclean. Judgement reserved.

BRUT CAP CLASSIQUE

Vintaged, méthode champenoise: 50% Chardonnay, 50% Pinot Noir

MUMM SOUTH AFRICA

See TWEE JONGEGEZELLEN

70 NEDERBURG

STELLENBOSCH

• 65,000 cases

This estate was founded in 1791 by Philip Wolvaart, but it is a brand, not an estate product. Nederburg is sourced from a large number of different properties (including Nederburg), to provide its collective ownership, Stellenbosch Farmers' Winery, with its flagship range. Nederburg produced South Africa's first *cuve close*, Première Cuvée, in 1945 and the Brut version of this wine is the country's best-selling fizz today. Paul Pontallier of Château Margaux has been Nederburg's consultant since 1989.

WINEMAKER

Newald Marais

HOUSE STYLE & RANGE

With the exception of the occasional Private Bin release, Blanquette is Nederburg's only *méthode champenoise* and it is not bad, but not special either. A soft, easy-drinking fizz, it gives the impression of a wine that finds it difficult to develop post-disgorgement aromas, although I cannot help admiring its fluffy freshness of fruit.

BLANQUETTE CAP CLASSIQUE DE CHARDONNAY

Vintaged, méthode champenoise: 100% Chardonnay

KAP SEKT

Vintaged, cuve close: 14% Chardonnay, 43% Cruchen, 43% Riesling

PREMIÈRE CUVÉE BRUT

Not vintaged, cuve close: 50% Chenin Blanc, 30% Cruchen, 20% Sauvignon Blanc

PREMIÈRE CUVÉE DOUX

Not vintaged, cuve close: 50% Chenin Blanc, 30% Cruchen, 20% Sauvignon Blanc

85 OAK VILLAGE

BELLVILLE

The primary label of an export-only organisation called Vinfruco, which itself is funded by Unifruco, South Africa's largest fruit exporter. Owned by Capespan, Vinfruco was established as recently as 1992, and has connections with flying MW winemaker Kym Milne, but only for still wines, the fizz being made by none other than Nicky Krone of Krone Borealis fame.

WINEMAKER

Nicky Krone

HOUSE STYLE & RANGE

If I was surprised to find a serious quality sparkling wine lurking behind the rather commercial name and presentation of Oak Village, I was half-expecting it to be the work of Nicky Krone, once I had tasted it. The creamy, walnutty mellowed richness of this *cuvée* makes Oak Village a sparkling wine of classic quality, and although this is Vinfruco's first attempt, Nicky Krone has such a track record that both the wine and this producer can be rated without hesitation.

★★ OAK VILLAGE CUVÉE BRUT NV CAP CLASSIQUE

Not vintaged, méthode champenoise: 55% Chardonnay, 45% Pinot Noir

LE PHANTOM

See SAXENBURG

PONGRÁCZ

See BERGKELDER

N/A RIEBEEK

RIEBEEK-KASTEEL, SWARTLAND

Another cooperative selling bicycle-pump Sauvignon Blanc.

WINEMAKER

Sias du Toit

HOUSE RANGE

SPARKLING BRUT

Not vintaged, carbonated: 100% Sauvignon Blanc

SPARKLING DEMI-SEC

Not vintaged, carbonated: 100% Riesling

JEAN ROI

See L'ORMARINS

N/A ROODEZANDT

ROBERTSON

More cooperative bicycle-pump jobs.

WINEMAKER

Christie Steytler

HOUSE RANGE

SPARKLING BRUT

Not vintaged, carbonated: Colombard, Sauvignon Blanc

SPARKLING DEMI-SEC

Not vintaged, carbonated: 100% Gewürztraminer

N/A ROOIBERG

ROBERTSON

This medal-winning cooperative enjoys a high reputation for its fortified wines. It also produces a carbonated Sauvignon Blanc.

WINEMAKER

Eben Rademeyer, Christo Pienaar

HOUSE RANGE

SPARKLING BRUT

Not vintaged, carbonated: 100% Sauvignon Blanc

VIN DOUX SPARKLING

Not vintaged, carbonated: 60% Chenin Blanc, 40% Gewürztraminer

J.C. LE ROUX

See BERGKELDER

N/A SAXENBURG

STELLENBOSCH

• 200 cases

Adrian and Brigit Bührer purchased this estate in 1989 and immediately began planting its 80 hectares of vineyards. These started to come on stream in the early 1990s since when Saxenburg has become one of the Cape's fastest-rising stars.

Sparkling wine was first produced in 1991 but Saxenburg is best-known for its reds. The Bührers also own the Domaine Capion in the Languedoc.

WINEMAKER

Nico van der Merwe

HOUSE STYLE & RANGE

One *cuvée* tasted just once, so an overall rating is not possible, but I found Le Phantom to be a highly acidic oddity with tangy fruit. Everything about it tells me it will develop if given longer post-disgorgement ageing, although along what lines I cannot tell.

LE PHANTOM

Vintaged, méthode champenoise: 60% Chardonnay, 40% Pinot Noir

SOLEIL DU MATIN

See MÔRESON

√A
SONOP WINERY
WINDEMEUL, PAARL
1,000 cases
Other labels - Cape Levant, Jacques
Germanier

The Sonop Winery was established in 1991
and is owned by SAVISA, a large export-
oriented company that was founded in the
same year by Jacques Germanier of
Switzerland. The first wines were produced
in 1992, although the first sparkling wine
was produced in 1993. In addition to the
sparkling wine labels indicated above, Sonop
markets wines under numerous other brands,
including Athlone, Bredasdorp, Cape Soleil,
Diemersdal, Imandi, Kumala, and Tulando.
WINEMAKER
Thierry Fontannaz
HOUSE STYLE & RANGE
Jacques Germanier Brut is also sold as Le
Brut du Levant under the Cape Levant label.
At the time of writing, only the first *cuvée*
produced was available for tasting, so it is
impossible to give an overall rating, but it
was a decent quality, sharp, fresh, zingy fizz
in an embossed skittle-shaped bottle.
JACQUES GERMANIER BRUT, CAP CLASSIQUE
Not vintaged, méthode champenoise: 100% Chardonnay

√A
STELLENBOSCH FARMERS' WINERY
STELLENBOSCH
The SFW, as it is known, owns half-a-dozen
different companies, makes Château Libertas
and markets the Nederburg and Sable View
ranges. Wine estates include Monis and
Zonnenbloem.
WINEMAKER
Woutar Pienaar
HOUSE RANGE
LOUIS CHAUVIN CHARDONNAY CAP CLASSIQUE
Vintaged, méthode champenoise: 100% Chardonnay
LOUIS CHAUVIN PINOT NOIR CAP CLASSIQUE
Vintaged, méthode champenoise: 100% Pinot Noir

TRADOUW
See BARRYDALE

√A
VAN LOVREN
KLAASVOOGDS, ROBERTSON
This winery is owned by Nico and Wynand
Retief, who are more interested in
innovative winemaking and unpretentious

STELLENBOSCH
• 8,000 cases
This estate is a
combination of two old
properties, the original
Simonsig, which was
part of the Nooitgedacht
farm, dating back to
1704, and De Hoop,
which was part of the
Koelenhof farm, dating back to 1682. Frans
Malan already owned De Hoop when in
1964 he purchased Simonsig and combined
the two properties. In 1971 Simonsig
became the first producer of South African
méthode champenoise when Frans Malan
made his debut vintage of Kaapse Vonkel
(which means 'sparkling wine').
WINEMAKER
Johan Malan
HOUSE STYLE & RANGE
Some vintages of Kaapse Vonkel have
suffered bottle variation, with an oxidative
style occasionally popping up, but since it
has gone from a Chenin-based *cuvée* to a
classic blend its track-record has mostly
been for a correctly lean, fruit-driven
sparkling wine that picks up classic biscuity
bottle-aromas after an additional year of

80
SIMONSIG

post-disgorgement
ageing. I have just
realised that I have
been guilty elsewhere
of condemning
Simonsig's 1991
Cuvée Royal, yet I
had tasted a pre-release
sample of this new
prestige *cuvée*, and I
should always give non-commercial
disgorgements the benefit of the doubt and
reserve judgement. While I found it rather
foursquare, I have experienced much worse
with pre-release samples of wines that have
ended up as stunners. Furthermore,
Simonsig's 1991 Kaapse Vonkel was
excellent (although not quite the quality of
the 1992) and South Africa's most
experienced *méthode champenoise* producer
should know what it is doing when
making a theoretically superior *cuvée* from
the same year.
★ KAAPSE VONKEL BRUT CAP CLASSIQUE
*Vintaged, méthode champenoise: 40% Chardonnay,
60% Pinot Noir*
CUVÉE ROYALE
*Vintaged, méthode champenoise: 85% Chardonnay,
15% Pinot Noir*

pricing than anything seriously fine, and can
be extremely successful in this niche.
WINEMAKER
Wynand & Bussell Retief
HOUSE RANGE
PAPILLON BRUT
Not vintaged, carbonated: Chardonnay, Colombard
PAPILLON DEMI-SEC
*Not vintaged, carbonated: 50% Colombard,
50% Riesling*
PAPILLON DOUX
Not vintaged, carbonated: 100% Muscadel

80
VILLIERA
KOELENHOF, PAARL
• 15,000 cases
Although this estate was once owned by
the De Villiers family, who made wine on
the property, no vines had grown here in
recent times until the Naudé family sold
Villiera to Helmut Ratz in 1975. The
owner of an entertainment complex at
Kärnten in Austria, Ratz purchased the
estate with the express aim of producing
wine to export back to his homeland. It
was Ratz who replanted the vineyard and

modernised the cellars, but in 1983 he
sold Villiera to its present owners, the
Grier family, who have established its
reputation. High-tech traditionalists with a
passion for sparkling wine, the Grier
family employed champenois Jean-Louis
Denois as consultant, producing the
estate's first *méthode champenoise* in 1984.
Hired on a ten-year contract that has now
expired, Denois was originally from
Cumières, but he moved to Limoux,
where he is one of the most innovative
winemakers.
WINEMAKER
Jeff Grier
HOUSE STYLE & RANGE
The basic non-vintage Carte Rouge is
definitely the best sparkling wine in the
Villiera range, which is a great compliment
because this is the least expensive *cuvée*, it is
produced in by far the largest volume, and it
contains Chenin Blanc and Pinotage. On
the other hand, it is also the youngest *cuvée*,
so it could merely be a reflection of how
these wines have improved in the last few
years. In any case, the Carte Rouge is a
classic *méthode champenoise*, with creamy, rich

87 VALUE

TWEE JONGEGEZELLEN

TULBAGH

- 16,000 cases
- Other labels - Krone Borealis

This old wine farm was founded in 1710 by two young Dutchmen who were apparently known as the *Twee Jonge Gezellen* or 'Two Young Bachelors', or so the story goes. Unfortunately, their names have never been discovered and little else is known about them.

The estate itself is often referred to as Twee Jonge Gezellen, although the wines are invariably labelled Twee Jongegezellen, joining up the last two words.

WINEMAKER

Nicky Krone

HOUSE STYLE & RANGE

While the presentation of Krone Borealis might look rather garish, and the price is certainly very reasonable, the wine that lurks beneath the label is no cheap and cheerful fizz. Krone Borealis is one of the world's classic sparkling wines and its vintages have demonstrated exceptional longevity.

Typically this *cuvée* is deceptively soft and

easy-drinking when first released, with delicious, gentle fruit that falls somewhere between the New and Old Worlds in character and structure. After one year's additional post-disgorgement age, it starts to pick up some biscuity complexity, and a year later this is enhanced and mellowed by lovely toasty aromas.

My favourite vintages so far are 1993 and 1990, the latter having extraordinarily fresh and breezy fruit underscored by classic creamy, biscuity complexity. With this sort of quality, it is little wonder that owner-winemaker Nicky Krone was chosen to make Cuvée Cap Mumm for the famous Reims-based Champagne house. This is a very fresh and zesty wine, with a long and elegant fruit-dominated palate that is softened by smooth mousse of tiny bubbles.

★★ KRONE BOREALIS BRUT CAP CLASSIQUE
Not vintaged, méthode champenoise: 50% Chardonnay, 50% Pinot Noir

★★ CAP CUVÉE FOR MUMM
Vintaged, méthode champenoise: 35% Chardonnay, 65% Pinot Noir

SUNRISE ON THE TULBAGH MOUNTAINS BEHIND THE VINEYARDS OF TWEE JONGEGEZELLEN, TULBAGH

fruit that is nicely mellowed by understated malolactic.

The Carte d'Or is also non-vintage, but produced exclusively from classic Champagne grapes (including barrel-fermentation for the Chardonnay) and twice the age of the Carte Rouge, but either the wine cannot take long yeast contact or Grier is making much better wine now, because it is rather foursquare and lacks the finesse of the basic blend.

The same applies to the Première Cuvée, although some vintages are better than others (eg., the 1990 is superior to the 1991), and they would certainly benefit

from being released earlier. The soft, perfumed aromas, plump fruit and perfect mousse of the Rosé Brut give it the edge over all but the best of Villiera's vintage *cuvées*, even though it contains a good splash of non-classic Pinotage, but there again it is a much more recent wine.

★★ TRADITION CARTE ROUGE BRUT, CAP CLASSIQUE
Not vintaged, méthode champenoise: 30% Chardonnay, 10% Chenin Blanc, 10% Pinotage, 50% Pinot Noir

TRADITION CARTE D'OR BRUT, CAP CLASSIQUE
Vintaged, méthode champenoise: 50% Chardonnay, 50% Pinot Noira

★ TRADITION PREMIÈRE CUVÉE BRUT, CAP CLASSIQUE
Vintaged, méthode champenoise: 40% Chardonnay, 60% Pinot Noira

⭑ VILLIERA TRADITION BRUT ROSÉ, CAP CLASSIQUE
Not vintaged, méthode champenoise: 30% Chardonnay, 10% Pinotage, 60% Pinot Noir

N/A

VREDENDAL

VREDENDAL, OLIFANTS RIVER

Formerly known as Olifantsrivier Koöp Wynkelder, this is the country's largest cooperative, processing the equivalent of the entire New Zealand harvest every year. Vredendal produces one of South Africa's best Ruby Cabernets, but I have not tasted its carbonated fizz.

WINEMAKER

François Weich

HOUSE RANGE

SPARKLING DRY
Not vintaged, carbonated: Chenin Blanc, Colombard Fernao Pires

SPARKLING SEMI-SWEET
Not vintaged, carbonated: Chenin Blanc, Colombard Fernao Pires

N/A

WELTEVREDE

BONNIEVALE, ROBERTSON

- 150 cases

Established in 1973, Weltevrede means 'well satisfied', which is an apt comment on this estate's white and dessert wines which are of good general quality. The first sparkling wine was produced in 1994 and released in December 1996.

WINEMAKER

Nicolas Rust, Philip Jonker

HOUSE RANGE

PHILIP JONKER BRUT CAP CLASSIQUE
Vintaged, méthode champenoise: 100% Sauvignon Blanc

N/A

ZANDVLIET

ASHTON, ROBERTSON

Famous for its Shiraz and recent dramatic improvement for Chardonnay. Cap Classique is only a very recent development in this winery's range.

WINEMAKER

Paul de Wet

HOUSE RANGE

MÉTHODE CAP CLASSIQUE BRUT
Vintaged, méthode champenoise: 10% Chardonnay, 90% Pinot Noir

REST OF AFRICA

IT IS OFTEN SAID THAT WINE CANNOT BE PRODUCED IN EQUATORIAL COUNTRIES BECAUSE THE HEAT PROMOTES EXCESSIVE FOLIAGE WITH FEW GRAPES, BUT THIS IS A BIT OF AN OLD WIVES' TALE. SPARKLING WINE IS PROBABLY THE LAST WINE STYLE ONE WOULD EXPECT TO BE PRODUCED IN EQUATORIAL COUNTRIES, YET IT IS PRODUCED IN TWO OF THEM: PERU AND KENYA.

KENYA

Grapes have been grown in Kenya since 1982, when John and Elli D'Olier first brought back cuttings from California. Their vineyards are located at **Lake Naivasha**, 1900 metres above sea level in the Rift Valley. This area is known as the Flower Garden of Africa and it is literally one vast flower garden, with blooms that are flown to florists all over the world on a daily basis. You can grow anything here, and you can grow it twice a year too and, as the D'Oliers discovered, you can certainly grow grapes on Lake Naivasha's rich volcanic soil: the cool nights give surprisingly high acidity levels.

John is a Kenyan from Huguenot stock, his father having come to East Africa from Ireland during the First World War, and Elli is a Californian. They produced their first grape wines in 1986, having won a silver medal at Lisbon in 1985 for their papaya wine. Papaya wine is a traditional Kenyan product that is very strong, thick and oily. Not the sort of thing that would go down well on international markets, but the grape wines are fresh, clean and drinkable with no baked or otherwise off-putting hot-climate characteristics.

In 1992 the D'Oliers produced their first bottle-fermented fizz, and I was so impressed that I wanted to taste it back in the UK, on a cold, dank day, as far removed as possible from the romance and beauty of Lake Naivasha, and side-by-side with other sparkling wines. However, I was not returning home but moving on, and I did not think a bottle would benefit from days of travelling in the heat of Kenya's bush. I am indebted, therefore, to Andrew Leach, a friend of the D'Oliers, who brought a bottle back and posted it to me from Drutton, Somerset, where he is the Deputy Headmaster of King's School.

TENDING A VINEYARD IN ZIMBABWE. DRIP IRRIGATION IS ESSENTIAL IN THIS HOT, DRY CLIMATE

Under blind conditions, the fizz did not live up to my first impressions, but that was to be expected. It remained, though, perfectly clean and adequate, and I have tasted worse first wines from the New World ventures of many famous Champagne houses, so I look forward to the second release of Lake Naivasha.

ZIMBABWE

The first wines were produced here in the mid-1960s, after Ian Smith's regime had made a unilateral declaration of independence. But the once familiar names of Philips and Monis have been superceded by African Distillers and Mukuyu, just as Rhodesia itself has long since been renamed Zimbabwe. Low-quality vines were dug up and replaced with more classic varieties, drip-irrigation was installed, and cool fermentation technology introduced.

There are still just two producers, although there are many small, privately-owned vineyards that supply these large firms. **African Distillers**, which is also known as **Stapleford Wines**, is situated north of Harare and owns 180 hectares of vineyards at Bulawayo, Odzi, and Gweru. Gweru is also the location of its large winery. **Mukuyu**, which took over Monis, is owned by Cairns Holdings, whose winery and 100 hectares of vineyards are situated south of a village called Marondera, 100 kilometres east of Harare.

Although the wine industry is relatively modern, it obviously relies on an antiquated bottle manufacturer because both producers bottle some *cuvées* in new bottles made with a *bague carré*, the squared-off glass rim around the neck of a Champagne bottle onto which the *agrafe* of old used to be fixed.

The best Zimbabwe fizz is **Mukuyu Chardonnay Brut de Brut**, a fresh, clean, fruity *méthode champenoise* that is comparable in quality to Veuve du Vernay in France. Le Grand Charlemagne Vin Sec from Stapleford Wines has a nasty plastic stopper, but might appeal to a glue-sniffer, although Bostick is cheaper and will probably give you less of a headache. Le Grand Charlemagne Vin Doux and Mukuyu Chardonnay Demi-Sec are not very nice at all. Presumably, the latter *cuvée* has the same base wine as the Mukuyu Chardonnay Brut de Brut, which makes me suspect that there is something amiss with the *dosage* process, particularly as the other undrinkable bubblies are all sweet to one degree or another. Bearing this in mind, and the great strides Zimbabwe has made in the quality of its still wines over the last ten years, the current state of affairs is not unduly alarming, and I expect a similar advance in the standard of this country's fizz over the next decade or so.

HUGE VINEYARDS IN THE CARNEROS REGION, NAPA, CALIFORNIA WHERE LINES OF VINES STRETCH ALMOST AS FAR AS THE EYE CAN SEE

UNITED STATES

THE FIRST AMERICAN SPARKLING WINE WAS MADE IN 1842 BY NICHOLAS LONGWORTH FROM VINEYARDS ALONG THE BANKS OF THE OHIO RIVER NEAR CINCINNATI. WHEN LONGWORTH ARRIVED IN CINCINNATI SOME 20 YEARS EARLIER HE WAS VIRTUALLY PENNILESS, BUT LIKE SO MANY OF HIS ERA WHO ASPIRED TO THE AMERICAN DREAM, HE QUICKLY WENT FROM RAGS TO RICHES.

After studying law for a mere six months, Longworth set up in a practice that made him a millionaire. As a hobby, he planted a vineyard in 1823 in a part of Cincinnati known as Tusculum, which later became the city's Frederick H. Alms Memorial Park. When many of the vines he imported from Europe died, Longworth turned to native American varieties and quickly discovered Catawba, the so-called 'wonder grape', which he planted in 1825. Three years later he made his first Catawba wine and was so impressed that he retired from law to devote his energy to viticulture and winemaking.

Longworth planted hundreds of acres of Catawba, and encouraged others to follow his example, buying their grapes to add to his own production. Initially he produced still wine, but it was his sparkling Catawba that really caught on. All native American grapes have a strangely exotic, cloying taste commonly described as foxy, but none more so than Catawba. Although not widely appreciated these days, it was adored by second and later generation east coast Americans, who grew up with the foxy taste. No European vines had at that time been able to withstand the bitterly cold east coast winters and imported European wines were in short supply and very expensive, thus not available to the majority of east coast Americans. Instead they were brought up on jellies and juice made from native grapes and so naturally took to the foxy taste of the wines these grapes made. In fact they became so used to it that in 1973 Leon D. Adams, author of *The Wines of America*, wrote 'To most Americans, "grape flavor" means that foxy taste, even though by that juncture most American wine enthusiasts were rejecting that 'grape flavor' in the wines they drank.

In 1854, the popular American poet Henry Longfellow even wrote an Ode to Catawba Wine in which he compared it to two of the most famous growths of Champagne:

*Very good in its way
Is the Verzenay,
Or the Sillery soft and creamy;
But Catawba wine
Has a taste more divine,
More dulcet, delicious and creamy.*

Not a great poem, perhaps, but an effective one.

By 1858 the fame of Catawba had spread as far as Europe where, according to the *Illustrated London News,* 'Sparkling Catawba, of the pure, unadulterated juice of the Catawba grape, transcends the Champagne of France'. Quite what jellies and juice that particular copy editor had been weaned on, goodness only knows - the only mitigating factor in his defence is that

NICHOLAS LONGWORTH, THE MAN WHO MADE AMERICA'S FIRST SPARKLING WINE IN 1842

THE OLD HOUSE, WERK CHAMPAGNE CELLARS, CINCINNATI

Champagne at that time was very sweet.

By 1860 one-third of all the vines in America were planted along the banks of the Ohio, which boasted twice the acreage of California's vineyards, making Ohio the wine-centre of the New World prior to the Civil War (1861-1865). At that juncture, Longworth was the country's largest wine producer, with half-a-million bottles in his cellars, yet in 1865, just two years after he died, his vineyards were abandoned. This was not due to battle damage, but to 'vine sickness', which today is presumed to have been powdery mildew and black rot. Had Longworth been alive, it would have been a huge setback, but not an insurmountable one. He had overcome much greater disasters, particularly in his prime, but after his death the estate was divided amongst his heirs, not one of which possessed Longworth's passion for the vine.

The irony is that this viticultural disaster, and the apathy of Longworth's heirs, paved the way for the next phase of America's sparkling wine development, namely the emergence of New York's fabled 'champagne', the first of which was made that very year, 1865, by Joseph Masson.

After training in France, Masson was employed by Werk Champagne Cellars in Cincinnati, then hired by Charles Davenport Champlin for the Pleasant Valley Wine Company in Hammondsport. Masson called his first New York fizz Sparkling Catawba, just as Longworth had, and it even won an honourable mention at the Paris Exposition in 1867. He was soon joined by his brother Jules, who had been in charge of one of Longworth's Cincinnati wineries until the vineyards were abandoned.

When in 1870 the two Masson brothers presented their latest *cuvée* to a meeting of Pleasant Valley growers, it was mistaken for a 'great champagne of the west' (meaning California) and so the Great Western

Champagne brand acquired its name.

Great Western Champagne was launched later that year, and in 1873 it became the first American sparkling wine to win a gold medal in Europe. This brand claimed to be made in 'Rheims, New York', and inside the winery, the post room was craftily named Rheims to facilitate this ruse. The entire Great Western range encompassed many other types of wine, but the so-called 'champagne' was its primary source of income. Furthermore it became the most important brand of sparkling wine in the country, a position maintained for no less than 50 years, with only the advent of Prohibition causing its demise.

The other famous New York champagne of the 19th century was Gold Seal, the primary brand of the Urbana Wine Company, which was founded in 1865 by the vine growers of Urbana in much the same way that the Pleasant Valley Wine Company had five years earlier. In fact, the Urbana Wine Company deliberately modelled itself on Pleasant Valley, right down to hiring a Frenchman, Charles le Breton, formerly of Louis Roederer, to make its sparkling wines. Le Breton was succeeded in 1871 by Jules Crance of Moët & Chandon, and the brand, which was initially called Imperial, changed to Gold Seal in 1887.

In more than 100 years Gold Seal employed only five winemakers, all French. Crance was followed by his son Eugene in 1923, who produced sacramental wines during Prohibition. After the Repeal, Charles Fournier of Veuve Clicquot was hired to recapture the brand's pre-Prohibition fame, and he did this by first pioneering hybrid vines over native *labrusca*, then working with Konstantin Frank to champion the cause for *vinifera* vines against the advice of local experts. When Fournier retired in 1967 he was replaced by the

WHO SOLD WINE BEFORE THE REPEAL?

A young English gentleman, hard up on his luck in New York in 1933 embarked upon an ephemeral career selling booze. In April of that year he heard that two acquaintances, Jack Kreindlar and his friend 'Charlie', were going into the wine business. They introduced him to one of the backers, Frank Hunter (of Tilden and Hunter, the world champion tennis doubles team).

The Englishman was duly enlisted and his first sale was a case of Champagne George Goulet to one Woolly Donahue. The deal was struck just before midnight on 4th December 1933 which, as Prohibition was not repealed until 5th December, was a crime. Who was he? None other than David Niven, who confessed to this little escapade in his autobiography *The Moon's a Balloon*.

As it happened Niven was an awful salesman. Hired on a wage of $40 a week based on sales of $400 at 10% commission, he rarely achieved this target and hardly ever exceeded it, unlike his colleague Harry Rantzman whose selling acumen was such that he ended up owning several apartment blocks in the Bronx. Niven was one of the founding sons of '21's' and to this day his photograph (an FBI mug-shot with a board around his neck bearing his registration number on it) adorns the offices bearing the caption 'First and worst salesman'.

DOMAINE MUMM WINERY IN SILVERADO, NAPA VALLEY

fifth and last French winemaker, Guy Devaux from Marne et Champagne. When Gold Seal was purchased by Seagram in 1979, Devaux launched the highly secret 'Project Lafayette', which culminated in 1987 with the opening of Mumm Napa Valley.

THE NOT-SO CRAZY UKRAINIAN

When Charles Fournier arrived at Gold Seal in 1934, he was alarmed by the highly aromatic character of the labrusca grapes planted in the Finger Lake vineyards. Accustomed to the classic concept of Champagne whereby the neutral base wines are enhanced by yeast autolysis, Fournier asked whether Chardonnay and Pinot Noir could be grown in New York State. Local wine-growers assured him that no vinifera vines could survive the harsh winters.

Accepting this as fact, he imported hybrid vines (crosses between French and native American varieties), which had originally been developed to combat phylloxera, and for 20 years contented himself with producing the best possible sparkling wines he could from these. However, he was never truly happy with the results he achieved, which was why he was so eager to place his faith in a Ukrainian immigrant, Konstantin Frank, who all the highly qualified New York 'experts' treated as a charlatan.

Frank had arrived in America in 1951 with no money and, unable to speak English, he washed dishes to support his wife and three children. As soon as he could speak a little English, he applied for a job at the New York State viticultural research station at Geneva, claiming he had studied viticulture at Odessa, organised collective farms in the Ukraine, taught viticulture and oenology at an agricultural institute and, after the war, managed farms in Austria and Bavaria for the occupying forces. They didn't believe him but employed him anyway, and set him to work hoeing blueberries. Soon the staff at Geneva were convinced that not only was Frank's previous employment record a work of fiction, but the man was plain crazy.

When Frank asked why they weren't growing recognised European vines, he was bluntly informed that the winters were too harsh, a fact he instantly dismissed as absurd. 'Cold?' he said. 'Where I come from, it's so cold that spit freezes before it hits the ground'. Konstantin Frank's English had indeed improved, and he used it to explain that 'back home' temperatures dropped to -40°F and entire vineyards of vinifera vines had to be buried under several feet of soil every year before the winter set in. He argued that if vinifera grapes could grow successfully in Russia, then their failure to do so in New York State must be due to diseases or pests that could be controlled, rather than winter temperatures.

Two years later, Fournier heard Frank's claims and, after talking with Frank, employed him. Frank's claims proved to be justified, particularly after the great freeze of February 1957. Later that year some of the hardiest labrusca vines failed to bear a single grape, yet less than ten per cent of the buds on Frank's Riesling and Chardonnay vines were damaged, and they went on to yield a bumper crop of ripe grapes.

HISTORIC SPARKLING WINE PRODUCTION AT BUENA VISTA, PHOTOGRAPHED BY EADWEARD MUYBRIDGE

CHARLES FOURNIER AND KONSTANTIN FRANK (LEFT), WHO PROVED THAT VINIFERA GRAPE VARIETIES COULD BE GROWN SUCCESSFULLY IN NEW YORK STATE (SEE BOX LEFT)

AGOSTON HARASZTHY, FOUNDER OF THE BUENA VISTA VINEYARD AND WINERY IN SONOMA

CALIFORNIA

THE EARLIEST CALIFORNIA SPARKLING WINE WAS PRODUCED CIRCA 1855 BY BENJAMIN DAVIS WILSON, THE FIRST MAYOR OF LOS ANGELES, AT THE SAN GABRIEL WINERY, FROM GRAPES GROWN AT HIS NEARBY LAKE VINEYARD. ACCORDING TO AN ISSUE OF *ALTA CALIFORNIA* IN MARCH 1855, 'MR WILSON'S EXPERIMENT OF MAKING A FIRST QUALITY CHAMPAGNE WINE PROMISES TO BE ENTIRELY SUCCESSFUL AND WE BELIEVE THE TIME IS NOT FAR DISTANT WHEN CALIFORNIA WILL BE AN EXPORTER OF WINE'.

Wilson did not pursue the elusive bubble, but achieved such fame for his still wines that 35 years later San Gabriel had become the world's largest winery, producing more than 15 million gallons.

Shortly after Wilson's ephemeral fizz, the quest was taken up by a neighbour, Pierre Sainsevain who, with his brother, owned El Aviso. Established by Jean-Louis Vignes in 1823, El Aviso was California's first commercial vineyard, and its location in Los Angeles is today marked as Aliso Street.

Leaving his brother in charge of El Aviso, Pierre Sainsevain travelled to France to learn the Champagne method and purchase the necessary equipment. When he returned in 1857, Sainsevain brought with him a French Champagne maker by the name of Pierre Debanne and set up a new winery at San Jose where they laid down 50,000 bottles for second fermentation that very same year. Labelled 'Sparkling California', they sold for $12 per dozen.

Sainsevain's return from France coincided with the founding of the historic Buena Vista vineyard and winery in Sonoma by Agoston Haraszthy, one of the most colourful characters in American history. Haraszthy had instructed his son Arpad to study Champagne production and through correspondence between the two we know that Sainsevain had tripled his production of sparkling wine to 150,000 bottles in 1858.

Haraszthy's two sons were married to the daughters

of General Mariano Vallejo, the former Mexican *comandante* of California. Vallejo made his first sparkling wine in 1859 with the help of a French winemaker called Dr. Faure. Since there was a friendly rivalry between these two wine producers, who were linked by marriage, it was probably the launch of Vallejo's sparkling wine which prompted Haraszthy to send Arpad to Champagne the following year.

Arpad worked at the house of de Venoge in Epernay in 1860 (nine years later, Arthur Bricout, the former technical director at de Venoge, married the daughter of Christian Adalbert Kupferberg, the Sekt producer in Mainz, and today Kupferberg, Champagne Bricout and Buena Vista are all under the same ownership), but when he returned to Buena Vista, his efforts to replicate sparkling wine proved disastrous.

At the time this was put down to the use of the Mission grape, which was thought to be unsuited to the process, but from the rate of failure it was obviously a fundamental flaw in the technique (such as failing to understand the margins for error when adding the bottling liquor). In 1864 alone, some 65,400 bottles were rejected out of 72,000 and Arpad was forced to leave Buena Vista that year. When his father employed Pierre Debanne, Sainsevain's former winemaker, the production problems were resolved, and 40,000 bottles were made in 1866, 90,000 in 1867 and 120,000 the following year. These sparkling wines sold at $12-15 per dozen, which was only just below the prices fetched by authentic French Champagne.

Dejected, but not defeated, and with the aid of new partners, Arpad Haraszthy pursued his attempt to master the techniques of sparkling wine production, and succeeded. Arpad Haraszthy & Company abandoned the Mission grape, experimented with numerous varieties, including Riesling, Muscat and Zinfandel, producing various sparkling wines, most successful of which was 'Dry Eclipse', which became nationally famous in the 1870s.

In 1878, a future pioneer of California fizz by the name of Paul Masson (not to be confused with Joseph and Jules Masson, who were already working on the east coast) arrived on the scene. He had left his native Burgundy at the age of 19 and travelled to Santa Clara where he was befriended by fellow Frenchman Charles Lefranc. Lefranc had inherited his father-in-law's vineyard at Los Gatos and he employed the young Masson, sending him back to France in 1884 to buy champagne-making equipment. In 1886 Masson married Lefranc's daughter Louise and the company changed its title to Lefranc & Masson. Lefranc was succeeded by his son Henry, who sold his share in the business to Masson in 1892, whereupon the Paul Masson Champagne Company was founded.

In 1896 Masson planted a mountain vineyard called La Cresta and later built his own production facility called Mountain Winery, which was dubbed 'the winery in the sky'. He won a string of awards for his sparkling wines, including an honourable mention at the Paris exposition in 1900. Masson was known for

FRANZ HAZEK, SEATED, AND CHARLES ZEDTWITZ (LEFT) WITH OTHER WINEMAKERS AT KORBEL

ROBERT LOUIS STEVENSON'S 'SILVERADO SQUATTERS', CHAPTER ON NAPA WINE

lavish parties, attended by celebrities such as Charlie Chaplin, but his most famous stunt was to give the singer Anna Held a champagne bath, which was perhaps the origin of this frivolous notion of the height of luxury.

During Prohibition, Masson maintained his lifestyle, producing sparkling wines for medicinal purposes, dispensed on doctor's prescription through pharmacies. In 1929, however, his Mountain Winery was raided by armed hijackers who claimed to be Federal agents, clearing out his cellars in four truckloads. It took a violent act such as this robbery to dishearten the 89 year old Masson, who semi-retired four years later and sold up everything in 1936.

The Mountain Winery and the Paul Masson brand were purchased by Martin Ray, who hired an ex-Jesuit Brother Oliver Goulet as winemaker. Goulet was the chief winemaker at the Jesuit Fathers Novitiate in Los Gatos, but had quit in order to get married, and under his guidance Paul Masson champagnes continued to pick up awards as they had prior to Prohibition.

At the same time that Masson began planting his mountain vineyard in 1896, a Czech immigrant winemaker by the name of Franz Hazek joined the firm of Korbel and started producing sparkling wine. Until this juncture, the Korbel brothers, who originally came from Bohemia (irrevocably tied to the history of Czechoslovakia) had made only still wine and brandy. In fact, the Korbel brothers were lumberjacks by trade, and had only started making wine in Sonoma's Russian River because they had chopped down every single tree on their land. They had to invest the money they had made selling timber by planting something reasonably quick-growing, and with California wine taking off, vines seemed the obvious choice.

Hazek had already launched his own sparkling wine, Grand Pacific, to compete with Paul Masson and Haraszthy's Dry Eclipse, but the Korbel brothers changed the Grand Pacific name to Korbel Sec, and sales increased. Hazek was succeeded by another Czech by the name of Jan Hanuska, who was so obsessive

THE FIRST CARBONATED, *CUVE CLOSE* AND TRANSFER METHOD

According to Professor George Husmann, by 1888 sparkling wines were being produced by carbonation and fetching $10 per dozen, compared to $16 for those made by bottle-fermentation. The first sparkling wine produced by *cuve close* was in 1933 when Chateau Gai, a Canadian firm, set up a specially equipped winery at Lewiston in New York State, which was called Chateau Gay (sic). It is uncertain when or who made the first California *cuve close*, but it was probably in the late 1940s by one of three producers: Padre Vineyards at Cucamonga, Roma Wine Company at Fresno, or Weibel at Warm Springs, each of whom made tank-fermented fizz at about this juncture.

Padre Vineyards also attempted the first American transfer method in the late 1940s, but it was not particularly successful. Most producers did not attempt this process until the technology had been perfected by the Germans in the 1950s, with Paul Masson the first notable changeover from *méthode champenoise* to transfer method in 1959.

about the secret of his *cuvées* that he would not allow even the Korbel brothers into their own winery when he was preparing them. Such arcane practices were not uncommon: in 1889 Adolphe Reiklen established the American Champagne Company in San Francisco, claiming that his 'Reiklen Process' was so advanced that it was conducted in a locked room, and to this day no one knows what this involved.

The Italian Swiss Colony is known to have produced sparkling wines at Asti, Sonoma, since at least the early 1890s, when its sparkling Muscat became known. But when Charles Jadeau from Saumur was employed, drier *cuvées* were introduced. In 1936, the Italian Swiss Colony was one of three important pre-Prohibition brands to make a successful comeback, the other three being Paul Masson, Almadén (which shared the same roots as Paul Masson) and Korbel.

That same year Alsatian-born Adolf Heck headed a group of investors to buy Cook's Imperial Champagne Cellars, which had produced sparkling wine in St. Louis, Missouri, as early 1859. Heck changed the name to the American Wine Company, but the purchase left him so financially overstretched that in 1939 he sought the backing of a silent partner. He found one via a Swiss investor, but it was none other than Joachim von Ribbentrop, Hitler's foreign minister.

There was probably no intrigue involved. Ribbentrop was genuinely interested in sparkling wine, but he was not a Sekt salesman as so many references claim. He was looked down upon by high-born Germans because he had no title or money, but had added 'von' to his name and married into a wealthy family. Since that family was Henkell, German nobility used to refer to him as 'that Sekt salesman' and this insult was such a common tag that it has been recorded as a fact (even by such otherwise meticulous references as the *Encyclopedia Britannica*). Ribbentrop thus had sufficient natural interest in sparkling wine to invest in Heck's company for perfectly legitimate reasons. Indeed, had the investment been for undercover purposes, we can be sure that his minions would have made sure the paper trail did not lead back to Ribbentrop himself. It was, however, an unwise and extremely untimely transaction, and led to the company's confiscation by the US government. After the war Adolf's eldest son, Adolf L Heck, moved to California, where he managed the Italian Swiss Colony until the opportunity arose to buy Korbel with his two younger brothers.

AFTER THE WAR

The problems that prevented sparkling wines from increasing in quality in the immediate post-war period were not only the same as those for still wines; they were complicated by the dumming-down effect of *cuve close* technology. The wine industry suffered on a worldwide scale following the First World War, which in many cases denied its producers the fresh impetus that a new generation always brings. In the USA, however, it was much worse in a sense, because there was less of a winemaking culture to fall back on than in Europe.

Yet before American producers had a chance to get

IMAGE FROM THE WINERY MUSEUM OF CORDORNÍU, NAPA VALLEY

back on their feet, the industry was forced to endure the debilitating effect of 13 years of Prohibition. Then, six years after Repeal, there was another world war and another generation lost. In the late 1940s there were few American vineyards left, hardly any containing quality wine varieties and none that were properly cared for, with no skilled labour for the vineyards or wineries. Little wonder then that in the 1950s the most technologically advanced country in the world possessed the most backward wine industry.

Apart from a few exceptions, still wines produced in California, the country's premier wine region, were made from substandard grape varieties, and were heavy and old-fashioned, often sweet or fortified. How America got out of that to achieve such an astonishing range of world quality wines has been nothing short of miraculous, and a testament to good old US 'can do' mentality (that and a bunch of crazy billionaires willing to throw away half their fortunes in pursuit of their dreams).

What gummed up the works for the sparkling wine sector of the industry was technology because America is a country where technology rules. If it can be automated, that's progress, and Americans just love progress. Before long California champagne was the *cuve close* product of inferior grape varieties.

When the word champagne was first coined by Americans in the 19th century, it was used because the wines aspired to the best that the French could produce. Whether it achieved this is subject to conjecture because no one alive today can say for sure, but we can be reasonably certain that the champagne name was used out of respect for the authentic French product, and that it was a term that expressed quality. By the 1950s, however, American champagne simply meant any wine that had bubbles, and the more the technology was applied, the cheaper the price became and the lower the quality dropped. For some reason, just because they had bubbles, these so-called champagnes were not considered to be wines *per se*, just products, and industrial ones at that.

American champagne was thus on the same downward spiral as German Sekt, although being a continent apart, there was no economic advantage to sourcing raw materials from other countries. When moves were underway to plant classic varieties for still wines, the sparkling wine situation got even worse, as

VINEYARDS, NAPA VALLEY

BOTTLE-CARBONATED!

In the 1960s, an English-born Californian-trained food technician devised a method whereby individual bottles of wine could be carbonated, rather than carrying out this process in huge tanks. He spent an enormous amount of time and his own personal fortune trying to change U.S. Federal labelling laws to take account of 'Miller's Way', but to no avail. A few producers adopted the process for a while, but it just became a passing fad.

the *cuve close* vats became convenient dustbins for the garbage the rest of the wine industry did not want.

Of course there were exceptions, and the instigator of a couple of these was Martin Ray, who owned Paul Masson between 1936 and 1943 (when it was taken over by Seagram). He made a sparkling wine from 100% Pinot Noir called Madame Pinot in 1949, when no one thought this variety had any potential in California. Then, in 1952, he produced a Champagne de Chardonnay. It was probably these two wines that spurred the late Jack Davies and his wife Jamie to establish Schramsberg, the first quality-oriented sparkling wine venture to appear after Prohibition.

Jack and Jamie Davies were shareholders in one of Ray's ventures and in the early 1980s Jack described his Madame Pinot and Champagne de Chardonnay as 'forerunners of the next wave of change', which suggests that these wines could well have had some impact on the couple's decision to buy the famous old

THE WINERY AT SCHRAMSBERG, BOUGHT BY JACK AND JAMIE DAVIES IN 1965

AMERICAN 'CHAMPAGNE'

It is perfectly legal to sell domestically produced sparkling wine as Champagne in the USA because the term has been used to describe American sparkling wine from very early days and is thus defined as a generic name under Federal Law. However, most serious sparkling wine producers have stopped using the term and it is now encountered only on cheap, tank-fermented fizz. Premium quality products can gain very little from using the Champagne name, as the more they lean on the reputation of others, the longer it will be before they can establish their own identity.

The one exception is Schramsberg, although you will not see 'Champagne' on any bottles of this wine exported to EU countries. I had more than a little sympathy with the late Jack Davies, who once offered to swap the name 'Champagne' for 'Champagne Style' on his Schramsberg label. The logic is indisputable; if it is Champagne Style, it cannot possibly be Champagne, yet the champenois turned him down flat.

Since the champenois have no hope of making Americans do anything they do not want to do, it would have been wise to accept this compromise, particularly if they could have used the Schramsberg case as a fulcrum for an industry-wide undertaking. At worst the champenois would be facing a far less objectionable term, and who knows where such a stepping-stone might have led once the American market had become accustomed to the absence of domestic wines claiming to be Champagne? And it is not as if the champenois can claim that they are forced to refuse a compromise on moral grounds, for they abuse their own appellation in South America, where companies such as Moët, Mumm and Piper sell domestic fizz as *Champaña* (the Spanish for Champagne). How hypocritical can you get?

Schramsberg winery in 1965. They devoted their time, energy and money to produce just one thing: quality sparkling wine made from Pinot Noir, Chardonnay and Pinot Blanc, using the *méthode champenoise*. Their efforts did not go unnoticed and just eight years later California received the champenois seal of approval when Moët & Chandon chose the Napa Valley for the location of its first premium quality winery outside Champagne. Schramsberg and Domaine Chandon were the twin catalysts that converted a sporadic production of California fizz into today's fully-fledged industry. In the 1980s a veritable flood of French-owned and Franco-American sparkling wine ventures appeared on the scene: Piper-Sonoma (1980), Maison Deutz (1981 but defunct since 1997), Roederer Estate (1982), Mumm Napa Valley (1985) and Taittinger's Domaine Carneros (1987). Pommery purchased shares in Scharffenberger in 1990, but a few years later this holding passed to Veuve Clicquot, a sister company in the LVMH group.

In the early 1990s Laurent-Perrier started a project with Iron Horse to produce a special *cuvée* from a single vineyard, but although the Champagne house still owns this land, and Iron Horse may one day release such a wine, Laurent-Perrier strategy has changed and it will no longer be the result of a joint-venture.

The two giant Spanish Cava houses have also invested in California's sparkling wine future. Freixenet was the first, when in 1982 it established its Sonoma-based Gloria Ferrer winery, which was named after the wife of Freixenet's president. Nearly a decade later Codorníu established its eponymous California operation in neighbouring Napa.

Technologically, California sparkling wine came of age in the early 1990s, when the acidity became less 'ribby' and more in tune with the fruit, which gave the wines much greater elegance than before. This was a surprising development because, as in all other New World sparkling wine areas where the climate is less than ideal for this style of wine, California's producers have been faced with two basic choices: pick ripe grapes that have too much sugar and insufficient acidity, or harvest much earlier, when acidity levels are much higher and the grapes have an almost ideal sugar level for the relatively low degree of alcohol required by sparkling wines. Naturally enough, early-harvesting seemed to be the obvious solution and most Californians took this route. But an early-harvested grape is by definition unripe, which creates all sorts of problems that are even more difficult to overcome.

Sparkling wine producers, not just in California but throughout the New World, often claim they harvest grapes at the same degree of ripeness as in Champagne. The crucial difference is, however, that grapes of 10% potential alcohol are not just ripe in Champagne, they are vintage-quality ripe, whereas California-grown grapes of the same potential alcohol are physiologically unripe. California grapes harvested at this level not only lack richness and depth, they have totally inappropriate acidity.

Take Champagne and California grapes with identical total acidity readings and the composition of the acidity in both will be radically different. At 10%, the coolest-climate California grapes are dominated by hard malic acid, whereas the acidity in a 10% potential alcohol Champagne grape is predominantly tartaric. Even at 9%, the acidity of a Champagne grape is still predominantly tartaric. This explains the apparent paradox of why sunny California initially produced so many thin, green, aggressively unripe sparkling wines. It also illustrates just how difficult it is to compensate for the seemingly insurmountable problems created by early harvesting. However, by and large California's sparkling wine producers have managed to do this.

A few producers like 'Mad Harry' Osborne of Kristone decided to go the opposite route to early-harvest. Instead he picked ripe grapes, challenging his critics with such undeniable logic as 'Why harvest unripe grapes when they have no flavour and the wrong acidity, when you can harvest a larger crop of ripe grapes and simply add the acidity?'. It is not as simple as that, of course, because ripe grapes invariably contain too much sugar. Between 11 and 11.5% potential alcohol is a sensible maximum for any producer seeking a trouble-free secondary fermentation, as this process adds a further one to 1.5% of alcohol and even specially cultured Champagne yeasts are impaired by osmotic pressure in the presence of 13.5% alcohol and above. Also, from an aesthetic point of view, most people would consider any sparkling wine with an alcoholic strength in excess of 13% to be too big and vulgar.

Well that's the theory and just as most California winemakers have defied logic to produce better and better early-harvest sparkling wines, so 'Mad Harry' has managed to create a first class product from truly ripe grapes (see Kristone). There is a long way for the California fizz industry to go, but it is already producing fine, international quality sparkling wine and its problems are at least being tackled from both ends.

THE WINERY AT CODORNÍU NAPA, CALIFORNIA

ARGYLE KNUDSEN VINEYARD IN THE RED HILLS OF DUNDEE.

The best California sparkling wine areas already proven are Mendocino (as exemplified by Roederer Estate and Scharffenberger), Carneros (Domaine Carneros and a source for Domaine Chandon and many other producers) and Sonoma (Piper Sonoma). But perhaps the most exciting potential for the future is Santa Maria Valley, which was first planted for the first sparkling wines in the 1960s and 1970s, long before it potential for silky Pinot Noir red wines was known. In those early days, the grapes went into pretty foul-tasting California champagne, but if I was asked to set up a top-quality sparkling wine venture anywhere in the world today, that is where I would put it.

PACIFIC NORTHWEST

Washington and Oregon are both slow developers in the field of sparkling wine production, yet it's possible they possess as much potential as California. In Washington, Château Ste. Michelle's sparkling wines showed great promise in the late 1970s, but they have been disappointing ever since and although renewed efforts are being made, Dr Michael Manz is currently making this state's most serious fizz at his Mountain Dome winery in Spokane.

With Oregon's reputation for Pinot Noir, it is surprising that the champenois have not invaded this state long ago. Laurent-Perrier purchased land with a view to planting a vineyard in the early 1990s, but since it began to rationalise its non-Champagne interests, the company has been looking to sell its Oregon holding. However, apart from that abortive attempt, and Bollinger's financial-only interest in Argyle, far and away Oregon's best sparkling wine, the interest shown by the champenois has been non-existent. Argyle in the Red Hills of Dundee is a joint venture between Cal Knudsen and Brian Croser (of Petaluma in Australia, hence the Bollinger connection). The quality is at least as good as Croser, the Australian sparkling wine, and the style is much softer and easier to appreciate.

THE MADONNA VINEYARD IN SPRING IN THE CARNEROS REGION, NAPA, WHERE THE ACACIA WINERY BUYS ITS GRAPES

70
ACACIA WINERY
NAPA, CALIFORNIA

A top-class Burgundian varietal specialist making a small but serious contribution to the California premium sparkling wine scene.

WINEMAKER
Dave Lattin

HOUSE STYLE & RANGE
Barrel-fermented, full malolactic fermentation, with little or no fining and a kiss of brandy in the *dosage*. Acacia is going for long yeast-ageing, which is not always as beneficial as some sparkling winemakers seem to think, but the *cuvées* so far have been much finer than the overly long yeast-aged Mondavi fizz. Extended yeast-ageing seems to be less of a problem for the quality of these sparkling wines than the toffee-caramel character produced by too much malolactic influence.

★ VINTAGE BRUT
  Vintaged, méthode champenoise: 20% Chardonnay, 80% Pinot Noir

N/A
ALBA VINEYARD
MILFORD, NEW JERSEY

Established in 1983 by Rudolf Marchesi who, as a child, watched his Italian grandparents make wine in New Jersey and grew up to open one of the first farm wineries in the state. He only started production of sparkling wines from *vinifera* varieties growing in the Musconetcong Valley relatively recently.

N/A
AMWELL VALLEY VINEYARD
RINGOES, NEW JERSEY

This producer shares the honour of being New Jersey's first farm winery with DelVista, both of which were licensed in August 1982. The production of sparkling wine is a relatively recent development for owner-winemaker Dr Michael Fisher.

80
S ANDERSON VINEYARD
YOUNTVILLE, CALIFORNIA

- 7,500 cases
- Other labels - Tivoli

A small winery producing Chardonnay and Cabernet from the Stags Leap District, plus some impressive *méthode champenoise* wines.

WINEMAKER
Carol Anderson

HOUSE STYLE & RANGE
The brut is a zesty, crisp, sherbety fizz with delicious, fine and delicate fruit, and a very long and fresh finish that is capable of achieving more complexity after an additional year or two of ageing.

The *blanc de blancs* comes from Stags Leap specifically, rather than Napa Valley generally, which is the source for all the other *cuvées*, and has always shown the greatest linear intensity of the range.

The salmon-coloured rosé has improved greatly over the years and is now showing off big aromas and real flavours that make it such a serious, potentially complex wine for its style.

★ BLANC DE BLANCS
  Vintaged, méthode champenoise: 100% Chardonnay
BLANC DE NOIRS
  Vintaged, méthode champenoise: 100% Pinot Noir
★ BRUT
  Vintaged, méthode champenoise: 40% Chardonnay, 60% Pinot Noir
★ ROSÉ
  Vintaged, méthode champenoise: 34% Chardonnay, 66% Pinot Noir

ANDRÉ
See E&J GALLO

N/A
ANTHONY ROAD
PENN YAN, NEW YORK

Located at the western shore at the north end of Seneca Lake, in the Finger Lakes AVA, this relatively recent producer of New York 'champagne' has yet to establish a track record.

ANTHONY WINERY
See AUGUSTA WINERY

82
ARGYLE WINERY
DUNDEE, OREGON

This is a joint venture between Cal Knudsen (formerly of Knudsen Erath) and Brian Croser (of Petaluma in Australia), with Allen Holstein, who runs Domaine Drouhin's vineyards as vineyard manager, and Rollin Soles who is in day-to-day charge. A great source for Riesling and Oregon's best sparkling

wine. Occasionally Chardonnay comes right, and Pinot Noir (once dire) has recently made dramatic progress. Argyle is, however, better known for Oregon's top sparkling wine.

WINEMAKER
Rollin Soles

HOUSE STYLE & RANGE
Softer and more fruit-driven than Croser's Australian sparkling wine, Argyle has been successful from its first vintage in 1987, but started to achieve more complexity from 1989 onwards. At the time of writing, Argyle was still selling the 1987 rosé which was rather too dark and too sweet for my liking. But no other vintages of this *cuvée* have been produced so far, although there is talk of one in the future. They are also still selling the 1987 *blanc de blancs*, but it has always been a more successful wine with its light, yet nicely structured style and exotic quality to the fruit. Look out for two single-vineyard sparkling wines; the first − vintage 1995 − will be released for the millenium. The Knudsen Vineyard Brut is 100% *barrique*-fermented and fully malolactic, while the Knudsen Vineyard Blanc de Blancs is made from a Dijon clone that has smaller clusters than all the other Chardonnay growing in Oregon. Quantities produced are very small, so the wines will not be cheap, but the only reason they have no star ratings is because I have not tasted them.

★ BLANC DE BLANCS
  Vintaged, méthode champenoise: 100% Chardonnay
★★ BRUT
  Vintage, méthode champenoise: 40% Chardonnay, 60% Pinot Noir
KNUDSEN VINEYARD BLANC DE BLANCS
  Vinatged, méthode champenoise: 100% Chardonnay
KNUDSEN VINEYARD BRUT
  Vintaged, méthode champenoise: 20% Chardonnay, 80% Pinot Noir
ROSÉ
  Vintaged, méthode champenoise: 100% Pinot Noir

ARMSTRONG RIDGE
See KORBEL

ARTERBERRY
See DUCK POND CELLARS

N/A
AUGUSTA WINERY
AUGUSTA, MISSOURI

- Other labels - Cedar Ridge, Anthony Winery

An up-and-coming producer of *méthode champenoise* sparklers.

BALLATORE
See E&J GALLO

60

BARBOURSVILLE

BARBOURSVILLE, VIRGINIA

Set in the foothills of the Blue Ridge Mountains and once the property of James Barbour, a former governor of Virginia, this property was purchased in 1976 by Zonin of Piedmont in Italy. Some of the still wines have been very good, but Barboursville has yet to establish a track-record for its fizz.

HOUSE RANGE

BARBOURSVILLE BRUT NATURAL

Not vintaged, charmat method: 80% Chardonnay, 20% Pinot Noir

55

BEAULIEU VINEYARD

RUTHERFORD, CALIFORNIA

● Other labels – BV, Domaine Beaulieu

Unexceptional fizz under the BV label.

HOUSE RANGE

BEAULIEU VINEYARD BRUT RESERVE

Vintaged, méthode champenoise: 62% Pinot Noir, 38% Chardonnay

N/A

BENMARL

MARLBORO, NEW YORK

● Other labels – Cuvée du Vigneron

Located in the Hudson River Region AVA, Benmarl is one of New York State's most successful wineries. Its Gaelic name refers to the vineyard's slate-marl soil, and although *vinifera* varieties are grown and *méthode champenoise* wines are made, Seyval Blanc made as a still wine is the preferred style here.

60

BENZIGER FAMILY WINERY

GLEN ELLEN, CALIFORNIA

After selling off its Glen Ellen and MG Vallejo brands, Benzinger has raised its standards, and now produces some brilliant value-for-money varietal wines, but its *blanc de blancs* could do with more finesse.

N/A

BILTMORE ESTATE

ASHEVILLE, NORTH CAROLINA

● 10,000 cases

The Vanderbilt's famous Biltmore estate in the Blue Ridge Mountains took 1,000 men six years to construct. When the magnificent 250-roomed mansion was completed in 1895, it not only contained an indoor gymnasium, bowling alley and swimming pool, but was so far advanced for the time that it boasted electricity, central heating, refrigeration and even indoor toilets. The first vines were planted in 1971 by the grandson of George Washington Vanderbilt, and today they amount to some 30 hectares. These vineyards grow at an altitude of 4,500 feet, which is cool enough to cultivate classic *vinifera* varieties, but sometimes too cold for them to ripen.

WINEMAKER

Bernard Delille

HOUSE STYLE & RANGE

I had hoped that I could wax so lyrical about Biltmore's fizz that I would be invited to stop over at America's grandest house, but however hard I try, I just cannot work up any enthusiasm for these wines. The Biltmore Estate Blancs de Blancs has no finesse, and although Chateau Biltmore Brut is fresher, it is merely amylic, thus uninteresting, and lacking acidity.

Note that the Biltmore Estate *cuvée* is not an estate-bottled wine, as it contains 95% California grapes.

HOUSE RANGE

BILTMORE ESTATE BLANC DE BLANCS BRUT

Not vintaged, méthode champenoise: 100% Chardonnay

CHATEAU BILTMORE BRUT

Vintaged, méthode champenoise: 100% Chardonnay

N/A

BOOKWALTER WINERY

PASCO, WASHINGTON STATE

After Jerry Bookwalter graduated from UC Davis in 1962, he gained more than 20 years' experience in viticulture and winemaking with Sagemoor Farms and various other vineyards in Washington and Oregon before starting up on his own in 1983. Bookwalter has produced fizz from a fairly early stage, but he has had much greater success with still wines, particularly Cabernet Sauvignon.

65

BOORDY VINEYARDS

HYDES, MARYLAND

Established at Riderwood in 1945 by journalist Philip Wagner, who introduced hybrids to the Atlantic northeast, and was thus responsible for a turning point in America's viticultural history. Wagner retired in 1980, when the winery was purchased by the Deford family, who moved it to the present location. The first sparkling wine was released in 1988, a crisp and clean fizz that has consistently been an above-average performer.

N/A

BOWERS HARBOUR VINEYARD

TRAVERSE CITY, MICHIGAN

This small boutique winery overlooking the picturesque Bowers Harbour produces sparkling wine on the Old Mission Peninsula AVA, but I have not yet tasted any examples.

50

BROTHERHOOD WINERY

WASHINGTONVILLE, NEW YORK

The oldest US winery in continuous operation, the Brotherhood Winery was established in 1839 by a shoemaker called Jean Jacques, who initially sold wine to the First Presbyterian Church of which he was an elder – hence the name. The wines used to be very much of the old school, but have become fresher and crisper since the winery was modernised in 1987. There is a *méthode champenoise*, but it is not the best style produced at this winery in the Hudson River Region AVA. A Bordeaux-style red called Marriage and a Riesling are much preferred.

GRAND MONARQUE 'CHAMPAGNE' RD

Not vintaged, méthode champenoise: 70% Pinot Noir, 30% Chardonnay

BROTHERHOOD BLANC DE BLANCS BRUT 'CHAMPAGNE'

Not vintaged: Seyval Blanc, Chardonnay

LA BUENA VIDA

See SMITH ESTATES

N/A

BULLY HILL

HAMMONDSPORT, NEW YORK

The *méthode champenoise* wines from this Keuka Lake producer in the Fingers Lakes AVA have not impressed.

BV

See BEAULIEU VINEYARDS

N/A

CAMAS WINERY

MOSCOW, IDAHO

● Other labels – Life Force

This producer buys in grapes from neighbouring Washington state for his fizz.

CAMELOT

See OLIVER WINE CO

N/A

CANANDAIGUA WINE CO

CANANDAIGUA, NEW YORK

● Other labels – Chase-Limogère, Cook's, Cribari, Cresta Blanca, La Domaine, Great Western, Paul Masson, J Pierrot, J Roget, Roma

Second in size only to Gallo, Canandaigua (which means 'chosen place' in the language of the Seneca Indians) has diversified its still-wine production into premium varietals, but Chase-Limogère is as good as it gets for fizz, and that could be a lot better.

HOUSE STYLE & RANGE

FOR CHASE-LIMOGÈRE *see* appropriate entry.

COOK'S is a dull, often over-heavy, *cuve close* 'champagne'.

CRIBARI is a sweetish, cheap *cuve close* fizz.

CRESTA BLANCA was once a famous mountain vineyard planted by Paul Masson who produced sparkling wines of legendary quality, but is now just a boring transfer method bubbly.

LA DOMAINE I have never tasted.

PAUL MASSON is a transfer-method fizz that has tried hard in the past, but has not really succeeded. Even if it turned out top-quality stuff, the brand has become so cheapened that it may never be taken seriously.

J PIERROT cannot be recommended.

J ROGET I have never tasted.

ROMA is a clumsy, over-sweet *cuve close*.

N/A
CAPROCK
LUBBOCK, TEXAS

Formerly known as Teysha Cellars, this winery has been under new ownership since 1992, when it changed its name to CapRock. Until recently, I was unaware that any fizz was produced here but, as Tony Soter of Etude in the Napa Valley consults, and I have tasted a number of good still wines from here, it should be worth keeping an eye out for it.

HOUSE RANGE

CAPROCK SPARKLING BRUT
Not vintaged, méthode champenoise:
50% Chardonnay, 50% Pinot Noir

CEDAR RIDGE
See AUGUSTA WINERY

N/A
THE CHADDSFORD WINERY
CHADDS FORD, PENNSYLVANIA

Since owner-winemaker Eric Miller established this operation in 1982, it has become one of the rising stars of the Atlantic Northeast, but it is a much more consistent producer of still wines, such as Chardonnay (Philip Roth Vineyard) and

Pinot Grigio, than for fizz.

HOUSE RANGE

CHADDSFORD BLANC DE BLANCS ET NOIR
Not vintaged, méthode champenoise: 80% Chardonnay
20% Pinot Noir

N/A
CHALET DEBONNÉ
MADISON, OHIO

Established in 1971 by Anthony Debevc, the production of fizz has been a relatively recent development and, as such, Chalet Debonné has yet to set a track record.

CHANDON
See DOMAINE CHANDON

CHANTAL
See CHATEAU CHANTAL

50
CHASE-LIMOGÈRE
WOODBRIDGE, CALIFORNIA

When this Canandaigua brand was launched, it was claimed to be the product of a blending philosophy that has created a 'multi-dimensional base *cuvée* that is at the forefront of winemaking innovation'. Using a 'proprietary blend of varietal grapes' from Northern California, Chase-Limogère combines free-run juice with a small proportion of intentionally oxidised juice, which the company believes to be a classic French blending technique that 'contributes body, complexity and soft tannins' while the free-run juice provides 'fresh and crisp qualities'. It is then aged for 12 to 15 months 'for additional complexity', and alembic pot-stilled brandy is used in the *dosage*, a method 'the French Champagne houses traditionally reserve for their top-of-the-line Champagnes'. The fact that most of this will be news to the *champenois* would be academic if the result were something special, but it is not.

HOUSE STYLE & RANGE

The brut is simply round and fizzy, while the brut rosé initially has a more attractive flowery nose, but is rather sweet and heavy.

BRUT
Not vintaged, cuve close: grape varieties not revealed
See CANANDAIGUA

N/A
CHATEAU BENOIT
CARLTON, OREGON

An occasional producer of *méthode champenoise*, Chateau Benoit has failed to impress.

N/A
CHATEAU CHANTAL
TRAVERSE CITY, MICHIGAN

Michigan's 'only bed & breakfast' winery

straddles a ridge at the northern end of the Old Mission Peninsula. A *méthode champenois* producer that has not impressed.

CHATEAU DE MONTE
See WIEDERKEHR WINERY

N/A
CHATEAU FRANK
HAMMONDSPORT, NEW YORK

The *méthode champenoise* from this Keuka Lake producer in the Fingers Lakes AVA has not impressed.

N/A
CHÂTEAU GRAND TRAVERSE
TRAVERSE CITY, MICHIGAN

- Other labels - O'Keefe Cellars, Old Mission Winery

Almost 50 hectares of vineyards planted exclusively with *vinifera* vines, Château Grand Traverse was established in 1975 by Ed O'Keefe, a former Green Beret colonel and FBI agent. Now run by the second-generation Ed O'Keefe, who continues to produce a sparkling wine that I encountered long ago. I found it to be clean and acceptable, but not special.

CHÂTEAU NAPOLEON
See WEIBEL

N/A
CHERRY VALLEY VINEYARDS
SAYLORSBURG, PENNSYLVANIA

- 200 cases

Established in 1980 by Mary and Dominic Sorrenti, Cherry Valley vineyard and winery are located in the Pocono Mountains. The first sparkling wine was produced in 1986.

WINEMAKER

Dominic Sorrenti

HOUSE RANGE

CHAMPAGNE
Vintaged, méthode champenoise; Seyval Blanc,
Vidal, Aurore

CHEURLIN
See GRUET

N/A
CHICAMA VINEYARDS
WEST TISBURY, MASSACHUSETTS

- Other labels - Sea Mist

It was the famous Konstantin Frank (*see p. 257*) who persuaded George and Catherine Mathiesen that they could grow *vinifera* grapes, and he even supplied the vine-cuttings with which to start off their vineyard. A *méthode champenoise* fizz is produced under the Sea Mist label.

HOUSE RANGE

EA MIST BRUT
Not vintaged, méthode champenoise: 100% Chardonnay

NA
CLINTON VINEYARDS
CLINTON CORNERS, NEW YORK
This Hudson River winery makes one of the best Seyval Blancs in New York State, but also produces *méthode champenoise* wines.
HOUSE RANGE
CLINTON VINEYARDS SEYVAL NATUREL HUDSON
  RIVER 'CHAMPAGNE'
Not vintaged, méthode champenoise: 100% Seyval Blanc
CLINTON VINEYARDS PEACH GALA
Not vintaged, méthode champenoise: 90% Seyval Blanc, 10% Peach

79
CODORNÍU NAPA
NAPA, CALIFORNIA
This winery is buried in a Carneros hillside with just a bunker-like protrusion visible from the road. At first, this might appear to be the siege mentality of a giant Cava company come to California to do battle with its old adversary, Freixenet. The latter had set up the California fizz firm of Gloria Ferrer almost ten years earlier. In fact, Codorníu's design is quite similar to that of its Raïmat winery in Spain.

Codorníu began construction in 1989 by completely removing a section of hillside and putting the topsoil to one side. After excavating and building the winery to just below the natural elevation of the knoll, the sloping sides of the building were packed with the indigenous soil and sown with local grasses. Visually, the effect is reminiscent of a section of the Maginot Line (albeit green, not grey), with a minimalist interior design.

Environmentally, the so-called berm system, as it is known, utilises earth to help insulate the building, thus significantly reducing energy consumption all year round.

The winery opened in 1991.
WINEMAKER
Todd Graffes
HOUSE STYLE & RANGE
The first few salvos Codorníu fired at the California arm of its Spanish rival were not up to much, but the biscuity bottle-aromas now build fairly quickly in the non-vintage brut and the vintaged Carneros Cuvée stands out for its lovely pincushion mousse.

Look out for the launch of Codorníu's prestige *cuvée*.
★ BRUT
Not vintaged, méthode champenoise: 50% Chardonnay, 50% Pinot Noir
★ CARNEROS CUVÉE
Vintaged, méthode champenoise: 25% Chardonnay, 75% Pinot Noir

COLORADO CELLARS
See VINELAND CORPORATION

COLORADO MOUNTAIN VINEYARDS
See VINELAND CORPORATION

COOK'S
See CANANDAIGUA

CORONATION
See FOUR CHIMNEYS FARM WINERY

CRESTA BLANCA
See CANANDAIGUA

CRIBARI
See CANANDAIGUA

CULBERTSON
See THORNTON WINERY

RICHARD CUNEO
See SEBASTIANI

DEUTZ
See MAISON DEUTZ

LA DOMAINE
See CANANDAIGUA

DOMAINE BEAULIEU
See BEAULIEU VINEYARDS

83
DOMAINE CARNEROS
NAPA, CALIFORNIA
● 60,000 cases
● Group ownership - Taittinger & Kobrand
Claude Taittinger began his search for a California property in the late 1970s, buying this 56-hectare estate in 1982, when its first vines were planted. There are now 45 hectares of vines, and a winery perched on top of a knoll with the pristine façade of Taittinger's 18th-century Château de la Marquetterie at Pierry in Champagne.

The visiting facility brought a new concept to California: instead of receiving a free tasting sample, visitors buy a full glass in an elegant flute, which a waitress serves at your own table with a few canapés. Through the French windows, you look across the formal gardens at the vineyards clinging to the rolling hillsides of Carneros. It is a far more civilised experience than sipping from a tiny sample glass while being jostled by tourists. The Americans love it, as do tourists, and Taittinger makes a healthy profit doing something other winery owners get grumpy about.
WINEMAKER
Eileen Crane
HOUSE STYLE & RANGE
The first couple of releases were among the worst that any French-owned venture had produced. (They were not actually bad wines in any technical sense, just plain boring, and lacking finesse). But the learning curve was very steep. It did not take long to adapt Taittinger's Old World expertise to New World grapes and technology, quickly elevating Domaine Carneros to one of the best California sparkling wines. Any all-American venture thinking of entering the fizz game should take heart from, but also heed the fact that even the *Champenois* need a year or two to get things right.

The brut is very fresh and elegant, with nice acidity and a crisp mousse of tiny bubbles. The *blanc de blancs* has a pale colour, creamy, flowery, sherbety aromas, and fine, light fruit on the palate, with very good acidity, and a soft mousse of ultrafine bubbles.
★★ BLANC DE BLANCS
Vintaged, méthode champenoise: 97% Chardonnay, 3% Pinot Blanc

THE GROUNDS OF CODORNÍU NAPA WINERY WHICH HAS BEEN BUILT INTO THE SIDE OF THE HILL

DOMAINE CHANDON

YOUNTVILLE, CALIFORNIA

- 412,500 cases
- Other labels - Étoile, Shadow Creek
  (export market)

Moët & Chandon is not just the brand leader
in Champagne, it is the trend-setter in
international sparkling wine ventures, having
purchased 324 hectares at Yountville in the
Napa Valley as early as 1973. This firm thus
saw the sparkling wine potential of California
in the '60s, a good ten to 20 years before any
other Champagne house, and effectively
gave Champagne's seal of approval on the
future of California sparkling wine.

Since Domaine Chandon's arrival, a
number of other famous Champagne houses
have set up their own California sparkling
wineries. At the time, there was a huge
demand for sparkling wine, which was
increasing at a rate that no one ever
imagined would stop. Then, just as all these
new ventures came to fruition, the market
began to decrease, due to the health and
neo-prohibitionist lobby, as well as general
economic factors. This left the established
brands fighting for a smaller slice of a
shrinking pie, and Domaine Chandon
responded by discounting its product to
maintain volume. It should have exported –
especially to the UK, where demand was still
on the rise and the exchange rate was
favourable. However, Domaine Chandon's
marketing people realised that the company
was almost unique in being able to afford
such a price war, as its capital costs had long
since been covered, whereas most of the other
new ventures were still operating on huge
loans at record interest rates. In a way,
Domaine Chandon was too successful because
although it kept its market share and probably
made a profit doing so, its reputation began
to tumble along with its price. Domaine
Chandon has tried to reverse this, but it has
proved somewhat difficult: once consumers
get used to a price point, it has a tendency to
stick. Why should they pay more?

The most important
reason is, of course,
quality. The quality of
Domaine Chandon has
improved over recent
years, particularly in those
wines that have come
on-stream in the last two
years. Its marketing,
however, has lagged
woefully behind, making

BOTTLES OF SPARKLING WINE IN PUPITRES IN THE
CELLARS AT DOMAINE CHANDON

it difficult to reposition the brand upmarket.

Of the various sources of grapes at
Domaine Chandon's disposal, Carneros has
traditionally been the most sought after, but
more recently Mount Veeder Chardonnay
has looked interesting, particularly when the
malolactic fermentation has been prevented.
The pity is that such wines have merely been
the backbone of non-vintage sparkling wines
uninspiringly labelled as Chandon Club
Cuvée. If instead of blending it with a
thumping great whack of Pinot Noir and
Pinot Blanc, this were marketed in its pure
form as Chandon Mount Veeder Chardonnay
and vintaged, it would have been a whole lot
more exciting.

Indeed, quite why Domaine Chandon
opted for an absence of vintaged sparkling
wines in its range is a mystery, and one that
has denied the brand an entire sector of the
market. It is one thing to promote the
philosophy of non-vintage blends, which are
more flexible and thus easier to transform
into top quality than the restricted single
vintage, but not to market any pure vintage
cuvées seems self-defeating.

I have long tried to point out, for
example, the great Champagnes that
Americans are missing because the market
there, apparently, demands a
vintage for all top-quality
wines. There is not a single
Champagne house that does
not sell at least one vintage
cuvée, but Domaine
Chandon insists on
restricting itself exclusively
to non-vintage sparkling
wines in the vintage-

CHANDON'S WINEMAKER DAWNINE DYER obsessed US.

WINEMAKER
Dawnine Dyer
HOUSE STYLE & RANGE
These sparkling wines have established a
track record for a full style that I have found
rather heavy and ponderous, with flavours that
are too broad, lacking freshness, finesse and a
certain raciness the French call *vif*. The reserve
wines have often taken on a petrolly character,
and the younger *cuvées* have always been
preferable. This, I think (I hope!) is changing
as the style has shifted to lighter and fresher,
with fluffy fruit and a sherbety finish. No
wine better displays this than the *blanc de noirs*
that Domaine Chandon chose to export under
its Shadow Creek label (once a completely
different secondary brand, but now merely an
export name for exactly the same wine sold
under the Domaine Chandon label in the US)

The case is not proven, yet; hence the 80-
point rating. Yet if this is the new direction
that Domaine Chandon is taking stylistically
across its entire range of *cuvées*, then it will
deserve 85 points at least. Note: the non-
vintage philosophy here usually involves
15-20% one-year-old reserve wine and two
to five per cent two-year-old reserve wines.
The last two figures of the three-digit *cuvée*
number indicated on the label reveal the year
of the primary vintage in a blend.

★ BRUT

*Not vintaged, méthode champenoise: 25% Chardonnay,
60% Pinot Noir, 5% Meunier, 10% Pinot Blanc*

BRUT RÉSERVE

*Not vintaged, méthode champenoise: 22% Chardonnay,
66% Pinot Noir, 6% Meunier, 6% Pinot Blanc*

★★ CARNEROS BLANC DE NOIRS

*Not vintaged, méthode champenoise: 1% Chardonnay,
85% Pinot Noir, 13% Meunier, 1% Pinot Blanc*

★★ ÉTOILE

*Not vintaged, méthode champenoise: 65% Chardonnay,
23% Pinot Noir, 5% Meunier, 7% Pinot Blanc*

★★ ÉTOILE

*Not vintaged, méthode champenoise: 60% Chardonnay,
30% Pinot Noir, 5% Meunier, 5% Pinot Blanc*

★ ROSÉ BRUT

*Not vintaged, méthode champenoise: 35% Chardonnay,
52% Pinot Noir, 10% Meunier, 3% Pinot Blanc*

★ **BRUT**
Vintaged, méthode champenoise: 30% Chardonnay, 62% Pinot Noir, 3% Meunier, 5% Pinot Blanc
BRUT ROSÉ
Vintaged, méthode champenoise: 25% Chardonnay, 75% Pinot Noir

DOMAINE MONTREAUX
See MONTICELLO VINEYARDS

DOMAINE ST GREGORY
See TAMUZZA VINEYARDS

60
DOMAINE STE MICHELLE
PATERSON, WASHINGTON
This winery is owned by Stimpson Lane, a large company which also owns Columbia Crest, Conn Creek and Villa Mount Eden among others. Apart from all the various other Washington brands its wines are sold under, the Domaine Ste Michelle label is used exclusively for sparkling wines, while the Château Ste Michelle label is used for still wines.
HOUSE STYLE & RANGE
These sparkling wines showed great promise in the late 1970s, but they have been disappointing ever since. Efforts are being renewed to rediscover the original potential for this style of wine. The *blanc de blancs* is a very amylic fizz with tart fruit, and the brut *dosage* quite separate on the palate. The brut is more serious in structure, with floral aromas that are more classic than those of the amylic *blanc de blancs*, and a certain scented complexity to the fruit.
COLUMBIA VALLEY BLANC DE BLANCS
Not vintaged, méthode champenoise: 100% Chardonnay
★ **COLUMBIA VALLEY BRUT**
Not vintaged, méthode champenoise: Pinot Noir, Chardonnay and other undisclosed varieties
COLUMBIA VALLEY EXTRA DRY
Not vintaged, méthode champenoise: Pinot Noir, Chardonnay and other undisclosed varieties

N/A
DUPLIN WINE CELLARS
ROSE HILL, NORTH CAROLINA
Established in 1976 by Dan and David Fussel, two brothers who were fed up with selling grapes to out-of-state wineries at knock-down prices, and decided to build their own winery which has since grown into something of a co-op, as neighbouring growers have joined in. Production includes *méthode champenoise* made from Scuppernong, a local oddity with loose-hanging grapes the size of cherry-tomatoes.

EDON ROC
See E&J GALLO

N/A
ELEPHANT BUTTE
TRUTH OR CONSEQUENCES, NEW MEXICO
• Other labels - Mont Jallon
A new entrant in the sparkling-wine sector. Not tasted and no information forthcoming.

N/A
EOLA HILLS
RICKREALL, OREGON
Established in 1988 by Tom Higgins, who planted Chenin Blanc, Sauvignon Blanc and Cabernet Sauvignon while everyone else was planting Pinot Noir and Chardonnay – because, he says, he didn't know any better! Sparkling-wine production commenced in the early 1990s

ÉTOILE
See DOMAINE CHANDON

EXCELSIOR
See MARKKO WINERY

N/A
FENN VALLEY VINEYARDS
FENNVILLE, MICHIGAN
Founded in 1973 by William Welsch, who bought an orchard (always a favoured location for vines), grubbed it up and planted a vineyard. He started growing hybrids, but now also includes *vinifera* varieties. A small amount of *méthode champenoise* is produced.
HOUSE RANGE
BRUT
Not vintaged, méthode champenoise: 60% Chardonnay, 20% Seyval, 20% Pinot Noir

CRÉMANT BRUT
Not vintaged, méthode champenoise: 80% Seyval Blanc, 17% Chardonel, 3% Marachel Foch
SILVER CUVÉE TÊTE DE CUVÉE
Not vintaged, méthode champenoise: 80% Chardonnay, 20% Pinot Noir

LA FERME MARTIN
See SAGPOND VINEYARDS

N/A
FILSINGER
TEMECULA, CALIFORNIA
Although this vineyard was established in 1974, and a winery built in 1980, the move into sparkling wine production has been relatively recent.

N/A
FIRELANDS WINE CO
SANDUSKY, OHIO
Established way back in 1880 by the Mantey family, who owned the winery until 1980, when it was purchased by a firm of distillers. I remember tasting a decent still Chardonnay in the late 1980s, but sparkling wine is a recent development.

65
FLYNNS VINEYARDS
RICKREALL, OREGON
Since Wayne Flynn established this venture in 1985, his primary ambition has been to produce world-class bottle-fermented sparkling wines from his family's vineyards at the southern end of the Eola Hills. However, he started off by selling most of his grapes to other wineries as well as making small amounts of varietal wines at Yamhill Valley Winery. He made his first sparkling wine in 1987, when his own winery was built.
WINEMAKER
Wayne Flynn
HOUSE STYLE & RANGE
The quality of the Blanc de Blancs started improving with the 1988 vintage, with the Cellar Select Brut catching up in 1989. These wines can show good autolysis, but need firmer structure before any more progress can be made.
★ **BLANC DE BLANCS BRUT**
Vintaged, méthode champenoise: 100% Chardonnay
CELLAR SELECT BRUT
Vintaged, méthode champenoise: 25% Chardonnay, 75% Pinot Noir

N/A
THOMAS FOGARTY
PORTOLA, CALIFORNIA
Established in 1982 by Dr Thomas Fogarty, a cardiovascular surgeon of some repute, this winery has relatively recently diversified into sparkling wine production.

N/A
FOUR CHIMNEYS FARM WINERY
HIMROD, NEW YORK
• Other labels - Coronation
In 1990, Walter Pederson, an editor for Macmillan Publishers, traded the buzz of working in the Big Apple for farm life at Four Chimneys, an Italian-style villa close to Lake Seneca in the Finger Lakes AVA. He found some vines growing on the farm and, after the Farm Winery Act was passed, planted some more and built a winery. He has, however, only recently started to produce sparkling wine.

N/A
GALENA CELLARS
GALENA, ILLINOIS

● Other labels - Lawlor Family

A relatively recent production of sparkling wine under the Lawlor Family label.

N/A
E&J GALLO
MODESTO, CALIFORNIA

● Other labels: Andre, Ballatore, Edon Roc, Indigo Hills

It is almost too much for the human mind to comprehend, but E&J Gallo has a total production under numerous different brands equal to one-and-a-half times the entire output of Australia, and although its latest fizzy offering just scrapes in, this is just the sort of producer that could, with a sufficient investment and the right consultant, produce a world-class sparkling wine.

This author waits to see whether Indigo Hills is as ambitious as Gallo gets, or becomes the blueprint for something altogether more serious.

65
GLENORA WINE CELLARS
DUNDEE, NEW YORK

Named after the nearby Glenora Waterfall, this winery was established in 1977 by four local growers who were among the first to take advantage of the passing of the Farm Winery Act (1976) to establish their own cooperative winery. Glenora consistently produces *méthode champenoise* wines that, relative to their Finger Lakes origin, are crisp and stylish, including a vintage brut and a vintage *blanc de blancs*.

75
GLORIA FERRER
SONOMA, CALIFORNIA

Established by Spanish Cava-giant Freixenet in 1982, and named after the wife of José Ferrer, the firm's president. Gloria Ferrer quickly made an acceptable, if unexciting, non-vintage brut, but started to excel with the odd vintage wine, such as the 1985 Carneros Cuvée. Since the mid-1990s, the quality has been more even, and the non-vintage brut now ranks, coincidentally, with Codorníu as equal second-best California fizz (behind Piper Sonoma) in the ready-to-drink stakes.

WINEMAKER
Bob Iantosca

HOUSE STYLE & RANGE

The brut is light and creamy with fat, sassy fruit and a sherbety finish, but in recent years the *cuvée* that has made the most progress has been the deliciously fresh, juicy and elegant *blanc de noirs*. There is little (if any) non-vintage philosophy here, as the effect that reserve wines have on the rate of maturation and potential complexity of a blend is not acknowledged. Reserve wines are perceived merely as levellers to even out the peaks and troughs of different harvests, which are not so acute in California as they are in Europe – hence most Gloria Ferrer non-vintage *cuvées* are pure vintage wines without any indication of the year in question. In all the breakdowns I have seen of these *cuvées*, the most reserve wine was three per cent in a 1991-based brut.

★★☆ BLANC DE NOIRS
Not vintaged, méthode champenoise: 8% Chardonnay, 92% Pinot Noir

★ SONOMA BRUT
Not vintaged, méthode champenoise: 10% Chardonnay, 90% Pinot Noir

SONOMA COUNTY ROSE
Not vintaged, méthode champenoise: 10% Chardonnay, 90% Pinot Noir

CARNEROS CUVÉE
Vintaged, méthode champenoise: 40% Chardonnay, 60% Pinot Noir

CARNEROS CUVÉE - LATE DISGORGED
As Carneros Cuvée but disgorged some five to six years later

ROYAL CUVÉE
Vintaged, méthode champenoise: 40% Chardonnay, 60% Pinot Noir

N/A
GOLD SEAL
HAMMONDSPORT, NEW YORK

● Other labels - Charles Fournier

Originally called the Imperial Winery, this historic firm built its reputation on 'New York Champagne'. The quality of this sparkling wine was based on 100 years of true Champagne expertise, in the form of Charles le Breton of Louis Roederer, Jules Crance of Moët & Chandon, Charles Fournier of Veuve Clicquot and Guy Devaux of Marne et Champagne, who all worked at Gold Seal. But of all of them, it is Charles Fournier who stands out.

It was Fournier who, after pioneering hybrids, had the courage to ignore local experts and employ New York's champion of *vinifera* vines, the irrepressible Konstantin Frank (*see p. 257*). This firm uses various methods of production today, but the transfer-method Charles Fournier Blanc de Noirs is the best sparkling wine here.

HOUSE STYLE & RANGE

CHARLES FOURNIER BLANC DE NOIRS
Not vintaged, transfer method: grape varieties not revealed

N/A
GOOD HARBOR VINEYARDS
LAKE LEE LANAU, MICHIGAN

Winemaker Bruce Simpson established this winery in 1980 and has a good local reputation for his wines, including a fizz. Not tasted.

GRAND MARK
See TABOR HILL

GRAND TRAVERSE
See CHATEAU GRAND TRAVERSE

GREAT WESTERN
See CANANDAIGUA

78
GRUET
ALBUQUERQUE, NEW MEXICO

The Gruet family are important growers in the Sézanne district of Champagne, and established one of the town's two local co-ops. Some of these wines have shown extraordinary acidity. Recommended *cuvées* include a non-vintage brut and a vintaged *blanc de blancs*.

HOUSE RANGE

GRUET BLANC DE BLANCS
Not vintaged, méthode champenoise: 100% Chardonnay

GRUET BRUT
Not vintaged, méthode champenoise: 75% Chardonnay, 25% Pinot Noir

GRUET BRUT BLANC DE NOIRS
Not vintaged, méthode champenoise: 75% Pinot Noir, 25% Chardonnay

N/A
HAIGHT VINEYARD
LITCHFIELD, CONNECTICUT

● 1,000 cases

Established in 1975 by Sherman Haight, who had wanted to grow vines but thought it would be impossible to cultivate *vinifera* varieties in Connecticut's climate, until he read an article by Konstantin Frank (*see p. 257*). I have not tasted the *méthode champenoise* produced here, but I have had decent Chardonnay and Riesling.

75
HANDLEY CELLARS
MENDOCINO, CALIFORNIA

I first came across the wines from this *méthode champenoise* specialist in the Anderson Valley during the mid-1980s, when it was out-performing Scharffenberger. Although the quality of Scharffenberger (now selling as Pacific Echo) has overtaken Handley, this is only because it has had the finance, facilities

THE HANDLEY WINERY IN THE ANDERSON VALLEY, MENDOCINO. FIFTY PER CENT OF THE WINES HERE ARE BARRIQUE-FERMENTED AND VIRTUALLY ALL OF THEM GO THROUGH MALOLACTIC FERMENTATION

...nd expertise of Champagne Veuve Clicquot to force a sprint in terms of the learning curve. Handley has not dropped back; indeed, the quality has been very consistent, and the cuvées have slowly improved from year to year.

WINEMAKER
Mila Handley

HOUSE STYLE & RANGE
About 45% to 50% of the wines are barrique-fermented and virtually all components go through full malolactic fermentation. They are not normally fined. The vintage brut always has good acidity and is softened by a fluffy mousse of tiny bubbles and a creamy, vanilla richness, whereas the blanc de blancs has occasionally lacked acidity, although its soft, creamy, lemony Chardonnay fruit stands out.

★ BLANC DE BLANCS
  Vintaged, méthode champenoise: 100% Chardonnay
★ BRUT
  Vintaged, méthode champenoise: 32% Chardonnay, 68% Pinot Noir
BRUT ROSÉ
  Vintaged, méthode champenoise: 10% Chardonnay, 90% Pinot Noir

N/A
HAZLITT
HECTOR, NEW YORK
Located on Sececa Lake in the Fingers Lakes, this relatively recent producer of New York 'champagne' has yet to establish a track record.

N/A
HERMANNHOF
HERMANN, MISSOURI
Hybrid méthode champenoise sparklers made from Seyval Blanc, Vidal and Villard in a converted pre-Prohibition brewery.

N/A
HILL COUNTRY CELLARS
AUSTIN, TEXAS
• Other labels - Moyer
The Moyers established a vineyard and winery for still wines in Manchester, Ohio (*see* MOYER VINEYARDS), before setting up this

sparkling-wine facility in 1980. But they sold the Texas venture in 1986 and it is now called Hill Country Cellars, although its sparkling wines are still sold under the Moyer label.

N/A
HOPKINS VINEYARD
NEW PRESTON, CONNECTICUT
This estate winery was established in 1979, but has relatively recently begun sparkling wine production.

N/A
HOSMER
OVID, NEW YORK
Located on Cayuga Lake in the Fingers Lakes, this relatively recent producer of New York 'champagne' has yet to establish a track record.

75
ROBERT HUNTER
SONOMA, CALIFORNIA
Unlike today, when Pinot Noir is a hot varietal, in the early 1980s Robert Hunter could not give the grapes away, which is why his friend Dan Duckhorn suggested that he should use them for sparkling wine.

WINEMAKER
Robert Hunter

HOUSE STYLE & RANGE
A richly flavoured cuvée that has plenty of complexity when released, yet is capable of further development in bottle.
★ SONOMA VALLEY BRUT DE NOIRS
  Vintaged, méthode champenoise: 34% Chardonnay, 66% Pinot Noir

INDIGO HILLS
See E&J GALLO

60
INGLESIDE PLANTATION
OAK GROVE, VIRGINIA
Ingleside produced Virginia's first sparkling wine in the early 1980s, but its Chardonnay and Cabernet Sauvignon are more interesting.

IRON HORSE
See PAGE 270

N/A
JAMESPORT VINEYARDS
JAMESPORT, NEW YORK
Located on Long Island, this sparkling wine producer uses transfer method and *cuve close*.

75
JEPSON
UKIAH, CALIFORNIA
Established in 1986 by Robert Jepson of the Jepson Corporation, a group of companies making a diverse range of products from sportswear to plane seats. The wines are produced from Jepson's own 50-hectare estate.

WINEMAKER
Kurt Lorenzi

HOUSE STYLE & RANGE
Forty per cent barrique-aged Chardonnay adds richness to the crisply-structured blanc de blancs brut, which receives a brandied dosage although the fruit is so pure it is not noticeable.
★ BLANC DE BLANCS BRUT
  Vintaged, méthode champenoise: 100% Chardonnay

85
J WINE COMPANY
HEALDSBURG, CALIFORNIA
Established in 1986 by Judy Jordan, the Jordan Sparkling Wine Company operated out of the back door of her father's Jordan winery until 1997, when she purchased Piper-Sonoma's specialist facility in Healdsburg. After his sojourn at Iron Horse, Claude Thibaut made the first two vintages of 'J' in 1987 and 1988, and was followed for one year by fellow Frenchman Roger Viron. Since 1990, however, the winemaker has been Israeli-born Oded Shakked, who assisted both Thibaut and Viron.

WINEMAKER
Oded Shakked

HOUSE STYLE & RANGE
The first releases of 'J' sparkling wine had a bit of a terpene character, but although this

THE 'J' WINE COMPANY VINEYARDS AT HEALDSBURG WHERE, AFTER TWO FRENCHMEN, THE CURRENT WINEMAKER IS AN ISRAELI

88
IRON HORSE VINEYARDS

SEBASTOPOL, CALIFORNIA

This was once the only railway stop in Sonoma Green Valley – hence the name, which has also given rise to Iron Horse's second label: Tin Pony! It was purchased in 1976 by Barry Sterling, an attorney and compulsive gardener with a love of wine and a life-long ambition to own a winery. Barry and his wife Audrey turned Iron Horse's derelict Victorian house into one of Sonoma's loveliest homes, surrounding it with thousands of flowers, shrubs and trees, including over 200 varieties of roses alone. The entire property runs to 130 hectares and when the Sterlings took over, it already had 45 hectares of vineyards, planted and managed in 1970 by Forrest Tancer, who also has vineyards in the Alexander Valley.

There are now 75 hectares of vineyard plus numerous orchards, but much of the property is wild and untamed and most of this will remain that way by design. The vineyards are broken up into numerous plots, each of which is separated by a chunk of uncultivated land, which Forrest considers vital for the health of his vines, as each one provides sufficient habitat for the necessary population of natural predators to the pests that would otherwise run riot. He could cultivate great swathes of land, but would only end up having to resort to chemical sprays to control the pests and Forrest is very green-minded, as indeed is Joy, Forrest's wife and Barry and Audrey's daughter.

Joy left a high-profile career as a TV journalist in 1986 to become a partner in and marketing director of Iron Horse. She has not, however, totally deserted her journalistic background, having written a book, *A Cultivated Life* (Villard Books), which received much critical acclaim for its insight into a year in the life of a California winery.

Forrest knew the vineyards like the back of his hand before Barry and Audrey arrived and this knowledge quickly established the basic quality of the wine. He is also a highly talented winemaker, having worked closely with two consultants: Claude Thibaut, who

IRON HORSE, WHERE VINES GROW SIDE BY SIDE WITH THOUSANDS OF FLOWERS, SHRUBS, AND TREES, INCLUDING 200 VARIETIES OF ROSES

went on to make Vve Devaux the most dynamic cooperative in Champagne, and Raphael Brisbois, the Alsatian genius who created the Indian fizz, Omar Khayyam.

WINEMAKER

Forrest Tancer, David Munksgard

HOUSE STYLE & RANGE

Nothing at Iron Horse is allowed to get in the way of its quest for textbook correctness of structure, acidity, low *dosage* and the all-important bottle-aromas of autolysis. It is these fine, acacia-like aromas that form an essential part of any great sparkling wine, but they require a relatively neutral base to build on, so Iron Horse avoids overt varietal character, which is easily achieved by Sonoma County Green Valley's climate. In steering this classic course with an unflinching discipline, Iron Horse has become one of California's most respected premium wine operations, but it has also attracted criticism for the austerity of its style. Indeed, some *cuvées* have been just a bit too correct to succeed – wines so clinically clean that they have not developed the potential complexity and finesse that is inherent in Iron Horse grapes. From 1987, however, the wines have softened, allowing the finesse to shine through and enabling a slow build-up of creamy, biscuity complexity.

The Iron Horse style is defiantly non-malolactic, although it would be interesting to see partial-malolactic on the Chardonnay

in cooler years. The vintage brut is a class act with deep, beautifully intense fruit, while the *blanc de blancs* is fat and weighty, with creamy-complex fruit of lovely finesse.

Vrais Amis (*True Friends*) is so named because it was conceived by Barry Sterling and his old French friend, Bernard de Nonancourt of Laurent-Perrier. It comes from a single vineyard, and Laurent-Perrier's oenologist Alain Terrier was involved in its early evolution, but since the Champagne house withdrew from all winemaking activities outside its own appellation, Vrais Amis has become exclusively a California product. It has such bright California fruit with just a touch of vanilla on the finish, and is bursting with beautiful acidity of great finesse, which is so hard to achieve with early-harvested grapes. It is as Californian as the beach, sun and roller-skating babes. I reckon that Brisbois, Iron Horse's one-time consultant, went because Forrest and Joy thought he would turn them into another Roederer Estate. I am sure I would love Iron Horse *à la* Roederer, but I also enjoy Vrais Amis and it is pure Iron Horse. You cannot help but admire Joy and Forrest for sticking to their guns. These are Iron Horse's finest *cuvées*, but the most wicked wine of all is the vividly coloured rosé, with fruit so brash it slaps you in the face. Although it is not in the same class, it deserves equal star-rating for its audacity alone.

★★ SONOMA-GREEN VALLEY BLANC DE BLANCS

   Vintaged, méthode champenoise: 100% Chardonnay

★★ SONOMA-GREEN VALLEY BRUT

   Vintaged, méthode champenoise: 25% Chardonnay, 75% Pinot Noir

★★ SONOMA-GREEN VALLEY BRUT ROSE

   Vintaged, méthode champenoise: 25% Chardonnay, 75% Pinot Noir

SONOMA-GREEN VALLEY LATE-DISGORGED BRUT

   As the Brut, but disgorged a few years later

★★ SONOMA-GREEN VALLEY VRAIS AMIS

   Vintaged, méthode champenoise: 30% Chardonnay, 70% Pinot Noir,

was eradicated by the 1990 vintage, it was not until the 1991 hit the shelves that this brand deserved world-class status. It is thus Shakked – not Thibaut – who has achieved the greatest success here, but that is no reflection on the diminutive Frenchman, whose record speaks for itself.

The first *cuvées* of any sparkling wine are

the most difficult, as the winemaker comes to grips with the unpredictable quality of grapes from an untested *terroir*. If, for whatever reason, the first winemaker does not stick around, someone else gets all the glory, but much of it will be as a direct result of the groundwork put in by his or her predecessor, as I am sure Shakked would

agree. Nonetheless, he is to be congratulated for removing the terpene character that denied the early *cuvées* their finesse, and for crafting an out-and-out California fizz that is lovely to drink when the fruit is young and elegant.

★★ J SONOMA COUNTY BRUT

   Vintaged, méthode champenoise: 55% Chardonnay, 45% Pinot Noir

N/A
KLEIN FAMILY VINTNERS
CALIFORNIA

• Other labels - Windsor Vineyards

Located in the Hudson River Region AVA, this producers's *méthode champenoise* have not yet impressed.

N/A
KINGS ROAD VINEYARD
ASBURY, NEW JERSEY

Although the founding in 1980 of this vineyard by John and Marie Abplanalp precedes that of Amwell Valley vineyard, its first vintage was not until 1983, one year later. The production of sparkling wine is a relatively recent development.

N/A
KLINGSHIRN
AVON LAKE, OHIO

The Klingshirn family have been growing grapes here since 1935 and built a winery in 1955, but sparkling wine is a relatively recent development.

N/A
KNAPP VINEYARDS
ROMULUS, NEW YORK

A *méthode champenoise* producer that has not impressed, Knapp Vineyards was established in 1982, and is located on Cayuga Lake in the Fingers Lakes AVA.

68
KORBEL
GUERNEVILLE, CALIFORNIA

California's leading sparkling wine specialist in the popular sector dates back to 1881, when the three Korbel brothers, Anton, Francis and Joseph, planted their first vineyard. Czech lumberjacks, the Korbels

THE IVY-CLAD CELLARS OF KORBEL IN GUERNEVILLE. THE FIRM DATES BACK TO 1881 WHEN IT WAS ESTABLISHED BY CZECH IMMIGRANTS. IT HAS BEEN IN THE HECK FAMILY POSSESSION SINCE THE 1950s

had purchased this property on the left bank of Sonoma's Russian River in the 1870s for its redwood forest. However, after chopping down all the trees, they had to plant a fairly rapid-growing crop to provide an income and, with over 100 thriving vineyards in the vicinity at that time, it is little surprise that the Korbels decided to follow suit.

The first few crops were sold as grapes, but then a winery was built and the Korbels embarked upon the more profitable business of making and selling wine, although the first fizz was not produced until 1896, when a winemaker by the name of Franz Hazek, another Czech, was hired. Hazek had already mastered the technique of bottle-fermentation, having launched his own brand, Grand Pacific, but it was not until he was succeeded by Jan Hanuska (yet another Czech winemaker), that Korbel's sparkling wine reputation really took off.

Korbel Champagne made a strong comeback after Prohibition, but the brand languished somewhat after the Second World War and did not pick up until the Korbels sold the company to another three brothers, this time from Alsace. Adolf L Heck, the eldest, had worked for his father, Adolf Heck Snr, at the famous Cook's Champagne Cellars in St Louis until 1944, when US government agents discovered that Joachim von Ribbentrop was a major shareholder, and promptly confiscated the firm. He then made sparkling wine for the Sweet Valley winery in Sandusky, Ohio, before moving to California in 1951 to manage the Italian Swiss Colony company. But he was merely biding his time until, he hoped, an opportunity would enable the Heck family to run their own business.

When Korbel came up for sale, with its history and reputation for California Champagne, it could not have been more heaven-sent for Adolf, who was one of the most experienced sparkling winemakers in the country. Together with his two brothers, Paul and Ben, Adolf Heck snapped it up and Korbel has remained in the family possession ever since.

HOUSE STYLE
Reliable rather than exciting, these sparkling wines are typically clean and rich, with fattish fruit. Armstrong Ridge is equally fattish, but longer flavoured. Styles include brut, *naturel*, *blanc de blancs*, *blancs de noirs*, Chardonnay, and rosé.

LA BUENA VIDA
See SMITH ESTATES

LA FERME MARTIN
See SAGPOND VINEYARDS

N/A
LAMOREAUX LANDING WINE CELLARS
LODI, NEW YORK

Located on Seneca Lake in the Fingers Lakes AVA, this is a relatively recent producer of New York 'champagne' and has yet to establish a track record.

60
LAUREL RIDGE
FOREST GROVE, OREGON

Best-known for Riesling and Pinot Noir fizz, but unexciting.

LAUREL RIDGE CUVÉE BLANC EXTRA DRY
Not vintaged, méthode champenoise: 100% Riesling

LAUREL RIDGE BRUT
Vintaged, méthode champenoise: 90% Pinot Noir, 10% Pinot Blanc

LAUREL RIDGE BRUT RESERVE
Vintaged, barrel-fermented méthode champenoise: 90% Pinot Noir, 10% Pinot Blanc

LAUREL SPUMANTE SEC
Not vintaged, méthode champenoise: 100% Muscat

LAWLOR FAMILY
See GALENA CELLARS

N/A
LENZ WINERY
PECONIC, NEW YORK

This Long Island producer was established in 1978, but has only recently started producing *méthode champenoise*, and has yet to establish a track record.

LIFE FORCE
See CAMAS WINERY

N/A
LONZ
MIDDLE BASS ISLAND, OHIO

An old, castle-like winery on Middle Bass Island, Lake Erie, hardly a stone's throw away from Canada's Pelee Island, which also grows vines. The Middle Bass vineyard was planted by Andrew Wehrle, an *emigré* from Alsace in 1884, who also built the winery, but he quickly sold it to Peter Lonz. It was Peter's son, George, who added the ramparts and other castle-like follies in the 1940s, and made Middle Bass the place to party in the 1950s when as many as 2,000 loose-living souls would fly or sail out to the island for a night's drinking and dancing. The wine they drank was Lonz, which George sold by the bottle, and rented glasses out to the party-goers. I've never tasted it, but I've met many people who have happy memories of those wild nights and everyone claims it was disgusting, yet they smile even more as they admit it! And they reckon it's

85
KRISTONE

• Group ownership - Kendall-Jackson Kendall-Jackson's prestige sparkling-wine project came to fruition in 1996 with the launch of a *blanc de blancs* and *blanc de noirs*, both from the 1991 vintage. Wines are made by 'Mad Harry' Osborne, who was Schramsberg's very first winemaker in the 1960s and also a consultant to the Veuve Clicquot-owned Cloudy Bay for the development of its Pelorus sparkling wine.

Mad Harry did not get his name for nothing; his only ambition is to make big, rich, complex sparkling wines and he'll go out on any limb to achieve it. On a very simplistic level, the basis of his sparkling-wine philosophy is that richness can only come from ripe grapes. He cannot understand why virtually every sparkling winemaker in the New World harvests grapes according to their acidity level, because you can always add acid but you can never add flavour to unripe grapes. Essentially, I agree with him, but he goes over the top.

Having got his big, rich wine from ripe grapes, he then decides to go all out for complexity in the wine prior to the second fermentation. Nothing could be simpler for Harry, who *barrique*-ferments as much as 40% of the base wines, then ages the lot in charred casks. This gives the base wines not so much a kiss of oak but a slap in the face with a two-by-four. However, true complexity in a sparkling wine takes a long time to evolve, and the longer the toastiness takes to develop, the greater the finesse it will have. This is the basic flaw in his philosophy, but I would much rather have one person like Mad Harry taking things to the limit than the plethora of winemakers whose technical correctness held back California's sparkling wines in the early days. And it is not as if Harry sees his philosophy as carved in stone; he is big enough to

'MAD HARRY' OSBORNE MADE WINES AT SCHRAMSBERG AND CONSULTED AT CLOUDY BAY BEFORE COMING TO KRISTONE

modify his own views, something I have seen him do in the middle of a discussion!

Already he has cut back on the big and blousy, bringing forth the fruit, and playing down the toasty, oaky aromas that dominated the first *cuvées* of Kristone. Knowing Harry, we have no worries about an over-compensatory swing into lean and mean sparkling wines – he's still Mad Harry, and richness is his game. But now that the winemaker has cut back on his excesses, it is time for Kendall-Jackson's marketing people to do the same. The bottle is fine, but the dressing is over-ornate and cheapens the presentation, which looks like Castellblanch Brut Zero Cava, right down to the kitsch ribbon around the neck. The packaging should be smart and stylish, but understated. Harry should tell the marketeers to let the wine do the talking.

WINEMAKER
Harold Osborne

HOUSE STYLE & RANGE
While the first vintage of *blanc de blancs* (1991) was far too fat, blousy and dominated by huge, toasty-oak aromas, the

first vintage of *blanc de noirs* (also 1991) was skilfully crafted, with less emphasis on oak and more on a succulence of fruit. The Blanc de Blancs did not lack quality intrinsically, the oaky toastiness just robbed it of finesse as a sparkling wine, but Mad Harry has had the last laugh because it has turned out much better than I imagined. The nose has developed an amazing cappuccino aroma. It reminded me very much of Billecart-Salmon's 1973 *blanc de blancs*, but the 20-year difference in age does underline my point about true complexity and finesse.

The second vintage of Blanc de blancs (1992) is like a classy oaked California Chardonnay on the nose, giving no hint that it might be sparkling. Although not as blousy as the 1991 was, it is still very toasty and too immediately oaky on the palate. Furthermore, Harry should have used more tartaric acid because the flavour here is just too rich for the balance of the wine.

The Blanc de Noirs is Harry's most consistent *cuvée* and unlike most California renditions of this style, except for a smattering of white grapes it an authentic *blanc de noirs*, which is to say it is white, not pink. Fruit-driven rather than oak-dominated, it has better acidity; thus the soft, creamy fruit shows more elegance.

Stylistically, the first vintage of Kristone's rosé (1992) falls between the other two *cuvées*, with toasty aromas on the nose, but rich, ripe and sweet strawberry fruit holding its own on the palate.

★ BLANC DE BLANCS CALIFORNIA CHAMPAGNE
  Vintaged, méthode champenoise: 70% Chardonnay, 30% Pinot Blanc

★★ BLANC DE NOIRS CALIFORNIA CHAMPAGNE
  Vintaged, méthode champenoise: 95% Pinot Noir, 5% Pinot Blanc

★★ BRUT ROSÉ CALIFORNIA 'CHAMPAGNE'
  Vintaged, méthode champenoise: 91% Pinot Noir, 7% Pinot Blanc, 2% Syrah

---

not much better today. I have no inclination to taste it because either way, it would take the shine off the story.

N/A
LUCAS VINEYARDS
INTERLAKEN, NEW YORK
Established in 1980, Lucas Vineyards is a relatively new producer of *méthode champenoise* wines and has yet to establish a track record.

MAISON DEUTZ
A joint venture between Beringer and Champagne Deutz, Maison Deutz was established in California's Arroyo Grande in 1985. I am in print as having said that I have been waiting for it to come right ever since. However, this brand became defunct at the end of 1997 after Beringer and Champagne Deutz parted ways. It was a pity, because I like the winemaker, Christian Roguenant, who is the hippest Frenchman anyone is

likely to meet and he has the most bizarre Gallo-California twang to his accent. He is not just likable, but highly knowledgeable, and probably would have succeeded with sparkling wine one day. However, although the Arroyo Grande does produce stunning fruit, particularly Pinot Noir, I think he was facing an uphill task given the *terroir* of the particular vineyard Maison Deutz was sourced from. Some critics rated his fizz very highly, so perhaps it is just a matter of taste, but somehow I think not.

MAISON DEUTZ: NO LONGER MAKING FIZZ

There was nothing technically wrong with the wines; they just failed to inspire, and virtually every *cuvée* had a rustic pepperiness that prevented any finesse developing.

N/A
MARKKO WINERY
CONNEAUT, OHIO

• Other labels - Excelsior
Established in 1968 by Arnulf Esterter, this was the first *vinifera* operation that started up in response to, and with the help of the legendary Konstantin Frank.

PAUL MASSON
See CANANDAIGUA

N/A
L MAWBY
SUTTONS BAY, MICHIGAN

• 1,000 cases
Larry Mawby planted his vineyard in 1973, producing his first wine in 1978. Since 1984, when he produced his first sparkling, he has been trying to craft a 'truly memorable, distinctive sparkling wine' that is 'unique' to his region, and hopes to achieve that goal within the next decade or so. In addition to the production from his own estate, for his *blanc de blancs* Larry buys in grapes from the Nitz Vineyard in Berrien County and Steele's Crossing Vineyard on the Leelanau Peninsula. Other products already bottled but not released include a Pinot Noir & Meunier blend (various *cuvées* of which have been laid down since 1992), a pure Chardonnay *cuvée* from the 1997 vintage and a blend of Riesling, Vignoles and Chardonnay.

The labelling of many of these wines – not just the fizz – is very tasteful, which suggests that Mawby has an eye for detail, yet he has overlooked the poor quality of the wire cage holding the sparkling-wine cork in place.

WINEMAKER
Lawrence Mawby

HOUSE STYLE & RANGE
With all the different *cuvées* already made or waiting in the wings, Larry Mawby is

obviously an ardent follower of the bubble, so I do not want to dull his enthusiasm. Furthermore, I have had just one tasting of three wines, which is insufficient to make a comprehensive judgement. However, from those wines I have tasted, it would appear they are too far advanced in their maturation prior to second fermentation, and have spent too long on yeast without gaining appreciably from it. Before making any comment on the sparkling wine potential here, I would like to see how pure varietal, single-vintage base wines react to being bottled within no more than six months of the harvest, and to being disgorged after 12, 24 and 36 months, which may well take up most of the 20 years or so that Larry has set aside for achieving his goal!

BLANC DE BLANCS
Not vintaged, méthode champenoise: 21% Chardonnay, 54% Seyval Blanc, 25% Vignoles

CRÉMANT BRUT
Not vintaged, estate-grown, méthode champenoise: 100% Vignoles

TALISMAN BRUT
Not vintaged, méthode champenoise: solera-blend of Chardonnay, Pinot Noir, Pinot Gris, Vignoles

BIEN DE VILLAGE BRUT
Vintaged, méthode champenoise: 70% Pinot Noir, 30% Pinot Gris

MIRABELLE
See SCHRAMSBERG

68
MIRASSOU VINEYARDS
SAN JOSE, CALIFORNIA

Established in 1854 by French goldminer Pierre Pellier, this company is best known today for its jug wines, but also makes simple, fruity fizz by *méthode champenoise* from its vineyards in Monterey County.

HOUSE RANGE
MIRASSOU BLANC DE NOIRS
Vintaged, méthode champenoise: 100% Pinot Noir

MIRASSOU BRUT RESERVE
Vintaged, méthode champenoise: 51% Pinot Noir, 27% Chardonnay, 22% Pinot Blanc

N/A
ROBERT MONDAVI
OAKVILLE, CALIFORNIA

This famous winery makes many great wines, but its sparkling wines are only available at the winery and are of fairly low quality.

N/A
MONTICELLO VINEYARDS
NAPA, CALIFORNIA

• 2,000 cases
• Other labels - Domaine Montreaux
Sparkling wines have been produced by Monticello Vineyards under the Domaine

Montreaux label since 1983.

HOUSE STYLE & RANGE
The 1985 was very fat, and the 1986 strangely metallic with odd aromas. Not tasted since.

DOMAINE MONTREAUX BRUT
Vintaged, méthode champenoise: 40% Chardonnay, 60% Pinot Noir

MONT JALLON
See ELEPHANT BUTTE

MONTREAUX
See MONTICELLO VINEYARDS

80
MOUNTAIN DOME
SPOKANE, WASHINGTON

• 2,500 cases
I first met Dr Michael Manz in 1994 and was immediately impressed by his enthusiasm. The meeting took place in Washington state, but in Seattle, not Spokane, and I have become fascinated by his venture, tasting the *cuvées* on a number of occasions, and corresponding with him on various points. There are half-a-dozen people dotted around the world who, I believe, will one day make exceptional sparkling wines, and Michael is one of them.

Mountain Dome is a family affair: in addition to Michael and his wife Patricia, there are three children and they all helped to build the winery. Now they all work in it, studies and other professions allowing. Michael Manz is an MD who specialises in child psychiatry, with his own practice at the Marycliff Institute, as well as being the medical director of the Psychiatric Center for Children and Adolescents. Quite how he finds time to put bubbles into bottles is beyond me, particularly as Patricia, who shares duties as winemaker and winery administrator, owns and runs Woodland Montessori School. They shame me into realising just how frivolous my occupation is compared to people whose jobs really matter, yet they can find time to build one of the most unusual wineries in the world.

Looking more like an observatory than a winery, a 4,000-square-foot geodesic dome forms part of the working facilities of Mount Dome, which is set in a 33-hectare forested property in the foothills of Mount Spokane. The winery is temperature-controlled, and by the year 2001, will boast an additional 15,000 square feet of underground cellars.

Michael's brother John assists in all the winemaking phases of Mountain Dome, while Michael and Patricia's son Erik has studied fermentation sciences and is destined to further his education in France – where no doubt he hopes to discover the secrets of Champagne. In the meantime, Mountain Dome has been relying on the consultancy

85
MUMM NAPA VALLEY

RUTHERFORD, CALIFORNIA

- 220,000 cases

When Seagram purchased Gold Seal in 1979, one of the founders of New York Champagne, its French-born winemaker, Guy Devaux, launched the highly secret 'Project Lafayette', which culminated in 1987 with the opening of Mumm Napa Valley.

The late Devaux guided this firm into the 1990s, hiring in 1987 Greg Fowler, who had been the winemaker at Schramsberg for the previous seven years. Fowler looks like an all-American farmer's hand, has the brain of a scientist, and comes across with the laid-back humour of a California surfer. Under his helm, Mumm Napa Valley has become one of the most impeccably run sparkling-wine operations I have seen.

While the winery is designed to run smoothly almost by itself (four full-time workers produce two million bottles a year), the vineyards are very much a labour-intensive operation. You can always tell a Mumm Napa Valley vineyard at harvest-time by the hundreds of FYBs or 'Funny Yellow Boxes' dotted about. Every grape picked for Mumm has to be delivered to the winery in one of these small plastic boxes, which have a maximum capacity of just 35lbs (less than 16 kilos) and have special air vents. The small size of the FYBs prevents crushing and the air circulating through their vents keeps the fruit cool. They are a great contrast to standard Napa Valley bins or gondolas, which contain between one and two tons of fruit.

It is the attention to details such as this that enabled Greg Fowler to produce sparkling wines in the late 1980s and early 1990s that were significantly superior to the authentic Champagne being churned out by Mumm in Reims. That was in Champagne Mumm's bad old days when the winemaker had lost it and the *cuvées* had the smell of sauerkraut. Greg knew as well as anyone that there is no comparison between the sparkling wine potential of the Napa Valley and the classic Champagne region, but he was over-achieving while Reims was under-achieving. However, Champagne Mumm is now giving Greg a run for his money.

WINEMAKER

Rob McNeill consulting with Greg Fowler

HOUSE STYLE & RANGE

The basic non-vintage brut prestige (known as Cuvée Napa by Mumm Brut on export markets) can sometimes be a bit young, and Winery Lake, one of Mumm Napa's finest *cuvées*, often does not travel. I'm not sure what upset Winery Lake, but if you have enjoyed it on an export market, you will love it in California.

Most of the grapes used in the vintaged DVX come from the Devaux vineyard in Carneros. It is a long, rich and tangy *cuvée* that retains an impressive purity of fruit for several years. Mumm Napa's *blanc de blancs* is not only brilliant quality, but consistently the greatest value *cuvée* in its range. The *blanc de noirs* is labelled 'rosé' on export markets and its soft, easy, ready-drinking style is certainly more of a traditional rosé than the Sparkling Pinot Noir.

The latter is not made on a regular basis, but when it is, you have to be prepared to take a trip on the wild side as you drink it. Greg Fowler's deep cerise-coloured fizz takes no prisoners; a single-vineyard *cuvée* from the Devaux vineyard in Carneros, it is so far over the top that more people will hate it than love it, but no one would argue its expressiveness. It's as Californian as the Beach Boys. I can hear waves from the Pacific Ocean crashing onto the edge of the vineyard, smell the wonderful aroma of wild strawberries, and taste the most outrageously perfumed Pinot fruit on the palate. It is not as serious as, say, DVX or even the *blanc de blancs*, but deserves equal rating as a fun wine.

★★ NAPA VALLEY BLANC DE BLANCS
   Not vintaged, méthode champenoise:
   70% Chardonnay, 30% Pinot Gris

★ NAPA VALLEY BLANC DE NOIRS
   Not vintaged, méthode champenoise:
   15% Chardonnay, 85% Pinot Noir

★ NAPA VALLEY BRUT PRESTIGE
   Not vintaged, méthode champenoise:
   45% Chardonnay, 52% Pinot Noir, 3% Meunier

★★ NAPA VALLEY SPARKLING PINOT NOIR
   Not vintaged, méthode champenoise:
   100% Pinot Noir

★★ NAPA VALLEY DVX
   Vintaged, méthode champenoise: 50% Chardonnay,
   50% Pinot Noir

★★ NAPA VALLEY WINERY LAKE
   Vintaged, méthode champenoise: 20% Chardonnay,
   80% Pinot Noir

of Raphael Brisbois (*see* IRON HORSE, p. 27 and OMAR KHAYYAM, p. 310).

Spokane is outside Washington's viticultura area, thus there are no vineyards at Mountai Dome. Grapes are sourced from a number o growers spread over the Columbia Valley, with whom Mountain Dome has long-term relationships. All grapes are harvested in small, 30-pound boxes to avoid bruising.

WINEMAKER

Michael Manz

HOUSE STYLE & RANGE

After an uncertain start (par for the course for every sparkling-wine venture), these wines became better focused with the 1990 and, particularly, 1991 vintage, but need less blatant oak and more acidity. Some *cuvées* could do with less time on yeast (two to three years rather than four to five), althoug this might need reversing once the acidity levels have been upped. Frankly, the only criticism is that Michael Manz has been tryin too hard to be too classic too early, but bett that he set his sights high and take such risks than be yet another relatively modest achieve Normally it's his Brut Vintage that stands ou although it can have too much coconutty oak (despite only French oak being used, never American, which is normally associated with such blatant coconut aromas but the non-vintage rosé, with its succulent *mélange* of strawberry-dominated red fruits, i improving with leaps and bounds. The new non-vintage brut is a blend of eight base wines from four vintages and is easily identified by its label depicting 'little people

★★ BRUT
   Not vintaged, méthode
   champenoise:
   35% Chardonnay,
   65% Pinot Noir

★★ BRUT ROSÉ
   Not vintaged, saignée
   method, méthode champenoise: 15% Chardonnay,
   85% Pinot Noir

★★ BRUT
   Vintaged, méthode champenoise: 35% Chardonnay,
   65% Pinot Noir

MOYER

See HILL COUNTRY CELLARS

N/A
MOYER VINEYARDS

MANCHESTER, OHIO

The Moyers established this vineyard and winery in 1972 to produce still wines, and i 1980 opened up a sparkling wine facility in Austin, Texas (*see* HILL COUNTRY CELLARS) They sold the Texas venture in 1986, since when the Moyers have begun sparkling-win production here.

NAPOLEON
See WEIBEL

O'KEEFE CELLARS
See CHATEAU GRAND TRAVERSE

70
OASIS
HUME, VIRGINIA
● 5,000 cases
Overlooked by the Blue Ridge Mountains, Oasis was established in 1977, when Israeli-born Dirgham Salahi and his wife Corinne planted some of the first Chardonnay, Cabernet Sauvignon and Merlot vines in the state of Virginia.

This is one of Virginia's more consistent producers, and one-third of the production is now devoted to sparkling wine.

WINEMAKER
Dirgham & Tareq Salahi

HOUSE STYLE & RANGE
The basic brut has a creamy, caramel, Devon-toffee nose, which suggests heavy-handed malolactic fermentation, and the wine certainly could do with more finesse. Even so, it is drinkable – eminently drinkable, in fact.

Although UC Davis-trained Dirgham and Tareq Salahi have produced *méthode champenoise* for a number of years, I am sure that with a few more *cuvées* devoted to fine-tuning the malolactic, they could craft a very classy little number.

✭ BRUT VIRGINIA SPARKLING WINE
Not vintaged, méthode champenoise: 60% Chardonnay, 40% Pinot Noir
EXTRA DRY VIRGINIA SPARKLING WINE
Not vintaged, méthode champenoise: 60% Chardonnay, 40% Pinot Noir
MILLENNIUM 2000 BRUT VIRGINIA SPARKLING WINE
Not vintaged, méthode champenoise: 60% Chardonnay, 40% Pinot Noir
CUVÉE D'OR BRUT VIRGINIA SPARKLING WINE
Vintaged, méthode champenoise: 60% Chardonnay, 40% Pinot Noir

OLD MISSION WINERY
See CHATEAU GRAND TRAVERSE

N/A
OLIVER WINE CO
BLOOMINGTON, INDIANA
● Other labels - Camelot
Established in 1972 by Bill Oliver, a law professor at Indiana University. I have tasted Oliver's Camelot Mead, but not his Camelot fizz, which must be a fairly recent venture.

PACIFIC ECHO
See SCHARFFENBERGER

PÈRE MARQUETTE
See THOMPSON WINERY

65
PINDAR VINEYARDS
PECONIC, NEW YORK
Dr Herodotus Damianos purchased a potato farm and, like so many others on Long Island, transformed it into a vineyard. His only intention was to sell grapes, but he suddenly had the urge to make wine and, in 1982, built a winery. In recognition of his Greek heritage, Damianos named the venture after the ancient Greek lyric poet, and Pindar is, today, Long Island's largest vineyard and winery. His premier *cuvée* sparkling wine is also one of the best *méthode champenoise* produced on Long Island.

75
PIPER-SONOMA
WINDSOR, CALIFORNIA
This brand dates back to 1980, when Piper-Heidsieck, the Reims-based Champagne house, joined forces with Sonoma Vineyards to build a sparkling-wine facility at Healdsburg. This was purchased by Judy Jordan of the J Wine Company in January 1997 and it no longer exists as a winery, only a brand. Piper-Sonoma wine continues to be produced here on a contract basis, under the supervision of winemaker, Rob McNeil.

WINEMAKER
Rob McNeil

HOUSE STYLE & RANGE
The wines in the early 1980s were a bit curious – resinous, even – but improved greatly towards the end of that decade and have taken on a lovely, zesty freshness since the early 1990s. A small proportion of most *cuvées* undergoes oak-fermentation and oak-ageing. Piper-Sonoma makes the best ready-to-drink non-vintage brut in California, while the vintaged Tête de Cuvée is a slow maturer.

BLANC DE NOIRS
Not vintaged, méthode champenoise: 92% Pinot Noir, 8% Meunier

✭✭ BRUT
Not vintaged, méthode champenoise: 15% Chardonnay, 70% Pinot Noir, 10% Meunier, 5% Pinot Blanc
BRUT ROSÉ
Vintaged, méthode champenoise: 92% Pinot Noir, 8% Meunier

✭✭ TÊTE DE CUVÉE
Vintaged, méthode champenoise: 25% Chardonnay, 70% Pinot Noir, 5% Pinot Blanc

N/A
POST FAMILIE WINERY
ALTUS, ARKANSAS
Established in 1880 by German *emigré* Jacob Post. Post's daughter Catherine defiantly continued to make wine during Prohibition, but she was jailed for serving it in her restaurant. Small amounts of *méthode champenoise* are sold under the Altus AVA.

N/A
PRINCE MICHAEL VINEYARDS
LEON, VIRGINIA
Owned by French industrialist Jean Leducq, who chose the name to honour various historic personages called Prince Michael. Located in the Monticello AVA, and set amid the foothills of the Blue Ridge Mountains, this is the largest vineyard in Virginia, although its production is supplemented with grapes from the company's own vineyards in Napa. Better known for its still wines, particularly its Chardonnay, Cabernet Sauvignon and a Bordeaux-style red called Le Ducq, Prince Michael has yet to establish a track record for sparkling wine.

N/A
REGENT CHAMPAGNE CELLARS
HIGHLAND, NEW YORK
Located in the Hudson River Region AVA, this relatively recent producer of New York 'champagne' has yet to establish a track record.

ROCKY MOUNTAIN VINEYARDS
See VINELAND CORPORATION

ROEDERER ESTATE
See PAGE 276

J ROGET
See CANANDAIGUA

N/A
RUTHERFORD BENCHMARKS
RUTHERFORD, CALIFORNIA
● 5,000 cases
● Other labels - Van der Kamp
The Van der Kamp label was established at Kenwood, Sonoma, in 1981 by Martin and Dixie Van der Kamp.

HOUSE STYLE & RANGE
Not tasted recently, but unimpressed in the early 1990s, when the brut was tired and one-dimensional, although the rosé showed simple varietal character.

VAN DER KAMP BRUT
Vintaged, méthode champenoise: 30% Chardonnay,

90
ROEDERER ESTATE

PHILO, CALIFORNIA

● Other labels - Quartet (export)

The founding of the first venture to achieve a quality of sparkling wine comparable not just to Champagne, but to very good Champagne, was indirectly the result of the election of French president François Mitterand in 1981.

The Rouzaud family, owners of Champagne Louis Roederer, were concerned about their cash reserves under the first Socialist government of France since the establishment of the Fifth Republic. At the very least, they feared that unearned money would be taxed to the hilt, and decided to get the money out of the country into a safer haven. The company had conducted a two-year study in the late 1970s to find the most suitable location for producing sparkling wine in California, and the approach of Socialist policies at home prompted Roederer to go ahead with the project sooner rather than later.

The study had pinpointed the Anderson Valley as the best place to grow grapes for sparkling wine, due to its proximity to the ocean and the maritime fogs and winds that provide a cooler climate than in the traditional regions of Napa and Sonoma further south. This microclimate lengthens the growing season in the Anderson Valley to 100 days, as in the Champagne region of France. Four ranches in three districts of the valley (Boonville, Philo and Navarro) were purchased between 1981 and 1982, comprising a property of 235 hectares in total. Some of the land was already planted with vines, but most has been planted since. The primary system of vine-training used is the lyre, which is not a surprising choice, as this method has been on trial in a dozen different villages in Champagne since 1985, and Roederer is one of the four houses involved with this experiment.

My first visit to Roederer Estate was in 1988. After a tour of the vineyard and cellars, we headed for the tasting room, where the general manager proceeded to open up a bottle of Champagne Roederer Brut Premier. When I explained that while a glass of Brut Premier might be very nice to finish off with, I would like to taste the Roederer Estate first, I was told that it was simply not possible: no one was allowed to taste the new product until its official launch in one month's time! I was not a happy man because, as the general manager of Roederer Estate knew, the reason

I was visiting the winery was to taste the new product. As it was, I did not even get to meet the winemaker. When I eventually tasted the wine in the UK, there was nothing special about it and I had no inkling of what was to come.

Set against this background, the fact that I later declared the second release of Roederer Estate to be the greatest non-Champagne sparkling wine really spoke volumes for the outstanding quality of the wine, for I certainly owed Roederer Estate no favours. However, my second and subsequent visits have all been a joy, accompanied not by an administrator, but by Michel Salgues, Roederer Estate's hugely talented, quietly spoken winemaker.

Following Louis Roederer's own house style, Michel used no malolactic fermentation until 1994, and since his second, 1987-based, release was a world-shattering success, this decision cannot be criticised – especially as he has maintained this exceptional quality ever since. However, even in the Anderson Valley the level of malic acidity is relatively high, thus in recent years he has been experimenting with between ten and 20 per cent malolactic fermentation.

There are lots of minute details involved in the crafting of a superior sparkling wine, but apart from the source of the grapes, the only major difference in Michel's vinification techniques is the addition of a little sulphur to the *liqueur de tirage* – something few California winemakers ever do. This has two desirable effects: firstly, it slows down the rate of second fermentation, and secondly, the sulphur itself acts as a precursor to slow-building post-disgorgement aromas. Like most quality sparkling-wine producers in the New World, Michel uses only the *cuvée*, never the *tailles*, but at the blending stage he also rejects ten to 25 per cent of the *vins de cuvée* on tasting, and I wonder how many others do that.

Note that the Roederer Estate uses the Quartet brand for export markets.

WINEMAKER
Michel Salgues

HOUSE STYLE & RANGE
The second and subsequent releases have been of a truly different order, not just for Roederer Estate, but for the international sparkling wine scene, although other New World producers have since joined Roederer in this new elite. The first time I tasted the second release, it had already been on the

THE ROEDERER ESTATE WINERY AND VINEYARDS

market long enough to have developed a beautifully rich flavour, with toasty, crumbly-biscuit complexity.

The shame is that most people who drink Roederer Estate today would not recognise this description because when first put onto the market, this wine can be very tight and green; it needs at least two years after disgorgement to mellow and for its true richness and complexity to emerge. A good tip is to buy magnums.

In Champagne, the qualitative difference of a magnum starts to be noticed at about five years after disgorgement and builds slowly, whereas for Roederer's California brew, the magnum effect kicks in after just one year and the difference in finesse of exactly the same wine is remarkable. The first release of the rosé was a 1989-based *cuvée*, the bottles of which have swung wildly from pure California fruit to examples that have been far too oxidative, although the magnums have all been elegant, gradually acquiring a delicate complexity, as have bottles and magnums of subsequent *cuvées* of this wine.

I was not as impressed as the US wine press obviously was by the first vintage (1989) of Roederer Estate's new prestige *cuvée*, L'Ermitage, although the 1990 immediately showed more finesse, and the style stabilised with the 1991: a full, yet soft and deliciously fruity wine with lots of youthful complexity which is highlighted by lovely acidity.

★★✫ ANDERSON VALLEY BRUT
  Not vintaged, méthode champenoise:
  55% Chardonnay, 45% Pinot Noir

★★✫ ANDERSON VALLEY BRUT ROSE
  Not vintaged, méthode champenoise:
  38% Chardonnay, 62% Pinot Noir

★★✫ ANDERSON VALLEY L'ERMITAGE
  Vintaged, méthode champenoise:
  65% Chardonnay, 35% Pinot Noir

MICHEL SALGUES

70% Pinot Noir

VAN DER KAMP MIDNIGHT CUVÉE ROSÉ
  Vintaged, méthode champenoise: 100% Pinot Noir

N/A
STE CHAPELLE WINERY
CALDWELL, IDAHO
Established in 1976 and named after the Gothic Ste Chapelle in Paris, Idaho's largest and oldest winery makes mostly *cuve close* fizz; the *blanc de noirs* stands out from the rest of the range.

HOUSE RANGE
STE CHAPELLE BLANC DE NOIRS
  Not vintaged, cuve close: 100% Pinot Noir
STE CHAPELLE BRUT
  *Not vintaged, cuve close: 80% Chardonnay,
  20% Pinot Noir*
STE CHAPELLE JOHANNISBERG RIESLING
  Not vintaged, cuve close: 100% Johannisberg Riesling
STE CHAPELLE SPECIAL HARVEST RIESLING
  Not vintaged, cuve close: 100% Johannisberg Riesling

STE MICHELLE
See DOMAINE STE MICHELLE

N/A
ST INNOCENT
SALEM, OREGON
Although I have not yet tasted the sparkling wine from St Innocent, I have high expectations from this producer, whose Freedom Hill Pinot Noir is one of Oregon's greatest wines.

N/A
ST JAMES
ST JAMES, MISSOURI
An up-and-coming producer of *méthode champenoise* sparklers.

N/A
ST JULIAN WINE COMPANY
PAW PAW, MICHIGAN
● 5,250 cases
The oldest and largest winery in Michigan, St Julian was originally established by an Italian in Canada in 1921 under the name of Meconi Wine Cellars. Later, it was moved to Detroit, where it was known as the Italian Wine Company. The business moved to its current location in 1938 and was once again renamed, this time as the St Julian Wine Company. Confusing as this might be, it was easier in those days to move the winery to the available vineyards than it was to transport the grapes back to the winery.

Another St Julian winery is located in Frankenmouth. Its sparkling wines, which are made from various fruit juices are well-liked, particularly the award-winning Raspberry 'Champagne'.

N/A
SAGPOND VINEYARDS
BRIDGEHAMPTON, NEW YORK
● Other labels - La Ferme Martin
Located on Long Island, this relatively recent producer of New York 'champagne' has yet to establish a track record.

80
SCHARFFENBERGER CELLARS
PHILO, CALIFORNIA
● Other labels – Pacific Echo
Established in 1981 by John Scharffenberger, who had grown grapes in Mendocino County for ten years before embarking on this sparkling wine venture. With investment from Pommery, the famous Champagne house, Scharffenberger acquired a 275-hectare property and built a stunning new winery, which was completed in time for the 1991 harvest. After Pommery became part of LVMH, Scharffenberger was transferred to Veuve Clicquot, which was also part of the group.

Technically, Scharffenberger is a sister company of Domaine Chandon, but in practice, the Veuve Clicquot portfolio (which includes Pelorus from New Zealand's Cloudy Bay) has always steered its own course. John Scharffenberger remained in day-to-day control until 1996, when he cashed in his residual shareholding to pursue a new career in property development.

The winery retained the Scharffenberger Cellars name, but in March 1998, its branding changed to Pacific Echo, although the full global conversion to this label will not be complete until late 1998, since various export markets had stocks of Scharffenberger to dispose of. The Scharffenberger label was distinctive and quite stylish, but a survey discovered that few consumers realised the product was from California – hence the new brand, which is very different, but also quite stylish. Indeed, my only criticism of the change is that the two vintaged *cuvées* (*blanc de blancs* and *brut rosé*) have lost their vintage status, even though the wines are exclusively from a single year. This is, I am sure, a mistake.

WINEMAKER
Tex Sawyer

HOUSE STYLE & RANGE
These wines have gained tremendous elegance and finesse since the early 1990s which, because of the lead-time involved, means an improvement in the wines made from the late 1980s, which coincides with the arrival of the current winemaker, Tex Sawyer. A second jump in quality was noticeable a couple of years later, and this probably coincided with the completion of Scharffenberger's high-tech winery in 1991.

The brut has steadily improved, having been transformed from a rather plodding fizz to something much fresher, finer and more elegant. It is lightly rich and smooth when first released, but builds up a lovely, creamy, biscuity complexity if kept for nine to 12 months.

The soft, silky, creamy *blanc de blancs* has always been the finest wine here, although its production has been infrequent. The last and most exciting was the 1991, although the 1995 (a pure vintage *cuvée*, but sold without vintage under the new Pacific Echo label) promises to be even better.

All *cuvées* now go through a full malolactic fermentation, whereas only a partial one used to be employed.

★★ PACIFIC ECHO ANDERSON VALLEY
  BLANC DE BLANCS
  Not vintaged, méthode champenoise: 100% Chardonnay
★★ PACIFIC ECHO ANDERSON VALLEY BRUT
  PRIVATE RESERVE
  *Not vintaged, méthode champenoise:
  50% Chardonnay, 50% Pinot Noir*
PACIFIC ECHO ANDERSON VALLEY CRÉMANT
  *Not vintaged, méthode champenoise:
  40% Chardonnay, 60% Pinot Noir*
★ PACIFIC ECHO BRUT
  *Not vintaged, méthode champenoise:
  33% Chardonnay, 67% Pinot Noir*
★ PACIFIC ECHO MENDOCINO BRUT ROSÉ
  *Not vintaged, méthode champenoise:
  40% Chardonnay, 60% Pinot Noir*

J SCHRAM
See SCHRAMSBERG

SCHRAMSBERG
See PAGE 278

N/A
SCHUG CARNEROS ESTATE
SONOMA, CALIFORNIA
Established in the Napa Valley in 1980 by Walter and Gertrude Schug, this estate transferred to the Carneros district in 1991.

HOUSE STYLE & RANGE
Very exuberant Rouge de Noir seems promising.
SCHUG CARNEROS ROUGE DE NOIR BRUT
  Vintaged, méthode champenoise: 100% Pinot Noir

SEA MIST
See CHICAMA VINEYARDS

70 VALUE
SEBASTIANI VINEYARDS
SONOMA, CALIFORNIA
● Other labels - Richard Cuneo
Established in 1896 by Italian *emigré* Samuele Sebastiani, whose son August made this the tenth largest winery in the US. Auguste died in 1980 and was succeeded by his son Sam, who modernised the winery and moved the production away from inexpensive wines to

80
SCHRAMSBERG VINEYARDS

**CALISTOGA,
CALIFORNIA**

- Other labels – J
  Schram, Mirabelle

This prestigious winery started the modern California sparkling-wine industry rolling in 1965. Until Domaine Chandon was set up some eight years later, Schramsberg was the only producer of serious quality bottle-fermented sparkling wine in the US. One indication of how owners Jamie and the late Jack Davies have been the precursors of development for other California producers is that Schramsberg employees have gone on to become the head winemakers of Codorníu, Franciscan, Kristone, Mumm Napa Valley and Piper-Sonoma.

Whatever possessed Jacob Schram to wander off the Silverado Trail at this particular point in 1862 and hack his way through an almost impenetrable tangle of undergrowth to the top of a rather minor, densely wooded hill on the edge of the Napa Valley has always been a mystery. It's not even the largest or the highest peak in the area: just a minor outcrop on the lower slopes of Diamond Mountain. But Schram came, saw and conquered the small hill he named Schramsberg. And it was on the broad veranda of his house that he entertained Robert Louis Stevenson, who described this property in *The Silverado Squatters* (1883).

By that time, however, the wines of Schramsberg were already enjoying an early success, even on an international basis, having been shipped to London in 1880, where they were available on the Carlton Club wine list. Schram's son sold the property during Prohibition and, apart from a couple of short-lived attempts to restart the business, the Schramsberg winery and vineyard were abandoned until 1965, when they were resurrected by Jack and Jamie Davies.

Schram had not made any sparkling wines, but Jack and Jamie had been partners of Martin Ray. The one-time owner of Paul Masson, Ray had been ahead of his time, making a couple of sparkling wines called Madame Pinot and Champagne de Chardonnay from classic Champagne varieties in the late 1940s and

THE HISTORIC HOUSE WHERE JACOB SCHRAM ENTERTAINED ROBERT LOUIS STEVENSON IN THE 1880s

early 1950s. When Schramsberg had established its reputation in the 1980s, Jack Davies would write that Ray's sparkling wines were 'forerunners of the next wave of change'; thus, they were probably the inspiration for him to do what he did: to bring back the glory days of California 'Champagne'.

WINEMAKER
Mike Reynolds

HOUSE STYLE & RANGE
I have followed Schramsberg for many years, and apart from the *blanc de blancs*, I did not take easily to the wines initially. I could understand and respect the philosophy – going for richness, concentration and complexity – but I just felt that more often than not the wines ended up clumsy and lacklustre.

Since the early 1990s, however, these wines have gradually become more fruit-driven. With less emphasis on substance and complexity, the fruit has been allowed to come to the fore – which is as it should be if a sparkling wine is to reflect the sunny clime of its Napa Valley origins. The result is that these *cuvées* are increasing in elegance and when they do develop complexity, they possess far more finesse.

Mirabelle is a lesser Schramsberg fizz blended from various north California wine growing areas.

MIRABELLE CALIFORNIA BRUT
*Not vintaged, méthode champenoise:
15% Chardonnay, 80% Pinot Noir, 5% Pinot Blanc*

★★☆ J SCHRAM NAPA VALLEY BRUT
*Vintaged, méthode champenoise: 80%
Chardonnay, 20% Pinot Noir*

★ NAPA VALLEY BLANC DE BLANCS
*Vintaged, méthode champenoise: 85%
Chardonnay, 15% Pinot Blanc*

★ NAPA VALLEY BLANC DE NOIRS
*Vintaged, méthode champenoise: 95% Pinot Noir,
5% Meunier*

NAPA VALLEY CRÉMANT
*Vintaged, méthode champenoise:
100% Flora*

NAPA VALLEY RESERVE
*Vintaged, méthode champenoise: 20%
Chardonnay, 80% Pinot Noir*

★ NAPA VALLEY ROSÉ CUVÉE DE PINOT
Vintaged, méthode champenoise: 95% Pinot Noir,

premium varietals – only to be fired by his mother! This producer now has a reputation for bargain varietal wines, but the quality has been variable. This inconsistency has not extended to Sebastiani's sparkling wines sold under the Richard Cuneo label.

HOUSE STYLE & RANGE
The Richard Cuneo Cuvée de Chardonnay is an attractive bargain that is surprisingly well-structured and capable of fine, biscuity complexity.

RICHARD CUNEO CUVÉE DE CHARDONNAY
Vintaged, méthode champenoise: 100% Chardonnay

SHADOW CREEK
See DOMAINE CHANDON

N/A
SHADY LANE CELLARS
SUTTON'S BAY, MICHIGAN
A recently established venture situated on the Leelanau Peninsula between Traverse City and Sutton's Bay, Shady Lane Cellars is the brainchild of neurosurgeon Joe O'Donnell and real-estate broker Bill Stouten. The original aim was to focus attention solely on the production of world-class *méthode champenoise* wines, which they commenced in 1992, but they got sidetracked in 1995, when they also produced still wines from Pinot Noir, Riesling and Chardonnay. These, and a 1992 fizz, were released in 1997, but 'a large inventory of sparkling wines' is promised soon.

N/A
SHARON MILLS WINERY
MANCHESTER, MICHIGAN
Located between Chelsea and Manchester in south-central Michigan, this winery has a good local reputation for its sparkling wines.

ROSE OF SHARON OLD MISSION PENINSULA
MICHIGAN CHAMPAGNE
*Not vintaged, saignée, méthode champenoise:
80% Chardonnay, 20% Pinot Noir*

SPARKLING CHARDONNAY OLD MISSION
PENINSULA MICHIGAN CHAMPAGNE
Not vintaged, méthode champenoise: 100% Chardonnay

SPARKLING RIESLING OLD MISSION PENINSULA
MICHIGAN CHAMPAGNE
Not vintaged, méthode champenoise: 100% Riesling

N/A
SILVERLAKE WINERY
WOODINVILLE, WASHINGTON
- 1,200 cases

Established in 1988, SilverLake is a sort of consumers' cooperative, where much of the shareholding is owned by a large number of customers who participate in the harvest and other production activities in order to qualify for special discount rates. The winemaking team is headed by Cheryl Barber-Jones, who was the senior winemaker for Chateau Ste Michelle and worked extensively with the legendary André Tchelistcheff.

WINEMAKER
Cheryl Barber-Jones

HOUSE STYLE & RANGE
Two wines tasted once does not entitle me to make an overall assessment, but to say I was not impressed would be an understatement. The first bottle of the brut was oxidative and tart, with free sulphur showing on the aftertaste. The back-up bottle was just as tart, although somewhat cleaner, yet this *cuvée* was eminently preferable to the *blanc de blancs*, which also had excessive sulphur, but it was fixed and smelly, not free and clean. In fact, its boiled-cabbage aroma suggested that the sulphur was not just fixed, but had produced mercaptans.

BLANC DE BLANCS
Not vintaged, méthode champenoise: 100% Chardonnay
BRUT
Not vintaged, méthode champenoise:
35% Chardonnay, 65% Pinot Noir
BRUT RESERVE
Same as brut, but disgorged at a later date

N/A
SMITH ESTATES
SPRINGTOWN, TEXAS
● Other labels – La Buena Vida
When Bobby Smith purchased an abandoned dairy farm in 1972 and planted a vineyard there two years later, he did not realise it was located in a 'dry' county (even today some counties still retain laws from the Prohibition era). He was saved by the Farm Winery Act, passed in 1977, and opened his winery the following year. This begs the question: where on earth did he go for a drink between 1972 and 1974? But that's the story, and Bobby Smith is sticking to it. Wines are sold under the La Buena Vida label and a *méthode champenoise* has been produced since the mid-1980s.

STANFORD
See WEIBEL

N/A
SWEDISH HILL VINEYARDS
ROMULUS, NEW YORK
Located on Cayuga Lake in the Fingers Lakes, this relatively recent producer of New York 'Champagne' has yet to establish a track record.

N/A
TABOR HILL
BUCHANAN, MICHIGAN
● Other labels - Grand Mark
Established by Leonard Olson and Carl Banholzer in 1970, this was Michigan's first *vinifera* operation. A large producer of *cuve close* bubblies, the best sparkling wine here is

Grand Mark, a Pinot Noir/Chardonnay *méthode champenoise* from the Lake Michigan Shore.

HOUSE RANGE
TABOR HILL GRAND MARK BRUT
Not vintaged, méthode champenoise: 70% Chardonnay, 30% Pinot Noir

50
TAMUZZA VINEYARDS
HOPE, NEW JERSEY
● Other labels - Domaine St Gregory
Established in 1985 by Paul and Susan Tamuzza, who produce sparkling wines from hybrids such as Aurore, Ravat and Seyval Blanc. Besides the more mainstream St Gregory, they also produce a range of 'real fruit Champagne' (fruit-and-grape sparkling blends) called Courtney's Sparklers.

HOUSE RANGE
DOMAINE ST GREGORY BLANC DE BLANCS
Not vintaged, méthode champenoise: 100% Chardonnay
DOMAINE ST GREGORY BRUT
Not vintaged, méthode champenoise: Chardonnay, Pinot Noir, Seyval Blanc

45
TEDESCHI VINEYARDS
MAUI, HAWAII
This property was originally known as the Torbert Plantation, when it was leased by King Kamehameha III in 1845 to LL Torbert, becoming Rose Ranch in 1856, after it was acquired by Captain James Makee. King Kalakaua, 'the Merrie Monarch', and his queen visited Rose Ranch so often that a cottage was built for them on the property, and it still stands. That this ranch, with its connection to King Kalakaua, should one day produce sparkling wine is indeed fitting; he was known as 'the Merrie Monarch' because of his legendary love of Champagne (and poker).

Since 1984, sparkling wines have been produced from Carnelian grapes grown at Tedeschi on the lower slopes of the dormant Haleakala volcano (sparkling pineapple wine was produced four years earlier). Wherever it might be grown, the Carnelian is too rustic a grape to produce a fine sparkling wine, but as Napa vintner Emile Tedeschi and his Hawaiian-based partner Pardee Erdman were lumbered with it after growing as many as 65 different varieties recommended for trials in the Hawaiian climate by a certain university on the mainland. The first vines were planted in 1977, and year after year the trials went on with no decision by the viticultural consultants as to which variety was best suited to the locality.

Erdman was running a business; not unreasonably, he felt that the university was using Tedeschi as an experimental station. When he could wait no longer for the experts

to decide, he grafted virtually all the vines over to one variety: Carnelian. He chose Carnelian because its grapes possessed the highest acidity, which was not altogether too surprising as it had been developed by Professor Olmo to provide exactly this quality in California's hot Central Valley. Astonishingly, the acidity turned out to be too high under tropical conditions.

Tedeschi *blanc de noirs* has been made in two consecutive vintages every five years or so (1984 & 1985, 1991 & 1992, and 1995 & 1996 so far). The grapes in the intervening years were used for still wines, which are made every year, and are much fresher, and hence better sellers. The biggest seller is, however, the still pineapple wine called Maui Blanc. It is cheaper and easier to make, involves no risk in the vineyard (or, indeed, in the winery). The only drawback is the vast amount of fibrous material left over after pressing.

Maui Blanc is such a profitable tourist gimmick that one wonders why Tedeschi bothers with anything else. If it is because of a real interest in making proper grape wine – particularly sparkling grape wine – then there are a lot of things that should have been tried long ago. There are, however, plans for growing other varieties, so it could be a whole different ball game in the future.

WINEMAKER
Dimitri Tchelistcheff (consultant)

HOUSE STYLE & RANGE
The *blanc de noirs* is a coarse and lacklustre fizz that could be fresher. Even though other varieties should be used, this sparkling Carnelian would be a lot better if it were bottled earlier and spent less time on yeast. The easy-going rosé (styled Rose Ranch Cuvée) is a much less ambitious, far more successful sparkling wine, but as far as I am aware has been made only once.

BLANC DE NOIRS BRUT
Vintaged, méthode champenoise: 100% Carnelian
✶ ROSE RANCH CUVÉE
Vintaged, méthode champenoise: 100% Carnelian

N/A
THOMPSON WINERY
MONEE, ILLINOIS
● Other labels - Père Marquette
Established in 1963, when Bern Ramey and Joseph Allen planted a vineyard here. They converted the former Illinois Central Railway station into a winery, and produced sparkling wine under the Ramey & Allen Champagne label in 1966. By 1968, however, the vines were dying from the effects of '2, 4-D' pesticide, which was being used on surrounding crops. Part of the vineyard was grubbed-up and the winery closed down, but it was saved by Dr John

Thompson, who purchased the property from Ramey, the surviving owner, in 1970. Thompson secured the agreement of neighbouring farmers not to use '2, 4-D', replanted the vineyard, and carried on making sparkling wine.

70
THORNTON WINERY
TEMECULA, CALIFORNIA
- 100,000 cases
- Other labels - Culbertson

John Culbertson established this winery in 1981, and has been making California sparkling wine ever since.

WINEMAKER
Jon Mepherson
HOUSE STYLE & RANGE
An eclectic range at times, from the middle-of-the-road brut through a very good blanc de noirs (the quality of which really came on stream in the late 1980s), to a sparkling red Burgundy style called Cuvée Rouge. Thornton has even produced a Cuvée de Frontignan.

TIVOLI
See S ANDERSON VINEYARD

60
TOMASELLO WINERY
HAMMONTON, NEW JERSEY
Farmer Frank Tomasello established this winery in 1933, immediately after Prohibition was repealed, and started making *méthode champenoise* sparkling wines in the 1940s. Traditionally, Tomasello has produced a number of different *cuvées* produced from a mixture of hybrid and native *labrusca* grapes, but he introduced pure *vinifera* fizz in 1987 with a Cuvée de Chardonnay.

N/A
VALLEY VINEYARDS
MORROW, OHIO
This vineyard and winery was established in 1970, but it started out as a mistake. Ken Schuster decided to plant a few vines around his family farm and sell grapes from a roadside stall. But he had no experience of vineyards and when the cuttings arrived he discovered that he had enough for 20 acres. Sparkling wines are a relatively recent development.

VAN DER KAMP
See RUTHERFORD BENCHMARKS

N/A
VINELAND CORPORATION
PALISADE, COLORADO
- Other labels - Colorado Cellars, Rocky Mountain Vineyards,

Colorado Mountain Vineyards
After 20 years of importing grapes from California for a spot of home winemaking, James Seewald established Colorado Mountain Cellars in 1978, initially supplementing locally-grown grapes with California fruit. Now part of Vineland Corporation, the winery produces sparkling wine under three different labels.

N/A
WAGNER VINEYARDS
LODI, NEW YORK
An established producer of *cuve close* New York 'champagne' located on Seneca Lake in the Fingers Lakes AVA.
HOUSE RANGE
WAGNER 1991 BRUT
> *Vintaged, méthode champenoise: 80% Pinot Noir, 20% Chardonnay*

N/A
NC WALDENSIAN
HICKORY, NORTH CAROLINA
A recent entrant in the field of North Carolina sparkling wines, NC Waldensian has yet to establish a track record.

N/A
WARNER VINEYARDS
PAW PAW, MICHIGAN
Situated on the riverbank in downtown Paw Paw, this company was established in 1938 by John Turner, who converted a pre-Prohibition winery into a grape-processing plant, producing juice from native Concord grapes. He also made a little Concord wine, but it was his son-in-law, James Warner, who built up this winery and planted vineyards with hybrid varieties.

Still owned by the Warner family, this company specialises in *méthode champenoise* wines, but although my experience of these wines has been sporadic, they have never impressed me.

WENTE VINEYARDS WINERY AND CELLARS IN LIVERMORE, CALIFORNIA

N/A
WEIBEL
MISSION SAN JOSE, CALIFORNIA
- Other labels - Stanford, Château Napoleon

Some *méthode champenoise* wines are made, but mostly vast volumes of crashingly boring *cuve close* wines are produced here.

N/A
WENTE VINEYARDS
LIVERMORE, CALIFORNIA
Carl Wente emigrated from Germany in 1880, and worked for fellow countryman Charles Krug before establishing his own winery in 1883. Small amounts of *méthode champenoise* have been produced since 1981.
HOUSE STYLE & RANGE
Fruity fizz at best, but some *cuvées* have had strange aromas which spoil any appeal.
BRUT
> *Vintaged, méthode champenoise: 60% Chardonnay, 30% Pinot Noir, 10% Pinot Blanc*

N/A
WIEDERKEHR WINERY
ALTUS, ARKANSAS
- Other labels - Chateau du Monte

The oldest winery in Arkansas, and the most successful, UC Davis-trained owner-winemaker Al Wiederkehr makes a decent Altus Spumante.

N/A
HERMANN J WIEMER VINEYARD
SENECA LAKE, FINGER LAKES
While working for a certain hybrid aficionado, Weimer produced some outstanding *vinifera* wines from his own vineyard. They received rave reviews and this vineyard has not looked back, although its *méthode champenoise* wine has not impressed.

N/A
WILLOW CREST
PROSSER, WASHINGTON STATE
I have not tasted the wines from this *méthode champenoise* producer.

WINDSOR VINEYARDS
See KLEIN FAMILY VINTNERS

N/A
WINERY OF THE LITTLE HILLS
ST CHARLES, MISSOURI
Up-and-coming *méthode champenoise* producer.

N/A
WOODBURY VINEYARDS
FREDONIA, NEW YORK
Located in the Lake Erie district, this *méthode champenoise* producer has not impressed.

CANADA

WHEN IN 1535 THE FRENCH EXPLORER JACQUES CARTIER SAILED DOWN THE ST. LAWRENCE RIVER TO NEW FRANCE, TO WHICH HE HAD LAID CLAIM THE YEAR BEFORE, HE DISCOVERED A LARGE ISLAND OVERRUN BY WILD VINES, WHICH HE ORIGINALLY CALLED THE ILE DE BACCHUS. HE LATER RENAMED THIS THE ILE D'ORLEANS IN A MOVE CALCULATED TO ENDEAR HIMSELF TO THE DUKE OF ORLEANS, SON OF KING FRANCIS I, BUT IT ILLUSTRATES THAT THE VINE HAS GROWN IN CANADA SINCE THE EARLIEST TIMES.

It is assumed that the Jesuit settlers who followed in the wake of Cartier's explorations were the first to make wine in Canada circa 1564, although the first commercial production did not occur until about 1860.

For the first 100 years or more, Canadian palates preferred the sweet, foxy-flavoured wines produced by the sort of native *labrusca* grape that Cartier encountered on the Ile d'Orleans. Sparkling versions of sweet *labrusca* emerged in the early 1950s, took a real grip on the market in the 1960s, yet became even more popular after 1971, when Andrés started the Baby Duck boom, a low alcohol fizz (seven per cent) that mimicked Cold Duck in the USA. Canadian customers displayed an even greater propensity for tacky sweet fizz than their American counterparts, lapping up vast volumes of lookalike products bearing names such as Daddy Duck, Luv-a-Duck, Fuddle Duck, Canada Duck, Cold Duckling, Baby Bear, Baby Deer, Golden Goose, Pink Flamingo, Pussycat and even Cold Turkey! According to Toronto-based wine writer Tony Aspler, sales of these products accounted for 90% of the Canadian wine industry's profit until as recently as the 1970s.

Although still a major earner, Canadians were gradually weaned off the Baby Duck boom from this juncture, as they took to more sophisticated products such as Mateus Rosé and purple polyester trousers.

Supposedly more serious styles of fizz had already come to prominence between 1964 and 1967, when the French authorities successfully sued Château-Gai, which was one of the four big Ontario wineries at the time, preventing it from selling Canadian 'champagne'. However, because the verdict was made in the French-speaking province of Quebec by a judge of French descent, a number of wineries have sought appeals in other Provinces.

Yet, with just one hopeful exception – Blue Mountain in British Columbia, the quality of Canada's bottle-fermented sparkling wine has hardly shown any improvement over the last 30 years. This is because Canadians themselves have not taken the sparkling wine style seriously, particularly in Ontario, which has been the industry's locomotive for 25 of those 30 years. The same could be said, however, for Canadian wine in general up to ten years ago, and the progress since has been nothing short of phenomenal, so there is still hope for Canadian fizz.

BLUE MOUNTAIN VINEYARDS, OKANAGAN VALLEY, BRITISH COLUMBIA

THE VQA SEAL OF QUALITY

With the North American Free Trade Agreement (NAFTA) looming, producers in Ontario and British Columbia realised that the Canadian market would be open to cheap American wines, with which they had no hope of competing. The only chance for their survival was to aim more upmarket (middle-market in international terms), and to achieve that they had to upgrade their vineyards, half of which were planted with *labrusca* grapes, while virtually all the rest were dominated by hybrids and crosses.

The problem was that there were (and still are) very few quality or authenticity regulations in Canada. If, for example, the label states 'Product of Canada', it does not necessarily mean the grapes used are Canadian, just that part of the production process was carried out on Canadian soil. This failing destroyed the incentive to upgrade the vineyards and thus stifled any chance of raising the quality – let alone authenticity – of Canadian wine, so a self-regulatory organisation called the Vintners Quality Alliance or VQA was formed in 1988.

The VQA encouraged the use of *vinifera* and 'preferred' hybrids, while the federal government banned the use of *labrusca* varieties for table wines, allowing them to be used only for fortified, aromatised and cheap sparkling products (*ie:* Baby Duck *et al*), and, at the same time, encouraging the uprooting of these vines through a subsidy scheme. More than a third of the vineyards in Ontario and British Columbia were pulled up, while quality-conscious wineries who wanted to see their own areas recognised internationally, planted premium varieties at a furious rate (and often at their own expense because they were seldom the same growers who farmed *labrusca* and benefited from subsidies).

Today the VQA seal guarantees the following:
1. Provincial appellations are 100% Canadian grown, a minimum of 85% from the province indicated and contain only classic *vinifera* or preferred hybrid varieties of a minimum ripeness level.
2. Specific appellations are 100% from the province indicated, a minimum of 85% from the area indicated and contain only classic *vinifera* or preferred hybrid varieties of a minimum ripeness level.
3. Estate bottled wines must be 100% from grapes owned or controlled by the winery.
4. Vineyard designated wines must be 100% from the vineyard indicated.

N/A
ANDRÉS WINES
WINONA, ONTARIO
The originator of Baby Duck, a popular and much-imitated sweet pink or red fizzy labrusca wine. More serious wines are sold under the Peller Estates label, named after Andrew Peller, the founder of Andrés, and is used exclusively for VQA wines.
WINEMAKER
Barry Poag
HOUSE STYLE & RANGE
Having established a plethora of cheap fizz from Baby Duck to Chante Blanc, Moody Blue, Kurhauser Trocken Sekt, Select Brut and Spumante, the rich, jammy Peller Cuvée Niagara comes as a relief, despite the exotic sweetness on the finish of this supposedly brut-style wine.

✶ PELLER CUVÉE NIAGARA BRUT
Not vintaged, cuve close: 85% Riesling, 15% Vidal Blanc

N/A
D'ANGELO ESTATE WINERY
AMHERSTBERG, ONTARIO
This estate was planted in 1984 and the winery opened in 1990, with plans to make the first sparkling wine in 1998.
WINEMAKER
Sal D'Angelo
HOUSE STYLE & RANGE
This wine will not be available to taste until sometime after publication, but is due to consist of Chardonnay and Pinot Noir grapes grown in the Lake Erie North Shore Region, and will be bottle-fermented.

76
BLUE MOUNTAIN
OKANAGAN FALLS, BRITISH COLUMBIA
This is one of British Columbia's most up-and-coming wineries, and owner-winemaker Ian Mavety has employed the talented Raphael Brisbois (formerly at Omar Khayyam in India and Iron Horse in California) to consult in the development of his sparkling wine.
WINEMAKER
Ian Matevy
HOUSE STYLE & RANGE
The Vintage Brut has a creamy, malo nose, high acidity and an oxidative hint on the finish. This wine merely needs a touch of fatness in the fruit to make it more generous in the mouth, and to pull back from its oxidative tendency, but it certainly shows enough promise to become a world-class fizz. Reserve Brut and Brut Rosé not yet tasted.

OKANAGAN VALLEY BRUT ROSÉ
Vintaged, méthode champenoise: grape varieties not revealed

OKANAGAN VALLEY RESERVE BRUT
Vintaged, méthode champenoise: 55% Chardonnay, 5% Pinot Gris, 40% Pinot Noir

★✶ OKANAGAN VALLEY VINTAGE BRUT
Vintaged, méthode champenoise: 35% Chardonnay, 5% Pinot Gris, 60% Pinot Noir

50
BRIGHTS WINES
NIAGARA FALLS, ONTARIO
Brights merged with Cartier to become Brights-Cartier and is now part of Vincor, Canada's largest wine producer, which also owns the pioneering Inniskillin winery, and sells wines under various brands, including the good value, upmarket Jackson-Triggs and Sawmill Creek labels.
WINEMAKER
Mira Ananicz
HOUSE STYLE & RANGE
The President Brut is not as clean as the President Rosé on the nose, but shows clean, commercial fruit on the palate. The mousse is a bit aggressive and the flavour somewhat concocted, but there are no flaws. The President Rosé has a simple but fresh aroma with exotic, grape-jelly fruit and a distinctly sweet palate (rosé obviously means sweet in Canada, whatever the technical description might be). Both President *cuvées* have old-fashioned labelling, and smarter presentation would help their image. The Bambino *cuvées* are both fairly nasty.

PRESIDENT CANADIAN CHAMPAGNE, GRANDE RESERVE BRUT
Not vintaged, cuve close: 15% Chardonnay and Chenin Blanc, 40% Seyval Blanc, 45% Vidal Blanc

PRESIDENT CANADIAN CHAMPAGNE, GRANDE RESERVE ROSÉ
Not vintaged, cuve close: 10% Baco Noir, 45% Seyval Blanc, 45% Vidal Blanc

ROSATO BAMBINO
Not vintaged, cuve close: 15% Baco Noir, 40% Elvira, 15% Muscat, 30% Vidal

SPUMANTE BAMBINO
Not vintaged, cuve close: 40% Elvira, 15% Muscat, 45% Vidal

N/A
CHÂTEAU DES CHARMES
ST DAVIDS, ONTARIO
Established in 1978 by Paul Bosc, a French-trained oenologist who had been the winemaker at Château-Gai. Today Château des Charmes is run by his son, Paul Bosc Jnr.
WINEMAKER
Paul Bosc
HOUSE STYLE & RANGE
The Brut has been a decent fizz in the past, but both samples of a recent *cuvée* were unclean, while the fruit in the Sec tasted unripe and extremely incongruous with the sweetness on the finish.

BRUT MÉTHODE TRADITIONELLE
Not vintaged, méthode champenoise: 50% Chardonnay, 50% Pinot Noir

SEC MÉTHODE TRADITIONELLE
Not vintaged, méthode champenoise: 25% Chardonnay, 25% Gamay, 50% Riesling

CIPES
See SUMMERHILL ESTATE

70
COLIO
HARROW, ONTARIO
Founded by a group of Italian businessmen who wanted to import Italian wines, but found it easier to build a winery and make their own.
WINEMAKER
Carlo Negri
HOUSE STYLE & RANGE
If you don't mind a fairly sweet fizz (and it really does taste as sweet as a *demi-sec*), this *cuve close* will be far more preferable than a number of more expensive Canadian *méthode champenoise*. It has a creamy, flowery aroma, with more-ish sweet fruit, although the mousse does tend to be a bit explosive in the mouth.

CHARDONNAY LILY, VIN MOUSSEUX
Vintaged, cuve close: 87% Chardonnay, 13% Goldburger

N/A
HAWTHORNE MOUNTAIN VINEYARDS
OKANAGAN FALLS, BRITISH COLUMBIA
Owned by Albert & Dixie LeComte, who wisely hired winemaker Eric von Krosig (Spock to his friends), who had to escape Planet Cipes to work here. Hawthorne Mountain Vineyards was originally called LeComte, and some wines are still produced under that label, but the emphasis now is firmly on establishing the new name.
WINEMAKER
Eric von Krosig
HOUSE STYLE & RANGE
Predictably, Spock has produced a bottle-fermented Riesling, but unfortunately he has chosen to make it in an oxidative style.

HMV Brut Dosage Zero
Not vintaged, méthode champenoise: 100% Riesling

N/A
HILLEBRAND ESTATES
NIAGARA-ON-THE-LAKE, ONTARIO
This winery was initially called Newark, after the original name of Niagara-on-the-Lake, but was changed to its present title in 1983, when it was purchased by Scholl & Hillebrand of Rüdesheim, Germany.
WINEMAKER
Jean Laurent Goux
HOUSE STYLE & RANGE
I have been impressed with the Trius Chardonnay and the blended red wine Trius Glenlake Vineyard, plus a sparkling wine called Mounier Brut, but I tasted the Trius Brut recently for the first time and found it had high acid, thin fruit and an unclean element.
TRIUS BRUT
Not vintaged, méthode champenoise: Chardonnay, Pinot Noir

N/A
MAGNOTTA WINERY
VAUGHAN, ONTARIO
This winery has vineyards on the famed Beamsville Bench, and has made some interesting Chardonnay and Icewine. However, I am puzzled by Magnotta's sparkling wines, which at one time tasted like sherry with bubbles, and have not improved, despite the quality elsewhere in the range and the general perception that this is a producer on the up.
WINEMAKER
Alejandero De Miguel, Bela Varga
HOUSE STYLE & RANGE
Recent *cuvées* of these wines, which are always sourced exclusively from the Niagara Peninsula, continue to baffle me. The Podámer Brut had an oxidative-toffee character, as did the Rossana Blanc de Blancs, which was patently old and had a deep yellow colour, whereas the Rosé was unclean with a bitter-sweet finish. I cannot understand what on earth Magnotta is trying to do with these sparkling wines, when the winemakers obviously have talent, producing such excellent still wines as Lenko Vineyards Chardonnay and Vidal Icewine.
PODÁMER BRUT
Not vintaged, méthode champenoise: Chardonnay
ROSSANA BLANC DE BLANC
Not vintaged, méthode champenoise: Chardonnay
ROSSANA ROSÉ
Not vintaged, méthode champenoise: Chardonnay, Pinot Noir

N/A
PELEE ISLAND WINERY
KINGSVILLE, ONTARIO
An hour by ferry, this is the most southerly location of any vineyard in Canada. It has the longest growing season and the warmest climate in the country – two good reasons why the first commercial winery in Canada was established here in 1860, when it was known as Vin Villa.
WINEMAKER
Walter Schmorantz
HOUSE RANGE
CANADIAN CHAMPAGNE CUVÉE RIESLING (DUE TO BE RENAMED)
Vintaged, cuve close: 35% Italico, 65% Riesling

65
PILLITTERI ESTATES WINERY
NIAGARA-ON-THE-LAKE, ONTARIO
• 250 cases
The Pillitteri family had been grape growers on the Niagara Peninsula for almost 50 years before they opened their own winery.
WINEMAKER
Joe Will
HOUSE STYLE & RANGE
Sweet, flowery-strawberry fruit that is more *demi-sec* than *sec* to taste, and is star-rated despite this sweetness.
✗ CLASSIQUE
Vintaged, cuve close: 100% Chardonnay

65
SUMAC RIDGE
SUMMERLAND, BRITISH COLUMBIA
Owned by Bob Wareham, but still very much run by one of his former partners, Harry McWatters. The latter has worked selflessly to establish and promote the British Columbia wine industry around the world. Harry's Private Reserve Gewürztraminer is one of the best examples of this variety found outside Alsace, and, after a rather disappointing start, his bottle-fermented fizz is beginning to show promise.

WINEMAKER
Marc Wendenburg, Harold Bates
HOUSE STYLE & RANGE
Steller's Jay Cuvée has excellent acidity and a classic, lean structure, but still needs cleaning up on the overly oxidative aromas and deciding whether to focus on the autolysis or malolactic fermentation. The Blanc de Noirs has a blush of apricot colour and a certain smokiness of Pinot fruit.
✗ BLANC DE NOIRS BRUT
Vintaged, méthode champenoise: 100% Pinot Noir
STELLER'S JAY CUVÉE BRUT
Vintaged, méthode champenoise: Chardonnay, Pinot Blanc, Pinot Noir

40
SUMMERHILL ESTATE WINERY
KELOWNA, BRITISH COLUMBIA
Eccentric owner Stephen Cipes insists that maturing his fizz in the 'Cheops' pyramid he has built on this property produces a significantly different product to the same wine that has not been subjected to this mystical power. I would not dispute that there is difference, but it is due to the build-up of heat in his wooden pyramid, and the change is not a favourable one.
WINEMAKER
Dr Alan Marks
HOUSE STYLE & RANGE
The world's only pyramid-aged 'Champagne' leaves a nasty chemical taste in the mouth, but it is not that special before being subjected to the forces of 'Cheops'. The Cipes Ice Wine Dosage sounds exciting, but is too coarse and oxidative.
CIPES BRUT
Not vintaged, bottle-fermented: 100% Johannisberg Riesling
CIPES ICE WINE DOSAGE DEMI-SEC
Not vintaged, bottle-fermented: 100% Johannisberg Riesling

SPARKLING WINE AGEING PYRAMID 'CHEOPS' AT THE SUMMERHILL ESTATE WINERY

CENTRAL & SOUTH AMERICA

MEXICO HAS SHOWN PROMISE FOR SPARKLING WINE PRODUCTION EVER SINCE FREIXENET ESTABLISHED A SPARKLING WINERY THERE IN 1982 AND THERE ARE SPARKLING WINES PRODUCED IN SUCH VITICULTURALLY INHOSPITABLE COUNTRIES AS PERU AND BOLIVIA, ALTHOUGH THEY CANNOT BE RECOMMENDED. GENERALLY SOUTH AMERICA LEAVES MUCH TO BE DESIRED, AND CHILE IN PARTICULAR SHOULD CERTAINLY BE DOING BETTER, AS ARGENTINA AND BRAZIL ARE DOING AT LEAST AS WELL, DESPITE THE OVERPRODUCTION OF THE FORMER, AND THE SIGNIFICANTLY LOWER POTENTIAL OF THE LATTER.

ARGENTINA

The fifth-largest wine country in the world, Argentina could be a major force in the premium quality sector of the New World market if only its excessive yields were curbed. Yet while Chile has strengthened its position as South America's premier wine country by significantly reducing its yield over the last ten years, Argentina has done the opposite.

Although total Argentinian production has been reduced by some ten per cent over the same period, one-third of its vineyards have been pulled up, thus increasing its yield per hectare from 66 to 88 hectolitres. This actually has a less harmful effect on fizz than it does on still wine, thus this country should and could do much better in the sparkling wine stakes than it does.

Argentina's **Domaine Chandon** is one of Moët & Chandon's oldest outposts, having been established in 1960, yet most of the fizz is simply fresh and clean and amylic, with a slightly bitter finish. However, Baron B stands out, especially the Extra Brut, which has better acidity and more finesse, and there are rumours of vast new plantations of Chardonnay and a swing from *cuve close* to *méthode champenoise* to improve the quality of future *cuvées*. On the local South American markets, Domaine Chandon unashamedly sells its bubbly as *Champaña*, as does Piper-Heidsieck with its Henri Piper brand, as does Mumm. In a nice ironic twist, José Orfila of St Martin makes sparkling wines in France, which it then exports to Argentina, where it is sold as *Champaña*!

BOLIVIA

It is believed that vines were first cultivated in this country in the 1560s, the vines coming from neighbouring Peru. Today vineyards are found at altitudes of between 1,600 and 2,400 metres in the high plateau country of La Paz in the north and around Tarija in the south. The soil is alluvial, the climate tropical, with rot-inducing humidity a greater problem than phylloxera, yet ironically most vines have to be irrigated.

Muscat is by far the most important variety, with more than half the wine produced being distilled into local *Pisco* brandy. But even the best of the remaining wines – from Chenin Blanc, Torrontes, Cabernet Sauvignon and Merlot grapes – are light-bodied and

VINEYARD IN MENDOZA, ARGENTINA, WITH THE ANDES MOUNTAIN RANGE BEHIND

uninteresting, with exports either negligible or non-existent. The only Bolivian fizz I have come across has been a non-vintage *demi-sec* called San Pedro Vino Espumante, and it was one of the most vile sparkling wines I have ever had the displeasure to taste.

BRAZIL

With ranches that are bigger than Belgium in a country that is large enough to encompass Western Europe twice-over, Brazil has enough room left over to plant the equivalent of Europe's entire vineyard area, not once, but several times over.

By far the largest wine region in Brazil is located in the southernmost state of Rio Grande do Sul, and borders Uruguay. Within its Palomas district is Santana do Livramento, Brazil's newest and most promising wine area where vineyards on the Campanha Gaùcha – the vast Gaucho plainlands – are planted with more than 20 *vinifera* varieties, while eight out of every ten vines in the rest of the country are *labrusca*.

Casa Moet & Chandon (Diamantina on export markets) produces both still and sparkling wines, the latter of which can be very good indeed, although it is brazenly sold on the Brazilian market as *Champaña*. **Mumm** does likewise with its Forestier brand. **De-Lantier** is a large, modern winery owned by Martini & Rossi, who produce some of Brazil's better wines, a bottle-fermented fizz sold under the De-Greville label.

CHILE

With a cheap and inexhaustible supply of irrigation water from the melting snows of the Andes, a perfect climate, and no phylloxera or other pests or diseases,

Chile has quickly become South America's best wine region – first for red wines and more recently for white, yet hardly ever has this country shown any potential for sparkling wine.

In certain respects Chile is like California, a strip of land along the western coast overlooking the Pacific. The first set of hills and small intersecting valleys encountered in both Chile and California are penetrated by cooling coastal air currents and the vineyards there provide the greatest potential for quality, while the wide valleys at the foot of the substantial mountain range beyond are better for producing larger volumes of lower quality wines.

It seems to me that the obvious place to start making an interesting quality of bottle-fermented fizz in Chile is Casablanca, after which producers should probably follow the Secano region – the first set of coastal hills – southwards as far as Concepcion, as soon as an infrastructure of roads can be built. Essentially Chilean sparkling wine producers should be hot on the trail of the best Sauvignon Blanc producers.

Champagne Mumm has recently seen fit to invest in Chile and, in the same hypocritical manner as its champenois colleagues in Argentina and Brazil, it calls these wines *Champaña* on the local market. Set up at Santiago in 1994, Mumm produces some 30,000 cases annually, and launched its first *cuvée* in 1995. The wines are dressed very much like Mumm Cuvée Napa, but they are made by *cuve close* and winemaker Daniel Maranesi has yet to come up with anything in the same class as his California counterpart Greg Fowler. Mumm produces a Brut (83% Chardonnay, 17% Pinot Noir) and Demi Sec (55% Chardonnay, 10% Pinot Noir, 35% Sauvignon Blanc).

Another Demi Sec is sold exclusively on the Chilean market under the **Maison Forestier** label. It is early days, but so far these wines, although clean, have been rather sweet and slightly amylic. Owner, Seagram, claims that it is the only Chilean fizz to be made from classic Champagne grapes, but another European interloper, Miguel Torres, has been making bottle-fermented sparkling wine from these grapes at Santiago long before Mumm decided to set up shop. Despite a substantial annual production of some 10,000 cases, **Torres** winemaker, Fernando Almeda O, unfortunately swings wildly between a deliciously light, elegant and refreshingly fruity style and a somewhat dull, boring wine that lacks finesse (70% Chardonnay, 30% Pinot Noir). Happily it has been of the former quality in recent times.

I have found **Santa Carolina** pure Chardonnay sparkling wine to have unripe fruit and substandard corks, while **Valdivieso**, which is an old hand at the sparkling wine business churns out fizz that is basic in quality and dominated by ferment odours. A recent tasting of **Concha y Toro** Champagne Extra Brut revealed a cheap smell and foursquare flavour, while the Brut had an almost foxy, floral aroma. The Grandier Brut by Santiago-based **Viña Manquehue** (called Darwin's Path on some export markets) has surprisingly succulent fruit on the nose, but needs a lighter hand on the palate for more freshness and elegance.

MEXICO

The Spanish brought wine to Mexico in 1521, making it the oldest wine-producing country in the Americas. Just three years later, the governor of New Spain (Mexico), Hernando Cortez, ordered all Spanish residents to plant 1,000 vines for every 100 Indian slaves they owned, and by 1595 the country was almost self-sufficient in wine. Shipments of Spanish wine had dwindled to such an extent that producers in the home country had to pressurise Philip II into forbidding the planting of further vineyards in the New World.

There is one competent sparkling wine producer in Mexico today, **Freixenet de Mexico** at Ezequiel Montes in Querétaro. Situated on a one-mile-high plateau north of Mexico City, Spanish Cava giant Freixenet produces 25,000 cases of Mexican fizz under the Sala Vivé label and this *cuvée* regularly outshines the company's famous Cordon Negro. Winemaker José Antonio Llaquet uses almost 50% Macabéo, a Cava grape, in its Brut, and this is supported by as much as 30% Ugni Blanc, plus 7% Chenin, 7% Sauvignon Blanc and 7% Pinot Noir. There is a Pétillant, which effectively reverses the proportion of Macabéo and Ugni Blanc, and Semi Seco and Petillan Extra (even sweeter) versions exist. Other fizz labels include **Ferrier**.

PERU

One of South America's oldest winegrowing countries, vineyards have been growing in Peru since at least 1563, when Francesco de Carabantes planted vines in the Ica valley. But many sources believe that Francisco Pizarro, the famous conquistador who built Lima, could have ordered the planting of vines as early as 1531. What is certain is that most Peruvian vineyards today are still located in the province of Ica.

Even though Ica is a fertile valley oasis surrounded by desert, it is hot and semi-arid, necessitating irrigation. With substantially cooler nights, the diurnal difference is such that crisp, vividly flavoured wines should be possible, but the achievements have yet to match this potential. **Tacama** in Ica is the only significant producer and although various wines are exported, to France of all places, only the Malbec is acceptable by international standards. The sparkling wines are unpleasantly explosive despite regular consultancy from famous Bordeaux professors Peynaud and Ribereau-Gayon.

THE TACAMA VINEYARD, NEAR ICA IN PERU

SEPPELT'S VINEYARD IN THE HILLS OF THE GREAT DIVIDING RANGE AT GREAT WESTERN, VICTORIA

AUSTRALIA

SALES OF AUSTRALIAN FIZZ PEAKED ON THE DOMESTIC MARKET IN THE LATE 1980S AND, BY 1989, SALES WERE IN SUCH A DECLINE THAT THE INDUSTRY, WITH MOUNTING STOCKS ON ITS HANDS, BECAME EXPORT HUNGRY. THIS COINCIDED WITH THE UK MARKET OPENING UP FOR AUSTRALIAN WINES IN GENERAL AND A SPARKLING WINE INITIATIVE BY ODDBINS, ONE OF THE MOST INNOVATIVE CHAINS OF WINE SHOPS IN THE COUNTRY, SERVED TO ESTABLISH ANGAS BRUT AND ANGAS ROSÉ AS FIRM FAVOURITES AMONG YOUNGER BRITISH CONSUMERS.

Angas was just one of many fruity bubblies, albeit an incredibly successful one, at the base of a vast range that included much finer Australian fizz. As Oddbins began to market these, and spread its wings to include *cuvées* from California, New Zealand *et al*, so the concept of premium sparkling wines evolved. As fizz from various 'New World' countries has filtered onto major international markets, so the global interest in these wines has grown, but it would not be an exaggeration to say that Australia and Oddbins laid down the foundations of today's premium sparkling wine market.

ORIGINS

The first Australian sparkling wine was produced by James King in 1843, just 55 years after Captain Arthur Phillip established Australia's earliest vineyard at Farm Cove in New South Wales. A free settler from Hertfordshire in England, King had established a vast grain and cattle ranch at Irrawing in the Hunter Valley, also in New South Wales, by 1826. He planted his first vineyard in 1836 and was primarily known for his 'Shepherd's Riesling', made from Sémillon, but was making sparkling wine by at least 1843.

Marketed as 'champagne', King's fizz won gold medals at the Sydney Horticultural Show in 1850 and 1852. Although another Hunter Valley grower by the name of W Burnett is recorded as having made a 'pink-and-white champagne', King was the only exhibitor of Australian sparkling wine at the Paris exposition of 1855, where it also won a medal. In their official report on the wines of New South Wales, the French judges magnanimously described the 'bouquet, body and flavour' of King's sparkling wine as 'equal to the finest champagnes', and it was chosen as one of only two wines to be served to Napoleon III at the exposition's final banquet.

In the late 1840s and throughout the 1850s several producers in South Australia took up sparkling winemaking, including Patrick Auld (Auldana), Thomas Hardy, Samuel Smith (Yalumba) and Joseph Ernest Seppelt (B. Seppelt & Sons, Seppeltsfield, and Chateau Tanunda). We know that the first sparkling wine made in the state of Victoria was before 1861 because a bottle is recorded as having been served at the Acclimatisation Society Dinner in October of that year, but its identity was not documented. According to *Sparkling Wines: The Technology of their Production in Australia*, the first Victorian

AUSTRALIA'S FAMED SPARKLING SHIRAZ, A GENERIC STYLE THAT CAN LOOSELY BE TAKEN TO INCLUDE SPARKLING RED WINES MADE FROM CABERNET SAUVIGNON, MERLOT AND OTHER RED GRAPE VARIETIES, WHETHER A PURE VARIETAL OR BLENDED

producer to be documented was Charles Braché, a German despite his French-sounding name. Braché initially made fizz in Melbourne, but later moved to Wahgunyah, where he continued production at a vineyard which he called Coblenz.

The most important development in Australia's emerging sparkling wine industry occurred when one Joseph Best died intestate in 1887, and his Great Western vineyard and cellars situated in South Australia were purchased by Hans Irvine. In the early 1890s, Irvine installed specialised equipment for the production of Sparkling wine, and employed Charles Pierlot, who had trained at Pommery. Irvine himself was knowledgeable about sparkling wine production, having made several study trips to France at a time when even one such journey was hazardous enough. In 1918, four years before his death, Irvine sold the business to his friend Benno Seppelt, thus creating Seppelt Great Western, which was destined to dominate Australia's sparkling wine industry.

In 1919 a French cook by the name of Edmund Mazure left his employ as manager of Auldana to set up his own vineyard and winery, making and selling fizz under the La Perouse label (later taken over by Wynns, becoming the now famous Seaview brand in 1975). A few years before Mazure went into business for himself, Leo Buring produced the first Minchinbury Champagne from the famous Minchinbury vineyard, which Penfold's took over in 1913. Today the brands of Seppelt, Seaview, Minchinbury and Wynns belong to Southcorp, which incidentally still uses the Laperouse name (albeit in a slightly modified form, and for still French wines).

Other notable firsts include the first so-called Sparkling Burgundy which was produced by the Victorian Champagne Company in 1881, and Minchinbury was the first sparkling wine to utilise the transfer method, although exactly when is unclear. It was, however, a milestone for the Australian sparkling wine industry because most of the country's bottle-fermented brands are currently produced in this manner.

The dubious honour of making the first Australian *cuve close* sparkling wine goes to Orlando, which produced its Barossa Pearl fizz by this method in 1956, while the even more questionable credit of the first carbonated wine belongs to Frederick Thomson, who made a light red fizz called Claretta, circa 1939.

THE SPARKLING WINE INDUSTRY TODAY

Australia does not have the largest sparkling wine industry in the New World, but it probably has the most diverse, and the proof of this is the key to Domaine Chandon's rapid success. Recognition of and investment in Australia's sparkling wine industry came almost ten years later than it did in California. As in other countries, it was Moët & Chandon who showed the pioneering spirit, its roving experts making repeated visits to virtually every wine area of southeastern Australia in the early 1980s. It was not until 1985, however, that the company established its luxurious Domaine Chandon at Green Point near Coldstream in Victoria's Yarra Valley.

Much of the success of this venture can be attributed to Dr Tony Jordan, one of Australia's most knowledgeable winemakers. Due to his efforts, the quality of Australia's Domaine Chandon effortlessly surged past that of California's Domaine Chandon, despite the latter's 12 year head start. In fact, it took this Australian outpost just four years to succeed, compared to 20 years for Domaine Chandon in California, but Jordan had three advantages. Firstly, he was able to draw upon the lessons learned at the Napa facility; secondly, Australia has a great number and diversity of potential sparkling wine areas to play with; thirdly, and most importantly, Jordan already knew where most of these areas were.

Jordan was one of the world's first two flying winemakers, hopping from one part of Australia to another with his former partner, Brian Croser. This dynamic duo followed the staggered harvesting dates around the massive continent of Australia, discovering more about its complex potential than any other individual. While Croser settled down in his chosen spot in the Adelaide Hills, Jordan used his accumulated knowledge to pinpoint as many of the most likely sparkling wine areas as possible.

Also in 1985, another Champagne house, Roederer, began investing in Australia, at Heemskerk in Pipers Brook, Tasmania, which the company owned until 1994. The launch of Roederer's first sparkling *cuvée*, a 1989 vintage called Jansz, was met with such hype on the local market that the entire production sold out within two weeks, despite the fact that it was poorly made and marred by an obvious fault. Subsequent releases have improved, although the wine has not been anywhere near as consistent as Roederer Estate in California, and when the company pulled out, Roederer's Jean-Claude Rouzaud claimed it was because they could not ripen the grapes properly in Tasmania.

This was unfair, as some of his own wines have demonstrated and, hopefully, future *cuvées* under the new owner, Samuel Smith & Sons, will prove it so. The truth was, I think, that Roederer was in the process of purchasing a property in the Douro Valley in Portugal, and although Rouzaud had a few million in spare cash in the US, the exchange rates were not favourable, thus he looked around to see what investments he could do without and found Heemskerk. For Rouzaud, borrowing from the bank is anathema, even on a temporary basis.

SPARKLING WINES IN PUPITRES IN THE DOMAINE CHANDON CELLARS AT GREEN POINT NEAR COLDSTREAM IN THE YARRA VALLEY

Bollinger has shown an interest in Australia' sparkling wine potential since the mid-1980s, when th famous Champagne house became a shareholder ir Petaluma. However, it has always been typically low key about the investment, allowing Brian Croser to 'do his own thing' as Bollinger's former chairman Christian Bizot, once put it. Bollinger is curious abou Croser's venture, but not concerned in any direct way with its production. Bollinger personnel will go there taste with Croser, and comment, but never interfere and do not want to see their name on the label, back o front, even in the most microscopic print.

Croser's first fizz was produced in 1984, but lik many Australian sparkling wines of this period, it was a hefty Chardonnay that just so happened to have bubbles, thus when this was released in 1986, it wa sold under Petaluma's second label – Bridgewater Mill Subsequent vintages have progressively approached Croser's style and have therefore been released under his own name, literally.

AUSTRALIA'S UNIQUE FIZZ

Auldana's Sparkling Burgundy was the precursor to Australia's famed Sparkling Shiraz, a generic style tha can loosely be taken to include sparkling red wine made from Cabernet Sauvignon, Merlot and other rec grape varieties, whether a pure varietal or blended.

But Australia's early Sparkling Burgundy was much lighter in both body and colour than today's Sparkling Shiraz which, as a product, could not be more differen from authentic sparkling red Burgundy (Bourgogne Mousseux), past or present. Sparkling Shiraz has a deep purple-red colour and is made in two basic styles, oaky or fruity, but both are stocky, pungently-flavoured full-throttle wines that invariably have a somewha sweet finish.

Many non-Australian sparkling wine drinkers do not take Sparkling Shiraz seriously, a prejudice born from being used to Champagne, which i predominantly white and occasionally pink, but never red. It is, however, a style that is taken very seriously by those who craft the wines, and the best *cuvées* have ar

THE MOST BASIC OBSERVATION TO MAKE ABOUT AUSTRALIAN FIZZ IS THAT MOST PREMIUM SPARKLING WINES ARE MADE BY THE TRANSFER METHOD, NOT *MÉTHODE CHAMPENOISE*. AND WHEN YOU CONSIDER THE QUALITY OF THESE WINES, YOU COULD WELL ASK WHO NEEDS THE *MÉTHODE CHAMPENOISE*?

enviable reputation among Australia's more wine-iterate consumers.

The most negative knee-jerk reaction to the sight of a frothing opaque-purple wine comes from European consumers and, ironically, the more experienced and knowledgeable the wine drinker, the more inclined he or she is to ridicule the product. Many will refuse to taste it and even those who do are not exactly immediate converts. It is, after all, a full-bodied red wine that just happens to be fizzy, and quite often it will have a sweetness that is as unexpected in a red wine as the bubbles. Furthermore, the tannin grates against the smoothness of the mousse. I know, I've been there. If, however, you approach this style not as something you expect to drink on a regular basis, but as a speciality, you can really get into the wines. They are serious, but they are also great fun.

PAST AND PRESENT QUALITY

As in other countries which have no geographically based sparkling wine appellations, the biggest stumbling block in Australia has always been the lack of specific sparkling wine vineyards. Most of the country's sparkling wine producers claim to grow grapes specifically for the purpose or, at the very least, to contract growers on this basis. But more times than not, this merely means the grapes have been harvested early, which is not the same thing. For cheap fizz, this may be okay, but not for premium quality sparkling wine. Ideally a vineyard should be planted with clones suited to sparkling wine production, and trained in an appropriate way. An established vineyard can be adapted with a certain degree of success by canopy management and adjusting yields, but it takes several years to achieve the required balance, and a similar period to convert it back. Thus, unless the vineyard owner also happens to be the wine producer, he is unlikely to make such a long-term commitment.

However, there are some sparkling wine-designated vineyards in Australia, and Croser and Domaine Chandon are among the oldest. These have been established by Brian Croser and Tony Jordan, former

CHATEAU REMY VINEYARDS IN THE HILLS OF THE GREAT DIVIDING RANGE, AT AVOCA, VICTORIA

partners in a wine consultancy called Oenotec, and it is interesting that, at the grass-roots level these vineyards represent, they should opt for opposing sparkling wine philosophies. Croser has gone the *terroir* route and is now able to distinguish the suitability for still wine or sparkling from plots which are adjacent to one another within a strictly limited area. Jordan has opted for the mainstream champenois concept, which utilises a patchwork of sites that fall within a broad spectrum of acceptable parameters and can thus be woven into a final product that is superior to any of its constituent parts.

As to the varieties cultivated, it is no surprise that virtually all premium quality brands are dominated by the two classic Champagne grapes, Chardonnay and Pinot Noir. The champenois workhorse, Meunier, is more prevalent in Australia, where producers often utilise 20% or more, than it is in California, where relatively few *cuvées* contain this variety, and those that do invariably have less than 5%.

The Petit Meslier has been tried in Australia by James Irvine. One of Champagne's long lost varieties, it is currently undergoing a minuscule resurgence, Jacquesson having made a pure Petit Meslier *cuvée* in 1997 from 40-year-old vines that were planted by the Chiquet family in their Dizy vineyards 'for fun' and have miraculously survived replantings all around them. Both Bollinger and Roederer have taken back cuttings from Irvine's vineyard. Cheap Aussie fizz can contain everything but the kitchen sink, but of the grapes not already mentioned that have been used in premium sparkling wine, Marsanne seems to be the most promising.

From a vinification point of view, there is a tendency to keep the wines in tank far too long before bottling, particularly among producers of cheaper *cuvées*, while a number of those trying to craft finer wines rely too heavily on malolactic for complexity. However, the most basic observation to make about Australian fizz is that most premium sparkling wines are made by the transfer method, not *méthode champenoise*. And when you consider the quality of these wines, you could well ask who needs the *méthode champenoise*?

ALDRIDGE
See CRANSWICK

N/A
ALKOOMI WINES
FRANKLAND, WESTERN AUSTRALIA
Sheep farmers Mervyn and Judy Lange
regularly produce a number of fine quality
wines, among these only one fizz – a
sparkling Shiraz.
WINEMAKER
Kim Hart
HOUSE STYLE & RANGE
This wine is not generally distributed, and I
have tasted it only once, at the winery, several
years ago. There is thus no overall rating and
my notes will not be applicable to the current
cuvée, but Kim Hart had already produced a
number of vintages, so she was not embarking
on a learning curve, and although the wine
was deeply coloured and richly flavoured, it
had unattractively strange aromas.
ALKOOMI
Vintaged, méthode champenoise: 100% Shiraz

75
ALL SAINTS
RUTHERGLEN, VICTORIA
This turreted winery was constructed by
George Sutherland Smith in 1880 and is
classified today by the National Trust. It is
not dissimilar to Hollywood's idea of a French
Foreign Legion fort, except that it is built
out of red-clay bricks. Apparently Smith
called it All Saints because a number of local
vineyards were named after saints. All Saints'
main claim to fame is its fortified wines,
which is why when it was taken over in 1992,
the new owners, Brown Brothers, made this
its specialist fortified wine label.

All Saints does, however, have a certain
history for sparkling wines, having produced
in the distant past a sweetish Chasselas
'champagne' under its top of the range
Lyrebird label.
WINEMAKER
Neil Jericho
HOUSE STYLE & RANGE
The elegantly rich Cabernet with its sweetish,
spicy-ripe fruit is by far the best fizz here.
MÉTHODE TRADITIONELLE
*Vintaged, méthode champenoise: grape varieties not
revealed*
★ CABERNET SAUVIGNON
*Not vintaged, bottle-fermented: 100% Cabernet
Sauvignon*

ANGAS BRUT
See YALUMBA

ARENBERG
See D'ARENBERG

N/A
ASHTON HILLS VINEYARD
ASHTON, SOUTH AUSTRALIA
This boutique winery was established in the
Adelaide Hills near Mount Lofty in 1982.
WINEMAKER
Stephen George
HOUSE STYLE & RANGE
Highly rated, but not tasted by this author.
SALMON BRUT
Vintaged, méthode champenoise: Chardonnay, Pinot Noir

BARRAMUNDI
See CRANSWICK

BLUE LAKE RIDGE
See YALDARA

75
BLUE PYRENEES
AVOCA, VICTORIA
• 25,000 cases
• Group ownership - Rémy-Cointreau
Formerly known as Chateau Remy (no
accents), this property started off in 1963 as
a joint venture between Rémy Martin and
its Australian importer, Nathan & Wyeth,
with the intention of producing Australian
brandy. It was thus planted with distillation
quality grapes such as Doradillo and
Trebbiano. Rémy Martin took full control of
the enterprise in 1969, and in the 1970s,
when sparkling wine consumption was
increasing as rapidly as brandy consumption
was declining, the decision was made to
switch production to fizz. This necessitated
pulling out all the Doradillo and, as the
production geared up to produce sparkling
wines from the classic Champagne varieties,
the Trebbiano eventually went too.
WINEMAKER
Vincent Gere, Kim Hart
HOUSE STYLE & RANGE
When Trebbiano formed the base wine,
these *cuvées* were fat and very plain, but they
have acquired a leaner structure since
Chardonnay, Pinot Noir and Meunier have
been used. Even so, these wines tend to be
on the sweet side, which deflects from the
fruit and complex aromas. However, the
quality has gradually improved, the style has
softened, and the wines have shown
increasing elegance. The Estate Reserve has
the largest proportion of Meunier of any
current Australian fizz and, in true

champenois fashion, it is blended from 38
different wines.

In fact, the wines come from six clones of
three varieties grown on four soil types
under three microclimates. These are the
new vineyards that the estate began planting
throughout the Pyrenees district in 1985.
Only the two *cuvées* that are sold under the
Chateau Remy label are exclusively from the
original Avoca estate (1,000 cases of Brut and
just 100 cases of Rosé); their distribution is
restricted to the Hong Kong market, and not
tasted by this author since the early 1990s.

Gere claims that his Midnight Cuvée is
'unique in the world' being 'the only *méthode
champenoise* picked by hand at night'. Many
cuvées are manually picked, of course, and a
number are harvested at night, but this is
probably the only one that can claim to be
both. Fiddler's Creek is one of Australia's
cheapest *méthode champenoises*, presumably
because it is made with 75% of the *tailles*
rejected from Blue Pyrenees best wines.
FIDDLER'S CREEK
*Not vintaged, méthode champenoise: 35% Chardonnay,
25% Pinot Noir, 10% Meunier, 15% Sauvignon
Blanc, 15% Sémillon*
CHATEAU REMY BRUT
*Not vintaged, méthode champenoise: 80% Chardonnay,
20% Pinot Noir*
CHATEAU REMY ROSÉ BRUT
*Not vintaged, méthode champenoise: 20% Chardonnay,
80% Pinot Noir*
★ ESTATE RESERVE
*Vintaged, 15% reserves, méthode champenoise: 55%
Chardonnay, 30% Pinot Noir, 15% Meunier*
★☆ MIDNIGHT CUVÉE
*Vintaged, méthode champenoise: 90% Chardonnay,
7% Pinot Noir, 3% Meunier*

BLUESTONE
See TATACHILLA

BRIDGEWATER MILL
See PETALUMA

78
BROWN BROTHERS
VICTORIA
Established in 1889 by John Francis Brown,
whose father had planted vines, but did not
make wine. However, it was John Brown II
who really created the foundations of Brown
Brothers' reputation. In the 1970s, this company
was almost on its own in trying to convince
export markets of Australia's exciting potential
in the quality wine sector. Based in Milawa
in the State of Victoria, Brown Brothers
continues to go from success to success with
a vast range of innovative wines.
WINEMAKER
Terry Barnett

HOUSE STYLE & RANGE

The non-vintage Pinot Noir/Chardonnay has greatly improved over the last couple of years, going from a fat, slightly oxidative style to a much fresher and crisper wine, with well-focused peachy fruit enhanced by ripe acidity.

★ PINOT NOIR CHARDONNAY BRUT

Not vintaged, méthode champenoise: 30-35% Chardonnay, 60-65% Pinot Noir, 5-10% Meunier

★★ PINOT NOIR CHARDONNAY BRUT

Vintaged, méthode champenoise: 20% Chardonnay, 80% Pinot Noir

72
BRL HARDY

ADELAIDE, SOUTH AUSTRALIA

Established in 1853, Hardys grew into a very large company with a vast estate of vineyards as a result of taking over Houghton, Château Reynella and the Stanley Wine Company. It was then purchased itself by Berri-Renmano, a huge combine of cooperatives producing twice as much wine as Hardys, with five times as many vineyards. The new business, BRL Hardy, was launched as a public company, and is now one of Australia's four largest wine producers.

WINEMAKER

Ed Carr (with Richard Lowe for Leasingham)

HOUSE STYLE & RANGE

There is nothing wrong with the Brut Reserve and Grand Reserve Brut, but there is nothing special about them either, although Hardys Grand Reserve Champagne was something of a trendsetter in the 1970s, when it was sourced from Clare Valley Riesling and Sémillon.

In the Sir James range, the Shiraz is by far the best, with its soft, spicy, red-fruit richness, although some *cuvées* have more obvious coconutty oak than others – a plus or a minus depending on your preference. The basic non-vintage Sir James Brut is rather weak, while the vintaged Brut tends to be fat, oxidative and overblown, lacking acidity and therefore without finesse, although it is sourced from Yarra Yarra and Tasmania, which should make it a lot crisper and finer. Leasingham is a classic sparkling Shiraz, with more cedary than coconutty, oaky character.

Omni is a cheap fizz that has more individual character than most at its price point, with a reasonable structure of firm, creamy fruit, but it is the Nottage Hill Chardonnay that is the real winner for the price, with its fresh, fluffy, gently rich and creamy fruit. The Yarra Burn Chardonnay Pinot Noir is very fresh and *vif*, with zesty, lemony fruit, which remains youthful beyond its years.

OMNI BRUT

Not vintaged, transfer method: grape varieties not revealed

SIR JAMES BRUT

Not vintaged, transfer method: Chardonnay, Pinot Noir and other unrevealed varieties

HARDYS BRUT RESERVE

Vintaged, transfer method: grape varieties not revealed

HARDYS GRAND RESERVE BRUT

Vintaged, transfer method: grape varieties not revealed

★ LEASINGHAM CLASSIC CLARE 1991 SPARKLING SHIRAZ

Vintaged, transfer method: 100% Shiraz

★ NOTTAGE HILL SPARKLING CHARDONNAY BRUT

Vintaged, transfer method: 100% Chardonnay

SIR JAMES BRUT

Vintaged, transfer method: Chardonnay, Pinot Noir, Meunier

★ SIR JAMES SPARKLING SHIRAZ

Vintaged, transfer method: 100% Shiraz

★ YARRA BURN CHARDONNAY PINOT NOIR BRUT

Vintaged, transfer method: Chardonnay, Pinot Noir

CARRINGTON

See ORLANDO

70
CASSEGRAIN

PORT MACQUARIE, NEW SOUTH WALES

John Cassegrain established this winery in 1980 at Port Macquarie in the Hastings River region which some believe to be too wet and windy for viticulture. However, although there have been highs and lows, some of the highs have been very exciting indeed. It was due to this uncertain climate that Cassegrain initially planted Chambourcin, and while the still wine from this obscure red hybrid has not been special, it might well make a more interesting fizz if D'Arenberg's *cuvée* is anything to go by.

WINEMAKER

John Cassegrain, Glen Goodall

HOUSE STYLE & RANGE

Sparkling wine production commenced as recently as 1992, with 1993 the first commercial vintage. The experimental *cuvée* produced in 1992 was very encouraging, the 1993 was an award-winning *cuvée* made with 17% Chardonnay and 83% Pinot Noir and the 1994 was a more traditional 40/60 blend.

In Cassegrain's case, I think the more Pinot included in the blend the better. The style is rich, smooth and full-bodied, but is sometimes spoilt by too much sulphur, although this is clean and thus free, not fixed, and will turn toasty if kept well-cellared for 12 months or so.

★ CASSEGRAIN HASTINGS BRUT

Vintaged, méthode champenoise: 40% Chardonnay, 60% Pinot Noir

CHANDON

See DOMAINE CHANDON

CHATEAU REMY

See BLUE PYRENEES

N/A
CLEVELAND WINERY

LANCEFIELD, VICTORIA

Established in 1984, when Keith and Lynette Brien restored this 19th century manor house in the heart of the Macedon Ranges, a developing district within the Central Victoria region. They own a four-hectare vineyard planted almost entirely with Chardonnay and Pinot Noir, although there is a small plot of Cabernet Sauvignon.

The early-June picking date for the Cabernet Sauvignon illustrates how cool the growing season is for a country where the first grapes are picked at midnight on New Year's Day (Château Hornsby, Alice Springs), although the fact that it grows at all, let alone ripens to a very high quality, contrasts the difference with the Champagne region, where Cabernet Sauvignon cannot ripen at all.

WINEMAKER

Keith & Lynette Brien

HOUSE STYLE & RANGE

Insufficient experience to give an overall rating, but the 1994 was rich and malty, with excellent high acidity, but it lacked finesse. Potential seems to be very good indeed.

MACEDON BRUT

Vintaged, méthode champenoise: 75% Chardonnay, 25% Pinot Noir

CLOVER HILL

See TALTARNI

75
COCKATOO RIDGE

SOUTH AUSTRALIA

A joint venture between Geoff Merrill, the 'flying moustache' of Mount Hurtle fame, and Yalumba. Mount Hurtle is built on a ridge, and there are always flocks of noisy cockatoos in the trees and gardens surrounding it, so in 1992 Merril released some wines under the Cockatoo Ridge label, and they literally took off, with annual sales reaching 200,000 cases by the second year.

88
DOMAINE CHANDON

COLDSTREAM, VICTORIA

- 60,000 cases
- Other labels - Green Point (used for export markets)

Under the auspices of Dr Tony Jordan, Domaine Chandon achieved an international standard in 1989, its third vintage, since when the wines have improved at an ever-faster rate. Prior to 1989, the only exceptional wine produced here was the 1986 Blanc de Blancs, which is probably why the first few vintages of Brut were all Chardonnay-dominated.

The early peak in Domaine Chandon's success can be put down to the blending of numerous base wines from many different areas. There are 50 hectares at Coldstream itself, in the Yarra Valley, as well as 40 hectares in the Strathbogie Ranges. Grapes are also purchased from these two districts plus such diverse areas as Coonawarra, Geelong, Mansfield, Macedon, Mornington Peninsula, Tasmania (Cool River) and Western Australia (King Valley and Pemberton).

The next turning point was one of style, and this started in 1993, since when the vintaged Brut has been Pinot-led, although this does not necessarily infer a greater percentage of that grape. Jordan admits he got the *modus operandi* wrong in the beginning, when he resolutely avoided malolactic, yet the wines are still around to show how good he was even then. The man has such a light touch that there was no danger of him making the mistake of overdoing the malolactic. So many New World sparkling wines are dominated by malolactic aromas, but Jordan puts just 30% of his base wines through the process, and the result is so beautifully understated that it merely adds a touch of softness and creaminess to the finish.

WINEMAKER
Tony Jordan, Wayne Donaldson

HOUSE STYLE & RANGE
Since the Brut came right with the 1989

vintage, each new release has been better than the last. The 1989 was dominated by exceptionally elegant Chardonnay. Despite Jordan's assertion that these *cuvées* became Pinot-dominated from the 1993 vintage, The 1990 has a wonderful Pinot richness. The 1991 was the first vintage to develop true biscuity finesse, but the 1992 was firmer with greater finesse, although it took longer to show it.

It is the brightness of the Pinot fruit that grips most about the 1993, while the 1994 has a firmness which keeps the wine quite tight as it slowly builds its biscuity richness. The 1995 is the best vintage so far, with a lovely understated richness, Pinot-led front and mid-palate, and creamy-smooth Chardonnay finesse on the finish plus a wonderful cushiony mousse.

The Rosé Brut is unashamedly upfront in every department; sumptuous on the nose, and even more delicious on the palate. The fruit is lovely when fresh, but with a little bottle-age develops a smooth vanilla finesse on the finish. At times it seems like pure Pinot Noir, but amazingly contains almost 60% Chardonnay.

The progress of the Blanc de Blancs has been strange. No one could deny that the 1986 Blanc de Blancs was a lovely wine and developed beautifully for several years. The mystery is why subsequent vintages were rather solid and foursquare, particularly as Jordan's Domaine Chandon has been so far ahead of the game. The 1993 is in a different class to all but the 1986, and probably has the edge over that too. A lovely elegant wine, with fresh fruit and good finesse.

The Cuvée Riche is the equivalent of a Champagne Doux (50g/l residual sugar) a very sweet style that is no longer produced in Champagne itself. Earlier bottlings have been amylic, but Jordan has since crafted a soft, sensuous, beautifully balanced dessert fizz.

★★ BLANC DE BLANCS BRUT
   Vintaged, méthode champenoise: 100% Chardonnay
★★ BLANC DE NOIRS BRUT
   Vintaged, méthode champenoise: 100% Pinot Noir
★★ BRUT
   Vintaged, méthode champenoise: 47% Chardonnay, 51% Pinot Noir, 2% Meunier
★ CUVÉE RICHE
   Not vintaged, méthode champenoise: 42% Chardonnay, 58% Pinot Noir
★★ ROSÉ BRUT
   Vintaged, méthode champenoise: 40% Chardonnay, 60% Pinot Noir

PANORAMIC VIEW FROM THE TASTING ROOM

WINEMAKER
Geoff Merrill

HOUSE STYLE & RANGE
The grapes are sourced from across regional and state boundaries, providing a fat, fresh fizz with a touch of vanilla on the finish. A serious wine at a silly price.

★ BRUT
   Not vintaged, méthode champenoise: Chardonnay, Pinot Noir, Sémillon

73
CRAIGMOOR

MUDGEE, NEW SOUTH WALES

- 1,000 cases
- Group ownership - Orlando

Established in 1858 by Adam Roth, a German émigré who planted the first Mudgee vineyards. In the 1930s Craigmoor became one of the first, some say the very first, to cultivate Chardonnay grapes in Australia. It was purchased in 1988 by Wyndham Estate, which itself was taken over by the huge Orlando group in 1990.

WINEMAKER
Robert Paul

HOUSE STYLE & RANGE
Big, rich and malty.

★ CRAIGMOOR VINTAGE CHARDONNAY 1994 BRUT
   Vintaged, transfer method: 85% Chardonnay, 15% Pinot Noir

72
THE CRANSWICK ESTATE

GRIFFITH, NEW SOUTH WALES

- Other labels - Aldridge Estate, Barramund

Originally built in 1976 by Cinzano for vermouth and bulk fortified wine production, this facility was vastly under-utilised until Graham Cranswick-Smith took over as genera manager in 1986 and instigated the bulk production of varietal wines. As sales of vermouth declined, Cranswick-Smith proposed the creation of its own branded range of wines to take advantage of the rapidl growing export market. However, logical as this was, Cinzano was not interested in developing an Australian wine brand and in 1990 decided to sell up. Cranswick-Smith led a successful management buy-out (completed in March 1991) and the winery, with its 90 hectares of vineyards, was renamed The Cranswick Estate. The new owners decided to keep out of the home market for the first five years, while they concentrated on exports. This was a fateful decision because from 1995 he company has won export awards by the bucket-load, and is now the seventh-largest Australian wine exporter. In addition to The Cranswick Estate's own vineyards, production is also sourced from 120 Riverina growers and, in 1994, the company began planting the 450-hectare Cocoparra vineyard (*Cocoparra* is Aboriginal for Kookaburra) which was developed using state-of-the-art technology, including satellite mapping.

WINEMAKER
Andrew Schulz, Ian Hongell

HOUSE STYLE & RANGE
Made from relatively inexpensive Riverina fruit, most of these wines can battle it out on price but offer good value for money, and some can rise above their station, particularly under The Cranswick Estate label. The Pinot/Chardonnay Brut, for instance, has a very creamy, almost oaky, smoothness underlying an impressive zesty, lemony flavour, but it is the Sparkling Shiraz that is truly out of Riverina's class, with a lovely ripeness of blackcurrant/raspberry fruit, and a drier style than most.

Barramundi has the edge over Aldridge Estate because of its ripe, raspberry-jam fruit, much to be expected from a Riverina product, and it develops a sweet, creamy, coffee-like complexity over six to 12 months. While toffee is to be avoided in a sparkling wine of any finesse, it's a real bonus in fizz this cheap. Aldridge Estate is not to be sniffed at; in fact, for off-the-shelf drinking, its light-bodied, gentle fruit offers more elegance for the price. And both Aldridge Estate and Barramundi are *cuve close*!

☆ ALDRIDGE ESTATE BRUT
Not vintaged, cuve close: Cabernet Sauvignon, Chardonnay, Colombard, Merlot, Sémillon

☆ BARRAMUNDI BRUT
Not vintaged, cuve close: Cabernet Sauvignon, Chardonnay, Colombard, Merlot, Sémillon

★ THE CRANSWICK ESTATE PINOT CHARDONNAY BRUT
Not vintaged, transfer method: 55% Chardonnay, 45% Pinot Noir

★☆ THE CRANSWICK ESTATE SPARKLING SHIRAZ
Not vintaged, transfer method: 100% Shiraz

CROSER
See PETALUMA

75
D'ARENBERG
MCLAREN VALE, SOUTH AUSTRALIA
2,000 cases
Established in 1912, D'Arenberg has made sparkling Shiraz on and off since the 1960s, but now mostly concentrates on Chambourcin, a hybrid of uncertain parentage. Fizzy Chambourcin might not be the greatest

sparkling wine in the world, but it is a good one, yet it is a wine that will never be sold in EU countries because the bureaucrats in Brussels have declared it illegal.

WINEMAKER
Chester Osborn

HOUSE STYLE & RANGE
The Chambourcin is a fresh, light and creamy fizzy red with a simple but enjoyable raspberry flavour and a dry style.

THE MCLAREN VALE MILLENNIUM MAGNUM
Not vintaged, transfer method: 100% Shiraz

★ THE PEPPERMINT PADDOCK CHAMBOURCIN
Vintaged, transfer method: 100% Chambourcin

DEAKIN ESTATE
See SUNNYCLIFF

70
DELATITE
MANSFIELD, VICTORIA
This small, family-owned venture planted its vineyard in 1968, contenting itself with selling grapes to start with, before building a winery between 1981 and 1982. The first table wines were produced in 1982 and the first sparkling wines in 1988.

WINEMAKER
Rosalind Ritchie

HOUSE STYLE & RANGE
Creamy richness of fruit.

DEMELZA BRUT
Not vintaged, bottle-fermented: 35% Chardonnay, 65% Pinot Noir

DEMELZA
See DELATITE

EDEN CREST
See IRVINE

EDWARDS & CHAFFEY
See SEAVIEW

'ELIZA'
See PADTHAWAY

FIDDLER'S CREEK
See BLUE PYRENEES

N/A
GRANT BURGE
TANUNDA, SOUTH AUSTRALIA
Established in 1988 by Grant Burge, co-founder of Krondorf (now part of Mildara Blass). He purchased this historic estate, formerly known as Jacob's Morooroo, through which he has rapidly created a brilliant reputation for consistency, quality and value for his eponymous brand.

WINEMAKER
Grant Burge

HOUSE STYLE & RANGE
Not yet established with anything like the same degree of consistency as Grant Burge's still wines, this fizz can sometimes have a green, malic edge; at other times it is softer with a touch of vanilla finesse on the finish.

METHODE TRADITIONELLE BRUT
Not vintaged, méthode champenoise: 50% Chardonnay, 50% Pinot Noir

GREEN POINT
See DOMAINE CHANDON

N/A
HANGING ROCK
NEWHAM, VICTORIA
Established in 1982 by John Ellis whose vineyards include blocks designated specifically for sparkling wine.

WINEMAKER
John Ellis

HOUSE STYLE & RANGE
Tasted just once, thus an overall rating is not possible, but it was clearly a full-bodied, richly flavoured sparkling wine that had been made in a oxidatively complexed style. Not cheap, but very distinctive and therefore divides opinion.

MACEDON BRUT
Not vintaged, méthode champenoise: Chardonnay, Pinot Noir

HARPER'S RIDGE
See SEAVIEW

80 VALUE
HASELGROVE
MCLAREN VALE, SOUTH AUSTRALIA
Established in 1980 by James Haselgrove.

WINEMAKER
Nick Haselgrove

HOUSE STYLE & RANGE
Full of deliciously tangy, bilberry and cranberry fruit, this lavishly flavoured fizz is marked by its fresh, billowy mousse. This is a *solera*-based sparkling wine that Nick Haselgrove laid down as recently as 1991. The first *cuvée* was drawn off in 1993 and if you search the label you should find the SG (Sparkling Garnet) code number that cracks the year of the primary base wine, as SG1 was effectively 1993-based, SG2 was 1994-based and so on.

The wine gets an added kick from the Australian 'port' used for the *dosage*. These *cuvées* are uncannily similar in style and quality, so the *solera* obviously works well, even if it has not been going that long. Indeed, a young *solera* should be preferable for sparkling wine production because old *soleras* have too many drawbacks in terms of terpenes and coarse oxidative characteristics.

HASELGROVE MCLAREN VALE SPARKLING GARNET
Not vintaged, méthode champenoise: 90% Shiraz, 10% Grenache

N/A
IRVINE
EDEN VALLEY, SOUTH AUSTRALIA
Also called Royal Champagne Enterprises, this small vineyard and winery was established in 1983 by James Irvine, who consulted for various wineries, and has single-handedly revived interest in one of Champagne's long-lost grape varieties, the Petit Meslier. It was on a trip to Champagne with his wife Marjorie that he first heard about this old vine. When he returned he discovered six Petit Meslier vines growing in a South Australian vineyard, believed to be the only examples of this variety in the entire country. He set up Royal Champagne Vineyards and cultivated his own small-holding with cuttings from these vines. He also grows Chardonnay and Merlot, but with the exception of an excellent still wine called Grand Merlot, Irvine specialises in sparkling wine and he obviously loves the style.
WINEMAKER
James Irvine
HOUSE STYLE & RANGE
The Merlot Brut is one of Australia's best sparkling red wines: a feast of a wine with the emphasis on rich, juicy Merlot fruit, and a backtaste of smooth, creamy, toasty-coffee oak. Irvine reckons that his Cuvée Royale needs six to ten years on its yeast, and will develop for a further five years after disgorgement. I'm not so sure. I was disappointed with the dull 1986 at six years old, but impressed by the lemony, toasty 1988 at 10 years old. At 15 years old the 1983 has some terpene character, softened by a honeyed finish. Without following these wines year in, year out as Irvine does, it is impossible to be sure, but perhaps he should put this *cuvée* on the market when its much younger, then we might be able to discover for ourselves.

Eden Crest Meslier, on the other hand, is always sold young, which suits the crisp, zesty varietal style. Who knows what Petit Meslier should taste like; this one has a lime and lavendar character. I can quite imagine it picking up terpenes so I think Irvine is right to make no attempt to induce any autolytic character, getting the wine off the yeast as soon as its secondary fermentation is complete.

★★☆ MERLOT BRUT
Not vintaged, méthode champenoise: 100% Merlot

☆★ BRUT ROYALE
Vintaged, méthode champenoise: 90% Chardonnay, 10% Petit Meslier

★ EDEN CREST MESLIER BRUT
Vintaged, méthode champenoise: 100% Petit Meslier

N/A
JANSZ
PIPER'S RIVER, TASMANIA
• 6,000 cases (16,000 when the new non-vintage comes on stream)

Formerly majority-owned by Louis Roederer, but sold to Joe Chromy in 1994, when it became part of the Heemskerk Group, along with Rochecombe Vineyard and Buchanans Vineyard. In February 1998, Chromy sold the Heemskerk Group to Dr Andrew Pirie of Piper's Brook, the most dynamic and successful wine producer in Tasmania. This sale did not, however, include the exciting new RV sparkling wine (*see* REBECCA VINEYARD), but it did include Jansz. However, fizz was not Pirie's game and within five weeks he sold Jansz brand to Samuel Smith & Son and entered into a long-term contract to supply grapes from the former Heemskerk vineyards. Jansz could not have found a better home, as Samuel Smith & Sons is famous for Yalumba premium sparkling wines, not to mention the ever-popular Angas Brut range. Geoff Linton stepped into the breach to make the 1998 vintage, but Tony Davis is due to become Jansz's permanent winemaker.
WINEMAKER
Tony Davis
HOUSE STYLE & RANGE
There are some high-powered people in the Australian fizz business who seriously doubt the potential of Tasmania in general and Heemskerk vineyards in particular, (Jean-Claude Rouzaud claimed the only reason he sold it was because he could not harvest ripe grapes here).

But some very good high points have been reached in certain vintages of Jansz and, under the smooth efficiency of the Yalumba fizz machine, time will tell whether it is a problem of climate or man. Certainly there have been some bad wines produced here, not least the first vintage, 1990, which had a blatant winemaking fault. But with such a highly prestigious Champagne house as Roederer giving its blessing to the sparkling wine potential of Tasmania, nobody dared suggest the first vintage was crap. Not locally anyway, because it received such rave reviews that a stocks sold out within 12 weeks.

The 1991 showed early promise, but I have not tasted it recently, and would not stake my reputation on it because the 1992 also showed early promise, yet it has developed an oxidised, malolactic taste of toffee that has robbed the wine of all finesse. The 1993 has thankfully developed nicely (so far!), with its classic lean structure and juicy fruit acidity, slowly yielding a lovely creamy, biscuity complexity.

A new non-vintage *cuvée* is due to be produced as from 1999. Its varietal composition will be the reverse of the original vintaged Jansz, and will consist of about one-third declassified vintage Jansz plus grapes sourced from cool-climate areas of South Australia.

BRUT CUVÉE
Not vintaged, méthode champenoise: 40% Chardonnay, 60% Pinot Noir

BRUT CUVÉE
Vintaged, méthode champenoise: 60% Chardonnay, 40% Pinot Noir

N/A
HILL OF HOPE
BROKE, NEW SOUTH WALES
Hill of Hope was established in 1996 at the former Saxonvale winery, in the Broke-Fordwich area, a recently designated district of the Hunter Valley. Owner Michael Hope owned 75 hectares of vineyards in the locality before he purchased Saxonvale, and he is due to plant a further 25 hectares.
WINEMAKER
Simon Gilbert
HOUSE STYLE & RANGE
It is impossible to judge the potential of any sparkling wine on a single vintage, particularly its first, but although I liked the ripe, sweet succulence on the finish of Hill of Hope's 1996, I was concerned by its deep yellow colour and the rapid evolution of the fruit.
BLANC DE NOIRS BRUT
Vintaged, méthode champenoise: 100% Pinot Noir

VIEW ACROSS THE EDEN VALLEY WHERE JAMES IRVINE IS EXPERIMENTING WITH PETIT MESLIER GRAPES IN HIS SPARKLING WINE CUVÉES

82
HOLLICK
COONAWARRA, SOUTH AUSTRALIA
• 1,000 cases
This small, high-quality winery was established in 1983 by Ian Hollick and began sparkling wine production in 1986, making a name for its vintaged Cornel Brut. It truly excels with its sparkling Merlot, first produced in 1993.
WINEMAKER
Ian Hollick, Matt Pellew
HOUSE STYLE & RANGE
The Merlot has huge fruity oak and floral aromas, with cherry, plum and blackberry fruit on the palate. A richly flavoured fizz, it can become jammy and very oaky with bottle-age, but always has some sweetness, although not sweet as most Australian sparkling reds.
★☆ SPARKLING MERLOT, COONAWARRA
Vintaged, méthode champenoise: 100% Merlot

JACOB'S CREEK
See ORLANDO

N/A
KATNOOK ESTATE
COONAWARRA, SOUTH AUSTRALIA
• Group ownership - part of the Wingara Wine Group, which also owns Sunnycliff
Established in 1980, this Coonawarra winery has deservedly won recognition for its stylish range of intensely flavoured wines, but has yet to earn a reputation for anything sparkling, although it has been producing this style since 1984.
WINEMAKER
Wayne Stehbens
HOUSE STYLE & RANGE
This blanc de blancs is made in a still wine style, with too much malolactic, but there is enough promise underneath to warrant keeping an eye on developments.

CHARDONNAY BRUT
Vintaged, transfer method: 86% Chardonnay, 8.5% Pinot Noir, 5.5% Meunier

75
KILLAWARRA
GREAT WESTERN VIA ARAFAT, VICTORIA
The Killawarra brand was established in 1969 by a Melbourne marketing company which, according to Len Evans' *Complete Book of Australian Wine*, purchased bulk supplies of gold medal-winning wines and sold them under the Killawarra label.
Perhaps Killawarra is best remembered for

its hexagonal-shaped bag-in-the-box wines (called cask wines in Australia), which became such an instant hit on the home market in 1977 that Killawarra quickly changed to a standard box shape in order to keep up with demand. The company was then sold to Swift & Moore, and eventually became part of Southcorp via Wynns.
WINEMAKER
Ian Shepherd
HOUSE STYLE & RANGE
The Brut style, whatever the *cuvée*, tends to be full to fat, relying on bubbles to provide crispness, and possessing more character than finesse, but decent enough. The Sparkling Shiraz/Cabernet is the winner: fruit-driven, not at all oaky, with lots of very fresh, fleshy fruit and the unmistakable peppery-spice varietal signature of Shiraz dominating.
★☆ PREMIER SPARKLING SHIRAZ CABERNET
Not vintaged, transfer method: 47% Cabernet Sauvignon, 53% Shiraz
CHARDONNAY BLANC DE BLANCS
Vintaged, transfer method: 100% Chardonnay
PREMIER BRUT
Vintaged, transfer method: 8% Chardonnay, 92% Pinot Noir

LEASINGHAM
See BRL HARDY

LISA CUVÉE
See BRIAN MCGUIGAN WINES

75
STEFANO LUBIANA
GRANTON, TASMANIA
• 1,600 cases
Small family-owned winery established in 1990 by Steve 'Stefano' and Monique Lubiana, whose first sparkling wine was made as recently as 1993.
WINEMAKER
Steve Lubiana
HOUSE STYLE & RANGE
Off the shelf, the non-vintage is definitely the best choice, with rich, tangy fruit and complex, malty aromas, but the vintage could be worth cellaring for a year or two. Although the vintage is spoiled by amylic aromas, these are likely to drop out after a while, and the fruit underneath is deliciously young and sherbety.
★ STEFANO LUBIANA NV BRUT
Not vintaged, méthode champenoise: 20% Chardonnay, 80% Pinot Noir
★ STEFANO LUBIANA 1995 BRUT
Vintaged, méthode champenoise: 40% Chardonnay, 60% Pinot Noir

MACEDON
See CLEVELAND, AND HANGING ROCK

75
MARIENBERG
MCLAREN VALE, SOUTH AUSTRALIA
• 500 cases
This winery was established in 1966 by Australia's first woman winemaker, Ursula Marie Pridham, who won numerous honours for her wines, including the first gold medal awarded to an Australian female winemaker. Pridham retired in 1990 and the new owners, Terry and Jill Hill, have gone from strength to strength under the guiding hand of one of the country's finest winemakers.
WINEMAKER
Grant Burge
HOUSE STYLE & RANGE
A fine quality of firm fruit, with some biscuity complexity, yet still age-worthy.
★ MARIENBERG PINOT CHARDONNAY NICOLLE BRUT
Not vintaged, méthode champenoise: 30% Chardonnay, 70% Pinot Noir

N/A
BRIAN MCGUIGAN WINES
CESSNOCK, NEW SOUTH WALES
Established in 1992, the famous McGuigan name is used in two different formats; the company trades under the title of Brian McGuigan Wines, while the wines are labelled McGuigan Brothers.
WINEMAKER
Peter Hall
HOUSE STYLE & RANGE
An interesting twist on the *méthode champenoise* theme here is that the yeast in the *liqueur d'expédition* is mixed with grape juice, not wine. The primary aim is to produce a much softer, richer style than most Australian fizz, which McGuigan believes to be too acidic and lacking flavour. How the quality and style of this wine will evolve in future *cuvées* is anyone's guess, since it was first produced as recently as 1996, but the bottle I tasted recently had a certain smoky complexity, although it is rather foursquare.
LISA CUVÉE BRUT
Not vintaged, méthode champenoise: Chardonnay, Sémillon

75
MITCHELTON
NAGAMBIE, VICTORIA
• Group ownership - Petaluma
Mitchelton's chief winemaker, Don Lewis, has produced sparkling wines here since the winery was established in 1973, when he had the legendary Colin Preece on call as consultant. After some 20 years' experience he had become convinced by the early 1990s that a small proportion of barrel-fermented Marsanne was an important breakthrough,

and Mitchelton's Nattier CH/MA was an excellent example of the promise this Rhône variety has for fattening up early-harvested Chardonnay. Yet just a few years later, the Nattier label is no longer used, and no Mitchelton sparkling wine contains any Marsanne, barrel-fermented or not. The Nattier label is now utilised by the firm's Melbourne distributor for an inexpensive own-label wine range produced under contract by Mitchelton, but Lewis has not given up on Marsanne, suggesting it might be used in future *cuvées*.

WINEMAKER
Don Lewis

HOUSE STYLE & RANGE
The sparkling wine produced here today is sold under the Preece label, named in honour of Colin Preece, and made from Goulburn Valley fruit. It is a good quality premium sparkling wine, but not an outstanding one, although it does possess some malolactic complexity. Perhaps this is a reflection of how our expectations have increased as sparkling wines have progressed, but Preece does not strike me as advanced for its time as Nattier was five years ago.

★ PREECE SPARKLING PINOT-CHARDONNAY
Vintaged, méthode champenoise: 50% Chardonnay, 50% Pinot Noir

75
MORRIS
RUTHERGLEN, VICTORIA
- 5,100 cases
- Group ownership – Orlando

Morris is a great old Australian wine name, established in 1897, and long since famous for its brilliant fortified wines. Although this winery belongs to one of Australia's four largest groups, the original owners are still involved.

WINEMAKER
David Morris

HOUSE STYLE & RANGE
Flavour-packed and definitely in the very creamy, oaky category, but then the Morris family has never done anything by halves.

★ MORRIS SHIRAZ-DURIF BRUT
Not vintaged, méthode champenoise: 25% Durif, 75% Shiraz

75
MOUNTADAM
EDEN VALLEY, SOUTH AUSTRALIA
- 1,000 cases

This venture in Eden Valley was established in 1972 by David Wynn, founder of the legendary Wynns Coonawarra Estate (now part of Southcorp). Since 1995 Mountadam has belonged to Wynn's son, Adam, who has been its chief winemaker since 1984.

WINEMAKER

Adam Wynn

HOUSE STYLE & RANGE
Wynn allows his sparkling wine a pale rosé hue because he believes that all the best non-rosé Champagnes are not decolourised and are thus 'usually pink'. In fact, they are not. Since Dom Pérignon invented the *coquard* press, all Champagne producers have taken pride in making the palest possible *cuvée* (without resorting to artificial means). Colour often creeps into the base wine, but will drop out prior to or during second fermentation. When the base wine possesses too much colour, a good producer will leave it, but its presence in the final product will be a reminder that he or she could have done better. However, colour is not intrinsically a quality problem; if Wynn wants a slight blush, that is his prerogative, and its pink tinge is visually attractive. The only dispute I have with Mountadam is that the malolactic influence is too dominant, layering the wine with creamy-toffee flavours which detract from its finesse. There is also a coconut character in the 1992 that is also too obvious. That said, the richness of these wines is outstanding, and the raw materials are high grade (helped along no doubt by crop thinning), which is why Mountadam deserves a good overall rating. However, a little fine-tuning of the malolactic would easily increase this to 85 points or more.

★ MOUNTADAM BRUT
Vintaged, méthode champenoise: Chardonnay, Pinot Noir

80
NORMANS
CLARENDON, SOUTH AUSTRALIA
The origins of this brand date back to 1853, when Jesse Norman, a brewer from Cambridge, planted his first vineyard. Normans remained a family business for five generations of owner-winemakers until 1982, when it was sold. It kept a low profile until becoming a publicly listed company in 1994, since when it has started to achieve the success it deserves.

WINEMAKER
Brian Light

HOUSE STYLE & RANGE
An underrated producer of sparkling wines, spoilt only by the amylic, Cava-styled basic non-vintage brut, which is not in the same class as the rest of the range. The Conquest has improved tremendously since the Chenin

Blanc has been dropped. It now has a nice *mélange* of fruit buoyed up by a lovely cushiony mousse. Normans Brut Pinot Noir is serious stuff indeed, with a lovely fluffy mousse and brilliant balance, which packs in plenty of real Pinot flavour despite the light-bodied structure. Pinot Noir (clone D2V5) obviously works well for this producer.

BRUT
Vintaged, bottle-fermented: Chenin Blanc, Sémillon, Trebbiano

★★ BRUT PINOT NOIR
Vintaged, bottle-fermented: 100% Pinot Noir

★ CONQUEST BRUT
Vintaged, bottle-fermented: 20% Grenache, 75% Pinot Noir, 5% Riesling

NOTTAGE HILL
See BRL HARDY

OMNI
See BRL HARDY

70
ORLANDO
ROWLAND FLAT, SOUTH AUSTRALIA
- 700,000 cases
- Group ownership – includes sparkling wines from Craigmoor, Jacob's Creek, Morris, Richmond Grove and Wyndham Estate (*see individual brands*)

This huge group, known both as Orlando Wines and Orlando Wyndham, started out in 1847 as G Gramp & Sons at Rowland Flat, the company's headquarters today. Now owned by the French Pernod-Ricard group, Orlando produces a quarter of Australia's wine production through a number of wineries and brands. Apart from the recently launched Trilogy, the brand most strongly linked to Orlando itself is Carrington, the full range of which is listed below.

Carrington was first produced in 1975, when almost all the brut-style sparkling wines in Australia were sold as so-called 'champagne' and even at the time of writing Carrington Brut was still being labelled as *Fine Champagne* on Australia's home market, although it must drop 'Champagne' from all its labels very soon, in accordance with the agreement between France and Australia.

WINEMAKER
Bernard Hickin

HOUSE STYLE & RANGE
Carrington Brut is a firm and flavourful wine with some creamy fruit on nose and palate. Carrington Rosé derives its colour from the addition of red wine in the *dosage*, which is legal in Champagne, but frowned upon because the red-wine character is disproportionately magnified by the process of disgorgement. At this inexpensive level,

however, Bernard Hickin seems to have mastered the trick, having created a fruity fizz for everyday drinking that has no overtly red-wine aromas. I have also been impressed by how this rosé picks up a touch of biscuity complexity if kept for six or nine months.

The vintaged Carrington Brut is a fresh, easy-drinking *cuvée* with soft, vanilla fruit. Trilogy is a blend of three different vintages with elegant fruit aromas and plenty of ripe acidity, but it could do with a firmer balance of alcohol to achieve a higher rating. Jacob's Creek Brut has a better alcohol structure, but it lacks acidity, is somewhat sweet, and although not exactly amylic, it definitely has cool-ferment fruit, such as softly ripe poached pears. This makes it an eminently commercial wine, but not really the sort of thing to excite the sparkling wine aficionado.

CARRINGTON BRUT
Not vintaged, transfer method: Chenin Blanc, Grenache, Sémillon and other unrevealed varieties

✭ CARRINGTON ROSÉ BRUT
Not vintaged, transfer method: Grenache, Sémillon and other unrevealed varieties

★ JACOB'S CREEK BRUT
Not vintaged, transfer method: Chardonnay, Pinot Noir

★ TRILOGY BRUT
Not vintaged, transfer method: 70% Chardonnay, 20% Pinot Noir, 10% Meunier

✭ CARRINGTON BRUT
Vintaged, transfer method: Chardonnay, Pinot Noir and other unrevealed varieties

N/A
PADTHAWAY ESTATE
PADTHAWAY, SOUTH AUSTRALIA
• 3,000 cases
This estate dates back to 1847, when Robert and Eliza Lawson settled here from Scotland. They named the 22,000-hectare property Padthaway Station, and it grew to 32,000 hectares in the 30 years they lived there. Padthaway Station remained in the Lawson family until the present owners purchased 50 hectares of the diminished property, including all the original buildings, in 1980, when it was renamed Padthaway Estate.

WINEMAKER
Nigel Catt

HOUSE STYLE & RANGE
I knew these sparkling wines better when they were made by Leigh Clarnette, who used more Chardonnay and, in 1990, introduced the overnight chilling of hand-picked grapes prior to pressing. The difference in finesse

between the 1990 and 1991 vintages and the previous two years was marked indeed. The Eliza and Sparkling Burgundy are produced in tiny quantities (250 cases each) and sold exclusively through the cellar door.

PINOT NOIR CHARDONNAY BRUT
Vintaged, méthode champenoise: 12% Chardonnay, 85% Pinot Noir, 3% Meunier

'ELIZA' PINOT NOIR BRUT
Vintaged, méthode champenoise: 100% Pinot Noir

SPARKLING BURGUNDY
Vintaged, méthode champenoise: 85% Pinot Noir, 15% Cabernet Sauvignon

75
PENLEY
COONAWARRA, SOUTH AUSTRALIA
• 500 cases
This Coonawarra winery was established in 1988 by Kym Tolley, whose mother was a Penfolds and father a Tolley, thus the name Penley. Historically, all grapes used were purchased, but Penley's own vineyards, planted especially for sparkling wine, came on stream in 1993 and have been used ever since.

WINEMAKER
Kym Tolley

HOUSE STYLE & RANGE
An interesting sparkling wine composed primarily of Coonawarra Pinot Noir, which is almost nonexistent these days, but provides a sharp and zesty fizz with a nice touch of malolactic complexity. Some vintages, like the 1990, have exceptional finesse indeed.

★ PINOT CHARDONNAY BRUT
Vintaged, méthode champenoise: 15% Chardonnay, 85% Pinot Noir

PEPPERMINT PADDOCK
See CASSEGRAIN

N/A
PLANTAGENET
MOUNT BARKER, WESTERN AUSTRALIA
Named after the shire in which it is situated, Plantagenet was once an apple-packing shed, but was converted into a winery in 1974 to process the grapes harvested from vineyards planted six years earlier. Initially the grapes had been sold to other wineries, but when Plantagenet started making its own wines, it became the first enterprise to market them under the Mount Barker appellation. The first sparkling wine was produced in 1990.

WINEMAKER
Gavin Berry, Tony Davis

HOUSE STYLE & RANGE
It is early days, and I have tasted only two of the four wines released so far, thus cannot give Plantagenet an overall rating. The 1992 was soft and ripe, while the 1993 had very high acidity which suggests these wines

should have been released in reverse order, but the common style factor is a maltiness that may or may not be to your liking, and should be toned down if Plantagenet wants more finesse in this wine. This fizz is interesting and deserves to be followed, but at the moment Plantagenet's still wines are better.

PLANTAGENET 1992 BRUT
Vintaged, méthode champenoise: 20% Chardonnay, 80% Pinot Noir

PREECE
See MITCHELTON

N/A
REBECCA VINEYARD
WEST TAMOR, TASMANIA
Just before Joe Chromy sold Heemskerk and Jansz in early 1998 to Dr Andrew Pirie of Piper's Brook (who shortly afterwards sold Jansz on to Samuel Smith & Sons of Yalumba fame), he launched a new single-vineyard sparkling wine called RV. These initials stood for Rochecombe Vineyard, which was part of the package sold to Pirie, but the deal did not include the RV brand itself. By chance, Chromy had another vineyard with the same initials – Rebecca Vineyard – which is where this wine will be sourced from in future and, of course, the R initial will stand for Rebecca, not Rochecombe, as from the 1998 vintage.

WINEMAKER
Gary Ford

HOUSE STYLE & RANGE
I cannot make an overall judgement of any wine that has released just one vintage, but the 1995 RV rates two stars in its own right, so I certainly hope that [a] the next two vintages from Rochecombe are every bit as good, and [b] if they are, that the same quality and style can be achieved with the fruit harvested from the Rebecca Vineyard. The most remarkable aspect of RV is that it is an easy-drinking, fruit-driven *cuvée*, yet scores so highly. It is utterly beguiling, with beautifully bright Pinot fruit and the most succulent of finishes. Hopefully Rebecca will be every bit as stunning.

★★ RV TASMANIA
Vintaged, méthode champenoise: 20% Chardonnay, 80% Pinot Noir

N/A
RICHMOND GROVE
TANUNDA, SOUTH AUSTRALIA
• 14,000 cases
• Group ownership - Orlando
This is the famous old Château Leonay winery, which was established in 1897 by Hermann Paul Leopold Buring, one of the great characters of Australia's early wine industry, but although the Leo Buring brand

88
PETALUMA

PICCADILLY, SOUTH AUSTRALIA
- Group ownership – also owns Mitchelton
- Other labels – Bridgewater Mill

This winery's origins can be traced back to 1976 and a classroom at Riverina College,

PETALUMA'S TIERED VINEYARD AT PICCADILLY

Wagga Wagga, where Brian Croser, a senior lecturer in oenology, made small batches of wine under the Petaluma label. The winery at Piccadilly was built in 1978 essentially to process the grapes from vineyards in Coonawarra and the Clare Valley belonging to the Evans Wine Company. But after the untimely death of one of its partners, Peter Fox, that company was broken up and its vineyards became part of Petaluma. But the vineyards at Piccadilly are the exclusive source for Petaluma's sparkling wine.

Indeed, it was Croser's gamble on planting the first Pinot Noir and Chardonnay in the Piccadilly Valley that served to be his biggest sparkling wine breakthrough; the style of fruit produced, and the balance of sugar and acidity yielded, was unlike that of any other region he had encountered in Australia. However, the south and west facing slopes have clearly delineated themselves as sparkling wine vineyards, because the vines between these areas produce grapes of radically different readings.

Although Bollinger has had a financial interest in Petaluma since 1985, the famous *grande marque* distances itself from any sparkling wines produced outside of Champagne: Croser is, as the name suggests, entirely Brian Croser's handiwork. Petaluma also carries out contract sparkling winemaking for numerous small and medium-sized companies, and their number has increased since the Southern Beverage Corporation, which specialised in this sector of the market, went into receivership in 1997.

WINEMAKER
Brian Croser

HOUSE STYLE & RANGE
The first sparkling wine was produced in 1984 from 100% Chardonnay, but although better than most Australian fizz at the time, it was still very much in the 'Chardonnay that happens to have bubbles' mode. Croser thought so too, which is why he released it

under his second label, Bridgewater Mill. The first Croser to be released was the 1985. It was 80/20 Chardonnay/Pinot Noir, but the Chardonnay was still dominant, although the structure was more classic. Within just three years it had developed some toastiness on the finish, turning into a mini Dom Ruinart, but its rate of maturation was too fast, and the Chardonnay too influential.

Croser tightened up the structure in the 1986 and dropped the Chardonnay to 70%, but it was still too much, so he lowered it further in 1987, then to 65% in 1988, according to assistant winemaker Andrew Hardy, and lower still to 50%, according to Croser, in 1998. The 1987 had excellent acidity and was a watershed year in my view.

Croser is better in some years than others because the vintages seem to differ in Piccadilly more than they do in most other Australian wine areas, but from 1987 the wine has had the correct lean structure. According to Croser himself, he continued fine-tuning the varietal balance for three reasons: firstly the learning curve (it is now evident that Piccadilly Pinot brings more intensity, finesse and longevity, although Chardonnay is necessary to fill out the middle palate - this is almost a complete reversal of the roles these grapes play in Champagne); secondly, the variation of vintage (cooler years benefit from more Pinot, and Piccadilly saw a succession of these from 1992 to 1996, when the amount of Pinot increased to between 65 and 90%); and thirdly, availability (Pinot tends to be more prolific).

Some vintages have gone through strangely foursquare developmental stages, and none suits being over-chilled, but generally the fruit has softened, although the structure is still classically lean. If a vintage of Croser does appear to flatten out, leave it in the cellar and forget about it for a couple of years because, when released, there should be an attractive Pinot plumpness, which after any developmental stage develops a smooth vanilla-finesse, and gradually builds up a biscuity complexity.

★★ CROSER BRUT
Vintaged, méthode champenoise: 10 to 50% Chardonnay, 50 to 90% Pinot Noir

now belongs to Southcorp, the winery itself was purchased by Orlando, who renamed it as part of their Richmond Grove operations. The first Richmond Grove wines originated from a vineyard of that name in the Upper Hunter Valley in 1977, but the winery moved to the Lower Hunter after its association with the Wyndham Group, which became part of the French-owned Orlando group in 1990.

WINEMAKER
John Vickery

HOUSE STYLE & RANGE
Tasted only once, when it showed a tart richness, with a slight excess of free sulphur showing. Opinion reserved.
PINOT NOIR/CHARDONNAY BRUT
Not vintaged, méthode champenoise: 35% Chardonnay, 65% Pinot Noir

80
PETER RUMBALL

GLEN OSMOND, SOUTH AUSTRALIA
Peter Rumball established this eponymous brand in 1988. He is a great advocate and, indeed, exponent of Australian sparkling Shiraz, which accounts for 90% of his production.

WINEMAKER
Peter Rumball

HOUSE STYLE & RANGE
The Shiraz is soft and luscious with intense, spicy varietal fruit that makes superb drinking upon purchase, but you will be even more pleased if you cellar it for a couple of years.
PINOT NOIR/CHARDONNAY
Not vintaged, méthode champenoise: 30% Chardonnay, 70% Pinot Noir
★★ SPARKLING SHIRAZ
Not vintaged, méthode champenoise: 100% Shiraz

RV
See REBECCA VINEYARD

SIR JAMES
See BRL HARDY

65
SAMUEL SMITH & SON

ANGASTON, SOUTH AUSTRALIA
- Group ownership - Nautilus (New Zealand) and Jansz (Tasmania)
- Other labels - Yalumba (*see individual entry for Yalumba*)

This firm was established in 1849 by Samuel Smith, a brewer from Dorset, England, who travelled to Australia with his wife and children. It has always been assumed that Smith did not have much money because he became a humble gardener in the orchards of George Fife Angas, the founder of Angaston, yet he managed to purchase 12 hectares of land almost immediately. Smith named this property Yalumba (Aboriginal for 'all the

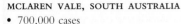

80 VALUE

SEAVIEW

MCLAREN VALE, SOUTH AUSTRALIA
- 700,000 cases
- Group ownership - Southcorp
- Other labels - Edwards & Chaffey

The Seaview name stems from vineyards planted in 1850, but the sparkling wines evolved through an entirely different route.

The vineyards were planted at Hope Farm by George Manning, an emigré from Cambridge. When Manning's son sold the farm in 1892, the new owner, Walter Craven, renamed the property Hope Vineyards. It was not until 1948, when this property was purchased by Ferguson & Chaffey (later Edwards & Chaffey) that the name of its vineyards was changed to Seaview.

Edwards & Chaffey sold the first wines (Seaview Cabernet Sauvignon 1951, one of Australia's first varietally-labelled wines) under this label in the 1950s, and Seaview Vineyards remained under their ownership until 1971, when they were taken over by Castlemaine Tooheys.

In 1972 Castlemaine Tooheys acquired Wynns and the twin roots of the Seaview brand's origins came together because Wynns owned the historic Romalo Champagne Cellars, which was renamed Seaview Champagne Cellars in 1975.

Romalo grew out of a sparkling wine operation started by one Edmond Mazure in 1919. Mazure was the winemaker at Auldana Champagne Cellars, which did not 'invent' Australian sparkling Burgundy, but was certainly the trail-blazer in the 1890s for the deep, dark, big, fat and intensely rich style that is accepted now. Under Mazure, who was hired by owner Josiah Symon in 1888 as manager-winemaker, became a partner in 1899 and managing director in 1903, Auldana became the most famous producer of sparkling wine in the country, sweeping up all the trophies in the first 15 years of the Adelaide Wine Show's existence.

In 1909, Mazure purchased a property at Magill, which had once been part of the Auld estate (the origins of Auldana), which he named La Perouse. It is not known when

VIEW ACROSS THE MCLAREN VALE

he made his very own first sparkling wine, but there is mention of one submitted to the Adelaide Wine Show in 1917 by Mrs H Mazure of Auldana, so it would appear that he was making wines from his own grapes under the Auldana label since at least 1915. By 1918, however, he was submitting wines to the Adelaide show under his own name without mention of Auldana, and in 1919 he resigned as managing director of Auldana.

By all accounts, the split with Josiah Symons was acrimonious. Furthermore, Mazure's relationship with a new partner, New Zealander Bertram Collins, was not a happy one. Collins' investment was sought to help fund the construction of a new winery, the products of which Mazure intended to market as La Perouse, but by 1920 the New Zealander was in full financial control, and he named it Romalo (after his daughter Roma and her friend, Lois). Occasionally wines were released under the La Perouse label, but Mazure and his wife lived out the rest of their lives in relative poverty and absolute obscurity, an ignominious end for one of Australia's pioneering winemakers.

Samuel Wynn became a partner in 1925, and the majority shareholder by 1929. In 1975, three years after Wynns had been taken over by Castlemaine Tooheys, Romalo Champagne Cellars was changed to Seaview Champagne Cellars, taking advantage of the soaring success of the Seaview wines. Penfolds purchased Wynns, then took over Lindemans before it was acquired by the owners of Seppelt, the South Australian Brewing

Company, which eventually formed Southcorp, under whose umbrella Seaview is marketed today, side-by-side with its arch rival Seppelt.

WINEMAKER
Steve Chapman

HOUSE STYLE & RANGE
The Brut and Rosé Brut generally have the edge over Seppelt's Brut and Rosé Brut, but Seaview lacks the depth of range of its sister brand, and consequently does not hit as many heights. The difference is, however, quite marked, particularly on Seaview's standard Brut, which is fresher, fluffier than the Seppelt Brut. The Brut Rosé has easy-drinking, strawberry/lavender fruit with a soft, creamy mousse. The Pinot Noir Chardonnay Brut offers real richness of flavour, with smooth, creamy fruit that gently builds in the mouth. Although completely fruit-driven when first released, when given a little more bottle-age, this *cuvée* can become increasingly big, rich and toasty.

The 1995 Blanc de Blancs has an oxidative style, but this is atypical for this otherwise creamy, fruity fizz. Lovers of toasty fizz should opt for the Edwards & Chaffey, Seaview's premium *cuvée*, a very toasty blockbuster that can maintain this peak thanks to very good acidity. The non-vinatge brut is *méthode champenoise* except on certain export markets where it is transfer method.

✫ BRUT
Not vintaged, méthode champenoise/transfer method: Grenache, Pinot Noir, Sémillon, Shiraz and other unrevealed varieties

✫ ROSÉ BRUT
Not vintaged, méthode champenoise: Grenache, Pinot Noir, Sémillon, Shiraz and other unrevealed varieties

★ BLANC DE BLANCS BRUT
Vintaged, méthode champenoise: 100% Chardonnay

★✫ EDWARDS & CHAFFEY PINOT NOIR CHARDONNAY BRUT
Vintaged, méthode champenoise: 72% Chardonnay, 28% Pinot Noir

★ PINOT NOIR CHARDONNAY BRUT
Vintaged, méthode champenoise: 75% Chardonnay, 25% Pinot Noir

country around') and in 1849 planted vines. He remained in the employ of Angas until 1852, when he joined the gold-rush in Victoria, struck modestly lucky, and returned home with sufficient capital to purchase two horses and another 32 hectares, putting the rest towards building cellars and a new house.

By the 1860s, medal-winning Yalumba

wines had a growing reputation in Australia and in 1878 Smith won a silver medal at the Paris exposition. One of Smith's grandsons, Walter 'Tiger' Smith, married Ida Hill, sister of Clem, the dashing left-hander who captained Australia's cricket team. When one of Walter's three sons, Wyndham, went to school he found himself in a class with

no fewer than 11 boys, all called Smith. The headmaster requested that the parents modify their childrens' surnames for the sake of the teacher's sanity. When it came to Wyndham they called him Hill Smith. The name stuck, and the firm has remained in the Hill-Smith family ever since.

continued on page 301

82 VALUE

SEPPELT

GREAT WESTERN VIA ARAFAT, VICTORIA
- 435,000 cases
- Group ownership - Southcorp

Like Seaview, the origin of Seppelt is divided between the name and the wine. The firm today considers that it was established in 1851, when Joseph Ernst Seppelt arrived in the Barossa Valley from Germany with his wife and two children. He had sufficient capital to start up almost any sort of business he might desire, having come from a wealthy German family. They were manufacturers of snuff amongst other things and naturally his initial idea was to grow tobacco, but the Barossa Valley was unsuitable. He grew grain and grapes instead, establishing Seppeltsfield, which grew rapidly.

In 1868 Seppelt died aged only 55, and the business was taken over by his son Benno, who was even more successful than his father. By 1875 Seppeltsfield possessed 225 hectares of vineyards and the winery had been extended to double its former size. A new winery was built in 1885 and by 1906 the vineyards had expanded to 600 hectares, yet this satisfied only one-third of the production demand for Seppelt's wines and brandies, forcing the purchase of grapes from other growers.

In 1914 Benno bought the Clydeside vineyard and cellars at Rutherglen in Victoria, and in 1916 he acquired Chateau Tanunda, a purchase that included more than half the country's stock of brandy. However, until he purchased the famous vineyards and cellars of Great Western in 1918, Seppelt was not involved in the production of sparkling wine.

The origins of Great Western (and thus Seppelt) sparkling wine dates back to the 1850s, when Joseph and Henry Best set up a slaughterhouse and butchery. Great Western was gold country, and the miners worked up ferocious appetites, making the Best brothers comfortably rich. In 1864, the gold rush had considerably diminished and, as the Bests considered what to invest their money in, so the first vineyards were being planted. Encouraged by the viticultural pioneers, the brothers each planted their own vineyard. What became of Henry is uncertain, but Joseph Best produced his first harvest in 1867 and excavated his own cellars a few years later. When Joseph Best died intestate in 1887, his estate was disposed of. This consisted of just over 200 hectares of land, including 22 hectares of vineyards, his cellars and stock, all purchased by Hans Irvine. Irvine's ambition was to make 'champagne'.

BOTTLES OF SALINGER SUR LATTES IN THE
UNDERGROUND CELLARS OF SEPPELT

He made several study trips to France and in the early 1890s he installed specialised equipment for sparkling wine production, and lured Frenchman Charles Pierlot from Pommery to be his winemaker. The resulting wines won awards all over Australia and, after offices and cellars were opened in London, the wines won awards in Europe too.

In 1918, at the age of 62, Irvine retired, selling his business to his friend Benno Seppelt, thus creating Seppelt Great Western. In 1923, a young assistant winemaker was transferred to Great Western from Seppeltsfield. His name was Colin Preece, and he turned out to be one of Australia's greatest winemakers, not just for fizz but across the entire spectrum of sparkling wine styles. Through the ascendancy of his star, Seppelt Great Western achieved great fame and respect.

WINEMAKER
Ian McKenzie

HOUSE STYLE & RANGE
Most of the grapes for all of these wines is sourced from Drumborg in Victoria and Tumbarumba in New South Wales. There are many better quality sparkling wines than Seppelt's Great Western Brut, which does not get even half a star, but none that offers better value. Clean, fresh and zesty, the Brut consistently makes a decent mouthful when released, although its citrussy fruit has a tendency to develop terpene-like characteristics, making it a *cuvée* to drink, not keep.

Although the Rosé gets equal star-rating to Seaview's Rosé, the Seppelt *cuvée* is easier to drink. The Pinot Noir Chardonnay is a good wine, but not a patch on Seaview's; its fat, sassy fruit being fine when fresh, but it is in fact simpler and less layered than Seaview, tending to become dominated by terpenes, rather than toasty bottle-aromas, if kept a while. The Show Reserve Drumborg Chardonnay Blanc de Blancs is produced in very small volumes, but Seppelt standard Chardonnay Blanc de Blancs is no longer marketed, although what appears to be the same wine is sold under own-labels such as

St. Michael (Marks & Spencer) in the UK. This is invariably of excellent value, with a soft mousse and succulent fruit that often hints of lime and is capable of developing intriguing smoky-honeyed complexity after age.

Salinger's austere, citrussy fruit needs time in bottle to develop finesse, and peaks at about seven years of age. When it was first released in the 1980s Salinger revolutionised everyone's concept of New World sparkling wine, but the fizz industry has progressed so quickly that, although good, it is only a one-star wine now.

The Sparkling Shiraz has a fresh fruity style with a nice touch of oak, and bags of rich, raisiny complexity. Not everyone will like the Show Sparkling Shiraz, but for devotees of this unique Australian style its massive, cassis-flavoured, blockbuster quality is unmistakable.

GREAT WESTERN BRUT
Not vintaged, transfer method: Colombard, Grenache, Tarrango, Thompson Seedless and other unrevealed varieties

GREAT WESTERN IMPERIAL RESERVE
Not vintaged, transfer method: Colombard, Grenache, Tarrango, other unrevealed varieties

GREAT WESTERN GRANDE RESERVE
Not vintaged, transfer method: Colombard, Grenache, Tarrango, other unrevealed varieties

★ GREAT WESTERN ROSÉ
Not vintaged, transfer method: Colombard, Grenache, Tarrango, Thompson Seedless and other unrevealed varieties

GREAT WESTERN ROSÉ RESERVE
Not vintaged, transfer method: Colombard, Grenache, Tarrango, other unrevealed varieties

SUNDAY CREEK PINOT NOIR CHARDONNAY
Not vintaged, transfer method: 42% Chardonnay, 44% Pinot Noir, 14% Meunier

HARPERS RANGE PINOT NOIR CHARDONNAY
Vintaged, méthode champenoise: 57% Chardonnay, 41% Pinot Noir, 2% Meunier

★ PINOT NOIR CHARDONNAY
Vintaged, méthode champenoise: 40% Chardonnay, 55% Pinot Noir, 5% Meunier

★ BLANC DE BLANCS BRUT
Vintaged, transfer method: 100% Chardonnay

SHOW RESERVE DRUMBORG CHARDONNAY BLANC DE BLANCS
Vintaged, transfer method: 100% Chardonnay

★ SALINGER BRUT
Vintaged, méthode champenoise: 58% Chardonnay, 42% Pinot Noir

★★ SPARKLING SHIRAZ
Vintaged, transfer method: 100% Shiraz

★★ SHOW SPARKLING SHIRAZ
Vintaged, méthode champenoise: 100% Shiraz

HOUSE STYLE & RANGE

Angas Brut can vary from shipment to shipment, but it is definitely fruity fizz. There is nothing wrong with this, but if you want more serious stuff, refer to the Yalumba entry. Angas Brut shows well initially, but easily tires into something that all too often should be avoided. When fresh, however, it is a fattish fizz with exotic tropical fruits on the finish, and recent shipments have shown an increasing amount of Chardonnay-like aromas. Angas Brut Rosé is an even more upfront fruity fizz, but rather too twee for me, with a talcum powder perfume that gets burdensome after just one glass.

⭐ ANGAS BRUT

Not vintaged, transfer method: Chardonnay, Chenin Blanc, Colombard, Grenache, Macabéo, Muscadelle, Palomino, Parellada, Pedro Ximénez, Pinot Noir, Sémillon, Shiraz, Trebbiano, Xarello

ANGAS BRUT ROSÉ

Not vintaged, transfer method: Cabernet Sauvignon, Cabernet Franc, Carignan, Cinsaut, Grenache, Merlot, Shiraz

SUNDAY CREEK

See SEPPELT

60
SUNNYCLIFF

IRAAK, VICTORIA

• Other labels - Deakin Estate

Under the same ownership as Katnook in South Australia, Sunnycliff was established in 1980 and produces budget fizz.

WINEMAKER

Mark Zeppel

HOUSE STYLE & RANGE

Soft, easy-drinking, fruity fizz, with a strange acidity balance. The Sunnycliff is not bad for a *cuve close* in global terms, but there are better Australian versions (Barramundi and Aldridge for example).

BRUT

Vintaged, cuve close: 40% Chardonnay, 20% Chenin Blanc, 40% Colombard

DEAKIN ESTATE BRUT

Vintaged, cuve close: 40% Chardonnay, 20% Chenin Blanc, 40% Colombard

80
TALTARNI

MOONAMBEL, VICTORIA

• 15,000 cases

This immaculate vineyard and winery in the beautiful Pyrenees was established in 1972 by Dominique Portet, whose brother Bernard runs Clos du Val in California.

Taltarni is where David Hohnen cut his winemaking teeth for five years, after qualifying from UC Davis, before taking over at Cape Mentelle. It is no coincidence

that both Portet and Hohnen have established a reputation for making wines of exceptional longevity because they both share the philosophy that complexity with finesse can only be achieved slowly, although Portet probably leans more towards complexity, and Hohnen finesse.

The breakthrough in the quality of Taltarni's sparkling wine came when Portet began sourcing some of his grapes from Tasmania, which accounts for at least 20% of every blend and, of course, is used for Clover Hill.

WINEMAKER

Dominique Portet, Shane Clohesy, Chris Markell

HOUSE STYLE & RANGE

The Chardonnay/Pinot Noir Brut has a lean structure that is on the austere side of correct, but has worked increasingly well with each release, and loosens up after 12 to 18 months additional bottle-age. The Brut Taché is the most immediately delightful *cuvée* in the Taltarni range, with deliciously soft fruit cushioned by a fresh, fluffy mousse, and an elegant balance between richness and acidity. This not simply an easy-drinking fizz, but an Australian sparkling rosé of rare finesse. Clover Hill is potentially Taltarni's most exciting *cuvée*, but I have been following it since the first vintage, 1991, and I have to confess that the jury is still out. The 1994 is considered the best vintage so far, but the autolysis is too malty, lacking finesse. That, however, is a one-off trait and may not be repeated in forthcoming vintages. What does disturb me, though, is the green, Chablis-like fruit that has typified all vintages of this Tasmanian *cuvée*. Why not leave the grapes on the vine a little longer?

⭐⭐ BRUT TACHÉ
CHARDONNAY PINOT NOIR BRUT

Not vintaged, méthode champenoise: 54% Chardonnay, 41% Pinot Noir, 5% Meunier

⭐ CHARDONNAY PINOT NOIR BRUT

Not vintaged, méthode champenoise: 56% Chardonnay, 40% Pinot Noir, 4% Meunier

CLOVER HILL 1994 TASMANIA BRUT

Vintaged, méthode champenoise: 50% Chardonnay, 45% Pinot Noir, 5% Meunier

80 VALUE
TATACHILLA

MCLAREN VALE, SOUTH AUSTRALIA

The Tatachilla vineyard was planted in 1887 by JG Kelly, but the winery was not established until 1901. It quickly became an important brand, after which it went through a chequered existence, ending up as a label belonging to the Southern Vales

Cooperative. The Tatachilla brand and the old cooperative winery, which is known as The Wattles, and built in 1901, were purchased in 1993 by a group of investors led by Vic Zerella and Keith Smith, Wolf Blass's former marketing manager. Keith Smith, who runs the winery on a day-to-day basis, enticed expatriate Australian winemaker Daryl Groom back from California to act as consultant to Michael Fragos, Tatachilla's senior winemaker. Between them, Fragos and Groom have rapidly built up a brilliant reputation for big, rich, intensely flavoured red wines, but have recently proved themselves adept at putting bubbles into bottles as well.

WINEMAKER

Michael Fragos (Daryl Groom consulting)

HOUSE STYLE & RANGE

The Bluestone Brut is soft and creamy, with the capacity to age and a testament to how well-selected Chenin Blanc can produce a premium-quality fizz in Australia. The Sparkling Malbec is, I think, a unique varietal sparkling wine. Made from the grape that was famous for the 'Black Wine' of Cahors in the 19th century, it is a highly perfumed, fruit-driven *cuvée* of some finesse, and has been made in a drier style than most Australian sparkling reds.

★ BLUESTONE BRUT

Not vintaged, méthode champenoise: 30% Chenin Blanc, 70% Pinot Noir

★ SPARKLING MALBEC

Not vintaged, méthode champenoise: 100% Malbec

TRILOGY

See ORLANDO

N/A
TUCK'S RIDGE AT RED HILL

DROMANA, VICTORIA

• 750 cases

A small winery with 23 hectares of vines on Red Hill, Tuck's Ridge was established in 1987 by Peter Hollick, the sole owner.

WINEMAKER

Daniel Greene

HOUSE STYLE & RANGE

The first sparkling wine was produced in 1993 and as that was the current release at the time of writing, and the only wine I have tasted, it would be unfair to draw any overall opinion. For the record, however, it was fat with sassy fruit, but had some excess free sulphur showing.

VUES BRUT

Vintaged, méthode champenoise: Chardonnay and Pinot Noir

VUES

See TUCK'S RIDGE AT RED HILL

N/A
WYNDHAM ESTATE
DALWOOD, NEW SOUTH WALES

- 15,000 cases
- Group ownership - Orlando

One of the oldest names in Australian wine history, this estate dates back to 1828, when it was purchased as a bankrupt property by George Wyndham, an Englishman who was educated at Eton and Harrow. He named the 485-hectare Hunter Valley estate Dalewood, and planted his first vines in 1830, but they died, so he planted more in 1931, and they survived.

Success, however, was not easy in those early days, and Wyndham's first harvest in 1935 was a write-off. He obviously had the sort of fatalistic humour that was required of any Outback pioneer worth his salt, having recorded that his first crop 'promised to make good vinegar'. Under Wyndham's son John, Dalewood Estate became the second largest vineyard in Australia and its wines were not only famous on the home market, but won awards around the world, including truly meaningful ones in London and Bordeaux.

After John Wyndham died in 1887, the recession of the 1890s took its toll and the estate ended up in the condition his father found it, bankrupt. The Commercial Banking Company ran the estate – not very well by all accounts – until it was sold in 1901 to JFM Wilkinson. Wilkinson split the property in two, selling the house almost immediately to a Mr McNamara and, in 1904, he sold the vineyards to the Penfolds family, who made Dalewood a top-selling brand once again.

And so it remained until 1971, when a consortium led by former Penfolds winemaker Percy McGuigan, purchased the Dalewood estate (but not the brand) and the original homestead, reuniting the property. The property was renamed Wyndham Estate and the wines achieved great success, particularly on export markets, until 1990, when the consortium sold out to the French-owned Orlando group (now also known as Orlando-Wyndham).

WINEMAKER
Philip Laffer
HOUSE STYLE & RANGE
Wyndham made its first fizz in 1994, and the 1995 was in circulation at the time of writing, so it is far too early to make any definitive judgement, but it appears as if the style Laffer is aiming for is broad and complex, and he is halfway there with the second vintage, but it needs more acidity.

BRUT CUVÉE

Vintaged, transfer method: Chardonnay, Pinot Noir and other unrevealed varieties

70
YALDARA
LYDOCH, SOUTH AUSTRALIA

- Other labels - Blue Lake Ridge

Chateau Yaldara was founded in 1947 by Herman Thumm, a German who had picked up his winemaking experience in Persia of all places. Initially the focus was on sweet reds that were peculiar to their time, then Thumm's son Robert concentrated on sparkling wines of various styles, from Champagne to Spumante, dry to sweet, red, white, rosé and everything between. Not inappropriately, the name 'Yaldara' is Aboriginal for 'sparkling',.

HOUSE STYLE & RANGE
Commercially soft, fruity fizz in general, the fruit in the Brut is rather too exotic for its own good, while the Brut Rosé has fresher, raspberry fruit, but both benefit from over- rather than under-chilling. These bubblies are the same as those sold under the Blue Lake Ridge label, and are firmly aimed at the budget end of the market, with no pretensions.

BRUT

Not vintaged, transfer method: grape varieties not revealed

BRUT ROSÉ

Not vintaged, transfer method: grape varieties not revealed

85
YALUMBA
ANGASTON, SOUTH AUSTRALIA

- 5,000 cases
- Group ownership - Samuel Smith & Sons

Yalumba is the winery where all Samuel Smith & Sons' sparkling wines are made. The Yalumba name has recently been removed from Angas Brut (see SAMUEL SMITH & SONS) to re-emphasise the quality of Yalumba's premium sparkling wines.

WINEMAKER
Geoff Linton
HOUSE STYLE & RANGE
The Cuvée One is Yalumba's best-value fizz; it quickly develops lovely biscuity aromas on the nose, but its lean structure demands more time to build up sufficient mellowing richness to balance this complexity on the palate. Cuvée Two is deep, dark and, according to its back label, mischievous. It is a fine, fizzy red with minty Cabernet flavour, and big oaky overtones.

Yalumba D is this company's top sparkling wine. The 'D' is a concatenation of LD, as in Late Disgorged; the original aim had been to produce a world-class sparkling wine through extended ageing on yeast. In the 1980s great emphasis was placed on extended yeast contact, but it has long since been widely appreciated that autolysis is not so much dependent on the duration of yeast contact as on the composition of the wine before it is bottled. With the right raw material and minimum processing, good autolysis can be achieved in one to three years; with the wrong raw material and too much processing, a wine could spend ten years on its yeast and pick up no autolytic character. This is why Yalumba D now spends three years rather than six on its lees, which is as it should be.

Its stylistic development showed promise with the 1987 vintage and seemed to peak in 1989, since when the quality has remained roughly the same, although its style has altered somewhat as its yeast-contact has been reduced. The structure is good and tight, with austere flavours and lean fruit. This can make the wine difficult to appreciate when it is first released, but it improves markedly with some gentle post-disgorgement ageing. However, some fine-tuning on the malolactic would loosen up the front palate and create a creaminess on the finish making Yalumba D more accessible between its release and the point at which the post-disgorgement maturation kicks in.

★★ CUVÉE ONE PINOT NOIR/CHARDONNAY NV BRUT

Not vintaged, transfer method: 30% Chardonnay, 70% Pinot Noir

★★ CUVÉE TWO PRESTIGE CABERNET SAUVIGNON

Not vintaged, méthode champenoise: 90% Cabernet Sauvignon, 10% Shiraz

★★ D BRUT

Vintaged, méthode champenoise: 20-35% Chardonnay, 55-70% Pinot Noir, 5-10% Meunier

N/A
YARRABANK
YARRA GLEN, VICTORIA

- 1,500 cases (7,000 projected)

This joint venture between Champagne Veuve Devaux and Yering Station (established 1988) began in 1993. Devaux's winemaker, Claude Thibaut, can now return to Victoria, where he once worked for Yellowglen prior to Iron Horse and Jordan in California.

WINEMAKER
Claude Thibaut
HOUSE STYLE & RANGE
With just the first vintage released and tasted, it is impossible to give this an overall rating, but the most impressive aspect of the 1993 is its exuberant acidity, which keeps the tangy, rich fruit very fresh and lively. This wine is labelled Cuvée No.1 and is 50/50 Yarra Valley and Mornington Peninsula. Grapes are hand-harvested into small baskets. No malolactic.

★★ BRUT

Vintaged, méthode champenoise: 50% Chardonnay, 50% Pinot Noir

YARRA BURN
See BRL HARDY

NEW ZEALAND

IT IS REALLY ONLY IN THE LAST TWENTY YEARS OR SO THAT WINEMAKERS IN NEW ZEALAND HAVE TURNED THEIR ATTENTION TO MAKING SPARKLING *CUVÉES*. HISTORICALLY THEY HAVE NOT HAD THE RIGHT GRAPE VARIETIES AVAILABLE TO MAKE WORLD-CLASS FIZZ, BUT AS MORE AND MORE VINEYARDS HAVE BEEN PLANTED WITH CLASSIC VARIETIES, SO WE HAVE SEEN THE EMERGENCE OF SOME EXCELLENT SPARKLING WINES.

Until as recently as 1981, only two wineries in New Zealand had dabbled with *méthode champenoise*: Mission and Selaks. The late Mate Selak is thought to have produced New Zealand's first sparkling wine at his winery in Kumeu near Auckland in 1956, when he used a Chasselas wine to produce an experimental *cuvée* called Champelle. Apparently the Chasselas did not work well with secondary fermentation and, without a skilled *remueur* to hand, Mate found the skills of riddling difficult to master. He also suffered an alarming loss of wine through exploding bottles, and it was not until 1971 that the Selaks winery was able to launch a bubbly of marketable quality. By this time, the Champelle name had been dropped and the wine was sold simply as Selaks Méthode Champenoise. Mate died in 1991, but he is remembered through Selaks Blanc de Blancs, the winery's top-of-the-range fizz, which is named after him.

Brother John of the Mission Vineyards, an old-established winery belonging to The Society of Mary, started his fizz-making career after Mate, but succeeded before him, making and marketing a sparkling wine called Fontanella in the mid-1960s. However, unlike Selaks, which has increased it range of sparkling wines to three different *cuvées*, Fontanella was dropped in the late 1970s, and Mission Vineyards no longer produces sparkling wines of any description.

Between Selaks and Mission, Corban's produced New Zealand's first *cuve close* sparkling wine to celebrate its 60th anniversary.

One factor responsible for the late development of sparkling wine in New Zealand has been the lack of suitable grapes. Few classic varieties were planted prior to 1980, and those that existed were in short supply for premium varietal wines. The most widely planted

variety was Müller-Thurgau, which was as unsuitable for brut-style sparkling wine as it was for classic table wine, yet accounted for 40% of the country's vineyards.

Sparkling wine became serious business in New Zealand in 1981, when industry giant Montana put its muscle behind the launch of Lindauer. For quite some time Montana's Lindauer Brut and Lindauer Rosé exemplified New Zealand's sparkling wine industry, yet these creamy, easy-drinking, transfer method bubblies were pretty damn good for their era, and in fact Lindauer still makes excellent value, unpretentious drinking today. However, it took the collaboration of Montana and Champagne Deutz in 1988 to put this country on the sparkling wine map, and it took one year longer for an expatriate champenois by the name of Daniel Le Brun to demonstrate Marlborough's potential for sparkling wines to rival good quality Champagne.

A year before the Montana-Deutz collaboration, Cloudy Bay produced its first vintage of Pelorus under the wandering eye of 'Mad Harry' Osborne, who was California's pioneering sparkling winemaker at Schramsberg back in the 1960s, and now makes Kristone (*see Kristone, p.272*). Australian Tony Jordan has produced a New Zealand *cuvée* of Domaine Chandon for several years by utilising Hunter's facilities in Marlborough. Coincident to this, Jordan has consulted for Jane Hunter as she has developed her own sparkling wine, which came of age in 1997 with the launch of an utterly beguiling export *cuvée* called Miru Miru.

New Zealand is viticulturally blessed in the number of different world-quality wine styles it can produce, and individually crafted sparkling wine is certainly one of them.

SHEEP AND VINEYARDS IN THE WAIRAU VALLEY AT BLENHEIM, MARLBOROUGH, WITH THE RICHMOND RANGE OF HILLS BEHIND

N/A
BENDIGO ESTATE
CROMWELL, CENTRAL OTAGO
- 2,000 cases
- Other labels - Chauvet

A partnership between Rudolf Bauer, who was the winemaker for Rippon vineyard until 1992 and then for Giesen until 1997, and Clotilde Chauvet, a champenois who succeeded Rudolf as winemaker at Rippon. We first met when at Rippon, when Chauvet was assisting Rudolf in 1992. I expect exciting *cuvées* from this new venture, not least because Bauer has already made the superb first release of Giesen's Voyage, while Chauvet has experience in Champagne, where she has made Champagne Marc Chauvet at Rilly-la-Montagne (her father is also president of Champagne Jacquart).

Bendigo is some 35 kilometres southeast of Rippon, by Lake Dunstan, and received its name from Australian gold-diggers from Bendigo in Victoria (which in turn received its name from William 'Bendigo' Thompson, a British pugilist famous for his peculiar crouching or bending style).

WINEMAKER
Rudolf Bauer, Clotilde Chauvet
HOUSE STYLE & RANGE
The first two vintages were produced from Marlborough grapes but, as from 1998, Bauer will start using grapes from his own Bendigo Estate. Not due to be released until this book is published, thus not tasted, so no overall rating is possible.

BRUT
> *Vintaged, méthode champenoise: 85% Chardonnay, 15% Pinot Noir*

N/A
BLUE ROCK
MARTINBOROUGH
Founded in 1985, Blue Rock produces fine Chardonnay and Sauvignon Blanc *cuvées*, with more than a little hope for its Riesling. However, it has yet to succeed with its sparkling wine.
WINEMAKER
Jenny Clarke
HOUSE STYLE & RANGE
The 1992 vintage is disappointingly thin and unfortunately attenuated with flavourless toasty bottle-aromas.

BRUT MÉTHODE TRADITIONELLE
> *Vintaged, méthode champenoise: 55% Chardonnay, 35% Pinot Noir, 10% Meunier*

CHARISMA
See MILLS REEF

CHANDON
See DOMAINE CHANDON

CHARD FARM, CENTRAL OTAGO, UNDER FROST

N/A
CHARD FARM
CENTRAL OTAGO
- Other labels - Roche

This property, with its spectacular mountain-side vineyard next to the famous bungy-jumping bridge at Kawarau Gorge, did not have its own winery until 1993, and embarked on sparkling wine production in 1997. This new fizz will be sold under the Roche label and has been produced with the help of consultant Owen J Bird, a Tasmanian who lives in Germany and whose other sparkling wine consultancies includes Ricci Curbastro in Franciacorta. Bird is an unassuming young man, a qualified oenologist and also a barrister-at-law.
WINEMAKER
Rob Hay, Owen J Bird
HOUSE STYLE & RANGE
Nothing to taste so early in the game, but these *cuvées* are blended from grapes grown in ten different locations in the Central Otago area (to jump on a steep learning curve) and some 80% of the wines are *barrique*-fermented (used barrels) using five different selected yeast strains plus some that have been vinified with indigenous yeast to give natural ferments. Some of the wines have undergone malolactic from one of two different cocktails.

ROCHE CUVÉE PRESTIGE BRUT
> *Not vintaged, méthode champenoise: 25% Chardonnay, 75% Pinot Noir*

ROCHE VINTAGE BRUT
> *Vintaged, méthode champenoise: 40% Chardonnay, 60% Pinot Noir*

CHAUVET
See BENDIGO ESTATE

N/A
CHIFNEY
MARTINBOROUGH
This small boutique winery in tranquil settings was established in 1984, but made its debut bubbly in 1994.
WINEMAKER
Michael Mebus
HOUSE RANGE
CHIFFONNAY
> *Vintaged, méthode champenoise: primarily Chenin Blanc, plus Sauvignon Blanc and Muscat*

N/A
COOPER'S CREEK
HUAPAI
- 300 cases

Award-winning winery founded in 1980 by Randy Weaver, a talented young winemaker from Oregon, and Andrew Henderson, an accountant. From its very first vintage, Cooper's Creek won critical acclaim and commercial success, so when Weaver returned to the US in 1988, this caused much concern, but Henderson's financial strategy remained on course and winemaker Kim Crawford has been every bit as successful as Weaver – until the Limeburners Bay case opened up a can of worms in 1998.

While suing Cooper's Creek over the processing of its grapes, Limeburners Bay found out that a Cooper's Creek Sauvignon Blanc exported to the UK contained only 55% of that variety, when it must be at least 85% by EC law. The NZ government ordered an audit which makes unsettling reading and Hendry was asked to resign from the New Zealand Wine Exports Board. This is sad news for the winery but it does explain why I have never received a sample of its fizz. The first sparkling wine, produced in 1992, was released in 1995.
WINEMAKER
Kim Crawford
HOUSE RANGE
FIRST EDITION BRUT
> *Vintaged, méthode champenoise: 50% Chardonnay, 50% Pinot Noir*

70
CORBAN'S
AUCKLAND
- 21,000 cases

Established by Assid Abraham Corban, a Lebanese stonemason who spent ten years in New Zealand trying different jobs before he decided to plant a vineyard in the Henderson area in 1902, only to discover that he was a natural born winemaker. It is now the second largest wine group in the country, having snapped up many wineries along the way.

In 1962 Corban's produced New Zealand's first *cuve close* bubbly to celebrate the company's 60th anniversary.
WINEMAKER
Kirsty Walton (for future vintages)
HOUSE STYLE & RANGE
The Verde, which is sold as non-vintage on some markets, is a perfectly acceptable firm fizz, but nothing special, and Amadeus has not been worthy of any note since the 1990 vintage. Indeed, the 1987 Amadeus, which was the first vintage I tasted, reminded me of a French *cuve close* of no fixed abode, and the 1993 has gone back to this anonymous style. Both are made with Hawkes Bay fruit.

AMADEUS CLASSIC RESERVE BRUT

Vintaged, méthode champenoise: 3% Chardonnay, 97% Pinot Noir

VERDE MÉTHODE CHAMPENOISE

Vintaged, méthode champenoise: 20% Chardonnay, 80% Pinot Noir

DEUTZ MARLBOROUGH

See MONTANA

75
DOMAINE CHANDON

MARLBOROUGH

Since Tony Jordan is Jane Hunter's consultant winemaker for her own Vintage Brut and Miru Miru, it is little surprise that Hunter's has also been the testing ground for this *cuvée*.

WINEMAKER

Tony Jordan

HOUSE STYLE & RANGE

The 1990 was an excellent debut, and early vintages captured the linear purity of Marlborough's fruit, but the very malty direction taken by the 1994 vintage has allowed the winemaking technique to dominate the style, and that has been a retrograde step.

VINTAGE MARLBOROUGH BRUT

Vintaged, méthode champenoise: 40% Chardonnay, 50% Pinot Noir, 10% Meunier

ELSTREE

See HIGHFIELD

N/A
GIESEN

BURNHAM, CHRISTCHURCH

Established in 1981 by the Giesen family, who had emigrated from Germany two years earlier. They now own the largest winery in the Canterbury area, surrounded by 35 hectares of vineyards, plus another ten in Marlborough.

WINEMAKER

Marcel Giesen

HOUSE STYLE & RANGE

Rudolf Bauer made the first few *cuvées*, and I really wish that I could give Giesen an overall rating of 85 points for the effort, but who is to know whether future releases will be just as stunning? I have not rated other newcomers, and it would be wrong to do so here. The fruit is sourced from Giesen's own vineyards in both Canterbury and Marlborough. I was bowled over by the sheer vivacity of the beautifully bright Pinot fruit in the first release of Voyage, and can only pray that the high proportion of reserves (30%) from previous vintages does indeed give future *cuvées* the high degree of consistency that Giesen believes it will.

★★ VOYAGE, SPECIAL CUVÉE BRUT

Vintaged, méthode champenoise: 3% Chardonnay, 97% Pinot Noir

MARLBOROUGH

- 7,000 cases (growing to 10,000)
- Other labels – Pelorus

Cloudy Bay was established by David Hohnen of Cape Mentelle, Western Australia, in 1985 and produced its first sparkling wine in 1987. The only sparkling wine in the world to be named after a dolphin, Hohnen named it after Pelorus Jack, who used to act as an unofficial pilot for ships entering the Marlborough Sounds (the mist from which gives rise to the origin of Cloudy Bay itself).

When Veuve Clicquot, which now owns controlling interest in Hohnen's business, first bought into the company in 1990, this *grande marque* was quick to point out that it had no intention of bringing out a New World fizz. However, Cloudy Bay was already five years and four vintages into a research and development programme that was due to give birth to Pelorus. Hohnen had no intention of wasting either this money or the experience he had accumulated, thus he continued with the project.

At first Veuve Clicquot maintained a discreetly low profile, but with a different man at the helm and its own corporate role in the LVMH group subtly changed, this famous Champagne house not only took an increasingly keen interest in the development of Cloudy Bay's sparkling wine, it also opened up its portfolio to include Scharffenberger (now Pacific Echo), which had previously come under the auspices of its sister company Pommery.

WINEMAKER

'Mad Harry' Osborne, Kevin Judd

HOUSE STYLE & RANGE

Pelorus maybe a mite too oaky for purists, but the oak is not so evident when the wine is consumed by itself, rather than tasted under clinical conditions against other sparkling wines. However, from the oak that is present, true aficionados of New World fizz will not be surprised to learn of 'Mad Harry' Osborne's role in this wine, as he pioneered California sparkling wine as Schramsberg's first winemaker and currently produces Kristone (*see p.272*).

Mad Harry was particularly pleased when I told him the 1993 Pelorus was excellent because, from his point of view, it was the Harvest from Hell. It was in October 1997 and I had just tasted back to 1987, the first

88
CLOUDY BAY

Pelorus vintage, with Edward Berry at Veuve Clicquot's London office. Not one wine was over the hill, although the 1989 had to be sidelined when both samples appeared to have the same corked aroma. The 1987, however, was still in very good condition; not in the same league as, say, the 1987 Roederer Estate (California), but miles better than Roederer's 1986.

The 1988 was even better than the 1987, with very toasty fruit and a creamy, smooth finish. The 1990 and 1992 were as good as Roederer's legendary 1987 and this surprised me because I knew they were high quality sparkling wines, but had not realised they were that good. The 1990 was initially heavy, and would have been an even better wine with higher acidity, but it benefited greatly from being poured a while, developing layers of classy, creamy, walnutty complexity over the rich, toasty fruit. The 1991 still has a small nugget of bitterness that promises to develop into a superior version of the 1990 by the year 2000.

The 1993 is the lightest Pelorus so far, yet it is potentially the best vintage so far, which illustrates what a strange blessing a cold, rainy harvest can be. Mad Harry complained that it was the worst picking he had endured, and that he and Kevin had to work very hard in the winery, especially with the *dosage*, to get the balance right. Well, it was worth the effort. Picking grapes in the rain is a regular if unwelcome occurrence in Champagne, but the finesse and perfume of Pelorus 1993 suggests that it might be worth praying for rain in some other New World wine areas.

Like all Pelorus vintages, the 1993 has a noticeably deeper colour than most other sparkling wines from New Zealand. When it was first released, it had a touch of pepperiness to the fruit, but it was lovely and ripe, with excellent acidity, and has since gained a certain fluffy finesse. As I write, the malolactic has just started to dominate the wine, although this will eventually be subsumed by the oakiness, when the two will be transformed into the creamy, toasty complexity that is the hallmark of Pelorus.

★★ PELORUS MARLBOROUGH BRUT

Vintaged, méthode champenoise: 45% Chardonnay, 55% Pinot Noir

N/A

GILLAN ESTATE

BLENHEIM, MARLBOROUGH

Established in 1992 by Terry and Toni Gillan, who made their first sparkling wine the same year, and now own 15 hectares of vineyards.

WINEMAKER

Sam Weaver

HOUSE STYLE & RANGE

Too early to make an overall judgement, but reports from down-under suggest a fresh, elegant, creamy, fruity style.

MÉTHODE CHAMPENOISE RESERVE BRUT

Vintaged, méthode champenoise: Chardonnay, Pinot Noir

N/A

HIGHFIELD

BLENHEIM, MARLBOROUGH

- 1,000 cases
- Other labels - Elstree

Shin Yokoi and Tom Tenuwera shared two passions – Champagne and the desire to own a New World winery. In 1991 they purchased Highfield as a going concern, and a friend, Neil Buchanan, took on the responsibility of running it. In 1993 they engaged another friend, Michel Drappier of Champagne Drappier, to oversee the production of a sparkling wine.

WINEMAKER

Tony Hooper, Michel Drappier

HOUSE STYLE & RANGE

Too early to make an overall judgement, but when the first vintage (1993) was released, it showed rich fruit with a lovely creamy, vanilla character, but it quickly took on a malty style that detracted from the wine's finesse. But Drappier and Hooper believe they have learned a lot since that first *cuvée*, so we must wait and see. They are going about it seriously, though, having planted sparkling wine designated vineyards with low-vigour clones and rootstock. Currently they ferment a quarter of the wine in old barrels and apply 100% malolactic, with three years on yeast, although they hope to extend this to five years in the future, if the style permits.

ELSTREE, MARLBOROUGH

Vintaged, méthode champenoise: 45% Chardonnay, 55% Pinot Noir

85 VALUE

HUNTER'S

BLENHEIM, MARLBOROUGH

- 1,000 cases

Established in 1982 by Ernie Hunter, a great ambassador for New Zealand wines who died in a tragic car accident in 1987. He left a 33-year-old widow and a business that had its share of financial problems. No one would have blamed Jane Hunter had she walked away, perhaps to return to her native South Australia. Instead she built up one of the country's most respected wineries. Jane Hunter was awarded an OBE for her services to New Zealand wine. Ernie would have been very proud of her achievements.

WINEMAKER

Gary Duke

HOUSE STYLE & RANGE

I have followed Hunter's sparkling wines on and off for ten years, and they have improved by leaps and bounds. The Marlborough Brut was quite austere in the early years, but it has gradually acquired the richness and intensity of flavour necessary to balance a correctly lean structure, and it is now capable of considerable complexity. But my favourite is Miru Miru, Hunter's lip-smacking export brand. This is a totally different kettle of fish; it is so vibrantly fresh, lusciously fruity, and easy to drink when first released, it can fool you into thinking that it is for immediate consumption only, but if kept a few months it develops a great depth of flavour, classic structure and makes a serious sparkling wine indeed. On the other hand, who cares? It's such a lovely guzzle, you would be a fool not to drink it straight away!

★ MARLBOROUGH BRUT

Vintaged, méthode champenoise: 38% Chardonnay, 50% Pinot Noir, 12% Meunier

★★ MIRU MIRU MARLBOROUGH BRUT

Vintaged, méthode champenoise: 60% Chardonnay, 40% Pinot Noir

80

JACKSON ESTATE

BLENHEIM, MARLBOROUGH

- 3,000 cases

The Jackson Estate was established in 1987 by John Stichbury, whose great-grandfather, Adam Jackson, first settled the area, giving his name to the road on which the estate is located. It had always been Stichbury's intention to specialise in sparkling wine, but the time-lag from planting vines to marketing a commercial product was such that he produced Sauvignon Blanc to generate some cash flow. Thus it was that Jackson Estate ended up with such a cult following – not just for Sauvignon Blanc, which some people rate as highly as Cloudy Bay, but also for the superb Chardonnay, Pinot Noir, and Botrytised Riesling that followed. Now the fizz, made by Aussie winemaker Martin Shaw, has come as a surprise!

WINEMAKER

Martin Shaw

HOUSE STYLE & RANGE

The 1993 was not as good as the inaugural 1992 vintage, having less New World ripeness and more of a Chablis-like greenness to the fruit (although the 1993 had one-third less Chardonnay than the 1992). The 1993 is still a good wine, and should benefit from additional bottle-age, to acquire a creamy, toasty complexity It seems this *cuvée* benefits from more Chardonnay and less yeast-contact.

★ JACKSON ESTATE 1993 MARLBOROUGH

Vintaged, méthode champenoise: 40-60% Chardonnay, 60-40% Pinot Noir

LINDAUER

See MONTANA

N/A

LINTZ ESTATE

MARTINBOROUGH

This ten hectare estate was established in 1988 by Geisenheim-trained Chris Lintz, who made his first wines in 1991, and I just happened to be travelling through when they were less than a year old. I was duly impressed; indeed I was amazed by his Cabernet Sauvignon, which displayed exceptional structure for the locality.

WINEMAKER

Chris Lintz

HOUSE STYLE & RANGE

Although fresh and floral when first released, this *cuvée* has a tendency to go toasty in bottle, rather than petrolly, as top German Sekts do.

RIESLING BRUT

Vintaged, méthode champenoise: Chardonnay and Pinot Noir

82

MATUA VALLEY

WAIMAUKU, KUMEU

- 3,000 cases

Matua Valley was established in 1974 by the Spence brothers, Ross and Bill, who started off in a leased tin-shed. They now have a superbly equipped winery and have long been well known and well liked for their expressive varietal wines. Started making fizz in 1989.

WINEMAKER

Mark Robertson

HOUSE STYLE & RANGE

It is virtually impossible to name this *cuvée*, which used to be known as 'M' and is still referred to as this by many of its followers. The vintage in a written form now constitutes this wine's name, the 1991 was in fact Matua Nineteen Ninety-One Brut, the 1992 Matua Nineteen Ninety-Two Brut, and so on. There has been an impressive learning curve for this *cuvée*, which is now rich and satisfying, with fresh, fluffy fruit. I have not tasted the new fizz from Matua's Shingle Peak winery in Marlborough, but Matua has an established track record for sparkling wine, and the Shingle Peak varietal wines have been excellent.

★★ BRUT

Vintaged, méthode champenoise: 40% Chardonnay, 60% Pinot Noir

SHINGLE PEAK BRUT

Vintaged, méthode champenoise: 40% Chardonnay, 60% Pinot Noir

CELLIER LE BRUN

RENWICK, MARLBOROUGH

• 150,000 cases

Established in 1980 by Daniel Le Brun, who was born in Monthélon, a few kilometres south of Epernay, in the hinterland of Champagne's Côte des Blancs. His family had been *vignerons* since 1648, passing on their viticultural skills from father to son for 12 generations. It was his great-grandfather who, at the turn of the century, decided to make and sell Champagne rather than just grapes.

Daniel's initial inclination was to carry on the family tradition, but during his studies at the Ecole de Viticulture et d'Oenologie d'Avize he realised how restraining and suppressive the system was in Champagne. So, while his brother settled in to the family groove helping his father make and sell Champagne René Le Brun, Daniel decided to travel. In 1975, he visited New Zealand, fell in love with the place and emigrated later that year. Three years later, he met and married Adele, they purchased some land just outside Renwick in Marlborough in order to plant a vineyard.

Without even thinking about it, Daniel planted Chardonnay, Pinot Noir and Pinot Meunier, his only concession to New Zealand being to plant these vines wide enough to take a Kiwi tractor. He did everything the champenois way. His natural instinct to burrow a cellar into the Renwick hillside to replicate the naturally cool and stable storage conditions of home was not as mad as the locals imagined, but they called him 'the mad Frenchman' all the same.

Daniel made his first non-vintage base wine in 1983, releasing it in 1986. His first vintage was a 1985 Blanc de Blancs, but it was his 1986 Blanc de Blancs that the New Zealand wine press hyped up. It was, however, far too big and fat to have any class, and although Le Brun was obviously pleased by its success, he knew it was wide of the mark. In Marlborough's verdant vineyards, he was experiencing a very steep learning curve. He decided to break with his roots by burying his champenois text books under a row of vines and go back to basics.

'The vigour of the vines,' he explains, 'has to be controlled. This is never a problem in Champagne, but in New Zealand the vine becomes a jungle if you do not cut it back savagely. I also have to harvest earlier to get

CELLIER LE BRUN CELLARS IN MARLBOROUGH

acceptable levels of acidity and pH. In Champagne, we had to warm the cellars in the winter to keep the fermentation going and there was no problem with precipitation of tartaric crystals, which happened naturally in the cold climate. Here in New Zealand I had to introduce refrigeration techniques in the cellar. I also tend to prevent the malolactic more often here than in Champagne and, whatever I do, the wines are ready to drink much earlier than back home and require less *dosage* – just five to six grams per litre of sugar, rather than eight to 12.'

It all worked, and quickly too. By the early 1990s, Daniel had become one of only two New World sparkling wine producers to rival not just Champagne, but good quality Champagne. Roederer Estate in California achieved this with its 1987-based release, while Le Brun came good with his 1989 Blanc de Blancs, and his 1990 Brut was an even greater success. By this juncture there really was nothing that Daniel Le Brun had to do to improve the quality of his wines.

In 1996, just as this Frenchman's star seemed well and truly established in the sparkling wine world's firmament, Le Brun dropped out of sight. His former business partner Tony Nightingale now owns 95% of Cellier Le Brun, but although there was obviously more to this than a simple takeover, all I can say is that Daniel Le Brun has since been involved in consultancy work, and there are rumours of a new venture in the offing.

Nightingale has expanded the vineyards from 14 to 30 hectares, and brought in winemaker Allan McWilliams, who has an impressive CV. Since McWilliams graduated from Roseworthy, Australia's premier wine school, he has gained worldwide experience before becoming chief winemaker for Negociants New Zealand,

where he developed the Nautilus, Twin Islands and Half Moon Bay ranges.

WINEMAKER
Allan McWilliams

HOUSE STYLE & RANGE

The early vintages were rather overblown but, as indicated above, since the 1989 Blanc de Blancs they have been outstanding. In fact, the 1989 was so good it started rumours that Daniel Le Brun had imported it direct from his family in Champagne! There is no denying the class, finesse and biscuity complexity of the Blanc de Blancs, although it is generally several years more precocious than a blanc de blancs Champagne of the same age.

Unusually the Vintage Brut has more of a tendency to go toasty than the Blanc de Blancs, but some coconutty character has crept into this wine since the 1992 Vintage Brut was released under new management. Hopefully this is the result of messing about with the *dosage*. I say hopefully because if this is so it can be rectified, whereas if it is something that Le Brun actually did to the original base-wine, it cannot.

The non-vintage Brut has been the most exported, yet least exciting wine in the range, and from the fresh, fruit-driven *cuvée* available at the time of writing, either Allan McWilliams has successfully manipulated this wine or Le Brun perfected it just before he left.

The Rosé, with its exuberant red-berry fruit, is utterly delicious, but occasionally the colour has dropped out or mellowed, which is why it was sometimes released as a Blanc de Noirs. However, the new management has renamed it Taché, which should cover all eventualities.

The following wines can be assessed on the basis of their track-record, but it will be some time before the new winemaker has put his own mark on Cellier Le Brun, thus judgement is reserved on an overall rating.

★ BRUT, MARLBOROUGH
Not vintaged, méthode champenoise: 30% Chardonnay, 60% Pinot Noir, 10% Meunier

★★ TACHÉ BRUT, MARLBOROUGH
Not vintaged, méthode champenoise: 100% Pinot Noir

★★ BLANC DE BLANCS BRUT, MARLBOROUGH
Vintaged, méthode champenoise: 100% Chardonnay

★★ VINTAGE BRUT, MARLBOROUGH
Vintaged, méthode champenoise: 50% Chardonnay, 50% Pinot Noir

---

75 VALUE
MILLS REEF
TAURANGA, BAY OF PLENTY

• 20,000 cases

This father and son operation was established in 1989 and produced its first sparkling wine in 1990, launching it three years later. In 1995 the Prestons moved into a brand new

winery complete with 150-seater restaurant.
WINEMAKER
Paddy & Tim Preston
HOUSE STYLE & RANGE

The Prestons have quickly built a reputation for the incredible consistency of their coconutty fizz. There is no denying the quality of fruit and beautifully ripe acidity, but the dominance of so much oak detracts from the finesse of the sparkling wines. The oak is supposedly 'older French' barrels, but they are obviously not old enough and the wine has too much contact with them. Furthermore, I am becoming increasingly alarmed at the number of French oak barrels that have the blatant coconutty character associated with American oak. I do not propose they should stop making this rich, coconutty, fruity fizz. Why should they when the wines regularly win awards and critical acclaim down-under? But now they have assured their own success, I would love to see the Prestons attempt a more classic style of sparkling wine, made from the same quality of fruit, with the same level of care and attention. In the meantime, true Champagne aficionados should knock ten points off the above rating, while lovers of four-by-two should add on another ten points!

The vintage *cuvée* changed from 100% Chardonnay to the blend indicated below with the 1994 vintage, but the earlier vintages were so successful that I suspect an additional Blanc de Blancs *cuvée* will be launched in the future.

★ CHARISMA MÉTHODE TRADITIONELLE, HAWKES BAY

    Not vintaged, méthode champenoise: 35% Chardonnay, 65% Pinot Noir

★★ BRUT MÉTHODE TRADITIONELLE, HAWKES BAY

    Vintaged, méthode champenoise: 45% Chardonnay, 55% Pinot Noir

MIRU MIRU
See Hunter's

85 VALUE
MONTANA
MARLBOROUGH, GISBORNE, HAWKES BAY, AUCKLAND
• 400,000 cases

I doubt that Ivan Yukich had an inkling of what he was starting when he planted a half-acre vineyard in the 1940s. Yukich called his tiny vineyard Montana because it was located high in the Waitakere Ranges, west of Auckland, and in his native Dalmation tongue *montana* meant mountain. He sold his first Montana wine in 1952, and from this seed this company has grown to become the largest wine producer in New Zealand.

Much of Montana's early expansion was due to a range of cheap sparkling wine products (Pearl, Cold Duck, Poulet Poulet), but the company was also responsible for pioneering the Marlborough district, which has not only quickly established New Zealand's position in the New World's wine hierarchy,

but later turned out to be the most promising region for high-quality sparkling wine.

Montana launched a more than decent fruity fizz under the Lindauer label in 1981, eight years before entering into a joint venture to produce Deutz Brut Marlborough Cuvée, but it was the Franco-Kiwi *cuvée* that put the country on the map as far as sparkling wine potential was concerned.

WINEMAKER
Jeff Clarke, Andy Frost
HOUSE STYLE & RANGE
The Lindauer Brut is always value for money and can often be surprisingly good quality, particularly when it is appreciated that this wine accounts for three-quarters of Montana's total fizz production. Lindauer normally has fresh and fluffy lemon meringue or juicy lime fruit, and is best drunk straight from the shelf, although occasionally you will come across a *cuvée* that can be aged into a soft, honeyed fizz. The Lindauer Rosé is produced in a much smaller volume (20,000 cases as opposed to 300,000), but is usually more straightforward. The premium Lindauer Special Reserve can sometimes outperform the Deutz Brut Marlborough Cuvée. It has exquisite finesse for such a satisfying flavour of soft fruit, with sweetish vanilla smoothness on the finish.

The first release of Deutz Brut Marlborough Cuvée was streaks ahead of the now defunct Maison Deutz in California, even though the American operation had a three year start. However, that first release was not exactly earth-shattering, although like so many New World ventures involving grande marque Champagne houses, there was a tendency by the wine media to hype it up.

With each new release, though, Deutz Brut Marlborough Cuvée has acquired more finesse, and now has a refreshing, fruity style with a serious edge when young, developing a toasty, high-acid, Chablis-like style with bottle-age, although I never keep it more than a year. On the other hand, the Deutz

HOT AIR BALLOONS DRIFT OVER MONTANA'S BRANCOTT ESTATE VINEYARDS

Blanc de Blancs is so young at six or seven years old that it may well repay cellaring for longer than its existence has allowed me to experiment with. Look out for a new Blanc de Noirs that Montana is launching just after this book is due to be published.

★ LINDAUER BRUT

    Not vintaged, transfer method: 'predominantly' Chardonnay, Pinot Noir, plus other unrevealed varieties

LINDAUER ROSÉ

    Not vintaged, transfer method: 'predominantly' Chardonnay, Pinot Noir, plus other unrevealed varieties

★★ LINDAUER SPECIAL RESERVE

    Not vintaged, transfer method: 30% Chardonnay, 70% Pinot Noir

★★ DEUTZ BRUT MARLBOROUGH CUVÉE

    Not vintaged, méthode champenoise: 50% Chardonnay, 50% Pinot Noir

★★ DEUTZ BLANC DE BLANCS MARLBOROUGH CUVÉE

    Vintaged, méthode champenoise: 100% Chardonnay,

N/A
MORTON ESTATE
KATIKATI, BAY OF PLENTY
• 55,000 cases

Established in 1978 by Morton Brown, a former Woolworths trainee and car salesman who made good in finance and marketing. In 1982 Brown erected this estate's famous white-plastered Cape Dutch-style winery, but it was the raw talent and extrovert personality of John Hancock, his partner-winemaker, who put Morton Estate on the map. In 1987, the winery was floated on the stock exchange and taken over a year later by Mildara Wines of Australia; it is now owned by John and Alison Coney. Hancock has left to pursue his own project (Trinity Hill, Hastings, but no fizz yet).

WINEMAKER
Evan Ward
HOUSE STYLE & RANGE
This excellent estate frustratingly produces one of New Zealand's finest and potentially complex sparkling wines. The frustrating element is the incidence of bad corks, which sometimes manifests itself merely as green apple on mild steel taste (as opposed to the softer fruit of ripe green apples), while other times it is more prominently corky.

I know Hancock had problems with wines I tasted back in 1992, so this cork business extends back into the 1980s. However, I do not read of any such problem in the New Zealand wine press, so maybe I've been unlucky.

MORTON ESTATE SPARKLING BRUT, METHOD TRADITIONELLE

    Vintaged, méthode champenoise: 33% Chardonnay, 47% Pinot Noir, 20% Meunier

NAUTILUS
See NEGOCIANTS NEW ZEALAND

80
NEGOCIANTS NEW ZEALAND
RENWICK, MARLBOROUGH

- 11,000 cases
- Other labels - Nautilus, Twin Islands

This company, which incorporates the Nautilus vineyard, was established in 1985, and in 1987 became a wholly owned subsidiary of Samuel Smith & Sons of Yalumba fame (Australia). There is a Nautilus vineyard with cellar-door sales, but no Nautilus winery as such, the wines being produced at Rapaura Vintners, which Negociants New Zealand has a shareholding in. The debut Nautilus *cuvée* was produced in 1991, with the first Twin Islands being made the following year.

WINEMAKER
Matt Harrop, Helena Lindberg

HOUSE STYLE & RANGE
Nautilus is extremely fruity and not at all complex, but delicious to drink. It is an estate-produced sparkling wine, whereas Twin Islands is produced from purchased grapes. The varietal composition of Twin Islands is virtually the reverse of Nautilus, and is described as 'commercial fruit driven', but it is so herbaceous that I thought it was mainly Sauvignon Blanc when I first tasted it. While there is something to be said for producing an herbaceous fizz to express the verdancy of its New Zealand origins, it is not true to its varietal roots. Hopefully later-picked fruit from less vigorous vineyards will allow Twin Islands to evolve into a better quality product.

★ NAUTILUS ESTATE CUVÉE BRUT
MARLBOROUGH
Not vintaged, méthode champenoise: 25% Chardonnay, 75% Pinot Noir

TWIN ISLANDS BRUT
Not vintaged, méthode champenoise: 70% Chardonnay, 30% Pinot Noir

N/A
PARKER MÉTHODE CHAMPENOISE
GISBORNE

You cannot miss Parker's winery; it's the one with a DC3 on the roof. Unfortunately he won't submit samples of his wines, even when I turn up virtually on his doorstep for a centralised tasting of New Zealand fizz.

WINEMAKER
Phil Parker

HOUSE RANGE
DRY FLINT
Not vintaged, méthode champenoise: 50% Chenin Blanc, 50% Sémillon

ROSÉ
Not vintaged, méthode champenoise: 100% Pinot Noir

CLASSICAL BRUT
Vintaged, méthode champenoise: 25% Chardonnay, 75% Pinot Noir

PELORUS
See CLOUDY BAY

N/A
RIPPON VINEYARD
LAKE WANAKA

- 100 cases

If a competition for the most photographic vineyard location in the world existed, Rippon would be on the short-list. The vineyard was established in 1986 by Rolfe and Lois Mills, and it was Rolfe's grandfather who brought the name of Rippon to Central Otago, where it is common, particularly in the Wanaka and Cromwell areas.

Rolfe's grandfather was Sir Percy Sargood, and his father, Sir Frederick Sargood, who was Minister of Defence for the newly-formed Australian Federation of States in 1901. But he named his house in Melbourne to honour the maiden name of his mother, Emma Rippon, who was the daughter of Thomas Rippon, the chief cashier of the Bank of England. Such are the convoluted origins of the name given to this sparkling wine.

WINEMAKER
Various

HOUSE STYLE & RANGE
Although Rolf and Lois sent me a bottle, it had not been disgorged. After it had travelled halfway around the world on its sediment, I crudely riddled it and tasted the wine without any *dosage*, thus it would be unfair to comment, but I certainly look forward to tasting the full commercial product.

EMMA RIPPON BRUT
Vintaged, méthode champenoise: 75% Chardonnay, 25% Pinot Noir

ROCHE
See CHARD FARM

N/A
SELAKS
KUMEU, AUCKLAND

Selaks consistently produces fine quality, stylish wines, particularly whites, but its sparkling wine has been uninspiring. This is curious because Selaks produced the first Kiwi fizz back in 1956, and with 40 years experience they should have the process licked by now.

WINEMAKER
Darryl Wooley

HOUSE STYLE & RANGE
The only sparkling wine which shows this producer's unique experience is its citrussy, toasty 'Mate I Selak' Blanc de Blancs. The other *cuvées* have an overpowering maltiness.

MÉTHODE TRADITIONELLE
Not vintaged, méthode champenoise: 30% Chardonnay, 70% Pinot Noir

★ 'MATE I SELAK' BLANC DE BLANCS

Vintaged, méthode champenoise: 100% Chardonnay
MÉTHODE TRADITIONELLE
Vintaged, méthode champenoise: 30% Chardonnay, 70% Pinot Noir

SHINGLE PEAK
See MATUA VALLEY

75
SOLJANS
HENDERSON

Established in 1937 by Frank Soljan, whose son Tony runs this immaculately equipped winery today. Soljans was primarily known for its dessert wines, particularly its matured sherries, but it is now firmly established as a producer of premium varietal wines. However, until the relatively recent launch of Legacy, the only sparkling wine Soljans was known for was a sweet, aromatic fizz called Vivace Spumante. Legacy is its first brut-style fizz.

WINEMAKER
Tony Soljans

HOUSE STYLE & RANGE
A fresh and sprightly fizz, totally fruit-driven, and probably best drunk as young as possible. No one has sufficient experience of this *cuvée* to know what its ageing potential might be.

★ LEGACY MÉTHODE TRADITIONNELLE
Vintaged, méthode champenoise: 72% Chardonnay, 28% Pinot Noir

TWIN ISLANDS
See NEGOCIANTS NEW ZEALAND

N/A
VIDAL
HASTINGS

This winery was founded by a Spaniard, but is now owned by George Fistonich, the son of a Dalmation immigrant and proprietor of Villa Maria. Vidal consistently produces some of the most exciting red wines in Hawke's Bay, but the whites often lack finesse, and the first sparkling wines, which were first produced in 1987, got off to a pretty shaky start.

WINEMAKER
Rod McDonald

HOUSE STYLE & RANGE
After the 1987s, these sparkling wines were cleaner and took on a soft, creamy, more delicate style.

MÉTHODE TRADITIONELLE BLANC DE BLANCS BRUT
Vintaged, méthode champenoise: 100% Chardonnay
MÉTHODE TRADITIONELLE BLANC DE NOIRS BRUT
Vintaged, méthode champenoise: 100% Pinot Noir
MÉTHODE TRADITIONELLE BRUT
Vintaged, méthode champenoise: 30% Chardonnay, 70% Pinot Noir

VOYAGE
See GIESEN

ASIA

ALTHOUGH AT LEAST ONE CHAMPAGNE HOUSE HAS EXPERIMENTED WITH SPARKLING WINE IN KOREA, IT HAS NOT BEEN A GREAT SUCCESS. NOR HAVE ANY OF THE BUBBLIES OCCASIONALLY PRODUCED IN JAPAN. INDEED, THE ONLY TWO ASIAN COUNTRIES WITH ANY REPUTATION FOR BUBBLES ARE CHINA AND INDIA.

CHINA

It is assumed that the first Chinese wines were made in 128BC, when General Chang planted *vinifera* seeds at the Imperial Palace in Chang An (now called Xian), some 600 miles south of Beijing, although there is no firm evidence of any winemaking, just viticulture. It is difficult to discern when the first Chinese sparkling wine was made, but most bubbly produced in this vast country today is artificially constructed from grape juice, apple juice, and alcohol, then injected with carbonic gas. Only two companies produce bottle-fermented sparkling wine: **Imperial Court** in Shanghai and **Dragon Seal** in Beijing.

Imperial Court is a joint venture with Rémy Martin and is a light, acidic fizz made from Ugni Blanc grapes. Dragon Seal started its sparkling wine production as recently as 1997, but using 1993 base wines, and is made by Frenchman Denis Degache, who has so far used Chardonnay exclusively.

INDIA

In 1982, self-made Bombay millionaire Sham Chougule asked Piper-Heidsieck to provide technical assistance in a project aimed at producing fine, sparkling *méthode champenoise* Indian wines. Piper-Heidsieck despatched to India a young oenologist called Raphael Brisbois, who was then attached to the firm's subsidiary Company, Champagne Technologie.

Brisbois chose a site at Narayangaon, in the state of Maharashtra, and constructed a £4 million high-tech winery set into the side of the Sahyadri Mountains.

The wine sold under the **Omar Khayyam** label was exceptional ten years ago, when hardly anyone in the New World was making a decent fizz. The vineyards are located on east-facing slopes of the Sahyadri Mountains, where the lime-rich clay soil and altitude of some 750 metres are well suited to growing wine grapes. The first *cuvées* were supposed to have contained 30% Chardonnay, the balance being Ugni Blanc for extra acidity, although the amount of Chardonnay has since increased and a small amount of Pinot Noir is also now used. However, when I met Brisbois at Iron Horse in California, he confessed to me that his first *cuvée* of Omar Khayyam was virtually 100% Thompson Seedless (sultana), although many experienced tasters in those days thought it was almost entirely Chardonnay.

Although the wine is as good now as it was then, it has not evolved while the rest of the New World sparkling wine industry has moved on. Consequently Omar Khayyam now seems rather dull and foursquare compared to the elegance and finesse of its more modern counterparts.

Apart from Omar Khayyam, there is a non-vintage Marquise de Pompadour Brut Royale, which tastes of Devon toffees and the vintaged Celebre Brut Royale, which is supposed to be the prestige *cuvée*, but tastes as it smells – ten years old. At the other extreme, Joie Demi Sec is a cheap *cuve close*. All these wines are marketed when they are much too old, and would greatly benefit from the light hand of a truly talented consultant, such as Brisbois himself.

IRRIGATION BY FLOODING ROWS OF VINES IN THE VINEYARD OF CHAMPAGNE INDIA – PRODUCER OF OMAR KHAYYAM

CHAMPAGNE VINTAGES

PRODUCERS ARE FREE TO MAKE AND SELL A VINTAGE CHAMPAGNE FROM ANY YEAR. A VINTAGE SHOULD DENOTE A SPECIAL QUALITY, AND IN SOME YEARS – 1996, 1990, 1985 AND 1982 FOR EXAMPLE – ALL THE PRODUCERS ARE IN AGREEMENT THAT IT DOES AND EACH ONE WILL INDEED PRODUCE A VINTAGE. AT THE OTHER END OF THE SPECTRUM THERE ARE YEARS WHEN, DUE TO APPALLING WEATHER CONDITIONS, THE QUALITY IS SO BAD THAT NO ONE IN THEIR RIGHT MIND WOULD WANT TO EMBLAZON THEIR BOTTLES WITH IT, THE LAST TWO BEING 1984 AND 1972. BETWEEN THESE TWO EXTREMES ARE MANY YEARS THAT ARE NOT BAD, BUT NOT SPECIAL, AND REALLY SHOULD NOT BE DECLARED. HOWEVER THERE ARE SOME PRODUCERS, MOSTLY COOPERATIVES AND RUN-OF-THE-MILL GROWERS, WHO DECLARE A VINTAGE VIRTUALLY EVERY YEAR, HENCE THE DEROGATORY TERM 'COOPERATIVE VINTAGE'.

Not so very long ago, old vintage Champagnes were the bargain buys of the auction circuit, but although they are not quite the giveaways they used to be, they remain relatively inexpensive compared to Bordeaux and Burgundy. It is always advisable to taste before bidding, even when the provenance is faultless, but if there is any doubt about how and where the wine has been stored from the moment it left the producer's cellars, pre-sale tasting is essential.

Key
No stars-   Poor to diabolical.
★   Average to good non-vintage quality.
★★   Very good non-vintage to borderline
              vintage quality.
★★★   Good vintage quality.
★★★★   Excellent vintage quality.
★★★★★   A rare classic.

1997 ★★★★
Contrary to fears leading up to the harvest, this year turned out to be a true vintage, particularly for Pinot Noir and Meunier. It will certainly prove to be better than anything from 1991 to 1994 inclusive, and superior to all but the Chardonnay-dominated *cuvées* of 1995.

1996 ★★★★★
Without doubt the best year since 1990, with an unprecedented ratio of acidity to sugar, it could even give that extraordinary vintage a run for its money. Only time will tell how great this vintage truly is, but the future will certainly look back on 1996 as the year that even Mumm returned to form.

1995 ★★★
After four years of sporadic successes, the champenois were relieved to have a universally declared vintage. Although, like 1988, this year did not achieve true vintage ripeness, it is indisputably very good in quality. The wines have good ageing potential and should turn out similar to the 1988s, although not quite in the same class, except for some Chardonnay-dominated *cuvées*, which could even have the edge.

1994 ★
A normal size harvest of good non-vintage quality.
THE BEST
Of the vintage Champagnes that will be declared Vilmart (Grand Cellier d'Or) should stand out. Charles Heidsieck's non-vintage Brut Réserve, Mis en Cave 1995, is primarily 1994-based and should start to drink well by the end of 1999.

FIZZ FOR THE MILLENNIUM

If money and rarity were no obstacle, I would crack a bottle of HEIDSIECK & CO 1907 GOÛT AMÉRICAIN, which has spent the last 80 years on the bottom of the Baltic courtesy of a German U-Boat in 1916. The bottles are incredibly consistent. With no trace of seawater penetration, the constant 2°C has put this wine through suspended animation and the result is a Champagne which is profoundly and succulently sweet, with impeccably balanced fruit of amazing purity and freshness.

Other rarities fit for the Millennium which I could not possibly afford, but have had the good fortune to taste would include 1921 MOËT & CHANDON (they transferred this vintage into the very first Dom Pérignon bottles so, without the detrimental effect of pouring from one bottle to another, this is in perfect condition whereas any surviving 1921 Dom Pérignon is not likely to be – this also happens to be the greatest Champagne that Moët has ever made); 1892 and 1914 POL ROGER (I cannot make up my mind which, since they are both in miraculously fizzy form); and 1955 VEUVE CLICQUOT (the greatest vintage I have tasted from this house, it even has the edge over the fabulous 1947).

I suppose the one *cuvée* specially produced for the Millennium I would recommend readers to buy would have to be the Jeroboam of PERRIER JOUËT 1995 BELLE EPOQUE because at $2,000 it is the biggest bargain, coming complete with an invitation for two to stay at the beautifully furnished Maison Belle Epoque in Epernay, where you will be lavishly wined and dined. I won't be buying it because staying at the Maison Belle Epoque is one of the perks of the job. Mind you, with two thousand couples staying there from the year 2000 on, it will probably be a long time before they can invite me again!

1993 ★
Normal size harvest of average non-vintage quality.
THE BEST
Pierre Gimonnet (Gastronome), Jacquesson (Signature), Jean-Michel Pelletier (Cuvée Anaëlle Brut), Roederer (Vintage) and Vilmart. Charles Heidsieck's 1993-based Brut Réserve Mis en Cave 1994 is already drinking beautifully.

1992 ★★
A fairly large harvest of very good non-vintage quality, which generally achieved vintage-quality ripeness, whereas 1991, 1993, 1994 and, indeed, 1995 did not.
THE BEST
Larmandier-Bernier (Grand Cru Blanc de Blancs) and Perrier-Jouët.
OTHER SUCCESSES
Nicolas Feuillatte (Blanc de Blancs), Jacquinet-Dumez (Cuvée L'Excellence), Moët & Chandon (Rosé), Pol Roger (Vintage), Pommery (Vintage), Ruinart (R) and Vilmart. Charles Heidsieck's 1992-based Brut Réserve Mis en Cave 1993 has already proved itself a winner and should continue to drink nicely through to the Millennium.

1991 ★
A large harvest of good non-vintage quality. Bollinger contemplated declaring a vintage, but finally did not.
THE BEST
Philipponnat (Clos des Goisses), Taittinger (Comtes de Champagne Rosé) and Vilmart (Grande Cellier d'Or and Coeur de Cuvée).
OTHER SUCCESSES
De Nauroy (Vintage) and Louis Roederer (Rosé).

1990 ★★★★★
The best all-round vintage since 1982, and the highest degree of ripeness since 1959. Although considerably riper than 1976, these rich and succulent wines have never tasted heavy due to their higher acidity, which has provided an impeccable balance from the moment they were first released.
THE BEST
Bollinger (Grande Année), Billecart-Salmon (Cuvée Nicolas-François), Gosset (Grand Millésimé), Charles Heidsieck (Vintage, Cuvée des Millénaires), Jacquart, Jacquesson (Blanc de Blancs, Signature Rosé), Laurent-Perrier (Grand Siècle Exceptionellement Millésimé), Moët & Chandon (Dom Pérignon), Pol Roger, Louis Roederer (Cristal, Cristal '2000', Blanc de Blancs), Ruinart (Dom Ruinart Blanc de Blancs), Salon, Veuve Clicquot (Vintage and Grande Dame) and Vilmart (Coeur de Cuvée). Krug 1990 Vintage had not been tasted at the time of writing.

1989 ★★★★

A vintage that was almost too spectacular to be true, the Krug tasted so luscious as soon as it had fermented that Henri Krug uncharacteristically encouraged journalists to taste from the barrel in November. Little wonder, then, that the 1989s initially promised to be generally superior to the 1988s, although the latter has since firmly established itself as the better vintage in general terms. Some of the first 1989s to be released were dire, but a few of the late-released 1989s will probably outperform even the best 1988s.

THE BEST

Billecart-Salmon (Blanc de Blancs, Cuvée Elizabeth Salmon Rosée), Bollinger (Grande Année, Vieilles Vignes Françaises), Drappier (Grand Sendrée), Alfred Gratien (Vintage), Charles Heidsieck, Piper-Heidsieck (Brut Sauvage), Jacquesson (Signature), Krug (Vintage, Clos du Mesnil), Philipponnat (Clos des Goisses), Ployez-Jacquemart (L. d'Harbonville), Pommery (Vintage), Veuve Clicquot (Vintage Réserve, Rich Réserve, Grande Dame).

OTHER SUCCESSES

Gosset (Grande Millésime), Bruno Paillard, Palmer, Pol Roger, Pommery (Vintage, Cuvée Louise Rosée), Louis Roederer (Blanc de Blancs, Rosée), Jacques Selosse (Grand Cru Blanc de Blancs) and Vilmart (Coeur de Cuvée).

1988 ★★★★

Although this normal-sized harvest did not quite reach the ripeness level of a true vintage, apart from some early-released, cheap Champagnes, 1988 has been of true vintage quality, as its slow-maturing wines have consistently demonstrated. Although they have nowhere near the massive malic content of the 1995s, it is the high malic content of the 1988s that made them firmer and less flamboyant than either the 1989s and 1990s, but has ensured their long-term potential. As with 1990, there are too many great 1988s to list, thus I have restricted the choice to the best of the best.

THE BEST

Billecart-Salmon (Cuvée Nicolas-François, Grande Cuvée, Cuvée Elizabeth Salmon Rosée), Bollinger (Grande Année, Vieilles Vignes Françaises), Pierre Gimonnet (Gastronome), Gosset (Celebris, Grand Millésime Rosée), Jacquesson (Perfection, Signature), Krug (Vintage, Clos du Mesnil), Lanson (Noble Cuvée), Laurent-Perrier (Vintage, Grand Siècle Alexandra Rosée), Moët & Chandon (Dom Pérignon), Perrier-Jouët (Belle Epoque, Belle Epoque Rosée), Philipponnat (Clos des Goisses), Ployez-Jacquemart (L. d'Harbonville), Pol Roger (Vintage, Rosée, Réserve Speciale PR, Cuvée Sir Winston Churchill), Pommery (Vintage, Cuvée Louise Rosée), Louis Roederer (Cristal, Cristal Rosée), Ruinart (Dom Ruinart Blanc de Blancs, Dom Ruinart Rosée), Salon, Taittinger (Comtes de Champagne Blanc de Blancs) and Veuve Clicquot (Grande Dame, Grande Dame Rosée).

1987 ★

Despite this being a large and ubiquitous 'cooperative vintage' of merely good non-vintage quality, a few truly exceptional vintage Champagnes were declared.

THE BEST

Baron Albert (Cuvée Jean de la Fontaine), Pommery (Cuvée Louise) and Jacques Selosse Cuvée d'Origine.

1986 ★★★

This was a large harvest, but not of true vintage quality. However, after the horrendously tiny 1985 vintage, which itself followed a string of poor or very small crops, the general mood in Champagne was to widely declare 1986 and a number of very good 1986s have emerged because they employed such exceptionally rigorous selection to enhance the quality.

THE BEST

Bollinger (Vieilles Vignes Françaises), Perrier-Jouët (Belle Epoque Rosée) and Philipponnat (Clos des Goisses).

OTHER TOP-PERFORMERS

*Billecart-Salmon (Cuvée Nicolas-François, Blanc de Blancs), Bollinger (Grande Année), De Castellane (Cuvée Florens), Pierre Gimonnet (Gastronome), Jacquart (Cuvée Mosaïque Rosée), Moët & Chandon (Brut Impérial), Pol Roger (Chardonnay, Cuvée Sir Winston Churchill, Réserve Spéciale PR), Louis Roederer (Vintage, Blanc de Blancs, Rosée), Ruinart (Dom Ruinart Rosée), Sugot Feneuil (Special Club) and Taittinger (Comtes de Champagne Blanc de Blancs, Comtes de Champagne Rosée).
This vintage should be consumed before the 1985s and 1982s.*

1985 ★★★★★

At the moment this vintage is not quite in the class of 1990 or 1982, but it is very close behind. Indeed, the 1985s have a very special character and the quality is improving at an unexpected rate, so they might eventually be on a par with 1990 and 1982. For the moment, what sets these two great vintages apart is their extraordinary consistency across all grape varieties and throughout all the districts of Champagne. Furthermore, the balance of the 1990s and 1982s has made them charming from the start. In comparison, the greatness of 1985 is very specific, focusing on the Pinot Noir, particularly from the northern montagne, where the savage frosts reduced production levels to minuscule amounts and consequently yielded phenomenally concentrated wines, and some wines still have a long way to go before the extract they contain opens up. This is definitely a vintage that future generations will be talking about and indeed tasting for decades to come.

THE BEST

Billecart-Salmon (Blanc de Blancs, Cuvée Nicolas-François, Grande Cuvée), Bollinger (Grande Année, Vieilles Vignes Françaises), De Castellane (Cuvée Florens), De Cazanove (Stradivarius), Charbaut (Certificate Blanc de Blancs, Certificate Rosée), Deutz (Cuvée William Deutz), Duval-Leroy (Cuvée des Roys), Nicolas Feuillatte (Cuvée Palmes d'Or), Gosset (Grand Millésime, Grand Millésime Rosée), Alfred Gratien (Vintage), Charles Heidsieck (Vintage, Rosée, Cuvée des Millénaires, Champagne Charlie), Heidsieck & Co Monopole (Diamant Bleu Rosée), Jacquart (La Cuvée Nominée Rosée), Jacquesson (Perfection, Dégorgement Tardive in magnum), Krug (Vintage, Clos du Mesnil), Lanson, Laurent-Perrier (Grand Siècle Exceptionellement, Grand Siècle Alexandra Rosée), Moët & Chandon (Brut Impérial, Rosée, Dom Pérignon), Perrier-Jouët (Belle Epoque, Belle Epoque Rosée), Philipponnat (Clos des Goisses), Piper-Heidsieck (Rare), Pol Roger (Vintage, Chardonnay, Rosée), Pommery (Cuvée Louise), Alain Robert (Sélection), Louis Roederer (Vintage, Blanc de Blancs, Rosée, Cristal, Cristal Rosée), Ruinart (Dom Ruinart Blanc de Blancs), Salon, Taittinger (Vintage, Comtes de Champagne Blanc de Blancs, Comtes de Champagne

Rosée), Vauversin, George Vesselle Blanc de Noirs, Veuve Clicquot (Vintage, Rosée, Grande Dame). Although some of these wines are approachable, they are best drunk after the 1986s, 1989s and 1990s.

1984 -

Uniformly diabolical, the only exception being the own-label vintage Champagne sold by the British supermarket Waitrose, which came from an unnamed grower on the Côte des Blancs who happened to purchase new oak barrels that year. There was no oakiness in the wine, but it was eminently drinkable. The mystery deepens because according to the Waitrose buyer, the same grower's 1985 was not a good wine at all, and I cannot think of anyone who made a hash of that year, let alone someone who was capable of making such a drinkable 1984.

1983 ★★★★

An underrated vintage that had a more classically lean structure than the 1982s, but was much less uniform. The best 1983s started to reach their peak in the mid-1990s, much as the 1979s did a few years ago and, interestingly, not in a dissimilar style.

THE BEST

Dom Pérignon

OTHER SUCCESSES

*Billecart-Salmon (Cuvée Nicolas-François), Bollinger (Grande Année), Charbaut (Certificate Blanc de Blancs), Gosset (Grand Millésime, Grand Millésime Rosée), Alfred Gratien (Vintage), Charles Heidsieck (Rosée, Cuvée des Millénaires), Henriot (Vintage, Cuvée Baccarat), Jacquesson (Perfection), Krug (Clos du Mesnil), Moët & Chandon (Brut Impérial, Cuvée 250ème Anniversaire), Orpale Blanc de Blancs, Perrier-Jouët (Belle Epoque), Philipponnat (Clos des Goisses), Pommery (Vintage, Cuvée Louise Rosée), Louis Roederer (Cristal, Cristal Rosée), Ruinart (Dom Ruinart Blanc de Blancs), De Venoge (Blanc de Blancs), Taittinger (Vintage, Comtes de Champagne Blanc de Blancs, Comtes de Champagne Rosée), Veuve Clicquot (Vintage, Grand Dame, Rosée).
Bottles of Charles Heidsieck (vintage) disgorged in mid-1998 far excel the perceived potential of this wine when it was originally released.*

1982 ★★★★★

A large crop of voluptuously rich Champagnes of an extraordinary consistency.

THE BEST

Krug Vintage, Krug Clos du Mesnil, Laurent-Perrier Cuvée Alexandre Rosée, Dom Pérignon, Dom Pérignon Rosée

OTHER SUCCESSES

Ayala Grande Cuvée, Billecart-Salmon (Blanc de Blancs, Cuvée Nicolas-François, Grande Cuvée), Bollinger (Grande Année, Rosée, Vieilles Vignes Françaises), De Castellane (Cuvée Florens), Charbaut (Certificate Rosée), Deutz (Cuvée William Deutz Rosée), Gosset (Grand Millésime Rosée), Alfred Gratien (Vintage), Charles Heidsieck (Champagne Charlie, Blanc de Blancs, Vintage), Heidsieck & Co Monopole (Diamant Bleu Rosée), Krug (Vintage, Clos du Mesnil), Laurent-Perrier (Grand Siècle Exceptionellement), Moët & Chandon (Brut Impérial), Mumm (Mumm de Mumm), Joseph Perrier (Cuvée Joséphine), Perrier-Jouët (Vintage, Belle Epoque), Philipponnat (Clos des Goisses), Ployez-Jacquemart (L. d'Harbonville), Pol Roger (Vintage, Chardonnay, Cuvée Sir Winston Churchill, Réserve Speciale PR, Rosée), Pommery (Cuvée Louise), Louis Roederer (Cristal,

Cristal Rosé), Dom Ruinart (R, Blanc de Blancs, Rosé), Salon, Taittinger (Vintage, Comtes de Champagne Blanc de Blancs, Comtes de Champagne Rosé) and Veuve Clicquot (Vintage).

1981 *****

A tiny crop that arrived when stocks were low and desperately needed for blending purposes, but small quantities of a number of vintages were declared and the most successful have great finesse and will outlast most 1982s.

THE BEST

Krug (one of the three greatest Champagnes produced between 1970 and 1990)

OTHER SUCCESSES

Billecart-Salmon (Blanc de Blancs), Bollinger (Vieilles Vignes Françaises), Charbaut (Certificate Blanc de Blancs), Deutz (Blanc de Blancs), Charles Heidsieck (Vintage), Krug (Clos du Mesnil), Lang-Biémont (Blanc de Blancs), Lanson (Vintage, Cuvée 225, Noble Cuvée), Laurent-Perrier, Pommery (Cuvée Louise), Louis Roederer (Cristal Rosé), Ruinart (Dom Ruinart Blanc de Blancs, Dom Ruinart Rosé).

1980 *

A small harvest overall, the yield in specific vineyards fluctuated wildly, from minuscule to quite prolific. The quality was average non-vintage, but within this context the wines were fresh and aromatic, with good acidity and satisfactory potential alcohol, proving extremely useful in maintaining the vigour of basic blends. Although generally not of sufficient calibre for a vintage, a number of houses actually declared this year. Most were foolish to do so, but time has thrown up some excellent exceptions

THE BEST

Moët & Chandon (Dom Pérignon Rosé), Philipponnat (Clos des Goisses) and Pommery (Cuvée Louise Rosé)

OTHER SUCCESSES

Billecart-Salmon (Blanc de Blancs), Bollinger (Vieilles Vignes Françaises), Moët & Chandon (Dom Pérignon), Pommery (Vintage en magnum, Cuvée Louise) and Veuve Clicquot.

HONOURABLE MENTIONS

Boizel (Vintage), Jacquart (Vintage, Blanc de Blancs), Lanson (Cuvée 225) and Palmer (Vintage)

1979 ****

A good sized harvest of excellent quality, picking commenced under ideal conditions, providing mature, healthy and wholesome grapes. Although persistent rain interposed, there was little sign of rot and the grapes remained high in sugar, with thin skins that pressed easily. Qualitatively on a par with 1975, the 1979s were delicious to drink when first released, but quickly firmed up. However, their elegance and finesse was so evident that it did not take any prescience in the mid-1980s to realise they would blossom into superb Champagnes by 1990. Some of them opened up almost overnight: it was fascinating to watch. This classic vintage is drinking beautifully now, with a style that is closer to 1983 than 1975, as the distinctive creamy, biscuity complexity of the Chardonnay begins to dominate the wines. The best will remain at their peak until they are 40 years of age or more.

THE BEST

Without doubt the greatest 1979 is Krug Clos du Mesnil, which comes as close to perfection as it is possible to get.

CLOSELY FOLLOWED BY

Billecart-Salmon (Blanc de Blancs), Deutz (Blanc de Blancs),

Charles Heidsieck (Cuvée Champagne Charlie), Krug (Vintage), Lanson (Vintage), Piper-Heidsieck (Rare), Pol Roger (Cuvée Sir Winston Churchill), Pommery (Cuvée Louise), Ruinart (Dom Ruinart Blanc de Blancs, Dom Ruinart Rosé) and Perrier-Jouët (Belle Epoque Rosé).

OTHER SUCCESSES

Bollinger (Vintage, Vieilles Vignes Françaises), Lanson (Noble Cuvée), Philipponnat (Clos des Goisses), Ployez-Jacquemart (L. d'Harbonville), Pol Roger (Vintage, Réserve Speciale PR), Pommery (Vintage) and Louis Roederer (Cristal)

FOURTH PLACE

Charbaut (Certificate Blanc de Blancs, Certificate Rosé), Deutz (Cuvée William Deutz), Gosset (Grand Millésimé), Alfred Gratien (Vintage), Laurent-Perrier (Vintage), Joseph Perrier (Vintage), Pol Roger (Chardonnay), Alain Robert (Tête de Cuvée), Louis Roederer (Vintage), Salon (Vintage), Taittinger (Comtes de Champagne Blanc de Blancs) and Veuve Clicquot (Vintage, Rosé).

FIFTH POSITION

Deutz (Blanc de Blancs), Drappier (Vintage, Grande Sendrée), George Goulet (Vintage, Rosé), Heidsieck & Co Monopole (Rosé), Henriot (Cuvée Baccarat), Bruno Paillard (Vintage), Perrier-Jouët (Vintage, Belle Epoque), Ployez-Jacquemart (Blanc de Blancs Spéciale), Pol Roger (Rosé), Louis Roederer (Blanc de Blancs), Jacques Selosse (Vintage), Taittinger (Comtes de Champagne Rosé) and Veuve Clicquot (Grande Dame).

1978 *

A near-fatal flowering that was one month late produced the lowest yield in recent history, dwarfing even 1981, and of an average non-vintage quality. The champenois cranked-up their propaganda machine so that the domestic French press accepted 1978 as a good, if not particularly special vintage. There was not much to choose between these wines and those of the 1980 harvest, yet both years were declared by a limited number of producers. At best the 1978s were generally fresh and fruity, but many were not fresh at all and over time have become flabby, even developing sweaty-armpit aromas in some cases. Generally the wines were far from complete, lacking the structure required for a good vintage Champagne, but as always there are exceptions

THE BEST

Perrier-Jouët (Belle Epoque)

SECOND BEST

Moët & Chandon (Dom Pérignon Rosé)

OTHER SUCCESSES

Billecart-Salmon (Cuvée Nicolas-François Billecart), Laurent-Perrier (Vintage), Moët & Chandon (Dom Pérignon), Perrier-Jouët (Belle Epoque Rosé), Alain Robert (Fleur de Mesnil Brut Rare) and Veuve Clicquot (Rosé).

Joseph Perrier (Vintage) deserves an honourable mention, but Louis Roederer (Cristal) was disappointing, particularly after its brilliant vintage-defying 1977.

1977 -

Not as bad as 1972 or 1984, but certainly a poor quality non-vintage year in which the health of the grapes was affected by mildew and grey rot. With an exceptional degree of selection in the vineyard, a small number of producers managed to elevate their wines above the norm to make interesting blending components due to their high acidity, mineral content and extract. With few

exceptions, however, they were low in sugar and consequently light in body and alcohol, but with high acidity most wines have tended to hold their mousse well. Meunier fared best in general, but isolated patches of Chardonnay produced some exceptionally fine blancs de blancs, although unfortunately they were lost in the non-vintage melting pot years ago.

THE BEST

Louis Roederer (Cristal), which might have the edge on the 1975 and 1981 of the same cuvée, is definitely on a par with the 1974 or 1982, and infinitely superior to the 1986 and 1987 Cristal.

1976 *****

A large harvest of true vintage quality, and some *cuvées* have turned out to be very special indeed. The crop was so plentiful that growers were unofficially encouraged by officials to harvest above the legal limit and press out only the *cuvée*, discarding the *taille*, resulting in the correct volume of juice per hectare, but from an illegally large volume of grapes. Some of the juice had a tendency to oxidise prior to, or during, the first fermentation, leaving an ungainly sherry-like aroma, but these were merely the unsuccessful products of a truly exceptional year, and the Champagnes they produced were the amongst the first to work their way out of the system. Generally the wines were rich in extract, high in alcohol, big and fat in character, with relatively low acidity. It was the low acidity that critics of this vintage latched onto, claiming that the 1976s would not last long, but the acidity was even lower in 1959, 1949, 1947 and 1945, and these turned out to be some of the greatest and longest-lived vintages that Champagne has produced. Acidity is not the sole factor affecting longevity – alcohol and extract play their part too. The best *cuvées* will outlive most of the 1975s, a vintage that most pundits describe as classic, and there is an opulence of fruit about the 1976s that makes them very special indeed.

THE BEST

The battle for the best of this vintage will go on for decades, but currently Taittinger (Comtes de Champagne Blanc de Blancs) is a whisker ahead of Krug (Vintage), followed by Heidsieck & Co Monopole (the last great Diamant Bleu), Philipponnat (Clos des Goisses) and Salon (Vintage), then Piper-Heidsieck (Rare), Louis Roederer (Cristal Rosé) and Taittinger (Comtes de Champagne Rosé), with Louis Roederer (Cristal), Ruinart (Dom Ruinart Blanc de Blancs, Dom Ruinart Rosé) and Veuve Clicquot (Grande Dame) close on their tail.

OTHER SUCCESSES

Henri Abelé (Impérial Club), Bollinger (Grande Année), Charbaut (Crémant Blanc de Blancs, Certificate Blanc de Blancs, Certificate Rosé), Deutz (Blanc de Blancs), Drappier (Grande Sendrée), Gosset (Grand Millésimé), George Goulet (Vintage, Rosé), Jeanmaire (Cuvée Elysée), Lanson (Vintage), Laurent-Perrier (Vintage), Moët & Chandon (Dom Pérignon), Perrier-Jouët (Vintage, Belle Epoque, Belle Epoque Rosé), Pol Roger (Réserve Speciale PR), De Venoge (Champagne des Princes) and Veuve Clicquot (Vintage).

1975 ****

A normal size harvest of excellent Champagnes, which virtually every house declared. The 1975s were very stylish from the moment they were released; beautifully soft and elegant, with the normally reticent Chardonnay aroma quickly dominating the wines for a change. Although 1975 was initially considered to be one of Champagne's most impressive post-war years, the champenois were caught on the hop when some highly-rated *cuvées* started to go over at the end of the 1980s. The most notable of these surprising failures was Pol Roger, but although it is unknown whether these wines will recover, the vintage as a whole has since stabilised, and there has been such a wealth of great 1975s that it is still difficult to be selective about the bulk of top performers.

THE BEST
Moët & Chandon (Dom Pérignon) and Philipponnat (Clos des Goisses – although it is going through an awkward developmental stage at the moment and is best left well cellared for another five years or so)

SECOND PLACE
Krug (Vintage), Moët & Chandon (Dom Pérignon Rosé) and Pol Roger (Cuvée Sir Winston Churchill).

THIRD PLACE
Bollinger (Grande Année), Jacquesson (Signature) and Lanson (Vintage)

FOURTH PLACE
Heidsieck & Co Monopole (Diamant Bleu), Moët & Chandon (Brut Impérial), Mumm (Cuvée René Lalou), Bruno Paillard (Vintage), Perrier-Jouët (Belle Epoque), Louis Roederer (Cristal Rosé), Taittinger (Vintage, Comtes de Champagne Rosé) and Veuve Clicquot (Vintage).

OTHER SUCCESSES
Henri Abelé (Grande Marque Impérial), Ayala (Blanc de Blancs), Besserat de Bellefon (Vintage), Billecart-Salmon (Cuvée N.F. Billecart), Boizel (Vintage), Bollinger Vieilles Vignes Françaises), Deutz (Vintage, Blanc de Blancs, Rosé), George Goulet (Vintage, Cuvée du Centenaire, Rosé), Alfred Gratien (Vintage), Heidsieck & Co Monopole (Vintage), Charles Heidsieck (Vintage), Jacquesson (Perfection, Late Disgorged), Abel Lepitre (Prince A. de Bourbon-Parme), Napoléon (Vintage), Perrier-Jouët (Vintage, Blason de France), Piper-Heidsieck (Cuvée Florens Louis), Pommery (Vintage), Louis Roederer (Vintage, Cristal) and Ruinart (Dom Ruinart Blanc de Blancs, Dom Ruinart Rosé), Taittinger (Comtes de Champagne Blanc de Blancs – however, two bottles uniquely disgorged in 1998 vie with Krug, Dom Pérignon and Cuvée Sir Winston Churchill for second best), De Venoge Champagnes des Princes and Veuve Clicquot Grande Dame

After these there is a big drop in quality.

1974 *
A normal size harvest of essentially good non-vintage quality that has also produced a few exceptionally good vintage Champagnes, particularly in the rosé style. The best wines come in full or good part from early picked grapes, the quality declining as the harvest progressed. Meunier generally fared best, but small lots of fine Chardonnay were also found in specific locations.

THE BEST
Louis Roederer (Cristal Rosé)

OTHER SUCCESSES
De Castellane (Rosé, Cuvée Commodore), George Goulet (Cuvée du Centenaire), Abel Lepitre (Prince A. de Bourbon-Parme), Bruno Paillard (Crémant Blanc de Blancs) and Louis Roederer (Cristal).

1973 ****
A typically large and difficult Champagne harvest, yet one that produced successful vintage wines. This was probably achieved through selection as much as by any intrinsic quality of the year. The average alcohol-acidity balance was somewhat low, but through a process of selection vintage *cuvées* of a much higher, far better balance were achieved. This is the ultimate expression of the Champagne-maker's art, and it resulted in wines of surprising uniformity, with a characteristic point of acidity that has kept them remarkably fresh and fragrant in their mature years.

THE BEST
Krug (Vintage) stands head and shoulders above the rest

SECOND PLACE
Billecart-Salmon (Blanc de Blancs), Jacquesson (Perfection), Moët & Chandon (Dom Pérignon, Dom Pérignon Rosé), Pol Roger (Vintage)

THIRD PLACE
Deutz (Cuvée William Deutz), Heidsieck & Co Monopole (Diamant Bleu), Laurent-Perrier (Vintage), Perrier-Jouët (Belle Epoque), Pommery (Vintage, Rosé), Taittinger (Comtes de Champagne Blanc de Blancs).

CLOSELY FOLLOWING
Bollinger (Grande Année, Vieilles Vignes Françaises), Charbaut (Certificate Blanc de Blancs), Collery (Rosé), Deutz (Blanc de Blancs), Gosset (Grand Millésimé), Alfred Gratien (Vintage), Henriot (Baron Philippe de Rothschild), Lanson (Vintage), Bruno Paillard (Blanc de Noirs), Joseph Perrier (91), Perrier-Jouët (Blason de France), Veuve Clicquot (Vintage).

BEST OF THE REST
Collery (Cuvée Herbillon, Cuvée Spécial Club), Deutz (Vintage), Heidsieck & Co Dry Monopole (Vintage), Jacquesson (Blanc de Blancs Late Disgorged), J. Lassalle (Blanc de Blancs), Moët & Chandon (Grand Impérial, Rosé), Mumm (Cuvée René Lalou), Napoléon (Vintage), Perrier-Jouët (Vintage), Philipponnat (Clos des Goisses), Pol Roger (Chardonnay), Louis Roederer (Vintage), Alfred Rothschild (Grand Trianon), Ruinart (Dom Ruinart Blanc de Blancs, Dom Ruinart Rosé), Salon (Vintage), Taittinger (Comtes de Champagne Rosé) and Veuve Clicquot (Grande Dame).

1972 -
A normal size harvest of uniformly diabolical quality. This year challenges 1984 for the dubious honour of producing the worst base wines in the last 30 years. Thin, acidic and thoroughly miserable, the 1972s severely taxed the skills of Champagne's greatest winemakers. Only through strict selection and a generous addition of rich reserve wines was it possible to hide the taint of 1972 in non-vintage blends of acceptable quality. There are no exceptions as far as I am aware.

1971 *****
A very small harvest of great vintage quality, the wines have fabulous extract and possess a specificity of style that has become very special over the years. A freak year in terms of the weather, which even included tornado damage, reduced the volume of the 1971 crop, but the lower yield increased sugar and acidity levels, concentrating this classic vintage. The wines have an excellent structure, great extract, exceptional finesse, and are very expressive of what is a remarkable and very special year. There can be no doubt that the best 1971s will continue to improve, providing some of the greatest Champagnes of the post-war period.

THE BEST
Salon (Vintage)

SECOND PLACE
Krug (Vintage), Moët & Chandon (Dom Pérignon, Dom Pérignon Rosé)

THIRD PLACE
Charbaut (Certificate Blanc de Blancs) and Taittinger (Comtes de Champagne Blanc de Blancs).

FOURTH PLACE
Billecart-Salmon (Cuvée N.F. Billecart), Gosset (Grand Millésimé), Lanson (Vintage), Perrier-Jouët (Belle Epoque) and Louis Roederer (Cristal), followed by Boizel (Vintage), Deutz (Cuvée William Deutz), Palmer (Vintage) and Pol Roger (Vintage, Chardonnay).

BEST OF THE REST
Collery (Cuvée Spécial Club), Alfred Gratien (Vintage), Jacquesson (Perfection), Moët & Chandon (Brut Impérial), Napoléon (Vintage), Joseph Perrier (Vintage), Perrier-Jouët (Vintage, Blason de France), Philipponnat (Clos des Goisses) and Louis Roederer (Vintage, Rosé).

1970 ***
A huge harvest of good vintage quality, the wines were surprisingly rich, albeit in a gentle fashion, and very satisfying from an early age. The largest Champagne crop on record, 1970 was widely declared, and the key to its uniformity was the exceptional quality of Meunier. The best are characterised by a completeness of style, but their precociousness has not made this a long-lasting vintage. All the more remarkable then that the top 1970 is Bollinger's Vieilles Vignes Françaises. According to Bollinger this Champagne is not expected to age particularly well because it is made from overripe Pinot Noir grapes, yet the 1970 was beautifully preserved the last time I tasted it at 27 years young.

THE BEST
Bollinger Vieilles Vignes Françaises

SECOND PLACE
Jacquesson (Late Disgorged), Moët & Chandon (Dom Pérignon), Louis Roederer (Cristal) and Taittinger (Comtes de Champagne Rosé)

THIRD PLACE
Bollinger (Grande Année), De Castellane (Cuvée Royale Chardonnay), George Goulet (Cuvée du Centenaire), Alfred Gratien (Vintage), Jacquesson (Perfection), Abel Lepitre (Prince A. de Bourbon-Parme), Moët & Chandon (Brut Impérial, Rosé), Philipponnat (Clos des Goisses), Taittinger (Comtes de Champagne Blanc de Blancs) and Veuve Clicquot (Vintage).

THE BEST PRE-1970 VINTAGES

***** 1966, 1964, 1961, 1959, 1953, 1952, 1949, 1947, 1928, 1921, 1911, 1904

**** 1969, 1962, 1955, 1945, 1943, 1934, 1933, 1929, 1926, 1923, 1920, 1919, 1914, 1915, 1906, 1900

SPARKLING GRAPE VARIETIES

SPARKLING WINE GRAPES FALL INTO TWO MAIN CATEGORIES: CLASSIC BRUT-STYLE (ESSENTIALLY NEUTRAL VARIETIES), AND SWEET-STYLE (PREFERABLY AROMATIC VARIETIES). WITHIN EACH CATEGORY, AN ELITE OF TOP QUALITY VARIETIES EXISTS, AFTER WHICH COME A NUMBER OF SUBSIDIARY GRAPES WHICH LACK A CERTAIN CLASS, YET CAN BE EXTREMELY USEFUL BLENDING COMPONENTS. BEYOND THESE TWO CATEGORIES AND THEIR SUBGROUPS, THERE IS A HOTCHPOTCH OF VARIETIES THAT ARE NOTHING MORE THAN FODDER FOR CHEAP FIZZ, USUALLY OF THE *CUVE CLOSE* KIND (SUCH WINES MAY INCLUDE SEEMINGLY CLASSIC GRAPES, BUT THE ACTUAL QUALITY USED IS UNLIKELY TO BE SUITABLE FOR A DECENT STILL WINE).

WHITE WINE VARIETIES

ALVARINHO
The classic Vinho Verde grape
Not a classic grape variety *per se*, this is, however, the finest Vinho Verde grape. This low-cropping variety is particularly successful in the northern part of the Minho province, between the Lima valley and the Spanish border, where it produces the fullest, most substantial Vinhos Verdes. Palacio da Brejoeira is the yardstick for this grape, a wine which is widely considered to be a class apart from any other Vinho Verde.

ALBALONGA
A one-off success in England
A Rieslaner x Sylvaner cross developed for its naturally high sugar level and early-ripening qualities. Roger Fisher made an extraordinarily successful sparkling wine in 1991 by blending this grape with Perle and Kerner to produce something uncannily like a Pouilly-Fumé, but with bubbles, of course. Subsequent vintages have not, however, been anywhere near as successful.

ALIGOTÉ
Third division Burgundian variety
A thin skinned grape of unexceptional quality, Aligoté makes tart wines of moderate alcoholic content, which sounds just right for fizz, yet seldom demonstrates any affinity for bubbles. However, it is permitted for Crémant de Bourgogne and may be used in Savoie for fizzy versions of Vin de Savoie and Vin du Bugey.

ARBANE
An ancient Champagne grape that is almost extinct
Champagne's other forgotten variety, although far more rare than Petit Meslier. Moutard Père et Fils has recently produced a Champagne Cuvée Arbane. Although this grape was renowned for its exceptional aromatic quality, this *cuvée* does not live up to expectations.

ARBOIS
Obscure, localised use in the Loire Valley
Capable of producing interesting still wines, particularly when blended with the Romorantin, this has yet to prove itself in sparkling wine terms, although it is permitted for Crémant de Loire, Touraine and Vouvray.

ARINTO
The same variety as Vinho Verde's Paderna
Portuguese variety of some potential for sparkling wine, albeit not realised as yet, the Arinto is most famous for producing still white wines in Bucelas, and has been used for fizz in Bucelas and Bairrada. See also PADERNA.

ATHIRI
Minor Greek variety
Used on the island of Rhodes by the CAIR cooperative for an aggressively strong, pure varietal sparkling wine, which has coarse fruit and a fiercely aggressive fizz.

AURORE
US East Coast hybrid
A cross of two hybrids, Seibel 788 x Seibel 29; always early picked because it ripens to a slight foxiness and the grapes tend to fall off the vine. Used in New Jersey (Tamuzza Vineyards), and Pennsylvania (Cherry Vineyards).

AUXERROIS
Underrated Alsace grape
Often confused with Pinot Blanc, this is most successful in Alsace and to a lesser, but improving extent, in England. Relatively neutral, it is well-suited to the *brut* style, but it is fatter than Pinot Blanc, thus benefits from cooler situations. Also used in Germany (Sektkellerei Möller).

AVESSO
A basic quality Vinho Verde grape
Thought to be a white variant of the Spanish variety Jaén, Avesso does not have the class of either the Alvarinho or Loureiro, but can be a useful blending component when grown in the southern Minho area.

AZAL
Acidic Vinho Verde grape
Another Vinho Verde grape that is not in the class of the Alvarinho and Loureiro, Azal does however contribute acidity to some Vinho Verde blends. Casa de Vilacetinho and Casa de la Boa are rare examples of pure Azal single-quinta Vinhos Verdes.

BACCHUS
An English oddity as far as sparkling wines go
A (Sylvaner x Riesling) x Müller-Thurgau cross; one of Germany's more superior viticultural breedings, but too aromatic for brut style sparkling wines. Barkham Manor in England blends Bacchus with Pinot Noir, which is an odd concept, yet quite successful in 1995.

BICAL
Secondary variety for Bairrada sparkling wine
Also known as *Borrado das Moscas* or 'Fly Droppings', this is usually blended with other Bairrada grapes such as Baga, Maria Gomes, Arinto and Rabo de Ovelha.

CERCEAL
Synonym for Madeira's famous Sercial grape
Not a serious fizz contender but Quinta das Bageiras has used it effectively as a component in its Bairrada Super Reserva sparkling wine.

CHARDONNAY
Classic Champagne variety
Famous for the finest white Burgundies and most of the world's other great dry white wines,. One of the two classic varieties used in Champagne, where it fetches a premium over Pinot Noir. Chardonnay is also the most successful brut style variety worldwide, adapting to a greater range of climates, soils and locations than any other grape. It has the greatest tendency to go toasty if aged after disgorgement, but can also develop finer, creamy, biscuity nuances, especially when from top growths of the Côte des Blancs in Champagne.

CHASSELAS
France's most popular table grape
Probably at its modest best in Alsace and Switzerland. Used for sparkling wine in the Savoie (Seyssel Mousseux, Vin de Savoie Mousseux).

CHENIN BLANC
A workhorse more than a true pedigree
Not a very fashionable grape, and only important because of its primary role in the sparkling wines of the Loire, particularly Saumur. Its naturally high acidity level is ideal for sparkling wine, but its aromatic qualities are too assertive, and this fights against the subtle effects of autolysis and prevents the development of mellow, bottle aromas of any true finesse. Its biggest problem, however, is the poor quality and underripeness of grapes harvested by many Loire producers. However, so much fizz is made from this variety that some exciting exceptions inevitably exist. Used in Australia (particularly for bulk-blended *cuve close*), South Africa (Cinzano, Franschhoek Vineyards, Môreson, Villiera), Mexico (Freixenet), and even Spain (Gran Caus from Can Ràfols dels Caus), although not officially permitted for Cava.

CHINURI
Minor Georgian variety
An obscure grape that is usually blended with Goruli, Mtsvane and Tasitska for Georgian sparkling wines.

CLAIRETTE
An historical mismatch for sparkling wine of any kind
Sugar-rich, intrinsically flabby grape that makes low-quality dry white still wines in southern France. The dry sparkling wine formerly known as Clairette de Die used to be a pure Clairette fizz, but its replacement, Crémant de Die, may now include up to 25% Muscat. Curiously, the sweet fizz formerly known as Clairette de Die Tradition (now called Clairette de Die Méthode Dioise Ancestrale) does not have to contain any Clairette whatsoever. In South Africa, the Chamonix Courchevel Cuvée Brut is 100% Clairette.

CÓDEGA
Mediocre Portuguese variety
An early-ripening Douro variety, also known as Roupeiro or Alva. Used effectively since 1994 in Schramsberg's Vertice joint venture, despite its generally poor still wine reputation and a very shaky sparkling wine debut.

COLOMBARD
A brandy grape
The requirements for brandy are similar to fizz: low alcohol and high acidity, making this a natural choice, if only for bulking up the base wine. Used

in cheaper blends in Australia (Aldridge, Angas, Barramundi, Seppelt Great Western, Sunnycliff) and South Africa (Roodezandt, Van Lovren, Vredendal). Also for Crémant de Bordeaux.

CORTESE
Famous Gavi grape
The effective use of this grape by Soldati La Scolca suggests it has more potential for sparkling Gavi than for the still wines.

CRUCHEN BLANC
A poor pretender to Riesling's crown
Also known as Cape Riesling or Paarl Riesling in South Africa; used for blending by Boschendal and Nederburg.

DEBINA
Obscure but capable Greek variety
Grown in Zitza, Epirus, where it makes fresh, delicately fruity perlant wines.

DOÑA BLANCA
A Galician variety
Some suggestion that this has interesting potential, but not for sparkling wine if the awful Don Perejón fizz by Vinos del Bierzo in León is anything to go by.

ELBLING
The grape that gave birth to Germany's Sekt industry.
Once held in high esteem in both Germany and France, the Elbling was the major Mosel grape in the 19th century. Now mostly confined to the Obermosel, where its very acid, neutral flavour makes it useful for the Sekt industry, but it is of little interest even to the most ardent devotees of German sparkling wine. Although known as Grossriesling and Kleiner Räuschling, it is not related in any way to the Riesling.

EZERGÓ
A declining, but still prolific Hungarian variety
A rot-prone grape used for cheap, bulk-blended, low quality fizz.

FERNAO PIRES
Portugal's most prolific white grape variety
Known as Maria Gomes in Bairrada, where it is usually blended with Baga, Bical, Arinto and Rabo de Ovelha. Also called Castelão Francês, and used to much greater effect when blended with Periquita in Loridos Bruto, one of Portugal's best sparkling wines. Also used in South Africa by the Vredendal cooperative.

FLORA
Gently aromatic variety
A Sémillon x Gewürztraminer cross produced by Professor Olmo, the only sparkling wine to use Flora is Schramsberg's Crémant Demi-Sec.

GOLDBURGER
A mediocre, somewhat aromatic variety
Welschriesling x Orangetraube cross developed in Austria, used for sparkling wine by Colio in Canada.

GORULI
Minor Georgian variety
An obscure grape that is usually blended with Chinuri, Mtsvane and Tasitska for Georgian sparkling wines.

GOUVEIO
Better known as Madeira's Verdelho
Not truly a sparkling wine grape, although Schramsberg has used it effectively for that purpose since 1994, for its Vertice joint venture in Portugal.

GRINGET
The Savagnin of Savoie
Apparently this is the same variety as the Savagnin in Jura. It is authorised for use in Vin de Savoie

Mousseux. *See* SAVAGNIN.

GRÜNER VELTLINER
The most important wine grape in Austria
One of the main varieties used for Austrian Sekt, it is hard to know whether it is not suited to sparkling wine or, simply, Austrian winemakers are no good at making fizz.

JACQUÈRE
Mainstay of the Savoie
Authorised for Vin de Savoie Mousseux and Vin du Bugey Mousseux. Typically makes light-bodied wines that are fresh, but without much intensity of flavour.

KERNER
Commonly used for German Sekt
Widely used for German Sekt, but this Trollinger x Riesling cross doesn't stand out as being particularly well-suited to the task. Hagnauer Burgstall Extra Trocken from the cooperative in Hagnau is a delightful exception. Kerner vies with Reichensteiner as the most prolific German cross used in England's embryonic fizz industry, where it has occasionally been surprisingly successful, particularly at Wickham. Roger Fisher also made an extraordinarily successful sparkling wine at his Bothy Vineyard in 1991 by blending this grape with Albalonga and Perle to produce something uncannily like a Pouilly-Fumé with bubbles. Subsequent vintages have not, however, been anywhere near as successful.

KIRÁLYLEÁNYKA
Hungarian synonym for Romania's Feteasca Regala
A Grasa x Feteasca Alba cross, used in cheap Hungarian bulk-blended fizz under the name of Királyleányka.

LABRUSCA
Native American species
Not to be confused with Lambrusco, *labrusca* is a species, not a variety. The oldest cultivated and best-known labrusca variety today is Concord. All lambrusca varieties and virtually all hybrids developed from this species have a distinctive foxy aroma which most wine drinkers find sickly sweet, unless they have been brought up on the stuff. Even then, most consumers tend to discriminate between the foxiness in Concord grape jelly, which can be agreeable, and the same character in a serious wine, which is increasingly becoming unacceptable even in labrusca heartland in America's northeastern states and Canada. This foxy character has long been recognised: one labrusca variety, Linnaeus, for example, has well-established synonyms such as the Fox grape and Northern Fox.

LEN DE L'EL
Distinctive, but lacks acidity
Traditional Gaillac variety sometimes spelt Len de l'Elh, and also known as Loin de l'Oeil – 'far from sight' in gaillaçoise. This sugar-rich grape is capable of producing flavoursome still wines, but sparkling wines generally lack sufficient freshness and acidity.

LOUREIRO
One of the two most important Vinho Verde grapes
Much heavier-cropping variety than the Alvarinho, Vinho Verde's other top-performing grape variety, consequently it produces a lighter wine. However, it has more aromatic quality, and the area best-suited to this variety is between the Lima and Cavado valleys.

MACABÉO
A neutral grape of moderate brut-style quality
Spanish variety supposedly used for its fruit, and

to 'lift' a Cava blend, giving it freshness. But the best that can be said for Macabéo is it is not as bad as the Parellada. Better known as the Viura in Rioja, where it is more usefully employed for still white wines. It has no truly distinguishing characteristics, although the giant Cava group Freixenet has successfully used it in Mexico, and Yalumba includes a little in its Angas Rosé in Australia.

MALVASIA
Classic sweet wine grape playing a minor role in Cava
Known as Subirat in Penedès where most Cava is produced, this is usually confined to Semi-Seco cuvées.

MALVASIA FINA
Posh synonym for lowly Portuguese variety called Vital
Not related to the true Malvasia in any way, this modest grape has been used surprisingly effectively for sparkling wine by Schramsberg since 1994 in its Portuguese joint venture called Vertice.

MARIA GOMES
Portugal's most prolific white grape variety
Better known throughout Portugal as Fernao Pires but called Maria Gomes in Bairrada, where it is used for sparkling wine. Usually blended with other local grapes such as Baga, Bical, Arinto and Rabo de Ovelha. *See also* FERNAO PIRES.

MARSANNE
One of two grapes responsible for sparkling St-Péray
In addition to St-Péray, the only dry sparkling wine in the Rhône Valley, Marsanne is an authorised variety for Vin de Savoie Mousseux. However, the best fizz containing this variety was called Mitchelton's Nattier. Made by Colin Preece in the early 1990s, Nattier possessed a small proportion of barrel-fermented Marsanne, and showed promise. Although Mitchelton has not totally abandoned all hope of using barrel-fermented Marsanne for sparkling wine, it has put it on the back-burner for the moment.

MAUZAC
Moderate brut style, surprisingly good for sweeter styles
Late-ripening grape grown in Limoux and Gaillac, west of Languedoc, France. In Limoux it has a natural tendency to evoke aromas of fresh-cut grass, although certain producers are quite successful at encouraging the flowery finesse of autolysis to dominate. Although the neutral character and good natural acidity would seem better suited to the *brut* style, rather than sweeter wines, its performance for dry wines is limited, and the re-emergence of Blanquette Méthode Ancestrale (formerly called Vin de Blanquette) is demonstrating the Mauzac's true potential for sweeter-styled bubbly, with deliciously rich, vibrantly fresh fruit, and fluffy sherbety finish. A Mauzac Rosé exists and its use is permitted in Gaillac's sparkling wines.

MELON DE BOURGOGNE
Infamous Muscadet variety
As the name suggests, the Muscadet grape originated in Burgundy, so it is not surprising that it is one of the varieties permitted for Crémant de Bourgogne, although the grapes lack acidity when ripe and are really not very pleasant when picked too early.

MOLETTE
Suitably neutral
Widely planted in the Savoie, where its light-bodied, neutral wines favour the sparkling process, although other varieties are required to construct a correctly balanced fizz of some interest. Authorised

for Seyssel Mousseux, Vin de Savoie Mousseux and Vin du Bugey Mousseux.

MOSCATO
The world's most sublime sweet sparkling wine grape
The king of Asti. *See* MUSCAT

MONDEUSE BLANCHE
Blending fodder
A lesser-quality variant of the Mondeuse Noire. Very little is grown, but it is authorised for Vin de Savoie Mousseux and Vin du Bugey Mousseux.

MTSVANE
Georgia's finest grape variety
An obscure grape that is usually blended with Chinuri, Goruli and Tasitska for Georgian sparkling wines.

MÜLLER-THURGAU
Ubiquitous German cross
Used more often and more successfully for sparkling wine in England than Germany.

MUSCADELLE
Bordeaux variety unrelated to Muscat
Muted aromatics compared to Muscat; better suited to slightly sweeter styles of fizz, although it is mostly used for dry *cuvées* of Crémant de Bordeaux and various sparkling Gaillac appellations. A blending component for Yalumba's Angas Rosé in Australia, Van Lovren's Papillon Brut in South Africa is the only pure varietal Muscadelle I have come across.

MUSCAT
Top quality aromatic grape
Apart from Asti and to a much lesser degree Clairette de Die Méthode Dioise Ancestrale, the Muscat is rarely used for sparkling wine.

The Moscato d'Asti, Moscato di Canelli or Moscato Bianco, as it is variously called in Italy is actually the Muscat Blanc à Petit Grains, otherwise known as Muscat d'Alsace, Muscat de Frontignan, and Muscat de Frontignac, to name but a few of the better identified synonyms.

Like all aromatic grapes, Moscato gains nothing from yeast-contact and is at its best as young as possible, when it has a fresh, grapey aroma, and light and lingering luscious sweetness. Its characteristic flowery-fruitiness can be intense and peachy, and may even have a hint of orange. The most important compound in the Moscato aroma is geraniol, which is wonderful when fresh, but assumes an unpleasantly pungent geranium odour with bottle-age.

Called Muskateller in Germany and some east European countries (where it is also called Muskotály). Muscat is a tiny blending component in Vin Doux Blush from Bon Courage in South Africa, and has even been found is some Cavas (Gran Caus from Can Ràfols dels Caus), although it is not officially allowed.

MUSKAT OTTONEL
Middle quality aromatic grape
An east-European variety that has replaced Muscat à Petits Grains in certain areas because of its relative hardiness. It has a lighter, crisper aromatic quality. At its best in Austria, where Szigeti produces a superb Muskat Ottonel Extra Dry at Gols in Neusiedlersee.

NOBLING
Good for acidity and ripeness
This Silvaner x Chasselas cross retains good acidity levels during the ripening process, which augers well for sparkling wine, but the only fizzy Nobling I have comes across, the Binzener Sonnhole Nobling Brut from Bezirkskellerei Markgräflerland

in Baden, Germany, was, unfortunately, not particularly well made.

ORION
Seldom encountered herbaceous hybrid
Hybrid Optima x Seyve-Villard 12/375 planted experimentally by Carter's Vineyard in England, where it is now grown organically for that producer's Lovejoy fizz.

ODENC
Crisp, acidic and fairly neutral
Once widely planted in southwest France, this was particularly popular in Bergerac, but is only authorised for Gaillac sparkling wines. Its intrinsically high acidity makes it useful for sparkling wines.

PADERNA
A Vinho Verde grape
Ranks alongside Trajadura as a good second division Vinho Verde grape, but it is more of an all-round variety, with no specific contribution to a blend. Also called Pederna and Pedernao, although outside the Minho it is better known as the Arinto. *See* ARINTO.

PALOMINO
Workhorse Sherry grape
Used by Yalumba in Australia for Angas Rosé, presumably because it is cheap and available.

PARELLADA
The least interesting of all Cava grapes
The major white grape variety in Catalonia, used for both still and sparkling wines. For Cava it is said to impart a distinctive aroma and soften the Xarel-lo, but the truth is almost the reverse because the vast majority of its base wines are so flabby they have to be propped up by Xarel-lo. Used by Yalumba for its Angas Rosé, again, presumably because it is cheap and available.

PEDRO XIMÉNEZ
Classic Sherry grape
The only sparkling wine I have found to contain this is Yalumba's Angas Rosé in Australia.

PERLE
A one-off success in England
Gewürztraminer x Müller-Thurgau cross grown primarily in Franken, Germany, where it can survive the coldest winter temperatures. Makes a light, fragrant and fruity wine in low yields. Roger Fisher made an extraordinarily successful sparkling wine at his Bothy Vineyard in 1991 by blending this grape with Albalonga and Kerner to produce something uncannily like a Pouilly-Fumé with bubbles. Subsequent vintages have not, however, been anywhere near as successful.

PETIT MESLIER
Rarely encountered ancient Champagne grape
Not as rare as Arbanne, there is, however, very little Petit Meslier remaining in Champagne today, although it was once fairly widely planted in the Aube region, where it was prized for its high acidity. The only two known examples of this grape are Irvine in Australia and, in 1997, Champagne Jacquesson, both of which are 100% pure varietals.

PINOT BLANC
Chardonnay's understudy
Principally found in sparkling wines from Alsace and Germany, but also widely used in English and Austrian *cuvées*. Common in Germany for so-called premium quality, *brut* style Sekt made by *méthode champenoise*, but not very successful, apart from a few individual exceptions. In Alsace, the further north the grapes are grown, the more often they

are blended with Auxerrois to bring a little fatness and generosity to the wines.

Small amounts of Pinot Blanc are found in numerous California sparkling wines (Domaine Carneros, Domaine Chandon, Kristone, Piper Sonoma, Schramsberg, Wente) and it is also one of the varieties permitted for Crémant de Bourgogne.

PROSECCO
Probably the most overrated sparkling wine grape in the world
Virtually all fizzy Prosecco wines today are dominated by bland amylic aromas.

RABO DE OVELHA
A minor Portuguese variety
Although a grape of no individual character, the use of Rabo de Ovelha in contributing to the structure of a sparkling wine blends should not be discounted.

REICHENSTEINER
Sugar-rich and Sylvaner-like
Müller-Thurgau x Madeleine Angevine x Calabreser-Fröhlich German cross. Fairly widely used for sparkling wine in England, where its mild, delicate, somewhat neutral wine is usually blended, and works better for some than others.

RIBOLLA
Very basic in Slovenia
A large Slovenian cooperative in Dubrovo called Kmetijska Zadruga Goriska Brda produces a rather bland pure Ribolla varietal fizz by *cuve close* called Peneca Rebula.

RIESLANER
Good Riesling-like potential
A Riesling x Silvaner cross that shares the hardiness of the Silvaner with more Riesling character than most German crosses. Schales (Rheinhessen) and Fürstlich Castell'sches Domänenamt (Franken) both make good Rieslaner Sekt, and the latter's leesy-rich Casteller Herrenberg is particularly successful, with classic petrolly aromas.

RIESLING
Classic Deutscher Sekt variety
Germany's best Riesling Sekte have steadily increased in both number and quality over the last five years, showing classic, petrolly aromas with rich, honeyed bottle aromas. Alsace makes some of the world's greatest Riesling, but its Crémant d'Alsace is disappointing because all the best grapes go into the still wines. A little Riesling is used as a blending component for sparkling wine in England (Denbies), but it has not been very successful. The grape is also a component in some of South Africa's cheaper bubblies (Nederburg, Van Lovren). The Riebeek cooperative in Swartland makes a pure Riesling fizz by carbonation. It is also used in Canada for Château des Charmes, Cipes, and Hawthorne.

RONDO
Siberian half-cast
Saperavi Serverny x Muscat Ottonel hybrid used by Sedlescombe in England in its Organic Rosé blend.

ROUSSETTE
Classic Savoie grape
Delicately aromatic variety used in Seyssel, Vin du Bugey Mousseux and Vin de Savoie Mousseux.

ROUSSANNE
Rhône companion to the Marsanne
Authorised for the flabby fizz of St.-Péray.

SACY
Minor Burgundian variety
Permitted for Crémant de Bourgogne, Sacy's high

acidity should make it very useful in the production of sparkling wines, but poor quality, over-production and slipshod winemaking have prevented this from happening.

SAUVIGNON BLANC
Too assertive for fine quality sparkling wine
Good Sauvignon is too assertive to make a decent sparkling wine and low-grade or underripe Sauvignon is even more disastrous. Most sparkling wines using this grape are produced in South Africa, where pure varietal *cuvées* are made by Boland, Franschhoek Vineyards, Morgennof, and Rooiberg, although they are mostly cheap carbonated products. The only Cap Classique (*méthode champenoise*) made from 100% Sauvignon Blanc that I am aware of is produced by Weltevrede.

Sauvignon is used as a component in blended South African fizz (Cinzano, Haute Provence, Nederburg, Roodezandt). It is also one of the two most commonly used varieties permitted for Crémant de Bordeaux, and Bordeaux Sauvignon is often the softest version of this variety. Cava giant Freixenet has used Sauvignon fairly successfully in Mexico, as has Blue Pyrenees in its Fiddlers Creek fizz. Also used by Barbara International in Slovenia.

SAVAGNIN
Oxidation-prone Traminer?
According to ampelographer Pierre Galet, Savagnin is the same variety as Traminer, which is more discreetly aromatic than the Gewürztraminer, yet genetically identical. The Traminer does not, however, make oxidatively-prone wines, whereas the Savagnin does. I refer not to the Jura's Vin Jaune, which undergoes an oxidative ageing process similar to Sherry, but simply to local dry white wines, which always have a niggling preponderance of acetaldehyde (created by the oxidation of alcohol, evoking a Sherry-like aroma) when even a small amount of Savagnin has been used. This grape is used for the sparkling wines of Arbois, Crémant de Jura, and L'Etoile Mousseux. *See* GRINGET.

SCHEUREBE
Best for late-harvest wines
The only predominantly Scheurebe fizz I have come across is the Dürkheimer Fronhof Scheurebe Brut from Katharinenhof in the Pfalz, Germany, and it had the unmistakable 'cat's pee' aroma that fouls any wine made by underripe grapes from this Sylvaner x Riesling cross.

SCHWARZRIESLING
See MEUNIER

SCUPPERNONG
Pungently musky grape
Produces large, bronze-coloured, loose-hanging cherry-like grapes. Extraordinarily distinctive and so pungent it has been used for the specific purpose of disguising the foxiness of *labrusca* varieties in some blends. Duplin Wine Cellars in North Carolina has made a Scuppernong fizz using *méthode champenoise*.

SÉMILLON
Classic white Bordeaux variety
Apart from some of the more herbaceous clones, Sémillon generally has a varietal character that is more conducive to sparkling wine than Sauvignon Blanc. What lets it down, however, is its acidity, which could be higher, and although acidity is a problem that can be overcome in the New World, where they merely add it by the bucketful, it is in the New World where the most aggressively herbaceous clones are to be found.

This is probably why Sémillon is usually found in cheaper Australian blends (Aldridge, Angas, Barramundi, Seppelt Grand Western, Sunnycliff). In South Africa, too, this variety is merely a blending component (Boschendal, Haute Provence) and far less popular for fizz than Sauvignon Blanc. It is one of the two most commonly used varieties permitted for Crémant de Bordeaux. Also used in various sparkling Gaillac wines.

SEYVAL BLANC
Prolific hybrid used for sparkling wine in England
This Seibel 5656 x Seibel 4986 hybrid is the most successful of the Seyve-Villard crosses. In England it has become more popular than any of the German crosses. In sparkling wine terms, however, as more vineyards are switching to classic Champagne varieties, Seyval Blanc is now found in fractionally fewer *cuvées* than Chardonnay, and both these lag well behind Pinot Noir, even though *vinifera* varieties are in a minority generally. Other sparkling wines using it include L Mawby in Michigan, USA; Cherry Vineyards in Pennsylvania, USA; and Brights in Ontario, Canada.

SILVANER
See SYLVANER

SMEDEREVKA
Prolific Serbian variety
High in both sugar and acidity, Smederevka is used in most blended white sparkling wines produced in Serbia.

SULTANA
See THOMPSON SEEDLESS

SYLVANER
Neutral but earthy
Originally from Austria, Sylvaner (spelt Silvaner in Germanic countries) is widely planted throughout Central Europe. A prolific, early maturing variety, it yields its best dry wines in Franken and Alsace. Most pure Sylvaner sparkling wine is made in Franken and the Nahe, but it is invariably too soft or fat, and simply provides a basic fizz with an uninteresting character, the exception being Schales' extraordinary Silvaner Eiswein Sekt from Rheinhessen.

TASITSKA
Minor Georgian variety
An obscure grape that is usually blended with Chinuri, Goruli and Mtsvane for Georgian sparkling wines.

THOMPSON SEEDLESS
The sultana grape!
According to Raphael Brisbois, the first vintage of Omar Khayyam, which grabbed headlines in the western wine press, was pure Thompson Seedless, even though it claimed to be a blend of Ugni Blanc and Chardonnay. Also used in cheaper Australian blends such as Seppelt Great Western.

TRAJADURA
Basic Vinho Verde grape
Contributes to the bouquet, and ranks alongside the Paderna as a good second division Vinho Verde grape. Also grown just across the Spanish border in Galicia, where it is known as the Treixadura.

TREBBIANO
Italian synonym for the Ugni Blanc
Used by Yalumba in Australia for Angas Rosé, presumably because it is cheap and available.

TRESSOT
See TROUSSEAU

UGNI BLANC
The Trebbiano of France

Usually makes light, thin, neutral wines ideal for making Armagnac and Cognac, and because the requirement for sparkling wine base wines is similar in several respects to distillation wines, Ugni Blanc certainly has some fizz potential. One of the varieties permitted for Crémant de Bordeaux, and successfully used by Freixenet in Mexico and Omar Khayyam in India. Also used by Imperial Court in China.

VERDESSE
Flabby, slightly aromatic variety
Authorised for Vin de Savoie Mousseux.

VERDISO
Speciality of Treviso
Zardetto in Treviso, Veneto, uses a little of this fresh, zippy variety in some of its Prosecco di Conegliano *cuvées*, which are among some of the better Prosecco produced.

VIDAL
Basic, but one of the more successful hybrids
This Ugni Blanc x Seibel 4986 hybrid produces fresh, lively, still white wines in Canada, where it is also used in some sparkling wines. Some American East Coast fizz, such as Cherry Vineyards in Pennsylvania, also use it as a blending component.

VIGNOLES
An uninteresting hybrid
Also known Ravat 51, this Seibel 6905 x Pinot de Corton hybrid often accounts for as much as a quarter of the sparkling wine blends produced by L Mawby in Michigan.

VIURA
See MACABÉO.

WELSCHRIESLING
Boring 'riesling' rip-off
One of the main varieties used for Austrian Sekt. Also used in Italy (Martini & Rossi's Oltrepó Pavese Brut is pure Welschriesling) and Canada (Pelee Island, where it is known as Italico).

XAREL-LO
The best of Cava's three 'traditional' varieties
According to Cava gospel Xarel-lo brings strength and body to sparkling wines and, indeed, it is quite useful in small amounts for adjusting the structure of an essentially Macabéo base wine. Also used by Yalumba in Australia for Angas Rosé.

BLACK GRAPE VARIETIES

AZAL TINTO
Dark skinned Vinho Verde grape
The black variant of Azal is just as acidic as the white, but used only for red Vinhos Verdes.

BACO NOIR
Successful red wine hybrid
A Folle Blanche x riparia cross that has no foxiness, making it one of the more acceptable hybrids, although its use in Canadian sparkling wine (Brights) has not so far been as successful as it has for red wine.

BAGA
Classic Bairrada red wine grape
The mainstay of most Bairrada, including its sparkling wines, but yet to demonstrate any finesse in fizzy format.

BLAUER WILDBACHER
Styrian variety used for Schilchersekt
Tends to produce rather nervy and ungenerous fizz with a dry, peppery-raspberry flavour.

BRACHETTO
Aromatic, dark-skinned counterpart to Moscato
Related to the Braquet of Provence, the Brachetto is believed to include Moscato somewhere in its

lineage, and certainly its sweet, frizzante and fully sparkling red wines boast hauntingly similar grapey aromas.

CABERNET FRANC
Raspberry flavouring

Most successful in the Loire, where it is well suited to rosé style fizz under the generic Crémant de Loire Anjou, Touraine and, most of all, Saumur appellations. Also used in various Gaillac sparkling wines for rosé *cuvées* and is one of the varieties permitted for Crémant de Bordeaux. Beyond France, the only other sparkling wine to use this variety is, as far as I am aware, Angas Rosé in Australia.

CABERNET SAUVIGNON
Blackcurrant flavouring

Arguably the greatest red wine grape in the world, Cabernet Sauvignon is relegated to a supporting role in the sparkling wine appellations of Crémant de Loire, Anjou, Saumur and Touraine. Confined to rosé *cuvées* under various Gaillac AOCs. Plays a more important role in Crémant de Bordeaux, but the best grapes obviously go into the famous red wines of the region. Sometimes plays a primary role in top-quality sparkling red wines such as Killawarra, and is even used in a pure varietal format by All Saints and Yalumba. Underripe and lesser quality wines from this grape can bulk up cheap white fizz such as Aldridge, Angas Rosé and Barramundi. Mauler in Switzerland also uses this variety.

CARIGNAN
Spanish workhorse

Grown extensively in Southern France and California, but use for sparkling wine is restricted to Spain, where it is known as the Cariñena and used in some Cavas (Mont Marçal), even though it is not officially permitted, and in Australia, in the blend for Angas Rosé.

CARMENÈRE
An obscure, ancient Bordeaux variety

Permitted for Crémant de Bordeaux, even though it is almost extinct in that region.

CARNELIAN
High acidity and low alcohol, but too rustic

A (Carignan x Cabernet Sauvignon) x Grenache cross developed by Professor Olmo in 1936 to provide good acidity levels in California's hot Central Valley, where it was hoped the grape might provide Cabernet-like wine, but leaned closer to the Grenache. Used by Tedeschi Vineyards on the Hawaiian island of Maui, it has generally proved too rustic for sparkling wine, although has shown some promise for rosé fizz.

CÉSAR
Ancient but minor Burgundian variety

Still found in some areas of Burgundy, most notably Irancy near Chablis, and permitted for red Bourgogne Mousseux. Modest blending quality only.

CHAMBOURCIN
Interesting red hybrid that has found success in Australia

Developed in France by Joannès Seves, this has only been available since 1963, and no one knows its parentage. Widely cultivated in France, especially in the Nantes district of the Loire, it can resist rot and cold, thus it has been tried in many marginal viticultural areas around the world. Its wines are generally perceived as herbaceous, although this is probably not intrinsic to the variety, but more likely due to the marginal climates under which it is grown. When ripe, Chambourcin wines can

have a marked raspberry style. A sparkling red of surprisingly good quality is made by D'Arenberg in South Australia.

CINSAULT
Blending fodder only

Too coarse and rustic in its own right, the Cinsault (also spelt Cinsaut) is a minor component of Veuve du Vernay Rosé in France and Angas Rosé in Australia.

DORNFELDER
Successful red wine cross

This Helfensteiner x Heroldrebe cross provides deeply coloured red wines in Germany, but rather curious fizz (Gebrüder Anselmann, Hambacher Schloss). At its sparkling best in England, where it has produced the beautiful, sunset-hued Aluric de Norschide fizz from the Chilford Hundred vineyard.

DURAS
Interesting Gaillac grape

Primary grape in Gaillac AOCs for rosé sparkling wines.

DURIF
The Petite Sirah of California

Morris in Australia blend this with true Shiraz to make a rich, creamy-oaky, flavour-packed red sparkling wine.

ESPADEIRO
Dark-skinned Vinho Verde grape

Important red Vinho Verde variety, also used in Spain's Rias Baixas, but not encountered elsewhere.

FER
Thought to be a naturalised clone of Malbec

Once widely used for full-bodied reds throughout Southwest France, but rarely encountered now, although still authorised for rosé *cuvées* in various Gaillac sparkling wine appellations.

GAMAY
Infamous Beaujolais grape

One of Champagne's old varieties, which is something the champenois would like to forget, but a small amount is still grown in the region today. It has even proved successful in England, where Thames Valley Vineyard has produced a pure Gamay *cuvée* under the Clocktower label. One of the varieties permitted for Crémant de Bourgogne and the red Bourgogne Mousseux. Also used for rosé *cuvées* in various Gaillac AOCs, and permitted in the sparkling wines of Loire (Anjou, Saumur) and Savoie (Vin du Bugey Mousseux, Vin du Bugey Mousseux). Has been used for fizz in Germany (Henkell), Canada (Château des Charmes) and even Serbia (Navip).

GELLEWZA
Obscure Maltese variety

Uniquely used for a Maltese medium-sweet *pétillant* rosé from Emmanuel Delicata.

GRENACHE
Classic Châteauneuf-du-Pape grape

Although this variety has jammy flavours when properly ripened in hotter New World areas, it is quite neutral when harvested early in cooler areas, and can make ideal blending fodder to bulk-up more classic varieties. Works particularly well in Normans Conquest in Australia, and is adequate for more run-of-the-mill *cuvées*, such as Angas, Orlando Carrington Rosé, Seaview, Seppelt Great Western.

GROLLEAU
Loire rosé warhorse

Not authorised for red wines in the Loire, but the staple for almost all the region's rosés and can be used for either white or rosé fizz in the Anjou,

Crémant de Loire, Saumur and Touraine appellations. A lighter-coloured Grolleau Gris exists, but its use is restricted to the generic Crémant de Loire appellation.

LAMBRUSCO
The Coca-Cola grape

Italian variety infamous for the production of a cheap fizz of the same name in the Emilia-Romagna area (overlapping a little into Lombardy). Most Lambrusco grapes are converted into a medium-sweet, purple-coloured unclassified wine and carbonated, but dry, white and rosé versions also exist. Some Lambrusco DOCs exist (Lambrusco Mantovano, Lambrusco di Sorbara, Lambrusco Grasparossa di Castelvetro, Lambrusco Reggiano and Salamino di Santa Croce), and the wines produced in some of these appellations can be more serious. A few are even bottle-fermented.

LIMBERGER
German red wine variety

Known as Lemberger in Washington state, USA, the Frankova in the Czech Republic, and the Blaufränkisch in Austria and Slovenia. Used, not very successfully, for sparkling wines by Bohemia Sekt in the Czech Republic, and the Brackenheim cooperative.

MALBEC
Surprisingly fine sparkling red potential

Permitted for Crémant de Bordeaux. Also used in the Loire (Anjou, Saumur, Touraine). The only pure Malbec *cuvée* I have come across is Tatachilla's excellent Sparkling Malbec from Australia.

MENCIA
Widely-planted, little-known Galician variety

Used by the Vinos del Bierzo co-op in León for the drinkable pink version of its Don Perejón sparkling wine.

MERLOT
King of the right-bank in Bordeaux

One of the varieties permitted for Crémant de Bordeaux, but the grapes used are usually low in quality. Also permitted for rosé *cuvées* in various Gaillac appellations. It has even been for used for some Cavas (Gran Caus from Can Ràfols dels Caus, Mont Marçal), although not officially allowed. The best sparkling wines to use Merlot are red pure varietals made in Australia (Hollick, Irvine), although most Aussie fizz using this variety contain small amounts of blending fodder made from low quality grapes for cheaper *cuvées* (Aldridge, Angas Rosé, Barramundi). In this respect the Australians treat Merlot like Cabernet Sauvignon.

MEUNIER
Champagne's understudy

Underrated in Champagne, where some producers still pretend they use less than they actually do, Also used in Germany, where it's called Schwarzriesling, although it is in no way related to Riesling (the logic being, presumably, that Riesling is widely acknowledged as Germany's greatest grape, thus calling Meunier 'Black Riesling' gives some sort of quality connotation). Used in a number of countries, including England (Meon Valley, Oldaker, Ridgeview, Woolings).

MONASTRELL
An underrated Spanish variety

Commonly used for Cava rosado, Freixenet is the first to experiment with Monastrell for white Cava.

MONDEUSE
Savoie's greatest red wine grape

Too distinctive for sparkling wine in general,

although a good splash can be a welcome relief for what would otherwise be rather bland fizz under the Vin de Savoie Mousseux and Vin du Bugey Mousseux appellations.

PERIQUITA
Portuguese red wine variety that makes good fizz
Blended with Fernao Pires to produce Loridos Bruto, one of Portugal's best sparkling wines.

PETIT VERDOT
Acidic black Bordeaux variety
Permitted for Crémant de Bordeaux.

PINEAU D'AUNIS
Black Loire grape of fading importance
A useful blending component which adds tingly-fruit sensation to sparkling wines in the Anjou, Crémant de Loire, Saumur and Touraine appellations. Can also be used to correct the structure of some *cuvées* that may not be as lean as they should be.

PINOTAGE
South African peculiarity
Pinot Noir x Cinsault cross developed in 1925, but only in the last few years has there been any attempt to hone the style of the red wines it produces. As far as its use in sparkling wine goes, a small percentage can work very well, as Villiera's Tradition Carte Rouge demonstrates.

PINOT NOIR
Classic Champagne variety
This Champagne variety does not retain its freshness for as many decades as Chardonnay, but it arguably provides a more complex wine. It goes biscuity (particularly crumbly digestive biscuits), rather than toasty, although toastiness is also a fairly common bottle aroma for this variety. Not generally as successful as Chardonnay outside Champagne, with few areas where it can lord it over its fellow champenois grapes (perhaps Canterbury in New Zealand, and Launceston in Tasmania, Willamette Valley in Oregon). It probably does have an edge over Chardonnay in England, where it is easily the most popular sparkling wine grape. Also extraordinarily successful for rosé style Sekt made by *méthode champenoise* in Germany.

PLECHISTIK
Minor Russian grape variety
Also spelt Plechistic, this indigenous Russian variety gives backbone to red Tsimlyanskoe sparkling wine, which primarily consists of Tsimlyansky, a local grape that lacks acidity and structure.

PROKUPAC
Prolific Serbian variety
Possibly related to the Syrah, this variety is used by Navip to make red sparkling wines by *cuve close* and carbonation in Serbia.

ST LAURENT
Thought to be related to Pinot Noir
Used by Chorherrenstift Klosterneuburg for sparkling wine in Austria and by Bohemia Sekt in the Czech Republic, but has not shown much aptitude for bubbles.

SAMROT
Apparently a mutation of Meunier
At least two producers make pure Samrot Sekt in Germany, and they are both from Württemberg. The Flein-Talheim cooperative *cuvée* is a basic commercial fizz, although it does have some Pinot-like character, which is not unexpected for a mutation of Meunier, and is preferable to the pink Samrot fizz produced by the Willsbach cooperative.

SYRAH
A great red wine grape

Although Syrah is permitted for rosé *cuvées* in various Gaillac appellations, it has not played a significant role in European sparkling wine production, and what little has been used is generally of mediocre quality and relegated to *cuve close* such as Veuve du Vernay Rosé. It does come into its own, however, in Australia under the guise of sparkling red Shiraz - huge, deeply coloured, intensely flavoured fizz that represents one of that country's best-hidden treasures.

TARRANGO
A better than Gamay lookalike
This Touriga x Thompson Seedless cross retains good acidity throughout ripening even in hot areas, and is only perceived to be Gamay-like because Brown Brothers produces a pure varietal by *macération carbonique*, which gives the wine the peardrop amylic aroma found in Beaujolais Nouveau. Underneath this ubiquitous aroma, however, the Tarrango offers far more fruit and generosity than Gamay of the same price ever does. Tarrango would seem to be a good bet for sparkling wine production, although the only fizz I know that contains even a small amount is Seppelt Great Western.

TEMPRANILLO
Rioja and Penedès red wine grape
Spanish variety not officially permitted for Cava, even though it is the top black grape in Penedès, where most Cava is produced. If only because it shares the same heritage, Cava producers should be experimenting with Tempranillo, but so far only Mont Marçal has used it, and that was for a Cava rosado.

TOURIGA FRANCESA
Classic Port grape and one-off fizz variety
Used effectively in Portugal since 1994 in Schramsberg's Vertice joint venture.

TRIOMPHE
Foxy red wine hybrid
This Knipperlé x 101-14 Millardet hybrid used to be called Triomphe d'Alsace and although it was developed in Alsace (by Kuhlmann, who also bred the Maréchal Foch and Léon Millot), it has never been grown in any Alsace vineyards. But the EU has not been content to merely ban this grape, it also insisted on banning Alsace from its name. Although it has a foxy aftertaste, this characteristic can be successfully hidden in a clever blend, which Peter Andrews has managed to do in his Welsh fizz called Cariad Blush, which has reduced the foxiness to jamminess.

TROLLINGER
Found mainly in Württemberg, Germany, where it produces fresh, fruity, but rather basic red wines. The Trollinger Rosé Sekt made by Gerhard Rienth cannot be recommended, although his Riesling Sekt is good, so it must be the grape rather than the winemaker.

TROUSSEAU
Dark, distinctive red wine grape
Authorised variety for Crémant du Jura and, as the Tressot, red Bourgogne Mousseux.

TSIMLYANSKY
Russian grape used for red sparkling wine
Indigenous Russian variety lacking acidity and structure, and usually requiring blending with Plechistik for backbone.

VINHAO
Common Vinho Verde grape
Used for red Vinhos Verdes, possibly the same as Sousao, one of the Port varieties, but not seen outside Portugal.

ZINFANDEL
America's do-it-all red wine grape
Of all the European people that have been absorbed into American culture, the Italians seem to be the most American of all, and so it is with the Italian Primitivo grape which, as the Zinfandel, has become more American than apple pie. Although best-known for its deep, dark, berry-flavoured red wine, the Zinfandel does not ripen evenly, consequently it is used for every style of wine imaginable. Underripe Zinfandel is usually blended into cheap *cuve close* California fizz, but some riper grapes from this variety are also used for higher quality sparkling wines such as Kristone, albeit in very small amounts.

RED GRAPE VARIETIES
GEWÜRZTRAMINER
World's most unlikely brut style sparkling wine grape
Genetically the same variety as Traminer, *gewürz* (spicy) was appended to those strains that had the most pungent aroma. Hardly the sort of grape one expects to find in a sparkling wine, yet there are at least two Sekte produced exclusively from this variety in Germany; the one from Martin Heim should impress, even if the other, from the Heuchelberg-Kellerei, won't. Murganheira makes a poor stab at fizzy Gewürztraminer in Portugal. Roodezandt has also produced one in South Africa while Rooiberg use 40% in one of its sparkling wine blends.

HANEPOOT
South African synonym for Muscat d'Alexandrie
Franschhoek Vineyard uses 50% Hanepoot in its La Clotte Demi-Sec sparkling wine.

MOSCHOFILERO
Top Greek sparkling wine grape
Late ripening, lightly aromatic with excellent acidity when picked early, no green hints, and muted aromatics. Used for Ode Panos. Also spelt Moschophilero.

PINOT GRIS
Dark horse amongst future sparkling wine classics
At its best for spicy still white wines in Alsace, and has shown excellent sparkling wine potential, although this inherent capability has been dashed by low quality fruit and poor handling. Nevertheless, top quality pure Pinot Gris Crémant d'Alsace will one day emerge on a consistent basis. Also relatively widely used for fizz in Germany, where it known as the Ruländer, and in England. A number of Slovenian sparklers benefit from a certain amount of Pinot Gris, and it is also used in the USA (L Mawby, Michigan), Canada (Blue Mountain, British Columbia), South Africa (Buitenverwachting, Laborie), as well as being one of the varieties permitted for Crémant de Bourgogne, various Loire wines, and Vin du Bugey Mousseux in Savoie.

POULSARD
Obscure and underrated
The Jura's pink-skinned grape is not widely cultivated, but can produce a fine and delicately aromatic sparkling wine under the L'Etoile Mousseux appellation. It is also an authorised variety for Vin du Bugey Mousseux in neighbouring Savoie.

GLOSSARY OF TECHNICAL TERMS

ACCESSIBLE Literally a wine that is easy to approach, with no great barriers of acidity or undeveloped extract to prevent immediate enjoyment and drinkability.

ACETIC ACID The most important volatile acid found in wine (apart from carbonic acid), small amounts of acetic acid contribute positively to the attractive flavour of a wine, but too much will taste like vinegar.

ACIDITY This usually refers to fixed acidity (as opposed to volatile acidity), which is essential for the life and vitality of all wines. Too much will make wine too sharp (not sour, which would be a fault), but insufficient acidity will make a sparkling wine taste flabby, and the flavour will not last in the mouth. Some people confuse acidity with bitterness: lemon juice is acidic, while lemon peel is bitter.

ADEGA (Port.) Commercial winery. Often used as part of a firm's title.

AFTERTASTE The flavour and aroma left in the mouth after the wine has been swallowed. When attractive, this adds a pleasurable dimension to a wine, and could be the reason why you prefer it to a similar wine which has no aftertaste as such.

AGES GRACEFULLY A wine that retains finesse as it matures and sometimes even increases in finesse.

AGGRESSIVE The opposite of soft and smooth.

AGRAFE (Fr.) An inverted U-shaped metal clip once used to secure the first corks during *prise de mousse*, but it is rarely used now as the advent of crown caps has seen the demise of bottles bearing *bague carré*.

ALCOHOL The product of fermentation, alcohol is essential to the flavour and body of any wine, and crucial to its balance.

ALCOHOLIC Usually used in the pejorative sense of wine having too much alcohol and thus being out of balance.

ALDEHYDE The midway stage between an alcohol and an acid, formed during the oxidation of an alcohol. Acetaldehyde is the most important of the common wine aldehydes, and it forms as wine alcohol oxidises into acetic acid (vinegar). Small amounts of acetaldehyde add to the complexity of a wine, but too much will make it smell like Sherry.

AMPELOGRAPHER An expert who studies, records and identifies grape-vines.

AMYLIC A first fermentation that is too cool can cause a preponderance of amyl acetate which has a peardrop or bubblegum aroma.

ANBAUGEBIET (Ger.) A wine region in Germany such as Rheinpfalz or Mosel-Saar-Ruwer that is divided into districts or Bereich. All QbA and QmP wines must show their Anbaugebiet of origin on the label.

ANO (Port.) Year

AÑO (Sp.) Year.

AOC (Fr.) Standing for Appellation d'Origine Contrôlée, which is the top-rung in the French wine quality system.

APERITIF Originally used exclusively to describe a beverage prescribed for laxative purposes, aperitif now describes any drink taken before a meal to stimulate the appetite. Generally the lightest sparkling wines are preferred as aperitifs, although for Champagne this is sometimes taken to mean that a *blanc de blancs* is ideal, whereas the best examples of this style need to be aged and can be the most intensely flavoured of all Champagnes.

APPELLATION This literally means a 'name', and usually refers to an official geographically-based designation.

ARE (Fr.) One-hundredth of an hectare.

AROMA In an ideal world, this should really be confined to the fresh and fruity smells reminiscent of grapes, rather than the more winey or bottle-mature complexities of bouquet, but a book is not an ideal world, and such correctness would merely result in a repetitiveness that would interrupt the flow of the text. It is thus inevitable that *aroma* and *bouquet* will be become synonymous, and the technically correct yet contradictory term 'bottle-aroma' is evidence of this.

AROMATIC GRAPE VARIETIES The most aromatic classic grapes are Muscat, Gewürztraminer and Riesling, due to their high terpene content. Sauvignon Blanc is also very aromatic, but in a more herbaceous style.

ASSEMBLAGE (Fr.) Blend of base wines that creates the final *cuvée*.

ATMOSPHERE A measurement of atmospheric pressure, one atmosphere equals 15lbs per square inch (psi), which is the pressure our bodies are subjected to at sea-level. A sparkling wine can be anything up to six atmospheres, which is 90lbs psi or the equivalent to the pressure of a double-decker bus tyre, but although care must always be taken when opening a pressurised container such as a Champagne bottle, it is not the same as pulling the plug from a bus tyre. Pressure is affected by temperature and the actual pressure a fully sparkling wine at serving temperature of, say, 6°C will be just 2.5 atmospheres. *See* PRESSURE.

ASSEMBLAGE (Fr.) The blending of base wines to create the final *cuvée*.

ASTI (It.) A town in Northern Italy that gives its name to the world's finest sweet sparkling wine.

AUSLESE (Ger.) Category of German QmP wine, (above Spätlese, but below Beerenauslese), that is very sweet, made from late-picked grapes and may contain some botrytized grapes.

AUSTERE A wine that lacks fruit.

AUTOLYSIS The enzymatic breakdown of yeast cells that increases the possibility of bacterial spoilage; the autolytic effect of aging a wine on its lees is therefore undesirable in most wines, exceptions being those bottled *sur lie* (mostly Muscadet) and, of course, sparkling wine. Autolysis creates the inimitable 'champagney' character, providing the potential for complexity, and determining how much finesse there will be after the complex bottle-aromas have built up. *See* BOTTLE-AROMAS.

AUTOLYTIC The smell of a freshly disgorged brut style sparkling wine, which is not 'yeasty' but has acacia-like flowery finesse.

AVA This stands for Approved Viticultural Area, the American equivalent of AOC, although it merely assures geographical integrity, with no regulations to control the grape varieties, how they are be grown or the style of wine that may be produced.

BACKWARD A wine that is slow to develop (the opposite of precocious).

BAGUE CARRÉ (Fr.) A squared-off glass rim around the neck of a Champagne bottle onto that the *agrafe* is fixed.

BAGUE COURONNE (Fr.) An exaggerated lip on the neck of a Champagne bottle is necessary if a crown-cap is to be used for the *prise de mousse*.

BALANCE Refers to the harmonious relationship between acids, alcohol, fruit, tannin and other natural elements. If you have two similar wines but you definitely prefer one of them, its balance is likely to be one of the two determining factors (length being the other).

BALTHAZAR Large bottle equivalent to 16 normal-sized 75cl bottles.

BARREL-FERMENTED A few Champagnes like Krug still ferment in oak barrels, which traditionally are well-used and do not contribute overt oakiness, although some producers such as Selosse and Vilmart use new oak, a fashion that has been picked up by a number of New World producers, such as Pelorus and Kristone.

BARRIQUE (Fr.) Literally means 'barrel', but generically used in English-speaking countries for any small oak cask and often denotes the use of new oak.

BASE WINES The fully-fermented dry wines that, when blended together, form the basis of a sparkling wine *cuvée*.

BEERENAUSLESE (Ger.) Category of German QmP wine that comes above Auslese, but beneath Trockenbeerenauslese and is made from botrytized grapes. It has more finesse and elegance than any other intensely sweet wine, with the possible exception of Eiswein.

BENCH OR BENCHLAND The flat land between two slopes, this term describes a natural, rather than man-made, terrace.

BENTONITE A fine clay containing a volcanic ash derivative called montromillonite, a hydrated silicate of magnesium that activates a precipitation in wine when used as a fining agent.

BIANCO (It., & Sp.) White.

BIO-DYNAMIC Wines produced bio-dynamically are grown without the aid of chemical or synthetic sprays or fertilisers and vinified with natural yeast and the minimum use of filtration, SO_2 and chaptalisation.

BISCUITY A desirable aspect of bouquet found in some Champagnes, particularly a well-matured, Pinot Noir dominated blend. (Chardonnay dominated Champagnes tend to go toasty).

BITE A very definite qualification of grip. Usually a desirable characteristic, but an unpleasant bite is possible.

BITTERNESS Can be good or bad. [1] An unpleasant aspect of a poorly made wine. [2] An expected characteristic of an as yet undeveloped concentration of flavours that should, with maturity, become rich and delicious.

BLIND, BLIND TASTING An objective tasting where the identity of wines is unknown to the taster until after he or she has made notes and given scores. All competitive tastings are blind.

BLOOM Yeast and bacteria adhering to the grape's *pruina* create a coating on all grapes, but is most noticeable on black varieties.

BLOWSY An overblown and exaggerated fruity aroma, such as fruit jam, which may be attractive in a cheap wine, but would indicate a lack of finesse in a more expensive product.

BLUSH WINE A rosé and probably cheap.

BOB An acronym for 'Buyer's Own Brand', under which numerous retailers and restaurants sell wine of increasingly good value, particularly in the supermarket sector where the selection process has been honed to a fine art since the early 1980s.

BODEGA (Sp.) Commercial winery.

BODY The extract of fruit and alcoholic strength together give an impression of weight in the mouth.

BOTRYTIS A generic term for rot, but often used synonymously with *Botrytis cinerea*.

BOTRYTIS CINEREA The technically correct name for noble rot, the only rot that is welcomed by winemakers, particularly in the sweet-wine areas, as it is responsible for the world's greatest sweet wines.

BOTRYTIZED GRAPES Literally 'rotten grapes', but commonly used for grapes that have been affected by *Botrytis cinerea*.

BOTTLE-AGE The length of time a wine spends in bottle before it is consumed. A wine that has good bottle-age is one that has sufficient time to mature properly. Bottle-ageing has a mellowing effect.

BOTTLE-AROMAS Mellowing aromas created after disgorgement, most typically described as toasty or biscuity, which take decades to form when the wine is still in contact with the yeast, but begin to blossom within just a few years of disgorgement. With time, far more profound aromas can build up, such as coconut, coffee, cocoa, honey, walnut and brazilnut.

BOTTLE-FERMENTED I use this without discrimination for any sparkling wine that has undergone a second fermentation in bottle, but when seen on a label, it invariably means the wine has been made by transfer method.

BOTTLE VARIATION As with all wines, bottle variation can occur with time, when the most minuscule differences in the environment of each bottle has had time to take effect. The older the wine, the greater the incidence of bottle variation, but Champagne is no more (or less) prone than, say, Bordeaux or Burgundy.

BOUQUET *See* AROMA.

BRANCO (Port.) White.

BREED The finesse of a wine that is due to the intrinsic quality of grape and terroir combined with the irrefutable skill and experience of a great winemaker.

BRUT (Fr.) Literally 'raw' or bone dry, but in practice a brut is usually merely dry and should never be austere (0-15g/l residual sugar).

BRUT ABSOLUT, BRUT INTÉGRAL, BRUT NON DOSAGE, BRUT ZÉRO (Fr.) *See* EXTRA BRUT.

BUTTERY Normally caused by diacetyl, which is produced during malolactic fermentation and which the food industry adds to margarine to make it taste more like butter. Although buttery is fine in a still Chardonnay, it detracts from the finesse of a sparkling wine, which is why the champenois have developed various special cocktails of low-diacetyl-producing of malolactic bacteria, which certain producers throughout the world could obviously benefit from.

CARAMEL An extreme version of buttery or a combination of diacetyl and oak.

CARBON DIOXIDE See Carbonic gas

CARBONIC ACID The correct term for carbon dioxide (CO2) when dissolved in the water content of wine (when it becomes H2CO3). Although sometimes referred to as a volatile acid, it is held in equilibrium with the gas in its dissolved state and cannot be isolated in its pure form.

CARBONIC GAS Synonymous with CO2 (carbon dioxide), this gas is naturally produced during the fermentation process (when the sugar is converted into almost equal parts of alcohol and carbonic gas), but is normally allowed to escape during fermentation, although a tiny amount will always be present in its dissolved form (carbonic acid) in any wine, even a still one. If the gas is prevented from escaping, it remains dissolved and the wine becomes sparkling.

CASES To harmonise the production details in this book, a case of wine is defined as twelve standard 75cl bottles, even for those wineries who ship in cases of six.

CAVA (Sp.) The generic appellation for *méthode champenoise* wines produced in various delimited areas of Spain.

CAVE, CAVES (Fr.) Literally 'cellar, cellars'.

CEDARWOOD, CEDARY A purely subjective word applied to a particular bouquet associated with the bottle-maturity of a wine previously stored or fermented in wood, usually oak. Often found in Australian sparkling Shiraz.

CELLAR PALATE When the winemaker and other people within a single winery taste their own product so often, usually in isolation from the wines of other producers, that they cannot see any faults. The classic case is when a cellar gradually becomes infested with a mould, which when absorbed through the casks into a wine may be harmless to humans, but which most seasoned consumers would find objectionable. It can creep up so slowly that no one inside the firm notices, yet to a visitor it is so obvious.

CHALLENGER BRAND A Champagne brand that is deliberately priced between the bottom end of *grande marque* prices and BOB or *premier prix*.

CHAMPAGNE Specifically a sparkling wine produced in a delimited area of northern France, the Champagne name is protected within the EU, and in various other countries. It is, however, abused elsewhere, especially in the USA, where it is perfectly legal to sell domestically-produced 'champagne', although the champenois do themselves no favours by abusing their own appellation on the fizz they produce in South America.

CHAMPENOIS (Fr.) The people of Champagne.

CHAPTALISATION (Fr.) Sugar added to grape must to raise a wine's alcoholic potential. Named after Jean-Antoine Chaptal, a brilliant chemist and technocrat who served Napoleon as minister of the interior and instructed vignerons on the advantages of adding sugar to grape juice.

CHARM A subjective term: if a wine charms, it appeals without blatantly attracting in an obvious fashion.

CHARMAT *See* CUVE CLOSE

CHÂTEAU (Fr.) Literally 'castle' or stately home. While many château-bottled wines do actually come from magnificent edifices that could truly be described as châteaux, many may be modest one-storey villas, some are no more than purpose-built *cuveries*, while a few are merely tin sheds! The legal connotation is the same as for any domain-bottled wine.

CHEF DE CAVES (Fr.) Literally the 'cellarmaster', but in Champagne the *chef de caves* is also the winemaker, to a greater or lesser extent (depending on the traditions of the house).

CHEVILLE (Fr.) A term commonly used to describe the straight tube-like shape of an old Champagne cork that has lost its capacity to swell once removed from the bottle. The opposite of *juponne*.

CHEWY An extreme qualification of meaty.

CHOCOLATY Chocolate in a red wine is a youthful characteristic of a high pH wine, often made from Pinot Noir, but in Champagne it is part of the complexity of a well-aged *cuvée* and usually Chardonnay, not Pinot.

CITRUS *Citrussy* indicates aromas and flavours of far greater complexity than the word *lemony* can suggest.

CIVC (Fr.) See Comité Interprofessionnel du Vin de Champagne.

CLARIFICATION, CLARIFY To remove any suspended matter that may cloud a wine (by fining or filtration) or grape juice (by *débourbage* or centrifuge).

CLASSIC, CLASSY Both subjective words to convey an obvious impression of quality. These terms are applied to wines that not only portray the correct characteristics for their type and origin, but possess the finesse and style indicative of only the most top-quality wines.

CLEAN A straightforward term applied to any wine devoid of any unwanted or unnatural undertones of aroma and flavour.

CLONE A genetically identical vine can be replicated an infinite number of times by microbiogenetic techniques. *See* LOCALISED CLONES.

CLOS (Fr.) A plot of land that was once enclosed by walls. However, only those that still are enclosed by walls are considered true clos, since it is the physical effect of these walls that cut off the vines from the surrounding area, creating its own, superior terroir.

CLOSED Refers to the nose or palate of a wine that fails to open or show much character. It also implies that the wine has some qualities, even if they are 'hidden' - these should open up as the wine develops in bottle.

CLOYING Applies to the sickly and sticky character of a poor sweet wine, where the finish is heavy and often unclean.

COARSE A term that should be applied to a 'rough and ready' wine, not necessarily unpleasant, but certainly not fine.

COLHEITA (Port.) Vintage.

COMITÉ INTERPROFESSIONNEL DU VIN DE CHAMPAGNE (CIVC) (Fr.) The semi-governmental interprofessional body that regulates the Champagne industry.

COMMERCIAL A diplomatic way for experts to say 'I don't like this, but I expect the masses will'! A commercial wine is blended to a widely acceptable formula; at its worst it may be bland and inoffensive, at its best it is probably fruity, quaffable and uncomplicated.

COMPLETE Refers to a wine which has everything (fruit, tannin, acidity, depth, length, etc) and thus feels satisfying in the mouth.

COMPLEXITY An overworked word that refers to many different nuances of smell or taste. Great wines in their youth may have a certain complexity, but it is only with maturity in bottle that a wine will eventually achieve full potential in terms of complexity.

COOL-FERMENTED An obviously cool-fermented wine is very fresh, with simple aromas of apples, pears and bananas, at best, but could be blighted by more oppressive aromas of peardrops, bubblegum or nail-varnish,

CORKED Nothing inherently wrong with the wine, the term corked applies to a penicillin infection inside the cork, which gives an unpleasant musty character, spoiling an otherwise good wine. Not too long ago it was highly improbable to have two consecutive corked bottles of the same wine, but every day scientists are discovering 'corky' smelling compounds that have nothing to do with the cork, so it is quite possible for entire batches of wine to smell or taste corked. Furthermore, the most common of these (*see* TCA) affects casks as much as cork, and the spores are highly volatile, thus one affected cork sitting in a plastic bag with thousands of other can infect the entire batch. However, no wine buyer should purchase such wines, let alone put them on the shelf.

CORRECT All the correct characteristics for its type and origin, but not necessarily an exciting wine.

COSECHA (Sp.) Vintage.

COULURE (Fr.) A physiological disorder of the vine that occurs as a result of alternating periods of warm and cold, dry and wet conditions after the bud-break. If this culminates in a flowering during which the weather is too sunny, the sap rushes past the embryo bunches to the shoot-tips, causing vigorous growth of foliage, but denying the clusters an adequate supply of essential nutrients. The barely formed berries dry up and drop to the ground.

CRAYÈRES (Fr.) Chalk-pits dug out in Gallo-Roman times.

CREAMY Dr Tony Jordan believes that creaminess in a sparkling wine is probably a combination of the finesse of the mousse (created by the most minuscule of bubbles and their slow release), an understated malolactic influence and a certain amount of Chardonnay flavour, the combined effect of which is picked up at the back of the throat on the finish of the wine.

CREAMY-BISCUITY See biscuity

CREAMY-CARAMEL MALO A lesser, more acceptable version of caramel.

CRÉMANT (Fr.) Although traditionally ascribed to a Champagne with a low-pressure and a soft, creamy mousse, the term has now been phased out in Champagne as part of the bargain struck with other French sparkling wines that have agreed to drop the term *Méthode Champenoise*. In return they have been exclusively permitted to use this old Champagne to create their own appellations, such as Crémant de Bourgogne, Crémant d'Alsace etc.

CRISP A clean wine, with good acidity showing on the finish, yielding a refreshing, clean taste.

CROSS A vine that has been propagated by crossing two or more varieties within the same species (*Vitis vinifera* for example), while a hybrid is a cross between two or more varieties from more than one species.

CROWN-CAP The common beer-bottle cap now widely used as the temporary closure while a sparkling wine undergoes its second fermentation.

CRU OR CRÛ (Fr.) Literally means 'growth', as in *Grand Cru* or 'great growth'.

CUSHIONY A beautifully soft, ultra-fine sensation caused by the minuscule bubbles of a first rate mousse.

CUVE (Fr.) A vat, *cuve* should not be confused with *cuvée*.

CUVE CLOSE (Fr.) Bulk production method of making inexpensive sparkling wine through a second fermentation in tank, *cuve close* was invented by Eugène Charmat in 1907, and is also commonly referred to as the Charmat method or process.

CUVÉE (Fr.) Originally the wine of one *cuve* or vat, this term now refers to a precise blend or specific product that could well be blended from several vats.

CUVERIE, CUVIER (Fr.) The room or building housing the fermenting vats.

DEACIDIFICATION The only methods of reducing acidity that fits well with the sparkling wine structure are tartrate precipitation and malolactic. Some producers in countries like England, where acidity levels can be very high, resort to chemical deacidification (adding calcium carbonate), but this should be avoided like the plague. Providing the wine is good enough, there is no such thing as having too much acidity in a sparkling wine, as this can always be balanced with the *dosage*. Some technically very sweet *demi-sec* Champagnes can taste almost dry when the acidity levels are exceptionally high.

DÉBOURBAGE (Fr.) The settling process that removes bits of skin, pips and other flotsam and jetsam from the freshly pressed grape juice.

DEFINITION A wine with good definition is one that is not just clean with a correct balance, but also has a positive expression of its grape variety and/or origin.

DELICATE Describes the quieter characteristics of quality that give a wine charm.

DÉGORGEMENT (Fr.) See Disgorgement

DEMI-SEC (Fr.) Literally 'semi-dry', but semi-sweet for all practical purposes (33-50g/l residual sugar).

DÉPARTEMENT (Fr.) Geopolitical division of France, similar to county in the UK or State in the USA.

DEPTH Refers first to a wine's depth of flavour and secondly to its depth of interest.

DISGORGEMENT The act of opening the bottle to remove the sediment after second fermentation.

DEUTSCHER QUALITÄTSSCHAUMWEIN (Ger.) Same as Deutscher Sekt.

DEUTSCHER QUALITÄTSSCHAUMWEIN BA (GER.) Same as Deutscher Sekt BA.

DEUTSCHER QUALITÄTSSCHAUMWEIN BESTIMMTER ANBAUGEBIETE (Ger.) Same as Deutscher Sekt BA.

DEUTSCHER SEKT (Ger.) A sparkling wine made by any method (though probably *cuve close*), exclusively comprising of wine from German-grown grapes. It may indicate a maximum of two grape names and should be at least ten months old when sold.

DEUTSCHER SEKT BA (Ger.) A sparkling wine made by any method (though probably *cuve close*), exclusively comprising of wine made from grapes grown in one of Germany's 13 specified regions, although it may indicate an even smaller denomination if 85 per cent of the grapes come from the named area.

DEUTSCHER SEKT BESTIMMTER ANBAUGEBIETE (Ger.) Same as Deutscher Sekt BA.

DISTINCTIVE A wine with a positive character. All fine wines are distinctive to one degree or another, but not all distinctive wines are necessarily fine.

DIURNAL RANGE The difference between the maximum daytime and minimum nightime temperatures. Generally, the greater the difference, the higher the retention of acidity during the ripening process.

DOC Confusingly this may stand for [1.] Italy's *Denominazione di Origine Controllata*; [2.] Portugal's *Denominaçao de Origem Controlada*; and [3.] Spain's *Denominacion de Origen Calificada*. [1.] and [2.] are theoretically the equivalent of the French AOC, while [3.] is comparable to Italy's DOCG.

DOCG Italy's *Denominazione di Origine Controllata e Garantita* is theoretically one step above the French AOC. Ideally it should be similar to, say, a *Premier* or *Grand Cru* in Burgundy or a *Cru Classé* in Bordeaux, but in reality, it is almost as meaningless as Italy's DOC, which is found on most of that country's worst wines.

DOSAGE (Fr.) Sugar added to sparkling wine after disgorgement, prior to shipping, via the *liqueur d'expédition*, the amount of which is controlled by the terminology used on the label (Extra-Brut, Brut, Sec,

Demi-Sec etc.). Since the sugar is used to balance the acidity, which is a necessary constituent of any sparkling wine, to keep it as fresh as possible throughout the lengthy production process, and the acidity slowly rounds out with age, obviously the older the wine, the less *dosage* required. *See* LIGHT DOSAGE

DOUX (Fr.) A very sweet sparkling wine with 50g/l or more of residual sugar, the last commercially available *doux* was made by Roederer in 1983, and sold under its famous Carte Blanche label. That wine had 60 grams of residual sugar, not really sweet by *doux* standards, although ten years earlier Roederer's Carte Blanche had 80g/l of residual sugar, and 100 years ago it was 180g. Roederer's Carte Blanche today is just 45 grams.

DRIP IRRIGATION Various forms exist, but at its most sophisticated, it is a computer-controlled watering system programmed with the vine's general water requirement and constantly amended by a continuous flow of data from soil sensors. The water is supplied literally drip by drip through a complex system of pipes with metered valves.

DRY STRAW *See* STRAW.

EISWEIN (Ger.) An Eiswein occurs through extremely unusual circumstances whereby grapes left on the vine to be affected by noble rot are frozen by frost or snow. They are harvested and rushed to the winery where they must be pressed in their frozen state so that the ice rises to the surface and can be skimmed off. This results in a fantastic concentration of juice, sugar, acidity, extract and minerals. Some so-called Ice Wines produced in other less fastidious countries are made from grapes that have been frozen, but not pressed in this state, therefore no ice is skimmed off and the wines are no more concentrated than they would have been if picked before they were frozen.

ELEGANT A subjective term applied to wines that may be described as stylish and possessing some finesse.

EN FOULE (Fr.) Literally 'in a crowd', *en foule* is the rather haphazard effect created when ungrafted vines are cultivated by various methods of layering.

ENGLISH AROMA A very fresh herbaceous character.

ENOLOGIST, ENOLOGY (Am.) American spelling of oenology, oenologist. *See* OENOLOGY

ESTERS Sweet-smelling compounds that are formed by the combination of acids and alcohols during fermentation and throughout maturation. In minute quantities, esters contribute to the aroma and bouquet of a wine, but an excess of esters can be oppressive, as in the common occurrence of too much amyl acetate (*see* AMYLIC).

EVERYDAY An inexpensive, easy-drinking wine.

EXPANSIVE A wine that is big, but open and accessible.

EXPRESSIVE A wine that is expressive is true to its grape variety and area of origin.

EXTRACT The term covers everything all the solid in a wine and literally gives the wine its body.

EXPLOSIVE The mousse of a sparkling wine can be explosive in the bottle or the mouth. If the wine is properly chilled and yet the mousse is so explosive when the bottle is opened that you have to pour out an undue amount before it stops gushing out of the neck, this will be due to imperfections on the inner surface of the vessel, which act as nuclei, forcing the wine to foam uncontrollably. This usually happens with cheap bottles, which are noticeably lighter in weight, often brighter green in colour, but can occasionally occur with a more expensive rogue bottles. If the explosive nature of the mousse occurs in the mouth to the point where it almost threatens to force the mouth open, this will be inherent in the wine, not the bottle. Normally a fizz that is explosive in the mouth is due to poor or cheap vinification techniques, such as carbonation, a second fermentation that is too warm and too short, or a wine that has not had enough yeast-contact following the second fermentation. As a result, much of the carbonic gas is left free (not bound to the wine) and free carbonic gas is the first to be released from a sparkling wine. However, the fixing or binding of carbonic gas in wine is not fully understood, and this explosive effect has been noted occasionally in the best Champagnes. Furthermore it can happen to some bottles in a batch and not others. Moët & Chandon has been researching the cause for more than a decade, and is still none the wiser!

EXTRA-BRUT (Fr.) Literally 'extra-raw' and actually bone-dry, this category incorporates all the non-dosage marketing terms such as *Brut Absolut, Brut Intégral, Brut Non Dosage, Brut Zéro* etc., plus the lower end of the brut spectrum (0-6g/l residual sugar).

EXTRA-SEC (Fr.) Literally 'extra-dry', but merely dry in most cases (12-20g/l residual sugar).

FAT A wine full in body and extract. It is good for any wine to have some fat, but fat in an unqualified sense can be derogatory and no wine should be too fat, as it will be flabby or too blowsy.

FEMININE Subjective term used to describe a wine with a preponderance of delicately attractive qualities, rather than weight or strength. A wine of striking beauty, grace and finesse with a silky texture and exquisite style.

FERMENTATION The biochemical process by which enzymes secreted by yeast cells convert sugar molecules into almost equal parts of alcohol and carbonic gas.

FERMENTACIÓN EN BOTELLA (Sp.) Literally 'bottle-fermented', thus actually transfer method.

FERMENTAZIONE NATURALE (It.) Literally 'naturally fermented', which should apply to every wine ever made - even a carbonated fizz must have been naturally fermented in the first place. What it is supposed to infer, however, is that a wine has been rendered sparkling by natural refermentation in a tank or bottle (usually the former).

FILTER, FILTRATION Most wines are filtered at various times throughout their production to remove suspended matter that either occurs naturally in the grape juice or is created through fermentation and maturation process. Some producers go to the trouble of not filtering their products because they believe it takes something out of the wine (flavour, body, stuffing - you name it) that should be there, whilst others are equally adamant in their belief that it literally polishes the wine, and that an unfiltered wine can be too diffuse, ill-defined and lacks focus, and therefore finesse. The jury is still out for any definitive answer, but certainly no wine should be filtered too many times or too aggressively. There are three basic methods of filtration: depth filtration (also known as earth filtration); pad filtration (also known as sheet filtration), and membrane filtration (also known as micro-porous filtration). There is also centrifugal filtration, which is not filtration in the pure sense but achieves the same objective by so-called centrifugal force.

FINESSE That elusive, indescribable quality that separates a fine wine from those of lesser quality.

FINE WINES Quality wines, representing only a small percentage of all wines produced.

FINING The clarification of fresh grape juice or wine is often speeded up by the use of various fining agents that operate by an electrolytic reaction to fine out oppositely charged matter.

FINISH The quality and enjoyment of a wine's aftertaste.

FIRM Refers to a certain amount of grip. A firm wine is a wine of good constitution, held up with a certain amount of tannin and acidity.

FIRST PRESSING The first pressing yields the sweetest, cleanest, clearest juice.

FIXED ACIDITY This is the total acidity less the volatile acidity. The main grape acids are tartaric (ripe acid) and malic (unripe acid), although a little citric will be present, plus traces of succinic and lactic. The amount of lactic (so-called milk acid because it is also found in sour milk) will be significant if the wine has undergone malolactic fermentation.

FIXED SULPHUR Added to wine primarily to prevent oxidation, which it does by fixing itself to the oxygen on a molecular basis. Once a molecule of sulphur is fixed, it stays fixed. It continues to do its job, keeping the oxygen prisoner, but it is no longer free to protect the wine against other molecules of oxygen: only free sulphur can do that. Sulphur can fix to all sorts of molecules in a wine, mostly harmless, but a few things are potentially hazardous in a smelly way. When sulphur fixes with hydrogen, for example, hydrogen sulphide (stink bombs, bad eggs) is formed. These are called fixed-sulphur faults. On the other hand, we are just beginning to understand that the toasty bottle-aroma most Champagne aficionados adores is in fact a fixed-sulphur fault!

FLABBY The opposite of crisp, referring to a wine lacking in acidity and consequently dull, weak and short.

FLASCHENGÄRUNG (Ger.) Bottle-fermented Sekt, but not necessarily *méthode champenoise*.

FLASCHENGÄRUNG NACH DEM TRADITIONELLEN VERFAHREN (Ger.) Same as Traditionelle Flashengärung.

FLESHY Refers to a wine with plenty of fruit and extract and infers a certain underlying firmness.

FLOWERY General floral aromas are found in young sparkling wines, and are the precursors to fuller, deeper, fruitier aromas. Specific acacia aromas are found in recently disgorged wines of any age.

FLYING WINEMAKER Nothing to do with levitation or the DTs, the concept of the flying winemaker was born in Australia where, due to the size of that continent and the staggered picking dates, highly sought-after consultants Brian Croser (now at Petaluma) and Tony Jordan (now at Green Point) would hop by plane from harvest to harvest.

FOAMY A less acute degree of *explosive*.

FOXY The very distinctive, highly perfumed character of various varieties and hybrids of *Vitis lambrusca*, an indigenous American species. This foxy character can be cloyingly sweet and sickly to European and Antipodean palates that are not unconditioned to methyl and ethyl anthranilate, the two esters responsible.

FREE SULPHUR The acrid odour of sulphur in a wine should, if detected, be akin to the smell of a recently extinguished match, and will go away with time in bottle, or a swirl of the glass.

FRIZZANTE (It.) Semi-sparkling or slightly fizzy, the equivalent of *pétillant*.

FRIZZANTINO (It.) Very lightly sparkling, the equivalent of *perlant*.

FRUITY Although wine is made from grapes, it will not have a fruity flavour unless the grapes used have the correct combination of ripeness and acidity.

FULL Usually refers to body, *eg*. full-bodied. But a wine can be light in body yet full in flavour.

FULLY FERMENTED A wine that is allowed to complete its natural course of fermentation and so yield a totally dry wine.

FULLY SPARKLING A wine with a pressure of 5-6 atmospheres.

GASIFICADO (Sp.) Artificially carbonated wine.

GENERIC A wine, usually blended, of a general appellation.

GENEROUS A generous wine gives its fruit freely on the palate, while an ungenerous wine is likely to have little or no fruit and, probably, an excess of tannin. All wines should have some degree of generosity.

GLUGGY Easy to guzzle.

GOOD GRIP A healthy structure of tannin supporting the fruit in a wine.

GOÛT AMÉRICAIN (Fr.) From the 19th century through to the 1920s, there was not an established regime of *dosage* for Champagne as there is today. Instead of *brut, sec, demi-sec* etc., the different market determined the *dosage* of Champagne. The American market was the third sweetest, and we know from the observation of Henry Vizetelly that in 1882 Champagnes labelled goût américain contained between 110 and 165 grams per litre of residual sugar.

GOÛT ANGLAIS (Fr.) Although the English market has demanded the driest Champagne, and the first Champagnes ever to be labelled *brut* were shipped to London sometime after 1876, at 10-30 grams per litre of residual sugar, the concept of *brut* was obviously relative to its times. Vizetelly recorded that the *gout anglais* varied between 22 and 66 grams, which was considered dry in its day, but would now be thought very sweet indeed.

GOÛT FRANÇAIS (Fr.) In the late-19th century, *goût français*, a style that was popular in both France and Germany, carried a *dosage* of between 165 and 200 grams, making it second only in sweetness to Champagnes destined for the Russian market (which did not have a designated 'goût', but according to Vizetelly contained between 200 and 300 grams, which is two to three times as sweet as Château d'Yquem).

GRAFT The joint between the rootstock and the scion of the producer vine.

GRAND CRU (Fr.) Literally 'great growth', in regions such as Burgundy, where its use is strictly controlled, it has real meaning (*ie* the wine should be great-relative to the quality of the year), but in other winemaking areas where there are no controls, it will mean little.

GRANDE MARQUE (Fr.) Literally a 'great brand' or 'famous brand', in the world of wine the term *grande marque* is specific to Champagne and until 1997 applied to members of a 'club' called the Syndicat de Grandes Marques, but this was disbanded when they could not agree on quality criteria for continued membership. The term will continue to be used, particularly in English-speaking countries, for the most famous brands, and a new 'club' could well appear in the future.

GRANVAS (Sp.) Same as *cuve close*.

GRAPEY Can be applied to an aroma or flavour that is reminiscent of grapes rather than wine, a particular characteristic of German wines and wines made from various Muscat or Muscat-like grapes.

GREEN Young and tart, as in Vinho Verde. It can be either a derogatory term, or simply an indication of youthful wine that might well improve.

GROWTH *See* CRU

HANDGERÜTTELT (Ger.) Hand-riddled (manual *remuage*), thus the wine has been bottle-fermented and not transferred, therefore this term can be taken to mean *méthode champenoise*.

HARSH A more derogatory form of *coarse*.

HEURIGE (Austrian) The name given to the new wine that, as from 11 November each year, may be sold in the small taverns of the same name that are owned by *vignerons* who made the wine. Vine branches are hung over the entrance to the Heurige when the new wine is available, and should be removed during the hours when the premises are not actually open. *See* STURM.

HIGH-DENSITY VINES This refers to vines that are planted closer together to force more competition with one another, yielding less fruit per vine, but of higher quality, and because there are more vines, the yield per hectare can be the same, or even more. High-density vines are not, however, a way of getting more for less, as the initial outlay for two, three or four times as many vines is considerable, as is the cost of additional posts and wires, not to mention the extra cost of tending the vines from pruning to harvest.

HIGH-TONE A term used in this book to describe aromas of bouquet that aspire to elegance, but that can become too exaggerated and be slightly reminiscent of vermouth.

HOLLOW A wine that appears to lack any real flavour in the mouth compared to the promise shown on the nose. Usually due to a lack of body, fruit or acidity.

HONEST Applied to any wine, but usually of a fairly basic quality, *honest* implies it is true in character and typical of its type and origin. It also infers that the wine does not give any indication of being souped-up or mucked about in any unlawful way. The use of the word honest is, however, a way of damning with feint praise for it does not suggest a wine of any special or truly memorable quality.

HONEYED Many Champagnes develop a honeyed character through bottle-age, as indeed can Riesling Sekte.

HORIZONTAL TASTING This is a tasting of different wines of the same style or vintage, as opposed to a vertical tasting, which consists of different vintages of the same wine.

HYBRID A cross between two or more grape varieties from more than one species.

JAHRGANGSWKT (Ger.) Literally 'vintage Sekt', this merely means a sparkling wine from a single year and does not infer any special connotation of quality.

JAMMY Commonly used to describe a fat and eminently drinkable red wine rich in fruit, if perhaps a bit contrived and lacking a certain elegance.

JEROBOAM Large bottle equivalent to four normal-sized 75cl bottles.

KABINETT The first rung of predication in Germany's QmP range, one below Spätlese and often drier than a QbA.

KLASSISCHE FLASHENGÄRUNG (Ger.) Same as Traditionelle Flashengärung.

LACTIC ACID The acid that develops in sour milk, which is also created in wine during the malolactic fermentation.

LAMBRUSCA A native American species of vine.

LAMBRUSCO (It.) A cheap, fizzy Italian wine.

LD A sparkling wine term that stands for 'late disgorged' and paradoxically means the same as 'recently disgorged'. The use of LD infers that the wine in question is of a mature vintage that has been kept on its yeast deposit for an extended period. *See* RD

LEES The sediment that accumulates in the bottom of a vat (or bottle) during the fermentation of a wine. Synonymous with sediment and to a certain degree yeast (as in yeast-contact).

LENGTH A wine that has length indicates that the flavour lingers in the mouth a long time after swallowing. If two wines taste the same, yet you definitely prefer one, but do not understand why, it is probably because the one you prefer has a greater length.

LIE (Fr.) The French for lees. *Sur lie* refers to a wine kept in contact with its lees.

LIEU-DIT (Fr.) A named site within a vineyard.

LIME This is the classic character of Sémillon and Riesling when grown in many areas of Australia, which explains why Sémillon from the Hunter Valley used to be sold as Hunter Riesling.

LINALOOL Found in some grapes, particularly Muscat and Riesling varieties. It contributes to the peachy-flowery fragrance that is the varietal characteristic of wines made from Muscat grapes.

LINGERING Normally applied to the finish of a wine - an aftertaste that literally lingers.

LIQUEUR DE TIRAGE (Fr.) The bottling liqueur: wine, yeast, sugar and yeast nutrients added to still Champagne to induce the mousse. A little bentonite (fining agent) will also be included at this juncture, to promote full sedimentation prior to *remuage*. The amount of sugar used determines how fizzy the wine will be. In theory between 4 and 4.3 grams of sugar per litre of wine will produce one atmosphere of pressure, the fluctuation being due to the alcoholic degree of the base wine (the more alcohol, the less efficient the yeast becomes). Between 24 and 25.8 grams of sugar are therefore required in theory to produce six atmospheres, but account must be taken of the potential loss of pressure at disgorgement, thus 27 grams is generally regarded as the rule-of-thumb dosage for a fully sparkling wine. Most Champagnes utilise 22-24 grams of sugar and are around five atmospheres, whereas most New World sparkling wines use 18-22 grams and are less fizzy at some 4.5 atmospheres.

LIGHT DOSAGE A personal term generally confined to Brut-style Champagnes that have no more than 8g/l of residual sugar (the maximum permitted being 15g/l).

MACERATION A term that is usually applied to the period during the vinification process when the fermenting juice is in contact with its skins.

MADERIZED The terms maderised and oxidised are sometimes erroneously believed to be synonymous, but Madeira is reductive, while Sherry is oxidative. All Madeiras are maderized by slowly heating the wines in specially constructed ovens, then slowly cooling them. Apart from Madeira itself, this maderised character is undesirable in all but certain Mediterranean wines that are deliberately made in a rancio style (the French tend to use rancio in preference to maderisé, which they all too often confuse with oxidise).

MAGNUM Large bottle equivalent to two normal-sized 75cl bottles, the ideal volume for ageing Champagne.

MALIC A tasting term that describes the green apple aroma and flavour found in some young wines, due to the presence of malic acid, the dominant acid found in apples.

MALIC ACID Although this very harsh-tasting (green apple on mild steel) acid diminishes during the ripening process, a significant quantity still persists in ripe grapes and, although reduced by fermentation, in the wine too.

MALOLACTIC A biochemical process that transforms the hard malic acid of unripe grapes into soft lactic acid and carbonic gas.

MANNOPROTEIN Nitrogenous matter secreted from yeast during autolysis.

MARQUE A brand or make.

MEAN An extreme qualification of *ungenerous*.

MELLOW A wine that is round and nearing its peak of maturity.

MERCAPTANS Methyl and ethyl alcohols can react with hydrogen sulphide to form mercaptans, foul-smelling compounds, often impossible to remove, which can ruin a wine. Mercaptans can smell of garlic, onion, burnt rubber or stale cabbage.

MÉTHODE CHAMPENOISE The process that converts a fully-fermented still wine into a sparkling wine by a second fermentation in the same bottle in which it is sold. In the EU this term is forbidden on the label of any wine other than Champagne, which never uses it anyway.

MÉTHODE GAILLACOISE (Fr.) A variant of *méthode rurale* involving *dégorgement*.

MÉTHODE RURALE (Fr.) The precursor of *méthode champenoise*, it involves no secondary fermentation. The wine is bottled before the first alcoholic fermentation has finished, and carbonic gas is produced during the continuation of fermentation in the bottle. There is also no *dégorgement*.

METODO CHAMPENOIS (It.) *See* MÉTHODE CHAMPENOISE.

METHUSELAH Large bottle equivalent to eight normal-sized 75cl bottles.

MICROCLIMATE Due to a combination of shelter, exposure, proximity to mountains, water mass and other topographical features unique to a given area, a vineyard can enjoy (or be prone to) a specific microclimate.

MID-PALATE [1] The centre-top of your tongue. [2] A subjective term to describe the middle of the taste sensation when taking a mouthful of wine. Could be hollow, if the wine is thin and lacking, or full, if rich and satisfying.

MILLERANDAGE (Fr.) A physiological disorder of the vine that occurs after cold or wet weather at the time of the flowering. This makes fertilization very difficult, and consequently many berries fail to develop. They remain small and seedless even when the rest of the bunch is full-sized and ripe.

MINERAL This is normally a positive term indicating a certain complexity and finesse, but some wines can have a minerally aftertaste that can sometimes be unpleasant. Vinho Verde has an attractive, almost tinny, mineral aftertaste.

MONOPOLE (Fr.) Single ownership of one vineyard.

MOUSSE (Fr.) The effervescence of a sparkling wine, which is best judged in the mouth; a wine may appear to be flat in one glass and vigorous in another due to the different surfaces. The bubbles of a good mousse should be small and persistent, the strength of effervescence depending on the style of wine.

MOUSSEUX *See* VIN MOUSSEUX

MOUTHFILL Good mouthfill infers a certain satisfaction or completeness, and is the opposite of hollow.

MUSHROOM Not a mustiness, but the attractive aroma of freshly peeled mushroom. This is quite common in old vintages of Champagne and, curiously, for some wines it affects just some bottles in a batch, yet not others, while for other wines this characteristic can be found in every single bottle. For the moment, no one knows its origin. At one time it was thought to be a characteristic of mature Meunier, but the instances where it affects only some bottles in a batch would seem to rule this out. One suggestion has been that it is a yeast-derived characteristic, the logic being that yeasts are a form of mushroom, but this explanation strikes many oenologists as being a bit too logical. The latest idea is that it could be a reaction between the yeast and the cork, when a little wine is trapped between the lip of the bottle and the top of the cork at bottling. Although not conclusive, since hearing this explanation, I have observed an unusually large deposit of dried wine on the lip of those bottles that have a fresh mushroom aroma.

NEBUCHADNEZZAR Large bottle equivalent to 20 normal-sized 75cl bottles.

NÉGOCIANT (Fr.) Commonly used to describe larger wine producing companies, the term is derived from the traditional practice of negotiating with growers to buy grapes and wholesalers or other customers to sell the wine produced.

NÉGOCE (Fr.) Collective form of *négociant*.

NERVY, NERVOUS Subjective term usually applied to a dry white wine that is firm and vigorous, but not quite settled down.

NEUTRAL GRAPE VARIETIES The opposite of aromatic grapes, these include virtually all the minor, nondescript varieties that produce bland tasting, low-quality wines, but also encompass better known varieties such as the Melon de Bourgogne, Aligoté, Pinot Blanc, Pinot Meunier and even classics like Chardonnay and Sémillon. Neutral varieties are for fine sparkling wines of the brut style because their characteristics are enhanced by the subtle effects of autolysis and mellowing bottle-aromas, whereas aromatic grapes fight against these processes.

NOBLE ROT A condition caused by the fungus Botrytis cinerea under certain conditions. *See* BOTRYTIS CINEREA.

NON-DOSAGE (Fr.) A sparkling wine that has received no dosage.

NON-VINTAGE In theory a blend of at least two different years, but many producers, particularly growers in Champagne, grade their *cuvées* on selection, often selling a pure vintage *sans année* (without year).

NOSE The smell or odour of a wine, encompassing both aroma and bouquet.

OAKY The aromatic qualities picked up from new oak, which usually consists of the creamy-vanilla aroma of vanillin, a natural oak aldehyde that also happens to be the principal aromatic component in vanilla pods. Sparkling wines seldom benefit from new oak characteristics, which are too overpowering for the subtle effects of autolysis, and deny the wines most of the finesse it might otherwise have had.

OENOLOGIST, OENOLOGY Pronounced 'enologist' and 'enology'(and spelt this way in the USA), oenology is the scientific study of wine, which is a branch of chemistry, and most winemakers today are qualified oenologists with practical, hands-on production experience and an

understanding of viticulture.
OFF VINTAGE OR YEAR A year in which many poor wines are produced due to adverse climatic conditions, such as very little sunshine during the summer, which can result in unripe grapes, or rain at the harvest, which can result in rot. Generally a vintage to be avoided, but approach any opportunity to taste the wines with an open mind because there are always good wines made in every vintage.
OPULENT Suggestive of a rather luxurious varietal aroma, very rich, but not quite blowsy.
ORGANIC WINES A generic term covering wines that are produced using the minimum amount of SO2, from grapes that have been grown without chemical fertilizers, pesticides or herbicides.
OSMOTIC PRESSURE When two solutions are separated by a semi-permeable membrane, water will leave the weaker solution for the other in an endeavour to equalize the differing solution strengths. In winemaking this is most usually encountered when yeast cells are expected to work in grape juice with an exceptionally high sugar content. Since water accounts for 65 per cent of a yeast cell, osmotic pressure causes the water to escape through its semi-permeable exterior. The cell caves in, (a phenomenon called plasmolysis), the yeast dries up and eventually dies.
OVERTONE A dominating element of nose and palate and often one that is not directly attributable to the grape or wine.
OXIDATIVE A wine that openly demonstrates the character of maturation on the nose or palate, which can range from various buttery, biscuity, spicy characteristics to a hint of nuttiness. Generally a positive term, although overly or too oxidative is negative.
OXIDATION, OXIDIZED These terms are ambiguous; from the moment grapes are pressed or crushed, oxidation sets in and the juice or wine will be oxidized to a certain and increasing extent. Oxidation is an unavoidable part of fermentation and an essential to the maturation process, but in order not to mislead, it is best to speak of a mature or, at the extreme, an oxidative wine because when 'oxidized' is used, even amongst experts, it will invariably be in an extremely derogatory manner, to highlight the Sherry-like odour of a wine that is in a prematurely advanced stage of oxidation.
PALATE The flavour or taste of a wine.
PEAK The so-called peak in the maturity of a wine is subject to the consumer's point of appreciation. Those liking fresher, crisper wines will perceive an earlier peak in the same wine than 'golden oldy' drinkers. A rule of thumb that applies to both extremes of taste is that a wine will remain at its peak for as long as it took to reach it.
PEARDROP *See* AMYLIC.
PEPPERY Applied to young wines whose various components are raw and not yet in harmony, sometimes quite fierce and prickly on the nose.
PERLANT (Fr.) Very slightly sparkling, less so than crémant and pétillant.
PERLWEIN (Ger.) Cheap, semi-sparkling wines made by carbonating a still wine. Mostly white, but can also be red or rosé.
PÉTILLANCE, PÉTILLANT (Fr.) A wine with enough carbonic gas to create a light sparkle.
PETROL, PETROLLY With some bottle-age, the finest Rieslings have a vivid and zesty bouquet that some refer to as petrolly. The petrolly character has an affinity with various zesty and citrussy odours, but many lemony, citrussy, zesty smells are totally different from one another and the Riesling's petrolly character is both singular and unmistakable. As great Riesling matures, so it also develops a honeyed character, bringing a classic, honeyed-petrol richness to the wine.
POST-DISGORGEMENT AGEING The period between disgorgement and when the wine is consumed. With the sudden exposure to air after an extended period of ageing under anaerobic conditions, the development of a sparkling wine after disgorgement is very different from that before.
PREMIER PRIX (Fr.) The cheapest Champagnes available in French supermarkets. Unlike British supermarket Champagnes, which can be very good buys indeed, premier prix are always purchased on price, usually with no regard to value, and are best avoided.
PHYLLOXERA Worldwide vine louse that spread from America to virtually every viticultural region in the late nineteenth century, destroying many vines. New vines had (and still have) to be grafted to phylloxera-resistant American rootstocks.
PRE-PHYLLOXERA VINE So-called because the vines have been planted *en foule* prior to Phylloxera. *See* EN FOULE.
PRESSURE The pressure inside a bottle of sparkling wine is affected by temperature and altitude. Pressure increases as the temperature rises, but decreases as the altitude climbs. To be uniform when comparing the pressure of different sparkling wines, oenologists around the world refer to pressures at 20°C and sea-level.
PRODUCER VINE Vines are usually grafted onto phylloxera-resistant rootstock, but the grapes produced are characteristic of the above-ground producer vine or scion, which is normally a variety of *Vitis vinifera*.
QBA (Ger.) Germany's *Qualitätswein bestimmter Anbaugebiete* is theoretically the equivalent of the French AOC.
QUAFFING An unpretentious wine that is easy and enjoyable to drink.
QUALITÄTSSCHAUMWEIN (Ger.) A so-called 'quality sparkling wine', this can be produced by any member state of the EU, but the term should be qualified by the country of origin (of the wine), thus only *Deutscher Qualitätsschaumwein* will necessarily be from Germany.
QUINTA (Port.) Literally 'farm', but used to indicate a wine estate.
RACKING Draining a wine off its lees into a fresh cask or vat.
RD A sparkling wine term that stands for 'recently disgorged', the initials RD are the trademark of Champagne Bollinger. See LD
RÉCOLTANT-MANIPULANT (Fr.) A grower who produces Champagne exclusively from his or her own vineyards.
REDUCTIVE The less exposure it has to air, the more reductive a wine will be. Different as they are in basic character, Champagne, Muscadet *sur lie* and Beaujolais Nouveau are all examples of a reductive, rather than oxidative, style. From the vividly autolytic Champagne, through Muscadet *sur lie* with its barest hint of autolytic character, to the amylic aroma of Beaujolais Nouveau.
REHOBOAM Large bottle equivalent to six normal-sized 75cl bottles.
REMUAGE (Fr.) The process whereby the sediment is encouraged down to the neck of the bottle in preparation for disgorgement.
RESERVE WINES Older wines added to a non-vintage blend.
RETICENT Suggests that the wine is holding back on its nose or palate, perhaps through youth, and may well develop with a little more maturity.
REVERSE SAIGNÉE In Champagne this involves a majority of Pinot Noir, commonly as much as 90%, which has undergone a light saignée, and is then blended with a small amount of Chardonnay for freshness.
RICH, RICHNESS A balanced wealth of fruit and depth on the palate and finish.
RIPE Grapes ripen, wines mature, although some of the constituents of a wine, such as fruit and even acidity, can be referred to as ripe. Tasters should however beware of mistaking a certain residual sweetness for ripeness.
ROASTED Describes the character of grapes subjected to the shrivelling or roasting of noble rot.
ROBUST A milder form of aggressive, which may often be applied to a mature product, ie., the wine is robust by nature, not aggressive through youth.
ROOTSTOCK The lower rooting part of a grafted vine, usually phylloxera-resistant.
ROOTY Usually refers to a certain rooty richness found in Pinot Noir. Although a connotation of root vegetables, rooty is a positive term, albeit a very distinctive one that people will love or hate, whereas vegetal is a negative term.
ROSÉ (Fr.) A pink wine.
ROSADO (Sp.) A pink wine.
ROSEWORTHY One of Australia's top colleges for viticulture and oenology (the other being Charles Stuart at Wagga Wagga).
SAIGNÉE (Fr.) The process of drawing off surplus liquid from the fermenting vat in order to produce a rosé wine from the free-run juice. In cooler wine regions, the remaining mass of grape pulp may be used to make a darker red wine than would normally be possible because of the greater ratio of solids to liquid, providing more colouring pigment.
SASSY Hopefully a less cringing version of the cheeky, audacious character found in a wine with bold, brash but not necessarily big flavour.
SBOCCATURA (It.) Disgorged.
SCHAUMWEIN (Ger.) Literally 'sparkling wine' and with no further qualification (such as *Qualitätsschaumwein*), this is merely the same as Sekt.
SCION The producer part of the vine, which is joined to the rootstock by grafting.
SEC (Fr.) Literally 'dry', but actually quite sweet (17-35g/l residual sugar).
SECOND FERMENTATION, SECONDARY FERMENTATION Strictly speaking this is the fermentation that occurs in bottle during the *méthode champenoise*, but the malolactic is sometimes erroneously referred to as the second fermentation.
SEKT (Ger.) Without qualification of Deutscher or BA, this term will be found on all the cheapest fizz produced in Germany by *cuve close* from a blend of wines from various EU countries.
SEKT BA (Ger.) A sparkling wine sourced from a single *Anbaugebiet* (German quality wine region), but like QbA these wines are often the product of an even smaller internal area.
SHERRY-LIKE Undesirable in sparkling wines, this refers to the odour in an advanced state of oxidised wine, and is caused by an excessive amount of acetaldehyde.
SHORT Refers to a wine that may have a good aroma and initial flavour, but falls short on the finish, its taste quickly disappearing after the wine has been swallowed.
SIN COSECHA (Sp.) Non-vintage.
SMOOTH The opposite of aggressive and more extreme than round.
SOFT Interchangeable with smooth, although it usually refers to the fruit on the palate, whereas smooth is more often applied to the finish. Soft is very desirable, but 'extremely soft' may be derogatory, inferring a weak and flabby wine.
SOLERA (Sp.) A system of continually refreshing an established blend with a small amount of new wine (equivalent in proportion to the amount extracted from the *solera*) to effect a wine of consistent quality and character.
SOLID Interchangeable with *firm*.
SOUPED UP OR SOUPY Implies a wine has been blended with something richer or more robust. A wine may well be legitimately souped-up, or it could mean that the wine has been played around with. The wine might not be correct, but it could still be very enjoyable.
SOUS MARQUE (Fr.) Second brand. An ancillary label under which second quality wines are sold, although the standard need not necessarily be inferior in any general sense.
SPARGING The introduction of carbonic gas into a wine prior to its bottling, often simply achieved through a valve in the pipe between the vat and the bottling line.
SPÄTLESE (Ger.) A QmP wine that is one step above Kabinett, but one below Auslese. It is fairly sweet and made from late-picked grapes.
SPRITZ, SPRITZIG (Ger.) Synonymous with *pétillant*.
SPRIGHTLY FRUITINESS I have deliberately used this expression instead of VA fruitiness because even though the latter is not a truly derogatory term, it has negative connotations, and would be taken the wrong way more times than not.
SPUMANTE (It.) Literally 'sparkling', but in practice *spumante* normally refers to a fully sparkling wine. *See* FULLY SPARKLING
STRAW Strawlike aromas often blight sparkling wines. Sometimes dry straw, other times wet straw, and others still are just strawlike. Producers say it is part of the complexity, but it strikes me as a very dull, ill-defined sort of complexity and one that is not completely clean. Perhaps it comes from the yeast, or maybe rotten grapes, or even the reaction of yeast-contact to wine made from a certain percentage of rotten grapes. In any case, this is not a positive attribute, although where it appears in this book the wines obviously have sufficient going for them to overcome these strawlike aromas, otherwise they would not be recommended.
STRETCHED Diluted by or cut with water or significantly inferior wine, which is usually illegal in official appellation. It can also refer to wine that has been produced from vines that have been stretched to yield a high volume of attenuated fruit.
STRUCTURE The structure of a wine is literally composed of its solids (acidity, sugar, and extract or density of fruit flavour) in balance with the alcohol, and how positively these elements feel in the mouth.
STURM (Aust.) A sweet, cloudy and *pétillant* wine that has not finished its fermentation.
STYLISH Wines possessing all the subjective qualities of charm, elegance and finesse. A wine might have the 'style' of a certain region or type, but a wine is either stylish or it is not. It defies definition.
SUBTLE Although this should mean a significant yet understated characteristic, it is often employed by wine snobs and frauds who taste a wine with a famous

label and know that it should be special, but cannot detect anything exceptional and need an ambiguous word to talk their way out of the hole they have dug for themselves. The most honest use of subtle in this book refers to the effect of autolysis.

SULPHUR An antioxidant with aseptic qualities used in the production of wine, sulphur should not be noticeable in the finished product, although sometimes a whiff may be detected on recently bottled wine. A good swirl of the glass should remove this and after a few months in bottle it ought to disappear. Eventually sulphur forms part of the toasty bottle-aromas in a sparkling wine.

SUPPLE Indicates a wine that is easy to drink, not necessarily soft, but a more graceful form of ease than the word *round* can manage.

SUR LIE (Fr.) Refers to wines, usually Muscadets, that have been kept on the lees and have not been racked or filtered prior to bottling. Although this increases the possibility of bacterial infection, the risk is worth taking for wines made from neutral grape varieties. It also avoids aeration and retains more of the carbonic gas created during fermentation imparting a certain liveliness and freshness. In the case of sparkling wines, it is better to keep reserve wines *sur lie* than to rack and filter them because it reduces the production of terpenes and helps to retain the nitrogenous matter that makes the wines more susceptible to autolysis.

TALENTO (It.) Since March 1996, producers of Italian *méthode champenoise* wines may utilise the new term of 'Talento', which has been registered as a trademark by the Instituto Talento Metado Classico, which was established in 1975 and formerly called the Instituto Spumante Classico Italiano. Talento is almost synonymous with the Spanish term Cava, although to be fully compatible it would have to assume the mantle of a DOC and to achieve that would require mapping all the areas of production. However, it will take all the Talento they can muster to turn most Italian *spumante brut* into an Internationally class of sparkling wine.

TANK METHOD Same as *cuve close*.

TARTARIC ACID The ripe acid of grapes that increases slightly when the grapes increase in sugar during the *véraison*.

TARTRATES, TARTRATE CRYSTALS Tartaric acid deposits look like sugar crystals at the bottom of a bottle and this may have been precipitated when a wine has experienced low temperatures. It can also happen naturally, deposited through the process of time, although seldom in a still or sparkling wine that has spent several months in contact with its lees, as this produces a mannoprotein called MP32, which prevents precipitation of tartrates. A fine deposit of glittering crystals can also be deposited on the base of a cork if it has been soaked in a sterilizing solution of metabisulphite prior to bottling. Both are harmless.

TCA Short for trichloroanisole, the prime but by no means only culprit responsible for corked wines, TCA is found in oak staves as well as cork. *See* CORKED

TERPENE Various terpenes and terpene alcohols are responsible for some of the most aromatic characteristics in wine, ranging from the floral aromas of Muscat to the petrol or kerosene character of a wonderfully mature Riesling. In sparkling wine a terpene character may indicate Riesling in the blend, but is more likely to be due to part or all the base wine being kept unduly long in tank prior to second fermentation.

TERROIR (Fr.) Literally 'soil', but in a viticultural sense terroir refers to the complete growing environment, which also includes altitude, aspect, climate and any other factors that may affect the life of a vine, and the quality of the grapes it produces.

TÊTE DE CUVÉE (Fr.) The first flow of juice during the pressing, the cream of the *cuvée*. It is the easiest to extract and the highest in quality with the best balance of acids, sugars and minerals.

THIN A wine lacking in body, fruit and other properties.

TIGHT A firm wine of good extract that gives the impression of being under tension, as if a wound spring waiting to uncoil, and thus has more obvious potential than either a reticent or a closed wine.

TINTO (Port., Sp.) Red.

TOAST [1] A slow-developing bottle-induced aroma commonly associated with the Chardonnay, but can develop in wines made from other grapes, including red wines. Toasty bottle-aromas are initially noticeable on the aftertaste, often with no indication on the nose. [2] A fast-developing oak-induced aroma. [3] Barrels are toasted during their construction to one of three grades: light or low, medium, and heavy or high.

TOTAL ACIDITY The total amount of acidity in a wine is usually measured in grams per litre and, because each acid is of a different strength, expressed either as sulphuric (in France) or tartaric acid (New World).

TRADITIONELLE FLASHENGÄRUNG (Ger.) The equivalent of *méthode champenoise*.

TRANSVASAGE (Fr.) Transfer method, whereby sparkling wines undergo a second fermentation in bottle, and are then decanted, filtered and re-bottled under pressure to maintain the mousse.

TROCKENBEERENAUSLESE OR TBA (Ger.) A QmP for wines produced from individually picked, botrytized grapes that have been left on the vine to shrivel. The wine is golden-amber to amber in colour, intensely sweet, viscous, very complex and as different from Beerenauslese as that wine is from Kabinett.

TYPICAL An over-used and less than honest form of honest.

TYPICITY A wine that shows good typicity is one that accurately reflects its grape and soil.

UC DAVIS Short for the University of California's enology department at Davis.

ULLAGE (Fr.) [1] The space between the top of the wine and the head of the bottle or cask. An old bottle of wine with an ullage beneath the shoulder of the bottle is unlikely to be any good. [2] The practice of topping up wine in a barrel to keep it full and thereby prevent excessive oxidation.

UNDERTONE Subtle and supporting, not dominating like an overtone. In a fine wine a strong and simple overtone of youth can evolve into a delicate undertone with maturity, adding to a vast array of other nuances that give it complexity.

UNGENEROUS A wine that lacks generosity has little or no fruit and far too much tannin (if red) or acidity for a correct and harmonious balance.

UNRIPE ACID Malic acid, as opposed to tartaric, which is ripe acid.

UP-FRONT Suggests an attractive, simple quality immediately recognised, which says it all. The wine may initially be interesting, but there would be no further development and the last glass would say nothing more than the first.

VA Abbreviation of volatile acidity.

VA FRUITINESS An ultra-fruitiness accentuated by volatile acidity, this can be a positive factor in the description of a wine, but the term VA (for volatile acidity) has such negative connotations that I have used 'sprightly fruitiness' so that the casual reader is not put off perfectly drinkable wines.

VALUE-FOR-MONEY The difference between penny-saving and penny-pinching. In theory true value-for-money exists at any price-point, whether five or five-hundred (pounds, dollars deutschemarks or whatever), and the decision to buy will depend on how deep your pocket is.

VANILLIN The aldehyde that gives vanilla pods their characteristic aroma, vanillin is also found naturally in oak, albeit on a smaller scale.

VARIETAL, VARIETAL AROMA, VARIETAL CHARACTER The character of a single grape variety as expressed in the wine it produces.

VDQS Commonly used abbreviation for *Vin Délimité de Qualité Supérieure*. Quality control system below AOC, but above *Vin de table* and *Vin de pays*.

VENDEMIA (Sp.) Harvest, often used to indicate vintage.

VERTICAL TASTING This is a tasting of different vintages of the same wine, as opposed to an horizontal tasting, which consists of different wines of the same style or vintage.

VIGNERON (Fr.) Vineyard worker.

VIGNOBLE (Fr.) Vineyard.

VIGOUR Although this term could easily apply to wine, it is invariably used when discussing the growth of a vine, particularly its canopy. To ripen grapes properly, a vine needs about 50 sq/cm of leaf surface to every gram of fruit, but if a vine is too vigorous (known as high vigour) and the canopy exceeds this optimum balance, the grapes will have an overly herbaceous character even when ripe.

VIN BOURRU (Fr.) *See* VIN MOUSTILLANT.

VIN DE CUVÉE (Fr.) Wine made from the first (and best) pressing only.

VIN DE GARDE (Fr.) Wine capable of significant improvement if allowed to age.

VIN DE PAYS (Fr.) A rustic style of country wine that is a step above *Vin de table*, but one beneath VDQS.

VIN DE TABLE (Fr.) Literally 'table wine', this is the lowest level of wine in France and is not allowed to give either the grape variety or the area of origin on the label. In practice it is likely to consist of various varieties from numerous areas that have been blended in bulk to produce a wine of consistent character, or lack of it, as the case may be.

VIN GRIS (Fr.) A delicate, pale version of rosé.

VINIFERA Species covering all varieties of vines providing classic wine-making grapes.

VINIFICATION Far more than simply fermentation, this involves the entire process of making wine, from the moment the grapes are picked to the point it is bottled.

VIN MOUSSEUX (Fr.) Literally means sparkling wine without any connotation of quality one way or the other, but because all fine sparkling wines in France utilise other terms, for all practical purposes it infers a cheap, low quality product.

VIN MOUSTILLANT (Fr.) Also called *vin bourru*. A slightly sweet, cloudy, *pétillant* wine that was traditionally drawn from the cask, off its less, when it was in the final phase of fermentation. This style of wine came into vogue in Paris when it was linked to the southwest of France by rail. Prior to the railway, growers in areas such as Gaillac traditionally despatched their new wines *sur lie* and just as tavern-owners conditioned live beer in their own cellars, so they would allow the *vins primeurs* to settle before serving. By the time the new wine reached Paris the fermentation would be complete and the wine would barely have a prickle, in much the same way as genuine Muscadet *sur lie*. With the advent of the railway, the wines arrived before the fermentation had finished, and had more of fizz – somewhere between a prickle and a pétillance. Fashion conscious Parisians lapped it up to such an extent that the railway owners had to guarantee the growers of Gaillac that they would deliver their wines within 56 hours to ensure the wines were indeed still fermenting.

VINO DE AGUJA (Sp.) A young, slightly sparkling or *perlant* wine.

VIN ORDINAIRE (Fr.) Literally 'an ordinary wine', this term is usually applied to a French *vin de table*, although it can be used in a derogatory way for any wine.

VINOUS Winey, characteristic of wine. When used to describe a wine, it infers basic qualities only.

VINTAGE The harvest or wine of a single year.

VIVID The fruit in some wines can be so fresh, ripe, clean-cut and expressive that it quickly gives a vivid impression of complete character in the mouth.

VOLATILE ACIDITY This has a sweet vinegary aroma, and if clearly detectable is usually deemed a fault, but a certain amount of volatile acidity (or VA for short) is essential to the fruitiness of every wine, and occasionally even high levels can be a positive factor. *See* VA FRUITINESS

WEISSHERBST (Ger.) A single-variety rosé wine produced from black grapes only.

WET STRAW *See* STRAW.

WINZERSEKT (Ger.,) Literally a 'grower Sekt', this can either be the product of a single grower or a cooperative of growers, but must be a Sekt bA.

YEAST A kind of fungus vital in all winemaking. Yeast cells excrete a number of enzymes, some 22 of which are necessary to complete the chain reaction known as fermentation.

YEAST ENZYMES Each enzyme acts as a catalyst for one activity and is specific for that task and no other in the fermentation process.

YEASTY Not a complimentary term for most wines, but a yeasty bouquet can be desirable in a good-quality sparkling wine, especially when young.

YIELD There are two forms of yield: [1] the quantity of grapes produced from a given area of land, [2] how much juice is pressed from it. Wine people in Europe use hl/ha or hectolitres per hectare, which is a combination of both, literally referring to how much juice has been extracted from the grapes harvested from an area of land. This is fine when the amount of juice that can be pressed from grapes is controlled by European-type appellation systems, but in the New World, where this seldom happens, they tend to talk in tons per acre.

ZESTY A lively characteristic that suggests a zippy tactile impression combined, maybe, with a hint of citrussy aroma.

ZING, ZINGY, ZIP, ZIPPY Terms all indicative of something refreshing, lively and vital, resulting from a high balance of ripe fruit acidity.

INDEX

PHOTOGRAPHIC CREDITS t = top, b = bottom, l = left, r = right, c = centre, h = half

CIVC Epernay: 16c, 22t, 44t; Valerie Dubois 19bl; Alain Fion 133r; John Hodder 22thc; Rohrscheid 12tr; Stuart Ziegler 43. Cephas: Jerry Alexander 259t; Mark Baynham 307; Nigel Blythe 96, 106; Fernando Briones 227; Andy Christodolo 15t, 212, 285, 288, 292, 294, 300; Bruce Fleming 15br, 266t, 271, 273; Christine Fleurent 22b; Christine Fleurent/Top 134; Kevin Judd 21ttr, 305, 308; Joris Luyten 59; Diana Mewes 19c; Diana Mewes/Mick Rock 3; R & K Muschenetz 284; Lars Nilsson 243; Janet Price 310; Alain Proust 30 (&5), 245 (&5), 247, 248, 252; John Rizzo 281, 283; Mick Rock 7, 10, 11, 14, 15bl, 18, 19t, 21thtl, bhtl, bhtr, bhbl, bhbr, 22thb, 24t, 25t, 41t, cl, cr, bl, br, 42tl, 42tr, 42b, 48, 55, 61, 66, 69, 75, 76, 81, 82, 87, 88t, 88bl, 98, 100, 103, 110l, 112, 113, 115, 117, 119, 126, 129, 133l, 135, 136t, 136b, 137, 145, 148, 152, 158, 165, 166, 167, 169, 171, 172, 175, 176, 178tl (&5), cr (&5), bl (&5),180b, 182, 184, 186, 187, 194, 204, 211, 214, 216, 220, 225, 226, 228, 230, 231, 232, 234, 235, 254 (&5), 256, 262, 270, 278, 280, 286 (&5), 289, 298, 303; Ted Stefanski 23 (&5), 259b, 261t; Stockfood 29, 35; Wine Magazine 39 (&5), 253. Tom Stevenson 16t, 17t, 22bht, 31b, 57t, b, 64t, b, 178br (&5), 209, 241. Veuve Clicquot Ponsardin: 9t, 12tl, 12b (&5), 13tl, 13tr (&5), 13b, 17b, 19br, 20t, 20b, 22bhc, 44b, 46, 47, 79, 130t, c, b, 131. Paul Bara 51. Cave Vinicole de Beblenheim 146. Billecart-Salmon 53. Billie Love Historical Collection 9b. O.J. Bird 304. Bollinger 54t, 54b, 56l. Buena Vista 257t, 257b. Casa da Tapada 178cl. Casal Branco 221. Caves Murganheira 222. Champagne Bureau/Jonathan Pollock & Stephen Wheeler 28. Champagne Cattier 68. Codorníu Napa 265. Domaine Chandon 21thbl, 266b. Tor Eigeland 16b. Frederick Frank 257c. Marie-Catherine Gault 56r. Richard Gillette 269t. R Grenéron 154. Richard Hadley 24b, 25b, 26, 102. Michel Horiot 160. J Wine Company 269b. JP Vinhos 223. Manfred Klimek 236. Korbel Bros 258t. Kristone 272. Krug 88br. Laurent-Perrier 90, 92l, r, 93, 122. Moët & Chandon: 73; Alain Mangin 72t; Richard Phelps Frueman 72l. Steven Morris 299. Bruno Paillard 107. Paramount Distillers, Inc. 255t, 255b. Perrier-Jouët 110r. Piper-Heidsieck 111. Pol Roger 116. Riedel 33, 34. Roederer Estate 276t, b. Royal Society 8. Ruinart 120t, b, 121. Schramsberg 258b, 260. Simonsig 251. Maison Albert Sounit 163. St & St 199. Studio Gartler Krems (RSV) 178bc. Taittinger 125. Union 128. Verband Deutscher Sektkellereien 179t, b, 180t, 181, 201. Vilmart & Cie 132. Wickham Vineyard 210 (&178tr) (&5). Doreen L Wynja 261b.